Street by Street

SOUTH YORKSHIRE

PLUS DRONFIELD, HEMSWORTH, HOLMFIRTH, WORKSOP

Enlarged Areas Barnsley, Doncaster, Rotherham, Sheffield

Ist edition May 2001

Published by AA Publishing (a trading name of Automobile Association Developments Limited, whose registered office is Norfolk House, Priestley Road, Basingstoke, Hampshire, RG24 9NY. Registered number 1878835).

Mapping produced by the Cartographic Department of The Automobile Association.

A CIP Catalogue record for this book is available from the British Library.

Printed by G. Canale & C. s.p.a., Torino, Italy

The contents of this atlas are believed to be correct at the time of the latest revision. However, the publishers cannot be held responsible for loss occasioned to any person acting or refraining from action as a result of any material in this atlas, nor for any errors, omissions or changes in such material. The publishers would welcome information to correct any errors or omissions and to keep this atlas up to date. Please write to Publishing, The Automobile Association, Fanum House, Basing View, Basingstoke, Hampshire, RG21 4EA.

Ref: MX073

Key to map pages	ii-iii
Key to map symbols	iv-1
Enlarged scale pages	2-9
Street by Street	10-199
Index – towns & villages	200-201
Index – streets	201-234
Index – featured places	234-238

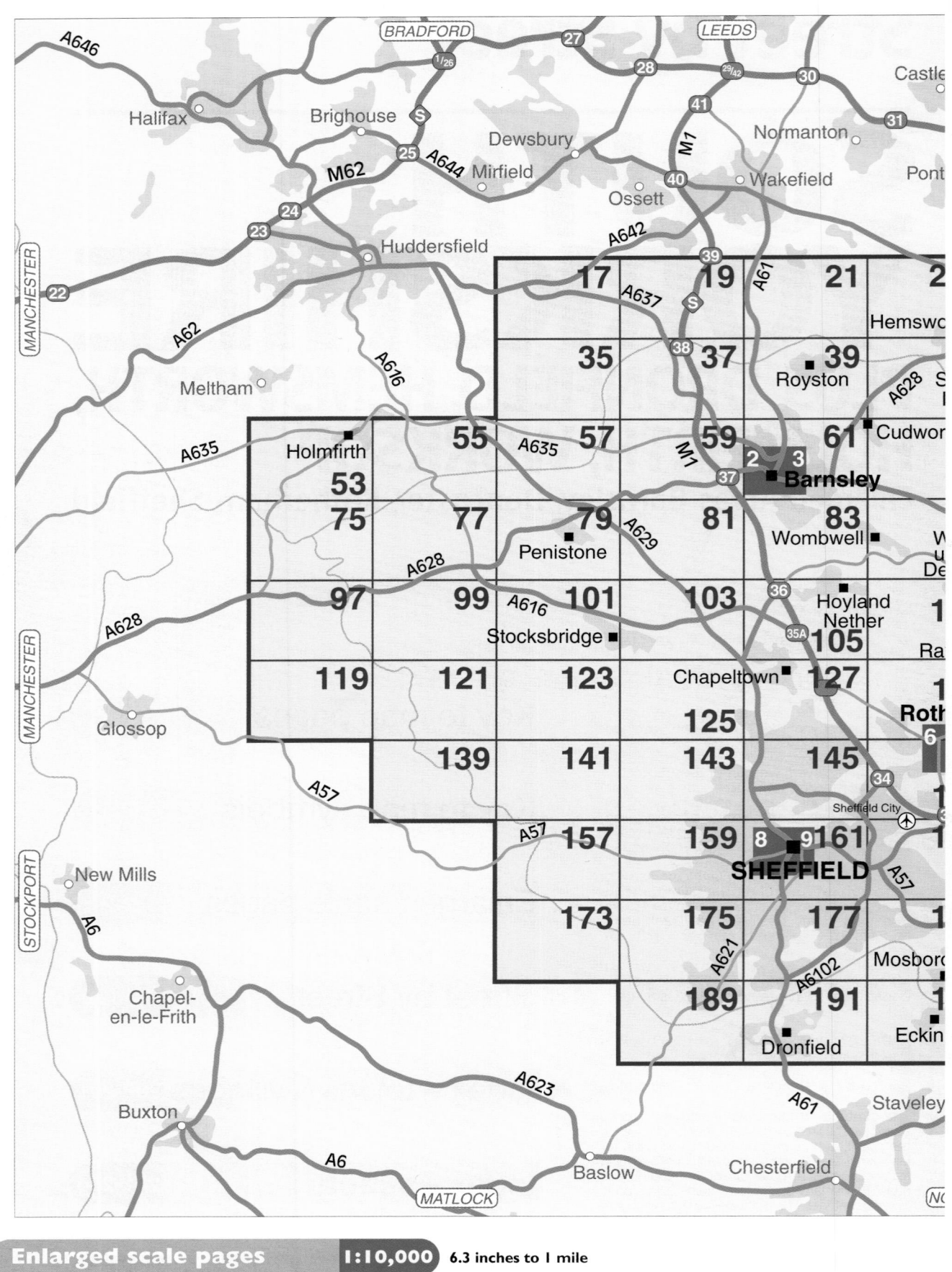

ii

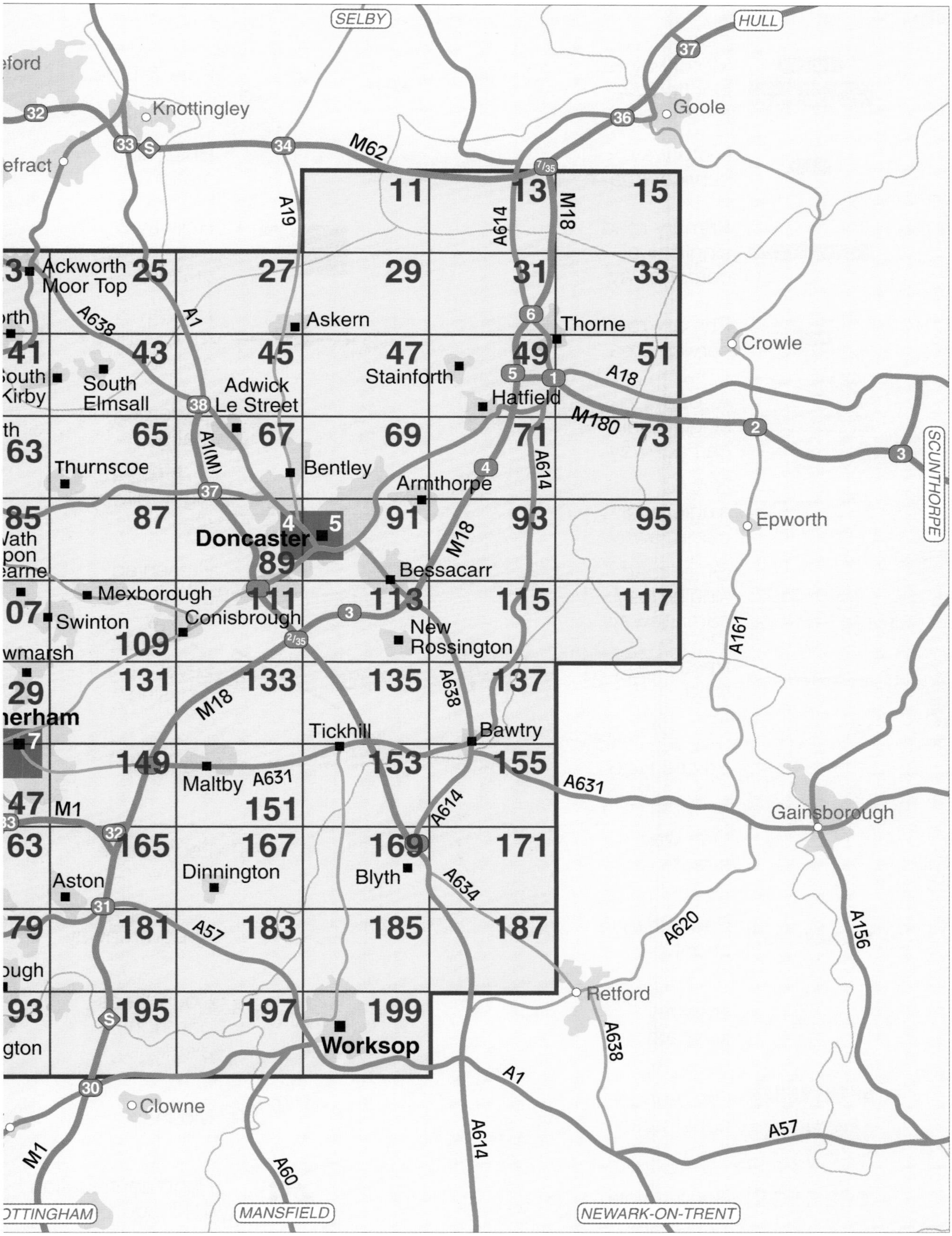

SELBY

HULL

37

32

Knottingley

36   Goole

33 S

34   M62   M18

efract

A19

A614

M18

11   13   15

eford

23 Ackworth   25   27   29   31   33
Moor Top

orth   A638   6

A1   Askern   Thorne

41   43   45   47   49   51

South   South   Adwick   Stainforth   5   1   A18   Crowle
Kirby   Elmsall   Le Street   38

th   65   67   69   Hatfield   71   M180   73   2   SCUNTHORPE

63   A1(M)   Bentley   A614   3

Thurnscoe   37   Armthorpe   4

85   87   4 5   91   93   95   Epworth

Wath   Doncaster   M18   A161
pon
earne   89

Mexborough   111   Bessacarr   113   115   117

07   Swinton   Conisbrough   3   New
    2/35   Rossington

wmarsh   109

29   131   133   135   137   A638
herham   M18

7   Tickhill   Bawtry   A631

47   149   153   155   A631   Gainsborough

M1   Maltby   A631   A614

33   32   151   A620   A156

63   165   167   169   171

Aston   Dinnington   Blyth   A634

31

79   181   183   185   187   A638

ough   A57

93   S 195   197   199   Retford
gton   Worksop

30   Clowne   A1

M1   A60   A614   A57

OTTINGHAM   MANSFIELD   NEWARK-ON-TRENT

3.6 inches to 1 mile   **Scale of main map pages 1:17,500**

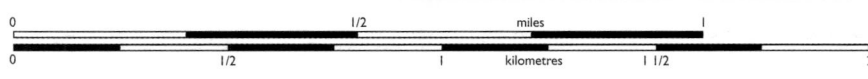

0   1/2   miles   1

0   1/2   1   kilometres   1 1/2   2

Junction 9	Motorway & junction	**P+🚌**	Park & Ride
Services	Motorway service area	🚌	Bus/coach station
	Primary road single/dual carriageway		Railway & main railway station
Services	Primary road service area		Railway & minor railway station
	A road single/dual carriageway	⊖	Underground station
	B road single/dual carriageway	⊖	Light railway & station
	Other road single/dual carriageway	+++++++++	Preserved private railway
	Restricted road	*LC*	Level crossing
	Private road	•—•—•—•	Tramway
	One way street	--------	Ferry route
	Pedestrian street	....	Airport runway
	Track/ footpath	—·—·—·—	Boundaries- borough/ district
	Road under construction	ꝟꝟꝟꝟ	Mounds
	Road tunnel	**93**	Page continuation 1:17,500
P	Parking	**7**	Page continuation to enlarged scale 1:10,000

River/canal
lake, pier

Aqueduct
lock, weir

465
▲
Winter Hill

Peak (with
height in
metres)

Beach

Coniferous
woodland

Broadleaved
woodland

Mixed
woodland

Park

Cemetery

Built-up
area

Featured building

City wall

A&E

Accident &
Emergency
hospital

Toilet

Toilet with
disabled facilities

Petrol station

PH Public house

PO Post Office

Public library

Tourist Information
Centre

Castle

Historic house/
building

Wakehurst
Place NT

National Trust
property

Museum/
art gallery

Church/chapel

Country park

Theatre/
performing arts

Cinema

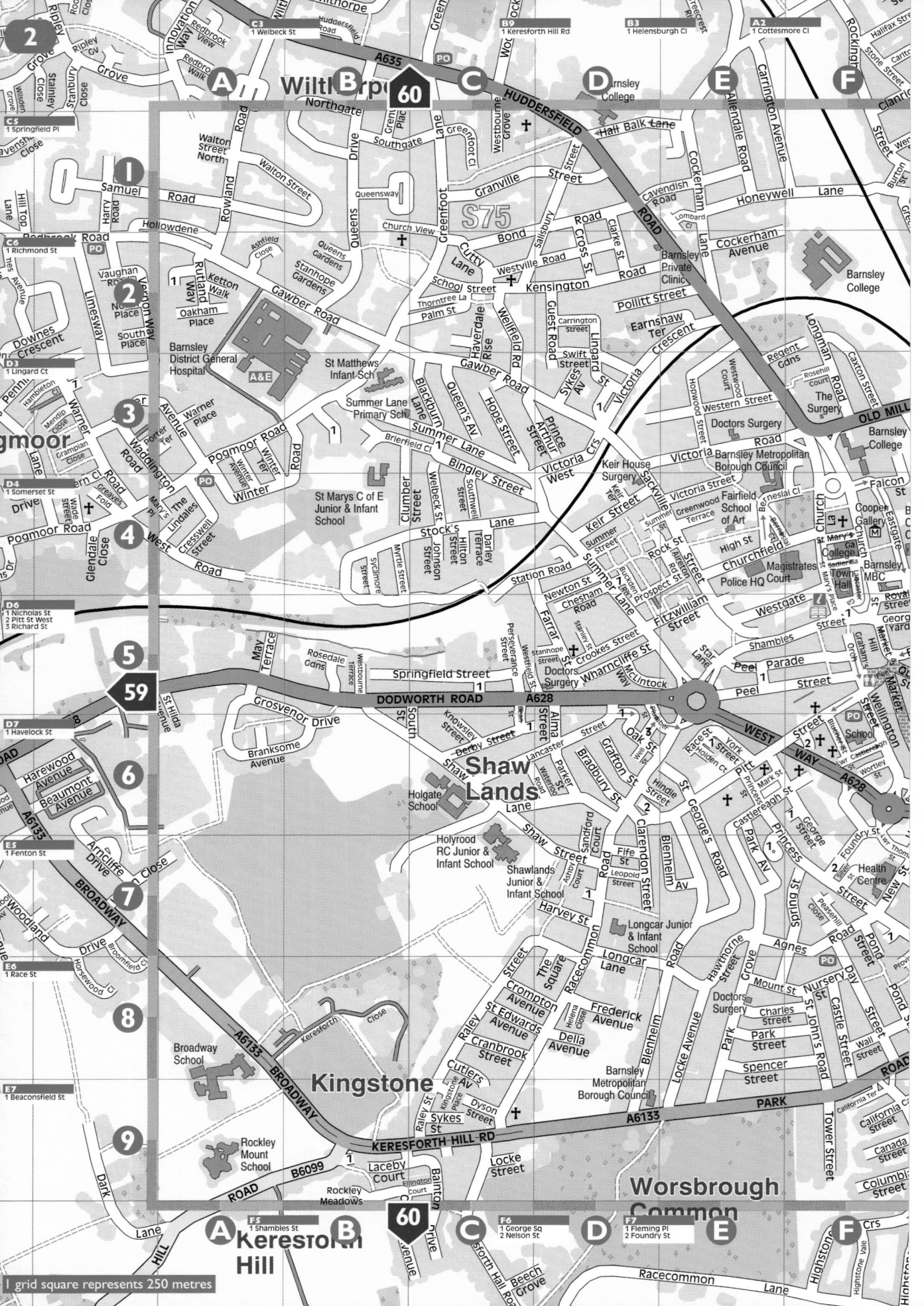
2
C3 1 Welbeck St
B9 1 Keresforth Hill Rd
B3 1 Helensburgh Cl
A2 1 Cottesmore Cl
C5 1 Springfield Pl
C6 1 Richmond St
D3 1 Lingard Ct
D4 1 Somerset St
D6 1 Nicholas St 2 Pitt St West 3 Richard St
D7 1 Havelock St
E5 1 Fenton St
E6 1 Race St
E7 1 Beaconsfield St
F5 1 Shambles St
F6 1 George Sq 2 Nelson St
F7 1 Fleming Pl 2 Foundry St
A
B
C
D
E
F
1
2
3
4
5
6
7
8
9
60
59
S75
A635
HUDDERSFIELD ROAD
Northgate
Southgate
Walton Street North
Walton Street
Samuel Road
Rowland Road
Queens Drive
Queensway
Greenfoot Lane
Greenfoot Cl
Granville Street
Westbourne Grove
Hall Balk Lane
Cockerham Lane
Allendale Road
Carrington Avenue
Cavendish Road
Honeywell Lane
Lombard Cl
Cockerham Avenue
Barnsley College
Barnsley Private Clinic
Church View
Bond Road
Salisbury
Cross St
Clarke St
Cutty Lane
Westville Road
Kensington Road
School Street
Thorntree La
Palm St
Pollitt Street
Earnshaw Ter
Victoria Crescent
Hollowdene
Redbrook Road
Vaughan Road
North Place
South Place
Vernon Way
Limesway
Downes Crescent
Ashfield Close
Queens Gardens
Stanhope Gardens
Gawber Road
Rutland Way
Ketton Walk
Oakham Place
Barnsley District General Hospital
A&E
St Matthews Infant Sch
Haverdale Rise
Wellfield Rd
Guest Road
Carrington Street
Swift Street
Lingard St
Sykes Av
Regent Gdns
Longman Road
Caxton Street
Rosehill Court
The Surgery
OLD MILL
Westwood Court
Hopwood Street
Western Street
Doctors Surgery
Victoria Road
Barnsley Metropolitan Borough Council
Summer Lane Primary Sch
Blackburn Lane
Queen's Av
Hope Street
Prince Arthur Street
Summer Lane
Brierfield Cl
Bingley Street
Pogmoor
Warner Place
Warner Lane
Pogmoor Road
Winter Road
Winter Avenue
Winter Ter
Waddington Road
Porter Ter
Grampian Close
Mendip Close
Hambleton Cl
Greaves Fold
Wade Street
Mary's Pl
The Lindales
Cresswell Street
West Road
Glendale Close
Keir House Surgery
Victoria Crs West
Sackville Street
Victoria Street
Keir Street
Fairfield School of Art
Greenwood Terrace
Bernesal Cl
Church Street
Falcon St
Cooper Gallery
Eastgate
St Mary's Gate
College
Barnsley MBC
Town Hall
St Marys C of E Junior & Infant School
Clumber Street
Welbeck St
Southwell Street
Stock's Lane
Johnson Street
Hilton Street
Darley Terrace
Sycamore Street
Myrtle Street
Station Road
Summer Street
Summer Lane
Rock St
Airedale Rd St
High St
Churchfield
Magistrates Court
Police HQ
Westgate
Royal Street
Newton St
Chesham Road
Buckden Road
Prospect St
Fitzwilliam Street
Farrar St
Stanley St
Crookes Street
Stanhope Street
Doctors Surgery
Wharncliffe St
McIntosh
Star Lane
Shambles Street
Peel Parade
Peel Street
Grahams Orch
Market Hill
Rosedale Gdns
Westbourne Terrace
May Terrace
Perseverance Street
Westfield St
Springfield Street
DODWORTH ROAD
A628
WEST WAY
Grosvenor Drive
Branksome Avenue
St Hilda Avenue
South St
Knowsley Street
Derby Street
Alma Street
Lancaster Street
Oak St
Well St
Race St
Holden Ct
York Street
Pitt Street
Mark St
Princess Street
Castlereagh St
Wellington Street
School
Wortley St
Shaw Lands
Shaw Lane
Holgate School
Waterloo Road
Parker St
Bradbury St
Crafton St
Hindle Street
St George's Road
Park Av
George Street
Foundry St
Health Centre
New St
Harewood Avenue
Beaumont Avenue
Arncliffe Drive
Close
A6133
BROADWAY
Woodland Drive
Broomfield Cl
Horsewood Cl
Holyrood RC Junior & Infant School
Shaw Street
Shawlands Junior & Infant School
Sandford Court
Ashby Court
Fife St
Leopold Street
Clarendon Street
Blenheim Av
Harvey St
Longcar Junior & Infant School
Spring St
Peasehill Close
Agnes Road
Pond Street
Longcar Lane
Racecommon Road
The Square
Crompton Avenue
St Edwards Avenue
Frederick Avenue
Helena Close
Della Avenue
Hawthorne Street
Grove Street
Mount St
Nursery St
Day Street
Doctors Surgery
Charles Street
Park Street
St John's Road
Castle Street
Wall Street
Spencer Street
Raley Street
Cranbrook Street
Cutlers Av
Kingstone Place
Dyson Street
Sykes St
Kingstone
Blenheim
Locke Avenue
Barnsley Metropolitan Borough Council
PARK ROAD
Tower Street
California Ter
California Street
Canada Street
Columbia Street
Keresforth Close
Broadway School
KERESFORTH HILL RD
Rockley Mount School
B6099
ROAD
Laceby Court
Ellington Court
Bainton Drive
Rockley Meadows
Locke Street
Worsbrough Common
Dark Lane
HILL
Keresforth Hill
Keresforth Hall Road
Beech Grove
Racecommon Lane
Highstone Vale
1 grid square represents 250 metres

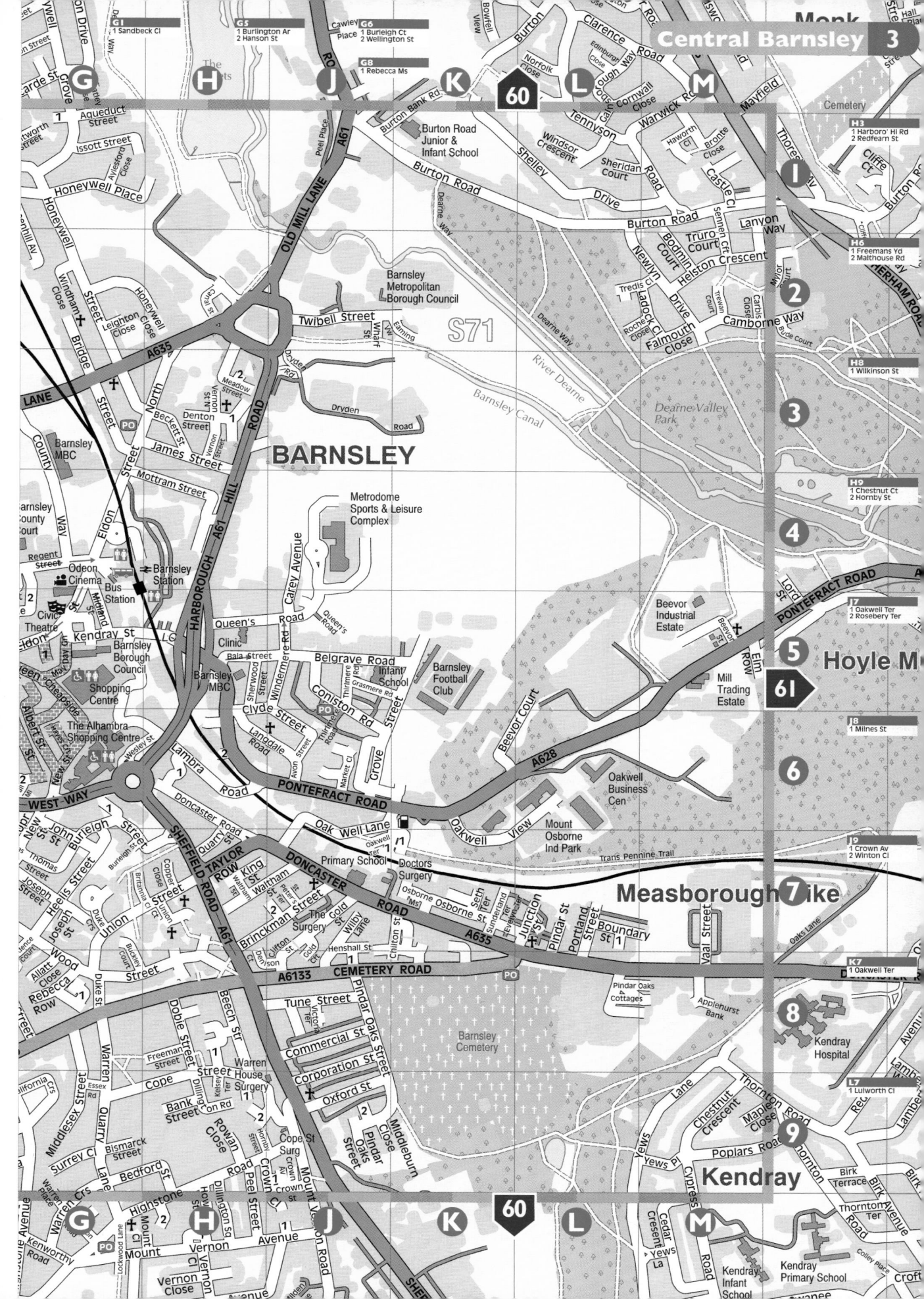

Monk

BARNSLEY

S71

Hoyle M

Measborough ike

Kendray

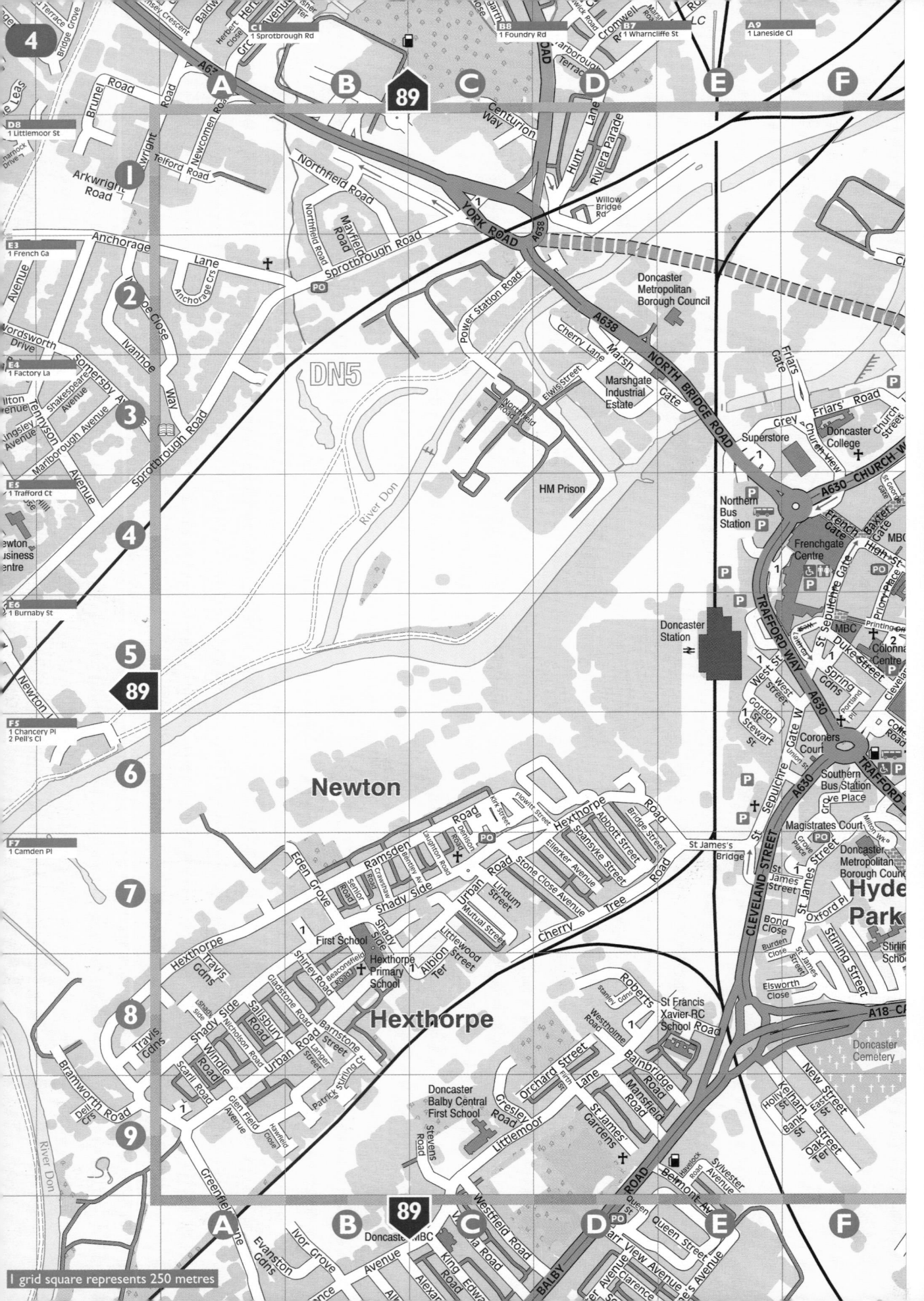
4
89
A
B
C
D
E
F
1
2
3
4
5
6
7
8
9
C1 1 Sprotbrough Rd
B8 1 Foundry Rd
B7 1 Wharncliffe St
A9 1 Laneside Cl
D8 1 Littlemoor St
E3 1 French Ga
E4 1 Factory La
E5 1 Trafford Ct
E6 1 Burnaby St
F5 1 Chancery Pl 2 Pell's Cl
F7 1 Camden Pl
Terrace
Bridge Grove
Herbert Close
Brunel Road
Newcomen Road
Telford Road
Arkwright Road
Northfield Road
Mayfield Road
Centurion Way
Hunt Lane
Riviera Parade
Willow Bridge Rd
YORK ROAD
A638
Anchorage Lane
Anchorage Crs
Sprotbrough Road
Power Station Road
Doncaster Metropolitan Borough Council
Cherry Lane
Marsh Gate
NORTH BRIDGE ROAD
Wordsworth Drive
Somersby Avenue
Ivanhoe Way
Tennyson Avenue
Shakespeare Avenue
Marlborough Avenue
DN5
River Don
Elwis Street
Marshgate Industrial Estate
HM Prison
Friars Gate
Friars' Road
Grey Friars' Road
Church View
Church Street
Doncaster College
Superstore
A630 CHURCH WAY
Northern Bus Station
French Gate
Frenchgate Centre
Baxter Gate
High St
St Sepulchre Gate
Priory Place
Doncaster Station
TRAFFORD WAY
MBC
Printing Office
Colonnades Centre
Duke Street
Spring Gdns
West St
West Street
Gordon St
Stewart St
Coroners Court
Southern Bus Station
Grove Place
Magistrates Court
Doncaster Metropolitan Borough Council
St James Street
Hyde Park
Oxford Pl
Stirling Street
Bond Close
Burden Close
Elsworth Close
CLEVELAND STREET
A630
A18
Doncaster Cemetery
Newton
Hexthorpe Road
Flowitt Street
Kirk Street
Denison Road
Laughton Road
Bentley Av
Ramsden Road
Eden Grove
Crawshaw Road
Shady Side
Urban Road
Lindum Street
Mutual Street
Stone Close Avenue
Ellerker Avenue
Spansyke Street
Abbott Street
Bridge Street
St James's Bridge
Cherry Tree Road
Littlewood Street
Albion Ter
First School
Hexthorpe Primary School
Shirley Road
Beaconsfield Road
Gladstone Road
Travis Gdns
Salisbury Road
Barnstone Street
Hexthorpe
Windle Road
Nicholson Road
Langer Street
Patrick Stirling Ct
Scarll Road
Glen Field Avenue
Hawfield Close
Bramworth Road
Dell Crs
Greenfield Lane
Roberts Road
Stanley Gdns
Westholme Road
St Francis Xavier RC School
Bainbridge Road
Mansfield Road
Orchard Street
Firth St
St James' Gardens
Doncaster Balby Central First School
Cresley Road
Littlemoor Lane
Stevens Road
Westfield Road
BALBY ROAD
Belmont Av
Sylvester Avenue
Havelock Road
Holly Bank St
Kelham St
East St
Oak Ter
New Street
Queen St
Queen Street
Ivor Grove
Evanston Gdns
Doncaster MBC
King Edward Road
Clarence
1 grid square represents 250 metres

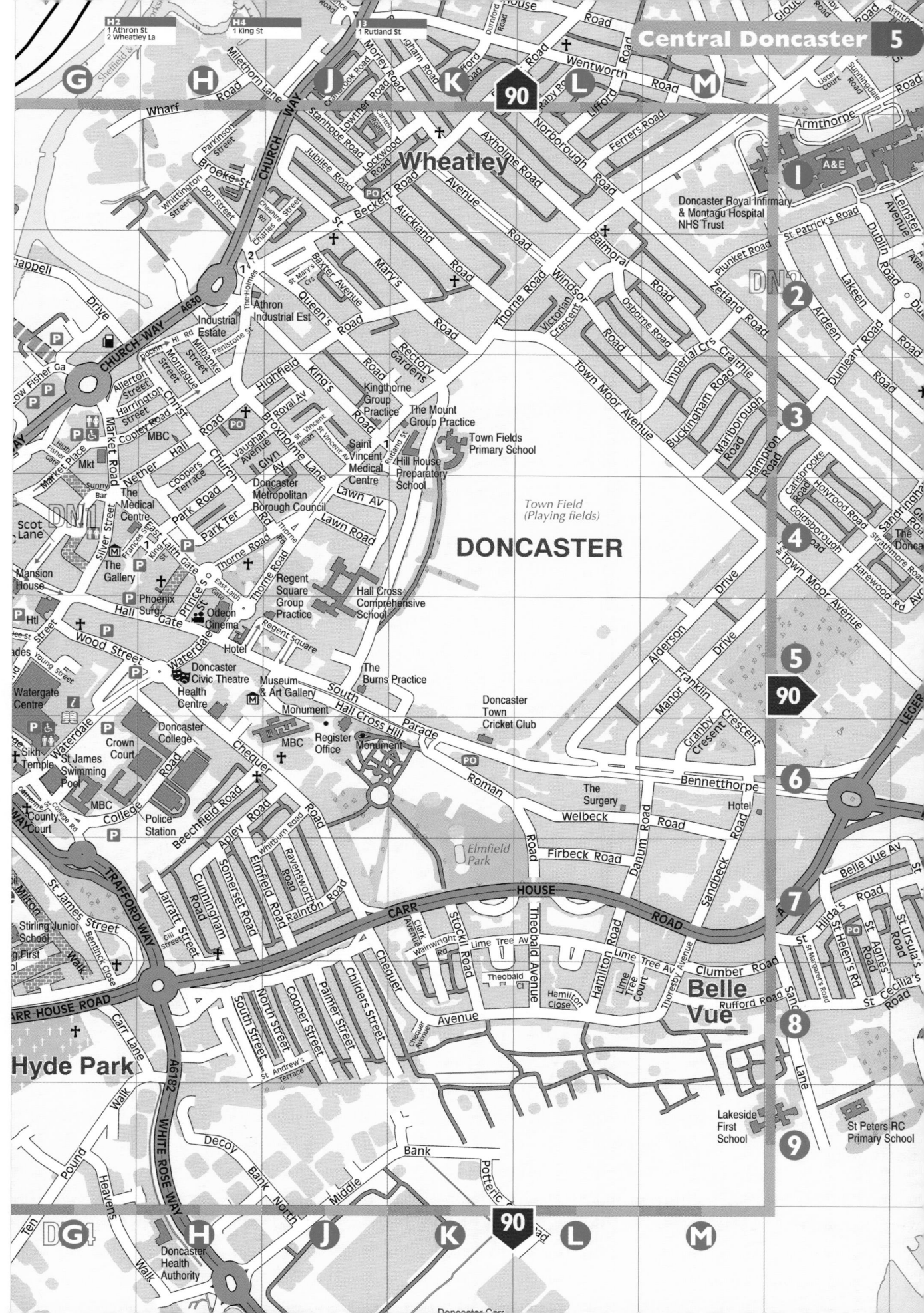
H2
1 Athron St
2 Wheatley La
H4
1 King St
J3
1 Rutland St
Wheatley
DONCASTER
Town Field
(Playing fields)
Doncaster Royal Infirmary & Montagu Hospital NHS Trust
Hall Cross Comprehensive School
Town Fields Primary School
Hill House Preparatory School
Doncaster Metropolitan Borough Council
Museum & Art Gallery
Doncaster Civic Theatre
Doncaster College
Doncaster Town Cricket Club
Elmfield Park
Belle Vue
Hyde Park
Lakeside First School
St Peters RC Primary School
Doncaster Health Authority
Stirling Junior School
Church Way
Carr House Road
Trafford Way
White Rose Way
Thorne Road
Town Moor Avenue
Bennetthorpe
South Parade
Hall Cross Hill
Roman Road
Chequer Road
90

E3
1 Amen Cnr
2 George St
D4
1 Railway Ter
D3
1 Chemist La
A4
1 Devonshire St
F5
1 The Crofts
128
146
S61
S60
Masbrough
Thorn Hill
Thornhill Industrial Estate
NEW WORTLEY ROAD
A629
CENTENARY WAY
A630
GREASBROUGH STREET
B6089
REASBROUGH ROAD
Greasbrough Road
Henley Way
Andrews Place
Henley Lane (Track)
Copley Pl
Avon Mount
Dovercourt Road
Mount St
Henley Rise
Mount Pleasant Rd
Henley Gv Road
Oates Street
Wortley Rd
Clough Bank
Clough Road
Clough Street
Clough Green
Rodger St
Hartley Lane
North Street
Hardy Street
Hope Street
Hope St Extension
Tenter Street
Joseph St
James St
Walter St
School
Primrose Hl
Milton Street
North Dr
Field Way
Lincoln Street
Northfield Road
Rawmarsh
Ashley Industr Est
Claire Ct
Amber Business Cen
Rotherham MBC
Drummond St
Baden Street
Neville Street
Glasshouse Street
Thames Street
Garden La
Mary St
Wortley Road
Henley Grove Road
Garden St
Alice Rd
Park Street
Brown St
Thornhill Edge
St John's Avenue
James Street
Falding St
Winifred Street
Fisher Close
Greaves Road
Midland Road
Woodstock Bower Group Practice
Rotherham Area Health Authority
Ferham Ho Clinic
Ferham Park
Amergate Clinics
Kimberworth Road
Union St
College Rd
Vine Cl
Chapel Wk
Mosque
Chapel Walk
Hall St
Cupola Yd
St
Central Rd
Forge Lane
George St
Bridge St
Frederick St
Bridgegate
PO
Frame Ga
Howard Street
College of Tech
Rotherham Central Station
Rotherham Magistrates Court
The Statutes
Central Business Park
Market St
Corporation St
The Business Centre
High St
College Street
Robert Street
Victoria St
Albert Street
St Bede's Road
Orchard Pl
Princes St
Station Road
Masbrough
Coronation Br
Masbrough Street
John Street
Providence Street
Lyme St
Main Street
Domine Lane
Moorgate St
Ship Hl
Snail Hl
Wellgate
Town Hall
Unity Pl
Burrell Street
Wilfred St
Westgate
Oil Mill Fold
Down's Rw
Rotherham MBC
Grove Road
Cavendish Road
Hartington Road
Hartington Cl
Joseph St
Belmont St
Infant School
Chatsworth Rd
Sarah Street
Devonshire Street
Florence Road
Tummon Street
Holmes Lane
Rotherham United Football Club
Millmoor Lane
Armer St
Brinsworth
Don Street
Water Lane
Coke La
Swan St
Maltkiln St
Contour Health Centre
Steel St
Trans Pennine Trail
LC
Sheffield Road
Wheathill St
Canklow Rd
Chapel La
A6021 ALMA ROAD
Nightingale
ROTH
CANKLOW RD
OLD SHEFFIELD ROAD
The Maltings
Marsh St
Riverside Way
River Don
Bradmarsh Business Park
Bow Bridge Close
The Business Centre
Templeborough Business Centre
Mill Close
Dodds Cl
Bradmar
Fullerton Road
Mill St
Robinson St
Town Street
Rother View Road
Canklow Road
Jubilee St
Moorgate Cemetery
Mountenoy Road
Reneville Cl
Rotherham
Sheffield
Besse
Way
pleborough
ROAD
A6178
Ickles Way
Warden Street
Bentley Street
Trans Pennine
River Rd
CENTENAR
1 grid square represents 250 metres

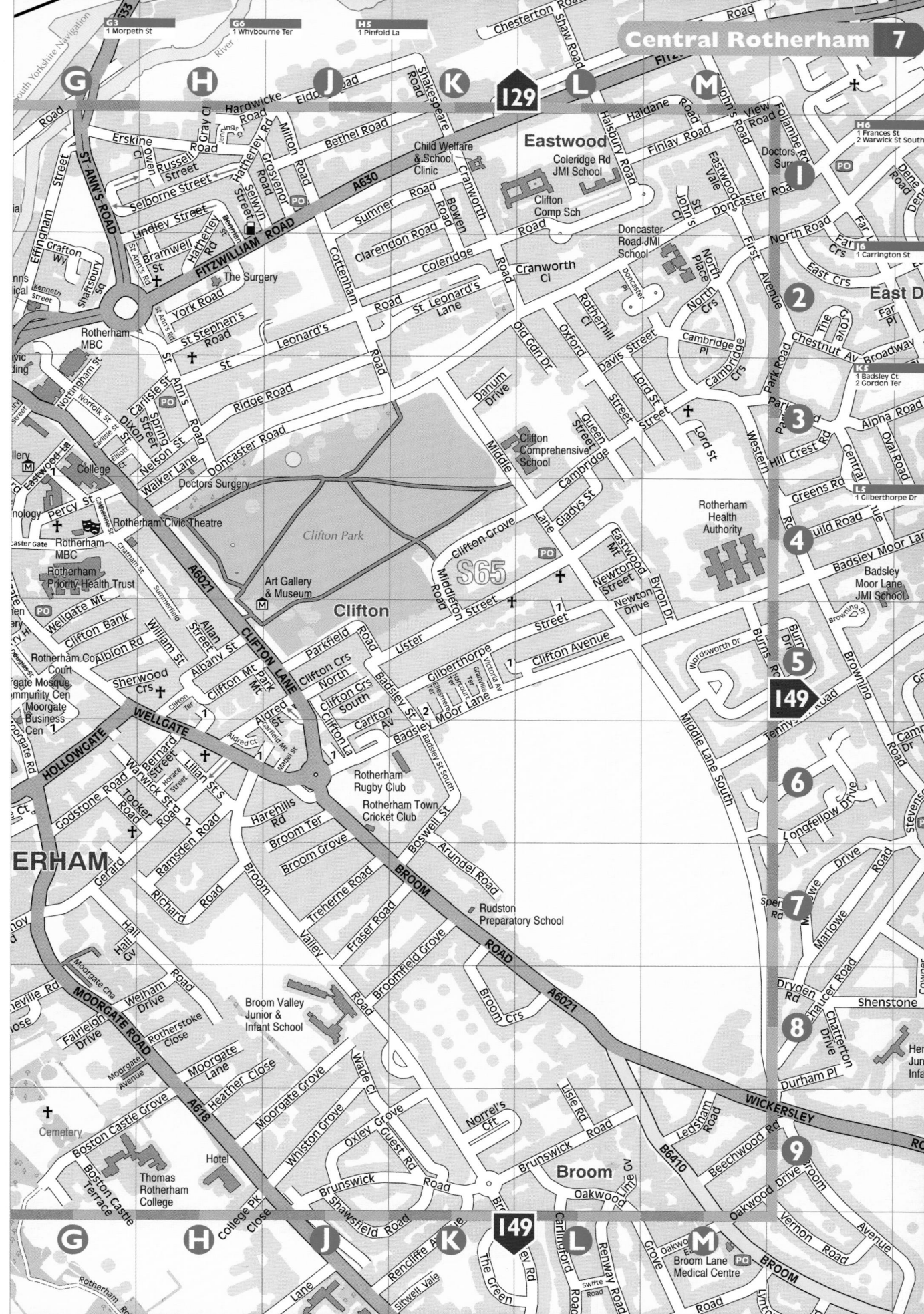
G3 1 Morpeth St
G6 1 Whybourne Ter
H5 1 Pinfold La
H6 1 Frances St 2 Warwick St South
J6 1 Carrington St
K5 1 Badsley Ct 2 Gordon Ter
L5 1 Gilberthorpe Dr
129
149
Eastwood
Clifton
Broom
Clifton Park
Rotherham Civic Theatre
Art Gallery & Museum
Rotherham Health Authority
Rotherham Rugby Club
Rotherham Town Cricket Club
Rudston Preparatory School
Broom Valley Junior & Infant School
Thomas Rotherham College
Broom Lane Medical Centre
Clifton Comprehensive School
Clifton Comp Sch
Coleridge Rd JMI School
Doncaster Road JMI School
Badsley Moor Lane JMI School
Child Welfare & School Clinic
The Surgery
Doctors Surgery
Rotherham MBC
Rotherham Priority Health Trust
Moorgate Business Cen
Cemetery
Hotel
College
S65
FITZWILLIAM ROAD
ST ANN'S ROAD
CLIFTON LANE
WELLGATE
HOLLOWGATE
BROOM ROAD
MOORGATE ROAD
WICKERSLEY ROAD
A630
A6021
A618
B6410

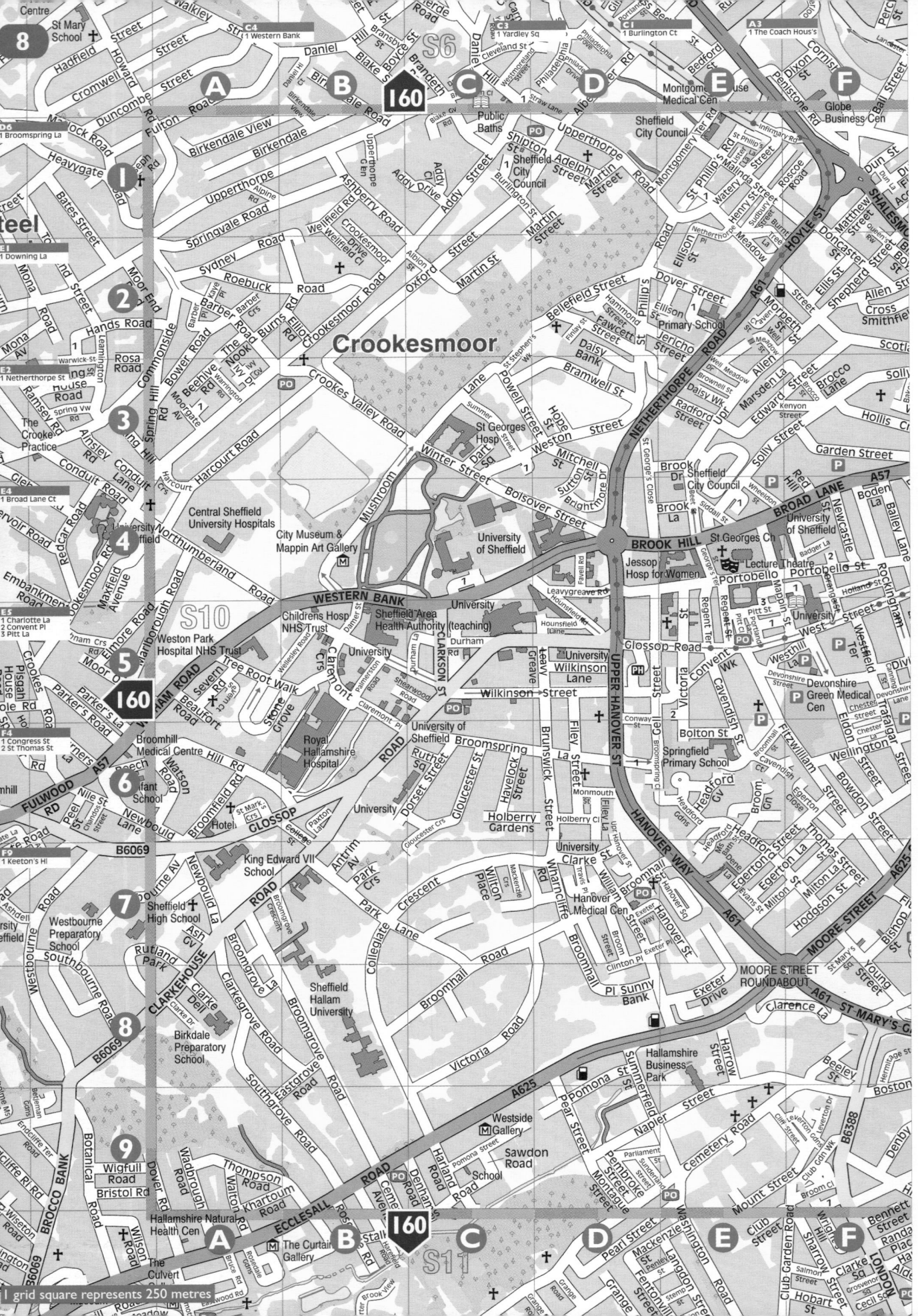

C4
1 Western Bank
C3
1 Yardley Sq
C1
1 Burlington Ct
A3
1 The Coach Hous's
D6
1 Broomspring La
E1
1 Downing La
E2
1 Netherthorpe St
E4
1 Broad Lane Ct
E5
1 Charlotte La
2 Convent Pl
3 Pitt La
F4
1 Congress St
2 St Thomas St
F9
1 Keeton's Hl
S6
160
A
B
C
D
E
F
1
2
3
4
5
6
7
8
9
S10
S11
Crookesmoor
St Mary School
Public Baths
Montgomery House Medical Cen
Globe Business Cen
Sheffield City Council
Sheffield City Council
Ellison Primary School
The Crookes Practice
St Georges Hosp
Central Sheffield University Hospitals
City Museum & Mappin Art Gallery
University of Sheffield
Jessop Hosp for Women
St Georges Ch
Lecture Theatre
Portobello
Childrens Hosp NHS Trust
Sheffield Area Health Authority
University (teaching)
Weston Park Hospital NHS Trust
Royal Hallamshire Hospital
Broomhill Medical Centre
University of Sheffield
Springfield Primary School
Devonshire Green Medical Cen
King Edward VII School
Sheffield High School
Westbourne Preparatory School
Birkdale Preparatory School
Sheffield Hallam University
Hanover Medical Cen
MOORE STREET ROUNDABOUT
Hallamshire Business Park
Westside Gallery
School
Hallamshire Natural Health Cen
The Curtain Gallery
The Culvert
WESTERN BANK
BROOK HILL
BROAD LANE
NETHERTHORPE ROAD
UPPER HANOVER ST
HANOVER WAY
MOORE STREET
ECCLESALL ROAD
CLARKEHOUSE ROAD
GLOSSOP ROAD
FULWOOD RD
BROCCO BANK
SHALESMOOR
A61
A57
A625
B6069
B6388
1 grid square represents 250 metres

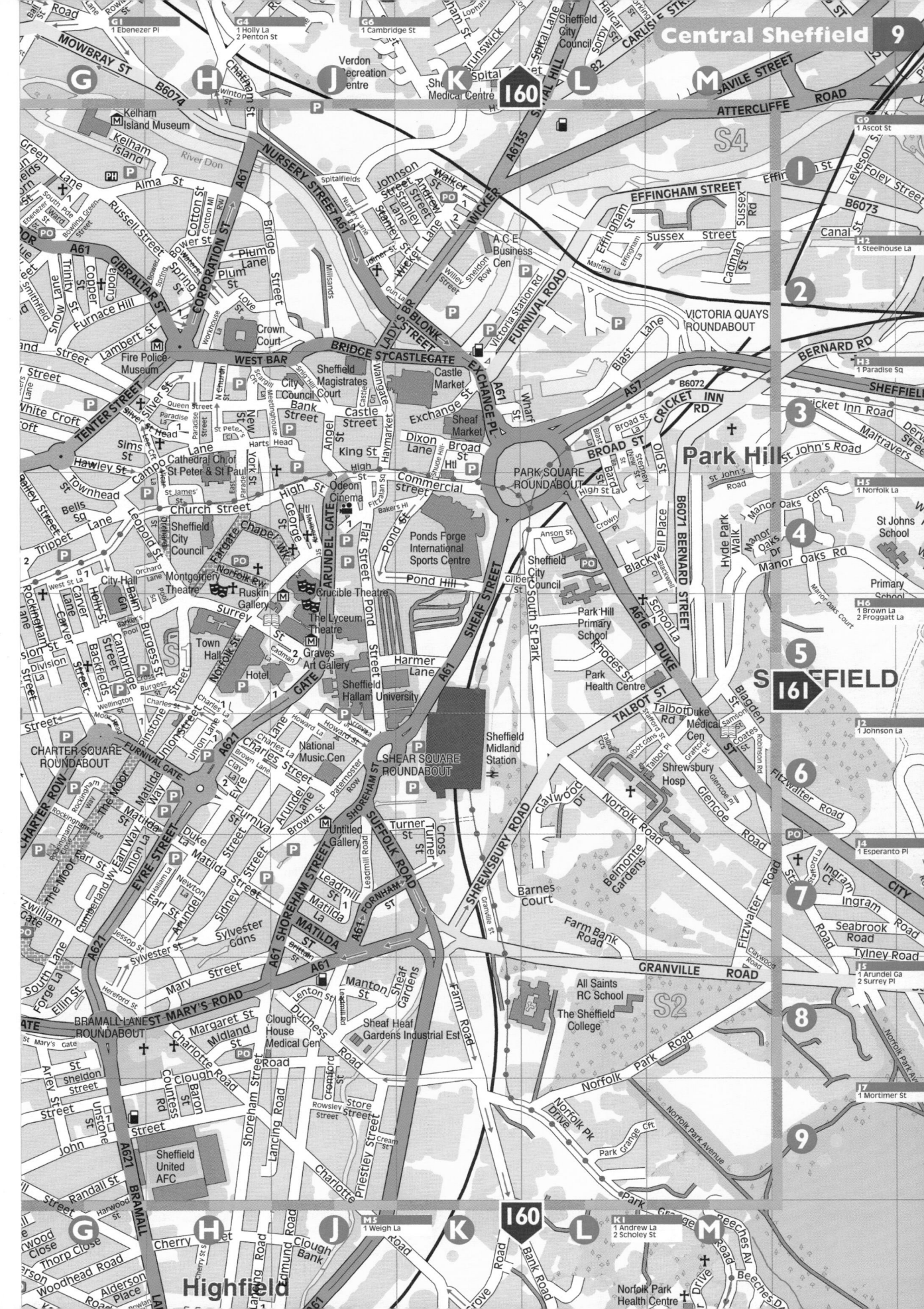
G1 1 Ebenezer Pl
G4 1 Holly La 2 Penton St
G6 1 Cambridge St
G9 1 Ascot St
H2 1 Steelhouse La
H3 1 Paradise Sq
H5 1 Norfolk La
H6 1 Brown La 2 Froggatt La
J2 1 Johnson La
J4 1 Esperanto Pl
J5 1 Arundel Ga 2 Surrey Pl
J7 1 Mortimer St
M5 1 Weigh La
K1 1 Andrew La 2 Scholey St
MOWBRAY ST
Verdon Recreation Centre
Sheffield City Council
Spital Hill
ATTERCLIFFE ROAD
SAVILE STREET
Kelham Island Museum
Kelham Island
River Don
NURSERY STREET A61
WICKER
EFFINGHAM STREET
B6073
Sussex Street
A.C.E. Business Cen
CORPORATION ST
GIBRALTAR ST
FURNIVAL ROAD
VICTORIA QUAYS ROUNDABOUT
Crown Court
Fire Police Museum
WEST BAR
BRIDGE ST
CASTLEGATE
BERNARD RD
Sheffield Magistrates Court
Castle Market
City Council
Bank Street
Castle Street
TENTER STREET
Cathedral Ch of St Peter & St Paul
Sheaf Market
CRICKET INN RD
Park Hill
PARK SQUARE ROUNDABOUT
Commercial Street
Odeon Cinema
Ponds Forge International Sports Centre
Church Street
Sheffield City Council
ARUNDEL GATE
Pond Hill
Crucible Theatre
Montgomery Theatre
Ruskin Gallery
The Lyceum Theatre
SHEAF STREET
Park Hill Primary School
Town Hall
Graves Art Gallery
Harmer Lane
Hotel
Sheffield Hallam University
Park Health Centre
SHEFFIELD
161
Duke Medical Cen
Shrewsbury Hosp
CHARTER SQUARE ROUNDABOUT
FURNIVAL GATE
National Music Cen
SHEAR SQUARE ROUNDABOUT
Sheffield Midland Station
CHARTER ROW
The Moor
EYRE STREET
Untitled Gallery
SHOREHAM STREET
SUFFOLK ROAD
SHREWSBURY ROAD
Norfolk Road
Barnes Court
Farm Bank Road
GRANVILLE ROAD
MATILDA ST
ST MARY'S ROAD
All Saints RC School
The Sheffield College
S2
BRAMALL LANE ROUNDABOUT
Clough House Medical Cen
Sheaf Heaf Gardens Industrial Est
Farm Road
Norfolk Park Road
Sheffield United AFC
BRAMALL
Norfolk Park Avenue
Highfield
Norfolk Park Health Centre
160

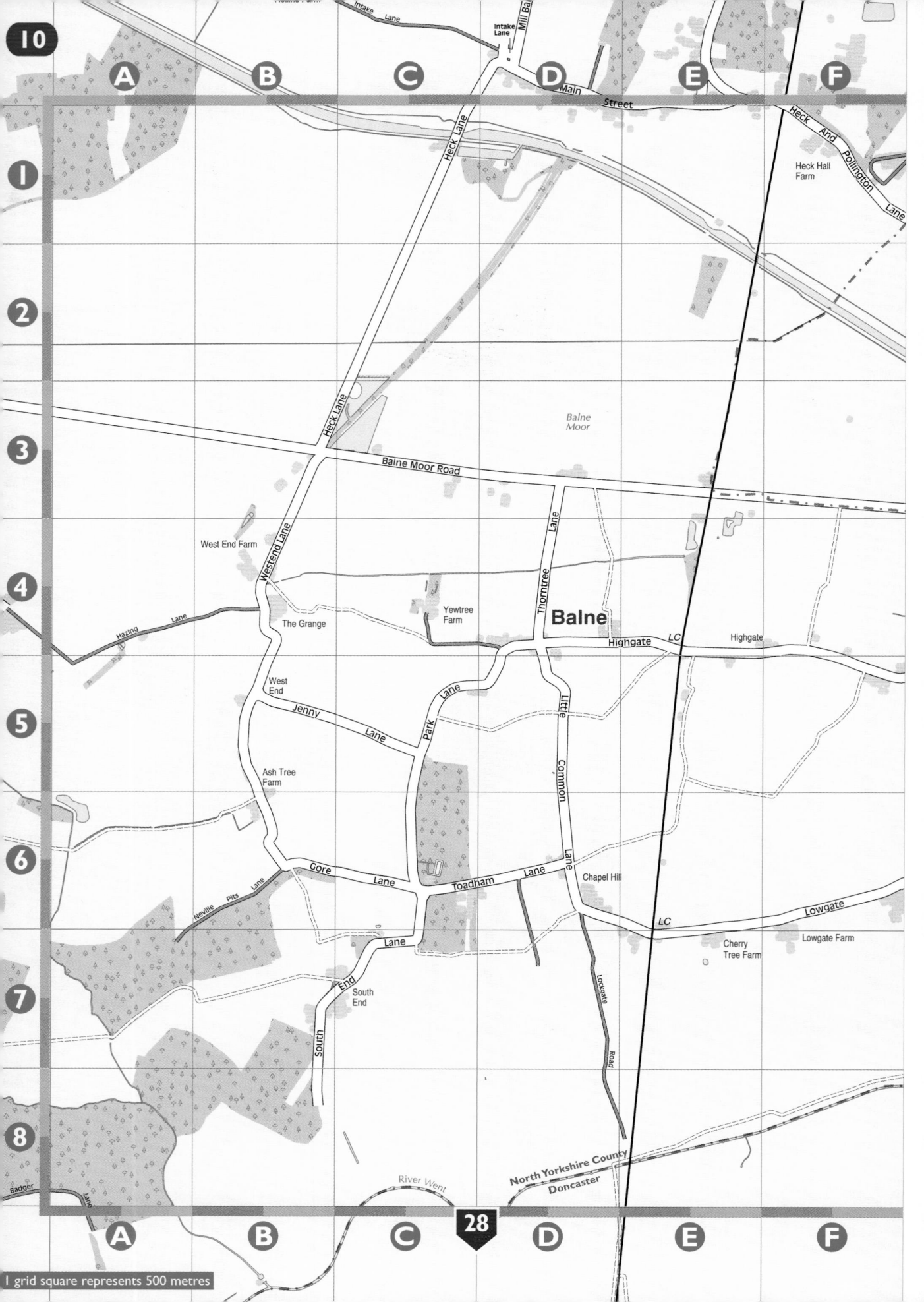

A
B
C
D
E
F
1
2
3
4
5
6
7
8
Intake Lane
Intake Lane
Mill Ba
Main Street
Heck And Pollington Lane
Heck Hall Farm
Heck Lane
Balne Moor
Balne Moor Road
West End Farm
Westend Lane
Thorntree Lane
Yewtree Farm
Balne
Hazing Lane
The Grange
Highgate
LC
Highgate
West End
Jenny Lane
Park Lane
Little Common Lane
Ash Tree Farm
Gore Lane
Toadham Lane
Chapel Hill
Neville Pits Lane
Lowgate
LC
Lowgate Farm
Cherry Tree Farm
South End Lane
South End
Lockgate Road
North Yorkshire County
Doncaster
River Went
Badger Lane
28
1 grid square represents 500 metres

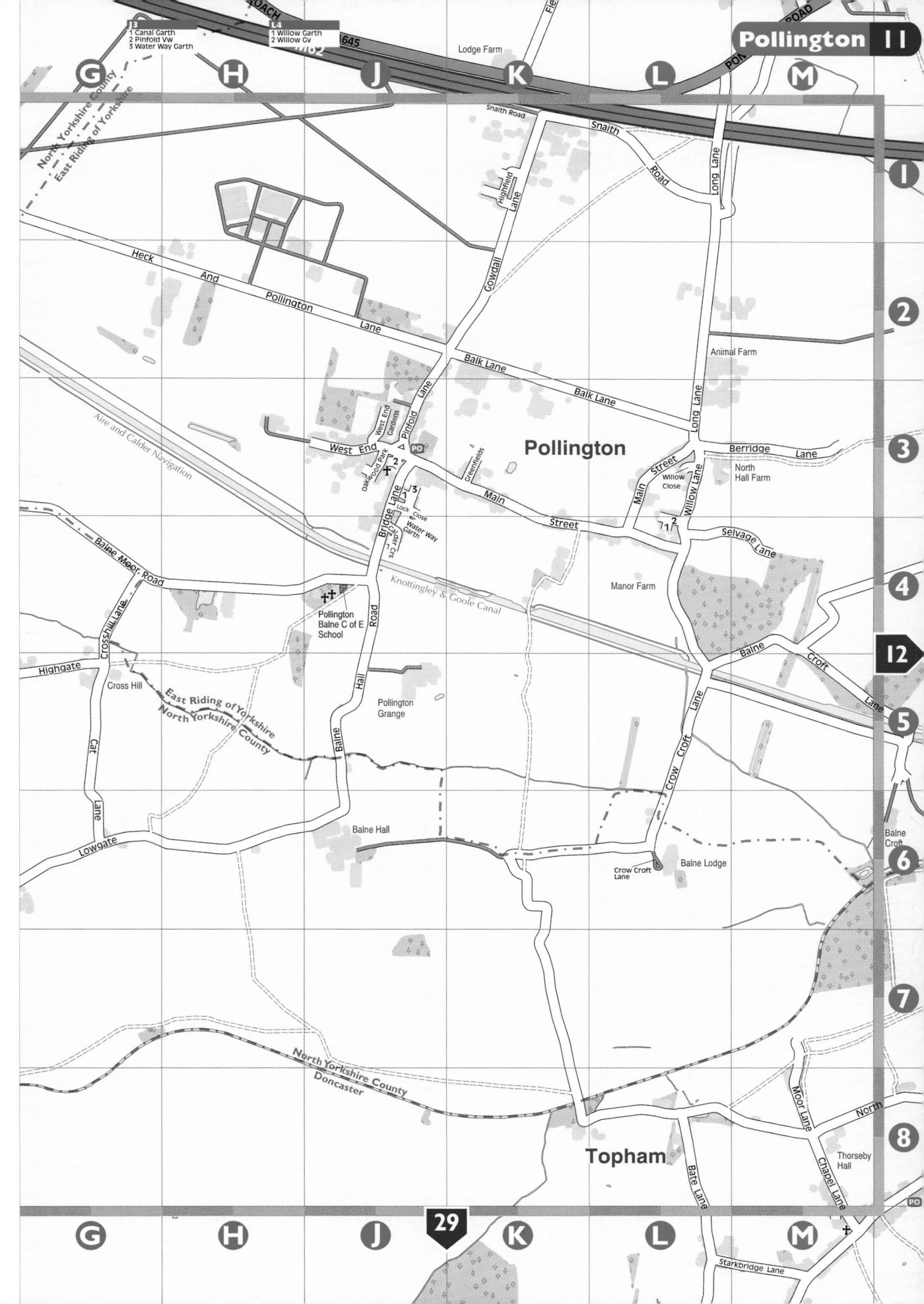

G H J K L M

1 Canal Garth
2 Pinfold Vw
3 Water Way Garth

1 Willow Garth
2 Willow Gv

1645

Lodge Farm

Snaith Road

Snaith Road

Long Lane

PO... ROAD

North Yorkshire County
East Riding of Yorkshire

Heck And Pollington Lane

Highfield Lane

Gowdall Lane

Balk Lane

Balk Lane

Animal Farm

Long Lane

Aire and Calder Navigation

West End Gardens

Pinfold Lane

Pollington

Berridge Lane

West End

PO

Greenfields

Main

Street

Willow Close

North Hall Farm

Oakwood Park

Bridge Lane

Lock

Calder Crs

Water Way Garth

Main

Street

Street

Willow Lane

Selvage Lane

Balne Moor Road

Crosshill Lane

Knottingley & Goole Canal

Pollington Balne C of E School

Manor Farm

Balne Croft Lane

Highgate

Cross Hill

East Riding of Yorkshire
North Yorkshire County

Balne Hall Road

Pollington Grange

Crow Croft Lane

Balne Croft Lane

Cat Lane

Lowgate

Balne Hall

Crow Croft Lane

Balne Lodge

North Yorkshire County
Doncaster

Moor Lane

North

Thorseby Hall

Topham

Bate Lane

Chapel Lane

PO

Starkbridge Lane

I 2 3 4 12 5 6 7 8

A   B   C   D   E   F

West Cowick

M62

Moor Hill

Camela House

Carr Lane

The Carr

Finnley's Lane

London Lane

Park Lane

Trans Pennine Trail

Phippin Parks

Park Farm

Southfield Reservoir

Lane

Trans Pennine Trail

Aire and Calder Navigation

Knottingley & Goole Canal

Balne Croft

New Ings

Eskholme

Plaice Hills Farm

Eskholme Lane

North Lane

New Junction Canal

North Lane

Broad Lane

Sykehouse Road

Marsh Hill Farm

Kirk Lane

Marsh Hill Lane

Warren Hall

Pincheon Green Lane

Pincheon Green

Thorseby Hall

PO

Mawson Green

Sykehouse

A   B   C   D   E   F

30

11

1 grid square represents 500 metres

East
Cowick

Butterfield
Close

Dowsons
Lane

High Stree

Back Lane

Goathead Lane

G   H   J   K   L   M

M62

A614(T)

Rivers Lane

Between Rivers Lane

Between

Oak Lane

Aire and Calder Navigation

M18

New Bridge

Greenland Lane

Greenland
Farm

Greenland

Lane

Greenland Farm

BARRIER BANK

A614(T)

BARRIER BANK

Beever's Bridge

Poplars
Farm

ng Lane

Johnny

I4

East Riding of Yorkshire

Doncaster

River Don

A614

SELBY ROAD

Chatterton
Farm

Reedholme Lane

Reedholme
Common

Bank House

Reedholme Lane

Oak Lane

Rudgate Lane

Banks Farm

Moorends Road

Dikes
Marsh

Rabbit Hill Farm

1
2
3
4
5
6
7
8

G   H   J   31   K   L   M

Hadds Lane

Bridge

A B C D E F

Bridge Lane

Paper Mill Road

Dutch

Moor   Road

Elms Farm

Johnny Moor Long Lane

Commons Farm

Moor Road

Hales

Hookmoor Farm

Top House

Moor Road

LC

Johnny Moor Long Lane

Greenland

Priory Farm

LC

LC

Snaith & Cowick Moors

Moorends Road

LC

Moor Ends

LC

A B C D E F

1 grid square represents 500 metres

I
2
3
4
13
5
6
7
8

G   H   J   St Helena   K   L   M

Hook Pastu

rfields

Goole
Grange

Park
Farm

I

2

3

4

Rawcliffe
Moors

5

6

7

Goole
Moors

8

G   H   J   33   K   L   M

ding of Yorkshire
Doncaster

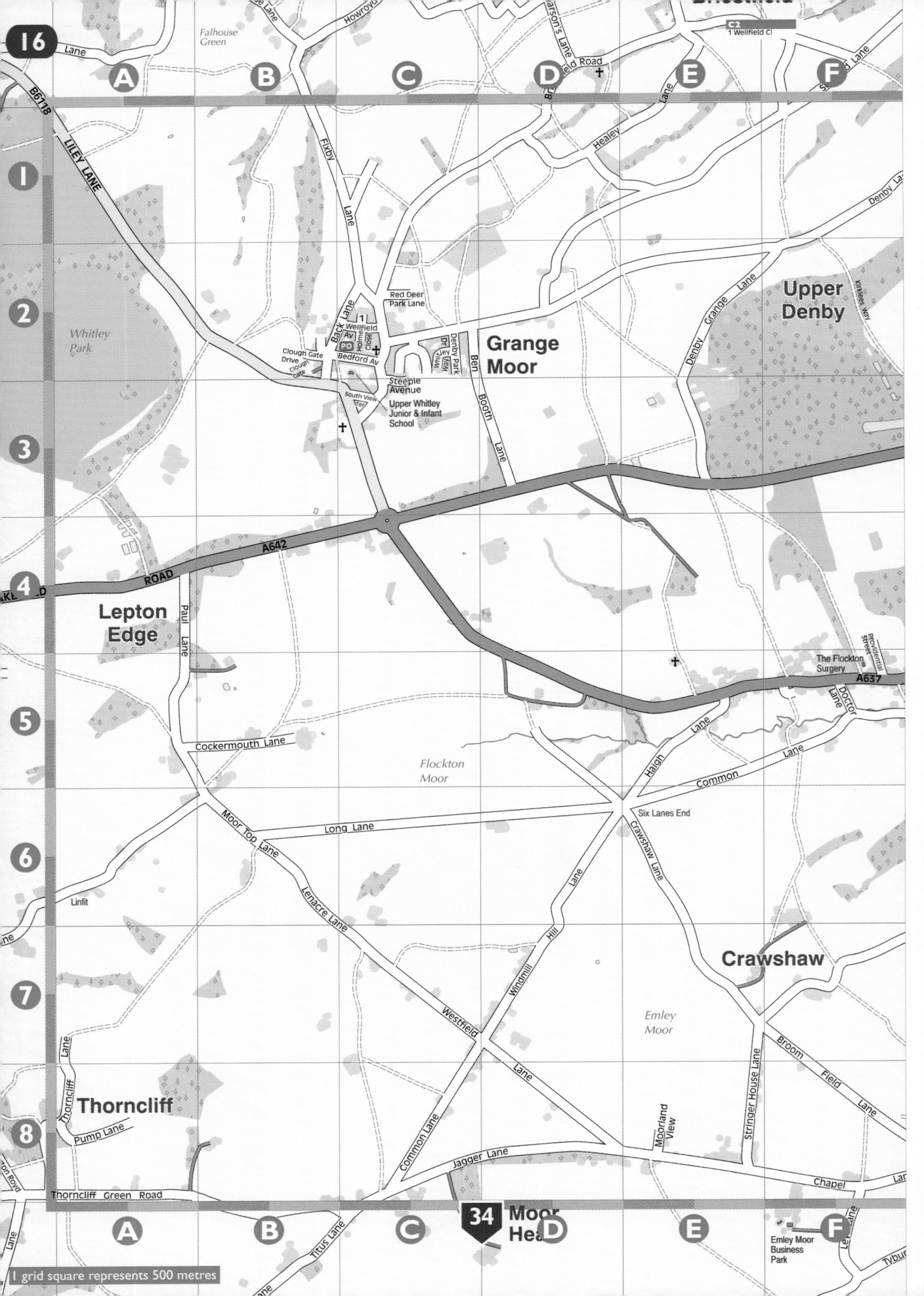

A B C D E F

I

2

3

4

5

6

7

8

A B C D E F

B6118

Lane

Falhouse Green

LILEY LANE

Howroyd Lane

Fixby Lane

Whitley Park

Red Deer Park Lane

Back Lane

Wellfield
Av
Holme
PO Liley
Cl
HM
View

Denby Park Dr

Grange Moor

Clough Gate Drive
Clough Gate

Bedford Av

South View Ter

Steeple Avenue

Upper Whitley Junior & Infant School

Ben Booth Lane

Healey Lane

Denby Lane

Upper Denby

Kirklees Way

Denby Grange Lane

C2
1 Wellfield Cl

A642

ROAD

KL D

Lepton Edge

Paul Lane

Providential Street

The Flockton Surgery

A637

Doctor Lane

Cockermouth Lane

Flockton Moor

Long Lane

Moor Top Lane

Lenacre Lane

Linfit

Haigh Lane

Common Lane

Six Lanes End

Lane

Crawshaw Lane

Crawshaw

Windmill Hill

Westfield Lane

Emley Moor

Stringer House Lane

Broom Field Lane

Lane

Thorncliff

Pump Lane

Common Lane

Moorland View

Jagger Lane

Chapel Lane

Thorncliff Green Road

34 **Moor Head**

Emley Moor Business Park

Tyburn

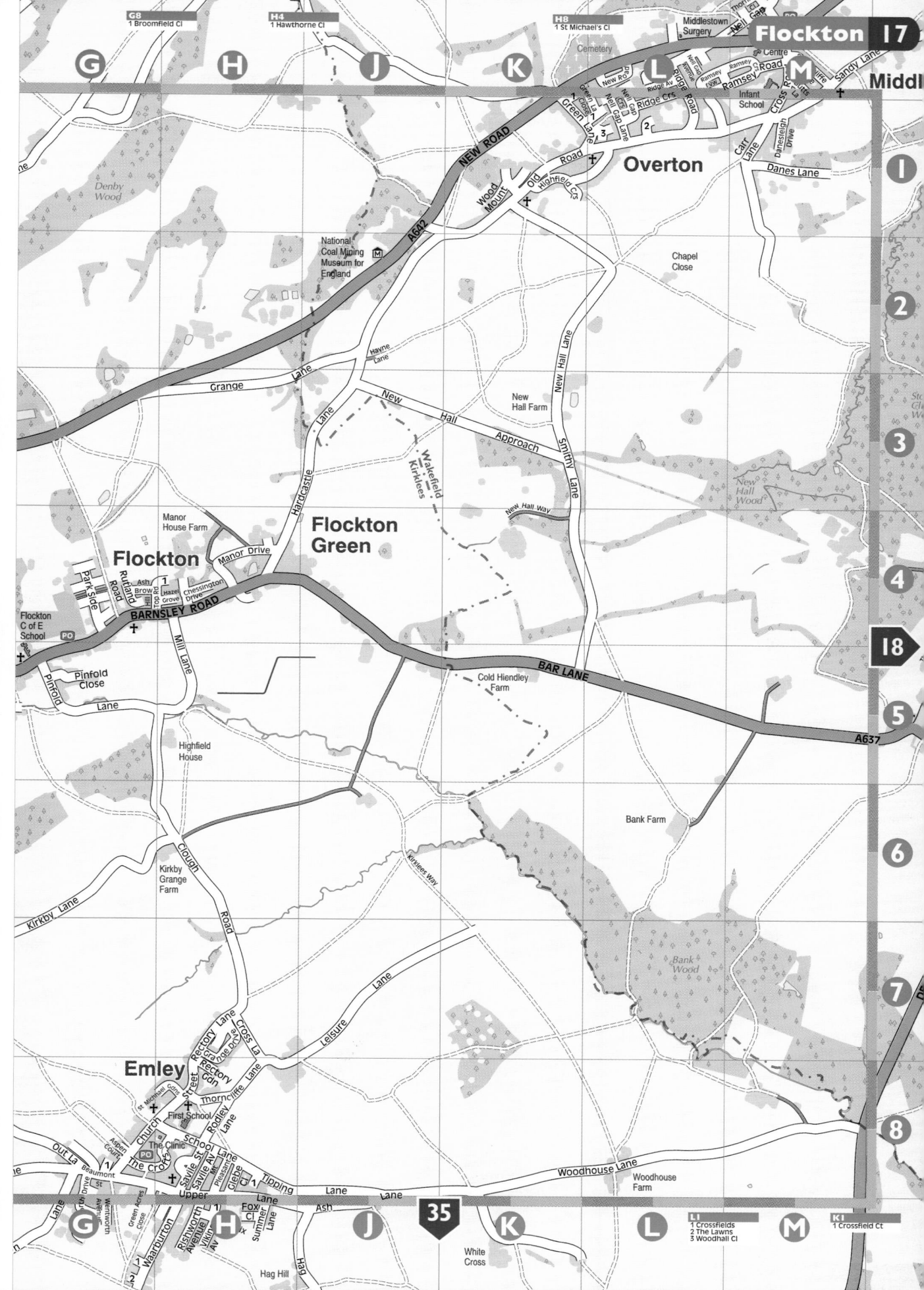
G8
1 Broomfield Cl
H4
1 Hawthorne Cl
H8
1 St Michael's Cl
Middlestown Surgery
Cemetery
Overton
Denby Wood
NEW ROAD
A642
National Coal Mining Museum for England
Chapel Close
Grange Lane
Hayne Lane
New Hall Approach
New Hall Farm
New Hall Lane
Smithy Lane
New Hall Wood
New Hall Way
Wakefield
Kirklees
Hardcastle Lane
Manor House Farm
Flockton
Flockton Green
Manor Drive
Chessington Drive
Rutland Road
Park Side
BARNSLEY ROAD
Flockton C of E School
Pinfold Close
Pinfold Lane
Mill Lane
Cold Hiendley Farm
BAR LANE
A637
Highfield House
Bank Farm
Kirkby Grange Farm
Kirkby Lane
Clough Road
Kirklees Way
Bank Wood
Leisure Lane
Emley
Rectory Lane
Cross La
Thorncliffe Lane
First School
The Clinic
School Lane
Woodhouse Lane
Woodhouse Farm
Tipping Lane
Upper Lane
White Cross
Hag Hill
L1
1 Crossfields
2 The Lawns
3 Woodhall Cl
K1
1 Crossfield Ct

18

35

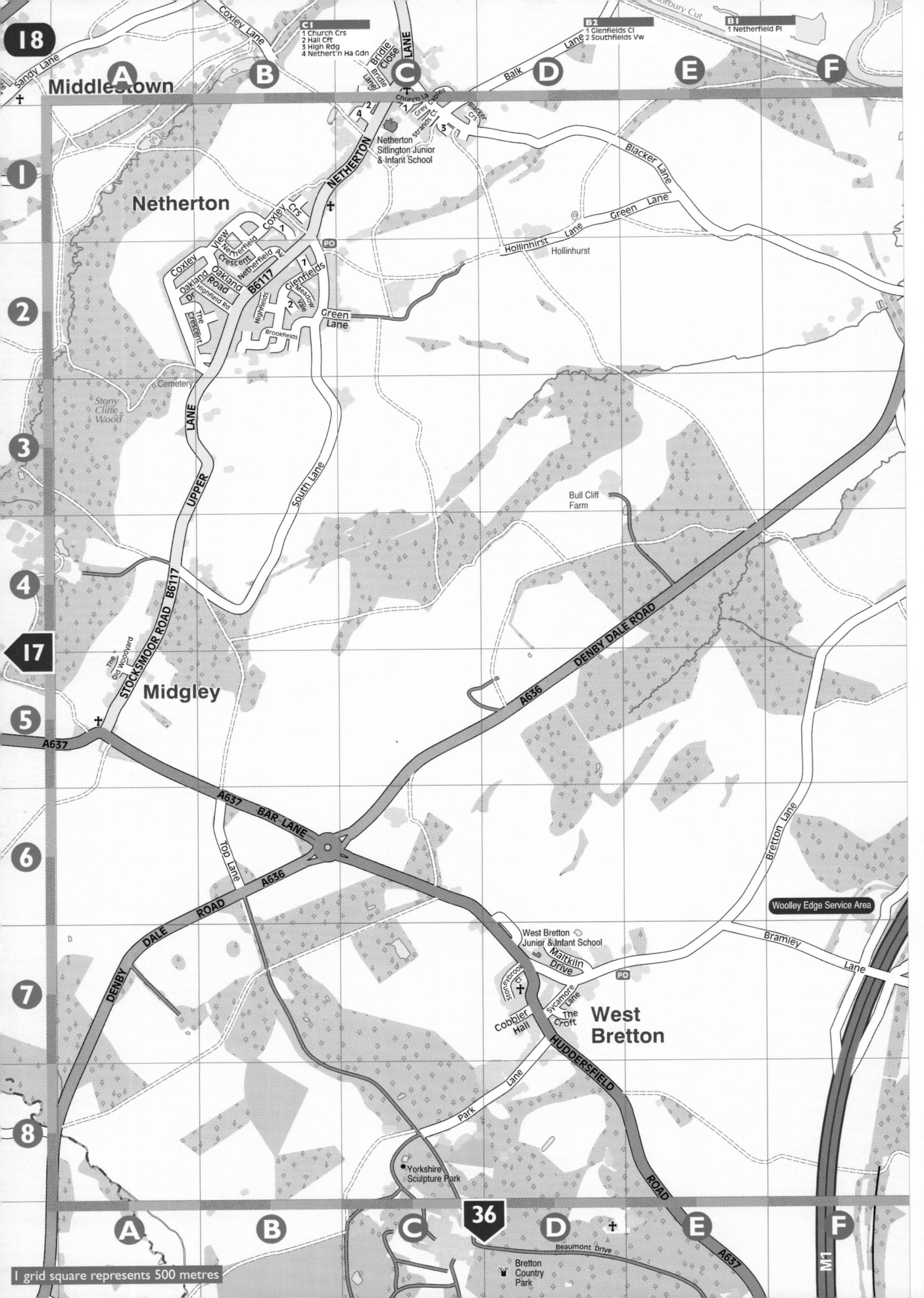
18
17
36
C1
1 Church Crs
2 Hall Cft
3 High Rdg
4 Nethert'n Ha Gdn
B2
1 Glenfields Cl
2 Southfields Vw
B1
1 Netherfield Pl
Middlestown
Sandy Lane
Coxley Lane
Bridle Close
Bridle Lane
LANE
Balk Lane
Church La
Grey Gables
Strands Ct
Blacker Crs
Netherton Sitlington Junior & Infant School
NETHERTON
Blacker Lane
Green Lane
Netherton
Coxley Crs
Coxley View
Netherfield Crescent
Netherfield Av
Coxley
Oakland Road
Oakland Dr
Highfield Rd
The Crescent
B6117
Glenfields
Meadow Vale
Highfields
Brookfields
Green Lane
Hollinhirst Lane
Hollinhurst
PO
Cemetery
Stony Cliffe Wood
UPPER LANE
South Lane
Bull Cliff Farm
STOCKSMOOR ROAD B6117
The Old Woodyard
Midgley
DENBY DALE ROAD
A636
A637
A637 BAR LANE
Top Lane
A636
DENBY DALE ROAD
Bretton Lane
Woolley Edge Service Area
Bramley Lane
West Bretton Junior & Infant School
Maltkiln Drive
Stoneybrook Cl
Sycamore Lane
The Croft
Cobbler Hall
West Bretton
HUDDERSFIELD ROAD
Park Lane
Yorkshire Sculpture Park
Beaumont Drive
Bretton Country Park
M1
A
B
C
D
E
F
1
2
3
4
5
6
7
8
1 grid square represents 500 metres

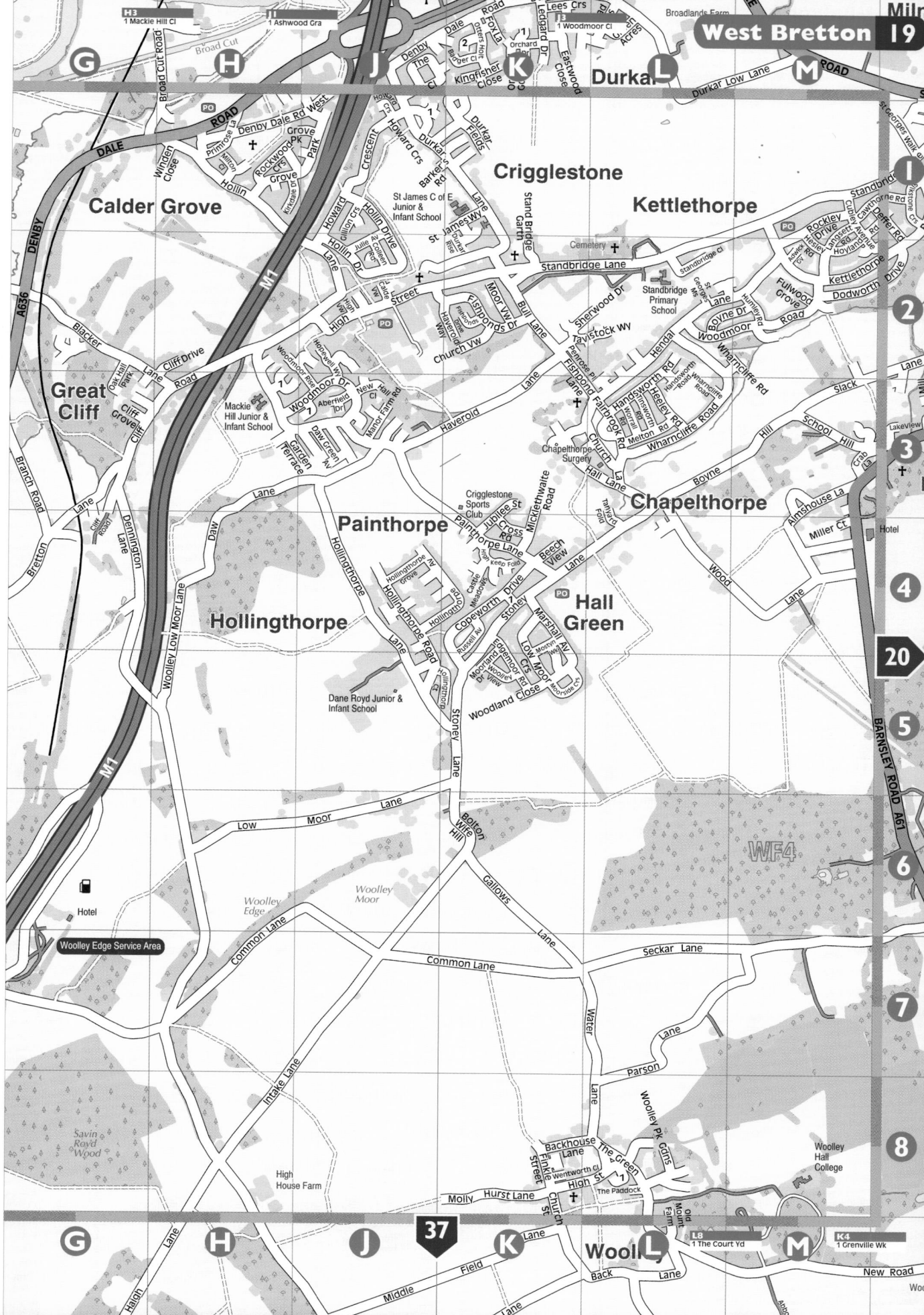
H3 1 Mackie Hill Cl
J1 1 Ashwood Gra
J3 1 Woodmoor Cl
Calder Grove
Crigglestone
Kettlethorpe
Great Cliff
Painthorpe
Chapelthorpe
Hollingthorpe
Hall Green
Durkar
St James C of E Junior & Infant School
Standbridge Primary School
Mackie Hill Junior & Infant School
Chapelthorpe Surgery
Crigglestone Sports Club
Dane Royd Junior & Infant School
Woolley Edge Service Area
Hotel
Woolley Moor
Woolley Edge
Savin Royd Wood
High House Farm
Woolley Hall College
WF4
Standbridge Lane
Denby Dale Road
Barnsley Road A61
M1
A636
Common Lane
Seckar Lane
Low Moor Lane
Woolley Low Moor Lane
Stoney Lane
Gallows Lane
Intake Lane
Water Lane
Parson Lane
Molly Hurst Lane
Backhouse Lane
High St
Wentworth Cl
Woolley Pk Gdns
The Green
The Paddock
Middle Field Lane
Back Lane
New Road
Haveroid Lane
Cliff Road
Blacker Lane
Denby Dale Rd West
Wharncliffe Road
Woodmoor Road
Dodworth Drive
L8 1 The Court Yd
K4 1 Grenville Wk
37
20

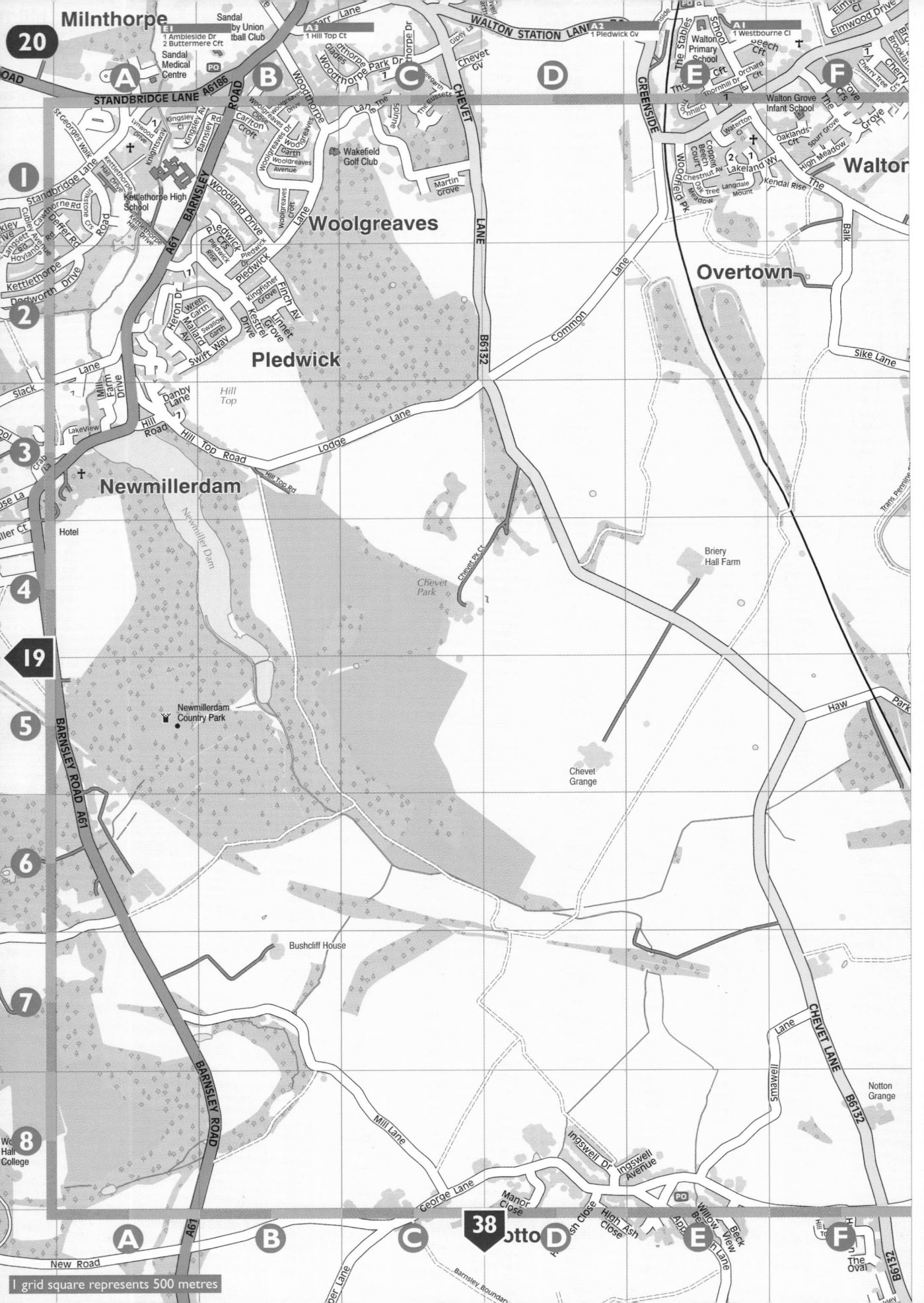

Milnthorpe
Sandal Medical Centre
Woolgreaves
Wakefield Golf Club
Kettlethorpe High School
Pledwick
Newmillerdam
Hotel
Newmillerdam Country Park
Chevet Park
Overtown
Walton
Walton Primary School
Walton Grove Infant School
Briery Hall Farm
Chevet Grange
Bushcliff House
Notton Grange
STANDBRIDGE LANE A6186
WALTON STATION LANE
BARNSLEY ROAD A61
CHEVET LANE B6132
Common Lane
Lodge Lane
Hill Top Road
Mill Lane
George Lane
New Road
Sike Lane
Haw Park
Smawell Lane
Ingswell Avenue
Newmiller Dam
Hill Top
E1 1 Ambleside Dr 2 Buttermere Cft
A3 1 Hill Top Ct
A2 1 Pledwick Gv
A1 1 Westbourne Cl
19
38
1 grid square represents 500 metres

N
Crofton

L6
1 Hooton Crs
2 Millward St

G   H   J   K   L

Thorntree
Hill

Hare
Park

Brooklands Rd

Brooklands Rd

Tree Road

Waterton
Park Golf
Club

Brockwood Ct

Hotel

Elland's Pennine Trail

Santingley Grange

Anglers
Country
Park

Wintersett

Santingley Lane

Wintersett Lane

Long Lane

Back Lane

Dam Lane

**Haw
Park**

Haw   Park   Lane

Ferry Top Lane

**Wintersett
Reservoir**

Cold
Hiendley
Reservoir

Lane

Lane

Lakeside

Estate

Nostell

Common Ing Lane

Brunswick

Churchfields

George St

Cemetery

**Havercro
Ryhill**

St James
Court

22

5

6

Cold

Hiendley

Ryhill Pits Lane

Cold Hiendley

Common

Lane

Station

Falkirk Drive

Westfield

Sunny Bank

Willowgarth
Close

Road

Charles

Charles
St

Market

Latfields La

Chapel St

St Ann's
Lane

Cemetery
Rd

Primary
School

PO

Mulberry Av

Quarry
Mount

Mill La

Top
Orch

Mulberry
Place

Havercroft
Health Centre

Havercroft
Junior
& Infant School

Greenside

Brier

Cowr

7

Barnsley   Canal (disused)

Lane

Barnsley   Boundary   Walk

Ten Lands Lane

Hall Field La

B6428

Navvy   Lane

Church

Lane

Ellis Laithe

Notton Lane

39

Barnsley   Boundary   Walk

LANE

B6428

High Well

Church

G   H   J   K   L   M

1

2

3

4

5

6

7

8

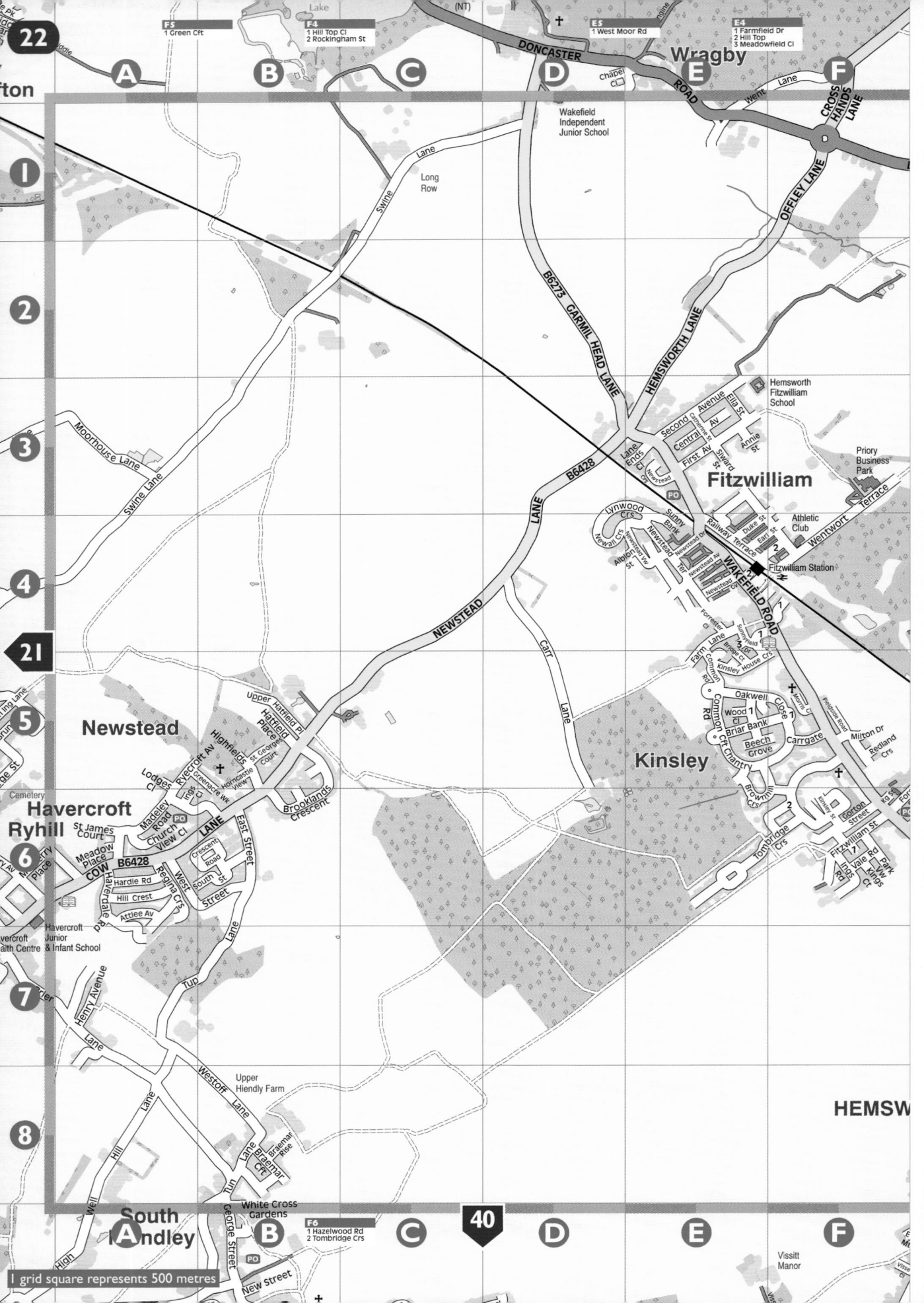

A B C D E F

F5
1 Green Cft

F4
1 Hill Top Cl
2 Rockingham St

E5
1 West Moor Rd

E4
1 Farmfield Dr
2 Hill Top
3 Meadowfield Cl

F6
1 Hazelwood Rd
2 Tombridge Crs

Lake
(NT)

DONCASTER

Wragby

ROAD

CROSS HANDS LANE

OFFLEY LANE

Chapel Cl

Wakefield Independent Junior School

Swine

Lane

Long Row

B6273 GARMIL HEAD LANE

HEMSWORTH LANE

Went Lane

Hemsworth Fitzwilliam School

Second Avenue

Central Av

Ella St

Catherine St

First Av

Sward

Annie St

Priory Business Park

B6428

Lane Ends

Newstead Ct

Fitzwilliam

Wentworth Terrace

Lynwood Crs

Newall Crs

Sunny Bank

Railway Terrace

Duke St

Earl St

Athletic Club

PO

NEWSTEAD

Albion St

Newstead Vw

Newstead Rd

Newstead Ter

Newstead

WAKEFIELD ROAD

Fitzwilliam Station

Carr

Lane

Forrester

Farm Lane

Common

Kinsley House Crs

Sunny Field

Bridge Cl

Morris Cl

Moorhouse Lane

Swine Lane

Newstead

Upper Hatfield Pl

Hatfield Place

Highfields

Greenacre Wk

Horncastle View

St Georges Court

Ryecroft Av

Lodges Cl

Madeley Road

Brooklands Crescent

Church View Cl

Crescent Road

East Street

South St

PO

LANE

Cemetery

Havercroft

Ryhill

St James Court

Meadow Place

COW

B6428

Hardie Rd

Hill Crest

Attlee Av

Haverdale Rd

West Lane

Regina Crs

Street

Berry Place

Havercroft Junior & Infant School

vercroft lth Centre

Kinsley

Common Rd

Oakwell Close

Wood Cl

Briar Bank

Beech Grove

Chantry

Carrgate

Brown

Milton Dr

Redland Crs

Tombridge Crs

Gorton Street

Fitzwilliam St

Vale Rd

Kings

Park

Henry Avenue

Lane

Westoft Lane

Tup Lane

Upper Hiendly Farm

HEMSW

Well Hill

Turn Lane

George Street

Braemar Rise

Braemar Cft

White Cross Gardens

South ndley

PO

New Street

Vissitt Manor

21

40

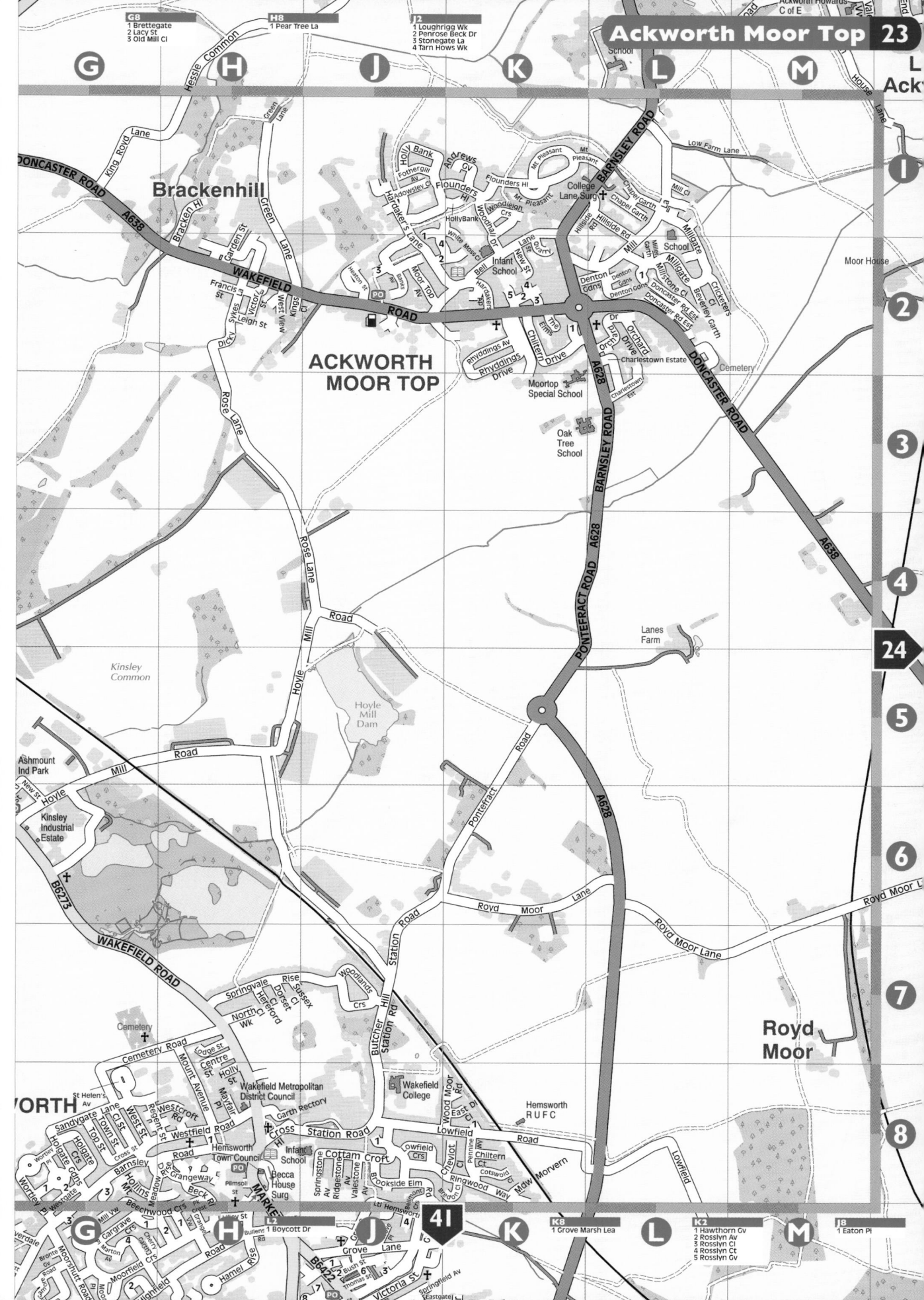
G8
1 Brettegate
2 Lacy St
3 Old Mill Cl
H8
1 Pear Tree La
J2
1 Loughrigg Wk
2 Penrose Beck Dr
3 Stonegate La
4 Tarn Hows Wk
Brackenhill
ACKWORTH MOOR TOP
DONCASTER ROAD
WAKEFIELD ROAD
BARNSLEY ROAD
PONTEFRACT ROAD
Kinsley Common
Hoyle Mill Dam
Ashmount Ind Park
Kinsley Industrial Estate
Lanes Farm
Moor House
Cemetery
Moortop Special School
Oak Tree School
Infant School
College Lane Surg
Charlestown Estate
Royd Moor Lane
Royd Moor
Wakefield College
Wakefield Metropolitan District Council
Hemsworth RUFC
Hemsworth Town Council
Becca House Surg
24
41
L2
1 Boycott Dr
K8
1 Grove Marsh Lea
K2
1 Hawthorn Gv
2 Rosslyn Av
3 Rosslyn Cl
4 Rosslyn Ct
5 Rosslyn Gv
J8
1 Eaton Pl

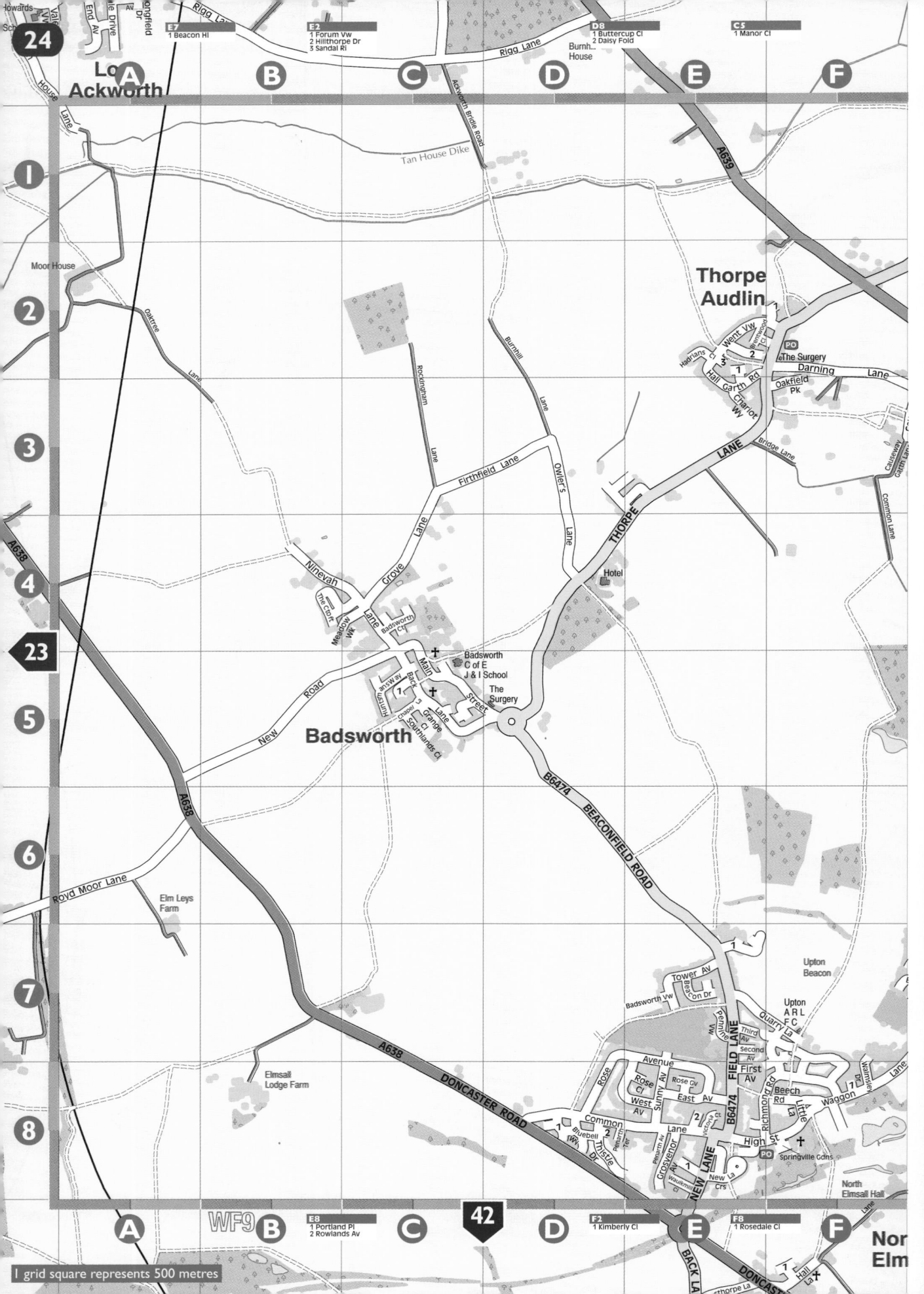

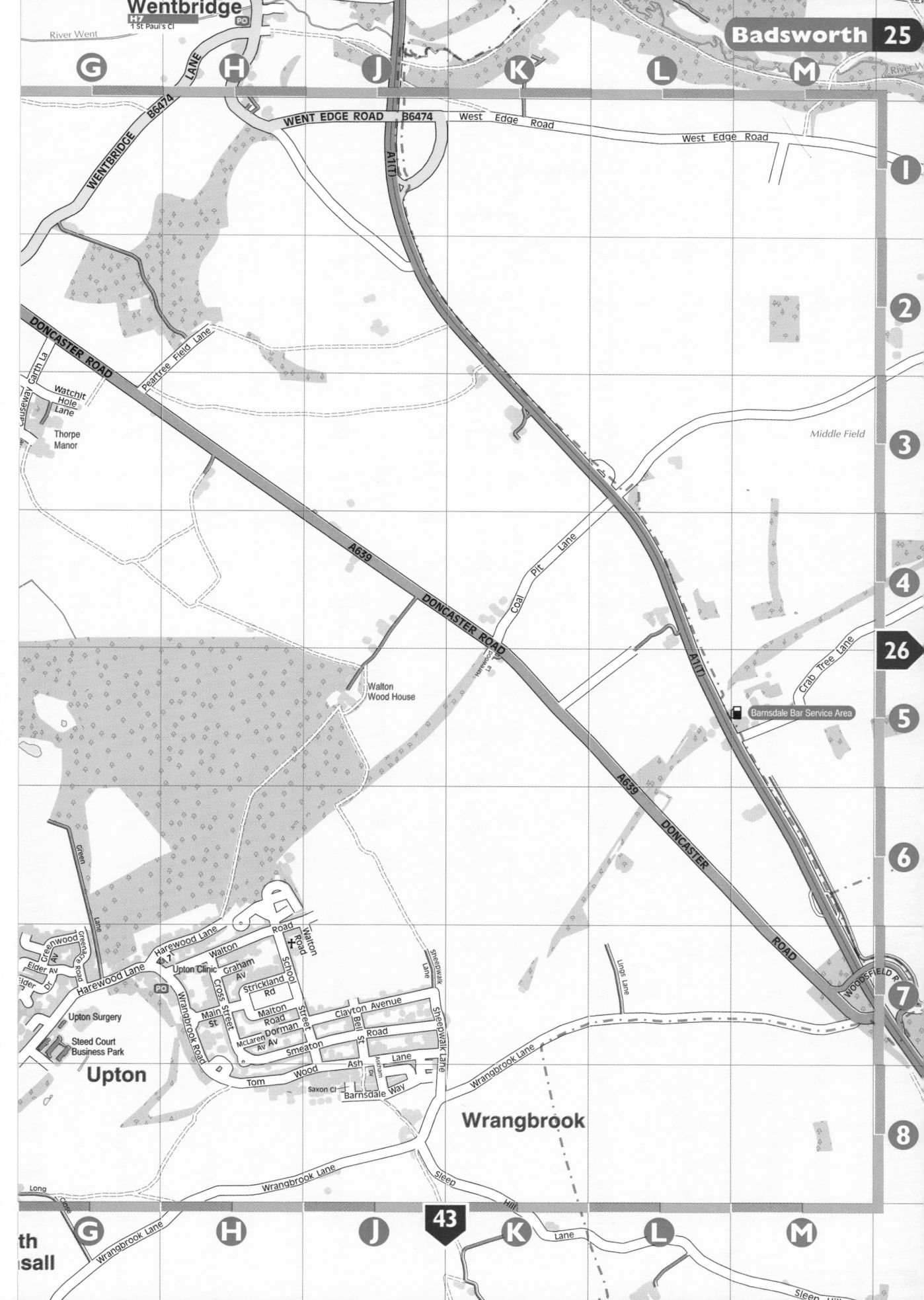

Wentbridge
H7
1 St Paul's Cl

River Went

G   H   J   K   L   M

WENT EDGE ROAD   B6474   West   Edge   Road

West Edge Road

WENTBRIDGE   B6474

A1(T)

1

DONCASTER ROAD

Peartree Field Lane

2

Causeway Garth La

Watchit
Hole
Lane

Thorpe
Manor

Middle Field

3

A639

Coal   Pit   Lane

DONCASTER ROAD

4

26

A1(T)

Walton
Wood House

Harewood La

Barnsdale Bar Service Area

5

A639

DONCASTER

Green

ROAD

6

Greenwood
AV

Greenacre Road

Elder AV

Eder dr

Harewood Lane

Road

Walton

Walton

Lane

Sheepwalk

Lane

WOODSFIELD R

7

Harewood Lane H7

Upton Clinic

Graham
AV

Strickland
Rd

Upton Surgery

Main
St

Cross
St

Malton
Road

McLaren
Av AV

Dorman
Av

Clayton Avenue

Bell
St

Road

Sheepwalk Lane

Lings Lane

Wrangbrook Road

PO

School Street

Smeaton

Tom
Wood

Ash
Lane

Lane

Aselum

Steed Court
Business Park

Upton

Saxon Cl

Barnsdale Way

Wrangbrook Lane

Wrangbrook

8

Long

Close

Wrangbrook Lane

Sleep

Hill

G   H   J   **43**   K   L   M

th

sall

Wrangbrook Lane

Lane

Sleep Hill

Crab Tree Lane

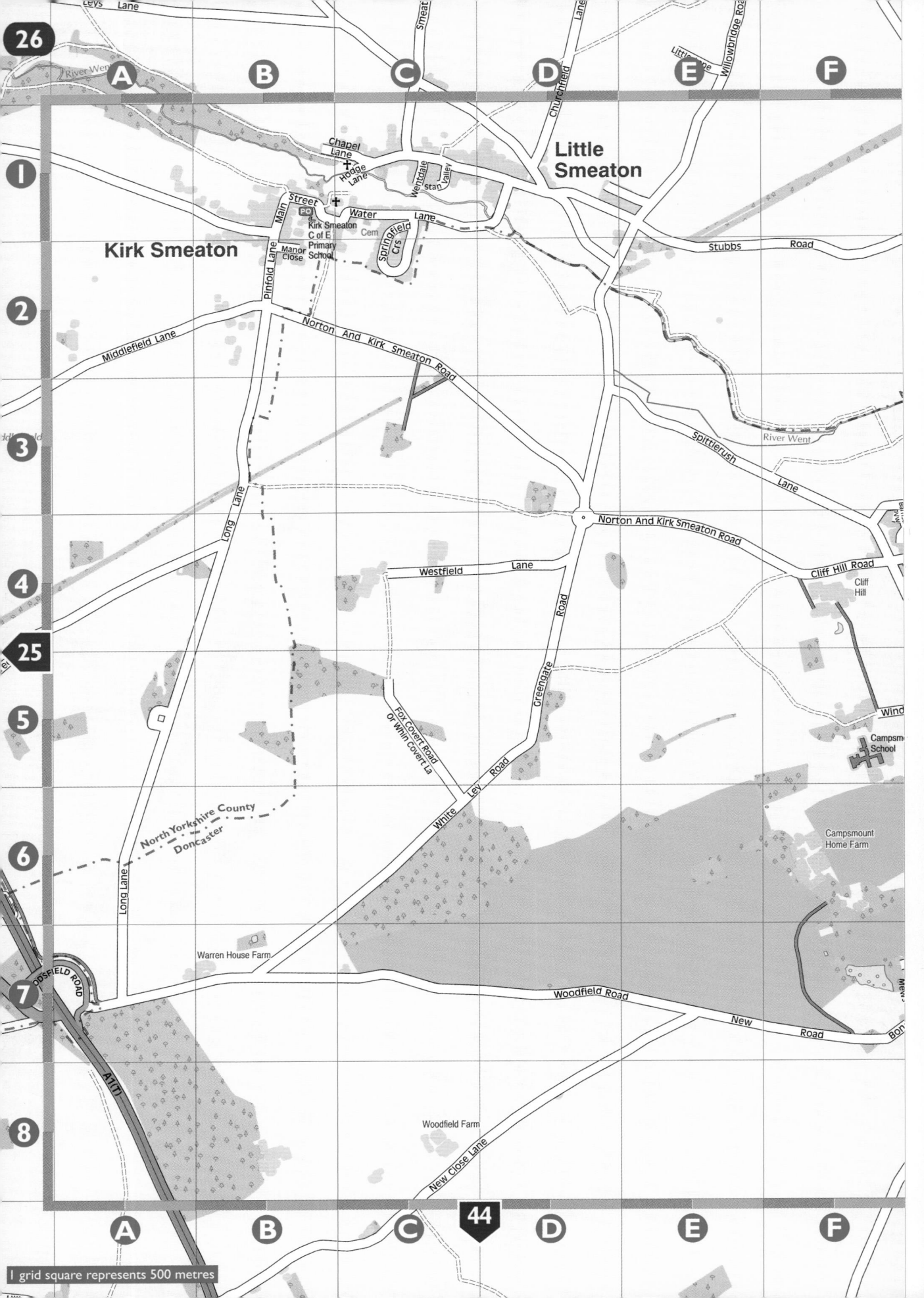

A B C D E F

River Went

Leys Lane

Smeat

Lane

Willowbridge Ro

Little Lane

Chapel
Lane

Little
Smeaton

1

Hodge
Lane

Wentdale
stan
Valley

Street

Main Street

PO

Water
Lane

Kirk Smeaton
C of E
Primary
School

Cem

Springfield
Crs

Stubbs   Road

Kirk Smeaton

Pinfold Lane

Manor
Close

2

Middlefield Lane

Norton And Kirk Smeaton Road

River Went

Spittlerush

3

ddlefield

Long Lane

Lane

Norton And Kirk Smeaton Road

Cliff Hill Road

4

Westfield   Lane

Cliff
Hill

Greengate

Road

Campsm
School

Wind

5

Fox Covert Road
Or Whin Covert La

North Yorkshire County
Doncaster

White   Ley   Road

Campsmount
Home Farm

6

Long Lane

ODSFIELD ROAD

Warren House Farm

7

Woodfield Road

New   Road

Bon

A1(T)

Woodfield Farm

New Close Lane

8

A B C   D E F

G6
1 Byron Av
2 Sherwood Cl

G7
1 Campsmount

H4
1 Linkway
2 Orchard Cl

G H J K L M

Common Lane

A19

SELBY ROAD

Badger Lane

Common Lane

Badger

Walden Stubbs

River Went

LC

LC

Went Bridge

LC

Wentbank House

Tanpit Lane

Stubbs Lane

North Yorkshire County
Doncaster

Norton Priory

Norton Mill Lane

Walden Stubbs Road

Priory Road Or Hall Lane

Norton Common Farm

Back Lane

Broc-O-Bank

Newthorpe Rd

Forrester's Cl Bse

West End

Ryecroft Av

Road

Fir Tree Drive

The Rd

Manor Close

Adelaide Rd

PO

Trafford Rd

Arundel Rd

Headingley

Orchard Dr

Arundel Dr

High Street

Station Road

Manor Garth

Quarry Road

Lyndhurst Close

Lyndhurst Dr

Ashburnham Close

Denver Road

Swan Syke Dr

Drynurst Close

Norton Common Lane

LC

New Road

Norton

Pinfold Lane

Common Lane

Lyndhurst Rise

Cridling Gardens

Norton County Junior & Infant School

Ryecroft

Balk

Stygate Lane

mill Lane

Road

Campsall Balk

Norton Common Road

28

Shakespeare Av

Tennyson Av

Wordsworth Av

Church Drive

Welling Drive

Chilla Drive

Glebe Road

East View

Grange Road

Willow Road

Field Road

Norton Common Road

LC

Willow Garth

6

DN6

Campsall

Cemetery

Woodlands Rise

Braytn Cl

Cedar Walk

Loxley Mount

The Avenue

Campsall Park Drive

Campsall Hall Road

Vaughan Road

Beech Road

Church View

Field Road

Askern Swimming Pool

Campsall Road

Hilton St

A19

High Street

Back Lane

Orchard Rd

Barnsdale Lane

Cherry Garth

Sutton

Woodgarth

Burghwallis Road

Woodgarth Road

Spa Ter

Hill

Chapel

Station Rd

PO

LC

Sunnymede Crs

Queen's Road

King's Road

Sunnymede Terrace

Sunnymede Av

King's Ter

Eastfield Drive

Thompson

Poplar Cl

Mayfield Ter

Marlborough

Bellevue

Beverley

Rd

Marlborough Av

Highfield Road

Blossom Av

Westfield Crs

Infant Sch

Rusty Moor Lane

Newmarc

Norbreck

7

ASKERN

8

Instoneville

Alan Crs

Sherwood Av

Davis Rd

Theodore

Llewelyn Crescent

Mary Rd

Anita Rd

Airstone Rd

Green Park

Manor Road

Victoria Road

The Avenue

Instone Terrace

Market Place

High Street

Askern Health Centre

Llewelyn Crs

Alfred Road

Manor Way

Askern Spa Junior School

45

G H J K L M

J4
1 Ashburnham Wk

H6
1 Langleys Rd

Rushy Moor

Rushy

BOW

I
2
3
4
5
6
7
8

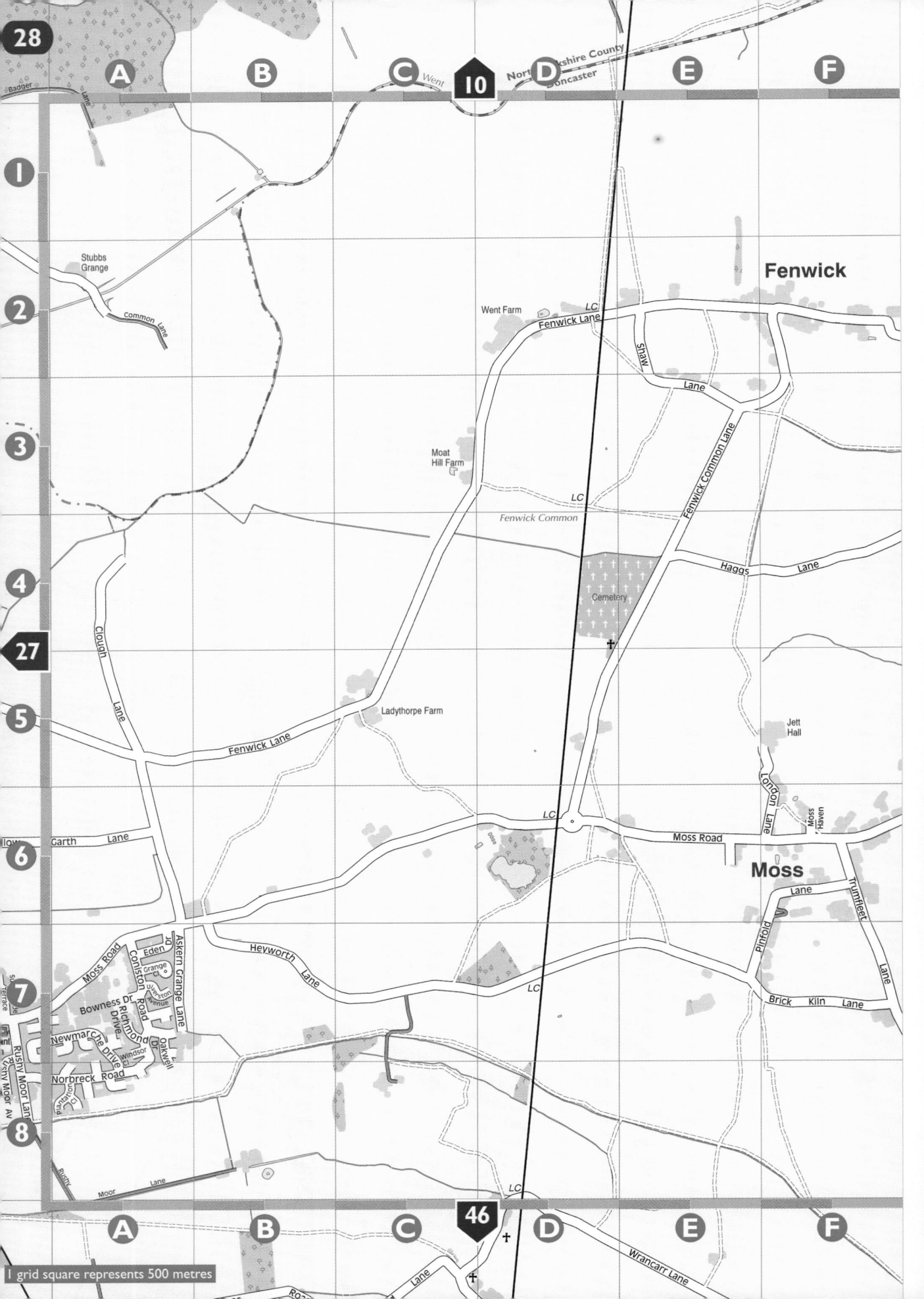

A   B   C   10   North Yorkshire County
Doncaster   D   E   F

1

Stubbs
Grange

Common Lane

2

Went Farm   LC   Fenwick
Fenwick Lane

Fenwick

Shaw

Lane

3

Moat
Hill Farm

LC

Fenwick Common   Fenwick Common Lane

Haggs   Lane

4

Clough

Cemetery

Lane

27

5

Ladythorpe Farm

Fenwick Lane

Jett
Hall

London Lane

Moss
Haven

LC

Garth   Lane

Moss Road

6

Moss

Lane

Trumfleet

Moss Road

Askern Grange Lane

Heyworth   Lane

Pinfold

Lane

Eden
Conliston   Grange
Road   Avenue

LC

7

Bowness Dr   Richmond
Road

Oakwell   Brick   Kiln   Lane

Newmar   Cne Drive
Windsor

Rusty Moor Lane

Norbreck Road

Plantation
CI

8

LC

Rusty   Moor   Lane

A   B   C   46   D   Wrancarr Lane   E   F

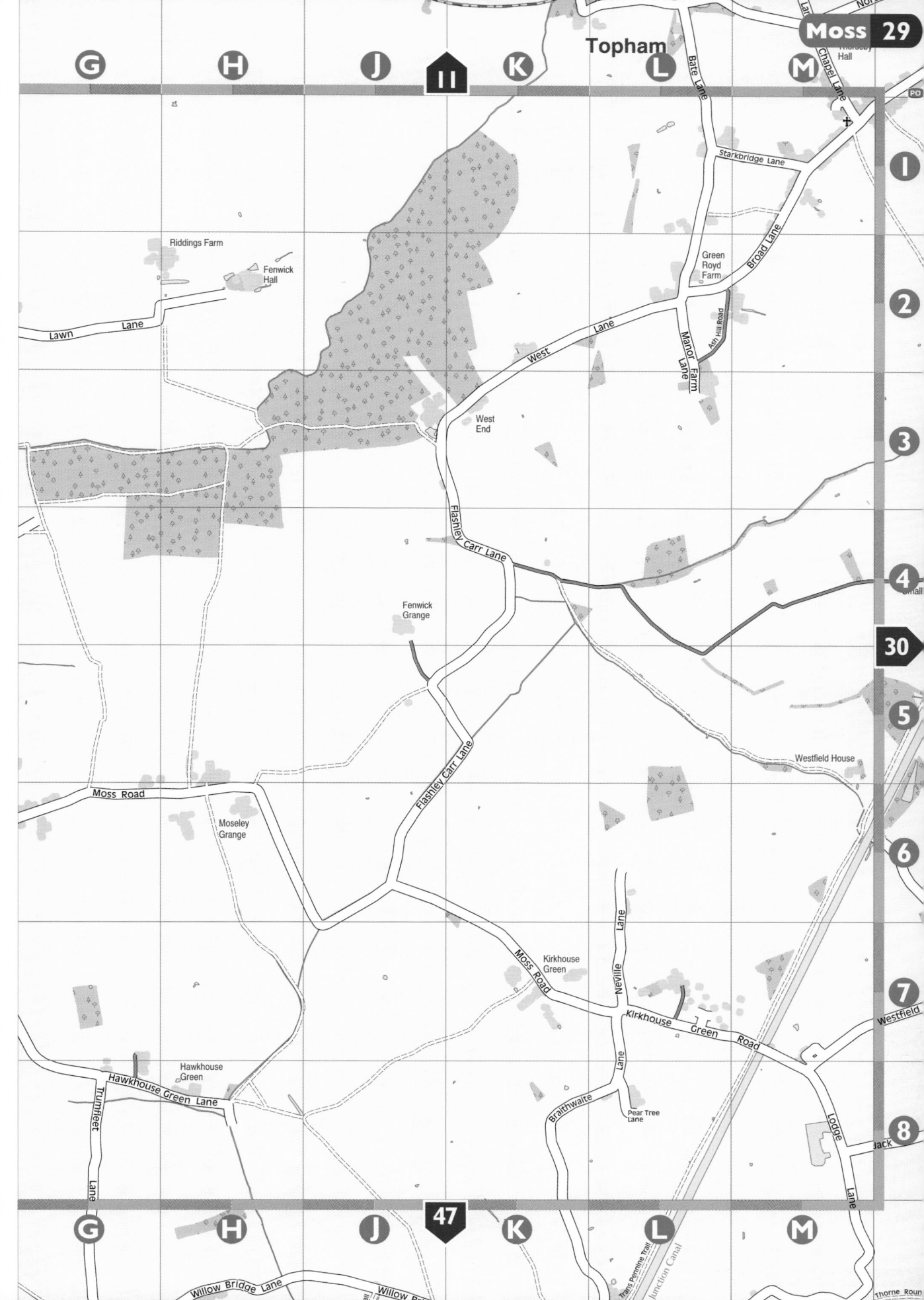

Topham

G H J I K L M

I
2
3
4
30
5
6
7
8

Thoresby
Hall

PO

Starkbridge Lane

Green
Royd
Farm

Broad Lane

Riddings Farm

Fenwick
Hall

Lawn Lane

West Lane

Manor Farm Lane

Ash Hill Road

Chapel Lane

Bate Lane

West
End

Flashley Carr Lane

Fenwick
Grange

Small

Westfield House

Westfield

Moss Road

Moseley
Grange

Flashley Carr Lane

Kirkhouse
Green

Neville Lane

Kirkhouse Green Road

Moss Road

Braithwaite Lane

Pear Tree
Lane

Hawkhouse
Green

Hawkhouse Green Lane

Trumfleet Lane

Lodge Lane

Jack

Trans Pennine Trail

Junction Canal

Thorne Roun

Willow Bridge Lane

Willow Bri

G H J K L M

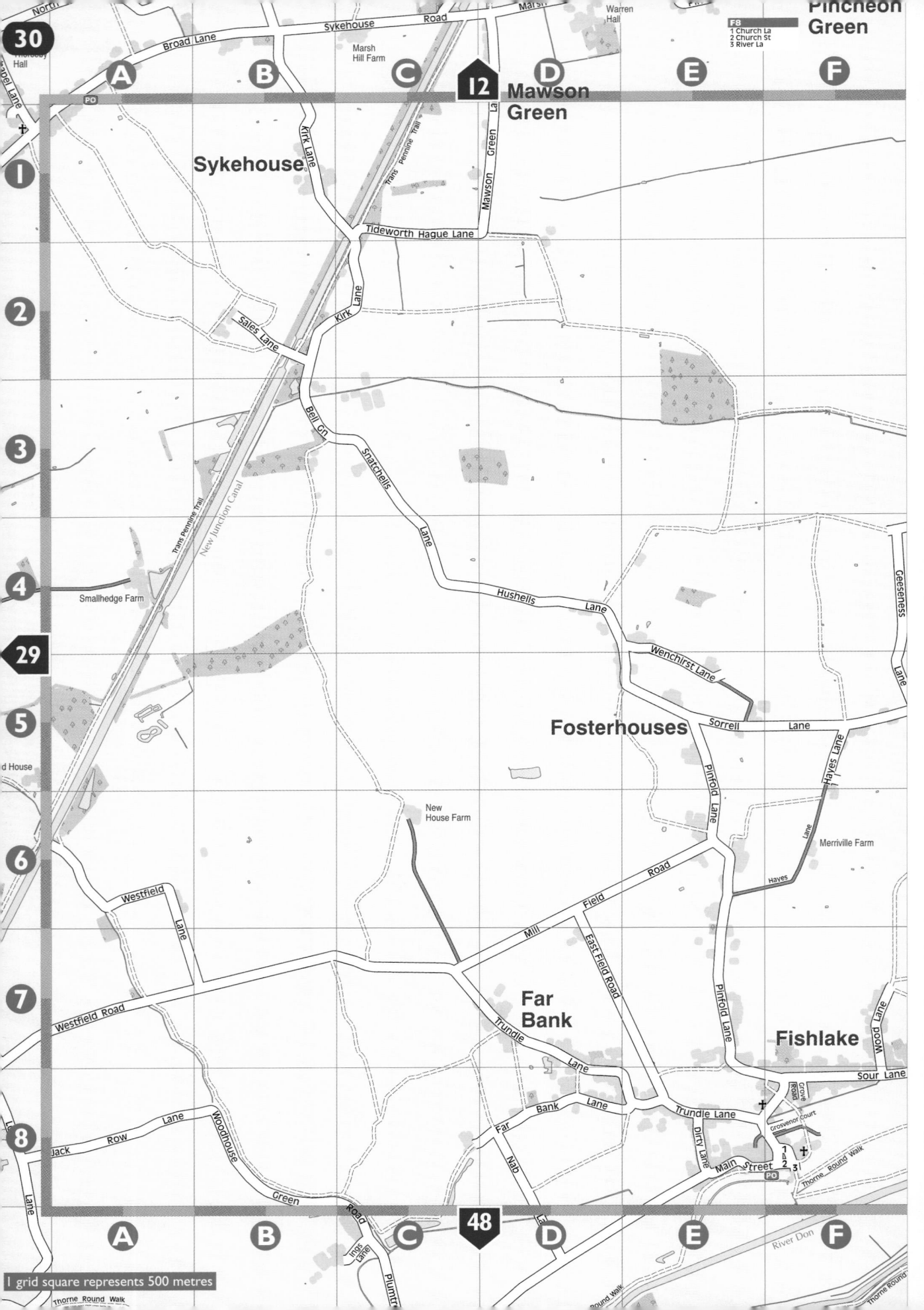

Sykehouse
Mawson Green
Fosterhouses
Far Bank
Fishlake
Pincheon Green
Broad Lane
Sykehouse Road
Marsh Hill Farm
Warren Hall
Kirk Lane
Mawson Green La
Trans Pennine Trail
Tideworth Hague Lane
Sales Lane
Bell Gn
Snatchells Lane
New Junction Canal
Smallhedge Farm
Hushells Lane
Wenchirst Lane
Sorrell Lane
Geeseness Lane
Pinfold Lane
Hayes Lane
Merriville Farm
New House Farm
Westfield Lane
Mill Field Road
East Field Road
Westfield Road
Trundle Lane
Bank Lane
Far Bank Lane
Nab La
Jack Row Lane
Woodhouse Green Road
Dirty Lane
Main Street
Grove Road
Grosvenor Court
Wood Lane
Sour Lane
Thorne Round Walk
River Don
Ings Lane
Plumtr
F8
1 Church La
2 Church St
3 River La
12
29
48
1 grid square represents 500 metres

K6
1 Quay Rd
2 Waterside Rd

K7
1 Dorothy Av
2 Lyndhurst Cl

L8
1 Browns La
2 Foundry La
3 Godfrey Rd

G   H   J   13   K   L   M

Dikes Marsh

Hadds   Lane

Bank Side

COWICK ROAD

SELBY ROAD

A614

M18

Wormley Hill

Wormley   Hill

Lane

Dikes Marsh Farm

Marsh Lane

River Don

Syke   Lane

Black

Hadds Nook Road

North Common Road

Thorne And Dikesmarsh Road

Mount Pleasant Road

Bloomhill Road

North Common

Bloomhill

4

32

5

The Elms

Cowick Road

A614

Ferry Rd

Wood   Lane

Thorninghurst Farm

Thorne Round Walk

Hangsman Hill

Land   Ends   Road

M18

Mount   Pleasant   Road

Land Ends Road

Alexandra

Ivy Road

Hawthorne Road

Oak Road

Oak Crs

Corona

Willow Crescent

Walnut Street

Cedar Street

Willow Rd

Willow Avenue

Willow Crs

5

6

Drive

Sour Lane

Lowhill

Junction 6

2

1

Quayside

Waterside

Waterside

Omega   Boulevard

M18

Highfield Crs

Lime Tree Grove

Millfield

North

Eastern   Road

Casson's Road

Marsden Grove

Benwood Crescent

2

Edward

King

Ingleno

PO

7

T

Thorne North Stn

Clifton Court

Brooke Street

Brookfield Close

Durham Avenue

Foster Road

Field Road

St Nicholas St

Mansion Court

Gardens

Thorne Grange School

SELBY ROAD A614

FIELD SIDE

A614

Pinfold Lane

White Lane

Queen Street

Rope Walk

Lock Lane

Boating Dyke Way

Lock Hill

Staniland Yacht Club

Stainforth and Keadby Canal

Thorne   Land Walk

3

Chestnut House Surgery

Thorne Health Centre

Thorne

Union   Street

Orchard Road

Ashburnham Road

Queen Street

Belle Vue Terrace

Fairtree

KING ST

PO

Bridge Street

SQ PL

CHURCH ST

Stonegate

Southfield

8

Middlebrook La

Green Top

Canal Side

G   H   J   49   K   L   M

M8
1 Chapel La
2 Horse Fair Gn

M6
1 Highfield Crs
2 Upper Kenyon St

1 Birchwood Cl
2 Cherry Tree Dr
3 Hawthorne Av
4 Hawthorne Gv

Park View

Park Crs

West Court

A8
1 Haynes Gn
2 Tennyson Av
3 Tithe Barn La

A6
1 Edward Ct
2 Henry Ct
3 King Edward Crs
4 Kings Court Rd

A4
1 Newholme Dr

A3
1 Bloomhill Cl
2 Micklethwaite Gv

A   B   LC   C   14   D   E   F

I

2

Moorends Road

3

Moorends

The Avenue
Micklethwaite Rd
The Green
Grange
Marshland Rd
Bloomhill Court
Chadwick Rd
The Fairway
Haig Road
Oakmoor Road
Richmond Road
High
Calford Road
Hazel Road
Northgate Road
Barnsley Rd

Grove
East Gate
Grove
Darlington
Belvedere Drive
Alexandra Rd
West Road
South Road
Park Road
Geneva Square
Kents Gardens
Locarno Rd
Locarno Road
Barnsley Road
Windlestone Sq
Eldon Grove
Shildon Grove

The Surgery
West Road First School
PO
Wembley Road
Orchard Lane
Dunelm Crescent
Vermuyden Rd
Silkstone Oval

4

Bloomhill   Road
Bloom Hill Grove
Laurel Avenue
Rowan Close
Laburnum Avenue
Mulberry Avenue
Moorends Clinic
Moorends Marshland First School

31

Ferndale   Drive
Newfields Avenue
Newfields Drive
Newfields Close

5

Marshland Rd
Moor Lane
Wilkinson Avenue
Willow Avenue
Willow Grove
Holly Rd
Maple Close
Cedar Road
Willow Crescent
Willow Rd
Willow Grove
Broadbent Gate Road

Dairy Farm

Tween Bridge Moors

Thorne Waste Drain Road

6

Walnut Road
Oak Road
Corona Drive
Road King Edward
Road
James Court
Charles Court
Orchard Rd
Coulman Road

PO
Inglenook Drive
King Edward First School
Kendon Gardens
Albert Street
Coulman Road

7

Low Kenyon St
Mansion Court
Gardens
Nicholas Road
Balk
Causeway Farm

THORNE
Thorne Grammar School
Thorne Swimming Baths
Church Street
Coventry Road
House
Littlewood Road
Danum Close
Alwyn
Lockwood Close
Moor   Edges   Road

Sand Moors or South Moors

DN8

Moor Owners Road

8

Thorne Health Centre
Elmhirst
Haynes Road
Haynes Gardens
Travis
Wike Gate Road
Sandmoor Farm

Filson Street
Stonegate
Middlebrook La
Bridge Street
WEST STREET
RIVER
Cemetery
Glebe Road
Southfield Road
Warren Road

Green Top First School
Cemetery
Thorne Comm First School
Ash Close
Tree Close
Peel Castle
Haynes Grove
Pasture

A   B   Lane   Middle School   C   50   D   E   F

B3
1 Grange Gv
2 Grange Sq
3 Thrislington Sq

B4
1 The Hermitage

St Michael's Dr

Nun

G H J **15** K L M

East Riding of Yorkshire
Doncaster

*Will
Pitts*

*Thorne Moors
or Waste*

Doncaster
North Lincolnshire

G H **51** J K L M

I
2
3
4
5
6
7
8

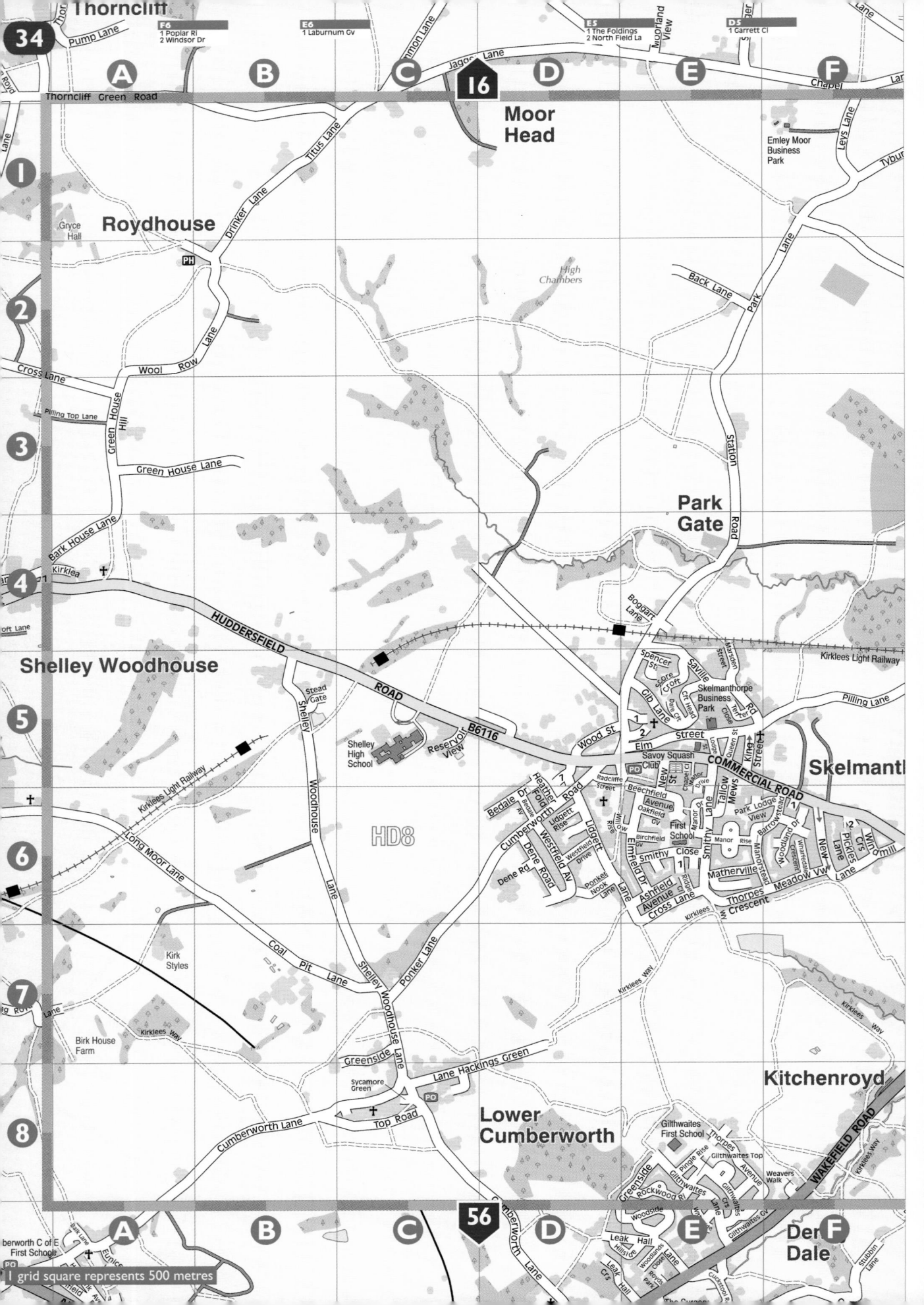

Thorncliff

A · B · C · D · E · F

F6
1 Poplar Rl
2 Windsor Dr

E6
1 Laburnum Gv

E5
1 The Foldings
2 North Field La

D5
1 Garrett Cl

Pump Lane

Thorncliff Green Road

16

Moor Head

Jagoe Lane

Cannon Lane

Chapel

Emley Moor Business Park

Levs Lane

Tyburn

I

Gryce Hall

Roydhouse

PH

Titus Lane

Drinker Lane

High Chambers

Back Lane

Park Lane

2

Wool Row Lane

Green House Hill

Cross Lane

Pilling Top Lane

3

Green House Lane

Station Road

Park Gate

Bark House Lane

4

Kirklea
1

HUDDERSFIELD

Boggart Lane

Shelley Woodhouse

ROAD

B6116

Kirklees Light Railway

Stead Gate

Shelley

Woodhouse Lane

Shelley High School

Reservoir View

Wood St

Spencer St
Score
Croft
Crt Head
Taiter
Closes

Skelmanthorpe Business Park

Pilling Lane

5

Kirklees Light Railway

Gib Lane

Savoy Squash Club

New St

Chapel

Commercial Road

King Street

Skelmanth

HD8

Long Moor Lane

Bedale Dr

Heathfield Road

Cumberworth Road

Westfield Av

Liggett La

Radcliffe Street

Beechfield Avenue
Oakfield Gv

First School

Tallow Mews

Park Lodge View

Manor Rise

Smithy Lane

Barrowstead

Windmill

Pickles Lane

New Lane

6

Dene Rd

Dene Road

Emfield Dr

Ashfield Avenue
Cross Lane

Smithy
Close
1

Matherville

Thorpes

Meadow Vw

Kirklees
Wy

Crescent

Coal Pit Lane

Kirk Styles

Shelley Woodhouse Lane

Ponker Lane

7

Kirklees Way

Birk House Farm

Kirklees Way

Greenside

Lane Hackings Green

Kitchenroyd

Greenside

Sycamore Green

PO

Lower Cumberworth

WAKEFIELD ROAD

Kirklees Wy

8

Cumberworth Lane

Top Road

Glithwaites First School

Thorpes

Pinfold Rise

Glithwaites Top

Greenside

Rockwood Rl

Glithwaites Lane

Avenue

Weavers Walk

Glithwaites Gv

Woodside

Leak Hall

Hillfield

Der Dale

berworth C of E
First School

A · B · C 56 D · E · F

1 grid square represents 500 metres

G   H   J   17   K   L   M

Woodhouse Lane

Woodhouse Farm

I

Thornicl...

St Mi...

School

Rodley Lane

The Crofs

The Clinic

PO

Aspen Court

Green Acres Close

Out...

Wentworth Avenue

Wentworth

Waarburton

Rishworth Avenue

Viking Av

Glo...

Phoenix Av

Viking Av

Upper

Savile Ros

Savile St

Tipping Lane

Fox Cl

Summer Lane

Ash Lane

2

Hag Hill

Hag Hill

Kiln Lane

White Cross

Low House Farm

Frank Lane

Emley Old Hall Farm

Old Hall Lane

Gillcar Farm

Emley Park

3

River Dearne

A636

Colliers Way

Manor Road

Park Mill

Langley Lane

Wakefield Road

Long Lane

Park Av

Pack Horse Close

Back Lane

Kirklees Way

Clayton Ha Far...

4

Emley Lodge

Park Road

Dearne Way

Park Mill Way

Ings Mill Av

Short Hill

The Royds

36

Pilling Lane

Riverside

Langley Lane

3

Dearne Park

5

Ings Mill

Albert Rd

Victoria St

Vinery Cl

Church Lane

First School

PO

Clayton West

Bilham Road

Bilham Grange

5

Pennine Rise

Pennine Dr

Sunnymead

The Bungalows

Grove House Drive

Scissett Swimming Baths.

5

Hill

Cliffe Vw

Newlands Av

Holmfield Rd

High Street

Moorland View

Ash Cl

Scissett Middle School

Riverside Business Park

4

7

Chapel

Duke

Springfield

Cliffe Street

Holmfield Cl

...horpe

Church Ter

Barnsley Road

PO

Holmfield Avenue

Wood

Oldfield Lane

6

Scissett

B6116

BUSKER LANE

Dearne Valley Health Centre

Marshall Mill Court

Kirklees Way

Bank End Lane

East Fold

Nortonthorpe Hall School

New St

Crown

Lower Common Lane

Cemetery

Highbridge Lane

A636

Nortonthorpe Industrial Estate

Wood Ter

Cuttlehurst

Upper Common Lane

House Lane

Hoyland

7

Bagden Lane

Dearne Way

Wheatley

Wheatley Hill Farm

Hill Lane

Hollin

High Road

Hotel

Bagden Hall

Kirklees Way

Kirklees Way

8

Clough House Lane

Bagden Lane

Ackin Royd

Defler Wood

New Road

K5
1 Cherry La
2 Clifton Vw
3 Holmfield
4 Holmfield Av
5 The Ings
6 Victoria Ter

Kirkb... Barnsley

A B C 18 D E F

I
2
3
4
35
5
6
7
8

Dearne Way

Bretton Country Park

Barnsley Boundary Walk

Wakefield Barnsley

Lower Lake

Beaumont Drive

ROAD

A637

Huddersfield Road

M1

F7
1 Oakwood Sq

Haigh Lane

Haigh

Junction 38

SWITHEN HILL

Clayton Hall Farm

Kirklees Barnsley

Church Lane

Barnsley Boundary Walk

Longsides

Jebb Lane

High Wood

PARK WALK ROYD HILL

A637

Ballfield Lane

High Hoyland

Upper Field Lane

Upper Field Lane

High Hoyland Lane

Darton High School

Home View Road

Highlands Road

Brookhill Rd

Birthwaite Rd

Junior School

Hawthorne Ct

Infant School

Upper Field Lane

Churchfield Close

Church

Cawthorne Park

High

Dean Hill

A B 58 C D E F

Barnsley Bour

1 Oakwood Sq

Cinder Hill

Barnsley Boundary Walk

G7
1 Churchfield Av
2 Highwood Cl
3 Jacobs Hall Ct
4 Lambe Flatt
5 Rushworth Cl

H6
1 High Cl
2 Sike Cl

H7
1 Carrfield Cl
2 Daykin Cl
3 Hedge La
4 Oak Tree La
5 Quarry Cl

H8
1 Richmond Av

G   H   J   **19**   K   L   M

Woolley

Savin Royd Wood

High House Farm

Haigh Lane

Moorhouse La

Near Moon Farm

Barnsley Boundary Walk

Middle Lane

Field Lane

Back Lane

Gipsy Lane

Hawton Lane

New Road

Woodhouse Lane

Abbot Lane

Old Mount Farm

The Paddock

Church Street

Holly Hall Lane

High Green

Haw Top

Woolley Edge Lane

Woolley Colliery Rd

Bluebell Road

Windhill Lane

Windhill Av

Windhill Crescent

Windhill Drive

Windhill Mount

River Dearne

Dearne Way

Woolley Colliery Road

Bloomhouse Lane

Cranborne Drive

Keswick Dr

Coniston Av

Pennine View

Sackup Lane

Edgehill Road

Staincross Head Rise

Newark Rise

Staincross

38
Staincross

Moorland Av

Moorland Cr

Lins View

Moorland View

Bourn Common

Thorne End Rd

Redland Grove

New Road

New Road

Oaklea

Orchard Cl

New Rd

Austwick

Bentham Wy

Harkstead

Eshton

Oaklea

Burnham

Withernsea

Princess St

Longsight Rd

Valley Rd

Skelton Av

George St

Zion Dr

Birthwaite Hall

A637 HUDDERSFIELD ROAD

Windsor Avenue

Bretton Close

Bretton Road

Strafford St

Airedale Rd

Swallow Cl

Allendale Road

Lynton

Barnsley MBC

Alan Rd

Agnes Rd

Richard Rd

Howden Close

Fountain Close

Ryan Rd

School St

Bridge St

Dearne St

Darton Hall Close

Montrose Avenue

Oaks Farm Dr

Bloomfield Road

Inglewood

Cherry Hills

Andrews Dr

Oaks Wood Dr

Willow Brook Road

Lwr High Royds

Uppr High Royds

Priest Royd Croft

Hill Brow Surgery

Croft Dr

Crossgate

Wellgate

Infant School

Kingsway

Alton Way

Appleby

Kingsway

Maple Rd

Alder

Broadway

New St

George St

New Street Av

Longfield Dr

Longlands Court

Mapplewell Health Cen

TOWNGATE

B6131

Nobberson Avenue

Pye Avenue

Darton Lane

Malincroft

Priestley Av

Cooper Rd

Uplands Av

Kexbrough

Churchfield

Churchfield Lane

Ballfield Lane

Beaumont Rd

Kexbrough Dr

Elsham

Dove

Kibroyd Dr

Bence Lane

Roman Rd

Lansdowne Crs

Hedge Lane

Meadow Lane

Meyrick Dr

Trivdale Dr

Bence Dr

CHURCH ST

Church Close

Darton

Wentworth Road

Darton Junior & Infant School

Darton Lane

Roberson

Spark Lane

B6428

Swallow Hill

Swallow Hill Road

Dearne Valley

M1

A637 BARNSLEY ROAD

Chedworth Close

59

DEARNE HALL ROAD

Low Barugh

Royal Court

M7
1 Broomhead Ct
2 Longlands Dr
3 Ravens Cl
4 Spark La

M5
1 Moorcrest Ri
2 Stamford Wy
3 Wheatley Ri

M6
1 Melford Cl

L4
1 Grasmere Crs

L5
1 Langcliffe Cl
2 Roeburn Cl

L6
1 Bloomfield Ri
2 Grove Rd
3 Sunningdale Av

K7
1 Lawndale Fold
2 Oaks Farm Dr
3 Oaks Wood Dr
4 Rockwood Cl

M7
1 Barnsley Rd
2 Wells St

K6
1 Cranborne Dr

PO

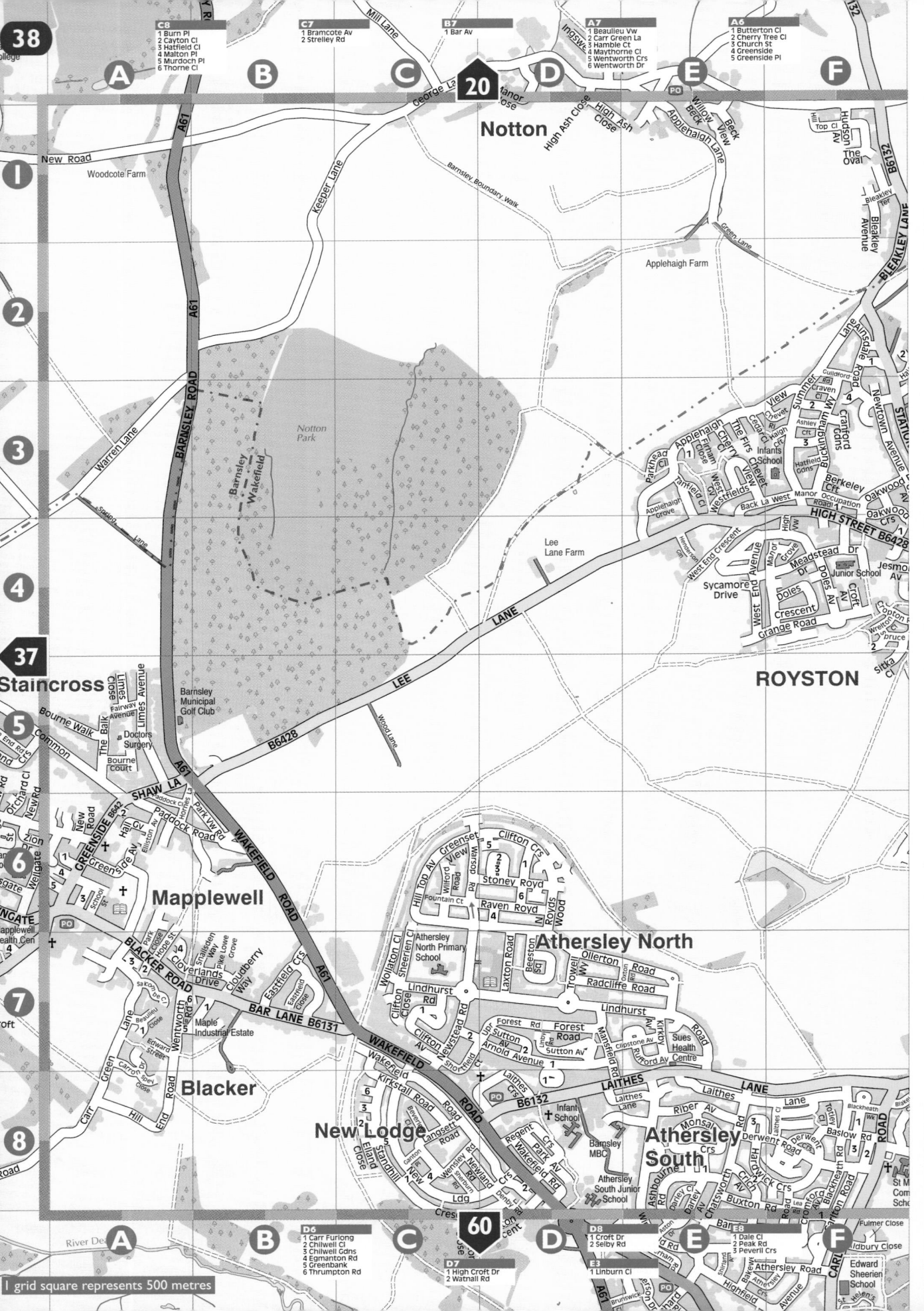
C8
1 Burn Pl
2 Cayton Cl
3 Hatfield Cl
4 Malton Pl
5 Murdoch Pl
6 Thorne Cl
C7
1 Bramcote Av
2 Strelley Rd
B7
1 Bar Av
A7
1 Beaulieu Vw
2 Carr Green La
3 Hamble Ct
4 Maythorne Cl
5 Wentworth Crs
6 Wentworth Dr
A6
1 Butterton Cl
2 Cherry Tree Cl
3 Church St
4 Greenside
5 Greenside Pl
20
Notton
ROYSTON
Staincross
Mapplewell
Blacker
New Lodge
Athersley North
Athersley South
Notton Park
Woodcote Farm
Applehaigh Farm
Lee Lane Farm
Barnsley Municipal Golf Club
Maple Industrial Estate
Barnsley MBC
Athersley South Junior School
Athersley North Primary School
Sues Health Centre
Infants School
Junior School
Doctors Surgery
Edward Sheerien School
BARNSLEY ROAD
WAKEFIELD ROAD
LEE LANE
B6428
HIGH STREET B6428
BAR LANE B6131
BLACKER ROAD
LAITHES LANE
B6132
BLEAKLEY LANE
New Road
Keeper Lane
Warren Lane
Mill Lane
George La
Barnsley Boundary Walk
Green Lane
Spring Lane
Wood Lane
37
60
D6
1 Carr Furlong
2 Chilwell Cl
3 Chilwell Gdns
4 Egmanton Rd
5 Greenbank
6 Thrumpton Rd
D7
1 High Croft Dr
2 Watnall Rd
D8
1 Croft Dr
2 Selby Rd
E3
1 Linburn Cl
E8
1 Dale Cl
2 Peak Rd
3 Peverll Crs
1 grid square represents 500 metres

G3
1 Kent Cl
2 Queensway
3 Well Hill Gv

G5
1 Brownroyd Av

G6
1 Lambecroft

G7
1 Springbank Cl

H3
1 Robin Hood Av
2 Rowland St

H7
1 Wharncliffe St
2 Woodmoor St

G   H   J   **21**   K   L   M

Ellis Laithe

Barnsley Boundary Walk

Church Lane

Felkirk
Kirkgate

Raven Lane   Slack Lane

Barnsley Boundary Walk

Wood Wk
Moor Wy
Winter Av
Syke Cft
Northlands
Monkton Way
Lane
Lidgett Way
Common
Warren Cl
Robin Lane

Royston Comprehensive School
Barnsley Metropolitan Borough Council

Victoria Rd
North Road
Filey Avenue
Milgate St
Park Crescent
West St
Poplar Ter
The Av

MIDLAND   **ROAD**

B6428
Infant School
Godley St
Alfred Street
Meadow Cres
Meadow St
Low Croft
Caldervale
Cross La
Bisley Cl

Railwaymens Sports Club

Royston Clinic
B6132 CHURCH ST
New St
Vicarage La
St John's Walk
Jack Cl Orch
Primary School
Park View
Meadow Rd
Meadow Av
Calder
Cross Lane
East End Crescent
Carlingray Cl

Sandybridge Lane

Greenside
The Green View
Henry Cl
Redthorne Way
Millside

Shafton
Felkirk View
Coronation Avenue
Queen's Dr
Dog Hill
Shafton View
Chaff

Cemetery
Redwood Av
Plantation Av
Park Crescent
Church Hill
Pools La
Pools Lane

Lidgate Lane

40

Kirkfield Wy
Fearnville
Cross La
East Pinfold
West Pinfold
Central Dr
South Dr
North La
Cooper Avenue
Kirk Cross Crs

Pinfold Lane

Shafton Two Gates

Bateman
Weet Shaw Lane
Sherwood Way
Royston Road

Three Nooks Av

Lynwood Drive
Woodroyd Av
Avondale
Grace's Rd
The Cl
Birdas Rd
Ridgeway
Francus Rd
Wood
Braham Street
Crookes St
Chapel Av
Chapel La

Boulder Br Lane

ROYSTON LANE B6132

Cronkhill Lane

Trans Pennine Trail

Shaw Lane

The Gv
King's Rd
Queen's
6

Carlton

Church St
Manor Farm Cl
Fish Dam Lane
Manor St

Carlton Junior & Infant School

Charles St
George St
7
Infant School
Cherry Cl
Horbury
Jacob Rd
Intake La

Carlton Industrial Estate
Albion Rd

Beech Avenue
Park Av
Oak Tree Av
Rose Tree Av
Victoria St
Almond Avenue
Rose Tree Ct

Silverstone Avenue

Industry Road
Carlton Industrial Estate
Michaels RC Comprehensive School
Barkston Rd
Shawfield
Barkston Road

Market St
Carlton Road
Prospect

ROAD
8

F2
1 Birkdale Rd
2 Cutts Field Vw

F3
1 Boswell Cl
2 Clevedon Wy
3 Petworth Cft
4 Summer Rd

F4
1 Hallcroft Rl
2 Whitewood Cl

F8
1 Blackheath Cl
2 Carlton Rd
3 Derwent Cl

M7
1 Crosby St
2 Newington Av
3 School St

M8
1 Baycliff Cl
2 Cartmel Ct
3 Kirkham Pl
4 St Francis Bvd

G   H   J   **61**   K   G **West**   L   M

Rain Dr
St Michael's Av
Poulton
Far Field
Bank St
Roberts St
School Hl
Sycamore Av
Willow Cl
Bloemfontein St
Jack Cl
BARNSLEY
Manor Rd
St John's

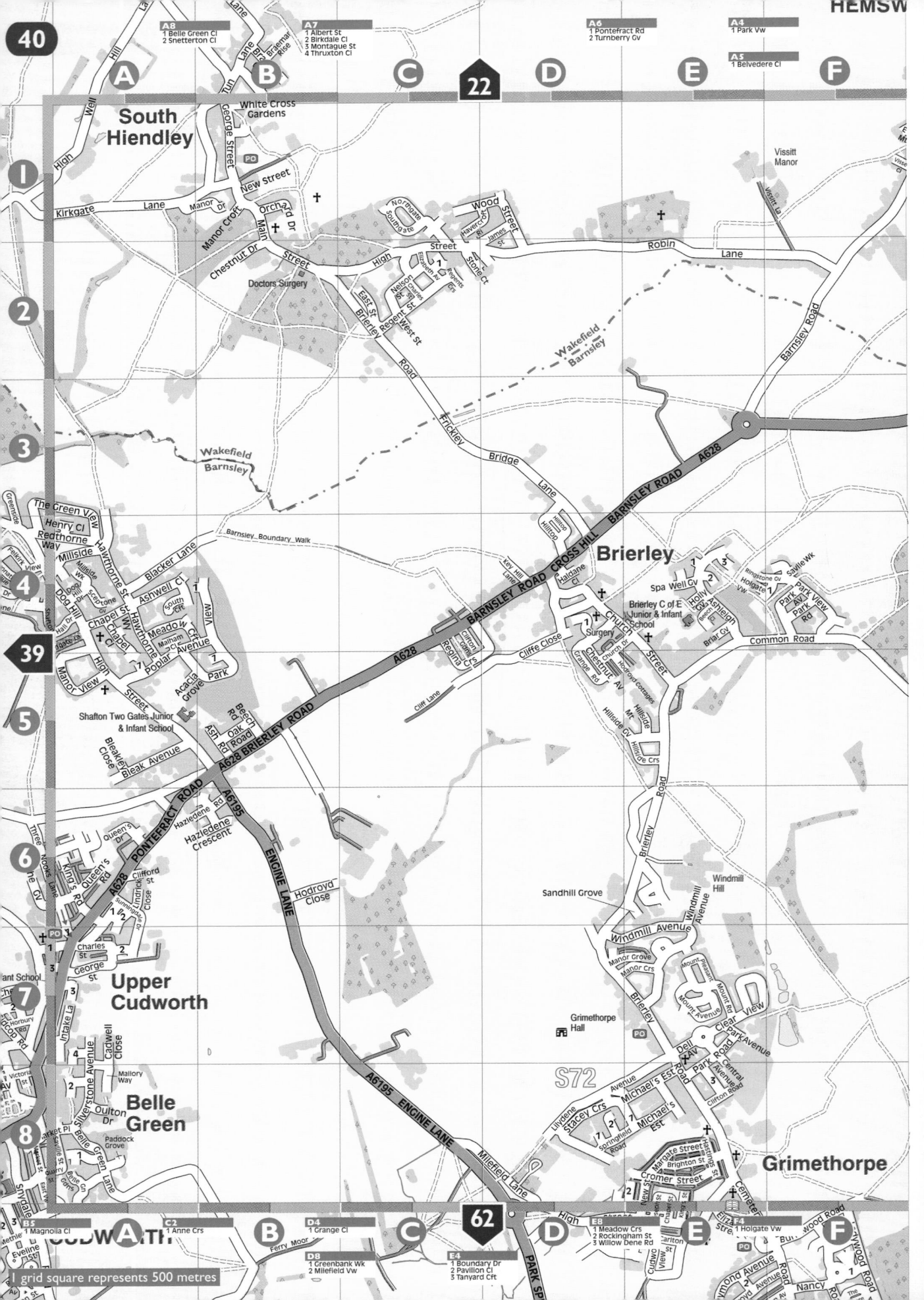
A8
1 Belle Green Cl
2 Snetterton Cl
A7
1 Albert St
2 Birkdale Cl
3 Montague St
4 Thruxton Cl
A6
1 Pontefract Rd
2 Turnberry Gv
A4
1 Park Vw
A5
1 Belvedere Cl
22
South Hiendley
White Cross Gardens
Vissitt Manor
Robin Lane
Doctors Surgery
Wakefield
Barnsley
Brierley
Brierley C of E Junior & Infant School
Common Road
Barnsley Road
A628 Barnsley Road
Cross Hill
Shafton Two Gates Junior & Infant School
A628 Brierley Road
A628 Pontefract Road
A6195 Engine Lane
Sandhill Grove
Windmill Hill
Grimethorpe Hall
S72
Upper Cudworth
Belle Green
Grimethorpe
39
62
B5
1 Magnolia Cl
C2
1 Anne Crs
D4
1 Grange Cl
D8
1 Greenbank Wk
2 Milefield Vw
E4
1 Boundary Dr
2 Pavilion Cl
3 Tanyard Cft
E8
1 Meadow Crs
2 Rockingham St
3 Willow Dene Rd
F4
1 Holgate Vw
1 grid square represents 500 metres

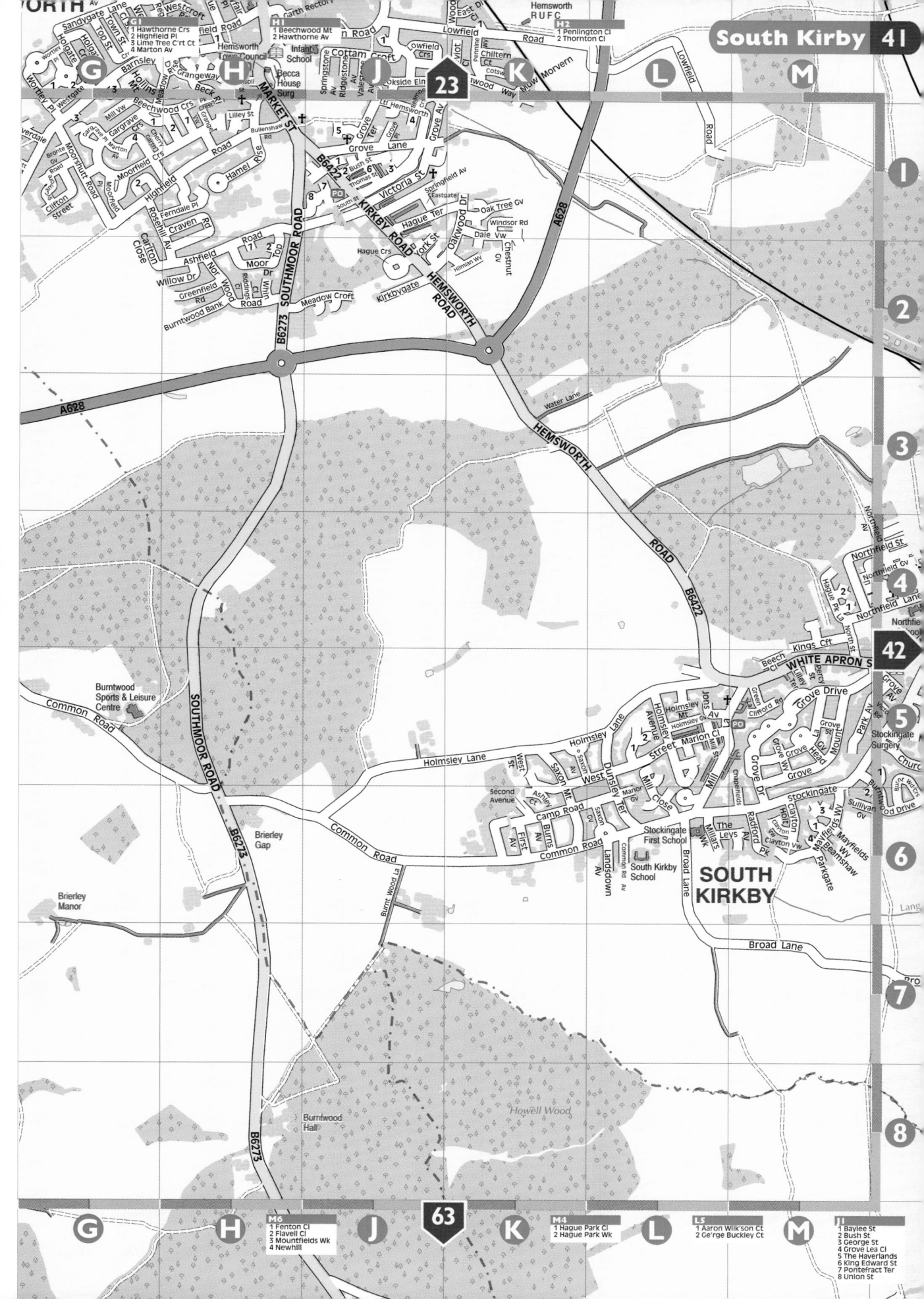

G1
1 Hawthorne Crs
2 Highfield Pl
3 Lime Tree C'rt Ct
4 Marton Av
H1
1 Beechwood Mt
2 Hawthorne Av
H2
1 Penlington Cl
2 Thornton Cl
Hemsworth R U F C
Hemsworth Town Council
Infant School
Becca House Surg
Sandygate Lane
Holgate
Town St
Top St
Barnsley
Hollins Mt
Grangeway
Beck Rd
MARKET ST
Cottam Croft
Lowfield Road
Chiltern Ct
Muw Morvern
Beechwood Crs
Mill Vw
Gargrave
Lilley St
Bullenshaw Rd
Grove Lane
Grove Av
Moorsnutt Road
Moorfield Crs
Highfield
Hamel Rise
Clifton Street
Ferndale Pl
Craven Rd
Rosehill Av
Carlton Close
Ashfield
Moor Dr
Willow Dr
Greenfield Rd
Nor Wood
Burntwood Bank
Road
B6422
KIRKBY ROAD
Victoria St
Springfield Av
Hague Ter
Oak Tree Gv
Windsor Rd
Dale Vw
Oakwood Dr
York St
Hague Crs
Chestnut Gv
Hilmian Wy
Kirkbygate
HEMSWORTH ROAD
Meadow Croft
SOUTHMOOR ROAD
B6273
A628
Water Lane
HEMSWORTH ROAD
B6422
Northfield Av
Northfield St
Northfield Gv
Northfield Lane
Hague Pk La
North St
Kings Cft
Beech Cl
WHITE APRON S
Grove Drive
Clifford Rd
Holmsley Mt
Jons Av
Holmsley Lane
Holmsley Avenue
Street
Marion Cl
Grove Dr
Park Av
Stockingate Surgery
Burntwood Drive
Stockingate
Sullivan Gv
Burnt Wood Drive
Burntwood Sports & Leisure Centre
Common Road
SOUTHMOOR ROAD
Holmsley Lane
West
Saxon Av
Dunsley Ter
Mill Close
Second Avenue
Camp Road
Burns Av
First Av
Common Road
Landsdown Av
Stockingate First School
The Levs
Radford Pk
Clayton Vw
Mayfields Wy
Beamshaw
Parkgate
South Kirkby School
Broad Lane
SOUTH KIRKBY
Brierley Gap
Brierley Manor
Burnt Wood La
Broad Lane
B6273
Burntwood Hall
Howell Wood
M6
1 Fenton Cl
2 Flavell Cl
3 Mountfields Wk
4 Newhill
M4
1 Hague Park Cl
2 Hague Park Wk
L5
1 Aaron Wilk'son Ct
2 Ge'rge Buckley Ct
J1
1 Baylee St
2 Bush St
3 George St
4 Grove Lea Cl
5 The Haverlands
6 King Edward St
7 Pontefract Ter
8 Union St

23
42
63

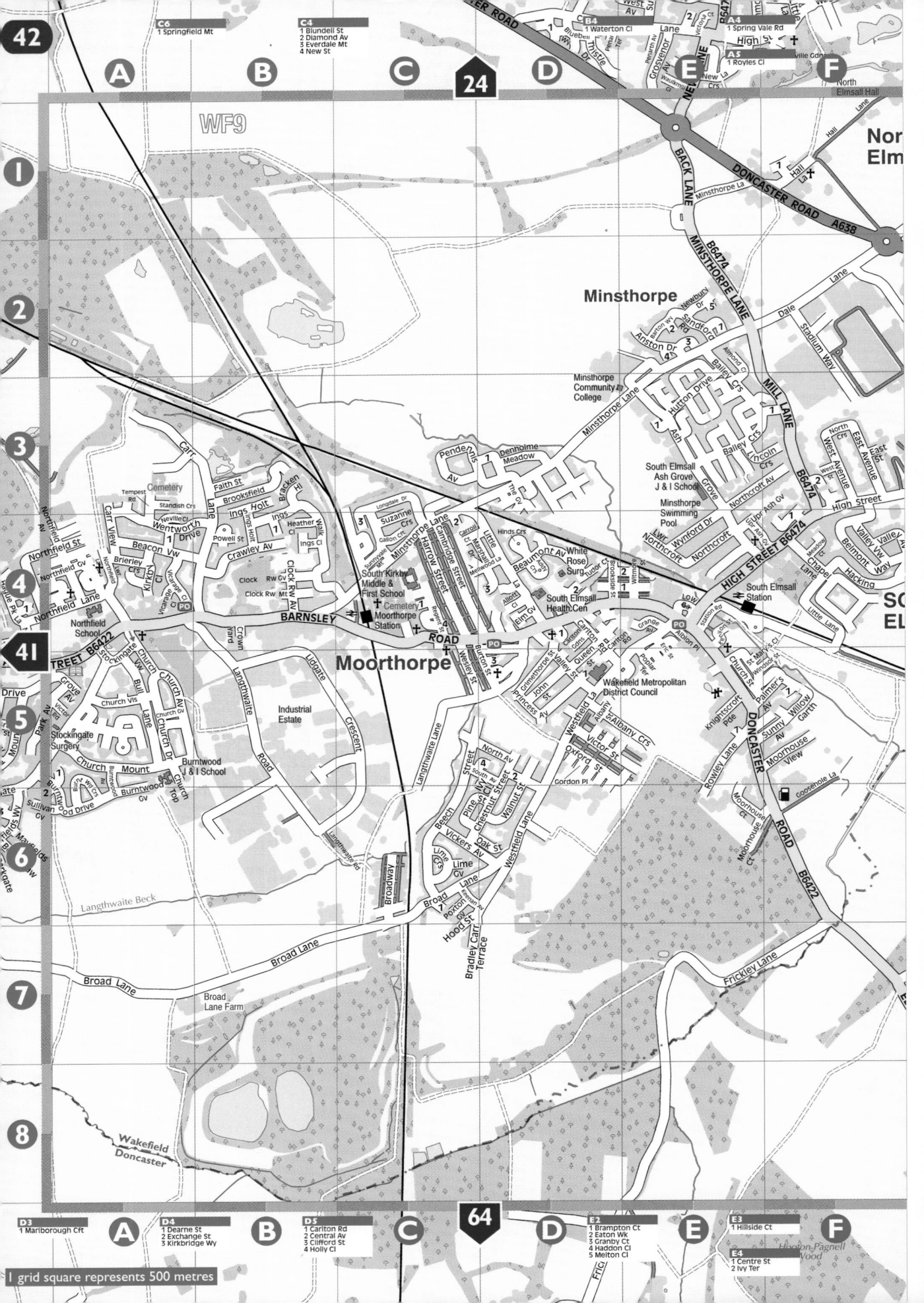
C6
1 Springfield Mt
C4
1 Blundell St
2 Diamond Av
3 Everdale Mt
4 New St
B4
1 Waterton Cl
A4
1 Spring Vale Rd
A5
1 Royles Cl
24
WF9
41
Minsthorpe
Moorthorpe
Minsthorpe Community College
South Elmsall Ash Grove J & I School
Minsthorpe Swimming Pool
South Kirkby Middle & First School
Moorthorpe Station
South Elmsall Station
South Elmsall Health Cen
Wakefield Metropolitan District Council
Northfield School
Stockingate Surgery
Burntwood J & I School
Industrial Estate
Broad Lane Farm
Langthwaite Beck
Wakefield
Doncaster
DONCASTER ROAD A638
BARNSLEY ROAD
HIGH STREET B6474
MINSTHORPE LANE B6474
DONCASTER ROAD B6422
MILL LANE
BACK LANE
Broad Lane
Frickley Lane
64
D3
1 Marlborough Cft
D4
1 Dearne St
2 Exchange St
3 Kirkbridge Wy
D5
1 Carlton Rd
2 Central Av
3 Clifford St
4 Holly Cl
E2
1 Brampton Ct
2 Eaton Wk
3 Granby Ct
4 Haddon Cl
5 Melton Cl
E3
1 Hillside Ct
E4
1 Centre St
2 Ivy Ter
1 grid square represents 500 metres

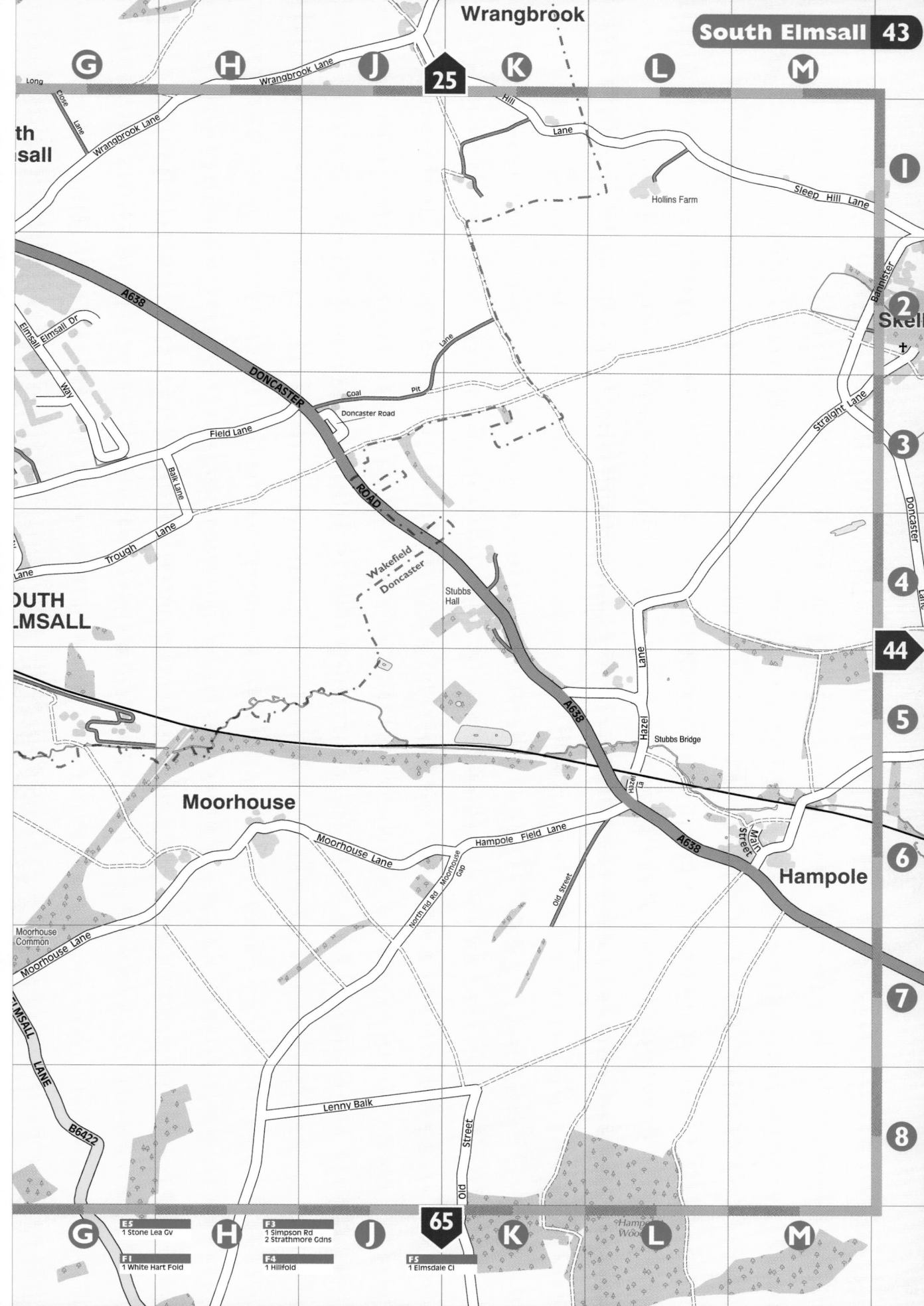

Wrangbrook

G   H   J   **25**   K   L   M

Wrangbrook Lane
Wrangbrook Lane
Long
Close
Lane

th
sall

Hill
Lane

Hollins Farm

Sleep Hill Lane

I

Barnister

2

Skell

A638

Elmsall Dr
Elmsall
Way

DONCASTER

Lane

Straight Lane

Doncaster Lane

3

Field Lane

Coal   Pit
Doncaster Road

Balk Lane

Trough   Lane

Lane

ROAD

4

Wakefield
Doncaster

Stubbs
Hall

44

OUTH
LMSALL

A638

Lane

Hazel

5

Stubbs Bridge

Moorhouse

Moorhouse Lane

Hampole Field Lane

Hazel La

Main Street

A638

Hampole

6

Moorhouse Lane
Moorhouse
Common

North Fld Rd

Moorhouse Gap

Old Street

A638

7

MSALL
LANE

B6422

Lenny Balk

Old Street

8

Hampole Wood

F6
1 Hobcroft Ter
E6
1 Buttercross
2 French St
3 Old Hall Rd
4 Windermere Cl
Woodfield Farm
E5
1 Buttercross Cl
2 Cromwell Gv
3 Crossfield H'se Cl
D6
1 Cromwell Ct
A
B
C
D
E
F
26
New Close Lane
1
2
3
4
5
6
7
8
43
66
Hill Lane
Lane
Bannister
Skelbrooke
A1(T)
Straight Lane
Doncaster Lane
Sixrood Lane
Scorcher Hills Lane
The Abbe's Close
Grange Lane
Burghwallis
Club House
Old Village Street
Stony Croft Lane
Burghwallis Grange
Green Lane
Doncaster Lane
Skellow
Mill Lane
Willowbrook
Fullerton Close
Cranfield Dr
Crossfield Dr
Crossfield La
Acacia Road
Ash Rd
Road
Lodge
Crabgate Lane
Crabgate Drive
Sherwood Drive
Newlands Av
Harmby Cl
Leyburn Road
Amberley Rise
Weatherall Place
Lavenham Pl
Waltham Dr
Hauxwell
Sherburn Close
Worsley Place
Appleby Place
Lawndale
Cross Hi Ct
Bridgewater Dr
Finghall Rd
Bellerby Road
Bellerby Pl
Spennithorne Road
Leys Lane
HAMPOLE BALK B1220
SKELLOW ROAD
B1220
Howden Avenue
Skellow Hall Farm
South Dr
Laurel
Elm
Mansfield Crs
George St
Charles
Edward Rd
Briar Road
Birch Av
Hawthorne Crs
Beech Road
Terrace
Poplar
Street
Chestnut
Ings Lane
PO
Humber Cl
Humber Ct
Ridgill Av
Willington Rd
Repton Rd
Sandyfields Vw
Dalecroft Rd
Victor St
Rolleston Road
Repton Road
Chapel Street
A1
npole
Hampole Grange
Junction 38
A638
Red House
Roman Ridge
Cemetery
Red House
Red House
CASTER BY-PASS
F8
1 Woodcock Wy
Elmwood
St. Vincent Av
Lawn Avenue
Great North
Bosworth Road
Whinfell Close
Lane
Kingfisher Rd
Osprey Close
Falcon Ct
Fern Bank
Merlin Cl
1 grid square represents 500 metres

ASKERN
G7
1 Croasdale Gdns
2 Martindale Wk
Sutton
Burghwallis Lane
Lady Gap Lane
Sutton Road
Rose Lane
Littlemoor First School
Askern Spa Junior School
Manor Way
Instone Terrace
HIGH STREET
Rushy Moor
DONCASTER ROAD
A19
Shirley Wood
The Abbe's Walk
Squirrel Wood
Owston
Rockley Lane
Stockbridge Lane
North Park La
North Park Lane
Robin Hood Golf Club
Brick Kiln Plantation
Holme
Holme Lane
Carcroft
Owston Lane
B1220
ASKERN ROAD
Owston Wood
Sixteen Acre Plantation
SKELLOW ROAD
STATION ROAD
Carcroft Health Centre
High Street
Carcroft Industrial Estate
Wellsyke Road
Brooklands Rd
Bentley Moor Lane
Hangthwaite Road
Holmeroyd Road
Tiltshills Lane
Tilts
Tilts Hills
CHURCH LANE
Planet Road
Special School
Alexandra Road

27
46
67

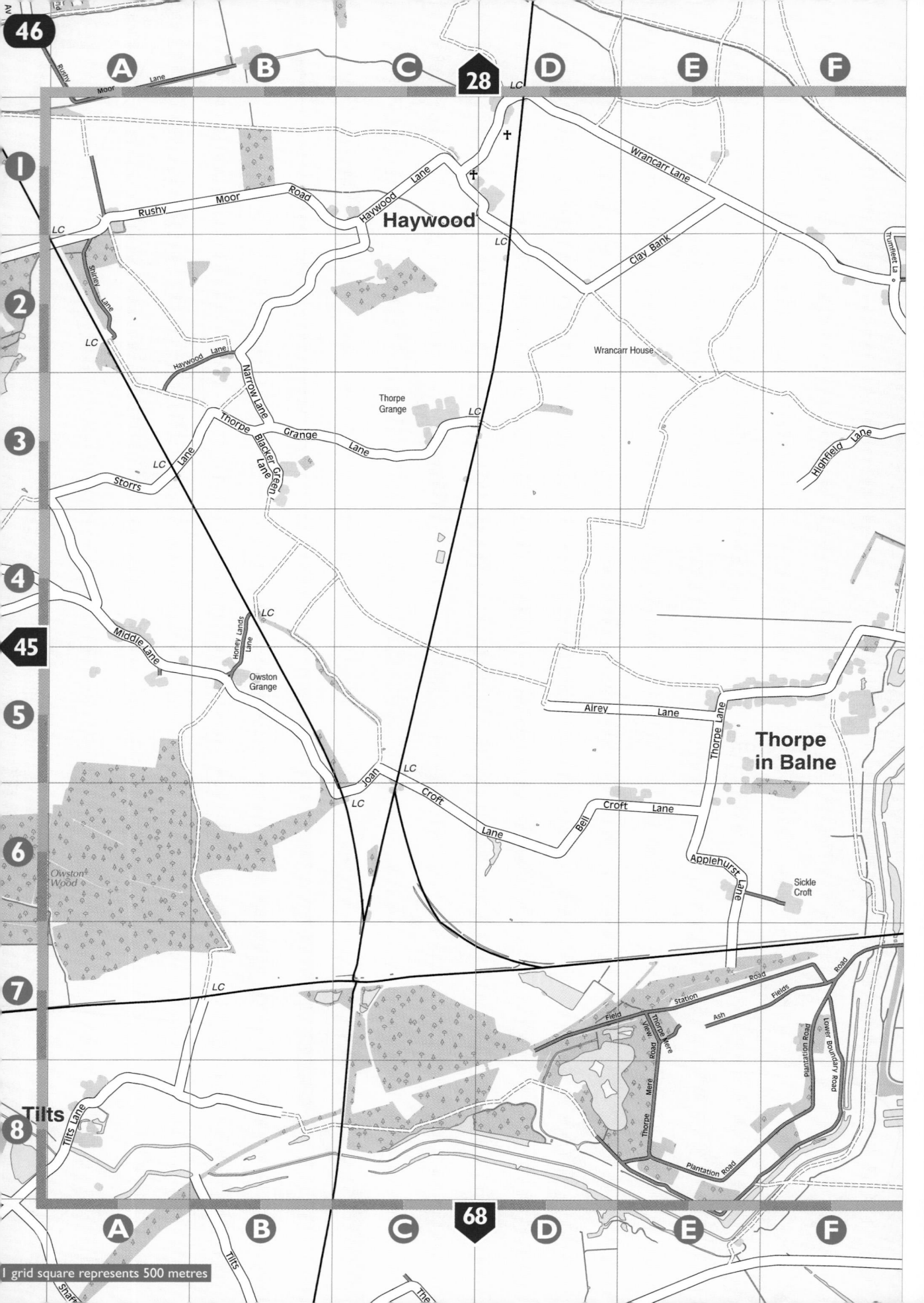

46
28
45
68
Haywood
Thorpe in Balne
Tilts
Rushy Moor Road
Haywood Lane
Wrancarr Lane
Clay Bank
Shirley Lane
Wrancarr House
Narrow Lane
Thorpe Grange
Thorpe Grange Lane
Blacker Green Lane
Storrs Lane
Highfield Lane
Trumfleet La
Middle Lane
Honey Lands Lane
Owston Grange
Airey Lane
Thorpe Lane
Joan Croft Lane
Bell Croft Lane
Applehurst Lane
Sickle Croft
Owston Wood
Field Station Road
Fields Road
Ash
Thorpe Mere View
Thorpe Mere Road
Plantation Road
Lower Boundary Road
Tilts Lane
LC
1 grid square represents 500 metres

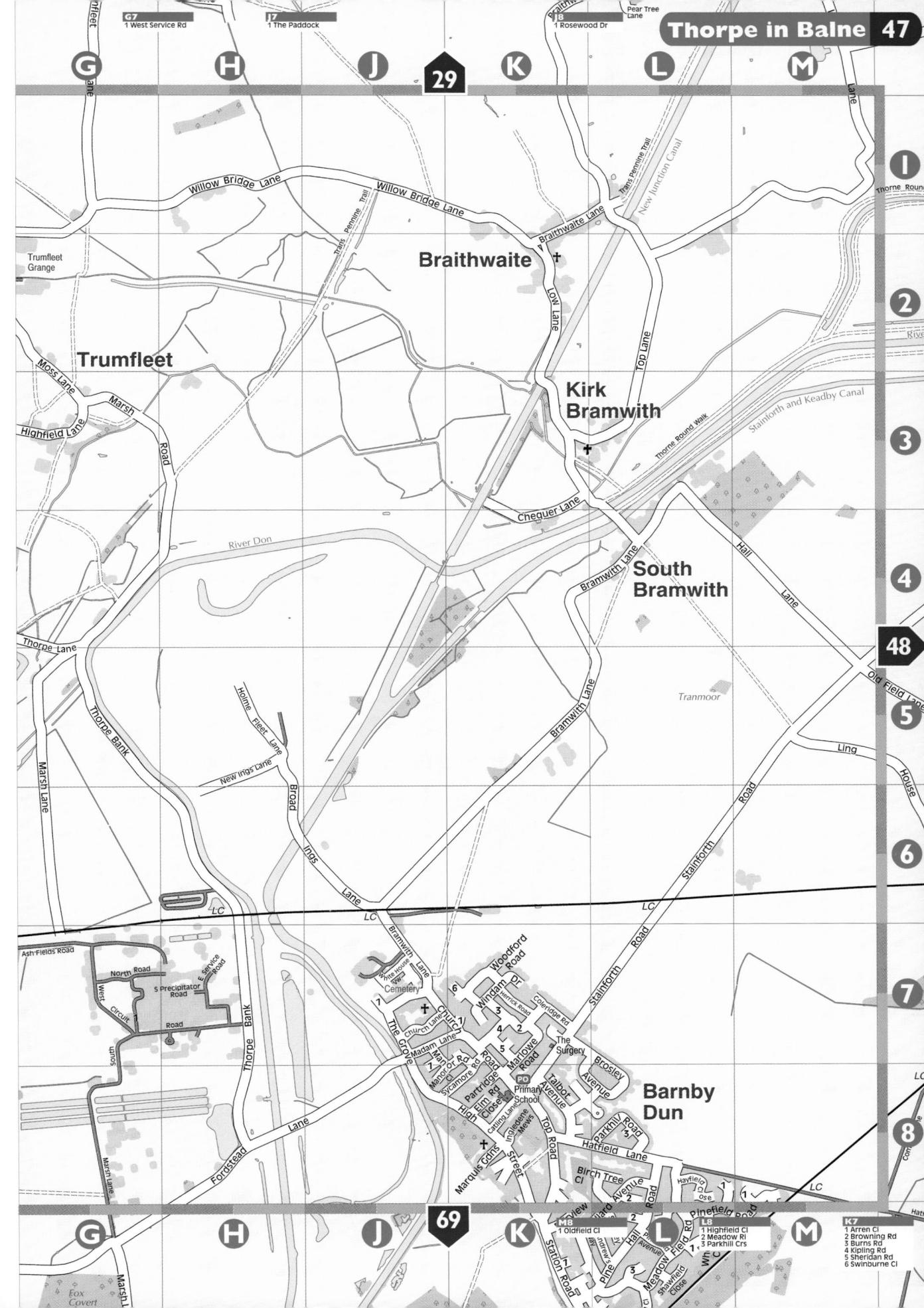

G7
1 West Service Rd

J7
1 The Paddock

B
1 Rosewood Dr

Pear Tree Lane

G   H   J   29   K   L   M

I

2

Trumfleet Grange

Braithwaite

Willow Bridge Lane

Willow Bridge Lane

Trans Pennine Trail

Trans Pennine Trail

Braithwaite Lane

New Junction Canal

3

Moss Lane

Trumfleet

Marsh Road

Highfield Lane

Kirk Bramwith

Low Lane

Top Lane

Thorne Round Walk

Stainforth and Keadby Canal

Rive

Chequer Lane

River Don

South Bramwith

Bramwith Lane

Hall Lane

4

48

Thorpe Lane

Tranmoor

Old Field Lane

5

Thorpe Bank

Holme Fleet Lane

New Ings Lane

Bramwith Lane

Ling

House

Marsh Lane

Broad Ings Lane

Stainforth Road

6

LC

LC

LC

7

Ash Fields Road

North Road

West Circuit

S Precipitator Road

E Service Road

Road

Thorpe Bank

Woodford Road

Cemetery

Three House WW?

Windam Dr

Herrick Road

Coleridge Rd

Brosley Avenue

The Surgery

Barnby Dun

Marsh Lane

Fordstead Lane

The Grove

Church Lane

Madam Lane

Manor Dr

Church Lane

Sycamore Rd

Malowe Road

Talbot Avenue

Top Road

Parkhill Road

Stainforth Road

LC

Partridge Road

Elm Rd

Close

Catling Lane

PO

Primary School

Inglebene Mews

High Avenue

Hatfield Lane

8

Marquis Gdns

Birch Tree Cl

Hayfield Close

Pinefield Road

LC

Fox Covert

G   H   J   69   K   L   M

M8
1 Oldfield Cl

L8
1 Highfield Cl
2 Meadow Rl
3 Parkhill Crs

K7
1 Arren Cl
2 Browning Rd
3 Burns Rd
4 Kipling Rd
5 Sheridan Rd
6 Swinburne Cl

Station Road

Pine Lane

Meadow View Rd

Shawfield Close

Marsh

Hat

48
30
47
70
A
B
C
D
E
F
1
2
3
4
5
6
7
8
D8
1 Ingram Gv
E2
1 Polton Toft
D3
1 Breezemount Ct
2 Crossways
3 Nutfields Gv
D6
1 Hazel Rd
C4
1 Duke St
2 Lord St
3 Queen's Crs
4 Stanley Rd
C2
1 Fleet La
2 New Inn La
3 White House Cl
C3
1 Bridge Hl
Trundle Lane
Dirty Lane
Far Bank
Nab Lane
Row
Lane
Green Road
Ings Lane
Plumtree Hill Road
Fishlake Nab
River Don
Thorne Round Walk
Stainforth and Keadby Canal
East Bank
West Bank
Water Lane
Silver St
Finkle Street
Fleets Close
Briars La
Thorne Road
Field Road
Old Carpenter's Yard
Ramskir Lane
New Park Estate
Polton Close
Holme Gardens
School
Kirton Lane Primary School
Measham Drive
Moira Cl
Mayfield Avenue
Kirton Lane
Hugh Hill Lane
PO
Ashfield Grove
Beech Crescent
Chestnut Avenue
Dr Anderson Av
West Avenue
Coronation Road
East Lane
Back Lane
New Green
Princess Avenue
Church Road
Kenneth Avenue
Junction Road
STAINFORTH
Bootham Lane
Crofts Lane
Doncaster Road
Stainforth Middle School
Cemetery
Oldfield Close
Oldfield Lane
WRCC Clinic
Kingsway
Stanley Gdns
Emerson Avenue
Bootham Crescent
Bootham Rd
Oldfield Crescent
Thomas Road
East Avenue
Old Field Lane
King Georges Court
Victoria Close
Station Road
Hatfield & Stainforth Station
DN7
Ling House Lane
Ling House
Parks
The Crescent
Bootham Lane Industrial Estate
Hop Hills La
The Oval
Cherry Tree Gv
Mitchell Cl
Orchard Grove
Cherry Tree Dr
Abbey Way
Norwood Road
Crabtree Road
Abbeyfield Road
Hampton Road
Parks Road
Craven Road
Myrtle Road
Poplar Road
Beechfield Road
Broadway
Canterbury Road
Durham Road
Prescott Gv
Lichfield Road
York Road
Winchester Road
Inverness Road
Hatfield County Primary School
Bootham Close
Nettleholme
Hund Oak Drive
Station Road
Menson Drive
King's Close
Grange
Cleveland Way
Millard Avenue
Ash Hill Crescent
St Edwins Close
Warrenne Road
Abbey Road
Broom Ct
Roseberry Av
Crookes Broom Avenue
Marton Dr
St Lawrence Road
Sheep Dip Lane
The Parks
Ashfield Road
Ingram Crs
Ingram Road
Primary School
Drive
Oakland Av
Crookes Broom Lane
The Surgery
Ash Hill Rd
Leverstock Green
Kinsbourne Gn
Ash Hill Middle School
High School
Hatfield Comprehensive School
Coppice Grove
Broadwater
Broadwater
Botany Bay
LC
Botany Bay Lane
Common Lane
Hatfield La
E3
1 Cedar Av
E7
1 Abbey Dr
2 Cherry Tree Dr
3 Glencoe Cl
E8
1 Broadwater Dr
2 Warrenne Cl
3 White House Cl
F3
1 Ellesmere Gv
2 Watsons Cft
F7
1 Grange Cl
2 Homestead Garth
3 Hund Oak Dr
4 Linden Cl
5 Milcroft Crs
6 Parkstone Gv
7 Thompson Nook
F8
1 Nunthorpe Cl
2 St Andrews Gv
3 Thompson Dr
Aston Gn
Norman Drive
Road
ROAD
The Lings
1 grid square represents 500 metres

G7
1 Bracken Heen Cl
2 Westfield Vls
G8
1 Manor Gdns
J7
1 Firth Field Rd
Stainforth and Keadby Canal
Staniland Yacht Club
Boating Dyke Way
Union Road
Canal Side
31
Thorne Round Walk
M18
Ashfields
Kirton Lane
Pennine Road
Cotswold Road
Quantock Close
Grampian Way
Thorne Golf Club
Ashfield Road
Hatfield Road A614
South Pde A614
Green Top First School
Burgar Road
Johnston's Road
Poffinder Wood Rd
Lane
Bailey Lane
Hatfield Road A1146
Tudworth Road A614
Cuckoo Lane
Doncaster North Service Area
Junction 1
M180
A18
50
Junction 5
Crook Tree Lane
Thorne Road A1146
Brierholme Close
Brierholme Carr Road
Stanhurst Lane
Brierholme Carr
Tudworth Green Farm
Manor Middle School
Victoria Av
Ambrose Av
Bullivant Rd
Station Road
HATFIELD
North Ings Road
Old Thorne Road
Firth Field Road
Brierholme Ings Road
Tudworth Road
Sandtoft Road
Travis County Primary School
High Street A18
Back Field La
Epworth Rd (West)
New Mill Field Rd
Old Epworth Rd (East)
Epworth Road
Acomb Common Road
Stone Hill Road
Stone Hill A614
Slay Pits
Cemetery Road
Churchill Avenue
Lane
Stone Hill
Far Common Road
Bull Moor Road
Manor Road A18
Hatfield Cemetery
71
Primary School
Warwick Close
Somerton Dr
Main Street
Laurold Avenue
Remple Avenue
Hatfield Woodhouse
M1
1 Elm Tree Gv
L1
1 Malvern Cl

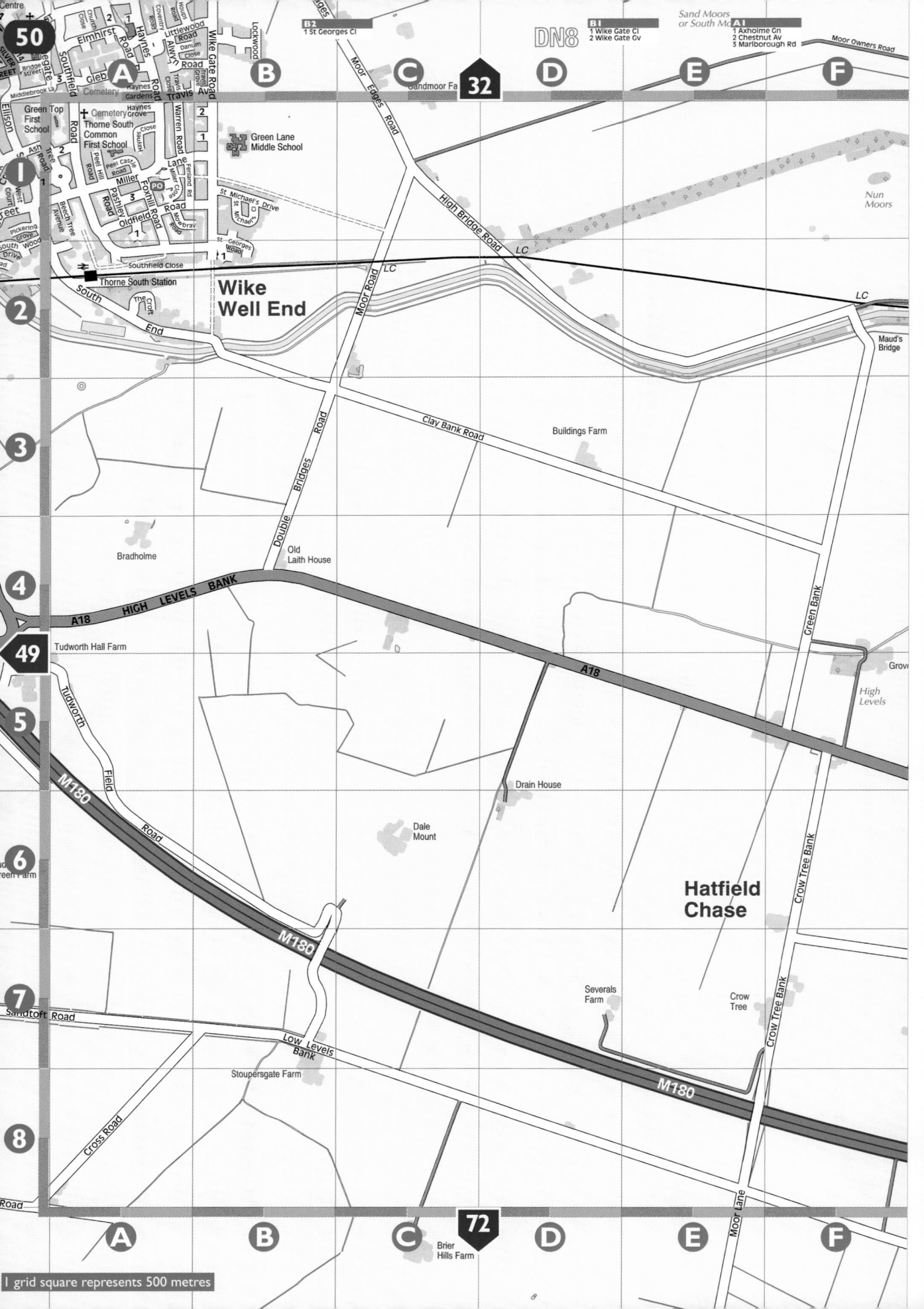

50
32
72
49
DN8
B2
1 St Georges Cl
B1
1 Wike Gate Cl
2 Wike Gate Gv
A1
1 Axholme Gn
2 Chestnut Av
3 Marlborough Rd
Sand Moors or South Moors
Moor Owners Road
Sandmoor Farm
Green Top First School
Thorne South Common First School
Green Lane Middle School
Cemetery
Southfield Close
Thorne South Station
Wike Well End
South End
Moor Edges Road
High Bridge Road
Moor Road
Double Bridges Road
Clay Bank Road
Buildings Farm
Nun Moors
Maud's Bridge
Bradholme
Old Laith House
A18 HIGH LEVELS BANK
A18
Tudworth Hall Farm
Tudworth Field Road
Green Bank
High Levels
Drain House
Dale Mount
M180
Hatfield Chase
Crow Tree Bank
Severals Farm
Crow Tree
Sandtoft Road
Low Levels Bank
Stoupersgate Farm
Cross Road
Moor Lane
Brier Hills Farm
1 grid square represents 500 metres

G H J **33** K L M

I

Medge Hall

LC

Stainforth & Keadby Canal

Sa
Far

2

Ol

3

Sandhill Farm

Dirtness
Levels

4

House

Red House

Boating Dike

Jaque's Bank

5

Popla

Hains Farm

Jacque's Farm

6

Bank
House Farm

A18

Smaque
Farm

HIGH LEVELS
BANK

A18

Elder
House

High Levels Bank

Dirtness
Bridge
Farm

7

Plains House
Farm

Doncaster
North Lincolnshire

8

M180

M180

Low Levels Bank

Lane

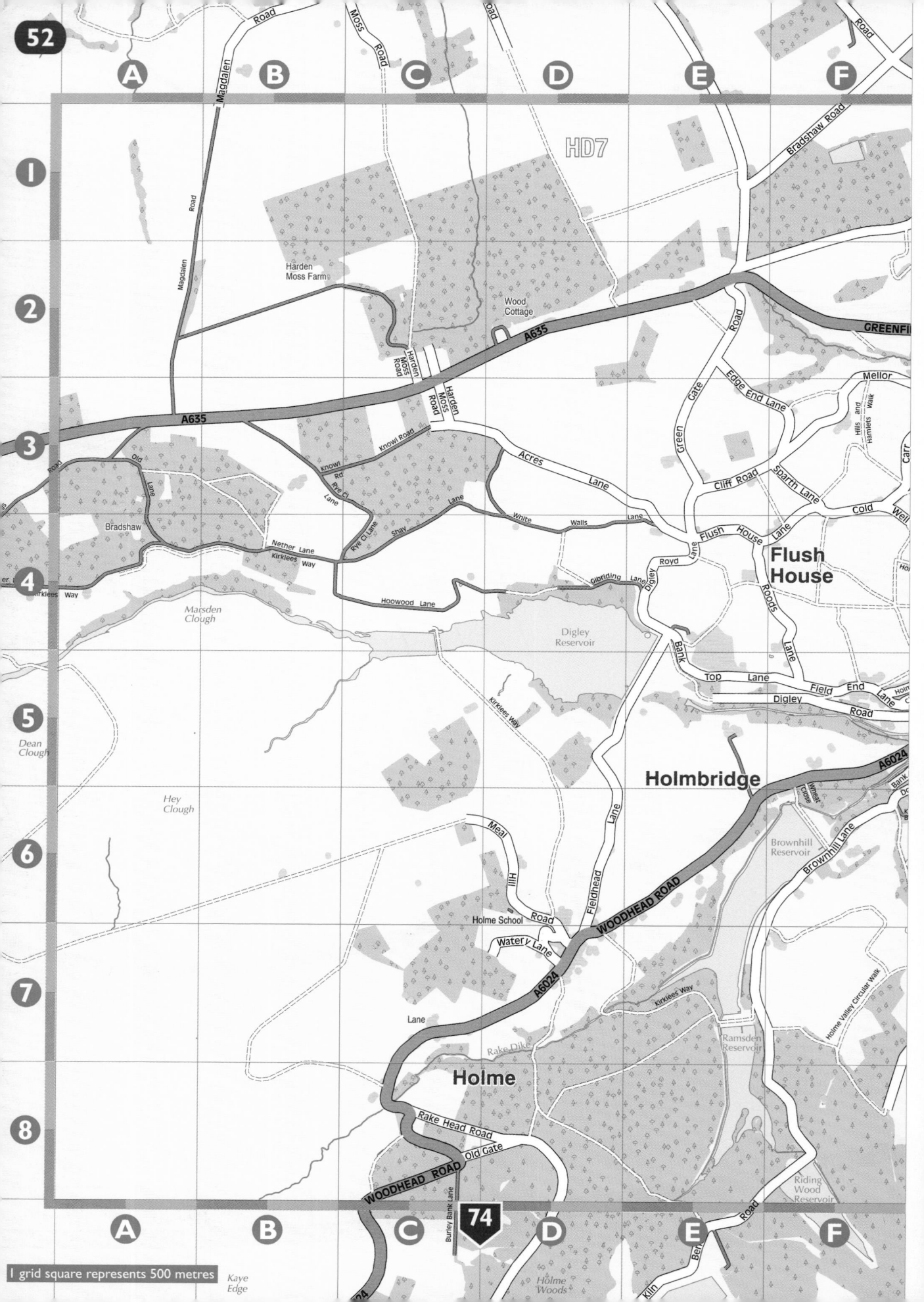

A
B
C
D
E
F
1
2
3
4
5
6
7
8
HD7
Magdalen Road
Moss Road
Bradshaw Road
Harden Moss Farm
Wood Cottage
A635
GREENFI
Harden Moss Road
Knowl Road
Knowl Rd
Rye Cl Lane
Old Road
Lane
Bradshaw
Nether Lane
Kirklees Way
Acres Lane
Shay Lane
White Walls Lane
Green Gate
Edge End Lane
Mellor
Hills and Hamlets Walk
Cliff Road
Sparth Lane
Cold Well
Carr
Flush House Lane
Royd Lane
Digley
Gibriding Lane
Flush House
Roods Lane
Hoowood Lane
Marsden Clough
Digley Reservoir
Bank Top Lane
Field End Lane
Digley Road
Dean Clough
Hey Clough
Holmbridge
A6024
Wheat Close
Meal Hill Road
Fieldhead Lane
Brownhill Reservoir
Brownhill Lane
Holme School
Watery Lane
WOODHEAD ROAD
Kirklees Way
Holme Valley Circular Walk
Lane
Rake Dike
Ramsden Reservoir
Holme
Rake Head Road
Old Gate
Riding Wood Reservoir
Burley Bank Lane
Road
Ben
Kiln
Holme Woods
Kaye Edge
1 grid square represents 500 metres

74

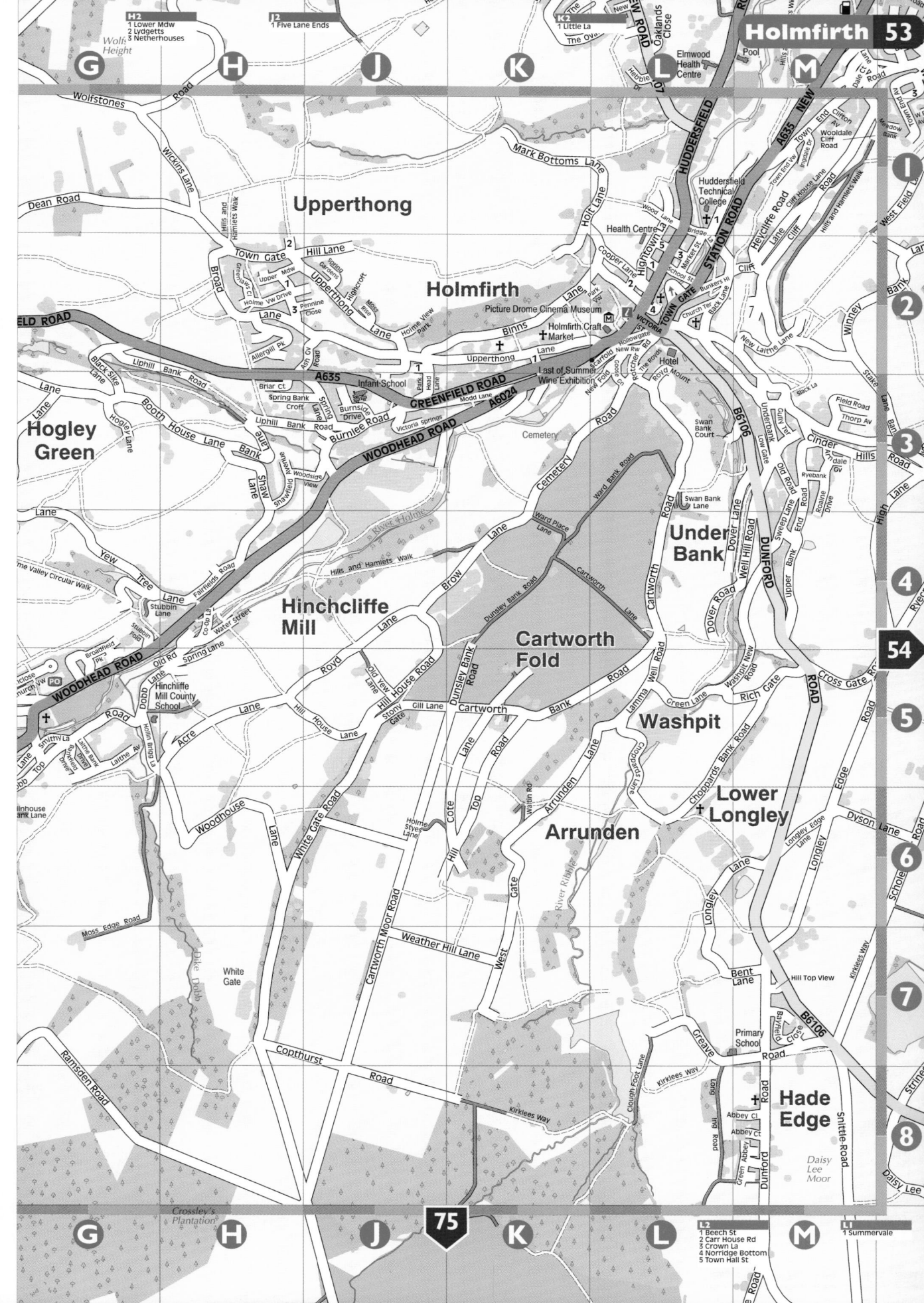

G H J K L M

H2
1 Lower Mdw
2 Lydgetts
3 Netherhouses

J2
1 Five Lane Ends

K2
1 Little La
The Oval

Elmwood
Health
Centre

Pool

I

Wolfstones

Wolf
Height

Dean Road

Wickins Lane

Broad

Road

Upperthong

Mark Bottoms Lane

Holt Lane

Hightown La

Huddersfield
Technical
College

Health Centre

STATION ROAD

HUDDERSFIELD

Town End Vw
Town End
Indsale Dr

Cliff House Lane

Heycliffe Road

Wooldale
Cliff
Road

West Field Rd

Winney

1

Town Gate
Upper Mdw
Greenvale
Holme Vw Drive
Pennine
Close

Hill Lane

Upperthong Lane

Highcroft
Moss
Gardens

Holmfirth

Picture Drome Cinema Museum

Cooper Lane

School
Market St

Church Ter

Back Lane

Cliff

Bank

Lane

2

Allergill Pk

A635

Infant School

GREENFIELD ROAD

Binns

Upperthong

Holmfirth Craft
Market

Last of Summer
Wine Exhibition

New Fold

Scarfold

Rotcher
The Royd
Roay Mount

Hotel

New Laithe Lane

Church

3

Hogley
Green

Liphill Bank Road

Booth House Lane

Spring Bank
Croft

Burnlee
Drive

Liphill Bank

Woodside
View

A6024

WOODHEAD ROAD

Victoria Springs

Mdd Lane

Cemetery

Road

Swan
Bank
Court

B6106

Underbank
Low Gate

Cinder
Hills

Thorp Av

Field Road

High Lane

3

Yew

Tree

Lane

Shaw Lane

Sharpfield

River Holme

Hills and Hamlets Walk

Cemetery Lane

Ward Bank Road

Ward Place
Lane

Swan Bank
Lane

Dover Lane

DUNFORD
Well Hill Road

**Under
Bank**

Old Road

Ryebank

4

Stubbin
Lane

Water Street

Fairfields

Road

**Hinchcliffe
Mill**

Brow
Lane

Dunsley Bank Road

Cartworth
Lane

Dover Road

Cartworth
Road

Upper

Lane

54

Broadfield
Pk

Old Rd

Spring Lane

Royd

Old Yew
Lane

**Cartworth
Fold**

Cartworth

Bank

Lamma Well Road

Green Lane

Rich Gate

Washpit New Rd

Cross Gate Rd

ROAD

5

WOODHEAD ROAD

Hinchcliffe
Mill County
School

Hill House Lane

Stony
Gate

Gill Lane

Cartworth

Road

Choppards Bank Road

Washpit

**Lower
Longley**

Longley Edge

5

Acre

Woodhouse Lane

White Gate Road

Hill House Lane

Cote Lane

Top Road

Arrunden Lane

Watin Rd

Longley Edge
Lane

Longley Lane

Dyson Lane

6

Holme
Styes Lane

Arrunden

River Ribble

Bent
Lane

Hill Top View

Kirklees Way

B6106

7

Cartworth Moor Road

Weather Hill Lane

West
Gate

Greave

Bayfield
Close

Primary
School

Dunford Road

7

White
Gate

Copthurst

Road

Kirklees Way

Clough Foot Lane

Abbey Cl
Green Abbey

Abbey Ct

Dunford Road

Snittle Road

**Hade
Edge**

8

Ramsden Road

Crossley's
Plantation

Dike Dokk

75

Kirklees Way

Daisy
Lee
Moor

String

Daisy Lee

8

G H J K L M

L2
1 Beech St
2 Carr House Rd
3 Crown La
4 Norridge Bottom
5 Town Hall St

L1
1 Summervale

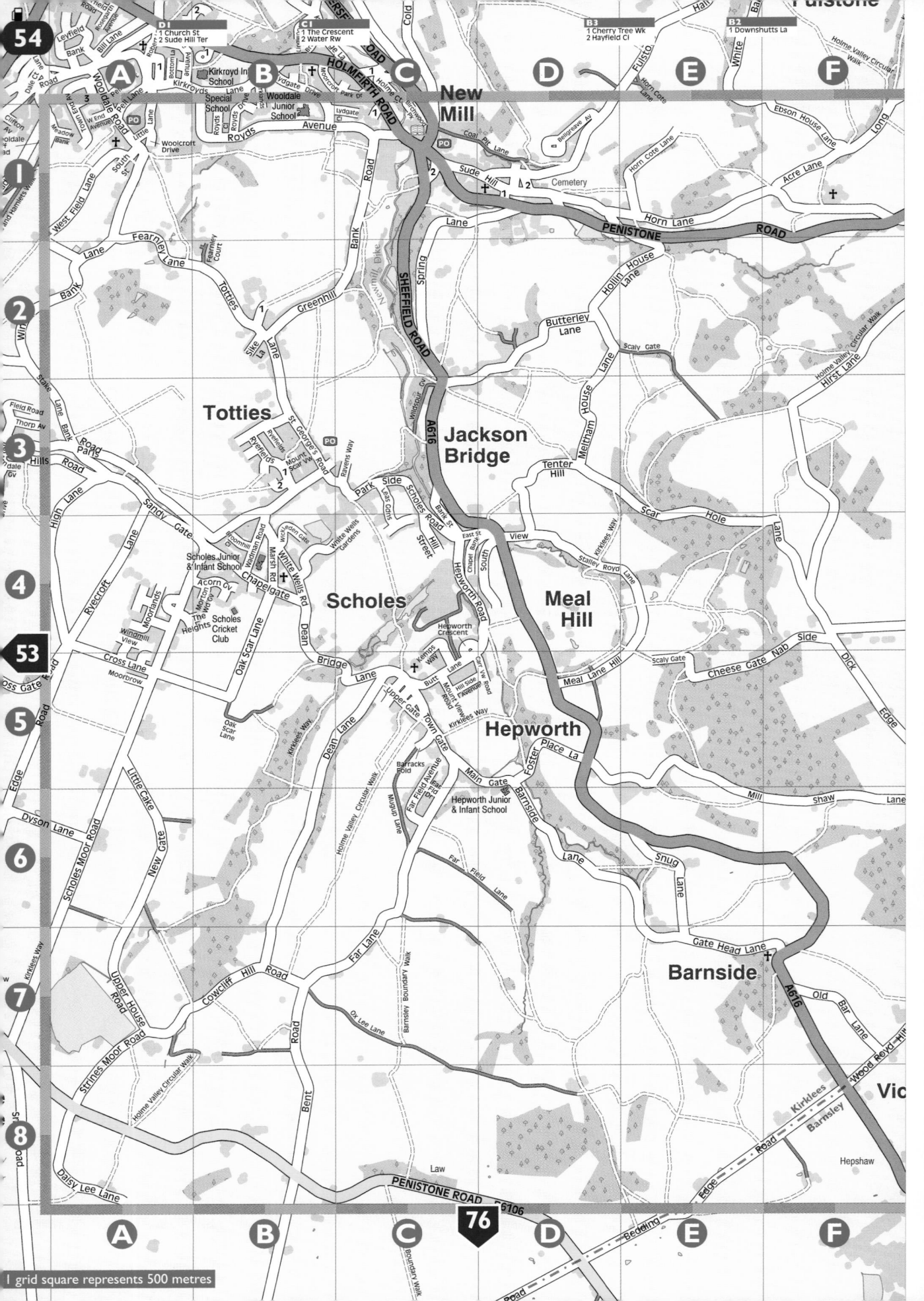

54
53
76
D1 1 Church St 2 Sude Hill Ter
C1 1 The Crescent 2 Water Rw
B3 1 Cherry Tree Wk 2 Hayfield Cl
B2 1 Downshutts La
New Mill
Totties
Jackson Bridge
Scholes
Meal Hill
Hepworth
Barnside
HOLMFIRTH ROAD
SHEFFIELD ROAD
A616
PENISTONE ROAD
PENISTONE ROAD B6106
Kirkroyd Inf School
Special School
Wooldale Junior School
Scholes Junior & Infant School
Scholes Cricket Club
Hepworth Junior & Infant School
Hepworth Crescent
Cemetery
Royds Avenue
Sude Hill
Coal Pit Lane
Spring Lane
Bank Road
Greenhill
Totties Lane
Fearnley Lane
Fearnley Court
West Field Lane
Sike La
St George's Road
Ryefields
Mount Scar Vw
Ravens Way
Park Side
Leas Gdns
Scholes Road
Bank St
Hill Street
East St
Chapel Bank
South
Hepworth Road
Sandy Gate
High Lane
Ryecroft Lane
Broomhill Cl
Wadman Road
Marsh Rd
White Wells Rd
White Wells Gardens
Wickleden Gate
Chapelgate
Acorn Gv
Morton Wd Gv
The Heights
Moorlands
Windmill View
Cross Lane
Moorbrow
Oak Scar Lane
Dean Bridge Lane
Dean Lane
Kemps Way
Butt Lane
Hill Side Avenue
Carr Vw Road
Mount View Road
Upper Gate
Town Gate
Kirklees Way
Main Gate
Barracks Fold
Far Field Avenue
Far Fld Dr
Mugup Lane
Far Field Lane
Foster Place La
Barnside Lane
Tenter Hill
Meltham House Lane
Butterley Lane
Hollin House Lane
Scaly Gate
Scar Hole Lane
Stalley Royd Lane
Meal Lane Hill
Cheese Gate Nab Side
Dick Edge Lane
Mill Shaw Lane
Snug Lane
Gate Head Lane
Old Bar Lane
Wood Royd Hill
Hirst Lane
Holme Valley Circular Walk
Horn Lane
Horn Cote Lane
Acre Lane
Ebson House Lane
Bellgreave Av
Long
Scholes Moor Road
Little Cake
New Gate
Dyson Lane
Edge Road
Upper House Road
Cowcliff Hill Road
Far Lane
Strines Moor Road
Ox Lee Lane
Barnsley Boundary Walk
Bent Road
Daisy Lee Lane
Law
Edge Road
Kirklees
Barnsley
Hepshaw
Bedding
Wooldale Road
Pell Lane
Little Lane
Woolcroft Drive
South St
Stake Lane
Bank
Field Road
Thorp Av
Paris Road
Hills Road
Wildspur Gv
Newmill Dike
Lydgate Cl
Moorcroft Park Dr
Holme Ct
Birchwood
PO
1 grid square represents 500 metres

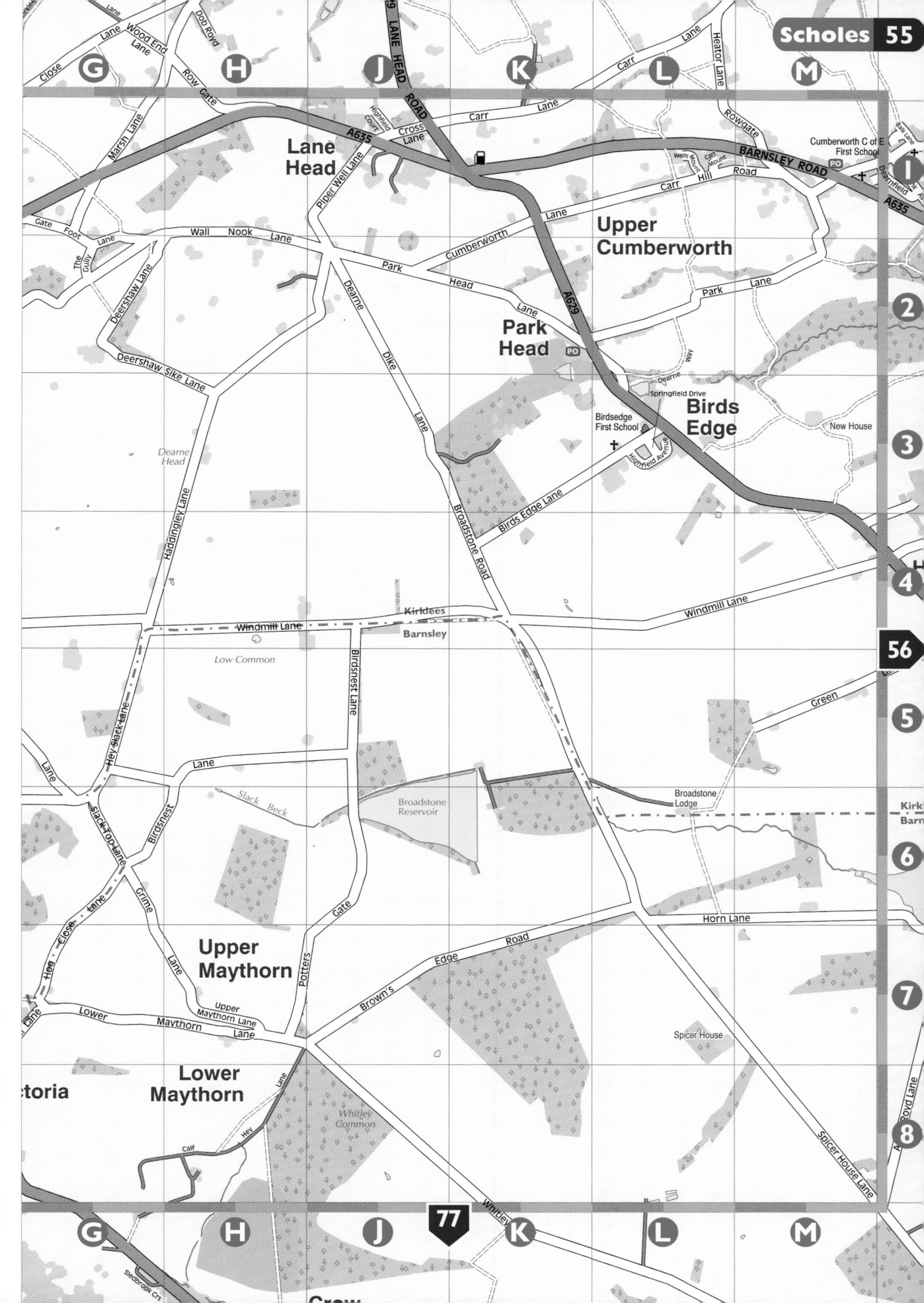

G H J K L M

Lane Head

Lane Head Road

A635

Piper Well Lane

Marsh Lane

Wood End Lane

Dob Royd

Row Gate

Close

Lane

Highfield Court

Cross Lane

Carr Lane

Carr Lane

Wells Mount

Carr Mount

Carr Hill Road

Rowgate

BARNSLEY ROAD

A635

Cumberworth C of E First School

PO

Deernfield

Park Lane

I

Gate Foot Lane

The Gully

Wall Nook Lane

Park Head Lane

Cumberworth Lane

Upper Cumberworth

Park Lane

Dearne Way

2

Deershaw Lane

Deershaw Sike Lane

Dearne Lane

A629

Park Head

PO

Springfield Drive

Dearne

Birds Edge

New House

Dearne Head

Birdsedge First School

Highfield Avenue

3

Haddingley Lane

Broadstone Road

Birds Edge Lane

H

4

Windmill Lane

Windmill Lane

Kirklees

Barnsley

56

Low Common

Birdsnest Lane

Green

5

Hey Slack Lane

Lane

Slack Beck

Broadstone Reservoir

Broadstone Lodge

Kirk Barn

6

Birdsnest Lane

Slack Top Lane

Grime Lane

Potters Gate

Brown's Edge Road

Horn Lane

7

Upper Maythorn

Heg Close Lane

Upper Maythorn Lane

Lower Maythorn Lane

Lane

Spicer House

...toria

Calf

Hey

Lower Maythorn

Whitley Common

Whitle...

Spicer House Lane

A Boyd Lane

8

G H J **77** K L M

Crow

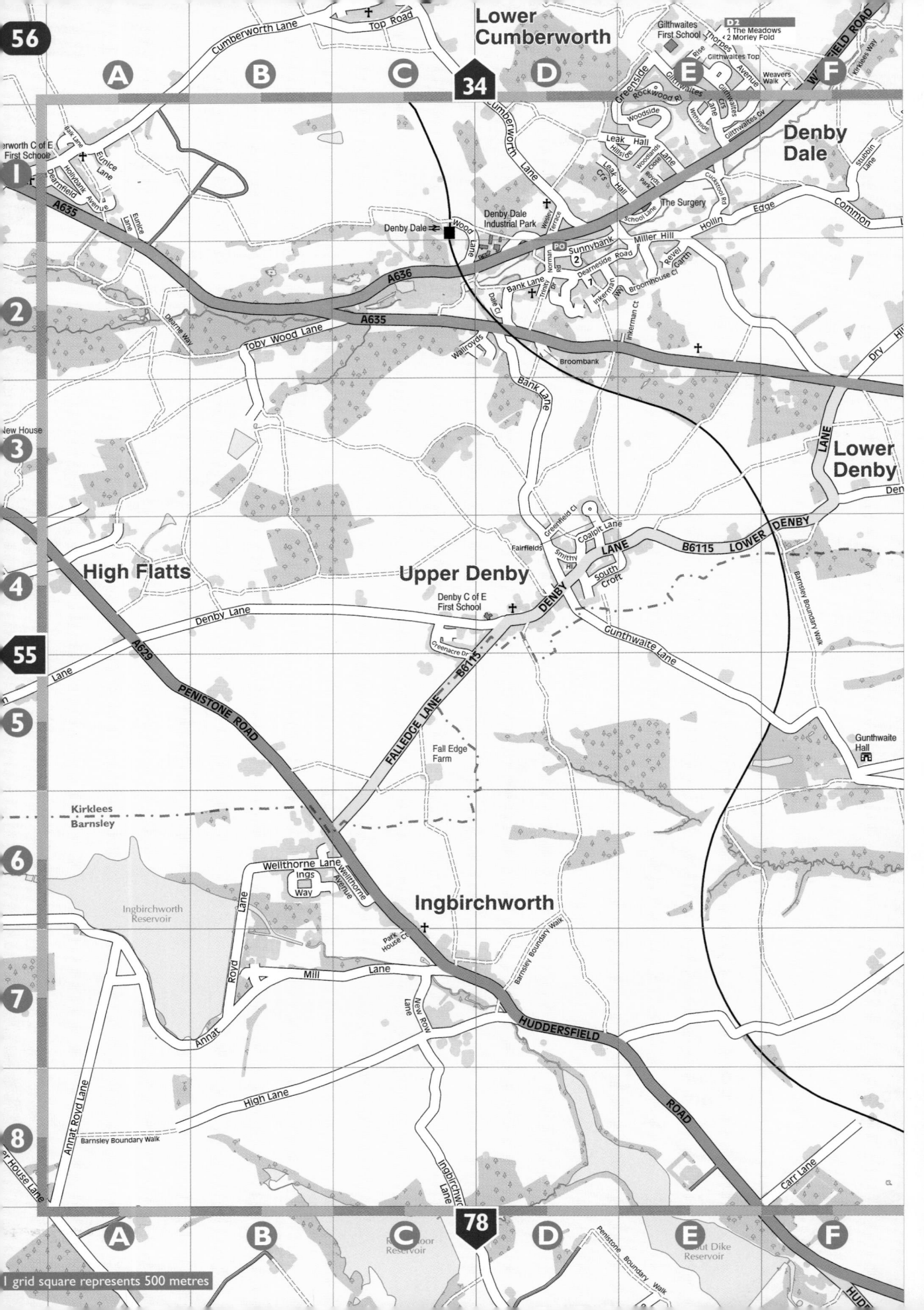

A   B   C   34   D   E   F

D2
1 The Meadows
2 Morley Fold

Lower
Cumberworth

Gilthwaites
First School

Denby
Dale

Cumberworth Lane

Top Road

Cumberworth C of E
First School

Eunice Lane

Dearnfield

A635

Eunice Lane

Deane Way

Toby Wood Lane

A636

A635

Denby Dale

Wood Lane

Denby Dale
Industrial Park

Greenside

Rockwood Rd

Woodside

Leak
Hall

Leak
Hall
Crs

Woodlands

Thorpes

Gilthwaites Top

Gilthwaites
Avenue

Gilthwaites Gv

Weavers
Walk

Kirklees Way

The Surgery

School Lane

Hollin

Edge

Common

Stubbin Lane

PO

Sunnybank

Norman Rd

Weaver
Terrace

Dearneside Road

Miller Hill

Revel
CT

Bank Lane

Dale Cl

Inkerman Rw

Inkerman Ct

Broomhouse Cl

Garth

Wallroyds

Bank Lane

Broombank

Dry Hill

New House

Lower
Denby

Den

High Flatts

Denby Lane

A629

PENISTONE ROAD

Greenacre Dr

B6115

Upper Denby

Denby C of E
First School

Fairfields

Greenfield Cl

Smithy
Hill

Coalpit Lane

DENBY LANE

South
Croft

B6115 LOWER DENBY

Gunthwaite Lane

Barnsley Boundary Walk

Gunthwaite
Hall

Kirklees
Barnsley

FALLEDGE LANE

Fall Edge
Farm

Ingbirchworth
Reservoir

Wellthorne Lane

Ings
Way

Wellthorne Avenue

Ingbirchworth

Royd Lane

Mill Lane

Annat

Park
House Ct

New Row Lane

Barnsley Boundary Walk

HUDDERSFIELD ROAD

Annat Royd Lane

High Lane

Barnsley Boundary Walk

House Lane

Ingbirchworth Lane

Carr Lane

Reservoir

Reservoir

Penistone Boundary Walk

Dike
Reservoir

HUD

1 grid square represents 500 metres

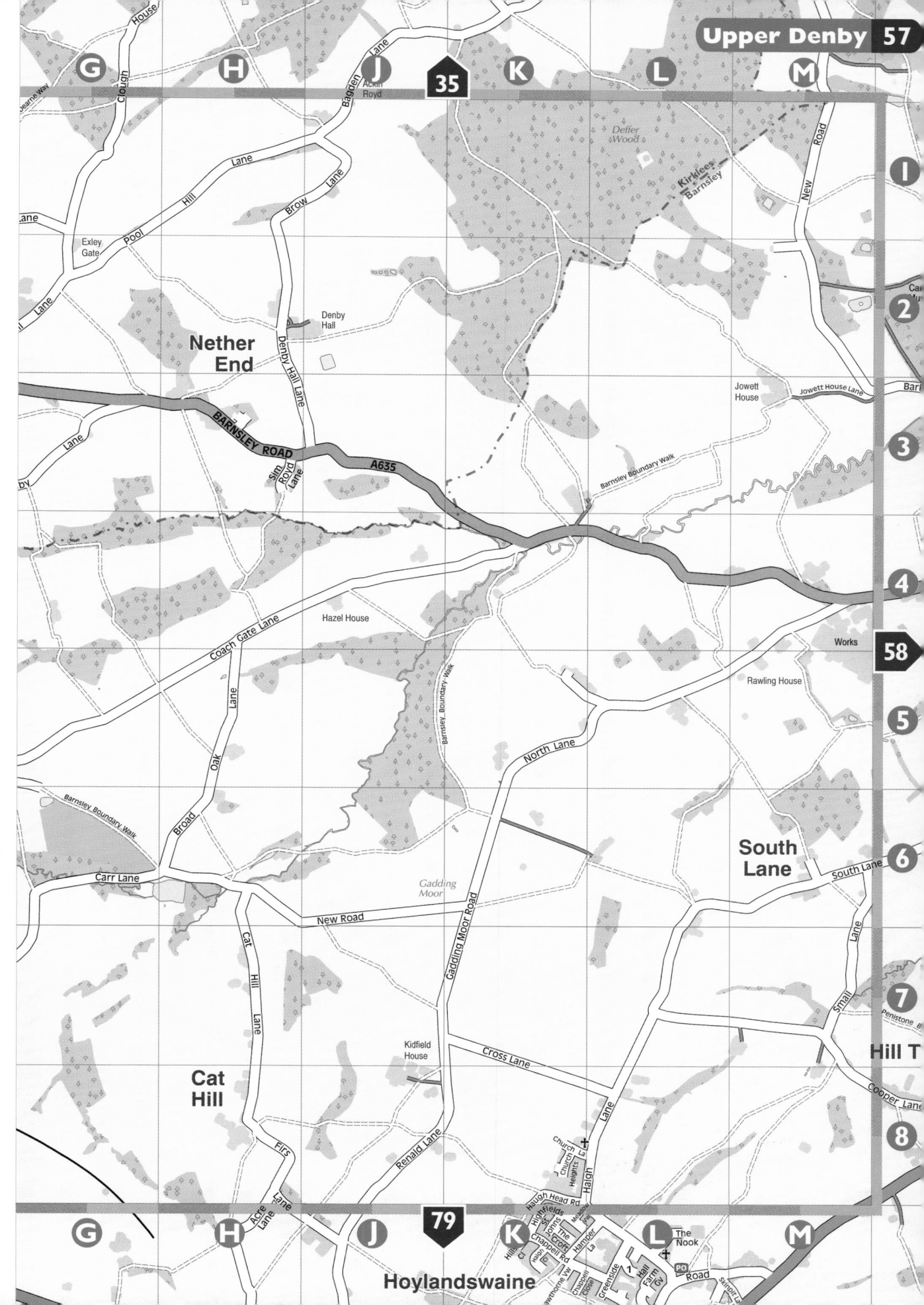

G H J 35 K L M

I

2

3

4

58

5

6

7

8

G H J 79 K L M

Deffer
Wood

Kirklees
Barnsley

New Road

Car

Bar

Jowett
House

Jowett House Lane

Bar

Barnsley Boundary Walk

Works

Rawling House

South
Lane

South Lane

Small Lane

Penistone B

Hill T

Cooper Lane

Nether
End

Denby
Hall

Denby Hall Lane

BARNSLEY ROAD

A635

Sim Royd Lane

Bagden Lane

Ackin
Royd

Hill

Brow

Lane

Lane

Pool

House

Clough

Dearne Way

Exley
Gate

Lane

Lane

Lane

Denby

Coach Gate Lane

Oak Lane

Broad Lane

Barnsley Boundary Walk

Carr Lane

Hazel House

Barnsley Boundary Walk

North Lane

Gadding
Moor

New Road

Gadding Moor Road

Cat Hill Lane

Cat
Hill

Firs Lane

Acre Lane

Renald Lane

Kidfield
House

Cross Lane

Haugh Head Rd

Highfields

Church Heights

Church La

Haigh Lane

St John's

The Croft

Hamper La

Meadow Vw

Hills Cl

Chappell Rd

Greenside

Hall Farm Fly

The
Nook

PO

Road

Sunpit La

Hoylandswaine

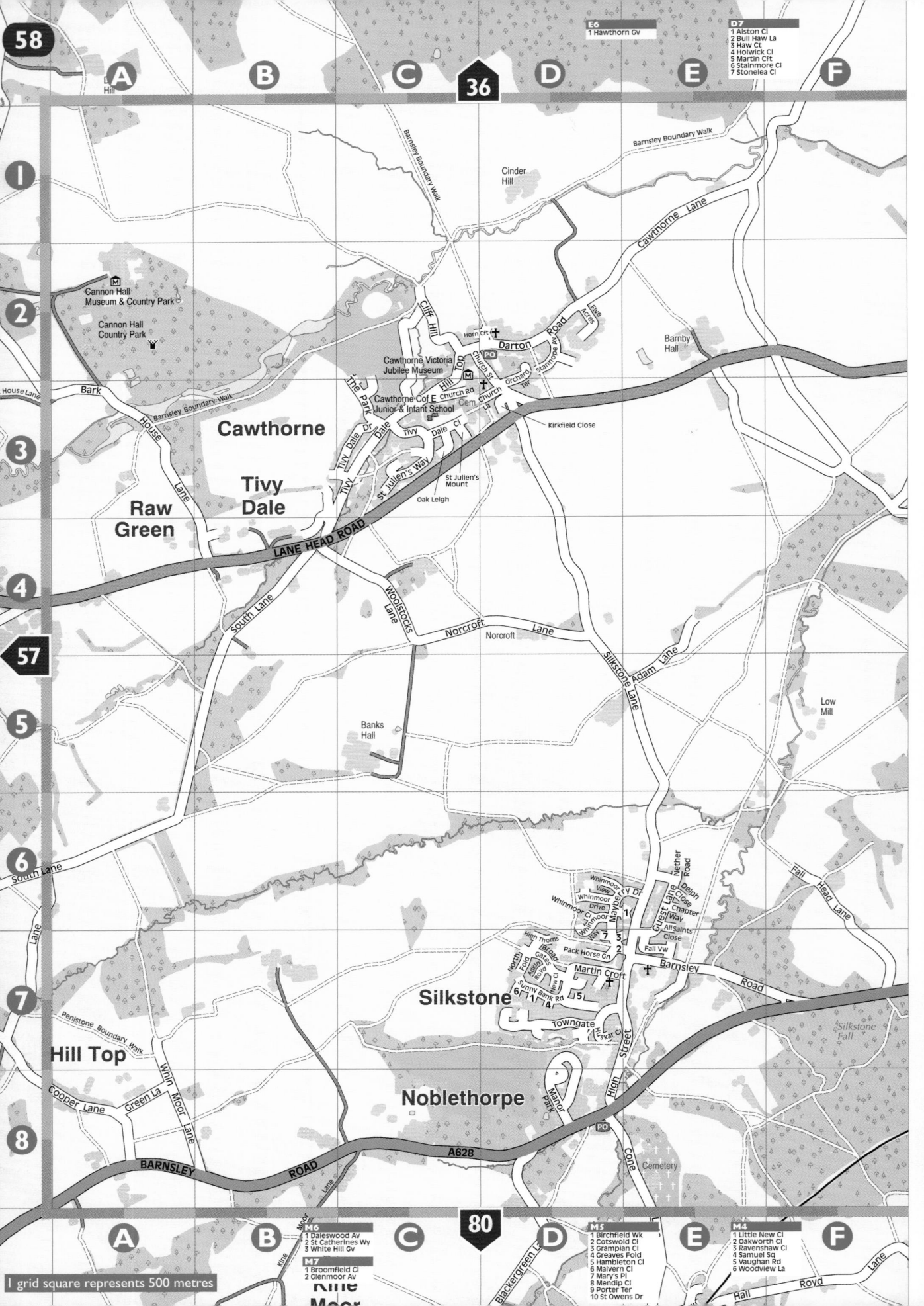

A B C D E F

D7
1 Alston Cl
2 Bull Haw La
3 Haw Ct
4 Holwick Cl
5 Martin Cft
6 Stainmore Cl
7 Stonelea Cl

I

Barnsley Boundary Walk

Cinder Hill

Hill

2

Cannon Hall Museum & Country Park

Cannon Hall Country Park

Barnsley Boundary Walk

Horn Cft

Darton

Cawthorne Victoria Jubilee Museum

Cliff Hill

Hill Top

Church St

Elbe Acres

Stanhope Way

Road

Barnby Hall

House Lane

Bark

Cawthorne

Cawthorne C of E Junior & Infant School

The Park

Church Rd

Orchard Ter

Church

Cem

Kirkfield Close

3

Raw Green

Tivy Dale

Tivy Dale Dr

Tivy Dale

Tivy Dale Cl

St. Julien's Way

St Julien's Mount

House Lane

Oak Leigh

4

LANE HEAD ROAD

South Lane

Woolstocks Lane

Norcroft Lane

Norcroft

Silkstone Lane

Adam Lane

Low Mill

5

Banks Hall

6

South Lane

Lane

Nether Road

Delph

Fall Head Lane

Whinmoor View

Mayberry Dr

Guest Lane

Chapter Way

Whinmoor Drive

Close

Whinmoor Cl

Allsaints Close

Whinmoor

High Thorns

Fall Vw

Briary Gate Road

Pack Horse Gn

Martin Croft

Barnsley

North Fold

Road

7

Penistone Boundary Walk

Silkstone

Sunny Bank Rd

Towngate

High Street

Manor Park

Silkstone Fall

Hill Top

Whin Moor Lane

Cooper Lane

Green La

Noblethorpe

8

BARNSLEY

ROAD

A628

Cone

Cemetery

PO

Lane

Blackergreen La

A

C

D
M5
1 Birchfield Wk
2 Cotswold Cl
3 Grampian Cl
4 Greaves Fold
5 Hambleton Cl
6 Malvern Cl
7 Mary's Pl
8 Mendip Cl
9 Porter Ter
10 St Owens Dr

E

F
M4
1 Little New Cl
2 Oakworth Cl
3 Ravenshaw Cl
4 Samuel Sq
5 Vaughan Rd
6 Woodview La

Kine Moor

Hall Royd

G H J K L M

37

DEARNE HALL ROAD

Low
Barugh

Royal
Court

Barugh

Barugh Lane B6428
BARUGH LANE
The Cft
Werner Cft
7
Eden
Cl
Medina
Midhurst
Gv
Elsfead
Cl
Annan
Cl
Way
Medway
Cl
CLAYCLIFFE ROAD

Claycliffe
Business
Park

Claycliffe
Business
Park

Cannon
Way

Whaley Road

Redbrook
Business
Park

LANE HEAD ROAD A635 CAWTHORNE ROAD BARUGH GREEN ROAD A635

PO

St Austell
Dr
Longley Street
Miller St
Nicholson
Av
St John's
Cl
Birtle
Cl

**Barugh
Green**

Mawfield
Rd
St
Thomas's
Road

WILTHORPE ROAD

The Leylands
The Crescent

Acres
Wd
Comber
Rd

Westbury Cl

Redcliffe
Ripley
Rookdale Close
Redbrook
Gv

3

Mary
St
Higham
Common
Coronation
Road

Stevenson
Drive

Havlock Cl

Lane

Royd

Royd Lane

S75

Redbrook Farm

Gawber

Redbrook
Road
Rainton Gv
Barden
Walton Street
North
Samuel Road
Hollowdene

4

Lane

Lawton
Cl
William Ct
Avon
Close
Weaver
Welland
Court

Higham

Church
Street
Beever St
Bakehouse
Lane

Craven Wd
Velvet
Wd
Colster
Close

Treelands
Rowan Dr
Lines
Downes
North
Place
South
Place

PO

60

Hugset
Wood

Pog Well Lane

Hermit   Lane

Gawber
Junior &
Infant School

Wharfedale
Rd
St Helena
Intake
Pentine Way
Oakfield
Walk
Drane
Wade St
Warner
Road
Haddington
Way
Warner
Place

Rutland Cl
Oakham

West
Road

5

PO

Higham Common

Farm House Lane
Harden
Cl
Longside
Law
Pogmoor
Road
St Martins Cl
10
Pogmoor
Lane
Pogmoor
Glendale
Close
West
Road

Crest
Stre

Higham
Lane
Midhope
West Moor Crs
Ewden Wy
Hunters
Rl

St Hilda
Avenue

6

Sh

Crown Hl Rd
White Hill
TAV
PO
A628
Hareswood
Avenue
Beaumont
Broadway School
BROADWAY

Junction 37

M1

Hunters
Avenue
Moorland Av
Woodland
Dr
Arncliffe Cl Linton Cl

A6133

7

Elmhirst
Lane
Ct
Cliffe
Road
Whinby Road
Upr
Cliffe
Rd
Galpharm
Wy
Hawthorne
Crescent
A628 BARNSLEY ROAD
Hill
Pk
Gro
Gate Crs
South Road
Wareham
Gv
South
Crs
Hollin
Cl
Low
Pasture
Close

Horse Wood
Close

Rockley Mou
School

Dark
Lane

8

Middle Field Rd

A628

Fall Bank Crescent

LC

Thornely
Av

Dodworth
Junior
School

Queen's
Drive

Bark Mdw
Damsteads
Roydd
Wd
Syke
Farrow
Close
Butterleys

KERESFORTH

Broadway School

Ke
Cou

LC

Dodworth
Station

STATION RD
MITCHELSON AV
Baslow Crs
BARNSLEY ROAD
Dodworth
Health
Centre
Pollyfox Wy

Park
Water
Jermyn Cft
Bowden

Bradshaw Cl

Langden
Close

B6449

Bamford
Haddon
Cl
Hayfield
B6449

Cemetery

Dodworth
B6099
PO

Primary
School

Ke
Hill

Rockley Mou
School

Ratten
Row

Dodw
C of E
School

81

**Dodworth
Bottom**

G H J K L M

Dodworth

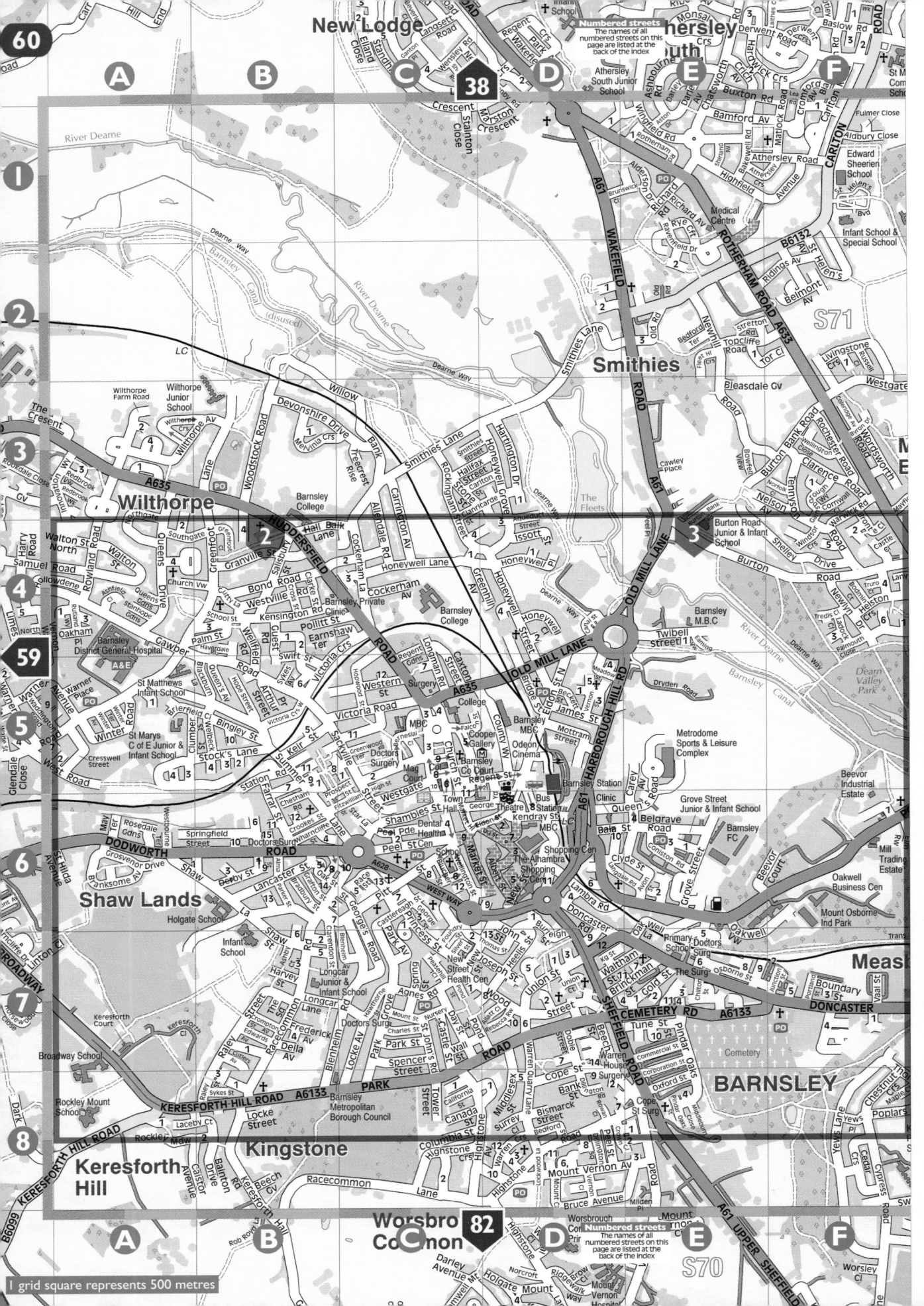

60
38
59
82
New Lodge
Athersley South
Numbered streets
The names of all numbered streets on this page are listed at the back of the index
Athersley South Junior School
Edward Sheerien School
Infant School & Special School
Medical Centre
River Dearne
Barnsley Canal (disused)
Smithies
S71
Wilthorpe
Wilthorpe Junior School
Barnsley College
Barnsley District General Hospital
Burton Road Junior & Infant School
Barnsley M.B.C
Dearn Valley Park
Metrodome Sports & Leisure Complex
Beevor Industrial Estate
Barnsley Station
Bus Station
Town Hall
Theatre
The Alhambra Shopping Cen
Grove Street Junior & Infant School
Barnsley FC
Mill Trading Estate
Oakwell Business Cen
Mount Osborne Ind Park
Shaw Lands
Holgate School
Longcar Junior & Infant School
Keresforth Court
Broadway School
Rockley Mount School
Barnsley Metropolitan Borough Council
Cemetery
BARNSLEY
Kingstone
Keresforth Hill
Worsbrough Common
S70
A61 WAKEFIELD ROAD
ROTHERHAM ROAD A633
HUDDERSFIELD ROAD
A635 OLD MILL LANE
A61 HARBOROUGH HILL RD
DODWORTH ROAD
WEST WAY
CEMETERY RD A6133
DONCASTER
KERESFORTH HILL ROAD A6133 PARK ROAD
SHEFFIELD ROAD
A61 UPPER SHEFFIELD ROAD
B6099 KERESFORTH HILL ROAD
1 grid square represents 500 metres

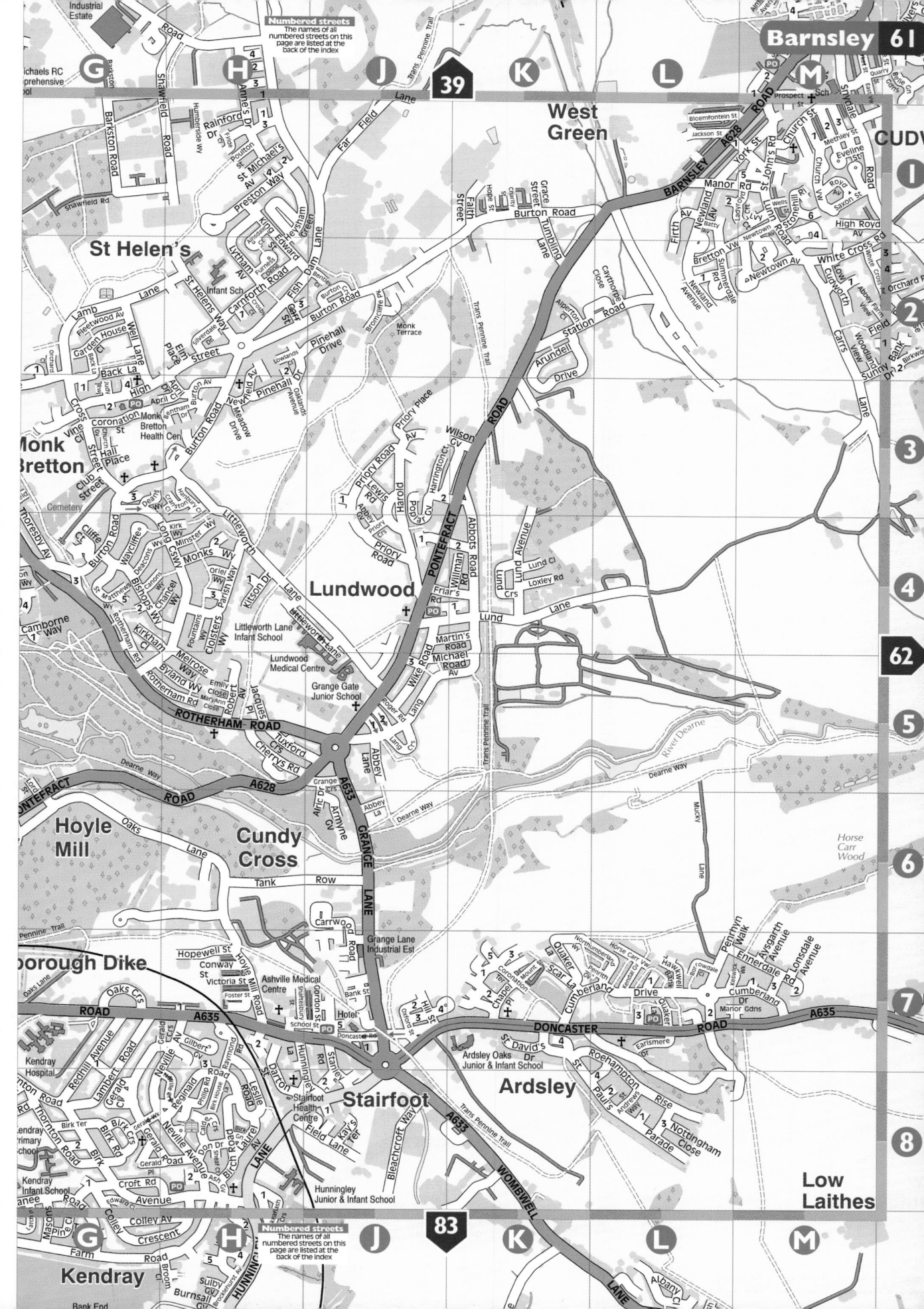

Barnsley 61
Numbered streets
The names of all numbered streets on this page are listed at the back of the index
39
62
83
West Green
St Helen's
Monk Bretton
Lundwood
Hoyle Mill
Cundy Cross
Stairfoot
Ardsley
Kendray
Low Laithes
Horse Carr Wood
River Dearne
Trans Pennine Trail
Dearne Way
PONTEFRACT ROAD
BARNSLEY ROAD
ROTHERHAM ROAD
GRANGE LANE
DONCASTER ROAD
WOMBWELL LANE
A628
A633
A635
Industrial Estate
Infant Sch
Littleworth Lane Infant School
Lundwood Medical Centre
Grange Gate Junior School
Grange Lane Industrial Est
Ashville Medical Centre
Ardsley Oaks Junior & Infant School
Stairfoot Health Centre
Hunningley Junior & Infant School
Kendray Hospital
Kendray Infant School
Monk Bretton Health Cen
Cemetery
Monk Terrace

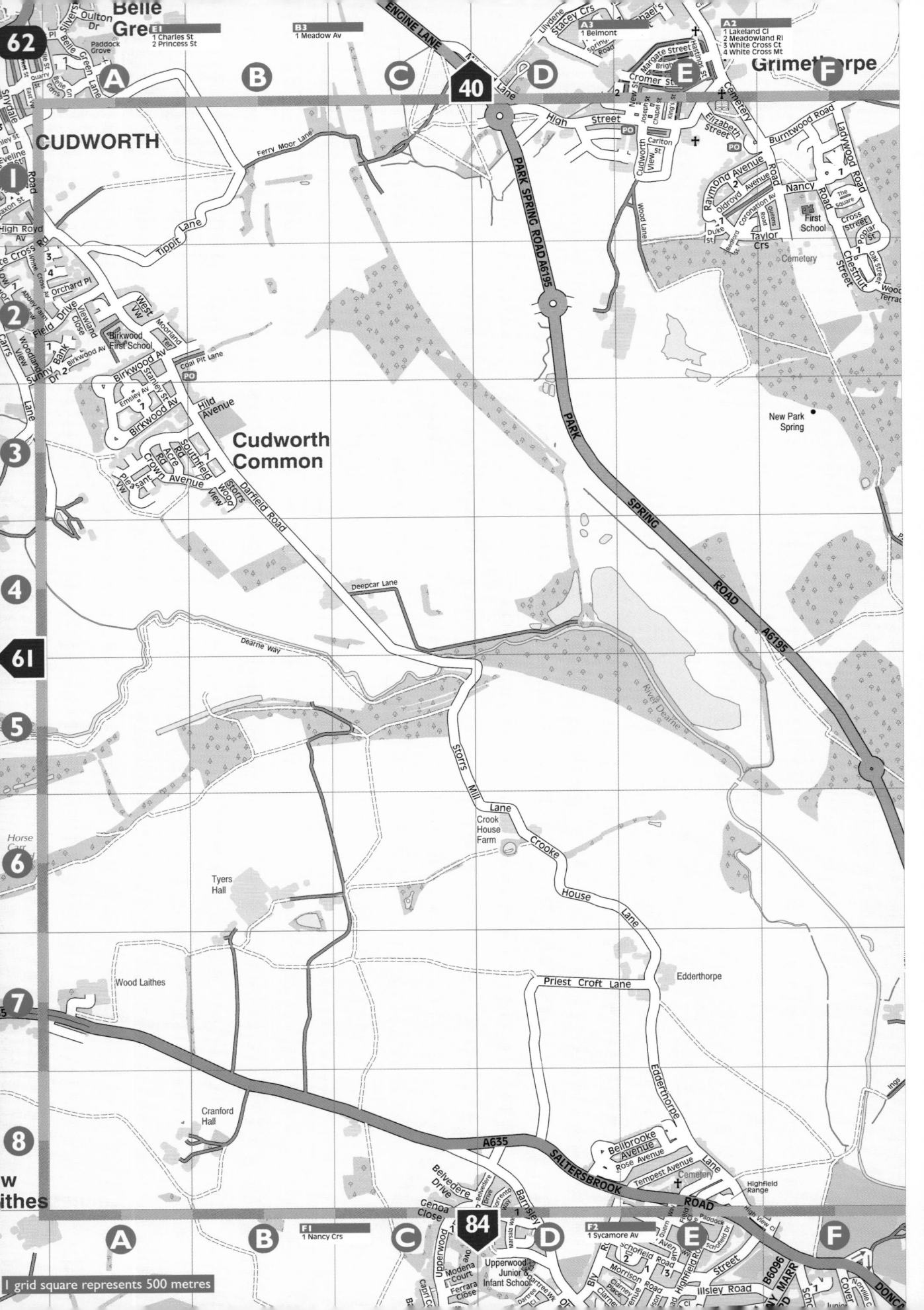

62
40
61
84
E1
1 Charles St
2 Princess St
B3
1 Meadow Av
A3
1 Belmont
A2
1 Lakeland Cl
2 Meadowland Ri
3 White Cross Ct
4 White Cross Mt
F1
1 Nancy Crs
F2
1 Sycamore Av
A
B
C
D
E
F
1
2
3
4
5
6
7
8
CUDWORTH
Cudworth Common
Grimethorpe
Belle Green
Oulton Dr
Paddock Grove
Belle Green Lane
Engine Lane
High Street
Ferry Moor Lane
Tippit Lane
Stacey Crs
Margate Street
Cromer St
Hastings St
Cemetery
Elizabeth Street
Burntwood Road
Ladywood Road
Carlton
Cudworth View
Wood Lane
PARK SPRING ROAD A6195
PARK SPRING ROAD A6195
Raymond Avenue
Oldroyd Avenue
Coronation Av
Queens Road
Nancy Road
First School
The Square
Cross Street
Poplar St
Chestnut Street
Oak Street
Taylor Crs
Duke St
Bedford Ct
Cemetery
New Park Spring
High Royd Av
White Cross Rd
Orchard Pl
Field Drive
Viewland Close
West Vw
Moorland Ter
Birkwood First School
Birkwood Av
Sunny Bank
Woodland View
Coal Pit Lane
PO
Stanley St
Emsley Av
Hild Avenue
Southfield Rd
Acre Rd
Crown Avenue
Pleasant Vw
Storrs Wood View
Darfield Road
Deepcar Lane
Dearne Way
River Dearne
Storrs Mill Lane
Crook House Farm
Crooke House Lane
Tyers Hall
Wood Laithes
Priest Croft Lane
Edderthorpe
Edderthorpe Lane
Cranford Hall
A635
SALTERSBROOK ROAD
Bellbrooke Avenue
Rose Avenue
Tempest Avenue
Cemetery
Highfield Range
Belvedere Drive
Genoa Close
Barnsley Road
Upperwood Road
Modena Court
Ferrara Close
Upperwood Junior School
Schofield Road
Morrison Road
Highfield Road
Illsley Road
B6096
Horse Carr
1 grid square represents 500 metres

G　H　J　**41**　K　L　M

I

2

3 Clay

4

64

5

6

7

8

H4
1 Mileswood Cl

J5
1 Woodlands Vw

J6
1 Oak Haven Av
2 Old Hall Wk

Howell Wood

West Haigh Wood

Howell Lane

Houghton Lodge

Howell House

Howell Lane

Shortwood Lane

Top Lane

Back Lane

Common Lane

Com Lane

Chapel Lane

Clayton Lane

B6273

MOOR LANE

Hoister Lane

Park Lane

Little Park

Crabtree Drive

Ashwood

Pinewood Close

Park Lane

Cemetery

Pear Tree Close

HIGH STREET B6273

Milton St

School St

Garraby

Normandale Rd

Springvale Road

Great Houghton

Stonebridge Lane

Spry Lane

PO

Church Lane

Pinfield Close

Potts Crescent

Pleasant Avenue

Mount Av

Stonebridge Lane

Clayton Lane

Thurnscoe Gooseacre J M School

Gooseacre Avenue

Rodds Avenue

Cross St

Great Houghton Clinic

Dearne St

Byron St

B6411 THURNSCOE LANE

John Street

Wescoe Avenue

Norfolk Road

Clayton Avenue
Clayton Drive

Westfield Crescent
Manor Square
Wensley Street

Manor Road

Sandhill

Primary School

Edward St

New Street

Turner Street

Chapel Lane

Little Houghton

ROTHERHAM ROAD

HOUGHTON ROAD

Rectory Close

Rectory Lane

Common Road

Lorne Road

Saint Helens Cl

Church Street

Southfield Lane

Sunday School

Little Theatre

Hickleton Court

Cemetery

Billingley

Mitchellcliff Lane

A6195

Buttercross Drive

Middlecliff Lane

Billingley Lane

Middlecliff Lane

Houghton Main Welfare & Sports Club

George Street

John St

Queen's Av

Windsor Crescent

Charles St

Mary Street

Sheffield Rd

B6273

West Kirk Lane

Back Lane

High Street

Pagnell Av

Burntwood Close

Middlewood Hall

H8
1 Hill Farm Cl

M7
1 Horsemoor Rd
2 Thornley Sq

K6
1 Ebenezer St

J8
1 Belmont Crs

Billingley

B8
1 Barley Vw
2 Hall Farm Ri
3 Wheatfield Dr

B7
1 Ashberry Cl

A8
1 Togo St

A7
1 Cross Butcher St
2 Edward St
3 Kingsway Gv
4 Marlborough Cl
5 Whyn Vw

A **B** **C** 42 **D** **E** **F**

1

Wakefie
Doncaster

Hooton Pagnell
Wood

Wink House

Frickley Hall

Common Lane

2

Lane

Top

Back Lane

Chapel Hill

Hall Bring

PO

Tan Pit Lane

Teapot Corner

Tan Pit Close

The Croft

Church Field Road

3 Clayton

Church Field Road

Stotfold Road

4

63

Watchley

Doncaster
Barnsley

5

Stotfold

6

Thurnscoe
Gooseacre
J M School

Primary
School

Whinside Crs

Burnside

Whingardens

Gooseacre Avenue

Challenger Crs

St Peter's St

Road

Pangbourne

Lingamore
Leys

Britton Street

Hanover Street

Brunswick Street

Chapel Lane

Cromwell Street

Lancaster Street

York Street

Hill
Primary
School

Stotfold

Thurnscoe East

Hickleton
Golf Club

7

Westfield Crescent

Manor
Square

Monsave
Street

Richmond
Road

Peartree Avenue

Wensley
Street

Merrill
Road

Basildon
Road

Low Grange
Square

Stotfold Drive

Willow
Road

Park
Ct

Oak
Road

School
Road

Orchard
Way

John Street

Garden Lane

Holly Bush Drive

Delightonby Street

Windsor
Square

Romar St

Britton
Square

Grange
Crs

Windsor Street

Stuart Street

Dane St

Granger
St

Norman
St

Hanover
Square

Brunswick
Street

George Street

Albion Drive

Chapel Lane

Tyton Dri
Avenue

Torne Road

Butcher Street

Albert
St

Chapel Street

Church Street

Kingsway

HOUGHTON ROAD

PO

Welfare
Road

Park Road

Shepherd Lane

Thurnscoe Station

STATION ROAD

PO

Saxon Street

Dane
St

Tudor
St

Coronation St

King St

Queen St

Princess Dr

Thurnscoe
Business
Centre

Phoenix Lane

Lidget Lane

LIDGET LANE B6411

Doncaster Road

Saint
Helens
Cl

Sunday
School

Little
Theatre

Hickleton
Court

High
Street

Walpert Av

Troutbeck

Billingley

Cemetery

Pagnell
Av

Burntwood
Close

Derry

Hillcrest

Hallgate
Grove

Lindley
Crescent

Crossdale

Turness
Grove

Farm
Hall
Dr

Barrowfield Road

The
Windings

Southfield Lane

Chestnut
Gv

8

THURNSCOE

A **B** C7
1 Chapman St
2 Clarke St **C** 86 **D** **E** **F**

A635

Goldthorpe
RC JMI
School

Doncaster Road

A635

Kathleen
Grove

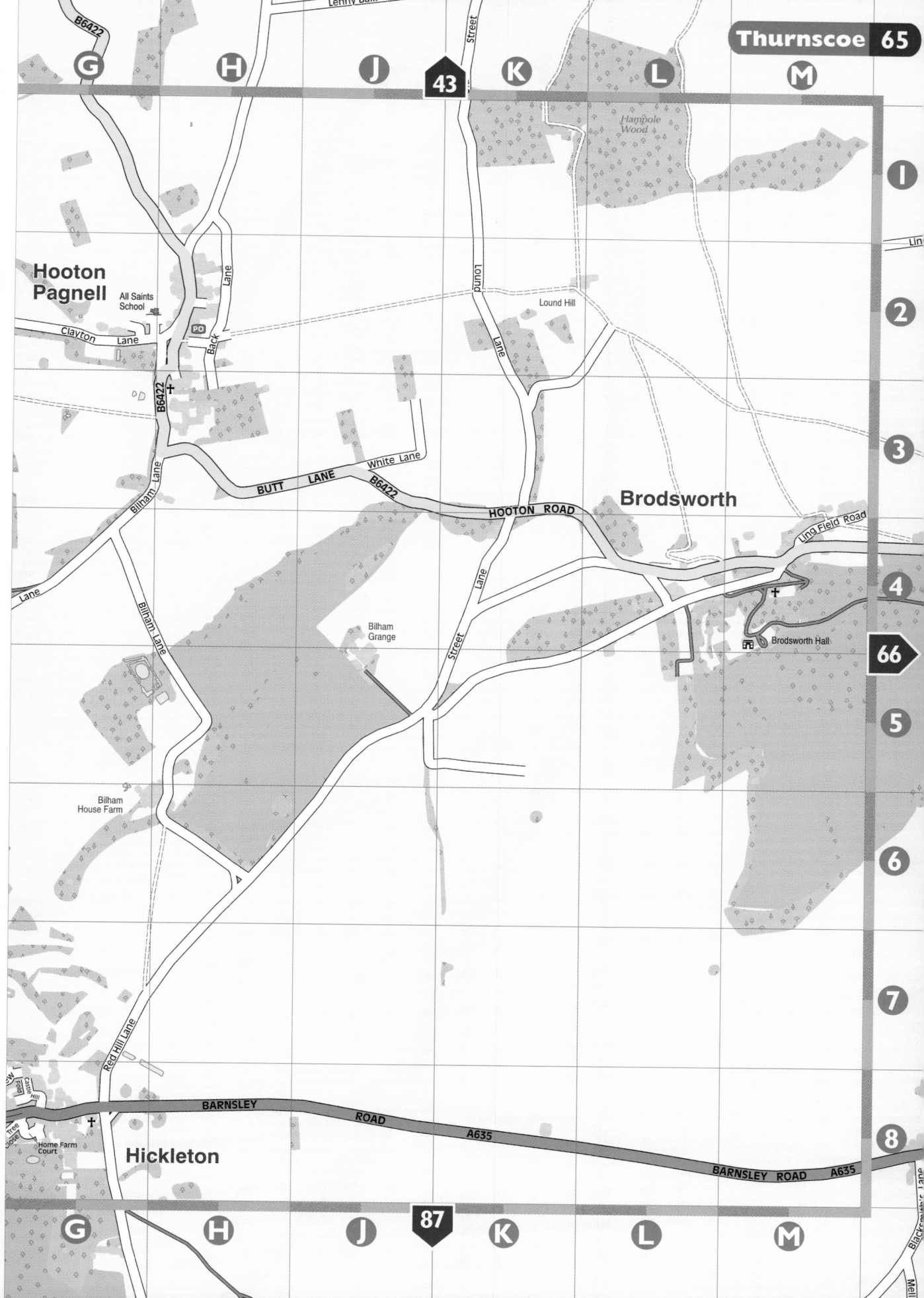

G H J 43 K L M

1

Hampole Wood

2

Hooton
Pagnell

Lound Hill

All Saints
School

PO

Clayton Lane

Back Lane

Lound Lane

3

B6422

BUTT LANE White Lane

Brodsworth

B6422

Bilham Lane

HOOTON ROAD

Ling Field Road

4

Lane

Street Lane

Bilham
Grange

Brodsworth Hall

66

Bilham Lane

5

6

Bilham
House Farm

7

Red Hill Lane

8

BARNSLEY ROAD

ROAD A635

Home Farm
Court

BARNSLEY ROAD A635

Hickleton

G H J 87 K L M

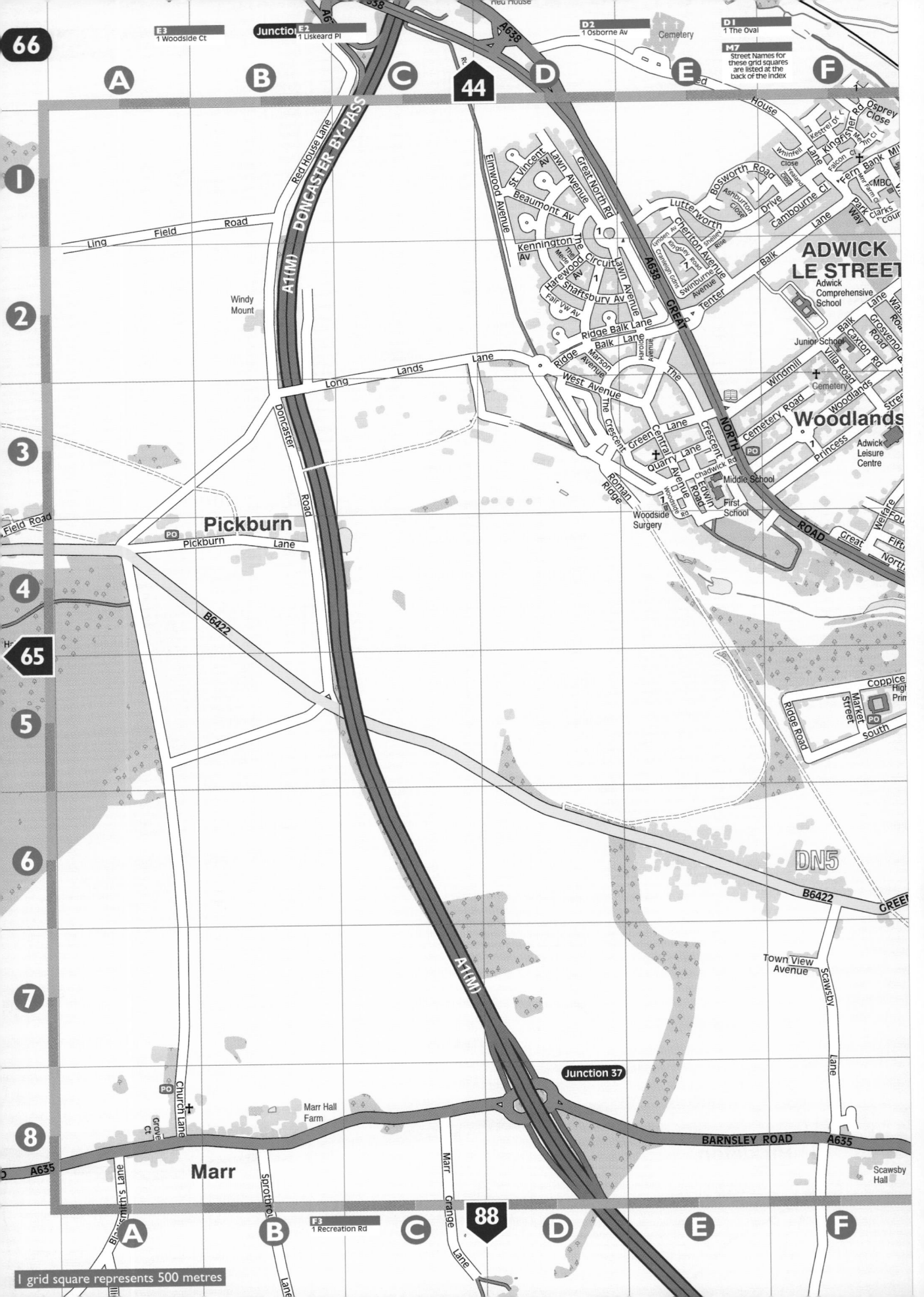
E3
1 Woodside Ct
E2
1 Liskeard Pl
D2
1 Osborne Av
D1
1 The Oval
M7
Street Names for these grid squares are listed at the back of the index
44
Cemetery
DONCASTER BY-PASS
A1(M)
Red House Lane
Ling Field Road
Long Lands Lane
Windy Mount
Doncaster Road
Pickburn
Pickburn Lane
Field Road
B6422
65
ADWICK LE STREET
Adwick Comprehensive School
Junior School
Woodlands
Adwick Leisure Centre
Middle School
First School
Woodside Surgery
Roman Ridge
GREAT NORTH ROAD
A638
Coppice
Ridge Road
Market Street
DN5
Town View Avenue
Scawsby Lane
Junction 37
BARNSLEY ROAD
A635
Marr Hall Farm
Church Lane
Grove Ct
Marr
Marr Grange Lane
Blacksmith's Lane
Scawsby Hall
F3
1 Recreation Rd
88
1 grid square represents 500 metres

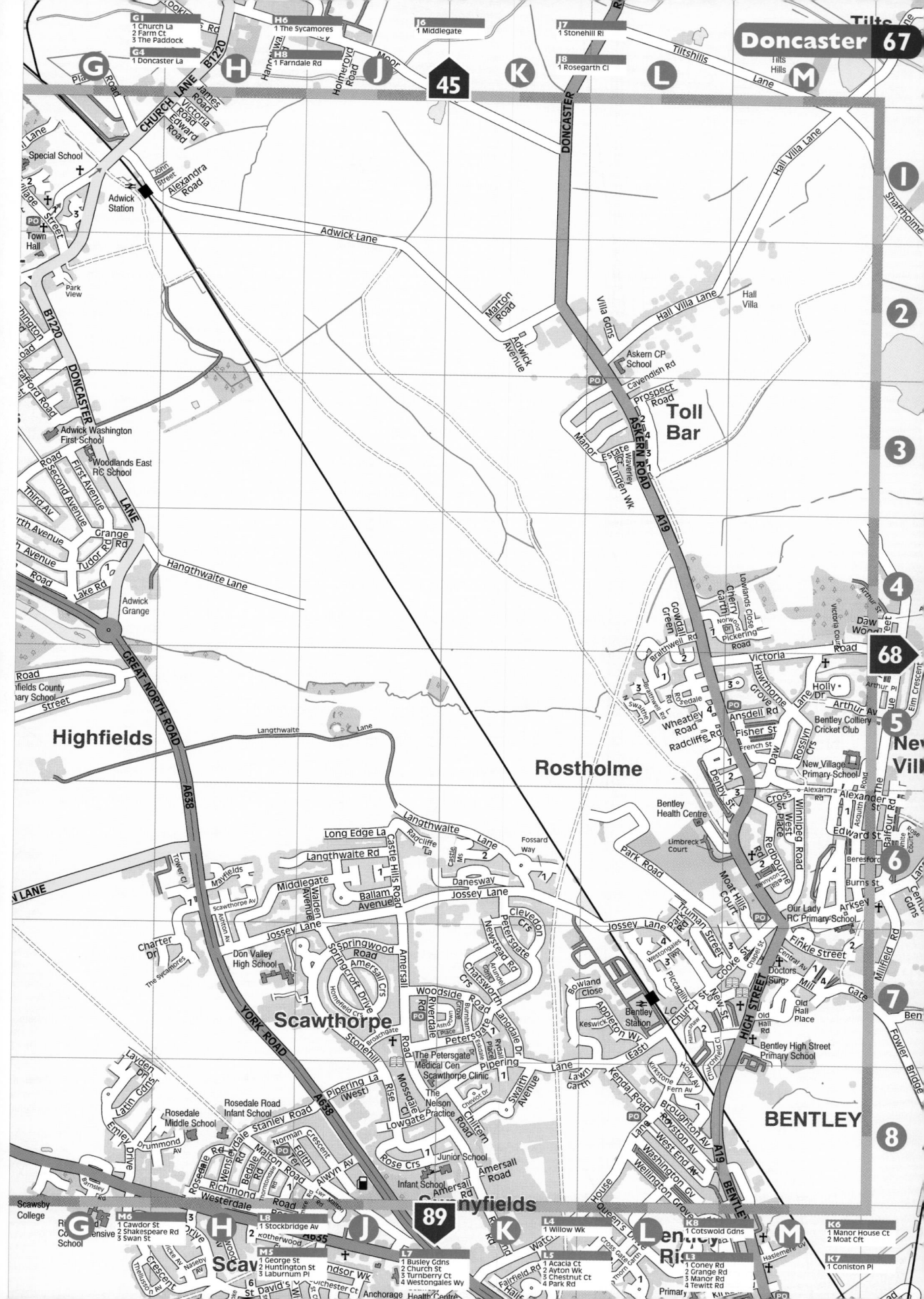
G1
1 Church La
2 Farm Ct
3 The Paddock
G4
1 Doncaster La
H6
1 The Sycamores
H8
1 Farndale Rd
J6
1 Middlegate
J7
1 Stonehill Ri
J8
1 Rosegarth Cl
45
68
89
Adwick Station
Town Hall
Special School
Adwick Lane
Hall Villa Lane
Toll Bar
Askern CP School
Adwick Washington First School
Woodlands East RC School
Adwick Grange
Hangthwaite Lane
Highfields
Rostholme
Scawthorpe
Don Valley High School
Bentley Health Centre
Bentley Station
Bentley High Street Primary School
Our Lady RC Primary School
New Village Primary School
Bentley Colliery Cricket Club
BENTLEY
Rosedale Road Infant School
Rosedale Middle School
The Petersgate Medical Cen
Scawthorpe Clinic
The Nelson Practice
Junior School
Infant School
Scawsby College
Sunnyfields
M6
1 Cawdor St
2 Shakespeare Rd
3 Swan St
L8
1 Stockbridge Av
M5
1 George St
2 Huntington St
3 Laburnum Pl
L7
1 Busley Gdns
2 Church St
3 Turnberry Ct
4 Westongales Wy
L4
1 Willow Wk
L5
1 Acacia Ct
2 Ayton Wk
3 Chestnut Ct
4 Park Rd
K8
1 Cotswold Gdns
L3
1 Coney Rd
2 Grange Rd
3 Manor Rd
4 Tewitt Rd
K6
1 Manor House Ct
2 Moat Cft
K7
1 Coniston Pl

Tilts

68

A   B   C   46   D   E   F

1

2   Shaftholme   Almholme

3

4   Amy Road   Marsh   The Croft
    Arthur St   Daw Wood
    Victoria
67   Holly Dr   Five Oaks
5   Arthur Av   Stockbridge   Arksey
    Elm Crescent   PO   Chadwick Gdns
    New Village   Arthur   Station
    New Village Primary School   Grosvenor Crs   Arksey   Common   Lane
    Alexandra Rd   Alexander Rd   Ings Way   Mastall Lane   Ings   Dog Croft Lane
    Edward St   Arksey County Junior & Infant School
6   Beresford St   Cemetery   Colvin Close   River Don
    Burns St   Brook   Kenrock Close
    Arksey   Century Gdns   Hemp   Pits
    Lady Primary School   LC
    Millfield Rd
7   kle Street   Bentley Common   Bentley   Common   Lane   LC   A630   Cromwell Road
    Gate   LC
    Fowler Bridge Road   Wheatley Hall Business Centre
8   River Don   Wheatley   Park   Hereford Road   Guildford Road
    Worcester Av   HALL   Kingfisher First School   Carlisle Road
    Norwich Road   Beckett   PO   Chestnut
    WHEATLEY   Road   Coventry
    90   ROAD
    A   B   C   90   D   E   Exeter   F
    Liverpool Av   Lichfield   Parkway   Beckett Road   Parkway   The
    Southwell   Ripon Avenue   Bristol   Winchester   Thornhill
    Harrowden   Infant School   Crossway
    Primary   DN2

1 grid square represents 500 metres

Kirk Sandall
69
Dun
G7
1 Sandalwood Cl
G8
1 Endcliffe Wy
2 Parkstone Wy
3 Woodlea Wy
J3
1 Orchard Cl
J5
1 Marian Rd
2 St Nicholas Cl
J6
1 Eleanor Ct
G
H
J
K
L
M
47
Marsh Lane
Fox Covert
River Dun Navigation
River Don
Station Road
Top Road
Fairview Court
Mallard Avenue
The Spinney
Hall Road
St Andrew's Way
Pine Hall
Pinefield Avenue
Pinefield Road
Meadow Field Rd
Wheatfield Close
Shawfield Close
Greenfield Cl
Hayfield Close
Parkwood Rise
Park Hill Grange
Armthorpe Lane
Doncaster Road
Thorold Place
Eccleston Rd
Longton Road
King George Sq
Sutton Road
Grange Pk
Moor Lane
Sandall Grove
Horton View
Maldwell Way
West Green Dr
Ashton Drive
Glade Vw
Lancaster Av
Harewood Av
Connaught Drive
Curzen Crs
Hesketh Drive
Kirk Sandall Station
Sandall Stones Rd
Sandall Lane
Works
The Beeches
Dentons Green La
Queen Mary Crs
Church Road
Brecks Lane
Redhall Close
Coniston Rd
Derwent Dr
Elizabeth Avenue
Newhall Road
Graham Road
Junior School
Stones Road
Guildhall Industrial Estate
Sandall Carr Road
Gardenia Rd
Lobelia Crs
Kirk Sandall Infant School
Denehall Road
Thorpehall Rd
Church Balk Gardens
Kirk Sandall
Long Sandall
Lyndhurst Crescent
Scott Crs
Church Balk
Bardon Road
Rockley Avenue
Athelstane Crs
Edencroft Drive
Edencroft Dr
Far Field Rd
Eden Fld Rd
Meadow Walk
Meadow Cft
Long Field Road
70
THORNE
Clay Lane
Doncaster Road
Lynton Drive
Doncaster MBC
Sunnyside
The Boulevard
St Oswald's Dr
Edenthorpe Surgery
Kingthorne Group Practice
Clovelly Road
Hartland Crs
Acre Cl
A18
ROAD
Gurth Av
The Drive
Lane
Thorn Lane
Dun Road
Plumb Estates
Hungerhill Lane
Hungerhill Comprehensive School
THORNE
The Crescent
Eden Grove
Cedric Road
County Primary School
Mere Lane
Hatfield Lane
Coningsburgh Road
Rowena Av
Ivanhoe Rd
Robin Hood Rd
Edenthorpe
Little Lane
Clay Lane West
Curlew Junior School
Barnby Dun Road
Shackleton Road
Wilberforce Road
Moffat Gardens
Jefferson Avenue
Livingstone Av
Herald Road
Bowes Road
Parklands
Birchdale Close
Ashdale Close
Fieldside
Emdale Drive
Lichen
Ridgewood Av
The Mt
Lyndale Avenue
Larkspur Cl
Chalmers Drive
WHEATLEY HALL RD
Clay Lane
A630
Derby Road
Barnby Dun Road
Truro Avenue
THORNE ROAD
Ogden Road
Shaw Lane Industrial Estate
Grange Farm
Mere Lane
Shaw Wood
Holly Dene
Fernbank Drive
Hawthorn
Pinewood Avenue
Oak Rd
Bevre Road
Avenue
Shaw Wood Junior & Infant School
Shaw Lane
Shaw Wood Way
A18
Thorne Road
Heath Bank Rd
Lowfield Rd
Grove V
Masefield Road
Greenleafe Av
Boundary Avenue
Hill Top Crs
Edgehill Road
Ennerdale Road
Sandall Park Drive
Linkswood
Silver Jubilee
Fernhurst
Wheatley
LEGER
Golf Course
Park Avenue
Elm Road
Basil Av
Mansfield St
Markham Avenue
Elm Place
Mere Lane
Briar Road
Armthorpe High School
Paxton Crescent
Edward St
Crescent
Doctors Surgery
Charles Crescent
Our Lady of Sorrows RC School
Laurel Road
Almond Av
Lime Tree
Chestnut Avenue
Beech
Ash Grove
Glebe
Road
91
L4
1 Fernhall Cl
L5
1 Holme Wood Ct
2 Worral Ct
L1
1 Heathfield Cl
2 Limedale Vw
3 Mill Field Ct
L3
1 Longton Rd
2 Tarleton Cl
3 Tynedale Cl
K6
1 Aspen Cl
2 Oakdale Cl
K4
1 Camellia Dr
2 Magnolia Cl
3 Thirlmere Gdns
K5
1 Milton Gv
2 Sherwood Av
K3
1 Cowley Pl
2 Prince's Sq
3 St Helen's Sq
4 St James Cl
5 Stanley Sq
6 Windermere Crs
7 Windle Sq
K1
1 Pinfold Ct
K2
1 Rainford Sq
Barton Lane
The Armthorpe Surgery
ARMTHORPE
Kingsley Crs
Danesthorpe Close
Rowan Court
Wellcroft
Road
1
2
3
4
5
6
7
8

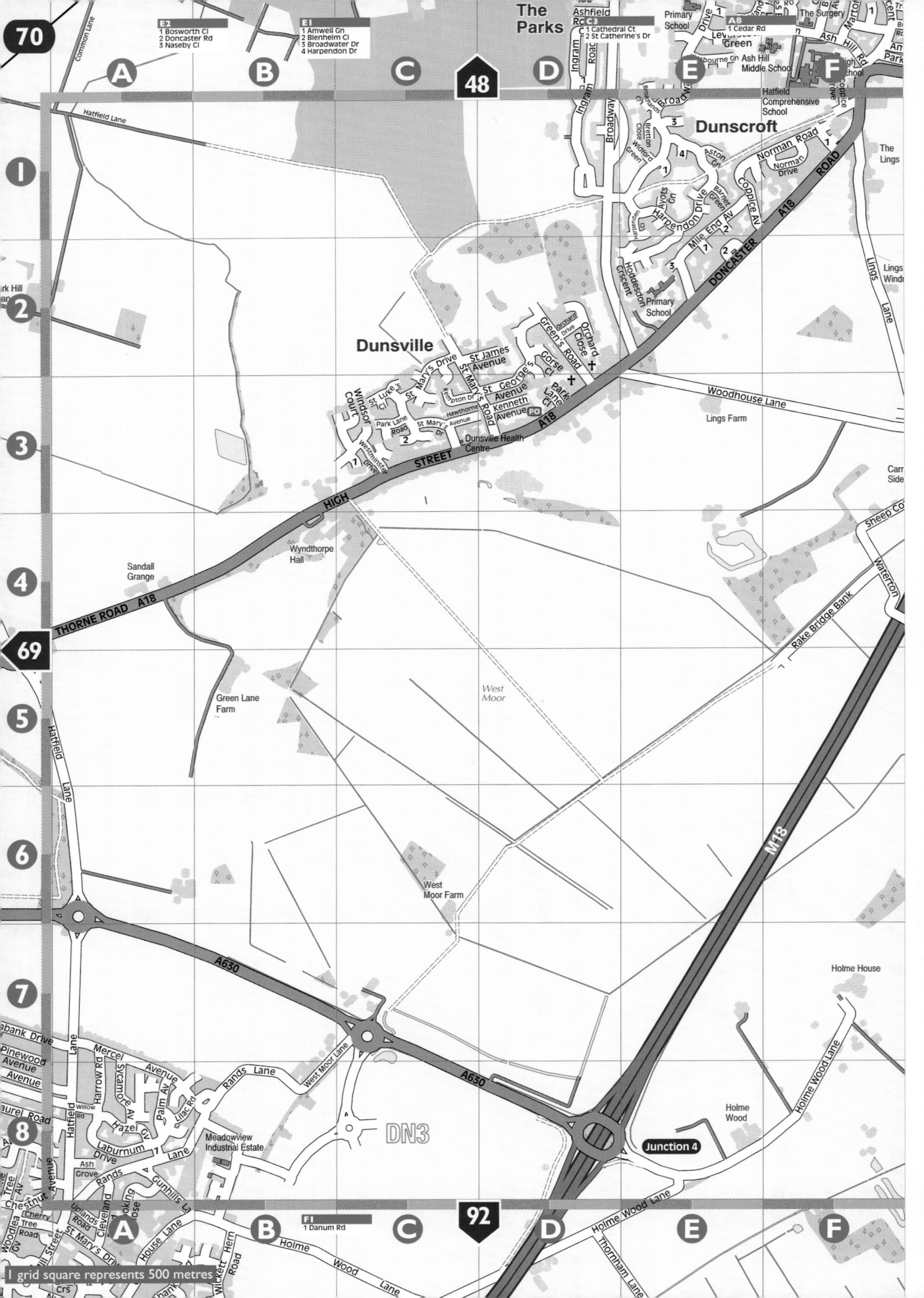
E2
1 Bosworth Cl
2 Doncaster Rd
3 Naseby Cl
E1
1 Amwell Gn
2 Blenheim Cl
3 Broadwater Dr
4 Harpendon Dr
C3
1 Cathedral Ct
2 St Catherine's Dr
A8
1 Cedar Rd
F1
1 Danum Rd
The Parks
Dunscroft
Dunsville
Hatfield Comprehensive School
Ash Hill Middle School
The Surgery
Primary School
Wyndthorpe Hall
Sandall Grange
Green Lane Farm
West Moor
West Moor Farm
Lings Farm
The Lings
Holme House
Holme Wood
Meadowview Industrial Estate
Dunsville Health Centre
Junction 4
DN3
THORNE ROAD A18
HIGH STREET
DONCASTER ROAD A18
A630
M18
Woodhouse Lane
Rake Bridge Bank
Holme Wood Lane
Hatfield Lane
Common Lane
West Moor Lane
Rands Lane
Thornham Lane
Lings Lane
1 grid square represents 500 metres

48
69
92

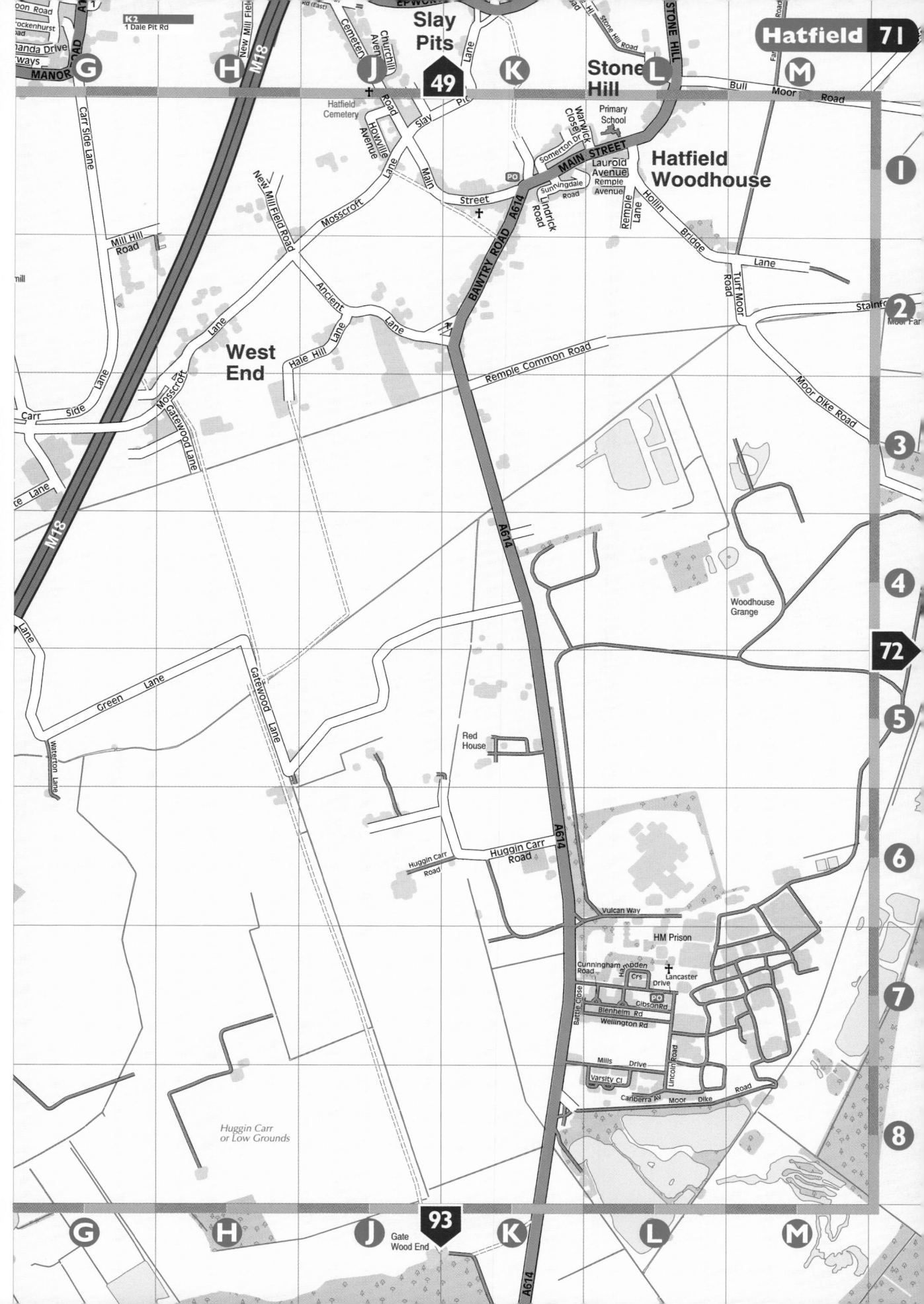

Slay Pits
Stone Hill
Hatfield Woodhouse
West End
Hatfield Cemetery
Primary School
Main Street
Bawtry Road A614
M18
Manor Road
Carr Side Lane
Mill Hill Road
New Mill Field Road
Mosscroft Lane
Ancient Lane
Hale Hill Lane
Remple Common Road
Gatewood Lane
Green Lane
Waterton Lane
Cemetery Road
Churchill Avenue
Howville Avenue
Slay Pit Lane
Stone Hill Road
Bull Moor Road
Warwick Close
Somerton Dr
Sunningdale Road
Lindrick Road
Laurold Avenue
Remple Avenue
Remple Lane
Hollin Bridge Lane
Turf Moor Road
Moor Dike Road
Woodhouse Grange
Red House
Huggin Carr Road
Vulcan Way
HM Prison
Cunningham Road
Hampden Crs
Lancaster Drive
Gibson Rd
Blenheim Rd
Wellington Rd
Battle Close
Lincoln Road
Mills Drive
Varsity Cl
Canberra Av
Huggin Carr or Low Grounds
Gate Wood End
K2 1 Dale Pit Rd

49
72
93

72

A   B   C   50   D   E   F

Cross Road

Road

Brier
Hills Farm

1

Stainforth   Moor   Road

2   Stainforth   Moor   Road

Moor Farm

Dike Road

3

4

71

Lindholme Bank Road

5

Lindholme   Bank   Road

6   Lindholme
Hall

Hatfield Moors

7

8

A   B   C   94   D   E   F

Moor Lane

1 grid square represents 500 metres

G '80
H
J
51
K
L
M

M180
M180
M180

Low Levels Bank

Doncaster
North Lincolnshire

Plains Lane

Goodcop Farm

Lindholme Grange

Low Levels

Sandtoft

West Hale Farm

Doncaster
North Lincolnshire

North Idle Drain

West Carr

West Carr Houses

Idle Bank

Roe Carr

I

2

3

4

5

6

7

8

G
H
J
95
K
L
Kinevah Farm
M

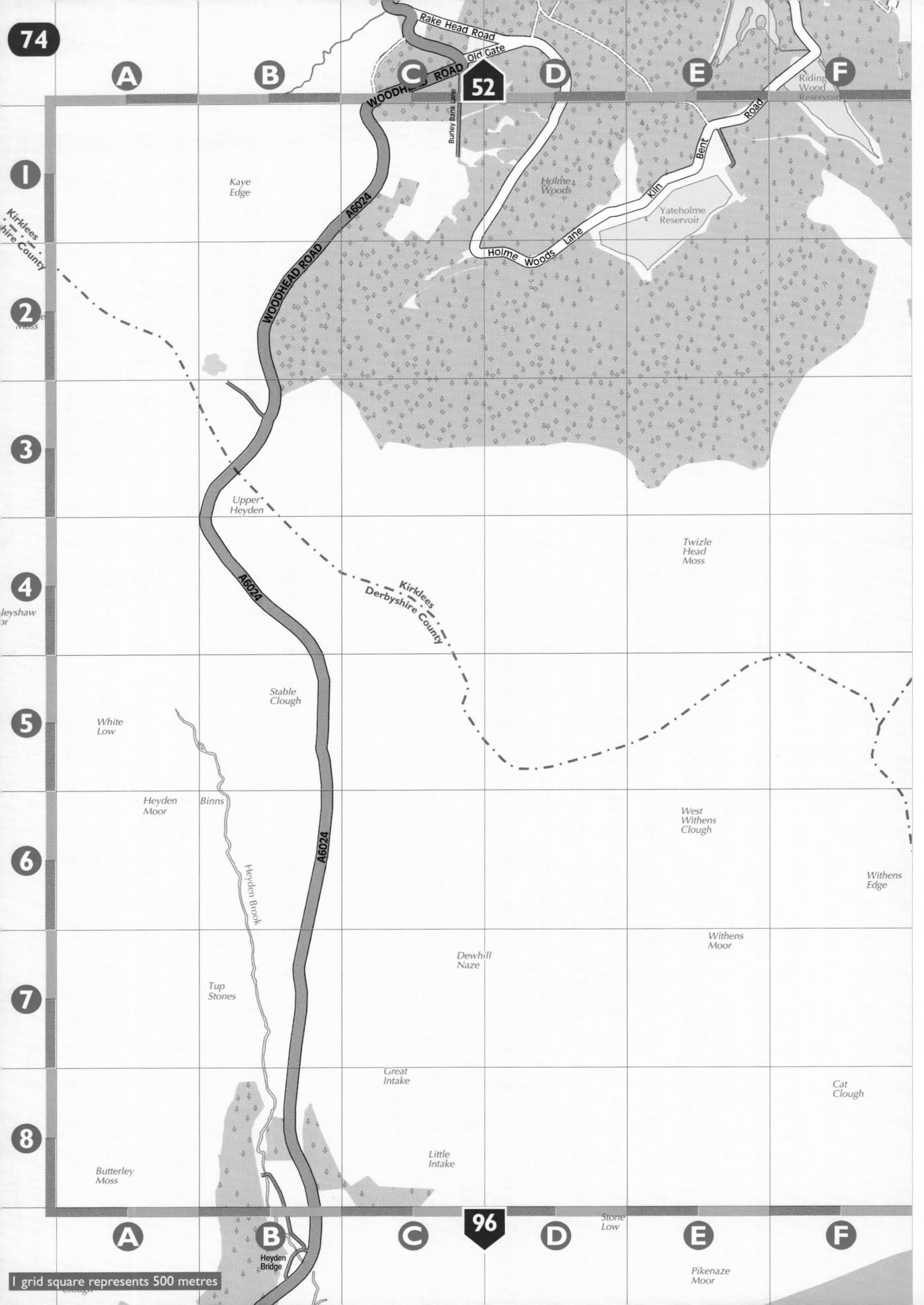

A   B   C   D   E   F

Rake Head Road

WOODHEAD ROAD   Old Gate

52

Riding Wood Reservoir

Burley Bank Lane

Bent Road

A6024

WOODHEAD ROAD

Kirklees Yorkshire County

Kaye Edge

Holme Woods

Kiln

Yateholme Reservoir

Holme Woods Lane

Moss

Upper Heyden

Kirklees Derbyshire County

Twizle Head Moss

A6024

Stable Clough

White Low

Heyden Moor   Binns

West Withens Clough

Withens Edge

Heyden Brook

A6024

Withens Moor

Dewhill Naze

Tup Stones

Great Intake

Cat Clough

Butterley Moss

Little Intake

A   B   C   D   E   F

Stone Low

Heyden Bridge

Pikenaze Moor

I grid square represents 500 metres

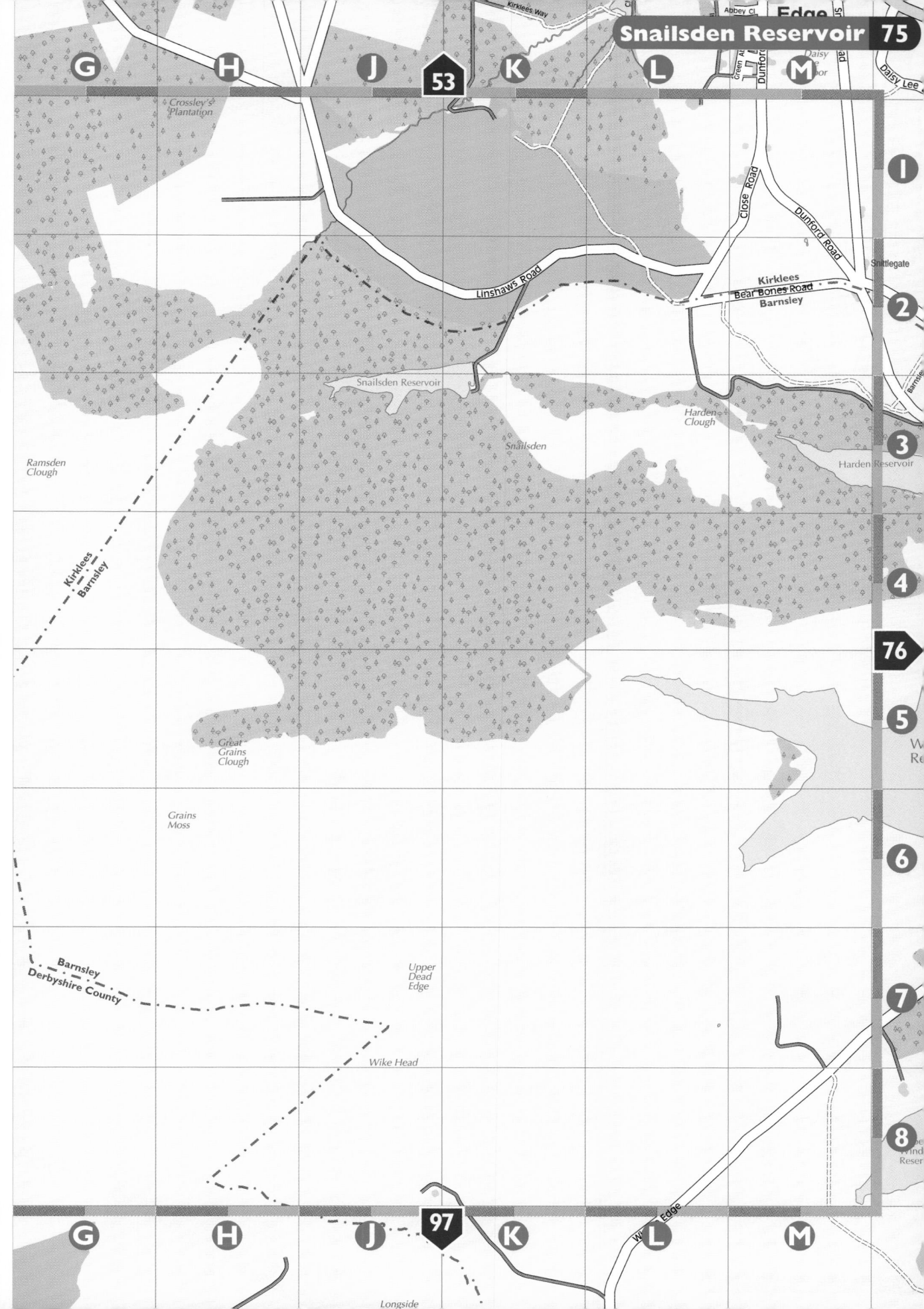

Kirklees Way

Abbey Cl.

Edge

Green A

Daisy

Dunfor

Daisy Lee

G

H

J

53

K

L

M

Crossley's
Plantation

Close Road

Dunford Road

Snittlegate

I

Linshaws Road

Kirklees

Bear Bones Road

Barnsley

2

Kirklees

Barnsley

Snailsden Reservoir

Harden
Clough

3

Harden Reservoir

Ramsden
Clough

Snailsden

4

76

5

W
Re

Great
Grains
Clough

6

Grains
Moss

Barnsley

Derbyshire County

Upper
Dead
Edge

7

8

ne
Wind
Reser

Wike Head

W
Edge

G

H

J

97

K

L

M

Longside

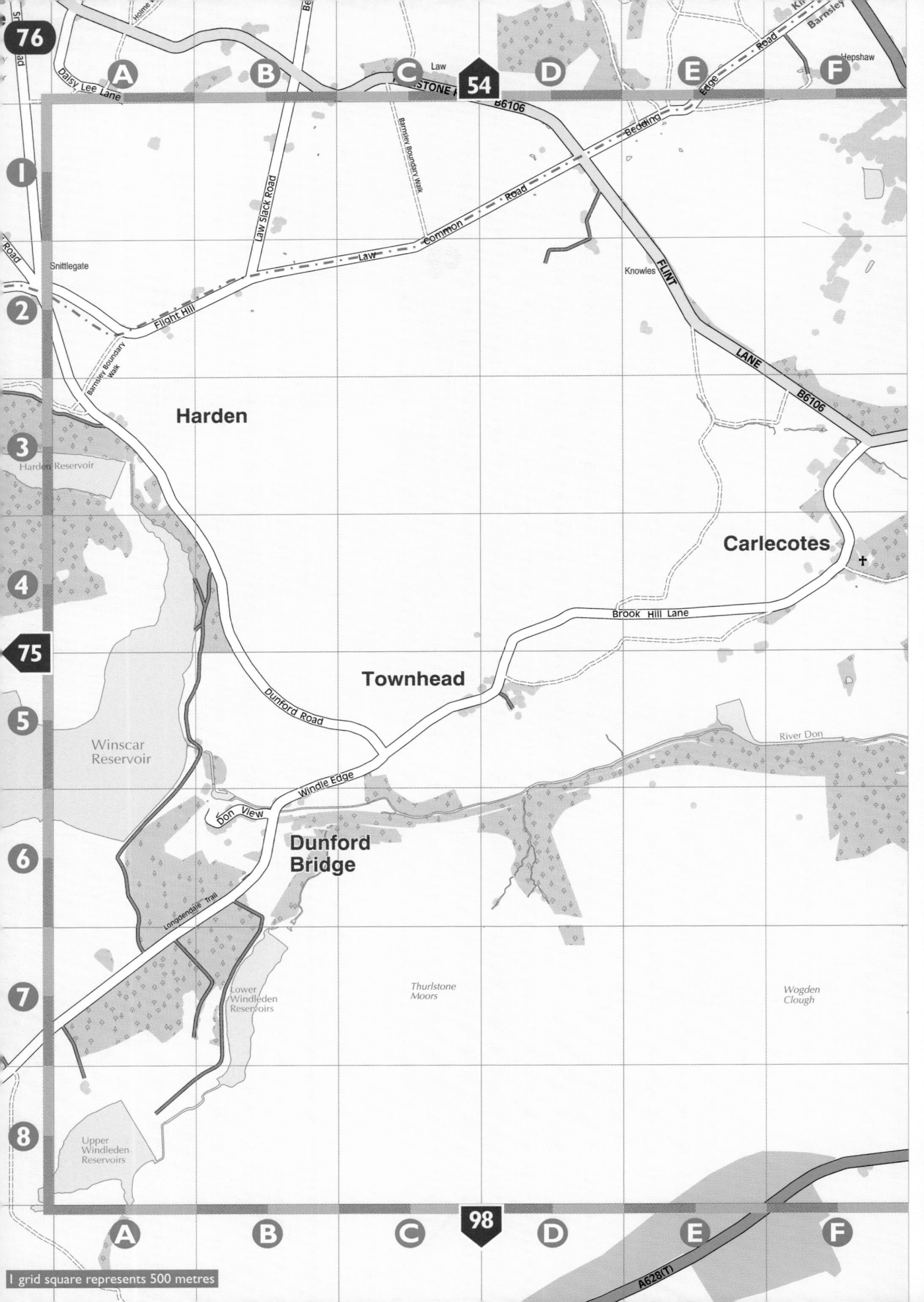

A B C D E F

Daisy Lee Lane

Holme

Law Slack Road

Barnsley Boundary Walk

B6106

Bedding

I

Law Common Road

Law

FLINT

Knowles

Road

Snittlegate

Barnsley Boundary Walk

2

Flight Hill

LANE B6106

Edge

Barnsley

Hepshaw

Harden

3

Harden Reservoir

Carlecotes

†

4

Brook Hill Lane

Dunford Road

Townhead

5

River Don

Winscar
Reservoir

Windle Edge

Don View

**Dunford
Bridge**

6

Longdendale Trail

7

Lower
Windleden
Reservoirs

Thurlstone
Moors

Wogden
Clough

8

Upper
Windleden
Reservoirs

A B C D E F

A628(T)

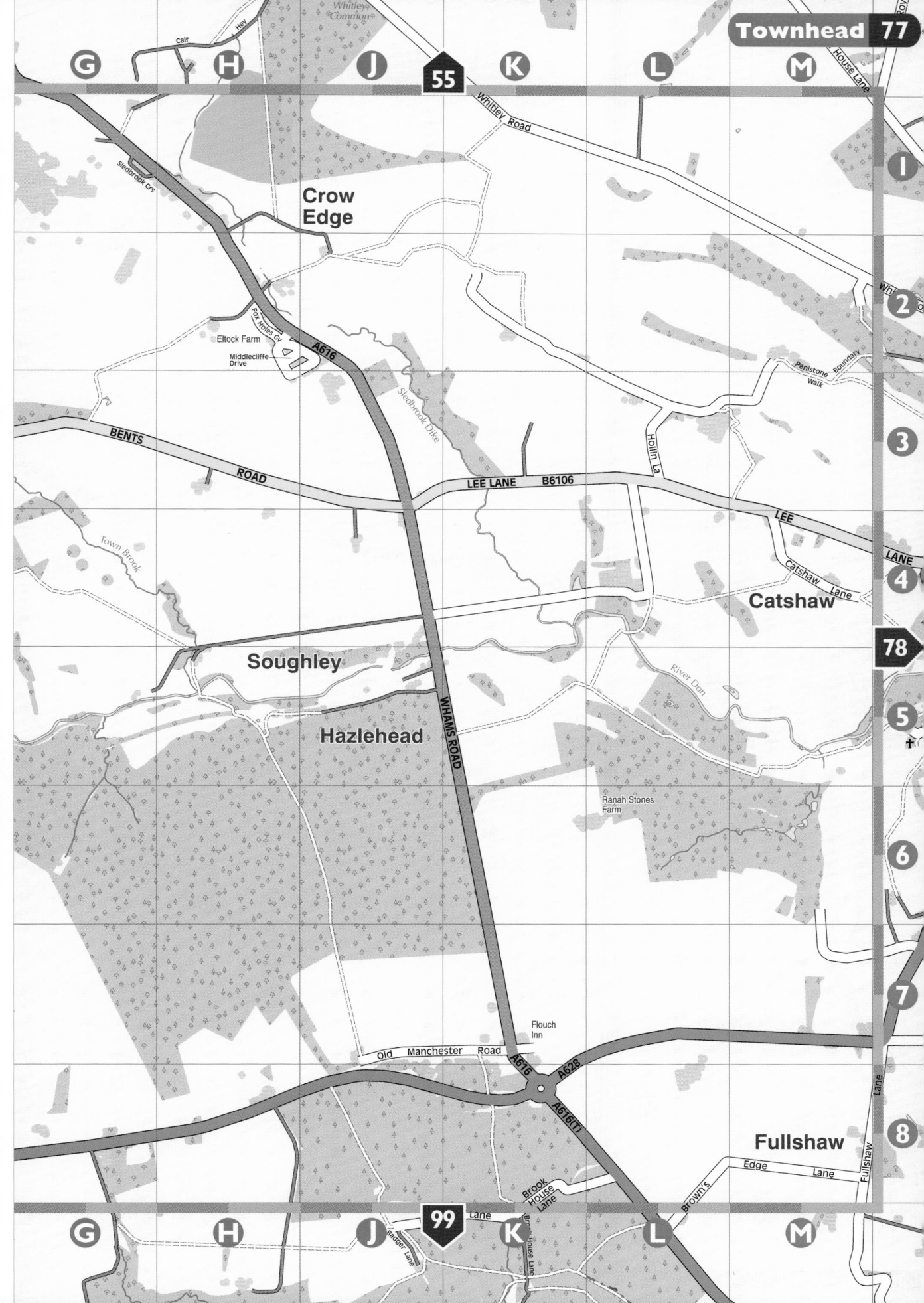

G H J **55** K L M

Whitley Common

Calf Hey

I

Whitley Road

Crow Edge

Sledbrook Crs

2

Fox Holes Gv

Eltock Farm A616

Middlecliffe Drive

Sledbrook Dike

Whi

Penistone Boundary Walk

3

BENTS ROAD

LEE LANE B6106

Hollin La

LEE

Town Brook

LANE

Catshaw Lane

4

Catshaw

Soughley

River Don

78

Hazlehead

5

†

Ranah Stones Farm

WHAMS ROAD

6

7

Flouch Inn

Old Manchester Road A616

A628

A616(T)

Fullshaw

8

Edge Lane

Fullshaw Lane

Brook House Lane

Brown's

Lane

G H J **99** K L M

Badger Lane

Brook House Lane

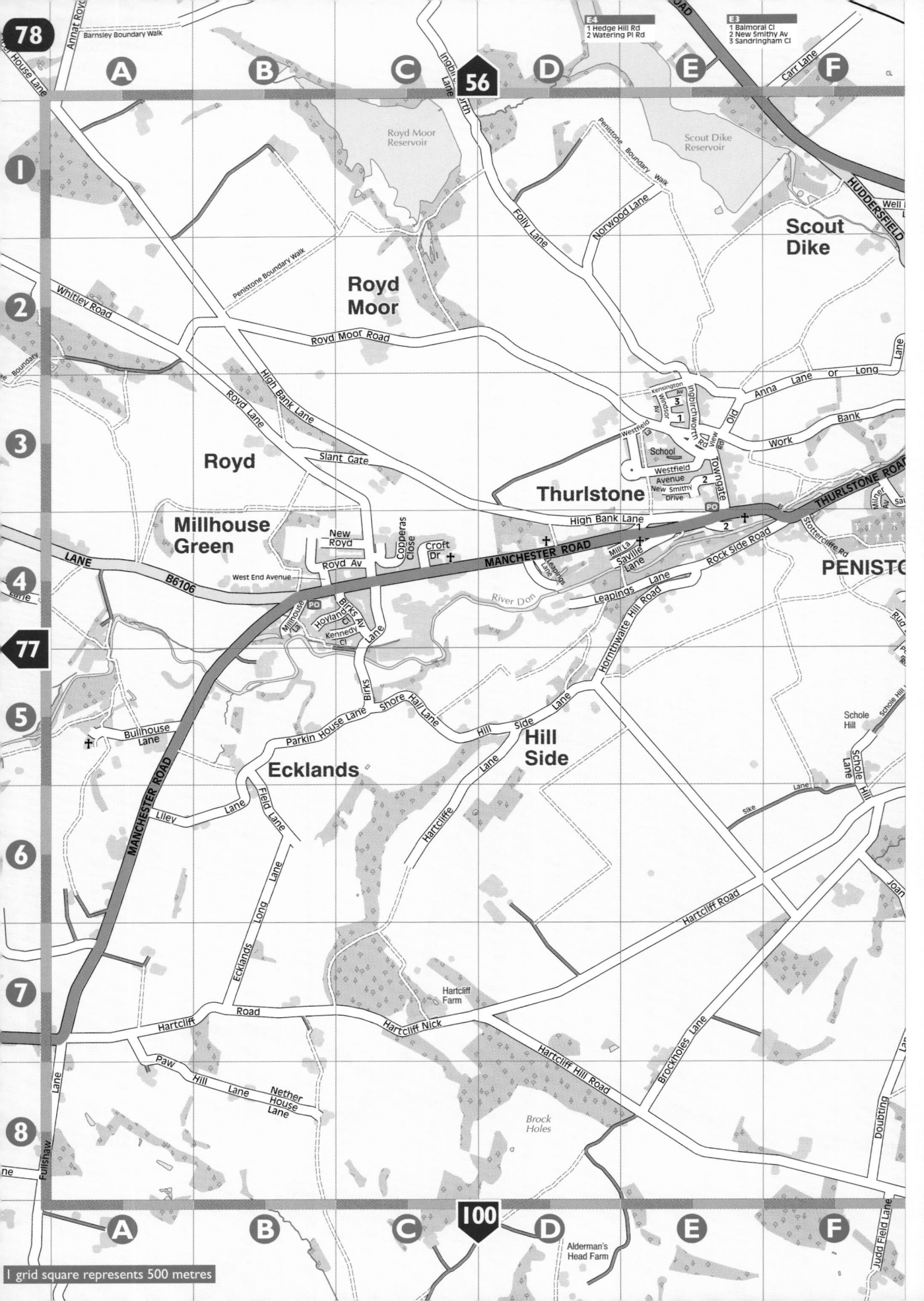
78
56
77
100
E4
1 Hedge Hill Rd
2 Watering Pl Rd
E3
1 Balmoral Cl
2 New Smithy Av
3 Sandringham Cl
Royd Moor Reservoir
Scout Dike Reservoir
Scout Dike
Royd Moor
Royd
Thurlstone
Millhouse Green
PENISTO
Ecklands
Hill Side
Barnsley Boundary Walk
Penistone Boundary Walk
Whitley Road
Royd Moor Road
High Bank Lane
Royd Lane
Slant Gate
Folly Lane
Norwood Lane
Ingbirchworth Lane
Carr Lane
HUDDERSFIELD
Anna Lane or Long Lane
Bank
Work
Old
School
Westfield Avenue
New Smithy Drive
Towngate
THURLSTONE ROAD
MANCHESTER ROAD
LANE
B6106
West End Avenue
New Royd
Royd Av
Copperas Close
Croft Dr
Birks Av
Hoyland Cl
Kennedy Cl
Millhouse La
River Don
Leapings Lane
Saville Lane
Mill La
Rock Side Road
Stottercliffe Rd
Hornthwaite Hill Road
Birks Lane
Shore Hall Lane
Parkin House Lane
Hill Side Lane
Bullhouse Lane
Liley Lane
Field Lane
Hartcliffe Lane
Ecklands Long Lane
Hartcliff Road
Hartcliff Nick
Hartcliff Farm
Hartcliff Hill Road
Paw Hill Lane
Nether House Lane
Fullshaw Lane
Brock Holes
Brockholes Lane
Sike Lane
Schole Hill
Schole Hill Lane
Doubting
Judd Field Lane
Alderman's Head Farm
1 grid square represents 500 metres

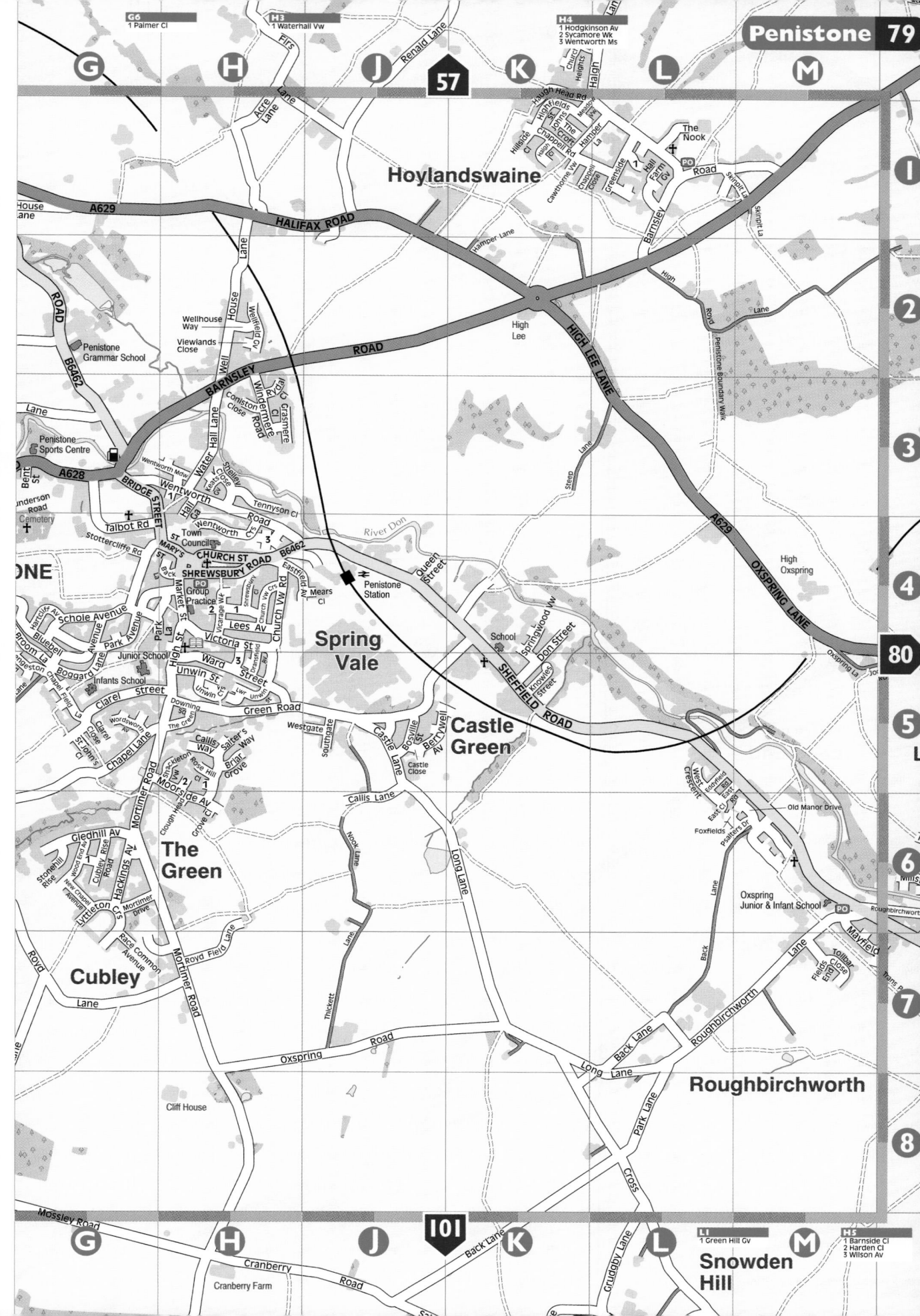
G6
1 Palmer Cl
H3
1 Waterhall Vw
H4
1 Hodgkinson Av
2 Sycamore Wk
3 Wentworth Ms
Hoylandswaine
Penistone
Spring Vale
Castle Green
The Green
Cubley
Roughbirchworth
Snowden Hill
High Oxspring
High Lee
Penistone Station
Penistone Grammar School
Penistone Sports Centre
Oxspring Junior & Infant School
Cliff House
Cranberry Farm
L1
1 Green Hill Gv
M5
1 Barnside Cl
2 Harden Cl
3 Wilson Av
57
80
101

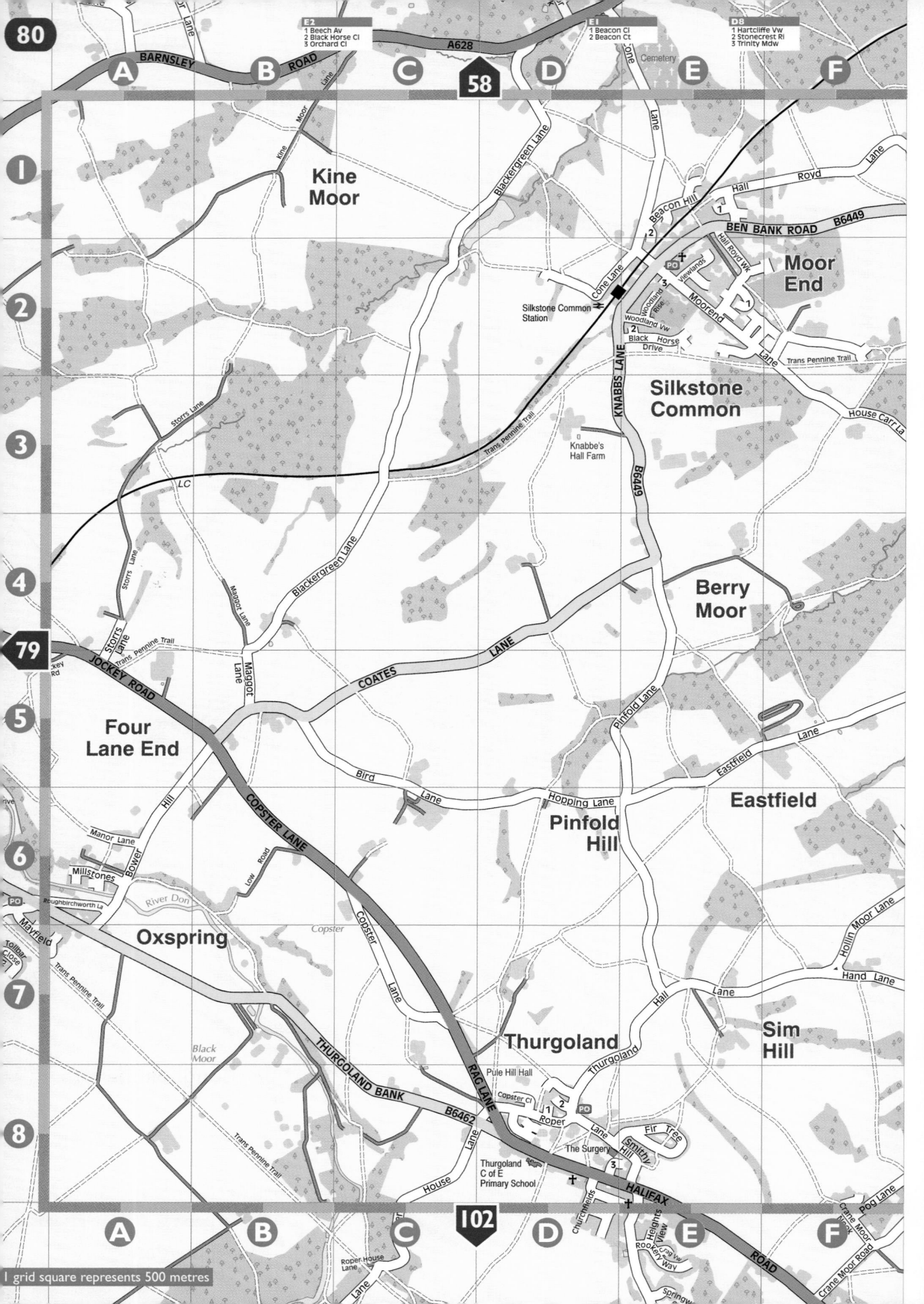

E2
1 Beech Av
2 Black Horse Cl
3 Orchard Cl
E1
1 Beacon Cl
2 Beacon Ct
D8
1 Hartcliffe Vw
2 Stonecrest Rl
3 Trinity Mdw
58
79
102
BARNSLEY ROAD
A628
Cemetery
Kine Moor
Blackergreen Lane
Moor Lane
Cone Lane
Hall Royd Lane
Beacon Hill
BEN BANK ROAD B6449
Hall Royd Wk
Viewlands
Moor End
Moorend Lane
Woodland Rise
Woodland Vw
Black Horse Drive
Silkstone Common Station
Trans Pennine Trail
KNABBS LANE
Silkstone Common
House Carr La
Storrs Lane
Knabbe's Hall Farm
B6449
LC
Maggot Lane
Berry Moor
COATES LANE
JOCKEY ROAD
Four Lane End
Pinfold Lane
Eastfield Lane
Bird Lane
Hopping Lane
Eastfield
Pinfold Hill
Manor Lane
COPSTER LANE
Low Road
Bower Hill
Millstones
River Don
Roughbirchworth La
Copster
Copster Lane
Oxspring
Mayfield
Tollbar Close
Hollin Moor Lane
Hand Lane
Hall Lane
Sim Hill
Black Moor
Thurgoland
Thurgoland Hall Lane
Pule Hill Hall
THURGOLAND BANK
RAG LANE
B6462
Copster Cl
Roper Lane
Fir Tree
Smithy Hill
The Surgery
Thurgoland C of E Primary School
House Lane
HALIFAX ROAD
Churchfields
Heights View
Rookery Way
Crag Vw
Springw
Roper House Lane
Pog Lane
Crane Moor Nook
Crane Moor Road

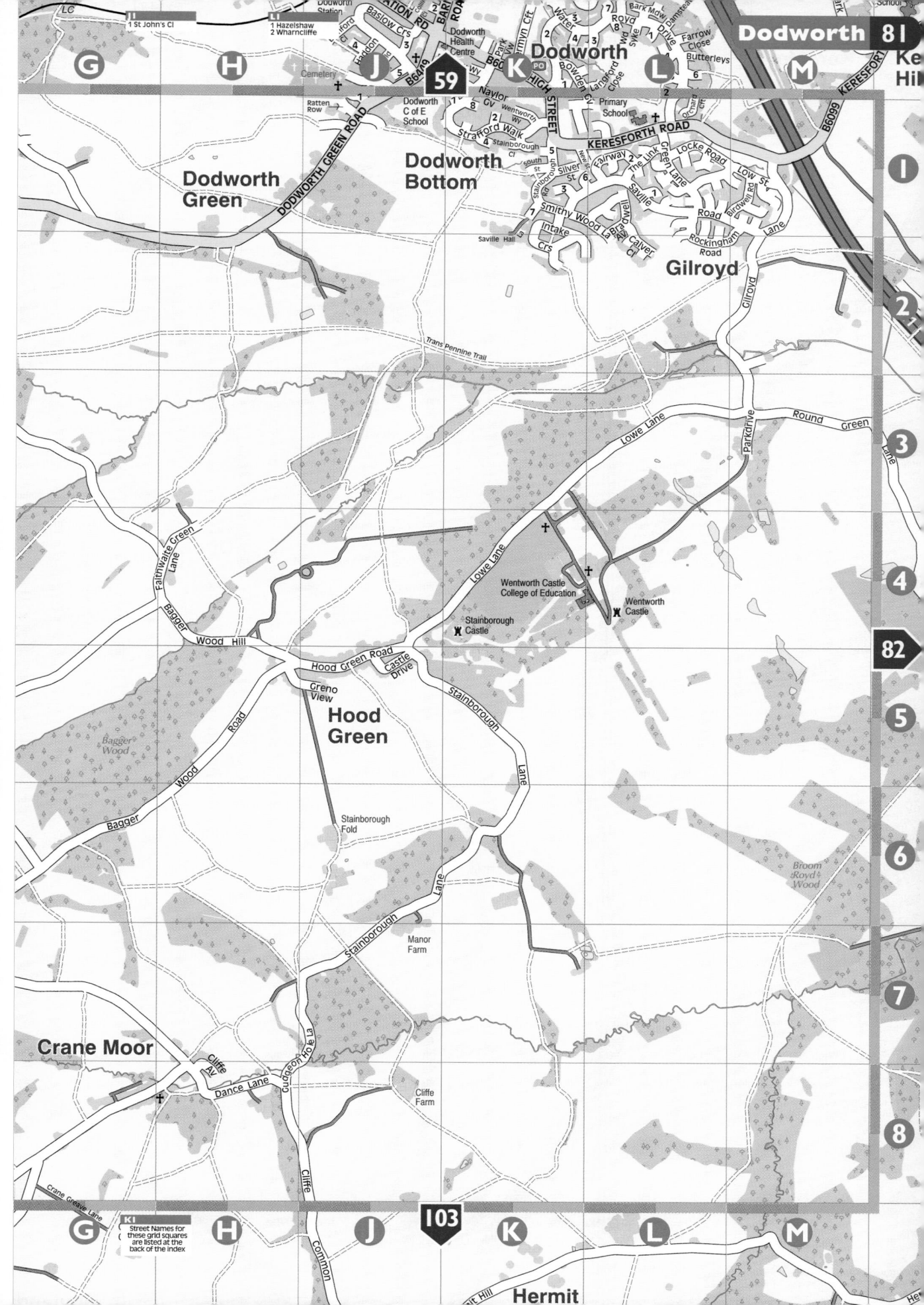

1 St John's Cl
1 Hazelshaw
2 Wharncliffe
Dodworth Station
Cemetery
Dodworth Health Centre
Dodworth
Baslow Crs
Haddon
Bark Mdw
Royd
Damstead
Farrow Close
Butterleys
Keresford
Ratten Row
Dodworth C of E School
Naylor Gv
Wentworth Wy
Strafford Walk
Stainborough Cl
HIGH STREET
Bowden Gv
Langford Close
Primary School
KERESFORTH ROAD
Orchard Cft
B6099
Dodworth Green
DODWORTH GREEN ROAD
Dodworth Bottom
South St
Stainborough Rd
Silver St
New St
Fairway
The Link
Green Lane
Locke Road
Low St
Saville
Bridwell Rd
Smithy Wood La
Bradwell Av
Intake Crs
Saville Hall
Calver Cl
Rockingham Road
Lane
Gilroyd
Trans Pennine Trail
Round Green
Lowe Lane
Parkdrive
Faithwaite Green Lane
Bagger Wood Hill
Wentworth Castle College of Education
Wentworth Castle
Stainborough Castle
Hood Green Road
Castle Drive
Greno View
Hood Green
Stainborough Lane
Bagger Wood
Bagger Wood Road
Stainborough Fold
Broom Royd Wood
Manor Farm
Crane Moor
Cliffe Av
Dance Lane
Cudgeon Hole La
Cliffe Farm
Cliffe Common
Crane Greave Lane
Street Names for these grid squares are listed at the back of the index
Hermit
G H J K L M
1 2 3 4 5 6 7 8
59
82
103

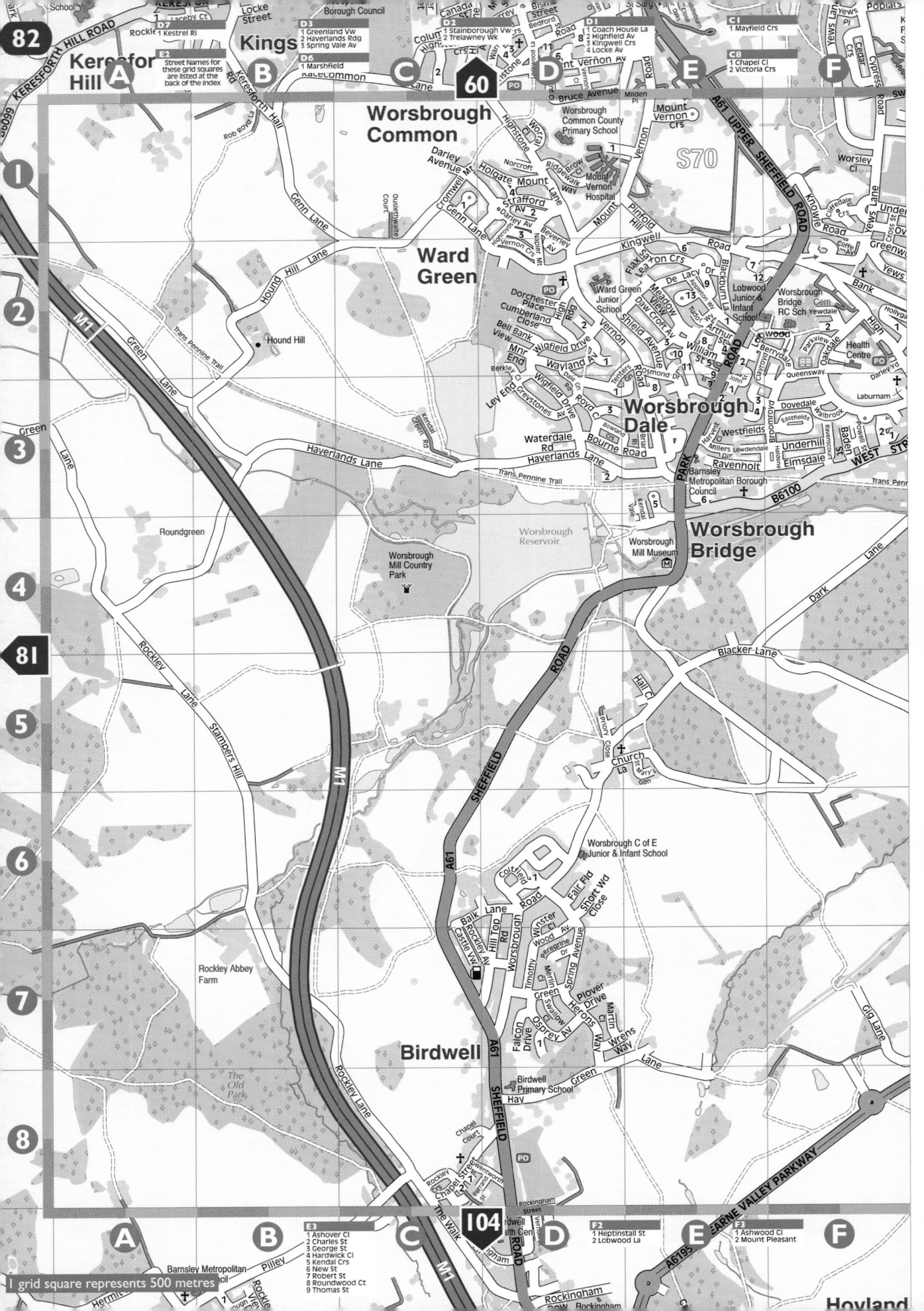
D7
1 Kestrel Ri
E2
Street Names for these grid squares are listed at the back of the index
D3
1 Greenland Vw
2 Haverlands Rdg
3 Spring Vale Av
D6
1 Marshfield
D2
1 Stainborough Vw
2 Trelawney Wk
D1
1 Coach House La
2 Highfield Av
3 Kingwell Crs
4 Locke Av
C1
1 Mayfield Crs
C8
1 Chapel Cl
2 Victoria Crs
Keresforth Hill
Kings
Borough Council
Locke Street
KERESFORTH HILL ROAD
Keresforth Hall Rd
Racecommon Lane
60
Bruce Avenue
Worsbrough Common
Worsbrough Common County Primary School
Mount Vernon Crs
A61 UPPER SHEFFIELD ROAD
S70
Worsley Cl
Rob Royd La
Darley Avenue
Holgate Mount
Strafford Av
Genn Lane
Cromwell Mt
Ousletwaite Court
Ridgewalk Way
Mount Vernon Hospital
Pinfold Hill
Kingwell Road
Vernon Road
Mount
Ward Green
Hound Hill Lane
Hound Hill
Trans Pennine Trail
Green Lane
M1
Saxon Crs
Flax Lea
De Lacy Dr
Blackburn La
Ward Green Junior School
Lobwood Junior & Infant School
Worsbrough Bridge RC Sch
Dorchester Place
Cumberland Close
Bell Bank View
Mnr End
Wigfield Drive
Wayland Av
Meadow View
Daw Croft Av
Shield Avenue
Osmond Dr
William St
Arthur St
Berrydale
Parkview
Oakdale
Queensway
Health Centre
Knowle Road
Yews Lane
Bank
High
Darley Yd
Laburnam
Dovedale
Walbrook
Eastfields
Westfields
Underhill
Elmsdale
Baden St
WEST ST
Ley End
Greystones Av
Royd Cl
Worsbrough Dale
Waterdale Rd
Haverlands Lane
Bourne Road
Kendal Green Rd
PARK ROAD
Ravenholt
Barnsley Metropolitan Borough Council
B6100
Green Lane
Roundgreen
Worsbrough Reservoir
Worsbrough Mill Country Park
Worsbrough Mill Museum
Worsbrough Bridge
Dark Lane
81
Blacker Lane
Hall Cl
Rockley Lane
Stampers Hill
Priory Close
Church La
St Mary's Gdn
SHEFFIELD ROAD
A61
Worsbrough C of E Junior & Infant School
Coltfield
Worsbrough Road
Fair Fld
Short Wd Close
Balk Lane
Hill Top Rd
Rockley Av
Castle Vw
Winster Cl
Wood Av
Peregrine Dr
Spring Avenue
Timothy Wood
Merlin Cl
Green
Swallow Cl
Plover Drive
Herons Way
Martin Cl
Wrens Way
Osprey Av
Falcon Drive
Rockley Abbey Farm
Birdwell
Birdwell Primary School
Hay Green Lane
Gig Lane
The Old Park
Chapel Court
Rockley Crs
Chapel Street
Wentworth
Rockingham Street
104
The Walk
Birdwell Health Cen
A6195 DEARNE VALLEY PARKWAY
E3
1 Ashover Cl
2 Charles St
3 George St
4 Hardwick Cl
5 Kendal Crs
6 New St
7 Robert St
8 Roundwood Ct
9 Thomas St
F2
1 Heptinstall St
2 Lobwood La
F3
1 Ashwood Cl
2 Mount Pleasant
Barnsley Metropolitan Council
Pilley
Rockingham
Hoyland
1 grid square represents 500 metres

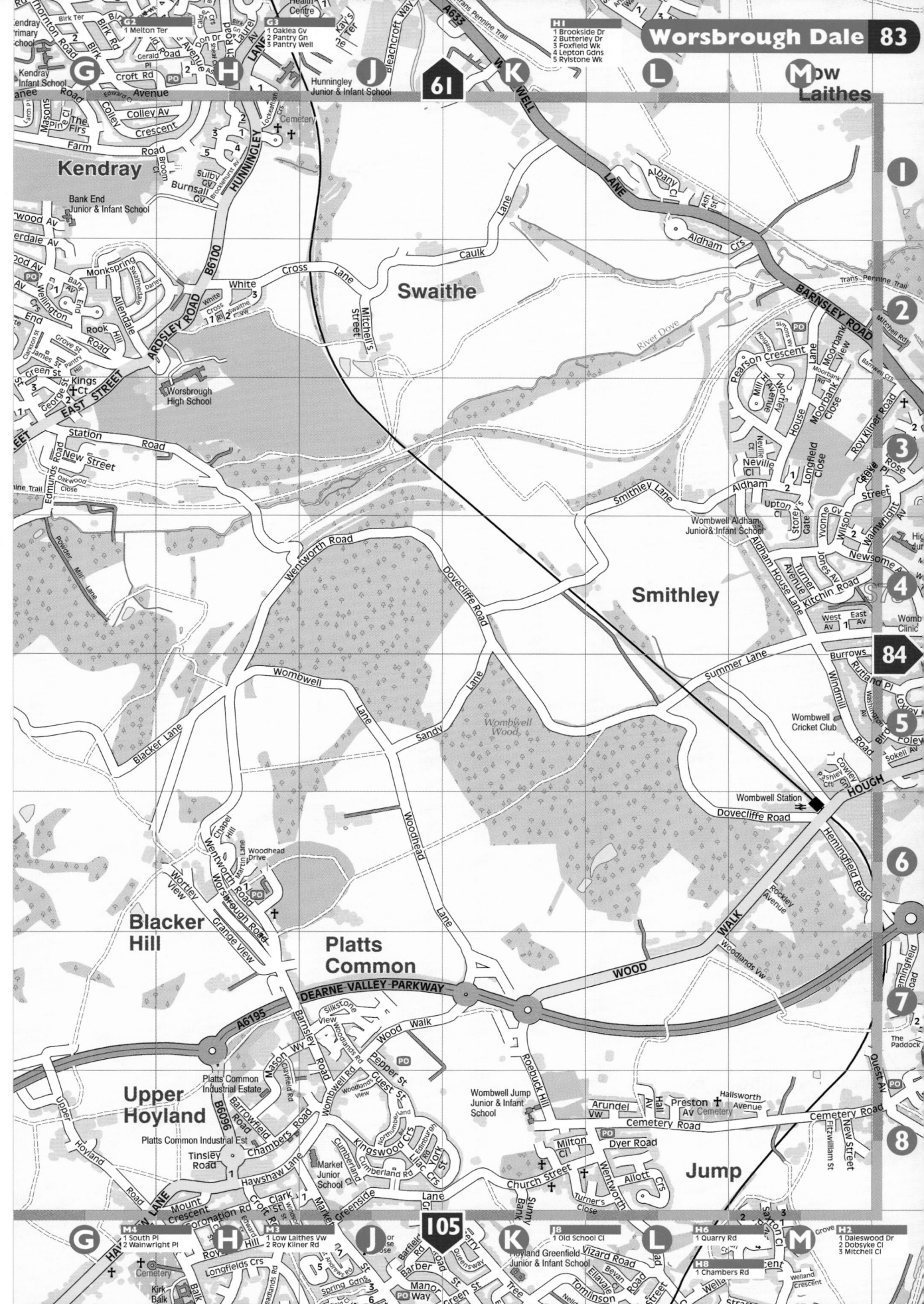
Kendray
Swaithe
Smithley
Blacker Hill
Platts Common
Upper Hoyland
Jump
Mow Laithes
Worsbrough High School
Wombwell Station
Wombwell Wood
Dearne Valley Parkway
Wombwell Cricket Club
Hunningley Junior & Infant School
Bank End Junior & Infant School
Wombwell Aldham Junior & Infant School
Wombwell Jump Junior & Infant School
Market Junior School
Platts Common Industrial Estate
Hoyland Greenfield Junior & Infant School
G2 1 Melton Ter
G3 1 Oaklea Gv 2 Pantry Gn 3 Pantry Well
H1 1 Brookside Dr 2 Butterley Dr 3 Foxfield Wk 4 Lepton Gdns 5 Rylstone Wk
M4 1 South Pl 2 Wainwright Pl
M3 1 Low Laithes Vw 2 Roy Kilner Rd
J8 1 Old School Cl
H6 1 Quarry Rd
H8 1 Chambers Rd
H2 1 Daleswood Dr 2 Dobsyke Cl 3 Mitchell Cl
61
84
105

A8
1 Burtop Cft
2 Old House Cl
3 Tingle Bridge Crs
A7
1 Ellis Ct
2 Mellwood Gv
E7, E8, F1, F2
Street Names for these grid squares are listed at the back of the index
A5
1 Copeland Rd
2 Roberts St
A4
1 Bradley Av
2 Frederick St
3 Princess St
4 William St
A3
1 Hammerton St
2 Sadler's Ga
D5, D6, E1, E2
Street Names for these grid squares are listed at the back of the index
Cranford Hall
62
83
106
SALTERSBROOK ROAD
Tempest Avenue
DONCASTER
Snape Hill
Low Valley
Darfield
Broomhill
WOMBWELL
Hemingfield
Brampton
S73
Barnsley Road
Upperwood Junior & Infant School
Oberon Crs
Schofield Road
Morrison Road
Illsley Road
East Street
North Street
NANNY MARR RD
B6096
School Street
Junior School
Cover Drive
Pinfold Lane
Foulstone School
Darfield Cricket Club
Meadow Lane
Church Street
Darfield Health Centre
Inkerman Rd
West Street
South View
GARDEN ST
Hill Street
SNAPE HILL ROAD B6096
New Street
Springbank
Springfield Crescent
Vicar Road
Upperwood Road
Lombard Crescent
Venetian Crs
Trans Pennine Trail
Netherwood Road
Balk Lane
Pitt Street
Bradberry
Mitchell Rd
Primary School
GEORGE STREET
Doveside Dr
Honeysuckle Close
Aspen Grove
Henry Street
Millmoor Rd
STONYFORD ROAD
St Michaels RC Junior & Infant School
Ings Road
Valley Road
Station Road Industrial Estate
Barnsley M B C
STATION ROAD
Edward Street
A633
Littlefield La
Rimington Road
Highfields Junior School
Newsome Av
Main Street
Bond Street
Cemetery
Summer Lane
Wombwell Clinic
Barnsley Metropolitan Borough Council
High St
Rectory Cl
The Gables School
Oakfield Junior School
Kingsway
CHURCH ST
Kelvin Grove Surgery
Hawson Street
Park Street Junior & Infant School
Doctors Surgery
Everill Gate Lane
Wombwell Public Baths
Foley Avenue
Bondfield Crs
Wright Crs
HOUGH LANE
Wood Street
Jardine Street
Hall Street
Roebuck Street
Wentworth View
Wombwell High School
Gypsy Lane
Wath Road
WATH ROAD A633
BRAMPTON ROAD
A6195
Barnsley
Rotherham
Lundhill Grove
Hoober View
Brampton Crescent
DEARNE VALLEY PARKWAY A6195
B6089
KNOLLBECK LANE
Primary School
Chapel Avenue
Rother Street
Brampton Health Cen
Garden Drive
PONTEFRACT ROAD
B6273
Highgate
Knollbeck Avenue
Wynmoor Crescent
Doctors Surgery
Manor Road
Westpit Hill
Fleet Close
Honister Close
BRAMPTON ROAD
Hemingfield Road
Infant School
School Street
Beech House Road
Tingle Bridge Lane
Lady Croft Lane
Quest Av
Barnsley Boundary Walk
NEW ROAD B6097
B4
1 Diamond St
2 Lower York St
3 Melville St
B5
1 Hoyland St
2 Kings Rd
3 Winders Pl
C1
1 Cortina Rl
C4
1 New St
2 Smith St
C5
1 Foulstone Rw
C6
1 Glenmore Rl
D1
1 Palermo Fold
D2
1 Amalfi Cl
D3
1 Providence St
1 grid square represents 500 metres

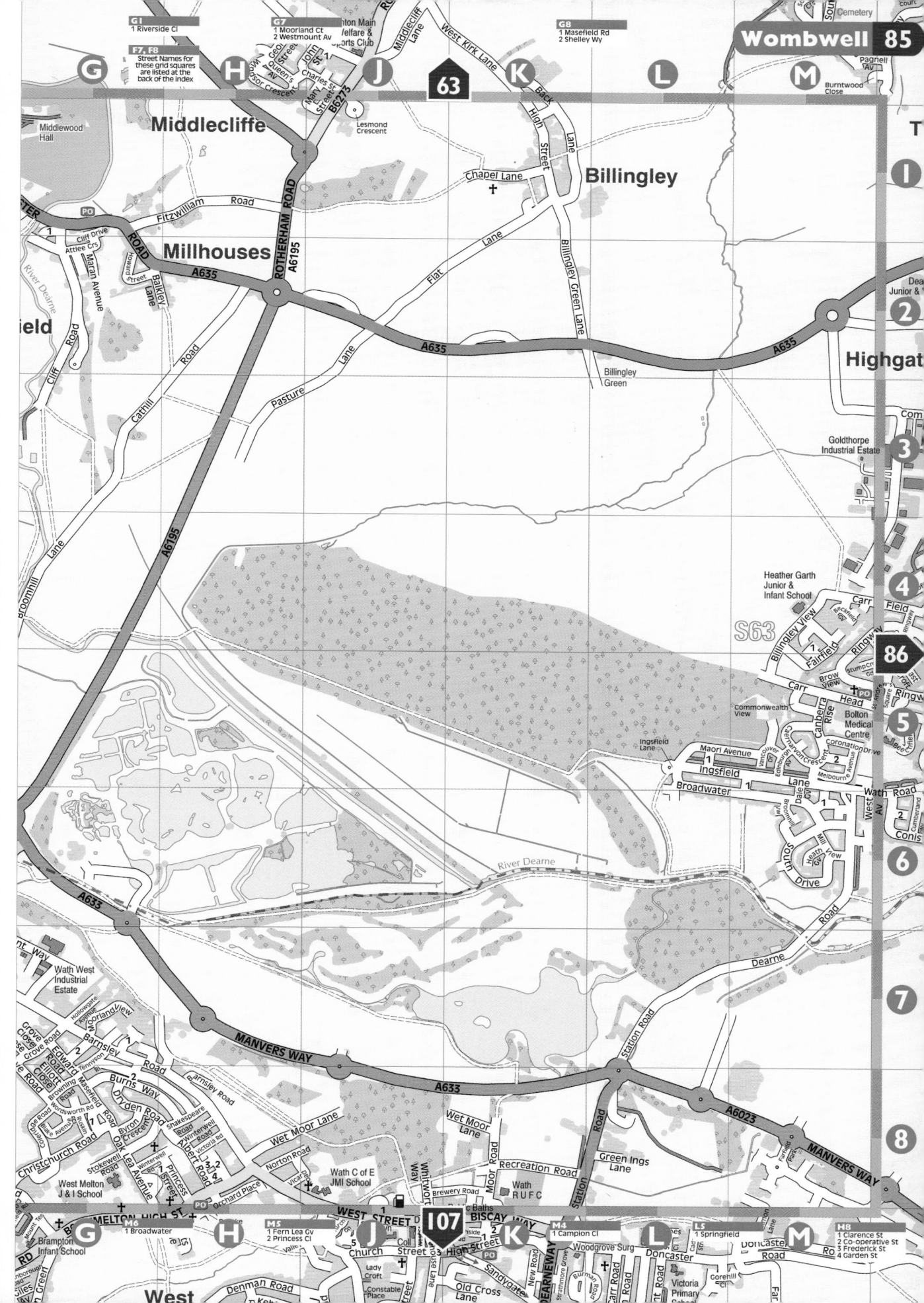
G1
1 Riverside Cl
F7, F8
Street Names for these grid squares are listed at the back of the index
G7
1 Moorland Ct
2 Westmount Av
G8
1 Masefield Rd
2 Shelley Wy
63
Middlecliffe
Middlewood Hall
Lesmond Crescent
Billingley
Chapel Lane
High Street
Back Lane
West Kirk Lane
Middlecliff Lane
ROTHERHAM ROAD
A6195
B6273
Fitzwilliam Road
Millhouses
Cliff Drive
Attlee Crs
Maran Avenue
Howard Street
Balkley Lane
A635
River Dearne
Cliff Road
Cathill Road
Broomhill Lane
Flat Lane
Pasture Lane
Billingley Green Lane
Billingley Green
Highgat
Goldthorpe Industrial Estate
Heather Garth Junior & Infant School
S63
86
Billingley View
Fairfield
Ringway
Carr Field
Brow View
Carr Head
Commonwealth View
Canberra Rise
Bolton Medical Centre
Coronation Drive
Ingsfield Lane
Maori Avenue
Vancouver Dr
Edinburgh Av
Caernarvon Crescent
Melbourne Avenue
Ingsfield Lane
Broadwater
Dale Cv
Broomhill Vw
Wath Road
West Av
Cumberland
Conis
Heath Gv
Mill View
South Drive
River Dearne
Dearne Road
A633
Wath West Industrial Estate
MANVERS WAY
Station Road
A6023
Barnsley Road
Moorland View
Grove Close
Grove Road
Edward Road
Elliott Close
Burns Way
Dryden Road
Byron Crescent
Shakespeare Road
Masefield Road
Browning Road
Wordsworth Rd
Tennyson
Winterwell Road
Victoria Rd
Albert Road
Princess Street
Oak Lea Avenue
Stokewell Road
Christchurch Road
West Melton J & I School
Orchard Place
Wet Moor Lane
Norton Road
Wath C of E JMI School
Whitworth Way
Moor Road
Recreation Road
Brewery Road
Wath RUFC
Station Road
Green Ings Lane
Fairfield Park
MELTON HIGH ST
WEST STREET
BISCAY WAY
107
M6
1 Broadwater
M5
1 Fern Lea Gv
2 Princess Cl
M4
1 Campion Cl
L5
1 Springfield
H8
1 Clarence St
2 Co-operative St
3 Frederick St
4 Garden St
Brampton Infant School
Church Street
High Street
Lady Croft
Constable Place
Sandygate
Old Cross Lane
New Road
DEARNEWAY
Woodgrove Surg
Doncaster Road
Victoria Primary School
Gorehill Cl
Denman Road
West
Cemetery
Pagnell Av
Burntwood Close

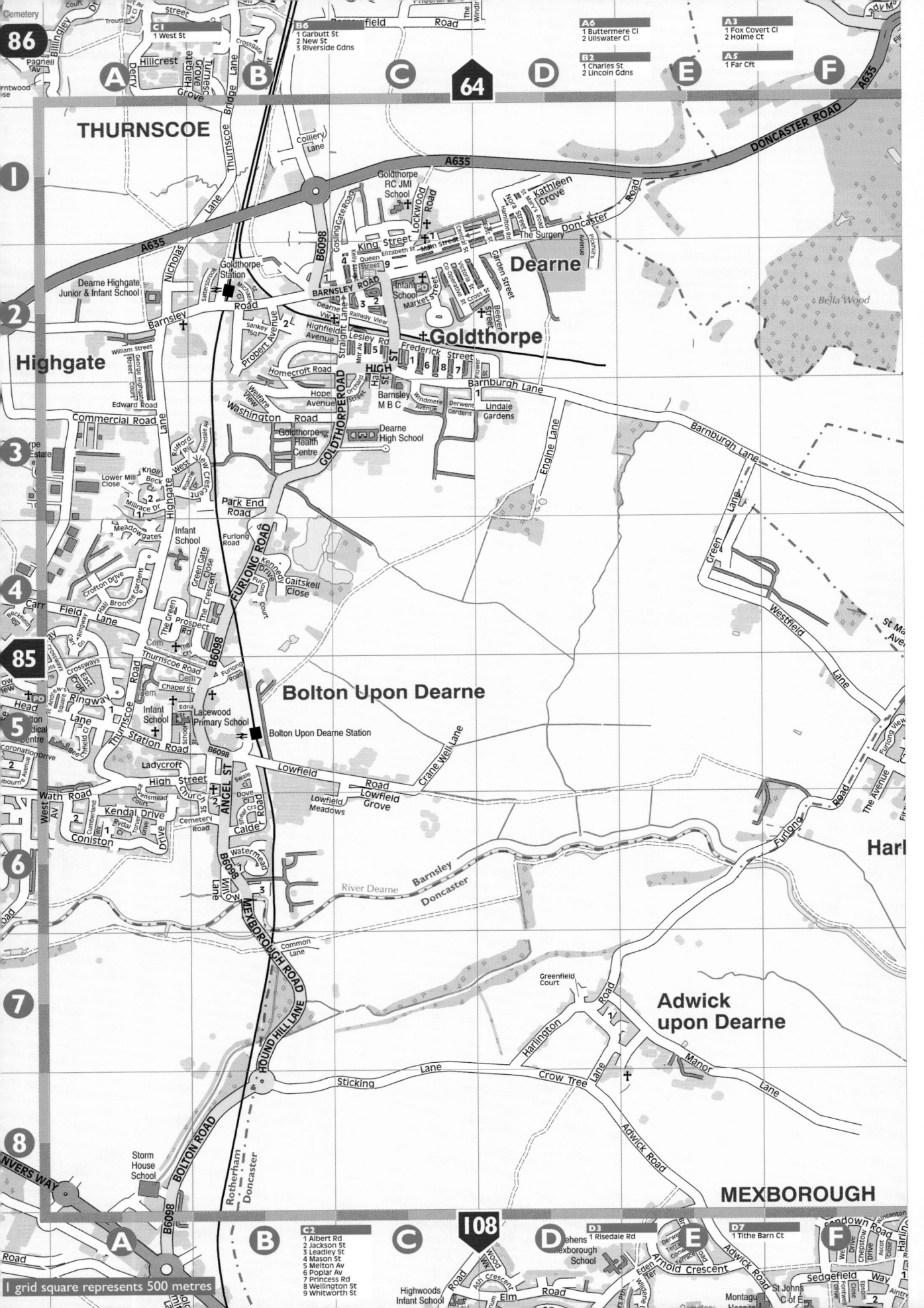

86
64
85
108
A
B
C
D
E
F
1
2
3
4
5
6
7
8
C1
1 West St
B6
1 Garbutt St
2 New St
3 Riverside Gdns
A6
1 Buttermere Cl
2 Ullswater Cl
B2
1 Charles St
2 Lincoln Gdns
A3
1 Fox Covert Cl
2 Holme Ct
A5
1 Far Cft
THURNSCOE
Highgate
Goldthorpe
Dearne
Bolton Upon Dearne
Adwick upon Dearne
MEXBOROUGH
Bella Wood
A635
DONCASTER ROAD
Doncaster Road
Thurnscoe Bridge Lane
Nicholas Lane
Hillcrest
Colliery Lane
Goldthorpe RC JMI School
Goldthorpe Station
Dearne Highgate Junior & Infant School
BARNSLEY ROAD
Barnsley Road
King Street
Queen Street
Elizabeth St
Main Street
Lockwood Road
Gosling Gate Road
Kathleen Grove
The Surgery
Garden Street
Market Street
Cross St
Beever Street
Railway View
Highfield Avenue
Lesley Rd
Frederick Street
HIGH ST
Probert Avenue
Sankey Sq
William Street
Edward Road
Commercial Road
Homecroft Road
Barnburgh Lane
Barnsley M B C
Windmere Avenue
Derwent Gardens
Lindale Gardens
Hope Avenue
Welfare View
Washington Road
Goldthorpe Health Centre
GOLDTHORPE ROAD
Dearne High School
Engine Lane
Lower Mill Close
Park End Road
Furlong Road
FURLONG ROAD
Kennedy Drive
Gaitskell Close
Meadowgates
Infant School
Green Gate Close
The Crescent
Crofton Drive
Broome Gardens
Carr Field Lane
Prospect Rd
The Green
Thurnscoe Road
B6098
Chapel St
Ringway
Crossways
Lacewood Primary School
Bolton Upon Dearne Station
Station Road
Lowfield Road
Lowfield Grove
Lowfield Meadows
Crane Well Lane
Ladycroft
High Street
ANGEL ST
Wath Road
Kendal Drive
Coniston
Cemetery Road
Calder Road
Watermead
Willow Lane
MEXBOROUGH ROAD
River Dearne
Barnsley Doncaster
Common Lane
HOUND HILL LANE
Sticking Lane
Crow Tree Lane
Harlington Road
Greenfield Court
Manor Lane
Adwick Road
Green Lane
Westfield Lane
Furlong Road
The Avenue
Storm House School
BOLTON ROAD
Rotherham Doncaster
C2
1 Albert Rd
2 Jackson St
3 Leadley St
4 Mason St
5 Melton Av
6 Poplar Av
7 Princess Rd
8 Wellington St
9 Whitworth St
D3
1 Risedale Rd
D7
1 Tithe Barn Ct
Mexborough School
Arnold Crescent
Highwoods Infant School
Sedgefield Way
1 grid square represents 500 metres

BARNSLEY ROAD A635

BARNSLEY A635

G4
1 St Margarets Av

Home Farm Court

Hickleton

G H J 65 K L M

I

2

3

Hangman Stone Road

4

88

5

Hickleton Road

St Peter's Close

Stables Lane

The Pinfold

The Poplars

Wadworth Close

High Street

Hall Street

PO

Cemetery

Windsor Drive

Balmoral Close

Belvoir Avenue

Caernarvon Drive

Conway Drive

Cresacre

Easton Rd

Fox Lane

Barnburgh

Doncaster Road

St Helen's Lane

Hangman Stone Road

Margarets Avenue

Hollowgate

Scott Avenue

Church Lane

Lane

Barnburgh Primary School

Far Moor Cl

North Drive

Sayers Close

Crane Moor Close

Manor Road

Windsor Drive

Cambridge Close

William Drive

Doncaster Road (Harlington)

Doncaster Road

Ludwell Hill

6

Ox Pa

ington

Mill Lane

Barnburgh Grange

Melton Mill Lane

Doncaster Road

Doncaster College

Hig'7
Melton

River Dearne

North Ings

Dearne Bridge

8

Windhill

Infant School

Ullswater Road

Oulton Rise

Coniston Road

A635

A   **Marr**   **B**   **C**   66   **D**   **E**   **F**

Marr Hall Farm
F7
1 Chestnut Gv
2 Field House Rd
3 Hillside Ct
4 Rectory Ms

F6
1 Castle Gv
2 Derwent Pl
3 Glendale Rd
4 Melton Wood Gv
5 Spring Hill Cl
6 Woodview

E6
1 Cambrian Cl
2 Kendal Cl

BARNSLEY ROAD   A635

Scawsby Hall

1

Marr Grange

2

3   Brand   Lane   Little Lane   Long Lane

Melton Wood   Burntwood Grange   Spring Lane

4   Ladyfield Farm   Melton Brand Farm

87

Sheep Lane Farm

5   Stone Cross Drive   Branstone Road   Roe Croft Cl

Ox Pasture   Toecroft Farm   Ambleside Crescent   Spring Crescent   Roe Croft Cl

6   Melton Road   Toecroft Lane   Westmorland Way   Melton Road   Thorpe Lane   Melton Gdns

Cotswold Drive   Folder Lane   Riverhead   Manor Gardens   Main Street   PO

New Lane   Orchard Infant School

7   **High Melton**   Cadeby Lane   Copley School   Scabba Wood   St Dominic's Close   Boat Lane   Spinney Hi

8   Garden Lane   Nursery   Lane   River Don

A   **B**   C   110   **D**   E   **F**

J2, K2, L7, M1
Street Names for these grid squares are listed at the back of the index

M3, M5, M6
Street Names for these grid squares are listed at the back of the index

M7
Street Names for these grid squares are listed at the back of the index

1 grid square represents 500 metres

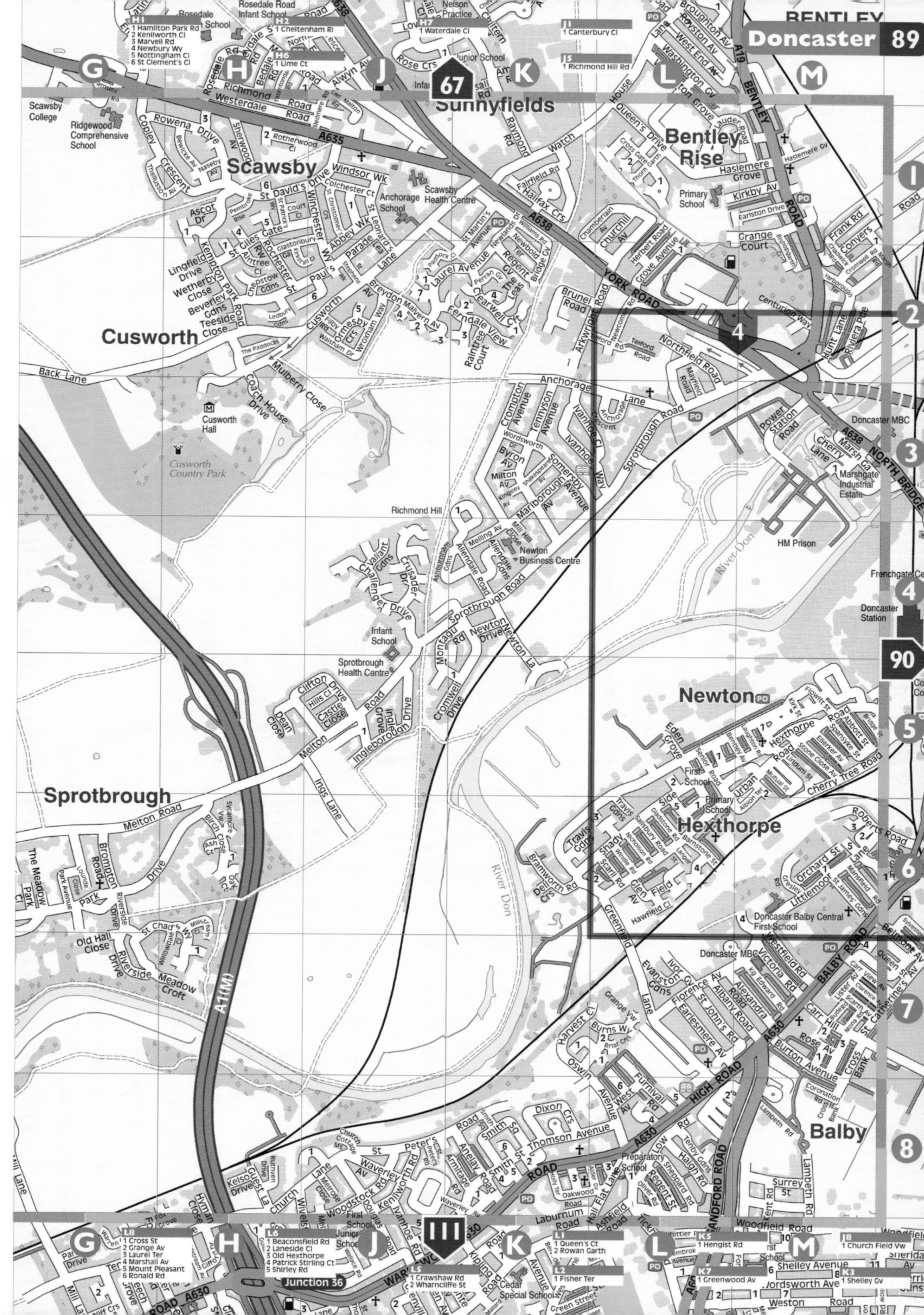

BENTLEY
Sunnyfields
Scawsby
Bentley Rise
Cusworth
Sprotbrough
Newton
Hexthorpe
Balby
Scawsby College
Ridgewood Comprehensive School
Rosedale School
Rosedale Road Infant School
Nelson Practice
Junior School
Anchorage School
Scawsby Health Centre
Primary School
Cusworth Hall
Cusworth Country Park
Richmond Hill
Newton Business Centre
Infant School
Sprotbrough Health Centre
Doncaster MBC
Marshgate Industrial Estate
HM Prison
Frenchgate Ce
Doncaster Station
First School
Doncaster Balby Central First School
Preparatory School
Cedar Special School
Junction 36
A635
A638
A19
A630
A1(M)
YORK ROAD
NORTH BRIDGE
BENTLEY ROAD
BALBY ROAD
HIGH ROAD
SANDFORD ROAD
Melton Road
Sprotbrough Road
Back Lane
Anchorage Lane
River Don
67
4
90
111
H1 1 Hamilton Park Rd 2 Kenilworth Cl 3 Marvell Rd 4 Newbury Wy 5 Nottingham Cl 6 St Clement's Cl
H2 1 Cheltenham Ri
H6 1 Lime Ct
H7 1 Waterdale Cl
J1 1 Canterbury Cl
J5 1 Richmond Hill Rd
L8 1 Cross St 2 Grange Av 3 Laurel Ter 4 Marshall Av 5 Mount Pleasant 6 Ronald Rd
L6 1 Beaconsfield Rd 2 Laneside Cl 3 Old Hexthorpe 4 Patrick Stirling Ct 5 Shirley Rd
L5 1 Crawshaw Rd 2 Wharncliffe St
L1 1 Queen's Ct 2 Rowan Garth
L2 1 Fisher Ter
K5 1 Hengist Rd
K7 1 Greenwood Av
J8 1 Church Field Vw
K3 1 Shelley Gv

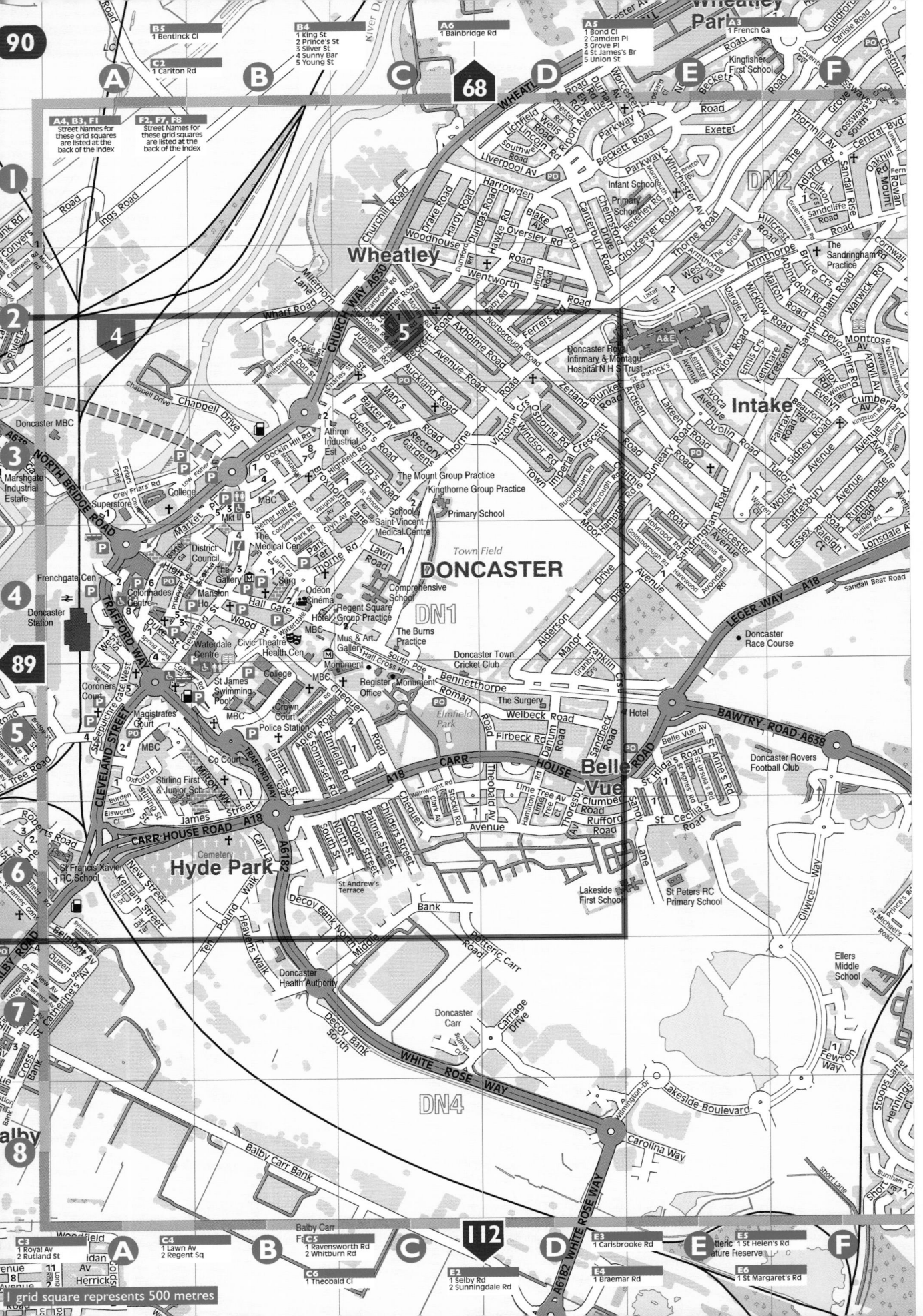
B5 1 Bentinck Cl
C2 1 Carlton Rd
B4 1 King St 2 Prince's St 3 Silver St 4 Sunny Bar 5 Young St
A6 1 Bainbridge Rd
A5 1 Bond Cl 2 Camden Pl 3 Grove Pl 4 St James's Br 5 Union St
A3 1 French Ga
A4, B3, F1 Street Names for these grid squares are listed at the back of the index
F2, F7, F8 Street Names for these grid squares are listed at the back of the index
68
Wheatley
DN2
Intake
DONCASTER
DN1
Town Field
Belle Vue
Hyde Park
DN4
Doncaster Station
Frenchgate Cen
Doncaster MBC
Marshgate Industrial Estate
North Bridge Road
Trafford Way
Cleveland Street
Church Way A630
Carr House Road A18
Bawtry Road A638
Leger Way A18
White Rose Way
A6182
Doncaster Royal Infirmary & Montagu Hospital N H S Trust
Doncaster Race Course
Doncaster Rovers Football Club
Doncaster Town Cricket Club
Comprehensive School
Regent Square Group Practice
The Burns Practice
The Mount Group Practice
Kingthorne Group Practice
Primary School
Saint Vincent Medical Centre
Waterdale Centre
Civic Theatre
Health Cen
Mus & Art Gallery
Mansion Ho
District Council
The Gallery
Odeon Cinema
Colonnades Centre
St James Swimming Pool
Magistrates Court
Police Station
Crown Court
Register Office
Monument
Elmfield Park
The Surgery
Hotel
Cemetery
St Francis Xavier RC School
Stirling First & Junior Sch
St Andrew's Terrace
Doncaster Health Authority
Doncaster Carr
Lakeside First School
St Peters RC Primary School
Ellers Middle School
Kingfisher First School
Infant School
Primary School
The Sandringham Practice
Athron Industrial Est
Coroners Court
Lakeside Boulevard
Carolina Way
Balby Carr Bank
Decoy Bank South
Decoy Bank North
Potteric Carr Road
Carriage Drive
Sandall Beat Road
Wheatley Park
Balby
89
112
1 grid square represents 500 metres
C3 1 Royal Av 2 Rutland St
C4 1 Lawn Av 2 Regent Sq
C5 1 Ravensworth Rd 2 Whitburn Rd
C6 1 Theobald Cl
E2 1 Selby Rd 2 Sunningdale Rd
E3 1 Carisbrooke Rd
E4 1 Braemar Rd
E5 1 St Helen's Rd
E6 1 St Margaret's Rd

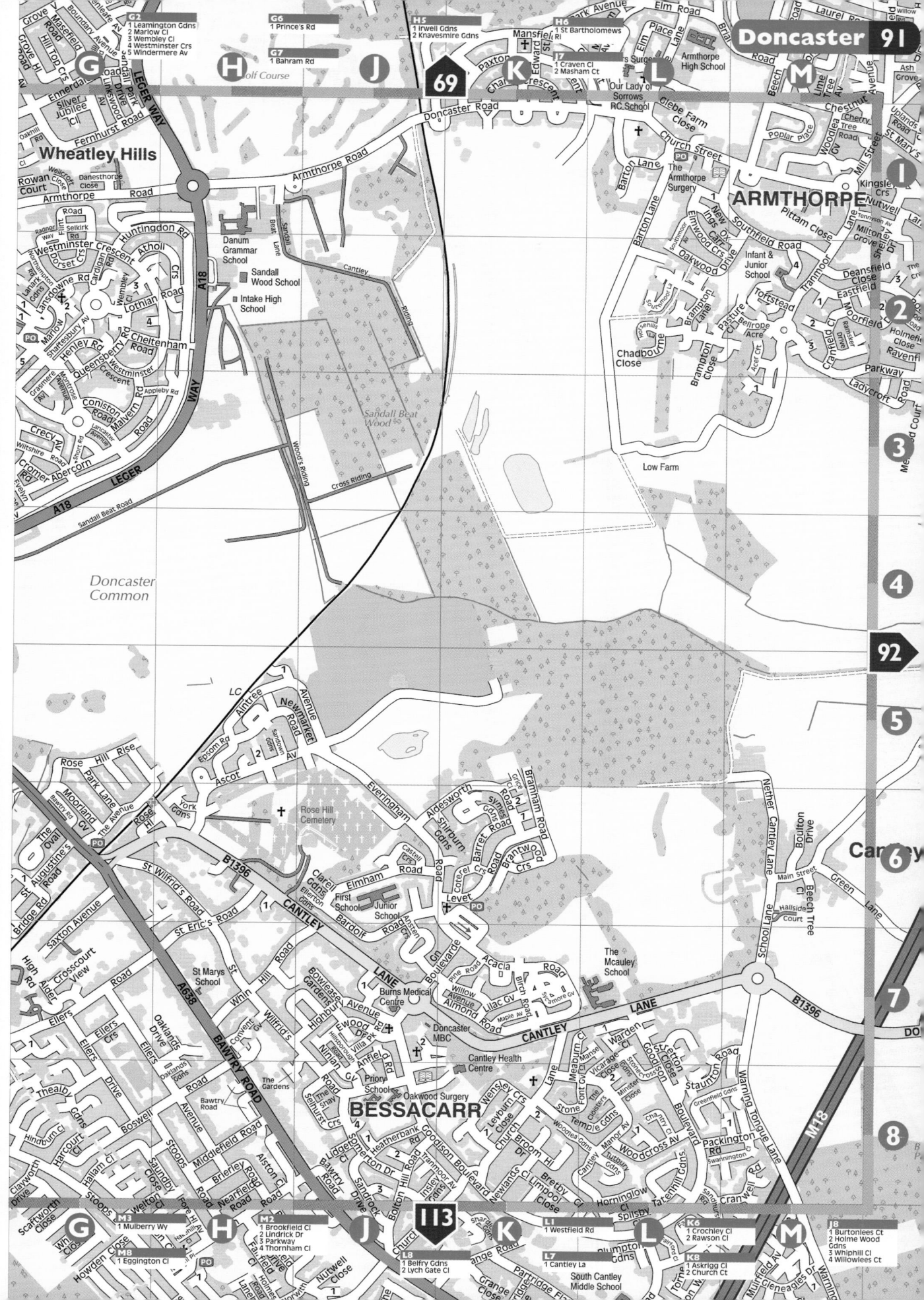
G2
1 Leamington Gdns
2 Marlow Cl
3 Wembley Cl
4 Westminster Crs
5 Windermere Av
G6
1 Prince's Rd
G7
1 Bahram Rd
H5
1 Irwell Gdns
2 Knavesmire Gdns
H6
1 St Bartholomews Rl
J7
1 Craven Cl
2 Masham Ct
69
Armthorpe High School
Our Lady of Sorrows RC School
Doncaster Road
Armthorpe Road
Church Street
Glebe Farm Close
The Armthorpe Surgery
ARMTHORPE
Barton Lane
Southfield Road
Pittam Close
Infant & Junior School
Wheatley Hills
Leger Way
A18
Danum Grammar School
Sandall Wood School
Intake High School
Huntingdon Rd
Westminster Crescent
Lansdowne Rd
Cheltenham Road
Queensberry Crescent
Coniston Road
Malvern Road
Abercorn
Sandall Beat Road
Sandall Beat Wood
Wood's Riding
Cross Riding
Cantley Riding
Chadbourne Close
Brampton Close
Parkway
Ladycroft
Low Farm
Doncaster Common
92
LC
Aintree
Newmarket Road
Avenue
Epsom Rd
Ascot
Rose Hill Rise
Park Lane
Moorland Gv
The Avenue
Rose Hill Cemetery
Everingham
Aldesworth
Shirburn Gdns
Bramham Road
Brantwood Crs
B1396
Cantley Lane
St Wilfrid's Road
St Eric's Road
Bardolf Road
Elmham Road
First School
Junior School
Levet
Boulevarde
Acacia Road
The Mcauley School
Nether Cantley Lane
School Lane
Boulton Drive
Main Street
Beech Tree Cl
Hallside Court
Green Lane
Cantley
M18
A638
Bawtry Road
St Marys School
Saxton Avenue
Crosscourt View
Ellers
Oaklands Drive
Burns Medical Centre
Doncaster MBC
Cantley Health Centre
Priory School
Oakwood Surgery
BESSACARR
The Gardens
Bawtry Road
Middlefield Road
Heatherbank
Goodison Boulevard
Woodcross Av
Packington Rd
Warning Tongue Lane
Staunton Road
Horninglow Cl
Tatenhill Gdns
Cranwell Rd
113
M3
1 Mulberry Wy
M2
1 Brookfield Cl
2 Lindrick Dr
3 Parkway
4 Thornham Cl
M8
1 Eggington Cl
L8
1 Belfry Gdns
2 Lych Gate Cl
L1
1 Westfield Rd
L7
1 Cantley La
K6
1 Crochley Cl
2 Rawson Cl
K8
1 Askrigg Cl
2 Church Ct
J8
1 Burtonlees Ct
2 Holme Wood Gdns
3 Whiphill Cl
4 Willowlees Ct
South Cantley Middle School
Scaftworth Close
Howden Close
Nutwell Close
Partridge Flatt

92
70
91
114
DN3
A
B
C
D
E
F
1
2
3
4
5
6
7
8
C6
1 Kingston Cl
B7
1 Oakwood Dr
2 Springwood Cl
A2
1 Ambass'dor Gdns
2 Greenfield Cl
3 Meltonfield Cl
4 Springfield Cl
A1
1 Handsworth Gdns
2 Ruskin Dr
Meadowview Industrial Estate
Junction 4
Holme Wood Lane
Thornham Lane
Thornham
Nutwell
Cow House Lane
Walbank Road
Wickett Hern Road
Haldynby Gdns
Hornsby Rd
Locking Dr
Regent Avenue
The Lings
Butterill Drive
Whiphill Lane
Granby Court
Alder Holt Cl
Holme View
Fiddlers Drive
Nutwell Lane
Kingsley Crs
Nutwell Lane
Tennyson Av
Milton Grove
Shelley Dr
Deansfield Close
Eastfield
The Crescent
Leyfield Court
Woodfield Road
Holmefield Close
Ravenfield
Parkway
Ladycroft
Melwood Court
Hallcroft Drive
Cranfield Dr
Mill Street
St Mary's Drive
Uplands Road
Cleveland Road
Nooking Close
Gunhills La
Laburnum Drive
Ash Grove
Hazel Gv
Laurel Rd
Willow Rd
Hatfield
Chestnut Av
Cherry Tree Road
Lime Tree Av
Woodlea Gv
South Woodfield Farm
M18
Branton Grange
Cockwood Farm
Gate Wood Lane
Cantley Common
Kilham Lane
Kilham Farm
River Torne
Cantley
Green Lane
Beech Tree
Branton
Branton Gate Road or Whiphill Top Lane
Bracken Close
Oak Tree Road
Poplar Close
Milton Road
St Wilfreds C of E (a) Junior & Infant School
Conway Drive
Valley Drive
Silverdale Close
Chapel Lane
Moor View
Rural Cres
Alliss Rd
Whiphill Top Lane
Carlton Close
Belmont Close
Kingsmead
The Close
PO
Green Lane
DONCASTER ROAD
SANDPIT HILL
MOOR GAP
B1396
DONCASTER ROAD
St Vincent's Avenue
Ashwood Cl
Poppyfields Wy
Quarry Lane
Brockholes Lane
Glen Rd
Brockhole
Black Carr Plantation
Torne View
Childers Drive
Common Lane
Ravenswood Dr
Ainsley Close
Sandhill Rise
River Way
Riverside Gdns
Dursley Ct
MAIN STREET
Norwood Avenue
Spey Drive
Nene Grove
Dart Grove
Avon Court
Myrtle Gv
Orchard Wk
Maple Drive
Ellers Lane
Auckley
Auckley County Primary School
School Lane
Eastfield Lane
The Hollows
Bell Lane
E8
1 Rossmoor Cl
2 Thorncliffe Gdns
C7
1 Langton Gdns
2 Sunnyside
River
Lidget
1 grid square represents 500 metres

Huggin Carr
or Low Grounds

G H J **71** K L M

Gate
Wood End

A614

Boston
Park

Great
Gate
Wood

Poor
Piece

I

2

3

Gate Wood Lane

Gate Farm

Gate Wood Lane

Torne Bridge

4

A614

Long
Plantation

God's

94

5

Common Lane

Acomb Farm

6

Levels Lane

Blaxton
Common

7

Auckley
Common

ROAD

8

G H J **115** K L M

TORNE

Finningly
Grange Far

Springban
Close

Shepherds
Croft

Blaxton

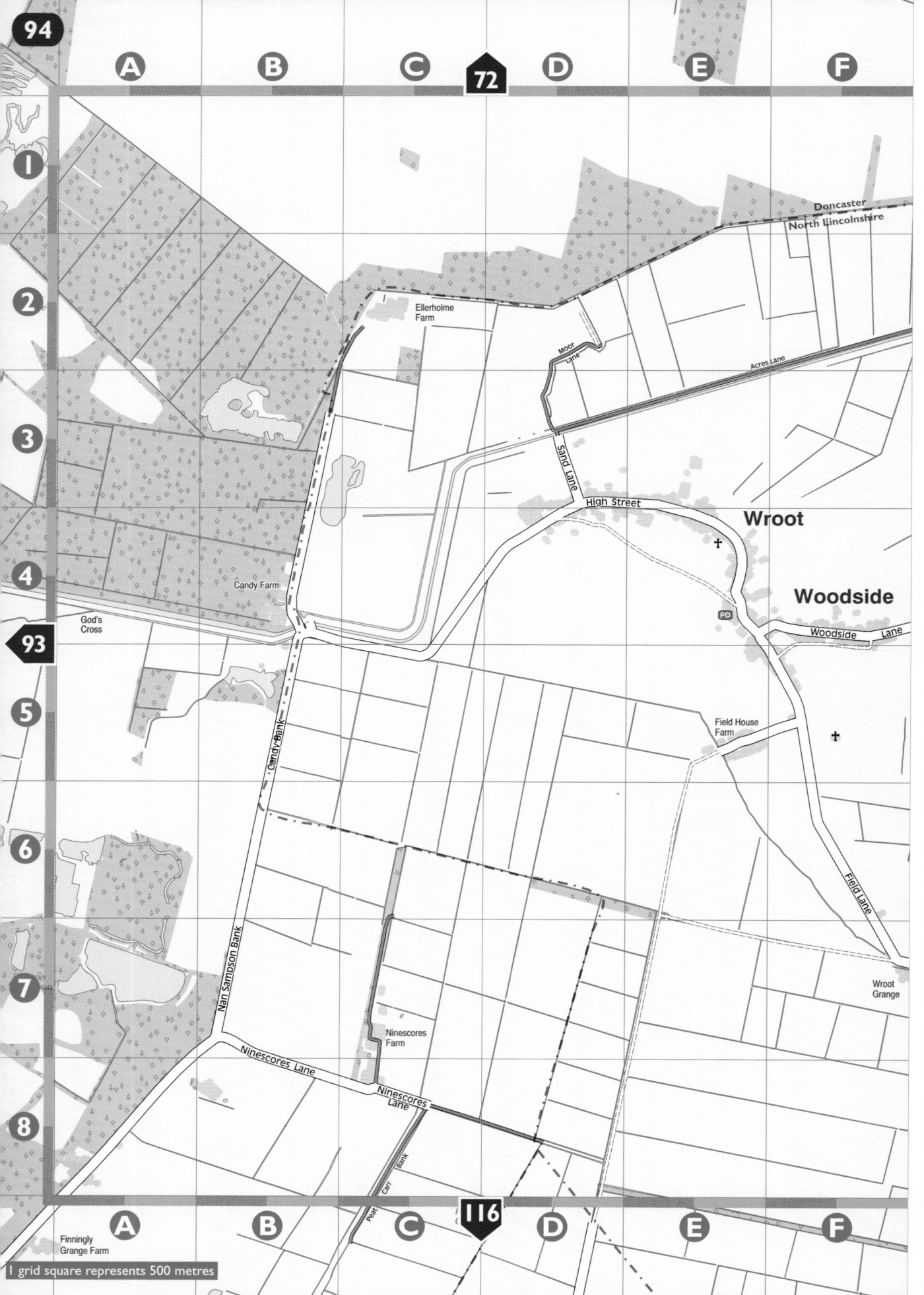

A   B   C   72   D   E   F

1

2

3

4

93

5

6

7

8

Doncaster
North Lincolnshire

Ellerholme
Farm

Moor
Lane

Acres Lane

Sand Lane

High Street

Wroot

Woodside

PO

Woodside   Lane

Candy Farm

God's
Cross

Field House
Farm

Candy Bank

Nan Sampson Bank

Field Lane

Wroot
Grange

Ninescores
Farm

Ninescores Lane

Ninescores
Lane

Peat   Carr   Bank

Finningly
Grange Farm

A   B   116   C   D   E   F

1 grid square represents 500 metres

G H J 73 K L M

I
2
3
4
5
6
7
8

Ninevah
Farm

Tunnel
Pits

River Torne

Poles Bank

Aucklands
Farm

Harvester
Farm

DN9

Greenholme
Bank

Water Bank

South Engine Drain

Thorn Bank

Greenholme
Bank Farm

Haxey
Turbary

Star
Carr

Charity Farm

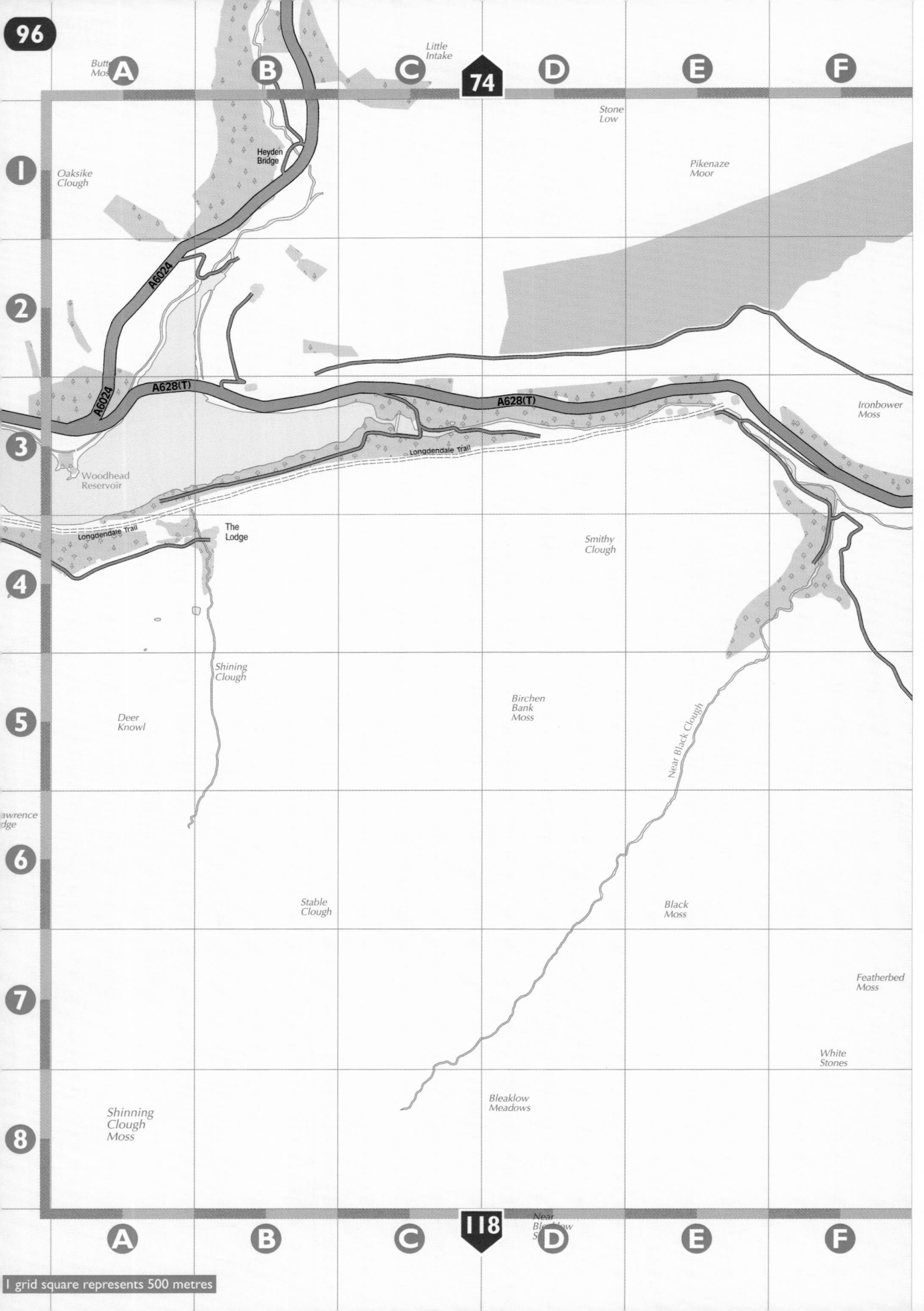

96

74

Butt...
Moss

A

Oaksike
Clough

B

Heyden
Bridge

Little
Intake

C

D

Stone
Low

E

Pikenaze
Moor

F

1

2

A6024

A6024

A628(T)

A628(T)

Ironbower
Moss

3

Woodhead
Reservoir

Longdendale Trail

Longdendale Trail

The
Lodge

Smithy
Clough

4

Shining
Clough

Deer
Knowl

Birchen
Bank
Moss

Near Black Clough

5

awrence
dge

6

Stable
Clough

Black
Moss

Featherbed
Moss

7

White
Stones

8

Shinning
Clough
Moss

Bleaklow
Meadows

Near
Bleaklow S...

118

A

B

C

D

E

F

1 grid square represents 500 metres

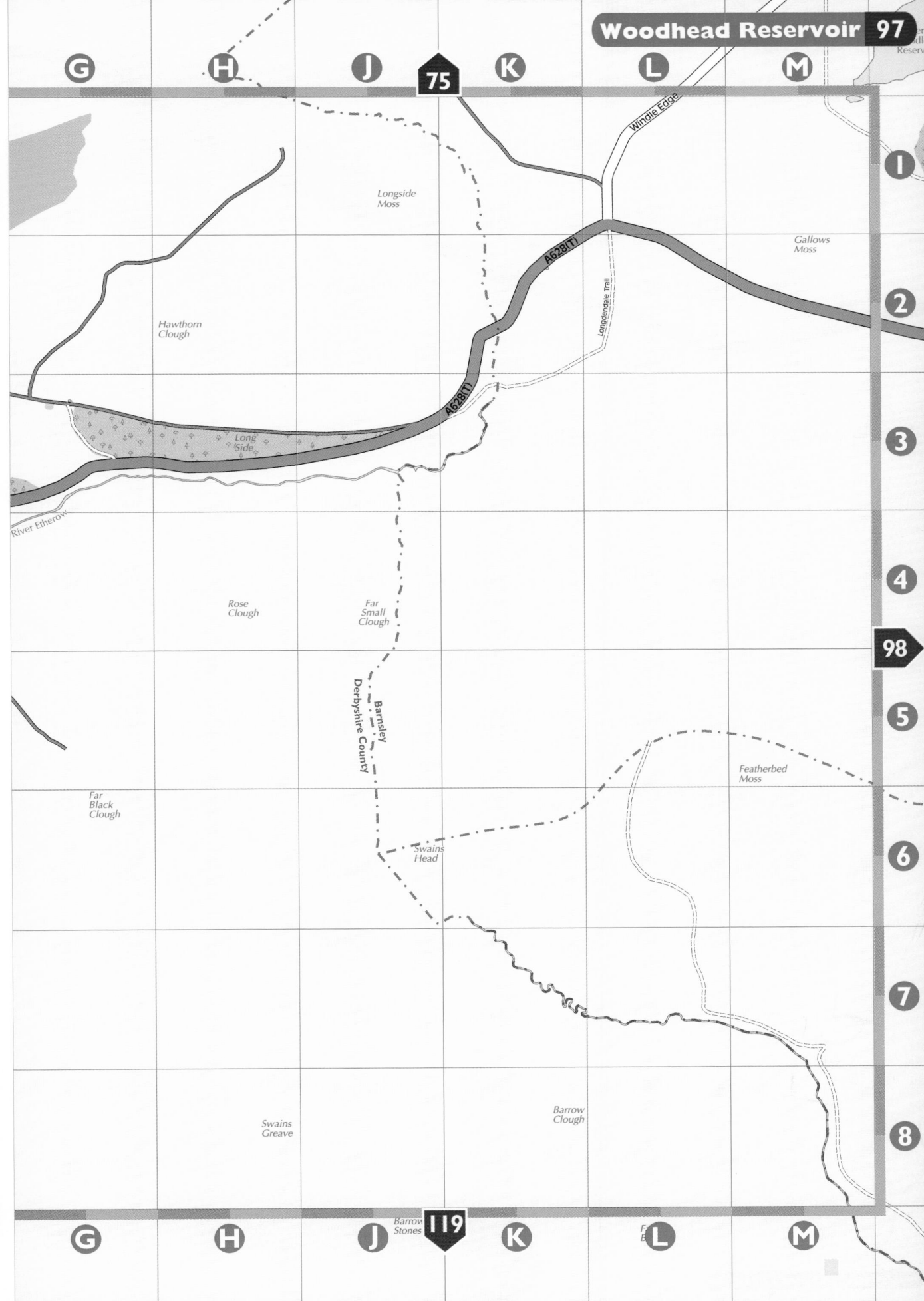

G   H   J   75   K   L   M

1

2

3

4

98

5

6

7

8

Longside Moss

Windle Edge

A628(T)

Longdendale Trail

Gallows Moss

Hawthorn Clough

A628(T)

Long Side

River Etherow

Rose Clough

Far Small Clough

Barnsley
Derbyshire County

Far Black Clough

Featherbed Moss

Swains Head

Swains Greave

Barrow Clough

G   H   J   *Barrow Stones* 119   K   L   M

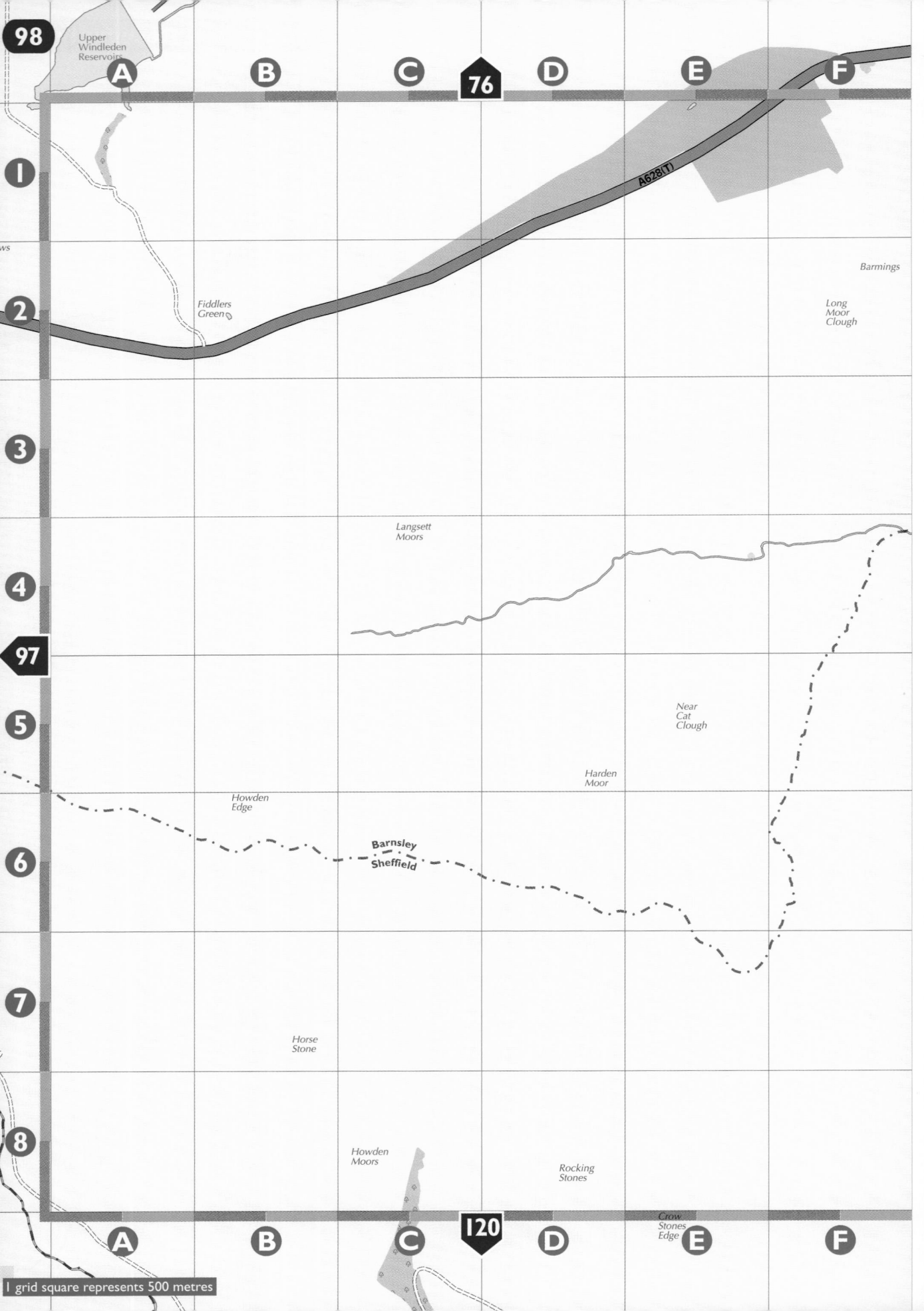

Upper
Windleden
Reservoirs

Ⓐ B C 76 D E F

I

ws

Fiddlers
Green ⌕

2

A628(T)

Barmings

Long
Moor
Clough

3

Langsett
Moors

4

97

Near
Cat
Clough

5

Harden
Moor

Howden
Edge

Barnsley
Sheffield

6

7

Horse
Stone

8

Howden
Moors

Rocking
Stones

Crow
Stones
Edge

Ⓐ B C 120 D E F

1 grid square represents 500 metres

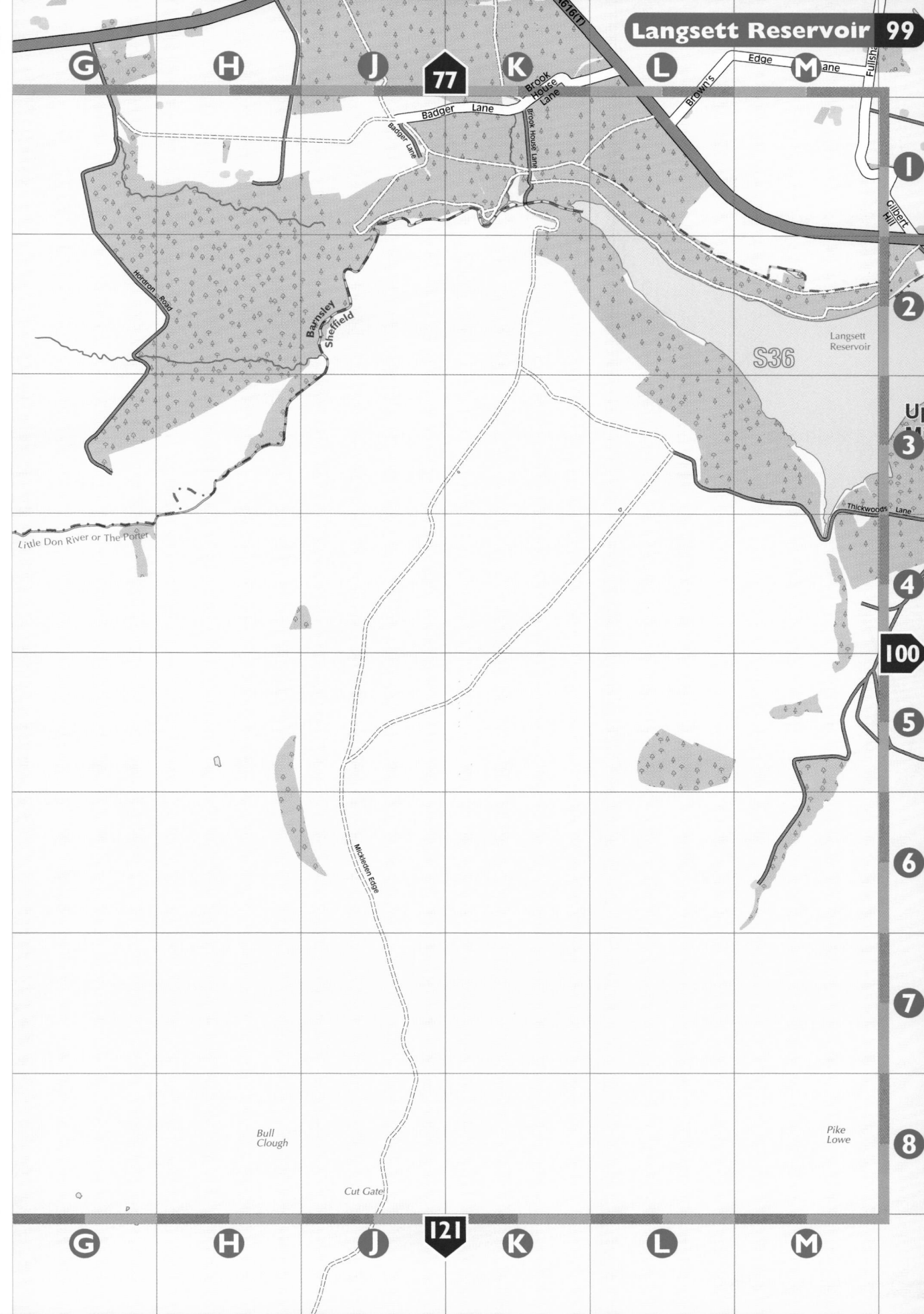

G H J **77** K L M

Edge ane

Brown's

Badger Lane

Badger Lane

Brook House Lane

Brook House Lane

Gilbert Hill

Hordron Road

Barnsley
Sheffield

Langsett
Reservoir

S36

Up
Mi

Thickwoods Lane

Little Don River or The Porter

Mickleden Edge

Bull
Clough

Cut Gate

Pike
Lowe

I

2

3

4

100

5

6

7

8

G H J **121** K L M

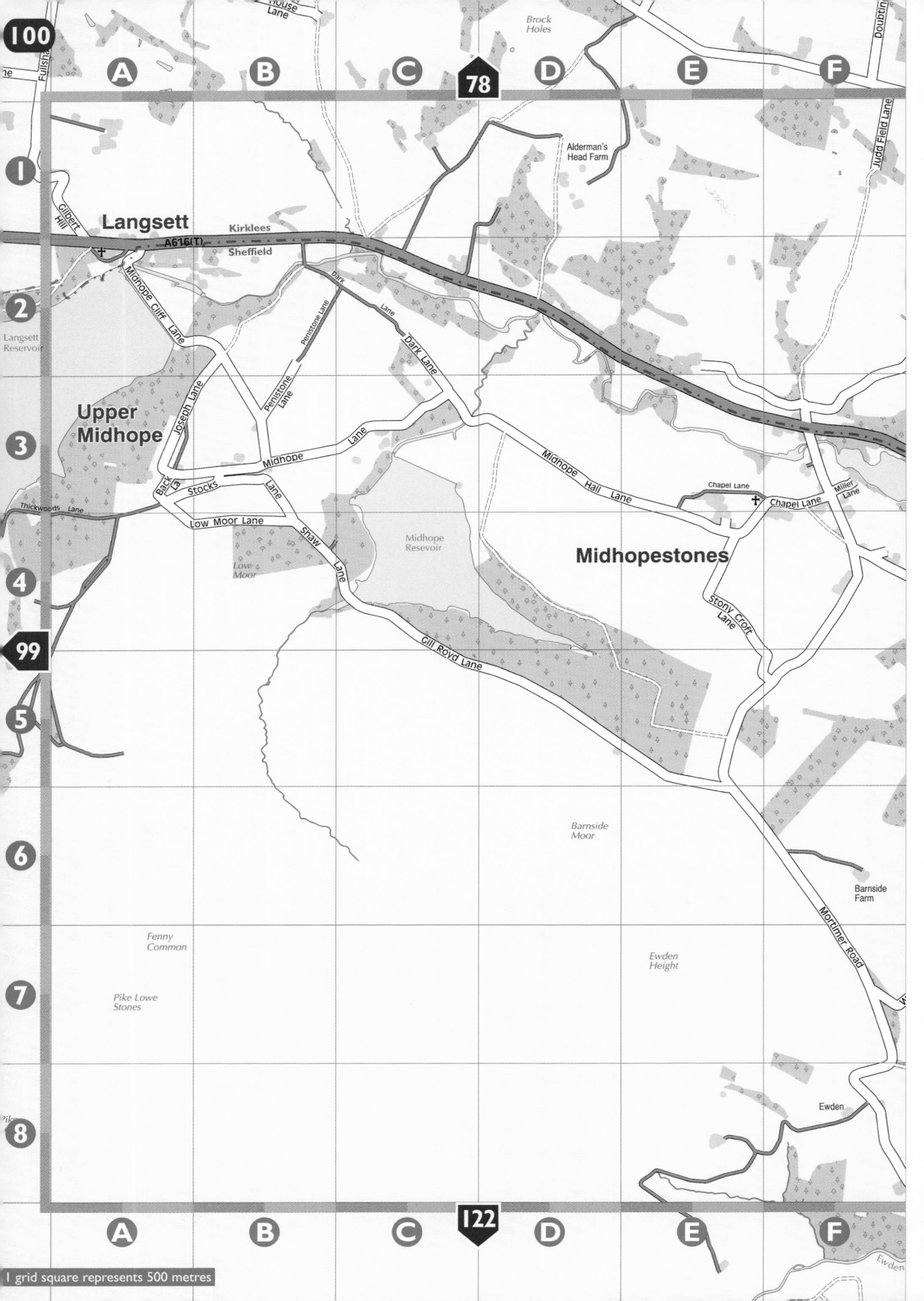

78
A B C D E F
Brock Holes
Alderman's Head Farm
Judd Field Lane
Langsett
Gilbert Hill
A616(T)
Kirklees
Sheffield
Langsett Reservoir
Midhope Cliff Lane
Dark Lane
Penistone Lane
Upper Midhope
Joseph Lane
Midhope Lane
Back La
Stocks Lane
Thickwoods Lane
Low Moor Lane
Shaw Lane
Low Moor
Midhope Reservoir
Midhope Hall Lane
Chapel Lane
Miller Lane
Midhopestones
Stony Croft Lane
Gill Royd Lane
99
Barnside Moor
Barnside Farm
Mortimer Road
Fenny Common
Ewden Height
Pike Lowe Stones
Ewden
122
1 2 3 4 5 6 7 8

1 grid square represents 500 metres

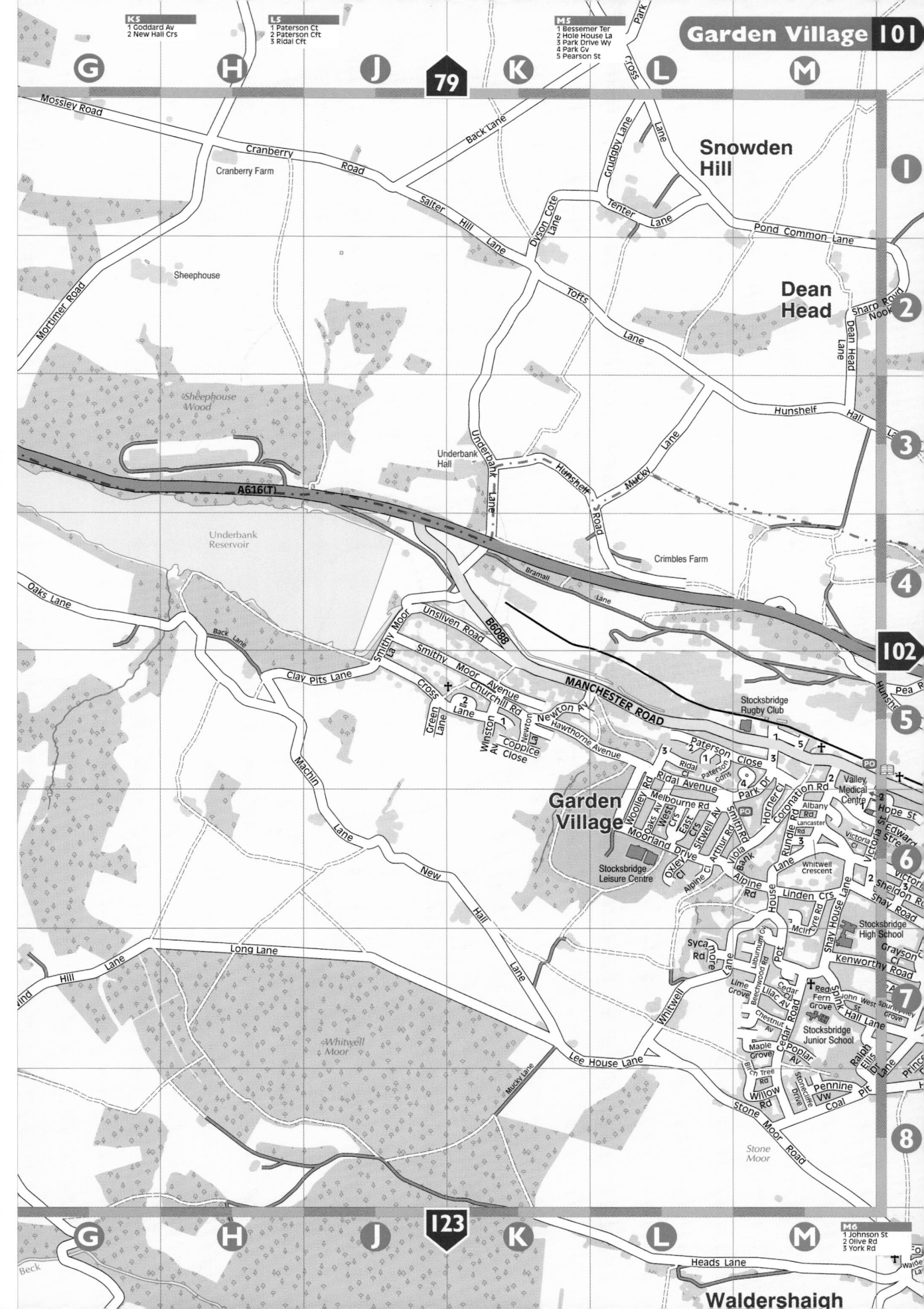

79

123

KS
1 Goddard Av
2 New Hall Crs

LS
1 Paterson Ct
2 Paterson Cft
3 Ridal Cft

MS
1 Bessemer Ter
2 Hole House La
3 Park Drive Wy
4 Park Gv
5 Pearson St

M6
1 Johnson St
2 Olive Rd
3 York Rd

G   H   J   K   L   M

I
2
3
102
4
5
6
7
8

Mossley Road

Cranberry Road

Cranberry Farm

Salter Hill Lane

Back Lane

Snowden Hill

Cruddgby Lane

Tenter Lane

Dyson Cote Lane

Pond Common Lane

Sharp Road

Nook

Dean Head

Dean Head Lane

Sheephouse

Tofts Lane

Hunshelf Hall

Sheephouse Wood

Mortimer Road

Underbank Hall

Underbank Lane

Hunshelf Road

Mucky Lane

A616(T)

Underbank Reservoir

Crimbles Farm

Bramall Lane

Oaks Lane

Back Lane

Clay Pits Lane

Smithy Moor La

Unsliven Road

B6088

MANCHESTER ROAD

Stocksbridge Rugby Club

Hunshe

Pea

Smithy Moor Avenue

Cross Lane

Green Lane

Churchill Rd

Winston Av

Coppice Close

Newton La

Newton Av

Hawthorne Avenue

Paterson Close

Ridal Cl

Paterson Gdns

Machin Lane

Garden Village

Ridal Avenue

Woolley Rd

Melbourne Rd

Oaks Av

West Crs

East St

Sitwell Av

Park Dr

Horner Cl

Coronation Rd

Albany Rd

Lancaster Rd

Victoria

Valley Medical Centre

Hope St

Edward

New Hall Lane

Stocksbridge Leisure Centre

Moorland Drive

Oxley Cl

Alpine Cl

Arthur Rd

Smith Rd

Viola Bank

Alpine Rd

Rundle Lane

House

Whitwell Crescent

Victoria

Sheldon Rd

Shay Road

Linden Crs

Long Lane

Hill Lane

Whitwell Lane

Syca more Rd

Laburnum G

McIlryre Rd

Shay House Lane

Spurley

Grove

Stocksbridge High School

Grayson Cl

Kenworthy Road

Lee House Lane

Whitwell Moor

Lime Grove

Beechwood Rd

Cedar Rd

Chestnut Av

Lilac Av

Fern Grove

John West St

Hall Lane

Stocksbridge Junior School

Maple Grove

Poplar Av

Birch Tree Rd

Willow Rd

Pennine VW

Coal

Stone Moor Road

Ralph Ellis Lane

Pit

Prince

Stone Moor

Mucky Lane

Heads Lane

Waldershaigh

Beck

Wind Hill Lane

G   H   J   K   L   M

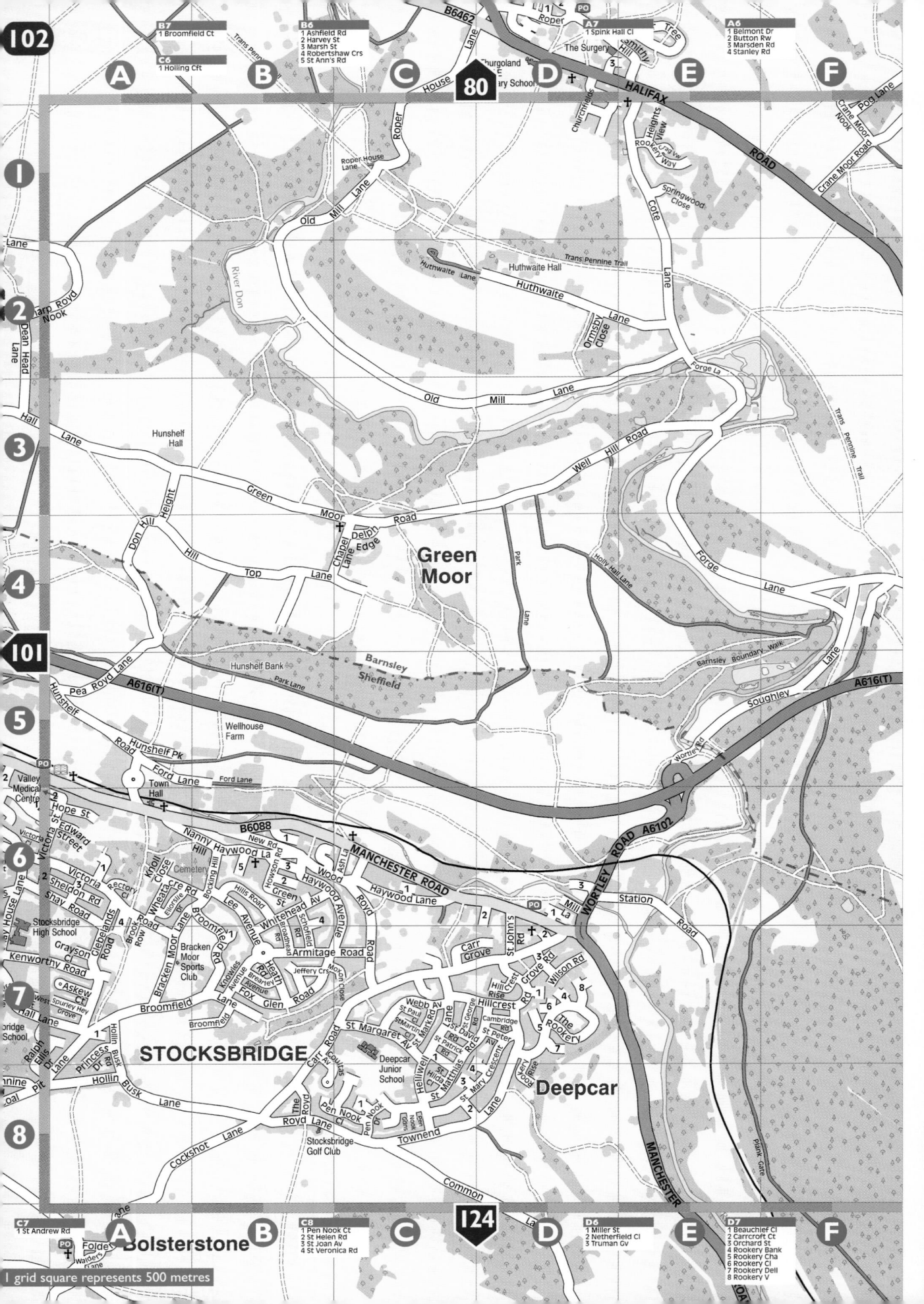

102
80
101
124
A
B
C
D
E
F
1
2
3
4
5
6
7
8
B7
1 Broomfield Ct
C6
1 Holling Cft
B6
1 Ashfield Rd
2 Harvey St
3 Marsh St
4 Robertshaw Crs
5 St Ann's Rd
A7
1 Spink Hall Cl
A6
1 Belmont Dr
2 Button Rw
3 Marsden Rd
4 Stanley Rd
B6462
Roper
The Surgery
Smithy Hill
Tree
Thurgoland
ary School
HALIFAX ROAD
Trans Pennine Trail
House Lane
Roper House Lane
Roper Lane
Churchfields
Heights View
Rookery Way
Springwood Close
Cote Lane
Pog Lane
Crane Moor Nook
Crane Moor Road
Old Mill Lane
River Don
Huthwaite Lane
Huthwaite Hall
Huthwaite Lane
Ormsby Close
Forge La
Sharp Royd Nook
Dean Head Lane
Hall Lane
Hunshelf Hall
Well Hill Road
Green Moor Road
Don Hill Height
Hill Top Lane
Chapel Lane
Delph Edge
Green Moor
Park Lane
Holly Hall Lane
Forge Lane
Barnsley
Sheffield
Hunshelf Bank
Park Lane
Barnsley Boundary Walk
Pea Royd Lane
A616(T)
Soughley Lane
Hunshelf Road
Wellhouse Farm
Hunshelf Pk
Ford Lane
Town Hall
Valley Medical Centre
Hope St
Edward Street
Victoria St
Wortley Rd
B6088
New Rd
Nanny Haywood La
Hill
MANCHESTER ROAD
WORTLEY ROAD A6102
Station Road
Mill La
Cemetery
Knoll Close
Rectory Cl
Victoria Rd
Sheldon Rd
Shay Road
Wheatacre Rd
Bocking Hill
Hills Road
Howson Rd
Green St
Wood
Ash La
Haywood Lane
Haywood Avenue
Royd Road
Whitehead Av
Schofield Rd
Broadhead Rd
Lee Avenue
Broomfield Rd
Brook Row
Road
Stocksbridge High School
Clegelands Road
Grayson Cl
Kenworthy Road
Bracken Moor Lane
Bracken Moor Sports Club
Heath Rd
Brearley Avenue
Knowles Avenue
Armitage Road
Jeffery Crs
Moor Close
Fox Glen Road
Askew Ct
West Spurley Hey Grove
Broomfield Lane
Hall Lane
Hollin Busk
Princess Dr
Ralph Ellis Dr
Lane
STOCKSBRIDGE
Hollin Busk Lane
Pit Lane
Carr Grove
St John's Rd
Hillcrest Rise
Grove Rd
Wilson Rd
Webb Av
St Paul Cl
St Martin Cl
St Mark Rd
St George Rd
St David Rd
Cambridge Rd
Hillcrest Rd
The Rookery
St Margaret Av
St Peter Av
St Patrick Rd
St Matthias Rd
St Mary Crescent
Carr Road
Coultas Av
Deepcar Junior School
Helliwell Ct
St Hilda Ct
Rookery Rise
Deepcar
The Royd
Royd Lane
Pen Nook Cl
Pen Nook Dr
Pen Nook Gdns
Townend
Lane
Cockshot Lane
Stocksbridge Golf Club
Common
MANCHESTER ROAD
Plank Gate
C7
1 St Andrew Rd
C8
1 Pen Nook Ct
2 St Helen Rd
3 St Joan Av
4 St Veronica Rd
D6
1 Miller St
2 Netherfield Cl
3 Truman Gv
D7
1 Beauchief Cl
2 Carrcroft Ct
3 Orchard St
4 Rookery Bank
5 Rookery Cha
6 Rookery Cl
7 Rookery Dell
8 Rookery V
Bolsterstone
Folder
1 grid square represents 500 metres

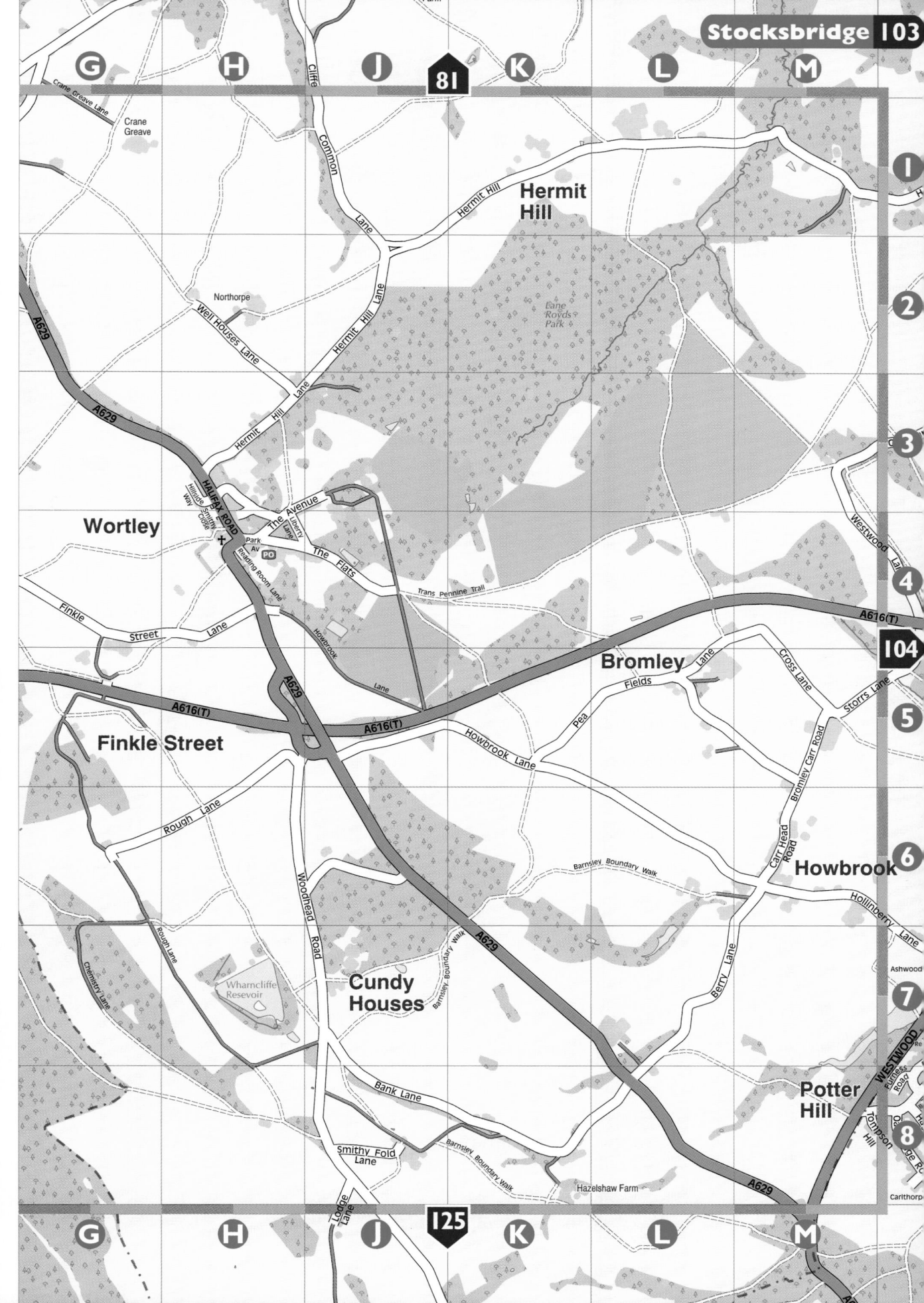

G H J **81** K L M

Crane Greave Lane

Crane
Greave

**Hermit
Hill**

Cliffe

Common

Lane

Hermit Hill

Lane

Northorpe

Well Houses Lane

Hermit Hill Lane

Lane
Royds
Park

A629

A629

Hermit Hill

Wortley

HALIFAX ROAD

Hillside
Way
Smithy
Close

The Avenue

The Liberty Lane

Park
Av

PO

Reading Room Lane

The Flats

Trans Pennine Trail

Howbrook

Lane

**Bromley
Fields**

Lane

Cross Lane

Westwood Lane

A616(T)

A616(T)

A629

A616(T)

Howbrook Lane

Pea

Storrs Lane

Finkle Street

Finkle

Street

Lane

Bromley Carr Road

Carr Head Road

Howbrook

Hollinberry Lane

Rough Lane

Barnsley Boundary Walk

Ashwood

Rough Lane

Chemistry Lane

Woodhead Road

Wharncliffe
Resevoir

**Cundy
Houses**

Barnsley Boundary Walk

A629

Berry Lane

WESTWOOD

Furness Road

**Potter
Hill**

Bank Lane

Tompson Hill

Smithy Fold
Lane

Barnsley Boundary Walk

Hazelshaw Farm

A629

Carlthorp

Lodge Lane

G H J **125** K L M

I

2

3

4

104

5

6

7

8

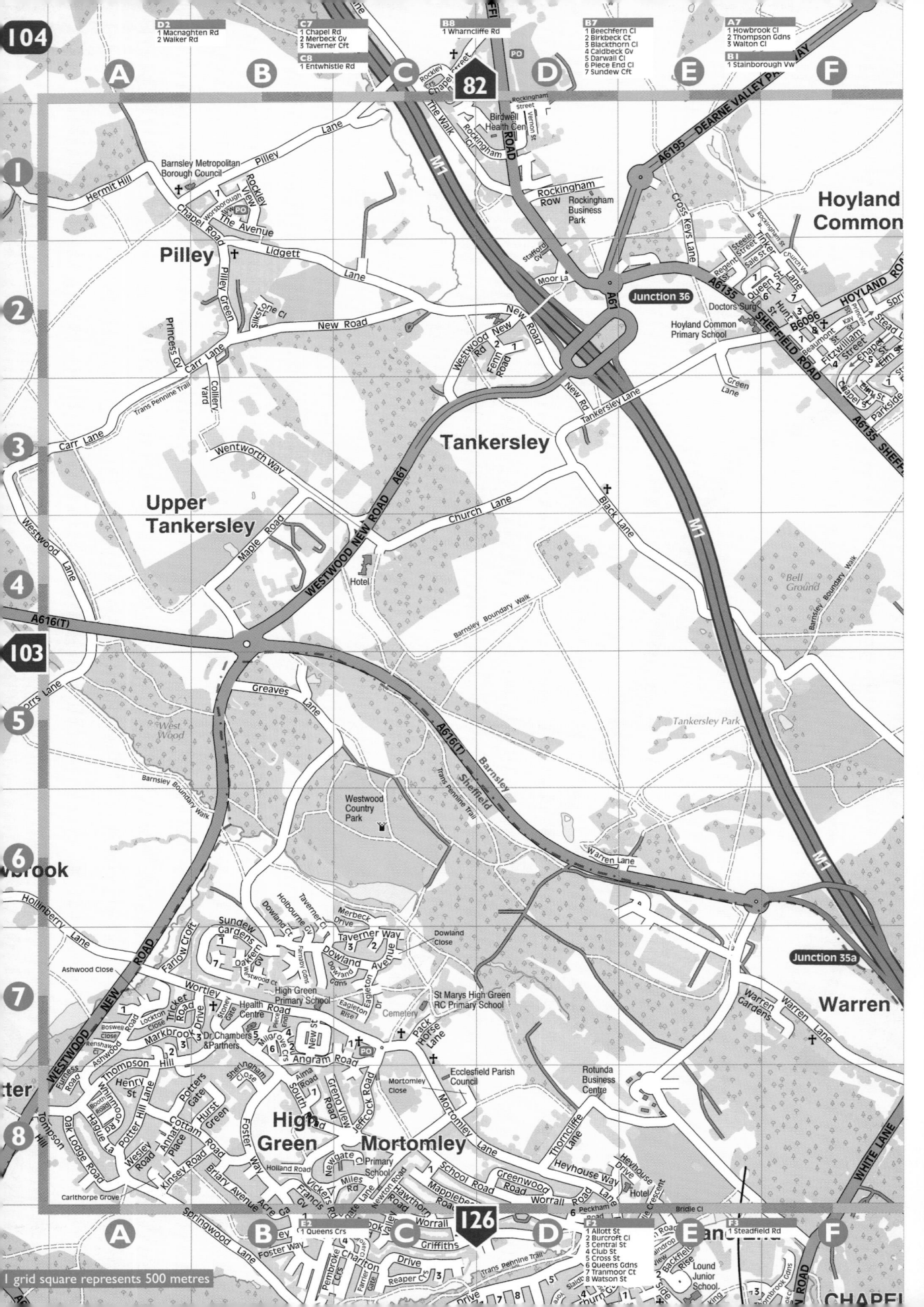
D2
1 Macnaghten Rd
2 Walker Rd
C7
1 Chapel Rd
2 Merbeck Gv
3 Taverner Cft
C8
1 Entwhistle Rd
B8
1 Wharncliffe Rd
B7
1 Beechfern Cl
2 Birkbeck Ct
3 Blackthorn Cl
4 Caldbeck Gv
5 Darwall Cl
6 Piece End Cl
7 Sundew Cft
A7
1 Howbrook Cl
2 Thompson Gdns
3 Walton Cl
B1
1 Stainborough Vw
82
Pilley
Hoyland Common
Tankersley
Upper Tankersley
Junction 36
Junction 35a
High Green
Mortomley
Warren
103
126
E2
1 Queens Crs
F2
1 Allott St
2 Burcroft Cl
3 Central St
4 Club St
5 Cross St
6 Queens Gdns
7 Tranmoor Ct
8 Watson St
F3
1 Steadfield Rd
1 grid square represents 500 metres

Hoyland
G2
1 Brentwood Cl
2 Pendlebury Gv
3 Sandcroft Cl
J1
1 Booth St
2 Hall St
3 Little Leeds
4 Milton Rd
5 St Andrews Crs
6 Tithe Laithe
7 Vicarage Cl
J2
1 Alder Ms
2 George St
J3
1 Primrose Wy
2 Roseberry Cl
Cemetery Road
Jump
G
H
J
K
L
M
83
Hawshaw Lane
Mount Crescent
Coronation Rd
Royston Hill
Longfields Crs
Cemetery
Kirk Balk School
Hoyland Sports Centre
West Street
Fearnley Road
Manor House Close
Hoyland Greenfield Junior & Infant School
Vizard Road
Welland Crescent
Fairburn Grove
Strafford Avenue
Tomlinson Rd
St Helen's Street
Cobcar Close
Cobcar St
Infant School
Town Hall
High St
Southgate
King Street
Royal Ct
Noble St
Hill St
Fitzwilliam St
Elsecar & Hoyland Station
Wilkinson Rd
Wood View
Foundry Street
Church Street
Elsecar
Infant School
Canal (dis)
B6097
Wath Rd
Hoyland
Milton
S74
Springwood Road
Skiers View Road
Clough Fields Road
Clough Fields Rd
Shaftesbury Drive
Infant School
Pendlebury Grove
Warren View
Bluebell Close
Wharncliffe Close
Sunnybrook Close
Meadowfield Drive
Church Lea
Milton Rd
Armroyd Lane
Elsecar Workshops
Forge Lane
Barnsley Boundary Walk
Elsecar Reservoir
Wentworth Road
Barnsley Rotherham Burying Lane
Trans Pennine Trail
Broadcarr Road
King's Wood
Water Lane
Barrow Field Lane
Mill Lane
106
Harley
Black Lane
Harley Road
B6090
Dike Hill
Barrow Hill
Barrow
Wentworth
Main Street
Clayfield Lane
Wentworth C of E School
The Little Gallery
The Square
Cricket View Road
Occupation Road
Viewtree Close
Lodge Drive
A6135
Hood Hill Plantation
Cover Close
Ashes Lane
Church Field Lane
Hood Hill
B6086
Kirby Lane
Barnsley Road
M1
Hague Lane
1
2
3
4
5
6
7
8
127
M1
1 Aberford Gv
2 Hambleton Cl
3 Ledsham Ct
4 Wendel Gv
L2
1 Beacon Vw
2 The Croft
L1
1 Stirling Cl
2 Sunny Bank Ri
K2
1 Southlea Cl
2 Wentworth Vw
K1
1 Rock Mt
Town
Little Lane
Peacock
Avocet Way
Raven Drive
Bittern View

106
84
105
128
A
B
C
D
E
F
1
2
3
4
5
6
7
8
Brampton
Cortworth
Hoober
SMITHY BRIDGE LANE
ELSECAR ROAD
WATH ROAD
Barnsley Rotherham
Barnsley Boundary Walk
Royds Farm
Royds Lane
Linthwaite Lane
Coley Lane
Coley Lane Farm
Rainborough Park
Hoober Hall
Hoober Hall Lane
Lea Brook
Lee Brook Lane
Rotherham Roundwalk
Street
Street Lane
Hoober Field
Hoober Stand
HOOBER LANE
ANGEL LANE
CORTWORTH LANE
B6091 CORTWORTH LANE
Rotherham Roundwalk
Wentworth Park
STUBBIN
Westfield
Manor Road
Westpit Hill
Hurley Croft
Fleet Close
Honister Close
Tingle Close
Brampton Road
Carnley Street
Packman Way
Quarry Bank
FIRTH
ROTHERHAM ROAD
Brookside Crescent
Bramble Way
PO
1 grid square represents 500 metres

G7 1 Thompson Cl
H7 1 Wharncliffe Cl 2 Woodhouse Cl
J1 1 Brook Farm Ms 2 Church La 3 Church St 4 Montgomery Rd 5 Thornhill Pl
H2 1 Wombwell Av
H8 1 Humphries Av 2 The Steadlands
85
WATH UPON DEARNE
West Melton
Newhill
Abdy
Ryecroft
Upper Haugh
West Street
Biscay Way
Church Street
High Street
Sandygate
Dearneway
Wath Wood Road
Warren Vale Rd
Rockingham Road
Blackamoor Road
Wentworth Road
Packman Road
Doncaster Road
Far Field Lane
Racecourse Road
Stump Cross Road
Festival Road
Quarry Hill Road
Wath Upon Dearne Comprehensive School
Wath Pope Pius R C Secondary School
Our Ladys & St Josephs RC JMI School
Victoria Primary School
Wath Park Infant School
Brampton Ellis Infant School
Swinton Fitzwilliam Infants School
Rawmarsh Thorogate Junior & Infant Sch
Rawmarsh Monkwood JMI School
Monkwood Health Centre
Wath Wood
Wath Cemetery
108
129
M8 1 Bennett Cl
K8 1 Pipe House La
L2 1 Hawthorne Rd
K4 1 Beechwood Cl
K7 1 Macmanus Av
K2 1 Cherry Tree Pl 2 Fir Cl 3 Marshall Gv 4 Sycamore Crs
J8 1 The Parade
K1 1 Moor Rd 2 Wharncliffe Av
S62

108
B5
1 Ash Rdg
2 Tiverton Cl
3 Woodhall Ri
B6
1 Benton Ter
B4
1 Charnwood St
2 King St
3 Poplar Gv
4 Temperance St
A8
1 Beechwood Cl
A6
1 Beechville Av
2 Hesley Ct
3 Low Wood Cl
A5
1 Rocklea Cl
D2, F3
Street Names for these grid squares are listed at the back of the index
86
MEXBOROUGH
Storm House School
Comprehensive Mexborough School
Highwoods Infant School
Park Road Infant School
Cemetery
Montagu Hospital
St Johns C of E School
Swinton Bridge
Whitelea Grove Trading Estate
Mexborough Bus Station
Cliff Street Industrial Cen
Mexborough Station
Mexborough Business Centre
Adwick Road Surgery
Doncaster Area Health Authority
Pinfold Lands
River Don
S64
Bow Broom
Queen Street J & I School
Swinton Swimming Pool
The Richmond Fellowship
Special School
Doctors Surgery
Rotherham MBC
Swinton Station
Swinton Meadows Business Park
Swinton Meadows Industrial Est
107
SWINTON
Swinton Comprehensive School
Primary School
Engine House Farm
Denaby Common
Hooton Common
Doncaster
Rotherham
Piccadilly
Doctors Surgery
Kilnhurst
Kilnhurst Junior & Infants School
A6022 CHURCH STREET
STATION STREET
BRIDGE STREET
A6022 ROWMS LANE
SWINTON ROAD
WATH ROAD
A6023
B6098
B6090
HOOTON ROAD
KILNHURST ROAD
VICTORIA ST
Golden Smithies Lane
Adwick Road
Cemetery Road
Bank Street
Church Street
Highwoods Road
Manvers Road
Queen Street
Whitelee Road
Talbot Road
Meadow Lane
Denaby Lane
Holmes Lane
Howdike Lane
Springfield Road
Wharf Road
Glasshouse Lane
Kilnhurst Road
130
B7
1 Fernvale Wk
C2
1 Highwoods Crs
C4
1 Broomville St
2 Wharf Cl
D3
1 Belmont St
2 Britain St
3 Cresswell St
4 Dodsworth St
E2
1 Bhatia Cl
2 Garden St
E3
1 Hope St
2 Market St
F1
1 Haydock Cl
2 Southwell Ri
F2
1 Tyas Pl
1 grid square represents 500 metres

A **B** **C** 88 **D** **E** **F**

B6
1 Camellia Cl

B5
1 Bentinick St
2 Doncaster Rd

B2
1 Rosemary Gv

B4
1 Duftons Cl

A6
1 Brookside

B1
1 Brackenbury Cl
2 The Paddocks

1

Cadeby

Warmsworth

Ings Road
Manor Drive
Hollow Gate

2

River Don

SHEFFIELD ROAD A630

Warmsworth

3

Trans Pennine Trail

Conisbrough Station

Trans Pennine Trail

Conisbrough Castle

River Don

SHEFFIELD

Edlington Victoria Primary School

Staveley

A6023 Road

4

Station Road Junior & Infant School

Burcroft Hill
Burcroft Hill
Windgate Hill
Milner Gate

Middle School

Church Road
Prince's Crescent
King's Crs
Queen's Crs

109

LOW ROAD
Station Road
Dale
Doncaster Metropolitan Borough Council

Milner Gate Court
Ravens Walk
Head Lane
A630

St John's Road
Auburn Road
Hazel Road
Nelson Road
Wellington Road
Gordon Road
Main Avenue
PO

5

Elm Green Lane
The Oval
Westgate

Chapter Gallery
Museum

Church Street
Waverley
West Street
March Gate

DONCASTER ROAD A630
Drake
Crookhill Road
Wheat
Hereward Court
Saxon Row

St Marys Catholic School
Bungalow Road
Market Place
Thompson Avenue
Baines Avenue
Dixon Road
Carr Road

Doctors' Surgery
The Health Centre
Cross Lane

6

March Gate
New Hill
Willow Street

Birch Grove
Avenue
Corn
Wood View
Common Road

Highbury Vale
Church View
Howbeck Drive
Broomvale Walk
Howbeck Close
Thornlea Close

Hill Top Junior & Infant School
Linden Grove
Violet Avenue
Lilac Crescent
Broomhouse

ROAD
B6094 CLIFTON HILL
Windmill
Roberts Avenue
Sheldon Avenue
Jasmine
Lavender
Snake Lane
Medley View

Conisbrough Common

Lichfield Gdns
Stone Riding

Hillside Drive
Mallin
Hill Top Crs
Clark Avenue
PO
Drive
Tait Avenue

7

DN12

Kearsley Lane

Snake Lane
Common Road

B6094 CARR LANE

Edlington School
Eccles Dr
Hatter Drive
Hill Top View

EDLINGTON LANE

8

Common Lane

B6376 School Walk

Rectory Gdns
Back Lane Wood

Old Edlington

B6094

B637

C5
1 Brook Rd
2 Butt Hole Rd
3 Templestowe Ga

E6
1 Bower V
2 Grainger Cl

F6
1 Mount Vw
2 Windermere Gra

I grid square represents 500 metres

Balby

89

Junction 36

WARMSWORTH A630

Warmsworth Primary School

Mayflower Rd

HIGH ROAD A630

Nightingale Primary School

Ambler Junior School

Cedar Special School

Westbourne Gardens

Broomhouse Lane

Cemetery

Alverley Grange

Broomhouse Lane

Broomhouse Lane

New Edlington

Edlington Wood

A1(M)

Wood Lane

Stump Cross

White Cross Lane

Junction 2/35

A1(M)

M18

Wadworth Wood

Springwell Lane

Grange Lane

Aldcliffe Crs

Gate

Downland Close

Clayfield Industrial Estate

Doncaster Health Authority

Doncaster & South Humber Healthcare NHS Trust

St Catherine's Well

TICKHILL ROAD

SANDFORD R

A630

A60

A60

Woodfield Road

Shelley Avenue

Wordsworth Avenue

Weston Road

Newbolt Road

Fulwood Drive

WADWORTH

Wadworth Hall Lane

Tofield Road

White Cross Lane

Gospel Well

Wadworth

Rockcliffe Drive

MAIN STREET A60

High Street

Gospel Well

112

133

112
90
111
134
A
B
C
D
E
F
1
2
3
4
5
6
7
8
Balby Carr Bank
Carolina Way
A1
1 Chesterton Rd
Balby Carr Farm
A6182 WHITE ROSE WAY
Potteric Carr Nature Reserve
Woodfield Rd
Sheridan Av
Herrick Gdns
Goldsmith Rd
Longfellow Rd
Stevenson Rd
Dryden Rd
Balby Carr School
Weston Road
Loversall Close
Doncaster & South Humber Healthcare NHS Trust
Hall Balk Lane
Whisperwood Dr
Coppicewood Court
Whisperwood Drive
Beeston Plantation
Loversall Carr
Potteric Carr
Hall Balk Lane
M18
Junction 3
A60
Rake's Lane
Skipwith Close
Bubup Hill
Loversall
The Surgery
Rake's Lane
Wadworth Hill
Junction 2/35
St Catherine's Well Stream
WADWORTH HILL A60
Mill Farm
Daw Lane
Wadworth Carr
Carr Bank
Egg Lane
Stancil Lane
MAIN STREET A60
Osberton Street
Street
Church Road
Old School Lane
Ratten Row
Beancroft Close
Well Lane
PO
Carr
Manor House
Manor Rise
Wadworth
Church View
Wadworth County Primary School
Grange Farm
1 grid square represents 500 metres

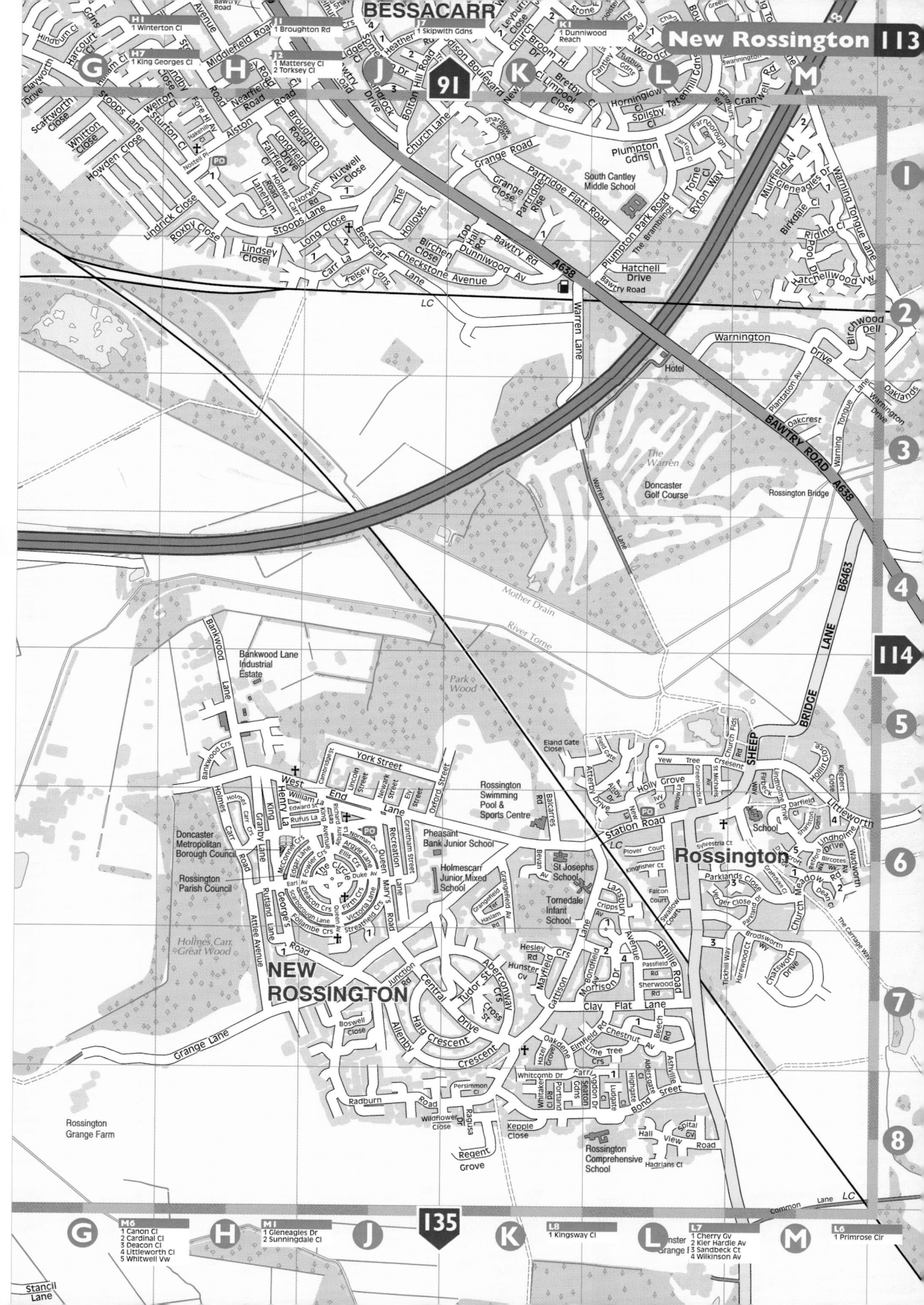
BESSACARR
H1
1 Winterton Cl
H7
1 King Georges Cl
J1
1 Broughton Rd
J2
1 Mattersey Cl
2 Torksey Cl
J7
1 Skipwith Gdns
K1
1 Dunniwood Reach
91
South Cantley Middle School
Hatchell Drive
Bawtry Road
A638
BAWTRY ROAD
Warren Lane
Hotel
Warnington Drive
The Warren
Doncaster Golf Course
Rossington Bridge
Mother Drain
River Torne
B6463
BRIDGE LANE
Bankwood Lane Industrial Estate
Park Wood
York Street
West End Lane
Rossington Swimming Pool & Sports Centre
Station Road
Rossington
Doncaster Metropolitan Borough Council
Rossington Parish Council
Pheasant Bank Junior School
Holmescarr Junior Mixed School
St Josephs School
Tornedale Infant School
Holmes Carr Great Wood
NEW ROSSINGTON
Grange Lane
Rossington Grange Farm
Rossington Comprehensive School
Common Lane
114
135
G
H
J
K
L
M
1
2
3
4
5
6
7
8
M6
1 Canon Cl
2 Cardinal Cl
3 Deacon Cl
4 Littleworth Cl
5 Whitwell Vw
M1
1 Gleneagles Dr
2 Sunningdale Cl
L8
1 Kingsway Cl
L7
1 Cherry Gv
2 Kier Hardie Av
3 Sandbeck Ct
4 Wilkinson Av
L6
1 Primrose Cir
Stancil Lane

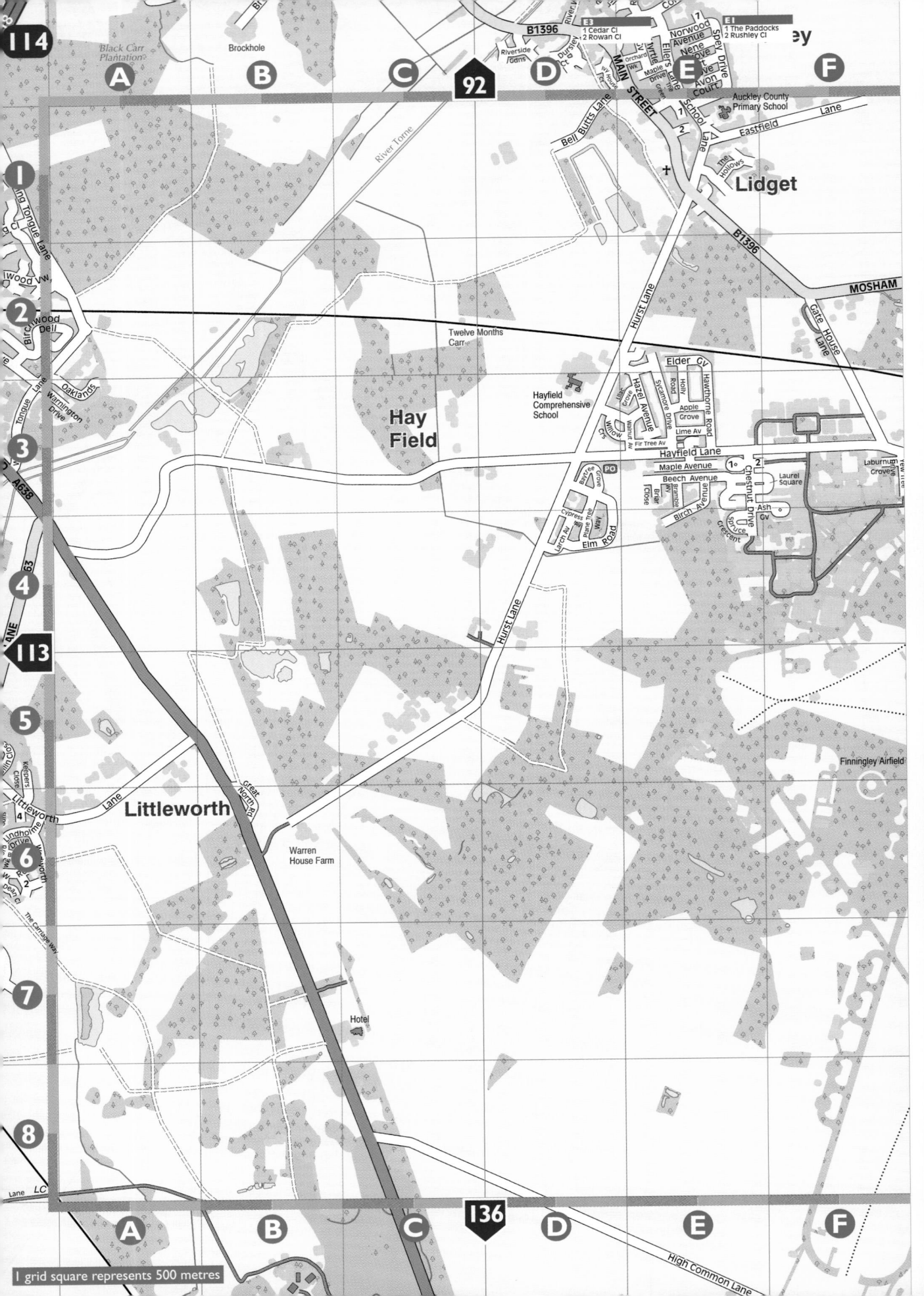

A   B   C   D   E   F

Black Carr
Plantation

Brockhole

River Torne

I

ng Tongue Lane

wood Vw

2
Birchwood
Dell

Twelve Months
Carr

Lidget

B1396

MOSHAM

B1396

Hurst Lane

Gate House Lane

Eastfield Lane

Auckley County
Primary School

MAIN STREET

Bell Butts Lane

Riverside
Gdns

Dursley
Ct

B1396

1 Cedar Cl
2 Rowan Cl

Norwood
Avenue
Nene

Ellers
Eadle

Spey Drive

Avon
Court

School Lane

The
Hollows

1 The Paddocks
2 Rushley Cl

Oaklands

Tongue

Warmington Drive

3

AG38

63

4

113

Hayfield
Comprehensive
School

Hay
Field

Elder Gv

Lilac Grove

Hazel Avenue

Holly Road

Sycamore Drive

Hawthorne Road

Apple Grove

Lime Av

Willow Crs

Walnut Av

Fir Tree Av

Hayfield Lane

Maple Avenue

Beech Avenue

Bay Tree Gv

Briar Close

Bramble Wy

Birch Av

Chestnut Drive

1

2

Laurel Square

Laburnum Gv

Yew Tree

Groves

Ash Gv

Spruce Crescent

Cypress
Av

Plane Tree Wy

Larch Av

Elm Road

Hurst Lane

5

Keepers
Close

Littleworth

Lindholme
Drive

4

6

2

Littleworth

Great North Rd

Warren
House Farm

Lane

PO

Finningley Airfield

The Carriage Way

7

Hotel

8

Lane LC

A   B   C   D   E   F

High Common Lane

1 grid square represents 500 metres

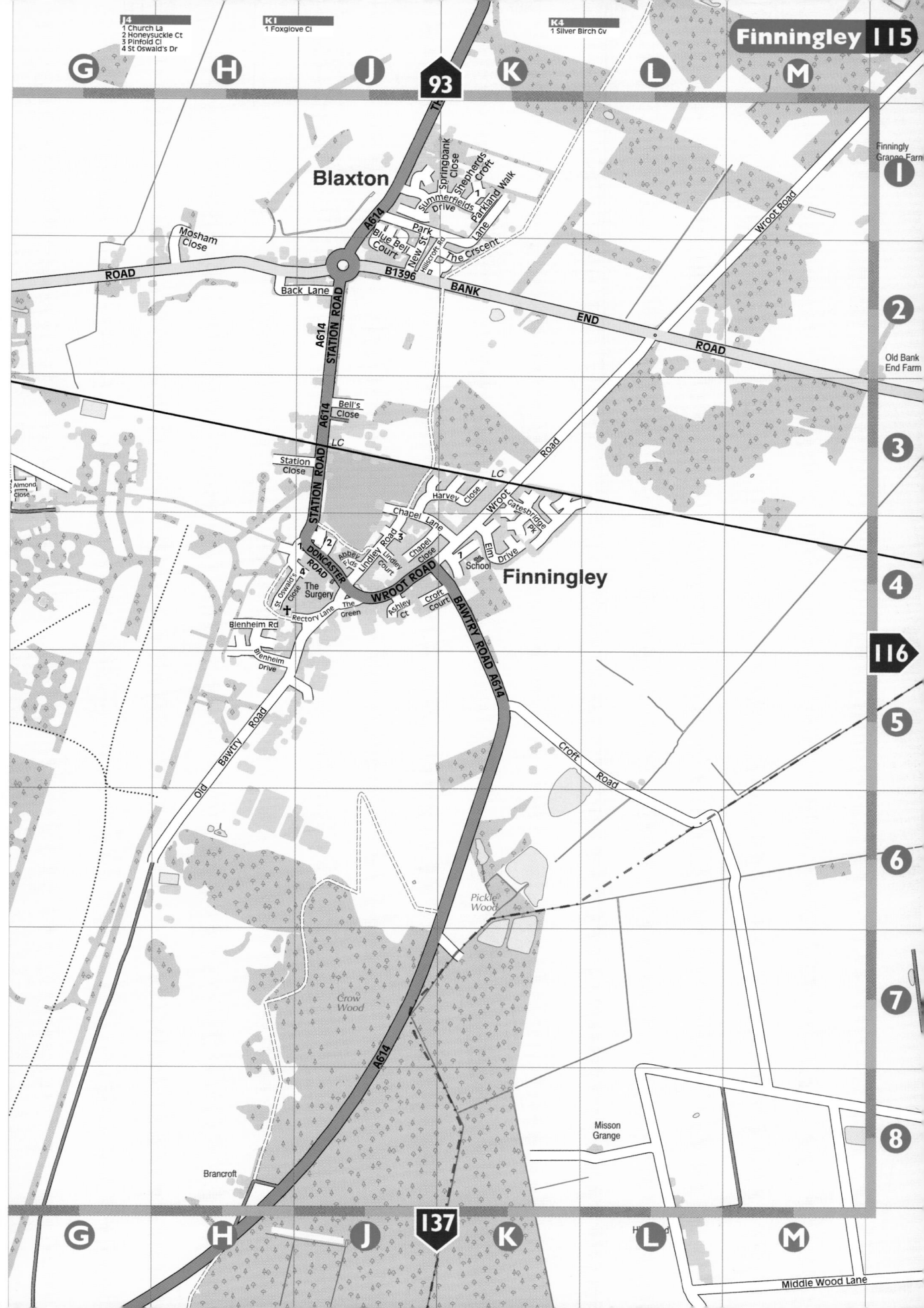

G H J K L M

93

J4
1 Church La
2 Honeysuckle Ct
3 Pinfold Cl
4 St Oswald's Dr

K1
1 Foxglove Cl

K4
1 Silver Birch Gv

Finningly
Grange Farm

I

2
Old Bank
End Farm

3

4

116

5

6

7

8

Blaxton

Mosham
Close

ROAD

Back Lane

Springbank
Close

Shepherds
Croft

Parkland Walk

Summerfields
Drive

Park
Lane

New St.

Blue Bell
Court

Hillscroft Rd

The Crscent

B1396

A614

STATION ROAD

BANK

END

ROAD

Bell's
Close

LC

Station
Close

Almond
Close

Harvey
Close

Chapel Lane

Wroot

Road

LC

Gatesbridge
Pk

Road

STATION ROAD

A614

Chapel
Road

Lindley
Court

Chapel
Close

Elm
Drive

Abbey
Cl.

St Oswald's
Close

DONCASTER

ROAD

The
Surgery

Rectory Lane

WROOT ROAD

The
Green

Ashley
Ct

Croft
Court

School

7

Finningley

Blenheim Rd

Blenheim
Drive

Bawtry

Road

Old

Bawtry

Road

BAWTRY ROAD

A614

Croft

Road

Pickle
Wood

Crow
Wood

A614

Brancroft

Misson
Grange

137

G H J K L M

Middle Wood Lane

94

115

A   B   C   D   E   F

1
2
3
4
5
6
7
8

Finningly
Grange Farm

Old Bank
End Farm

Whin
Covert

BANK END ROAD   B1396

Peat
Carr

Scores
Lane

Peat Carr

Doncaster
Nottinghamshire County

Misson Bank

North Lincolnshire
Nottinghamshire County

Misson Bank

B1396   SANDERSON'S BANK

Springs Road

Beech
Hill Farm

LC

Fitzwilliams Road

LC

Newlands
Farm

Low Deeps Lane

Chapel Baulk

Springs Road

Levels
Farm

Springs Farm

Spring
Hill

Deeps Lane

Red House

Springs Road

Levels Lane

grid square represents 500 metres

Wood Farm

95

G H J K L M

I
2
3
4
5
6
7
8

M3
1 Colleywell Cl

Trinity Farm

Bull Hassocks
Farm

Cove Road

Cove Rd
Upperthorpe
HI
Lane
Amcote
Rd
Well Road
Weir
CI
The
Fir
Birches
Park
Park
Dr
Park
Cl
Commonside
The Meadows
Weavers
Croft
Drew La
Moorlands
B1396

Westwoodside

DONCASTER ROAD

North Lincolnshire
Nottinghamshire County

Idle Bank

Broomston Lane

Thimholme Lane

LC

LC

LC

LC

Broomston Lane

Broomston

Fountain
Farm

Idle Bank

Tindale Bank Road

Langholme

Tindale Bank Road

Haxey
Grange

Star
Carr

New

HOl

We

G H J K L M

South Carr
Farm

LC

Mother Drain

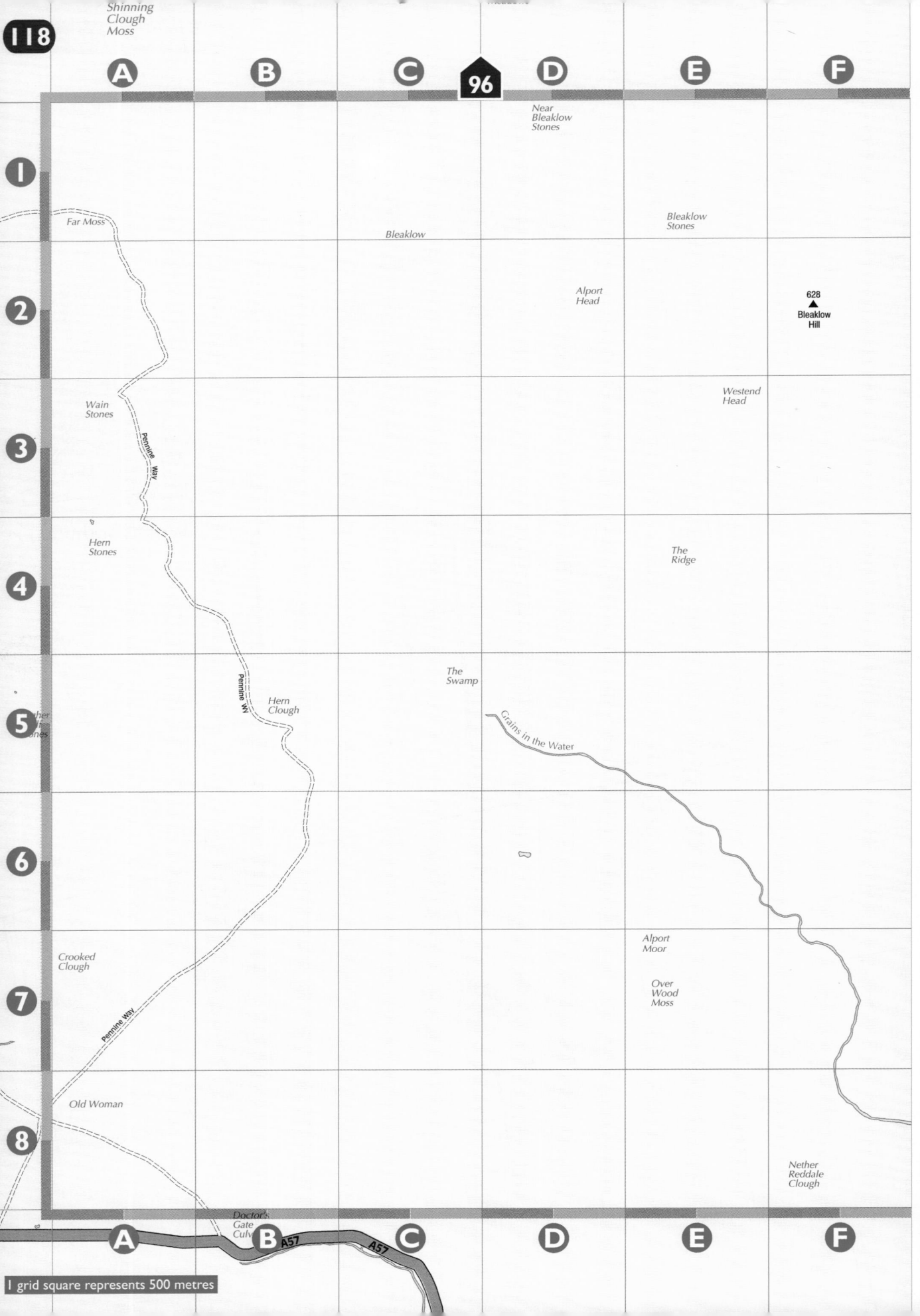

A   B   C   96   D   E   F

Shinning Clough Moss

Near Bleaklow Stones

1

Far Moss

Bleaklow

Bleaklow Stones

2

Alport Head

628
▲
Bleaklow Hill

Wain Stones

Westend Head

Pennine Way

3

Hern Stones

The Ridge

4

The Swamp

Pennine W

Hern Clough

5

Grains in the Water

ther
ones

6

Crooked Clough

Alport Moor

Over Wood Moss

Pennine Way

7

Old Woman

8

Nether Reddale Clough

Doctor's Gate Culv

A   B A57   A57   C   D   E   F

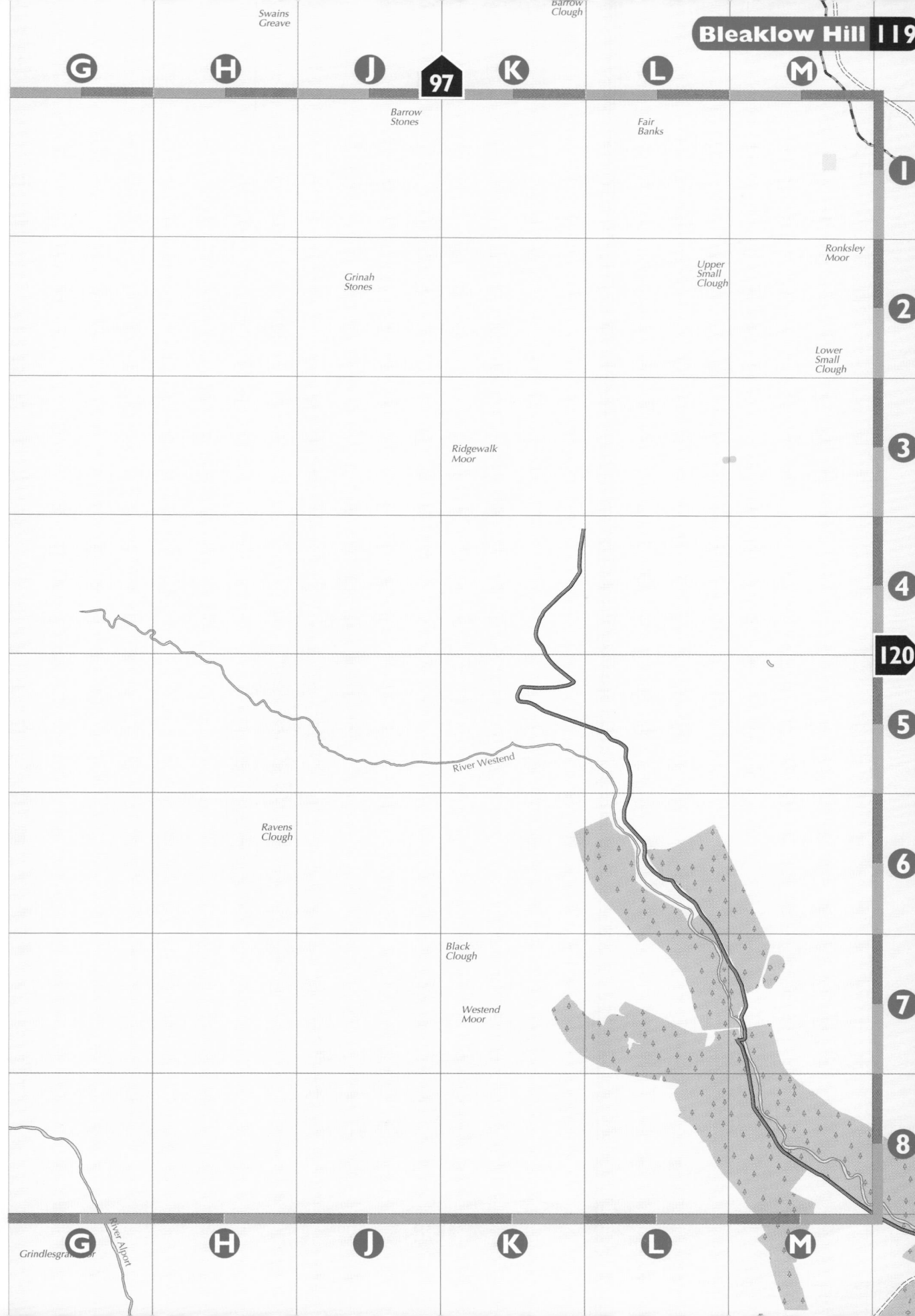

G   H   J   97   K   L   M

I

2

3

4

120

5

6

7

8

G   H   J   K   L   M

Swains
Greave

Barrow
Clough

Barrow
Stones

Fair
Banks

Grinah
Stones

Upper
Small
Clough

Ronksley
Moor

Lower
Small
Clough

Ridgewalk
Moor

River Westend

Ravens
Clough

Black
Clough

Westend
Moor

Grindlesgrain oor

River Alport

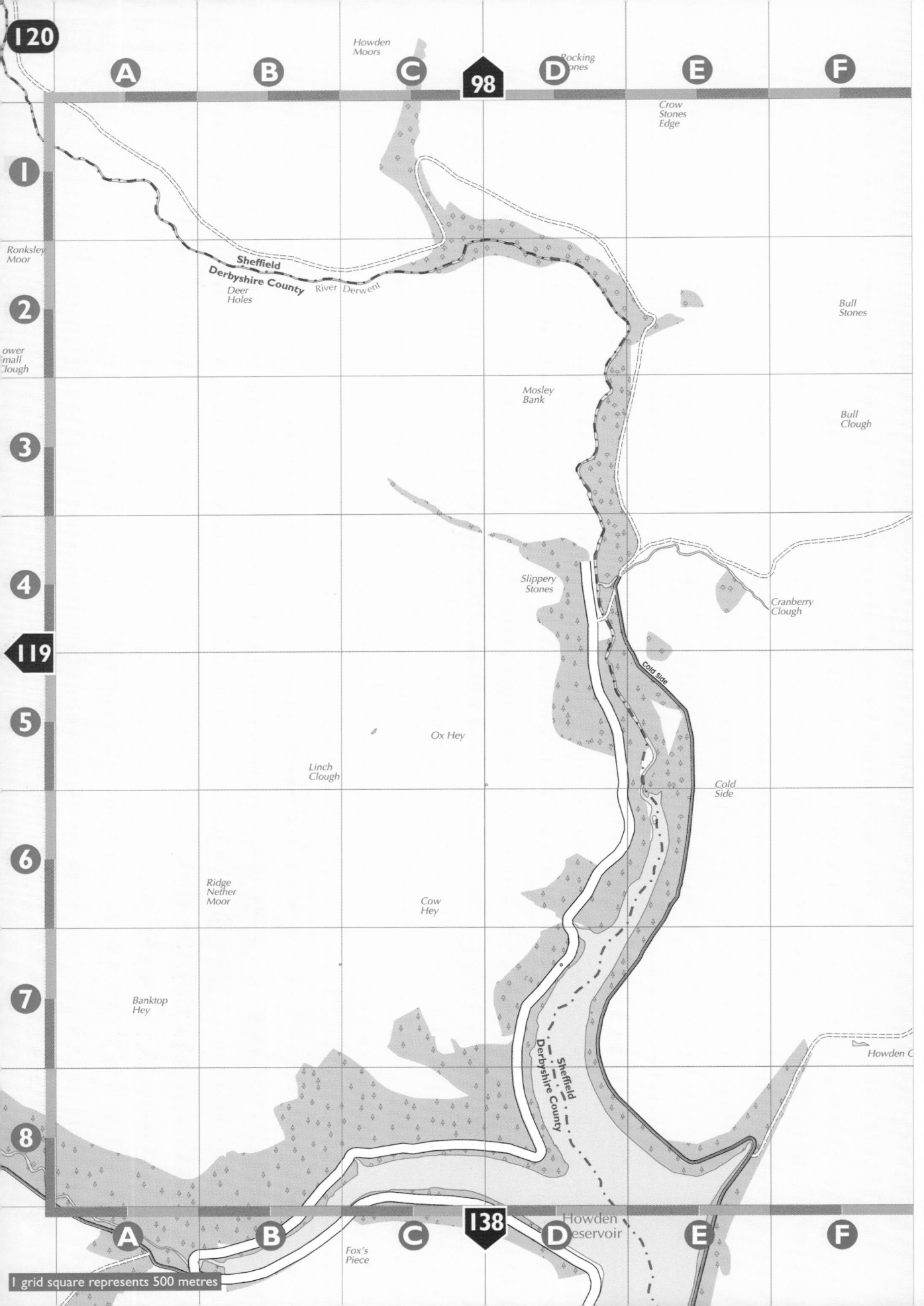

120

A
B
C
98
D
E
F

1

Ronksley
Moor

Sheffield
Derbyshire County River Derwent

Deer
Holes

Howden
Moors

Rocking
Stones

Crow
Stones
Edge

Bull
Stones

2

ower
mall
lough

Mosley
Bank

Bull
Clough

3

Slippery
Stones

Cranberry
Clough

4

119

Cold Side

Ox Hey

5

Linch
Clough

Cold
Side

6

Ridge
Nether
Moor

Cow
Hey

7

Banktop
Hey

Sheffield
Derbyshire County

Howden C

8

A
B
C
138
D

Fox's
Piece

Howden
Reservoir

E
F

1 grid square represents 500 metres

G H J 99 K L M

I
2
3
4
122
5
6
7
8

Bull
Clough

Cut

Upper
Commons

546
▲
Margery
Hill

Stainery
Clough

Middle
Moss

Penistone
Stile

Featherbed
Moss

Clough

G H J 139 K L M

Howden
Moors

Abbey Brook

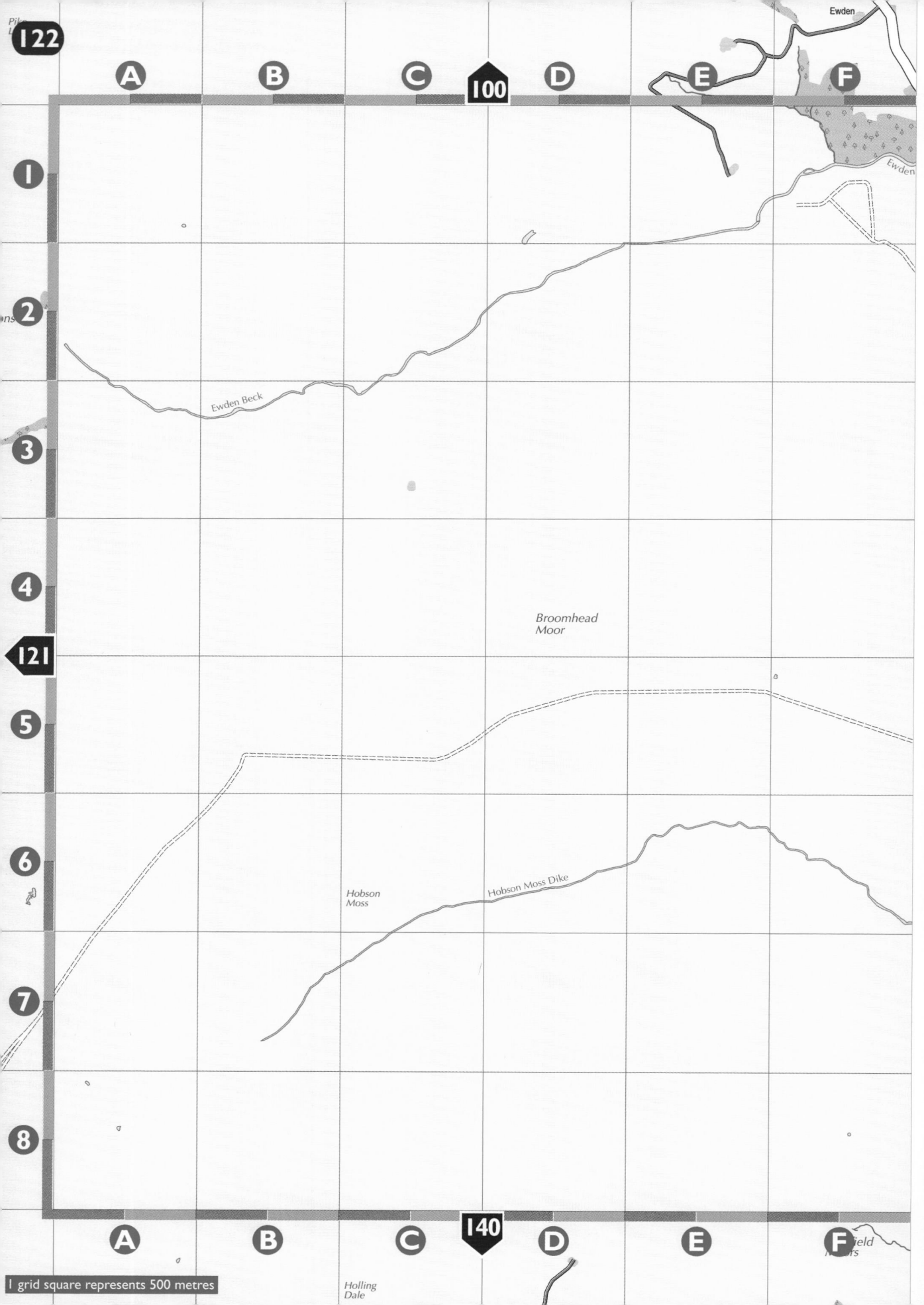

Ⓐ Ⓑ Ⓒ **100** Ⓓ Ⓔ Ⓕ

Ewden

Ⅰ

Ewden

2

ns

3

Ewden Beck

Pike

4

Broomhead
Moor

121

5

6

Hobson
Moss   Hobson Moss Dike

7

8

Ⓐ Ⓑ Ⓒ **140** Ⓓ Ⓔ Ⓕ field
                                                  rs

1 grid square represents 500 metres

Holling
Dale

Beck

Heads Lane

Waldershaigh

Yewtrees Lane

New

Broomhead
Hall

Lane

Allas Allas Dike Lane

Wigtwizzle

Broomhead
Reservoir

Rushy Lane

Mill Lane

New Road

Moor Lane

Lee

Lane

Dwarriden

Lane

Canyards

White Lee Lane

White Lee
Farm

Walker Edge

Canyards

Hills Lane

Field Road

White
Lee
Moor

Mortimer Road

Penistone Road

Load

Smallfield

Agden
Bridge

Agden Side Road

Smallfield Lane

West
Nab

Bolsterstone Road

Penistone Road

Onesac

Mortimer Road

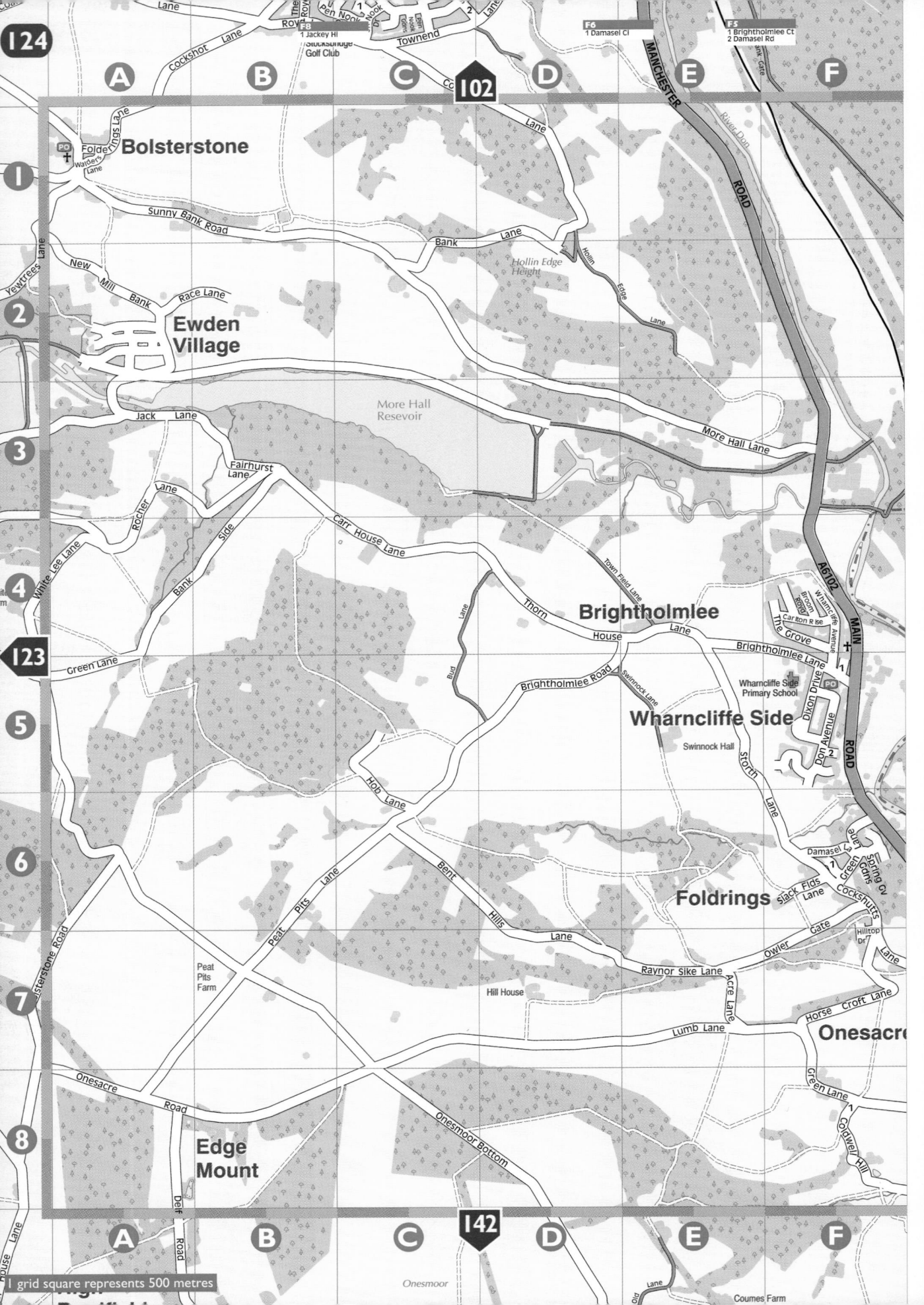

A B C 102 D E F

I **Bolsterstone**
PO
Folderings Lane
Watsers
Lane
Yewtrees Lane
Sunny Bank Road
Bank Lane
Hollin Edge Height
Hollin
2 New Mill Bank
Race Lane
Ewden Village
Edge Lane

Jack Lane
More Hall Resevoir
More Hall Lane
3 Fairhurst Lane
Rocher Lane
Carr House Lane
MANCHESTER ROAD
River Don

4 White Lee Lane
Bank Side
Town Field Lane
Thorn House
Brightholmlee
Wharncliffe Avenue
Broom Royd
Carlton R Ise
The Grove
Brightholmlee Lane
A6102

Green Lane
Bud Lane
Brightholmlee Road
Swinnock Lane
Wharncliffe Side Primary School
PO
Dixon Drive
MAIN ROAD

5
Swinnock Hall
Wharncliffe Side
Storth Lane
Don Avenue

6 Hob Lane
Peat Pits Lane
Bent Hills Lane
Foldrings
Slack Flds Lane
Cockshutts
Damasel La
Green Gdns
Spring Gv
Owler Gate Lane
Hilltop Dr

7 Onesacre Road
Peat Pits Farm
Hill House
Raynor Sike Lane
Acre Lane
Lumb Lane
Horse Croft Lane
Onesacre
Green Lane
Coldwell Hill

8 Onesacre Road
Edge Mount
Delf Road
Onesmoor Bottom

A B 142 C D E F

Onesmoor
Coumes Farm

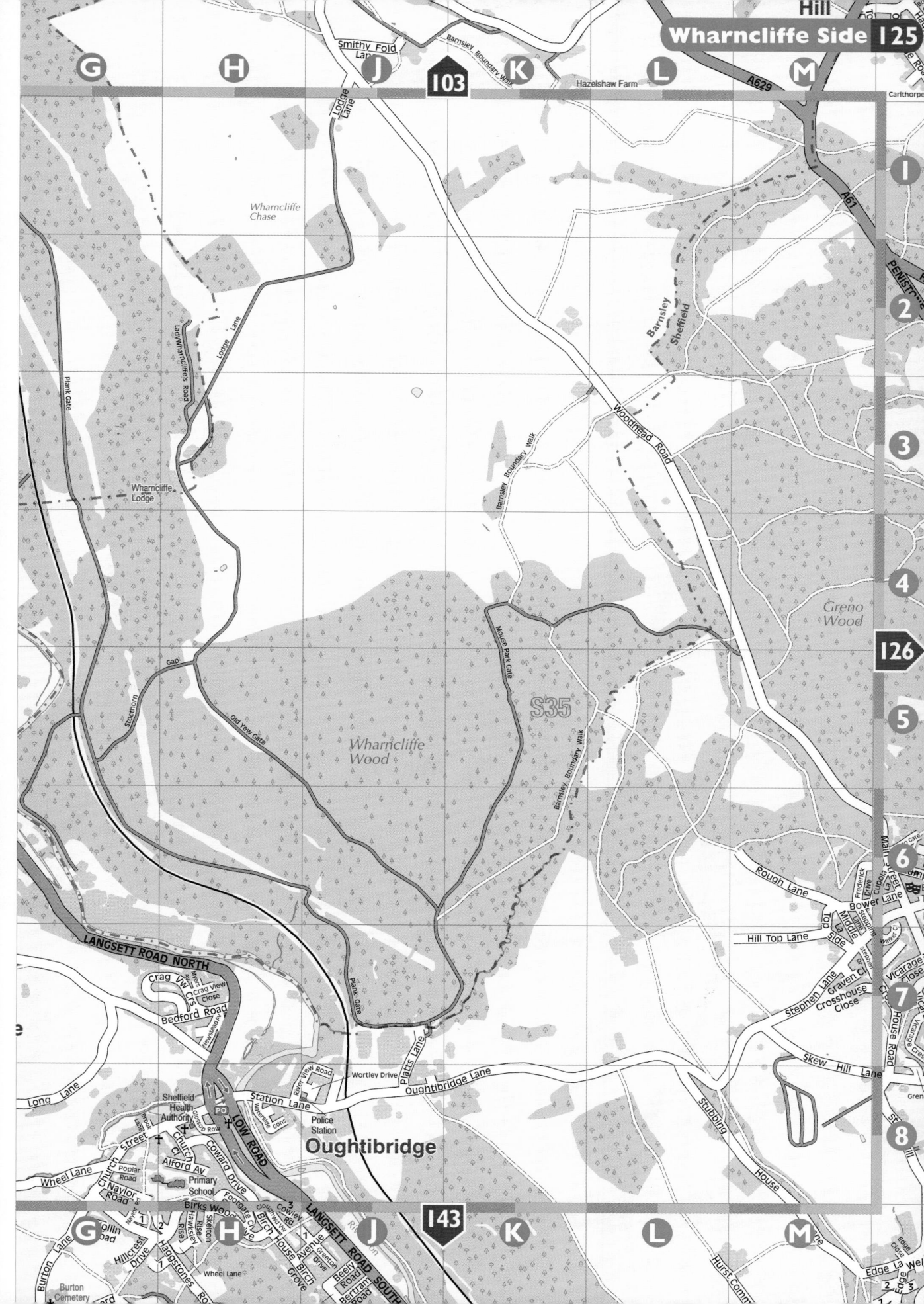

103
126
143
G
H
J
K
L
M
1
2
3
4
5
6
7
8
Hill
Smithy Fold Lane
Barnsley Boundary Walk
Hazelshaw Farm
A629
Carlthorpe
A61
Penistone
Lodge Lane
Wharncliffe Chase
Ladywharncliffe's Road
Plank Gate
Wharncliffe Lodge
Barnsley
Sheffield
Woodhead Road
Greno Wood
Mouse Park Gate
Gap
Stocthorn
Old Yew Gate
S35
Wharncliffe Wood
Main Street
Rough Lane
Frederick Drive
Cupola
Bower Lane
Top Side
Middle Lane
Hill Top Lane
Stephen Lane
Craven Cl
Crosshouse Close
Vicarage Close
House Road
Skew Hill Lane
Stubbing
House
Langsett Road North
Crag Vw Crs
Crag View Close
Bedford Road
Platts Lane
River View Road
Wortley Drive
Oughtibridge Lane
Long Lane
Station Lane
Sheffield Health Authority
PO
Low Road
Police Station
Oughtibridge
Church Street
Church Cl
Alford Av
Coward Drive
Wheel Lane
Poplar Road
Naylor Road
Primary School
Birks Wood
Footgate Cl
Cowley Rd
Langsett Road South
Collin Road
Burton Lane
Hillcrest Drive
Haggstones Road
Hawksley Rise
Skelton
Birch House Avenue
Greeton Drive
Beely Road
Bertram Road
Grove
Wheel Lane
Burton Cemetery
Hurst Comm
Edge Close
Edge La
Edge

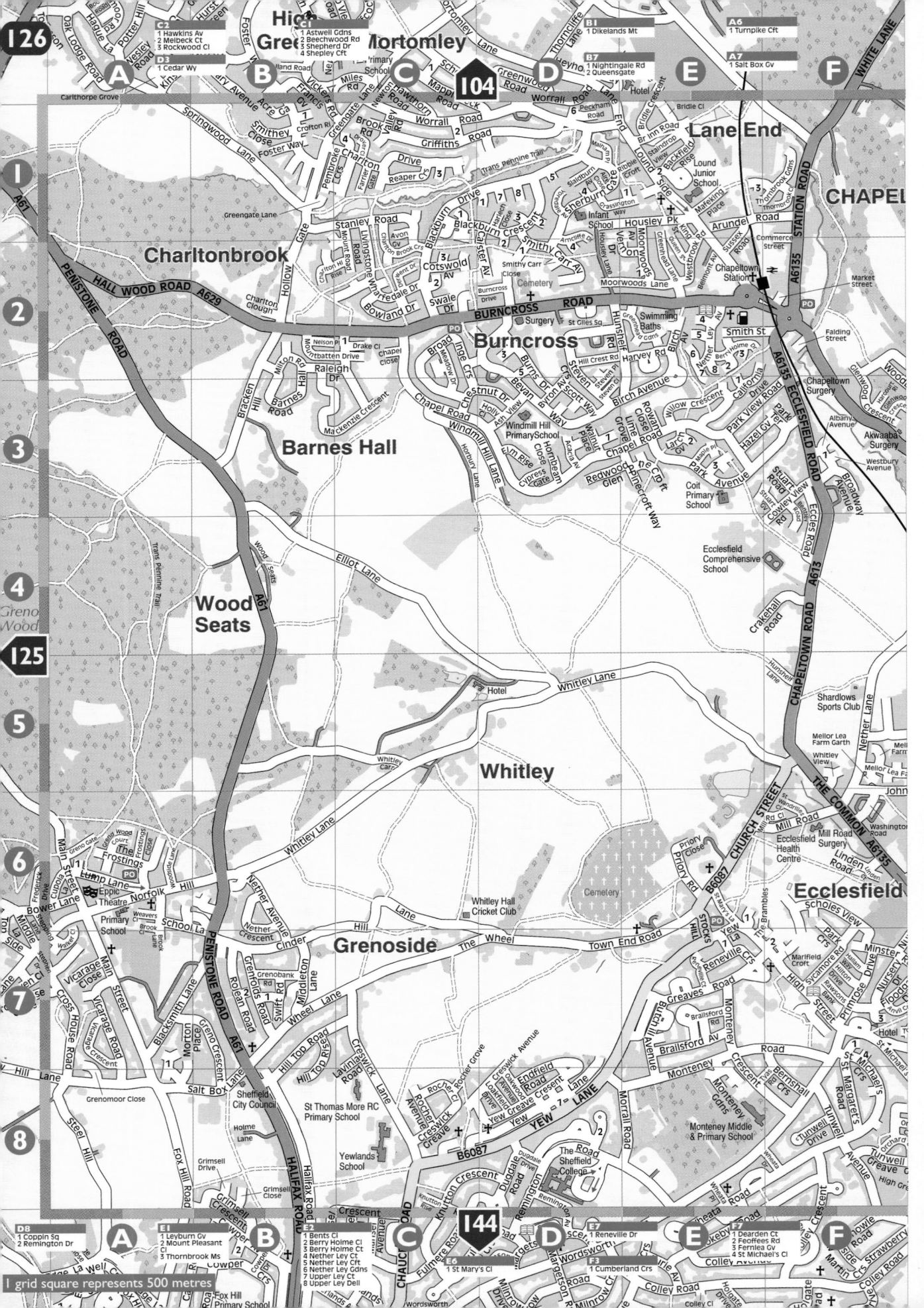

126
104
125
144
A
B
C
D
E
F
1
2
3
4
5
6
7
8
C2
1 Hawkins Av
2 Melbeck Ct
3 Rockwood Cl
D3
1 Cedar Wy
C1
1 Astwell Gdns
2 Beechwood Rd
3 Shepherd Dr
4 Shepley Cft
B1
1 Dikelands Mt
B7
1 Nightingale Rd
2 Queensgate
A6
1 Turnpike Cft
A7
1 Salt Box Gv
High Green
Mortomley
Lane End
CHAPEL
Charltonbrook
Burncross
Barnes Hall
Wood Seats
Whitley
Grenoside
Ecclesfield
Greno Wood
Carlthorpe Grove
Springwood Lane
Smithey Close
Foster Way
Greengate Lane
Pembroke Crs
Charlton Drive
Worrall Road
Griffiths Road
Trans Pennine Trail
Stanley Road
Blackburn Crescent
Smithy Carr Av
Housley Pk
Arundel Road
Station Road
White Lane
A6135
Chapeltown Station
Market Street
Hall Wood Road A629
Penistone Road
Burncross Road
Chapel Road
Windmill Hill Lane
Windmill Hill Primary School
Coit Primary School
Ecclesfield Road
Chapeltown Road
A613
Ecclesfield Comprehensive School
Elliot Lane
Whitley Lane
Hotel
Shardlows Sports Club
Church Street
B6087
The Common
Mill Road
Ecclesfield Health Centre
Mill Road Surgery
Cemetery
Whitley Hall Cricket Club
Town End Road
The Wheel
Cinder Hill
Nether Avenue
Main Street
Lump Lane
Eppic Theatre
Norfolk Hill
Bower Lane
Primary School
School La
Wheel Lane
Hill Top Road
Cresswick Lane
Yew Lane
Greaves Road
Brailsford Av
Monteney Road
Monteney Middle & Primary School
St Thomas More RC Primary School
Yewlands School
Sheffield City Council
The Sheffield College
Halifax Road
Salt Box Lane
Hill Lane
Steel Hill
Fox Hill Road
Grenomoor Close
Morrall Road
Tunwell Avenue
High Street
Chapeltown Surgery
Akwaaba Surgery
D8
1 Coppin Sq
2 Remington Dr
E1
1 Leyburn Gv
2 Mount Pleasant Cl
3 Thornbrook Ms
E2
1 Bents Cl
2 Berry Holme Cl
3 Berry Holme Ct
4 Nether Ley Ct
5 Nether Ley Cft
6 Nether Ley Gdns
7 Upper Ley Ct
8 Upper Ley Dell
E6
1 St Mary's Cl
E7
1 Reneville Dr
F3
1 Cumberland Crs
F7
1 Dearden Ct
2 Feoffees Rd
3 Fernlea Gv
4 St Michael's Cl
1 grid square represents 500 metres

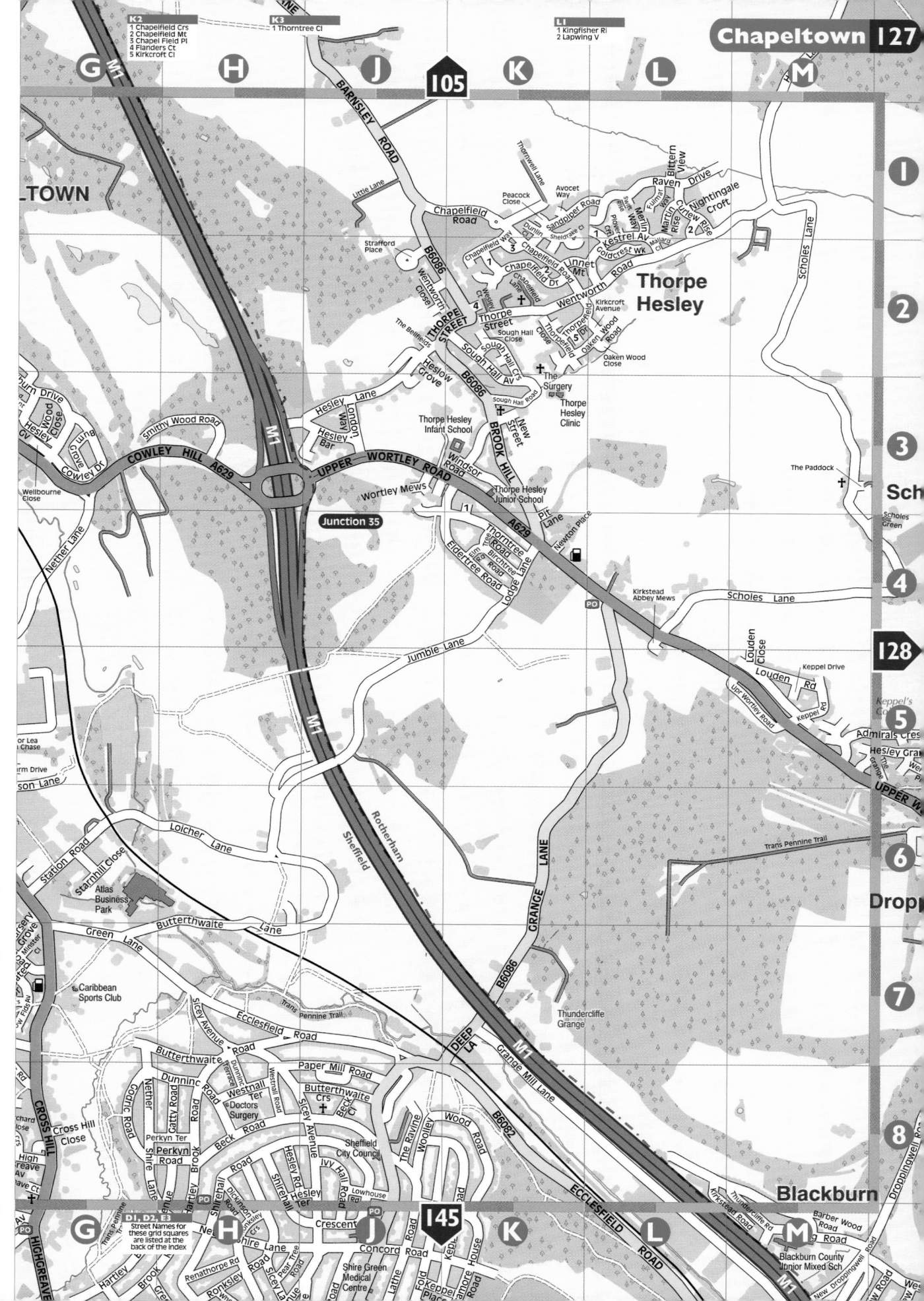
K2
1 Chapelfield Crs
2 Chapelfield Mt
3 Chapel Field Pl
4 Flanders Ct
5 Kirkcroft Cl
K3
1 Thorntree Cl
L1
1 Kingfisher Ri
2 Lapwing V
105
128
145
D1, D2, E3 Street Names for these grid squares are listed at the back of the index
Thorpe Hesley
Blackburn
Barnsley Road
Chapelfield Road
Wentworth Road
Thorpe Street
Sough Hall Av
Brook Hill
Hesley Lane
Cowley Hill
Upper Wortley Road
Junction 35
Jumble Lane
Scholes Lane
Grange Lane
Loicher Lane
Station Road
Butterthwaite Lane
Green Lane
Ecclesfield Road
Grange Mill Lane
Deep La
Cross Hill
Thorpe Hesley Infant School
Thorpe Hesley Junior School
The Surgery
Thorpe Hesley Clinic
Atlas Business Park
Caribbean Sports Club
Thundercliffe Grange
Sheffield City Council
Doctors Surgery
Shire Green Medical Centre
Blackburn County Junior Mixed Sch
Trans Pennine Trail
Rotherham
Sheffield

C6
1 Burgen Rd
2 Kent Rd
C5
1 Sidons Cl
J8, K1
Street Names for these grid squares are listed at the back of the index
B7
1 Hill View East
2 Webster Cl
B5
1 Remount Wy
B6
1 Dr'pp'gwell Fm Cl
106
127
146
Scholes
Wingfield
Kimberworth Park
Dropping Well
Kimberworth
Bradgate
Masbrough
Morley Pond
Dog Kennel Pond
Scholes Coppice
Keppel's Column
S61
Rotherham Roundwalk
Church Street
Town Lane
Roughwood Road
UPPER WORTLEY ROAD
A629
WORTLEY ROAD
A629 NEW WORTLEY
WILTON GARDENS
Rockingham Junior & Infant School
Greasbrough Health Centre
Wingfield Comprehensive School
Redscope Junior & Infant School
Kimberworth Park Clinic
Kimberworth Park Medical Centre
Superbowl Two Thousand
Abbey School
Old Hall Comprehensive School
Primary School
Infants School
D6
1 Barber Balk Cl
2 Raybould Rd
3 Wainwright Rd
D8
1 Dycott Rd
2 Kimb'rw'th Pk Rd
E8
1 Broadgate Ho Cl
2 Wortley Rd
1 grid square represents 500 metres

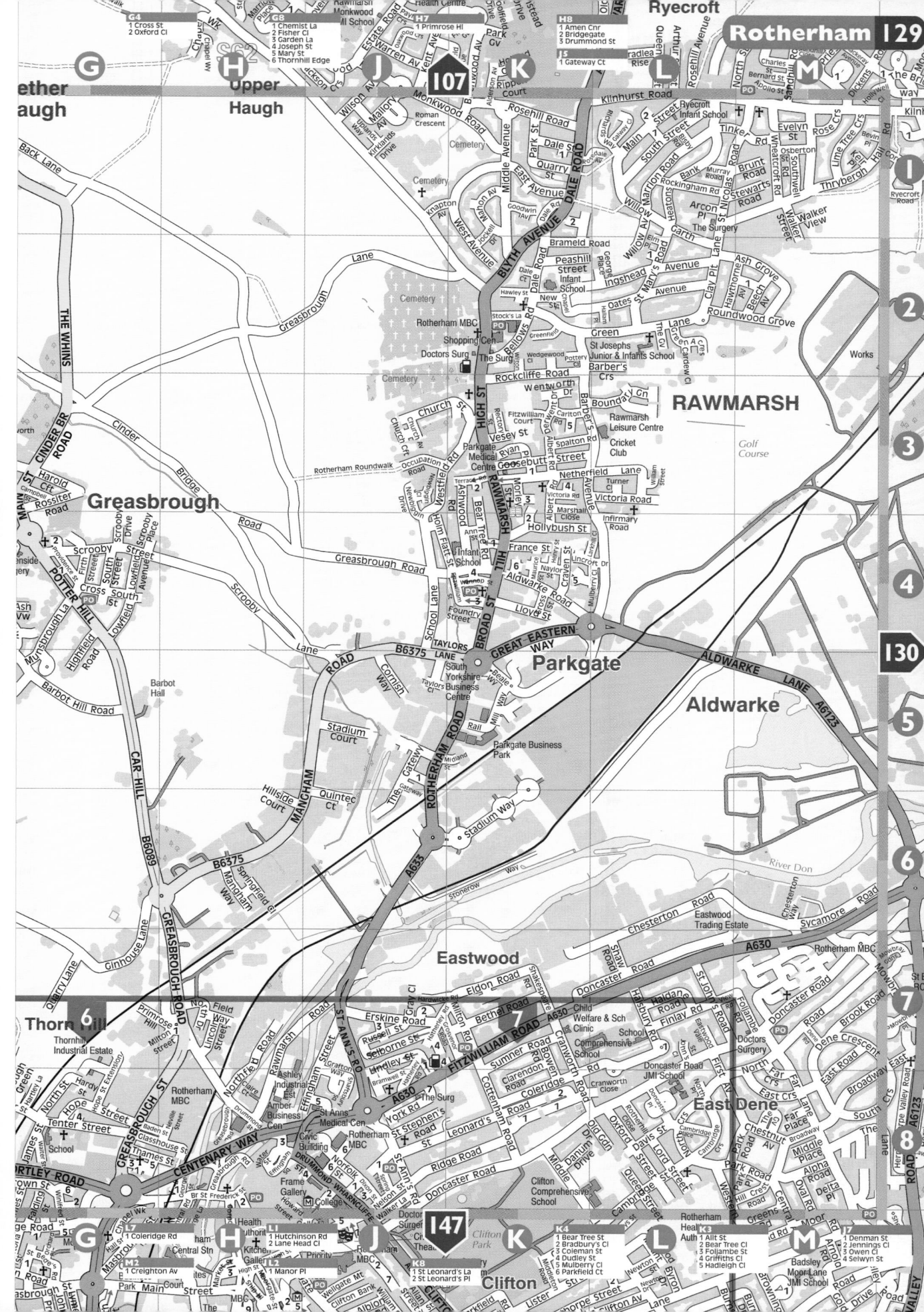
G4
1 Cross St
2 Oxford Cl
G8
1 Chemist La
2 Fisher Cl
3 Garden La
4 Joseph St
5 Mary St
6 Thornhill Edge
H7
1 Primrose Hl
H8
1 Amen Cnr
2 Bridgegate
3 Drummond St
J5
1 Gateway Ct
Ryecroft
Upper Haugh
107
Kilnhurst Road
Rosehill Road
Monkwood Road
Roman Crescent
Cemetery
Back Lane
THE WHINS
CINDER BR ROAD
Cinder Bridge Road
Greasbrough Lane
Greasbrough
Greasbrough Road
Scrooby Lane
POTTER HILL
Barbot Hall
Barbot Hill Road
CAR HILL
B6089
GREASBROUGH ROAD
MANGHAM ROAD
B6375
Ginhouse Lane
Quarry Lane
BLYTH AVENUE
DALE ROAD
HIGH ST
BROAD ST
RAWMARSH HILL
Rotherham MBC
Shopping Cen
Doctors Surg
The Surg
Rockcliffe Road
Church St
Rotherham Roundwalk
Occupation Road
Parkgate Medical Centre
Goosebutt Street
Netherfield Lane
Victoria Road
Hollybush St
Infant School
Peashill Street Infant School
St Josephs Junior & Infants School
Barber's Crs
RAWMARSH
Rawmarsh Leisure Centre
Cricket Club
Golf Course
Works
Ryecroft Infant School
The Surgery
Walker View
Thrybergh Hall Rd
Roundwood Grove
GREAT EASTERN WAY
TAYLORS LANE
Parkgate
South Yorkshire Business Centre
Parkgate Business Park
Stadium Way
ROTHERHAM ROAD
A633
ALDWARKE LANE
A6123
Aldwarke
River Don
Stonerow Way
Chesterton Road
Eastwood Trading Estate
Sycamore Road
Eastwood
A630
Doncaster Road
Rotherham MBC
Thorn Hill
6
Thornhill Industrial Estate
7
FITZWILLIAM ROAD
Child Welfare & Sch Clinic
Comprehensive School
Doncaster Road JMI School
Doctors Surgery
East Dene
CENTENARY WAY
GREASBROUGH ST
ST ANN'S RD
Ashley Industrial Est
Amber Business Cen
St Anns Medical Cen
Rotherham MBC
Civic Building
DRUMMOND WHARNCLIFFE
Frame Gallery
College
Clifton Comprehensive School
Clifton Park
Clifton
130
147
L7
1 Coleridge Rd
M2
1 Creighton Av
L1
1 Hutchinson Rd
2 Lane Head Cl
L2
1 Manor Pl
K8
1 St Leonard's La
2 St Leonard's Pl
K4
1 Bear Tree St
2 Bradbury's Cl
3 Coleman St
4 Dudley St
5 Mulberry Cl
6 Parkfield Ct
K3
1 Allt St
2 Bear Tree Cl
3 Foljambe St
4 Griffiths Cl
5 Hadleigh Cl
J7
1 Denman St
2 Jennings Cl
3 Owen Cl
4 Selwyn St
Rotherham Health Auth
Badsley Moor Lane JMI School
Central Stn

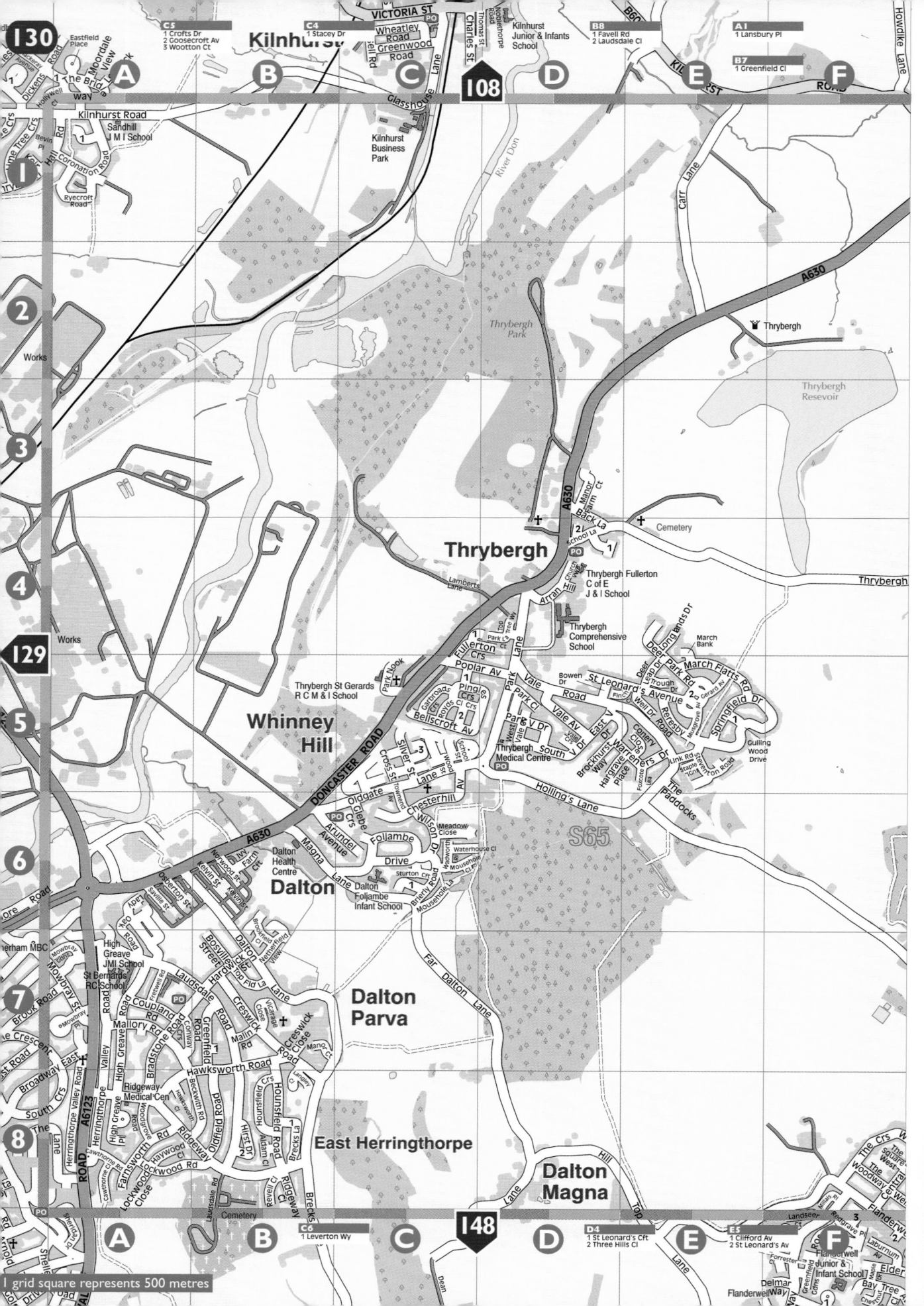

A B C 108 D E F

Eastfield Place

C5
1 Crofts Dr
2 Goosecroft Av
3 Wootton Ct

Kilnhurst

C4
1 Stacey Dr

VICTORIA ST

Wheatley Road
Greenwood Road

Charles St
Thomas St

Kilnhurst Junior & Infants School

B8
1 Favell Rd
2 Laudsdale Cl

A1
1 Lansbury Pl

B7
1 Greenfield Cl

Lime Tree Crs
Dickens Avenue
A1
The Bridleway

Hollywell
Bevin Rd

Kilnhurst Road

Sandhill J M I School

Coronation Road

Ryecroft Road

Kilnhurst Business Park

Glasshouse Lane

River Don

KILNHURST ROAD

Carr Lane

I

2

Works

Thrybergh Park

Thrybergh

Thrybergh Resevoir

3

Works

129

A630

Manor Ct
Back La
School La
Arran Hill
PO
2 1

Cemetery

Thrybergh

Thrybergh Reservoir

4

Lamberts Lane

Thrybergh

Thrybergh Fullerton C of E J & I School

Thrybergh

5

Thrybergh St Gerards R C M & I School

Park Nook

Fullerton Crs
Poplar Av

Pingles Crs
Carlyoads Rds
Crs

Bellscroft Av

Whinney Hill

DONCASTER ROAD

Silver St
Cross St
Oldgate
Glebe Crs
Chesterhill

School Lane

Park Lt
Tree W
Park Lane
Vale
Park Cl
Vale Av
East Dr
West Vale Dr

Thrybergh Comprehensive School

Bowen Dr

St Leonard's Avenue
Deer Leap Dr
Long Lands Dr
Park Rd
March Flatts Rd
March Bank

Springfield Dr

Thrybergh South Medical Centre
PO

Conery Way
Brodhurst
Hargrave
Trenchers Place
Reresby
Well Dr
Gerard Av
Fincroft
Midgrove Av

Link Rd
Staple Croft
Norton Road

Guilling Wood Drive

The Paddocks

6

A630

Farm Cft
Lidget Lane
Kelvin St
Norwood St

Magna Lane
Arundel Avenue
Foljambe Drive

Wilson Road
Sturton Road
Brierly Road
Mousehole

Meadow Close
Waterhouse Cl
Wadworth
Mousehole Lane

Holling's Lane

S65

Dalton

Dalton Health Centre

Dalton Foljambe Infant School

7

Rotherham MBC

Mowbray St
Brook Road

High Greave JMI School
St Bernards RC School

Laudsdale Road
Coupland Rd
Mallory Rd
Bradstone Rd

Hardwick Lane
Greenfield Rd
Creswick Road
Conway Crs
Malin Rd

Bosville St
Hawksworth Road
Freeland Rd
Nethershield View

Creswick Close
Vicarage Lane
Manor

Far Dalton Lane

Dalton Parva

Broadway East

South Crs
The

Herringthorpe Valley Road
A6123
St Bernards
Farnsworth Rd
Ridgeway Pl
High Greave
Ridgeway Medical Cen
Ridgeway Rd
Lockwood Rd
Beckwith Rd
Hirst Dr
Hounsfield Road
Aldam Cl
Brecks La

Langley

East Herringthorpe

Dalton Magna

Hill Lane
Dean Lane
Top Lane

8

Cawthorne Rd
Lockwood Close
Laudsdale Rd
Cemetery

C6
1 Leverton Wy

148

D4
1 St Leonard's Cft
2 Three Hills Cl

E5
1 Clifford Av
2 St Leonard's Av

C6
1

The Crs
The Square West
The Woodway West
Flanderwell Central

Flanderwell Junior & Infant School

Landseer
Redgrave Pl
Elder
Laburnum Av
Bay Tree
Delmar Way
Flanderwell Lane
Greenfield Gdns
Maple Pl

A B C D E F

DONCASTER ROAD
H4
1 Bosvile Cl
H8
1 Grasby Ct
2 Moorfield Av
3 Moorfield Gv
J7
1 Ranfield Ct
Hooton Roberts
109
The Wapping
Back Lane
Firsby Lane
B6093
RAVENFIELD LANE
Park Lane
Conisbrough Parks
Ravenfield Park
Firsby Hall Farm
Arbour Lane
Conisbrough Lodge
Lane
HOOTON LANE
Church Cl
Church La
St James View
Ravenfield
Garden Lane
Dovecote La
St James Dr
MAIN STREET
Pingle Lane
Lime Cl
Birk Lodge
Doncaster Rotherham
132
B6093
MOOR LANE NORTH
Ravenfield Junior & Infant School
Ravenfield Common
Ravenfield Grange
Holly's
House Road
Radford Cl
Cedar Dr
Road
Common
Lane
Moor
Lane
Sandringham Place
Allott Cl
Moor La N
Braithwell
Osborne Close
Westby Close
Birchwood Drive
Doctors Surgery
PO
Holling's Lane
Smeaton Cl
Poplar Cl
Howson Cl
Barberry Way
Grayson Cl
Longfield Drive
Hazel Ct
Firethorn Rise
Blackthorn Rise
Reasby Av
Wood Close
Silvermoor Drive
Common Farm Close
Bramley Lane
Lidget Lane
M18
Hellaby Lane
Spencer Dr
Sandeby Dr
Stone Close
Vincent Rd
Hurlfield Rd
MOOR LANE SOUTH
Sunnyside
St Andrew's Close
Laceby Cl
Bigby Way
Elsham Cl
Searby Rd
Moorfield Cl
St Johns Av
St Francis Close
Fairfield Close
Belvedere Parade
Blenheim Close
Hellaby View
Belford Cl
Belford Dr
St John's Cl
Wellcliffe Cl
Windsor Close
Holyrood Rd
Harewood Grove
B6093
Rosedale Way
Nidderdale Pl
Ferndale Dr
Balmoral Way
Coppins Cl
Frogmore Close
Brook
Copse
Askam Ct
Gaunt Cl
Milner Way
Lidget Lane
Braithwell Way
Micklebring Way
Bramley Way
Hellaby Industrial Estate
Rother W
Birk Grange Farm
149
G
H
J
K
L
M
1
2
3
4
5
6
7
8

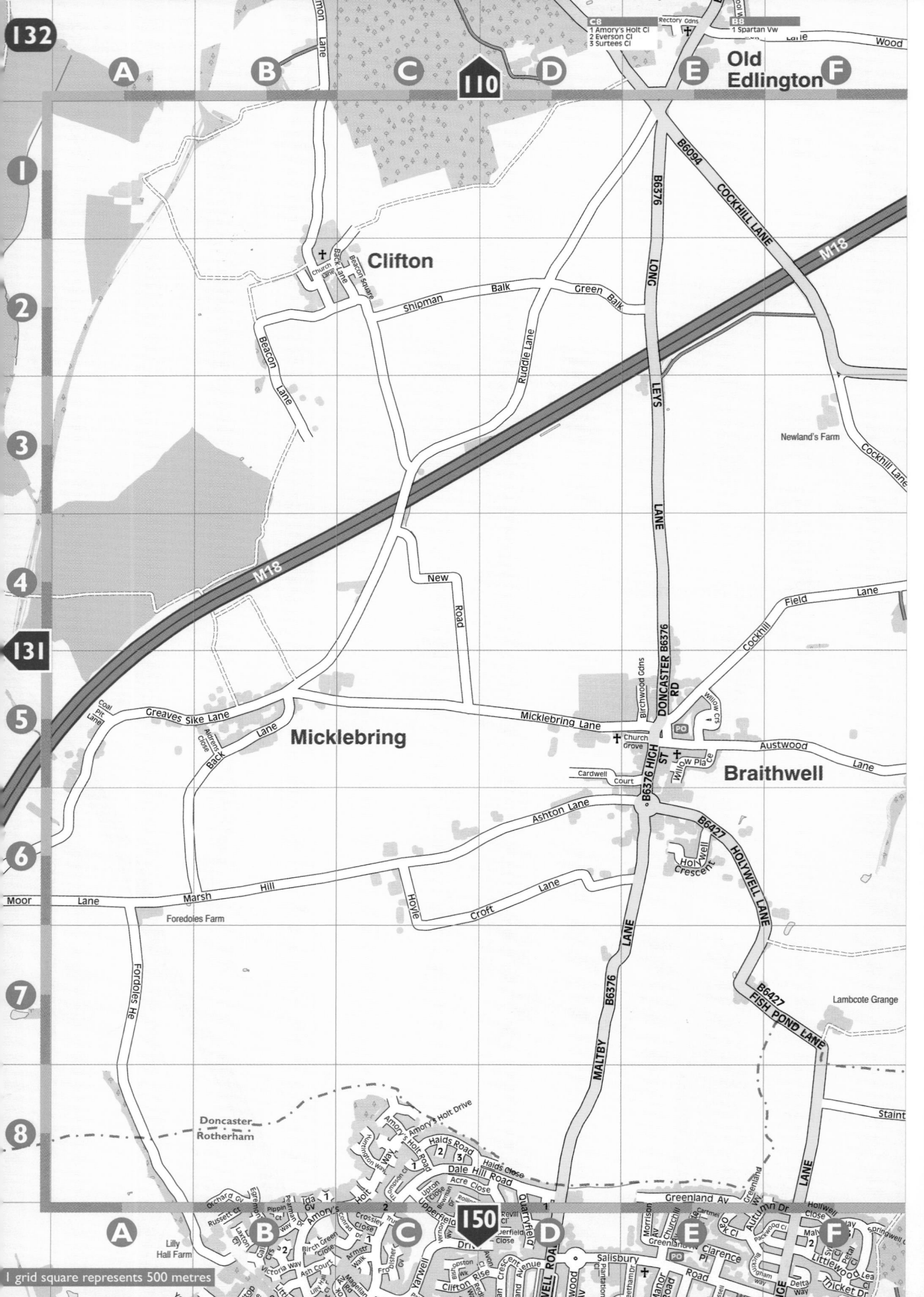

Old Edlington
Clifton
Micklebring
Braithwell
M18
B6376
LONG LEYS LANE
B6094 COCKHILL LANE
Shipman Balk
Green Balk
Ruddie Lane
Beacon Lane
Beacon Square
Back Lane
Church Lane
New Road
Newland's Farm
Cockhill Lane
Field Lane
Cockhill
Greaves Sike Lane
Coal Pit Lane
Aldrens Close
Back Lane
Micklebring Lane
Birchwood Gdns
DONCASTER RD B6376
Willow Crs
PO
Church Grove
Cardwell Court
B6376 HIGH ST
Willow Place
Austwood Lane
Ashton Lane
B6427 HOLYWELL LANE
Holywell Crescent
Moor Lane
Marsh Hill
Hoyle
Croft Lane
Foredoles Farm
Fordoles He
MALTBY B6376 LANE
B6427 FISH POND LANE
Lambcote Grange
Doncaster
Rotherham
Amory's Holt Drive
Haids Road
Haids Close
Dale Hill Road
Greenland Av
Autumn Dr
Lilly Hall Farm
Salisbury Road
Clarence Pl
Littlewood
Thicket Dr
C8
1 Amory's Holt Cl
2 Everson Cl
3 Surtees Cl
B8
1 Spartan Vw
Rectory Gdns
Wood Lane
Stainton
1 grid square represents 500 metres

110
131
150

G H J III K L M

J7
1 Old Scotch
Spring La

M1
1 St Johns Cft

Lane

1

CHURCH ROAD

Short Gate

B6094

WILSIC ROAD

Green
Lane

Manor Rise

Old
School
Lane

PO

Church
View

2

Cockhill Farm

B6094

LONG GATE

B6094

Wilsic
Road

3

Woodlands Farm

Stainton Lane

Wilsic Hall
School

Wilsic

Home Farm

Rakes Lane

4

Lodge Farm

134

Hole
Lane

Cockhill Lane

Tickhill Back Lane

5

Chapel
Lane

Limekiln Lane

Ruddle Mill Lane

The Ruddle Mill

Hirst Lane

Wood Lane

Broad   Riding

Stainton
Little
Wood

6

Holme
Hall Farm

Raw
Lane

Holme Hall Lane

Stainton

Stainton
Woodhouse Farm

7

The
Avenue

Stainton
1

School Lane

on Lane

Limekiln Lane

8

G H J 151 K L M

Scotch Spring

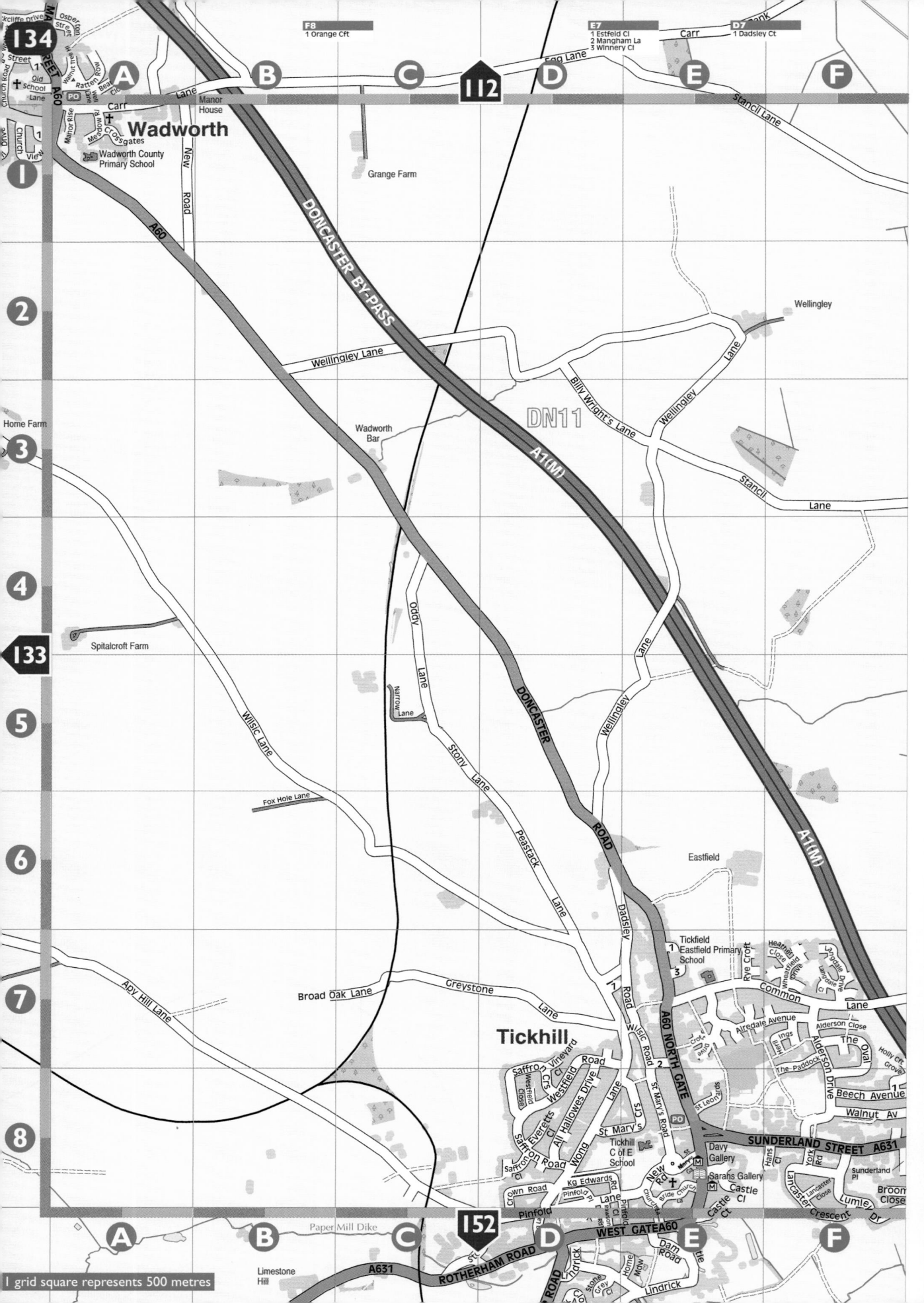

134

A60
Church Road
Osberton Street
Walnut Road
Ratten Row
Mews
Carr
Manor Rise
Beal Cl
PO
Old School Lane
Church View
A60
1 Drive

Wadworth
Crossgates
Wadworth County Primary School

Manor House
Lane
New Road
A60

F8
1 Orange Cft

E7
1 Estfield Cl
2 Mangham La
3 Winnery Cl

Carr

D7
1 Dadsley Ct

Stancil Lane

112

Egg Lane

A
B
C
D
E
F

1

Grange Farm

DONCASTER BY-PASS

2

Wellingley Lane

Wellingley

Wellingley Lane

3

Home Farm

Wadworth Bar

A1(M)

DN11

Billy Wright's Lane

Wellingley Lane

Stancil

Lane

133

4

Spitalcroft Farm

Oddy Lane

Wellingley Lane

5

WILSIC LANE

Narrow Lane

Stony Lane

DONCASTER ROAD

6

Fox Hole Lane

Peastack Lane

Dadsley Road

Eastfield

A1(M)

Tickfield
1 Eastfield Primary School
3

Rye Croft
Common Lane
Hearnshaw Close
Wheatfield
Argyle Drive
Lancaster Close

7

APY HILL LANE

Broad Oak Lane

Greystone Lane

Tickhill

Wilsic Road
Vineyard Road
Westfield Road
Saffron Crs
Westfield Close
New Road

Airedale Avenue
Alderson Close
The Paddock
Ings
Herrings
Alderson Drive
The Oval
Holly Crt Grove
Beech Avenue
1
Walnut Av

8

Saffron Road
Saffron Cl
Everetts
All Hallowes Drive
Wong
St Mary's Road
St Leonards
A60 NORTH GATE
PO
2

Davy Gallery
Hans Ings
SUNDERLAND STREET A631
York Rd
Sunderland Pl
Lancaster Crescent
Lumley
Broom Close

St Mary's
Tickhill C of E School
Kg Edwards
Own Road
Pinfold
Pinfold Lane

St Bride Church

Sarahs Gallery
Castle Cl
Castle Ct

152

Paper Mill Dike

A
B
C
D
E
F

Limestone Hill
A631
ROTHERHAM ROAD
WEST GATE A60
Dam Road
Lindrick
Grey Cl
Lindrick

1 grid square represents 500 metres

Rossington
Grange Farm

Wildflower
Close

Ragusa

Kepple
Close

Regent
Grove

Rossington
Comprehensive
School

Hall
View
Road

Spital
Gv

Hadrians Cl

Common
Lane
L.C.

G

H

J

113

K

L

M

I

Hunster
Grange Farm

Stancil
Lane

New
Lodge

2

Park
Wood

Stancil

3

Hesley
Hall
School

4

Bog
Wood

Goole Dike or River Torne

136

Martin
Beck

5

Hopyard Lane

Limpool Farm

6

Dumpling
Castle

Tickhill
High
Common

Beck Lane

Lane

Sheepwash Lane

Martin

High

Common

Lane

7

Common

Tickhill
Grange

Paper Mill Lane

Vine
Rd

Nettle
Cft

8

Meadow
Dirve

**Spital
Hill**

A631

G

H

BLYTH ROAD

J

153

K

BAWTRY ROAD

L

M

Don

Moorhouse Farm

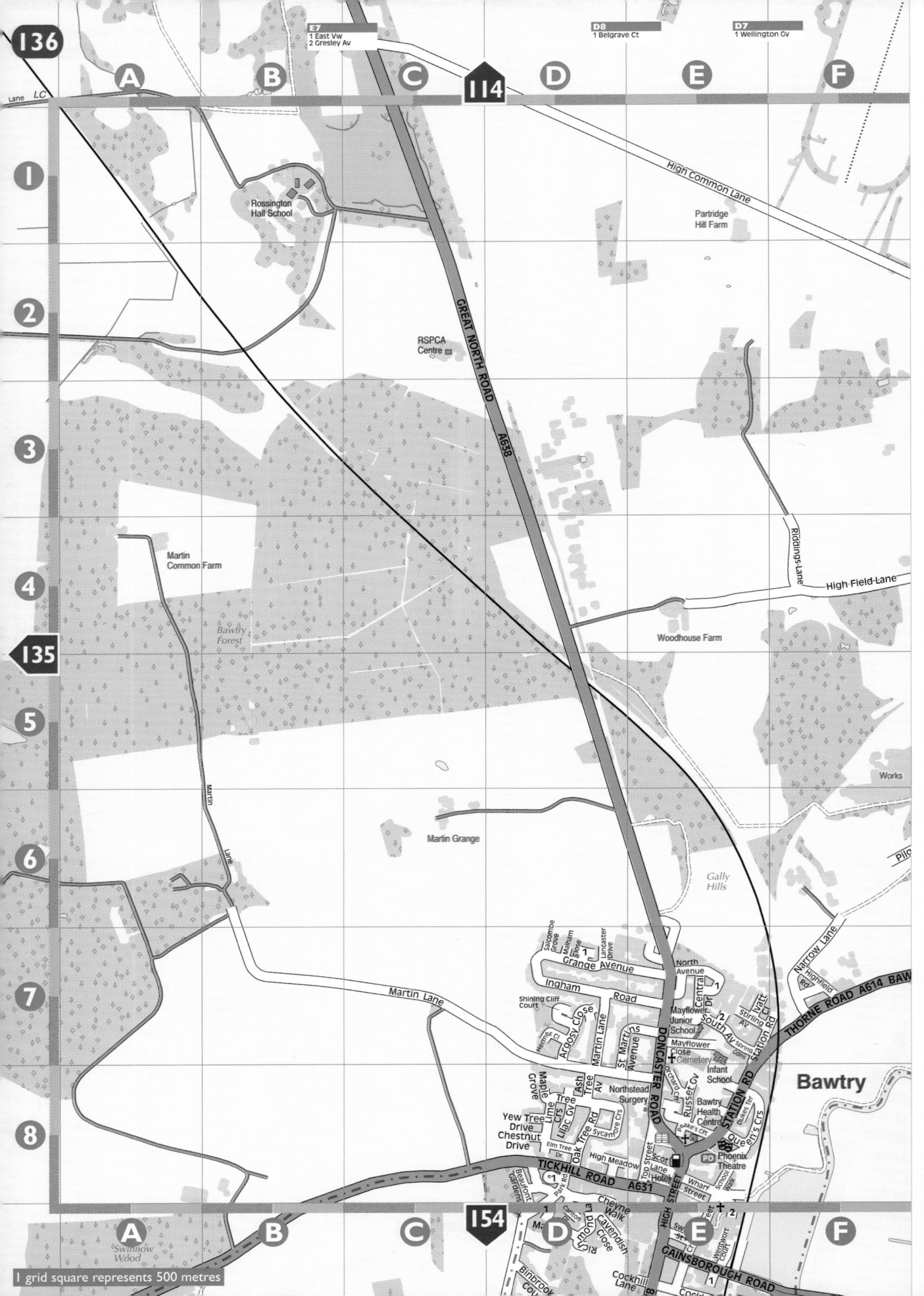
136
E7
1 East Vw
2 Gresley Av
D8
1 Belgrave Ct
D7
1 Wellington Gv
114
135
154
A
B
C
D
E
F
1
2
3
4
5
6
7
8
Rossington Hall School
High Common Lane
Partridge Hill Farm
GREAT NORTH ROAD
A638
RSPCA Centre
Riddings Lane
High Field Lane
Martin Common Farm
Bawtry Forest
Woodhouse Farm
Works
Martin Lane
Martin Grange
Gally Hills
Narrow Lane
THORNE ROAD A614
Grange Avenue
Ingham Road
North Avenue
Mayflower Junior School
Mayflower Close
Cemetery
Infant School
DONCASTER ROAD
STATION RD
Bawtry
Bawtry Health Centre
Phoenix Theatre
Northstead Surgery
Yew Tree Drive
Chestnut Drive
TICKHILL ROAD A631
High Meadow
HIGH STREET
Cheyne Walk
Cavendish Close
GAINSBOROUGH ROAD
Cockhill Lane
Swinnow Wood
1 grid square represents 500 metres

G H J **115** K L M

I

2

3

4

5

6

7

8

Misson Grange

Highwood Farm

Middle Wood Lane

Bracken Hill Lane

Cross Lane

Austerfield Park Golf Club

Austerfield Drain

Doncaster
Nottinghamshire County

Low Common

Bryans Close Lane

Rugged Butts La

Bawtry Road

Coronation Avenue

Jubilee Cl

Station Road

Manor Cl

Vicar La

Middle Street

Primary School

Back Lane

West Street

High Street

Misson

Butten Meadow

Austerfield

Low Field La

A614

Grim Rise

South View

William Bradford Close

Newington Road

Newington

Norwith Hill

Hagg Lane

Slaynes Lane

River Idle

Clay Bank Lane

G H J **155** K L M

Scaftworth Grange

re Farm

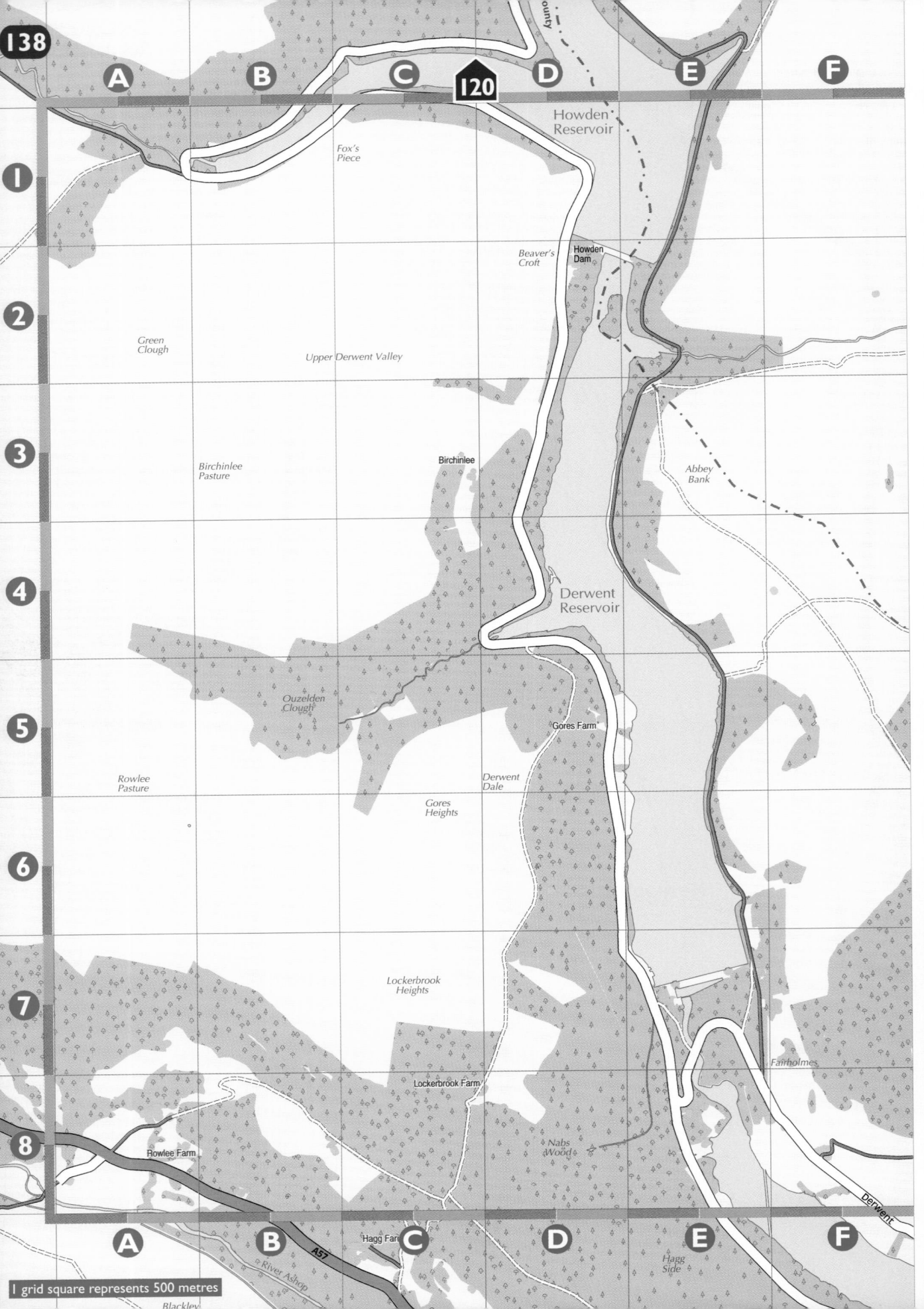

138

120

A   B   C   D   E   F

1
2
3
4
5
6
7
8

Fox's
Piece

Howden
Reservoir

Beaver's
Croft

Howden
Dam

Green
Clough

Upper Derwent Valley

Birchinlee
Pasture

Birchinlee

Abbey
Bank

Derwent
Reservoir

Ouzelden
Clough

Gores Farm

Rowlee
Pasture

Derwent
Dale

Gores
Heights

Lockerbrook
Heights

Fairholmes

Lockerbrook Farm

Nabs
Wood

Rowlee Farm

Hagg Farm

A57

River Ashop

Hagg
Side

Derwent

Blackley

A   B   C   D   E   F

1 grid square represents 500 metres

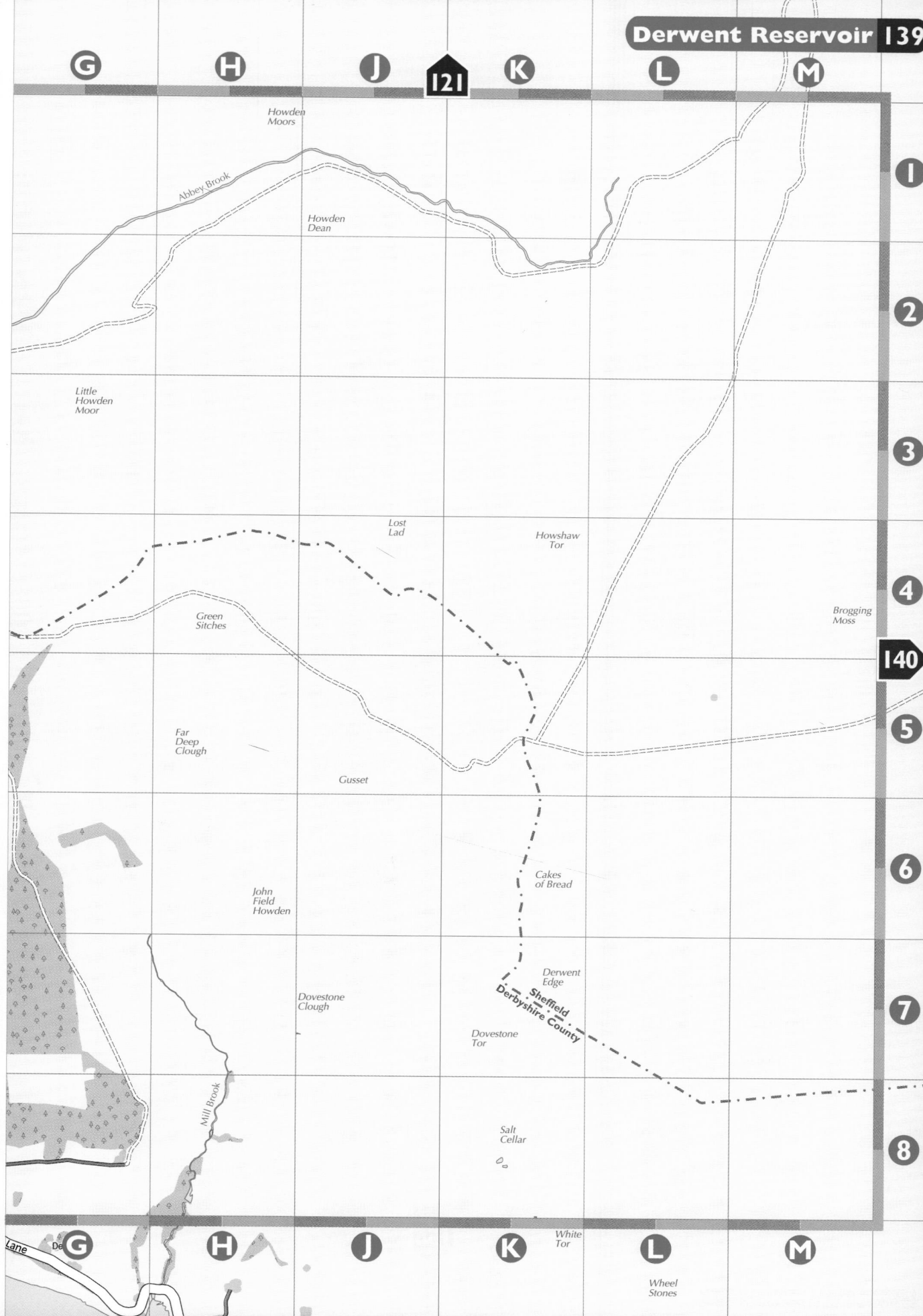

G H J **121** K L M

I
2
3
4
140
5
6
7
8

Howden
Moors

Abbey Brook

Howden
Dean

Little
Howden
Moor

Lost
Lad

Howshaw
Tor

Brogging
Moss

Green
Sitches

Far
Deep
Clough

Gusset

John
Field
Howden

Cakes
of Bread

Dovestone
Clough

Derwent
Edge

Sheffield
Derbyshire County

Dovestone
Tor

Mill Brook

Salt
Cellar

White
Tor

Wheel
Stones

Lane   De   G   H   J   K   L   M

A   B   C   **122**   D   E   F

I

2

3

4

139

5

6

7

8

A   B   **156**   D   E   F

Bradfield
Moors

Holling
Dale

Thornseat
Delf

Thornseat Road

Mortimer Road

Thompson House
Green

Holling
Dale
Plantation

Bole Edge
Plantation

Lane Head
Road

Hall
Lane

Hallfield

Dale Dike
Resevoir

Brogging
Moss

Strines Dike

Foulstone
Dell

Foulstone
Moor

PH

Strines

Strines
Resevoir

Strines
Moor

Sugworth
Hall

Bents
House

Moor
Lodge

Strines
Edge

Sheffield
Derbyshire County

Sugworth Road

Rising
Clough

G H J 123 K L M

1
High
Brad
Kirk Edge

2

Brown House Lane

Woodfall Lane

Mortimer Road

Windy Bank

Agden
Resevoir

Woodseats

Thornseat

Dale Road

The Sands

Fair
House
Lane

PO Low
Bradfield

Walker House

Annet Lane

Smithy
Bridge
Rd

Dale
Croft

Lamb

3

Hill

Bradfield
Dale

Plumpton Lane

Edgefield Farm

Mill Lee Lane

Mill Lee Road

Blindside Lane

Tor Farm

New Roa

4

142

5

F

Hoar stones Road

Ughill Road

Wet
Shaw Lane

Ughill

Tinker Bottom

6

Sugworth
Road

Bradfield
Moors

West Lane

Platts Farm

Platts
Lane

Corker
Walls

Corker

7

Hall
Broom

Lane

Stake Hill Road

Ughill Moors

8

G H J 157 K L M

Crawshaw
m

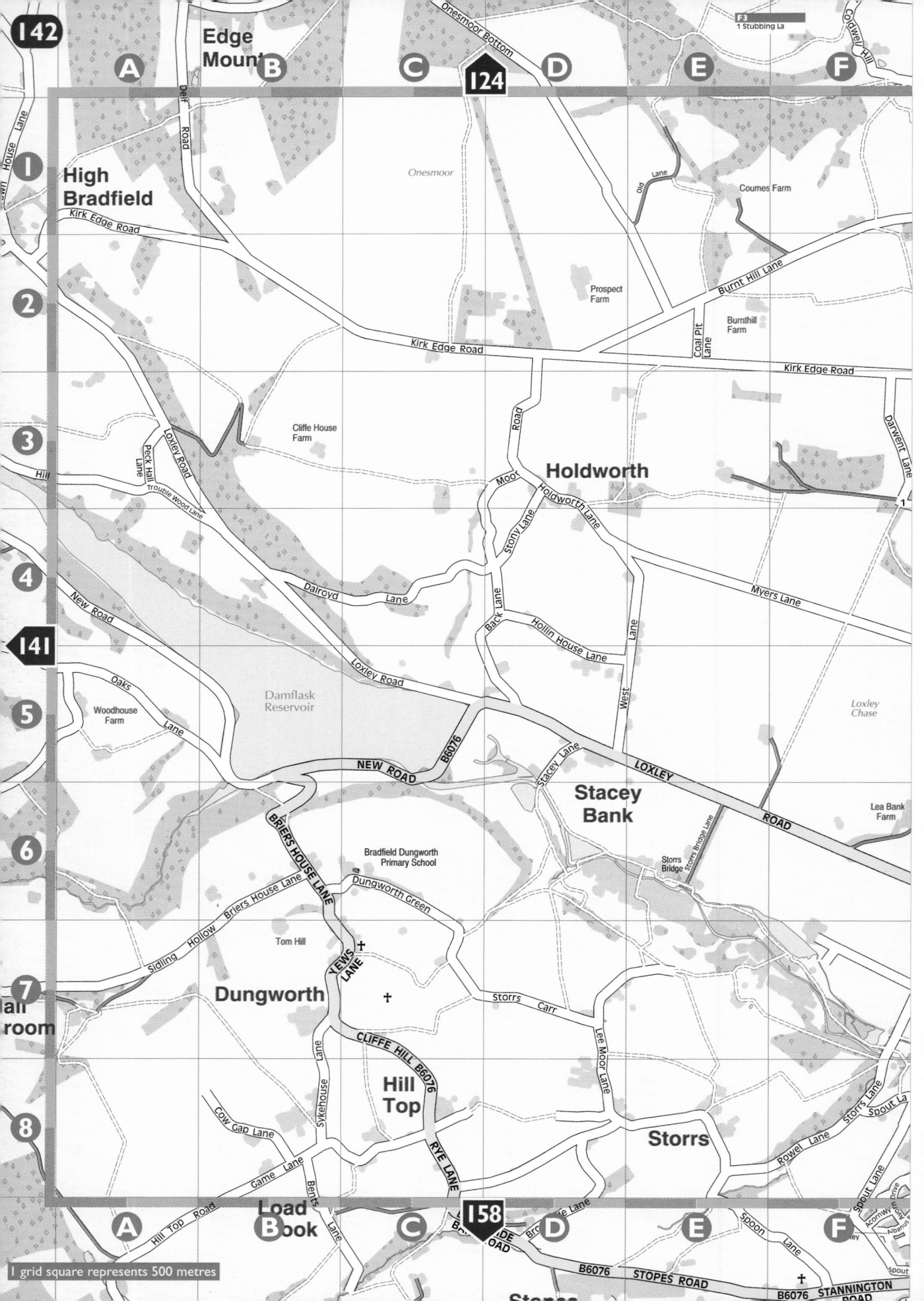

A Edge **B** Mount **C** 124 **D** **E** **F**

1 High Bradfield

Kirk Edge Road

Onesmoor

Coumes Farm

Old Lane

Burnt Hill Lane

2 Kirk Edge Road Prospect Farm

Coal Pit Lane

Burnthill Farm

Kirk Edge Road

3 Cliffe House Farm

Hill

Peck Hall Lane

Loxley Road

Trouble Wood Lane

Moor Road

Stony Lane

Holdworth Lane

Holdworth

Darwent Lane

4 Dalroyd Lane

New Road

Back Lane

Hollin House Lane

Myers Lane

Loxley Road

West Lane

Loxley Chase

5 Oaks Lane

Woodhouse Farm

Damflask Reservoir

New Road B6076

Stacey Lane

LOXLEY

Lea Bank Farm

Stacey Bank

6 BRIERS HOUSE LANE

NEW ROAD

Bradfield Dungworth Primary School

Dungworth Green

Storrs Bridge

Storrs Bridge Lane

ROAD

Sidling Hollow

Briers House Lane

Tom Hill

YEWS LANE

†

7 **Dungworth**

†

Storrs Carr

Lee Moor Lane

Hall room

8 Cow Gap Lane

Sykehouse Lane

CLIFFE HILL B6076

Hill Top

RYE LANE

Rowel Lane

Storrs Lane

Spout Lane

Storrs

Game Lane

Bents Lane

A Hill Top Road **B** Load Book **C** 158 **D** Browside Road **E** Spoon Lane **F**

B6076 STOPES ROAD

Coldwell Hill Road

F3 1 Stubbing La

B6076 STANNINGTON

G1 1 Naylor Gv
H1 1 Haggstones Dr 2 Highcliffe Dr 3 Holmesfield
J1 1 Ashbourne Gv
L5 1 Wadsley La
G8 1 Red Oak La
125
144
159
M7 1 Avondale Rd 2 Greenock St
M5 1 Ganton Rd
L8 1 Stannington Ri
L7 1 Findon Pl
L6 1 Wade Meadow
Worrall
Middlewood
Wadsley
Hillsborough
Loxley
Malinbridge
Birley
Stannington
LANGSETT ROAD SOUTH A6102
MIDDLEWOOD RD NORTH
MIDDLEWOOD ROAD
LOXLEY ROAD
B6077
HOLME LANE
A6101
B6076
B6079
Bradfield School
Burton Cemetery
Yews Day Hospital
Low Ash Farm
Beeley Wood
Loxley Common
Merlin Theatre
Wisewood Secondary School
Wisewood Cemetery
River Loxley
River Don
Myers Grove School
Shooters Grove Primary School
Nook Lane Junior School
Rivelin Primary School
Dykeshall Medical Cen
Far Lane Medical Cen
Cupola Gallery
Hurst
Long Lane
Stubbing Lane
Worrall Road
Stockarth Lane
Beeley Wood Lane
Hurst Common Lane
Boggard Lane
Mowson Lane
Rural Lane
Wadsley Lane
Ben Lane
Rodney Hill
Black Lane
Greaves Lane
Myers Grove Lane
Rivelin Bank
Watersmeet Road
Wisewood Road
Dykes Hall Road
Findon Road
Hallowmoor Road
Dial House Road
Laird Road
Aldene Road
Cox Road
Studfield Road

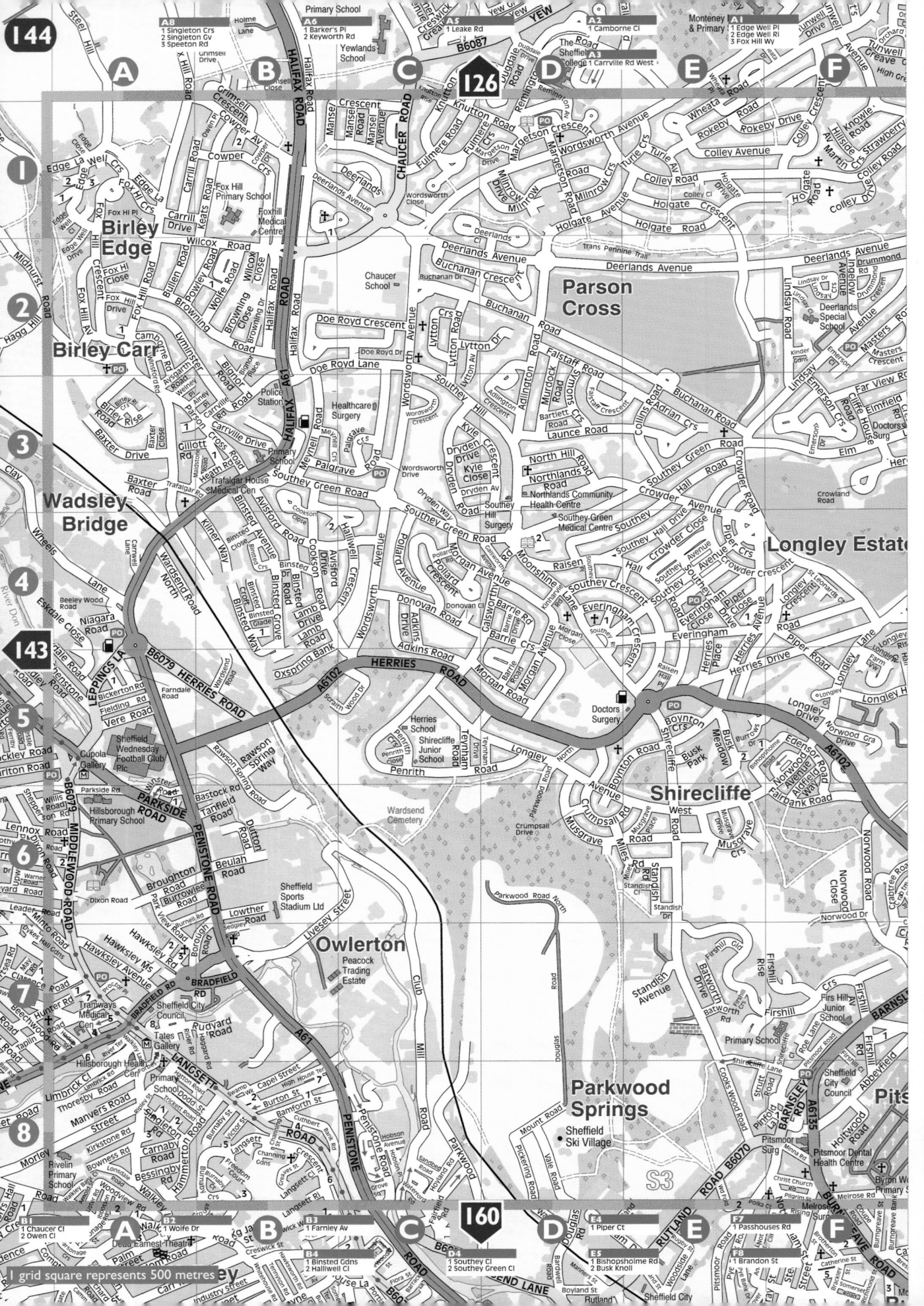

144
126
143
160
A8
1 Singleton Crs
2 Singleton Gv
3 Speeton Rd
A6
1 Barker's Pl
2 Keyworth Rd
A5
1 Leake Rd
A2
1 Camborne Cl
A3
1 Carrville Rd West
A1
1 Edge Well Pl
2 Edge Well Rl
3 Fox Hill Wy
Primary School
Yewlands School
The Sheffield College
Monteney & Primary
B6087
YEW
Birley Edge
Birley Carr
Wadsley Bridge
Parson Cross
Longley Estate
Shirecliffe
Owlerton
Parkwood Springs
Sheffield Ski Village
S3
Fox Hill Primary School
Foxhill Medical Centre
Chaucer School
Deerlands Special School
Police Station
Healthcare Surgery
Primary School
Trafalgar House Medical Cen
Northlands Community Health Centre
Southey Green Medical Centre
Southey Hill Surgery
Doctors Surgery
Herries School
Shirecliffe Junior School
Sheffield Wednesday Football Club Plc
Cupola Gallery
Hillsborough Primary School
Wardsend Cemetery
Sheffield Sports Stadium Ltd
Peacock Trading Estate
Tramways Medical Cen
Sheffield City Council
Tates Gallery
Hillsborough Health Cen
Rivelin Primary School
Firs Hill Junior School
Pitsmoor Surg
Pitsmoor Dental Health Centre
Sheffield City Council
Halifax Road
Chaucer Road
Deerlands Avenue
Buchanan Road
Southey Green Road
Herries Road
A6102
B6079 Herries Road
A61
Penistone Road
Middlewood Road
B6079
Parkside Road
Bradfield Rd
Langsett Road
Barnsley Rd
A6135
Burngreave Road
Rutland Road B6070
Trans Pennine Trail
B1
1 Chaucer Cl
2 Owen Cl
B2
1 Wolfe Dr
B3
1 Farnley Av
B4
1 Binsted Gdns
2 Halliwell Cl
D4
1 Southey Cl
2 Southey Green Cl
E4
1 Piper Ct
E5
1 Bishopsholme Rd
2 Busk Knoll
F7
1 Passhouses Rd
F8
1 Brandon St
Dead Earnest Theatre
Sheffield City
1 grid square represents 500 metres

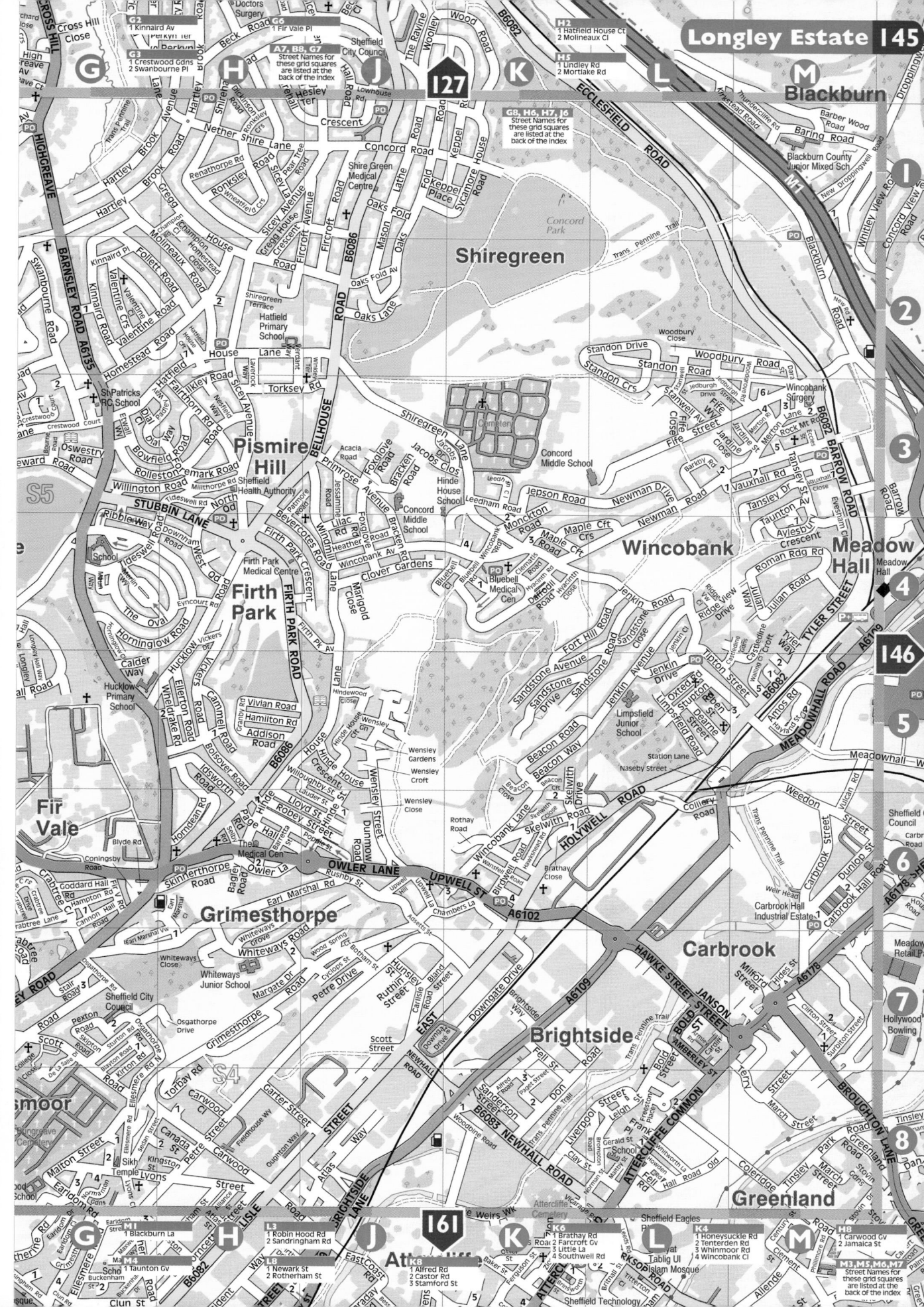
G2
1 Kinnaird Av
G3
1 Crestwood Gdns
2 Swanbourne Pl
G6
1 Fir Vale Pl
A7, B8, G7
Street Names for these grid squares are listed at the back of the index
H2
1 Hatfield House Ct
2 Molineaux Cl
H5
1 Lindley Rd
2 Mortlake Rd
G8, H6, H7, J6
Street Names for these grid squares are listed at the back of the index
127
146
161
Blackburn
Blackburn County Junior Mixed Sch
Shiregreen
Concord Park
Shire Green Medical Centre
Hatfield Primary School
St Patricks RC School
Pismire Hill
Sheffield Health Authority
Concord Middle School
Hinde House School
Cemetery
Wincobank Surgery
Wincobank
Meadow Hall
Firth Park
Firth Park Medical Centre
Bluebell Medical Cen
Hucklow Primary School
Limpsfield Junior School
Fir Vale
The Medical Cen
Grimesthorpe
Whiteways Junior School
Sheffield City Council
Carbrook
Carbrook Hall Industrial Estate
Meadowhall Retail Park
Hollywood Bowling
Brightside
Greenland
Attercliffe Cemetery
Sheffield Eagles
Islam Mosque
Sheffield Technology
S4
S5
HIGHCREAVE
BARNSLEY ROAD A6135
ECCLESFIELD ROAD
BELLHOUSE ROAD
FIRTH PARK ROAD
STUBBIN LANE
OWLER LANE
UPWELL ST
HOLYWELL ROAD
MEADOWHALL ROAD
TYLER STREET
BARROW ROAD
HAWKE STREET
JANSON STREET
BROUGHTON LANE
ATTERCLIFFE COMMON
B6083 NEWHALL ROAD
BRIGHTSIDE LANE
M1
A6102
A6109
A6178
B6086
B6082
M1
1 Blackburn La
M4
1 Taunton Gv
L3
1 Robin Hood Rd
2 Sandringham Rd
L8
1 Newark St
2 Rotherham St
K8
1 Alfred Rd
2 Castor Rd
3 Stamford St
K6
1 Brathay Rd
2 Farcroft Gv
3 Little La
4 Southwell Rd
K4
1 Honeysuckle Rd
2 Tenterden Rd
3 Whinmoor Rd
4 Wincobank Cl
H8
1 Carwood Gv
2 Jamaica St
M3, M5, M6, M7
Street Names for these grid squares are listed at the back of the index

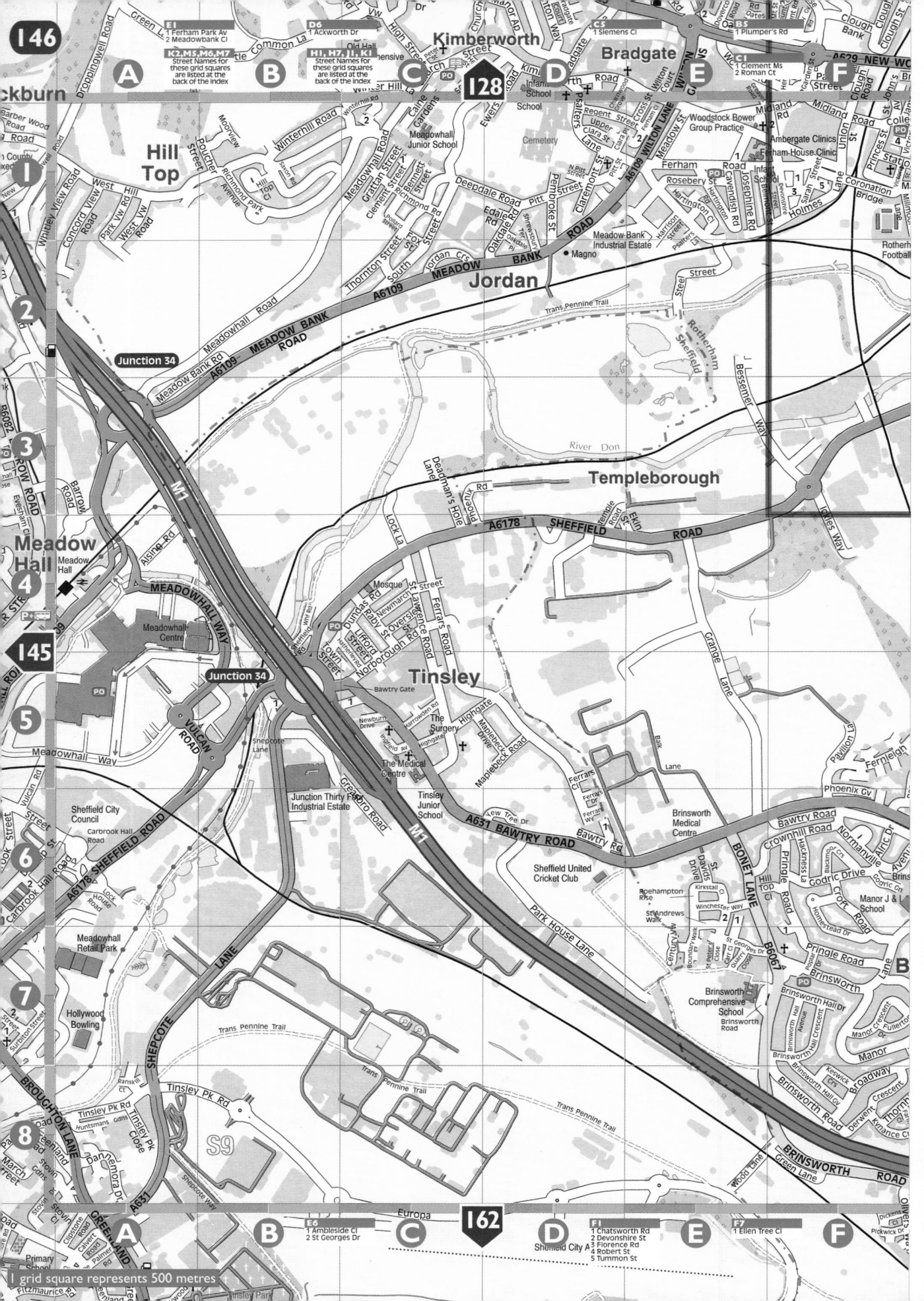
146
145
128
162
E1
1 Ferham Park Av
2 Meadowbank Cl
K2,M5,M6,M7
Street Names for these grid squares are listed at the back of the index
D6
1 Ackworth Dr
H1, H7, J1, K1
Street Names for these grid squares are listed at the back of the index
C5
1 Siemens Cl
B5
1 Plumper's Rd
C1
1 Clement Ms
2 Roman Ct
Kimberworth
Bradgate
Hill Top
Jordan
Templeborough
Meadow Hall
Tinsley
Ferham
Junction 34
M1
A6109 MEADOW BANK ROAD
A6178 SHEFFIELD ROAD
A631 BAWTRY ROAD
A6109 WILTON LANE
A629 NEW WO
MEADOWHALL WAY
VULCAN ROAD
SHEPCOTE LANE
BROUGHTON LANE
BONET LANE
B6067
BRINSWORTH ROAD
Meadowhall Road
Meadow Bank Rd
Winterhill Road
Richmond Park Avenue
Whitley View Road
Concord View Road
Park Vw Rd
West Vw Road
West Hill
Poucher Street
Meadowhall Junior School
Deepdale Road
Pitt Street
Pembroke St
Claremont St
Wilton Lane
Meadow St
Woodstock Bower Group Practice
Ambergate Clinics
Ferham House Clinic
Midland Road
Coronation Bridge
Meadow Bank Industrial Estate
Magno
Trans Pennine Trail
River Don
Rotherham Sheffield
Steel Street
Bessemer Way
Ickles Way
Deadman's Hole Lane
Lock La
Grange Lane
Meadowhall Centre
Meadowhall Way
Mosque
St Lawrence Road
Ferrars Road
Norborough Rd
Town Street
The Surgery
The Medical Centre
Tinsley Junior School
Highgate
Maplebeck Road
Junction Thirty Four Industrial Estate
Greasbro Road
Sheffield City Council
Carbrook Hall Road
Meadowhall Retail Park
Hollywood Bowling
Sheffield United Cricket Club
Park House Lane
Balk Lane
Brinsworth Medical Centre
Brinsworth Comprehensive School
Bawtry Road
Crownhill Road
Pringle Road
Godric Drive
Manor J & I School
Brinsworth
Tinsley Pk Rd
Tinsley Pk Close
Shepcote Way
Europa
S9
Green Lane
Wood Lane
Phoenix Gv
Fernleigh
E6
1 Ambleside Cl
2 St Georges Dr
F1
1 Chatsworth Rd
2 Devonshire St
3 Florence Rd
4 Robert St
5 Tummon St
F7
1 Ellen Tree Cl
1 grid square represents 500 metres

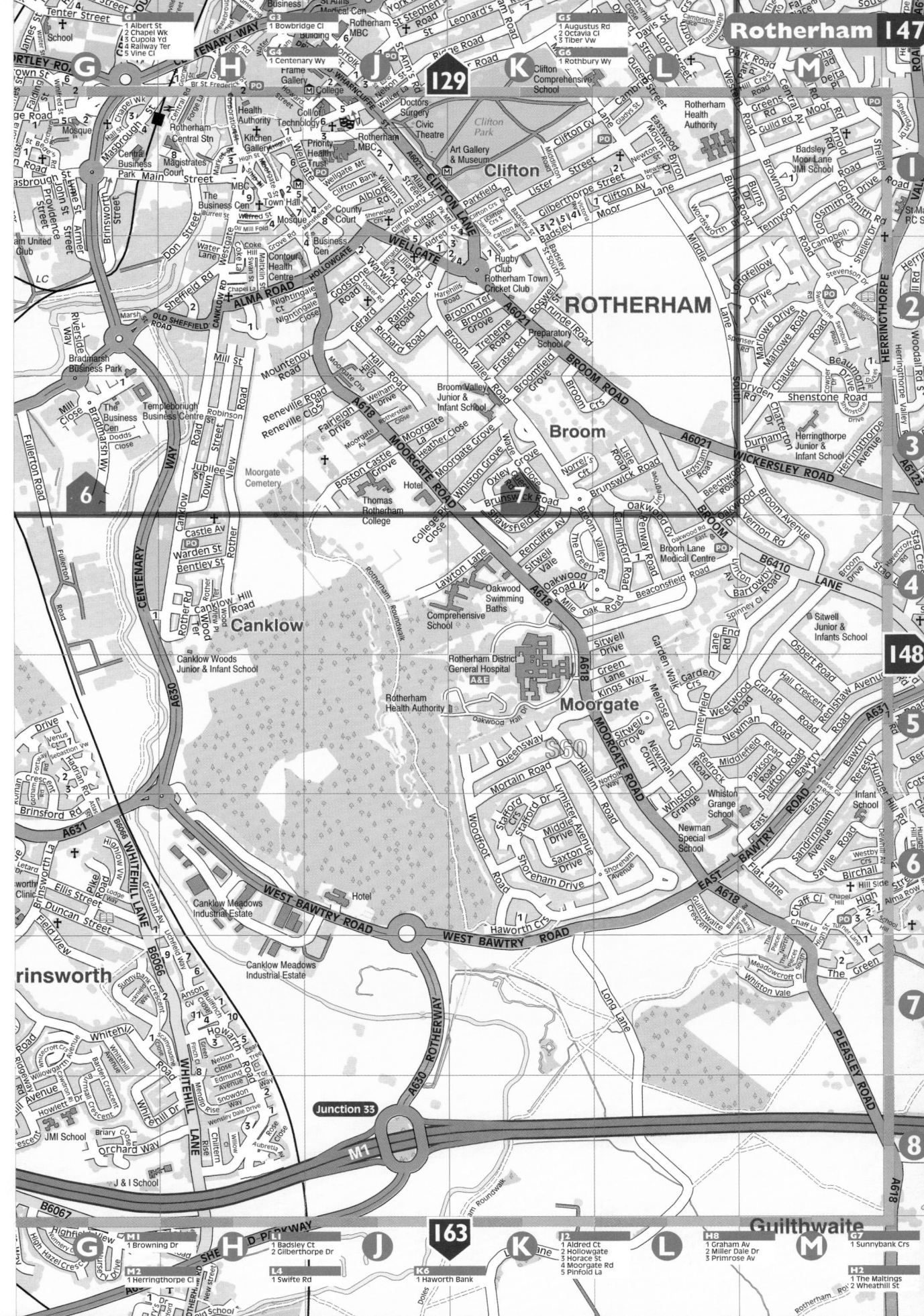
G1
1 Albert St
2 Chapel Wk
3 Cupola Yd
4 Railway Ter
5 Vine Cl
G3
1 Bowbridge Cl
G4
1 Centenary Wy
G5
1 Augustus Rd
2 Octavia Cl
3 Tiber Vw
G6
1 Rothbury Wy
129
Clifton
Clifton Park
Art Gallery & Museum
Clifton Comprehensive School
Rotherham Health Authority
Badsley Moor Lane JMI School
Rotherham Central Stn
Magistrates Court
Town Hall
County Court
Rugby Club
Rotherham Town Cricket Club
ROTHERHAM
Preparatory School
Bradmarsh Business Park
Templeborough Business Centre
Broom Valley Junior & Infant School
Broom
Herringthorpe Junior & Infant School
Moorgate Cemetery
Thomas Rotherham College
Broom Lane Medical Centre
Oakwood Swimming Baths
Comprehensive School
Canklow
Canklow Woods Junior & Infant School
Rotherham District General Hospital
A&E
Rotherham Health Authority
Moorgate
Sitwell Junior & Infants School
148
Whiston Grange School
Newman Special School
Infant School
Canklow Meadows Industrial Estate
Canklow Meadows Industrial Estate
WEST BAWTRY ROAD
MOORGATE ROAD
WICKERSLEY ROAD
BROOM ROAD
CENTENARY WAY
WHITEHILL LANE
PLEASLEY ROAD
ROTHERWAY
Junction 33
M1
rinsworth
JMI School
J & I School
Guilthwaite
163
M1
1 Browning Dr
M2
1 Herringthorpe Cl
L1
1 Badsley Ct
2 Gilberthorpe Dr
L4
1 Swifte Rd
K6
1 Haworth Bank
J2
1 Aldred Ct
2 Hollowgate
3 Horace St
4 Moorgate Rd
5 Pinfold La
H8
1 Graham Av
2 Miller Dale Dr
3 Primrose Av
G7
1 Sunnybank Crs
H2
1 The Maltings
2 Wheathill St

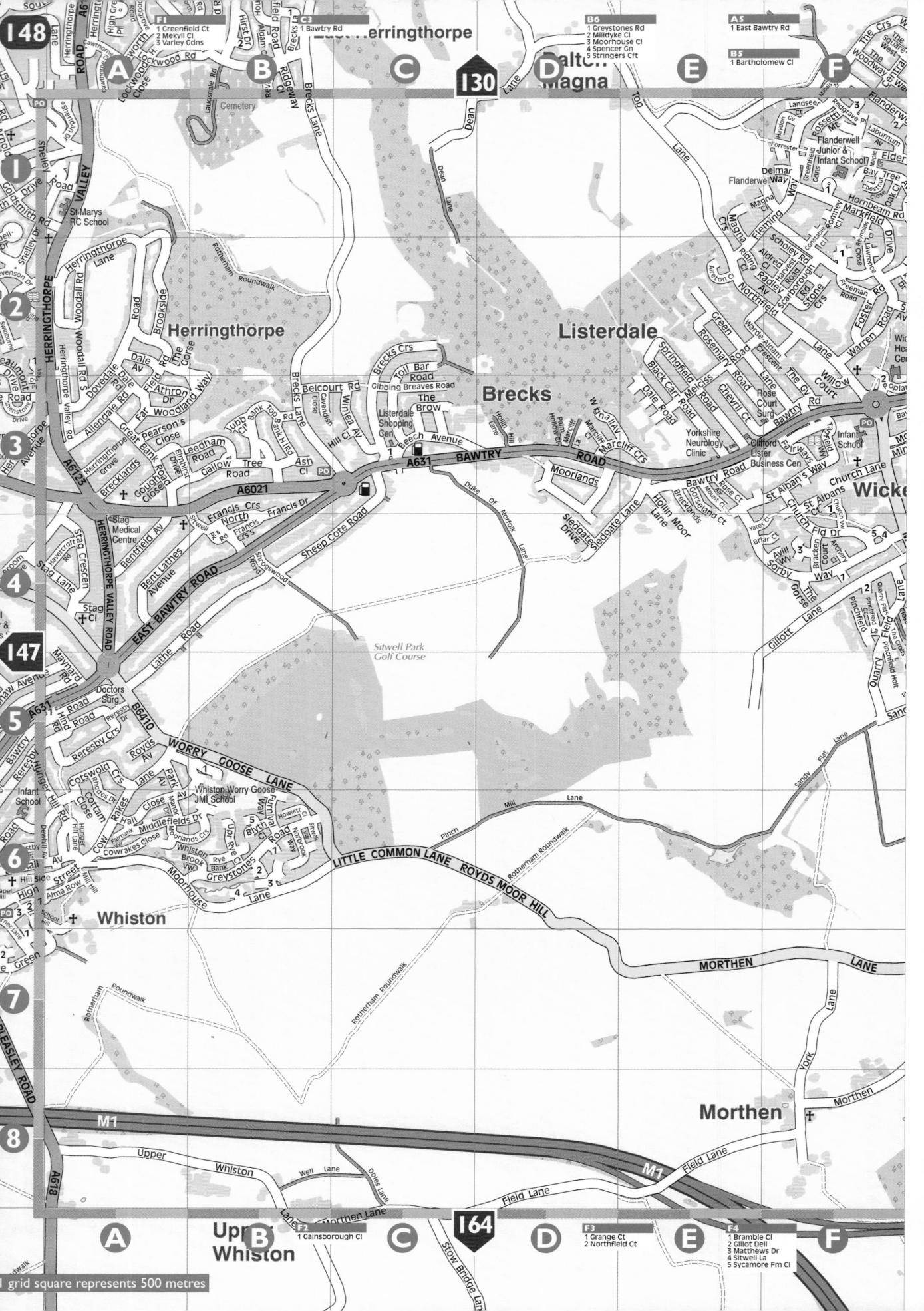
F1
1 Greenfield Ct
2 Mekyll Cl
3 Varley Gdns
C3
1 Bawtry Rd
B6
1 Greystones Rd
2 Milldyke Cl
3 Moorhouse Cl
4 Spencer Gn
5 Stringers Cft
A5
1 East Bawtry Rd
B5
1 Bartholomew Cl
130
Herringthorpe
Listerdale
Brecks
Whiston
Morthen
Sitwell Park
Golf Course
Herringthorpe Valley Road
East Bawtry Road
Bawtry Road
Worry Goose Lane
Little Common Lane
Royds Moor Hill
Morthen Lane
Brecks Lane
Sheep Cote Road
Lathe Road
Dean Lane
Top Lane
Stag Medical Centre
St Marys RC School
Whiston Worry Goose JMI School
Flanderwell Junior & Infant School
Yorkshire Neurology Clinic
Clifford Lister Business Cen
Listerdale Shopping Cen
Doctors Surg
Rose Court Surg
Cemetery
147
M1
A618
Pleasley Road
Upper Whiston Lane
Field Lane
Upper Whiston
164
F2
1 Gainsborough Cl
F3
1 Grange Ct
2 Northfield Ct
F4
1 Bramble Cl
2 Gillot Dell
3 Matthews Dr
4 Sitwell La
5 Sycamore Fm Cl
1 grid square represents 500 metres

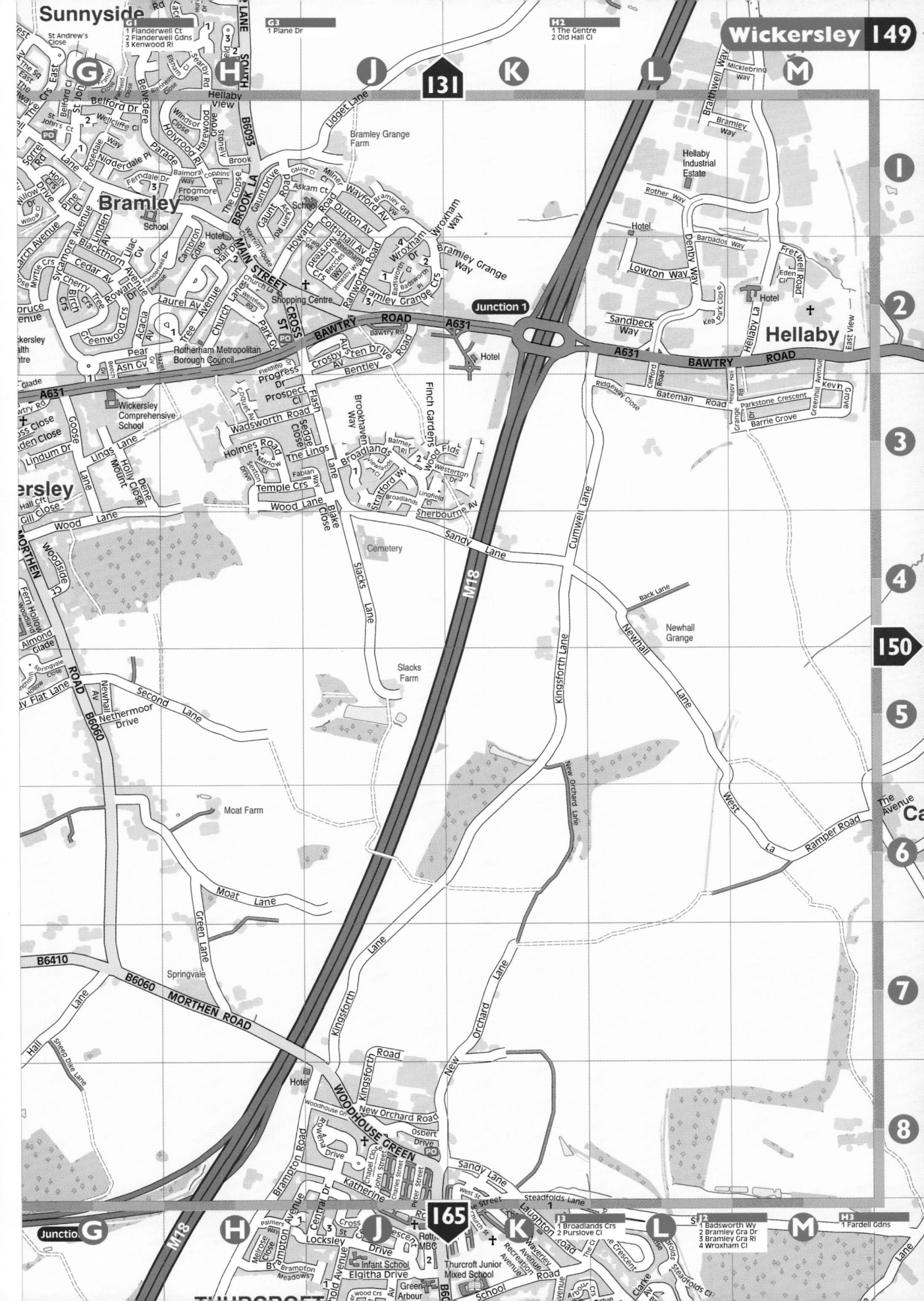

Sunnyside
G1
1 Flanderwell Ct
2 Flanderwell Gdns
3 Kenwood Rl
G3
1 Plane Dr
H2
1 The Gentre
2 Old Hall Cl
131
Bramley Grange Farm
Hellaby Industrial Estate
Bramley
School
Hotel
Shopping Centre
Rotherham Metropolitan Borough Council
Junction 1
BAWTRY ROAD
A631
Hellaby
Wickersley Comprehensive School
Cemetery
Newhall Grange
150
Slacks Farm
Moat Farm
Springvale
Hotel
M18
B6060 MORTHEN ROAD
B6410
WOODHOUSE GREEN
Sandy Lane
Wood Lane
Newhall Lane
Kingsforth Lane
Cumwell Lane
Back Lane
Moat Lane
Green Lane
New Orchard Lane
Ramper Road
Slacks Lane
Lidget Lane
MAIN STREET
BROOK LA
B6093
SOUTH LANE
Infant School
Thurcroft Junior Mixed School
165
J3
1 Broadlands Crs
2 Purslove Cl
J2
1 Badsworth Wy
2 Bramley Gra Dr
3 Bramley Gra Rl
4 Wroxham Cl
H3
1 Fardell Gdns

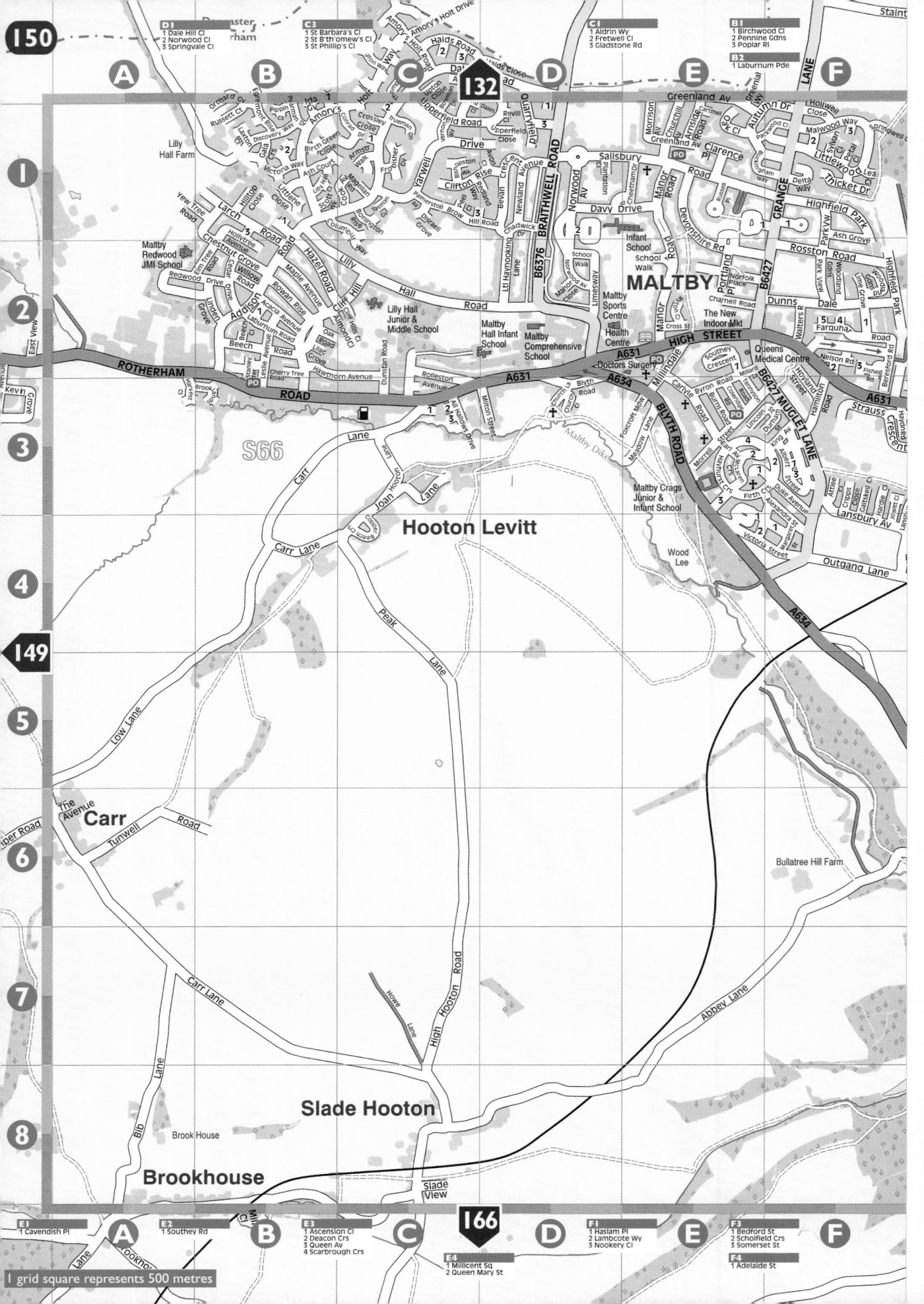
D1
1 Dale Hill Cl
2 Norwood Cl
3 Springvale Cl
C3
1 St Barbara's Cl
2 St B'th'omew's Cl
3 St Phillip's Cl
C1
1 Aldrin Wy
2 Fretwell Cl
3 Gladstone Rd
B1
1 Birchwood Cl
2 Pennine Gdns
3 Poplar Rl
B2
1 Laburnum Pde
132
149
166
A
B
C
D
E
F
1
2
3
4
5
6
7
8
MALTBY
Hooton Levitt
Carr
Slade Hooton
Brookhouse
S66
ROTHERHAM ROAD
A631
A634
B6376
B6427
HIGH STREET
BLYTH ROAD
BRAITHWELL ROAD
MUGLET LANE
GRANGE LANE
Lilly Hall Farm
Lilly Hall Road
Maltby Redwood JMI School
Lilly Hall Junior & Middle School
Maltby Hall Infant School
Maltby Comprehensive School
Maltby Sports Centre
Health Centre
Doctors Surgery
The New Indoor Mkt
Queens Medical Centre
Infant School
Maltby Crags Junior & Infant School
Maltby Dike
Wood Lee
Bullatree Hill Farm
Brook House
Carr Lane
Low Lane
Tunwell Road
The Avenue
Peak Lane
High Hooton Road
Howe Lane
Bib Lane
Abbey Lane
Joan Hooton Lane
Slade View
Outgang Lane
Greenland Av
Salisbury Road
Davy Drive
Devonshire Rd
Highfield Park
Rosston Road
Dunns Dale
Strauss Crescent
Lansbury Av
Victoria Street
E1
1 Cavendish Pl
E2
1 Southey Rd
E3
1 Ascension Cl
2 Deacon Crs
3 Queen Av
4 Scarbrough Crs
E4
1 Millicent Sq
2 Queen Mary St
F1
1 Haslam Pl
2 Lambcote Wy
3 Nookery Cl
F3
1 Bedford St
2 Scholfield Crs
3 Somerset St
F4
1 Adelaide St
1 grid square represents 500 metres

133

G H J K L M

I
2
3
4
152
5
6
7
8

Scotch Spring Lane

Maltby Colliery

Doncaster
TICKHILL ROAD
Rotherham

Carr House

Lumley Crescent

Elgar Drive
Quilter
Purcel Stanford Cl Road
Cl
Sousa St
Mortimer Novello
Road St

Lee Croft

Birks Holt
Drive

Stoney Well Lane

Sandbeck Lodge

Woolthwaite Farm

Sandbeck Lane

Sandbeck Lane

Rough Park

The Grove

A634

Gipsy Lane

Sandbeck Hall

Abbey House

• Roche Abbey

A634

Stone

King's Wood Lane

Horseshoe Lane

Flat Lane

New Road

King's Wood

G H J **167** K L M

King's Wood Lane

Flat Lane

134
168
151
A
B
C
D
E
F
1
2
3
4
5
6
7
8
SUNDERLAND STREET A631
Walnut Av
St Mary's
Tickhill C of E School
Davy Gallery
Sarahs Gallery
Castle Cl
Sunderland Pl
Lancaster Crescent
Lumley Dr
Broom Close
Kg Edwards Rd
Crown Rd
Pinfold
Pinfold Cl
West Gate A60
Rotherham Road
Stone La
Dam Road
Castle Ct
Lindrick Close
Stone Grey Cl
Home Mdw
Lindrick
Lindrick Lane
Paper Mill Dike
Limestone Hill
A631
A60 Worksop Road
Crooked Head Lane
Water Lane
Whinny Haugh Lane
Bagley Farm
Blyth Gate Lane
A60
Folds Lane
South Wongs Farm
Folds Farm
Doncaster
Nottinghamshire County
Styrrup Carr
A60 Malpas Hill A60
Styrrup Lane
Thornbury Hill Lane
Park House
Rotherham
Nottinghamshire County
B6463
Oldcotes
A634 Maltby Road
Wynlea Drive
Elmsmere Drive
Blyth

1 grid square represents 500 metres

Spital
Hill

J3
1 Common La

K2
1 Rutland Dr

K3
1 Cambridge Rd
2 Dorset Dr
3 Melbourne Gv
4 Windermere Av

Meadow
Drive

Moorhouse Farm

BLYTH ROAD

TICKHILL ROAD B6463

BAWTRY ROAD

Doncaster
Nottinghamshire County

Plumtree
Farm

North Border County
Secondary School

Tickhill
Low
Common

Harworth

Common Lane

A1(M)

Common

Bracken Way

Bramble
Way

Thornhill Rd

Church Wk

Briar Ct

Holly
Ct

Gregory
Cres

Church La

PO

MAIN STREET

The
Green

B6463

STYRRUP ROAD

Moor
Top
Rd

Meadow Way

Crescent
Avenna

Sherwood
Road

Grange View

Grange Dr

Bawtry
Road

West Street

East Street

Dorchester Road

Woodside
View

Sandrock Road

Bauk

Oxford Drive

Smith
Sq

Thompson
Av

Amanda
Road

Beech Rd

Whitby Road

Lindsey Road

Greenwood
Av

Harworth
Medical
Centre

Sandymount

Grange View

St Patricks
Primary
School

Bircotes
Sports
Centre

Snipe Park Rd

Crewe
Rd

Waterslack Rd

Howard
Rd

Norfolk
Drive

Wh

Lane

Devonshire
Rd

Saxon
Way

Mayfair
Cl

Festival Avenue

Beverley Road

Grosvenor

Herriot
Rd

Talbot Road

Gilbert Road

Infant
School

Junior
School

Alexandra Road

Shrewsbury Road

PO

Scrooby Road

Colley
Rd

Cemetery

Bawtry
Road

Russell
Av

Top
Court

Scrooby
Close

Khan Medical
Centre

Harworth C of E
Primary School

Blyth Road

Snape Lane

154

Brunel Close

Brunel
Gate

Harworth Park
Industrial Estate

Oaklands
Drive

Serlby Road

Paddin

Pinfold Lane

MAIN STREET

Styrrup

B6463

Styrrup Lane

Styrrup Lane

Whitewater Lane

A1(M)

DONCASTER BY-PASS

169

Blyth Road

BAWTRY ROAD

A614

Nook
Flatt
Wood

Holme Farm

Whitewater
Common

Harworth
Avenue

L3
1 Holderness Cl
2 Sandymount East
3 Sandymount W

L2
1 Welbeck Rd

River

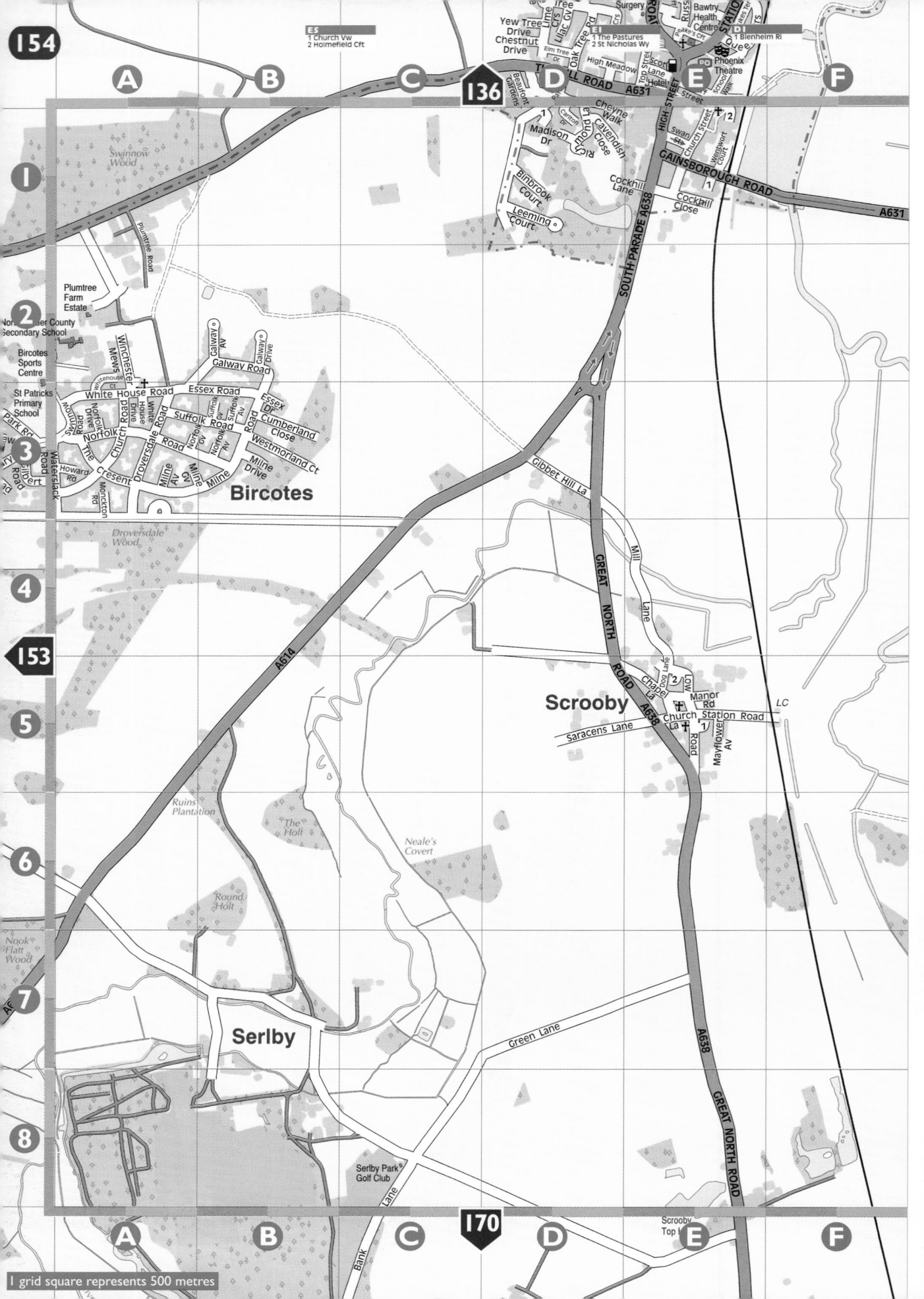
154
153
136
170
E5
1 Church Vw
2 Holmefield Cft
E1
1 The Pastures
2 St Nicholas Wy
D1
1 Blenheim Ri
A
B
C
D
E
F
1
2
3
4
5
6
7
8
Yew Tree Drive
Chestnut Drive
Lime Crs
Lilac Gv
Oak Tree Rd
Elm Tree Dr
High Meadow
Top Street
Scot Lane
Hotel
Surgery
Bawtry Health Centre
Phoenix Theatre
School Walk
Peake's Cft
STATION
Beaufont Gardens
ROAD
A631
HIGH STREET
Street
Cheyne Walk
Cavendish Close
Madison Dr
Carlton Dr
Binbrook Court
Leeming Court
Cockhill Lane
Cockhill Close
Swan St
Church Street
Wentworth Court
GAINSBOROUGH ROAD
SOUTH PARADE A638
Swinnow Wood
Plumtree Road
Plumtree Farm Estate
Secondary School
Bircotes Sports Centre
St Patricks Primary School
Winchester Mews
Whitehouse Ct
White House Road
Essex Road
Galway Av
Galway Drive
Galway Road
Essex Dr
Cumberland Close
Westmorland Ct
Suffolk Road
Suffolk Gv
Suffolk Av
Norfolk Gv
Norfolk Av
Norfolk Drive
Norfolk
Swinnow Road
Church Road
White House Drive
Droversdale Road
Road
The Cresent
Howard Rd
Moncton Rd
Milne Av
Milne Gv
Milne Drive
Milne
Watersiack Road
Park Rd
Bircotes
Droversdale Wood
Gibbet Hill La
Mill Lane
GREAT NORTH ROAD
A614
A638
Dog Lane
Low Road
Chapel La
Manor Rd
Church La
Station Road
LC
Scrooby
Saracens Lane
Mayflower Av
Ruins Plantation
The Holt
Neale's Covert
Round Holt
Nook Flatt Wood
Serlby
Green Lane
Serlby Park Golf Club
Lane
Bank
Scrooby Top
1 grid square represents 500 metres

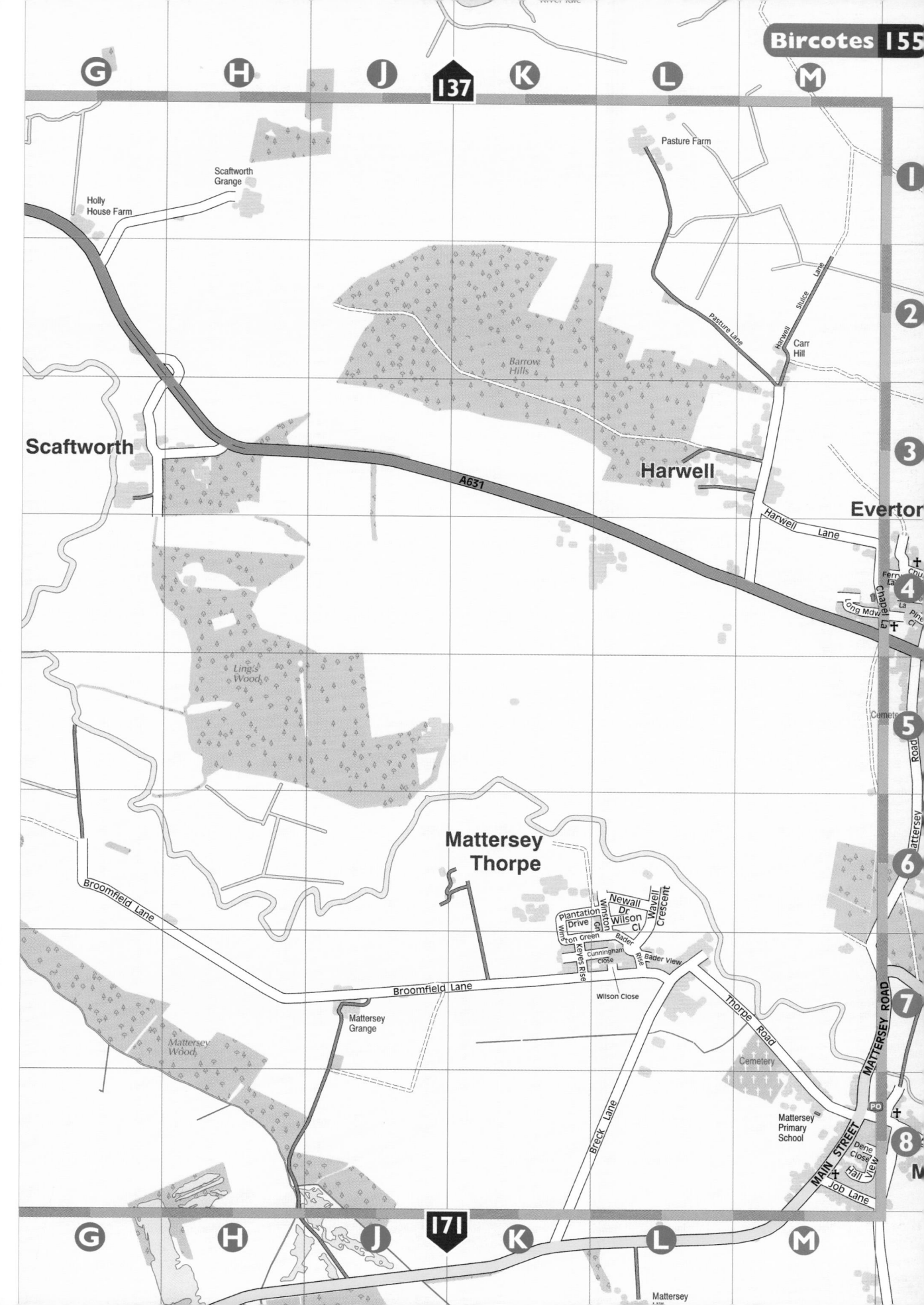

137

G H J K L M

1

Pasture Farm

2

Pasture Lane

Harwell
Sluice Lane

Carr
Hill

Scaftworth Grange

Holly
House Farm

Barrow
Hills

Scaftworth

A631

Harwell

3

Harwell Lane

Everton

Ferry La
Long Mdw
Chapel La
Pine Cl

4

Ling's
Wood

Cemetery

5

Mattersey Road

6

**Mattersey
Thorpe**

Plantation
Drive
Winston Green
Keyes Rise
Cunningham Close
Winston Cl
Newall Dr
Wilson Cl
Wavell Crescent
Bader Rise
Bader View
Wilson Close

Broomfield Lane

Thorpe Road

7

Broomfield Lane

Mattersey
Grange

Mattersey
Wood

Cemetery

Mattersey Road

Breck Lane

Mattersey
Primary
School

PO

Main Street
Dene Close
Hall View
Job Lane

8

171

G H J K L M

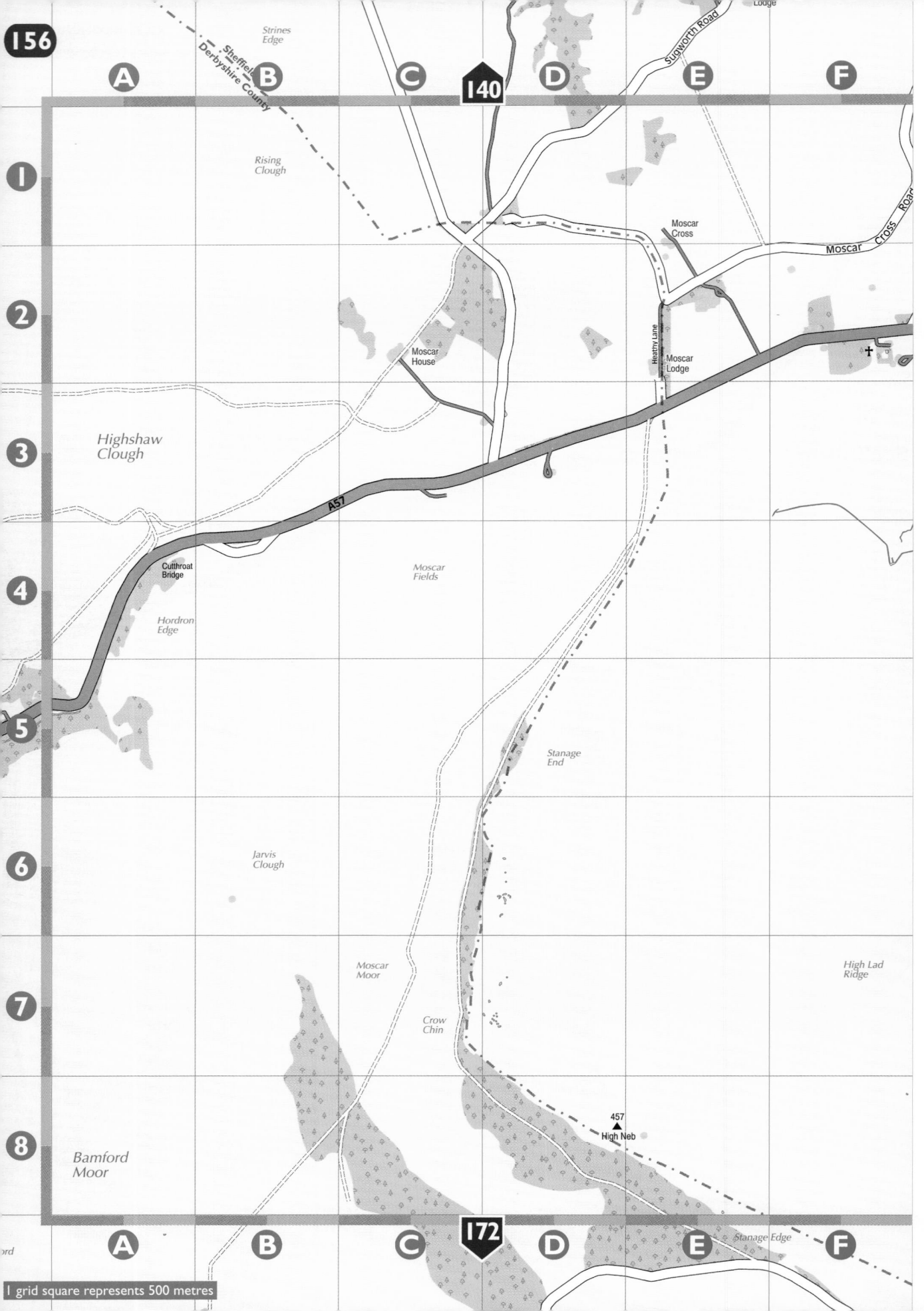

Strines
Edge

Sheffield
Derbyshire County

Rising
Clough

Sugworth Road

Lodge

Moscar
Cross

Moscar Cross Road

Moscar
House

Heathy Lane

Moscar
Lodge

Highshaw
Clough

A57

Cutthroat
Bridge

Moscar
Fields

Hordron
Edge

Stanage
End

Jarvis
Clough

High Lad
Ridge

Moscar
Moor

Crow
Chin

457
High Neb

Bamford
Moor

Stanage Edge

1 grid square represents 500 metres

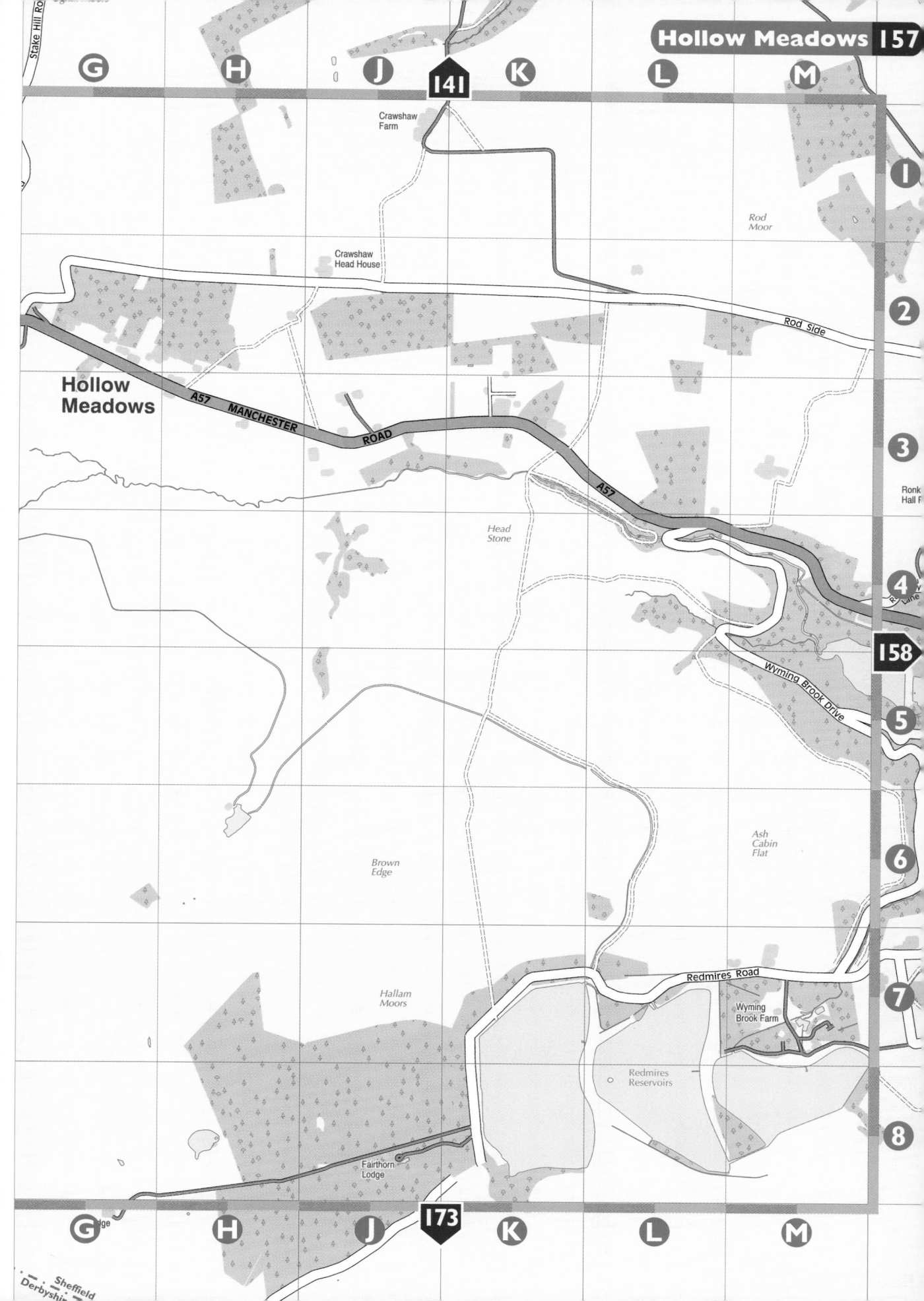

G   H   J   **141**   K   L   M

I

Crawshaw
Farm

Rod
Moor

2

Crawshaw
Head House

Rod Side

**Hollow
Meadows**

A57 MANCHESTER   ROAD

A57

3

Ronk
Hall F

Head
Stone

4

R Line

158

Wyming Brook Drive

5

Ash
Cabin
Flat

6

Brown
Edge

Redmires Road

7

Wyming
Brook Farm

Hallam
Moors

Redmires
Reservoirs

8

Fairthorn
Lodge

Sheffield
Derbyshi

Stake Hill Ro

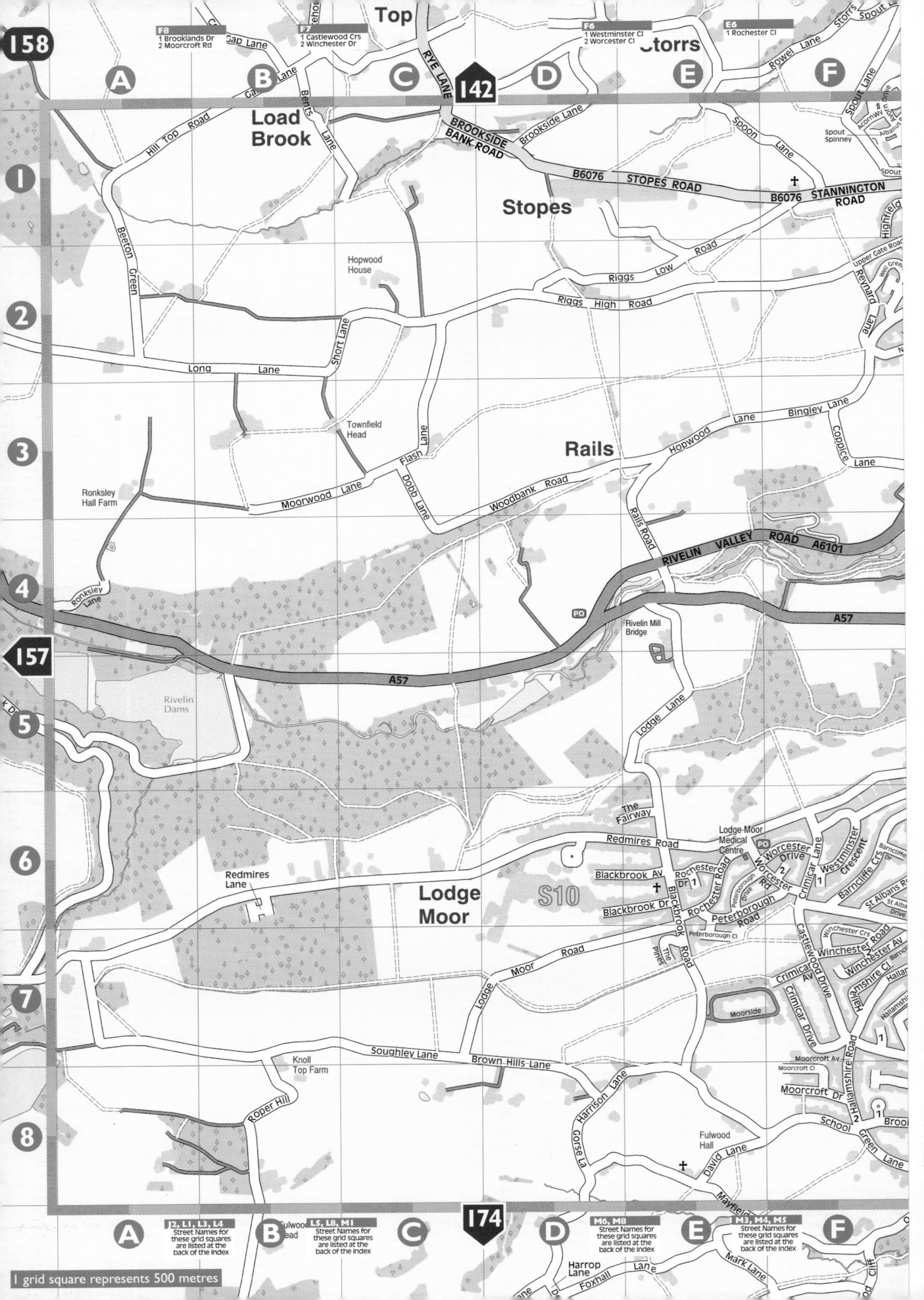
F8
1 Brooklands Dr
2 Moorcroft Rd
F7
1 Castlewood Crs
2 Winchester Dr
F6
1 Westminster Cl
2 Worcester Cl
E6
1 Rochester Cl
Top
Storrs
142
Load
Brook
Stopes
Rails
Lodge
Moor
S10
Hill Top Road
Gap Lane
Bents Lane
Rye Lane
Brookside Bank Road
Brookside Lane
B6076 Stopes Road
B6076 Stannington Road
Spoon Lane
Spout Lane
Rowel Lane
Spout Spinney
Beeton Green
Hopwood House
Riggs Low Road
Riggs High Road
Short Lane
Long Lane
Townfield Head
Flash Lane
Hopwood Lane
Bingley Lane
Coppice Lane
Moorwood Lane
Dobb Lane
Woodbank Road
Ronksley Hall Farm
Rails Road
Rivelin Valley Road A6101
Ronksley Lane
A57
Rivelin Mill Bridge
Rivelin Dams
Lodge Lane
The Fairway
Redmires Road
Lodge Moor Medical Centre
Redmires Lane
Blackbrook Av
Blackbrook Dr
Blackbrook Road
Rochester Road
Rochester Dr
Worcester Drive
Worcester Rd
Peterborough Drive
Peterborough Road
Peterborough Cl
Crimicar Lane
Westminster Crescent
Barncliffe Crs
St Albans Rd
The Pines
Lodge Moor Road
Castlewood Drive
Winchester Crs
Winchester Road
Winchester Av
Crimicar Av
Crimicar Drive
Hallamshire Cl
Hallamshire Road
Moorside
Soughley Lane
Brown Hills Lane
Knoll Top Farm
Moorcroft Av
Moorcroft Cl
Moorcroft Dr
School Green Lane
Roper Hill
Harrison Lane
Gorse La
Fulwood Hall
David Lane
Mayfield
157
174
J2, L1, L3, L4 Street Names for these grid squares are listed at the back of the index
L5, L8, M1 Street Names for these grid squares are listed at the back of the index
M6, M8 Street Names for these grid squares are listed at the back of the index
M3, M4, M5 Street Names for these grid squares are listed at the back of the index
Harrop Lane
Foxhall Lane
Mark Lane
A B C D E F
1 2 3 4 5 6 7 8
1 grid square represents 500 metres

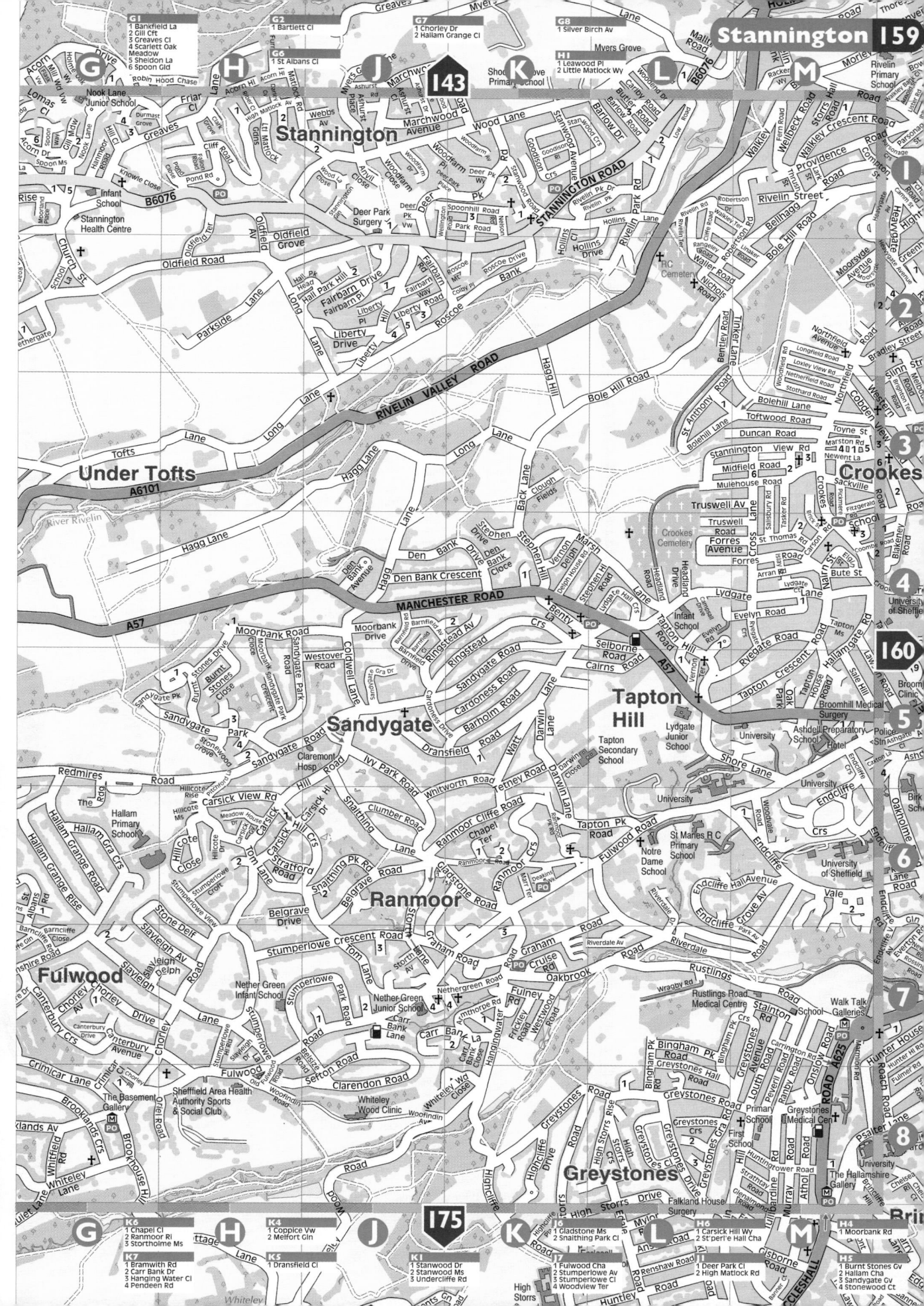

Stannington 159
G1
1 Bankfield La
2 Gill Cft
3 Greaves Cl
4 Scarlett Oak Meadow
5 Sheldon La
6 Spoon Gld
G2
1 Bartlett Cl
G6
1 St Albans Cl
G7
1 Chorley Dr
2 Hallam Grange Cl
G8
1 Silver Birch Av
H1
1 Leawood Pl
2 Little Matlock Wy
143
Stannington
Under Tofts
Sandygate
Tapton Hill
Crookes
Ranmoor
Fulwood
Greystones
STANNINGTON ROAD
RIVELIN VALLEY ROAD
MANCHESTER ROAD
A6101
A57
B6076
A625
River Rivelin
Nook Lane Junior School
Infant School
Stannington Health Centre
Deer Park Surgery
RC Cemetery
Crookes Cemetery
Infant School
Tapton Secondary School
Lydgate Junior School
Claremont Hosp
Hallam Primary School
University
Ashdell Preparatory School
Broomhill Medical Surgery
St Maries R C Primary School
Notre Dame School
University of Sheffield
Nether Green Infant School
Nether Green Junior School
Rustlings Road Medical Centre
Walk Talk Galleries
Whiteley Wood Clinic
Sheffield Area Health Authority Sports & Social Club
The Basement Gallery
Greystones Medical Cen
First School
Primary School
Falkland House Surgery
The Hallamshire Gallery
Rivelin Primary School
160
175
G
H
J
K
L
M
1
2
3
4
5
6
7
8
K6
1 Chapel Cl
2 Ranmoor Ri
3 Storthholme Ms
K7
1 Bramwith Rd
2 Carr Bank Dr
3 Hanging Water Cl
4 Pendeen Rd
K4
1 Coppice Vw
2 Melfort Gln
K5
1 Dransfield Cl
K1
1 Stanwood Dr
2 Stanwood Ms
3 Undercliffe Rd
J6
1 Gladstone Ms
2 Snaithing Park Cl
J7
1 Fulwood Cha
2 Stumperlowe Av
3 Stumperlowe Cl
4 Woodview Ter
H6
1 Carsick Hill Wy
2 St Peri'e Hall Cha
J1
1 Deer Park Cl
2 High Matlock Rd
H4
1 Moorbank Rd
H5
1 Burnt Stones Gv
2 Hallam Cha
3 Sandygate Gv
4 Stonewood Ct

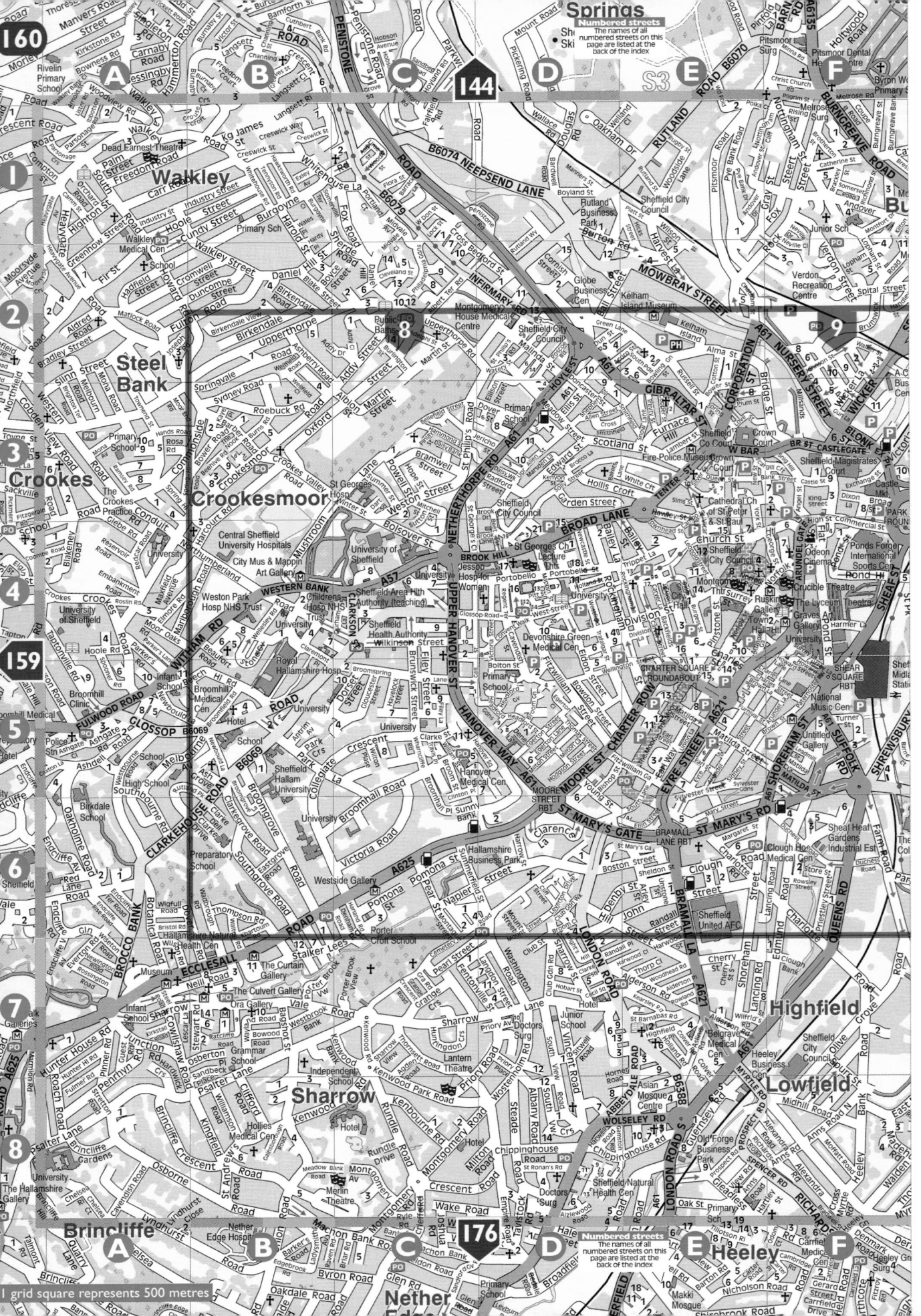

160
144
159
176
A
B
C
D
E
F
1
2
3
4
5
6
7
8
Springs
Numbered streets
The names of all numbered streets on this page are listed at the back of the index
S3
Walkley
Steel Bank
Crookes
Crookesmoor
Highfield
Lowfield
Sharrow
Brincliffe
Heeley
Nether Edge
B6074 NEEPSEND LANE
INFIRMARY RD
MOWBRAY STREET
A61 NURSERY STREET
A61 CORPORATION ST
GIBRALTAR ST
BROAD LANE
BROOK HILL
WESTERN BANK
A57
UPPER HANOVER ST
HANOVER WAY A61
MOORE ST
CHARTER ROW
EYRE STREET
A621
ST MARY'S GATE
ST MARY'S RD
SHOREHAM ST
SUFFOLK RD
QUEENS RD
BRAMALL LA
LONDON ROAD
ABBEYDALE ROAD
WOLSELEY RD
A625
ECCLESALL ROAD
GLOSSOP ROAD B6069
FULWOOD ROAD
WITHAM RD
CLARKEHOUSE ROAD
BROCCO BANK
NETHERTHORPE RD A61
HOYLE ST
RUTLAND ROAD B6070
BURNGREAVE ROAD
SHEAF ST
SHREWSBURY
University of Sheffield
Royal Hallamshire Hosp
Central Sheffield University Hospitals
Weston Park Hosp NHS Trust
Sheffield City Council
Kelham Island Museum
Crucible Theatre
The Lyceum Theatre
Sheffield United AFC
Sheffield Magistrates Court
Cathedral Ch of St Peter & St Paul
Ponds Forge International Sports Cen
Sheffield Hallam University
Sheffield Midland Station
CHARTER SQUARE ROUNDABOUT
MOORE STREET RBT
BRAMALL LANE RBT
SHEAF SQUARE RBT
1 grid square represents 500 metres

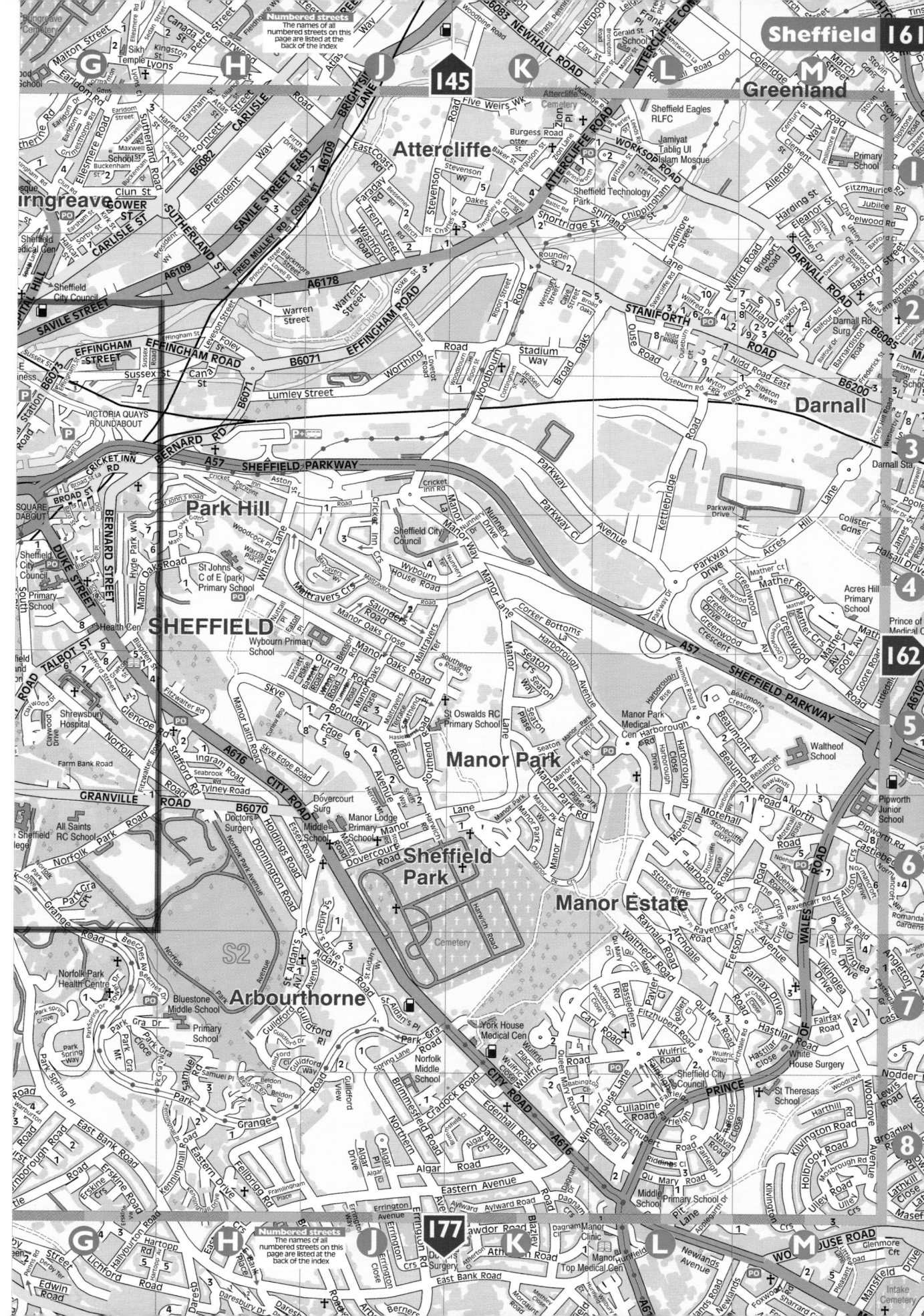
Numbered streets
The names of all numbered streets on this page are listed at the back of the index
145
177
162
G
H
J
K
L
M
1
2
3
4
5
6
7
8
Burngreave Cemetery
Greenland
Attercliffe
Attercliffe Cemetery
Sheffield Eagles RLFC
Jamiyat Tablig Ul Islam Mosque
Sheffield Technology Park
Primary School
Darnall
Darnall Sta
Darnall Rd Surg
Sheffield City Council
VICTORIA QUAYS ROUNDABOUT
Park Hill
SHEFFIELD
St Johns C of E (park) Primary School
Wybourn Primary School
Health Cen
Shrewsbury Hospital
St Oswalds RC Primary School
Manor Park
Manor Park Medical Cen
Waltheof School
Pipworth Junior School
Acres Hill Primary School
All Saints RC School
Doctors Surgery
Dovercourt Surg
Manor Lodge Primary School
Middle School
Sheffield Park
Cemetery
Manor Estate
S2
Arbourthorne
Norfolk Park Health Centre
Bluestone Middle School
Primary School
York House Medical Cen
Norfolk Middle School
Sheffield City Council
St Theresas School
White House Surgery
Middle School
Primary School
Manor Clinic
Top Medical Cen
Doctors Surgery
Intake Cemetery
SAVILE STREET
SAVILE STREET EAST
A6109
A6178
B6082
SUTHERLAND ST
CARLISLE ST
GOWER ST
EFFINGHAM ROAD
EFFINGHAM STREET
B6071
B6073
A57
SHEFFIELD PARKWAY
BERNARD RD
CRICKET INN RD
BROAD ST
DUKE STREET
BERNARD STREET
TALBOT ST
A616
CITY ROAD
B6070
GRANVILLE ROAD
ATTERCLIFFE ROAD
WORKSOP ROAD
STANIFORTH ROAD
DARNALL ROAD
B6085
B6200
NEWHALL ROAD
B6083
WALES ROAD
PRINCE OF WALES ROAD
A6102
WOODHOUSE ROAD
Lumley Street
Manor Lane
Manor Oaks Road
Harborough Avenue
Eastern Avenue
East Bank Road
Norfolk Park Road

162
146
161
178
C6
1 Richmond Park Cl
B8, C7
Street Names for these grid squares are listed at the back of the index
B7
1 Richmond Hall Dr
A3, A6, A7
Street Names for these grid squares are listed at the back of the index
B3
1 High Hazels Cl
2 High Hazels Mead
A5
1 Bowden Wood Cl
2 Bowden Wood Pl
A2
1 Basford Ms
2 Boden Pl
3 Craven Cl
4 Fulford Cl
5 Fulford Pl
6 Greenland Cl
7 Whitby Rd
A
B
C
D
E
F
1
2
3
4
5
6
7
8
Europa Link
Sheffield City Airport
Tinsley Park Cemetery
Tinsley Park
Trans Pennine Trail
Coleford Road
Catley Road
Infield Lane
Darnall Health Centre
Darnall Cemetery
Greenland Road
Greenland Way
GREENLAND ROAD
A631
A6102
MAIN RD
MAIN ROAD
B6085
B6200
Tates Gallery
Sheffield City Council
Darnall Sta.
Senior Rd
Elmham Road
Bannham Road
Olivers Mount
Poole Place
Poole Road
PRINCE OF WALES RD
Handsworth Avenue
Houstead Road
Handsworth Crescent
Lound Road
HANDSWORTH ROAD B6200
Willow Drive
Maple Grove
Chestnut Avenue
Alder Lane
Larch Hill
Hall Road
Clifton Crs
Clifton Lane
SHEFFIELD PARK WAY
A630
SHEFFIELD PARKWAY
Halsall Drive
Halsall Av
Prince of Wales Road Medical Centre
Bowden Wood Crescent
POPLAR WAY
B6533
B6066
HIGH FIELD SPRING
HIGHFIELD LANE
Quarry Road
Halesworth Road
HANDSWORTH ROAD
Finchwell Road
Finchwell Close
Enfield Place
Handsworth
Portland Business Park
Birklands Avenue
Birklands Drive
Richmond Park Road
Richmond Park Drive
Medical Cen
St Joseph's Rd
Fitzalan Rd
Handsworth Branch Clinic
Cemetery
Medlock Crescent
Medlock Drive
Medlock Close
ORGREAVE LANE
Orgreave Lane
ROTHERHAM ROAD
Kirkdale Crescent
Kirkdale Drive
RETFORD ROAD
S13
Ballifield Road
Ballifield Crescent
Handsworth Grange Road
Handsworth Grange Close
Ballifield Primary School
B6066 BEAVER HILL
Beaver Avenue
Beaver Close
Beaver Drive
Pipworth Junior School
Pipworth Rd
Castlebeck Av
Danewood Gardens
Danewood Av
Romandale Gardens
Athelstan Road
Wheatley Grove
RICHMOND ROAD
Richmond Avenue
Bramley Lane
Bramley Avenue
Sundown Road
Richworth Road
A57
Richmond
Ravenscroft Crescent
Ravenscroft Avenue
Ravenscroft Drive
Ravenscroft Road
Glenholme Drive
Glenholme Road
Spinkhill Drive
Wainwright Av
Wainwright Crs
Car View
Hastilar Road South
Castlebeck Drive
Angleton Av
Vikinglea Drive
Woodrove Avenue
Nodder Rd
Lewis Road
Fishponds Road
Aughton Crs
Stradbroke Primary School
Stradbroke Road
Stradbroke Avenue
Stradbroke Way
Smelter Wood Road
Smelter Wood Drive
Smelter Wood Crescent
Woodthorpe Community Primary School
Doctors Surgery
Richmond Medical Centre
Broadley Road
Chadwick Road
Lowburn Road
Audrey Road
Lathkill Close
Lathkill Rd
Masefield Road
Hastilar Road South
Mason Grove
Cardwell Avenue
Cardwell Drive
Severnside Drive
Severnside Place
Hardcastle Gardens
Coisley
Mauncer Lane
Vicar Lane
New Cross Drive
C8
1 Smelter Wood Cl
D6
1 Ashbourne Gv
2 Parsley Hay Cl
3 Parsley Hay Dr
4 Wenlock St
D8
1 Glenholme Pl
E6
1 Medlock Rd
E8
1 Hardcastle Dr
1 grid square represents 500 metres
NORMANTON HILL
B6064
Normanton
SHEFFIELD RD
TANNERY

G1 1 Church La
G8 1 Brockwood Cl
H2 1 Mappin's Rd
H8 1 David Cl 2 Greenwood La 3 Sylvia Cl
G2 1 California Dr 2 South View Ter
H1 1 Harmony Wy
J2 1 Burntwood Crs
147
Guilthwaite
Catcliffe
Treeton
Treeton C of E Junior & Infant School
Spa House
Burnt Wood
AUGHTON
164
Orgreave
Woodhouse Mill
Woodhouse
Woodhouse Station
Ironbridge Industrial Estate
Aston Fence Junior & Infant School
Aston Comprehensive School
Aston Swallownest Junior & Infant School
Fence
SHEFFIELD PARKWAY
A630
B6067
M1
A618
TREETON LANE
MILL LANE
ORGREAVE ROAD
POPLAR WAY
FRONT ST
WOOD LANE
RETFORD ROAD
SHEFFIELD ROAD
B6200
STATION ROAD
FURNACE LANE
Long Lane
Bole Hill
Flatts Lane
Doles Lane
Rotherham Roundwalk
Falconer Lane
Smallage Lane
West Lane
Park Hill
179
K8 1 John Hibbard Av
K4 1 Bradshaw Wy
J8 1 John Hibbard Cl 2 John Hibbard Ri
J7 1 Harbury St 2 Hudson Rd
J3 1 Arundel Rd

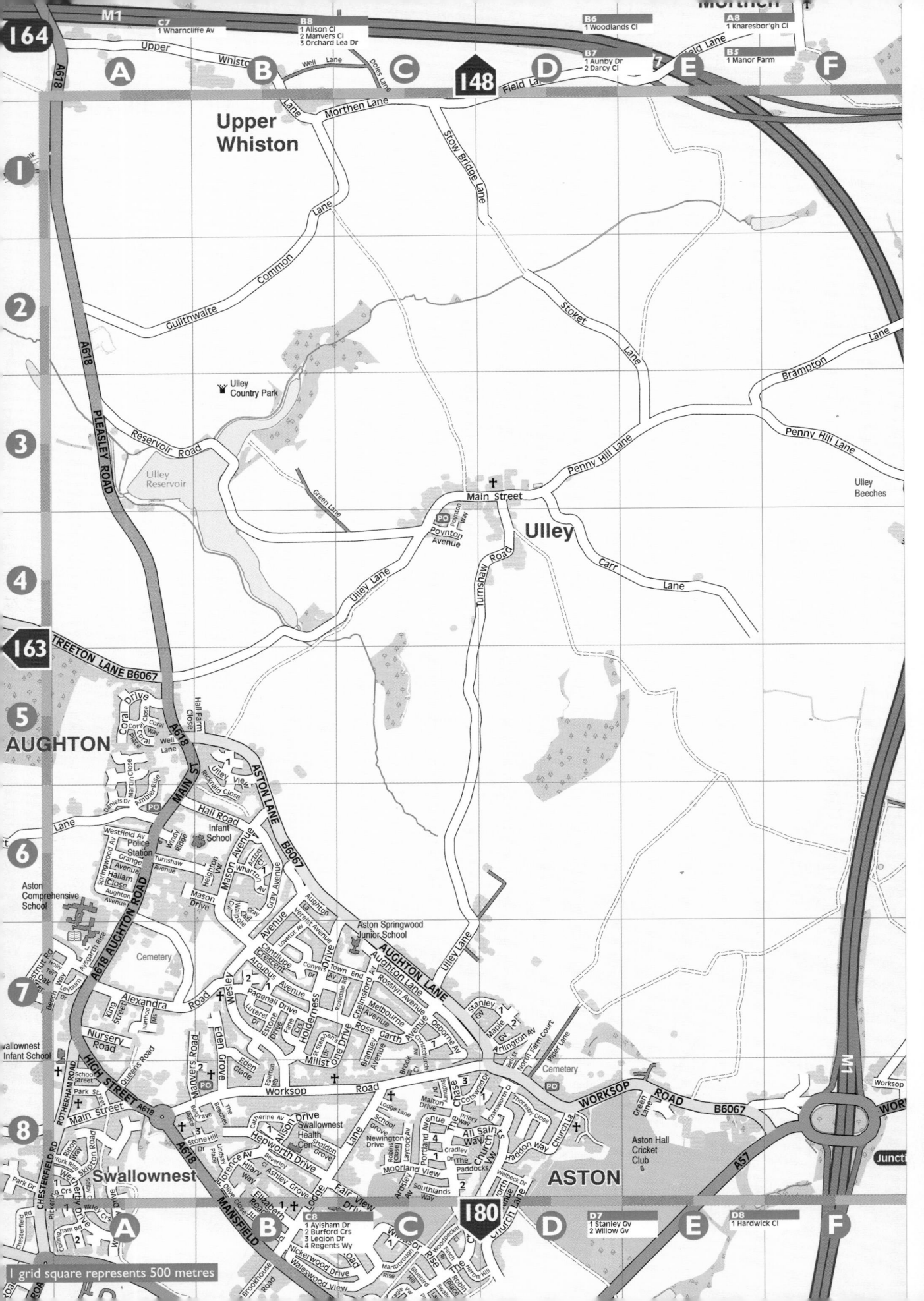

164
148
163
180
M1
Upper Whiston
Ulley Country Park
Ulley Reservoir
Ulley
Ulley Beeches
AUGHTON
Aston Comprehensive School
Aston Springwood Junior School
Swallownest
ASTON
Aston Hall Cricket Club
Cemetery
C7 1 Wharncliffe Av
B8 1 Alison Cl 2 Manvers Cl 3 Orchard Lea Dr
B6 1 Woodlands Cl
A8 1 Knaresbor'gh Cl
B7 1 Aunby Dr 2 Darcy Cl
B5 1 Manor Farm
C8 1 Aylsham Dr 2 Burford Crs 3 Legion Dr 4 Regents Wy
D7 1 Stanley Gv 2 Willow Gv
D8 1 Hardwick Cl
1 grid square represents 500 metres

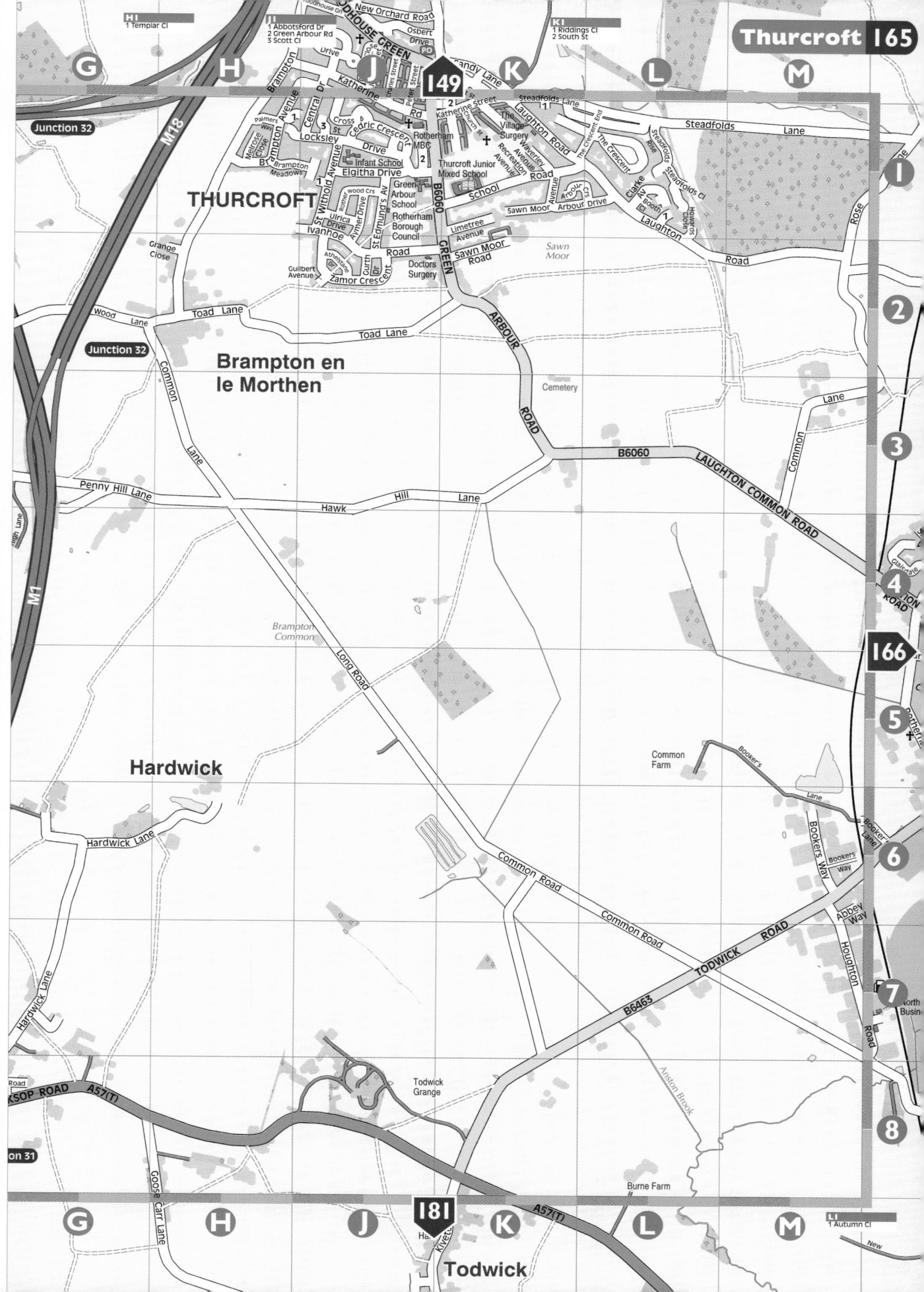
THURCROFT
Brampton en le Morthen
Hardwick
Todwick
Junction 32
M18
M1
B6060
ARBOUR ROAD
B6060 LAUGHTON COMMON ROAD
B6463 TODWICK ROAD
A57(T)
Toad Lane
Wood Lane
Common Lane
Penny Hill Lane
Hawk Hill Lane
Long Road
Common Road
Hardwick Lane
Goose Carr Lane
Steadfolds Lane
Laughton Road
Sawn Moor
Cemetery
Brampton Common
Common Farm
Bookers Lane
Bookers Way
Abbey Way
Houghton Road
Anston Brook
Todwick Grange
Burne Farm
Thurcroft Junior Mixed School
Infant School
Green Arbour School
Rotherham Borough Council
Rotherham MBC
Doctors Surgery
The Village Surgery
H1 1 Templar Cl
J1 1 Abbotsford Dr 2 Green Arbour Rd 3 Scott Cl
K1 1 Riddings Cl 2 South St
L1 1 Autumn Cl
149
166
181

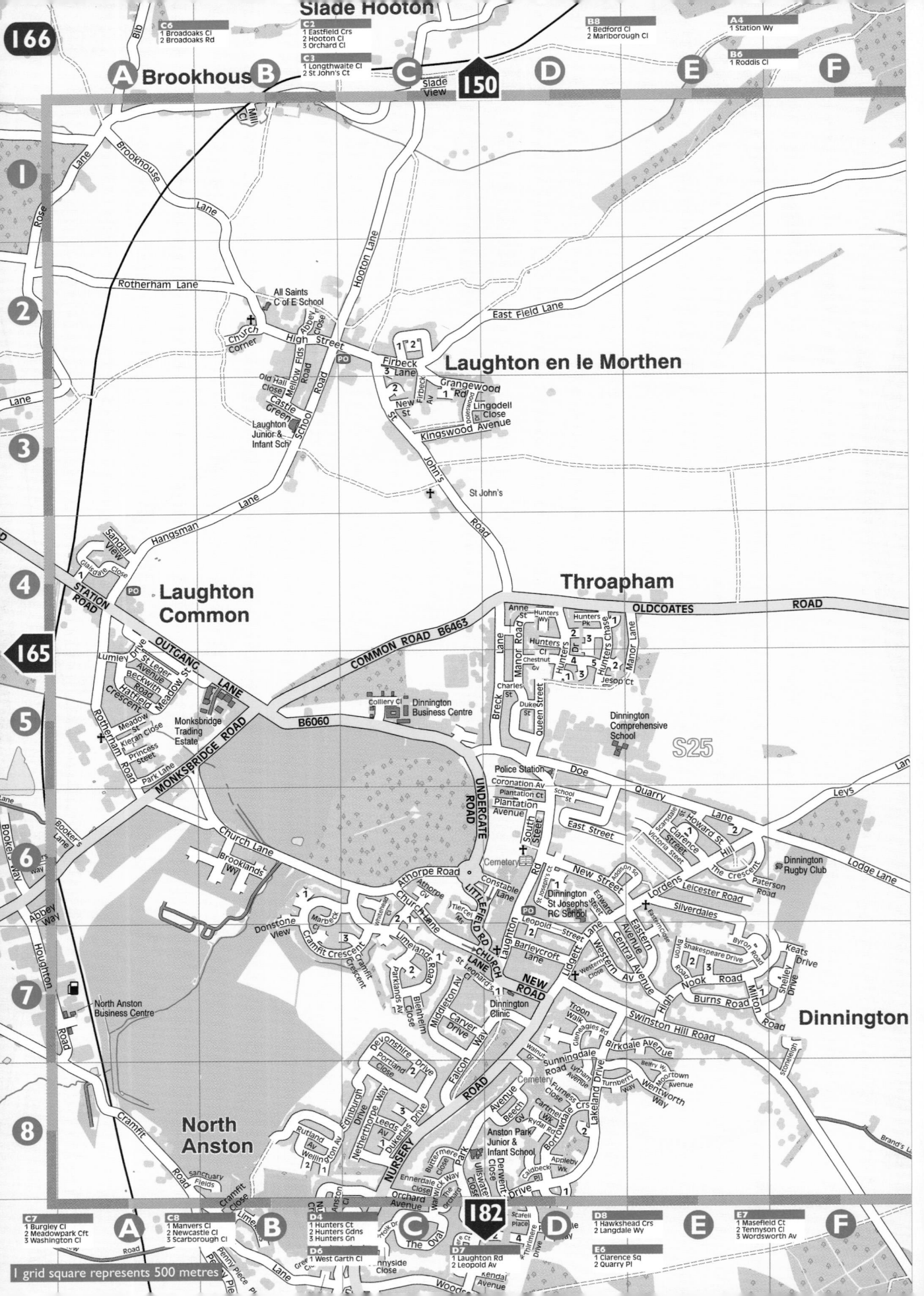

166
150
165
182
Slade Hooton
Brookhouse
Laughton en le Morthen
Laughton Common
Throapham
Dinnington
North Anston
S25
C6
1 Broadoaks Cl
2 Broadoaks Rd
C2
1 Eastfield Crs
2 Hooton Cl
3 Orchard Cl
C3
1 Longthwaite Cl
2 St John's Ct
B8
1 Bedford Cl
2 Marlborough Cl
A4
1 Station Wy
B6
1 Roddis Cl
C7
1 Burgley Cl
2 Meadowpark Cft
3 Washington Cl
C8
1 Manvers Cl
2 Newcastle Cl
3 Scarborough Cl
D4
1 Hunters Ct
2 Hunters Gdns
3 Hunters Gn
D6
1 West Garth Cl
D7
1 Laughton Rd
2 Leopold Av
D8
1 Hawkshead Crs
2 Langdale Wy
E6
1 Clarence Sq
2 Quarry Pl
E7
1 Masefield Ct
2 Tennyson Cl
3 Wordsworth Av
1 grid square represents 500 metres
All Saints C of E School
Laughton Junior & Infant Sch
St John's
Monksbridge Trading Estate
Dinnington Business Centre
Dinnington Comprehensive School
Police Station
Cemetery
Dinnington St Josephs RC School
Dinnington Rugby Club
Dinnington Clinic
North Anston Business Centre
Anston Park Junior & Infant School
Rotherham Lane
Brookhouse Lane
Hooton Lane
East Field Lane
High Street
School Road
St John's Road
Hangsman Lane
Station Road
Outgang Lane
Common Road B6463
Oldcoates Road
Monksbridge Road
B6060
Undercgate Road
Doe Quarry Lane
Lodge Lane
Church Lane
Athorpe Road
Littlefield Rd
New Road
Swinston Hill Road
Nursery Road
Cramfit Road
Houghton Road
Kingswood Avenue
Grangewood Rd
Lingodell Close
Firbeck Lane
Queen Street
Manor Road
Breck Lane
Plantation Avenue
East Street
New Street
Leicester Road
Silverdales
Central Avenue
Western Av
Eastern Avenue
Burns Road
Nook Road
Milton Road
Shakespeare Drive
Keats Drive
Birkdale Avenue
Sunningdale Road
Wentworth Way
Lakeland Drive
Carver Drive
Falcon Way
Middleton Av
Devonshire Drive
Edinburgh Drive
Netherthorpe Way
Dukeries Drive
Rutland Av
Wellington Av
Orchard Avenue
The Oval
Kendal Avenue
Cramfit Crescent
Donstone View
Brooklands Wy
Booker's Lane
Abbey Way
Rotherham Road
Park Lane
Princess Street
Sandall View
Glaisdale Close

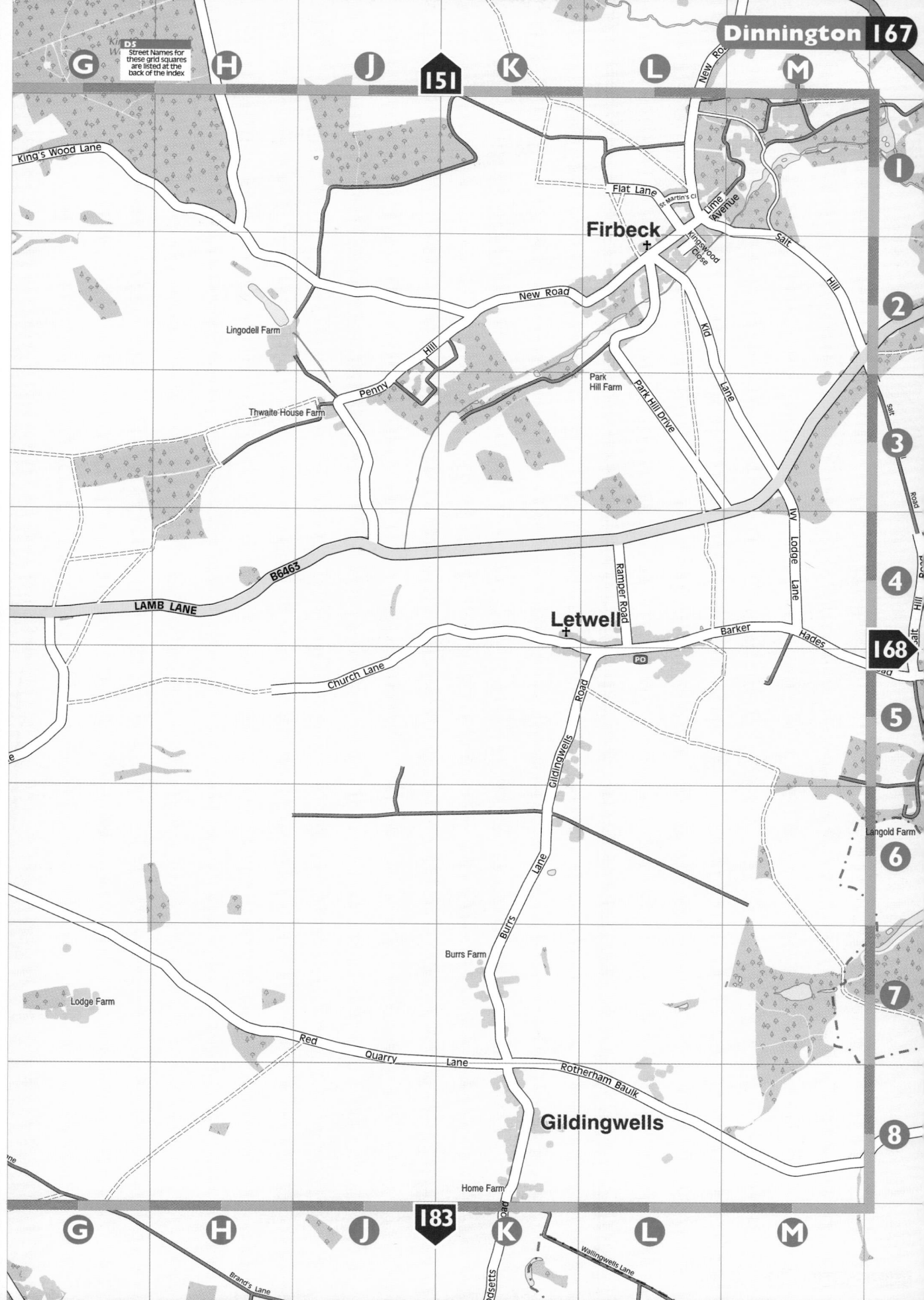
D5
Street Names for these grid squares are listed at the back of the index
G
H
J
151
K
L
M
1
2
3
4
168
5
6
7
8
183
King's Wood Lane
Lingodell Farm
Thwaite House Farm
Penny Hill
New Road
Firbeck
Flat Lane
St Martin's Cl
Lime Avenue
Kingswood Close
Salt Hill
Kid Lane
Park Hill Farm
Park Hill Drive
Ivy Lodge Lane
B6463
LAMB LANE
Ramper Road
Letwell
Barker
Hades
Church Lane
PO
Gildingwells Road
Langold Farm
Burrs Lane
Burrs Farm
Lodge Farm
Red Quarry Lane
Rotherham Baulk
Gildingwells
Home Farm
Wallingwells Lane
Brand's Lane
Salt Hill Road

168
D8
1 Harvest Cl
2 North Wy
3 Plough Dr
4 Ramsden Crs
D7
1 Sutherland Cl
D4
1 Wembley Rd
C8
1 Cedar Cl
2 Chiltern Wy
3 Hambleton Ct
4 Lowther Sq
5 Pentland Dr
152
A
B
C
D
E
F
Oldcotes
A634 MALTBY ROAD
BLYTH ROAD
A634
B6463
Wynlea Drive
Elmsmere Drive
Weirside
Main Street
Haven Hill
LAMB LANE B6463
Hermeston Hall
Goldthorpe Farm
Salt Hill Road
Dyscarr Wood
Langold
Chestnut Rd
Laburnum Road
Harrison Drive Business Centre
Harrison Drive
Langold Dyscarr Junior School
School Road
White Avenue
Markham Road
Firbeck Crescent
Dyscarr Cl
Goldthorpe Av
Knott End
Riddell Avenue
Cemetery
Hodsock Plantation
Hodsock Park
167
Road
Williams Street
Ramsden
Cross Street
Road
Avenue
Mellish
Church Street
Langold Health Centre
Hodsock Grange
A60 DONCASTER ROAD
The Lakeside Surgery
Langold Farm
Langold Lake
Langold Country Park
Hodsock Woodhouse
Costhorpe Industrial Estate
Woodhouse Lane
Costhorpe
Lawn Road
Northumberland Avenue
Willow Holt
Lawn Road Industrial Estate
Westmorland Dr
Cumberland Close
Lilac Lodge
Rotherham Baulk
Cleveland Close
Lilac Grove
Oak Tree Rise
Pinfold Drive
Coppice Way
Pasture Close
Hawthorn Way
Willow Av
Lime Tree Av
Sycamore Rd
Le Brun Square
Beckett Avenue
Dadley Road
Queens Road
Beech Gv
Knaton Road
Kingston Road
Mulberry Crs
Lindrick Close
184
Stewart Road
Oxford Road
Long Lane
Health Clinic
Granary
The Green
Hodsock Lane
Windsor Gardens
Balmoral Close
Kenilworth Drive
Warwick
North Carlton
1 grid square represents 500 metres

Holme Farm

Lane

Whitewater
Common

Whitewater Lane

DONCASTER BY-PASS

Harworth
Avenue

The
Woodlands

BAWTRY

A614

153

Junction 34

Blyth Service Area

A634

BAWTRY ROAD

Nornay
Close

Nornay

Common Lane

A1(T)

Meadow Lane

River Ryton

Hotel

B6045

A634

Blyth Cricket
Club

Park Drive

Priory
Close

The Maltings

The
Surgery

Mill Meadow View

RETFORD ROAD

170

A63

Blyth

SHEFFIELD ROAD

The Mews

PO

A634 HIGH STREET

High Street

St
Martins

Ryton
Close

Ryton Fields

Blyth C of E
Primary School

WORKSOP ROAD

Sherwood
Cls

Briber Road

Spitalfields

TWO
Acres

A1(T)

BRIBER HILL

Spital
Farm

B6045

SPITAL Rd

Hodsock
Lodge Farm

Plantation

Lane

Long
Plantation

Elm
Wood

Hodsock
Red Bridge

Hodsock
Plantation

Hodsock

Hodsock Lane

185

River Ryton

Damings
Wood

Black
Screed

170
154
169
186
A
B
C
D
E
F
1
2
3
4
5
6
7
8
Serlby Park Golf Club
F2 1 Spinneymead
GREAT NORTH ROAD
Scrooby Top House
River Ryton
Roman Bank Lane
Bishopfield Farm
Folly Nook Lane
Arundel Drive
Oaks Close
Stonehill Close
Southfall Cl.
Whitton Close
MATTERSEY
Ranskill Primary School
Station Road
Ravenshill Close
Bishopfield Lane
A638
Brecks Wood
Roman Bank
PO
Mayflower Gallery
Ranskill
Back Lane
Birk Hill
BLYTH ROAD
B6045
The Mantles
Huntsman Place
Underwood Avenue
Holds Lane
Blacksmith Lane
A634
Moor Lane
Baulk Lane
Torworth
Low Street
Blyth C of E Primary School
Graves Moor Lane
A1(T)
Jubilee Farm
SPITAL ROAD
College Farm
Lane
Long Plantation
Beech Farm
Damings Wood
Tinker Lane
1 grid square represents 500 metres

G H J 155 K L M M

I
2
3
4
5
6
7
8

Mattersey
Hall View
Job Lane

Mattersey Primary

Mattersey
Hill

Retford

Matt Road

ROAD B6045

Bridge House

Cherry Tree
Walk

AVENUE

Headlands
Lane

LC

Common Lane

Loundfield
Farm

The
Paddocks

Little Lane

Highfield House

PO
Ch

LC

Daneshill Road

Mattersey Road

Lound Low Road

G H J 187 K L M

Lane

Town Street

Ch
PO

School

Sutton

Bamford Moor
E8
1 Roslyn Crs
E7
1 The Crofts
2 Ibbotsons Cft
D7
1 Cannon Flds
156
Stanage Edge
Buck Stone
The Cough
Sheepwash Bank
Dennis Knoll
Greens House
Bamford County School
Taggs Knoll
Fidlers Cl
Gatehouse
Upper Hurst Farm
North Lees
Joan Lane
Hurstclough Lane
Nether Hurst
Brookfield Manor
Birley Lane
Lane
Saltergate
Sickleholme Golf Club
Bamford Station
Kimber Court Farm
Thorpe Farm
Cunliffe House
Birley Farm
Car Head
Towers Lane
Coggers Lane
Baulk Lane
Church Bank
Hill Lane
Ranmoor Hill
Church Bank
Hungry Lane
Banmoor Lane
Derwent Lane
Higger Lane
Dale Crs
Jagger's Lane
Hathersage
School La
River Derwent
Castleton Road
Cliffe Lane
Park Edge
Hotel
St Michaels C of E School
HATHERSAGE ROAD
CASTLETON ROAD
A6187
Barnfield Drive
Crossland Road
Oddfellows Road
Roslyn Road
Mill La
Hathersage Swimming Pool
Moorland Rd
Back Lane
Ninelands Rd
SHEFFIELD ROAD
Offerton Hall
Nether Hall
Dore Lane
Station App
Hathersage Station
A6187
STATION ROAD
Broadhay Farm
Callow Farm
1 grid square represents 500 metres

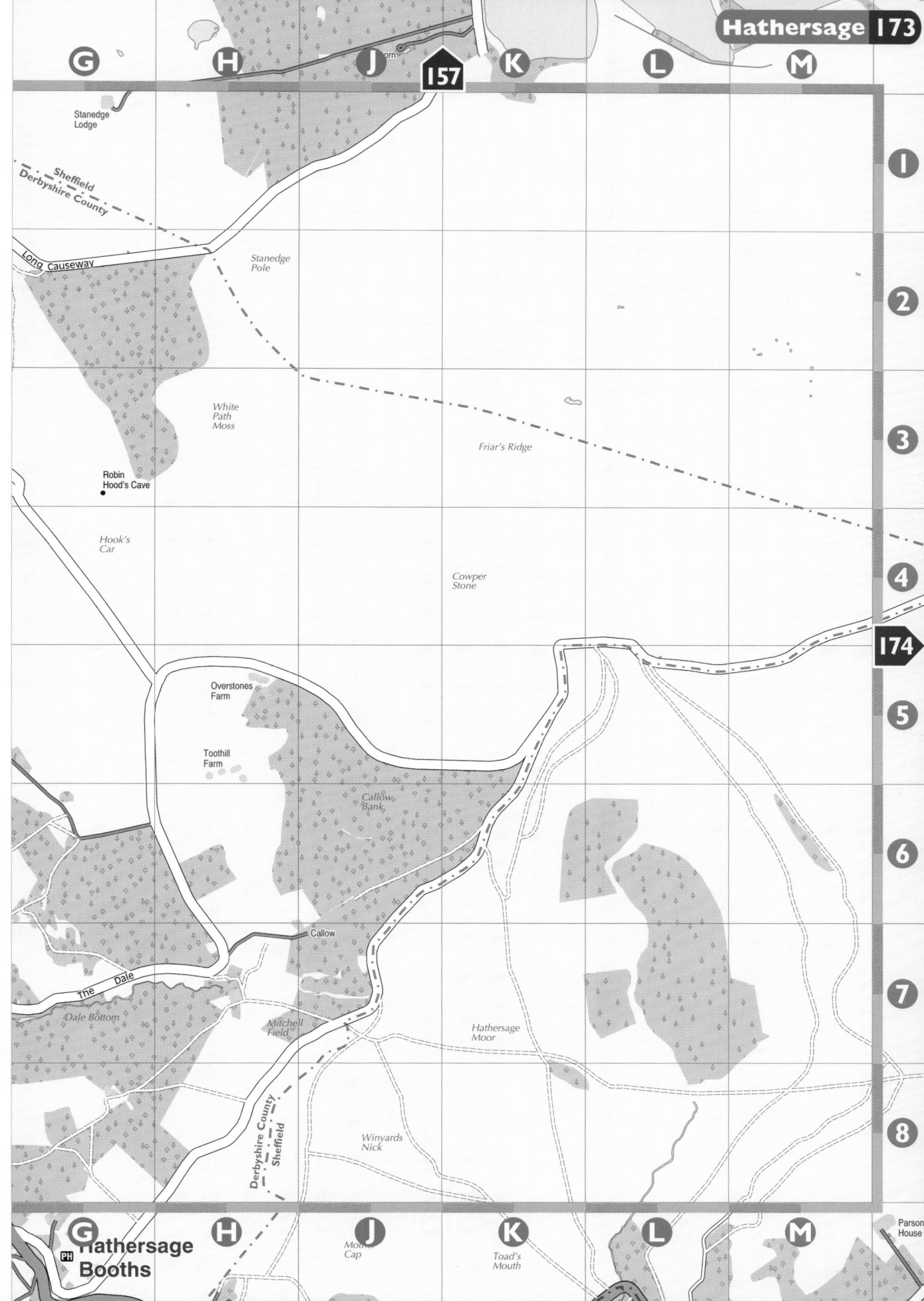

G   H   J   157   K   L   M

Stanedge
Lodge

Sheffield
Derbyshire County

Long Causeway

Stanedge
Pole

White
Path
Moss

Friar's Ridge

Robin
Hood's Cave

Hook's
Car

Cowper
Stone

174

Overstones
Farm

Toothill
Farm

Callow
Bank

Callow

The   Dale

Dale Bottom

Mitchell
Field

Hathersage
Moor

Derbyshire County
Sheffield

Winyards
Nick

I

2

3

4

5

6

7

8

G   H   J   K   L   M

Hathersage
Booths
PH

Mother
Cap

Toad's
Mouth

Parson
House

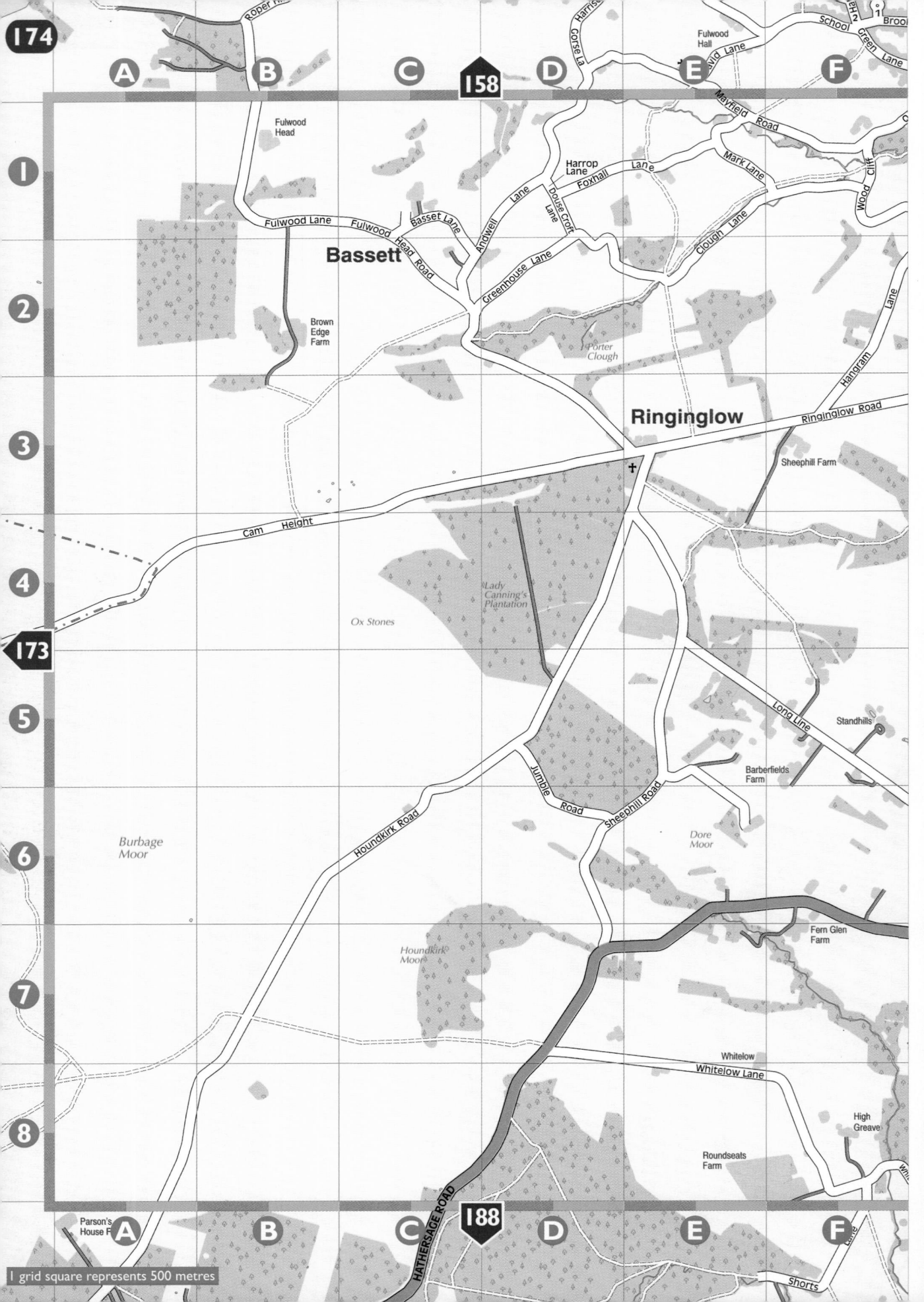

174
158
173
188
A
B
C
D
E
F
1
2
3
4
5
6
7
8
Fulwood Head
Fulwood Lane
Fulwood Head Road
Basset Lane
Bassett
Brown Edge Farm
Andwell Lane
Harrop Lane
Foxhall Lane
Douse Croft Lane
Greenhouse Lane
Clough Lane
Mark Lane
Mayfield Road
Fulwood Hall
School Green Lane
Wood Cliff
Porter Clough
Ringinglow
Ringinglow Road
Hangram Lane
Sheephill Farm
Cam Height
Ox Stones
Lady Canning's Plantation
Long Line
Standhills
Barberfields Farm
Jumble Road
Sheephill Road
Houndkirk Road
Dore Moor
Burbage Moor
Houndkirk Moor
Fern Glen Farm
Whitelow
Whitelow Lane
High Greave
Roundseats Farm
Hathersage Road
Parson's House F
Shorts
1 grid square represents 500 metres

G7
1 Causeway Gdns
H8
1 Dore Hall Cft
J2
1 Bents Green Pl
2 Moor View Ter
J8
1 Burlington Gln
2 Moorwinstow Cft
K3
1 Broad Elms Cl
K4
1 Almshill Crs
2 Broomcroft Pk
3 Croft Cl
4 Whirlow La
5 Whirlow Ms
159
Greystones
Ecclesall
Parkhead
Whirlow Brook
Whirlow
Abbeydale
Brick Houses
Townhead
Dore
S11
High Storrs School
Ecclesall Infant School
Bents Green Special School
Silverdale School
Broad Elms School
Doctors Surgery
Ecclesall Medical Centre
Dobcroft Infant School
Dobcroft Junior School
Hollis Hospital
HSBC Sports Club
The Moss
Moorside Farm
Castle Dyke
Whiteley Wood
Ecclesall Wood
Beauchief Golf Club House
Hotel
Dore Station
Abbeydale Park Sports Club
King Ecgbert Secondary School
Rowan School
Doctors Surg
Ringinglow Road
Cottage Lane
Common Lane
Coit Lane
Fenney Lane
Limb Lane
Ecclesall Road South
Hathersage Road
Whirlowdale Road
Abbey Lane
Abbeydale Road South
Dobcroft Road
Millhouses Lane
Dore Road
Long Line
Ash House Lane
Brickhouse Lane
Cross Lane
176
189
M3
1 Millhouses Gln
2 Silverdale Gdns
M2
1 Weetwood Dr
2 Woodholm Pl
M1
1 Banner Cross Dr
L5
1 Harewood Wy
2 Russell Ct
3 Wentworth Av
L8
1 Ladies Spring Gv
L2
1 Blenheim Gdns
2 Ecclesall Rd South
L3
1 Silverdale Gld
K5
1 Holkham Ri
2 Whirlowdale Cl
3 Whirlowdale Ri

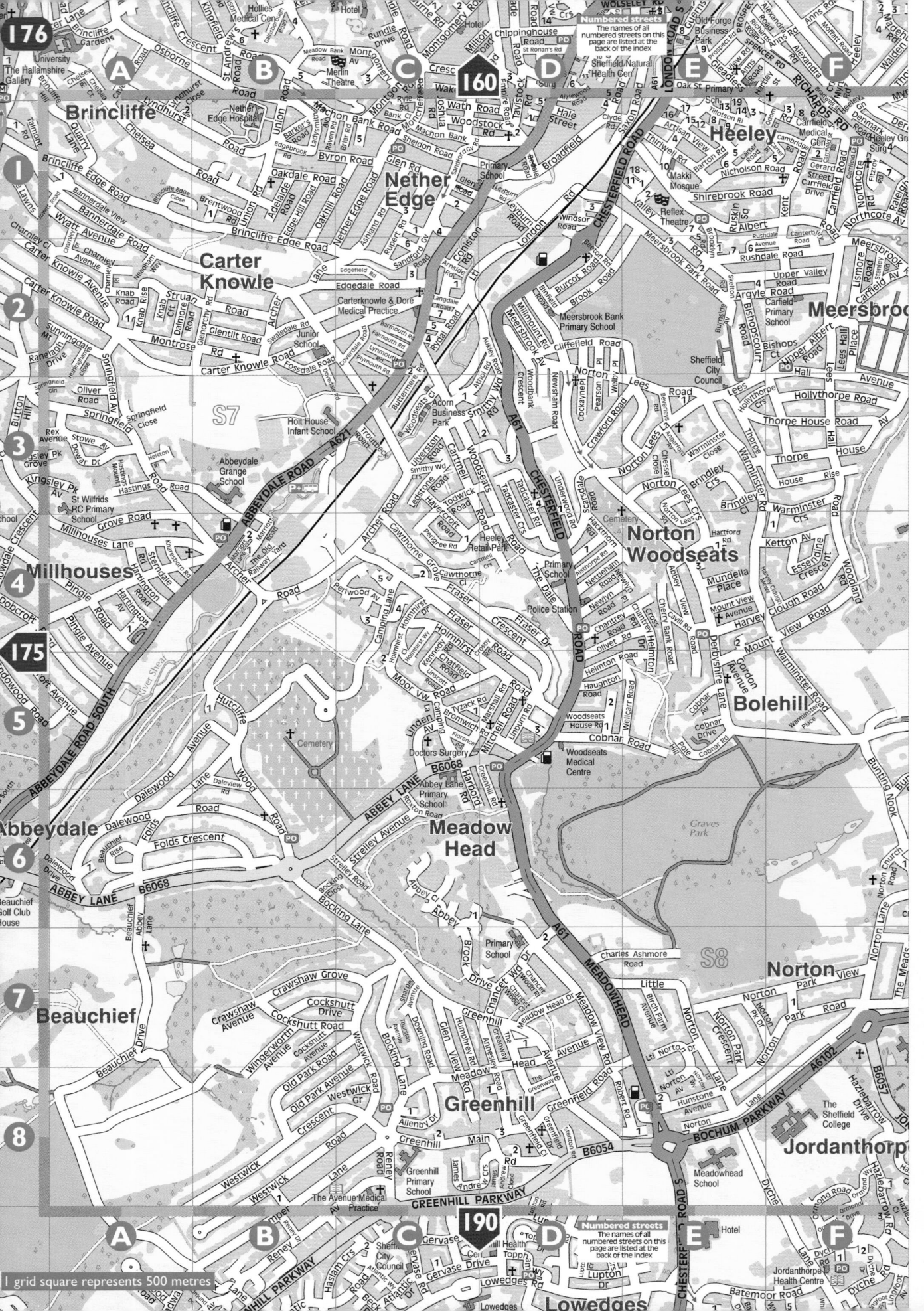

176
160
175
190
A
B
C
D
E
F
1
2
3
4
5
6
7
8
Numbered streets
The names of all numbered streets on this page are listed at the back of the index
Brincliffe
Nether Edge
Heeley
Carter Knowle
Meersbrook
Millhouses
Norton Woodseats
Bolehill
Abbeydale
Meadow Head
Beauchief
Norton
Greenhill
Jordanthorpe
Lowedges
S7
S8
University
The Hallamshire Gallery
Brincliffe Gardens
Hollies Medical Cen
Merlin Theatre
Nether Edge Hospital
Sheffield Natural Health Cen
Old Forge Business Park
Makki Mosque
Reflex Theatre
Carterknowle & Dore Medical Practice
Junior School
Meersbrook Bank Primary School
Carfield Primary School
Carfield Medical Cen
Sheffield City Council
Acorn Business Park
Holt House Infant School
Abbeydale Grange School
St Wilfrids RC Primary School
Heeley Retail Park
Primary School
Police Station
Cemetery
Woodseats Medical Centre
Doctors Surgery
Abbey Lane Primary School
Graves Park
River Sheaf
Beauchief Golf Club House
Greenhill Primary School
The Avenue Medical Practice
Meadowhead School
The Sheffield College
Hotel
Jordanthorpe Health Centre
ABBEYDALE ROAD
ABBEYDALE ROAD SOUTH
A621
A61
CHESTERFIELD ROAD
CHESTERFIELD ROAD S
LONDON ROAD S
MEADOWHEAD
ABBEY LANE
B6068
B6054
GREENHILL PARKWAY
BOCHUM PARKWAY
A6102
B6057
Charles Ashmore Road
Bocking Lane
Hutcliffe Wood Road
Millhouses Lane
Carter Knowle Road
Springfield Av
Mount View Road
Warminster Road
Norton Lees Lane
1 grid square represents 500 metres

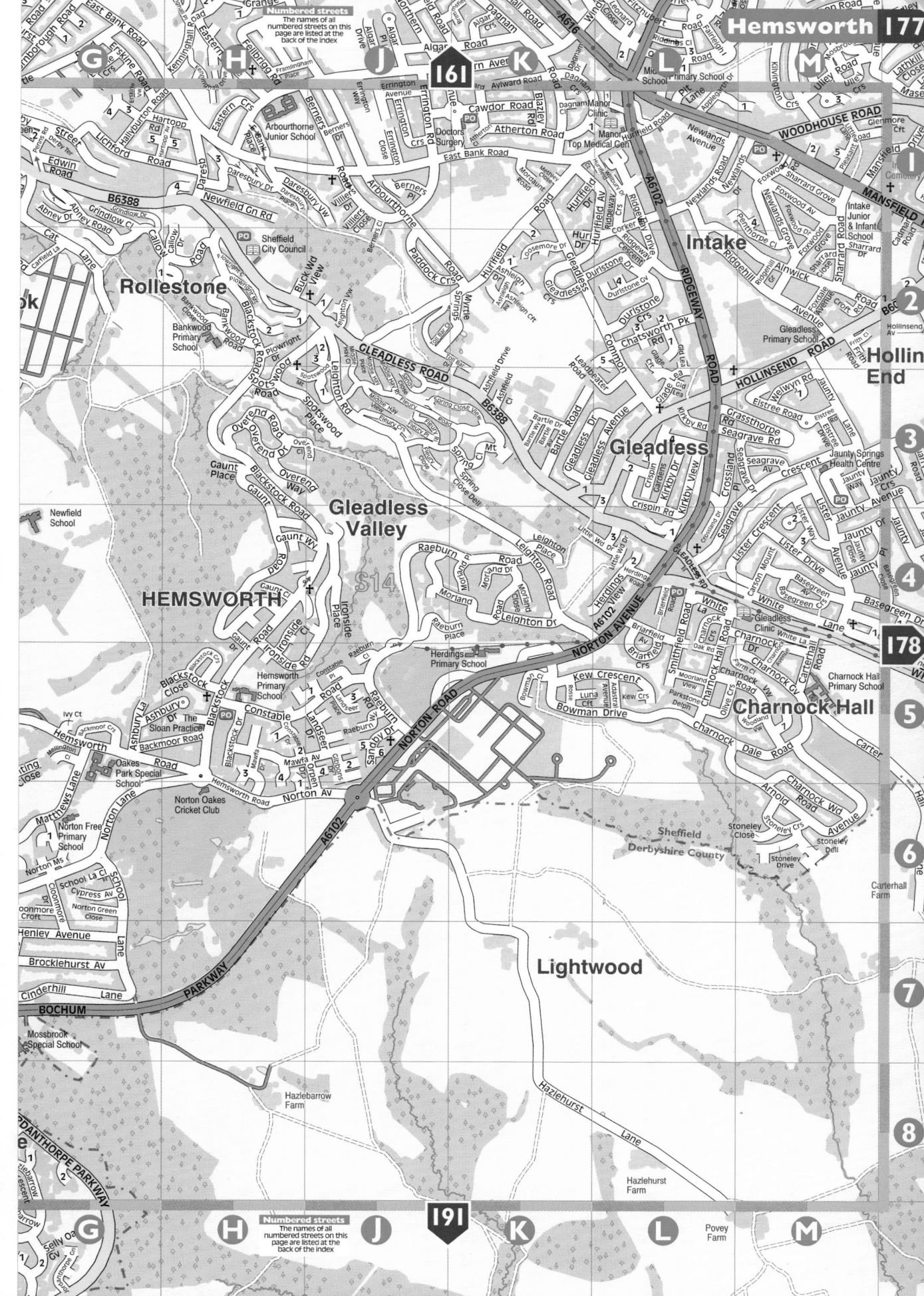
Numbered streets
The names of all numbered streets on this page are listed at the back of the index
161
178
191
G
H
J
K
L
M
1
2
3
4
5
6
7
8
Rollestone
Intake
Gleadless
Gleadless Valley
HEMSWORTH
Hollin End
Charnock Hall
Lightwood
S14
East Bank Road
Erskine Road
Lichford Road
Edwin Road
B6388
Newfield Gn Rd
Abney Rd
Cat Lane
Callow Rd
Arbourthorne Junior School
Arbourthorne
Berners Pl
Daresbury Dr
Villiers Dr
Paddock Crs
Sheffield City Council
Buck Wd View
Bankwood Primary School
Bankwood Road
Blackstock Road
Plowright
Spotswood Road
Spotswood Place
Leighton Rd
GLEADLESS ROAD
Hurlfield Road
Myrtle Springs
Ashfield Drive
Errington Rd
Cawdor Road
Atherton Road
Doctors Surgery
Manor Clinic
Top Medical Cen
Ridgeway Crescent
RIDGEWAY ROAD
A6102
A616
Mid School
Primary School
WOODHOUSE ROAD
MANSFIELD
Newlands Road
Foxwood Rd
Sharrard Road
Intake Junior & Infant School
Ridgehill
Alnwick
Gleadless Primary School
HOLLINSEND ROAD
Hollinsend Av
Elstree Road
Seagrave Rd
Crescent
Jaunty Springs Health Centre
Jaunty Avenue
Lister Crescent
Basegreen Av
Basegreen Dr
White Lane
Gleadless Clinic
Charnock Hall Road
Charnock Hall Primary School
Carter
Charnock Dale Road
Arnold Road
Stoneley Crs
Stoneley Close
Stoneley Dell
Stoneley Drive
Carterhall Farm
Durlstone Crs
Chatsworth Pk
Common
Leadbeater Road
Bartle Road
Gleadless Avenue
Kirkby View
Crispin Rd
Crossland
Seagrave
Overend Road
Gaunt Place
Blackstock Road
Newfield School
Gaunt Wy
Ironside Place
Raeburn Road
Morland
Leighton Dr
Leighton Place
Herdings Primary School
Herdings View
NORTON AVENUE
Kew Crescent
Bowman Drive
Briarfield Crs
Smithfield Road
Hemsworth Primary School
Constable
Landseer Dr
Sandby Dr
Blackstock Close
Ashbury Dr
The Sloan Practice
Backmoor Road
Hemsworth Road
Oakes Park Special School
Norton Oakes Cricket Club
Norton Av
NORTON ROAD
Mawfa Av
Matthews Lane
Norton Free Primary School
Norton Lane
School Lane
Cypress Av
Norton Green Close
Henley Avenue
Brocklehurst Av
Cinderhill Lane
BOCHUM
PARKWAY
Mossbrook Special School
Hazlebarrow Farm
Hazlehurst Lane
Hazlehurst Farm
Sheffield
Derbyshire County
JORDANTHORPE PARKWAY
Povey Farm

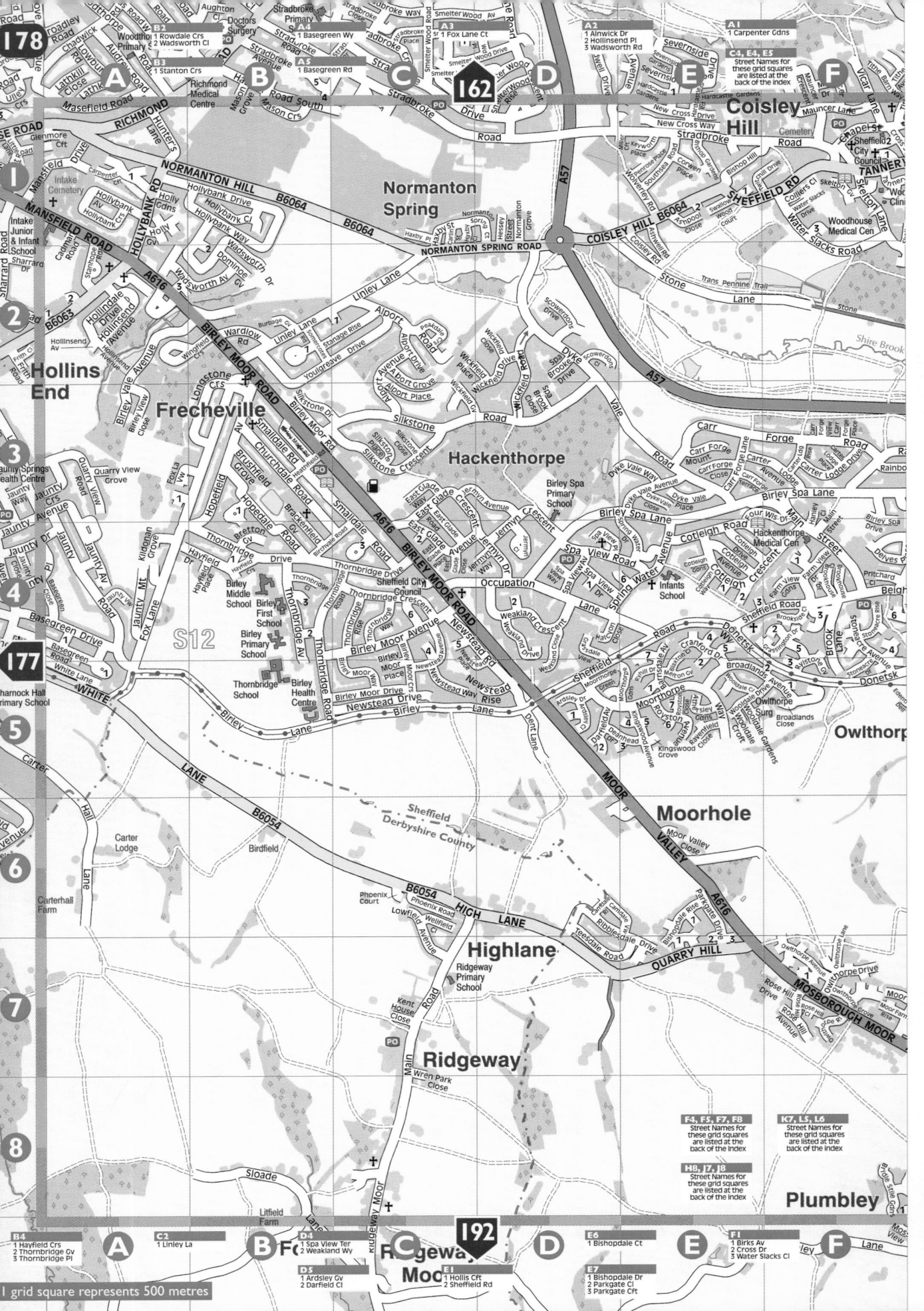

178
162
177
192
A
B
C
D
E
F
1
2
3
4
5
6
7
8
B2
1 Rowdale Crs
2 Wadsworth Cl
B3
1 Stanton Crs
A4
1 Basegreen Wy
A5
1 Basegreen Rd
A3
1 Fox Lane Ct
A2
1 Alnwick Dr
2 Hollinsend Pl
3 Wadsworth Rd
A1
1 Carpenter Gdns
C4, E4, E5
Street Names for these grid squares are listed at the back of the index
Coisley Hill
Normanton Spring
Hollins End
Frecheville
Hackenthorpe
Moorhole
Owlthorpe
Highlane
Ridgeway
Plumbley
S12
Masefield Road
Richmond Road
Normanton Hill
Mansfield Road
Birley Moor Road
Normanton Spring Road
Coisley Hill
Sheffield Rd
Stradbroke Road
Linley Lane
Silkstone Road
Dyke Vale Road
Birley Spa Lane
Carr Forge Road
Sheffield Road
Donetsk Way
Birley Lane
White Lane
Carter Hall Lane
High Lane
Quarry Hill
Moor Valley
Mosborough Moor
Stone Lane
Trans Pennine Trail
Shire Brook
Sheffield
Derbyshire County
Birley Spa Primary School
Hackenthorpe Medical Cen
Infants School
Sheffield City Council
Birley Middle School
Birley First School
Birley Primary School
Thornbridge School
Birley Health Centre
Ridgeway Primary School
Woodhouse Medical Cen
Richmond Medical Centre
Intake Cemetery
Intake Junior & Infant School
Carter Lodge
Birdfield
Carterhall Farm
Phoenix Court
Litfield Farm
Owlthorpe Surg
F4, F5, F7, F8
Street Names for these grid squares are listed at the back of the index
K7, L5, L6
Street Names for these grid squares are listed at the back of the index
H8, J7, J8
Street Names for these grid squares are listed at the back of the index
B4
1 Hayfield Crs
2 Thornbridge Gv
3 Thornbridge Pl
C2
1 Linley La
D4
1 Spa View Ter
2 Weakland Wy
D5
1 Ardsley Gv
2 Darfield Cl
E1
1 Hollis Cft
2 Sheffield Rd
E6
1 Bishopdale Ct
E7
1 Bishopdale Dr
2 Parkgate Cl
3 Parkgate Cft
F1
1 Birks Av
2 Cross Dr
3 Water Slacks Cl
1 grid square represents 500 metres

Mosborough 179
G1 1 Market St
G4 1 Delves Ter
G5 1 Lindholme Gdns 2 Lundwood Cl
G7 1 Moor Farm Garth
G8 1 Bridle Stile Cl 2 Plumbley Hall Rd
H5 1 Deane Field Vw 2 Purbeck Ct 3 Roydfield Cl 4 Thorpe Gn
163
180
193
Beighton
Drakehouse
Waterthorpe
Sothall
Holbrook
Westfield
Halfway
MOSBOROUGH
S20
Crystal Peaks
Sheffield City Council
UC Cinema
Police Station
Beighton Health Centre
Reignhead Primary School
Sothall Snooker & Leisure Centre
Brook House Junior School
Beighton Cemetery
Sothall Medical Centre
The Sheffield College
Health Centre
Primary School
Halfway Infant School
Junior School
Mosborough Medical Centre
Mosborough Primary School
River Rother
Trans Pennine Trail
A57
ECKINGTON WAY
STATION ROAD
B6058
HIGH STREET
A616
CHESTERFIELD ROAD
ROTHERHAM ROAD
L4 1 Ashdown Gdns 2 Broomwood Cl 3 Manor Farm Ct 4 Manor Farm Ms
L3 1 Marcham Dr
M5, M6, M8 Street Names for these grid squares are listed at the back of the index
K8 1 Deveron Rd 2 Eastcroft Vw 3 Rotherham Rd N
K3 1 Sycamore St
K4 1 Drake Ho La West 2 Primrose Crs 3 Sothall Ct 4 Sothall Ms
J6 1 May Tree Cft 2 Middlecliff Ct 3 Pedley Cl 4 Waterfield Ms
H6 1 Redfern Ct 2 Saddler Gn
J5 1 Ochre Dike Cl 2 Raseby Pl

180
164
179
194

Swallownest
ASTON
Aston Hall Cricket Club
Aston Lodge School
Nickerwood Farm
Waleswood
Rother Valley Lake
Rother Valley
Rother Valley Country Park
Water Sports Centre
Wales
Wales Bar
S26
Wales Junior & Infant School
Cemetery
High House Farm Court
Norwood
Killamarsh County J & I School
Killamarsh Medical Centre
Killamarsh Leisure Centre
MANSFIELD ROAD
ROTHERHAM ROAD
SCHOOL ROAD
SHEFFIELD ROAD
Delves Lane
Waleswood Road
Pithouse Lane
Rotherham
Derbyshire County
C1 1 Clumber Rl 2 Osprey Rd
B8 1 Nethergreen Ct 2 Nethergr'n Gdns 3 Nethermoor Av 4 Nethermoor Cl 5 Valley Dr
B1 1 Margaret Cl
A1 1 Harrogate Rd 2 Helmsley Cl
C8 1 Murray Rd
grid square represents 500 metres

G4
1 Horseshoe Cl

H5
1 Fathers Gdns

J2
1 De Houton Cl
2 Furnival Cl
3 Horbiry End

G5
1 Lambrell Gn
2 Lestermoor Av

G H J 165 K L M

on 31

I

Old Hall

A57(T)

Kiveton Lane

Todwick

Burne Farm

Upper Common Farm

Todwick JMI School

Mortains

Osborne Drive

2

The Pastures

Barber Close

Storth Lane

Ravis Road

Osborne Road

Osborne Road

Ravis

Manor Way

Stannern End

Roche End

Furnival Road

St Pauls Close

Wasteneys Road

Church Way

Manor Dr

Lindens

A57(T)

Low Laithes Farm

Road

St Pauls Crescent

2

The Guildway

Tortmayns

Meadows

Mill Hills

Rectory Gdns

3

3

Sandpit

Mill Fields

Mill Close

Kiveton Lane

Kiveton Park

Todwick Court

Kiveton Park

Am

182

Wales Junior School

Meadows Junior School

Wales High School

Highfield Av

Anston Av

Park View

Kiveton Gdns

Keeton Hall Road

Storth Lane

Chestnut Avenue

Wesley Road

Pevell

Waverley Av

Shoe Avenue

Meadow Dr

Garden House Dr

High Thorne

Chantry Place

4

Ash Grove

Hill Drive

Limetree Avenue

Stone Avenue

1

Danby Road

Essex

Barry Drive

Rookery Close

Maple Road

Myrtle Grove

Kiveton Park Infant School

B6059

1

2

Keeton Hall Road

ALES ROAD

STATION ROAD

Thomas St

Colliery Road

Kiveton Bridge Station

Stoney Bank

Stone Close

Broadbridge Cl

Broad Bridge Dr

RED HILL

5

more Avenue

2

Rothermoor Avenue

Littlemoor Avenue

Highmoor Avenue

Festival Close

Chapel Way

Greenway

1

Mackenzie Way

Osborne Road

Broad Dyke Close

Lather Close

Saxon Road

Pennythorne Close

1

Kiveton Park Group Practice

Walesmoor

Queens Av

Longlands Avenue

Lambrell Avenue

Ledger

Greenside Av

Norwood

1

Cuckoo Way

RED HILL

Stockwell Av

Coronation Cl

Cuckoo Way

Kiveton-Park Station

6

Way

Cuckoo Way

Peck Mill View

Lady Fl

Hard Lane

Manor Road

Packman Lane

7

Manor Road

Manor Farm

8

Walseker Lane

Northlands

Glebe Avenue

Casson Dr

North Farm Close

1

Thorpe Road

Thorpe Road

K5
1 Trinity Rd

K4
1 Berry Dr
2 Viking Wy

K2
1 Manor Cl

J8
1 Hudson Cl

J5
1 Victoria Cl
2 Victoria Ct

Union Street

Jackys Lane

North Farm Close

Doctors Surgery

Orchard Lee

Glebe Farm Close

Woodall Lane

Woodall Lane

Killamarsh Lane

Greystones Court

1

Woodall Lane

Harthill

Woodall

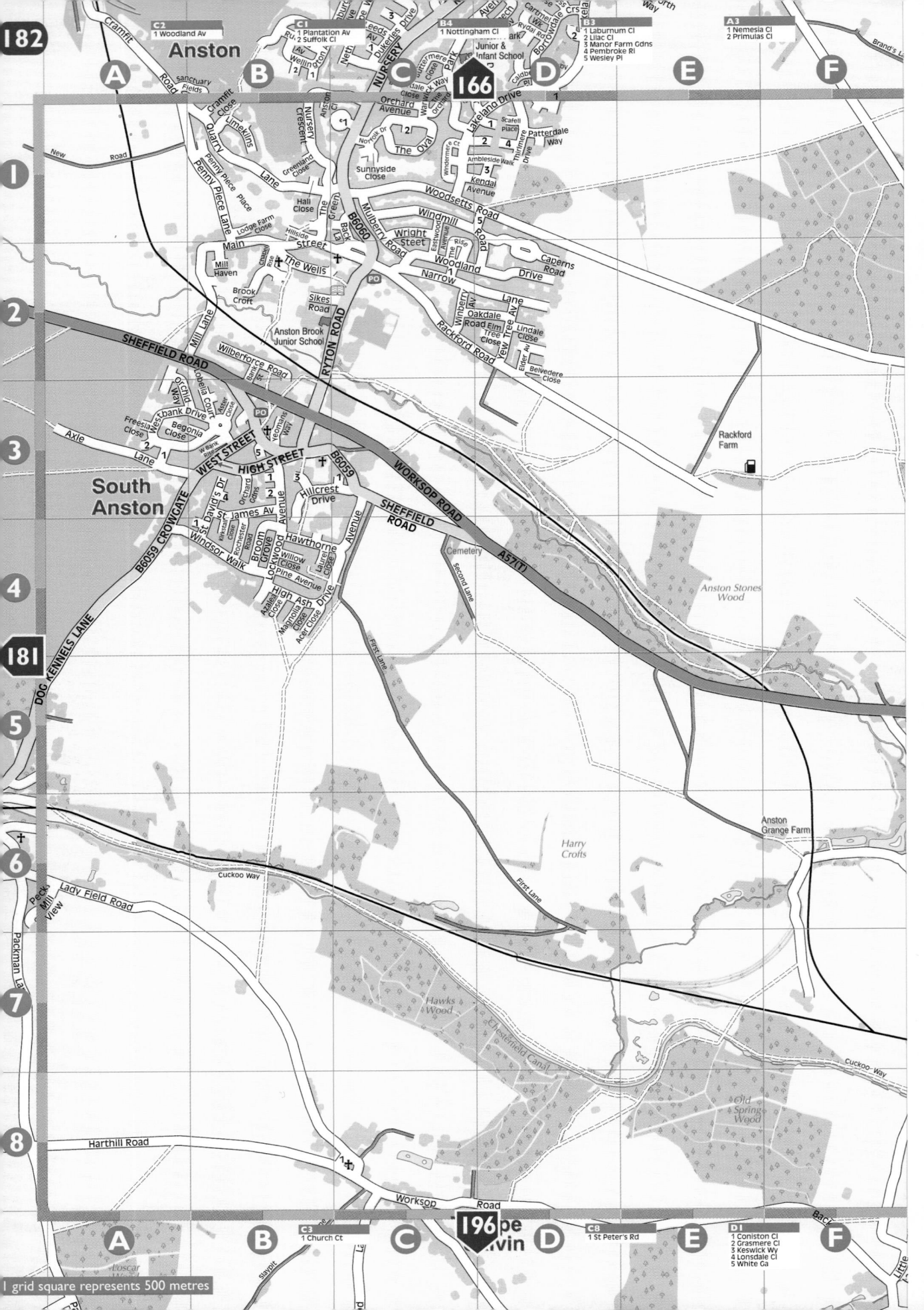

Anston

C2
1 Woodland Av

C1
1 Plantation Av
2 Suffolk Cl

B4
1 Nottingham Cl

B3
1 Laburnum Cl
2 Lilac Cl
3 Manor Farm Gdns
4 Pembroke Ri
5 Wesley Pl

A3
1 Nemesia Cl
2 Primulas Cl

166

Sanctuary
Fields

New Road

Cramfit Close

Limekilns

Quarry Lane

Penny Piece Lane

Penny Piece Place

Nursery Crescent

Greenland Close

The Green

Hall Close

The Green

Lodge Farm Close

Hillside Close

Mill Lane

Main Street

Chapel Place

The Wells

Mill Haven

Brook Croft

Back Lane

B6060

Mulberry Road

Wright Steet

Orchard Avenue

Warwick Way

Lakeland Drive

Junior & Infant School

Scafell Place

Thirlmere Drive

Patterdale Way

Ambleside Walk

Kendal Avenue

Sunnyside Close

Woodsetts Road

Windmill Road

The Woodland Drive

Caperns Road

Eastwood Cl

The Rise

Norfolk Dr

The Oval

Windermere Ct

Sikes Road

Anston Brook Junior School

PO

Narrow Lane

Winberry Av

Oakdale Road

Elm Tree Close

Lindale Close

New Tree Av

Elder Av

Belvedere Close

Rackford Road

Ryton Road

SHEFFIELD ROAD

Wilberforce Road

Bank Street

PO

Axle Lane

Orchid Way

Westbank Drive

Freesia Close

Begonia Close

Lobelia Court

WEST STREET

HIGH STREET

B6059

WORKSOP ROAD

SHEFFIELD ROAD

A57(T)

South Anston

B6059 CROWGATE

Windsor Walk

David's Dr

St James Av

Kirkstall Cl

Rochester Close

Broom Grove

Lockwood

Willow Close

Laurel Close

Pine Avenue

Hillcrest Drive

Hawthorne

Azalea Close

Magnolia Close

Acer Close

High Ash Drive

Avenue

Second Lane

Cemetery

First Lane

Rackford Farm

Anston Stones Wood

DOG KENNELS LANE

181

Pecks Mill View

Lady Field Road

Cuckoo Way

First Lane

Harry Crofts

Anston Grange Farm

Packman La

Hawks Wood

Chesterfield Canal

Old Spring Wood

Harthill Road

Worksop Road

Cuckoo Way

196

C3
1 Church Ct

C8
1 St Peter's Rd

D1
1 Coniston Cl
2 Grasmere Cl
3 Keswick Wy
4 Lonsdale Cl
5 White Ga

1 grid square represents 500 metres

J3
1 Pear Tree Cl
2 Worksop Rd
K8
1 Cherry Tree Av
2 Pembroke Rd
3 Pilgrim Ct
4 Potters Nook
5 York Pl
Gildingwells
167
Home Farm
Wallingwells Lane
Brand's Lane
Swinston Hill Road
Woodsetts Road
Brand's Farm
Oakland Close
Brandsmere Drive
Brands Close
Wallingwe
Dinnington Road
Hoads Avenue
Northfield Drive
Gildingwells
Springfield Close
Woodsetts Infant School
Berne Sq
Whitfield Gdns
Woodsetts
Worksop Road
Infant School
Warren Close
Cross Lane Close
Cross Field Drive
Nottinghamshire County
Rotherham
Wellfield Crs
Scholey Avenue
Limestone Close
Rockfield Dr
Stambers Close
Grange Avenue
Lindrick Road
Taylor Crescent
Taylor Drive
Cotterhill Woods
184
Worksop Road
Owday Lane
Rough Piece
Lindrick Common
Lindrick Golf Club
Lindrick Dale
Woodsetts Lane
GATEFORD ROAD
Brancliffe Grange
St Lukes C of E School
Moses View
Brancliffe Lane
Monks Way
Shireoaks
Shireoaks Common
Cartwright Street
Glenthorn Close
Leeds Road
Woodside Road
Elmtree Close
Cornwall Road
Walnut Avenue
Gateford Common
Turnerwood
Shireoaks Station
Cuckoo Way
Shireoaks Business Centre
Claylands Avenue
197
Thorpe Lane
Stadium

A8
1 Chaffinch Ms
2 Cuckoo Holt
3 Greenfinch Dl
4 Heron Gld
5 Magpie Cl
6 The Mallards

A   B   C   168   D   E   F

168

1 Stewart Cl

I

North Carlton

Oxford Road
Nottingham
County Health
Clinic

Long Lane
Stewart Road

Windsor Gardens

Carlsbrook Road
Craithie Road
Craigston Road
Stirling
Glamis
Pembroke Drive
Richmond
Conway
Corway
Balmoral Close
Strathaven Road
Strathmore Drive
Kenilworth Drive
Warwick Avenue
Windsor Road

Windsor Road   Arundel Drive

The Green

Granary Court

Hodsock Lane

Water Lane

2   Carlton in   The Cross   Highfield Grove
Lindrick

Wallingwells
Wood

S81

PO   Low Street

HIGH ROAD

2   Carlton in
Lindrick

Wallingwells

Carlton Hall Lane   Church Lane   South
Carlton

3

Carlton
Lake

ire County   Wigthorpe Lane   Liquorice Lane

Tinker's

Hill

Lane

Wigthorpe

4   Holme House   Owday Lane
Farm

A60

Technical
College

183   Broom Farm

Red   Lane

5   Owday
Wood

CARLTON ROAD

A60

6

7   Ashes Park Avenue   Eastwood Court
Applewood   Eddison   Morton   Ash Holt
Close   Mitchell Cv   Grove   Drive
Beaufort Way   Broomhill Av
Lancaster Walk   Halifax Dr
Manston Way   Park   Westerdale
St Mark's   Alexander Drive   Avenue   Rosedale   Bedale   Bransdale
Close   Keswick   Eskdale Dr   Appleby   Winter Grove   Kingsdale
Cromwell   Road   Court   Whatfedale
Wellesley Close   Rydal   Farndale
Coniston   Kendal Cl   Grasmere   Eddison   Wensleydale   Costerdale
Road   Ambleside Gra   Road   Road   Field   Close   Farndale   Coverdale
Gateford   Keswick Road   Landale   Meade   Close   Coverdale   Lane
Road   Carlton Close   Road   Drive   Hemmingfield   Whitsun
St Johns   Hemmingfield Road   Thievesdale
C of E   RAYMOTH LANE   B6041   THIEVESDALE LANE   Farm

8   GATEFORD ROAD   Gateford   Primary School
B6041   Buckingham Rise   Chatsworth   Durham Cl   Westminster
Sandmartins   Windsor   Dove Close   Road   Cl   Winchester   Thievesdale
Fieldfare   Road   Welland Close   Harewood Cl   Mercia Close   Canterbury Cl   Farm
Kestrel   Nene Walk   Curzon   Coppice   Gloucester   Fallow
Kingfisher Walk   Sheaf   Maple   Rochester Cl   View
Plover Drive   Gateford Rise   Vessey Road   Drive   Prospect Hill   BLYTH ROAD
Fulmar Way   Dawber Street   Prospect   3   Kilton Forest
Gateford Drive   Carlton Avenue   Drive   Golf Club

D8   A   B   E7   C   198   D   E8   E   F8   F
1 Thievesdale Av   1 Chapel Ga   1 Hemmingfield Wy   1 Bishopdale   1 Thornton Dl
2 Church Field Cl   2 Mossdale   2 Close Barn   2 Wheat Cft
3 Ribblesdale   3 Forest Hill Rd
4 Uttondale
5 Mercia Cl
6 Stable Cl
7 Worcester Cl

G   H   J   K   L   M

I

Red Bridge

Hodsock
Plantation

River Ryton

Damings
Wood

Forest
Farm

Elm
Wood

Black
Screed

Alder
Plantation

Forest
Plantation

Hodsock
Manor Farm

Ash
Holt

1

2

3

4

186

5

6

7

8

Crossley
Hill
Wood

Crossley Hill Lane

Fifty
Acres

Broom
Covert

Hundred Acre Lane

Broom
Hill
Wood

Hundred
Acre
Wood

B6045

Red Lane

Cowlishaw
Plantation

Carlton
Forest Farm

Thievesdale Lane

East
Thievesdale
Wood

Thievesdale Lane

Rayton
Angle

Scofton
Wood

186

A　B　C　170　D　E　F

Beech Farm

Damings Wood

Steeple Plantation

Tinker Lane

Tinker Lane

Forest Farm

A1(T)

BLYTH ROAD

Ranby Cottage Farm

River Ryton

Firs Farm

Ranby Hall

185

Bilby

A1(T)

Green Mile Lane

The Barracks

Old Blyth Road

Thievesdale Lane

Coachroad Plantation

Chequer Bridge

Hatchet Flat

A1(T)

Ranby C of E Primary School

Ranby House Preparatory School

Ranby

Strawberry Mile

Chequer Close

BLYTH ROAD

Beech Wood Farm

A　B　C　D　E　F

I grid square represents 500 metres

1　2　3　4　5　6　7　8

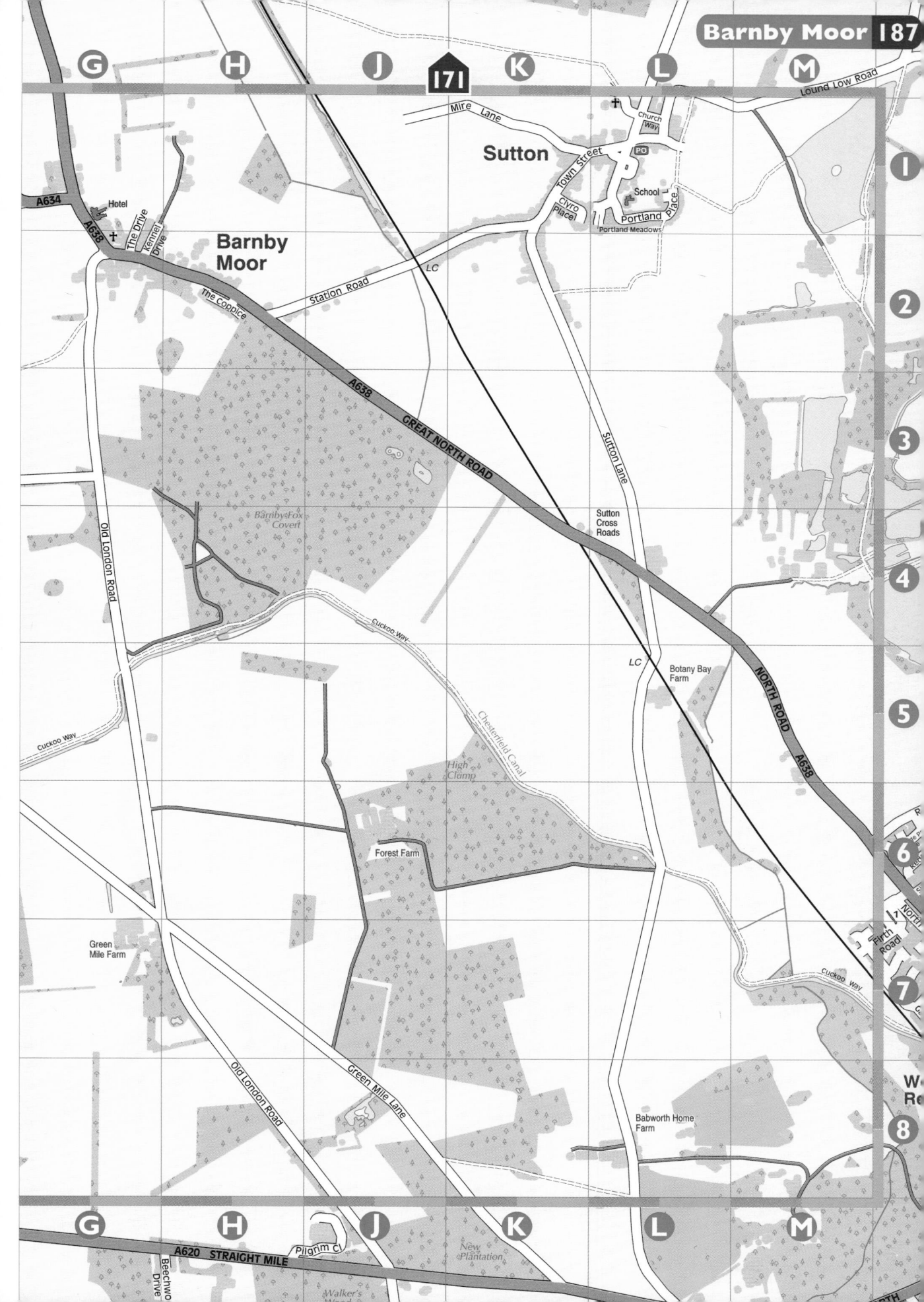

G H J 171 K L M

I
2
3
4
5
6
7
8

Lound Low Road

Mire Lane

Sutton

Church Way
PO
Town Street
School
Clyro Place
Portland Place
Portland Meadows

A634
A638
Hotel
The Drive
Kennel Drive

Barnby Moor

The Coppice
Station Road
LC

A638 GREAT NORTH ROAD

Sutton Lane

Sutton Cross Roads

Old London Road

Barnby Fox Covert

Cuckoo Way

LC

Botany Bay Farm

NORTH ROAD A638

Chesterfield Canal

Cuckoo Way

High Clamp

Forest Farm

Green Mile Farm

North

Firth Road

Cuckoo Way

Green Mile Lane

Old London Road

Babworth Home Farm

We
Re

New Plantation

G H J K L M

A620 STRAIGHT MILE
Pilgrim Cl
Beechwo
Drive

Walker's

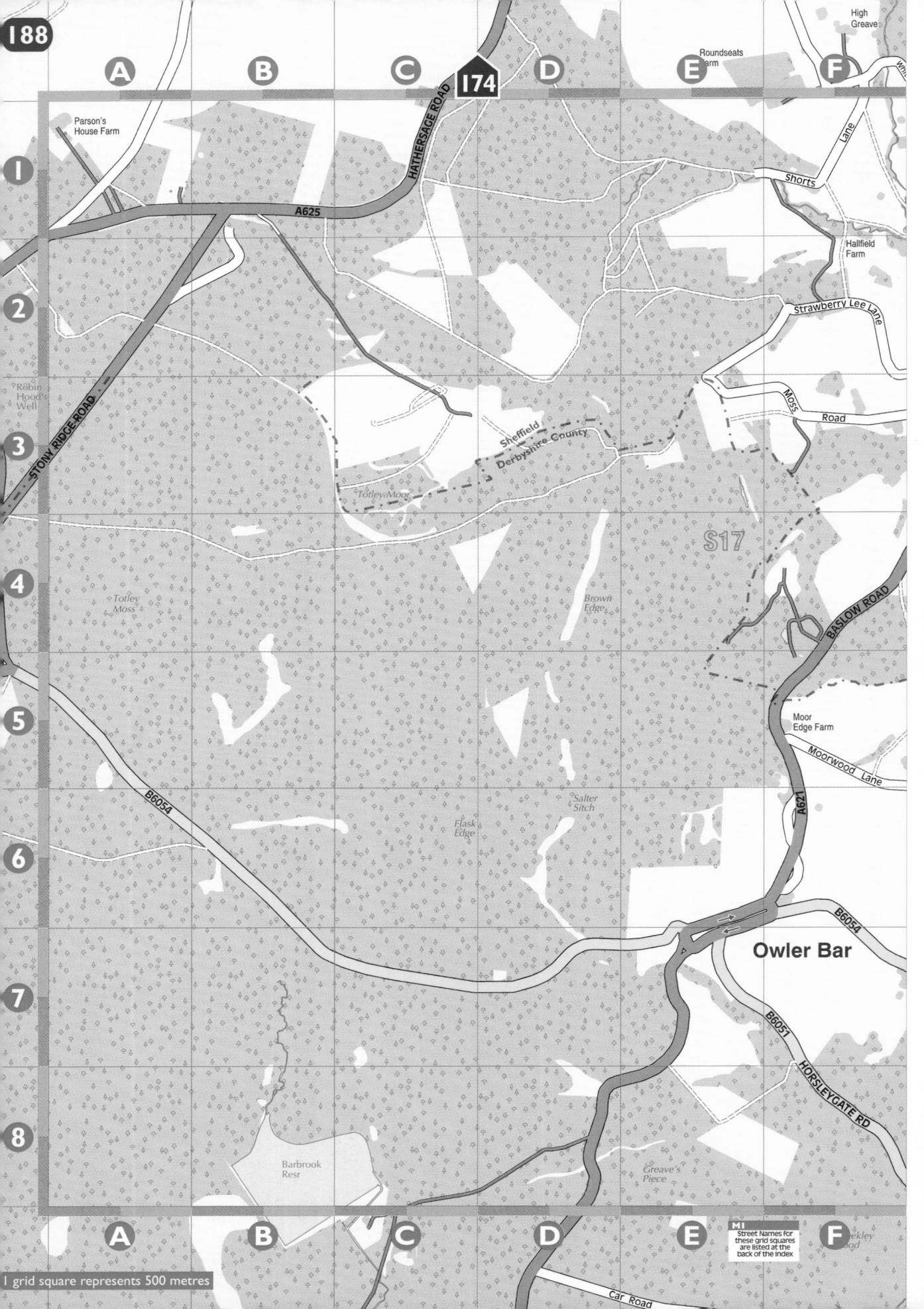

174

A   B   C   D   E   F

1   Parson's House Farm   High Greave

Roundseats Farm

Shorts Lane

Hallfield Farm

A625   HATHERSAGE ROAD

Robin Hood's Well   Strawberry Lee Lane

2

STONY RIDGE ROAD

Moss Road

3   Sheffield
                               Derbyshire County

Totley Moor   S17

4   Totley Moss   Brown Edge   BASLOW ROAD

Moor Edge Farm

5   Moorwood Lane

B6054   A621

Salter Sitch

6   Flask Edge

B6054

Owler Bar

7   B6051

HORSLEYGATE RD

8

Barbrook Resr   Greave's Piece

A   B   C   D   E   F

Car Road

1 grid square represents 500 metres

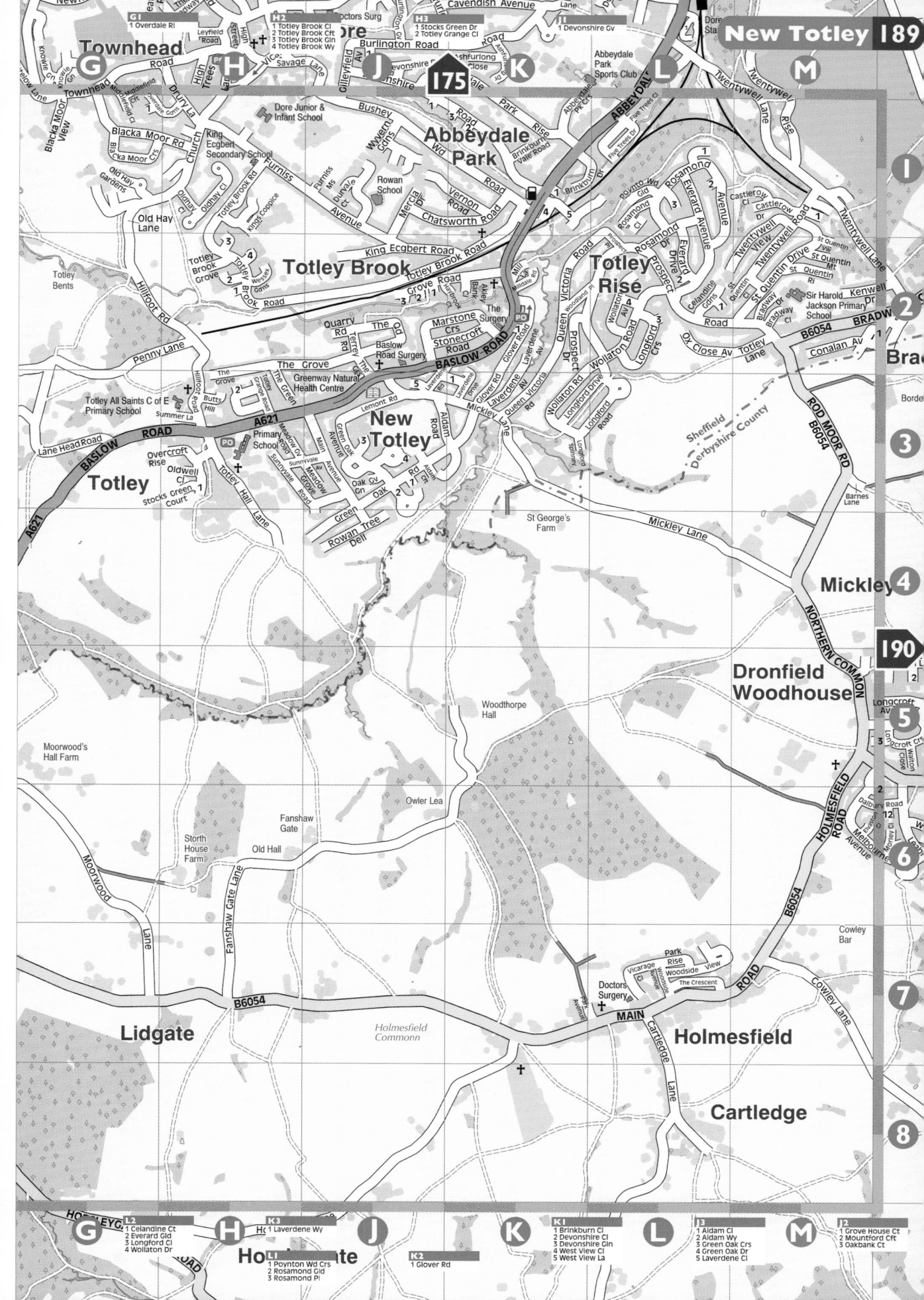

Townhead

Abbeydale Park

Totley Brook

Totley Rise

Totley Bents

New Totley

Totley

Sheffield
Derbyshire County

Mickley

Dronfield
Woodhouse

Woodthorpe
Hall

Moorwood's
Hall Farm

Owler Lea

Fanshaw
Gate

Storth House
Farm

Old Hall

Lidgate

Holmesfield
Commonn

Cowley
Bar

Holmesfield

Cartledge

St George's
Farm

G		
G1		
1 Overdale Ri		

H2		
1 Totley Brook Cl		
2 Totley Brook Cft		
3 Totley Brook Gln		
4 Totley Brook Wy		

H3		
1 Stocks Green Dr		
2 Totley Grange Cl		

I1		
1 Devonshire Gv		

G		
L2		
1 Celandine Ct		
2 Everard Gld		
3 Longford Cl		
4 Wollaton Dr		

H		
K3		
1 Laverdene Wy		

J		
L1		
1 Poynton Wd Crs		
2 Rosamond Gld		
3 Rosamond Pl		

K2		
1 Glover Rd		

K		
K1		
1 Brinkburn Cl		
2 Devonshire Cl		
3 Devonshire Gln		
4 West View Cl		
5 West View La		

L		

M		
J3		
1 Aldam Cl		
2 Aldam Wy		
3 Green Oak Crs		
4 Green Oak Dr		
5 Laverdene Cl		

M		
J2		
1 Grove House Ct		
2 Mountford Cft		
3 Oakbank Ct		

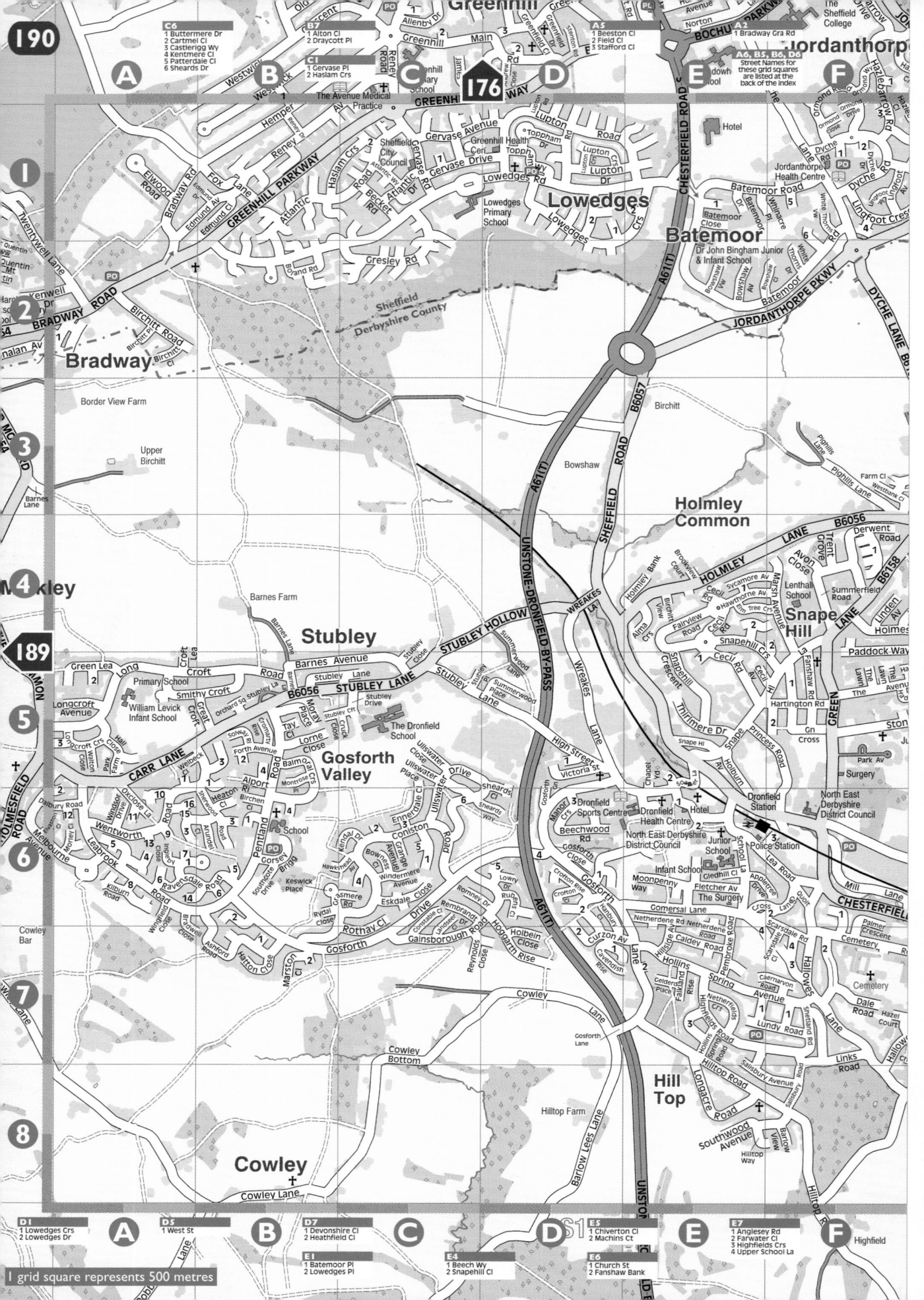

190
C6
1 Buttermere Dr
2 Cartmel Cl
3 Castlerigg Wy
4 Kentmere Cl
5 Patterdale Cl
6 Sheards Dr
B7
1 Alton Cl
2 Draycott Pl
C1
1 Gervase Pl
2 Haslam Crs
A5
1 Beeston Cl
2 Field Cl
3 Stafford Cl
A2
1 Bradway Gra Rd
A6, B5, B6, D6
Street Names for these grid squares are listed at the back of the index
176
189
Greenhill
Jordanthorpe
The Sheffield College
The Avenue Medical Practice
Lowedges
Lowedges Primary School
Greenhill Health Centre
Sheffield City Council
Batemoor
Dr John Bingham Junior & Infant School
Jordanthorpe Health Centre
Hotel
GREENHILL PARKWAY
BRADWAY ROAD
CHESTERFIELD ROAD
JORDANTHORPE PKWY
DYCHE LANE
Bradway
Sheffield
Derbyshire County
Border View Farm
Upper Birchitt
Birchitt
Bowshaw
Holmley Common
HOLMLEY LANE
B6056
B6057
SHEFFIELD ROAD
A61(T)
UNSTONE-DRONFIELD BY-PASS
Barnes Farm
Stubley
STUBLEY HOLLOW
STUBLEY LANE
CARR LANE
Primary School
William Levick Infant School
The Dronfield School
Gosforth Valley
Snape Hill
Lenthall School
Surgery
Dronfield Station
North East Derbyshire District Council
Police Station
Dronfield Sports Centre
Dronfield Health Centre
North East Derbyshire District Council
Junior School
Infant School
The Surgery
CHESTERFIELD
Cemetery
HOLMESFIELD ROAD
Cowley Bar
Cowley Bottom
Cowley
Cowley Lane
Hilltop Farm
Hill Top
Barlow Lees Lane
Highfield
D1
1 Lowedges Crs
2 Lowedges Dr
D5
1 West St
D7
1 Devonshire Cl
2 Heathfield Cl
E1
1 Batemoor Pl
2 Lowedges Pl
E4
1 Beech Wy
2 Snapehill Cl
E5
1 Chiverton Cl
2 Machins Ct
E6
1 Church St
2 Fanshaw Bank
E7
1 Anglesey Rd
2 Farwater Cl
3 Highfields Crs
4 Upper School La
1 grid square represents 500 metres

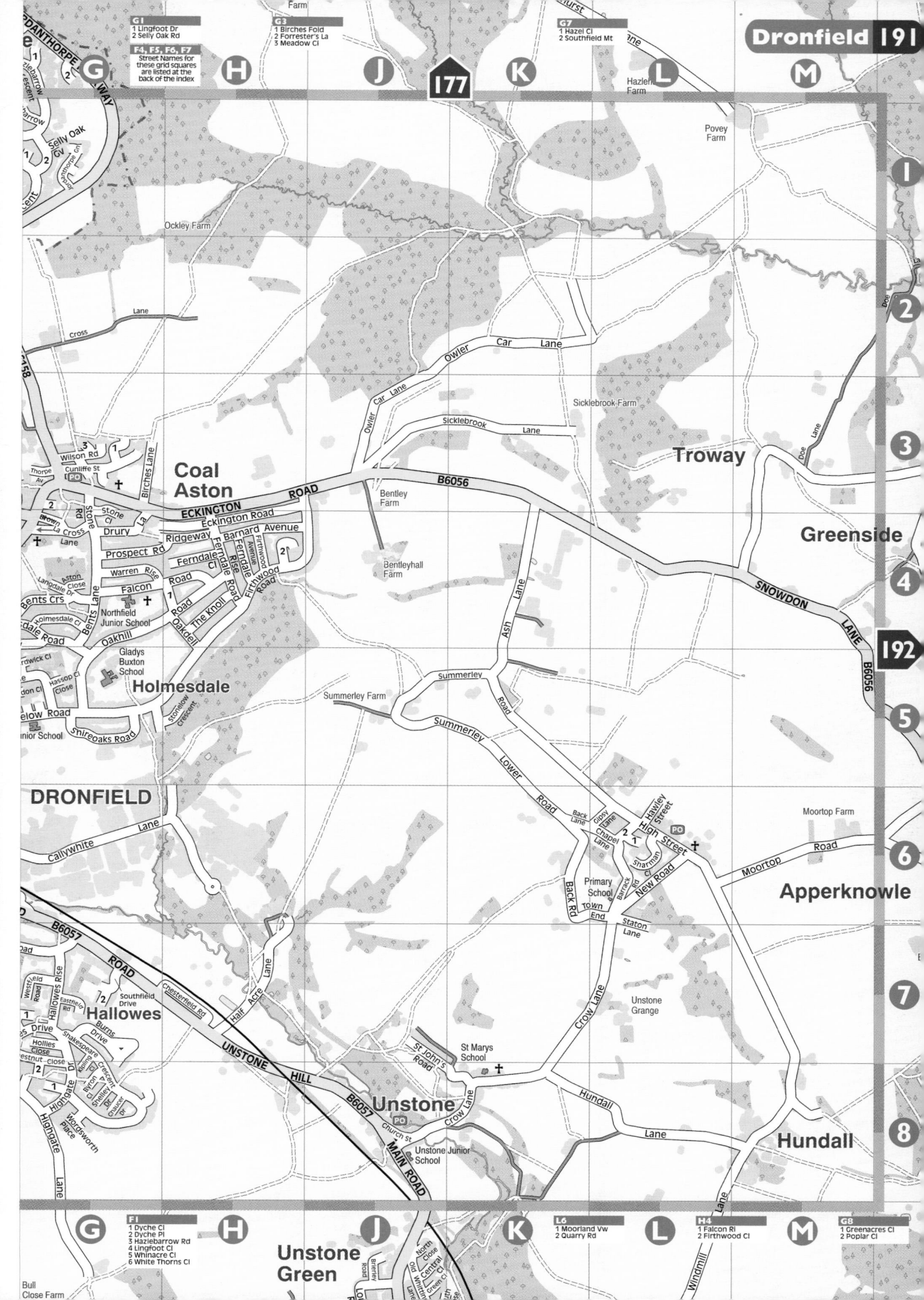
G1
1 Lingfoot Dr
2 Selly Oak Rd
F4, F5, F6, F7
Street Names for these grid squares are listed at the back of the index
G3
1 Birches Fold
2 Forrester's La
3 Meadow Cl
177
G7
1 Hazel Cl
2 Southfield Mt
Coal Aston
Ockley Farm
Povey Farm
Owler Car Lane
Sicklebrook Lane
Sicklebrook Farm
Troway
Greenside
Eckington Road
B6056
Bentley Farm
Bentleyhall Farm
Snowdon Lane
192
Holmesdale
Northfield Junior School
Gladys Buxton School
Ash Lane
Summerley Farm
Summerley Road
Summerley Lower Road
DRONFIELD
Callywhite Lane
High Street
Moortop Farm
Moortop Road
Apperknowle
Primary School
Staton Lane
Crow Lane
Unstone Grange
Hallowes
Unstone Hill
B6057
Chesterfield Rd
Half Acre Lane
St Marys School
St John's Road
Unstone
Hundall Lane
Hundall
Main Road
Church St
Unstone Junior School
Windmill Lane
F1
1 Dyche Cl
2 Dyche Pl
3 Hazlebarrow Rd
4 Lingfoot Cl
5 Whinacre Cl
6 White Thorns Cl
L6
1 Moorland Vw
2 Quarry Rd
H4
1 Falcon Ri
2 Firthwood Cl
G8
1 Greenacres Cl
2 Poplar Cl
Unstone Green
Bull Close Farm

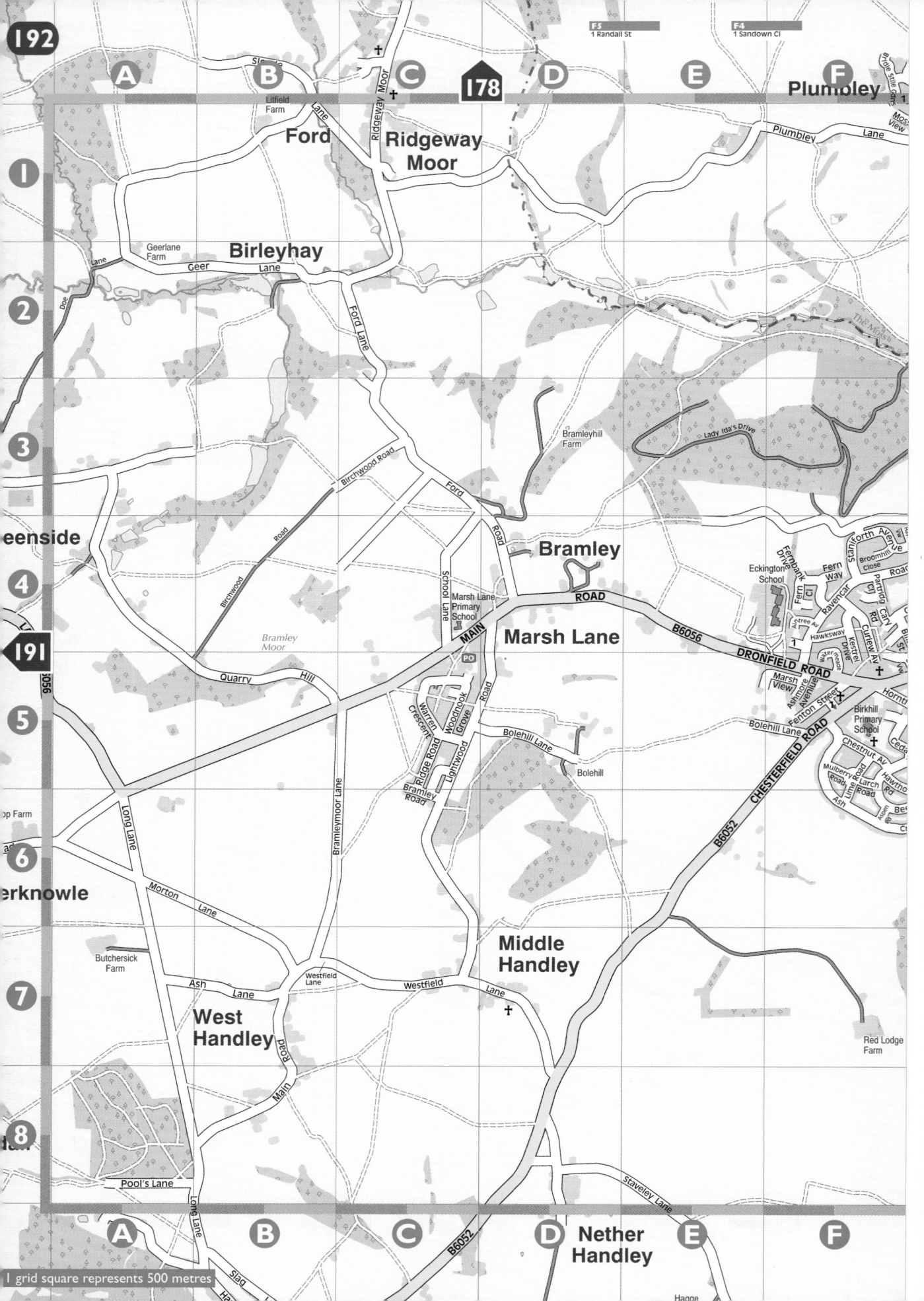
F5 1 Randall St
F4 1 Sandown Cl
178
A
B
C
D
E
F
1
2
3
4
5
6
7
8
Plumbley
Litfield Farm
Ford
Ridgeway Moor
Ridgeway Moor
Ford Lane
Plumbley Lane
Geerlane Farm
Birleyhay
Geer Lane
Doe Lane
The Moss
Lady Ida's Drive
Bramleyhill Farm
Birchwood Road
Ford Road
eenside
Bramley
Eckington School
Fernbank Drive
Fern Cl
Fern Way
Stanforth Avenue
Broomhill Close
Ravencar
Partridge Cl
Cary Rd
Curlew Av
Kestrel Drive
Hawksway
Watermeade
Birchwood Road
School Lane
Marsh Lane Primary School
MAIN ROAD
B6056
DRONFIELD ROAD
Marsh Lane
Bramley Moor
191
Quarry Hill
Marsh View
Ashmore Avenue
Fenton Street
Birkhill Primary School
Bolehill Lane
Warren Crescent
Woodnook Grove
Road
Bolehill Lane
Bolehill
CHESTERFIELD ROAD
B6052
Chestnut Av
Mulberry Road
Lime Road
Larch Rd
Ash
Ridge Road
Lightwood
Bramley Road
Long Lane
Bramleymoor Lane
p Farm
erknowle
Morton Lane
Butchersick Farm
Ash Lane
Westfield Lane
Westfield Lane
Middle Handley
West Handley
Road
Main
Red Lodge Farm
Pool's Lane
Long Lane
Staveley Lane
B6052
Nether Handley
Slag
Hagge
1 grid square represents 500 metres

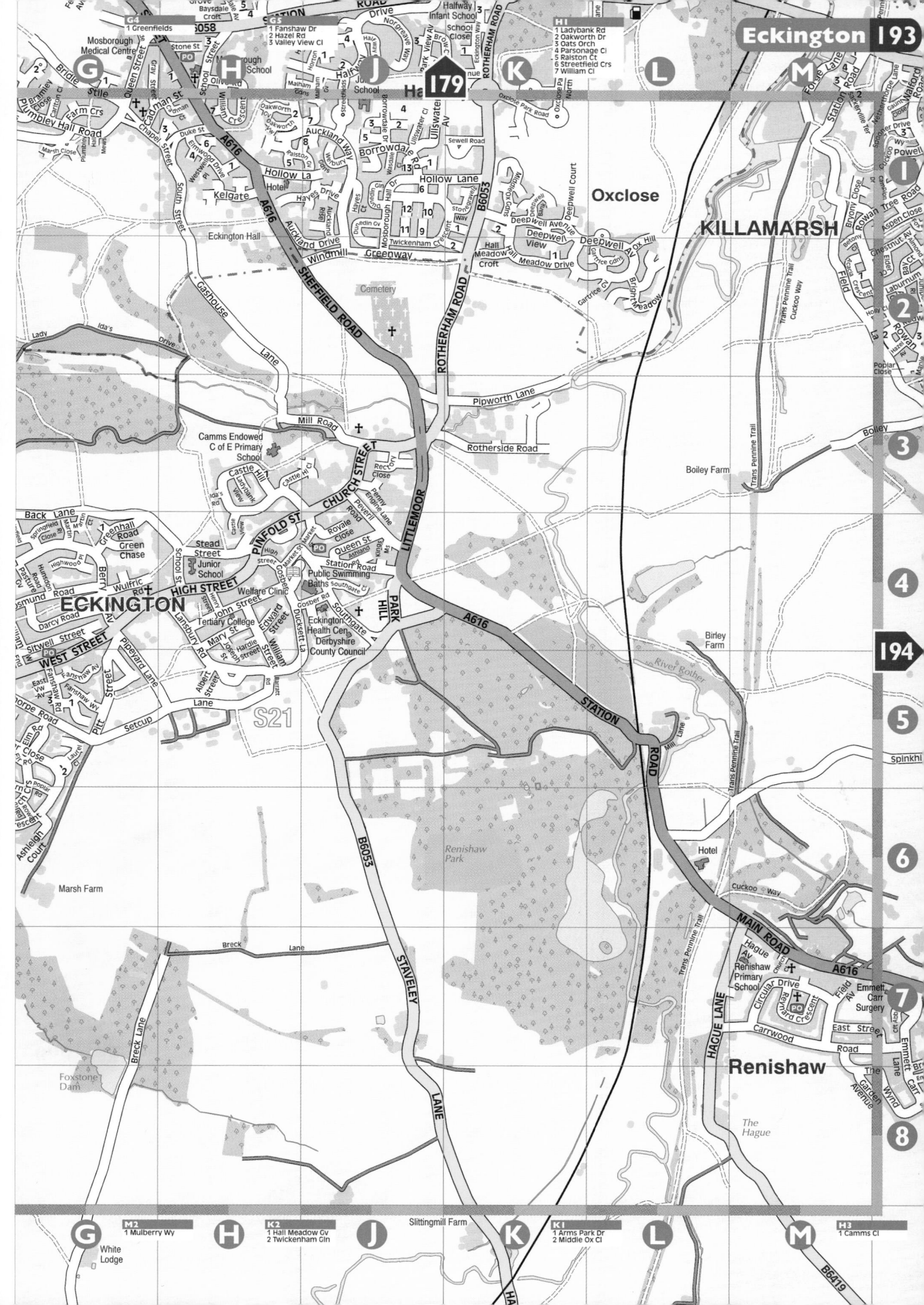
G4
1 Greenfields
G5
1 Fanshaw Dr
2 Hazel Rd
3 Valley View Cl
H1
1 Ladybank Rd
2 Oakworth Dr
3 Oats Orch
4 Parsonage Cl
5 Ralston Ct
6 Streetfield Crs
7 William Cl
Mosborough Medical Centre
Halfway Infant School
School Close
Mosborough School
179
Oxclose
KILLAMARSH
Eckington Hall
Cemetery
Camms Endowed C of E Primary School
Boiley Farm
Birley Farm
River Rother
194
ECKINGTON
Junior School
Public Swimming Baths
Welfare Clinic
Tertiary College
Eckington Health Cen
Derbyshire County Council
S21
Renishaw Park
Marsh Farm
Hotel
Renishaw Primary School
Emmett Carr Surgery
Renishaw
The Hague
Foxstone Dam
White Lodge
Slittingmill Farm
SHEFFIELD ROAD
ROTHERHAM ROAD
LITTLEMOOR
STATION ROAD
MAIN ROAD
STAVELEY LANE
HAGUE LANE
HIGH STREET
WEST STREET
CHURCH STREET
PINFOLD ST
Trans Pennine Trail
Pipworth Lane
Rotherside Road
Mill Road
Gashouse Lane
Breck Lane
Setcup Lane
Cuckoo Way
A616
B6053
B6419
B6058
M2
1 Mulberry Wy
K2
1 Hall Meadow Gv
2 Twickenham Gln
K1
1 Arms Park Dr
2 Middle Ox Cl
H3
1 Camms Cl

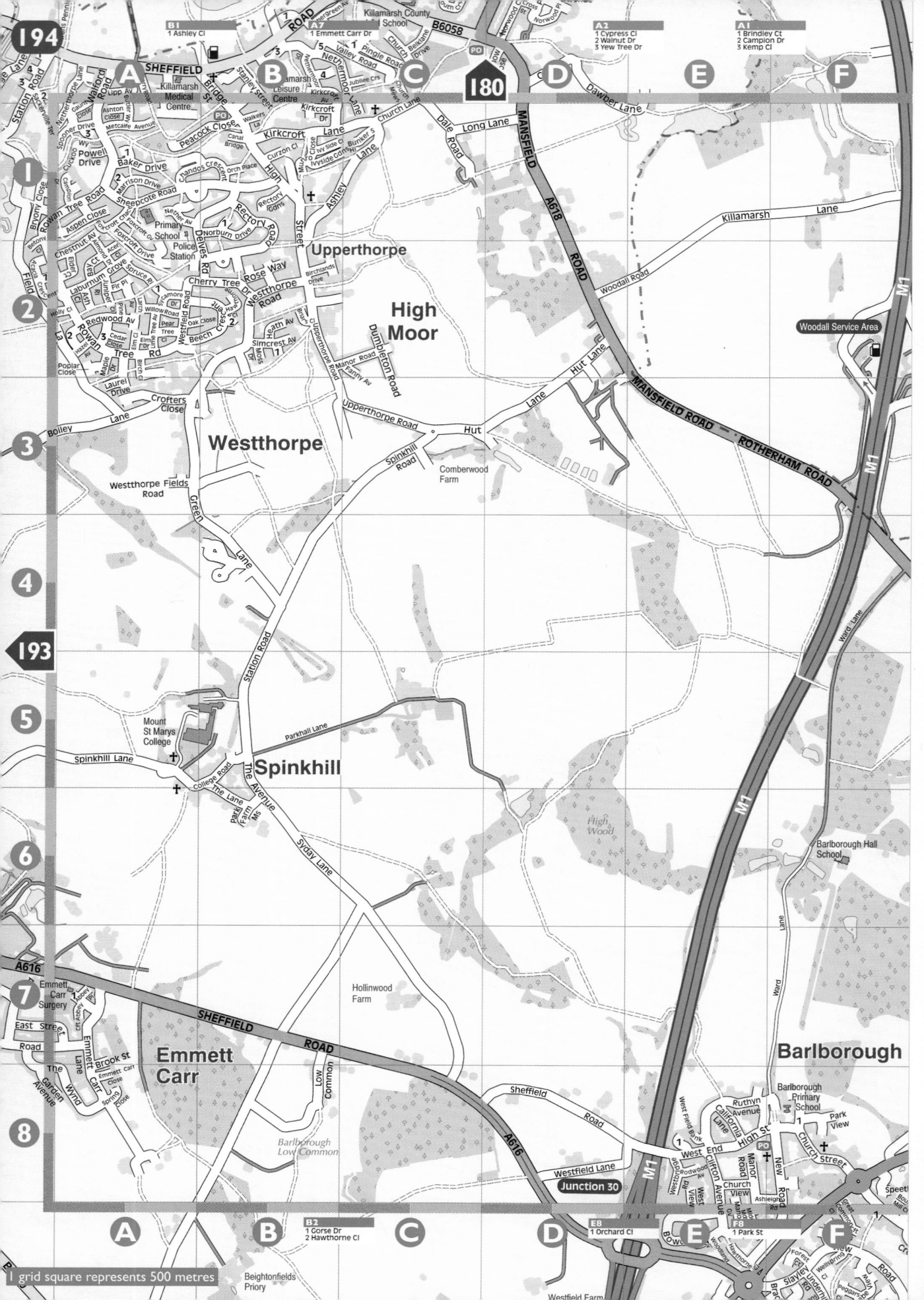

194
180
193
B1
1 Ashley Cl
A7
1 Emmett Carr Dr
A2
1 Cypress Cl
2 Walnut Dr
3 Yew Tree Dr
A1
1 Brindley Ct
2 Campion Dr
3 Kemp Cl
Killamarsh County Junior School
B6058
SHEFFIELD
Killamarsh Medical Centre
Killamarsh Leisure Centre
Primary School
Police Station
Upperthorpe
High Moor
Westthorpe
Westthorpe Fields Road
Comberwood Farm
Woodall Service Area
Mount St Marys College
Spinkhill
High Wood
Barlborough Hall School
Hollinwood Farm
Emmett Carr
Emmett Carr Surgery
Barlborough Low Common
Barlborough
Barlborough Primary School
Junction 30
Beightonfields Priory
Westfield Farm
B2
1 Gorse Dr
2 Hawthorne Cl
E8
1 Orchard Cl
F8
1 Park St
MANSFIELD ROAD
ROTHERHAM ROAD
SHEFFIELD ROAD
A618
A616
M1
Killamarsh Lane
Woodall Road
Hut Lane
Upperthorpe Road
Spinkhill Road
Station Road
Green Lane
Spinkhill Lane
Parkhall Lane
Sydday Lane
The Avenue
College Road
Ward Lane
Sheffield Road
Westfield Lane
Dawber Lane
Long Lane
Dale Road
Boiley Lane
Crofters Close
High Street
Church Street
West End
1 grid square represents 500 metres

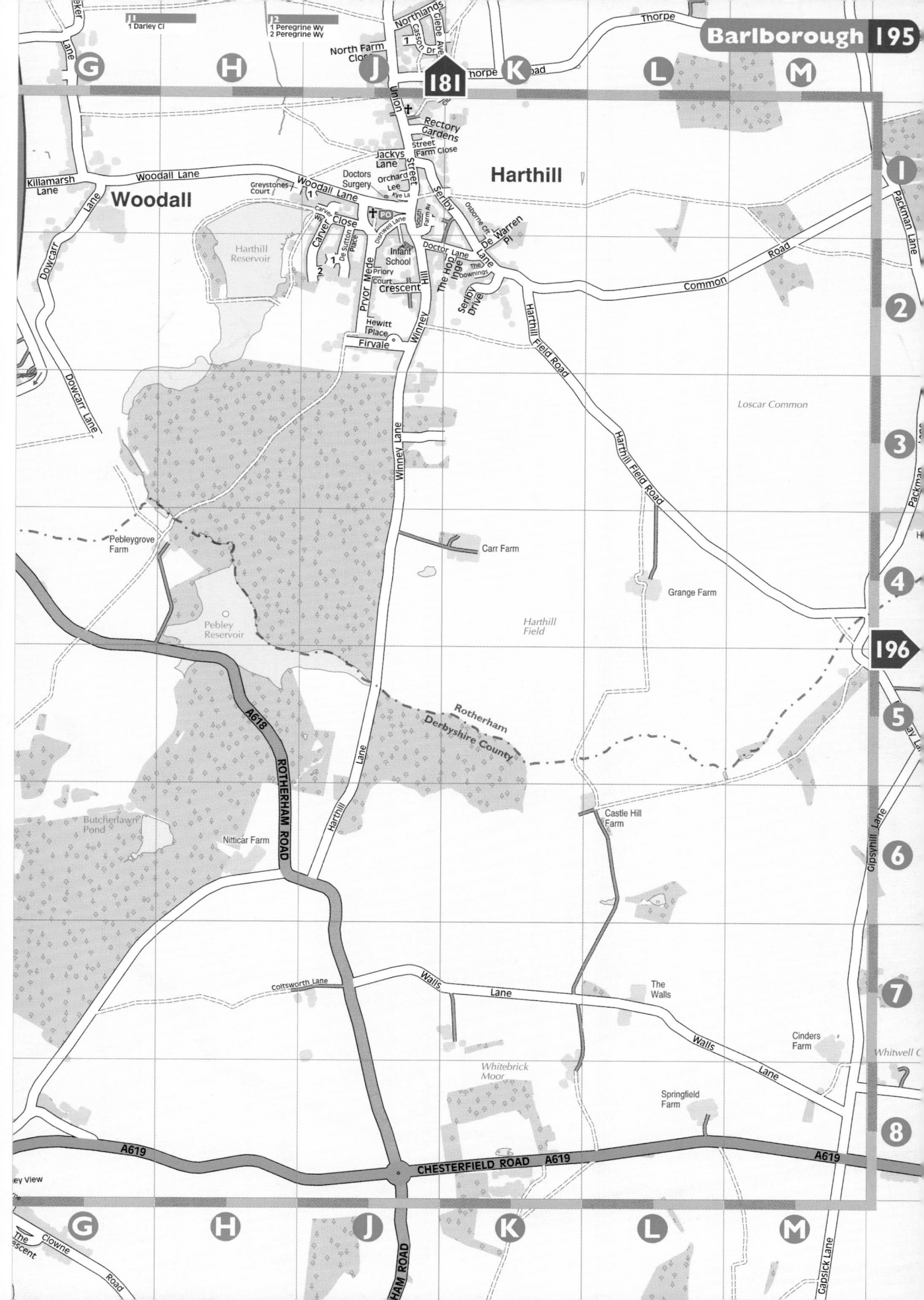

1 Darley Cl
1 Peregrine Wy
2 Peregrine Wy
Northlands
Glebe Ave
Casson Dr
North Farm Close
Thorpe Road
181
G
H
J
K
L
M
Union
Rectory Gardens
Street Farm Close
Jackys Lane
Street
Doctors Surgery
Orchard Lee
Kye La
Harthill
Woodall Lane
Killamarsh Lane
Greystones Court
Woodall
Carver Wy
Carver Close
De Sutton Place
Dishwell Lane
South Farm Av
Serlby Lane
Osborne Cft
De Warren Pl
Doctor Lane
The Hop Inge
The Downings
Infant School
Priory Court
Crescent
Pryor Mede
Winney Hill
Serlby Drive
Hewitt Place
Firvale
Harthill Reservoir
Dowcarr Lane
Common Road
Packman Lane
Harthill Field Road
Loscar Common
Winney Lane
Pebleygrove Farm
Carr Farm
Grange Farm
Harthill Field
Pebley Reservoir
196
Rotherham
Derbyshire County
A618
ROTHERHAM ROAD
Harthill Lane
Castle Hill Farm
Butcherlawn Pond
Nitticar Farm
Gipsyhill Lane
Coltsworth Lane
Walls Lane
The Walls
Cinders Farm
Whitebrick Moor
Springfield Farm
A619
CHESTERFIELD ROAD
The Crescent
Clowne Road
Gapsick Lane
2
3
4
5
6
7
8

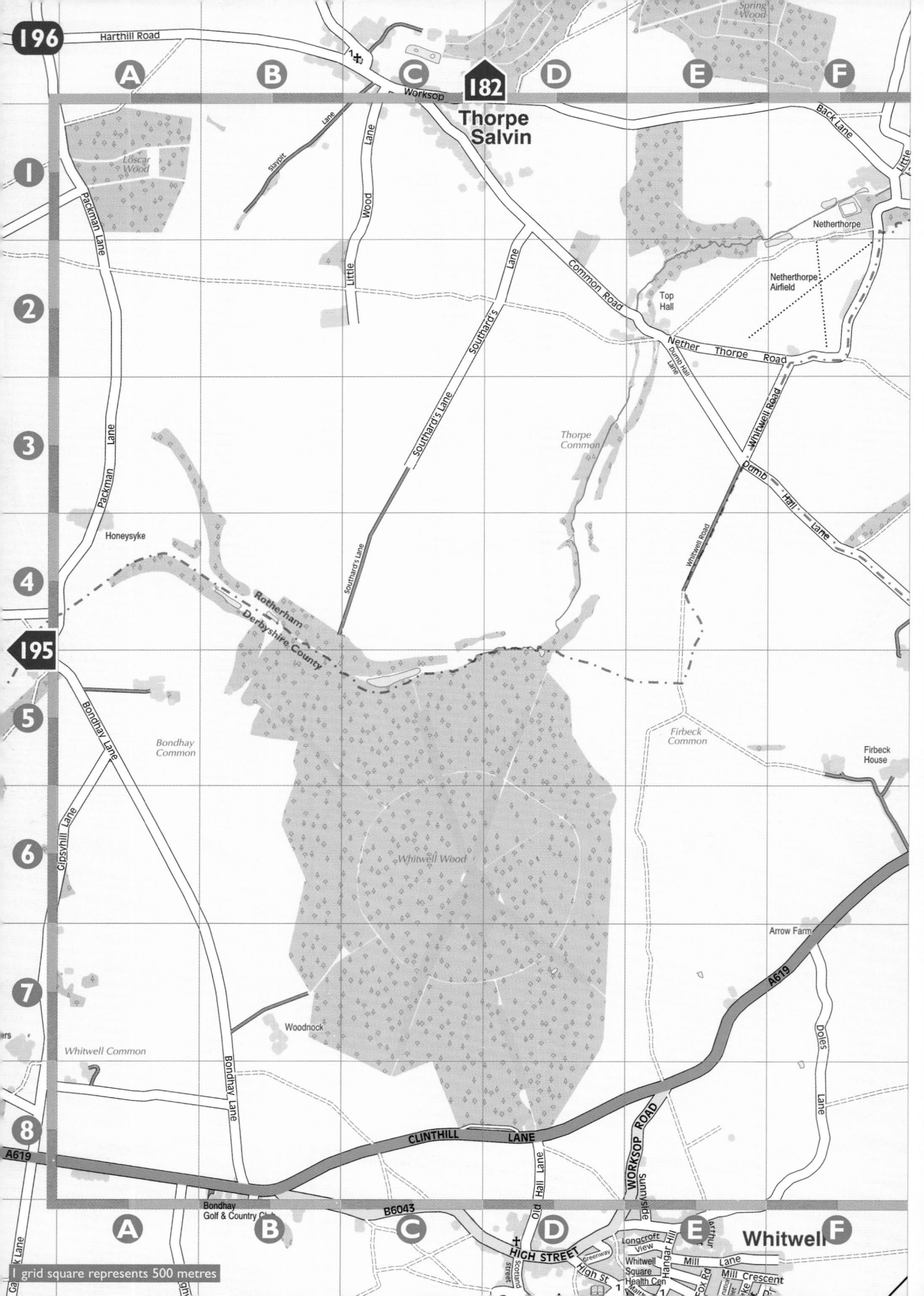

196
182
195
Harthill Road
Worksop
Thorpe Salvin
Spring Wood
Loscar Wood
Slaypit Lane
Little Wood Lane
Packman Lane
Back Lane
Netherthorpe
Netherthorpe Airfield
Common Road
Southard's Lane
Top Hall
Nether Thorpe Road
Dumb Hall Lane
Whitwell Road
Thorpe Common
Honeysyke
Rotherham
Derbyshire County
Bondhay Lane
Bondhay Common
Firbeck Common
Firbeck House
Gipsyhill Lane
Whitwell Wood
Arrow Farm
A619
Woodnock
Whitwell Common
Doles Lane
Worksop Road
Clinthill Lane
Old Hall Lane
Sunnyside
Bondhay Golf & Country Club
B6043
High Street
Greenway
Longcroft View
Whitwell Square
Health Cen
Hangar Hill
Mill Lane
Mill Crescent
High St
Scotland Street
Whitwell
1 grid square represents 500 metres

Turnerwood
Rhodesia
Darfoulds
Hodthorpe
Shireoaks Station
183
198
Shireoaks Business Centre
Dukeries Industrial Estate
The Hall
Shireoaks Miners Welfare & Sports Club
Thorpe Lane
Spring Lane
Shireoaks Road
Tranker Lane
A57(T)
Steetley Lane
Tylden Road
Boughton Road
Royds Crs
Primary School
Cecil Close
Marjorie St
Mable St
Mary Street
Winifred St
Elizabeth Crs
Holme Carr
Lady Lee Farm
High Grounds Way
Lodge Farm
Ladylea Close
Ashwood Rd
Scratta Lane
Featherbed Lane
MANSFIELD ROAD
A60
A619
West Wood
Harness Grove
Burnt Leys Farm
Ratcliffe Grange
Claylands Avenue
Cornwall Road
Leeds Road
Walnut Avenue
Elmtree Close
Glenthorn Close
Cuckoo Way
L2 1 Tylden Wy
M2 1 Tylden Rd
G H J K L M
1 2 3 4 5 6 7 8

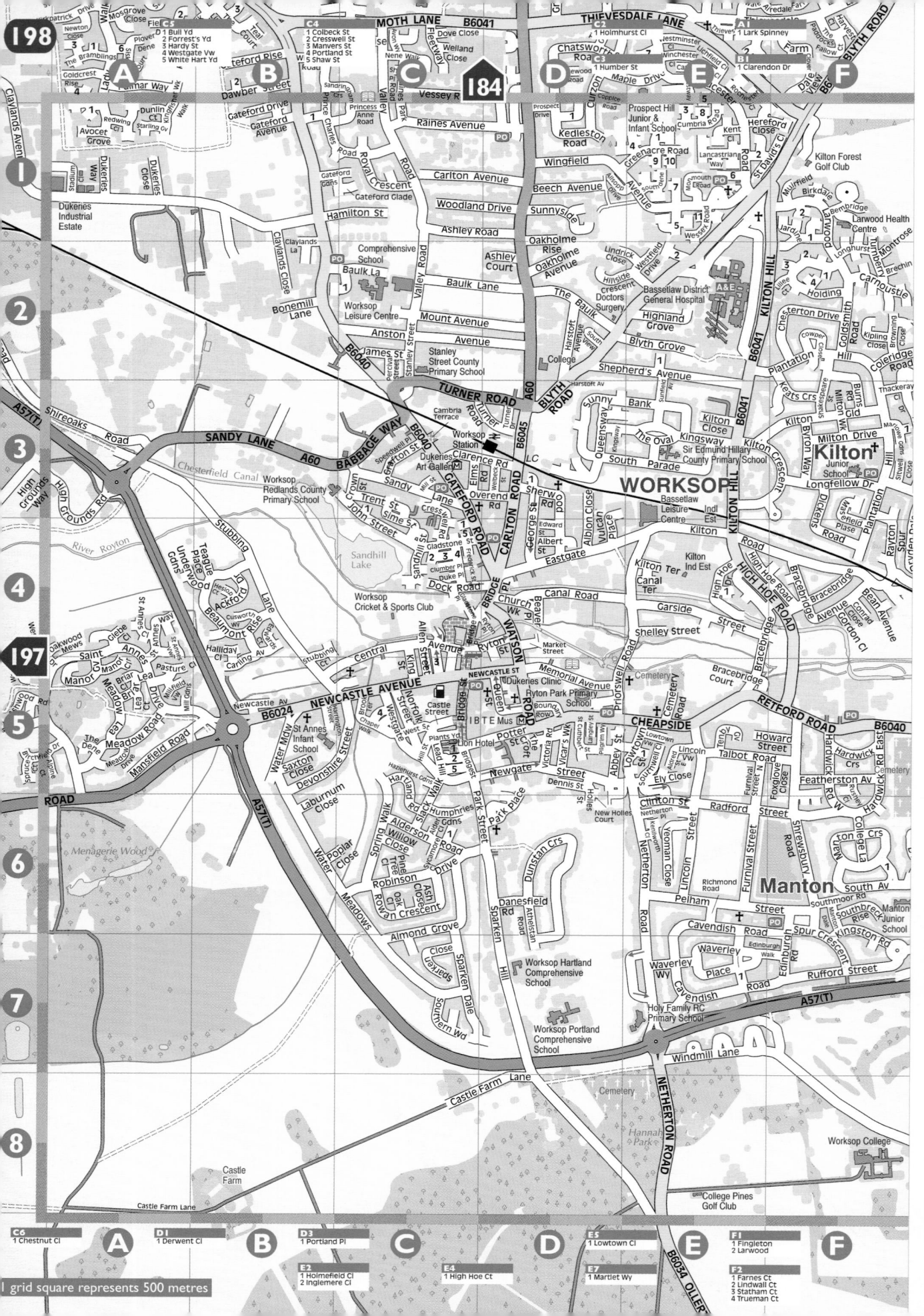

198
184
197
A
B
C
D
E
F
1
2
3
4
5
6
7
8
C5
1 Bull Yd
2 Forrest's Yd
3 Hardy St
4 Westgate Vw
5 White Hart Yd
C4
1 Colbeck St
2 Cresswell St
3 Manvers St
4 Portland St
5 Shaw St
C2
1 Holmhurst Cl
C3
1 Humber St
A1
1 Lark Spinney
B1
1 Clarendon Dr
MOTH LANE
B6041
THIEVESDALE LANE
BLYTH ROAD
Dove Close
Welland Close
Fleetway
Vessey Rd
Chatsworth Road
Maple Drive
Gateford Rise
Dawber Street
Gateford Drive
Gateford Avenue
Mosgrove Close
The Bramblings
Goldcrest Rise
Fulmar Way
Dunlin Ct
Redwing Cl
Starling Gv
Kingfisher Wk
Avocet Grove
Claylands Avenue
Dukeries Way
Dukeries Close
Stadium
Dukeries Industrial Estate
Princess Anne Road
Prince Charles Road
Raines Avenue
Royal Crescent
Gateford Gdns
Gateford Glade
Hamilton St
Carlton Avenue
Woodland Drive
Ashley Road
Ashley Court
Claylands La
Claylands Close
Comprehensive School
Baulk La
Baulk Lane
Valley Road
Bonemill Lane
Worksop Leisure Centre
Mount Avenue
Anston Avenue
James St
Stanley Street
Percival Street
Stanley Street County Primary School
Prospect Drive
Kedleston Road
Curzon Street
Coppice Road
Prospect Hill Junior & Infant School
Cumbria Road
Kent Cl
Hereford Close
St David's Cl
Greenacre Road
Lancastrian Way
Monmouth Road
Wessex Road
Wingfield
Beech Avenue
Sunnyside
Oakholme Rise
Oakholme Avenue
Allsopp Drive
Lindrick Close
Westfield Drive
Hillside Crescent
Doctors Surgery
Bassetlaw District General Hospital
A&E
Highland Grove
Blyth Grove
The Baulk
Harstoft Avenue
South View
College
Shepherd's Avenue
Harstoft Av
KILTON HILL
Kilton Forest Golf Club
Muirfield
Birkdale
Bembridge
Larwood Health Centre
Jardine
Larwood
Longhurst
Turnberry
Montrose
Brechin
Carnoustie
Holding
Chesterton Drive
Goldsmith Road
Kipling Close
Browning Close
Plantation Hill
Coleridge Road
Cowper Close
Keats Crs
Shakespeare
Burns Rd
Milton Gld
Thackeray Cl
Kilton Gld
Milton Wk
Milton Drive
Byron Way
Kilton
Junior School
Hill
Sitwell Close
Longfellow Dr
Dickens Road
Masefield Plase
Plantation
Rayton
Dryden Dale
TURNER ROAD
Turner Road
BLYTH ROAD
A60
B6045
Cambria Terrace
Worksop Station
Sunny Bank
Queensway
Kingsway
The Oval
Kilton Close
Sir Edmund Hillary County Primary School
South Parade
Kilton Crescent
B6041
WORKSOP
Bassetlaw Leisure Centre
Indl Est
A57(T)
Shireoaks Road
SANDY LANE
A60
BABBAGE WAY
B6040
Chesterfield Canal
Speedwell Pl
Grafton St
Dukeries Art Gallery
Clarence Rd
Elms Rd
Welbeck St
Worksop Redlands County Primary School
Crown St
Sandy Lane
Mill St
Trent St
Sime St
John Street
Cresswell Rd
Overend Rd
GATEFORD ROAD
CARLTON ROAD
Sherwood Rd
George St
Edward St
Albert St
Albion Close
Vulcan Place
Kilton Road
High Grounds Way
High Grounds Rd
River Ryton
Stubbing Lane
Teague Place
Underwood Gdns
Sandhill St
Gladstone St
Clumber Pl
Duke Pl
Frederick St
Sandhill Lake
Eastgate
Kilton Ter
Canal Ter
Kilton Ind Est
High Hoe Dr
HIGH HOE ROAD
Bracebridge
Bracebridge Avenue
Conrad Close
Bean Avenue
Gordon Cl
Hesiod Cl
Ackford Dr
Cusworth Wy
Beaumont Rise
Edwards Ct
Halliday Cl
Carling Av
Worksop Cricket & Sports Club
Dock Road
Bridge Pl
Church Wk
Beaver Pl
Canal Road
Garside Street
Shelley Street
St Annes Way
St Annes Dr
Glebe Cl
Oakwood Mews
Saint Annes
Manor Gv
Briar Cl
Lea Cl
Pasture Cl
Millfield Way
Mill Gdns
Stubbing Ct
Central Avenue
King St
Allen Street
Bridge St
Ryton St
WATSON ROAD
Market Street
Memorial Avenue
Priorswell Road
Cemetery
Cemetery Road
Bracebridge Court
RETFORD ROAD
B6040
Meadow Road
Lea Drive
Mansfield Road
The Dene
Meadow Drive
Spruce Cl
Larchfield Dr
Alpine Ct
Newcastle Av
B6024
NEWCASTLE AVENUE
NEWCASTLE ST
St Annes Infant School
Harrington Street
Brook St
Chapel Walk
Westgate
Norfolk Street
Castle Street
Dukeries Clinic
Queen St
Ryton Park Primary School
Boundary Row
CHEAPSIDE
Water Mdw
Saxton Close
Devonshire Street
West St
Plants Yd
Lion Hotel
IBTE Mus
Potter St
The Croft
Victoria Rd
Vicar's Wk
St Cuthbert St
Langley St
Pilgrim Wy
Abbey St
Lowtown St
Lowtown
Southwell Cl
Alfred Ct
Lincoln Vw
Tenby Gv
Howard Street
Talbot Road
Hardwick Crs
Hardwick Rd East
Hardwick Rd W
Featherston Av
Cemetery
Hill St
Lead Hill
Bridgegate
Newgate
Dennis St
Holles St
New Holles Court
Ely Close
Clinton St
Netherton Pl
Kenilworth Ct
Radford Street
Furnival Street N
Foxglove Close
Rushey Cl
College La
Laburnum Close
Hazlehurst Gdns
Hartland Rd
Slack Walk
Humphries Gdns
Alder Cl
Alderson Rd
Willow Close
Spring Walk
Sycamore Cl
Pine Tree Cl
Park Street
Park Place
Water Meadows
Poplar Close
Robinson Drive
Ash Close
Oak Cl
Rowan Crescent
Dunstan Crs
Netherton Road
Yeoman Close
Lincoln Street
Richmond Road
Furnival Street
Shrewsbury Road
Manton
Norton Crs
South Av
Southmoor Rd
Manton Dale
Southbreck Rise
Manton Junior School
Kingston Rd
Pelham Street
Cavendish Road
Edinburgh Walk
Edinburgh Rd
Spur Crescent
Rufford Street
Waverley Place
Waverley Wy
Cavendish Road
Danesfield Rd
Athelstan Road
Almond Grove
Sparken Close
Sparken Dale
Sparken Hill
Southern Wd
Worksop Hartland Comprehensive School
Holy Family RC Primary School
A57(T)
Menagerie Wood
Worksop Portland Comprehensive School
Windmill Lane
Castle Farm Lane
Cemetery
NETHERTON ROAD
Hannah Park
Castle Farm
Castle Farm Lane
College Pines Golf Club
Worksop College
ROAD
C6
1 Chestnut Cl
D1
1 Derwent Cl
D3
1 Portland Pl
E5
1 Lowtown Cl
F1
1 Fingleton
2 Larwood
E2
1 Holmefield Cl
2 Inglemere Cl
E4
1 High Hoe Ct
E7
1 Martlet Wy
F2
1 Farnes Ct
2 Lindwall Ct
3 Statham Ct
4 Trueman Ct
B6034 OLLER
1 grid square represents 500 metres

E1 Street Names for these grid squares are listed at the back of the index

I

Rayton Angle

Scofton Wood

Scofton

2

Gravel Pit Wood

Coleridge Road

Osberton Hall

Scott Close
Nash Close
Macaulay Close
Brooke Close

Tennyson Drive

Sitwell Road

3

Herrick Drive

Black Hill Clump

Rossetti Gardens

Chesterfield Canal

Osberto Grange

4

Rayton Lane

Rayton Farm

B6079

RETFORD ROAD

5

Cemetery

Forest Lane

Manton Villas

B6040

6

Highfield Crs
La Bukeries

Gorselands Avenue

South Av

Manton Infant School

Roebuck Way

Kingston Road

A57(T)

A57(T)

Manton Lodge

7

Kingston Close

Windmill Lane

Old Coach Road

8

Limetree Ave

Abbeydale 175 M6
Abbeydale Park 189 J1
Abdy 107 H5
Ackworth Moor Top 23 J2
Adwick Le Street 66 F2
Adwick upon Dearne 86 E7
Aldwarke 129 L5
Almholme 68 E2
Apperknowle 191 M6
Arbourthorne 161 H7
Ardsley 61 K8
Arksey 68 C5
Armthorpe 91 M1
Arrunden 53 K6
Askern 27 L8
Aston 164 D8
Athersley North 38 D7
Athersley South 38 E8
Attercliffe 161 J1
Auckley 92 E8
Aughton 163 M5
Austerfield 137 G5
Badsworth 24 B5
Balby 89 M8
Balne 10 D4
Barlborough 194 F7
Barnburgh 87 H4
Barnby Dun 47 L8
Barnby Moor 187 H2
Barnes Hall 126 B3
Barnside 54 E7
Barnsley 3 J3
Barrow 105 K6
Barugh 59 J1
Barugh Green 59 J3
Bassett 174 B2
Batemoor 190 E2
Bawtry 136 F8
Beauchief 175 M7
Beighton 179 K3
Belle Green 40 A8
Belle Vue 5 M8
Bentley 67 M8
Bentley Rise 89 L1
Berry Moor 80 E4
Bessacarr 91 J8
Bilby 186 B5
Billingley 85 K1
Bircotes 154 B3
Birds Edge 55 L3
Birdwell 82 C7
Birley Carr 143 M2
Birley Edge 144 A1
Birleyhay 192 A2
Blackburn 127 M8
Blacker 38 A8
Blacker Hill 83 G6
Blaxton 115 J1
Blyth 169 L4
Bolehill 176 E5
Bolsterstone 124 A1
Bolton Upton Dearne 86 B5
Bow Broom 108 A3
Bradgate 128 D8
Bradway 190 A2
Braithwaite 47 J2
Braithwell 132 E5
Brakenhill 23 G1
Bramley 149 G1
Bramley 192 D4
Brampton 84 D8
Brampton en le Morthen 165 H2
Branton 92 B6
Brecks 148 D3
Brick Houses 175 G7
Brierholme Carr 49 L6
Brierley 40 D4
Brightholmlee 124 D4
Brightside 145 K7
Brincliffe 176 A1
Brodsworth 65 L3
Bromley 103 L5
Brookhouse 150 A8
Broom 7 L9
Broomhill 84 F5
Burghwallis 44 F3
Burncross 126 C2
Burngreave 160 F1
Cadeby 110 B1
Calder Grove 19 G1
Campsall 27 H7
Canal Side 31 L8
Canklow 147 H4
Cantley 91 M6
Carbrook 145 L7
Carcroft 45 G5
Carlecotes 76 E4
Carlton 39 H6
Carlton in Lindrick 184 D2
Carr 150 A6
Carter Knowle 176 B2
Cartledge 189 L8
Cartworth Fold 53 K4
Castle Green 79 K5
Catcliffe 163 H1
Cat Hill 57 H8
Catshaw 77 M4
Cawthorne 58 B3
Chapeltorpe 19 L3
Chapeltown 126 F1
Charltonbrook 126 A2
Charnock Hall 177 L5
Clayton 64 A3
Clayton West 35 L5
Clifton 7 J5
Clifton 132 C2
Coal Aston 191 H3
Coisley Hill 178 E1
Cold Hiendley 21 H6
Conanby 109 K5
Conisbrough 109 L4
Cortworth 106 C6
Costhorpe 168 C7
Cotterhill Woods 183 J4
Cowley 190 B8
Crane Moor 81 G7
Crawshaw 16 E7
Crigglestone 19 K1
Crookes 159 M3
Crookesmoor 8 A3
Crow Edge 77 J1
Cubley 79 G7
Cudworth 61 M1
Cudworth Common 62 B3
Cundy Cross 61 H6
Cundy Hos 103 J7
Cusworth 89 G2
Dalton 130 B6
Dalton Magna 130 D8
Dalton Parva 130 C7
Darfield 84 F2
Darfoulds 197 J6
Darnall 161 M3
Darton 37 J7
Dean Head 101 M2
Dearne 86 D2
Deepcar 102 D8
Denaby Main 109 J3
Denby Dale 56 F1
Dinnington 166 F7
Dodworth 59 K8
Dodworth Bottom 81 J1
Dodworth Green 81 H1
Doncaster 5 K4
Dore 175 J8
Drakehouse 179 H4
Dronfield 191 G6
Dronfield Woodhouse 189 M5
Dropping Well 127 M6
Dunford Bridge 76 B6
Dungworth 142 B7
Dunscroft 70 E1
Dunsville 70 C2
Eastfield 80 E6
East Herringthorpe 130 B8
Eastwood 7 L1
Eastwood 129 J7
Ecclesall 175 L2
Ecclesfield 126 F6
Eckington 193 G4
Ecklands 78 B5
Edenthorpe 69 L6
Edge Mount 124 B8
Elscar 105 L2
Emley 17 G8
Emmett Carr 194 A7
Eskholme 12 A7
Everton 155 M3
Ewden Village 124 A2
Far Bank 30 D7
Felkirk 39 L1
Fenwick 28 F2
Finkle Street 103 G5
Firbeck 167 L2
Firth Park 145 H4
Fir Vale 145 G6
Fishlake 30 F8
Fitzwilliam 22 E3
Flockton 17 G4
Flockton Green 17 J4
Flush House 52 F4
Foldrings 124 E6
Ford 192 B1
Fosterhouses 30 D5
Four Lane End 80 A5
Frecheville 178 A3
Fullshaw 77 M8
Fulwood 159 G7
Garden Village 101 K6
Gateford 184 B7
Gateford Common 183 M8
Gawber 59 L4
Gildingwells 167 K8
Gilroyd 81 L2
Gleadless 177 L3
Gleadless Valley 177 J4
Goldthorpe 86 C2
Gosforth Valley 190 B5
Grange Moor 16 D2
Greasbrough 129 G3
Great Cliff 19 G3
Great Houghton 63 J5
Greenhill 176 C8
Greenland 145 M8
Green Moor 102 C4
Greenside 191 M4
The Green 79 H6
Grenoside 126 B7
Greystones 159 K8
Grimesthorpe 145 H6
Grimethorpe 40 E8
Guilthwaite 163 M1
Hackenthorpe 178 C3
Hade Edge 53 M8
Haigh 36 E3
Halfway 179 J8
Hall Broom 141 M7
Hall Green 19 K4
Hallowes 191 G7
Hampole 43 M6
Handsworth 162 C5
Hangsman Hill 31 K5
Harden 76 A3
Hardwick 165 G5
Harley 105 H6
Harlington 86 F6
Harthill 195 K1
Harwell 155 L3
Harworth 153 J3
Hatfield 49 G7
Hatfield Chase 50 E6
Hatfield Woodhouse 71 L1
Hathersage 172 D7
Havercroft 21 M6
Hay Field 114 C3
Haywood 46 C1
Hazlehead 77 J5
Heeley 176 E1
Hellaby 149 M2
Hemingfield 84 A8
Hemsworth 22 F8
Hemsworth 177 G4
Hepworth 54 D5
Hermit Hill 103 K1
Herringthorpe 148 A2
Hexthorpe 4 B8
Hickleton 65 G8
Higham 59 J4
Higham Common 59 J5
High Bradfield 142 A1
Highfield 160 F7
Highfields 67 G5
High Flatts 56 A4
Highgate 85 M2
High Green 104 B8
High Hoyland 36 B6
Highlane 178 C7
High Melton 87 M7
High Moor 194 C2
Hillsborough 143 K5
Hill Side 78 D5
Hill Top 57 M7
Hill Top 109 K8
Hill Top 142 C8
Hill Top 146 A1
Hill Top 190 E8
Hinchcliffe Mill 53 H4
Hodsock 169 J8
Hogley Green 53 G3
Holbrook 179 L7
Holdworth 142 D3
Hollingthorpe 19 H4
Hollins End 177 M2
Hollow Meadows 157 G3
Holmbridge 52 E5
Holme 52 C8
Holmesdale 191 G5
Holmesfield 189 L7
Holmfirth 53 J2
Holmley Common 190 E3
Hoober 106 E6
Hood Green 81 J5
Hood Hill 105 H7
Hooton Levitt 150 C4
Hooton Pagnell 65 G2
Hooton Roberts 109 H8
Howbrook 103 M6
Hoyland 105 H2
Hoyland Common 104 F1
Hoylandswaine 79 J1
Hoyle Mill 61 G6
Hundall 191 M8
Hyde Park 4 F7
Ingbirchworth 56 C6
Instoneville 27 K7
Intake 90 E3
Intake 177 L2
Jackson Bridge 54 C3
Jordanthorpe 176 F8
Jordon 146 C2
Jump 83 L8
Kendray 3 M9
Kendray 83 G1
Keresforth Hill 60 A8
Kettlethorpe 19 L1
Kexbrough 37 G7
Killamarsh 193 L1
Kilnhurst 108 B8
Kilton 198 F3
Kimberworth 128 C8
Kimberworth Park 128 D5
Kine Moor 80 B1
Kingstone 2 B9
Kinsley 22 E5
Kirk Bramwith 47 K3
Kirk Sandall 69 K4
Kirk Smeaton 26 A2
Kitchenroyd 34 E8
Kiveton Park 182 A5
Kiveton Park 181 J4
Lane End 126 E1
Lane Head 55 H1
Langold 168 C3
Langsett 100 A1
Laughton Common 166 A4
Laughton en le Morthen 166 C2
Lepton Edge 16 A4
Letwell 167 K4
Lidgate 189 G7
Lidget 114 E1
Lightwood 177 K7
Listerdale 148 D2
Little Houghton 63 H7
Little Smeaton 26 D1
Littleworth 114 A6
Load Brook 158 B1
Lodge Moor 158 C6
Longley Estate 144 F4
Long Sandall 69 H4
Loversall 112 B5
Low Barugh 59 K1
Low Bradfield 141 L3
Lowedges 190 D1
Lower Cumberworth 34 D8
Lower Denby 56 F3
Lower Longley 53 L6
Lower Maythorn 55 H8
Lowfield 160 E8
Low Laithes 61 M8
Low Valley 84 D3
Loxley 143 G7
Lundwood 61 J4
Malinbridge 143 L8
Maltby 150 E2
Manor Estate 161 K6
Manor Park 161 J5
Manton 198 E6
Mapplewell 38 A6
Marr 66 A8
Marsh Lane 192 D4
Masbrough 6 A3
Mattersey Thorpe 155 J6
Mawson Green 12 D8
Meadow Hall 145 M4
Meadow Head 176 C6
Meal Hill 54 D4
Measborough Dike 3 L7
Meersbrook 176 F2
Mexborough 86 E8
Micklebring 132 B5
Mickley 189 M4
Middlecliffe 85 G1
Middle Handley 192 D7
Middlewood 143 K3
Midgley 18 A5
Midhopestones 100 D4
Millhouse Green 78 A4
Millhouses 85 H2
Millhouses 175 M4
Milton 105 J2
Minsthorpe 42 D2
Misson 137 M5
Monk Bretton 60 F3
Moor End 80 F2
Moorends 32 B2
Moorgate 147 K5
Moor Head 34 D1
Moorhole 178 E6
Moorhouse 43 H6
Moorthorpe 42 D4
Morthen 148 E8
Mortomley 104 C8
Mosborough 179 G7
Moss 28 E6
Nether Edge 176 C1
Nether End 57 H2
Nether Haugh 106 F8
Netherton 18 A1
New Edlington 111 G6
Newhill 107 J3
Newington 137 H6
New Lodge 38 B8
Newmillerdam 20 A3
New Rossington 113 H7
Newstead 22 A5
Newton 4 B6
New Totley 189 J3
New Village 68 A5
Noblethorpe 58 C8
Normanton Spring 178 C1
North Anston 166 A8
North Carlton 184 E1
North Elmsall 42 F1
Norton 27 G4
Norton 176 F7
Norton Woodseats 176 E4
Norwood 180 D7
Notton 38 D1
Nutwell 92 B2
Oldcotes 168 D1
Old Denaby 109 G4
Old Edlington 110 E8
Onesacre 124 F7
Orgreave 163 G6
Oughtibridge 125 J8
Overton 17 L1
Overtown 20 E2
Owler Bar 188 E7
Owlerton 144 B7
Owlthorpe 178 F5
Owston 45 J4
Oxclose 193 L1
Oxspring 80 A7
Painthorpe 19 J4
Park Gate 34 E3
Parkgate 129 K5
Park Head 55 K2
Parkhead 175 K4
Park Hill 9 M3
Park Mill 35 L3
The Parks 48 D8
Parkwood Springs 144 D8
Parson Cross 144 D2
Penistone 78 F4
Piccadilly 107 M6
Pickburn 66 B4
Pilley 104 A2
Pincheon Green 12 F8
Pinfold Hill 80 D6
Pismire Hill 145 H3
Pitsmoor 144 F8
Platts Common 83 J7
Pledwick 20 B2
Plumbley 178 F8
Pogmoor 59 L5
Pollington 11 K3
Potter Hill 103 M8
Rails 158 D3
Ranby 186 E8
Ranmoor 159 J6
Ranskill 170 F3
Ravenfield 131 H4
Raw Green 58 A3
Rawmarsh 129 L3
Renishaw 193 L8
Rhodesia 197 K3
Richmond 162 C7
Ridgeway 178 C7
Ridgeway Moor 192 C1
Ringinglow 174 E3
Rollestone 177 G2
Rossington 113 L6
Rostholme 67 K5
Rotherham 6 F7
Roughbirchworth 79 L8
Royd 78 B3
Roydhouse 34 A1
Royd Moor 23 M7
Royd Moor 78 C2
Royston 38 E5
Ryecroft 107 L8
Ryhill 21 M6
St Helen's 61 G2
Sandhill 63 H6
Sandtoft 73 K3
Sandygate 159 J5
Scaftworth 155 C3
Scawsby 89 H1
Scawthorpe 67 H7
Scholes 54 B4
Scholes 128 A3
Scissett 35 G6
Scofton 199 M1
Scout Dike 78 F1
Scrooby 154 D5
Serlby 154 B7
Shafton 39 L4
Shafton Two Gates 39 L5
Sharrow 160 B8
Shaw Lands 2 C6
Sheffield 9 M5
Sheffield Park 161 J6
Shirecliffe 144 E6
Shiregreen 145 K2
Shireoaks 183 J8
Silkstone 58 C7
Silkstone Common 80 E3
Sim Hill 80 E7
Skelbrooke 44 A2
Skellow 44 E5
Skelmanthorpe 34 F5
Slade Hooton 150 B8
Slay Pits 49 J8
Smithies 60 D2
Smithley 83 L4
Snape Hill 84 D2
Snape Hill 190 F4
Snowden Hill 101 L1
Sothall 179 K6
Soughley 77 H5
South Anston 182 A3
South Bramwith 47 L4
South Carlton 184 E3
South Elmsall 42 F4
South Hiendley 40 A1
South Kirkby 41 L6
South Lane 57 M6
Spinkhill 194 B5
Spital Hill 135 J8
Spring Vale 79 J4
Sprotbrough 89 G6
Stacey Bank 142 D6
Staincross 37 M5
Stainforth 48 D3
Stainton 133 J7
Stairfoot 61 J8
Stannington 159 H1
Steel Bank 160 A2
Stockbridge 68 A5
Stocksbridge 102 A7
Stone 151 K7
Stone Hill 49 L8
Stopes 158 D1
Storrs 142 E8
Stubbley 190 B4
Styrrup 153 H6
Sunnyfields 89 J1
Sunnyside 131 G8
Sutton 45 H1
Sutton 187 K1
Swaithe 83 J2
Swallow Hill 37 L8
Swallownest 164 A8
Swinton 107 M5
Swinton Bridge 108 C3
Sykehouse 30 B1
Tankersley 104 C3
Tapton Hill 159 L5
Templeborough 146 D3
Thorncliff 16 A8
Thorne 32 A7
Thorn Hill 6 D2
Thornseat 141 G2
Thorpe Audlin 24 E2
Thorpe Hesley 127 L2
Thorpe in Balne 46 E5
Thorpe Salvin 196 C1
Throapham 166 D4
Thrybergh 130 C4
Thurcroft 165 H1
Thurgoland 80 D7
Thurlstone 78 D3
Thurnscoe 86 A1
Thurnscoe East 64 D7
Tickhill 134 D7
Tilts 45 M8
Tinsley 146 A5
Tinsley 146 C5
Tivy Dale 58 B3
Todwick 181 K1
Toll Bar 67 L3
Topham 11 K8
Torworth 170 E5
Totley 189 G3
Totley Brook 189 H2
Totley Rise 189 K2
Totties 54 B3
Townhead 76 C5
Townhead 175 G8
Treeton 163 J3
Troway 191 L3
Trumfleet 47 G2
Turnerwood 183 G8
Ughill 141 K6
Ulley 164 D4
Under Bank 53 L4
Under Tofts 159 G3
Unstone 191 J8
Upper Cudworth 40 A7
Upper Cumberworth 55 L1
Upper Denby 16 F2
Upper Denby 56 C4
Upper Haugh 107 H8
Upper Hoyland 83 G8
Upper Maythorn 55 H7
Upper Midhope 100 A3
Upper Tankersley 104 A3
Upperthong 53 H1
Upperthorpe 194 B2
Upper Whiston 164 B1
Upton 25 G8
Victoria 54 F8
Wadsley 143 J5
Wadsley Bridge 143 M3
Wadworth 134 A1
Walden Stubbs 27 J1
Waldershaigh 123 L1
Wales 180 F4
Wales Bar 180 E4
Walkley 160 A1
Wallingwells 183 M2
Walton 20 F1
Ward Green 82 C2
Warmsworth 110 F2
Warren 104 F7
Washpit 53 L5
Waterside 31 H7
Waterthorpe 179 H5
Wath upon Dearne 107 L1
Wentworth 105 M6

West Bretton 18 D7
West End 71 H2
Westfield 179 J8
West Green 61 K1
West Handley 192 A7
West Melton 107 G1
Westthorpe 194 B3
Westwoodside 117 M4
Wharncliffe Side 124 E5
Wheatley 5 K1
Wheatley 90 C2
Wheatley Hills 91 G1
Wheatley Park 68 E8
Whinney Hill 130 B5
Whirlow 175 K5
Whirlow Brook 175 G4
Whiston 148 A6
Whitley 126 D5
Wickersley 148 F3
Wigthorpe 184 E4
Wigtwizzle 123 H3
Wike Well End 50 B2
Wilsic 133 M3
Wilthorpe 60 A3
Wincobank 145 L4
Windhill 109 G1
Wingfield 128 C4
Wintersett 21 L3
Wombwell 84 A6
Woodall 195 G1
Woodhouse 163 G8
Woodhouse Mill 163 J7
Woodlands 66 F3
Wood Seats 126 B4
Woodsetts 183 J3
Woodside 94 F4
Woolgreaves 20 B1
Woolley 37 L1
Worksop 198 D3
Worrall 143 H3
Worsbrough Bridge 82 E4
Worsbrough Common 2 D9
Worsbrough Common 82 C1
Worsbrough Dale 82 E3
Wortley 103 G4
Wrangbrook 25 K8
Wroot 94 E4

USING THE STREET INDEX

Street names are listed alphabetically. Each street name is followed by its postal town or area locality, the Postcode District, the page number, and the reference to the square in which the name is found.

Aaron Wilkinson Ct *HEM/SK/SE* WF9 .... **41** L5 1

Some entries are followed by a number in a blue box. This number indicates the location of the street within the referenced grid square. The full street name is listed at the side of the map page.

GENERAL ABBREVIATIONS

Abbreviation	Meaning
ACC	ACCESS
ALY	ALLEY
AP	APPROACH
AR	ARCADE
ASS	ASSOCIATION
AV	AVENUE
BCH	BEACH
BLDS	BUILDINGS
BND	BEND
BNK	BANK
BR	BRIDGE
BRK	BROOK
BTM	BOTTOM
BUS	BUSINESS
BVD	BOULEVARD
BY	BYPASS
CATH	CATHEDRAL
CEM	CEMETERY
CEN	CENTRE
CFT	CROFT
CH	CHURCH
CHA	CHASE
CHYD	CHURCHYARD
CIR	CIRCLE
CIRC	CIRCUS
CL	CLOSE
CLFS	CLIFFS
CMP	CAMP
CNR	CORNER
CO	COUNTY
COLL	COLLEGE
COM	COMMON
COMM	COMMISSION
CON	CONVENT
COT	COTTAGE
COTS	COTTAGES
CP	CAPE
CPS	COPSE
CR	CREEK
CREM	CREMATORIUM
CRS	CRESCENT
CSWY	CAUSEWAY
CT	COURT
CTRL	CENTRAL
CTS	COURTS
CTYD	COURTYARD
CUTT	CUTTINGS
CV	COVE
CYN	CANYON
DEPT	DEPARTMENT
DL	DALE
DM	DAM
DR	DRIVE
DRO	DROVE
DRY	DRIVEWAY
DWGS	DWELLINGS
E	EAST
EMB	EMBANKMENT
EMBY	EMBASSY
ESP	ESPLANADE
EST	ESTATE
EX	EXCHANGE
EXPY	EXPRESSWAY
EXT	EXTENSION
F/O	FLYOVER
FC	FOOTBALL CLUB
FK	FORK
FLD	FIELD
FLDS	FIELDS
FLS	FALLS
FLS	FLATS
FM	FARM
FT	FORT
FWY	FREEWAY
FY	FERRY
GA	GATE
GAL	GALLERY
GDN	GARDEN
GDNS	GARDENS
GLD	GLADE
GLN	GLEN
GN	GREEN
GND	GROUND
GRA	GRANGE
GRG	GARAGE
GT	GREAT
GTWY	GATEWAY
GV	GROVE
HGR	HIGHER
HL	HILL
HLS	HILLS
HO	HOUSE
HOL	HOLLOW
HOSP	HOSPITAL
HRB	HARBOUR
HTH	HEATH
HTS	HEIGHTS
HVN	HAVEN
HWY	HIGHWAY
IMP	IMPERIAL
IN	INLET
IND EST	INDUSTRIAL ESTATE
INF	INFIRMARY
INFO	INFORMATION
INT	INTERCHANGE
IS	ISLAND
JCT	JUNCTION
JTY	JETTY
KG	KING
KNL	KNOLL
L	LAKE
LA	LANE
LDG	LODGE
LGT	LIGHT
LK	LOCK
LKS	LAKES
LNDG	LANDING
LTL	LITTLE
LWR	LOWER
MAG	MAGISTRATE
MAN	MANSIONS
MD	MEAD
MDW	MEADOWS
MEM	MEMORIAL
MKT	MARKET
MKTS	MARKETS
ML	MALL
ML	MILL
MNR	MANOR
MS	MEWS
MSN	MISSION
MT	MOUNT
MTN	MOUNTAIN
MTS	MOUNTAINS
MUS	MUSEUM
MWY	MOTORWAY
N	NORTH
NE	NORTH EAST
NW	NORTH WEST
O/P	OVERPASS
OFF	OFFICE
ORCH	ORCHARD
OV	OVAL
PAL	PALACE
PAS	PASSAGE
PAV	PAVILION
PDE	PARADE
PH	PUBLIC HOUSE
PK	PARK
PKWY	PARKWAY
PL	PLACE
PLN	PLAIN
PLNS	PLAINS
PLZ	PLAZA
POL	POLICE STATION
PR	PRINCE
PREC	PRECINCT
PREP	PREPARATORY
PRIM	PRIMARY
PROM	PROMENADE
PRS	PRINCESS
PRT	PORT
PT	POINT
PTH	PATH
PZ	PIAZZA
QD	QUADRANT
QU	QUEEN
QY	QUAY
R	RIVER
RBT	ROUNDABOUT
RD	ROAD
RDG	RIDGE
REP	REPUBLIC
RES	RESERVOIR
RFC	RUGBY FOOTBALL CLUB
RI	RISE
RP	RAMP
RW	ROW
S	SOUTH
SCH	SCHOOL
SE	SOUTH EAST
SER	SERVICE AREA
SH	SHORE
SHOP	SHOPPING
SKWY	SKYWAY
SMT	SUMMIT
SOC	SOCIETY
SP	SPUR
SPR	SPRING
SQ	SQUARE
ST	STREET
STN	STATION
STR	STREAM
STRD	STRAND
SW	SOUTH WEST
TDG	TRADING
TER	TERRACE
THWY	THROUGHWAY
TNL	TUNNEL
TOLL	TOLLWAY
TPK	TURNPIKE
TR	TRACK
TRL	TRAIL
TWR	TOWER
U/P	UNDERPASS
UNI	UNIVERSITY
UPR	UPPER
V	VALE
VA	VALLEY
VIAD	VIADUCT
VIL	VILLA
VIS	VISTA
VLG	VILLAGE
VLS	VILLAS
VW	VIEW
W	WEST
WD	WOOD
WHF	WHARF
WK	WALK
WKS	WALKS
WLS	WELLS
WY	WAY
YD	YARD
YHA	YOUTH HOSTEL

POSTCODE TOWNS AND AREA ABBREVIATIONS

Abbreviation	Town/Area
ABRD	Abbeydale Road
ARMTH	Armthorpe
ATT	Attercliffe
AU/AST/KP	Aughton/Aston/Kiveton Park
AWLS/ASK	Adwick le Street/Askern
BSLY	Barnsley
BSLYN/ROY	Barnsley north/Royston
BSVR	Bolsover
BTLY	Bentley
BWTY	Bawtry
CHPT/GREN	Chapeltown/Grenoside
CONI	Conisbrough
CUD/GR	Cudworth/Grimethorpe
DARN/MH	Darnall/Meadowhall
DEARNE	Wath upon Dearne/Bolton upon Dearne
DOD/DAR	Dodworth/Darton
DON	Doncaster
DONS/BSCR	Doncaster south/Bessacarr
DRON	Dronfield
EARL	Earlsheaton
ECC	Ecclesall
ECK/KIL	Eckington/Killamarsh
EDL/UDV	Edale/Upper Derwent Valley
EPW	Epworth
FEA/AMT	Featherstone/Ackworth Moor Top
FUL	Fulwood
GLE	Goole
GLSP	Glossop
GLV	Gleadless Valley
HACK//IN	Hackenthorpe/Intake
HAN/WDH	Handsworth/Woodhouse
HATH/EY	Hathersage/Eyam
HEM/SK/SE	Hemsworth/SouthKirby/South Elmsall
HOLM/MEL	Holmfirth/Meltham
HOR/CROF	Horbury/Crofton
HOY	Hoyland
HTFD	Hatfield
KBTN	Kirkburton
KIMB	Kimberworth
MALT	Maltby
MEX/SWTN	Mexborough/Swinton
MOS	Mosborough
NROS/TKH	New Rossington/Tickhill
OWL	Owlerton
PONT	Pontefract
RAW	Rawmarsh
RHAM	Rotherham
RHAM/THRY	Rotherham/Thrybergh
RTFD	Retford
SCSW/CWLE	Scunthorpe southwest/Crowle
SHEF	Sheffield
SHEFN	Sheffield north
SHEFP/MNR	Sheffield Park/Manor
SHEFS	Sheffield south
ST/HB/BR	Stannington/Hillsborough/Bradfield
STKB/PEN	Stocksbridge/Penistone
STV/CWN	Staveley/Clowne
THNE	Thorne
TOT/DORE	Totley/Dore
WHHL	Wheatley Hills
WKFDW/WTN	Wakefield west/Walton
WMB/DAR	Wombwell/Darfield
WRKN	Worksop north
WRKS	Worksop south

A

Aaron Wilkinson Ct
HEM/SK/SE WF9 **41** L5 1
The Abbe's Cl *AWLS/ASK* DN6 **44** F2
The Abbe's Wk *AWLS/ASK* DN6 **45** H3
Abbey Brook Ct *SHEFS* S8 **176** C6 1
Abbey Brook Dr *SHEFS* S8 **176** C6
Abbey Cl *DIN* S25 **166** B2
HOLM/MEL HD7 **53** L8
SHEFS S8 **176** C6
Abbey Ct *HOLM/MEL* HD7 **53** L8
Abbey Crs *ABRD* S7 **175** M6
Abbey Cft *ABRD* S7 **175** M6
Abbeydale Park Crs
TOT/DORE S17 **189** K1
Abbeydale Park Ri
TOT/DORE S17 **175** J8
Abbeydale Rd *SHEFS* S8 **160** D8
SHEFS S8 **176** B4
Abbeydale Rd South *SHEFS* S8 **175** M6
TOT/DORE S17 **189** L1
Abbey Dr *HTFD* DN7 **48** E7 1
Abbey Farm Vw *CUD/GR* S72 **61** M2
Abbeyfield Rd *ATT* S4 **144** F8
HTFD DN7 **48** D7
Abbey Flds *EPW* DN9 **115** J4
Abbey Gra *ABRD* S7 **175** M6
Abbey Gv *BSLYN/ROY* S71 **61** J3
Abbey La *BSLYN/ROY* S71 **61** J5
ECC S11 **175** L4
MALT S66 **150** E7
SHEFS S8 **176** C6
Abbey Lane Dell *SHEFS* S8 **175** M6
Abbey Pl *ECK/KIL* S21 **194** A7
Abbey Rd *HTFD* DN7 **48** E8
Abbey Sq *BSLYN/ROY* S71 **61** J3 1
Abbey St *WRKS* S80 **198** D5
Abbey View Rd *SHEFS* S8 **176** E4
Abbey Wk *BTLY* DN5 **89** J2
Abbey Wy *DIN* S25 **165** M6
HTFD DN7 **48** E6
Abbot La *HOR/CROF* WF4 **37** M1
Abbotsford Dr *MALT* S66 **165** J1 1
Abbots Meadow *MOS* S20 **179** L6 1
Abbots Rd *BSLYN/ROY* S71 **61** K4
Abbott St *DONS/BSCR* DN4 **4** D6
Abdy Rd *KIMB* S61 **128** B5
RAW S62 **107** H5
Aberconway Crs
NROS/TKH DN11 **113** K7
Abercorn Rd *WHHL* DN2 **91** G3
Aberfield Dr *HOR/CROF* WF4 **19** J3
Aberford Gv *HOY* S74 **105** M1 1
Abingdon Gdns *KIMB* S61 **128** F4
Abingdon Rd *WHHL* DN2 **90** F2
Abney Cl *SHEFS* S8 **177** G1 1
Abney Dr *SHEFS* S8 **177** G1
Abney Rd *SHEFS* S8 **177** G1
Acacia Av *CHPT/GREN* S35 **126** D3
MALT S66 **149** G2
MALT S66 **150** B2
Acacia Ct *BTLY* DN5 **67** L5 1
Acacia Crs *ECK/KIL* S21 **193** M2
Acacia Gv *CONI* DN12 **109** L7
CUD/GR S72 **40** A5
Acacia Rd *AWLS/ASK* DN6 **44** E5
DONS/BSCR DN4 **91** K7
SHEFN S5 **145** J3
Acer Cl *DIN* S25 **182** B4
ECK/KIL S21 **194** A2
Acer Cft *ARMTH* DN3 **91** M2
Ackford Dr *WRKS* S80 **198** B4
Ackworth Dr *DARN/MH* S9 **146** D6 1
Acomb Common Rd *HTFD* DN7 **49** K7
Acorn Cft *KIMB* S61 **128** F5
Acorn Dr *ST/HB/BR* S6 **158** F1
Acorn Gv *HOLM/MEL* HD7 **54** B4
Acorn Hl *ST/HB/BR* S6 **143** H8
Acorn St *OWL* S3 **8** F1
Acorn Wy *ST/HB/BR* S6 **158** F1
Acre Cl *ARMTH* DN3 **69** K5
MALT S66 **132** C8
Acre Ga *CHPT/GREN* S35 **104** B8
Acre La *CHPT/GREN* S35 **124** E7
HOLM/MEL HD7 **53** H5
HOLM/MEL HD7 **54** F1
STKB/PEN S36 **79** H1
Acre Rd *CUD/GR* S72 **62** A3
Acres Hill La *DARN/MH* S9 **161** M4
Acres Hill Rd *DARN/MH* S9 **161** M3
Acres La *EPW* DN9 **94** E2
HOLM/MEL HD7 **52** D3
Acton Cl *AU/AST/KP* S26 **164** B6
Adam La *DOD/DAR* S75 **58** E5
Adastral Av *HACK/IN* S12 **177** L5
Addison Rd *MALT* S66 **150** B2
MEX/SWTN S64 **108** F2
SHEFN S5 **145** H5
Addison Sq *DIN* S25 **166** D6
Addy Cl *ST/HB/BR* S6 **8** C1
Addy Crs *HEM/SK/SE* WF9 **42** D4
Addy Dr *ST/HB/BR* S6 **8** B1
Addy St *ST/HB/BR* S6 **8** C1
Adelaide Rd *AWLS/ASK* DN6 **27** H4
ECC S11 **176** B1
Adelaide St *MALT* S66 **150** F4 1
Adelphi St *ST/HB/BR* S6 **8** D1
Adkin Royd *DOD/DAR* S75 **58** D7
Adkins Dr *SHEFN* S5 **144** C4
Adkins Rd *SHEFN* S5 **144** C4
Adlard Rd *WHHL* DN2 **90** F1 1
Adlington Crs *SHEFN* S5 **144** D3
Adlington Rd *SHEFN* S5 **144** D3
Admirals Crest *KIMB* S61 **127** M5
Adowsley Cl *FEA/AMT* WF7 **23** J1
Adrian Crs *SHEFN* S5 **144** E3
Adsetts St *ATT* S4 **145** J6
Adwick Av *BTLY* DN5 **67** K2
Adwick Ct *MEX/SWTN* S64 **108** F3 1
Adwick Gv *WKFDW/WTN* WF2 **19** M2
Adwick La *AWLS/ASK* DN6 **67** J1
Adwick Pk *DEARNE* S63 **108** B1
Adwick Rd *MEX/SWTN* S64 **86** D8
MEX/SWTN S64 **108** F3 2
Agden Br *ST/HB/BR* S6 **123** G7
Agden Rd *ABRD* S7 **160** C7
Agden Side Rd *ST/HB/BR* S6 **123** H6
Agnes Rd *BSLY* S70 **2** E7
DOD/DAR S75 **37** H7
Ainsdale Av *DEARNE* S63 **86** B3
Ainsdale Ct *BSLYN/ROY* S71 **61** H2
Ainsdale Rd *BSLYN/ROY* S71 **38** F2
Ainsley Cl *EPW* DN9 **92** D8
Ainsley Rd *FUL* S10 **160** A3 1
Ainsty Rd *ABRD* S7 **160** D8 1
Aintree Av *DONS/BSCR* DN4 **91** H5
ECK/KIL S21 **192** F4
Aintree Cl *BTLY* DN5 **89** H2
Aintree Dr *MEX/SWTN* S64 **108** F1
Aire Cl *CHPT/GREN* S35 **126** D1
Airedale *WRKN* S81 **184** E8
Airedale Av *NROS/TKH* DN11 **134** E7
Airedale Rd *DOD/DAR* S75 **37** G7
ST/HB/BR S6 **145** L5
Aireton Cl *MALT* S66 **148** E2
Aireton Rd *BSLY* S70 **2** E4
Airey La *AWLS/ASK* DN6 **46** D5
Air Mount Cl *MALT* S66 **148** E3
Airstone Rd *AWLS/ASK* DN6 **27** K8
Aisby Dr *NROS/TKH* DN11 **113** L5
Aisthorpe Rd *SHEFS* S8 **176** D4
Aitken Rd *MEX/SWTN* S64 **108** B7
Aizlewood Rd *SHEFS* S8 **160** D8 2
Akley Bank Cl *TOT/DORE* S17 **189** K2
Alan Rd *DOD/DAR* S75 **37** H7
Alba Cl *WMB/DAR* S73 **84** C1
Albanus Rdg *ST/HB/BR* S6 **158** F1
Albany Av *CHPT/GREN* S35 **126** F3
Albany Cl *WMB/DAR* S73 **83** L1
Albany Crs *HEM/SK/SE* WF9 **42** D5
Albany La *NROS/TKH* DN11 **113** J6
Albany Rd *ABRD* S7 **160** D8
DONS/BSCR DN4 **89** L7
MEX/SWTN S64 **108** B6
STKB/PEN S36 **101** M6
Albany St *HEM/SK/SE* WF9 **42** D5
RHAM/THRY S65 **7** H5
Albert Rd *DEARNE* S63 **85** H8
DEARNE S63 **86** C2 1
HACK/IN S12 **178** F4
KBTN HD8 **35** J4
MEX/SWTN S64 **108** E2
RAW S62 **129** K3
SHEFS S8 **176** E1
Albert St *BSLY* S70 **3** G5
CUD/GR S72 **40** A7 1
DEARNE S63 **64** A7
ECK/KIL S21 **193** H5
MALT S66 **150** F3
MEX/SWTN S64 **108** B3
RHAM S60 **6** C4
THNE DN8 **32** A7

WRKS S80 198 D4
Albert Terrace Rd ST/HB/BR S6 8 D1
Albion Cl WRKS S80 198 D4
Albion Dr DEARNE S63 64 D7
Albion Pl HEM/SK/SE WF9 42 E4
Albion Rd BSLYN/ROY S71 39 G8
RHAM/THRY S65 7 G5
Albion St HEM/SK/SE WF9 22 D4
ST/HB/BR S6 8 C2
Albion Ter DONS/BSCR DN4 4 C8
Alcester Rd ABRD S7 160 D8
Aldam Cl RHAM/THRY S65 130 B8
TOT/DORE S17 189 J3
Aldam Cft TOT/DORE S17 189 J3
Aldam Rd DONS/BSCR DN4 111 J1
TOT/DORE S17 189 J3
Aldam Wy TOT/DORE S17 189 J3
Aldbury Cl BSLYN/ROY S71 60 F1
Aldcliffe Crs DONS/BSCR DN4 111 K3
Aldene Av ST/HB/BR S6 143 K6
Aldene Gld ST/HB/BR S6 143 K6
Aldene Rd ST/HB/BR S6 143 K5
Alder Cl DOD/DAR S75 37 L6
WRKS S80 198 C6
Alder Gv DONS/BSCR DN4 89 L8
THNE DN8 32 A4
WMB/DAR S73 84 D3
Alder Holt Cl ARMTH DN3 92 A2
Alder La DARN/MH S9 162 C4
Alder Ms HOY S74 105 J2
Alderney Rd SHEFP/MNR S2 160 E8
Aldersgate Cl NROS/TKH DN11 113 L7
Alderson Av RAW S62 129 K1
Alderson Cl NROS/TKH DN11 134 F7
Alderson Dr BSLYN/ROY S71 60 E1
NROS/TKH DN11 134 F7
WHHL DN2 5 M5
Alderson Pl SHEFP/MNR S2 160 E7
Alderson Rd SHEFP/MNR S2 160 D7
WRKS S80 198 C6
Alderson Rd North
SHEFP/MNR S2 160 E7
Aldervale Cl MEX/SWTN S64 108 B7
Aldesworth Rd
DONS/BSCR DN4 91 J6
Aldfield Wy SHEFN S5 144 F6
Aldham Crs WMB/DAR S73 83 L1
Aldham House La
WMB/DAR S73 83 M4
Aldred Cl ECK/KIL S21 180 C7
MALT S66 148 E2
Aldred Ct RHAM/THRY S65 7 H6
Aldred Rd FUL S10 160 A2
Aldred St RHAM/THRY S65 7 H6
Aldred St East WRKS S80 198 E5
Aldrens Cl CONI DN12 132 B5
Aldrin Wy MALT S66 150 C1
Aldwarke La RHAM/THRY S65 129 L5
Aldwarke Rd RAW S62 129 K4
Alexander Dr WRKN S81 184 B7
Alexander St BTLY DN5 67 M6
Alexandra Cl KIMB S61 128 C7
Alexandra Rd AU/AST/KP S26 164 A7
AWLS/ASK DN6 67 H1
BTLY DN5 67 M6
DONS/BSCR DN4 89 M7
DRON S18 190 F5
MEX/SWTN S64 108 F2
NROS/TKH DN11 153 M3
SHEFP/MNR S2 160 E8
THNE DN8 32 B3
Alexandra St MALT S66 150 E3
THNE DN8 31 M6
Alexandra Ter
BSLYN/ROY S71 61 K7
Alford Av CHPT/GREN S35 125 H8
Alfred Rd AWLS/ASK DN6 27 J8
DARN/MH S9 145 K8
Alfred St BSLYN/ROY S71 39 J3
Algar Cl SHEFP/MNR S2 161 J8
Algar Crs SHEFP/MNR S2 161 K8
Algar Dr SHEFP/MNR S2 161 J8
Algar Pl SHEFP/MNR S2 161 J8
Algar Rd SHEFP/MNR S2 161 J8
Alice Rd KIMB S61 6 B3
Alison Cl AU/AST/KP S26 164 B8
Alison Crs SHEFP/MNR S2 161 M6
Alison Dr AU/AST/KP S26 164 B8
Allan St RHAM/THRY S65 7 H5
Allas Dike La STKB/PEN S36 123 J3
Allas La STKB/PEN S36 123 J3
Allatt Cl BSLY S70 3 G8
Alldred Crs MEX/SWTN S64 108 A6
Allenby Cl SHEFS S8 176 C8
Allenby Crs NROS/TKH DN11 113 J7
Allenby Dr SHEFS S8 176 C8
Allendale BSLY S70 83 G2
Allendale Gdns BTLY DN5 89 K4
Allendale Rd BTLY DN5 89 K4
DOD/DAR S75 37 H7
DOD/DAR S75 60 C3
HOY S74 105 H2
RHAM/THRY S65 148 A3
Allende Wy DARN/MH S9 161 M1
Allen Rd MOS S20 179 K5
Allen St OWL S3 8 F2
WRKS S80 198 C4
Allergill Pk HOLM/MEL HD7 53 H2
Allerton St DON DN1 5 G3
Allestree Dr DRON S18 190 A6
All Hallows Dr
NROS/TKH DN11 134 D8
All Hallows Dr MALT S66 150 C3
Alliance St ATT S4 161 H1
Alliss Rd ARMTH DN3 92 C7
Allott Cl HEM/SK/SE WF9 42 D4
RHAM/THRY S65 131 H7
Allott Crs HOY S74 83 L8
Allott St HOY S74 104 F2
All Saints Cl DOD/DAR S75 58 E7
All Saints Wy AU/AST/KP S26 164 C8
Allsopp Dr WRKN S81 198 D1
Allt St RAW S62 129 K3
Alma Crs DRON S18 190 E4
Alma Rd CHPT/GREN S35 104 B8
RHAM S60 6 F6
Alma Rw RHAM S60 148 A6
Alma St BSLY S70 2 D5
OWL S3 9 G1
WMB/DAR S73 84 B5
Almholme La BTLY DN5 68 D2
Almond Av ARMTH DN3 69 M8
CUD/GR S72 39 M8
Almond Cl EPW DN9 115 G3
HEM/SK/SE WF9 42 E2
MALT S66 150 B2
Almond Dr ECK/KIL S21 194 A2
Almond Gld MALT S66 149 G4
Almond Gv WRKS S80 198 C7
Almond Rd DONS/BSCR DN4 91 K7
Almond Tree Rd
AU/AST/KP S26 180 D5
Almshill Crs ECC S11 175 K4
Almshill Dr ECC S11 175 K4
Alms Hill Rd ECC S11 175 K4
Almshill Gld ECC S11 175 K4
Almshouse La
WKFDW/WTN WF2 19 M4
Alney Pl ST/HB/BR S6 144 B3
Alnwick Dr HACK/IN S12 178 A2
Alnwick Rd HACK/IN S12 177 M2
Alperton Cl BSLYN/ROY S71 61 K2
Alpha Rd RHAM/THRY S65 129 M8
Alpine Cl STKB/PEN S36 101 L6
Alpine Ct WRKS S80 197 M5
Alpine Rd ST/HB/BR S6 8 A1
STKB/PEN S36 101 L6
Alport Av HACK/IN S12 178 C3
Alport Dr HACK/IN S12 178 C2
Alport Gv HACK/IN S12 178 C2
Alport Pl HACK/IN S12 178 C3
Alport Ri DRON S18 190 B5
Alport Rd HACK/IN S12 178 C2
Alric Dr BSLYN/ROY S71 61 J6
RHAM S60 146 F6
Alsing Rd DARN/MH S9 146 A4
Alston Cl DOD/DAR S75 58 D7
DONS/BSCR DN4 91 H8
Alston Rd DONS/BSCR DN4 113 H1
Alton Cl DRON S18 190 B7
ECC S11 175 L5
Alton Wy DOD/DAR S75 37 L6
Alverley La DONS/BSCR DN4 111 L3
Alwyn Av BTLY DN5 67 J8
Alwyn Rd THNE DN8 32 A8
Amalfi Cl WMB/DAR S73 84 D2
Amanda Av WRKN S81 184 D1
Amanda Dr HTFD DN7 48 F8
Amanda Rd NROS/TKH DN11 153 K3
Ambassador Gdns
ARMTH DN3 92 A2
Amberley Ri AWLS/ASK DN6 44 D5
Amberley St DARN/MH S9 145 L7
Ambler Ri AU/AST/KP S26 164 A6
Ambleside Cl MOS S20 193 J1
RHAM S60 146 E6
Ambleside Crs BTLY DN5 88 E6
Ambleside Dr
WKFDW/WTN WF2 20 E1
Ambleside Gra WRKN S81 184 D7
Ambleside Gv BSLYN/ROY S71 61 L7
Ambleside Wk DIN S25 182 C1
Ambrose Av HTFD DN7 49 G7
Amen Cnr RHAM S60 6 E3
America La DEARNE S63 107 G4
Amersall Crs BTLY DN5 67 J7
Amersall Rd BTLY DN5 67 J7
Amory's Holt Cl MALT S66 132 C8
Amory's Holt Dr MALT S66 132 C8
Amory's Holt Rd MALT S66 132 C8
Amory's Holt Wy MALT S66 150 B1
Amos Rd DARN/MH S9 145 M5
Amwell Gn HTFD DN7 70 E1
Amy Rd BTLY DN5 68 A4
Anchorage Crs BTLY DN5 4 A2
Anchorage La BTLY DN5 89 K3
Ancient La HTFD DN7 71 J2
Ancona Ri WMB/DAR S73 84 D2
Ancote Cl DOD/DAR S75 59 L6
Andover Dr OWL S3 160 E1
Andover St OWL S3 160 E1
Andrew La OWL S3 9 K1
Andrews Gv FEA/AMT WF7 23 K1
Andrews Pl KIMB S61 128 E7
Andrew St OWL S3 9 K1
Andwell La FUL S10 174 C2
Anelay Rd DONS/BSCR DN4 89 K8
Anfield Rd DONS/BSCR DN4 91 J8
Angel La RAW S62 106 D6
Angel St DEARNE S63 86 B6
SHEF S1 9 J3
Angerford Av SHEFS S8 176 E3
Anglesey Rd DRON S18 190 E7
Angleton Av SHEFP/MNR S2 162 A7
Angleton Cl SHEFP/MNR S2 162 A7
Angleton Gdns
SHEFP/MNR S2 162 A7
Angleton Gn SHEFP/MNR S2 162 A7
Angleton Ms SHEFP/MNR S2 162 A7
Angram Rd CHPT/GREN S35 104 B7
Annan Cl DOD/DAR S75 59 J2
Anna Rd AWLS/ASK DN6 27 K8
Annat Pl CHPT/GREN S35 104 A8
Annat Royd La STKB/PEN S36 56 A8
Anne Crs CUD/GR S72 40 C2
Annesley Cl SHEFS S8 176 D8
Annesley Rd SHEFS S8 176 D7
Anne St DIN S25 166 D4
Annet La ST/HB/BR S6 141 K3
Annie St HEM/SK/SE WF9 22 E3
Anns Rd SHEFP/MNR S2 160 E8
Anns Rd North SHEFP/MNR S2 160 F8
Ann St RAW S62 129 K4
Ansdell Rd BTLY DN5 67 M5
Ansell Rd ECC S11 175 L1
Anson Cl WRKN S81 184 C7
Anson Gv RHAM S60 147 H7
Anson St SHEFP/MNR S2 9 L4
Ansten Crs DONS/BSCR DN4 91 J6
Anston Av AU/AST/KP S26 181 J4
WRKN S81 198 C2
Anston Cl DIN S25 182 B1
Anston Dr HEM/SK/SE WF9 42 E2
Antrim Av FUL S10 8 B7
Anvil Cl ST/HB/BR S6 159 J1
Anvil Crs CHPT/GREN S35 126 F7
Apley Rd DON DN1 5 H7
Apollo St RAW S62 107 M8
Apostle Cl DONS/BSCR DN4 111 J1
Appleby Cl DOD/DAR S75 37 K6
Appleby Ct WRKN S81 184 D7
Appleby Pl AWLS/ASK DN6 44 D5
Appleby Rd WHHL DN2 91 G3
Appleby Wk DIN S25 166 D8
Applegarth Cl
HAN/WDH S13 177 M1
Applegarth Dr HACK/IN S12 177 L1
Apple Gv EPW DN9 114 E3
Applehaigh Gv BSLYN/ROY S71 38 E3
Applehaigh La HOR/CROF WF4 38 E1
Applehaigh Vw BSLYN/ROY S71 38 E3
Applehirst Bank BSLY S70 3 M8
Applehurst La BTLY DN5 46 E6
Appleton Wy BSLY S70 82 E2
BTLY DN5 67 L7
Appletree Dr DRON S18 190 E6
Applewood Cl WRKN S81 184 B7
April Cl BSLYN/ROY S71 61 G3
April Dr BSLYN/ROY S71 61 H3
Apy Hill La NROS/TKH DN11 134 A7
Aqueduct St BSLYN/ROY S71 3 G1
Arbour Crs MALT S66 165 K1
Arbour Dr MALT S66 165 K1
Arbour La CONI DN12 131 J3
RHAM/THRY S65 131 J4
Arbourthorne Rd
SHEFP/MNR S2 177 J1
Archdale Cl SHEFP/MNR S2 161 M7
Archdale Pl SHEFP/MNR S2 161 L7
Archdale Rd SHEFP/MNR S2 161 L6
Archer Ga ST/HB/BR S6 143 H6
Archer La ABRD S7 176 B2
Archer Rd SHEFS S8 176 B4
Archery Cl MALT S66 148 F4
Archibald Rd ABRD S7 176 C1
Arcon Pl RAW S62 129 L1
Arcubus Av AU/AST/KP S26 164 B7
Ardeen Rd WHHL DN2 90 E3
Arden Ga DONS/BSCR DN4 111 K3
Ardmore St DARN/MH S9 161 L2
Ardsley Av AU/AST/KP S26 180 C1
Ardsley Cl MOS S20 178 D5
Ardsley Dr MOS S20 178 D5
Ardsley Gv MOS S20 178 D5
Ardsley Rd BSLY S70 83 G2
Argosy Cl BWTY DN10 136 D7
Argyle La NROS/TKH DN11 113 J6
Argyle Rd SHEFS S8 176 E2
Argyle St MEX/SWTN S64 108 E2
Argyll Av WHHL DN2 90 F2
Arklow Rd WHHL DN2 90 E3
Arksey Common La BTLY DN5 68 C5
Arksey La BTLY DN5 67 M6
Arkwright Rd BTLY DN5 89 K2
Arley St SHEFP/MNR S2 9 G8
Arlington Av AU/AST/KP S26 164 D7
Arlott Wy CONI DN12 111 G4
Armer St RHAM S60 6 C5
Armitage Rd DONS/BSCR DN4 89 K8
STKB/PEN S36 102 B7
Armley Rd DARN/MH S9 145 L7
Armroyd La HOY S74 105 K3
Arms Park Dr MOS S20 193 K1
Armstead Rd MOS S20 179 K4
Armstrong Wk MALT S66 150 C1
Armthorpe La ARMTH DN3 69 L2
WHHL DN2 90 E2
Armthorpe Rd ECC S11 159 K7
WHHL DN2 90 E2
Armyne Gv BSLYN/ROY S71 61 J6
Arncliffe Dr BSLY S70 59 M6
CHPT/GREN S35 126 D2
Arndale Gv HOLM/MEL HD7 53 M3
Arnold Av BSLYN/ROY S71 38 D7
HACK/IN S12 177 M6
Arnold Crs MEX/SWTN S64 108 A8
Arnold Rd RHAM/THRY S65 147 M1
Arnold St ST/HB/BR S6 160 A1
Arnside Rd MALT S66 150 E1
SHEFS S8 176 C2
Arran Hl RHAM/THRY S65 130 D4
Arran Rd FUL S10 159 M4
Arras St DARN/MH S9 161 K2
Arren Cl ARMTH DN3 47 K7
Arrunden La HOLM/MEL HD7 53 K6
Arthington St SHEFS S8 176 E1
Arthur Av BTLY DN5 67 M5
Arthur Pl BTLY DN5 67 M5
Arthur Rd STKB/PEN S36 101 L6
Arthur St BSLY S70 82 E2
BTLY DN5 67 M4
RAW S62 107 L8
Artisan Vw SHEFS S8 176 E1
Arundel Av RHAM S60 163 J3
RHAM/THRY S65 130 B6
Arundel Cl DRON S18 190 B6
Arundel Cottages RHAM S60 163 J3
Arundel Crs RHAM S60 163 H3
Arundel Dr RTFD DN22 170 F2
WRKN S81 184 D1
Arundel Gdns BTLY DN5 67 K7
Arundel Ga SHEF S1 9 J5
Arundel La SHEF S1 9 J6
Arundell Dr BSLYN/ROY S71 61 K3
Arundel Rd AWLS/ASK DN6 27 H4
CHPT/GREN S35 126 E1
RHAM S60 163 J3
RHAM/THRY S65 7 K7
Arundel St RHAM S60 163 H3
SHEF S1 9 H7
Arundel Vw HOY S74 83 L8
Ascension Cl MALT S66 150 E3
Ascot Av DONS/BSCR DN4 91 H6
Ascot Cl MEX/SWTN S64 108 F1
Ascot Dr BTLY DN5 89 H1
Ascot St SHEFP/MNR S2 9 G9
Ashberry Cl DEARNE S63 64 B7
Ashberry Rd ST/HB/BR S6 8 B1
Ashbourne Gv
CHPT/GREN S35 143 J1
HAN/WDH S13 162 D6
Ashbourne Rd BSLYN/ROY S71 38 E8
HAN/WDH S13 162 D6
Ash Brow HOR/CROF WF4 17 G4
Ashburnham Cl AWLS/ASK DN6 27 J4
Ashburnham Gdns BTLY DN5 89 J4
Ashburnham Rd THNE DN8 31 L8
Ashburnham Wk
AWLS/ASK DN6 27 J4
Ashburton Cl AWLS/ASK DN6 66 E1
Ashbury Dr SHEFS S8 177 G5
Ashbury La SHEFS S8 177 G5
Ashby Ct BSLY S70 2 D7
Ash Cl ECK/KIL S21 194 A2
RHAM/THRY S65 148 B3
WRKS S80 198 C6
Ash Ct BTLY DN5 89 H6
MALT S66 150 B1
Ash Crs ECK/KIL S21 192 F6
MEX/SWTN S64 108 C1
Ashdale Cl ARMTH DN3 69 K6
Ash Dale Rd CONI DN12 110 F3
Ashdell ECC S11 160 A5
Ashdell La ECC S11 160 A5
Ashdell Rd ECC S11 160 A5
Ashdene Ct MEX/SWTN S64 108 B7
Ashdown Gdns MOS S20 179 L4
Ashdown Pl BTLY DN5 67 J7
Ash Dyke Cl DOD/DAR S75 37 H8
Asher Rd ABRD S7 160 D7
Ashes La RAW S62 105 K7
Ashes Park Av WRKN S81 184 B7
Ashfield Av KBTN HD8 34 E6
THNE DN8 49 L1
Ashfield Cl DOD/DAR S75 2 A2
HACK/IN S12 177 K3
Ashfield Dr HACK/IN S12 177 K3
Ashfield Gv HTFD DN7 48 D3
Ashfield Rd DONS/BSCR DN4 111 L1
HEM/SK/SE WF9 41 H2
HTFD DN7 48 D8
STKB/PEN S36 102 B6
THNE DN8 49 J2
Ash Fields Rd ARMTH DN3 47 G7
BTLY DN5 46 E7
Ashford Rd DRON S18 190 B7
ECC S11 160 B7
Ashfurlong Cl TOT/DORE S17 175 K8
Ashfurlong Dr TOT/DORE S17 175 K8
Ashfurlong Pk TOT/DORE S17 175 K8
Ashfurlong Rd TOT/DORE S17 175 J8
Ashgate Cl ECC S11 160 A5
Ashgate La FUL S10 160 A5
Ashgate Rd ECC S11 160 A5
Ash Gv ARMTH DN3 70 A8
AU/AST/KP S26 181 G4
BSLY S70 61 H8
CONI DN12 109 L6
EPW DN9 114 E4
FUL S10 8 A7
HEM/SK/SE WF9 42 E3
MALT S66 149 G2
MALT S66 150 F1
RAW S62 129 L2
Ash Grove Rd HOLM/MEL HD7 53 J2
Ash Hill Crs HTFD DN7 48 F8
Ash Hill Rd GLE DN14 29 L2
HTFD DN7 48 F8
Ash Holt Dr WRKN S81 184 D7
Ash House La TOT/DORE S17 175 H6
Ashland Rd ABRD S7 176 C2
ECK/KIL S21 193 J4
Ash La DRON S18 191 K4
ECK/KIL S21 192 A7
KBTN HD8 35 J1
STKB/PEN S36 102 C6
Ashleigh CUD/GR S72 40 E4
Ashleigh Av HACK/IN S12 177 K2
Ashleigh Ct ECK/KIL S21 193 G6
Ashleigh Cft HACK/IN S12 177 K2
Ashleigh Dr HACK/IN S12 177 K2
Ashleigh Pl HACK/IN S12 177 K2
Ashleigh Rd STV/CWN S43 194 E8
Ashley Cl ECK/KIL S21 194 B1
Ashley Ct EPW DN9 115 J4
HEM/SK/SE WF9 41 K6
WRKN S81 198 D2
Ashley Cft BSLYN/ROY S71 38 F3
Ashley Gv AU/AST/KP S26 164 B8
Ashley La ECK/KIL S21 194 B1
Ashley Rd WRKN S81 198 C1
Ashmore Av ECK/KIL S21 192 F5
Ashover Cl BSLY S70 82 E3
Ashpool Cl HAN/WDH S13 178 E1
Ash Rdg MEX/SWTN S64 108 B5
Ash Rd AWLS/ASK DN6 44 F5
CUD/GR S72 40 B5
DEARNE S63 107 K2
Ash St MOS S20 179 G8
ST/HB/BR S6 160 C1
WMB/DAR S73 83 L1
Ashton Av BTLY DN5 67 H6
Ashton Cl ECK/KIL S21 194 A1
Ashton Dr ARMTH DN3 69 J3
Ashton La MALT S66 132 D6
Ash Tree Av BWTY DN10 136 D8
Ash Tree Rd THNE DN8 49 M1
Ashurst Cl ST/HB/BR S6 143 J8
Ashurst Dr ST/HB/BR S6 143 J8
Ashurst Pl ST/HB/BR S6 143 J8
Ashurst Rd ST/HB/BR S6 143 J8
Ash Vw CHPT/GREN S35 126 D3
KIMB S61 128 F4
Ashville NROS/TKH DN11 113 L7
Ashwell Cl CUD/GR S72 40 A4
Ashwell Rd HAN/WDH S13 178 E1
Ashwood Cl ARMTH DN3 92 A8
BSLY S70 82 F3
CHPT/GREN S35 104 A7
Ashwood Gra HOR/CROF WF4 19 J1
Ashwood Gv CUD/GR S72 63 H4
Ashwood Rd CHPT/GREN S35 104 A7
RAW S62 129 K3
WRKS S80 197 M5
Ashworth Dr KIMB S61 128 B5
Askam Ct MALT S66 149 H1
Askam Rd MALT S66 149 H1
Askern Grange La
AWLS/ASK DN6 28 A7
Askern Rd AWLS/ASK DN6 45 J6
BTLY DN5 67 L3
Askew Ct STKB/PEN S36 102 A7
Askham Gv HEM/SK/SE WF9 25 J7
Askrigg Cl DONS/BSCR DN4 91 K8
Asline Rd SHEFP/MNR S2 160 E7
Aspen Cl ARMTH DN3 69 K6
ECK/KIL S21 194 A1
Aspen Ct KBTN HD8 17 G8
Aspen Gv WMB/DAR S73 84 E3
Aspen Rd ECK/KIL S21 192 F6
Aspen Wy MEX/SWTN S64 108 A7
Asquith Rd BTLY DN5 67 M6
DARN/MH S9 145 M3
Aster Cl DIN S25 182 B3
MOS S20 179 K4
Aston Cl DRON S18 191 G4
Aston Dr BSLYN/ROY S71 60 E1
Aston Gn HTFD DN7 70 E1
Aston La AU/AST/KP S26 164 B5
Aston St SHEFP/MNR S2 161 H3
Astwell Gdns
CHPT/GREN S35 126 C1
Athelstan Cl HAN/WDH S13 162 C6
Athelstane Crs ARMTH DN3 69 K4
Athelstane Dr MALT S66 165 J2
Athelstane Rd CONI DN12 109 M5
Athelstan Rd HAN/WDH S13 162 C6
WRKS S80 198 D6
Athersley Crs BSLYN/ROY S71 60 E1
Athersley Gdns MOS S20 178 E5
Athersley Rd BSLYN/ROY S71 60 E1
Atherton Cl SHEFP/MNR S2 177 K1
Atherton Rd SHEFP/MNR S2 177 K1
Atholl Crs WHHL DN2 91 G2
Athol Rd SHEFS S8 176 C3
Athorpe Gv DIN S25 166 C6
Athorpe Rd DIN S25 166 C6
Athron Dr RHAM/THRY S65 148 A3
Athron St DON DN1 5 H2
Atkin Pl SHEFP/MNR S2 160 E7
Atlantic Dr SHEFS S8 190 C1
Atlantic Rd SHEFS S8 190 B1
Atlantic Wy SHEFS S8 190 C1
Atlas St ATT S4 161 H1
RHAM S60 147 G6
Atlas Wy ATT S4 145 J8
Atterby Dr NROS/TKH DN11 113 L5
Attercliffe Common
DARN/MH S9 145 L8
Attercliffe Rd ATT S4 9 M1
DARN/MH S9 161 K1
Attlee Av HOR/CROF WF4 22 A6
NROS/TKH DN11 113 H6
Attlee Cl MALT S66 150 F3
Attlee Crs WMB/DAR S73 85 G2
Aubretia Av RHAM S60 147 H8
Auburn Rd CONI DN12 110 F5
Auckland Av ST/HB/BR S6 143 J7
Auckland Dr MOS S20 193 H1
Auckland Ri MOS S20 193 J1
Auckland Rd DON DN1 5 K1
MEX/SWTN S64 108 F2
Auckland Wy MOS S20 193 J1
Audrey Rd HAN/WDH S13 162 A8
Aughton Av AU/AST/KP S26 164 A6
Aughton Cl HAN/WDH S13 162 B8
Aughton Crs HAN/WDH S13 162 A7
Aughton Dr HAN/WDH S13 162 A7
Aughton La AU/AST/KP S26 164 C7
Aughton Rd AU/AST/KP S26 164 A7
Augustus Rd RHAM S60 147 G5
Aukley Rd SHEFS S8 176 D2
Aunby Dr AU/AST/KP S26 164 B7
Austen Av DONS/BSCR DN4 111 J1
Austen Dr MALT S66 149 J2
Austin Cl ST/HB/BR S6 143 J7
Austin Ct ST/HB/BR S6 143 J6
Austwick Cl DOD/DAR S75 37 L5
DONS/BSCR DN4 111 K3
Austwood La MALT S66 132 E5
Autumn Cl MALT S66 165 L1
Autumn Dr MALT S66 150 E1
Avenue Rd AWLS/ASK DN6 27 K8
DEARNE S63 107 L1
WHHL DN2 5 K1
The Avenue AWLS/ASK DN6 27 K8
AWLS/ASK DN6 27 G6
BSLYN/ROY S71 39 J3
BTLY DN5 68 A6
BTLY DN5 86 F6
CHPT/GREN S35 103 H4
DARN/MH S9 162 A3
DOD/DAR S75 104 B1
DONS/BSCR DN4 91 G6
DRON S18 190 F5
ECK/KIL S21 194 B5
MALT S66 133 J7
MALT S66 150 A6
MOS S20 179 K3
THNE DN8 32 A3
Aviemore Rd DONS/BSCR DN4 111 J1
Avill Wy MALT S66 148 F4
Avisford Dr SHEFN S5 144 B4
Avisford Rd SHEFN S5 144 B3
Avoca Av WHHL DN2 90 E3
Avocet Gv WRKN S81 198 A1
Avocet Wy KIMB S61 127 K1
Avon Cl DOD/DAR S75 59 J4
DRON S18 190 F4
MALT S66 150 D1
WMB/DAR S73 84 D6
Avon Ct EPW DN9 92 E8
Avondale Dr BSLYN/ROY S71 39 G6
Avondale Rd KIMB S61 128 E8
ST/HB/BR S6 143 M7
WHHL DN2 90 E4
Avon Gv CHPT/GREN S35 126 C1
Avon Mt KIMB S61 128 E8
Avon St BSLYN/ROY S71 3 J6
Avon Wy WRKN S81 184 C8
Axholme Gn THNE DN8 50 A1
Axholme Rd EPW DN9 117 M3
WHHL DN2 5 K1
Axle La DIN S25 182 A3
Aylesbury Crs DARN/MH S9 145 M4
Aylesbury Rd WHHL DN2 90 F3
Aylesford Cl BSLYN/ROY S71 3 G1
Aylsham Dr AU/AST/KP S26 164 C8
Aylward Cl SHEFP/MNR S2 161 K8
Aylward Rd SHEFP/MNR S2 161 K8

Aymer Dr MALT S66 165 J2
Ayots Gn HTFD DN7 70 E1
Aysgarth Av BSLYN/ROY S71 61 M7
Aysgarth Ri AU/AST/KP S26 164 A7
Aysgarth Rd ST/HB/BR S6 144 A3
Ayton Wk BTLY DN5 67 L5 2
Azalea Cl DIN S25 182 B4

B

Babbage Wy WRKS S80 198 B3
Babington Cl SHEFP/MNR S2 161 K8
Babington Ct
SHEFP/MNR S2 161 K8 1
Babur Rd ATT S4 161 H1 1
Back Field La HTFD DN7 49 H8
Backfield Ri CHPT/GREN S35 126 E1
Backfields SHEF S1 9 G5
Backhouse La HOR/CROF WF4 19 K8
Back La AWLS/ASK DN6 27 G7
AWLS/ASK DN6 27 G3
BSLYN/ROY S71 61 G2
BTLY DN5 64 A3
BTLY DN5 65 H2
BTLY DN5 89 G2
BWTY DN10 137 M5
CONI DN12 110 E8
CUD/GR S72 63 K8
DIN S25 182 C1
DRON S18 191 K6
ECK/KIL S21 193 G4
EPW DN9 115 H2
FUL S10 159 K3
HATH/EY S32 172 E8
HEM/SK/SE WF9 24 C5
HEM/SK/SE WF9 42 E1
HOLM/MEL HD7 53 L2
HOR/CROF WF4 16 B2
HOR/CROF WF4 21 M3
HOR/CROF WF4 37 L1
HTFD DN7 48 C3
KBTN HD8 34 E2
KBTN HD8 35 L4
MALT S66 132 B2
MALT S66 132 B5
MALT S66 149 L4
RAW S62 129 G1
RHAM/THRY S65 130 D3
RHAM/THRY S65 131 H1
RTFD DN22 170 E3
ST/HB/BR S6 142 D4
STKB/PEN S36 79 H4
STKB/PEN S36 79 L7
STKB/PEN S36 100 A3
STKB/PEN S36 101 K1
STKB/PEN S36 101 H4
WRKS S80 196 F1
Back La West BSLYN/ROY S71 38 E3
Backmoor Crs SHEFS S8 177 G5
Backmoor Rd SHEFS S8 177 G5
Back Rd DRON S18 191 K6
Back St HAN/WDH S13 179 G1
Bacon La DARN/MH S9 161 J2
Baden St BSLY S70 82 F3
RHAM S60 6 D2
Bader Ri BWTY DN10 155 L7
Bader Vw BWTY DN10 155 L7
Badger Cl HAN/WDH S13 163 G8
Badger Dr HAN/WDH S13 163 G8
Badger La AWLS/ASK DN6 27 L1
SHEF S1 8 F4
STKB/PEN S36 99 J1
Badger Pl HAN/WDH S13 163 G8
Badger Ri HAN/WDH S13 163 G8
Badger Rd HAN/WDH S13 163 G8
Badsley Ct RHAM/THRY S65 7 K5 1
Badsley Moor La
RHAM/THRY S65 7 K6
Badsley St RHAM/THRY S65 7 J5
Badsley St South
RHAM/THRY S65 7 K6
Badsworth Cl MALT S66 149 J2
WMB/DAR S73 84 D5 1
Badsworth Ct
HEM/SK/SE WF9 24 C4
Badsworth Pl MALT S66 149 J2
Badsworth Rd
DONS/BSCR DN4 111 G2
Badsworth Vw
HEM/SK/SE WF9 24 E7
Badsworth Wy MALT S66 149 J2 1
Bagden La KBTN HD8 6 G1
Bagger Wood Hl DOD/DAR S75 81 H4
Bagger Wood Rd DOD/DAR S75 81 G6
Bagley Rd ATT S4 145 H6
Bagshaw's Rd HACK/IN S12 177 M1 2
Bagshot St ECC S11 160 B7
Bahram Rd DONS/BSCR DN4 91 G7 1
Bailey Crs HEM/SK/SE WF9 42 E2
Bailey Dr ECK/KIL S21 180 C7
Bailey La HTFD DN7 49 H3
SHEF S1 8 F4
Bailey St SHEF S1 8 F4
Bainbridge Rd DONS/BSCR DN4 4 D8
Baines Av CONI DN12 110 E6
Bainton Dr BSLY S70 2 C9
Bakehouse La DOD/DAR S75 59 L4
Baker Dr ECK/KIL S21 194 A1
Bakers Hl SHEF S1 9 J4
Bakers La SHEF S1 8 F3
Baker St DARN/MH S9 161 K1
Bakewell Rd BSLYN/ROY S71 60 E1
Bala St BSLYN/ROY S71 3 H5
Balby Carr Bank
DONS/BSCR DN4 90 B8
Balby Rd DONS/BSCR DN4 89 M7
Balcarres Rd NROS/TKH DN11 113 K6
Baldwin St DARN/MH S9 161 J2 1
Balfour Dr DARN/MH S9 161 M2
Balfour Rd BTLY DN5 68 A6
DARN/MH S9 161 M2
Balk La BSLY S70 82 C6
GLE DN14 11 K3
HEM/SK/SE WF9 43 H3
KBTN HD8 56 A1
RHAM S60 146 E5
Balkley La WMB/DAR S73 85 G2
The Balk BTLY DN5 68 C1
DOD/DAR S75 38 A5
WKFDW/WTN WF2 20 F1
Ballam Av BTLY DN5 67 J6
Ballfield La DOD/DAR S75 37 G7
Ballifield Av HAN/WDH S13 162 E6
Ballifield Cl HAN/WDH S13 162 E6
Ballifield Crs HAN/WDH S13 162 F6
Ballifield Dr HAN/WDH S13 162 F6
Ballifield Pl HAN/WDH S13 162 E6
Ballifield Ri HAN/WDH S13 162 F6
Ballifield Rd HAN/WDH S13 162 E6
Ballifield Wy HAN/WDH S13 162 E6
Ball Rd ST/HB/BR S6 143 M8
Ball St OWL S3 8 F1
Balmain Dr ST/HB/BR S6 143 M6
Balmain Rd ST/HB/BR S6 143 M6
Balmer Ri MALT S66 149 J3
Balm Gn SHEF S1 9 G4
Balmoral Cl BTLY DN5 87 G4
STKB/PEN S36 78 E3 1
WRKN S81 184 D1
Balmoral Crs DRON S18 190 B5
Balmoral Rd HAN/WDH S13 179 G1
WHHL DN2 5 L2
Balmoral Wy MALT S66 149 H1
Balne Croft La GLE DN14 11 M5
Balne Hall Rd GLE DN14 11 H1
Balne Moor Rd GLE DN14 10 C3
GLE DN14 11 G4
Baltic Rd DARN/MH S9 161 K1
Bamford Av BSLYN/ROY S71 60 E1
Bamford Cl DOD/DAR S75 59 J8
Bamforth St ST/HB/BR S6 144 B8
Bank Cl ABRD S7 176 C1
KIMB S61 128 D6
Bank End Av BSLY S70 83 G2
Bank End La KBTN HD8 35 L6
Bank End Rd BSLY S70 82 F2
BWTY DN10 116 A3
EPW DN9 115 K2
Bankfield Dr HOLM/MEL HD7 53 G5
Bankfield La ST/HB/BR S6 159 G1 1
Bankfield Rd ST/HB/BR S6 143 L8
Bank House Rd FUL S10 160 A2 1
Bank La CHPT/GREN S35 103 J8
HOLM/MEL HD7 52 F5
HOLM/MEL HD7 53 H3
KBTN HD8 56 D3
STKB/PEN S36 124 C2
Banks Av FEA/AMT WF7 23 J2
Bank Side CHPT/GREN S35 124 A4
Bank St BSLY S70 3 H9
BSLYN/ROY S71 61 J7
CUD/GR S72 39 M8 1
DIN S25 182 B3
DON DN1 4 F9
HOLM/MEL HD7 54 C3
HOY S74 105 H2
MEX/SWTN S64 108 E3
SHEF S1 9 J3
Bank Top La HOLM/MEL HD7 52 E4
Bank Top Rd RHAM/THRY S65 148 B3
Bank Vw RHAM S60 147 M6
Bankwood Cl SHEFS S8 177 H2
Bankwood Crs
NROS/TKH DN11 113 H5
Bankwood La NROS/TKH DN11 113 H4
Bankwood Rd SHEFP/MNR S2 177 H2
Banmoor La HATH/EY S32 172 C7
Banner Ct ECC S11 175 M1
Banner Cross Dr ECC S11 175 M1 1
Bannerdale Cl ECC S11 176 A1 1
Bannerdale Rd ECC S11 176 A1
Bannerdale Vw ECC S11 176 A1
Bannham Rd DARN/MH S9 162 B3
Bannister La AWLS/ASK DN6 44 A2
Bar Av DOD/DAR S75 38 B7 1
Barbados Wy MALT S66 149 L2
Barber Balk Cl KIMB S61 128 D6 1
Barber Balk Rd KIMB S61 128 D7
Barber Cl AU/AST/KP S26 181 J2
Barber Crs ST/HB/BR S6 8 A2
Barber Pl FUL S10 8 A2
Barber Rd FUL S10 8 A2
Barberry Wy RHAM/THRY S65 131 J7
Barber's Av RAW S62 129 K3
Barber's Crs RAW S62 129 K2
Barber's La ECK/KIL S21 180 B7
Barbers Pth MEX/SWTN S64 108 D1
Barber St HOY S74 105 J1
Barber Wood Rd KIMB S61 145 M1
Barbot Hill Rd KIMB S61 129 G5
Barcroft DOD/DAR S75 59 L3 1
Barden Crs RHAM S60 147 G7
Barden Dr DOD/DAR S75 59 M4
Bardolf Rd DONS/BSCR DN4 91 J6
Bardon Rd ARMTH DN3 69 K5
Bard St SHEFP/MNR S2 9 L3
Bardwell Rd OWL S3 160 D1
Barfield Av RHAM S60 147 L6
Barfield Rd HOY S74 105 J1
Barholm Rd FUL S10 159 K5
Bari Cl WMB/DAR S73 84 C1
Baring Rd KIMB S61 145 M1
Barkby Rd DARN/MH S9 145 L3
Barker Hades Rd WRKN S81 167 L4
Barker's Pl ST/HB/BR S6 144 A6 1
Barker's Pool SHEF S1 9 G5
Barker's Rd ECC S11 176 B1
HOR/CROF WF4 19 J1
Barker St MEX/SWTN S64 108 C2
Bark House La DOD/DAR S75 58 A3
Bark Mdw DOD/DAR S75 59 L8
Barkston Rd BSLYN/ROY S71 39 G8
BSLYN/ROY S71 61 G1
Bar La DOD/DAR S75 38 B7
HOR/CROF WF4 17 K5
Barlborough Rd WMB/DAR S73 84 C6
Barlby Gv HACK/IN S12 179 G4
Barleycroft La DIN S25 166 D7
Barley Ms DRON S18 190 A6 2
Barley Vw DEARNE S63 64 B8 1
Barleywood Rd DARN/MH S9 162 A1
Barlow Dr ST/HB/BR S6 159 L1
Barlow Lees La DRON S18 190 D8
Barlow Rd ST/HB/BR S6 143 L8
Barlow Vw DRON S18 190 F8
Barmouth Rd ABRD S7 176 C2
Barnard Av DRON S18 191 H4
Barnardiston Rd DARN/MH S9 161 M2
Barnburgh La DEARNE S63 86 C3
Barnby Dun Rd WHHL DN2 69 G7
Barncliffe Cl FUL S10 159 G7
Barncliffe Crs FUL S10 158 F6
Barncliffe Dr FUL S10 158 F6
Barncliffe Gln FUL S10 158 F7
Barncliffe Rd FUL S10 159 G7
Barnes Av DRON S18 190 B5
Barnes Ct SHEFP/MNR S2 9 K7
Barnes Hall Rd
CHPT/GREN S35 126 B3
Barnes La DRON S18 189 M3
DRON S18 190 B5
Barnet Av ECC S11 175 J2
Barnet Gn HTFD DN7 70 E1
Barnet Rd ECC S11 175 J2
Barnfield Av FUL S10 159 J4
Barnfield Cl FUL S10 159 J5
Barnfield Dr FUL S10 159 J5
HATH/EY S32 172 D8
Barnfield Rd FUL S10 159 J4
Barnfields HATH/EY S32 172 D8
Barnsdale Av MOS S20 178 E5
Barnsdale Ms AWLS/ASK DN6 27 G7
Barnsdale Vw AWLS/ASK DN6 26 F3
Barnsdale Wy HEM/SK/SE WF9 25 J8
Barnside Cl STKB/PEN S36 79 H5 1
Barnside La HOLM/MEL HD7 54 D6
Barnsley Av CONI DN12 109 L5
Barnsley Boundary Wk
CHPT/GREN S35 102 E5
CHPT/GREN S35 125 K6
DOD/DAR S75 58 A3
HOLM/MEL HD7 76 C1
HOR/CROF WF4 21 J7
HOY S74 105 K3
KBTN HD8 56 F4
STKB/PEN S36 56 A8
WMB/DAR S73 84 B8
Barnsley Rd ATT S4 144 F7
BTLY DN5 65 H8
CUD/GR S72 40 D1
CUD/GR S72 61 L1
DEARNE S63 85 H8
DEARNE S63 86 B2
DOD/DAR S75 37 J7 1
DOD/DAR S75 58 E7
DOD/DAR S75 59 J8 1
FEA/AMT WF7 23 L3
HEM/SK/SE WF9 42 B4
HOR/CROF WF4 17 G4
HOY S74 83 H7
KBTN HD8 35 J6
KBTN HD8 56 A1
KIMB S61 105 J8
OWL S3 144 F8
SHEFN S5 145 G2
STKB/PEN S36 79 H3
THNE DN8 32 B4
WKFDW/WTN WF2 20 A1
WMB/DAR S73 62 D8
WMB/DAR S73 84 A3
Barnstone St DONS/BSCR DN4 4 B8
Barnwell Crs WMB/DAR S73 83 M2
Baron St SHEF S1 9 H9
Barrack Rd DRON S18 191 L6
Barracks Fold HOLM/MEL HD7 54 C5
Barratt Rd ECK/KIL S21 193 H5
Barrel La DONS/BSCR DN4 111 H1
Barret Rd DONS/BSCR DN4 91 K6
Barretta St ATT S4 145 H6
Barrie Crs SHEFN S5 144 D4
Barrie Dr SHEFN S5 144 D4
Barrie Gv MALT S66 149 M3
Barrier Bank GLE DN14 13 H3
Barrie Rd DONS/BSCR DN4 111 M1 1
SHEFN S5 144 D5
Barrowby Rd RHAM S60 147 L4
Barrow Field La RAW S62 105 L5
Barrowfield Rd DEARNE S63 64 C4
HOY S74 83 H8
Barrow Hl RAW S62 105 K6
Barrow Rd DARN/MH S9 145 M3
Barrowstead KBTN HD8 34 E6
Bartholomew Cl RHAM S60 148 B5 1
Bartholomew St WMB/DAR S73 84 A4
Bartle Av HACK/IN S12 177 K3
Bartle Dr HACK/IN S12 177 K3
Bartle Rd HACK/IN S12 177 K3
Bartlett Cl ST/HB/BR S6 159 G2 1
Bartlett Rd SHEFN S5 144 D3
Bartle Wy HACK/IN S12 177 K3
Barton La ARMTH DN3 91 L1
Barton Pl CONI DN12 109 M6
Barton Rd SHEFS S8 176 E1
Barton Wy HEM/SK/SE WF9 42 E2
Barugh Green Rd DOD/DAR S75 59 J3
Barugh La DOD/DAR S75 59 J2
Basegreen Av HACK/IN S12 177 M4
Basegreen Cl HACK/IN S12 178 A4
Basegreen Crs HACK/IN S12 177 M4
Basegreen Dr HACK/IN S12 177 M4
Basegreen Pl HACK/IN S12 177 M4 1
Basegreen Rd HACK/IN S12 178 A5 1
Basegreen Wy HACK/IN S12 178 A4 1
Basford Cl DARN/MH S9 161 M2
Basford Dr DARN/MH S9 161 M2
Basford Ms DARN/MH S9 162 A2 1
Basford Pl DARN/MH S9 161 M2 1
Basford St DARN/MH S9 161 M2
Basil Av ARMTH DN3 69 J8
Basildon Rd DEARNE S63 64 A6
Baslow Crs DOD/DAR S75 59 J8
Baslow Rd BSLYN/ROY S71 38 F8
TOT/DORE S17 188 F4
Bassett La FUL S10 174 C1
Bassett Pl SHEFP/MNR S2 161 H5
Bassett Rd SHEFP/MNR S2 161 J5
Bassingthorpe La KIMB S61 128 F5
Bassledene Rd SHEFP/MNR S2 161 L7
Bastock Rd ST/HB/BR S6 144 B6
Bate La GLE DN14 11 L8
Bateman Cl CUD/GR S72 39 L5
Bateman Rd MALT S66 149 L3
Batemoor Cl SHEFS S8 190 E1
Batemoor Dr SHEFS S8 190 E1
Batemoor Pl SHEFS S8 190 E1 1
Batemoor Rd SHEFS S8 190 E1
Batesquire MOS S20 179 K5
Bath St OWL S3 8 E7
Battison La DEARNE S63 107 H3
Battle Cl HTFD DN7 71 K7
Batt St SHEFP/MNR S2 160 E7 3
Batty Av CUD/GR S72 61 L1
Batworth Dr ATT S4 144 E7
Batworth Rd SHEFN S5 144 E7
Baulk Farm Cl RAW S62 128 F3
Baulk La HATH/EY S32 172 E7
NROS/TKH DN11 153 K2
RTFD DN22 170 D5
WRKN S81 198 C2
The Baulk WRKN S81 198 D2
Bawtry Cl NROS/TKH DN11 153 K3
Bawtry Ga DARN/MH S9 146 C5
Bawtry Rd BWTY DN10 137 L4
BWTY DN10 154 B5
BWTY DN10 155 K3
DARN/MH S9 146 D6
DONS/BSCR DN4 90 E5
DONS/BSCR DN4 113 K2
HTFD DN7 71 K2
MALT S66 148 F3
NROS/TKH DN11 153 K3
RHAM S60 146 F6
RHAM/THRY S65 148 C3 1
WRKN S81 153 M8
WRKN S81 169 L3
Baxter Av DON DN1 5 J2
Baxter Cl ST/HB/BR S6 144 A3
Baxter Dr ST/HB/BR S6 144 A3
Baxter Ga DON DN1 4 F4
Baxter Rd ST/HB/BR S6 144 A3
Baycliff Cl BSLYN/ROY S71 39 H8 1
Bay Ct ECK/KIL S21 194 A2
Bayfield Cl HOLM/MEL HD7 53 M7
Baylee St HEM/SK/SE WF9 41 J1 1
Baysdale Cft MOS S20 179 H8
Bay Tree Av MALT S66 148 F1
Baytree Gv EPW DN9 114 D3
Beacon Cl DARN/MH S9 145 K5
DOD/DAR S75 80 E1 1
Beacon Ct DOD/DAR S75 80 E1 2
Beacon Cft DARN/MH S9 145 K5
Beacon Dr HEM/SK/SE WF9 24 E7
Beaconfield Rd
HEM/SK/SE WF9 24 D6
Beacon Hl DOD/DAR S75 80 E1
HEM/SK/SE WF9 24 E7 1
Beacon La MALT S66 132 B2
Beacon Rd DARN/MH S9 145 K5
Beaconsfield Rd
DONS/BSCR DN4 4 B8
RHAM S60 147 L4
Beaconsfield St BSLY S70 2 E7 1
MEX/SWTN S64 108 D2 1
Beacon Sq MALT S66 132 C2
Beacon Vw HEM/SK/SE WF9 42 A4
HOY S74 105 L2 1
Beacon Wy DARN/MH S9 145 K5
Beale Wy RAW S62 129 K5
Beamshaw HEM/SK/SE WF9 41 M6
Bean Av WRKS S80 198 F4
Beancroft Cl NROS/TKH DN11 112 A8
Bear Bones Rd HOLM/MEL HD7 75 M2
Bear Tree Cl RAW S62 129 K3 2
Bear Tree Rd RAW S62 129 K3
Bear Tree St RAW S62 129 K4 1
Beauchamp Rd KIMB S61 128 D6
Beauchief Abbey La SHEFS S8 176 A7
Beauchief Cl STKB/PEN S36 102 D7 1
Beauchief Dr SHEFS S8 176 A8
Beauchief Ri SHEFS S8 176 A6
Beaufont Gdns BWTY DN10 136 D8
Beaufort Rd FUL S10 8 A5
WHHL DN2 90 F3
Beaufort Wy WRKN S81 184 C7
Beaulieu Cl DOD/DAR S75 38 A7
Beaulieu Vw DOD/DAR S75 38 A7 1
Beaumont Av AWLS/ASK DN6 66 D1
BSLY S70 59 M6
HEM/SK/SE WF9 42 D4
SHEFP/MNR S2 161 L5
Beaumont Cl SHEFP/MNR S2 161 M5
Beaumont Crs
SHEFP/MNR S2 161 L5 1
Beaumont Dr HOR/CROF WF4 36 D1
RHAM/THRY S65 147 M2
Beaumont Ms
SHEFP/MNR S2 161 M6 1
Beaumont Ri WRKS S80 198 B4
Beaumont Rd DOD/DAR S75 37 G8
Beaumont Rd North
SHEFP/MNR S2 161 L5
Beaumont St HOY S74 104 F2
KBTN HD8 17 G8
Beaumont Wy
SHEFP/MNR S2 161 L5 2
Beaver Av HAN/WDH S13 162 F7
Beaver Cl HAN/WDH S13 162 F7
Beaver Dr HAN/WDH S13 162 F7
Beaver Hill Rd HAN/WDH S13 162 F7
Beaver Pl WRKS S80 198 D4
Beccles Wy MALT S66 149 J2
Beck Cl MEX/SWTN S64 108 B6
SHEFN S5 127 J8
Becket Crs KIMB S61 128 B5
Becket Rd SHEFS S8 190 C1
Beckett Av WRKN S81 168 D8
Beckett Rd DON DN1 5 J1
WHHL DN2 68 E8
Beckett St BSLYN/ROY S71 3 H3
Beckfield Gv DEARNE S63 85 M4
Becknoll Rd WMB/DAR S73 84 E7
Beck Ri HEM/SK/SE WF9 23 H8
Beck Rd SHEFN S5 127 H8
Beckton Av MOS S20 179 J5
Beckton Ct MOS S20 179 K5
Beckton Gv MOS S20 179 J5
Beck Vw HOR/CROF WF4 35 E1
Beckwith Rd DIN S25 166 A5
RHAM/THRY S65 130 A8
Bedale WRKN S81 184 E7
Bedale Av KBTN HD8 34 D6
Bedale Dr KBTN HD8 34 D6
Bedale Rd BTLY DN5 67 H8
SHEFS S8 176 D1
Bedding Edge Rd
HOLM/MEL HD7 76 E1
Bedford Av HOR/CROF WF4 16 C2
Bedford Cl DIN S25 166 B8 1
Bedford Rd CHPT/GREN S35 125 H7
Bedford St BSLY S70 3 G9
CUD/GR S72 62 E2
MALT S66 150 F3 1
ST/HB/BR S6 160 D2 1
Bedford Ter BSLYN/ROY S71 60 E2
Bedgebury Cl MOS S20 179 M6 1
Bedgrave Cl ECK/KIL S21 180 D7
Beecham Ct MEX/SWTN S64 108 A6
Beech Av CUD/GR S72 39 M7
DOD/DAR S75 80 E2 1
EPW DN9 114 E3
NROS/TKH DN11 134 F8
RAW S62 129 M2
RHAM/THRY S65 148 C3
WRKN S81 198 D1
Beech Cl CUD/GR S72 40 E4
HEM/SK/SE WF9 41 M5
MALT S66 150 B2
WMB/DAR S73 84 A7
Beech Crs ECK/KIL S21 192 F6
ECK/KIL S21 194 A2
HTFD DN7 48 D3
MEX/SWTN S64 108 C2
Beechcroft WRKN S81 198 E1 1
Beechcroft Rd
DONS/BSCR DN4 111 J2 1
Beeches Av SHEFP/MNR S2 161 G7
Beeches Dr SHEFP/MNR S2 161 G7
Beeches Gv MOS S20 179 L4
Beeches Rd AU/AST/KP S26 180 F4
The Beeches ARMTH DN3 69 K3
AU/AST/KP S26 164 B8
MEX/SWTN S64 108 A5
Beechfern Cl
CHPT/GREN S35 104 B7 1
Beechfield Av KBTN HD8 34 E6
Beechfield Cl DEARNE S63 86 A5
Beechfield Rd DON DN1 5 H7
HTFD DN7 48 D8
Beech Gv BSLY S70 60 B8
BTLY DN5 67 M7 1
CONI DN12 109 M6
DIN S25 166 D8
DONS/BSCR DN4 111 G1
HEM/SK/SE WF9 22 E5
MALT S66 149 G2
WRKN S81 168 C8
Beech Hl CONI DN12 110 A6
Beech Hill Rd FUL S10 160 A5
Beech House Rd WMB/DAR S73 84 B7
Beech Rd ARMTH DN3 69 M8
AWLS/ASK DN6 27 H6
AWLS/ASK DN6 44 E6
CUD/GR S72 40 B5
DEARNE S63 107 L1
HEM/SK/SE WF9 24 F8
MALT S66 150 B2
NROS/TKH DN11 113 L7
NROS/TKH DN11 153 L2
Beech St BSLY S70 3 H8
HEM/SK/SE WF9 42 C6
HOLM/MEL HD7 53 L2 1
Beech Tree Av THNE DN8 50 A1
Beech Tree Cl ARMTH DN3 91 M6
Beech Vw HOR/CROF WF4 19 K4
Beechville Av
MEX/SWTN S64 108 A6 1
Beech Wy AU/AST/KP S26 163 M7
DRON S18 190 E4 1
Beechwood Cl ARMTH DN3 69 L6 1
DEARNE S63 107 K4 1
RAW S62 108 A8 1
Beechwood Crs
HEM/SK/SE WF9 41 G1
Beechwood Mt
HEM/SK/SE WF9 41 H1 1
Beechwood Rd
CHPT/GREN S35 126 C1 2
DRON S18 190 D6
RHAM/THRY S65 7 M9
ST/HB/BR S6 143 M7
STKB/PEN S36 101 M7
Beehive Rd FUL S10 8 A3
Beeley St SHEFP/MNR S2 8 F8
Beeley Wood La ST/HB/BR S6 143 L3
Beeley Wood Rd ST/HB/BR S6 144 A4
Beely Rd CHPT/GREN S35 143 J1
Beeston Cl DRON S18 190 A5 1
Beeston Sq BSLYN/ROY S71 38 D7
Beeton Gn ST/HB/BR S6 158 A1
Beeton Rd SHEFS S8 176 D2
Beet St OWL S3 8 E4
Beever La DOD/DAR S75 59 L4
Beevers Rd KIMB S61 128 B5
Beever St DEARNE S63 86 D2
Beevor Ct BSLYN/ROY S71 3 K6
Beevor St BSLYN/ROY S71 3 M5
Begonia Cl DIN S25 182 A3
Beighton Rd HACK/IN S12 178 F4
HAN/WDH S13 179 H1
MEX/SWTN S64 108 C7
Beighton Rd East MOS S20 179 G4
Belcourt Rd RHAM/THRY S65 148 B3
Beldon Cl SHEFP/MNR S2 161 H8
Beldon Pl SHEFP/MNR S2 161 H8
Beldon Rd SHEFP/MNR S2 161 H8
Belford Cl MALT S66 149 G1
Belford Dr MALT S66 149 G1
Belfry Gdns DONS/BSCR DN4 91 L8 1
Belfry Wy DIN S25 166 E8
Belgrave Ct BWTY DN10 136 D8 1
Belgrave Dr FUL S10 159 H6
Belgrave Pl AU/AST/KP S26 164 A8
Belgrave Rd BSLYN/ROY S71 3 J5
FUL S10 159 J6
Belgrave Sq SHEFP/MNR S2 160 E7 1
Belklane Dr ECK/KIL S21 180 C8
Bell Bank Vw BSLY S70 82 D2
Bellbrooke Av WMB/DAR S73 62 D8

Bell Butts La EPW DN9 114 D1
Bell Croft La BTLY DN5 46 D6
Bellefield St OWL S3 8 D2
Belle Green Cl CUD/GR S72 40 A8 1
Belle Green Gdns CUD/GR S72 40 A8
Belle Green La CUD/GR S72 40 A8
Bellerby Pl AWLS/ASK DN6 44 D5
Bellerby Rd AWLS/ASK DN6 44 D5
Belle Vue Av DONS/BSCR DN4 90 E5
Belle Vue Rd MEX/SWTN S64 108 E3
Belle Vue Ter THNE DN8 31 M8
The Bellfields KIMB S61 127 J2
Bellgreave Av HOLM/MEL HD7 54 D1
Bell Gn GLE DN14 30 B3
Bellhagg Rd ST/HB/BR S6 159 M1
Bellhouse Rd SHEFN S5 145 J3
Bell La FEA/AMT WF7 23 K2
Bellmont Crs HEM/SK/SE WF9 41 J1
Bellows Rd RAW S62 129 K2
Bellrope Acre ARMTH DN3 91 M2
Bell's Cl EPW DN9 115 J3
Bellscroft Av RHAM/THRY S65 130 C5
Bells Sq SHEF S1 9 G4
Bell St AU/AST/KP S26 164 D8
HEM/SK/SE WF9 25 J7
Bellwood Crs HOY S74 105 G2
THNE DN8 31 L7
Belmont CUD/GR S72 62 A3 1
Belmont Av BSLYN/ROY S71 60 F2
CHPT/GREN S35 126 E2
DONS/BSCR DN4 4 E9
Belmont Cl ARMTH DN3 92 C7
Belmont Crs CUD/GR S72 63 J8 1
Belmont Dr STKB/PEN S36 102 A6 1
Belmonte Gdns SHEFP/MNR S2 9 L7
Belmont St KIMB S61 146 E1
MEX/SWTN S64 108 D3 1
Belmont Wy HEM/SK/SE WF9 42 F4
Belper Rd SHEFS S8 176 D1 1
Belridge Cl DOD/DAR S75 59 M3 1
Belsize Rd ECC S11 159 H7
Belton Cl DRON S18 190 A6 3
Belvedere DONS/BSCR DN4 111 K1
Belvedere Cl AWLS/ASK DN6 27 M7
CUD/GR S72 40 A5 1
DIN S25 182 D2
Belvedere Dr THNE DN8 32 A4
WMB/DAR S73 62 C8
Belvedere Pde MALT S66 131 G8
Belvoir Av BTLY DN5 87 G4
Bembridge WRKN S81 198 F1
Ben Bank Rd DOD/DAR S75 80 E1
Ben Booth La HOR/CROF WF4 16 C2
Bence Cl DOD/DAR S75 37 J8
Bence La DOD/DAR S75 37 G8
Ben Cl ST/HB/BR S6 143 K6
Benita Av MEX/SWTN S64 109 G3
Ben La ST/HB/BR S6 143 K6
Benmore Dr MOS S20 179 M6 2
Bennett Cl RAW S62 107 M8 1
Bennetthorpe WHHL DN2 5 M6
Bennett St KIMB S61 146 C1
SHEFP/MNR S2 160 D7 2
Benson Rd SHEFP/MNR S2 161 J5
Bentfield Av RHAM/THRY S65 148 A4
Bentham Dr BSLYN/ROY S71 61 H3
Bentham Wy DOD/DAR S75 37 L5
Bent Hills La CHPT/GREN S35 124 C6
Bentinck Cl DON DN1 5 G7
Bentinick St CONI DN12 110 B5 1
Bent La HOLM/MEL HD7 53 L7
Bent Lathes Av RHAM S60 148 A4
Bentley Av DONS/BSCR DN4 4 B7
Bentley Cl BSLYN/ROY S71 61 J2
Bentley Common La BTLY DN5 68 A7
Bentley Moor La
AWLS/ASK DN6 45 H8
Bentley Rd BTLY DN5 67 M8
CHPT/GREN S35 126 F3
FUL S10 159 L2
MALT S66 149 J3
Bentley St RHAM S60 147 H4
Benton Ter MEX/SWTN S64 108 B6 1
Benton Wy KIMB S61 128 D8
Bent Rd HOLM/MEL HD7 54 B8
Bents Cl CHPT/GREN S35 126 E2 1
ECC S11 175 J2
Bents Crs DRON S18 191 G4
ECC S11 175 K3
Bents Dr ECC S11 175 J2
Bents Green Av ECC S11 175 J1
Bents Green Pl ECC S11 175 J2 1
Bents Green Rd ECC S11 175 K2
Bents La DRON S18 191 G4
ST/HB/BR S6 142 B8
Bents Rd ECC S11 175 K2
KIMB S61 128 D6
STKB/PEN S36 77 G3
Bent St STKB/PEN S36 79 G3
Benty La FUL S10 159 K4
Beresford Rd MALT S66 150 F3
Beresford St BTLY DN5 67 M6
Berkeley Cft BSLYN/ROY S71 38 F3
Berkley Cl BSLY S70 82 D2
Bernard Rd ATT S4 161 H3
CONI DN12 110 F6
Bernard St RAW S62 107 M8
RHAM/THRY S65 7 H6
SHEFP/MNR S2 9 M4
Berners Cl SHEFP/MNR S2 177 J2
Berners Dr SHEFP/MNR S2 177 J1
Berners Pl SHEFP/MNR S2 177 J1
Berners Rd SHEFP/MNR S2 177 H1
Berneslai Cl BSLY S70 2 E4
Berneslai Ct BSLY S70 2 E4
Berne Sq DIN S25 183 H3
Bernshall Crs SHEFN S5 126 F8
Berresford Rd ECC S11 160 B7 2
Berridge La GLE DN14 11 L3
Berrington Cl DONS/BSCR DN4 111 L3
Berry Av ECK/KIL S21 193 G4
Berrydale BSLY S70 82 E2
Berry Dr AU/AST/KP S26 181 K4 1
Berry Holme Cl
CHPT/GREN S35 126 E2 2
Berry Holme Ct
CHPT/GREN S35 126 E2 3
Berry Holme Dr
CHPT/GREN S35 126 E2
Berry La CHPT/GREN S35 103 L7
Berrywell Av STKB/PEN S36 79 J5
Bertram Rd CHPT/GREN S35 143 J1
Bessacarr La DONS/BSCR DN4 113 J1
Bessemer Pl DARN/MH S9 161 J2 2
Bessemer Rd DARN/MH S9 161 J1
Bessemer Ter
STKB/PEN S36 101 M5 1
Bessemer Wy RHAM S60 146 E2
Bessingby Rd ST/HB/BR S6 144 A8
Bethel Rd RHAM/THRY S65 7 J1
Bethel St HOY S74 105 K1
Betjeman Gdns ECC S11 160 A6 1
Betony Cl ECK/KIL S21 193 M2
Between Rivers La GLE DN14 13 G3
Beulah Rd ST/HB/BR S6 144 B6
Bevan Av NROS/TKH DN11 113 K6
Bevan Cl HOY S74 105 L1
Bevan Crs MALT S66 150 D1
Bevan Wy CHPT/GREN S35 126 D3
Bevercotes Rd SHEFN S5 145 H4
Beverley Av BSLY S70 82 D1
Beverley Cl AU/AST/KP S26 164 B8
BSLYN/ROY S71 38 C8
Beverley Gdns BTLY DN5 89 H2
Beverley Garth FEA/AMT WF7 23 L2
Beverley Rd NROS/TKH DN11 153 L3
WHHL DN2 90 E1
Beverleys Rd SHEFS S8 176 E3
Beverley St DARN/MH S9 161 L1
Bevin Pl RAW S62 129 M1
Bevre Rd ARMTH DN3 69 L7
Bewicke Av BTLY DN5 89 H1
Bhatia Cl MEX/SWTN S64 108 E2 1
Bib La DIN S25 150 A8
Bickerton Rd ST/HB/BR S6 144 A5
Bierlow Cl WMB/DAR S73 84 E6
Bigby Wy RHAM/THRY S65 131 G8
Bignor Pl ST/HB/BR S6 144 B3
Bignor Rd ST/HB/BR S6 144 B2
Bilham La BTLY DN5 65 G4
Bilham Rd KBTN HD8 35 L5
Billam Pl KIMB S61 128 C6
Billam St ECK/KIL S21 192 F4
Billingley Dr DEARNE S63 64 A8
Billingley Green La CUD/GR S72 85 K1
Billingley La CUD/GR S72 63 K7
Billingley Vw DEARNE S63 85 M5
Billy Wright's La
NROS/TKH DN11 134 D3
Bilston St ST/HB/BR S6 144 B8 1
Binbrook Ct BWTY DN10 154 D1
Binders Rd KIMB S61 128 C6
Binfield Rd SHEFS S8 176 D2
Bingham Park Crs ECC S11 159 L7
Bingham Park Rd ECC S11 159 L8
Bingham Rd SHEFS S8 176 D5 1
Bingley La ST/HB/BR S6 158 F3
Bingley St DOD/DAR S75 2 C3
Binns La HOLM/MEL HD7 53 K2
Binsted Av SHEFN S5 144 B3
Binsted Cl SHEFN S5 144 B4
Binsted Crs SHEFN S5 144 B4
Binsted Cft SHEFN S5 144 B4
Binsted Dr SHEFN S5 144 B4
Binsted Gdns SHEFN S5 144 B4 1
Binsted Gld SHEFN S5 144 B4
Binsted Gv SHEFN S5 144 B4
Binsted Rd SHEFN S5 144 B4
Binsted Wy SHEFN S5 144 B4
Birchall Av RHAM S60 147 M6
Birch Av AWLS/ASK DN6 44 E6
CHPT/GREN S35 126 D3
EPW DN9 114 E4
Birch Cl BTLY DN5 89 H6
ECK/KIL S21 194 A2
Birch Crs MALT S66 149 G2
Birchdale Cl ARMTH DN3 69 K6
Birchen Cl DONS/BSCR DN4 113 J2
DRON S18 190 B6
Birches Fold DRON S18 191 G3 1
Birches La DRON S18 191 G3
The Birches EPW DN9 117 M3
Birch Farm Av SHEFS S8 176 E7
Birchfield Crs DOD/DAR S75 59 L7 1
Birchfield Dr WRKS S80 197 M5
Birchfield Gv KBTN HD8 34 E6
Birchfield Wk DOD/DAR S75 59 M5 1
Birch Green Cl MALT S66 150 B1
Birch Gv CHPT/GREN S35 143 H1
CONI DN12 110 B5
Birch House Av
CHPT/GREN S35 143 H1
Birchitt Cl TOT/DORE S17 190 A2
Birchitt Pl TOT/DORE S17 190 A2
Birchitt Rd TOT/DORE S17 190 A2
Birchitt Vw DRON S18 190 E4
Birchlands Dr ECK/KIL S21 194 B2
Birch Rd BSLY S70 61 H8
DARN/MH S9 161 J1
DONS/BSCR DN4 91 K7
Birch Tree Cl ARMTH DN3 47 K8
Birchtree Rd KIMB S61 127 K4
Birch Tree Rd STKB/PEN S36 101 M7
Birchvale Rd HACK/IN S12 178 B4
Birchwood Av RAW S62 129 K1
Birchwood Cl MALT S66 150 B1 1
MOS S20 179 J7 1
THNE DN8 31 M6 1
Birchwood Cft MOS S20 179 J7
Birchwood Dell
DONS/BSCR DN4 113 M2
Birchwood Dr
RHAM/THRY S65 131 G7
Birchwood Gdns MALT S66 132 E5
MOS S20 179 J7 2
Birchwood Gv MOS S20 179 J7
Birchwood Pk HOLM/MEL HD7 54 C1
Birchwood Ri MOS S20 179 J7 3
Birchwood Rd ECK/KIL S21 192 B4
Birchwood Vw MOS S20 179 J7
Birchwood Wy MOS S20 179 J7 4
Bircotes Wk NROS/TKH DN11 113 M6
Bird Av WMB/DAR S73 84 A5
Bird La STKB/PEN S36 80 C5
Birds Edge La KBTN HD8 55 K4
Birdsnest La HOLM/MEL HD7 55 G6
KBTN HD8 55 J5
Birdwell Rd ATT S4 145 K6
DOD/DAR S75 81 L1
MEX/SWTN S64 108 B7
Birk Av BSLY S70 61 G8
Birkbeck Ct CHPT/GREN S35 104 B7 2
Birk Crs BSLY S70 61 G8
Birkdale WRKN S81 198 F1
Birkdale Av DIN S25 166 D7
Birkdale Cl CUD/GR S72 40 A7 2
DONS/BSCR DN4 113 M1
Birkdale Ri MEX/SWTN S64 108 B5
Birkdale Rd BSLYN/ROY S71 38 F2 1
Birkendale ST/HB/BR S6 8 A1
Birkendale Rd ST/HB/BR S6 160 B2
Birkendale Vw ST/HB/BR S6 160 B2 2
Birk Gn BSLY S70 61 H8
Birk House La BSLY S70 61 H8
Birklands Av HAN/WDH S13 162 C6
Birklands Cl HAN/WDH S13 162 C6
Birklands Dr HAN/WDH S13 162 C6
Birk Rd BSLY S70 61 G8
Birks Av HAN/WDH S13 178 F1 1
STKB/PEN S36 78 C4
Birks Holt Dr MALT S66 150 F4
Birks La STKB/PEN S36 78 C5
Birks Rd KIMB S61 128 C6
Birks Wood Dr
CHPT/GREN S35 143 H1
Birk Ter BSLY S70 61 G8
Birkwood Av CUD/GR S72 62 A2
Birley La HACK/IN S12 178 B5
HATH/EY S32 172 D5
Birley Moor Av HACK/IN S12 178 C4
Birley Moor Cl HACK/IN S12 178 C4 1
Birley Moor Crs HACK/IN S12 178 C4
Birley Moor Dr HACK/IN S12 178 C5
Birley Moor Pl HACK/IN S12 178 C5
Birley Moor Rd HACK/IN S12 178 B3
Birley Moor Wy HACK/IN S12 178 C4
Birley Rise Crs ST/HB/BR S6 144 A3
Birley Rise Rd ST/HB/BR S6 144 A3
Birley Spa Dr HACK/IN S12 178 F3
Birley Spa La HACK/IN S12 178 D3
Birley Vale Av HACK/IN S12 178 A3
Birley Vale Cl HACK/IN S12 178 A3
Birley Vw CHPT/GREN S35 143 H2
Birthwaite Rd DOD/DAR S75 36 F7
Bisby Rd RAW S62 129 L1
Biscay Wy DEARNE S63 107 K1
Bishopdale WRKN S81 184 E8 1
Bishopdale Ct MOS S20 178 E6 1
Bishopdale Dr HACK/IN S12 178 E7 1
Bishopdale Ri HACK/IN S12 178 E7
Bishopfield La RTFD DN22 170 E2
Bishop Gdns HAN/WDH S13 178 E1
Bishopgarth Cl BTLY DN5 89 M1
Bishop Hl HAN/WDH S13 178 E1
Bishops Ct SHEFS S8 176 E2
Bishopscourt Rd SHEFS S8 176 E2
Bishopsholme Rd SHEFN S5 144 E5 1
Bishopston Wk MALT S66 150 C1
Bishop St SHEF S1 8 F7
Bishops Wy BSLYN/ROY S71 61 G4
Bisley Cl BSLYN/ROY S71 39 J4
Bismarck St BSLY S70 3 G9
Bittern Vw KIMB S61 127 L1
Blacka Moor Crs
TOT/DORE S17 189 G1
Blackamoor Rd RAW S62 107 K6
Blacka Moor Rd
TOT/DORE S17 189 G1
Blacka Moor Vw
TOT/DORE S17 189 G1
Blackbird Av RHAM S60 147 H7 1
Blackbrook Av FUL S10 158 D6
Blackbrook Dr FUL S10 158 D6
Blackbrook Rd FUL S10 158 E6
Blackburn Crs CHPT/GREN S35 126 C1
Blackburn Cft
CHPT/GREN S35 126 D1 1
Blackburn Dr CHPT/GREN S35 126 C2
Blackburne St ST/HB/BR S6 144 B8 2
Blackburn La BSLY S70 82 E2
DOD/DAR S75 2 C3
KIMB S61 145 M1 1
Blackburn Rd KIMB S61 145 M1
Blackburn St BSLY S70 82 E2 1
Black Carr Rd MALT S66 148 E2
Blackdown Av MOS S20 179 H5
Blacker Crs HOR/CROF WF4 18 C1
Blacker Green La BTLY DN5 46 B3
Blackergreen La STKB/PEN S36 80 B4
Blacker La BSLY S70 82 E5
CUD/GR S72 40 A4
HOR/CROF WF4 18 E1
Blacker Rd DOD/DAR S75 38 A7
Blackheath Cl BSLYN/ROY S71 38 F8 1
Blackheath Rd BSLYN/ROY S71 38 F8
Blackheath Wk BSLYN/ROY S71 38 F8
Black Hill Rd RHAM/THRY S65 148 B3
Black Horse Cl STKB/PEN S36 80 E2 2
Black Horse Dr STKB/PEN S36 80 E2
Black La HOY S74 104 D3
ST/HB/BR S6 143 H8
Blackmoor Crs RHAM S60 146 F6
Blackmore St ATT S4 161 H2
Black Sike La HOLM/MEL HD7 53 G2
Blacksmith La CHPT/GREN S35 126 A7
RTFD DN22 170 F5
Blacksmith's La BTLY DN5 88 A1
Blackstock Cl SHEFS S8 177 H5
Blackstock Crs GLV S14 177 H5
Blackstock Dr SHEFS S8 177 H5
Blackstock Rd SHEFP/MNR S2 177 H2
SHEFS S8 177 H5
Black Syke La GLE DN14 31 G4
Blackthorn Av MALT S66 149 G2
Blackthorn Cl
CHPT/GREN S35 104 B7 3
Blackthorne Cl CONI DN12 110 E6
Blackthorn Ri RHAM/THRY S65 131 J7
Blackwell Cl SHEFP/MNR S2 9 M4
Blackwell Pl SHEFP/MNR S2 9 L4
Blackwood Av
DONS/BSCR DN4 111 K1 1
Blagden St SHEFP/MNR S2 9 M5
Blair Athol Rd ECC S11 175 M1
Blake Av DEARNE S63 85 G8
WHHL DN2 90 D1
Blake Cl MALT S66 149 J3
Blake Grove Rd ST/HB/BR S6 8 C1
Blakeley Cl BSLYN/ROY S71 38 F8
Blakeney Rd FUL S10 160 A4
Blake St ST/HB/BR S6 160 B2
Bland La ST/HB/BR S6 143 K6
Bland St ATT S4 145 J7
Blast La ATT S4 9 L3
SHEFP/MNR S2 9 L3
Blaxton Cl MOS S20 178 E5
Blayton Rd ATT S4 145 G8
Blazley Rd SHEFP/MNR S2 177 K1
Bleachcroft Wy BSLY S70 61 J8
Bleak Av CUD/GR S72 40 A5
Bleakley Av HOR/CROF WF4 38 F1
Bleakley Cl CUD/GR S72 40 A5
Bleakley La BSLYN/ROY S71 38 F2
Bleakley Ter HOR/CROF WF4 38 F1
Bleasdale Gv BSLYN/ROY S71 60 E3
Blenheim Av BSLY S70 2 E7
Blenheim Cl DIN S25 166 C7
HTFD DN7 70 E1 2
MALT S66 131 G8
Blenheim Crs
MEX/SWTN S64 108 D2 2
Blenheim Dr EPW DN9 115 H4
Blenheim Gdns ECC S11 175 L2 1
Blenheim Ri BWTY DN10 154 D1 1
WRKN S81 184 C7 2
Blenheim Rd BSLY S70 2 D8
EPW DN9 115 H4
HTFD DN7 71 L7
Blindside La ST/HB/BR S6 141 H4
Bloemfontein St CUD/GR S72 61 L1
Blonk St OWL S3 9 K2
Bloomfield Ri DOD/DAR S75 37 L6 1
Bloomfield Rd DOD/DAR S75 37 K6
Bloomhill Cl THNE DN8 32 A3 1
Bloomhill Ct THNE DN8 32 A3
Bloom Hill Gv THNE DN8 32 A4
Bloomhill Rd THNE DN8 31 L4
Bloomhouse La DOD/DAR S75 37 J5
Blossom Av AWLS/ASK DN6 27 M8
Blow Hall Crs CONI DN12 111 G6
Blucher St BSLY S70 2 F6
Bluebell Av STKB/PEN S36 79 G4
Bluebell Cl HOY S74 105 G3
SHEFN S5 145 J4
Blue Bell Ct EPW DN9 115 J1
Bluebell Rd DOD/DAR S75 37 J4
SHEFN S5 145 K4
Bluebell Wy HEM/SK/SE WF9 24 D8
Bluebird Hl AU/AST/KP S26 180 C1
Blue Boy St OWL S3 8 F2
Blundell Ct BSLYN/ROY S71 61 H2 1
Blundell St HEM/SK/SE WF9 42 C4 1
Blyde Rd SHEFN S5 145 G6
Bly Rd WMB/DAR S73 84 D1
Blyth Av RAW S62 129 K2
Blyth Cl RHAM S60 148 B6
Blythe St WMB/DAR S73 84 A4
Blyth Gate La NROS/TKH DN11 152 C3
Blyth Gv WRKN S81 198 E2
Blyth Rd MALT S66 150 D3
NROS/TKH DN11 153 K4
RTFD DN22 170 B4
RTFD DN22 186 D5
WRKN S81 168 D1
WRKN S81 184 F8
WRKN S81 198 D3
Boardman Av RAW S62 107 G7
Boating Dyke Wy THNE DN8 31 L8
Boat La BTLY DN5 88 F7
Bochum Pkwy SHEFS S8 177 G7
Bocking Cl SHEFS S8 176 B6
Bocking Hl STKB/PEN S36 102 B6
Bocking La SHEFS S8 176 B6
Bocking Ri SHEFS S8 176 C7 1
Boden La SHEF S1 8 F4
Boden Pl DARN/MH S9 162 A2 2
Bodmin Ct BSLYN/ROY S71 3 M2
Bodmin St DARN/MH S9 161 K1 1
Boggard La CHPT/GREN S35 143 G1
STKB/PEN S36 79 G5
Boggart La KBTN HD8 34 E4
Boiley La ECK/KIL S21 193 M3
Boland Rd TOT/DORE S17 190 B2
Bold St DARN/MH S9 145 L7
Bole Cl WMB/DAR S73 84 D3
Bole Hl RHAM S60 163 J2
Bolehill La ECK/KIL S21 192 D5
FUL S10 159 L3
Bole Hill Rd FUL S10 159 K3
Bolsover Rd SHEFN S5 145 H5
Bolsover Rd East ATT S4 145 H6 1
Bolsover St OWL S3 8 C4
Bolsterstone Rd ST/HB/BR S6 123 M7
Bolton Hill Rd
DONS/BSCR DN4 113 J1
Bolton Rd DEARNE S63 86 A8
Bolton St CONI DN12 109 K5
OWL S3 8 E6
Bolton Wife Hl HOR/CROF WF4 19 K6
Bond Cl DON DN1 4 E7
Bondfield Av NROS/TKH DN11 113 L7
Bondfield Crs WMB/DAR S73 84 A5
Bondhay La WRKS S80 196 A5
Bond Rd DOD/DAR S75 2 C2
Bond St NROS/TKH DN11 113 L8
WMB/DAR S73 84 A4
Bone La AWLS/ASK DN6 26 F7
Bonemill La WRKN S81 198 B2
Bonet La RHAM S60 146 E6
Bonington Ri MALT S66 150 C1
Booker Rd SHEFS S8 176 C5 1
Booker's La DIN S25 165 M6
Bookers Wy DIN S25 165 M6
Bootham Cl HTFD DN7 48 F7
Bootham Crs HTFD DN7 48 D4
Bootham La HTFD DN7 48 E5
Bootham Rd HTFD DN7 48 D4
Booth Cl MALT S66 165 L1
MOS S20 179 H5
Booth Cft MOS S20 179 H5
Booth House La
HOLM/MEL HD7 53 G3
Booth Pl RAW S62 107 J7
Booth Rd CHPT/GREN S35 104 A8
Booth St HOY S74 105 J1 1
KIMB S61 128 F3
Borough Rd ST/HB/BR S6 144 B7
Borrowdale Av MOS S20 193 J1 2
Borrowdale Cl AWLS/ASK DN6 45 G6
BSLYN/ROY S71 61 L7
MOS S20 193 J1 3
Borrowdale Crs DIN S25 166 D8
Borrowdale Dr MOS S20 179 J8
Borrowdale Rd MOS S20 193 J1
Boston Castle Gv RHAM S60 7 G9
Boston Castle Ter RHAM S60 7 G9
Boston St SHEFP/MNR S2 8 F9
Bosvile Cl RHAM/THRY S65 131 H4 1
Bosville Rd FUL S10 159 M4 1
Bosville St RHAM/THRY S65 130 B7
STKB/PEN S36 79 J5
Boswell Cl BSLYN/ROY S71 38 F3 1
CHPT/GREN S35 104 A7
NROS/TKH DN11 113 J7
Boswell Rd DEARNE S63 107 K3
DONS/BSCR DN4 91 G8
Boswell St RHAM/THRY S65 7 K7
Bosworth Cl HTFD DN7 70 E2 1
Bosworth Rd AWLS/ASK DN6 66 E1
Bosworth St FUL S10 159 M3 1
Botanical Rd FUL S10 160 A6
Botany Bay La ARMTH DN3 48 A8
Botham St ATT S4 145 J7
Boughton Rd WRKS S80 197 L2
Boulder Bridge La CUD/GR S72 39 K5
The Boulevard ARMTH DN3 69 J5
Boulton Dr ARMTH DN3 91 M6
Boundary Av WHHL DN2 69 G8
Boundary Cl CONI DN12 111 G4 1
Boundary Dr CUD/GR S72 40 E4 1
Boundary Gn RAW S62 129 K3
Boundary Rd SHEFP/MNR S2 161 J5
Boundary Rw WRKS S80 198 D5
Boundary St BSLY S70 3 L7
Boundary Wk RHAM S60 146 E7
Bourne Ct DOD/DAR S75 38 A5
Bourne Mill Cl STV/CWN S43 194 F8
Bourne Rd BSLY S70 82 D3
SHEFN S5 145 G3
Bourne Wk DOD/DAR S75 37 M5
Bow Bridge Cl RHAM S60 6 D8
Bowden Gv DOD/DAR S75 59 K8
Bowden Wood Av
DARN/MH S9 162 A5
Bowden Wood Cl
DARN/MH S9 162 A5 1
Bowden Wood Crs
DARN/MH S9 162 A5
Bowden Wood Dr
DARN/MH S9 162 A5
Bowden Wood Pl
DARN/MH S9 162 A5 2
Bowden Wood Rd
DARN/MH S9 162 A5
Bowdon St SHEF S1 8 F6
Bowen Dr RHAM/THRY S65 130 D5
Bowen Rd RHAM/THRY S65 7 K1
Bower Cl KIMB S61 128 C6
Bower Hl STKB/PEN S36 80 A6
Bower La CHPT/GREN S35 125 M6
Bower Rd FUL S10 8 A3
MEX/SWTN S64 108 B3
Bower Spring OWL S3 9 H2
Bower St OWL S3 9 H2
Bower V CONI DN12 110 E6 1
Bowes Rd ARMTH DN3 69 J6
Bowfell Vw BSLYN/ROY S71 60 E3
Bowfield Rd SHEFN S5 145 G3
Bowland Cl BTLY DN5 67 K7
Bowland Crs BSLY S70 82 D3
Bowland Dr CHPT/GREN S35 126 C2
Bowlease Gdns
DONS/BSCR DN4 91 J7
Bowling Green St OWL S3 9 G2
Bowman Cl HACK/IN S12 177 K5
Bowman Dr HACK/IN S12 177 K5
MALT S66 150 C1
Bowness Cl DRON S18 190 C6
Bowness Dr AWLS/ASK DN6 28 A7
Bowness Rd ST/HB/BR S6 144 A8
Bowood Rd ECC S11 160 B7
Bowshaw Av SHEFS S8 190 E2
Bowshaw Cl SHEFS S8 190 E2
Bowshaw Vw SHEFS S8 190 E2
Bow St CUD/GR S72 39 M8
Boyce St ST/HB/BR S6 160 B2
Boycott Dr FEA/AMT WF7 23 L2 1
Boyd Rd DEARNE S63 107 K4
Boyland St OWL S3 160 D1
Boyne Dr WKFDW/WTN WF2 19 L2
Boyne Hl HOR/CROF WF4 19 L3
Boynton Crs SHEFN S5 144 E5
Boynton Rd SHEFN S5 144 D6
Brabbs Av HTFD DN7 49 G7
Bracebridge WRKS S80 198 E5
Bracebridge Av WRKS S80 198 F4
Bracebridge Ct WRKS S80 198 E5
Brackenbury Cl BTLY DN5 110 B1 1
Bracken Cl ARMTH DN3 92 C6
Bracken Ct MALT S66 148 F4
Brackenfield Gv HACK/IN S12 178 B3
Bracken Heen Cl HTFD DN7 49 G7 1
Bracken Hl CHPT/GREN S35 126 B3
FEA/AMT WF7 23 H2
HEM/SK/SE WF9 42 B3
Bracken Hill La BWTY DN10 137 L1
Bracken Moor La
STKB/PEN S36 102 A7
Bracken Rd SHEFN S5 145 J3
Bracken Wy NROS/TKH DN11 153 H3
Brackley St OWL S3 160 F1
Bradberry Balk La
WMB/DAR S73 84 A3
Bradbury's Cl RAW S62 129 K4 2
Bradbury St BSLY S70 2 D6
SHEFS S8 176 E1 2
Bradfield Rd ST/HB/BR S6 144 A7
Bradgate Cl KIMB S61 128 E8

Bradgate Ct KIMB S61 128 D8
Bradgate La KIMB S61 128 D8
Bradgate Pl KIMB S61 128 E7
Bradgate Rd KIMB S61 128 E8
Bradlea Ri RAW S62 107 L8
Bradley Av WMB/DAR S73 84 A4 1
Bradley Carr Ter
HEM/SK/SE WF9 42 C7
Bradley St FUL S10 159 M2
Bradmarsh Wy RHAM S60 6 D8
Bradshaw Av RHAM S60 163 K3
Bradshaw Cl DOD/DAR S75 59 L5 1
Bradshaw Rd HOLM/MEL HD7 52 F1
Bradshaw Wy RHAM S60 163 K4 1
Bradstone Rd
RHAM/THRY S65 130 A8
Bradway Cl TOT/DORE S17 189 M2
Bradway Dr TOT/DORE S17 189 M2
Bradway Grange Rd
TOT/DORE S17 190 A2 1
Bradway Rd TOT/DORE S17 189 M2
Bradwell Av DOD/DAR S75 81 L2
Bradwell Cl DRON S18 190 A6
Bradwell St SHEFP/MNR S2 160 F8
Braemar Cft CUD/GR S72 22 B8
Braemar Ri CUD/GR S72 22 B8
Braemar Rd WHHL DN2 90 E4 1
Braemore Rd ST/HB/BR S6 143 L6
Brailsford Av SHEFN S5 126 E7
Brailsford Rd SHEFN S5 126 E7
Braithwaite La HTFD DN7 29 K8
HTFD DN7 47 K2
Braithwell Rd BTLY DN5 67 L5
MALT S66 150 D1
RHAM/THRY S65 131 J7
Braithwell Wy MALT S66 149 L1
Bramah St BSLYN/ROY S71 39 G6
Bramall La SHEFP/MNR S2 9 G9
STKB/PEN S36 101 K4
Bramall Lane Rbt SHEF S1 9 G8
Bramble Cl MALT S66 148 F4 1
The Brambles CHPT/GREN S35 126 E7
Bramble Wy DEARNE S63 106 F1
EPW DN9 114 E3
NROS/TKH DN11 153 J3
The Bramblings
DONS/BSCR DN4 113 L2
WRKN S81 184 A8
Bramcote Av BSLYN/ROY S71 38 C7 1
Brameld Rd MEX/SWTN S64 107 M4
RAW S62 129 K2
Bramham Ct DARN/MH S9 161 M2 2
Bramham Rd DARN/MH S9 161 M2 3
DONS/BSCR DN4 91 K5
Bramley Av AU/AST/KP S26 164 C8
HAN/WDH S13 162 D7
Bramley Cl MOS S20 193 G1
Bramley Dr HAN/WDH S13 162 D6
Bramley Grange Crs MALT S66 149 J2
Bramley Grange
Dr MALT S66 149 J2 2
Bramley Grange Ri MALT S66 149 J2 3
Bramley Grange Vw MALT S66 149 J1
Bramley Grange Wy MALT S66 149 J2
Bramley Hall Rd
HAN/WDH S13 162 D7
Bramley La HAN/WDH S13 162 D6
HOR/CROF WF4 18 E7
MALT S66 131 L7
Bramleymoor La ECK/KIL S21 192 C6
Bramley Park Cl
HAN/WDH S13 162 D7
Bramley Park Rd
HAN/WDH S13 162 D6
Bramley Rd ECK/KIL S21 192 C6
Bramley Wy MALT S66 149 L1
Brampton Av MALT S66 165 H1
Brampton Cl ARMTH DN3 91 L3
Brampton Ct
HEM/SK/SE WF9 42 E2 1
MOS S20 178 E5 1
Brampton Crs WMB/DAR S73 84 D6
Brampton La ARMTH DN3 91 L2
AU/AST/KP S26 164 F3
Brampton Mdw MALT S66 165 H1
Brampton Rd DEARNE S63 84 F8
MALT S66 149 H8
WMB/DAR S73 84 D6
Brampton St WMB/DAR S73 84 F7
Brampton Vw WMB/DAR S73 84 D6 1
Bramshill Cl MOS S20 179 L6
Bramshill Ct MOS S20 179 L6 2
Bramwell St OWL S3 8 D3
RHAM/THRY S65 7 H2
Bramwith La ARMTH DN3 47 J7
HTFD DN7 47 K5
Bramwith Rd ECC S11 159 K7 1
Bramworth Rd
DONS/BSCR DN4 89 K6
Branch Rd HOR/CROF WF4 19 G3
Brancliffe La WRKN S81 183 K7
Brandeth Rd ST/HB/BR S6 160 C2 2
Brand La BTLY DN5 88 D3
Brandon St OWL S3 144 F8 1
Brandreth Cl ST/HB/BR S6 160 C2 3
Brands Cl WRKN S81 183 J2
Brand's La DIN S25 166 F8
Brandsmere Dr WRKN S81 183 J2
Branksome Av BSLY S70 2 A6
Bransby St ST/HB/BR S6 160 B2 3
Bransdale WRKN S81 184 E7
Branstone Rd BTLY DN5 88 F5
Branton Gate Rd
Or Whiphill Top La
ARMTH DN3 92 C5
Brantwood Crs
DONS/BSCR DN4 91 K6
Brathay Cl ATT S4 145 K6
Brathay Rd ATT S4 145 K6 1
Bray St DARN/MH S9 161 L2 1
Brayton Gdns AWLS/ASK DN6 27 G6
Brearley Av STKB/PEN S36 102 B7
Brechin WRKN S81 198 F2
Brecklands MALT S66 148 E3
RHAM/THRY S65 148 A3
Breck La BWTY DN10 155 L8
DIN S25 166 D5
ECK/KIL S21 193 G7
Brecks Crs RHAM/THRY S65 148 C2
Brecks La ARMTH DN3 69 L3
RHAM/THRY S65 130 B8
Brecon Cl MOS S20 179 L5
Bredon Cl HEM/SK/SE WF9 23 J8
Breezemount Ct HTFD DN7 48 D3 1
Brendon Cl WMB/DAR S73 84 D6
Brentwood Av ECC S11 176 B1 1
Brentwood Cl HOY S74 105 G2 1
PONT WF8 24 E2
Brentwood Rd ECC S11 176 B1
Bressingham Cl ATT S4 161 G1 1
Bressingham Rd ATT S4 160 F1
Bretby Cl DONS/BSCR DN4 91 K8
Brett Cl RAW S62 107 G7
Brettegate HEM/SK/SE WF9 23 G8 1
Bretton Cl DOD/DAR S75 37 G7
HTFD DN7 70 E1
Bretton Gv HACK/IN S12 178 B4
Bretton La HOR/CROF WF4 18 F6
Bretton Rd DOD/DAR S75 37 H7
Bretton Vw CUD/GR S72 61 L2
Brewery Rd DEARNE S63 85 J8
Breydon Av BTLY DN5 89 J2
Briar Bank HEM/SK/SE WF9 22 E5
Briar Cl EPW DN9 114 E3
WRKS S80 198 A5
Briar Ct HOLM/MEL HD7 53 H3
MALT S66 148 E4
NROS/TKH DN11 153 J3
Briar Cft DONS/BSCR DN4 89 L7
Briarfield Av HACK/IN S12 177 L4
Briarfield Crs HACK/IN S12 177 L5
Briarfields La CHPT/GREN S35 143 G2
Briar Gv CUD/GR S72 40 E4
STKB/PEN S36 79 H5
Briar Lea WRKS S80 198 A5
Briar Ri BSLY S70 82 E3
Briar Rd ABRD S7 176 C1
ARMTH DN3 69 L8
AWLS/ASK DN6 44 E6
Briars Cl ECK/KIL S21 194 B2
Briars La HTFD DN7 48 D2
Briary Av CHPT/GREN S35 104 B8
Briary Cl RHAM S60 147 G8
Briber Hl WRKN S81 169 L6
Briber Rd WRKN S81 169 L5
Brickhouse La TOT/DORE S17 175 G7
Brick Kiln La AWLS/ASK DN6 28 F7
Brick St FUL S10 159 M3
Bridby St HAN/WDH S13 179 G1
Bride Church La
NROS/TKH DN11 134 E8
Bridge Cl KBTN HD8 35 J5 1
Bridge Ct HEM/SK/SE WF9 22 E4
Bridgegate RHAM S60 6 F3
Bridge Gv BTLY DN5 89 K2
Bridge Hl HTFD DN7 48 C3 1
Bridge Inn Rd CHPT/GREN S35 126 E1
Bridgelake Dr
DONS/BSCR DN4 111 M3
Bridge La GLE DN14 11 J4
HOLM/MEL HD7 53 L1
PONT WF8 24 E3
Bridge Pl WRKS S80 198 D4
Bridge Rd DONS/BSCR DN4 91 G7
Bridge St BSLY S70 61 J7 1
BSLYN/ROY S71 3 G2
DOD/DAR S75 37 J6
DONS/BSCR DN4 4 D6
ECK/KIL S21 180 B8
MEX/SWTN S64 108 C4
OWL S3 9 J2
RHAM S60 6 E3
STKB/PEN S36 79 G3
THNE DN8 31 M8
WRKS S80 198 C5
Bridgewater Park Dr
AWLS/ASK DN6 44 D5
Bridle Cl CHPT/GREN S35 126 E1
Bridle Crs CHPT/GREN S35 126 E1
Bridle Stile MOS S20 179 G8
Bridle Stile Cl MOS S20 179 G8 1
Bridle Stile Gdns MOS S20 178 F8
The Bridleway RAW S62 108 A8
Bridport Rd DARN/MH S9 161 M2
Brier Cl MOS S20 179 H6
Brierey Cl DOD/DAR S75 37 L7
Brierfield Cl DOD/DAR S75 2 B3
Brierfield Rd HACK/IN S12 177 L4
Brierholme Carr Rd HTFD DN7 49 K7
Brierholme Cl HTFD DN7 49 J6
Brierholme Ings Rd HTFD DN7 49 K7
Brier La HOR/CROF WF4 21 M7
Brierley Crs HEM/SK/SE WF9 42 A4
Brierley Rd CUD/GR S72 40 B5
DONS/BSCR DN4 91 H8
Brierly Rd RHAM/THRY S65 130 C6
Briers House La ST/HB/BR S6 142 B6
Brier St ST/HB/BR S6 144 A7 1
Briggs Rd BSLYN/ROY S71 39 G6
Brightholmlee Ct
CHPT/GREN S35 124 F5 1
Brightholmlee La
CHPT/GREN S35 124 E4
Brightholmlee Rd
CHPT/GREN S35 124 D5
Bright Meadow MOS S20 193 L2
Brightmore Dr OWL S3 8 D4
Brighton St CUD/GR S72 40 E8
Brighton Terrace Rd FUL S10 160 A3
Brightside La DARN/MH S9 161 J1
Brightside Wy ATT S4 145 K7
Brimmesfield Dr
SHEFP/MNR S2 161 J7 1
Brimmesfield Rd
SHEFP/MNR S2 161 J8
Brimmsfield Cl SHEFP/MNR S2 161 K8
Brinckman St BSLY S70 3 H7
Brincliffe Crs ECC S11 160 A8
Brincliffe Edge Cl ECC S11 176 A1
Brincliffe Edge Rd ECC S11 175 M1
Brincliffe Gdns ECC S11 160 A8
Brincliffe Hl ECC S11 159 M8
Brindley Cl SHEFS S8 176 E3
Brindley Ct ECK/KIL S21 194 A1 1
Brindley Crs SHEFS S8 176 E3
Brinkburn Cl TOT/DORE S17 189 K1 1
Brinkburn Dr TOT/DORE S17 189 K1
Brinkburn Vale Rd
TOT/DORE S17 189 K1
Brinsford Rd RHAM S60 147 G6
Brinsworth Hall Av RHAM S60 146 F7
Brinsworth Hall Crs RHAM S60 146 F7
Brinsworth Hall Dr RHAM S60 146 F7
Brinsworth Hall Gv RHAM S60 146 F7
Brinsworth La RHAM S60 146 F7
Brinsworth Rd RHAM S60 146 E7
RHAM S60 163 G1
Brinsworth St DARN/MH S9 161 K1
RHAM S60 6 D6
Bristol Gv WHHL DN2 90 E1
Bristol Rd ECC S11 160 A6
Britain St MEX/SWTN S64 108 D3 2
Britannia Cl BSLY S70 3 G7
Britannia Rd DARN/MH S9 162 A3
Britland Cl DOD/DAR S75 59 L5 2
Britnall St DARN/MH S9 161 L1
Briton Sq DEARNE S63 64 C6
Briton St DEARNE S63 64 C6
Brittain St SHEF S1 9 J7
Broachgate BTLY DN5 67 J7
Broadbent Gate Rd THNE DN8 32 A6
Broad Bridge Cl
AU/AST/KP S26 181 J5
Broadcarr Rd HOY S74 105 H5
Broadcroft Cl MOS S20 179 L4
Broad Cut Rd HOR/CROF WF4 19 H1
Broad Dyke Cl AU/AST/KP S26 181 K5
Broad Elms Cl ECC S11 175 K3 1
Broad Elms La ECC S11 175 J4
Broadfield Pk HOLM/MEL HD7 53 G5
Broadfield Rd SHEFS S8 176 D1
Broadgate House Cl
KIMB S61 128 E8 1
Broad Gates DOD/DAR S75 58 D7
Broadhead Rd STKB/PEN S36 102 B6
Broad Inge Crs CHPT/GREN S35 126 C2
Broad Ings La ARMTH DN3 47 H5
Broadlands MALT S66 149 J3
Broadlands Av MOS S20 178 E5
Broadlands Cl HTFD DN7 48 E8
MOS S20 178 F5
Broadlands Crs MALT S66 149 J3 1
Broadlands Cft MOS S20 178 F5 1
Broadlands Ri HACK/IN S12 178 F5 2
Broad La GLE DN14 29 M2
HEM/SK/SE WF9 41 L6
HOLM/MEL HD7 53 H2
SHEF S1 8 E4
Broad Lane Ct SHEF S1 8 E4 1
Broadley Rd HAN/WDH S13 161 M8
Broad Oak La NROS/TKH DN11 134 B7
STKB/PEN S36 57 H6
Broad Oaks DARN/MH S9 161 K2
Broadoaks Cl DIN S25 166 C6 1
Broadoaks Rd DIN S25 166 C6 2
Broad Riding MALT S66 133 J6
Broadstone Rd KBTN HD8 55 K3
Broad St HOY S74 105 H1
RAW S62 129 K4
SHEF S1 9 K3
SHEFP/MNR S2 9 L3
Broad Street La SHEFP/MNR S2 9 L3
Broadwater DEARNE S63 85 M6 1
Broadwater Dr HTFD DN7 48 E8 1
HTFD DN7 70 E1 3
Broadway BSLY S70 2 A8
DOD/DAR S75 37 M6
HEM/SK/SE WF9 42 C6
HTFD DN7 48 E7
HTFD DN7 70 D1
MEX/SWTN S64 107 M5
RHAM S60 146 F8
RHAM/THRY S65 129 M8
Broadway Av CHPT/GREN S35 126 F3
Broadway Cl MEX/SWTN S64 107 M5
Broadway East
RHAM/THRY S65 129 M8
The Broadway
DONS/BSCR DN4 111 K2
Brocco Bank ECC S11 160 A7
Brocco La OWL S3 8 F3
Brocco St OWL S3 8 F3
Brockenhurst Rd HTFD DN7 48 F8
Brockfield Cl BSLY S70 82 E2 2
Brockholes La ARMTH DN3 92 B8
STKB/PEN S36 78 E8
Brockhurst Wy
RHAM/THRY S65 130 D5
Brocklehurst Av BSLY S70 83 H1
SHEFS S8 177 G7
Brockswood Ct
WKFDW/WTN WF2 21 G2
Brockwood Cl
HAN/WDH S13 163 G8 1
Broc-o-bank AWLS/ASK DN6 27 G4
Brodsworth Wy
NROS/TKH DN11 113 M7
Bromcliffe Pk BSLYN/ROY S71 61 J2
Bromley Carr Rd
CHPT/GREN S35 103 M6
Brompton Rd BTLY DN5 89 G6
DARN/MH S9 145 L8
Bromwich Rd SHEFS S8 176 C5
Bronte Av DONS/BSCR DN4 111 K1
Bronte Cl BSLYN/ROY S71 3 M1
Bronte Gv HEM/SK/SE WF9 41 G1
MEX/SWTN S64 108 F1
Bronte Pl RAW S62 107 M8
Brook Cl AU/AST/KP S26 164 C8
CHPT/GREN S35 126 A6
Brook Cft DIN S25 182 B2
Brook Dr OWL S3 8 E3
Brooke Cl WRKN S81 199 G3
Brooke Dr DEARNE S63 107 H1
Brooke St DON DN1 5 H1
HOY S74 105 H1
THNE DN8 31 L7
Brook Farm Ms DEARNE S63 107 J1 1
Brookfield Av MEX/SWTN S64 108 B5
Brookfield Cl ARMTH DN3 91 M2 1
RHAM/THRY S65 130 B6
THNE DN8 31 L7
Brookfield Rd SHEFS S8 160 D8 4
Brookfields HOR/CROF WF4 18 B2
Brookhaven Wy MALT S66 149 J3
Brook Hl KIMB S61 127 K3
OWL S3 8 D4
Brook Hill La STKB/PEN S36 76 D4
Brookhill Rd DOD/DAR S75 36 F7
Brookhouse Cl HACK/IN S12 178 F4
Brookhouse Dr HACK/IN S12 178 F4
Brookhouse Hl ECC S11 159 G8
Brookhouse La DIN S25 166 A1
Brook House La STKB/PEN S36 77 K8
STKB/PEN S36 99 K1
Brookhouse Rd
AU/AST/KP S26 180 B1
Brooklands MALT S66 150 A3
Brooklands Av FUL S10 158 F8
Brooklands Crs FUL S10 159 G8
HOR/CROF WF4 22 B6
Brooklands Dr FUL S10 158 F8 1
Brooklands Rd AWLS/ASK DN6 45 G8
Brooklands Wy DIN S25 166 B6
Brook La CHPT/GREN S35 125 G8
CHPT/GREN S35 126 A7
HACK/IN S12 178 F4
MALT S66 149 H1
OWL S3 8 D4
Brooklyn Pl SHEFS S8 176 E2 1
Brooklyn Rd SHEFS S8 176 E2 2
Brook Rd CHPT/GREN S35 126 C1
CONI DN12 110 C5 1
RHAM/THRY S65 129 M7
SHEFS S8 176 D2
Brook Rw STKB/PEN S36 102 A7
Brooksfield HEM/SK/SE WF9 42 B3
Brookside CONI DN12 110 A6 1
HEM/SK/SE WF9 23 J8
MEX/SWTN S64 107 M6
RHAM/THRY S65 148 A2
Brookside Bank Rd
ST/HB/BR S6 158 C1
Brookside Cl HACK/IN S12 178 F4
Brookside Crs DEARNE S63 106 F2
Brookside Dr BSLY S70 83 H1 1
Brookside La ST/HB/BR S6 158 D1
Brookside St HEM/SK/SE WF9 42 D4
Brook St ECK/KIL S21 194 A8
RHAM S60 147 M6 1
Brook Ter WRKS S80 198 C5
Brookvale BSLYN/ROY S71 61 H4 1
Brookview Ct DRON S18 190 E4
Brook Wy BTLY DN5 68 B6
Broom Av RHAM/THRY S65 147 M3
Broombank KBTN HD8 56 D2
Broom Cl BSLY S70 83 H1
DEARNE S63 107 L3
DOD/DAR S75 37 L6
ECC S11 8 F9
NROS/TKH DN11 134 F8
Broom Ct HTFD DN7 48 E8
Broom Crs RHAM/THRY S65 7 K8
Broomcroft Pk ECC S11 175 K4 2
Broom Dr RHAM S60 147 M4
Broome Av MEX/SWTN S64 108 B4
Broomfield Cl BSLY S70 59 M7 1
KBTN HD8 17 G8 1
Broomfield Ct
STKB/PEN S36 102 B7 1
Broomfield Gv RHAM S60 7 J8
STKB/PEN S36 102 A7
Broom Field La KBTN HD8 16 F7
Broomfield La BWTY DN10 155 G6
STKB/PEN S36 102 A7
Broomfield Rd FUL S10 8 A6
STKB/PEN S36 102 B6
Broom Gn OWL S3 8 E6
Broom Gv DIN S25 182 B4
RHAM/THRY S65 7 J7
Broomgrove Crs FUL S10 8 A7
Broomgrove La FUL S10 8 A7
Broomgrove Rd FUL S10 8 B8
Broomhall Pl FUL S10 8 D7
Broomhall Rd FUL S10 8 C8
Broomhall St OWL S3 8 D7
Broomhead Ct DOD/DAR S75 37 M7 1
Broomhead Rd WMB/DAR S73 84 D6
Broomhey Av KBTN HD8 35 H1 1
Broomhill Av WRKN S81 184 C7
Broomhill Cl ECK/KIL S21 192 F4
HOLM/MEL HD7 54 B4
Broom Hill Dr DONS/BSCR DN4 91 K8
Broomhill La DEARNE S63 85 G4
Broomhill Vw DEARNE S63 85 M6
Broomhouse Cl KBTN HD8 56 E2
Broomhouse La CONI DN12 110 F6
DONS/BSCR DN4 111 K2
Broom Riddings KIMB S61 128 F5
Broom Rd RHAM/THRY S65 7 K7
Broomroyd BSLY S70 82 F3
Broom Royd CHPT/GREN S35 124 F4
Broomspring Cl OWL S3 8 D6
Broomspring La FUL S10 8 C6
OWL S3 8 D6 1
Broomston La EPW DN9 117 J5
Broom St FUL S10 8 D7
Broom Ter RHAM/THRY S65 7 J7
Broomvale Wk CONI DN12 110 E6
Broom Valley Rd RHAM S60 7 K9
RHAM/THRY S65 7 H7
Broomville St
MEX/SWTN S64 108 C4 1
Broomwood Cl MOS S20 179 L4 2
Broomwood Gdns MOS S20 179 L4
Brosley Av ARMTH DN3 47 K8
Brotherton St OWL S3 160 F1
Broughton Av BTLY DN5 67 L8
Broughton La DARN/MH S9 145 M8
Broughton Rd
DONS/BSCR DN4 113 J1 1
ST/HB/BR S6 144 A6
Brow Cl BSLY S70 82 D1
Brow Crs MOS S20 179 J8
Brow Hill Rd MALT S66 150 C1
Brow La HOLM/MEL HD7 53 J4
KBTN HD8 57 H1
Brownell St OWL S3 8 E3
Brownhill Crs HEM/SK/SE WF9 22 E5
Brownhill La HOLM/MEL HD7 52 F6
Brown Hills La FUL S10 158 C7
Brown House La ST/HB/BR S6 141 M1
Browning Av
DONS/BSCR DN4 111 M1 2
Browning Cl BSLYN/ROY S71 60 F2 1
ST/HB/BR S6 144 B2
WRKN S81 198 F2
Browning Dr
RHAM/THRY S65 147 M1 1
ST/HB/BR S6 144 B2
Browning Rd ARMTH DN3 47 K7 2
DEARNE S63 85 G8
MEX/SWTN S64 108 E1
RHAM/THRY S65 147 M1
ST/HB/BR S6 144 A2
Brown La DRON S18 191 G4
SHEF S1 9 H6 1
Brownroyd Av
BSLYN/ROY S71 39 G5 1
Brown's Edge La STKB/PEN S36 99 L1
Brown's Edge Rd
STKB/PEN S36 55 J7
Browns La THNE DN8 31 L8 1
Brown St RHAM S60 6 B3
SHEF S1 9 J7
The Brow RHAM/THRY S65 148 C3
Brow Vw DEARNE S63 85 M5
Broxholme La DON DN1 5 H3
Broxholme Rd SHEFS S8 176 D4 1
Bruce Av BSLY S70 82 D1
Bruce Crs WHHL DN2 90 F2
Bruce Rd ECC S11 160 B7 3
Brunel Cl NROS/TKH DN11 153 K5
Brunel Ga NROS/TKH DN11 153 K5
Brunel Rd BTLY DN5 89 K2
Brunswick HOR/CROF WF4 21 M5
Brunswick Cl BSLYN/ROY S71 60 D1
Brunswick Rd RHAM S60 7 J9
Brunswick St DEARNE S63 64 C6
FUL S10 8 D6
Brunt Rd RAW S62 129 M1
Brushfield Gv HACK/IN S12 178 B3
Bryans Close La BWTY DN10 137 K4
Bryony Cl ECK/KIL S21 193 M1
Bubup Hl NROS/TKH DN11 112 A5
Bubwith Rd DARN/MH S9 145 M5 1
Buchanan Crs SHEFN S5 144 C2
Buchanan Dr SHEFN S5 144 C2
Buchanan Rd SHEFN S5 144 D2
Buckden Rd BSLY S70 2 D4
Buckenham St ATT S4 161 G1
Buckingham Cl DRON S18 190 B5 1
Buckingham Ri WRKN S81 184 B8
Buckingham Rd CONI DN12 109 M4
WHHL DN2 5 M3
Buckingham Wy
BSLYN/ROY S71 38 F3
MALT S66 150 E1
RHAM S60 147 H7 2
Buckleigh Rd DEARNE S63 107 J3
Buckley Ct BSLY S70 3 G7
Buckthorn Cl MEX/SWTN S64 108 A7
Buck Wood Vw
SHEFP/MNR S2 177 H2
Bude Ct BSLYN/ROY S71 61 G4 1
Bude Rd DONS/BSCR DN4 89 M7
Bud La CHPT/GREN S35 124 C5
Bullcroft Cl AWLS/ASK DN6 45 G6
Bullen Rd ST/HB/BR S6 144 A2
Bullenshaw Rd
HEM/SK/SE WF9 41 H1
Bullfinch Cl RHAM S60 147 H7
Bull Haw La DOD/DAR S75 58 D7 2
Bullhouse La STKB/PEN S36 78 A5
Bullivant Rd HTFD DN7 49 G7
Bull La HEM/SK/SE WF9 42 A5
HOR/CROF WF4 19 K2
Bull Moor Rd HTFD DN7 49 M8
Bull Yd WRKS S80 198 C5 1
Bungalow Rd CONI DN12 110 F5
The Bungalows KBTN HD8 35 J5
RHAM S60 163 J3
Bunker S Hl ECK/KIL S21 194 C1
Bunkers Hl HOLM/MEL HD7 53 L2
Bunting Cl SHEFS S8 176 F6
Bunting Nook SHEFS S8 176 F5
Burbage Cl DRON S18 190 B5 2
Burbage Gv HACK/IN S12 178 B2
Burcot Rd SHEFS S8 176 D2
Burcroft Cl HOY S74 104 F2 2
Burcroft Hl CONI DN12 110 B4
Burden Cl DON DN1 4 E7
Burford Av DONS/BSCR DN4 111 J2
Burford Crs AU/AST/KP S26 164 C8 2
Burgar Rd THNE DN8 49 M2
Burgen Rd KIMB S61 128 C6 1
Burgess Rd DARN/MH S9 161 K1
Burgess St SHEF S1 9 G5
Burghwallis La AWLS/ASK DN6 45 G2
Burghwallis Rd AWLS/ASK DN6 27 G8
Burgley Cl DIN S25 166 C7 1
Burgoyne Cl ST/HB/BR S6 160 B1
Burgoyne Rd ST/HB/BR S6 160 B1
Burkinshaw Av RAW S62 107 K7
Burleigh Ct BSLY S70 3 G6 1
Burleigh St BSLY S70 3 G7
Burley Bank La HOLM/MEL HD7 74 C1
Burlington Ar BSLY S70 3 G5 1
Burlington Ct ST/HB/BR S6 8 C1 1
Burlington Gln TOT/DORE S17 175 J8 1
Burlington Gv TOT/DORE S17 175 J8
Burlington Rd TOT/DORE S17 175 J8
Burlington St ST/HB/BR S6 8 C1
Burman Rd DEARNE S63 107 K1
Burnaby Ct ST/HB/BR S6 144 B8
Burnaby Crs ST/HB/BR S6 144 B8
Burnaby Gn ST/HB/BR S6 144 B8 3
Burnaby St DON DN1 4 E6 1
ST/HB/BR S6 144 B8
Burnaston Cl DRON S18 190 A6 4
Burncross Dr CHPT/GREN S35 126 D2
Burncross Rd CHPT/GREN S35 126 C2
Burnell Rd ST/HB/BR S6 144 A7
Burngreave Bank ATT S4 160 F1
Burngreave Rd ATT S4 144 F8
Burngreave St ATT S4 160 F1
Burn Gv CHPT/GREN S35 127 G3
Burnham Av DOD/DAR S75 37 M6
Burnham Cl DONS/BSCR DN4 90 F8
Burnham Gv BTLY DN5 67 K7

Burnham Wy WMB/DAR S73 84 D2
Burnhill La HEM/SK/SE WF9 24 D2
Burnlee Rd HOLM/MEL HD7 53 J3
Burn Pl BSLY/ROY S71 38 C8 1
Burnsall Crs RHAM S60 147 G7
Burnsall Gv BSLY S70 83 H1
Burns Av HEM/SK/SE WF9 41 K6
Burns Dr CHPT/GREN S35 126 D2
DRON S18 191 G7
RHAM/THRY S65 147 M1
Burnside DEARNE S63 64 A6
Burnside Av SHEFS S8 176 E2
Burnside Dr HOLM/MEL HD7 53 J3
Burns Rd ARMTH DN3 47 K7 3
DIN S25 166 E7
DONS/BSCR DN4 111 M1 5
MALT S66 150 E3
RHAM/THRY S65 7 M5
ST/HB/BR S6 8 A2
WRKN S81 198 F3
Burns St BTLY DN5 67 M6
Burns Wy DEARNE S63 85 G8
DONS/BSCR DN4 89 L7
Burnt Hill La CHPT/GREN S35 142 E2
Burnt Stones Cl FUL S10 159 H5
Burnt Stones Dr FUL S10 159 H5
Burnt Stones Gv FUL S10 159 H5 1
Burnt Tree La OWL S3 8 E1
Burntwood Av HEM/SK/SE WF9 42 A5
Burntwood Bank
HEM/SK/SE WF9 41 H2
Burntwood Cl DEARNE S63 63 M8
Burnt Wood Crs
HEM/SK/SE WF9 42 A6
Burntwood Crs RHAM S60 163 J2 1
Burntwood Dr HEM/SK/SE WF9 41 M5
Burntwood Gv HEM/SK/SE WF9 42 A6
Burnt Wood La CUD/GR S72 41 J6
Burntwood Rd CUD/GR S72 62 F1
Burrell St RHAM S60 6 E5
Burrowlee Rd ST/HB/BR S6 144 A6
Burrows Dr SHEFN S5 144 E5
Burrows Gv WMB/DAR S73 83 M5
Burrs La WRKN S81 167 K7
Burton Av BSLYN/ROY S71 61 H3
DONS/BSCR DN4 89 M7
Burton Bank Rd BSLYN/ROY S71 3 J1
Burton Crs BSLYN/ROY S71 61 J2
Burton La CHPT/GREN S35 143 G1
Burtonlees Ct
DONS/BSCR DN4 91 J8 1
Burton Rd BSLYN/ROY S71 61 G4
Burton St BSLYN/ROY S71 2 F1
HEM/SK/SE WF9 42 C4
ST/HB/BR S6 144 B8
Burton Ter DONS/BSCR DN4 89 M7 1
Burtop Cft WMB/DAR S73 84 A8 1
Burying La RAW S62 105 J4
Bushey Wood Rd
TOT/DORE S17 189 J1
Bushfield Rd DEARNE S63 107 H2
Bush St HEM/SK/SE WF9 41 J1 2
Busker La KBTN HD8 35 H6
Busk Knoll SHEFN S5 144 E5 2
Busk Meadow SHEFN S5 144 E5
Busk Pk SHEFN S5 144 E5
Busley Gdns BTLY DN5 67 L7 1
Butcher Hill Station Rd
HEM/SK/SE WF9 23 J7
Butcher St DEARNE S63 64 A7
Butchill Av SHEFN S5 126 E7
Bute St FUL S10 159 M4
Butler Rd ST/HB/BR S6 143 L8
Butler Wy ECK/KIL S21 180 A8
Butten Meadow BWTY DN10 137 G5
Butterbusk CONI DN12 110 C5
Buttercross AWLS/ASK DN6 44 E6 1
Buttercross Cl AWLS/ASK DN6 44 E5 1
Buttercross Dr CUD/GR S72 63 G7
Buttercup Cl HEM/SK/SE WF9 24 D8 1
Butterfield Cl GLE DN14 13 G1
Butterfield Ct WMB/DAR S73 84 E7 1
Butterill Dr ARMTH DN3 92 B2
Butterley Dr BSLY S70 83 H1 2
Butterley La HOLM/MEL HD7 54 D2
Butterleys DOD/DAR S75 59 L8
Buttermere Cl AWLS/ASK DN6 44 F6
DEARNE S63 86 A6 1
DIN S25 166 C8
Buttermere Cft
WKFDW/WTN WF2 20 E1 2
Buttermere Dr DRON S18 190 C6 1
Buttermere Rd SHEFS S8 176 C3
Buttermere Wy
BSLYN/ROY S71 61 M7 1
Butterthwaite Crs SHEFN S5 127 J8
Butterthwaite La
CHPT/GREN S35 127 G7
Butterthwaite Rd SHEFN S5 127 G7
Butterton Cl DOD/DAR S75 38 A6 1
Butt Hole Rd CONI DN12 110 C5 2
Butt La BTLY DN5 65 H3
HOLM/MEL HD7 54 C5
Button Hl ECC S11 175 M3
Button Rw STKB/PEN S36 102 A6 1
Butts Hl TOT/DORE S17 189 H3
Buxton Rd BSLYN/ROY S71 38 E8
Byland Wy BSLYN/ROY S71 61 G5
Byrley Rd KIMB S61 128 C6
Byrne Cl DOD/DAR S75 59 J3
Byron Av AWLS/ASK DN6 27 G6 1
BTLY DN5 89 K3
CHPT/GREN S35 126 D3
DONS/BSCR DN4 111 L1 1
Byron Cl DRON S18 191 G8
Byron Crs DEARNE S63 85 G8
Byron Dr BSLYN/ROY S71 60 F3
RHAM/THRY S65 7 M4
Byron Rd ABRD S7 176 B1
DIN S25 166 E7
MALT S66 150 E3
MEX/SWTN S64 108 F2
MOS S20 179 L5 1
Byron St CUD/GR S72 63 J6
Byron Wy WRKN S81 198 F3

C

Cadeby Av CONI DN12 109 L5
Cadeby La BTLY DN5 88 A7
Cadman Ct MOS S20 193 H1
Cadman La SHEF S1 9 H5
Cadman Rd HACK/IN S12 178 A2
Cadman St ATT S4 9 M2
DEARNE S63 107 L1
MOS S20 193 G1
Cadwell Cl CUD/GR S72 40 A7
Caernarvon Crs DEARNE S63 85 M5
Caernarvon Dr BTLY DN5 87 G4
Caernarvon Rd DRON S18 190 E7
Caine Gdns KIMB S61 146 C1
Cairns Rd FUL S10 159 K5
MOS S20 179 K3
Caister Av CHPT/GREN S35 126 D1
Caistor Av BSLY S70 2 B9
BSLY S70 60 A8
Calcot Park Av MEX/SWTN S64 108 B5
Caldbeck Gv
CHPT/GREN S35 104 B7 2
Caldbeck Pl DIN S25 166 D8
Calder Av BSLYN/ROY S71 39 J4
Calder Crs BSLY S70 61 H8
GLE DN14 11 J4
Calder Rd DEARNE S63 86 B6
KIMB S61 128 D5
Caldervale BSLYN/ROY S71 39 J3
Calder Vw HOR/CROF WF4 19 J2
Calder Wy SHEFN S5 145 G5
Caldey Rd DRON S18 190 E7
Calf Hey La STKB/PEN S36 55 H8
California Crs BSLY S70 2 F9
California Dr CHPT/GREN S35 126 E3
RHAM S60 163 G2 1
California La STV/CWN S43 194 E8
California St BSLY S70 2 F9
California Ter BSLY S70 2 F9
Calladine Wy MEX/SWTN S64 108 A6
Callis La STKB/PEN S36 79 J6
Callis Wy STKB/PEN S36 79 H5
Callow Dr SHEFP/MNR S2 177 H2
Callow Mt SHEFS S8 177 G2 1
Callow Rd SHEFP/MNR S2 177 G2
Callywhite La DRON S18 191 G6
Calner Cft MOS S20 179 M5
Calver Cl DOD/DAR S75 81 L2
Calvert Rd DARN/MH S9 162 A1
Camborne Cl ST/HB/BR S6 144 A2 1
Camborne Rd ST/HB/BR S6 144 A2
Camborne Wy BSLYN/ROY S71 3 M2
BSLYN/ROY S71 61 G4
Cambourne Cl AWLS/ASK DN6 66 F1
Cambria Dr DONS/BSCR DN4 111 J1 2
Cambrian Cl BTLY DN5 88 E6 1
Cambria Ter WRKS S80 198 C3
Cambridge Cl BTLY DN5 86 F5
Cambridge Crs RHAM/THRY S65 7 M3
Cambridge Pl RHAM/THRY S65 7 M2
Cambridge Rd
NROS/TKH DN11 153 K3 1
SHEFS S8 176 F1
STKB/PEN S36 102 D7
Cambridge St HEM/SK/SE WF9 42 C4
MEX/SWTN S64 108 C2
NROS/TKH DN11 113 J5
RHAM/THRY S65 7 L4
SHEF S1 9 G6 1
Cambron Gdns MALT S66 149 H2
Camdale Ri HACK/IN S12 178 D6
Camdale Vw HACK/IN S12 178 D6
Camden Pl DON DN1 4 F7 1
Camellia Cl CONI DN12 110 B6 1
Camellia Dr ARMTH DN3 69 K4 1
Cam Height ECC S11 174 B4
Cammell Rd SHEFN S5 145 H5
Camms Cl ECK/KIL S21 193 H3 1
Camm St ST/HB/BR S6 160 A1
Campbell Cl WRKN S81 184 D7 1
Campbell Dr RHAM/THRY S65 147 M2
Campbell St RAW S62 129 G3
Camping La SHEFS S8 176 C4
Campion Cl DEARNE S63 85 M4 1
Campion Dr ECK/KIL S21 194 A1 2
MEX/SWTN S64 108 B6
Campo La SHEF S1 9 G4
Camp Rd HEM/SK/SE WF9 41 K6
Campsall Balk AWLS/ASK DN6 27 H5
Campsall Dr FUL S10 159 L4
Campsall Field Cl DEARNE S63 107 J3
Campsall Field Rd
DEARNE S63 107 J2
Campsall Hall Rd
AWLS/ASK DN6 27 G6
Campsall Park Rd
AWLS/ASK DN6 27 G6
Campsall Rd AWLS/ASK DN6 27 K7
Campsmount AWLS/ASK DN6 27 G7 1
Canada St ATT S4 145 H8
BSLY S70 2 F9
Canal Br ECK/KIL S21 194 B1
Canal Garth GLE DN14 11 J3 1
Canal Rd WRKS S80 198 D4
Canal St ATT S4 161 H3
BSLYN/ROY S71 3 H2
Canal Ter WRKS S80 198 E4
Canberra Av HTFD DN7 71 L8
Canberra Ri DEARNE S63 85 M5
Candy Bank EPW DN9 94 B5
Canklow Hill Rd RHAM S60 147 H4
Canklow Rd RHAM S60 6 E6
Canning St SHEF S1 8 F5
Cannock St ST/HB/BR S6 144 A7 2
Cannon Flds HATH/EY S32 172 D7 1
Cannon Hall Rd SHEFN S5 145 G7
Cannon Wy DOD/DAR S75 59 K2
Canon Cl NROS/TKH DN11 113 M6 1
Canons Wy BSLYN/ROY S71 61 G4
Canterbury Av FUL S10 159 G7
Canterbury Cl BTLY DN5 89 J1 1
WRKN S81 184 E8
Canterbury Crs FUL S10 159 G7
Canterbury Dr FUL S10 159 G7
Canterbury Rd HTFD DN7 48 E7
SHEFS S8 176 F2
WHHL DN2 90 D1
Cantilupe Crs AU/AST/KP S26 164 B7
Cantley La DONS/BSCR DN4 91 L7 1
DONS/BSCR DN4 91 H6
Cantley Manor Av
DONS/BSCR DN4 91 L8
Cantley Riding WHHL DN2 91 J2
Canyards Hills La ST/HB/BR S6 123 J4
Capel St ST/HB/BR S6 144 B8
Caperns Rd DIN S25 182 D2
Capri Ct WMB/DAR S73 84 C1
Caraway Gv MEX/SWTN S64 108 B7
Carbis Cl BSLYN/ROY S71 3 M2
Carbrook Hall Rd
DARN/MH S9 145 M6
Carbrook St DARN/MH S9 145 M6
Cardew Cl RAW S62 129 L2
Cardiff St DARN/MH S9 145 L7
Cardigan Rd WHHL DN2 91 G2
Cardinal Cl NROS/TKH DN11 113 M6 2
Cardoness Dr FUL S10 159 J5
Cardoness Rd FUL S10 159 K5
Cardwell Av HAN/WDH S13 162 D8
Cardwell Ct MALT S66 132 D5
Cardwell Dr HAN/WDH S13 162 D8
Carey Av BSLYN/ROY S71 3 J5
Carfield Av SHEFS S8 176 F2
Carfield La SHEFS S8 177 G2
Car Hl KIMB S61 129 G5
Carisbrooke Rd WHHL DN2 90 E3 1
Carisbrook Rd WRKN S81 184 C1
Carlby Rd ST/HB/BR S6 143 L8
Carley Dr MOS S20 179 K6
Carling Av WRKS S80 198 B5
Carlin St HAN/WDH S13 178 C2
Carlisle Rd ATT S4 145 J7
WHHL DN2 68 F8
Carlisle St MEX/SWTN S64 108 B6
RHAM/THRY S65 7 G3
Carlisle St East ATT S4 161 H1
Carlthorpe Gv CHPT/GREN S35 104 A8
Carlton Av RHAM/THRY S65 7 J6
WRKN S81 198 C1
Carlton Cl ARMTH DN3 92 C7
HEM/SK/SE WF9 41 G1
MOS S20 193 G1
WRKN S81 184 C8
Carlton Cft WKFDW/WTN WF2 20 B1
Carlton Dr BWTY DN10 154 D1
Carlton Gdns HEM/SK/SE WF9 42 D4
Carlton Hall La WRKN S81 184 D2
Carlton Ri CHPT/GREN S35 124 F4
Carlton Rd BSLYN/ROY S71 38 F8 2
BSLYN/ROY S71 60 F1
HEM/SK/SE WF9 42 D5 1
RAW S62 129 K3
ST/HB/BR S6 143 M5
WHHL DN2 5 J1
WRKN S81 184 D6
WRKN S81 198 D3
WRKS S80 198 D4
Carlton St BSLYN/ROY S71 60 C3
CUD/GR S72 39 M8
CUD/GR S72 62 E1
Carlyle Rd MALT S66 150 E3
Carlyle St MEX/SWTN S64 108 E2
Carnaby Rd ST/HB/BR S6 144 A8
Carnarvon St ST/HB/BR S6 160 C2 5
Carnforth Rd BSLYN/ROY S71 61 H2
Carnley St DEARNE S63 106 F1
Carnoustie WRKN S81 198 F2
Carnoustie Cl MEX/SWTN S64 108 C5
Carolina Wy DONS/BSCR DN4 90 E8
Carpenter Cft HACK/IN S12 178 A1
Carpenter Gdns
HACK/IN S12 178 A1 1
Carr Bank NROS/TKH DN11 112 E8
Carr Bank Cl ECC S11 159 K7
Carr Bank Dr ECC S11 159 K7 2
Carr Bank La ECC S11 159 J7
Carr Cl RHAM S60 146 E7
Carrcroft Ct STKB/PEN S36 102 D7 2
Carrfield Cl DOD/DAR S75 37 H7 1
Carrfield Dr SHEFS S8 176 F1
Carr Field La DEARNE S63 85 M4
Carrfield La SHEFP/MNR S2 176 F1
Carrfield Rd SHEFS S8 176 F1
Carrfield St SHEFP/MNR S2 176 F1
Carr Forge Cl HACK/IN S12 178 E3
Carr Forge La HACK/IN S12 178 E3
Carr Forge Mt HACK/IN S12 178 E3
Carr Forge Pl HACK/IN S12 178 F3
Carr Forge Rd HACK/IN S12 178 E3
Carr Forge Ter HACK/IN S12 178 E3
Carr Forge Vw HACK/IN S12 178 F3
Carr Furlong BSLYN/ROY S71 38 D6 1
Carrgate HEM/SK/SE WF9 22 F5
Carr Gn DEARNE S63 86 A4
Carr Green La DOD/DAR S75 38 A7 2
Carr Gv STKB/PEN S36 102 C7
Carr Head La DEARNE S63 85 M5
Carr Head Rd CHPT/GREN S35 103 M6
Carr Hl DONS/BSCR DN4 89 M7
Carr Hill Rd KBTN HD8 55 L1
Carr House La CHPT/GREN S35 124 B4
Carr House Rd DON DN1 4 F8
DONS/BSCR DN4 5 K7
HOLM/MEL HD7 53 L2 2
Carriage Dr DONS/BSCR DN4 90 D7
The Carriage Wy
NROS/TKH DN11 113 M6
Carrill Dr ST/HB/BR S6 144 A1
Carrill Rd ST/HB/BR S6 144 A1
Carrington Av DOD/DAR S75 60 C3
Carrington Rd ECC S11 159 M7
Carrington St DOD/DAR S75 2 D2
RHAM/THRY S65 7 J6 1
Carr La AU/AST/KP S26 164 D4
CHPT/GREN S35 104 A3
CONI DN12 110 C7
DOD/DAR S75 104 A2
DON DN1 5 G8
DONS/BSCR DN4 113 J2
DRON S18 190 A5
GLE DN14 12 C2
HEM/SK/SE WF9 22 D4
HEM/SK/SE WF9 42 A3
HOLM/MEL HD7 52 F3
HOR/CROF WF4 17 M1
KBTN HD8 55 K1
MALT S66 150 A7
NROS/TKH DN11 134 A1
RHAM/THRY S65 130 E1
STKB/PEN S36 56 F8
Carr Mt KBTN HD8 55 L1
Carroll Ct HEM/SK/SE WF9 42 C4
Carron Dr DOD/DAR S75 38 A7
Carr Rd CONI DN12 110 E6
DEARNE S63 107 L1
ST/HB/BR S6 160 A1
STKB/PEN S36 102 B8
Carr Side La HTFD DN7 71 G3
Carrs La CUD/GR S72 61 M2
Carr St BSLYN/ROY S71 61 H2
Carr Vw HEM/SK/SE WF9 42 A3
Carr View Av DONS/BSCR DN4 89 M7
Carr View Rd HOLM/MEL HD7 54 C5
KIMB S61 128 B7
Carrville Dr ST/HB/BR S6 144 B3
Carrville Rd ST/HB/BR S6 144 B3
Carrville Rd West
ST/HB/BR S6 144 A3 1
Carrwell La ST/HB/BR S6 144 A4
Carrwood Rd BSLY S70 61 J6
ECK/KIL S21 193 M7
Carsick Gv FUL S10 159 H6
Carsick Hill Crs FUL S10 159 H6
Carsick Hill Dr FUL S10 159 J6
Carsick Hill Rd FUL S10 159 H6
Carsick Hill Wy FUL S10 159 H6 1
Carsick View Rd FUL S10 159 H6
Carson Mt HACK/IN S12 177 M4
Carson Rd FUL S10 159 M4
Carter Hall La HACK/IN S12 177 M5
Carterhall Rd HACK/IN S12 177 M5
Carter Knowle Av ECC S11 175 M2
Carter Knowle Rd ECC S11 175 M2
Carter Lodge Av HACK/IN S12 178 E3
Carter Lodge Dr HACK/IN S12 178 F3
Carter Lodge Pl HACK/IN S12 178 F3
Carter Lodge Ri HACK/IN S12 178 F3
Carter Pl SHEFS S8 176 F1
Carter Rd SHEFS S8 176 E1
Cartledge La DRON S18 189 L7
Cartmel Cl DRON S18 190 C6 2
MALT S66 150 E1
Cartmel Ct BSLYN/ROY S71 39 H8 2
Cartmell Crs SHEFS S8 176 C4
Cartmell Rd SHEFS S8 176 C3
Cartmel Wk DIN S25 166 D8
Cartworth Bank Rd
HOLM/MEL HD7 53 K5
Cartworth La HOLM/MEL HD7 53 K4
Cartworth Moor Rd
HOLM/MEL HD7 53 J7
Cartworth Rd HOLM/MEL HD7 53 L4
Cartwright St WRKN S81 183 J8
Car Vale Dr SHEFP/MNR S2 162 A7
Car Vale Vw SHEFP/MNR S2 162 A7
Carver Cl AU/AST/KP S26 195 J2
Carver Dr DIN S25 166 C7
Carver La SHEF S1 9 G4
Carver St SHEF S1 9 G5
Carver Wy AU/AST/KP S26 195 J1
Carwood Cl ATT S4 145 H8
Carwood Gv ATT S4 145 H8 1
Carwood Rd ATT S4 145 H8
Cary Rd ECK/KIL S21 192 F4
SHEFP/MNR S2 161 K7
Casson Dr AU/AST/KP S26 181 J8
Casson's Rd THNE DN8 31 L7
Castell Crs DONS/BSCR DN4 91 J6
Castle Av CONI DN12 110 A5
RHAM S60 147 H4
Castlebeck Av SHEFP/MNR S2 161 M6
Castlebeck Cft
SHEFP/MNR S2 162 A6 1
Castlebeck Dr SHEFP/MNR S2 162 A7
Castle Cl BSLYN/ROY S71 3 M1
BTLY DN5 89 J5
NROS/TKH DN11 134 E8
STKB/PEN S36 79 J5
Castle Ct NROS/TKH DN11 152 E1
Castle Crs CONI DN12 110 A4
Castledale Cft
SHEFP/MNR S2 161 M7 1
Castledale Gv SHEFP/MNR S2 161 M7
Castledale Pl
SHEFP/MNR S2 161 M7 2
Castledine Ct DONS/BSCR DN4 111 M3
Castledine Cft DARN/MH S9 145 M4
Castledine Gdns DARN/MH S9 145 L5
Castle Dr DOD/DAR S75 81 J5
Castle Farm La WRKS S80 198 C8
Castle Ga NROS/TKH DN11 152 E1
Castlegate OWL S3 9 J3
Castle Gn DIN S25 166 B3
SHEF S1 9 J3
Castle Gv BTLY DN5 88 F6 1
Castle Hl CONI DN12 110 A5
ECK/KIL S21 193 H3
Castle Hill Av MEX/SWTN S64 109 G3
Castle Hill Cl ECK/KIL S21 193 H3
Castle Hill Fold BTLY DN5 65 G8
Castle Hills Rd BTLY DN5 67 J6
Castle La STKB/PEN S36 79 J5
Castle Mdw HOR/CROF WF4 19 K4
Castle Ms BTLY DN5 67 K6
Castlereagh St BSLY S70 2 E6
Castlerigg Wy DRON S18 190 C6 3
Castlerow Cl TOT/DORE S17 189 L1
Castlerow Dr TOT/DORE S17 189 M1
Castle St BSLY S70 2 D5 2
CONI DN12 110 A5
SHEF S1 9 J3
WRKS S80 198 C5
Castle Ter CONI DN12 110 A5
Castleton Rd HATH/EY S32 172 C7
Castle Vw BSLY S70 82 C7
CONI DN12 110 F6
ECK/KIL S21 193 H4
Castlewood Crs FUL S10 158 F7 1
Castlewood Dr FUL S10 158 F7
Castor Rd DARN/MH S9 145 K8 2
Catania Ri WMB/DAR S73 84 C1
Catcliffe Rd DARN/MH S9 162 A3 2
Cathedral Ct HTFD DN7 70 C3 1
Catherine Av AU/AST/KP S26 164 B8
Catherine Rd ATT S4 160 F1
Catherine St DON DN1 5 G6
HEM/SK/SE WF9 22 E3
MEX/SWTN S64 108 D2 3
OWL S3 160 F1
RHAM/THRY S65 7 G4
Cat Hill La STKB/PEN S36 57 H7
Cathill Rd WMB/DAR S73 85 G3
Cat La GLE DN14 11 G5
SHEFS S8 177 G2
Catley Rd DARN/MH S9 162 A2
Catling La ARMTH DN3 47 K8
Catshaw La STKB/PEN S36 77 M4
Cattal St DARN/MH S9 161 L2 2
Catterick Cl CONI DN12 109 J5
Caulk La BSLY S70 83 K2
Causeway Gdns
TOT/DORE S17 175 G7 1
Causeway Garth La PONT WF8 24 F3
Causeway Gld TOT/DORE S17 175 G7
Causeway Head Rd
TOT/DORE S17 175 G7
The Causeway TOT/DORE S17 175 H8
Cavendish Av ST/HB/BR S6 143 J6
TOT/DORE S17 175 J8
Cavendish Cl BWTY DN10 154 D1
RHAM/THRY S65 148 B3
Cavendish Ct OWL S3 8 E6
Cavendish Pl MALT S66 150 E1 1
Cavendish Ri DRON S18 190 D7
Cavendish Rd BTLY DN5 67 L3
DOD/DAR S75 2 D1
ECC S11 160 A8
KIMB S61 146 E1
WRKS S80 198 E7
Cavendish St OWL S3 8 E5
Cave St DARN/MH S9 161 K2
Cavill Rd SHEFS S8 176 E4
Cawdor Rd SHEFP/MNR S2 177 K1
Cawdor St BTLY DN5 67 M6 1
Cawdron Ri RHAM S60 147 G7
Cawley Pl BSLYN/ROY S71 60 E3
Cawston Rd ATT S4 145 G7 1
Cawthorne Cl RHAM/THRY S65 130 A8
SHEFS S8 176 C4
Cawthorne Gv SHEFS S8 176 C4
Cawthorne La DOD/DAR S75 58 E2
Cawthorne Rd DOD/DAR S75 59 H3
RHAM/THRY S65 130 A8
WKFDW/WTN WF2 19 M1
Cawthorne Vw STKB/PEN S36 79 K1
Caxton La ECC S11 159 M5
Caxton Rd AWLS/ASK DN6 66 F2
ECC S11 160 A5 4
Caxton St BSLY S70 2 F3
Caythorpe Cl BSLYN/ROY S71 61 L2
Cayton Cl BSLYN/ROY S71 38 C8 2
Cecil Av DONS/BSCR DN4 111 G2
DRON S18 190 E5
Cecil Cl WRKS S80 197 L3
Cecil Rd DRON S18 190 E5
Cecil Sq SHEFP/MNR S2 160 D7
Cedar Av HTFD DN7 48 E3 1
MALT S66 149 G2
MEX/SWTN S64 108 D1
Cedar Cl BSLYN/ROY S71 38 E3
DONS/BSCR DN4 111 J2
ECK/KIL S21 192 F5
ECK/KIL S21 194 A2
EPW DN9 114 E3 1
STKB/PEN S36 101 M7
WRKN S81 168 C8 1
Cedar Crs BSLY S70 60 F8
Cedar Dr MALT S66 150 B2
RHAM/THRY S65 131 K6
Cedar Gv CONI DN12 109 L7
Cedar Rd ARMTH DN3 70 A8 1
DONS/BSCR DN4 111 J1
STKB/PEN S36 101 M7
THNE DN8 32 A6
Cedar Wk AWLS/ASK DN6 27 G7
Cedar Wy CHPT/GREN S35 126 D3 1
Cedric Av CONI DN12 109 L6
Cedric Crs MALT S66 165 J1
Cedric Rd ARMTH DN3 69 K5
Celandine Ct TOT/DORE S17 189 L2 1
Celandine Gdns TOT/DORE S17 189 L2
Celandine Gv WMB/DAR S73 84 E3
Celandine Ri MEX/SWTN S64 108 B7
Cemetery Av FUL S10 8 B9
Cemetery Rd AWLS/ASK DN6 66 E3
BSLY S70 3 J8
CUD/GR S72 40 E8
DEARNE S63 86 A6
DEARNE S63 107 J2
DRON S18 190 F7
ECC S11 8 E9
HEM/SK/SE WF9 23 G8
HOLM/MEL HD7 53 K3
HOR/CROF WF4 21 M6
HOY S74 83 L8
HTFD DN7 49 J8
MEX/SWTN S64 108 E2
WMB/DAR S73 84 B4
WRKS S80 198 E5
Centenary Wy RHAM S60 6 D3
RHAM S60 147 G4 1
Central Av AWLS/ASK DN6 66 E3
BTLY DN5 67 M7
CUD/GR S72 40 E8
DIN S25 166 D7
HEM/SK/SE WF9 22 E3
HEM/SK/SE WF9 42 D5 2
MALT S66 130 F8
MEX/SWTN S64 107 M5
RHAM/THRY S65 129 M8
WRKS S80 198 C5
Central Bvd WHHL DN2 90 F1
Central Dr BSLYN/ROY S71 39 G4
BWTY DN10 136 E7
MALT S66 165 J1
NROS/TKH DN11 113 J7
RAW S62 107 G7
Central Rd RHAM S60 6 E4
Central St DEARNE S63 86 C1

HOY S74 104 F2 3
Centre St HEM/SK/SE WF9 23 H8
HEM/SK/SE WF9 42 E4 1
Centurion Wy BTLY DN5 89 M2
Century Ct CONI DN12 111 G4 2
Century Gdns BTLY DN5 68 A6
Century St DARN/MH S9 161 M1
Century Vw RHAM S60 146 E7
Chadbourne Cl ARMTH DN3 91 L2
Chaddesden Cl DRON S18 190 A6 5
Chadwick Dr MALT S66 150 D1
Chadwick Gdns BTLY DN5 68 C5
Chadwick Rd AWLS/ASK DN6 66 E3
BTLY DN5 89 M2
HAN/WDH S13 162 A8
THNE DN8 32 B3
Chaff Cl RHAM S60 147 M6
Chaffinch Av RHAM S60 147 H7 3
Chaffinch Ms WRKN S81 184 A8 1
Chaff La RHAM S60 147 M6
Challenger Crs DEARNE S63 64 A6
Challenger Dr BTLY DN5 89 J4
Challoner Gn MOS S20 179 J7 5
Challoner Wy MOS S20 179 J7
Chalmers Dr WHHL DN2 69 H6
Chamberlain Av BTLY DN5 89 K1
Chamberlain Ct
CHPT/GREN S35 126 D1 2
Chambers Av CONI DN12 109 L5
Chambers La ATT S4 145 J6
Chambers Rd HOY S74 83 H8 1
KIMB S61 128 D6
Champion Cl SHEFN S5 145 H1
Champion Rd SHEFN S5 145 G1
Chancel Wy BSLYN/ROY S71 61 G4
Chancery Pl DON DN1 4 F5 1
Chancet Wood Cl SHEFS S8 176 D7
Chancet Wood Dr SHEFS S8 176 D7
Chancet Wood Ri SHEFS S8 176 D7
Chandos Crs ECK/KIL S21 194 A1
Chandos St FUL S10 160 A5 3
Channing Gdns ST/HB/BR S6 144 B8
Channing St ST/HB/BR S6 144 B8
Chantrey Rd SHEFS S8 176 D4
Chantry Cl DONS/BSCR DN4 91 L8
Chantry Gv BSLYN/ROY S71 39 G4
Chantry Pl AU/AST/KP S26 181 K4
Chapel Av BSLYN/ROY S71 39 G6
WMB/DAR S73 84 E7
Chapel Bank HOLM/MEL HD7 54 C4
Chapel Baulk BWTY DN10 116 F6
Chapel Cl BSLY S70 82 C8 1
CHPT/GREN S35 126 C2
CUD/GR S72 40 A4
EPW DN9 115 J4
FUL S10 159 K6 1
MALT S66 149 J8
Chapel Ct BSLY S70 82 C8
Chapelfield Crs KIMB S61 127 K2 1
Chapelfield Dr KIMB S61 127 K2
Chapelfield La KIMB S61 127 K2
Chapel Field La STKB/PEN S36 79 G5
Chapelfield Mt KIMB S61 127 K2 2
Chapel Field Pl KIMB S61 127 K2 3
Chapelfield Rd KIMB S61 127 J1
Chapelfields HEM/SK/SE WF9 41 M5
Chapelfield Wy KIMB S61 127 K2
Chapel Garth FEA/AMT WF7 23 L1
Chapelgate HOLM/MEL HD7 54 B4
Chapel Ga WRKN S81 184 E2 1
Chapel Hl AWLS/ASK DN6 27 L7
BTLY DN5 64 A3
HOY S74 83 H6
KBTN HD8 35 J5
MEX/SWTN S64 108 A4
RHAM S60 147 M6
Chapel Hole La MALT S66 133 G5
Chapel La ARMTH DN3 92 C7
BSLYN/ROY S71 39 G7
BWTY DN10 154 E5
BWTY DN10 155 M4
CHPT/GREN S35 102 C4
CONI DN12 110 A6
CUD/GR S72 63 H6
CUD/GR S72 85 K1
DARN/MH S9 161 L1 1
DEARNE S63 64 C6
DRON S18 191 L6
EPW DN9 115 J3
GLE DN14 11 M8
HEM/SK/SE WF9 24 C5
HEM/SK/SE WF9 42 F4
KBTN HD8 16 F8
PONT WF8 26 B1
RHAM S60 6 F6
STKB/PEN S36 79 G5
STKB/PEN S36 100 F3
THNE DN8 31 M8 1
Chapel Pl BSLYN/ROY S71 61 K7
Chapel Ri DIN S25 182 B2
Chapel Rd CHPT/GREN S35 104 C7 1
CHPT/GREN S35 126 C3
DOD/DAR S75 104 A1
Chapel St AWLS/ASK DN6 44 F7
BSLY S70 82 C8
BSLYN/ROY S71 61 K7 2
BTLY DN5 67 M7
CUD/GR S72 40 A4
CUD/GR S72 62 E1
DEARNE S63 64 A7
DEARNE S63 86 A5
DEARNE S63 107 J2
HAN/WDH S13 178 F1
HOR/CROF WF4 21 L6
HOY S74 104 F2
KIMB S61 128 F3
MEX/SWTN S64 108 B4
MOS S20 193 G1
RAW S62 129 K2
Chapel Ter FUL S10 159 K6
Chapeltown Rd
CHPT/GREN S35 126 F5
Chapel Wk RAW S62 107 H8
RHAM S60 6 C4
SHEF S1 9 H4
WRKS S80 198 C5
Chapel Wy AU/AST/KP S26 181 H5
RAW S62 107 H8
Chapelwood Rd DARN/MH S9 161 M1
Chapel Yd DRON S18 190 E5
Chapman St DARN/MH S9 145 M3 2
DEARNE S63 64 C7 1
Chappell Cl STKB/PEN S36 79 K1
Chappell Dr BTLY DN5 4 F2
Chappell Rd STKB/PEN S36 79 K1
Chapter Wy BSLYN/ROY S71 61 G4 2
DOD/DAR S75 58 E6
Chariot Wy PONT WF8 24 E3
Charity St BSLYN/ROY S71 61 K1
Charles Ashmore Rd SHEFS S8 176 D7
Charles Ct THNE DN8 32 A6
Charles Crs ARMTH DN3 69 K8
Charles La SHEF S1 9 H6
Charles Rd DEARNE S63 107 K2
Charles St AWLS/ASK DN6 44 F5
BSLY S70 2 E8
BSLY S70 82 E3 2
CUD/GR S72 40 A7
CUD/GR S72 40 C2
CUD/GR S72 62 E1 1
CUD/GR S72 63 H8
DEARNE S63 86 B2 1
DIN S25 166 D5
DON DN1 5 H2
HOR/CROF WF4 21 L6
MALT S66 165 J1
MEX/SWTN S64 108 B5
RAW S62 107 M8
SHEF S1 9 H6
Charlestown Est FEA/AMT WF7 23 L3
Charlotte La SHEF S1 8 E5 1
Charlotte Rd SHEF S1 9 H8
SHEFP/MNR S2 9 J9
Charlton Brook Crs
CHPT/GREN S35 126 C1
Charlton Clough
CHPT/GREN S35 126 B2
Charlton Dr CHPT/GREN S35 126 C1
Charlton Hill Ri
CHPT/GREN S35 126 B2
Charnell Rd MALT S66 150 E2
Charnley Av ECC S11 176 A2
Charnley Cl ECC S11 175 M1
Charnley Dr ECC S11 176 A2
Charnley Ri ECC S11 176 A2
Charnock Av HACK/IN S12 177 M5
Charnock Crs HACK/IN S12 177 L4
Charnock Dale Rd
HACK/IN S12 177 L5
Charnock Dr BTLY DN5 89 K2 1
HACK/IN S12 177 L4
Charnock Gv HACK/IN S12 177 M5
Charnock Hall Rd HACK/IN S12 177 L5
Charnock View Rd
HACK/IN S12 177 L5
Charnock Wood Rd
HACK/IN S12 177 M5
Charnwood Ct MOS S20 179 L5 2
Charnwood Dr
DONS/BSCR DN4 111 J2
Charnwood Gv KIMB S61 146 D1
Charnwood St
MEX/SWTN S64 108 B4 1
Charter Dr BTLY DN5 67 G7
Charter Rw SHEF S1 9 G7
Charter Square Rbt SHEF S1 9 G6
Chase Rd ST/HB/BR S6 143 H7
The Chase AU/AST/KP S26 180 C1
Chatfield Rd SHEFS S8 176 C5
Chatham St OWL S3 160 E2
RHAM/THRY S65 7 G4
Chatsworth Av
MEX/SWTN S64 109 H2
Chatsworth Cl AU/AST/KP S26 164 D8
Chatsworth Crs BTLY DN5 67 K7
Chatsworth Dr
NROS/TKH DN11 113 M7
Chatsworth Park Av
HACK/IN S12 177 L2 1
Chatsworth Park Dr
HACK/IN S12 177 L2 2
Chatsworth Park Gv
HACK/IN S12 177 L2 3
Chatsworth Park Rd
HACK/IN S12 177 L2
Chatsworth Pl DRON S18 190 B5 3
Chatsworth Ri DOD/DAR S75 81 K1 1
RHAM S60 147 H7 4
Chatsworth Rd BSLYN/ROY S71 60 E1
KIMB S61 6 A5
TOT/DORE S17 189 J1
WRKS S81 184 D8
Chatterton Dr
RHAM/THRY S65 147 M3
Chaucer Cl SHEFN S5 144 B1 1
Chaucer Dr DRON S18 191 G8
Chaucer Rd MEX/SWTN S64 108 F2
RHAM/THRY S65 147 M3
SHEFN S5 144 C1
Cheadle St ST/HB/BR S6 144 A7 3
Cheapside BSLY S70 3 G5
WRKS S80 198 E5
Checkstone Av
DONS/BSCR DN4 113 J2
Chedworth Cl DOD/DAR S75 37 J8
Cheese Gate Nab Side
HOLM/MEL HD7 54 E5
Cheetham Dr MALT S66 150 E1
Chelmsford Av AU/AST/KP S26 164 C7
Chelmsford Dr WHHL DN2 90 D1
Chelsea Ct ECC S11 160 A8
Chelsea Ri ECC S11 160 A8
Chelsea Rd ECC S11 176 A1
Cheltenham Ri BTLY DN5 89 H2 1
Cheltenham Rd WHHL DN2 91 G2
Chemist La RHAM S60 6 D3 1
Chemistry La CHPT/GREN S35 103 G7
Chepstow Dr MEX/SWTN S64 108 F1
Chepstow Gdns BTLY DN5 89 H2
Chequer Av DONS/BSCR DN4 5 J7
Chequer Br RTFD DN22 186 D7
Chequer La HTFD DN7 47 K4
Chequer Rd DON DN1 5 H6
Cheriton Av AWLS/ASK DN6 66 E1
Cherry Bank Rd SHEFS S8 176 E4
Cherry Cl BSLYN/ROY S71 38 E3
CUD/GR S72 39 M7
Cherry Garth AWLS/ASK DN6 27 G7
BTLY DN5 67 M4
HEM/SK/SE WF9 41 G1
Cherry Gv CONI DN12 109 K7
NROS/TKH DN11 113 L7 1
Cherry Hills DOD/DAR S75 37 L6
Cherry La BTLY DN5 4 D2
KBTN HD8 35 K5 1
Cherrys Rd BSLYN/ROY S71 61 H5
Cherry St SHEFP/MNR S2 160 E7
Cherry St South
SHEFP/MNR S2 160 E7
Cherry Tree Av WRKN S81 183 K8 1
Cherry Tree Cl DOD/DAR S75 38 A6 2
ECC S11 160 B8 1
RHAM S60 147 H7 5
Cherry Tree Crs MALT S66 149 G2
Cherry Tree Dell ECC S11 160 B8 2
Cherry Tree Dr ABRD S7 160 B8 3
ECK/KIL S21 194 A2
HTFD DN7 48 E7 2
THNE DN8 31 M6 2
Cherry Tree Gv HTFD DN7 48 E6
Cherry Tree Pl DEARNE S63 107 K2 1
Cherry Tree Rd ABRD S7 160 B8 4
ARMTH DN3 91 M1
AU/AST/KP S26 180 E5
DONS/BSCR DN4 4 D7
MALT S66 150 B2
Cherry Tree St HOY S74 105 K1
Cherry Tree Wk
HOLM/MEL HD7 54 B3 1
RTFD DN22 171 G2
Cherry Wk CHPT/GREN S35 126 E3 1
Chesham Rd BSLY S70 2 D5
Cheshire Rd DON DN1 5 H1
Chessel Cl SHEFS S8 176 E3
Chessington Dr HOR/CROF WF4 17 H4
Chesterfield Rd
AU/AST/KP S26 179 M1
DRON S18 190 F6
ECK/KIL S21 192 E6
SHEFS S8 176 D1
Chesterfield Rd South
SHEFS S8 190 E1
Chesterhill Av
RHAM/THRY S65 130 C6
Chester La SHEF S1 8 F6
Chester Rd WHHL DN2 68 D8
Chester St SHEF S1 8 F5
Chesterton Dr WRKN S81 198 F2
Chesterton Rd
DONS/BSCR DN4 112 A1 1
Chesterton Wy
RHAM/THRY S65 129 M6
Chesterwood Dr FUL S10 159 M5 1
Chestnut Av ARMTH DN3 91 M1
AU/AST/KP S26 181 G5
AWLS/ASK DN6 44 F6
CUD/GR S72 40 D4
DARN/MH S9 162 C4
DEARNE S63 107 K3
ECK/KIL S21 192 F5
ECK/KIL S21 193 M2
HTFD DN7 48 E3
MOS S20 179 K2
NROS/TKH DN11 113 L7
RHAM/THRY S65 129 M8
STKB/PEN S36 101 M7
THNE DN8 50 A1 2
WHHL DN2 68 F8
WKFDW/WTN WF2 20 E1
Chestnut Cl DRON S18 190 F7
MALT S66 148 F1
WRKS S80 198 C6 1
Chestnut Ct BSLY S70 3 H9 1
BTLY DN5 67 L5 3
Chestnut Crs BSLY S70 3 M9
Chestnut Dr BWTY DN10 136 D8
CHPT/GREN S35 126 C3
CUD/GR S72 40 B2
EPW DN9 114 E3
Chestnut Gv BTLY DN5 88 F7 1
CONI DN12 109 L6
DEARNE S63 64 B8
DIN S25 166 D5
HEM/SK/SE WF9 41 K2
MALT S66 150 B1
Chestnut Rd AU/AST/KP S26 163 M7
WRKN S81 168 D3
Chestnut St CUD/GR S72 62 F2
HEM/SK/SE WF9 42 D6
Chevet La HOR/CROF WF4 20 F7
Chevet Park Ct
WKFDW/WTN WF2 20 C4
Chevet Ri BSLYN/ROY S71 38 E3
Chevet Vw BSLYN/ROY S71 38 E3
Cheviot Cl HEM/SK/SE WF9 23 K8
THNE DN8 49 L1
Cheviot Dr BTLY DN5 67 K8
Chevril Ct MALT S66 148 E3
Cheyne Wk BWTY DN10 136 D8
Chichester Rd FUL S10 159 M3 2
Childers Dr EPW DN9 92 E8
Childers St DONS/BSCR DN4 5 J8
Chiltern Ct HEM/SK/SE WF9 23 K8
Chiltern Crs BTLY DN5 88 E6
Chiltern Dr FEA/AMT WF7 23 K2
Chiltern Ri RHAM S60 147 H8
Chiltern Rd BTLY DN5 67 K8
ST/HB/BR S6 143 M7
Chiltern Wy WRKN S81 168 C8 2
Chilton St BSLY S70 3 K8
Chilwell Cl BSLYN/ROY S71 38 D6 2
Chilwell Gdns BSLYN/ROY S71 38 D6 3
Chinley St DARN/MH S9 161 L2 3
Chippingham Pl
DARN/MH S9 161 K1 2
Chippingham St DARN/MH S9 161 L1
Chippinghouse Rd ABRD S7 160 D8
SHEFS S8 160 D8
Chiverton Cl DRON S18 190 E5 1
Choppards Bank Rd
HOLM/MEL HD7 53 L6
Choppards La HOLM/MEL HD7 53 L5
Chorley Av FUL S10 159 G7
Chorley Dr FUL S10 159 G7 1
Chorley Pl FUL S10 159 G8
Chorley Rd FUL S10 159 H7
Christchurch Av
AU/AST/KP S26 164 C7
Christchurch Rd DEARNE S63 85 G8
Christ Church Rd DON DN1 5 H3
OWL S3 144 F8
Church Av HEM/SK/SE WF9 42 A5
RAW S62 129 J3
Church Balk ARMTH DN3 69 K4
THNE DN8 32 A8
Church Balk Gdns ARMTH DN3 69 K4
Church Bank HATH/EY S32 172 E7
Church Cl AU/AST/KP S26 180 F5
CHPT/GREN S35 125 H8
DOD/DAR S75 37 J7
ECK/KIL S21 193 M7
MALT S66 150 D3
MEX/SWTN S64 108 A4
RHAM/THRY S65 131 G4
THNE DN8 32 A8
Church Cnr DIN S25 166 B2
Church Cottage Ms
DONS/BSCR DN4 89 J8
Church Ct DIN S25 182 C3 1
DONS/BSCR DN4 91 K8 2
Church Crs HOR/CROF WF4 18 C1 1
Church Cft RAW S62 129 J3
Churchdale Rd HACK/IN S12 178 B3
Church Dr CUD/GR S72 40 D5
HEM/SK/SE WF9 42 A5
Churchfield BSLY S70 2 E4
Churchfield Av CUD/GR S72 61 M1 1
DOD/DAR S75 37 G7 1
Churchfield Cl BTLY DN5 67 L8
DOD/DAR S75 36 F7
Church Field Cl WRKN S81 184 E2 2
Churchfield Crs CUD/GR S72 61 M1 2
Church Field Dr MALT S66 148 F3
Churchfield La DOD/DAR S75 36 F7
Church Field La RAW S62 105 K7
Church Field Rd AWLS/ASK DN6 27 H6
BTLY DN5 64 A3
Churchfields CHPT/GREN S35 102 D1
HOR/CROF WF4 21 M5
Church Flds KIMB S61 128 C8
Church Fields Rd
NROS/TKH DN11 113 M5
Churchfield Ter CUD/GR S72 61 M1 3
Church Field Vw
DONS/BSCR DN4 89 J8 1
Church Gn DEARNE S63 107 J1
Church Gv BSLYN/ROY S71 61 G3
HEM/SK/SE WF9 42 A5
MALT S66 132 E5
Church Hts STKB/PEN S36 57 K8
Church Hl BSLYN/ROY S71 39 H4
Churchill Av BTLY DN5 89 L2
HTFD DN7 49 J8
MALT S66 150 E1
Churchill Rd FUL S10 160 A4 1
STKB/PEN S36 101 K5
WHHL DN2 90 C1
Church La ARMTH DN3 47 J7
AU/AST/KP S26 164 D8
AWLS/ASK DN6 67 G1 1
BSLY S70 2 F4
BSLY S70 82 D5
BTLY DN5 66 A8
BTLY DN5 87 G5
BWTY DN10 154 E5
CUD/GR S72 39 L1
DEARNE S63 107 J1 2
DIN S25 166 B6
DIN S25 166 C7
DIN S25 167 J5
DOD/DAR S75 36 B4
DOD/DAR S75 58 D3
DONS/BSCR DN4 91 K8
DONS/BSCR DN4 111 H1
DONS/BSCR DN4 113 J1
ECK/KIL S21 194 C1
EPW DN9 115 J4 1
HACK/IN S12 179 G4
HAN/WDH S13 178 F1
HOR/CROF WF4 19 L3
HOR/CROF WF4 21 J8
HOY S74 104 C4
HTFD DN7 30 F8 1
KBTN HD8 35 K5
MALT S66 132 B2
MALT S66 148 F3
MALT S66 149 H2
MALT S66 150 D3
MOS S20 179 L4
NROS/TKH DN11 133 M1
NROS/TKH DN11 134 E8
NROS/TKH DN11 153 J3
RHAM S60 163 G1 1
RHAM S60 163 J3
RHAM/THRY S65 131 H4
STKB/PEN S36 57 K8
TOT/DORE S17 189 H1
WRKN S81 184 D3
Church Lane Ms MALT S66 149 H2
Church Lea HOY S74 105 J3
Church Meadow Rd
NROS/TKH DN11 113 M7
Church Ms ECK/KIL S21 180 C8
MEX/SWTN S64 109 G3
MOS S20 179 H8 1
Church Mt HEM/SK/SE WF9 42 A5
Church Rein Cl
DONS/BSCR DN4 111 G1 1
Church Rd ARMTH DN3 47 J7
ARMTH DN3 69 K3
CONI DN12 109 L3
CONI DN12 110 F4
DOD/DAR S75 58 C3
HTFD DN7 48 C3
NROS/TKH DN11 133 M1
NROS/TKH DN11 154 A3
Church St ARMTH DN3 91 L1
AU/AST/KP S26 180 F5
BSLY S70 2 F3
BSLYN/ROY S71 39 G4
BSLYN/ROY S71 39 H6
BTLY DN5 67 L7 2
BWTY DN10 154 E1
CHPT/GREN S35 125 G8
CHPT/GREN S35 126 E6
CONI DN12 110 A5
CUD/GR S72 40 D4
CUD/GR S72 61 M1
CUD/GR S72 63 J5
DEARNE S63 64 A7
DEARNE S63 86 A5
DEARNE S63 107 J1 3
DOD/DAR S75 37 J7
DOD/DAR S75 38 A6 3
DOD/DAR S75 58 C2
DOD/DAR S75 59 L4
DON DN1 4 F3
DRON S18 190 E6 1
DRON S18 191 J8
ECK/KIL S21 193 J3
HEM/SK/SE WF9 42 E5
HOLM/MEL HD7 54 D1 1
HOR/CROF WF4 19 K3
HOY S74 83 K8
HOY S74 105 L2
HTFD DN7 30 F8 2
KBTN HD8 17 G8
KIMB S61 128 C8
KIMB S61 128 E3
MALT S66 165 K1
MEX/SWTN S64 108 F3
MEX/SWTN S64 108 A4
MEX/SWTN S64 109 H3 1
RAW S62 129 J3
SHEF S1 9 H4
ST/HB/BR S6 159 G2
STKB/PEN S36 79 H4
STV/CWN S43 194 F8
THNE DN8 31 M8
WMB/DAR S73 84 F2
WRKN S81 168 C5
Church Ter HOLM/MEL HD7 53 L2
KBTN HD8 35 H6
Church Top HEM/SK/SE WF9 42 A5
Church Vw AU/AST/KP S26 164 C8
AU/AST/KP S26 181 K2
AWLS/ASK DN6 27 G7
BWTY DN10 154 E5 1
CONI DN12 110 E6
CUD/GR S72 61 M1
DOD/DAR S75 2 B1
DON DN1 4 F3
ECK/KIL S21 180 C8
HAN/WDH S13 179 G1
HEM/SK/SE WF9 42 A4
HOLM/MEL HD7 52 F5
HOR/CROF WF4 19 J2
HOY S74 104 F2
MALT S66 148 F3
NROS/TKH DN11 133 M1
RHAM/THRY S65 130 D4
STV/CWN S43 194 E8
Church View Cl HOR/CROF WF4 22 A6
Church View Crs STKB/PEN S36 79 H4
Church View Rd STKB/PEN S36 79 H4
Church Vls HEM/SK/SE WF9 42 A5
Church Wk CONI DN12 109 L3
NROS/TKH DN11 153 J3
WRKS S80 198 D4
Church Wy DON DN1 5 J1
RTFD DN22 187 L1
Cinder Bridge Rd RAW S62 129 G3
Cinder Hill La CHPT/GREN S35 126 B7
Cinderhill La SHEFS S8 177 G7
Cinderhill Rd KIMB S61 128 C5
Cinder Hills Rd HOLM/MEL HD7 53 M3
Cinder Hills Wy DOD/DAR S75 59 L8 1
Cinder La ECK/KIL S21 180 D8
Circle Cl SHEFP/MNR S2 161 M7
The Circle NROS/TKH DN11 113 J6
SHEFP/MNR S2 161 M6
The Circuit AWLS/ASK DN6 66 D1
Circular Dr ECK/KIL S21 193 M7
City Rd SHEFP/MNR S2 161 H5
Claire Ct RHAM S60 6 F2
Clanricarde St BSLYN/ROY S71 2 F1
Clara Pl KIMB S61 146 D1
Clarehurst Rd WMB/DAR S73 84 E1 1
Clarel Cl STKB/PEN S36 79 G5
Clarell Gdns DONS/BSCR DN4 91 J6
Clarel St STKB/PEN S36 79 G5
Claremont Crs FUL S10 8 B5
Claremont Pl FUL S10 8 B5
Claremont St KIMB S61 146 D1
Clarence Av DONS/BSCR DN4 89 M7
Clarence La SHEFP/MNR S2 8 E8
Clarence Pl MALT S66 150 E1
Clarence Rd BSLYN/ROY S71 60 F3
ST/HB/BR S6 143 M7
WRKS S80 198 C3
Clarence Sq DIN S25 166 E6 1
Clarence St DEARNE S63 85 H8 1
DIN S25 166 E6
Clarendon Dr WRKN S81 198 B1 1
Clarendon Rd ECC S11 159 J8
RHAM/THRY S65 7 J2
Clarendon St BSLY S70 2 D6
Clark Av CONI DN12 110 F7
DONS/BSCR DN4 5 K7
Clarke Av MALT S66 165 L1
Clarke Ct DIN S25 166 D5 1
Clarke Dell FUL S10 8 A8
Clarke Dr FUL S10 8 A8
Clarkegrove Rd FUL S10 8 A8
Clarkehouse Rd FUL S10 160 A6
Clarke Sq SHEFP/MNR S2 160 D7
Clarke St DEARNE S63 64 C7 2
DOD/DAR S75 2 D1
FUL S10 8 D7
Clark Gv ST/HB/BR S6 159 H1
Clarks Ct AWLS/ASK DN6 66 F1
Clarkson St BSLY S70 83 G2
FUL S10 8 C5
Clark St HOY S74 83 H8
Clarney Av WMB/DAR S73 84 D1
Clarney Pl WMB/DAR S73 84 D1
Clay Bank AWLS/ASK DN6 46 E2
Clay Bank Rd THNE DN8 50 C3
Claycliffe Av DOD/DAR S75 59 K3
Claycliffe Rd DOD/DAR S75 59 K2

Clayfield Av MEX/SWTN S64 109 H2
Clayfield La RAW S62 105 M6
Clayfield Rd MEX/SWTN S64 109 H2
Clayfields DONS/BSCR DN4 111 L2
Clayfield Vw MEX/SWTN S64 109 H2
Clay Flat La NROS/TKH DN11 113 K7
Claylands Av WRKN S81 183 M8
Claylands Cl WRKN S81 198 B1
Claylands La WRKN S81 198 B2
Clay La SHEF S1 9 H6
WHHL DN2 69 H7
Clay La West WHHL DN2 69 G6
Clay Pit La RAW S62 129 L2
Clay Pits La STKB/PEN S36 101 H5
Clayroyd BSLY S70 82 E3
Clay St DARN/MH S9 145 K8
Clayton Av DEARNE S63 63 M6
HEM/SK/SE WF9 25 J7
Clayton Crs MOS S20 179 J5
Clayton Dr DEARNE S63 63 M7
Clayton Hollow MOS S20 179 J5
Clayton Holt HEM/SK/SE WF9 41 M6
Clayton La BTLY DN5 65 G2
DEARNE S63 63 M6
Clayton Vw HEM/SK/SE WF9 41 M6
Clay Wheels La ST/HB/BR S6 143 M3
Claywood Dr SHEFP/MNR S2 9 L6
Claywood Rd SHEFP/MNR S2 9 M7
Clayworth Dr
DONS/BSCR DN4 90 F8 1
Clear Vw CUD/GR S72 40 E7
Clearwell Cft BTLY DN5 89 K2
Cleeve Hill Gdns MOS S20 179 H5
Clematis Rd SHEFN S5 145 K4
Clement Ms KIMB S61 146 C1 1
Clementson Rd FUL S10 160 A3 2
Clement St DARN/MH S9 161 M1
KIMB S61 146 C1
Clevedon Crs BTLY DN5 67 K6
Clevedon Wy BSLYN/ROY S71 38 F3 2
Cleveland Rd ARMTH DN3 92 A1
Cleveland St DON DN1 4 E7
ST/HB/BR S6 160 C2
Cleveland Wy HTFD DN7 48 F7
Clevland Cl WRKN S81 168 C8
Cliff Crs DONS/BSCR DN4 111 G1
Cliff Dr HOR/CROF WF4 19 H2
WMB/DAR S73 85 G2
Cliffe Av BSLY S70 82 F2
CHPT/GREN S35 81 H7
Cliffe Bank MEX/SWTN S64 108 B5
Cliffe Cl CUD/GR S72 40 D5
Cliffe Common La
CHPT/GREN S35 81 J8
Cliffe Ct BSLYN/ROY S71 61 G4
Cliffe Crs DOD/DAR S75 59 J8 2
Cliffedale Crs BSLY S70 82 F1
Cliffe Farm Dr ECC S11 159 L8 1
Cliffefield Rd MEX/SWTN S64 108 B5
SHEFS S8 176 D2
Cliffe Hl ST/HB/BR S6 142 C7
Cliffe House Rd SHEFN S5 144 F3
Cliffe La BSLYN/ROY S71 61 G4 3
HATH/EY S32 172 D7
Cliffe Rd ST/HB/BR S6 159 L2
WMB/DAR S73 84 F7
Cliffe St KBTN HD8 35 K5
Cliffe Vw KBTN HD8 35 K5
Cliffewood Ri KBTN HD8 35 J5 2
Cliff Gv HOR/CROF WF4 19 G3
Cliff Hl DOD/DAR S75 58 C2
MALT S66 150 B2
Cliff Hill Rd AWLS/ASK DN6 26 F4
Cliff Hills Cl MALT S66 150 C2
Cliff House La HOLM/MEL HD7 53 M1
Cliff La CUD/GR S72 40 C5
HOLM/MEL HD7 53 M2
Clifford Av RHAM/THRY S65 130 E5 1
Clifford Rd ECC S11 160 B8
HEM/SK/SE WF9 41 M5
KIMB S61 128 C6
MALT S66 149 L3
Clifford St CUD/GR S72 40 A6
HEM/SK/SE WF9 42 D5 3
Cliff Rd HOLM/MEL HD7 52 E3
HOLM/MEL HD7 53 M2
HOR/CROF WF4 19 G4
ST/HB/BR S6 159 H1
WMB/DAR S73 85 G3
Cliff St ECC S11 8 E9
MEX/SWTN S64 108 E3
Cliff Vw CONI DN12 109 K3
Clifton Av BSLYN/ROY S71 38 C7
DARN/MH S9 162 C4
HOLM/MEL HD7 53 M1
RHAM/THRY S65 7 L5
STV/CWN S43 194 E8
Clifton Bank RHAM/THRY S65 7 G5
Clifton Cl BSLYN/ROY S71 38 C7
Clifton Ct THNE DN8 31 L7
Clifton Crs BSLYN/ROY S71 38 D6
DARN/MH S9 162 B4
WHHL DN2 90 F1
Clifton Crs North
RHAM/THRY S65 7 J5
Clifton Crs South
RHAM/THRY S65 7 J5
Clifton Dr BTLY DN5 89 H5
Clifton Gdns CUD/GR S72 40 C4
Clifton Gv RHAM/THRY S65 7 K4
Clifton Hl CONI DN12 110 B6
Clifton La DARN/MH S9 162 C5
RHAM/THRY S65 7 H5
Clifton Mt RHAM/THRY S65 7 H5
Clifton Ri MALT S66 150 C1
Clifton Rd CUD/GR S72 40 E8
Clifton St BSLY S70 3 J8
DARN/MH S9 145 M7
HEM/SK/SE WF9 41 G1
Clifton Ter RHAM/THRY S65 7 H5
Clifton Vw KBTN HD8 35 K5 2
Clinthill La WRKS S80 196 C8
Clinton Pl FUL S10 8 D8
Clinton St WRKS S80 198 E6
Clipstone Av BSLYN/ROY S71 38 D7
Clipstone Gdns DARN/MH S9 162 A1
Clipstone Rd DARN/MH S9 162 A1
Clock Row Av HEM/SK/SE WF9 42 B4
Clock Row Gv HEM/SK/SE WF9 42 B4
Clock Row Mt HEM/SK/SE WF9 42 B4
The Cloisters DONS/BSCR DN4 91 L8
Cloisters Wy BSLYN/ROY S71 61 H5
Cloonmore Cft SHEFS S8 176 F6
Cloonmore Dr SHEFS S8 177 G6
Close Barn WRKN S81 184 E8 2
Close St HEM/SK/SE WF9 23 G8
The Close ARMTH DN3 92 B7
AWLS/ASK DN6 27 H4
BSLYN/ROY S71 39 G6
BSLYN/ROY S71 61 K4 1
BTLY DN5 64 A3
KBTN HD8 35 J5 3
Cloudberry Wy DOD/DAR S75 38 B7
Clough Bank KIMB S61 6 A2
SHEFP/MNR S2 160 F7
Clough Flds FUL S10 159 K3
Clough Fields Rd HOY S74 105 G2
Clough Foot La HOLM/MEL HD7 53 L8
Clough Ga HOR/CROF WF4 16 B2
Clough Gate Dr HOR/CROF WF4 16 B2
Clough Gn KIMB S61 6 B2
Clough Head STKB/PEN S36 79 H6
Clough House La KBTN HD8 57 G1
Clough La AWLS/ASK DN6 28 A4
ECC S11 174 E2
Clough Rd HOR/CROF WF4 17 H6
HOY S74 105 H2
KIMB S61 6 B4
SHEF S1 9 H9
Clough St KIMB S61 6 B3
The Clough EDL/UDV S33 172 B2
Clough Wood Vw
CHPT/GREN S35 143 H1
Clovelly Rd ARMTH DN3 69 K5
Clover Cl WRKN S81 184 F8
Clover Gdns SHEFN S5 145 J4
Clover Gn KIMB S61 128 B5
Cloverlands Dr DOD/DAR S75 38 A7
Club Garden Rd ECC S11 160 D7
Club Garden Wk SHEFP/MNR S2 8 F9
Club Mill Rd ST/HB/BR S6 144 C7
Club St BSLYN/ROY S71 61 G3
ECC S11 160 D7
HOY S74 104 F2 1
Clumber Pl WRKS S80 198 C4
Clumber Ri AU/AST/KP S26 180 C1 1
Clumber Rd DONS/BSCR DN4 5 M8
FUL S10 159 J6
Clumber St DOD/DAR S75 2 B4
Clun Rd ATT S4 161 G1
Clun St ATT S4 161 G1
Clyde Rd SHEFS S8 176 D1
Clyde St BSLYN/ROY S71 3 H6
Clyro Pl RTFD DN22 187 K1
Coach Gate La STKB/PEN S36 57 H5
Coach House Dr BTLY DN5 89 H2
Coach House La BSLY S70 82 D1 1
The Coach Houses FUL S10 8 A3 1
Coach Rd KIMB S61 128 F3
Coalbrook Av HAN/WDH S13 163 H7
Coalbrook Gv HAN/WDH S13 163 H7
Coalbrook Rd HAN/WDH S13 163 H7
Coalpit La KBTN HD8 56 D4
Coal Pit La CHPT/GREN S35 142 E2
CONI DN12 132 A5
CUD/GR S72 62 A2
HEM/SK/SE WF9 43 J3
HOLM/MEL HD7 54 C1
KBTN HD8 34 B7
PONT WF8 25 K4
STKB/PEN S36 101 M8
Coalpit Rd CONI DN12 109 J4
Coates La STKB/PEN S36 80 C5
Coates St SHEFP/MNR S2 9 M6
Cobb Ct MEX/SWTN S64 108 B6
Cobb Dr MEX/SWTN S64 108 A6
Cobbler Hall HOR/CROF WF4 18 D7
Cobcar Av HOY S74 105 M2
Cobcar Cl HOY S74 105 L1
Cobcar La HOY S74 105 L1
Cobcar St HOY S74 105 L2
Cobden Av MEX/SWTN S64 108 F2
Cobden Pl FUL S10 160 A3 3
Cobden View Rd FUL S10 159 M3
Cobnar Av SHEFS S8 176 E5
Cobnar Dr SHEFS S8 176 E5
Cobnar Gdns SHEFS S8 176 D5 2
Cobnar Rd SHEFS S8 176 D5
Cockayne Pl SHEFS S8 176 D3
Cockerham Av DOD/DAR S75 2 E2
Cockerham La DOD/DAR S75 2 E1
Cockermouth La
HOR/CROF WF4 16 A5
Cockhill Cl BWTY DN10 154 E1
Cockhill Field La MALT S66 132 E5
Cock Hill La BWTY DN10 154 D1
Cockhill La CONI DN12 132 F3
Cockshot La STKB/PEN S36 102 A8
Cockshutt Av SHEFS S8 176 B7
Cockshutt Dr SHEFS S8 176 B7
Cockshutt Rd SHEFS S8 176 B7
Cockshutts La CHPT/GREN S35 124 F6
Coggers La HATH/EY S32 172 D6
Coisley Hl HAN/WDH S13 178 D2
Coisley Rd HAN/WDH S13 178 E1
Coit La ECC S11 175 H4
Coke Hl RHAM S60 6 F6
Coke La RHAM S60 6 F6
Colbeck St WRKS S80 198 C4 1
Colby Pl ST/HB/BR S6 159 K2
Colchester Ct BTLY DN5 89 J1
Colchester Rd FUL S10 159 M3 3
Cold Hiendley Common La
HOR/CROF WF4 21 G6
Cold Side EDL/UDV S33 120 E5
Coldstream Av
DONS/BSCR DN4 111 H1
Coldwell Hl CHPT/GREN S35 124 F8
Coldwell La FUL S10 159 J4
Cold Well La HOLM/MEL HD7 52 F3
Coleford Rd DARN/MH S9 162 B2
Coleman St RAW S62 129 K4 3
Coleridge Av BSLYN/ROY S71 60 F3
Coleridge Rd ARMTH DN3 47 K7
DARN/MH S9 145 M8
DEARNE S63 85 G8
MALT S66 150 E3
RHAM/THRY S65 7 K2
WRKN S81 198 F2
Coley La RAW S62 106 B5
Colister Dr DARN/MH S9 161 M3
Colister Gdns DARN/MH S9 161 M4
Colleen Rd HOR/CROF WF4 19 J2
College La WRKS S80 198 F6
College Park Cl RHAM S60 147 J4
College Rd DON DN1 4 F6
ECK/KIL S21 194 A6
MEX/SWTN S64 108 F2
RHAM S60 6 C4
College St FUL S10 8 B6
RHAM/THRY S65 6 F4
Collegiate Crs FUL S10 8 B8
Colley Av BSLY S70 83 G1
SHEFN S5 144 E1
Colley Cl SHEFN S5 144 E1
Colley Crs BSLY S70 83 G1
SHEFN S5 144 F1
Colley Dr SHEFN S5 144 F1
Colley Pl BSLY S70 61 G8 1
Colley Rd SHEFN S5 144 E1
Colleywell Cl EPW DN9 117 M3 1
Colliers Cl HAN/WDH S13 178 F1
Colliers Wy KBTN HD8 35 K3
Colliery Cl DIN S25 166 C5
Colliery La DEARNE S63 86 B1
Colliery Rd ATT S4 145 L6
AU/AST/KP S26 181 H5
NROS/TKH DN11 153 M4
Colliery Yd DOD/DAR S75 104 B3
Collin Av ST/HB/BR S6 143 L6
Collindridge Rd WMB/DAR S73 84 B5
Collingbourne Av MOS S20 179 L6
Collingbourne Dr MOS S20 179 L6 3
Collingham Rd AU/AST/KP S26 180 A1
Collins Cl DOD/DAR S75 59 J8
Collins Rd SHEFN S5 144 E3
Colonel Ward Dr
MEX/SWTN S64 108 C4
Colster Cl DOD/DAR S75 59 L5
Colsterdale WRKN S81 184 F8
Coltfield BSLY S70 82 D6
Coltishall Av MALT S66 149 J1
Coltsworth La STV/CWN S43 195 H7
Columbia St BSLY S70 2 F9
Columbus Wy MALT S66 150 B1
Colver Rd SHEFP/MNR S2 160 E7
Colvin Cl BTLY DN5 68 C6
Colwall St DARN/MH S9 161 K1
Commerce St CHPT/GREN S35 126 E2
Commercial Rd DEARNE S63 86 A3
KBTN HD8 34 E5
Commercial St BSLY S70 3 J8
SHEF S1 9 K4
Common Farm Cl
RHAM/THRY S65 131 H7
Common Ing La
HOR/CROF WF4 21 M5
Common La ARMTH DN3 48 A8
AWLS/ASK DN6 27 L1
AWLS/ASK DN6 27 H4
BSLYN/ROY S71 39 G3
BTLY DN5 64 A2
BTLY DN5 68 E3
CONI DN12 110 B8
DEARNE S63 86 B7
DEARNE S63 107 M1
DIN S25 165 M3
DONS/BSCR DN4 111 H2
ECC S11 175 H2
EPW DN9 92 E8
GLE DN14 28 A2
HEM/SK/SE WF9 24 D8
HOR/CROF WF4 16 E6
HOR/CROF WF4 19 H7
KBTN HD8 16 C8
KBTN HD8 56 F1
MALT S66 165 H2
NROS/TKH DN11 134 E7
NROS/TKH DN11 135 G7
NROS/TKH DN11 135 M1
NROS/TKH DN11 153 H3
NROS/TKH DN11 153 J3 1
PONT WF8 24 F3
RHAM/THRY S65 131 L6
RTFD DN22 171 G3
STKB/PEN S36 102 C8
WKFDW/WTN WF2 20 D2
WRKN S81 169 M3
Common Rd AU/AST/KP S26 165 K6
AU/AST/KP S26 195 L2
CONI DN12 110 C7
CUD/GR S72 40 E4
DEARNE S63 63 M7
DIN S25 166 C5
HEM/SK/SE WF9 22 E5
WRKS S80 196 D2
Common Road Av
HEM/SK/SE WF9 41 L6
Commonside EPW DN9 117 M3
FUL S10 160 A3
The Common CHPT/GREN S35 126 F5
Commonwealth Vw
DEARNE S63 85 M5
Compton St ST/HB/BR S6 159 M1
Conalan Av TOT/DORE S17 189 M2
Conan Rd CONI DN12 109 M5
Concord Rd SHEFN S5 145 J1
Concord View Rd KIMB S61 146 A2
Conduit La FUL S10 160 A3 4
Conduit Rd FUL S10 160 A3
Cone La DOD/DAR S75 58 E8
STKB/PEN S36 80 D2
Conery Cl RHAM/THRY S65 130 E5
Coney Rd BTLY DN5 67 L3 1
Congress St SHEF S1 8 F4 1
Coningsburgh Rd ARMTH DN3 69 K5
Coningsby Rd SHEFN S5 145 G6
Coniston Av DOD/DAR S75 37 L5
Coniston Cl DIN S25 182 D1 1
STKB/PEN S36 79 H3
Coniston Dr DEARNE S63 86 A6
Coniston Pl BTLY DN5 67 K7 1
Coniston Rd ARMTH DN3 69 K3
AWLS/ASK DN6 28 A7
BSLYN/ROY S71 3 J5
DRON S18 190 C6
MEX/SWTN S64 109 G1
SHEFS S8 176 C2
WHHL DN2 91 G3
WRKN S81 184 C7
Coniston Ter SHEFS S8 176 C2 1
Connaught Dr ARMTH DN3 69 K3
Conrad Cl WRKS S80 198 F4
Conrad Dr MALT S66 150 C1
Constable Cl DRON S18 190 C7
GLV S14 177 J5 1
MALT S66 148 F2
Constable Dr SHEFS S8 177 H5
Constable La DIN S25 166 C6
Constable Pl DEARNE S63 107 J1
GLV S14 177 J5
Constable Rd SHEFS S8 177 H5
Constable Wy SHEFS S8 177 H5 1
Convent Gv DONS/BSCR DN4 91 H7
Convent Pl OWL S3 8 E5 2
Convent Wk OWL S3 8 E5
Conway Crs RHAM/THRY S65 130 A7
Conway Dr ARMTH DN3 92 B7
BTLY DN5 87 G4
WRKN S81 184 D1
Conway Pl WMB/DAR S73 84 D6
Conway St BSLY S70 61 H7
OWL S3 8 D6
Conway Ter MEX/SWTN S64 108 E1
Conyers Dr AU/AST/KP S26 164 B7
Conyers Rd BTLY DN5 89 M2
Coo Hl HAN/WDH S13 179 G1
Cook Av MALT S66 150 C1
Cooke St BTLY DN5 67 L7
Cookson Cl SHEFN S5 144 B3
Cookson Rd SHEFN S5 144 B4
Cookson St DONS/BSCR DN4 89 M7 2
Cooks Rd MOS S20 179 L5
Cooks Wood Rd OWL S3 144 E8
Coombe Pl FUL S10 160 A4 2
Coombe Rd FUL S10 159 M4
Co-operative St CUD/GR S72 61 L1 1
DEARNE S63 85 H8 2
Cooper La HOLM/MEL HD7 53 L2
STKB/PEN S36 57 M8
Cooper Rd DOD/DAR S75 37 G7
Coopers Ter DON DN1 5 H4
Cooper St DONS/BSCR DN4 5 J8
Co-op La HOLM/MEL HD7 53 H4
Copeland Rd WMB/DAR S73 84 A5 1
Cope St BSLY S70 3 H9
Copeworth Dr HOR/CROF WF4 19 K4
Copley Av CONI DN12 109 L5
Copley Crs BTLY DN5 89 G1
Copley Pl KIMB S61 128 E8
Copley Rd DON DN1 5 G3
Copperas Cl STKB/PEN S36 78 C4
Copper Beech Ct
WKFDW/WTN WF2 20 E1
Copper Cl BSLY S70 3 H7
Copper St OWL S3 9 G2
Coppice Av DOD/DAR S75 59 M3
HTFD DN7 70 E1
Coppice Cl STKB/PEN S36 101 K5
Coppice Gdns KIMB S61 128 F5
Coppice Gv HTFD DN7 48 F8
Coppice La ST/HB/BR S6 158 F3
Coppice Rd AWLS/ASK DN6 66 F5
WRKN S81 184 D8
The Coppice KIMB S61 128 A5
RTFD DN22 187 H2
Coppice Vw FUL S10 159 K4 1
Coppice Wy WRKN S81 168 D8
Coppicewood Ct
DONS/BSCR DN4 112 A3
Coppins Cl MALT S66 149 H1
Coppin Sq SHEFN S5 126 D8 1
The Copse MALT S66 149 H1
Copster Cl CHPT/GREN S35 80 D8
Copster La STKB/PEN S36 80 C6
Copthurst Rd HOLM/MEL HD7 53 H7
Coquet Av MALT S66 149 H3
Coral Cl AU/AST/KP S26 164 A5
Coral Dr AU/AST/KP S26 164 A5
Coral Pl AU/AST/KP S26 164 A5
Coral Wy AU/AST/KP S26 164 A5
Corby St ATT S4 161 H1
Corker Bottoms La
SHEFP/MNR S2 161 K4
Corker La ST/HB/BR S6 141 L7
Corker Rd HACK/IN S12 177 L1
Corn Hl CONI DN12 110 B6
Cornish St OWL S3 160 D2
Cornish Wy RAW S62 129 J5
Cornwall Cl BSLYN/ROY S71 60 F3
Cornwall Rd WHHL DN2 90 F2
WRKN S81 183 K8
Cornwell Cl RAW S62 107 G7
Corona Dr THNE DN8 31 M7
Coronation Av AU/AST/KP S26 181 G5
BWTY DN10 137 M4
CUD/GR S72 39 M4
CUD/GR S72 62 E1
DIN S25 166 D5
Coronation Br KIMB S61 6 A5
Coronation Dr DEARNE S63 85 M5
Coronation Gdns
DONS/BSCR DN4 111 G1 2
Coronation Rd DEARNE S63 107 L1
DOD/DAR S75 59 H3
DONS/BSCR DN4 89 M8
HOY S74 105 H1
HTFD DN7 48 D3
MEX/SWTN S64 108 C4
RAW S62 130 A1
STKB/PEN S36 101 M6
Coronation St BSLYN/ROY S71 61 G3
DEARNE S63 64 C8
WMB/DAR S73 84 F1
Coronation Ter BSLYN/ROY S71 61 K7
Corporation St BSLY S70 3 J9
OWL S3 9 H2
RHAM S60 6 E4
Cortina Ri WMB/DAR S73 84 C1 1
Cortworth La RAW S62 106 B6
Cortworth Rd ECC S11 175 L3
Corwen Pl HAN/WDH S13 178 E1
Cossey Rd ATT S4 161 G1
Cote La CHPT/GREN S35 102 E1
HOLM/MEL HD7 53 L7
Coterel Crs DONS/BSCR DN4 91 K6
Cotleigh Av HACK/IN S12 178 E4
Cotleigh Cl HACK/IN S12 178 E4 1
Cotleigh Crs HACK/IN S12 178 E4
Cotleigh Dr HACK/IN S12 178 E4
Cotleigh Gdns HACK/IN S12 178 E4
Cotleigh Pl HACK/IN S12 178 E4 2
Cotleigh Rd HACK/IN S12 178 E4
Cotleigh Wy HACK/IN S12 178 E4
Cotswold Av CHPT/GREN S35 126 C2
Cotswold Cl DOD/DAR S75 59 M5 2
HEM/SK/SE WF9 23 K8
Cotswold Crs RHAM S60 148 A5
Cotswold Dr AU/AST/KP S26 164 C8
BTLY DN5 88 E6
Cotswold Gdns BTLY DN5 67 K8 1
Cotswold Rd ST/HB/BR S6 143 M6
THNE DN8 49 L1
Cottage La ECC S11 175 G2
Cottam Cl RHAM S60 148 A6
Cottam Cft HEM/SK/SE WF9 23 J8
Cottam Rd CHPT/GREN S35 104 A8
Cottenham Rd RHAM/THRY S65 7 J2
Cottesmore Cl DOD/DAR S75 2 A2 1
Cottingham St DARN/MH S9 161 K3
Cotton Mill Rw OWL S3 9 H2
Cotton St OWL S3 9 H2
Coulman Rd THNE DN8 32 B7
Coulman St THNE DN8 32 A6
Coultas Av STKB/PEN S36 102 B7
Countess Rd SHEF S1 9 H8
County Wy BSLY S70 3 G3
Coupe Rd ATT S4 160 F1
Coupland Rd RHAM/THRY S65 130 A7
Court Cl BTLY DN5 89 H1
The Courtyard CONI DN12 109 G4
The Court Yd HOR/CROF WF4 19 L8 1
Coventry Dr WRKN S81 198 E1 2
Coventry Gv WHHL DN2 68 F8
Coventry Rd DARN/MH S9 162 A2
THNE DN8 32 A8
Cover Cl RAW S62 105 H6
Coverdale WRKN S81 184 F8
Coverdale Rd ABRD S7 176 C2
Cover Dr WMB/DAR S73 84 F1
Coverleigh Rd DEARNE S63 107 K3
Cove Rd EPW DN9 117 K2
Coward Dr CHPT/GREN S35 125 H8
Cowcliff Hill Rd HOLM/MEL HD7 54 B7
Cow Gap La ST/HB/BR S6 142 B8
Cow House La ARMTH DN3 92 A1
Cowick Rd GLE DN14 31 J1
Cow La ECC S11 175 L4
HOR/CROF WF4 22 A6
Cowley Bottom DRON S18 190 C7
Cowley Dr CHPT/GREN S35 127 G3
Cowley Gdns MOS S20 179 J7
Cowley Gn WMB/DAR S73 83 M5
Cowley Hl CHPT/GREN S35 127 G3
Cowley La DRON S18 189 M7
Cowley Pl ARMTH DN3 69 K3 1
Cowley Rd CHPT/GREN S35 143 H1
Cowley View Rd
CHPT/GREN S35 126 F4
Cowlishaw Rd ECC S11 160 A7
Cowood St MEX/SWTN S64 108 D2 4
Cowper Av ST/HB/BR S6 144 B1
Cowper Cl WRKN S81 198 F2
Cowper Crs ST/HB/BR S6 144 B1
Cowper Dr RHAM/THRY S65 147 M3
ST/HB/BR S6 144 B1
Cowper Rd MEX/SWTN S64 109 G2
Cowrakes Cl RHAM S60 148 A6
Cow Rakes La RHAM S60 148 A6
Coxley Crs HOR/CROF WF4 18 B1
Coxley Vw HOR/CROF WF4 18 A2
Cox Pl ST/HB/BR S6 143 K6
Cox Rd ST/HB/BR S6 143 K7
Crabgate Dr AWLS/ASK DN6 44 C5
Crabgate La AWLS/ASK DN6 44 C5
Crab La WKFDW/WTN WF2 19 M3
Crabtree Cl SHEFN S5 145 G6
Crabtree Crs SHEFN S5 145 G6
Crabtree Dr CUD/GR S72 63 H4
SHEFN S5 145 G6
Crab Tree La PONT WF8 25 M5
Crabtree La SHEFN S5 144 F7
Crabtree Pl SHEFN S5 144 F6
Crabtree Rd HTFD DN7 48 D6
SHEFN S5 144 F6
Cradley Dr AU/AST/KP S26 164 C8
Cradock Ms SHEFP/MNR S2 161 J8 1
Cradock Rd SHEFP/MNR S2 161 J8
Cragdale Gv MOS S20 179 H8
Crags Rd CONI DN12 109 M3
Crag Vw CHPT/GREN S35 102 E1
Crag View Cl CHPT/GREN S35 125 H7
Crag View Crs CHPT/GREN S35 125 G7
Craigston Rd WRKN S81 184 C1
Craig Wk MALT S66 149 J2
Craithie Rd WHHL DN2 5 M2
WRKN S81 184 C1
Crakehall Rd CHPT/GREN S35 126 E4
Cramfit Cl DIN S25 182 B1
Cramfit Crs DIN S25 166 B7
Cramfit Rd DIN S25 166 A8
Cramlands DOD/DAR S75 59 L8 2
Cranberry Rd STKB/PEN S36 101 H1
Cranborne Dr DOD/DAR S75 37 K6 1
Cranbrook St BSLY S70 2 C8
Crane Dr KIMB S61 128 C8
Crane Greave La
CHPT/GREN S35 81 G8
Crane Moor Cl BTLY DN5 87 G5
Crane Moor Nook
CHPT/GREN S35 102 F1
Crane Moor Rd
CHPT/GREN S35 102 F1
Crane Rd KIMB S61 128 C5
Crane Well La DEARNE S63 86 C5
Cranfield Cl ARMTH DN3 91 M2
Cranfield Dr AWLS/ASK DN6 44 D5
Cranford Ct MOS S20 178 E5 2
Cranford Dr HACK/IN S12 178 E4
Cranford Gdns BSLYN/ROY S71 38 F3

Cranleigh Gdns *AWLS/ASK* DN6.... **66** E2
Cranston Cl *BSLYN/ROY* S71 .... **61** H3
Cranwell Rd *DONS/BSCR* DN4 .... **113** M1
Cranworth Cl *RHAM/THRY* S65.... **7** K2
Cranworth Pl *OWL* S3 .... **160** F1 ⬚
Cranworth Rd *OWL* S3 .... **160** F1 ⬚
   RHAM/THRY S65.... **7** K1
Craven La *BSLYN/ROY* S71 .... **38** F3
   DARN/MH S9 .... **162** A2 ⬚
   DONS/BSCR DN4 .... **91** J7 ⬚
Craven Rd *HEM/SK/SE* WF9.... **41** H1
   HTFD DN7 .... **48** D7
Craven St *OWL* S3 .... **8** C2
   RAW S62 .... **129** K4
Craven Wood Cl *DOD/DAR* S75.... **59** L4
Crawford Rd *SHEFS* S8 .... **176** D3
Crawley Av *HEM/SK/SE* WF9.... **42** B4
Crawshaw Gv *SHEFS* S8 .... **176** B7
Crawshaw La *HOR/CROF* WF4.... **16** C1
Crawshaw Rd *DONS/BSCR* DN4 .... **4** B7
Cream St *SHEFP/MNR* S2 .... **9** J9
Crecy Av *WHHL* DN2 .... **91** G3
Creighton Av *RAW* S62 .... **129** M2 ⬚
Cresacre Av *BTLY* DN5 .... **87** G4
The Crescent East *MALT* S66 .... **149** C1
The Crescent End *MALT* S66 .... **165** K1
Crescent Rd *ABRD* S7 .... **160** C8
   HOR/CROF WF4 .... **22** A6
The Crescent *ARMTH* DN3.... **69** K5
   ARMTH DN3.... **92** A2
   AWLS/ASK DN6 .... **66** D3
   CONI DN12.... **109** L5
   CONI DN12 .... **110** F5
   DEARNE S63.... **86** A4
   DIN S25 .... **166** E6
   DOD/DAR S75 .... **59** M3
   DRON S18 .... **189** L7
   EPW DN9 .... **115** K2
   HOLM/MEL HD7 .... **54** C1 ⬚
   HOR/CROF WF4 .... **18** B2
   HTFD DN7 .... **48** D6
   MALT S66 .... **165** L1
   MEX/SWTN S64.... **107** M5
   NROS/TKH DN11 .... **154** A3
   TOT/DORE S17 .... **189** J2
The Crescent West *MALT* S66 .... **130** F8
Cresswell Rd *DARN/MH* S9 .... **162** A3 ⬚
   MEX/SWTN S64 .... **108** E3
   WRKS S80 .... **198** C3
Cresswell St *DOD/DAR* S75 .... **2** A4
   MEX/SWTN S64 .... **108** D3 ⬚
   WRKS S80 .... **198** C4 ⬚
Crest Rd *SHEFN* S5 .... **144** F3
Crestwood Ct *SHEFN* S5 .... **145** G3
Crestwood Gdns *SHEFN* S5 .... **145** G3 ⬚
Creswick Av *SHEFS* S8 .... **126** C8
Creswick Cl *RHAM/THRY* S65.. **130** B7
Creswick Greave *SHEFN* S5 .... **126** C8
Creswick La *CHPT/GREN* S35.. **126** C7
Creswick Rd *RHAM/THRY* S65.. **130** B7
Creswick St *ST/HB/BR* S6 .... **160** B1
Creswick Wy *SHEFS* S8 .... **160** B1
Crewe Rd *NROS/TKH* DN11 .... **153** M8
Crich Av *BSLYN/ROY* S71 .... **38** E8
Cricketers Cl *FEA/AMT* WF7 .... **23** L2
Cricket Inn Cr *SHEFP/MNR* S2 .. **161** J5
Cricket Inn Rd *SHEFP/MNR* S2 .. **9** H5
Cricket View Rd *RAW* S62 .... **105** H6
Cridling Gdns *AWLS/ASK* DN6 .... **27** J7
Crimicar Av *FUL* S10 .... **158** F7
Crimicar Cl *FUL* S10 .... **158** F7
Crimicar Dr *FUL* S10 .... **158** F7
Crimicar La *FUL* S10 .... **159** C8
Cripps Av *MEX/SWTN* DN11 .... **113** L6
Cripps Cl *MALT* S66 .... **150** F3
Crispin Cl *HACK/IN* S12 .... **177** L3 ⬚
Crispin Gdns *HACK/IN* S12 .... **177** L3 ⬚
Crispin Rd *HACK/IN* S12 .... **177** L3 ⬚
Croasdale Gdns
   AWLS/ASK DN6 .... **45** G7 ⬚
Crochley Cl *DONS/BSCR* DN4 .... **91** K6 ⬚
Croft Abbey *ECK/KIL* S21 .... **194** A7
Croft Av *BSLYN/ROY* S71 .... **38** D3 ⬚
Croft Chantry *HEM/SK/SE* WF9 .. **22** E5
Croft Cl *DOD/DAR* S75 .... **37** L6
   ECC S11 .... **175** K4 ⬚
Croft Ct *ARMTH* DN3.... **69** K4
   EPW DN9 .... **115** K4
Croft Dr *BSLYN/ROY* S71 .... **38** D3 ⬚
   DOD/DAR S75 .... **37** M6
   NROS/TKH DN11 .... **134** E7
   STKB/PEN S36.... **78** E2
Crofters Cl *WRKS* S80 .... **194** A3
Croft Head *KBTN* HD8.... **34** E5
Croft La *ECC* S11 .... **175** K4
Croft Lea *DRON* S18 .... **190** D6
Crofton Av *ST/HB/BR* S6 .... **143** M5
Crofton Cl *DRON* S18 .... **190** D6
Crofton Dr *DEARNE* S63.... **86** A4
Crofton Ri *CHPT/GREN* S35 .... **126** B3
   DRON S18 .... **190** D6
Croft Rd *BSLY* S70 .... **61** C8
   BWTH DN10 .... **115** K5
   DONS/BSCR DN4.... **111** J2
   HACK/IN S12 .... **177** M2
   HOY S74 .... **83** H8
   RHAM S60 .... **146** F6
Crofts Dr *RHAM/THRY* S65 .... **130** C5 ⬚
Crofts La *HTFD* DN7 .... **48** A3
The Crofts *HATH/EY* S32 .... **172** E7 ⬚
   KBTN HD8.... **17** C8
   MALT S66 .... **148** F4
   RHAM S60 .... **6** F5 ⬚
Croft St *BSLY* S70 .... **82** E2 ⬚
   KIMB S61 .... **128** F4
The Croft *BTLY* DN5 .... **68** C4
   CONI DN12.... **110** A6
   DOD/DAR S75 .... **59** J2
   HEM/SK/SE WF9.... **24** B4
   HOR/CROF WF4 .... **18** D7
   HOY S74 .... **105** L2 ⬚
   MEX/SWTN S64 .... **107** M5
   RHAM S60 .... **163** C3
   STKB/PEN S36.... **79** K1
   THNE DN8.... **50** A2
   WRKS S80 .... **198** D5

Cromarty Ri *DRON* S18.... **190** B5
Cromer Cl *RAW* S62 .... **129** K1 ⬚
Cromer Rd *WHHL* DN2.... **91** G3
Cromer St *CUD/GR* S72.... **40** F8
Cromford Av *BSLYN/ROY* S71.... **60** F1
Cromford St *SHEFP/MNR* S2.... **9** J9
   BTLY DN5.... **89** K3
Crompton Av *BSLY* S70 .... **2** C8
Crompton Rd *WHHL* DN2.... **68** F7
Cromwell Cl *WRKS* S80.... **184** B7
Cromwell Ct *AWLS/ASK* DN6.... **44** D6 ⬚
Cromwell Dr *BTLY* DN5.... **89** J3
Cromwell Gv *AWLS/ASK* DN6.... **44** E5 ⬚
Cromwell Mt *BSLY* S70.... **82** C1
Cromwell Rd *BTLY* DN5.... **89** M2
   MEX/SWTN S64.... **108** E3
Cromwell St *DEARNE* S63.... **64** C6
   ST/HB/BR S6.... **160** A2
Cronkhill La *BSLYN/ROY* S71.... **39** H6
Crooke La *CONI* DN12.... **109** H8
Crooked Lane Head
   NROS/TKH DN11.... **152** C2
Crooke House La
   BSLYN/ROY S71.... **62** D6
Crookes Cl *FUL* S10.... **159** M3
Crookes Broom Av *HTFD* DN7... **48** F8
Crookes Broom La *HTFD* DN7.... **48** F8
Crookes La *BSLYN/ROY* S71.... **39** G6
Crookesmoor Dr *ST/HB/BR* S6 .. **8** B1
Crookes Rd
   DONS/BSCR DN4.... **111** M1 ⬚
   FUL S10.... **160** A4
Crookes St *BSLY* S70.... **2** C5
Crookes Valley Rd *FUL* S10.... **8** B3
Crookhill Rd *CONI* DN12.... **110** B5
Crook Tree La *HTFD* DN7.... **49** J5
Cropton Rd *BSLYN/ROY* S71.... **38** F4
Crosby Av *MALT* S66.... **149** J2
Crosby Cl *BSLYN/ROY* S71.... **61** H2
Crosby Rd *SHEFS* S8.... **176** B5
Crosby St *CUD/GR* S72.... **39** M7 ⬚
Cross Allen Rd *MOS* S20.... **179** K5
Cross Bank *DONS/BSCR* DN4.... **89** M7
Cross Burgess St *SHEF* S1.... **9** G5
Cross Butcher St *DEARNE* S63 .. **64** A7 ⬚
Cross Chantry Rd *SHEFS* S8.... **176** E4
Crosscourt Vw
   DONS/BSCR DN4.... **91** G7
Cross Dr *HAN/WDH* S13.... **178** F1 ⬚
Crossfield Ct *HOR/CROF* WF4.... **17** K1 ⬚
Crossfield Dr *AWLS/ASK* DN6.... **44** E5
   DEARNE S63.... **107** J2
Cross Field Dr *WRKN* S81.... **183** K4
Crossfield House Cl
   AWLS/ASK DN6.... **44** E5 ⬚
Crossfield La *AWLS/ASK* DN6.... **44** E6
Crossfields *HOR/CROF* WF4.... **17** L1 ⬚
Cross Ga *BTLY* DN5.... **89** L1
Crossgate *DEARNE* S63.... **64** B8
   DOD/DAR S75.... **37** M6
Cross Ga *MEX/SWTN* S64.... **109** G3
Cross Gate Rd *HOLM/MEL* HD7 .. **53** M5
Crossgates *NROS/TKH* DN11.... **134** A1
Cross Hands La *HOR/CROF* WF4 .. **22** F1
Cross HI *CHPT/GREN* S35.... **127** G8
   CUD/GR S72.... **40** D4
   HEM/SK/SE WF9.... **23** H8
Cross Hill Cl *SHEFP/MNR* S2.... **127** G8
Cross Hill Ct *AWLS/ASK* DN6.... **44** D5
Crosshill La *GLE* DN14.... **11** G5
Crosshouse Cl *CHPT/GREN* S35 .. **125** M7
Cross House Rd
   CHPT/GREN S35.... **126** A7
Cross Keys La *SHEFP/MNR* S2 .... **104** F1
Crossland Dr *HACK/IN* S12.... **177** L4
Crossland Pl *HACK/IN* S12.... **177** L3
Crossland Rd *HATH/EY* S32.... **172** E8
Crossland St *MEX/SWTN* S64.... **108** B5
Cross La *BSLYN/ROY* S71.... **39** J4
   BWTH DN10.... **137** G2
   CHPT/GREN S35.... **103** M5
   DRON S18.... **190** E6
   DRON S18.... **191** G4
   FUL S10.... **159** M4
   HOLM/MEL HD7.... **54** A5
   KBTN HD8.... **17** H7
   KBTN HD8.... **34** E6
   KBTN HD8.... **55** J1
   SHEFS S8.... **191** G2
   STKB/PEN S36.... **57** K7
   STKB/PEN S36.... **79** L8
   STKB/PEN S36.... **101** J5
   TOT/DORE S17.... **189** J2
Cross Lane Cl *WRKS* S81.... **183** K3
Crossley Cl *MALT* S66.... **150** C1
Crossley Hill La *WRKN* S81.... **185** G3
Cross Myrtle Rd
   SHEFP/MNR S2.... **160** F8
Cross Park Rd *SHEFS* S8.... **176** E2 ⬚
Cross Riding *DONS/BSCR* DN4.... **91** J3
Cross Rd *HOR/CROF* WF4.... **17** M1
   HOR/CROF WF4.... **19** K4
   HTFD DN7.... **50** A8
Cross Road Banner *ECC* S11.... **175** M2
Cross Smithfield *OWL* S3.... **8** F2
Cross South St *KIMB* S61.... **129** G4
Cross St *BSLY* S70.... **82** F2
   BSLYN/ROY S71.... **61** G3
   BTLY DN5.... **67** M6
   CONI DN12.... **110** F5
   CUD/GR S72.... **62** F1
   CUD/GR S72.... **63** J6
   DEARNE S63.... **86** C2
   DEARNE S63.... **107** J1
   DOD/DAR S75.... **2** D1
   DONS/BSCR DN4.... **89** L8 ⬚
   ECK/KIL S21.... **180** D8
   HAN/WDH S13.... **178** F1
   HEM/SK/SE WF9.... **23** G8
   HEM/SK/SE WF9.... **25** H7
   HOY S74.... **104** F2 ⬚
   KIMB S61.... **129** G4 ⬚
   KIMB S61.... **146** E1
   MALT S66.... **149** H2
   MALT S66.... **150** E2
   MALT S66.... **165** J1
   NROS/TKH DN11.... **113** K7

RAW S62.... **129** K4
RHAM/THRY S65.... **130** C5
WRKN S81.... **168** C5
The Cross *WRKN* S81.... **184** E1
Cross Turner St *SHEFP/MNR* S2 .. **9** K6
Crossway *MEX/SWTN* S64.... **107** M5
Crossways *DEARNE* S63.... **86** A5
   HTFD DN7.... **48** D3 ⬚
   WHHL DN2.... **68** F8
Crossways North *WHHL* DN2.... **68** F8
Crossways South *WHHL* DN2 .... **90** F8
The Crossways
   SHEFP/MNR S2.... **161** M6 ⬚
Crow Croft La *GLE* DN14.... **11** L6
Crowden Wk *DOD/DAR* S75.... **59** L6 ⬚
Crowder Av *SHEFN* S5.... **144** E3
Crowder Cl *SHEFN* S5.... **144** E4
Crowder Crs *SHEFN* S5.... **144** E4
Crowder Rd *SHEFN* S5.... **144** E3
Crowgate *DIN* S25.... **182** A4
Crowland Rd *SHEFN* S5.... **144** F3
Crowley Dr *DEARNE* S63.... **107** J3
Crow La *DRON* S18.... **191** K8
Crowley Dr *DEARNE* S63.... **107** J3
Crown Av *BSLY* S70.... **3** J9 ⬚
   CUD/GR S72.... **62** A3
Crown Cl *BSLY* S70.... **3** H9
Crown Hill Rd *DOD/DAR* S75.... **59** L6
Crownhill Rd *RHAM* S60.... **146** E6
Crown La *HOLM/MEL* HD7.... **53** L2 ⬚
Crown Pl *SHEFP/MNR* S2.... **9** L4
Crown Rd *NROS/TKH* DN11.... **134** D8
Crown St *BSLY* S70.... **60** E8 ⬚
   HOY S74.... **105** H1
   KBTN HD8.... **35** H6
   MEX/SWTN S64.... **108** D3
   WRKS S80.... **198** C3
Crown Well HI
   BSLYN/ROY S71.... **61** K7 ⬚
Crown Yd *HEM/SK/SE* WF9.... **42** B4
Crowther Pl *SHEFP/MNR* S2.... **160** D7 ⬚
Crow Tree Bank *THNE* DN8.... **50** F7
Crow Tree La *MEX/SWTN* S64.... **86** D8
Croydon St *ECC* S11.... **160** D7 ⬚
Cruck Cl *DRON* S18.... **190** C5
Cruise Rd *ECC* S11.... **159** K7 ⬚
Crummock Rd *SHEFS* S8.... **176** C2 ⬚
Crummock Wy
   BSLYN/ROY S71.... **61** M7 ⬚
Crumpsall Dr *ST/HB/BR* S6.... **144** D6
Crumpsall Rd *SHEFN* S5.... **144** D6
Crumwell Rd *KIMB* S61.... **128** B5
Crusader Dr *BTLY* DN5.... **89** J4
Cubley Av *WKFDW/WTN* WF2.... **19** M1
Cubley Rise Rd *STKB/PEN* S36 .. **79** G6
Cuckoo Holt *WRKN* S81.... **184** A8 ⬚
Cuckoo La *HTFD* DN7.... **49** G7
Cuckoo Wy *AU/AST/KP* S26.... **182** B6
   ECK/KIL S21.... **193** M2
   RTFD DN22.... **187** C5
Cuckstool Rd *KBTN* HD8.... **56** E1
Cudworth Vw *CUD/GR* S72.... **62** E1
Cullabine Rd *SHEFP/MNR* S2.... **161** L8
Cumberland Av *WHHL* DN2.... **90** F3
Cumberland Cl *BSLY* S70.... **82** D2
   HOY S74.... **83** J8
   NROS/TKH DN11.... **154** B3
   WRKN S81.... **168** D8
Cumberland Crs
   CHPT/GREN S35.... **126** F3 ⬚
Cumberland Dr *BSLYN/ROY* S71 .. **61** K7
Cumberland Rd *HOY* S74.... **83** J8
Cumberland Wy *DEARNE* S63.... **86** A6
   SHEF S1.... **9** G7
Cumberworth La *KBTN* HD8.... **34** B8
   KBTN HD8.... **55** J2
Cumberworth Rd *KBTN* HD8.... **34** D6
Cumbria Rd *WRKN* S81.... **198** E1
Cumwell La *MALT* S66.... **149** K4
Cundy St *ST/HB/BR* S6.... **160** A2
Cunliffe St *DRON* S18.... **191** G3
Cunningham Cl *BWTY* DN10.... **155** K7
Cunningham Rd *DON* S18.... **5** H7
   HTFD DN7.... **71** K7
Cupola *OWL* S3.... **9** G2
Cupola La *CHPT/GREN* S35.... **126** A6
Cupola Yd *RHAM* S60.... **6** E2
Curlew Av *ECK/KIL* S21.... **192** F4
Curlew Rdg *SHEFP/MNR* S2.... **161** H5
Curlew Ri *KIMB* S61.... **127** L1
Curzen Crs *ARMTH* DN3.... **69** L3
Curzon Av *DRON* S18.... **190** D7
Curzon Cl *ECK/KIL* S21.... **194** B1
Curzon Dr *WRKN* S81.... **198** D1
Cusworth La *BTLY* DN5.... **89** J2
Cusworth Wy *WRKS* S80.... **198** B4
Cuthbert Bank Rd
   ST/HB/BR S6.... **144** B8
Cuthbert Rd *ST/HB/BR* S6.... **144** B8
Cutler Cl *ECK/KIL* S21.... **179** M8 ⬚
Cutlers Av *BSLY* S70.... **2** C8
Cutthroat Br *EDL/UDV* S33.... **156** A4
Cuttlehurst *KBTN* HD8.... **35** H6
Cutts Av *DEARNE* S63.... **107** H2
Cutts Field Vw
   BSLYN/ROY S71.... **38** F2 ⬚
Cutts Ter *SHEFS* S8.... **160** D8 ⬚
Cutty La *DOD/DAR* S75.... **2** C2
Cyclops St *ATT* S4.... **145** J7
Cypress Av *EPW* DN9.... **114** D4
   SHEFS S8.... **177** G6
Cypress Cl *ECK/KIL* S21.... **194** A2 ⬚
Cypress Ga *CHPT/GREN* S35.... **126** D3
Cypress Gv *CONI* DN12.... **109** K7
Cypress Rd *BSLY* S70.... **3** M9
   BSLY S70.... **60** F8
Cyprus Rd *SHEFS* S8.... **176** E2 ⬚

D

Dadley Rd *WRKN* S81.... **168** D8
Dadsley Ct *NROS/TKH* DN11 .... **134** D7 ⬚
Dadsley Rd *NROS/TKH* DN11.... **134** D8
Daffodil Rd *SHEFN* S5.... **145** K4
Dagnam Cl *SHEFP/MNR* S2.... **177** K1
Dagnam Crs *SHEFP/MNR* S2.... **161** K8

Dagnam Dr *SHEFP/MNR* S2.... **161** K8
Dagnam Pl *SHEFP/MNR* S2 .... **177** K1 ⬚
Dagnam Rd *SHEFP/MNR* S2.... **161** K8
Daisy Bank *OWL* S3.... **8** D2
Daisy Lee La *HOLM/MEL* HD7.... **54** A8
Daisy Fold *HEM/SK/SE* WF9.... **24** D7 ⬚
Daisy Wk *MOS* S20.... **179** J4
   OWL S3.... **8** E3
Dalbury Rd *DRON* S18.... **189** M6
Dalby Gdns *MOS* S20.... **179** L6
Dalby Gv *MOS* S20.... **179** L5
Dale Av *RHAM/THRY* S65.... **148** A3
Dale Cl *BSLYN/ROY* S71.... **38** E8 ⬚
   KBTN HD8.... **56** D7
Dale Crs *HATH/EY* S32.... **172** F7
Dale Cft *KBTN* HD8.... **34** E5
   ST/HB/BR S6.... **141** L3
Dalecroft Rd *AWLS/ASK* DN6.... **44** F7
Dale Green Rd *BSLY* S70.... **82** D2
Dale Gv *DEARNE* S63.... **85** M6
Dale Hill Cl *MALT* S66.... **150** D1 ⬚
Dale Hill Rd *MALT* S66.... **132** C8
Dale La *HEM/SK/SE* WF9.... **42** E7
Dale Pit Rd *HTFD* DN7.... **71** K2 ⬚
Dale Rd *CONI* DN12.... **110** A5
   DRON S18.... **190** F7
   ECK/KIL S21.... **194** C1
   MALT S66.... **148** E3
   RAW S62.... **129** K1
   RHAM/THRY S65.... **148** A2
   ST/HB/BR S6.... **141** D4
Dale St *RAW* S62.... **129** K1
Dalestorth Av *SHEFS* S8.... **176** D4
Daleswood Av *BSLY* S70.... **59** M6 ⬚
Daleswood Dr *BSLY* S70.... **83** H2 ⬚
The Dale *HATH/EY* S32.... **173** C7
   SHEFS S8.... **176** D4
Dale Vw *HEM/SK/SE* WF9.... **41** K1
   WRKN S81.... **184** F8
Daleview Rd *SHEFS* S8.... **176** B5
Dalewood Av *SHEFS* S8.... **176** A6
Dalewood Dr *SHEFS* S8.... **175** M6
Dalewood Rd *SHEFS* S8.... **176** A6
Dalmore Rd *ECC* S11.... **176** A2
Dalroyd La *ST/HB/BR* S6.... **142** B4
Dalton Ct *SHEFS* S8.... **160** D8 ⬚
Dalton La *RHAM/THRY* S65.... **130** B7
Damasel Cl *CHPT/GREN* S35 .. **124** F6 ⬚
Damasel La *CHPT/GREN* S35.... **124** F6
Damasel Rd *CHPT/GREN* S35 .. **124** F5 ⬚
Dame La *BWTY* DN10.... **137** M4
Damer St *FUL* S10.... **8** B5
Dam Rd *NROS/TKH* DN11.... **152** E1
Damsteads *DOD/DAR* S75.... **58** E8
Danby La *WKFDW/WTN* WF2.... **20** A3
Danby Rd *AU/AST/KP* S26.... **181** K4
Dance La *CHPT/GREN* S35.... **81** H8
Danebrook Cl
   SHEFP/MNR S2.... **162** A6 ⬚
Danebrook Dr
   SHEFP/MNR S2.... **162** A6 ⬚
Danesfield Rd *WRKS* S80.... **198** D6
Daneshill Rd *RTFD* DN22.... **171** J7
Danes La *HOR/CROF* WF4.... **17** M1
Danesleigh Dr *HOR/CROF* WF4 .. **17** M1
Danesthorpe Cl *WHHL* DN2.... **91** G1
Dane St *DEARNE* S63.... **64** C7
Dane St North *DEARNE* S63.... **64** C7
Dane St South *DEARNE* S63.... **64** C7
Danesway *BTLY* DN5.... **67** K6
Danethorpe Wy *CONI* DN12.... **109** L7 ⬚
Danewood Av *SHEFP/MNR* S2 .. **162** A7
Danewood Cft *SHEFP/MNR* S2 .. **162** A6
Danewood Gdns
   SHEFP/MNR S2.... **162** A6
Daniel Hl *ST/HB/BR* S6.... **160** C2
Daniel Hill Ct *ST/HB/BR* S6.... **160** B2 ⬚
Daniel Hill St *ST/HB/BR* S6.... **160** B2
Daniel Hill Ter *ST/HB/BR* S6 .. **160** C2 ⬚
Daniel La *RAW* S62.... **128** F1
Daniels Dr *AU/AST/KP* S26.... **164** A6
Dannemora Dr *DARN/MH* S9 .. **146** A8
Danum Cl *THNE* DN8.... **32** A8
Danum Dr *RHAM/THRY* S65.... **7** K3
Danum Rd *DONS/BSCR* DN4.... **5** F1 ⬚
   HTFD DN7.... **70** F1 ⬚
Dara St *DARN/MH* S9.... **145** M2
Darcy St *AU/AST/KP* S26.... **164** B7 ⬚
Darcy Rd *ECK/KIL* S21.... **193** G4
Daresbury Dr *SHEFP/MNR* S2 .. **177** H1
Daresbury Pl *SHEFP/MNR* S2 .. **177** H1
Daresbury Rd *SHEFP/MNR* S2 .. **177** H1
Daresbury Vw *SHEFP/MNR* S2 .. **177** H1 ⬚
Darfield Av *MOS* S20.... **178** D5 ⬚
Darfield Cl *MOS* S20.... **178** D5 ⬚
   NROS/TKH DN11.... **113** M6
Darfield Rd *CUD/GR* S72.... **62** B3
Dargle Av *WHHL* DN2.... **90** E2
Dark La *BSLY* S70.... **59** M8
   BSLY S70.... **82** K4
   STKB/PEN S36.... **100** B2
Darley *BSLY* S70.... **83** G3
Darley Av *BSLY* S70.... **82** C1
Darley Cl *AU/AST/KP* S26.... **195** J1 ⬚
   BSLYN/ROY S71.... **60** E1
Darley Gv *ST/HB/BR* S6.... **143** H8
Darley Ter *DOD/DAR* S75.... **3** C4
Darley Yd *BSLY* S70.... **82** F3
Darlington Gv *THNE* DN8.... **32** A4
Darnall Dr *DARN/MH* S9.... **161** M2
Darnall Rd *DARN/MH* S9.... **161** M2
Darning La *PONT* WF8.... **24** F2
Darrington Dr
   DONS/BSCR DN4.... **111** H2
Darrington Pl *BSLYN/ROY* S71 .. **61** K4
Dart Gv *EPW* DN9.... **92** E8
Darton Hall Cl *DOD/DAR* S75.... **37** K4
Darton La *DOD/DAR* S75.... **37** L7
Darton Rd *DOD/DAR* S75.... **58** D2
Darton St *BSLY* S70.... **61** H7
Dartree Wk *WMB/DAR* S73.... **84** D1
Dart Sq *OWL* S3.... **8** C3
Darwall Cl *CHPT/GREN* S35.... **104** B7 ⬚
Darwent La *CHPT/GREN* S35.... **142** F3
Darwin Cl *FUL* S10.... **159** K5
Darwin La *FUL* S10.... **159** K5

Darwin Rd *ST/HB/BR* S6.... **143** M5
Darwynn Av *MEX/SWTN* S64.... **107** L4
David Cl *HAN/WDH* S13.... **163** H8 ⬚
David La *FUL* S10.... **158** C8
Davies Dr *MEX/SWTN* S64.... **108** B6
Davis Rd *AWLS/ASK* DN6.... **27** J8
   RHAM/THRY S65.... **7** L3
Davy Dr *MALT* S66.... **150** D1
Davy Rd *CONI* DN12.... **109** J4
Dawber La *ECK/KIL* S21.... **180** D8
Dawber St *WRKN* S81.... **184** B8
Daw Croft Av *BSLY* S70.... **82** E2
Daw Green Av *HOR/CROF* WF4 .. **19** J3
Dawlands Cl *SHEFP/MNR* S2 .. **161** M6 ⬚
Dawlands Dr
   SHEFP/MNR S2.... **161** M6 ⬚
Daw La *BTLY* DN5.... **67** M3
   HOR/CROF WF4.... **19** H4
   NROS/TKH DN11.... **112** B7
Dawson Dr *RAW* S62.... **107** G7
Daw Wd *BTLY* DN5.... **67** M4
Daykin Cl *DOD/DAR* S75.... **37** H7 ⬚
Daylands Av *CONI* DN12.... **109** L6
Day St *BSLY* S70.... **2** F8
Deacon Cl *NROS/TKH* DN11 .... **113** M6 ⬚
Deacon Crs *MALT* S66.... **150** E3 ⬚
   NROS/TKH DN11.... **113** M6
Deacons Wy *BSLYN/ROY* S71.... **61** G4
Deadman's Hole La
   DARN/MH S9.... **146** C3
Deakins Wk *FUL* S10.... **159** K6
Deane Field Vw *MOS* S20.... **179** H5 ⬚
Deanhead Dr *MOS* S20.... **178** E5 ⬚
Deanhead Dr *MOS* S20.... **178** D5
Dean Head La *STKB/PEN* S36.... **101** M2
Dean La *HOLM/MEL* HD7.... **54** B5
   RHAM/THRY S65.... **148** C1
Dean Rd *HOLM/MEL* HD7.... **53** C1
Deansfield Ct *ARMTH* DN3.... **91** M2
Dean St *BSLY* S70.... **2** C5
Deans Wy *BSLYN/ROY* S71.... **61** G3
Dearden Ct *CHPT/GREN* S35 .. **126** F7 ⬚
Dearne Br *BTLY* DN5.... **87** K8
Dearne Dike La *DOD/DAR* S75 .. **32** J2
Dearne Hall Fold *DOD/DAR* S75 .. **59** J4
Dearne Hall Rd *DOD/DAR* S75 .. **59** K1
Dearne Pk *KBTN* HD8.... **35** J5
Dearne Rd *DEARNE* S63.... **85** M7
   WMB/DAR S73.... **84** E7
Dearne Royd *KBTN* HD8.... **35** J5 ⬚
Dearneside Rd *KBTN* HD8.... **56** D2
Dearne St *CONI* DN12.... **110** A4
   CUD/GR S72.... **63** J6
   DARN/MH S9.... **145** L5
   DOD/DAR S75.... **37** J5
   HEM/SK/SE WF9.... **42** D4 ⬚
Dearne Valley Pkwy
   WMB/DAR S73.... **84** A7
Dearne Vw *DEARNE* S63.... **86** B2
Dearneway *DEARNE* S63.... **107** K1
Dearne Wy *DOD/DAR* S75.... **37** G4
   KBTN HD8.... **35** J4
   KBTN HD8.... **55** L3
Dearnfield *KBTN* HD8.... **56** A1
Dearnley Vw *DOD/DAR* S75.... **60** B3 ⬚
Decoy Bank North
   DONS/BSCR DN4.... **5** H9
Decoy Bank South
   DONS/BSCR DN4.... **90** B7
Deepcar La *CUD/GR* S72.... **62** C4
Deepdale Rd *KIMB* S61.... **146** C1
Deep La *SHEFN* S5.... **127** K7
Deepwell Av *MOS* S20.... **193** J5
Deepwell Bank *MOS* S20.... **193** K1
Deepwell Ct *MOS* S20.... **193** K5
Deepwell Vw *MOS* S20.... **193** K1
Deerlands Av *SHEFN* S5.... **144** A1
Deerlands Cl *SHEFN* S5.... **144** C1
Deerlands Mt *SHEFN* S5.... **144** C1
Deer Leap Dr *RHAM* S60.... **130** E5
Deer Park Cl *ST/HB/BR* S6.... **159** J1 ⬚
Deer Park Pl *ST/HB/BR* S6.... **159** J1
Deer Park Rd *RHAM/THRY* S65.. **130** E4
   ST/HB/BR S6.... **159** J1
Deer Park Vw *ST/HB/BR* S6.... **159** J1
Deer Park Wy *ST/HB/BR* S6.... **159** K1
Deershaw La *KBTN* HD8.... **55** G2
Deershaw Sike La *KBTN* HD8.... **55** G2
Deffer Rd *WKFDW/WTN* WF2.... **19** M1
De Houton Cl *AU/AST/KP* S26 .. **181** J2 ⬚
Deightonby St *DEARNE* S63.... **64** C7
De Lacy Dr *BSLY* S70.... **82** C2
Delamere Cl *MOS* S20.... **179** L5
De La Salle Dr *ATT* S4.... **145** G8
Delf Rd *ST/HB/BR* S6.... **124** A8
Delf St *SHEFP/MNR* S2.... **160** F8 ⬚
Della Av *BSLY* S70.... **2** D8
Dell Av *CUD/GR* S72.... **40** E7
Dell Crs *DONS/BSCR* DN4.... **89** K6
Delmar Wy *MALT* S66.... **148** E1
Delph Cl *DOD/DAR* S75.... **58** E6
Delph Edge *CHPT/GREN* S35.... **102** C4
Delph House Rd *FUL* S10.... **159** K4
Delta Pl *RHAM/THRY* S65.... **129** M8
Delta Wy *MALT* S66.... **150** F1
Delves Av *HACK/IN* S12.... **179** G3
Delves Cl *HACK/IN* S12.... **179** G3
Delves Dr *HACK/IN* S12.... **179** G4
Delves La *AU/AST/KP* S26.... **180** B4
Delves Pl *HACK/IN* S12.... **178** F4
Delves Rd *ECK/KIL* S21.... **194** A1
   HACK/IN S12.... **179** G4
Delves Ter *HACK/IN* S12.... **179** G4 ⬚
Denaby Av *CONI* DN12.... **109** G4
Denaby La *CONI* DN12.... **108** F6
Den Bank Av *FUL* S10.... **159** J4
Den Bank Cl *FUL* S10.... **159** K4
Den Bank Crs *FUL* S10.... **159** J4
Den Bank Dr *FUL* S10.... **159** K4
Denby Dale Rd *HOR/CROF* WF4 .. **18** C3
   HOR/CROF WF4.... **19** G2
Denby Dale Rd West
   HOR/CROF WF4.... **19** H1

Denby Grange La
HOR/CROF WF4 16 E2
Denby Hall La KBTN HD8 57 H2
Denby La HOR/CROF WF4 16 F1
KBTN HD8 56 B4
Denby Park Dr HOR/CROF WF4 16 C2
Denby Rd BSLYN/ROY S71 38 D8
Denby St BTLY DN5 67 L5
SHEFP/MNR S2 8 F9
Denby Wy MALT S66 149 L1
Dene Cl BWTY DN10 155 M8
MALT S66 149 G3
Dene Crs RHAM/THRY S65 129 M7
Denehall Rd ARMTH DN3 69 L4
Dene La OWL S3 8 E7
Dene Rd KBTN HD8 34 D6
RHAM/THRY S65 129 M7
The Dene WRKS S80 198 A5
Denham Rd ECC S11 8 C9
Denholme Cl OWL S3 160 F2 2
Denholme Meadow
HEM/SK/SE WF9 42 D3
Denison Ct BSLY S70 3 H8
Denison Rd DONS/BSCR DN4 4 C6
Denman Rd DEARNE S63 107 H1
Denman St RHAM/THRY S65 7 H1
Denmark Rd SHEFP/MNR S2 176 F1
Dennington La HOR/CROF WF4 19 G4
Dennis St WRKS S80 198 D5
Dent La MOS S20 178 D5
Denton Gdns FEA/AMT WF7 23 K2
Denton Rd SHEFS S8 176 D3 1
Dentons Green La ARMTH DN3 69 K3
Denton St BSLYN/ROY S71 3 H3
Denver Rd AWLS/ASK DN6 27 J4
Derby Pl SHEFP/MNR S2 177 G1 2
Derby Rd WHHL DN2 69 G7
Derbyshire La SHEFS S8 176 E4
Derby St BSLY S70 2 C6
SHEFP/MNR S2 176 F1
Derby Ter SHEFP/MNR S2 177 G1
Derriman Av ECC S11 175 M3
Derriman Cl ECC S11 175 M3
Derriman Dr ECC S11 175 M3
Derriman Gln ECC S11 175 L3
Derriman Gv ECC S11 175 M3
Derry Gv DEARNE S63 64 A8
Derwent Cl BSLYN/ROY S71 38 F8 1
DIN S25 166 D8
DRON S18 190 F4 1
WRKN S81 198 D1 1
Derwent Crs BSLYN/ROY S71 38 F8
RHAM S60 146 F8
Derwent Dr ARMTH DN3 69 K4
CHPT/GREN S35 126 C2
MEX/SWTN S64 109 G1 1
RAW S62 129 K3
Derwent Gdns DEARNE S63 86 C3
Derwent La EDL/UDV S33 138 F8
HATH/EY S32 172 C7
Derwent Pl BTLY DN5 88 F6 2
WMB/DAR S73 84 D6 2
Derwent Rd BSLYN/ROY S71 38 E8
DRON S18 190 F4
KIMB S61 128 E4
MEX/SWTN S64 109 G1
Derwent St SHEFP/MNR S2 161 H3
Derwent Ter MEX/SWTN S64 108 E1
Derwent Wy DEARNE S63 84 F7
De Sutton Pl AU/AST/KP S26 195 J2
Deveron Rd MOS S20 179 K8 1
Devonshire Cl DRON S18 190 D7 2
TOT/DORE S17 189 K1 2
Devonshire Dr DIN S25 166 C8
DOD/DAR S75 60 B3
TOT/DORE S17 175 J8
Devonshire Gln
TOT/DORE S17 189 K1 3
Devonshire Gv
TOT/DORE S17 189 J1 1
Devonshire La SHEF S1 8 F5
Devonshire Rd MALT S66 150 E1
NROS/TKH DN11 153 K3
TOT/DORE S17 175 J8
WHHL DN2 90 F2
Devonshire St KIMB S61 6 A4 1
SHEF S1 8 E5
WRKS S80 198 B5
Dewar Dr ABRD S7 176 A3
De Warren Pl AU/AST/KP S26 195 K2
Dewhill Av RHAM S60 147 M6
Dial Cl SHEFN S5 145 G3
Dial House Rd ST/HB/BR S6 143 L7
Dial Wy SHEFN S5 145 G3
Diamond Av HEM/SK/SE WF9 42 C4 2
Diamond St WMB/DAR S73 84 B4 1
Dick Edge La HOLM/MEL HD7 54 F5
Dickens Cl RHAM S60 162 F1
Dickenson Ct
CHPT/GREN S35 126 D2 1
Dickens Rd RAW S62 107 M8
WRKN S81 198 F3
Dickinson Pl BSLY S70 60 D8 3
Dickinson Rd BSLY S70 60 D8 4
SHEFN S5 127 H8
Dicky Sykes La FEA/AMT WF7 23 H2
Digby Cl KIMB S61 128 C7
Digley Rd HOLM/MEL HD7 52 F5
Digley Royd La HOLM/MEL HD7 52 E4
Dike Hl RAW S62 105 J6
Dikelands Mt
CHPT/GREN S35 126 B1 1
Dillington Rd BSLY S70 3 H9
Dillington Sq BSLY S70 3 H9
Dinmore Cl DONS/BSCR DN4 111 L3
Dinnington Rd DIN S25 183 H3
SHEFS S8 176 D3 2
Dirleton Dr DONS/BSCR DN4 111 H1 1
Dirty La HTFD DN7 30 E8
Discovery Wy MALT S66 150 B1
Dishwell La AU/AST/KP S26 195 J2
Disraeli Gv MALT S66 150 C1
Ditchingham St ATT S4 161 G1 2
Division La SHEF S1 9 G5
Division St SHEF S1 8 F5
Dixon Crs DONS/BSCR DN4 89 K8
Dixon Dr CHPT/GREN S35 124 F5
Dixon La SHEF S1 9 K3
Dixon Rd CONI DN12 110 E6
ST/HB/BR S6 143 M6
Dixon St OWL S3 160 D2 2
RHAM/THRY S65 7 G3
Dobbin Hl ECC S11 175 L1
Dobb La HOLM/MEL HD7 53 G5
ST/HB/BR S6 158 C3
Dobb Top Rd HOLM/MEL HD7 52 F6
Dobcroft Av ABRD S7 175 M5
Dobcroft Cl ECC S11 175 L3
Dobcroft Rd ECC S11 175 L3
Dobie St BSLY S70 3 H8
Dobsyke Cl BSLY S70 83 H2 2
Dockin Hill Rd DON DN1 5 H3
Dock Rd WRKS S80 198 C4
Doctor La AU/AST/KP S26 195 J2
HOR/CROF WF4 16 F5
Dodds Cl RHAM S60 6 D8
Dodd St ST/HB/BR S6 144 A8
Dodson Dr HAN/WDH S13 162 D5
Dodsworth St
MEX/SWTN S64 108 D3 2
Dodworth Dr
WKFDW/WTN WF2 19 M2
Dodworth Green Rd
DOD/DAR S75 81 H1
Dodworth Rd BSLY S70 2 B5
Doe La ECK/KIL S21 191 M3
SHEFS S8 192 A2
Doe Quarry La DIN S25 166 D5
Doe Royd Crs SHEFN S5 144 B2
Doe Royd Dr SHEFN S5 144 C2
Doe Royd La SHEFN S5 144 B3
Dog Croft La BTLY DN5 68 E6
Dog Hl CUD/GR S72 39 M4
Dog Hill Dr CUD/GR S72 40 A4
Dog Kennels La
AU/AST/KP S26 181 M5
Dog La BWTY DN10 154 E5
Dolcliffe Rd MEX/SWTN S64 108 E3
Doles Av BSLYN/ROY S71 38 F4
Doles Crs BSLYN/ROY S71 38 F4
Doles La RHAM S60 148 C8
RHAM S60 163 J1
WRKS S80 196 F7
Doleswood Dr DIN S25 166 C3
Domine La RHAM S60 6 E4
Dominoe Gv HACK/IN S12 178 B2
Don Av CHPT/GREN S35 124 F5
ST/HB/BR S6 143 L4
Doncaster Ga RHAM/THRY S65 6 F4
Doncaster La AWLS/ASK DN6 44 A3
AWLS/ASK DN6 67 G2
AWLS/ASK DN6 67 G4 1
Doncaster Pl RHAM/THRY S65 7 L2
Doncaster Rd ARMTH DN3 69 J5
ARMTH DN3 91 J1
AWLS/ASK DN6 27 L4
AWLS/ASK DN6 45 K5
BSLY S70 3 H6
BSLY S70 61 H7 1
BSLYN/ROY S71 61 J7
BTLY DN5 66 B3
BTLY DN5 67 K1
BTLY DN5 87 H4
BWTY DN10 136 E7
CONI DN12 109 K3
CONI DN12 110 B5 2
DEARNE S63 86 D1
DEARNE S63 107 L1
EPW DN9 115 J4
EPW DN9 117 J4
FEA/AMT WF7 23 L2
HEM/SK/SE WF9 42 E1
HTFD DN7 48 B4
HTFD DN7 70 E2 2
MALT S66 132 E5
MEX/SWTN S64 108 F3
NROS/TKH DN11 134 D5
RHAM/THRY S65 7 H4
RHAM/THRY S65 130 B6
WMB/DAR S73 84 F1
WRKN S81 168 D5
WRKN S81 184 D7 2
Doncaster Road Est
FEA/AMT WF7 23 L2
Doncaster Rd (Harlington)
BTLY DN5 87 G6
Doncaster St OWL S3 8 F1
Don Dr BSLY S70 61 H8
Donetsk Wy HACK/IN S12 178 E4
Don Hill Height STKB/PEN S36 102 A4
Donnington Rd
MEX/SWTN S64 109 H1
SHEFP/MNR S2 161 H6
Donovan Cl SHEFN S5 144 C4
Donovan Rd SHEFN S5 144 C4
Don Rd DARN/MH S9 145 K8
Donstone Vw DIN S25 166 B7
Don St CONI DN12 110 B4
DON DN1 5 H1
RHAM S60 6 E6
STKB/PEN S36 79 K5
Don Vw STKB/PEN S36 76 B6
Dorchester Pl BSLY S70 82 D2
Dorchester Rd
NROS/TKH DN11 153 M2
Dore Cl TOT/DORE S17 175 L8
Dore Hall Cft TOT/DORE S17 175 H8 1
Dore La HATH/EY S32 172 D8
Dore Rd TOT/DORE S17 175 J7
Dorking St ATT S4 161 G2 1
Dorman Av HEM/SK/SE WF9 25 H7
Dorothy Av THNE DN8 31 K7 1
Dorothy Rd ST/HB/BR S6 143 M6
Dorset Cl HEM/SK/SE WF9 23 H7
Dorset Crs WHHL DN2 91 G2
Dorset Dr NROS/TKH DN11 153 K3 2
Dorset St FUL S10 8 B6
Double Bridges Rd THNE DN8 50 B4
Doubting La STKB/PEN S36 78 F8
Douglas Rd DONS/BSCR DN4 89 J8
OWL S3 144 D8
OWL S3 160 D1
Douglas St RHAM S60 6 F5
Douse Croft La FUL S10 174 D1
Dovecliffe Rd WMB/DAR S73 83 J4
Dove Cl DEARNE S63 86 B6
WMB/DAR S73 84 D6
WRKN S81 184 C8
Dovecote La RHAM/THRY S65 131 G4
Dovecott Lea MOS S20 179 M4
Dovedale BSLY S70 82 F3
Dovedale Rd ABRD S7 176 B2
RHAM/THRY S65 148 A3
Dove La AU/AST/KP S26 180 C2
Dovercourt Rd KIMB S61 128 E8
SHEFP/MNR S2 161 J6
Dover La HOLM/MEL HD7 53 M4
Dove Rd WMB/DAR S73 84 D6
Dover Rd FUL S10 160 A6
HOLM/MEL HD7 53 L4
Dover St OWL S3 8 D2
Doveside Dr WMB/DAR S73 84 E2
Dowcarr La AU/AST/KP S26 195 G3
Dowland Av CHPT/GREN S35 104 B7
Dowland Cl CHPT/GREN S35 104 C7
Dowland Ct CHPT/GREN S35 104 B6
Dowland Gdns
CHPT/GREN S35 104 B7
Downes Crs DOD/DAR S75 59 M4
Downgate Dr ATT S4 145 J7
Downham Rd SHEFN S5 145 H4
Downing La OWL S3 8 E1 1
Downing Rd SHEFS S8 176 C7
Downing Sq STKB/PEN S36 79 H5
The Downings AU/AST/KP S26 195 K2
Downland Cl DONS/BSCR DN4 111 K3
Downshutts La
HOLM/MEL HD7 54 B2 1
Down's Rw RHAM S60 6 F5
Drake Cl CHPT/GREN S35 126 C2
Drake Head La CONI DN12 110 C5
Drake House Crs MOS S20 179 H4
Drake House La MOS S20 179 K4
Drake House La West
MOS S20 179 K4 1
Drake House Wy MOS S20 179 J4
Drake Rd WHHL DN2 90 C1
Dr Anderson Av HTFD DN7 48 D3
Dransfield Av STKB/PEN S36 79 H5
Dransfield Cl FUL S10 159 K5 1
Dransfield Rd FUL S10 159 J5
Draycott Pl DRON S18 190 B7 2
Drewry La EPW DN9 117 M3
Drinker La KBTN HD8 34 B1
Driver St HAN/WDH S13 163 H8
The Drive ARMTH DN3 69 L5
RTFD DN22 187 G2
ST/HB/BR S6 143 M5
Dronfield Rd ECK/KIL S21 192 E5
Droppingwell Farm Cl
KIMB S61 128 B6 1
Droppingwell Rd KIMB S61 128 A8
Drover Cl CHPT/GREN S35 126 C1
Droversdale Rd
NROS/TKH DN11 154 A3
Drummond Av BTLY DN5 67 G8
Drummond Crs SHEFN S5 144 F2
Drummond Rd SHEFN S5 144 F2
Drummond St RHAM S60 6 F2
Drury Farm Ct DOD/DAR S75 59 L6 3
Drury La DRON S18 191 G4
TOT/DORE S17 175 H8
Dryden Av SHEFN S5 144 C3
Dryden Dl WRKN S81 199 G4
Dryden Dr SHEFN S5 144 C3
Dryden Rd BSLYN/ROY S71 3 J3
DEARNE S63 85 G8
DONS/BSCR DN4 112 A1
MEX/SWTN S64 108 F2
RHAM/THRY S65 147 M3
SHEFN S5 144 C3
Dryden Wy SHEFN S5 144 C3
Dry Hill La KBTN HD8 56 F2
Dryhurst Cl AWLS/ASK DN6 27 J4
Dublin Rd WHHL DN2 90 E3
Duchess Rd SHEFP/MNR S2 9 J8
Duckham Dr AU/AST/KP S26 180 C1
Ducksett La ECK/KIL S21 193 H4
Dudley Rd ST/HB/BR S6 143 M5
WHHL DN2 90 F4
Dudley St RAW S62 129 K4 4
Duftons Cl CONI DN12 110 B4 1
Dugdale Dr SHEFN S5 126 D8
Dugdale Rd SHEFN S5 126 D8
Duke Av MALT S66 150 F3
NROS/TKH DN11 113 J6
Duke Crs BSLY S70 3 G7
KIMB S61 128 C6
Duke La SHEF S1 9 H6
Duke of Norfolk La MALT S66 148 C3
Duke Pl WRKS S80 198 C4
Dukeries Cl WRKN S81 198 A1
Dukeries Crs WRKS S80 198 F6
Dukeries Dr DIN S25 166 C8
Dukeries Wy WRKN S81 198 A1
Duke's Crs CONI DN12 110 F4
Dukes Pl RHAM/THRY S65 147 M3
Dukes Ter BWTY DN10 136 E8
Duke St BSLY S70 3 G8
CUD/GR S72 62 E1
DIN S25 166 D5
DON DN1 4 F5
HEM/SK/SE WF9 22 E4
HOY S74 105 J1
HTFD DN7 48 C4 1
MEX/SWTN S64 108 B3
MOS S20 193 H1
SHEFP/MNR S2 9 M5
Duke Wood Rd KBTN HD8 35 J5
Dumb Hall La AU/AST/KP S26 196 E3
WRKS S80 196 E2
Dumbleton Rd ECK/KIL S21 194 C2
Duncan Rd FUL S10 159 M3
Duncan St RHAM S60 147 G6
Duncombe St ST/HB/BR S6 160 B2
Dundas Rd DARN/MH S9 146 C4
WHHL DN2 90 C2
Dunedin Gln MOS S20 193 J1
Dunedin Gv MOS S20 193 J1
Dunella Dr ST/HB/BR S6 143 M6
Dunella Pl ST/HB/BR S6 143 L6
Dunella Rd ST/HB/BR S6 143 L6
Dunelm Crs THNE DN8 32 B4
Dun Flds OWL S3 8 F1
Dunford Rd HOLM/MEL HD7 53 M8
HOLM/MEL HD7 75 M1
Dungworth Gn ST/HB/BR S6 142 C6
Dunkeld Rd ECC S11 175 M2
Dunkerley Rd ST/HB/BR S6 143 H6
Dun La OWL S3 8 F1
Dunleary Rd WHHL DN2 90 E3
Dunlin Cl KIMB S61 127 K1
Dunlin Ct WRKN S81 198 A1
Dunlop St DARN/MH S9 145 M6
Dunmere Cl BSLYN/ROY S71 60 E2 1
Dunmow Rd ATT S4 145 J6
Dunninc Rd SHEFN S5 127 H8
Dunninc Ter SHEFN S5 127 H8
Dunniwood Av
DONS/BSCR DN4 113 K2
Dunniwood Reach
DONS/BSCR DN4 113 K1 1
Dunns Dl MALT S66 150 F2
Dunscroft Gv NROS/TKH DN11 113 M6
Dunsley Bank Rd
HOLM/MEL HD7 53 K5
Dunsley Ter HEM/SK/SE WF9 41 L5
Dunstan Crs WRKS S80 198 D6
Dunstan Rd MALT S66 150 C3
Dun St MEX/SWTN S64 108 C5
OWL S3 8 F1
Durham Av THNE DN8 31 L7
Durham Cl WRKN S81 184 E8
Durham La FUL S10 8 C5
Durham Pl RHAM/THRY S65 147 M3
Durham Rd FUL S10 8 C5
HTFD DN7 48 E7
WHHL DN2 68 D8
Durham St MALT S66 150 F3
Durkar Flds HOR/CROF WF4 19 K1
Durkar La HOR/CROF WF4 19 J1
Durkar Ri HOR/CROF WF4 19 K1
Durlstone Cl HACK/IN S12 177 L2 2
Durlstone Crs HACK/IN S12 177 L2
Durlstone Dr HACK/IN S12 177 K2
Durlstone Gv HACK/IN S12 177 L2
Durmast Gv ST/HB/BR S6 159 G1
Durnan Gv RAW S62 107 G7
Durnford Rd WHHL DN2 90 C2
Dursley Ct EPW DN9 92 D8
Durvale Ct TOT/DORE S17 189 J1
Dutton Rd ST/HB/BR S6 144 B6
Dwarriden La STKB/PEN S36 123 K3
Dyche Cl SHEFS S8 190 F1 1
Dyche Dr SHEFS S8 190 F1
Dyche La SHEFS S8 176 E8
Dyche Pl SHEFS S8 190 F1 1
Dyche Rd SHEFS S8 190 F1
Dycott Rd KIMB S61 128 D8 1
Dyer Rd HOY S74 83 L8
Dykes Hall Gdns ST/HB/BR S6 143 M7
Dykes Hall Pl ST/HB/BR S6 143 M6
Dykes Hall Rd ST/HB/BR S6 143 L6
Dykes La ST/HB/BR S6 143 L7
Dyke Vale Av HACK/IN S12 178 E3
Dyke Vale Cl HACK/IN S12 178 E3
Dyke Vale Pl HACK/IN S12 178 E3
Dyke Vale Rd HACK/IN S12 178 D2
Dyke Vale Wy HACK/IN S12 178 D3
Dykewood Dr ST/HB/BR S6 143 K4
Dyscarr Cl WRKN S81 168 D4
Dyson Cote La STKB/PEN S36 101 K2
Dyson La HOLM/MEL HD7 53 M6
Dyson Pl ECC S11 160 B7 4
Dyson St BSLY S70 2 C9

E

Eaden Crs HOY S74 105 K1
Eagleton Dr CHPT/GREN S35 104 C7
Eagleton Ri CHPT/GREN S35 104 C7
Eagle Vw AU/AST/KP S26 180 C1
Eaming Vw BSLYN/ROY S71 3 K2
Earl Av MALT S66 150 E3
NROS/TKH DN11 113 H6
Earldom Cl ATT S4 161 G1
Earldom Dr ATT S4 161 G1
Earldom Rd ATT S4 145 G8
Earldom St ATT S4 161 G1
Earlesmere Av DONS/BSCR DN4 89 L7
Earl Marshal Cl ATT S4 145 H6
Earl Marshal Dr ATT S4 145 H7 1
Earl Marshal Rd ATT S4 145 H6
Earl Marshal Vw ATT S4 145 G7
Earlsmere Dr BSLYN/ROY S71 61 L7
Earlston Dr BTLY DN5 89 M1
Earl St HEM/SK/SE WF9 22 E4
SHEF S1 9 H7
Earl Wy SHEF S1 9 G7
Earnshaw Ter DOD/DAR S75 2 D2
Earsham St ATT S4 161 G2
East Av HEM/SK/SE WF9 24 E8
HEM/SK/SE WF9 42 F3
HTFD DN7 48 D5
MEX/SWTN S64 107 M5
RAW S62 129 K1
WMB/DAR S73 83 M4
East Bank HTFD DN7 48 C2
East Bank Cl SHEFP/MNR S2 177 H1 1
East Bank Pl SHEFP/MNR S2 177 H1
East Bank Rd SHEFP/MNR S2 161 G8
East Bank Vw
SHEFP/MNR S2 177 H1 2
East Bank Wy
SHEFP/MNR S2 177 H1 3
East Bawtry Rd RHAM S60 147 M5 1
RHAM S60 148 A5 1
East Cl STKB/PEN S36 79 L6
East Coast Rd DARN/MH S9 161 J1
East Crs RHAM/THRY S65 129 M8
STKB/PEN S36 101 L6
East Cft DEARNE S63 86 A5
Eastcroft Cl MOS S20 179 K7
Eastcroft Dr MOS S20 179 J8
Eastcroft Gln MOS S20 179 K7 1
Eastcroft Vw MOS S20 179 K8 2
Eastcroft Wy MOS S20 179 K7 2
East Dale Cl HEM/SK/SE WF9 23 K8
East End Crs BSLYN/ROY S71 39 J4
Eastern Av DIN S25 166 E6
SHEFP/MNR S2 161 J8
Eastern Cl DIN S25 166 E6
Eastern Crs SHEFP/MNR S2 177 H1
Eastern Dr SHEFP/MNR S2 161 H8
Eastfield Av STKB/PEN S36 79 H4
Eastfield Cl DOD/DAR S75 38 B7
Eastfield Crs DIN S25 166 C2 1
DOD/DAR S75 38 B7
Eastfield Dr AWLS/ASK DN6 27 L7
Eastfield La CHPT/GREN S35 80 E5
East Field La DIN S25 166 D2
Eastfield Pk EPW DN9 114 E1
Eastfield Pl RAW S62 108 A8
Eastfield Rd ARMTH DN3 91 M2
DRON S18 191 G7
FUL S10 160 A2 2
East Field Rd HTFD DN7 30 D7
Eastfields BSLY S70 82 F3
East Fold KBTN HD8 35 G6
Eastgate BSLY S70 2 F4
HEM/SK/SE WF9 41 J1
East Ga THNE DN8 32 A3
Eastgate WRKS S80 198 D4
East Glade Av HACK/IN S12 178 C4
East Glade Cl HACK/IN S12 178 C4
East Glade Crs HACK/IN S12 178 C3
East Glade Pl HACK/IN S12 178 C4
East Glade Rd HACK/IN S12 178 C3
East Glade Sq HACK/IN S12 178 C4 2
East Glade Wy HACK/IN S12 178 C3
Eastgrove Rd FUL S10 8 A9
East Laith Ga DON DN1 5 H4
East La HTFD DN7 48 C3
East Pde SHEF S1 9 H4
East Pinfold BSLYN/ROY S71 39 G4
East Rd RHAM/THRY S65 129 M8
SHEFP/MNR S2 160 F8
STKB/PEN S36 79 L6
East Service Rd ARMTH DN3 47 H7
East St BSLY S70 83 G3
CUD/GR S72 40 C2
DEARNE S63 86 D1
DIN S25 166 D6
DON DN1 4 F9
ECK/KIL S21 193 M7
HEM/SK/SE WF9 42 F3
HOLM/MEL HD7 54 C4
HOR/CROF WF4 22 B6
NROS/TKH DN11 153 L2
WMB/DAR S73 84 E1
East Vale Dr RHAM/THRY S65 130 D5
East Vw AWLS/ASK DN6 27 H6
BWTY DN10 136 E7 1
CUD/GR S72 39 M8
MALT S66 149 M2
East View Av ECK/KIL S21 193 G5
Eastwood Av DIN S25 182 C2
Eastwood Ct WRKN S81 184 D6
Eastwood La RHAM/THRY S65 7 G4
Eastwood Mt RHAM/THRY S65 7 L4
Eastwood Rd ECC S11 160 B7 5
Eastwood V RHAM/THRY S65 7 M1
Eaton Pl HEM/SK/SE WF9 23 J8 1
SHEFP/MNR S2 161 H4
Eaton Sq BTLY DN5 87 H4
Eaton Wk HEM/SK/SE WF9 42 E2 2
Ebenezer Pl OWL S3 9 G1 1
Ebenezer St CUD/GR S72 63 K6 1
OWL S3 9 G1
Eben St DARN/MH S9 145 L5
Ebson House La
HOLM/MEL HD7 54 F1
Ecclesall Rd ECC S11 159 M8
Ecclesall Rd South ECC S11 175 L2 2
Eccles Dr CONI DN12 110 F7
Ecclesfield Rd CHPT/GREN S35 126 F3
DARN/MH S9 127 K8
SHEFN S5 127 H7
Eccles St DARN/MH S9 145 M3
Eccleston Rd ARMTH DN3 69 L2
Eckington Rd DRON S18 191 H4
MOS S20 179 K7
Eckington Wy MOS S20 179 H3
Ecklands Long La
STKB/PEN S36 78 B7
Edale Ri DOD/DAR S75 59 J8 3
Edale Rd ECC S11 175 L1
KIMB S61 146 C1
Edderthorpe La WMB/DAR S73 62 E7
Eddison Cl WRKN S81 184 E8
Eddison Park Av WRKN S81 184 C6
Eddyfield Rd STKB/PEN S36 79 L6
Eden Cl DOD/DAR S75 59 J2
MALT S66 149 M2
Edencroft Dr ARMTH DN3 69 K4
Eden Dr AWLS/ASK DN6 28 A7
ST/HB/BR S6 143 J7
Edenfield Cl BSLYN/ROY S71 61 H1 1
Eden Field Rd ARMTH DN3 69 L5
Eden Gld AU/AST/KP S26 164 B8
Eden Gv AU/AST/KP S26 164 B7
DONS/BSCR DN4 4 B7
Eden Grove Rd ARMTH DN3 69 L5
Edenhall Rd SHEFP/MNR S2 161 K8
Edensor Rd SHEFN S5 144 F5
Eden Ter MEX/SWTN S64 108 E1
Edenthorpe Dell HACK/IN S12 178 F5
Edenthorpe Gv MOS S20 179 G5
Edgar La NROS/TKH DN11 113 H6
Edgbaston Wy CONI DN12 111 G4
Edgebrook Rd ECC S11 176 B1
Edgecliffe Pl BSLYN/ROY S71 60 E2 2
Edge Cl ST/HB/BR S6 144 A1
Edgedale Rd ABRD S7 176 C2
Edge End La HOLM/MEL HD7 52 E2
Edgefield Rd ABRD S7 176 C2
Edge Hill Rd ABRD S7 176 B1
Edgehill Rd DOD/DAR S75 37 L5
WHHL DN2 69 G8
Edgelands Ri CUD/GR S72 61 M2 1
Edge La ST/HB/BR S6 143 M1
Edgemoor Rd HOR/CROF WF4 19 K4
Edgemount Rd ABRD S7 176 C2 3
Edge Well Cl ST/HB/BR S6 144 A1
Edge Well Crs ST/HB/BR S6 144 A1
Edge Well Dr ST/HB/BR S6 144 A2
Edge Well Pl ST/HB/BR S6 144 A1 1
Edge Well Ri ST/HB/BR S6 144 A1 2

Edinburgh Av DEARNE S63 .... 85 M5
Edinburgh Cl BSLYN/ROY S71 ... 60 F3 1
Edinburgh Dr DIN S25 ... 166 C8
Edinburgh Rd HOY S74 ... 83 J8
WRKS S80 ... 198 F7
Edinburgh Wk WRKS S80 ... 198 E7
Edith Ter BTLY DN5 ... 67 H8
Edlington La CONI DN12 ... 110 E7
DONS/BSCR DN4 ... 111 G2
Edmonton Cl DOD/DAR S75 ... 59 L5 3
Edmund Av RHAM S60 ... 147 H8
TOT/DORE S17 ... 190 A1
Edmund Cl TOT/DORE S17 ... 190 B1
Edmund Dr TOT/DORE S17 ... 190 A1
Edmund Rd SHEFP/MNR S2 ... 160 F7
Edmunds Rd BSLY S70 ... 83 G3
Edna St DEARNE S63 ... 86 A5
Edward Cl BSLY S70 ... 61 G8
Edward Ct THNE DN8 ... 32 A6 1
Edward Rd AWLS/ASK DN6 ... 44 F6
AWLS/ASK DN6 ... 67 H1
DEARNE S63 ... 85 G7
DEARNE S63 ... 86 A3
Edwards Ct WRKS S80 ... 198 B4
Edward St ARMTH DN3 ... 69 K8
BTLY DN5 ... 67 M6
CUD/GR S72 ... 63 J6
DEARNE S63 ... 64 A7 2
DIN S25 ... 166 D6
DOD/DAR S75 ... 38 A7
ECK/KIL S21 ... 193 H4
HOY S74 ... 105 H1
MEX/SWTN S64 ... 108 B3
NROS/TKH DN11 ... 113 H6
OWL S3 ... 8 E3
STKB/PEN S36 ... 102 A6
WMB/DAR S73 ... 84 C4
WMB/DAR S73 ... 84 E2
WRKS S80 ... 198 D4
Edwin Rd AWLS/ASK DN6 ... 66 E3
SHEFP/MNR S2 ... 177 G1
Effingham La ATT S4 ... 9 L2
Effingham Rd DARN/MH S9 ... 161 J2
Effingham Sq RHAM S60 ... 6 F3
Effingham St ATT S4 ... 9 L1
RHAM/THRY S65 ... 7 G2
Egerton Cl SHEF S1 ... 8 F6
Egerton La OWL S3 ... 8 E7
Egerton Rd AU/AST/KP S26 ... 164 B8
DRON S18 ... 190 F5 2
Egerton St OWL S3 ... 8 E7
Eggington Cl ARMTH DN3 ... 91 M8 1
Egg La NROS/TKH DN11 ... 112 D8
Egmanton Rd
BSLYN/ROY S71 ... 38 D6 1
Egremont Ri MALT S66 ... 132 B8
Eilam Cl KIMB S61 ... 128 C7
Eilam Rd KIMB S61 ... 128 C7
Ekin St RHAM S60 ... 146 E3
Eland Gate Cl NROS/TKH DN11 .. 113 J5
Elcroft Gdns MOS S20 ... 179 K4
Elder Av DIN S25 ... 182 D2
HEM/SK/SE WF9 ... 25 G7
Elder Ct ECK/KIL S21 ... 194 A2
Elder Dr HEM/SK/SE WF9 ... 24 F7
MALT S66 ... 148 F1
Elder Gv CONI DN12 ... 109 L6
EPW DN9 ... 114 E2
Eldertree Rd KIMB S61 ... 127 K4
Eldon Gv THNE DN8 ... 32 C4
Eldon Rd RHAM/THRY S65 ... 129 K7
Eldon St BSLY S70 ... 2 F5
SHEF S1 ... 8 F5
Eldon St North BSLY S70 ... 3 G4
Eleanor Ct ARMTH DN3 ... 69 J6 1
Eleanor St DARN/MH S9 ... 161 M1
Elgar Dr MALT S66 ... 151 G3
Elgin St FUL S10 ... 159 M4
Elgitha Dr MALT S66 ... 165 J1
Elizabeth Av ARMTH DN3 ... 69 L3
CUD/GR S72 ... 40 C2
Elizabeth Rd AU/AST/KP S26 ... 164 B8
Elizabeth St CUD/GR S72 ... 62 E1
DEARNE S63 ... 85 J3
Elland Cl BSLYN/ROY S71 ... 38 C8
Ella Rd ATT S4 ... 145 G8 1
Ella St HEM/SK/SE WF9 ... 22 E3
Ellavale HOY S74 ... 105 L1
Ellenbro Rd ST/HB/BR S6 ... 143 M7
Ellen Tree Cl RHAM S60 ... 146 F7 1
Ellerker Av DONS/BSCR DN4 ... 4 D7
Ellers Av DONS/BSCR DN4 ... 91 G7
Ellers Crs DONS/BSCR DN4 ... 91 G7
Ellers Dr DONS/BSCR DN4 ... 91 G7
Ellershaw La CONI DN12 ... 109 L6
Ellershaw Rd CONI DN12 ... 109 M6
Ellers La EPW DN9 ... 92 E8
Ellers Rd DONS/BSCR DN4 ... 91 G7
Ellerton Gdns DONS/BSCR DN4 ... 91 J6
Ellerton Rd SHEFN S5 ... 145 H5
Ellesmere Gv HTFD DN7 ... 48 F3 1
Ellesmere Rd ATT S4 ... 145 G8
ATT S4 ... 161 G1
Ellesmere Rd North ATT S4 ... 145 G8
Ellesmere Ter RHAM/THRY S65 ... 7 K5
Ellington Ct BSLY S70 ... 2 B9
BSLY S70 ... 60 B8 2
Ellin St SHEF S1 ... 9 G8
Elliot La CHPT/GREN S35 ... 126 C4
Elliot Rd ST/HB/BR S6 ... 8 B2
Elliott Av WMB/DAR S73 ... 84 B6
Elliott Cl DEARNE S63 ... 85 G8
Elliott Ct RHAM/THRY S65 ... 7 G3
Elliott Dr KIMB S61 ... 128 D5
Elliottville St ST/HB/BR S6 ... 160 A1 1
Ellis Av DEARNE S63 ... 107 H3
Ellis Ct WMB/DAR S73 ... 84 A7 1
Ellis Crs NROS/TKH DN11 ... 113 J6
WMB/DAR S73 ... 84 E8
Ellisons Rd ECK/KIL S21 ... 180 C7
Ellison St OWL S3 ... 8 E2
THNE DN8 ... 49 M1
Ellis St OWL S3 ... 8 F2
RHAM S60 ... 147 G6
Elliston Av DOD/DAR S75 ... 38 A6
Ellmont Av KBTN HD8 ... 35 G1
Ellorslie Dr STKB/PEN S36 ... 102 A6
Elmbridge Cl BSLYN/ROY S71 ... 39 J4
Elm Cl ARMTH DN3 ... 47 K8
ECK/KIL S21 ... 194 A2
Elm Crs BTLY DN5 ... 68 A5
MOS S20 ... 179 G7
Elmdale Cl MEX/SWTN S64 ... 108 B7
Elmdale Dr ARMTH DN3 ... 69 K6
Elm Dr ECK/KIL S21 ... 194 A2
EPW DN9 ... 115 K4
Elmfield Av SHEFN S5 ... 144 F3
Elmfield Dr KBTN HD8 ... 34 E6
Elmfield Rd DON DN1 ... 5 H7
NROS/TKH DN11 ... 113 K7
Elm Green La CONI DN12 ... 110 A5
Elm Gv HEM/SK/SE WF9 ... 42 D4
KIMB S61 ... 128 F4
Elmham Rd DARN/MH S9 ... 162 B3
DONS/BSCR DN4 ... 91 J6
Elmhirst Dr RHAM/THRY S65 ... 148 A3
Elmhirst La DOD/DAR S75 ... 59 H7
Elmhirst Rd THNE DN8 ... 32 A8
Elm La SHEFN S5 ... 144 F3
Elmore Rd FUL S10 ... 160 A4
Elm Pl ARMTH DN3 ... 69 L8
BSLYN/ROY S71 ... 61 H2
RAW S62 ... 129 L2
Elm Ri CHPT/GREN S35 ... 126 D3
Elm Rd ARMTH DN3 ... 69 L8
AWLS/ASK DN6 ... 44 E5
ECK/KIL S21 ... 193 G5
EPW DN9 ... 114 D4
HEM/SK/SE WF9 ... 23 J8
MEX/SWTN S64 ... 108 D1
MOS S20 ... 179 L3
Elm Rw BSLYN/ROY S71 ... 3 M5
Elmsall Dr HEM/SK/SE WF9 ... 43 G2
Elmsall La AWLS/ASK DN6 ... 42 F7
Elmsall Wy HEM/SK/SE WF9 ... 43 G2
Elmsdale BSLY S70 ... 82 F3
Elmsdale Cl HEM/SK/SE WF9 ... 42 F5 1
Elmsmere Dr WRKN S81 ... 168 E1
Elms Rd WRKS S80 ... 198 C3
The Elms FEA/AMT WF7 ... 23 K2
Elm St HOY S74 ... 104 F2
KBTN HD8 ... 34 E5
Elm Tree Cl DIN S25 ... 182 D2
Elmtree Cl WRKN S81 ... 183 K8
Elm Tree Crs DRON S18 ... 190 E4
Elm Tree Dr BWTY DN10 ... 136 D8
Elm Tree Gv THNE DN8 ... 49 M1 1
Elm Tree Rd KIMB S61 ... 127 K4
MALT S66 ... 150 B2
Elmview Rd DARN/MH S9 ... 145 M3 3
Elmville Av MEX/SWTN S64 ... 108 A6
Elm Wy DEARNE S63 ... 107 L3
Elmwood Av AWLS/ASK DN6 ... 66 D1
Elmwood Crs ARMTH DN3 ... 91 L1
Elmwood Dr MOS S20 ... 193 H1
Elsecar Rd RAW S62 ... 106 D2
Elsham Cl RHAM/THRY S65 ... 131 H8
Elstead Cl DOD/DAR S75 ... 59 J2
Elstree Dr HACK/IN S12 ... 177 M3
Elstree Rd HACK/IN S12 ... 177 M3
Elsworth Cl DON DN1 ... 4 E8
Elvaston Cl DRON S18 ... 189 M6
Elwin Ct DONS/BSCR DN4 ... 111 M3
Elwis St BTLY DN5 ... 4 D3
Elwood Rd TOT/DORE S17 ... 190 A1
Ely Cl WRKS S80 ... 198 E5
Ely Rd WHHL DN2 ... 68 D8
Ely St NROS/TKH DN11 ... 113 J6
Embankment Rd FUL S10 ... 160 A4
Emerson Av HTFD DN7 ... 48 D4
Emerson Cl SHEFN S5 ... 144 F2
Emerson Crs SHEFN S5 ... 144 F3
Emerson Dr SHEFN S5 ... 144 F3
Emily Cl BSLYN/ROY S71 ... 61 H5
Emley Dr BTLY DN5 ... 67 G8
Emmett Carr Cl ECK/KIL S21 ... 194 A8
Emmett Carr Dr ECK/KIL S21 ... 194 A7 1
Emmett Carr La ECK/KIL S21 ... 194 A7
Empire Rd ABRD S7 ... 160 D8
SHEFS S8 ... 176 D1 2
Emsley Av CUD/GR S72 ... 62 A3
Endcliffe Av ECC S11 ... 159 M6
Endcliffe Crs ECC S11 ... 159 M6
Endcliffe Edge FUL S10 ... 159 M6 1
Endcliffe Glen Rd ECC S11 ... 160 A6
Endcliffe Grove Av FUL S10 ... 159 L6
Endcliffe Hall Av FUL S10 ... 159 L6
Endcliffe Rise Rd ECC S11 ... 160 A6
Endcliffe Terrace Rd ECC S11 ... 160 A6
Endcliffe Vale Av ECC S11 ... 160 A7
Endcliffe Vale Rd FUL S10 ... 159 M6
Endcliffe Wy WHHL DN2 ... 69 G8 1
Endfield Rd SHEFN S5 ... 126 D8
Endowood Rd ABRD S7 ... 175 M5
Enfield Pl HAN/WDH S13 ... 162 D5
Engine La CUD/GR S72 ... 40 B6
DEARNE S63 ... 86 D3
Ennerdale Av MOS S20 ... 193 J1 1
Ennerdale Cl DIN S25 ... 166 C8
DRON S18 ... 190 C6
MEX/SWTN S64 ... 109 G1
Ennerdale Dr MOS S20 ... 193 J1 3
Ennerdale Rd BSLYN/ROY S71 ... 61 M7
WHHL DN2 ... 91 G1
Ennis Crs WHHL DN2 ... 90 E2
Entwhistle Rd
CHPT/GREN S35 ... 104 C8 1
Epping Gdns MOS S20 ... 179 L5
Epping Gv MOS S20 ... 179 L5
Epsom Cl MEX/SWTN S64 ... 108 F1
Epsom Rd DONS/BSCR DN4 ... 91 H5
Epworth Rd HTFD DN7 ... 49 J8
Epworth Rd (West) HTFD DN7 ... 49 H8
Eric St HEM/SK/SE WF9 ... 42 E4
Errington Av SHEFP/MNR S2 ... 161 J8
Errington Cl SHEFP/MNR S2 ... 177 J1
Errington Crs SHEFP/MNR S2 ... 177 J1
Errington Rd SHEFP/MNR S2 ... 161 J8
Errington Wy SHEFP/MNR S2 ... 161 J8
Erskine Crs SHEFP/MNR S2 ... 161 G8
Erskine Rd RHAM/THRY S65 ... 7 G1
SHEFP/MNR S2 ... 161 G8
Erskine Vw SHEFP/MNR S2 ... 177 G1
Eshton Ct DOD/DAR S75 ... 37 L5
Eskdale Cl DRON S18 ... 190 C6
ST/HB/BR S6 ... 143 M4
Eskdale Dr BTLY DN5 ... 67 K7
WRKN S81 ... 184 C7
Eskdale Rd BSLYN/ROY S71 ... 61 L7 2
KIMB S61 ... 128 D4
ST/HB/BR S6 ... 143 M4
Eskholme La GLE DN14 ... 12 B7
Esperanto Pl SHEF S1 ... 9 J4 1
Essendine Crs SHEFS S8 ... 176 F4
Essex Av WHHL DN2 ... 90 F4
Essex Cl AU/AST/KP S26 ... 181 K5
Essex Dr NROS/TKH DN11 ... 154 B3
Essex Rd BSLY S70 ... 3 G9
NROS/TKH DN11 ... 154 A3
SHEFP/MNR S2 ... 161 H6
Estate Rd RAW S62 ... 107 J8
Estfeld Cl NROS/TKH DN11 ... 134 E7 1
Estone Dr AU/AST/KP S26 ... 164 B7
Etwall Wy SHEFN S5 ... 145 G3
Eunice La KBTN HD8 ... 56 A1
Europa Link DARN/MH S9 ... 162 C1
Evans St OWL S3 ... 8 E7
Evanston Gdns
DONS/BSCR DN4 ... 89 L7
Eveline St CUD/GR S72 ... 61 M1
Evelyn Av WHHL DN2 ... 90 F3
Evelyn Rd FUL S10 ... 159 L4
Evelyn St RAW S62 ... 129 M1
Evelyn Ter BSLY S70 ... 3 K7
Everard Av TOT/DORE S17 ... 189 L1
Everard Dr TOT/DORE S17 ... 189 L2
Everard Gld TOT/DORE S17 ... 189 L2 2
Everdale Mt HEM/SK/SE WF9 ... 40 F1
HEM/SK/SE WF9 ... 42 C4 3
Everetts Cl NROS/TKH DN11 ... 134 D8
Everill Cl WMB/DAR S73 ... 84 D6
Everill Gate La WMB/DAR S73 ... 84 D5
Everingham Cl SHEFN S5 ... 144 E4
Everingham Crs SHEFN S5 ... 144 D4
Everingham Rd
DONS/BSCR DN4 ... 91 J6
SHEFN S5 ... 144 E4
Everson Cl MALT S66 ... 132 C8 2
Everton Rd ECC S11 ... 160 A7
Evesham Cl DARN/MH S9 ... 145 M3
Ewden Rd WMB/DAR S73 ... 84 D6
Ewden Wy DOD/DAR S75 ... 59 L6
Ewers Rd KIMB S61 ... 146 D1
Ewood Dr DONS/BSCR DN4 ... 91 J7
Exchange Pl ATT S4 ... 9 K3
Exchange St HEM/SK/SE WF9 .. 42 D4 2
SHEF S1 ... 9 K3
Exeter Dr OWL S3 ... 8 E8
Exeter Pl FUL S10 ... 8 D7
Exeter Rd WHHL DN2 ... 90 E1
Exeter Wy OWL S3 ... 8 D7
Exley Av ST/HB/BR S6 ... 160 B1
Eyam Cl DOD/DAR S75 ... 59 J8 4
Eyam Rd FUL S10 ... 159 M4 2
Eyncourt Rd SHEFN S5 ... 145 H4
Eyre La SHEF S1 ... 9 H6
Eyre St SHEF S1 ... 9 G7

F

Fabian Wy MALT S66 ... 149 H3
Factory La DON DN1 ... 4 E4 1
Fairbank Rd SHEFN S5 ... 144 F6
Fairbank Vw RHAM S60 ... 148 A6
Fairbarn Cl ST/HB/BR S6 ... 159 J2 1
Fairbarn Dr ST/HB/BR S6 ... 159 J2
Fairbarn Pl ST/HB/BR S6 ... 159 J2
Fairbarn Rd ST/HB/BR S6 ... 159 J2
Fairbarn Wy ST/HB/BR S6 ... 159 J2
Fairbrook Rd HOR/CROF WF4 ... 19 L3
Fairburn Gdns RHAM S60 ... 147 H7 5
Fairburn Gv HOY S74 ... 105 M1
Fairfax Dr SHEFP/MNR S2 ... 161 M7
Fairfax Rd SHEFP/MNR S2 ... 161 M7
WHHL DN2 ... 90 F3
Fair Fld BSLY S70 ... 82 D6
Fairfield DEARNE S63 ... 85 M5
Fairfield Cl DONS/BSCR DN4 ... 113 H1
MALT S66 ... 131 G8
Fairfield Rd BTLY DN5 ... 89 K1
OWL S3 ... 160 C1
Fairfields KBTN HD8 ... 56 D4
Fairfields Rd HOLM/MEL HD7 ... 53 H4
Fairford Cl DONS/BSCR DN4 ... 113 L1
Fair Holme Vw ARMTH DN3 ... 92 A3
Fair House La ST/HB/BR S6 ... 141 L3
Fairhurst La CHPT/GREN S35 ... 124 B3
Fairleigh SHEFP/MNR S2 ... 161 L8
Fairleigh Dr RHAM S60 ... 7 G8
Fairmount Gdns
HACK/IN S12 ... 178 E4 3
Fairthorn Rd SHEFN S5 ... 145 H3
Fairtree Wk THNE DN8 ... 31 M8
Fair View Av AWLS/ASK DN6 ... 66 D2
Fairview Cl HOY S74 ... 105 G2
Fairview Ct ARMTH DN3 ... 69 K1
Fair View Dr AU/AST/KP S26 ... 164 B8
Fairview Rd DRON S18 ... 190 E4
Fairway DOD/DAR S75 ... 81 L1
Fairway Av DOD/DAR S75 ... 38 A5
Fairways MALT S66 ... 148 F3
The Fairway FUL S10 ... 158 E6
THNE DN8 ... 32 B3
Faith St BSLYN/ROY S71 ... 61 K1
HEM/SK/SE WF9 ... 42 B3
Falcon Cl AWLS/ASK DN6 ... 66 F1
Falcon Ct NROS/TKH DN11 ... 113 L6
Falcon Dr BSLY S70 ... 82 D7
RHAM S60 ... 163 K4
Falconer La HAN/WDH S13 ... 163 K6
Falcon Ri DRON S18 ... 191 H4 1
Falcon Rd DRON S18 ... 191 G4
Falcon St BSLY S70 ... 2 F4
Falcon Wy DIN S25 ... 166 C8
Falding St CHPT/GREN S35 ... 126 F2
RHAM S60 ... 6 C4
Falkland Ri DRON S18 ... 190 E7
Falkland Rd ECC S11 ... 175 L1
Fall Bank Crs DOD/DAR S75 ... 59 H7
Falledge La STKB/PEN S36 ... 56 C5
Fall Head La DOD/DAR S75 ... 58 F6
Fallon Rd ST/HB/BR S6 ... 159 H1
Fallow Ct WRKN S81 ... 184 F8
Fall Vw DOD/DAR S75 ... 58 E7
Falmouth Cl BSLYN/ROY S71 ... 3 M2
Falmouth Rd ABRD S7 ... 176 C2
Falstaff Crs SHEFN S5 ... 144 D3
Falstaff Rd SHEFN S5 ... 144 D2
Falthwaite Green La
DOD/DAR S75 ... 81 H4
Fane Crs AU/AST/KP S26 ... 164 B7
Fanny Av ECK/KIL S21 ... 194 C2
Fanshaw Av ECK/KIL S21 ... 193 G5
Fanshaw Bank DRON S18 ... 190 E6 2
Fanshaw Dr ECK/KIL S21 ... 193 G5 1
Fanshaw Gate La DRON S18 ... 189 H7
Fanshaw Rd DRON S18 ... 190 F5
ECK/KIL S21 ... 193 G5
Fanshaw Wy ECK/KIL S21 ... 193 G5
Faraday Rd DARN/MH S9 ... 161 J1
Faranden Rd DARN/MH S9 ... 161 L2 2
Far Bank La HTFD DN7 ... 30 D8
Farcliff BTLY DN5 ... 88 F6
Far Common Rd HTFD DN7 ... 49 M8
Far Crs RHAM/THRY S65 ... 129 M8
Far Cft DEARNE S63 ... 86 A5 1
Farcroft Gv ATT S4 ... 145 K6 2
Far Dalton La RHAM/THRY S65 .. 130 C7
Fardell Gdns MALT S66 ... 149 H3 1
Far Field Av HOLM/MEL HD7 ... 54 C6
Far Field Dr HOLM/MEL HD7 ... 54 C5
Far Field La BSLYN/ROY S71 ... 61 J1
DEARNE S63 ... 107 M1
HOLM/MEL HD7 ... 54 C6
Farfield Pk DEARNE S63 ... 85 M8
Far Field Rd ARMTH DN3 ... 69 L4
RHAM/THRY S65 ... 148 A3
Fargate SHEF S1 ... 9 H4
Far Golden Smithies
MEX/SWTN S64 ... 108 A3
Farish Pl SHEFP/MNR S2 ... 176 F1 1
Far La HOLM/MEL HD7 ... 54 C7
RHAM/THRY S65 ... 129 M8
ST/HB/BR S6 ... 143 M6
Farlow Cft CHPT/GREN S35 ... 104 A7
Farm Bank Rd SHEFP/MNR S2 ... 9 L7
Farm Cl ARMTH DN3 ... 69 L6 2
BSLYN/ROY S71 ... 61 G3 1
DRON S18 ... 190 F3
HACK/IN S12 ... 177 L5
RHAM S60 ... 146 F8
Farm Ct AWLS/ASK DN6 ... 67 G1 2
Farm Crs MOS S20 ... 193 G1
Farmfield Dr HEM/SK/SE WF9 .. 22 E4 1
Farm Fields Cl MOS S20 ... 179 H6
Farmhill Cl BTLY DN5 ... 89 J2 1
Farm House La DOD/DAR S75 ... 59 L5
Farm La HEM/SK/SE WF9 ... 22 E5
Far Moor Cl BTLY DN5 ... 87 G5
Farmoor Gdns MOS S20 ... 179 M6 3
Farm Rd BSLY S70 ... 83 G1
SHEFP/MNR S2 ... 9 K8
Farmstead Cl
SHEFP/MNR S2 ... 177 H2 1
Farm View Cl HACK/IN S12 ... 178 F4 1
KIMB S61 ... 128 B7
Farm View Dr HACK/IN S12 ... 178 F4
Farm View Gdns HACK/IN S12 .. 178 F4
Farm View Rd KIMB S61 ... 128 A7
Farm Wy WMB/DAR S73 ... 84 E1
Farnaby Gdns CHPT/GREN S35 .. 104 B7
Farnborough Dr
DONS/BSCR DN4 ... 113 L1
Farndale WRKN S81 ... 184 F8
Farndale Rd BTLY DN5 ... 67 H8 1
ST/HB/BR S6 ... 144 A5
Farndon Gv WRKN S81 ... 184 B8 1
Farnes Ct WRKN S81 ... 198 F2 1
Farnley Av ST/HB/BR S6 ... 144 B3 1
Farnsworth Rd
RHAM/THRY S65 ... 130 A8
Far Pl RHAM/THRY S65 ... 129 M8
Farquhar Rd MALT S66 ... 150 F2
Farrar Rd SHEFS S8 ... 160 D8 7
Farrar St BSLY S70 ... 2 D5
Farrier Ga CHPT/GREN S35 ... 126 C1
Farringdon Dr
NROS/TKH DN11 ... 113 K8
Farrow Cl DOD/DAR S75 ... 59 L8
Farthing Gale Ms BTLY DN5 ... 89 K2 2
Far Townend DOD/DAR S75 ... 59 L8 3
Far View Rd SHEFN S5 ... 144 F3
Farwater Cl DRON S18 ... 190 E7 2
Farwater La DRON S18 ... 190 D6 1
Fathers Gdns
AU/AST/KP S26 ... 181 H5 1
Favell Rd OWL S3 ... 8 D4
RHAM/THRY S65 ... 130 B8 1
Fawcett St OWL S3 ... 8 D2
Fearnehough St
DARN/MH S9 ... 161 L2 3
Fearn House Crs HOY S74 ... 105 G2
Fearnley Ct HOLM/MEL HD7 ... 54 B2
Fearnley La HOLM/MEL HD7 ... 54 A2
Fearnley Rd HOY S74 ... 105 G2
Fearnville Gv BSLYN/ROY S71 ... 39 G4
Featherbed La WRKS S80 ... 197 J5
Featherston Av WRKS S80 ... 198 F5
Felkirk Dr HOR/CROF WF4 ... 21 L6
Felkirk Vw CUD/GR S72 ... 39 M4
Fellbrigg Rd SHEFP/MNR S2 ... 161 H8
Fellowsfield Wy KIMB S61 ... 128 C8
Fell Rd DARN/MH S9 ... 145 L8
Fell St DARN/MH S9 ... 145 L8
Fellview Cl HATH/EY S32 ... 172 E8
Fenland Rd THNE DN8 ... 50 A1
Fenney La ECC S11 ... 175 J5
Fenn Rd DOD/DAR S75 ... 104 D2
Fensome Wy WMB/DAR S73 ... 84 E1 2
Fenton Cl HEM/SK/SE WF9 ... 41 M6 1
Fenton Cft KIMB S61 ... 128 E7
Fenton Flds KIMB S61 ... 128 E7
Fenton Rd KIMB S61 ... 128 E5
Fenton St BSLY S70 ... 2 E5 1
ECK/KIL S21 ... 192 F5
KIMB S61 ... 128 D8
Fentonville St ECC S11 ... 160 C7
Fenton Wy KIMB S61 ... 128 F5
Fenwick Common La
AWLS/ASK DN6 ... 28 E4
Fenwick La AWLS/ASK DN6 ... 28 B5
Feoffees Rd CHPT/GREN S35 .. 126 F7 2
Ferguson St DARN/MH S9 ... 161 K1
Ferham Cl KIMB S61 ... 146 E1
Ferham Park Av KIMB S61 ... 146 E1 1
Ferham Rd KIMB S61 ... 146 E1
Fern Av BTLY DN5 ... 67 L8
MOS S20 ... 179 K3
Fern Bank AWLS/ASK DN6 ... 66 F1
Fernbank Dr ARMTH DN3 ... 69 M7
ECK/KIL S21 ... 192 F4
Fern Cl ECK/KIL S21 ... 192 F4
WHHL DN2 ... 90 F1
WMB/DAR S73 ... 84 E3
Ferncroft Av MOS S20 ... 179 G8
Ferndale Cl DRON S18 ... 191 H4
Ferndale Dr MALT S66 ... 149 G1
THNE DN8 ... 32 A5
Ferndale Pl HEM/SK/SE WF9 ... 41 G1
Ferndale Ri DRON S18 ... 191 H4
Ferndale Rd CONI DN12 ... 109 M5
DRON S18 ... 191 H4
Ferndale Vw BTLY DN5 ... 89 J2
Fernhall Cl ARMTH DN3 ... 69 L4 1
Fern Hollow MALT S66 ... 149 G4
Fernhurst Rd WHHL DN2 ... 91 G1
Fernlea Cl BTLY DN5 ... 89 K2 3
Fernlea Gv CHPT/GREN S35 ... 126 F7 3
Fern Lea Gv DEARNE S63 ... 85 M5 1
Fernleigh Dr RHAM S60 ... 146 F5
Fern Rd ST/HB/BR S6 ... 159 M1
Fernvale Wk MEX/SWTN S64 .. 108 B7 1
Fern Wy ECK/KIL S21 ... 192 F4
Ferrand St BSLY S70 ... 82 C8
Ferrara Cl WMB/DAR S73 ... 84 C1
Ferrars Cl DARN/MH S9 ... 146 D5
Ferrars Dr DARN/MH S9 ... 146 D6
Ferrars Rd DARN/MH S9 ... 146 C4
Ferrars Wy DARN/MH S9 ... 146 D6
Ferrers Rd WHHL DN2 ... 5 L1
Ferriby Rd ST/HB/BR S6 ... 143 M5
Ferry Boat La MEX/SWTN S64 ... 109 G3
Ferry La CONI DN12 ... 110 A4
Ferry Moor La CUD/GR S72 ... 62 B1
Ferry Rd THNE DN8 ... 31 J5
Ferry Top La HOR/CROF WF4 ... 21 L4
Festival Av NROS/TKH DN11 ... 153 L3
Festival Cl AU/AST/KP S26 ... 181 G5
Festival Rd DEARNE S63 ... 107 K2
Fewton Wy DONS/BSCR DN4 ... 90 F7
Fiddlers Dr ARMTH DN3 ... 92 A3
Field Av ECK/KIL S21 ... 193 M7
Field Cl DRON S18 ... 190 A5 2
WMB/DAR S73 ... 84 E1
WRKN S81 ... 184 E8
Field Dr CUD/GR S72 ... 61 M2
Field End La HOLM/MEL HD7 ... 52 F5
Fielders Wy CONI DN12 ... 111 G4 3
Fieldfare Dr WRKN S81 ... 184 A8
Field Ga NROS/TKH DN11 ... 113 L5
Fieldhead La HOLM/MEL HD7 ... 52 D6
Field Head Rd HOY S74 ... 105 J2
Fieldhead Rd
SHEFP/MNR S2 ... 160 E8 2
Field House Rd BTLY DN5 ... 88 F7 2
Fieldhouse Wy ATT S4 ... 145 H8
Fielding Dr MALT S66 ... 149 H3
Fielding Gv RAW S62 ... 107 K8
Fielding Rd ST/HB/BR S6 ... 144 A5
Field La BSLY S70 ... 61 J8
ECK/KIL S21 ... 193 M2
EPW DN9 ... 94 F6
HEM/SK/SE WF9 ... 24 E8
HEM/SK/SE WF9 ... 43 H3
RHAM S60 ... 148 D8
STKB/PEN S36 ... 78 B6
Field Rd HOLM/MEL HD7 ... 53 M3
HTFD DN7 ... 48 C3
THNE DN8 ... 31 M8
Fields End STKB/PEN S36 ... 79 M7
Fieldside ARMTH DN3 ... 69 K6
Field Side THNE DN8 ... 31 L7
Fieldside Rd HEM/SK/SE WF9 ... 22 F5
Field Station Rd BTLY DN5 ... 46 D7
Field Vw RHAM S60 ... 147 G6
Field Wy RHAM S60 ... 6 E1
Fife Cl DARN/MH S9 ... 145 L3
Fife St BSLY S70 ... 2 D7
DARN/MH S9 ... 145 L3
Fife Wy DARN/MH S9 ... 145 L3
Fifth Av AWLS/ASK DN6 ... 66 F4
Fiftyeights Rd BWTY DN10 ... 116 B4
Filby Rd BTLY DN5 ... 89 J2
Filey Av BSLYN/ROY S71 ... 39 H3
Filey La OWL S3 ... 8 D6
Filey St FUL S10 ... 8 D6
Finch Av WKFDW/WTN WF2 ... 20 B2
Finch Cl RHAM/THRY S65 ... 130 D5
Finch Gdns MALT S66 ... 149 J3
Finch Ri AU/AST/KP S26 ... 180 C1
Finch Rd DONS/BSCR DN4 ... 111 K1 2
Finchwell Cl HAN/WDH S13 ... 162 D5
Finchwell Crs HAN/WDH S13 ... 162 D5
Finchwell Rd HAN/WDH S13 ... 162 D5
Findon Crs ST/HB/BR S6 ... 143 L7
Findon Pl ST/HB/BR S6 ... 143 L7 1
Findon Rd ST/HB/BR S6 ... 143 L7
Findon St ST/HB/BR S6 ... 143 M7
Finghall Rd AWLS/ASK DN6 ... 44 D5
Fingleton WRKN S81 ... 198 F1 1
Finkle St BTLY DN5 ... 67 M7
HOR/CROF WF4 ... 19 K8
HTFD DN7 ... 48 C2
Finkle Street La
CHPT/GREN S35 ... 103 G4
Finlay Rd RHAM/THRY S65 ... 7 M1
Finlay St OWL S3 ... 8 D2
Finnley's La GLE DN14 ... 12 D1
Firbeck Av DIN S25 ... 166 C3
Firbeck Crs WRKN S81 ... 168 C4
Firbeck La DIN S25 ... 166 C2
Firbeck Rd DONS/BSCR DN4 ... 5 L7
SHEFS S8 ... 176 C4 1
Firbeck Wy NROS/TKH DN11 ... 113 M5
Fir Cl DEARNE S63 ... 107 K2 2
Fircroft Av SHEFN S5 ... 145 H2
Fircroft Rd SHEFN S5 ... 145 J2
Firethorn Ri RHAM/THRY S65 ... 131 J7

Firham Cl BSLYN/ROY S71 38 E3
Fir Pl ECK/KIL S21 194 A2
Fir Rd ECK/KIL S21 192 F5
Firsby La CONI DN12 109 J8
Firshill Av ATT S4 144 F7
Firshill Cl ATT S4 144 F7
Firshill Crs ATT S4 144 E7
Firshill Gld ATT S4 144 E7
Firshill Ri ATT S4 144 F7
Firshill Rd ATT S4 144 F7
Firs La STKB/PEN S36 57 H8
First Av AWLS/ASK DN6 67 G3
HEM/SK/SE WF9 22 E3
HEM/SK/SE WF9 24 E8
HEM/SK/SE WF9 41 K6
RHAM/THRY S65 7 M2
The Firs BSLY S70 83 G1
BSLYN/ROY S71 38 E3
First La DIN S25 182 C4
Fir St FUL S10 160 A2
Firth Av CUD/GR S72 61 L2
Firth Crs MALT S66 150 E3
NROS/TKH DN11 113 J6
Firth Dr ATT S4 161 H1
Firthfield La HEM/SK/SE WF9 24 C3
Firth Field Rd HTFD DN7 49 J7 1
Firth Park Av SHEFN S5 145 H4
Firth Park Crs SHEFN S5 145 H4
Firth Park Rd SHEFN S5 145 H4
Firth Rd DEARNE S63 106 F1
Firth St DONS/BSCR DN4 4 D8
KIMB S61 129 G4
Firthwood Av DRON S18 191 H4
Firthwood Cl DRON S18 191 H4 2
Firthwood Rd DRON S18 191 H4
Fir Tree CHPT/GREN S35 80 E8
Fir Tree Av EPW DN9 114 E3
Fir Tree Cl BTLY DN5 64 F8
Fir Tree Dr AU/AST/KP S26 180 E5
AWLS/ASK DN6 27 G4
Firtree Ri CHPT/GREN S35 126 E3 2
Firvale AU/AST/KP S26 195 J2
Fir Vale Pl SHEFN S5 145 G6 1
Fir Vale Rd SHEFN S5 145 G6
Fish Dam La BSLYN/ROY S71 39 H7
Fisher Cl RHAM S60 6 C4
Fisher La DARN/MH S9 162 A2
Fisher Rd MALT S66 150 F2
Fisher St BTLY DN5 67 M5
Fisher Ter BTLY DN5 89 L2 1
Fishlake Nab HTFD DN7 48 C1
Fishpond La HOR/CROF WF4 19 K2
Fish Pond La MALT S66 132 E7
Fishponds Dr HOR/CROF WF4 19 K2
Fishponds Rd HAN/WDH S13 162 A7
Fishponds Rd West
HAN/WDH S13 162 A8
Fitzalan Rd HAN/WDH S13 162 D6
Fitzalan Sq SHEF S1 9 J4
Fitzgerald Rd FUL S10 159 M3
Fitzhubert Rd SHEFP/MNR S2 161 L7
Fitzmaurice Rd DARN/MH S9 161 M1
Fitzroy Rd SHEFP/MNR S2 176 F1
Fitzwalter Rd SHEFP/MNR S2 9 M7
Fitzwilliam Av CONI DN12 109 K5
DEARNE S63 107 J2
Fitzwilliam Ct RAW S62 129 K3
Fitzwilliam Dr BTLY DN5 86 F6
Fitzwilliam Ga SHEF S1 8 F7
Fitzwilliam Rd RHAM/THRY S65 7 H2
WMB/DAR S73 85 G1
Fitzwilliam Sq RAW S62 128 F3
Fitzwilliam St BSLY S70 2 D5
HEM/SK/SE WF9 22 F6
HOY S74 104 F2
HOY S74 105 L2
MEX/SWTN S64 108 A5
RAW S62 129 K4
SHEF S1 8 E6
WMB/DAR S73 83 M8
Five Acres DOD/DAR S75 58 D2
Five Lane Ends
HOLM/MEL HD7 53 J2 1
Five Oaks BTLY DN5 68 C4
Five Trees Cl TOT/DORE S17 189 L1
Five Trees Dr TOT/DORE S17 189 L1
Five Weirs Wk DARN/MH S9 161 K1
Fixby La EARL WF12 16 B1
Flanders Ct KIMB S61 127 K2 4
Flanderwell Av MALT S66 149 G2
Flanderwell Ct MALT S66 149 G1 1
Flanderwell Gdns MALT S66 149 G1 2
Flanderwell La MALT S66 130 F8
Flash La MALT S66 149 J3
ST/HB/BR S6 158 C3
Flashley Carr La AWLS/ASK DN6 29 J6
Flask Vw ST/HB/BR S6 143 G8
Flat La CUD/GR S72 85 J2
DIN S25 167 L1
MALT S66 151 J7
RHAM S60 147 M6
The Flats CHPT/GREN S35 103 J4
Flat St SHEF S1 9 J4
Flatts Cl RHAM S60 163 J2
Flatts La DEARNE S63 107 H1
RHAM S60 163 J2
Flavell Cl HEM/SK/SE WF9 41 M6 2
Flaxby Rd DARN/MH S9 161 M2 4
Flax Lea BSLY S70 82 E2
Fleet Cl DEARNE S63 84 E8
Fleet Hill Crs BSLYN/ROY S71 60 E2
Fleet La HTFD DN7 48 C2 1
Fleets Cl HTFD DN7 48 C2
Fleet St KBTN HD8 35 H6
Fleetway WRKN S81 184 C8
Fleetwood Av BSLYN/ROY S71 61 G2
Fleming Pl BSLY S70 2 F7 1
Fleming Wy MALT S66 148 E2
Fletcher Av DRON S18 190 E6
Fleury Cl GLV S14 177 J3
Fleury Crs GLV S14 177 J3
Fleury Pl GLV S14 177 J3
Fleury Ri GLV S14 177 J3
Fleury Rd GLV S14 177 J3
Flight Hl HOLM/MEL HD7 76 A2
Flint La HOLM/MEL HD7 76 E2
Flint Rd WHHL DN2 91 G2
Flintway DEARNE S63 107 K4
Flockton Av HAN/WDH S13 162 F7
Flockton Crs HAN/WDH S13 162 F7
Flockton Dr HAN/WDH S13 163 G7
Flockton Rd HAN/WDH S13 163 G7
Flodden St FUL S10 159 M3 1
Floodgate Dr CHPT/GREN S35 126 F7
Flora St ST/HB/BR S6 160 C1
Florence Av AU/AST/KP S26 164 B8
DONS/BSCR DN4 89 L7
Florence Ri WMB/DAR S73 84 D2
Florence Rd KIMB S61 6 A5
SHEFS S8 176 C5
Flounders Hl FEA/AMT WF7 23 J1
Flower St DEARNE S63 86 D2
Flowitt St DONS/BSCR DN4 4 C6
MEX/SWTN S64 108 D2
Flowright Cl SHEFP/MNR S2 177 H2
Flush House La HOLM/MEL HD7 52 E4
Folderings La STKB/PEN S36 124 A1
Folder La BTLY DN5 88 E6
The Foldings KBTN HD8 34 E5 1
Folds Crs SHEFS S8 176 A6
Folds Dr SHEFS S8 176 A6 1
Folds La NROS/TKH DN11 152 B4
SHEFS S8 176 A6
Foley Av WMB/DAR S73 84 A5
Foley St ATT S4 161 H2
Foljambe Crs NROS/TKH DN11 113 H6
Foljambe Dr RHAM/THRY S65 130 C6
Foljambe Rd RHAM/THRY S65 129 M7
Foljambe St RAW S62 129 K3 3
Follett Rd SHEFN S5 145 G2
Folly La STKB/PEN S36 78 D1
Folly Nook La RTFD DN22 170 F1
Fontwell Dr MEX/SWTN S64 108 F1
Footgate Cl CHPT/GREN S35 125 H8
Forbes Rd ST/HB/BR S6 144 A8
Ford La HACK/IN S12 192 C2
STKB/PEN S36 102 A5
Fordoles Head La MALT S66 132 A7
Ford Rd ECC S11 175 M1
ECK/KIL S21 192 C3
RHAM S60 163 G2
Fordstead La ARMTH DN3 47 H8
Ford St HEM/SK/SE WF9 22 F6
Fore Hill Av DONS/BSCR DN4 113 H1
Foremark Rd SHEFN S5 145 H3
Forest Hill Rd WRKN S81 184 E8 3
Forest La WRKS S80 199 G5
Forest Ri DONS/BSCR DN4 111 J2
Forest Rd BSLYN/ROY S71 38 D7
Forge La CHPT/GREN S35 102 E2
ECK/KIL S21 179 M8
HOY S74 105 L3
RHAM S60 6 E4
SHEF S1 9 G8
Forge Rd AU/AST/KP S26 180 F4
Formby Ct BSLYN/ROY S71 61 H1 2
Forncett St ATT S4 161 H1
Fornham St SHEF S1 9 J7
Forres Av FUL S10 159 L4
Forres Rd FUL S10 159 M4
Forrester Cl HEM/SK/SE WF9 22 E4
MALT S66 148 F1
Forrester's Cl AWLS/ASK DN6 27 G4
Forrester's La DRON S18 191 G3 2
Forrest's Yd WRKS S80 198 C5 2
Forster Rd DONS/BSCR DN4 111 M1
Forth Av DRON S18 190 B5
Fort Hill Rd DARN/MH S9 145 K5
Fortway Rd RHAM S60 147 G5
Forum Vw PONT WF8 24 E2 1
Fossard Cl WHHL DN2 90 E1
Fossard Wy BTLY DN5 67 K6
Fossdale Rd ABRD S7 176 B2
Foster Place La
HOLM/MEL HD7 54 D5
Foster Rd MALT S66 148 F2
THNE DN8 31 L7
Foster's Cl MEX/SWTN S64 108 A4
Foster St BSLY S70 61 H7
Foster Wy CHPT/GREN S35 104 B8
Fothergill Av FEA/AMT WF7 23 J1
Foulstone Rw WMB/DAR S73 84 C5 1
Foundry La THNE DN8 31 L8 2
Foundry Rd DONS/BSCR DN4 4 B8 1
Foundry St BSLY S70 2 F7 2
HOY S74 105 L2
RAW S62 129 K4
Fountain Cl DOD/DAR S75 37 J6
Fountain Ct BSLYN/ROY S71 38 C6
Fountains Wy BSLYN/ROY S71 61 H4
Four Lanes Cl DOD/DAR S75 59 J2 1
Fourth Av AWLS/ASK DN6 66 F4
Four Wells Dr HACK/IN S12 178 E4
Fowler Bridge Rd BTLY DN5 68 A7
Fowler Crs NROS/TKH DN11 113 J6
Fox Cl KBTN HD8 35 H1
KIMB S61 128 B5
Foxcote Lea RHAM/THRY S65 130 E5
Fox Ct MEX/SWTN S64 108 B6
Fox Covert Cl DEARNE S63 86 A3 1
Fox Covert Rd
Or Whin Covert La PONT WF8 26 C5
Foxcroft Cha ECK/KIL S21 194 A1
Foxcroft Dr ECK/KIL S21 194 A1
Foxcroft Gv ECK/KIL S21 194 A1
Foxcroft Mdw MALT S66 150 E3
Foxfields STKB/PEN S36 79 L6
Foxfield Wk BSLY S70 83 H1 3
Fox Glen Rd STKB/PEN S36 102 B7
Foxglove Cl EPW DN9 115 K1 1
WRKS S80 198 F6
Foxglove Rd SHEFN S5 145 J3
Fox Gv DONS/BSCR DN4 111 G1
Foxhall La FUL S10 174 D1
Fox Hill Av ST/HB/BR S6 144 A2
Fox Hill Cl ST/HB/BR S6 144 A2
Fox Hill Crs ST/HB/BR S6 144 A1
Fox Hill Dr ST/HB/BR S6 144 A2
Fox Hill Pl ST/HB/BR S6 144 A1
Fox Hill Rd ST/HB/BR S6 126 A8
Foxhill Rd THNE DN8 50 A1
Fox Hill Wy ST/HB/BR S6 144 A1 3
Fox Hole La NROS/TKH DN11 134 B6
Fox Holes Gv STKB/PEN S36 77 H2
Foxland Av MEX/SWTN S64 107 L5
Fox La BTLY DN5 87 G4
HACK/IN S12 178 A4
TOT/DORE S17 190 B1
Fox Lane Ct HACK/IN S12 178 A3 1
Fox Lane Vw HACK/IN S12 178 A3
Fox Rd ST/HB/BR S6 160 C1
Foxroyd Cl BSLYN/ROY S71 61 K7 4
Fox St KIMB S61 146 C1
OWL S3 160 F1
Foxwood Av HACK/IN S12 177 M1
Foxwood Dr HACK/IN S12 177 M1
Foxwood Gv HACK/IN S12 177 M2
Foxwood Rd HACK/IN S12 177 M1
Framlingham Pl
SHEFP/MNR S2 161 H8
France Rd ST/HB/BR S6 143 H6
Frances St DON DN1 5 G4
RHAM/THRY S65 7 H6 1
France St RAW S62 129 K4
Francis Crs North
RHAM/THRY S65 148 B4
Francis Crs South
RHAM/THRY S65 148 B4
Francis Dr RHAM/THRY S65 148 B4
Francis Gv CHPT/GREN S35 104 B8
Francis St FEA/AMT WF7 23 H2
Francus Rd BSLYN/ROY S71 39 G6
Frank La KBTN HD8 35 G2
Franklin Crs WHHL DN2 5 M5
Frank Pl DARN/MH S9 145 L8
Frank Rd BTLY DN5 89 M1
Fraser Cl SHEFS S8 176 C4 2
Fraser Crs SHEFS S8 176 C4
Fraser Dr SHEFS S8 176 D4
Fraser Rd RHAM/THRY S65 7 J7
SHEFS S8 176 C4
Frederick Av BSLY S70 2 D8
Frederick Dr CHPT/GREN S35 125 M6
Frederick St DARN/MH S9 161 M3
DEARNE S63 85 H8 3
DEARNE S63 86 C2
MEX/SWTN S64 108 D2
RHAM S60 6 E3
RHAM S60 163 G2
WMB/DAR S73 84 A4 2
WRKS S80 198 C4
Frederic Pl BSLY S70 60 D8 1
Fred Mulley Rd ATT S4 161 H2
Freedom Ct ST/HB/BR S6 144 B8
Freedom Rd ST/HB/BR S6 160 A1
Freeman Rd MALT S66 148 F2
Freeman St BSLY S70 3 H8
Freemans Yd BSLY S70 3 H6 1
Freesia Cl DIN S25 182 A3
Freeston Pl DARN/MH S9 145 L8
French Ga DON DN1 4 E3 1
French St AWLS/ASK DN6 44 E6 2
BTLY DN5 67 M5
Fretson Rd SHEFP/MNR S2 161 L7 2
Fretwell Cl MALT S66 150 C1 2
Fretwell Rd MALT S66 149 M2
RHAM/THRY S65 130 A7
Friar Cl ST/HB/BR S6 159 H1
Friars Ga BTLY DN5 4 F2
Friar's Rd BSLYN/ROY S71 61 J4
Frickley Bridge La CUD/GR S72 40 C3
Frickley La BTLY DN5 64 D1
Frickley Rd ECC S11 159 K7
Frith Cl HACK/IN S12 177 M2
Frith Rd HACK/IN S12 177 M2
Frobisher Gv MALT S66 150 C1
Froggatt La SHEF S1 9 H6 2
Frogmore Cl MALT S66 149 H1
Front St RHAM S60 163 J3
Frostings Cl CHPT/GREN S35 126 A6
The Frostings CHPT/GREN S35 126 A6
Fulford Cl DARN/MH S9 162 A2 1
Fulford Pl DARN/MH S9 162 A2 3
Fullerton Av CONI DN12 109 K5
Fullerton Cl AWLS/ASK DN6 44 D5
Fullerton Crs RHAM/THRY S65 130 C5
Fullerton Dr RHAM S60 146 F7
Fullerton Rd RHAM S60 6 C8
RHAM S60 147 G4
Fullshaw La STKB/PEN S36 77 M8
Fulmar Wy KIMB S61 127 L1
WRKN S81 184 A8
Fulmer Cl BSLYN/ROY S71 60 F1
Fulmere Crs SHEFN S5 144 C1
Fulmere Rd SHEFN S5 144 C1
Fulmer Rd ECC S11 160 A8
Fulney Rd ECC S11 159 K7
Fulton Rd FUL S10 160 A2
Fulwood Cha FUL S10 159 J7 1
Fulwood Dr DONS/BSCR DN4 111 M3
Fulwood Gv WKFDW/WTN WF2 19 M2
Fulwood Head Rd FUL S10 174 C1
Fulwood La FUL S10 174 B1
Fulwood Rd ECC S11 159 H8
FUL S10 159 L6
Furlong Ct DEARNE S63 86 B4
Furlong Rd BTLY DN5 86 F6
DEARNE S63 86 B4
Furlong Vw BTLY DN5 86 F5
Furnace Hl OWL S3 9 G2
Furnace La HAN/WDH S13 163 H8
Furness Cl DIN S25 166 D8
ST/HB/BR S6 143 H8
Furness Dene BSLYN/ROY S71 61 H2
Furness Rd CHPT/GREN S35 104 A8
Furniss Av TOT/DORE S17 189 H1
Furniss Ms TOT/DORE S17 189 J1
Furnival Cl AU/AST/KP S26 181 J2 2
Furnival Ga SHEF S1 9 G6
Furnivall Rd DONS/BSCR DN4 89 L7
Furnival Rd ATT S4 9 K2
AU/AST/KP S26 181 J2
Furnival St SHEF S1 9 H6
WRKS S80 198 E6
Furnival St North WRKS S80 198 E5
Furnival Wy RHAM S60 148 B6
Fylde Cl BSLYN/ROY S71 61 H1

G

Gadding Moor Rd
STKB/PEN S36 57 K7
Gainford Rd THNE DN8 32 B3
Gainford Sq THNE DN8 32 B4
Gainsborough Cl MALT S66 148 F2 1
Gainsborough Rd ABRD S7 160 B8
BWTY DN10 154 E1
DRON S18 190 C7
Gainsborough Wy
BSLYN/ROY S71 3 L1
Gaitskell Cl DEARNE S63 86 B4
MALT S66 150 F3
Gala Crs MALT S66 150 B1
Galley Dr MOS S20 179 H6
Gallon Cft HEM/SK/SE WF9 42 C4
Gallows La HOR/CROF WF4 19 K6
Gallow Tree Rd
RHAM/THRY S65 148 B3
Galpharm Wy DOD/DAR S75 59 J7
Galsworthy Av SHEFN S5 144 D4
Galsworthy Cl
DONS/BSCR DN4 111 K2
Galsworthy Rd SHEFN S5 144 D4
Galway Av NROS/TKH DN11 154 B2
Galway Cl RAW S62 129 L1
Galway Dr NROS/TKH DN11 154 B2
Galway Rd NROS/TKH DN11 154 B2
Game La ST/HB/BR S6 142 B8
Gamston Rd SHEFS S8 160 D8
Gannow Cl ECK/KIL S21 180 D8
Ganton Pl BSLYN/ROY S71 38 C8
Ganton Rd ST/HB/BR S6 143 M5 1
Garbroads Crs
RHAM/THRY S65 130 C5
Garbutt St DEARNE S63 86 B6 1
Garden Av ECK/KIL S21 193 M8
Garden Crs RHAM S60 147 L5
Garden Dr WMB/DAR S73 84 E7
Garden Gv WMB/DAR S73 84 A7
Garden House Cl
BSLYN/ROY S71 61 G2
Garden House Dr
AU/AST/KP S26 181 K4
Gardenia Rd ARMTH DN3 69 J4
Garden La BTLY DN5 88 B8
RHAM S60 6 D3
RHAM/THRY S65 131 H4
Gardens La CONI DN12 109 M5
The Gardens DONS/BSCR DN4 91 H8
Garden St DEARNE S63 64 B7
DEARNE S63 85 H8 4
DEARNE S63 86 D2
FEA/AMT WF7 23 H2
KIMB S61 6 A3
MEX/SWTN S64 108 E2 2
SHEF S1 8 F3
WMB/DAR S73 84 E2
Garden Ter HOR/CROF WF4 19 H3
Garden Wk RHAM S60 147 L4
Gardom Cl DRON S18 190 B6 1
Garfield Mt RHAM/THRY S65 7 H6
Gargrave Crs HEM/SK/SE WF9 41 G1
Gargrave Pl HEM/SK/SE WF9 41 G1
Garland Cl MOS S20 179 J8
Garland Cft MOS S20 179 J8
Garland Dr ST/HB/BR S6 143 H6
Garland Mt MOS S20 179 J7 1
Garland Wy MOS S20 179 J8
Garmil Head La
HEM/SK/SE WF9 22 D2
Garraby Cl CUD/GR S72 63 J5
Garrett Cl KBTN HD8 34 D5 1
Garry Rd ST/HB/BR S6 143 M6
Garside St WRKS S80 198 E4
Garter St ATT S4 145 H8
Garth Cl DARN/MH S9 161 L2 1
Garth Rectory HEM/SK/SE WF9 23 H8
Garth Wy DRON S18 190 D6 2
Gartrice Gdns MOS S20 193 L2
Gartrice Gv MOS S20 193 K2
Gashouse La MOS S20 193 H2
Gate Crs DOD/DAR S75 59 K7
Gatefield Rd ABRD S7 176 C1 2
Gate Foot La KBTN HD8 55 G1
Gateford Av WRKN S81 198 B1
Gateford Cl WRKN S81 184 B8 2
Gateford Dr WRKN S81 198 B1
Gateford Gdns WRKN S81 198 B1
Gateford Gld WRKN S81 198 C1
Gateford Ri WRKN S81 184 B8
Gateford Rd WRKN S81 183 L6
WRKN S81 198 C2
WRKS S80 198 C3
Gate Head La HOLM/MEL HD7 54 E7
Gate House La EPW DN9 114 F2
Gatesbridge Pk EPW DN9 115 K3
Gateway Cl RAW S62 129 J5
Gateway Ct RAW S62 129 J5 1
The Gateway RAW S62 129 J6
Gate Wood La ARMTH DN3 93 H3
Gatewood La HTFD DN7 71 H5
Gattison La NROS/TKH DN11 113 K7
Gatty Rd SHEFN S5 127 H8
Gaunt Cl ECK/KIL S21 194 A1
GLV S14 177 H4
MALT S66 149 H1
Gaunt Dr GLV S14 177 H4
MALT S66 149 H1
Gaunt Pl GLV S14 177 H3
Gaunt Rd GLV S14 177 H3
MALT S66 149 H1
Gaunt Wy GLV S14 177 H4
Gawber Rd DOD/DAR S75 2 A2
Gayton Cl DONS/BSCR DN4 111 L2
Gayton Rd ATT S4 145 G7 2
Geer La HACK/IN S12 192 A2
Geeseness La GLE DN14 30 F4
Gelderd Pl DRON S18 190 E7
Gell St OWL S3 8 E6
Geneva Sq THNE DN8 32 B4
Genn La BSLY S70 82 B1
Genoa Cl WMB/DAR S73 62 C8
Genoa St MEX/SWTN S64 108 F2
The Gentre MALT S66 149 H2 1
George Buckley Ct
HEM/SK/SE WF9 41 L5 2
George La HOR/CROF WF4 38 C1
George Pl MEX/SWTN S64 109 G3 1
RAW S62 129 L2
George Sq BSLY S70 2 F6 1
George St AWLS/ASK DN6 44 F5
BSLY S70 2 F6
BSLY S70 82 E3 3
BSLY S70 83 G3
BTLY DN5 67 M5 1
CUD/GR S72 40 A7
CUD/GR S72 63 H8
DEARNE S63 64 D8
DEARNE S63 86 A2
DOD/DAR S75 37 M6
HEM/SK/SE WF9 41 J1 3
HOR/CROF WF4 21 M6
HOY S74 105 J2 2
RHAM S60 6 E3 2
SHEF S1 9 J4
WMB/DAR S73 84 B5
WMB/DAR S73 84 D3
WRKS S80 198 D4
George Yd BSLY S70 2 F5
Gerald Cl BSLY S70 61 G8
Gerald Crs BSLY S70 61 H7
Gerald Pl BSLY S70 61 G8
Gerald Rd BSLY S70 61 G8
Gerald St DARN/MH S9 145 L8
Gerald Wk BSLY S70 61 G8
Gerard Av RHAM/THRY S65 130 E5
Gerard Cl SHEFP/MNR S2 176 F1 2
Gerard Rd RHAM S60 7 G7
Gerard St SHEFS S8 176 F1
Gervase Av SHEFS S8 190 C1
Gervase Dr SHEFS S8 190 C1
Gervase Pl SHEFS S8 190 C1 1
Gervase Rd SHEFS S8 190 C1
Gibbet Hill La BWTY DN10 154 D3
Gibbing Greaves Rd
RHAM/THRY S65 148 C3
Gibbons Dr SHEFS S8 177 J5
Gibbons Wy SHEFS S8 177 J5 2
Gib La KBTN HD8 34 E5
Gibraltar St OWL S3 9 G2
Gibriding La HOLM/MEL HD7 52 D4
Gibson Rd HTFD DN7 71 L7
Gifford Dr DONS/BSCR DN4 111 H1
Gifford Rd SHEFP/MNR S2 160 E8 3
Gig La HOY S74 82 F7
Gilbert Gv BSLY S70 61 H7
Gilbert Hl STKB/PEN S36 100 A1
Gilberthorpe Dr
RHAM/THRY S65 7 L5 1
Gilberthorpe Rd
DONS/BSCR DN4 89 K8 1
Gilberthorpe St RHAM/THRY S65 7 K5
Gilbert Rd NROS/TKH DN11 153 M3
Gilbert St SHEFP/MNR S2 9 K4
Gildingwells Rd WRKN S81 167 K6
WRKN S81 183 J3
Giles Av DEARNE S63 107 G1
Gill Cl MALT S66 149 G4
Gill Cft ST/HB/BR S6 159 G1 2
Gilleyfield Av TOT/DORE S17 175 J8
Gillion Crs HOR/CROF WF4 19 J2
Gill La HOLM/MEL HD7 53 J5
Gill Mdw ST/HB/BR S6 159 G1
Gillot Dell MALT S66 148 F4 1
Gillott La MALT S66 148 F4
Gillott Rd ST/HB/BR S6 144 A3
Gill Royd La STKB/PEN S36 100 C4
Gill St DON DN1 5 H7
HOY S74 105 K2
Gilpin La ST/HB/BR S6 160 C2 7
Gilpin St ST/HB/BR S6 160 C1 1
Gilroyd La DOD/DAR S75 81 M2
Gilthwaites Crs KBTN HD8 34 E8
Gilthwaites Gv KBTN HD8 56 E1
Gilthwaites La KBTN HD8 34 E8
Gilthwaites Top KBTN HD8 34 E8
Ginhouse La KIMB S61 129 G7
Gipsy Green La DEARNE S63 107 K3
Gipsyhill La WRKS S80 196 A6
Gipsy La DOD/DAR S75 37 K2
DRON S18 191 L6
MALT S66 151 G6
Gisborne Rd ECC S11 175 M1
Glade Cft HACK/IN S12 177 L2
Glade Lea HACK/IN S12 177 L3
Glade Vw ARMTH DN3 69 K3
Gladstone Ms FUL S10 159 J6 1
Gladstone Pl WRKS S80 198 C4
Gladstone Rd DONS/BSCR DN4 4 A8
FUL S10 159 J6
MALT S66 150 C1 3
Gladstone St WRKS S80 198 C4
Gladys St RHAM/THRY S65 7 L4
Glaisdale WRKN S81 184 F8
Glaisdale Cl DIN S25 166 A4
Glamis Rd WHHL DN2 90 E4
WRKN S81 184 C1
Glasshouse La MEX/SWTN S64 108 C8
Glasshouse St RHAM S60 6 D3
Glastonbury Ga BTLY DN5 89 H2
Gleadless Av HACK/IN S12 177 K3
Gleadless Bank HACK/IN S12 177 K3 1
Gleadless Common
HACK/IN S12 177 K2
Gleadless Ct SHEFP/MNR S2 176 F1 3
Gleadless Crs HACK/IN S12 177 K2
Gleadless Dr HACK/IN S12 177 K3
Gleadless Mt HACK/IN S12 177 L4 1
Gleadless Rd HACK/IN S12 177 J2
SHEFP/MNR S2 177 H1 4
SHEFS S8 160 E8
SHEFS S8 176 E1 3
Glebe Av AU/AST/KP S26 181 J8
Glebe Cl KBTN HD8 17 H8
MEX/SWTN S64 108 A6
WRKS S80 198 A4
Glebe Crs RHAM/THRY S65 130 C6
Glebe Farm Cl ARMTH DN3 91 L1
AU/AST/KP S26 181 J8
Glebeland Cl RAW S62 107 J7
Glebelands Rd STKB/PEN S36 102 A7
Glebe Rd AWLS/ASK DN6 27 H6
FUL S10 160 A3
MEX/SWTN S64 108 A6
THNE DN8 32 A8
Glebe St DONS/BSCR DN4 111 H1
Gledhill Av STKB/PEN S36 79 G6
Gledhill Cl DRON S18 190 E6
Glenalmond Rd ECC S11 159 M8

Glencoe Cl HTFD DN7 48 E7
Glencoe Pl SHEFP/MNR S2 9 M6
Glencoe Rd SHEFP/MNR S2 9 M6
Glendale Cl DOD/DAR S75 59 M6
Glendale Rd BTLY DN5 88 F6
Gleneagles Dr ARMTH DN3 113 M1
DONS/BSCR DN4 113 M1
Gleneagles Ri MEX/SWTN S64 108 B5
Gleneagles Rd DIN S25 166 D7
Glen Field Av DONS/BSCR DN4 4 A9
Glenfields HOR/CROF WF4 18 B2
Glenfields Cl HOR/CROF WF4 18 B2
Glenholme Dr HAN/WDH S13 162 C8
Glenholme Pl HAN/WDH S13 162 D8
Glenholme Rd HAN/WDH S13 162 D8
Glenholme Wy HAN/WDH S13 162 C7
Glenmoor Av BSLY S70 59 M7
Glenmore Cft HACK/IN S12 177 M1
Glenmore Ri WMB/DAR S73 84 C6
Glenorchy Rd ABRD S7 176 B2
Glen Rd ABRD S7 176 C1
ARMTH DN3 92 C7
The Glen ECC S11 159 M6
Glenthorn Cl WRKN S81 183 J8
Glentilt Rd ABRD S7 176 B2
Glen View Rd SHEFS S8 176 C7
Glenville Cl HOY S74 105 H2
Glenwood Crs CHPT/GREN S35 126 F2
Gliwice Wy DONS/BSCR DN4 90 F6
Glossop Rd FUL S10 8 A6
FUL S10 160 A5
OWL S3 8 D5
Glossop Rw CHPT/GREN S35 125 H8
Gloucester Crs FUL S10 8 B7
Gloucester Rd KIMB S61 128 D6
WHHL DN2 90 E2
WRKN S81 184 E8
Gloucester St FUL S10 8 C6
Glover Rd SHEFP/MNR S2 160 E8
TOT/DORE S17 189 K2
Glyn Av DON DN1 5 H3
Goathland Dr HAN/WDH S13 163 G8
Goathland Pl HAN/WDH S13 163 H8
Goathland Rd HAN/WDH S13 163 H8
Goddard Av STKB/PEN S36 101 K5
Goddard Hall Rd SHEFN S5 145 G6
Godfrey Rd THNE DN8 31 L8
Godley St BSLYN/ROY S71 39 H3
Godric Dr RHAM S60 146 F6
Godric Gn RHAM S60 146 F6
Godric Rd SHEFN S5 127 G8
Godstone Rd RHAM S60 7 G6
Goldcrest Ri WRKN S81 184 A8
Goldcrest Wk KIMB S61 127 L2
Gold Cft BSLY S70 3 J8
Golden Smithies La
MEX/SWTN S64 107 M4
Goldsborough Rd WHHL DN2 90 E4
Goldsmith Dr RHAM/THRY S65 147 M1
Goldsmith Rd DONS/BSCR DN4 112 A1
RHAM/THRY S65 147 M1
WRKN S81 198 F2
Gold St BSLY S70 3 J7
Goldthorpe Av WRKN S81 168 D4
Goldthorpe Rd DEARNE S63 86 B3
Gomersal La DRON S18 190 E6
Gomersall Av CONI DN12 109 K5
Gooder Av BSLYN/ROY S71 39 G4
Goodison Bvd DONS/BSCR DN4 91 J8
Goodison Crs ST/HB/BR S6 159 K1
Goodison Ri ST/HB/BR S6 159 K1
Goodwin Av RAW S62 129 K1
Goodwin Crs MEX/SWTN S64 108 B3
Goodwin Rd KIMB S61 128 E3
SHEFS S8 176 E1
Goodyear Crs WMB/DAR S73 84 B5
Goore Av DARN/MH S9 161 M5
Goore Dr DARN/MH S9 161 M4
Goore Rd DARN/MH S9 161 M5
Gooseacre Av DEARNE S63 64 A6
Goosebutt St RAW S62 129 K3
Goose Carr La AU/AST/KP S26 165 H8
Goosecroft Av
RHAM/THRY S65 130 C5
Goose Gn HOLM/MEL HD7 53 L2
Goosehole La HEM/SK/SE WF9 42 F6
Goose La MALT S66 149 G3
Gordon Av SHEFS S8 176 E5
Gordon Cl WRKS S80 198 F4
Gordon Pl HEM/SK/SE WF9 42 D5
Gordon Rd CONI DN12 110 F5
ECC S11 160 B7
Gordon St BSLY S70 61 J7
DON DN1 4 E5
Gordon Ter RHAM/THRY S65 7 K5
Gorehill Cl DEARNE S63 107 L1
Gore La GLE DN14 10 B6
Gorse Cl HTFD DN7 70 D2
Gorse Dr ECK/KIL S21 194 B2
Gorseland Ct MALT S66 148 E3
Gorselands Av WRKS S80 199 G6
Gorse La FUL S10 158 D8
The Gorse MALT S66 148 F4
RHAM/THRY S65 148 A2
Gorsey Brigg DRON S18 190 B6
Gorton St HEM/SK/SE WF9 22 F6
Gosber Rd ECK/KIL S21 193 H4
Gosber St ECK/KIL S21 193 H4
Gosforth Cl DRON S18 190 D6
Gosforth Crs DRON S18 190 D6
Gosforth Dr DRON S18 190 D6
Gosforth Gn DRON S18 190 D6
Gosforth La DRON S18 190 D6
Gosling Gate Rd DEARNE S63 86 C2
Gotham Rd RHAM S60 147 G6
Gough Cl RHAM/THRY S65 148 A3
Goulding St MEX/SWTN S64 108 D3
Gowdall Gn BTLY DN5 67 L4
Gowdall La GLE DN14 11 K2
Gower St ATT S4 161 G1
WMB/DAR S73 84 C5
Grace Rd CONI DN12 111 G4
Grace St BSLYN/ROY S71 61 K1
Graftdyke Cl NROS/TKH DN11 113 M6
Grafton St BSLY S70 2 D6
SHEFP/MNR S2 9 M6
WRKS S80 198 C3
Grafton Wy RHAM/THRY S65 7 G2
Graham Av HEM/SK/SE WF9 25 H7
RHAM S60 147 H8
Graham Rd ARMTH DN3 69 K4
ECC S11 159 K7
FUL S10 159 J7
Graham's Orch BSLY S70 2 F5
Grainger Cl CONI DN12 110 E6
Grampian Cl BTLY DN5 89 J2
DOD/DAR S75 59 M5
Grampian Wy THNE DN8 49 L2
Granary Ct WRKN S81 184 E1
Granby Ct ARMTH DN3 92 A2
HEM/SK/SE WF9 42 E2
Granby Crs WHHL DN2 5 M6
Granby La NROS/TKH DN11 113 H6
Granby Rd CONI DN12 111 G5
SHEFN S5 145 H5
Grange Av AU/AST/KP S26 164 A6
BWTY DN10 136 D7
DONS/BSCR DN4 89 L8
DRON S18 190 C6
HEM/SK/SE WF9 42 E4
HTFD DN7 48 F7
WRKN S81 183 J4
Grange Cliffe Cl ECC S11 175 M3
Grange Cl AWLS/ASK DN6 28 A7
CUD/GR S72 40 D4
DONS/BSCR DN4 113 K1
HEM/SK/SE WF9 24 C5
HTFD DN7 48 F7
MALT S66 165 G2
WRKN S81 184 E1
Grange Ct BTLY DN5 89 L1
MALT S66 148 F3
Grange Crs BSLYN/ROY S71 61 J5
DEARNE S63 64 C7
ECC S11 160 C7
Grange Crescent Rd ECC S11 160 C7
Grange Dr KBTN HD8 17 H7
KIMB S61 128 B6
MALT S66 149 M3
NROS/TKH DN11 153 L2
Grange Farm DONS/BSCR DN4 111 L3
Grange Farm Dr
CHPT/GREN S35 143 H3
Grangefield Av
NROS/TKH DN11 113 K6
Grangefield Ter
NROS/TKH DN11 113 K6
Grange Gv THNE DN8 32 B3
Grange La AWLS/ASK DN6 44 E3
BSLYN/ROY S71 61 J6
DONS/BSCR DN4 111 J3
HOR/CROF WF4 17 H3
KIMB S61 127 K7
MALT S66 150 F1
NROS/TKH DN11 113 H7
RHAM S60 146 E4
Grange Mill La SHEFN S5 127 K7
Grange Pk ARMTH DN3 69 L2
Grange Rd AWLS/ASK DN6 27 H6
AWLS/ASK DN6 67 G4
BSLYN/ROY S71 38 E4
BTLY DN5 67 L3
CUD/GR S72 40 D5
DEARNE S63 107 H2
DONS/BSCR DN4 113 K1
ECC S11 160 C7
MEX/SWTN S64 107 M5
MOS S20 179 L4
RAW S62 107 L8
RHAM S60 147 M5
THNE DN8 32 B3
Grange Sq THNE DN8 32 B3
Grange St DEARNE S63 64 C7
The Grange KIMB S61 128 A5
Grange Vw DONS/BSCR DN4 89 L7
HEM/SK/SE WF9 41 H1
HOY S74 83 H6
NROS/TKH DN11 153 L2
Grange View Crs KIMB S61 128 B7
Grange View Rd KIMB S61 128 B7
Grangeway HEM/SK/SE WF9 23 H8
Grangewood Rd DIN S25 166 C3
Grantham St NROS/TKH DN11 113 J6
Grantley Cl WMB/DAR S73 84 D7
Granville Rd SHEFP/MNR S2 9 L8
Granville St DOD/DAR S75 2 C1
SHEFP/MNR S2 9 K7
Granville Ter RHAM/THRY S65 7 K5
Grasby Ct RHAM/THRY S65 131 H8
Grasmere Av WHHL DN2 91 G3
Grasmere Cl DIN S25 182 D1
STKB/PEN S36 79 H3
Grasmere Crs DOD/DAR S75 37 L4
Grasmere Rd AWLS/ASK DN6 45 G6
BSLYN/ROY S71 3 J5
CONI DN12 109 M5
DRON S18 190 C6
SHEFS S8 176 C2
WRKN S81 184 D8
Grassdale Vw HACK/IN S12 178 D4
Grassington Cl HACK/IN S12 178 F4
Grassington Dr HACK/IN S12 178 E4
Grassington Wy
CHPT/GREN S35 126 D1
Grassmoor Cl HACK/IN S12 177 K2
Grassthorpe Rd HACK/IN S12 177 L3
Grattan St KIMB S61 146 C1
Graven Cl CHPT/GREN S35 125 M7
Graves Moor La WRKN S81 170 B6
Gray Av AU/AST/KP S26 164 B6
Gray Cl RHAM/THRY S65 7 H1
Gray Gdns DONS/BSCR DN4 111 M1
Grays Ct CONI DN12 109 L3
Grayson Cl RHAM/THRY S65 131 H7
STKB/PEN S36 102 A7
Grayson Rd KIMB S61 128 E3
Gray's Rd BSLYN/ROY S71 39 G6
Gray St HOY S74 105 L2
MOS S20 179 G8
OWL S3 160 F1
Greasbro Rd DARN/MH S9 146 B5
Greasbrough La RAW S62 129 H2
Greasbrough Rd RAW S62 129 J4
RHAM S60 6 E1
Greasbrough St RHAM S60 6 D2
Great Bank Rd
RHAM/THRY S65 148 A3
Great Central Av
DONS/BSCR DN4 89 M7
Great Cliffe Rd DOD/DAR S75 59 J7
Great Common Cl
STV/CWN S43 194 F8
Great Cft DRON S18 190 B5
Great Eastern Wy RAW S62 129 K5
Great North Rd AWLS/ASK DN6 66 E2
BWTY DN10 136 C2
BWTY DN10 154 E8
NROS/TKH DN11 114 B5
Great Park Rd KIMB S61 128 C7
Greave Rd HOLM/MEL HD7 53 L7
Greaves Cl ST/HB/BR S6 159 G1
Greaves Fold DOD/DAR S75 59 M5
Greaves La CHPT/GREN S35 104 B5
ST/HB/BR S6 143 J8
ST/HB/BR S6 159 G1
Greaves Rd KIMB S61 128 E8
SHEFN S5 126 E7
Greaves Sike La CONI DN12 132 A5
Greaves St ST/HB/BR S6 144 B8
Greenacre Dr KBTN HD8 56 C4
Greenacre Rd HEM/SK/SE WF9 25 G7
WRKN S81 198 E1
Green Acres HOY S74 105 J2
RAW S62 129 L2
Greenacres Cl DRON S18 191 G8
Green Acres Cl KBTN HD8 35 G1
Greenacre Wk HOR/CROF WF4 22 A5
Green Arbour Rd MALT S66 165 J1
Green Balk CONI DN12 132 D2
Greenbank BSLYN/ROY S71 38 D6
Green Bank THNE DN8 50 F4
Greenbank Wk CUD/GR S72 40 D8
Green Boulevarde
DONS/BSCR DN4 91 J7
Green Cha ECK/KIL S21 193 G4
Green Cft HEM/SK/SE WF9 22 F5
Green Cross DRON S18 190 F5
Greenfield RAW S62 129 K2
Greenfield Cl ARMTH DN3 69 L1
ARMTH DN3 92 A2
KBTN HD8 56 D4
RHAM/THRY S65 130 B7
SHEFS S8 176 D8
Greenfield Ct MALT S66 148 F1
MEX/SWTN S64 86 D7
Greenfield Dr SHEFS S8 176 D8
Greenfield Gdns
DONS/BSCR DN4 91 L8
MALT S66 148 F1
Greenfield La DONS/BSCR DN4 4 A9
Greenfield Rd HEM/SK/SE WF9 41 H2
HOLM/MEL HD7 52 F2
HOY S74 83 J8
RHAM/THRY S65 130 B7
SHEFS S8 176 D8
Greenfields ECK/KIL S21 193 G4
GLE DN14 11 K3
Green Finch Cl RHAM S60 147 H7
Greenfinch Dl WRKN S81 184 A8
Greenfoot Cl DOD/DAR S75 2 C1
Greenfoot La DOD/DAR S75 2 C2
Green Gate Cl DEARNE S63 86 B4
Greengate La CHPT/GREN S35 126 B1
HAN/WDH S13 179 G1
Green Gate Rd HOLM/MEL HD7 52 E3
Greengate Rd HAN/WDH S13 179 H1
PONT WF8 26 D5
Greenhall Rd ECK/KIL S21 193 G4
Greenhead Gdns
CHPT/GREN S35 126 E2
Greenhead La CHPT/GREN S35 126 E1
Greenhill Av BSLYN/ROY S71 2 F1
MALT S66 149 M3
SHEFS S8 176 C7
Greenhill Bank Rd
HOLM/MEL HD7 54 B2
Green Hill Gv STKB/PEN S36 79 L1
Greenhill Main Rd SHEFS S8 176 E8
Greenhill Pkwy SHEFS S8 190 C1
TOT/DORE S17 190 B1
Greenhill Rd SHEFS S8 176 C5
Green House Hl KBTN HD8 34 A3
Greenhouse La FUL S10 174 D2
Green House La KBTN HD8 34 A3
Green House Rd WHHL DN2 90 F1
Greenhow St FUL S10 160 A2
Green Ings La DEARNE S63 85 L8
Greenland Av MALT S66 132 E8
MALT S66 150 E1
Greenland Cl DARN/MH S9 162 A2
DIN S25 182 B1
Greenland Ct DARN/MH S9 162 A1
Greenland Dr DARN/MH S9 162 A1
Greenland La GLE DN14 13 L3
Greenland Rd DARN/MH S9 162 A1
Greenlands Av
NROS/TKH DN11 113 L5
Greenland Vw BSLY S70 82 D3
DARN/MH S9 162 A2
Greenland Wy DARN/MH S9 162 A1
MALT S66 150 E1
Green La ARMTH DN3 91 M6
AU/AST/KP S26 164 B3
AU/AST/KP S26 164 E8
AWLS/ASK DN6 27 K8
AWLS/ASK DN6 44 C4
AWLS/ASK DN6 66 E3
BTLY DN5 66 F6
BTLY DN5 86 E4
BWTY DN10 154 D7
CHPT/GREN S35 124 F6
CHPT/GREN S35 124 A5
CHPT/GREN S35 127 G7
DEARNE S63 107 H4
DOD/DAR S75 81 L1
DOD/DAR S75 82 A2
DRON S18 190 F5
ECK/KIL S21 194 A3
FEA/AMT WF7 23 H1
HEM/SK/SE WF9 25 G6
HEM/SK/SE WF9 41 M5
HOLM/MEL HD7 53 L5
HOR/CROF WF4 17 K1
HOR/CROF WF4 18 D1
HOR/CROF WF4 18 B2
HOR/CROF WF4 38 E1
HOY S74 104 E3
HTFD DN7 71 G5
KBTN HD8 55 M5
KIMB S61 128 A8
MALT S66 148 E2
MALT S66 149 H6
NROS/TKH DN11 133 L1
OWL S3 8 F1
RAW S62 129 K2
RHAM S60 146 F8
RHAM S60 147 L5
STKB/PEN S36 58 A8
STKB/PEN S36 101 J5
Greenlaws Cl HOLM/MEL HD7 53 H2
Green Lea DRON S18 190 A5
Greenleafe Av WHHL DN2 69 G8
Green Mile La RTFD DN22 187 J8
Green Moor Rd STKB/PEN S36 102 B3
Green Oak Av TOT/DORE S17 189 J3
Green Oak Crs
TOT/DORE S17 189 J3
Green Oak Dr AU/AST/KP S26 180 E5
TOT/DORE S17 189 J3
Green Oak Rd TOT/DORE S17 189 J4
Greenock St ST/HB/BR S6 143 M7
Green Ri RAW S62 107 H8
Green Rd STKB/PEN S36 79 H5
Greenset Vw BSLYN/ROY S71 38 C6
Greenside CUD/GR S72 39 M3
DOD/DAR S75 38 A6
HOR/CROF WF4 21 M7
KBTN HD8 34 C8
KBTN HD8 56 E1
KIMB S61 128 F4
STKB/PEN S36 79 L1
Greenside Av AU/AST/KP S26 181 G5
DOD/DAR S75 38 A6
Greenside La HOY S74 105 J1
Greenside Ms HACK/IN S12 178 F4
Greenside Pl DOD/DAR S75 38 A6
Green Spring Av BSLY S70 82 D7
Green's Rd HTFD DN7 70 D2
RHAM/THRY S65 147 M1
Green St BSLY S70 83 G3
DONS/BSCR DN4 111 K1
HOY S74 105 K1
KIMB S61 128 F3
STKB/PEN S36 102 B6
The Green CONI DN12 109 G4
DEARNE S63 86 A4
DIN S25 182 B1
EPW DN9 92 E8
EPW DN9 115 J4
HOR/CROF WF4 19 L8
MEX/SWTN S64 107 M5
NROS/TKH DN11 153 J4
RHAM S60 147 K4
STKB/PEN S36 79 H5
THNE DN8 31 M8
THNE DN8 32 B3
TOT/DORE S17 189 H3
WRKN S81 184 E1
The Green Vw CUD/GR S72 39 M3
Greenway AU/AST/KP S26 181 H5
WRKN S81 184 E1
The Greenway SHEFS S8 176 D7
Greenwood Av BSLY S70 82 F2
DARN/MH S9 161 L4
DONS/BSCR DN4 89 K7
HEM/SK/SE WF9 25 G7
NROS/TKH DN11 153 K2
Greenwood Cl DARN/MH S9 161 M4
Greenwood Crs DARN/MH S9 161 L4
MALT S66 149 G2
Greenwood Dr DARN/MH S9 161 L4
Greenwood La
HAN/WDH S13 163 H8
Greenwood Rd
CHPT/GREN S35 104 D8
DARN/MH S9 161 M4
MEX/SWTN S64 108 C8
Greenwood Ter BSLY S70 2 E4
Greenwood Wy DARN/MH S9 161 L4
Greeton Dr CHPT/GREN S35 143 J1
Gregg House Crs SHEFN S5 145 H2
Gregg House Rd SHEFN S5 145 G1
Gregory Crs NROS/TKH DN11 153 J3
Gregory Rd SHEFS S8 176 E1
Grend Wood Ct
CHPT/GREN S35 126 A6
Grenfell Av MEX/SWTN S64 108 F2
Grenfolds Rd CHPT/GREN S35 126 B7
Grenobank Rd
CHPT/GREN S35 126 B7
Greno Crs CHPT/GREN S35 126 B7
Greno Ga CHPT/GREN S35 126 A6
Grenomoor Cl CHPT/GREN S35 126 A8
Greno Rd MEX/SWTN S64 108 B6
Greno Vw DOD/DAR S75 81 J5
HOY S74 105 G2
Greno View Rd
CHPT/GREN S35 104 B8
Grenville Pl DOD/DAR S75 2 B1
Grenville Rd DONS/BSCR DN4 111 J1
Grenville Wk HOR/CROF WF4 19 K4
Gresham Av RHAM S60 147 G6
Gresham Rd ST/HB/BR S6 160 A1
Gresley Av BWTY DN10 136 E7
Gresley Rd DONS/BSCR DN4 4 C9
SHEFS S8 190 C2
Grey Friars' Rd DON DN1 4 E3
Grey Gables HOR/CROF WF4 18 C1
Greystock St ATT S4 161 J1
Greystone La NROS/TKH DN11 134 C7
Greystones Av BSLY S70 82 D3
ECC S11 159 M8
Greystones Cl ECC S11 159 L8
Greystones Ct AU/AST/KP S26 195 H1
Greystones Crs ECC S11 159 L8
Greystones Dr ECC S11 159 L8
Greystones Grange Crs
ECC S11 159 L8
Greystones Grange Rd
ECC S11 159 L8
Greystones Hall Rd ECC S11 159 L8
Greystones Ri ECC S11 159 L8
Greystones Rd ECC S11 159 K8
RHAM S60 148 B6
Grice Cl DONS/BSCR DN4 91 K5
Griffin Rd MEX/SWTN S64 107 M4
Griffiths Cl RAW S62 129 K3
Griffiths Rd CHPT/GREN S35 126 C1
Grime La HOLM/MEL HD7 55 G6
Grimesthorpe Rd ATT S4 145 G8
ATT S4 145 H7
ATT S4 161 G1
Grimethorpe St
HEM/SK/SE WF9 42 D5
Grimsell Cl ST/HB/BR S6 126 B8
Grimsell Crs ST/HB/BR S6 126 B8
Grimsell Dr ST/HB/BR S6 126 B8
Grindlow Cl SHEFS S8 177 G1
Grindlow Dr SHEFP/MNR S2 177 G1
Grizedale Av MOS S20 179 L5
Grizedale Cl MOS S20 179 L5
Grosvenor Av HEM/SK/SE WF9 24 E8
Grosvenor Ct HTFD DN7 30 F8
Grosvenor Crs BTLY DN5 68 B5
DONS/BSCR DN4 111 H1
Grosvenor Dr BSLY S70 2 A5
Grosvenor Rd AWLS/ASK DN6 66 F2
NROS/TKH DN11 153 M3
RHAM/THRY S65 7 H1
Grosvenor Sq
SHEFP/MNR S2 160 D7
Grosvenor Ter
DONS/BSCR DN4 111 H1
Grouse Cft ST/HB/BR S6 160 A1
Grove Av BTLY DN5 89 L2
HEM/SK/SE WF9 41 J1
HEM/SK/SE WF9 42 A5
ST/HB/BR S6 143 L5
Grove Cl DEARNE S63 85 G7
STKB/PEN S36 79 H6
Grove Ct BTLY DN5 66 A8
Grove Dr HEM/SK/SE WF9 41 M5
Grove Farm WRKN S81 184 F8
Grove Head HEM/SK/SE WF9 41 M5
Grove Hill Rd WHHL DN2 68 F8
Grove House Ct
TOT/DORE S17 189 J2
Grove La HEM/SK/SE WF9 24 C4
HEM/SK/SE WF9 41 J1
HEM/SK/SE WF9 41 M5
Grove Lea Cl HEM/SK/SE WF9 41 J1
Grove Marsh Lea
HEM/SK/SE WF9 23 K8
Grove Mt HEM/SK/SE WF9 41 M5
Grove Pk HOR/CROF WF4 19 H1
Grove Pl DON DN1 4 F6
HEM/SK/SE WF9 41 J1
Grove Rd ABRD S7 176 A4
DEARNE S63 84 F7
DOD/DAR S75 37 L6
HTFD DN7 30 F8
RHAM S60 6 F6
STKB/PEN S36 102 D7
TOT/DORE S17 189 J2
Grove Sq ST/HB/BR S6 144 C8
Grove St BSLY S70 83 G2
BSLYN/ROY S71 3 J6
HEM/SK/SE WF9 41 M5
Grove Ter HEM/SK/SE WF9 41 J1
The Grove ARMTH DN3 47 J7
CHPT/GREN S35 124 F4
CUD/GR S72 39 M6
HEM/SK/SE WF9 42 D3
HOR/CROF WF4 21 L6
MALT S66 148 F2
RAW S62 129 L2
RHAM/THRY S65 129 M8
ST/HB/BR S6 143 J7
TOT/DORE S17 189 H2
WHHL DN2 90 E2
WRKN S81 184 D8
Grove V WHHL DN2 69 G8
Grove Wy HEM/SK/SE WF9 41 M5
Grudgby La STKB/PEN S36 101 L1
Gudgeon Hole La
CHPT/GREN S35 81 H8
Guernsey Rd SHEFP/MNR S2 160 E8
Guest La DOD/DAR S75 58 E7
DONS/BSCR DN4 89 H8
Guest Rd DOD/DAR S75 2 D2
ECC S11 160 A7
RHAM S60 7 J9
Guest St HOY S74 83 J8
Guilbert Av MALT S66 165 H2
Guildford Av SHEFP/MNR S2 161 H7
Guildford Cl SHEFP/MNR S2 161 H7
Guildford Dr SHEFP/MNR S2 161 H7
Guildford Ri SHEFP/MNR S2 161 H7
Guildford Rd BSLYN/ROY S71 38 F3
WHHL DN2 68 F8
Guildford Vw
SHEFP/MNR S2 161 J7
Guildford Wy SHEFP/MNR S2 161 H8
Guild Rd RHAM/THRY S65 147 M1
Guildway AU/AST/KP S26 181 J2
Guilthwaite Common La
AU/AST/KP S26 164 A2
Guilthwaite Crs RHAM S60 147 L6
Gullane Dr DONS/BSCR DN4 111 H1
Gulling Wood Dr
RHAM/THRY S65 130 E5
Gully Ter HOLM/MEL HD7 53 M3
The Gully KBTN HD8 55 G2
Gunhills La ARMTH DN3 70 A8
Gun La OWL S3 9 J2
Gunthwaite La KBTN HD8 56 D4
Gurney Rd DONS/BSCR DN4 111 M1
Gurth Av ARMTH DN3 69 L5
Gurth Dr MALT S66 165 J2
Gypsy La WMB/DAR S73 84 C6

H

Habershon Dr
CHPT/GREN S35 126 D1
Habershon Rd KIMB S61 128 D6
Hacking La HEM/SK/SE WF9 42 F4

Hackings Av STKB/PEN S36 79 G6
Hackness La RHAM S60 146 F6
Hackthorn Rd SHEFS S8 176 D4
Haddingley La KBTN HD8 55 H4
Haddon Cl DOD/DAR S75 59 J8
DRON S18 190 F5
HEM/SK/SE WF9 42 E2 4
Haddon Ri MEX/SWTN S64 109 H1
Haddon Rd BSLYN/ROY S71 60 F1 1
Haddon St OWL S3 160 D1 1
Haddon Wy AU/AST/KP S26 164 D8
Hadds La THNE DN8 31 J1
Hadds Nook Rd THNE DN8 31 K3
Haden St ST/HB/BR S6 144 A7
Hadfield St FUL S10 160 A2
WMB/DAR S73 84 C6
Hadleigh Cl RAW S62 129 K3 5
Hadrian Rd RHAM S60 147 G5
Hadrians Cl NROS/TKH DN11 113 L8
PONT WF8 24 E2
Haggard Rd ST/HB/BR S6 144 B7
Hagg Hl FUL S10 159 K2
ST/HB/BR S6 143 M2
Hagg La BWTY DN10 137 J7
FUL S10 159 H4
Haggs La AWLS/ASK DN6 28 E4
Haggstones Dr
CHPT/GREN S35 143 H1 1
Haggstones Rd
CHPT/GREN S35 143 G1
Hag Hill La KBTN HD8 35 H1
Hague Av ECK/KIL S21 193 M7
RAW S62 107 J7
Hague Crs HEM/SK/SE WF9 41 J2
Hague La CHPT/GREN S35 104 A8
ECK/KIL S21 193 L7
KIMB S61 105 M8
Hague Park Cl
HEM/SK/SE WF9 41 M4 1
Hague Park La HEM/SK/SE WF9 41 M4
Hague Park Wk
HEM/SK/SE WF9 41 M4 2
Hague Ter HEM/SK/SE WF9 41 J1
Haids Cl MALT S66 132 D8
Haids Rd MALT S66 132 C8
Haig Crs NROS/TKH DN11 113 J7
Haigh Cl STKB/PEN S36 79 K1
Haigh Cft BSLYN/ROY S71 38 F3
Haigh La DOD/DAR S75 36 F3
HOR/CROF WF4 16 E5
STKB/PEN S36 57 L8
Haigh Moor Cl HAN/WDH S13 162 C7
Haigh Moor Rd HAN/WDH S13 162 D7
Haigh Moor Wy BSLYN/ROY S71 38 F3
Haigh Rd DONS/BSCR DN4 89 L8
Haig Rd THNE DN8 32 B3
Hail Mary Dr HAN/WDH S13 163 H7
Haise Mt DOD/DAR S75 37 L6
Hakehill Cl DONS/BSCR DN4 113 H1
Halcyon Cl HACK/IN S12 178 D4
Haldane Cl CUD/GR S72 40 D4
Haldane Rd RHAM/THRY S65 7 L1
Haldene BSLY S70 82 F3
Haldynby Gdns ARMTH DN3 92 A1
Hale Hill La HTFD DN7 71 H2
Hale St SHEFS S8 176 D1
Halesworth Rd HAN/WDH S13 162 C5
Half Acre La DRON S18 191 H7
Halfway Dr MOS S20 179 J8
Halfway Gdns MOS S20 179 J8
Halifax Av CONI DN12 109 L5
Halifax Crs BTLY DN5 89 K1
Halifax Dr WRKN S81 184 C7
Halifax Rd CHPT/GREN S35 80 E8
CHPT/GREN S35 103 H3
CHPT/GREN S35 126 B8
SHEFN S5 144 B2
ST/HB/BR S6 144 B3
STKB/PEN S36 79 G1
Halifax St BSLYN/ROY S71 60 C3
Hallam Cha FUL S10 159 H5 2
Hallam Cl AU/AST/KP S26 164 A6
DONS/BSCR DN4 91 G8
Hallamgate Rd FUL S10 159 M5
Hallam Grange Cl FUL S10 159 G7 2
Hallam Grange Crs FUL S10 159 G6
Hallam Grange Ri FUL S10 159 G6
Hallam Grange Rd FUL S10 159 G6
Hallam La SHEF S1 9 H7
Hallam Pl RAW S62 129 L2
Hallam Rd RHAM S60 147 K5
Hallamshire Cl FUL S10 158 F7
Hallamshire Dr FUL S10 158 F7
Hallamshire Rd FUL S10 158 F8
Hallam Wy CHPT/GREN S35 126 F7
Hall Av HOY S74 83 L8
MEX/SWTN S64 108 F2
Hall Balk La DOD/DAR S75 2 D1
DONS/BSCR DN4 112 B3
NROS/TKH DN11 112 A4
Hall Brig BTLY DN5 64 A3
Hall Broome Gdns DEARNE S63 86 A4
Hallcar St ATT S4 161 G2
Hall Cl BSLY S70 82 E5
DEARNE S63 84 F8 1
DIN S25 182 B1
DRON S18 190 A5
Hall Close Av RHAM S60 148 A6
Hall Crs RHAM S60 147 M5
Hall Cft HOR/CROF WF4 18 C1 2
MALT S66 149 G3
Hallcroft Dr ARMTH DN3 92 A3
Hallcroft Ri BSLYN/ROY S71 38 F4 1
Hall Cross Hl DON DN1 5 J5
Hall Dr DEARNE S63 107 H2
Hall Farm Cl AU/AST/KP S26 164 B5
Hall Farm Dr DEARNE S63 64 B8
Hall Farm Gv STKB/PEN S36 79 L1
Hall Farm Ri DEARNE S63 64 B8 2
Hall Field La HOR/CROF WF4 21 L8
Hall Flat La DONS/BSCR DN4 111 L1
Hall Garth Rd PONT WF8 24 E2
Hallgate DEARNE S63 64 B8
Hall Ga DON DN1 5 G5
MEX/SWTN S64 109 G2
STKB/PEN S36 79 H4
Hallgate Rd FUL S10 159 L4 1
Hall Gv DOD/DAR S75 38 A6
RHAM S60 7 G7
Halliday Cl WRKS S80 198 B4
Halliwell Cl SHEFN S5 144 B4 2
Halliwell Crs SHEFN S5 144 C4
Hall La HEM/SK/SE WF9 42 F1
HOR/CROF WF4 19 K3
HTFD DN7 47 M4
ST/HB/BR S6 140 F3
Hall Meadow Cft MOS S20 193 K2
Hall Meadow Dr MOS S20 193 K2
Hall Meadow Gv MOS S20 193 K2 1
Hallowes Ct DRON S18 190 F6 1
Hallowes Dr DRON S18 190 F7
Hallowes La DRON S18 190 F7
Hallowes Ri DRON S18 191 G7
Hallowmoor Rd ST/HB/BR S6 143 L7
Hall Park Head ST/HB/BR S6 159 H2
Hall Park Hl ST/HB/BR S6 159 J2
Hall Park Mt ST/HB/BR S6 159 J2 2
Hall Pl BSLYN/ROY S71 61 G3
Hall Rd AU/AST/KP S26 164 B6
DARN/MH S9 162 C4
HAN/WDH S13 162 C5
RHAM S60 7 G7
Hall Road Old DARN/MH S9 145 L8
Hall Royd La DOD/DAR S75 80 E1
Hall Royd Wk DOD/DAR S75 80 E1
Hallside Ct ARMTH DN3 91 M6
Hall St BTLY DN5 87 H4
DEARNE S63 86 C3
HOY S74 105 J1 2
RHAM S60 6 D4
WMB/DAR S73 84 C5
Hallsworth Av HOY S74 83 L8
Hall Vw BWTY DN10 155 M8
Hall View Rd NROS/TKH DN11 113 L8
Hall Villa La BTLY DN5 67 L2
Hall Wood Rd CHPT/GREN S35 126 A2
Hallyburton Cl
SHEFP/MNR S2 177 G1 3
Hallyburton Dr
SHEFP/MNR S2 177 G1 4
Hallyburton Rd
SHEFP/MNR S2 177 G1
Halmshaw BTLY DN5 67 L7
Halsall Av DARN/MH S9 162 A4
Halsall Dr DARN/MH S9 161 M4
Halsall Rd DARN/MH S9 162 A4
Halsbury Rd RHAM/THRY S65 129 L7
Halstead Gv DOD/DAR S75 37 L5
Halton Ct HACK/IN S12 179 G4
Hamble Ct DOD/DAR S75 38 A7 3
Hambleton Cl DOD/DAR S75 59 M5 3
HOY S74 105 M1 2
Hambleton Ct WRKN S81 168 C8 3
Hameline Rd CONI DN12 109 M5
Hamel Ri HEM/SK/SE WF9 41 H1
Hamilton Cl DONS/BSCR DN4 5 L8
MEX/SWTN S64 109 G1 2
Hamilton Park Rd BTLY DN5 89 H1 1
Hamilton Rd DEARNE S63 86 D1
DONS/BSCR DN4 5 L8
MALT S66 150 F3
SHEFN S5 145 H5
Hamilton St WRKN S81 198 B1
Hammerton Rd ST/HB/BR S6 144 A8
Hammerton St
WMB/DAR S73 84 A3 1
Hammond St OWL S3 8 D2
Hampden Crs HTFD DN7 71 L7
Hampden Rd MEX/SWTN S64 108 E3
Hamper La STKB/PEN S36 79 K1
Hampole Balk AWLS/ASK DN6 44 D6
Hampole Field La
AWLS/ASK DN6 43 K6
Hampton Rd HTFD DN7 48 D7
SHEFN S5 145 G6
WHHL DN2 5 M4
Hanbury Cl BSLYN/ROY S71 61 H3
DONS/BSCR DN4 111 L3
DRON S18 190 D6
Hand La CHPT/GREN S35 80 F7
Handley St OWL S3 9 K1
Hands Rd FUL S10 160 A3
Handsworth Av DARN/MH S9 162 A4
Handsworth Crs DARN/MH S9 162 B4
Handsworth Gdns
ARMTH DN3 92 A1 1
Handsworth Grange Cl
HAN/WDH S13 162 E7
Handsworth Grange Crs
HAN/WDH S13 162 E6
Handsworth Grange Rd
HAN/WDH S13 162 E6
Handsworth Rd DARN/MH S9 162 B4
WKFDW/WTN WF2 19 L3
Hanging Water Cl FUL S10 159 K7 3
Hangingwater Rd ECC S11 159 K8
Hangman Stone Rd BTLY DN5 87 K5
Hangram La ECC S11 174 F3
Hangsman La DIN S25 166 A4
Hangthwaite La
AWLS/ASK DN6 67 H4
Hangthwaite Rd
AWLS/ASK DN6 45 H8
Hanley Cl HACK/IN S12 178 F4
Hanmoor Rd ST/HB/BR S6 159 G1
Hannah Rd HAN/WDH S13 163 H8
Hannas Royd DOD/DAR S75 59 L8 4
Hanover Sq DEARNE S63 64 C7
OWL S3 8 E7
Hanover St DEARNE S63 64 C6
OWL S3 8 D7
Hanover Wy OWL S3 8 D6
Hansby Cl NROS/TKH DN11 134 F8
Hanson Rd ST/HB/BR S6 143 H7
Hanson St BSLY S70 3 G5 2
Harbord Rd SHEFS S8 176 C5
Harborough Av
SHEFP/MNR S2 161 K4
Harborough Cl SHEFP/MNR S2 161 L5
Harborough Dr
SHEFP/MNR S2 161 L5
Harborough Hill Rd
BSLYN/ROY S71 3 H3 1
Harborough Ri SHEFP/MNR S2 161 L5
Harborough Rd
SHEFP/MNR S2 161 L5
Harborough Wy
SHEFP/MNR S2 161 L6
Harbury St HAN/WDH S13 163 J7 1
Harcourt Cl DONS/BSCR DN4 91 G8
Harcourt Crs FUL S10 8 A3
Harcourt Ri CHPT/GREN S35 126 F3
Harcourt Rd FUL S10 8 A4
Harcourt Ter RHAM/THRY S65 7 K5
Hardakers Ap FEA/AMT WF7 23 K2
Hardaker's La FEA/AMT WF7 23 J1
Hardcastle Dr HAN/WDH S13 162 E8 1
Hardcastle Gdns
HAN/WDH S13 162 E8
Hardcastle La HOR/CROF WF4 17 H4
Hardcastle Rd HAN/WDH S13 178 E1
Harden Cl DOD/DAR S75 59 L5
STKB/PEN S36 79 H5 2
Hardie Cl MALT S66 150 F4
Hardie Pl RAW S62 129 K1 3
Hardie Rd HOR/CROF WF4 22 A6
Hardie St ECK/KIL S21 193 H5
Harding Av RAW S62 107 H7
Harding Cl RAW S62 107 H8
Harding St DARN/MH S9 161 M1
Hard La AU/AST/KP S26 181 J6
Hardwick Cl AU/AST/KP S26 164 D8 1
BSLY S70 82 E3 4
DRON S18 190 F5
Hardwick Crs BSLYN/ROY S71 38 E8
ECC S11 160 A7
WRKS S80 198 F5
Hardwicke Rd RHAM/THRY S65 7 H1
Hardwick Gv DOD/DAR S75 81 K1 2
Hardwick La AU/AST/KP S26 165 G7
Hardwick Rd East WRKS S80 198 F6
Hardwick Rd West WRKS S80 198 F5
Hardwick St RHAM/THRY S65 130 B7
Hardy Pl ST/HB/BR S6 160 B2
Hardy Rd WHHL DN2 90 C1
Hardy St KIMB S61 6 C2
WRKS S80 198 C5 3
Harefield Rd ECC S11 160 B7 7
Harehills Rd RHAM/THRY S65 7 H6
Harewood Av ARMTH DN3 69 K3
AWLS/ASK DN6 66 D2
BSLY S70 59 M6
Harewood Ct NROS/TKH DN11 113 M7
Harewood Gv MALT S66 149 H1
Harewood La HEM/SK/SE WF9 25 G7
PONT WF8 25 K5
Harewood Rd WHHL DN2 90 E4
WRKN S81 184 D8
Harewood Wy ECC S11 175 L5 1
Hargrave Pl RHAM/THRY S65 130 D5
Harland Rd FUL S10 8 C9
Harlech Cl CHPT/GREN S35 126 D1
Harleston St ATT S4 161 G1 3
Harley Rd ECC S11 175 K2
RAW S62 105 H6
Harlington Ct CONI DN12 109 L3
Harlington Rd MEX/SWTN S64 86 D7
MEX/SWTN S64 108 F2
Harmby Cl AWLS/ASK DN6 44 D5
Harmer La SHEF S1 9 J5
Harmony Wy RHAM S60 163 H1 1
Harney Cl DARN/MH S9 162 A2
Harold Av AWLS/ASK DN6 66 E2
BSLYN/ROY S71 61 J3
Harold Cft RAW S62 129 G3
Harold St ST/HB/BR S6 160 B1
Harpenden Cl HTFD DN7 70 E2
Harpendon Dr HTFD DN7 70 E1 4
Harriet Cl BSLY S70 60 E8 3
Harrington Ct BSLYN/ROY S71 61 J3
Harrington Rd
SHEFP/MNR S2 160 E7 5
Harrington St DON DN1 5 G3
WRKS S80 198 B5
Harrison Dr WRKN S81 168 C4
Harrison La FUL S10 158 D8
Harrison Rd ST/HB/BR S6 143 M8
Harrison St KIMB S61 146 E2
Harris Rd ST/HB/BR S6 143 M5
Harrogate Dr CONI DN12 109 J4
Harrogate Rd
AU/AST/KP S26 180 A1 1
Harrop Dr MEX/SWTN S64 108 A6
Harrop La FUL S10 174 D1
Harrowden Rd DARN/MH S9 146 C5
WHHL DN2 90 D1
Harrow Rd ARMTH DN3 70 A8
Harrow St ECC S11 8 E8
HEM/SK/SE WF9 42 C4
Harry Firth Cl DARN/MH S9 161 L2 7
Harry Rd DOD/DAR S75 59 M4
Harstoft Av WRKN S81 198 D3
Hartcliff Av STKB/PEN S36 79 G4
Hartcliffe La STKB/PEN S36 78 C6
Hartcliffe Vw
CHPT/GREN S35 80 D8 1
Hartcliff Hill Rd STKB/PEN S36 78 D7
Hartcliff Nick STKB/PEN S36 78 C7
Hartcliff Rd STKB/PEN S36 78 A7
Hartford Cl SHEFS S8 176 E4 1
Hartford Rd SHEFS S8 176 E4
Hart Hl RAW S62 107 H7
Harthill Field Rd
AU/AST/KP S26 195 L3
Harthill La STV/CWN S43 195 J6
Harthill Rd AU/AST/KP S26 182 A8
CONI DN12 109 L6
HAN/WDH S13 161 M8
Hartington Av ABRD S7 176 A4
Hartington Cl KIMB S61 146 E1
Hartington Dr BSLYN/ROY S71 60 D3
Hartington Rd ABRD S7 176 A4
DRON S18 190 F5
KIMB S61 146 E1
Hartland Av MOS S20 179 L5 4
Hartland Ct MOS S20 179 L5 5
Hartland Crs ARMTH DN3 69 K5
Hartland Dr MOS S20 179 L5
Hartland Rd WRKS S80 198 C5
Hartley Brook Av SHEFN S5 145 G1
Hartley Brook Rd SHEFN S5 145 G1
Hartley La KIMB S61 6 C2
Hartley St MEX/SWTN S64 108 D3
SHEFP/MNR S2 160 E8
Hartopp Av SHEFP/MNR S2 177 G1
Hartopp Cl SHEFP/MNR S2 177 G1 5
Hartopp Dr SHEFP/MNR S2 177 H1 5
Hartopp Rd SHEFP/MNR S2 177 G1
Harts Head SHEF S1 9 J3
Harvest Cl BSLY S70 82 E3
DONS/BSCR DN4 89 K7
MALT S66 150 A3
WRKN S81 168 D8 1
WRKN S81 184 F8
Harvest La OWL S3 160 E1
Harvest Rd MALT S66 148 F2
Harvey Cl EPW DN9 115 J3
Harvey Clough Ms SHEFS S8 176 E4
Harvey Clough Rd SHEFS S8 176 E4
Harvey Rd CHPT/GREN S35 126 E2
Harvey St BSLY S70 2 D7
STKB/PEN S36 102 B6 2
Harwell La BWTY DN10 155 M3
Harwell Rd SHEFS S8 160 D8
Harwell Sluice La BWTY DN10 155 M2
Harwich Rd SHEFP/MNR S2 161 J6
Harwood Cl SHEFP/MNR S2 160 D7
Harwood Dr MOS S20 179 H6
Harwood Gdns MOS S20 179 J6
Harwood St SHEFP/MNR S2 160 E7
Harwood Ter BSLYN/ROY S71 61 J5 1
Harworth Av WRKN S81 153 L8
Haslam Crs SHEFS S8 190 C1 2
Haslam Pl MALT S66 150 F1 1
Haslam Rd NROS/TKH DN11 113 K6
Haslehurst Rd SHEFP/MNR S2 161 J5
Haslemere Gv BTLY DN5 89 L1
Hassop Cl DRON S18 191 G5
Hastilar Cl SHEFP/MNR S2 161 M7
Hastilar Rd SHEFP/MNR S2 161 L7 3
Hastilar Rd South
HAN/WDH S13 162 A8
SHEFP/MNR S2 162 A7
Hastings Mt ABRD S7 176 A3
Hastings Rd ABRD S7 176 A3
Hastings St CUD/GR S72 40 E8
Hatchell Dr DONS/BSCR DN4 113 L2
Hatchellwood Vw
DONS/BSCR DN4 113 M2
Hatfield Cl BSLYN/ROY S71 38 C8 3
Hatfield Crs DIN S25 166 A5
Hatfield Gdns BSLYN/ROY S71 38 F3
Hatfield House Ct SHEFN S5 145 H2 1
Hatfield House Cft SHEFN S5 145 H2
Hatfield House La SHEFN S5 145 G3
Hatfield La ARMTH DN3 47 K8
ARMTH DN3 70 A8
Hatfield Pl HOR/CROF WF4 22 B5
Hatfield Rd HTFD DN7 49 K3
Hatherley Rd DARN/MH S9 146 B4
MEX/SWTN S64 108 B3
RHAM/THRY S65 7 H1
Hathersage Rd HATH/EY S32 172 B7
TOT/DORE S17 175 G6
TOT/DORE S17 188 C1
Hatter Dr CONI DN12 110 F7
Hatton Cl DRON S18 190 B7
Hatton Rd ST/HB/BR S6 144 A8
Haugh Gn RAW S62 107 H7
Haugh Head Rd STKB/PEN S36 79 K1
Haugh La ECC S11 175 K2
Haugh Rd RAW S62 107 G7
Haughton Rd SHEFS S8 176 D5
Hauxwell Cl AWLS/ASK DN6 44 D5
Havelock Rd DONS/BSCR DN4 4 E9
Havelock St BSLY S70 2 D7 1
FUL S10 8 C6
WMB/DAR S73 84 E2 1
Haven Hl WRKN S81 168 B1
Havercroft Ri CUD/GR S72 40 C1
Havercroft Rd RHAM S60 148 A4
SHEFS S8 176 C3
Havercroft Ter ECK/KIL S21 179 M8 2
Haverdale Ri DOD/DAR S75 2 C3
Haverdale Rd HOR/CROF WF4 22 A6
Haverlands La BSLY S70 82 B3
Haverlands Rdg BSLY S70 82 D3 2
The Haverlands
HEM/SK/SE WF9 41 J1 5
Haveroid La HOR/CROF WF4 19 K3
Haveroid Wy HOR/CROF WF4 19 J2
Haw Ct DOD/DAR S75 58 D7 3
Hawes Cl MEX/SWTN S64 109 G1
Hawfield Cl DONS/BSCR DN4 4 A9
Hawke Cl RAW S62 107 G8
Hawke Rd WHHL DN2 90 D2
Hawke St DARN/MH S9 145 L7
Hawk Hill La MALT S66 165 J4
Hawkhouse Green La
AWLS/ASK DN6 29 G8
Hawkins Av CHPT/GREN S35 126 C2 1
Hawkshead Av DRON S18 190 B6
Hawkshead Crs DIN S25 166 D8 1
Hawkshead Rd ATT S4 145 K6
Hawksley Av ST/HB/BR S6 144 A7
Hawksley Ms ST/HB/BR S6 144 A7
Hawksley Ri CHPT/GREN S35 143 H1
Hawksley Rd ST/HB/BR S6 144 A7
Hawksway ECK/KIL S21 192 F4
Hawksworth Cl
RHAM/THRY S65 130 A8
Hawksworth Rd
RHAM/THRY S65 130 A8
ST/HB/BR S6 160 B1
Hawkwell Bank BSLYN/ROY S71 61 L7
Hawley St DRON S18 191 L6
RAW S62 129 K2
SHEF S1 9 G3
Haworth Bank RHAM S60 147 K6 1
Haworth Cl BSLYN/ROY S71 3 M1
Haworth Crs RHAM S60 147 K6
Haw Park La HOR/CROF WF4 21 J4
WKFDW/WTN WF2 20 F5
Hawshaw La HOY S74 105 G1
Hawson St WMB/DAR S73 84 C5
Hawson Wy WRKN S81 184 A8
Hawthorn Av ARMTH DN3 69 M7
MALT S66 150 B2
MOS S20 179 H6
Hawthorne Av DIN S25 182 B4
DRON S18 190 E4
HEM/SK/SE WF9 41 H1 2
HTFD DN7 70 C3
RAW S62 129 L2
STKB/PEN S36 101 K5
THNE DN8 31 M6 3
Hawthorne Cl ECK/KIL S21 194 B2 2
HOR/CROF WF4 17 H4 1
Hawthorne Ct DOD/DAR S75 36 F7
Hawthorne Crs AWLS/ASK DN6 44 E6
DOD/DAR S75 59 J7
HEM/SK/SE WF9 41 G1 1
MEX/SWTN S64 108 C2
Hawthorne Gv BTLY DN5 67 M5
THNE DN8 31 M6 4
Hawthorne Rd DEARNE S63 107 L2 1
EPW DN9 114 E3
THNE DN8 31 M6
The Hawthornes MOS S20 179 K3
Hawthorne St BSLY S70 2 E8
CUD/GR S72 40 A4
ST/HB/BR S6 159 M1 1
Hawthorne Wy CUD/GR S72 40 A4
Hawthorn Gv CONI DN12 109 L7 2
DOD/DAR S75 58 E6 1
FEA/AMT WF7 23 K2 1
Hawthorn Rd CHPT/GREN S35 104 C8
ECK/KIL S21 192 F5
ST/HB/BR S6 143 M7
Hawthorn Wy WRKN S81 168 C8
Hawtop La DOD/DAR S75 37 K1
Haxby Cl HAN/WDH S13 178 C1
Haxby Pl HAN/WDH S13 178 C1
Haxby St HAN/WDH S13 178 C2
Haybrook Ct TOT/DORE S17 189 J2
Haydn Rd MALT S66 150 F3
Haydock Cl MEX/SWTN S64 108 F1 1
Haydon Gv MALT S66 148 F1
Hayes Ct MOS S20 193 J1
Hayes Cft BSLY S70 3 G6
Hayes Dr MOS S20 193 H1
Hayes La HTFD DN7 30 F5
Hayfield Cl ARMTH DN3 47 L8
DOD/DAR S75 59 J8
DRON S18 190 B6 2
HOLM/MEL HD7 54 B3 2
Hayfield Crs HACK/IN S12 178 B4 1
Hayfield Dr HACK/IN S12 178 A4
Hayfield La EPW DN9 114 E3
Hayfield Pl HACK/IN S12 178 B4
Hayfield Vw ECK/KIL S21 192 F4
Hay Green La BSLY S70 82 D8
Hayhurst Crs MALT S66 150 E3
Hayland St DARN/MH S9 145 M5
Haylock Cl DOD/DAR S75 59 J4
Haymarket SHEF S1 9 J3
Hayne La HOR/CROF WF4 17 J2
Haynes Cl THNE DN8 50 A1
Haynes Gdns THNE DN8 32 A8
Haynes Gn THNE DN8 32 A8 1
Haynes Gv THNE DN8 50 A1
Haynes Rd THNE DN8 32 A8
Haythorne Wy MEX/SWTN S64 108 B6
Haywood Av STKB/PEN S36 102 B6
Haywood Cl RHAM/THRY S65 130 A8
Haywood La BTLY DN5 46 C1
STKB/PEN S36 102 B6
Hazel Av ECK/KIL S21 194 A2
EPW DN9 114 E3
Hazelbadge Crs
HACK/IN S12 178 C4 3
Hazel Cl DRON S18 191 G7 2
Hazel Ct DRON S18 190 F7
RHAM/THRY S65 131 J7
Hazel Gv ARMTH DN3 70 A8
CHPT/GREN S35 126 E3
CONI DN12 109 M6
HOR/CROF WF4 17 H4
MALT S66 149 G2
NROS/TKH DN11 113 K7
Hazel La AWLS/ASK DN6 43 L5
Hazel Rd CONI DN12 110 F5
ECK/KIL S21 193 G5 2
HTFD DN7 48 D6 1
MALT S66 150 B2
Hazelshaw DOD/DAR S75 81 L1 1
Hazelwood Cl DRON S18 190 A6 6
Hazelwood Dr MEX/SWTN S64 108 B7
Hazelwood Rd
HEM/SK/SE WF9 22 F6 1
Hazing La GLE DN14 10 A4
Hazlebarrow Cl SHEFS S8 176 F8
Hazlebarrow Ct SHEFS S8 176 F8 1
Hazlebarrow Crs SHEFS S8 176 F8
Hazlebarrow Dr SHEFS S8 176 F8
Hazlebarrow Gv SHEFS S8 177 G8 1
Hazlebarrow Rd SHEFS S8 190 F1 3
Hazledene Crs CUD/GR S72 40 A6
Hazledene Rd CUD/GR S72 40 A6
Hazlehurst Gdns WRKS S80 198 C5
Hazlehurst La SHEFS S8 177 K8
Headford Gdns OWL S3 8 E6
Headford Gv OWL S3 8 E6
Headford Ms OWL S3 8 E7
Headford St OWL S3 8 E6
Headingley Rd AWLS/ASK DN6 27 H4
Headingley Wy CONI DN12 111 G4
Headland Dr FUL S10 159 L4
Headland Rd FUL S10 159 L4
Headlands La RTFD DN22 171 G3
Headlands Rd HOY S74 105 H1
Heads La STKB/PEN S36 123 L1
Healey La EARL WF12 16 D1
Heath Av ECK/KIL S21 194 B2
Heath Bank Rd WHHL DN2 69 G8
Heathcote St ATT S4 145 H6 2
Heatherbank Rd
DONS/BSCR DN4 91 J8
Heather Cl HEM/SK/SE WF9 42 B4
NROS/TKH DN11 134 F7
RHAM S60 7 H9
Heatherdale Rd MALT S66 150 F2 1
Heather Fold KBTN HD8 34 D5
Heather Knowle
DOD/DAR S75 59 L8 5
Heather Lea Av TOT/DORE S17 175 G8
Heather Lea Pl TOT/DORE S17 175 G8
Heather Rd SHEFN S5 145 J4
Heathfield Cl ARMTH DN3 69 L1 1
DRON S18 190 D7 2

Heathfield Rd HACK/IN S12 178 B3
Heath Gv DEARNE S63 85 M6
Heath Rd ST/HB/BR S6 144 B3
STKB/PEN S36 102 B7
Heathy La ST/HB/BR S6 156 E2
Heaton Cl DRON S18 190 B6
Heaton Gdns CONI DN12 111 G5
Heatons Bank RAW S62 129 L1
Heaton St FEA/AMT WF7 23 J2
Heavens Wk DONS/BSCR DN4 5 G9
Heavygate Av FUL S10 160 A2
ST/HB/BR S6 160 A1
Heavygate Rd ST/HB/BR S6 160 A1
Heck & Pollington La GLE DN14 10 F1
Heck La GLE DN14 10 B3
Hedge Hill Rd STKB/PEN S36 78 E4 1
Hedge La DOD/DAR S75 37 H7 3
Heeley Bank Rd
SHEFP/MNR S2 160 F8
Heeley Gn SHEFP/MNR S2 176 F1
Heeley Rd WKFDW/WTN WF2 19 L3
Heelis St BSLY S70 3 G7
Heighton Vw AU/AST/KP S26 164 B6
The Heights HOLM/MEL HD7 54 A4
Heights Vw CHPT/GREN S35 102 E1
Helena Cl BSLY S70 2 D8
Helena St MEX/SWTN S64 108 E2
Helensburgh Cl DOD/DAR S75 2 B3 1
Hellaby Hall Rd MALT S66 149 M3
Hellaby La MALT S66 131 M7
MALT S66 149 M2
Hellaby Vw RHAM/THRY S65 131 H8
Helliwell La STKB/PEN S36 102 C8
Helmsley Av MOS S20 179 H8
Helmsley Cl AU/AST/KP S26 180 A1 2
Helmton Dr SHEFS S8 176 E4
Helmton Rd SHEFS S8 176 D5
Helston Crs BSLYN/ROY S71 3 M2
Helston Ri ABRD S7 176 A3
Hemingfield Rd WMB/DAR S73 83 M6
Hemmingfield Cl WRKN S81 184 D7 3
Hemmingfield Crs WRKN S81 184 D7
Hemmingfield Ri WRKN S81 184 D7 4
Hemmingfield Rd WRKN S81 184 D8
Hemmingfield Wy
WRKN S81 184 E7 1
Hemper Gv SHEFS S8 176 B8 1
Hemper La SHEFS S8 190 B1
Hemp Pits Rd BTLY DN5 68 B6
Hemsworth La HEM/SK/SE WF9 22 E3
Hemsworth Rd
HEM/SK/SE WF9 41 J2
SHEFS S8 177 G5
Hendal La WKFDW/WTN WF2 19 L2
Henderson Gln BSLYN/ROY S71 38 E4
Hendon St HAN/WDH S13 162 D6
Hengist Rd BTLY DN5 89 K5 1
Henley Av SHEFS S8 176 F7
Henley Grove Rd KIMB S61 6 A3
Henley La KIMB S61 128 E7
Henley Ri KIMB S61 6 A2
Henley Rd WHHL DN2 91 G2
Henley Wy KIMB S61 128 E8
Hennings Cl DONS/BSCR DN4 90 F8
Henry Av HOR/CROF WF4 22 A7
Henry Cl CUD/GR S72 39 M4
Henry Ct THNE DN8 32 A6 2
Henry La NROS/TKH DN11 113 H5
Henry Pl MEX/SWTN S64 109 G3 2
Henry Rd DEARNE S63 107 K1
Henry St BSLY S70 82 E2 4
CHPT/GREN S35 104 A8
ECK/KIL S21 193 H4
OWL S3 8 E1
RAW S62 129 K4
RHAM/THRY S65 6 F3
WMB/DAR S73 84 D3
Henshall St BSLY S70 3 J8
Heppenstall La DARN/MH S9 161 K1 3
Heptinstall St BSLY S70 82 F2 1
Hepworth Crs HOLM/MEL HD7 54 C4
Hepworth Dr AU/AST/KP S26 164 B8
Hepworth Rd DONS/BSCR DN4 89 K8 2
HOLM/MEL HD7 54 C4
Herald Rd ARMTH DN3 69 J6
Herbert Rd ABRD S7 176 C1 3
BTLY DN5 89 L2
Herbert St KIMB S61 128 C8
MEX/SWTN S64 108 F2
Herdings Ct HACK/IN S12 177 L4 2
Herdings Rd HACK/IN S12 177 L4
Herdings Vw HACK/IN S12 177 L4
Hereford Cl HEM/SK/SE WF9 23 H7
WRKN S81 198 E1
Hereford Rd WHHL DN2 68 F8
Hereford St SHEF S1 9 G8
Hereward Ct CONI DN12 110 C5
Hereward Rd SHEFN S5 144 F3
Hermes Cl BWTY DN10 136 D7
Hermitage St SHEFP/MNR S2 8 F8
The Hermitage THNE DN8 32 B4 1
Hermit Hl CHPT/GREN S35 103 K1
Hermit Hill La CHPT/GREN S35 103 J2
Hermit La DOD/DAR S75 59 K5
Heron Dr WKFDW/WTN WF2 20 A2
Heron Gld WRKN S81 184 A8 3
Heron Hl AU/AST/KP S26 180 C1
Heron Mt SHEFP/MNR S2 161 J5
Herons Wy BSLY S70 82 D7
Herrick Dr WRKN S81 199 G4
Herrick Gdns DONS/BSCR DN4 112 A1
Herrick Rd ARMTH DN3 47 K7
Herries Av SHEFN S5 144 E5
Herries Dr SHEFN S5 144 E5
Herries Pl SHEFN S5 144 E5
Herries Rd SHEFN S5 144 C5
ST/HB/BR S6 144 A5
Herril Ings NROS/TKH DN11 134 F7
Herringthorpe Av
RHAM/THRY S65 147 M3
Herringthorpe Cl
RHAM/THRY S65 147 M2 1
Herringthorpe Gv
RHAM/THRY S65 148 A3
Herringthorpe La
RHAM/THRY S65 148 A2
Herringthorpe Valley Rd
RHAM/THRY S65 130 A7
RHAM/THRY S65 148 A4
Herriot Gv NROS/TKH DN11 153 L3
Herschell Rd SHEFS S8 160 D8 3
Hesketh Dr ARMTH DN3 69 L3
Hesley Bar KIMB S61 127 J3
Hesley Ct MEX/SWTN S64 108 A6 2
Hesley Gra KIMB S61 127 M5
Hesley Gv CHPT/GREN S35 127 G3
Hesley La KIMB S61 127 J3
Hesley Rd NROS/TKH DN11 113 K7
SHEFN S5 127 H8
WKFDW/WTN WF2 19 M1
Hesley Ter SHEFN S5 145 H1
Heslop Ct WRKS S80 198 B4
Heslow Gv KIMB S61 127 J2
Hessey St HAN/WDH S13 178 D1
Hessle Rd ST/HB/BR S6 143 M5
Hewitt Pl AU/AST/KP S26 195 J2
Hewitt St MEX/SWTN S64 109 G2
Hexthorpe Rd DONS/BSCR DN4 4 D6
Heycliffe Rd HOLM/MEL HD7 53 M2
Heyden Br GLSP SK13 96 B1
Heyhouse Dr CHPT/GREN S35 104 E8
Heyhouse Wy CHPT/GREN S35 104 D8
Heysham Gn BSLYN/ROY S71 61 H2
Hey Slack La KBTN HD8 55 G5
Heyworth La AWLS/ASK DN6 28 B7
Hibberd Pl ST/HB/BR S6 143 L7
Hickleton Ct DEARNE S63 64 A8
Hickleton Rd BTLY DN5 87 G3
Hickleton St CONI DN12 109 K4
Hickmott Rd ECC S11 160 B7 3
Hickson Dr BSLYN/ROY S71 61 J3 2
Hicks St OWL S3 160 E1
Hides St DARN/MH S9 145 M7
Higger La HATH/EY S32 172 D7
High Alder Rd DONS/BSCR DN4 91 G7
Higham Common Rd
DOD/DAR S75 59 J3
Higham La DOD/DAR S75 59 J6
Higham Vw DOD/DAR S75 37 H8
High Ash Av KBTN HD8 35 K5
High Ash Cl HOR/CROF WF4 38 D1
High Ash Dr DIN S25 182 B4
High Bank La STKB/PEN S36 78 D4
Highbridge La KBTN HD8 35 G6
High Bridge Rd THNE DN8 50 C1
Highbury Av DONS/BSCR DN4 91 J7
Highbury V CONI DN12 110 E6
Highcliffe Ct MEX/SWTN S64 108 C4
Highcliffe Dr
CHPT/GREN S35 143 H1 2
ECC S11 159 K8
MEX/SWTN S64 108 B4
Highcliffe Pl ECC S11 175 K1
Highcliffe Rd ECC S11 159 K8
High Cl DOD/DAR S75 37 H6 1
High Common La BWTY DN10 136 E1
NROS/TKH DN11 135 K7
Highcroft HOLM/MEL HD7 53 J2
High Cft HOY S74 105 J2
High Croft Dr BSLYN/ROY S71 38 D7 1
Highfield GLE DN14 11 K1
Highfield Av AU/AST/KP S26 181 J4
BSLY S70 82 D1 2
BSLYN/ROY S71 60 E1
DEARNE S63 86 B2
KBTN HD8 55 L3
Highfield Cl ARMTH DN3 47 L8 1
Highfield Ct KBTN HD8 55 J1
Highfield Crs HOR/CROF WF4 17 K1
THNE DN8 31 M7 1
Highfield Gv DEARNE S63 84 E8
WRKN S81 184 F2
Highfield La AWLS/ASK DN6 46 F3
High Field La BWTY DN10 136 F4
Highfield La HAN/WDH S13 162 F5
RHAM S60 163 G3
WRKS S80 199 G6
Highfield Pk MALT S66 150 F1
Highfield Pl HEM/SK/SE WF9 41 G1 2
SHEFP/MNR S2 160 E7
Highfield Range WMB/DAR S73 62 E8
Highfield Ri ST/HB/BR S6 158 F2
Highfield Rd AWLS/ASK DN6 27 M7
BWTY DN10 136 F7
CONI DN12 110 B6
DON DN1 5 H3
HEM/SK/SE WF9 41 G1
HOR/CROF WF4 18 B2
KIMB S61 129 G5
MEX/SWTN S64 107 M4
WMB/DAR S73 84 E1
Highfields HOR/CROF WF4 18 B2
HOR/CROF WF4 18 C2
STKB/PEN S36 79 K1
Highfields Crs DRON S18 190 E7 3
High Field Spring
HAN/WDH S13 162 E3
Highfields Rd DOD/DAR S75 36 F7
DRON S18 190 E7
Highfield Vw RHAM S60 163 G1
High Fisher Ga DON DN1 5 G3
Highgate DARN/MH S9 146 C5
DEARNE S63 84 F5
GLE DN14 10 D4
Highgate Cl NROS/TKH DN11 113 L8
Highgate Ct DEARNE S63 86 A2
Highgate Dr DRON S18 191 G8
Highgate La DEARNE S63 86 A4
DRON S18 191 G8
Highgreave SHEFN S5 145 G1
High Greave Av SHEFN S5 127 G8
High Greave Ct SHEFN S5 126 F8
High Greave Pl
RHAM/THRY S65 130 A8
High Greave Rd
RHAM/THRY S65 130 A8
High Grounds Rd WRKS S80 198 A3
High Grounds Wy WRKS S80 197 M3
High Hazel Crs RHAM S60 163 G1
High Hazel Rd THNE DN8 32 B3
High Hazels Cl DARN/MH S9 162 B3 1
High Hazels Rd
DARN/MH S9 162 B3 2
High Hoe Ct WRKS S80 198 E4 1
High Hoe Dr WRKS S80 198 E4
High Hoe Rd WRKS S80 198 E4
High Hooton Rd DIN S25 150 C7
High House Farm Ct
AU/AST/KP S26 180 F5
High House Ter ST/HB/BR S6 144 B8
High Hoyland La DOD/DAR S75 35 M8
High Keep Fold HOR/CROF WF4 19 K4
Highland Gv WRKN S81 198 E2
High La HACK/IN S12 178 C6
HOLM/MEL HD7 54 A4
MALT S66 165 G4
STKB/PEN S36 56 B8
High Lee La STKB/PEN S36 79 K2
High Levels Bank THNE DN8 50 A4
THNE DN8 51 L7
Highlow Vw RHAM S60 147 G6
High Matlock Av ST/HB/BR S6 159 H1
High Matlock Rd
ST/HB/BR S6 159 J1 2
High Meadow BWTY DN10 136 D8
High Mdw WKFDW/WTN WF2 20 F1
Highmill Av MEX/SWTN S64 107 L4
Highmoor Av AU/AST/KP S26 181 G5
Highnam Crescent Rd
FUL S10 160 A4 3
High Nook Rd DIN S25 166 E7
High Rdg BSLY S70 82 D2
HOR/CROF WF4 18 C1 3
High Rd CONI DN12 110 F6
DONS/BSCR DN4 89 L8
DONS/BSCR DN4 111 G1
WRKN S81 184 E2
High Royd Av CUD/GR S72 61 M1
High Royd La STKB/PEN S36 79 L2
Highroyds BSLY S70 82 D2
Highstone Av BSLY S70 60 C8
Highstone Crs BSLY S70 60 C8
Highstone La BSLY S70 82 D1
Highstone Rd BSLY S70 60 D8
Highstone V BSLY S70 60 C8 2
High Storrs Cl ECC S11 175 K1
High Storrs Crs ECC S11 159 L8
High Storrs Dr ECC S11 175 K1
High Storrs Ri ECC S11 159 L8
High Storrs Rd ECC S11 175 K1
High St ARMTH DN3 47 K8
AU/AST/KP S26 164 A7
AWLS/ASK DN6 27 G7
AWLS/ASK DN6 27 L8
AWLS/ASK DN6 27 H4
AWLS/ASK DN6 45 G7
BSLY S70 2 E4
BSLY S70 82 F2
BSLYN/ROY S71 38 F4
BSLYN/ROY S71 61 G3
BTLY DN5 67 M7
BTLY DN5 68 B5
BTLY DN5 87 G4
BWTY DN10 137 M5
BWTY DN10 154 E1
CHPT/GREN S35 126 F7
CONI DN12 110 A5
CUD/GR S72 40 A5
CUD/GR S72 40 C2
CUD/GR S72 62 D1
CUD/GR S72 63 H5
CUD/GR S72 85 A1
DEARNE S63 64 A8
DEARNE S63 86 C2
DEARNE S63 86 A5
DEARNE S63 107 K1
DIN S25 166 B2
DIN S25 182 B3
DOD/DAR S75 37 L5
DOD/DAR S75 58 D8
DOD/DAR S75 59 K8
DON DN1 4 F4
DRON S18 190 D5
DRON S18 191 L6
ECK/KIL S21 193 H4
ECK/KIL S21 194 B1
EPW DN9 94 D3
HEM/SK/SE WF9 24 E8
HEM/SK/SE WF9 42 F4
HOR/CROF WF4 19 J2
HOR/CROF WF4 19 K8
HOY S74 105 J1
HTFD DN7 49 H8
HTFD DN7 70 B3
KBTN HD8 35 K5
KIMB S61 128 C8
MALT S66 132 E5
MALT S66 150 E2
MEX/SWTN S64 108 E3
MOS S20 179 G8
MOS S20 179 L3
NROS/TKH DN11 111 M8
RAW S62 129 K3
RHAM S60 6 F4
RHAM S60 147 M6
SHEF S1 9 J3
STKB/PEN S36 79 H5
STV/CWN S43 194 E8
TOT/DORE S17 175 H8
WMB/DAR S73 84 B4
WRKN S81 169 M5
High Street La SHEFP/MNR S2 9 L4
High Thorne Wy
AU/AST/KP S26 181 K4
Highthorn Rd MEX/SWTN S64 108 B6
High Thorns DOD/DAR S75 58 D7
Highton St FUL S10 160 A1
Hightown La HOLM/MEL HD7 53 L2
High Trees TOT/DORE S17 175 H8
High Vw BSLYN/ROY S71 38 F4
HOR/CROF WF4 19 J2
High View Cl WMB/DAR S73 84 E1
High Well Hill La CUD/GR S72 40 A1
Highwood Cl DOD/DAR S75 37 G7 2
Highwood Pl ECK/KIL S21 193 G4
Highwoods Crs
MEX/SWTN S64 108 C2 1
Highwoods Rd MEX/SWTN S64 108 C2
High Wray Cl ECC S11 175 M3
Hilary Wy AU/AST/KP S26 164 B8
Hild Av CUD/GR S72 62 B3
Hill Cl RHAM/THRY S65 148 B3
ST/HB/BR S6 159 G1
Hillcote Cl FUL S10 159 H6
Hillcote Dr FUL S10 159 H6
Hillcote Ms FUL S10 159 H6
Hillcote Ri FUL S10 159 H6
Hillcrest DEARNE S63 64 A8
Hill Crest HOR/CROF WF4 22 A6
HOY S74 105 G2
Hillcrest Dr CHPT/GREN S35 143 G1
DIN S25 182 B3
Hillcrest Ri STKB/PEN S36 102 D7
Hill Crest Rd CHPT/GREN S35 126 D2
RHAM/THRY S65 129 M8
Hillcrest Rd STKB/PEN S36 102 D7
WHHL DN2 90 E1
Hill End Rd DOD/DAR S75 38 A8
Hill Farm Cl DEARNE S63 63 M8 1
Hillfold HEM/SK/SE WF9 42 F4 1
Hillfoot Rd TOT/DORE S17 189 G2
Hill House La HOLM/MEL HD7 53 H5
Hill House Rd HOLM/MEL HD7 53 J5
Hill La HATH/EY S32 172 C7
HOLM/MEL HD7 53 J2
Hill Park Gv DOD/DAR S75 59 K7
Hill Rd WKFDW/WTN WF2 20 A3
Hills and Hamlets Wk
HOLM/MEL HD7 53 J4
Hillsborough Pl
ST/HB/BR S6 144 A7 4
Hillsborough Rd
DONS/BSCR DN4 91 J7
ST/HB/BR S6 144 A7 5
Hills Cl BTLY DN5 89 J5
Hillscroft Rd EPW DN9 115 J2
Hillside BSLYN/ROY S71 61 L7 3
DIN S25 182 B1
KBTN HD8 56 D1
MOS S20 179 G8
Hill Side RHAM S60 147 M6
Hill Side Av HOLM/MEL HD7 54 C5
Hillside Av DRON S18 190 E7
SHEFN S5 144 F1
Hillside Cl STKB/PEN S36 79 K1
Hillside Ct BTLY DN5 88 F7 3
HEM/SK/SE WF9 42 E3 1
KIMB S61 129 H6
Hillside Crs CUD/GR S72 40 E5
WRKN S81 198 D2
Hillside Dr CONI DN12 110 E6
HOY S74 105 K2
Hillside Gv CUD/GR S72 40 D5
Hill Side La STKB/PEN S36 78 C5
Hillside Mt CUD/GR S72 40 E5
Hillside Rd FEA/AMT WF7 23 K1
Hillside Wy CHPT/GREN S35 103 H3
Hills Rd STKB/PEN S36 102 B6
Hill St BSLYN/ROY S71 61 J7
HOLM/MEL HD7 54 C4
HOY S74 105 L2
SHEFP/MNR S2 8 F9
WMB/DAR S73 84 E2
WRKS S80 198 C5
Hillthorpe Dr PONT WF8 24 E2 2
Hilltop CUD/GR S72 40 D4
Hill Top DOD/DAR S75 58 C3
HEM/SK/SE WF9 22 E4 2
Hill Top Av BSLYN/ROY S71 38 C6
Hilltop Cl MALT S66 150 B1
Hill Top Cl HEM/SK/SE WF9 22 F4 1
HOR/CROF WF4 38 F1
KIMB S61 146 B1
RHAM S60 146 E6
Hill Top Ct NROS/TKH DN11 153 L3
WKFDW/WTN WF2 20 A3 1
Hill Top Crs CONI DN12 110 F6
MOS S20 179 H6
WHHL DN2 69 G8
Hilltop Dr CHPT/GREN S35 124 F7
Hilltop Gdns CONI DN12 109 K5
Hill Top La CHPT/GREN S35 125 M7
DOD/DAR S75 59 M4
RHAM/THRY S65 130 D8
STKB/PEN S36 102 A4
Hill Top Ri CHPT/GREN S35 126 B8
Hilltop Rd DRON S18 190 E7
Hill Top Rd BSLY S70 82 D7
CHPT/GREN S35 126 B8
CONI DN12 109 K6
HOLM/MEL HD7 53 K6
HOR/CROF WF4 17 H4
ST/HB/BR S6 158 A1
WKFDW/WTN WF2 20 A3
Hill Top Vw HOLM/MEL HD7 53 M7
Hilltop Wy DRON S18 190 E8
Hill Turrets Cl ECC S11 175 K3
Hill Vw East KIMB S61 128 B7 1
Hill View Rd KIMB S61 128 B7
Hillwood Cl WRKS S80 197 M5
Hilmian Wy HEM/SK/SE WF9 41 K2
Hilton Dr CHPT/GREN S35 126 F7
Hilton St AWLS/ASK DN6 27 L7
DOD/DAR S75 2 C4
Hindburn Cl DONS/BSCR DN4 91 G8
Hinde House Crs ATT S4 145 J5
Hinde House Cft ATT S4 145 J5
Hinde House La ATT S4 145 H6
Hinde St ATT S4 145 J6
Hindewood Cl ATT S4 145 J5
Hindle St BSLY S70 2 D6
Hind Rd RHAM S60 148 A5
Hinds Crs HEM/SK/SE WF9 42 D4
Hirst Common La
ST/HB/BR S6 143 L1
Hirst Dr RHAM/THRY S65 130 B8
Hirst Ga MEX/SWTN S64 109 G2
Hirst La HOLM/MEL HD7 54 F3
MALT S66 133 J6
Hoads Av WRKN S81 183 J3
Hoar Stones Rd ST/HB/BR S6 141 J4
Hobart St ECC S11 160 D7
Hobcroft Ter AWLS/ASK DN6 44 F6 1
Hob La CHPT/GREN S35 124 C5
Hobson Av ST/HB/BR S6 144 C8
Hobson Pl ST/HB/BR S6 144 C8
Hodder Ct CHPT/GREN S35 126 D1 4
Hoddesdon Crs HTFD DN7 70 E2
Hodge La PONT WF8 26 C1
Hodgkinson Av
STKB/PEN S36 79 H4 1
Hodgson St OWL S3 8 F7
Hodroyd Cl CUD/GR S72 40 B6
Hodroyd Cottages CUD/GR S72 40 D5
Hodsock La WRKN S81 169 H8
WRKN S81 184 E1
Hodsock Red Br WRKN S81 169 L8
Hodster La CUD/GR S72 63 H3
Hog Close La HOLM/MEL HD7 55 G7
Hoggarth Ri DRON S18 190 D6
Hogley La HOLM/MEL HD7 53 G3
Holbein Cl DRON S18 190 D7
Holberry Cl FUL S10 8 D6
Holberry Gdns FUL S10 8 C6
Holbourne Gv CHPT/GREN S35 104 B6
Holbrook Av MOS S20 179 K7
Holbrook Dr HAN/WDH S13 177 M1 3
Holbrook Gn MOS S20 179 K7
Holbrook Ri MOS S20 179 K6
Holbrook Rd HAN/WDH S13 161 M8
Holburn Av DRON S18 190 E5
Holden Ct BSLY S70 2 E6
Holderness Cl
NROS/TKH DN11 153 L3 1
Holderness Dr AU/AST/KP S26 164 B7
Holding WRKN S81 198 F2
Holdings Rd SHEFP/MNR S2 161 H6
Holds La RTFD DN22 170 F5
Holdworth La ST/HB/BR S6 142 D3
Hole House La STKB/PEN S36 101 M5 2
Holgate WMB/DAR S73 83 M2
Holgate Av SHEFN S5 144 D1
Holgate Crs HEM/SK/SE WF9 23 G8
SHEFN S5 144 E1
Holgate Dr SHEFN S5 144 E1
Holgate Gdns HEM/SK/SE WF9 23 G8
Holgate Mt BSLY S70 82 D1
Holgate Rd SHEFN S5 144 E1
Holgate Vw CUD/GR S72 40 F4 1
Holiwell Cl MALT S66 150 F1
Holkham Ri ECC S11 175 K5 1
Holland Cl RAW S62 107 K8
Holland Pl SHEFP/MNR S2 160 E7 6
Holland Rd CHPT/GREN S35 104 B8
SHEFP/MNR S2 160 E7
Holland St SHEF S1 8 F4
Holles St WRKS S80 198 D5
Hollies Cl DRON S18 191 G7
Hollinberry La CHPT/GREN S35 103 M6
Hollin Bridge La HTFD DN7 71 L1
Hollin Brigg La HOLM/MEL HD7 53 G5
Hollin Busk La STKB/PEN S36 102 A8
Hollin Busk Rd STKB/PEN S36 102 A7
Hollin Cl NROS/TKH DN11 113 M5
Hollin Cft DOD/DAR S75 59 L7
Hollindale Dr HACK/IN S12 178 A2
Hollin Dr HOR/CROF WF4 19 J2
Hollin Edge KBTN HD8 56 E1
Hollin Edge La STKB/PEN S36 124 D2
Holling Cft STKB/PEN S36 102 C6 1
Holling's La RHAM/THRY S65 130 D5
Hollingthorpe Av
HOR/CROF WF4 19 J4
Hollingthorpe Ct
HOR/CROF WF4 19 J5
Hollingthorpe Gv
HOR/CROF WF4 19 J4
Hollingthorpe La
HOR/CROF WF4 19 J4
Hollingthorpe Rd
HOR/CROF WF4 19 J4
Hollin Hill La RHAM/THRY S65 148 D3
Hollinhirst La HOR/CROF WF4 18 D2
Hollin House La
HOLM/MEL HD7 54 D2
KBTN HD8 35 K8
ST/HB/BR S6 142 D4
Hollin La HOR/CROF WF4 19 H1
STKB/PEN S36 77 L3
Hollin Moor La CHPT/GREN S35 80 F7
MALT S66 148 E3
Hollin Rd CHPT/GREN S35 143 G1
Hollins Cl ST/HB/BR S6 159 K2
Hollins Dr ST/HB/BR S6 159 K2
Hollinsend Av HACK/IN S12 178 A2
Hollinsend Pl HACK/IN S12 178 A2 2
Hollinsend Rd HACK/IN S12 177 L3 3
Hollins La ST/HB/BR S6 159 L1
Hollins Mt HEM/SK/SE WF9 23 G8
Hollins Spring Av DRON S18 190 E7
Hollins Spring Rd DRON S18 190 E7
Hollis Cl RAW S62 107 G7
Hollis Cft HAN/WDH S13 178 E1 1
SHEF S1 8 F3
Hollowdene DOD/DAR S75 59 M4
Hollow Ga BTLY DN5 110 A2
CHPT/GREN S35 126 B2
RHAM S60 147 M6 2
Hollowgate BTLY DN5 87 G5
HOLM/MEL HD7 53 L2
RHAM S60 7 G6
Hollowgate Av DEARNE S63 85 G7
Hollow La MOS S20 193 H1
The Hollows DONS/BSCR DN4 113 J1
EPW DN9 114 E1
Holly Av BTLY DN5 67 L8
Holly Bank FEA/AMT WF7 23 J1
Hollybank Av HACK/IN S12 178 A1
KBTN HD8 56 A1
Hollybank Cl HACK/IN S12 178 B1
Hollybank Crs HACK/IN S12 178 A1
Hollybank Dr HACK/IN S12 178 A1
Hollybank Rd HACK/IN S12 178 A2
Hollybank Wy HACK/IN S12 178 B1
Holly Bush Dr DEARNE S63 64 B7
Hollybush St RAW S62 129 K4
Holly Cl CHPT/GREN S35 126 D3
ECK/KIL S21 193 M2
HEM/SK/SE WF9 42 D5 4
Holly Ct NROS/TKH DN11 153 J3
Holly Crs MALT S66 149 G1
Holly Croft Gv
NROS/TKH DN11 134 F7
Holly Dene ARMTH DN3 69 L7
Holly Dr BTLY DN5 67 M5
Holly Gdns HACK/IN S12 178 A1
Hollygate BSLY S70 82 F2
Holly Gv CUD/GR S72 40 E4
DEARNE S63 107 K3
HACK/IN S12 178 A1

NROS/TKH DN11 113 L6
Holly Hall La CHPT/GREN S35 102 D4
Holly La SHEF S1 9 G4 1
Holly Mt MALT S66 149 G3
Holly Rd EPW DN9 114 E3
THNE DN8 32 A6
Holly's House Rd
RHAM/THRY S65 131 K6
Holly St DON DN1 4 E9
HEM/SK/SE WF9 23 H8
SHEF S1 9 G4
Holly Ter AU/AST/KP S26 163 M7
DONS/BSCR DN4 89 K8
Hollythorpe Crs SHEFS S8 176 E3
Hollythorpe Rd SHEFS S8 176 F3
Hollytree Av MALT S66 150 B1
Hollywell Cl RAW S62 129 M1
Holmclose HOLM/MEL HD7 52 F5
Holme Cl HOR/CROF WF4 16 C2
ST/HB/BR S6 144 A7 6
Holme Ct DEARNE S63 86 A3 2
Holmefield Cl ARMTH DN3 92 A2
WRKN S81 198 E2 1
Holmefield Cft BWTY DN10 154 E5 2
Holme Fleet La HTFD DN7 47 H5
Holme Gdns HTFD DN7 48 D2
Holme Hall La MALT S66 133 J6
Holme La BTLY DN5 45 M5
CHPT/GREN S35 126 B8
ST/HB/BR S6 143 M8
Holme Oak Wy ST/HB/BR S6 143 G8
Holmeroyd Rd AWLS/ASK DN6 45 J8
Holmes Carr Crs
NROS/TKH DN11 113 H6
Holmes Carr Rd
DONS/BSCR DN4 113 H1
NROS/TKH DN11 113 H5
Holmes Crs RHAM S60 163 J3
Holmesdale Cl DRON S18 191 G4
Holmesdale Rd DRON S18 190 F4
Holmesfield CHPT/GREN S35 143 H1 3
Holmesfield Rd DRON S18 189 M6
Holmes La CONI DN12 108 F7
KIMB S61 6 A5
Holmes Rd MALT S66 149 H3
The Holmes DON DN1 5 H2
Holme Styes La
HOLM/MEL HD7 53 K7
Holme Valley Circular Wk
HOLM/MEL HD7 52 F7
Holme View Dr HOLM/MEL HD7 53 H2
Holme View Pk HOLM/MEL HD7 53 J2
Holme View Rd DOD/DAR S75 36 F7
Holme Wood Ct ARMTH DN3 69 L5 1
Holme Wood Gdns
DONS/BSCR DN4 91 J8 2
Holme Wood La ARMTH DN3 92 B1
Holme Woods La
HOLM/MEL HD7 74 D2
Holmfield KBTN HD8 35 K5 3
Holmfield Av KBTN HD8 35 K5 5
Holmfield Cl KBTN HD8 35 K5
Holmfield Rd KBTN HD8 35 K5
Holm Flatt St RAW S62 129 J4
Holmhirst Cl SHEFS S8 176 C5
Holmhirst Dr SHEFS S8 176 C4
Holmhirst Rd SHEFS S8 176 C4
Holmhirst Wy SHEFS S8 176 C5
Holmhurst Cl WRKN S81 198 C2 1
Holmley Bank DRON S18 190 E4
Holmley La DRON S18 190 E4
Holmoak Cl MEX/SWTN S64 108 B6
Holmshaw Dr HAN/WDH S13 162 C7
Holmshaw Gv HAN/WDH S13 162 C7
Holmsley Av HEM/SK/SE WF9 41 L5
Holmsley Gv HEM/SK/SE WF9 41 L5
Holmsley La CUD/GR S72 41 J5
Holmsley Mt HEM/SK/SE WF9 41 L5
Holt La HOLM/MEL HD7 53 K1
Holtwood Rd ATT S4 144 F8
Holwick Cl DOD/DAR S75 58 D7 6
Holyoake Av HAN/WDH S13 162 C6
Holyrood Ri MALT S66 149 H1
Holyrood Rd WHHL DN2 90 E4
Holywell Crs MALT S66 132 E6
Holywell La CONI DN12 110 A6
MALT S66 132 E6
Holywell Rd ATT S4 145 K6
MEX/SWTN S64 108 B6
Homecroft Rd DEARNE S63 86 B2
Home Farm Ct BTLY DN5 65 G8
Homefield Crs BTLY DN5 67 J7
Home Mdw NROS/TKH DN11 152 E1
Homestead Cl SHEFN S5 145 H2
Homestead Dr RAW S62 107 K8
RHAM S60 146 F6
Homestead Garth HTFD DN7 48 F7 2
Homestead Rd SHEFN S5 145 G3
Honey Lands La BTLY DN5 46 B5
Honeysuckle Cl WMB/DAR S73 84 E3
Honeysuckle Ct EPW DN9 115 J4 2
Honeysuckle Rd SHEFN S5 145 K4 1
Honeywell Cl BSLYN/ROY S71 3 G2
Honeywell Gv BSLYN/ROY S71 60 D3
Honeywell La DOD/DAR S75 2 E1
Honeywell Pl BSLYN/ROY S71 3 G1
Honeywell St BSLYN/ROY S71 3 G1
Honister Cl DEARNE S63 84 E8
Hoober Av ECC S11 175 L2
Hoober Ct RAW S62 107 H7
Hoober Fld RAW S62 106 F5
Hoober Hall La RAW S62 106 D4
Hoober La RAW S62 106 E6
Hoober Rd ECC S11 175 L2
Hoober St DEARNE S63 106 F1
Hoober Vw RAW S62 107 H7
WMB/DAR S73 84 D6
Hood Green Rd DOD/DAR S75 81 J5
Hood St HEM/SK/SE WF9 42 C7
Hoole La FUL S10 160 A5 5
Hoole Rd FUL S10 160 A4
Hoole St ST/HB/BR S6 160 A1
Hooton Cl DIN S25 166 C2 2
Hooton Crs HOR/CROF WF4 21 L6 1
Hooton La DIN S25 166 C2
MALT S66 150 C3
RHAM/THRY S65 131 G4
Hooton Rd BTLY DN5 65 K4
MEX/SWTN S64 108 D8
Hoowood La HOLM/MEL HD7 52 C4
Hope Av DEARNE S63 86 B3
Hopedale Rd HACK/IN S12 178 B3
Hopefield Av HACK/IN S12 178 B3
Hope Rd CHPT/GREN S35 143 J1
Hope St BSLYN/ROY S71 61 K1
DOD/DAR S75 2 C3
DOD/DAR S75 38 A7
MEX/SWTN S64 108 E3 1
OWL S3 8 D3
RHAM S60 6 C2
STKB/PEN S36 102 A6
WMB/DAR S73 84 C5
Hope Street Extension
RHAM S60 6 D2
Hopewell St BSLY S70 61 H7
Hopewell Wy HOR/CROF WF4 19 J2
Hop Hills La HTFD DN7 48 E6
The Hop Inge AU/AST/KP S26 195 J2
Hopping La CHPT/GREN S35 80 D6
Hopwood La ST/HB/BR S6 158 E3
Hopwood St BSLY S70 2 E3
Hopyard La NROS/TKH DN11 135 G6
Horace St RHAM/THRY S65 7 H6
Horbiry End AU/AST/KP S26 181 J2 3
Horbury La CHPT/GREN S35 126 C3
Horbury Rd CUD/GR S72 39 M7
Hordron Rd STKB/PEN S36 99 G2
Hornbeam Cl CHPT/GREN S35 126 D3
Hornbeam Rd MALT S66 148 F1
Hornby St BSLY S70 3 H9 2
Horncastle Vw HOR/CROF WF4 22 B6
Horn Cote La HOLM/MEL HD7 54 E1
Horn Cft DOD/DAR S75 58 C2
Horndean Rd SHEFN S5 145 H6
Horner Cl STKB/PEN S36 101 M6
Horner Rd SHEFS S8 160 D8
Hornes La DOD/DAR S75 38 A6
Horninglow Cl
DONS/BSCR DN4 113 L1
SHEFN S5 145 G4
Horninglow Rd SHEFN S5 145 G4
Horn La HOLM/MEL HD7 54 E1
STKB/PEN S36 55 L6
Hornsby Rd ARMTH DN3 92 A2
Hornthorpe Rd ECK/KIL S21 192 F5
Hornthwaite Hill Rd
STKB/PEN S36 78 D5
Horse Carr Vw BSLYN/ROY S71 61 L7
Horse Croft La
CHPT/GREN S35 124 F7
Horse Fair Gn THNE DN8 31 M8 2
Horsehills La ARMTH DN3 91 L2
Horsemoor Rd DEARNE S63 63 M7 1
Horseshoe Cl
AU/AST/KP S26 181 G4 1
Horseshoe La MALT S66 151 J7
Horsewood Cl BSLY S70 59 M7
Horsewood Rd HAN/WDH S13 163 H7
Horsleygate Rd TOT/DORE S17 188 F7
Horton Cl MOS S20 179 J8 1
Horton Dr MOS S20 179 J8
Horton Vw ARMTH DN3 69 J2
Hough La WMB/DAR S73 83 M6
Houghton Rd DEARNE S63 63 L7
DIN S25 165 M7
Hound Hill La DOD/DAR S75 82 B2
MEX/SWTN S64 86 B8
Houndkirk Rd ECC S11 174 C6
Hounsfield Crs
RHAM/THRY S65 130 B8
Hounsfield La OWL S3 8 D5
Hounsfield Rd OWL S3 8 D4
RHAM/THRY S65 130 B8
Houps Rd THNE DN8 32 A8
House Carr La DOD/DAR S75 80 F3
House Grove Dr KBTN HD8 35 J5
Housley La CHPT/GREN S35 126 D1
Housley Pk CHPT/GREN S35 126 E1
Houstead Rd DARN/MH S9 162 B4
Howard Crs HOR/CROF WF4 19 J1
Howard La SHEF S1 9 J6
Howard Rd MALT S66 149 H2
MALT S66 150 F2 2
NROS/TKH DN11 154 A3
ST/HB/BR S6 160 A2
Howards Cl DIN S25 165 L1
Howard St BSLY S70 3 H9
BSLY S70 60 D8 6
DIN S25 166 E6
RHAM/THRY S65 6 F3
SHEF S1 9 J6
WMB/DAR S73 85 G2
WRKS S80 198 E5
Howarth Rd RHAM S60 147 H7
Howbeck Cl CONI DN12 110 E6
Howbeck Dr CONI DN12 110 E6
Howbrook Cl
CHPT/GREN S35 104 A7 1
Howbrook La CHPT/GREN S35 103 K5
Howden Av AWLS/ASK DN6 44 C6
Howden Cl DOD/DAR S75 37 K6
DONS/BSCR DN4 113 G1
Howden Rd DARN/MH S9 145 L8
Howdike La CONI DN12 108 F8
Howe La MALT S66 150 C7
Howell La CUD/GR S72 63 J1
Howlett Cl RHAM S60 148 B6
Howlett Dr RHAM S60 147 G8
Howse St HOY S74 105 L1
Howson Cl RHAM/THRY S65 131 J7
Howson Rd STKB/PEN S36 102 B6
Howville Av HTFD DN7 71 J1
Hoylake Dr MEX/SWTN S64 108 B6
Hoyland Cl STKB/PEN S36 78 E6
Hoyland Rd HOY S74 104 F2
OWL S3 144 C8
WKFDW/WTN WF2 19 M2
Hoyland St MALT S66 150 F2
WMB/DAR S73 84 B5 1
Hoyle Croft La MALT S66 132 C6
Hoyle Mill Rd BSLY S70 61 H7
HEM/SK/SE WF9 23 H5
Hoyle St OWL S3 8 F2
Hucklow Rd SHEFN S5 145 H5
Huddersfield Rd DOD/DAR S75 36 F2
DOD/DAR S75 60 A3 1
HOR/CROF WF4 18 D7
KBTN HD8 34 B4
KBTN HD8 35 G6
STKB/PEN S36 78 F1
Hudson Av HOR/CROF WF4 38 F1
Hudson Cl AU/AST/KP S26 181 J8 1
Hudson Rd HAN/WDH S13 163 J7 2
KIMB S61 128 C5
Huggin Carr Rd HTFD DN7 71 J6
Hugh Hill La HTFD DN7 48 F3
Humber Cl AWLS/ASK DN6 44 E6
Humber Ct AWLS/ASK DN6 44 E6
Humberside Wy
BSLYN/ROY S71 61 H1
Humber St WRKS S80 198 C3 1
Humley Rd WKFDW/WTN WF2 19 M2
Humphrey Rd SHEFS S8 176 C7
Humphries Av RAW S62 107 H8 1
Humphries Gdns WRKS S80 198 C6
Hundall La DRON S18 191 K8
Hund Oak Dr HTFD DN7 48 F7 3
Hundred Acre La WRKN S81 185 G4
Hungerhill Cl KIMB S61 128 B7
Hungerhill La ARMTH DN3 69 H5
Hunger Hill La RHAM S60 148 A6
Hungerhill Rd KIMB S61 128 B6
Hunger Hill Rd RHAM S60 147 M5
Hungry La HATH/EY S32 172 F7
Hunningley La BSLY S70 61 H8 1
Hunsdon Rd ECK/KIL S21 193 G4
Hunshelf Hall La
STKB/PEN S36 101 M3
Hunshelf La CHPT/GREN S35 126 F5
Hunshelf Pk STKB/PEN S36 102 A5
Hunshelf Rd CHPT/GREN S35 126 D2
STKB/PEN S36 101 M5
Hunsley St ATT S4 145 J7
Hunster Gv NROS/TKH DN11 113 K7
Hunstone Av SHEFS S8 176 E8
Hunt Cl BSLYN/ROY S71 61 G3 2
Hunter Hill Rd ECC S11 160 A8
Hunter House Rd ECC S11 159 M8
Hunter Rd ST/HB/BR S6 143 M7
Hunter's Av BSLY S70 59 L7
Hunters Cha DIN S25 166 D5
Hunters Cl DIN S25 166 D4
Hunters Ct DIN S25 166 D4 1
Hunters Dr DIN S25 166 D5
Hunters Gdns DIN S25 166 D4 2
ST/HB/BR S6 143 H6
Hunters Gn DIN S25 166 D4 3
Hunter's La HAN/WDH S13 178 A1
Hunters Pk DIN S25 166 D4
Hunters Ri DOD/DAR S75 59 L6
Hunters Wy DIN S25 166 D4
Huntingdon Crs ECC S11 160 C7
Huntingdon Rd WHHL DN2 91 G2
Huntington St BTLY DN5 67 M5 2
Huntington Wy MALT S66 132 C8
Huntingtower Rd ECC S11 159 M8
Hunt La BTLY DN5 4 D1
Huntley Gv ECC S11 175 K1
Huntley Rd ECC S11 175 L1
Huntsman Pl RTFD DN22 170 F4
Huntsman Rd DARN/MH S9 162 B3
Huntsmans Gdns
DARN/MH S9 146 A8
Huntsmans Wy
HEM/SK/SE WF9 24 C5
Hunt St HOY S74 104 F2
Hurl Dr HACK/IN S12 177 K2
Hurley Cft DEARNE S63 84 E8 1
Hurlfield Av HACK/IN S12 177 L2
Hurlfield Ct HACK/IN S12 177 K1
Hurlfield Dr HACK/IN S12 177 K1
RHAM/THRY S65 131 H8
Hurlfield Rd HACK/IN S12 177 K2
Hurlingham Cl ABRD S7 176 A3
Hursley Cl MOS S20 179 L6 5
Hursley Dr MOS S20 179 L6
Hurstclough La HATH/EY S32 172 B5
Hurst Gn CHPT/GREN S35 104 B8
Hurst La EPW DN9 114 E2
Hushells La GLE DN14 30 D4
Huskar Cl DOD/DAR S75 58 D7
Hutchinson La SHEFS S8 176 B4 1
Hutchinson Rd RAW S62 129 L1 1
SHEFS S8 176 B4 2
Hutcliffe Dr SHEFS S8 176 B5 1
Hutcliffe Wood Rd SHEFS S8 176 B5
Huthwaite La CHPT/GREN S35 102 D2
Hut La ECK/KIL S21 194 C3
Hutton Dr HEM/SK/SE WF9 42 E3
Hutton Rd KIMB S61 128 C6
Hyacinth Cl DARN/MH S9 145 K4
Hyacinth Rd SHEFN S5 145 K4
Hyde Park Wk SHEFP/MNR S2 9 M4
Hyland Crs DONS/BSCR DN4 111 J1 1
Hyman Cl DONS/BSCR DN4 89 H8

I

Ibberson Av DOD/DAR S75 37 L7
Ibbotson Rd ST/HB/BR S6 160 A1
Ibbotsons Cft HATH/EY S32 172 E7 2
Ickles Wy RHAM S60 6 A9
Icknield Wy RHAM S60 147 G7
Ida Gv MALT S66 150 B1
Ida's Rd ECK/KIL S21 193 H3
Idle Bank EPW DN9 73 K7
EPW DN9 117 G8
Idsworth Rd SHEFN S5 145 H5
Ilkley Crs AU/AST/KP S26 180 A1
Ilkley Rd SHEFN S5 145 H3
Illsley Rd WMB/DAR S73 84 E1
Imperial Crs WHHL DN2 5 M3
Industry Rd BSLYN/ROY S71 39 G8
DARN/MH S9 162 A2
Industry St ST/HB/BR S6 160 A1
Infield La DARN/MH S9 162 A3
Infirmary Rd OWL S3 8 E1
RAW S62 129 L4
ST/HB/BR S6 160 C2
Ingbirchworth La
STKB/PEN S36 56 C8
Ingbirchworth Rd
STKB/PEN S36 78 E3
Ingdale Dr HOLM/MEL HD7 53 M1
Ingelow Av SHEFN S5 144 F2
Ingfield Av DARN/MH S9 146 C5
Ingham Rd BWTY DN10 136 D7
Ingleborough Cft
CHPT/GREN S35 126 D1 5
Ingleborough Dr BTLY DN5 89 J5
Ingleby Cl DRON S18 190 A6
Ingledene Ms ARMTH DN3 47 K8
Ingle Gv BTLY DN5 89 J5
Inglemere Cl WRKN S81 198 E2 2
Inglenook Dr THNE DN8 32 A7
Inglewood DOD/DAR S75 37 K6
Inglewood Av MOS S20 179 L6 3
Inglewood Ct MOS S20 179 L6 6
Inglewood Dell MOS S20 179 L6 7
Ingram Ct SHEFP/MNR S2 161 H5 1
Ingram Crs HTFD DN7 48 D8
Ingram Gv HTFD DN7 48 D8 1
Ingram Rd HTFD DN7 70 D1
SHEFP/MNR S2 161 H5
Ings Cl HEM/SK/SE WF9 42 B4
HOR/CROF WF4 22 A6
Ingsfield La DEARNE S63 85 L5
Ingshead Av RAW S62 129 L2
Ings Holt HEM/SK/SE WF9 42 B4
Ings La AWLS/ASK DN6 44 E6
BTLY DN5 68 C5
BTLY DN5 68 E5
BTLY DN5 89 J5
CUD/GR S72 62 F8
HTFD DN7 48 C1
Ings Mill Av KBTN HD8 35 K4
Ings Mill Dr KBTN HD8 35 K5
Ings Rd BTLY DN5 90 A1
BTLY DN5 110 B1
HEM/SK/SE WF9 22 F6
WMB/DAR S73 84 E3
The Ings KBTN HD8 35 K5 5
Ings Wk HEM/SK/SE WF9 42 B4
Ings Wy BTLY DN5 68 B5
STKB/PEN S36 56 B6
Ingswell Av HOR/CROF WF4 20 D8
Ingswell Dr HOR/CROF WF4 20 D8
Inkerman Rd WMB/DAR S73 84 E2
Inkerman Wy KBTN HD8 56 D2
Inkersall Dr MOS S20 179 J7
Innovation Wy DOD/DAR S75 60 A3
Insley Gdns DONS/BSCR DN4 91 J8
Instone Ter AWLS/ASK DN6 45 K1
Intake Crs DOD/DAR S75 81 K1
Intake La CUD/GR S72 40 A7
DOD/DAR S75 59 M5
HOR/CROF WF4 19 H8
Inverness Rd HTFD DN7 48 E7
Ironside Cl GLV S14 177 H5
Ironside Pl GLV S14 177 J4
Ironside Rd GLV S14 177 H5
Irving St DARN/MH S9 162 A3
Irwell Gdns DONS/BSCR DN4 91 H5 1
Islay St FUL S10 159 M4
Issott St BSLYN/ROY S71 3 G1
Ivan Brook Cl DRON S18 190 A6 7
Ivanhoe Av AU/AST/KP S26 181 J5
Ivanhoe Cl BTLY DN5 89 K3
Ivanhoe Ms AU/AST/KP S26 164 A7
Ivanhoe Rd ARMTH DN3 69 K6
CONI DN12 109 M5
CONI DN12 110 F6
DONS/BSCR DN4 89 J8
MALT S66 165 J1
ST/HB/BR S6 159 L1 1
Ivanhoe Wy BTLY DN5 89 K3
Ivatt Cl BWTY DN10 136 E7
Ivor Gv DONS/BSCR DN4 89 L7
Ivy Cl HEM/SK/SE WF9 42 D6
HTFD DN7 49 H7
NROS/TKH DN11 113 L6
Ivy Cottage La ECC S11 175 G1
Ivy Ct SHEFS S8 177 G5
Ivy Dr FUL S10 8 A3
Ivy Farm Cl BSLYN/ROY S71 39 H6
Ivy Farm Cft RHAM/THRY S65 130 B6
Ivy Gv FUL S10 8 A3
Ivy Hall Rd SHEFN S5 127 J8
Ivy House Ct EPW DN9 92 D8
Ivy La MOS S20 179 L3
Ivy Lodge La WRKN S81 167 M3
Ivy Park Rd FUL S10 159 J5
Ivy Rd THNE DN8 31 M6
Ivy Side Cl ECK/KIL S21 194 B1
Ivyside Gdns ECK/KIL S21 194 B1
Ivy Ter HEM/SK/SE WF9 42 E4 2

J

Jack Close Orch BSLYN/ROY S71 39 G3
Jackey Hl CHPT/GREN S35 124 F8 1
Jack La CHPT/GREN S35 124 A3
Jack Row La HTFD DN7 29 M8
Jackson Crs RAW S62 107 H8
Jackson St CUD/GR S72 61 L1
DEARNE S63 86 C2 2
Jackys La AU/AST/KP S26 195 J1
Jacobs Cl SHEFN S5 145 J3
Jacobs Dr SHEFN S5 145 J3
Jacobs Hall Ct DOD/DAR S75 37 G7 3
Jacques Pl BSLYN/ROY S71 61 H5
Jagger La KBTN HD8 16 C8
Jagger's La HATH/EY S32 172 C7
Jamaica St ATT S4 145 H8 2
James Andrew Cl SHEFS S8 176 D8
James Andrew Crs SHEFS S8 176 C8
James Andrew Cft SHEFS S8 176 D8 2
James Ct THNE DN8 32 A6
James Rd AWLS/ASK DN6 45 H8
James St BSLY S70 83 G2
BSLYN/ROY S71 3 H3
CUD/GR S72 40 D2
DARN/MH S9 162 A4
MEX/SWTN S64 109 H2
RHAM S60 6 B4
WRKN S81 198 C2
Janson St DARN/MH S9 145 L7
Jaque's Bank THNE DN8 51 L4
Jardine WRKN S81 198 F1
Jardine Cl DARN/MH S9 145 L3
Jardine St DARN/MH S9 145 M3
WMB/DAR S73 84 B5
Jarratt St DON DN1 5 H7
Jarrow Rd ECC S11 160 B7 9
Jasmine Av MOS S20 179 K4
Jasmine Cl CONI DN12 110 B6
Jaunty Av HACK/IN S12 177 M4
Jaunty Cl HACK/IN S12 177 M4
Jaunty Crs HACK/IN S12 177 M3
Jaunty Dr HACK/IN S12 177 M4
Jaunty La HACK/IN S12 177 M3
Jaunty Mt HACK/IN S12 178 A4
Jaunty Pl HACK/IN S12 177 M4
Jaunty Rd HACK/IN S12 178 A4
Jaunty Vw HACK/IN S12 178 A4
Jaunty Wy HACK/IN S12 177 M3
Jay La AU/AST/KP S26 180 C1
Jebb La DOD/DAR S75 36 D3
Jedburgh Dr DARN/MH S9 145 L3
Jedburgh St DARN/MH S9 145 L3
Jeffcock Rd CHPT/GREN S35 104 C8
DARN/MH S9 162 A3 3
Jefferson Av WHHL DN2 69 H6
Jeffery Crs STKB/PEN S36 102 B7
Jeffery St SHEFP/MNR S2 176 F1 1
Jenkin Av DARN/MH S9 145 L5
Jenkin Cl DARN/MH S9 145 L4
Jenkin Dr DARN/MH S9 145 L5
Jenkin Rd DARN/MH S9 145 L4
Jennings Cl RHAM/THRY S65 7 H1
Jenny La GLE DN14 10 B5
Jepson Rd SHEFN S5 145 K3
Jericho St OWL S3 8 D2
Jermyn Av HACK/IN S12 178 C3
Jermyn Cl HACK/IN S12 178 D4
Jermyn Crs HACK/IN S12 178 D4
Jermyn Cft DOD/DAR S75 59 K8
Jermyn Dr HACK/IN S12 178 D4
Jermyn Wy HACK/IN S12 178 C4
Jersey Rd SHEFP/MNR S2 160 E8 6
Jesmond Av BSLYN/ROY S71 38 F4
Jesop Ct DIN S25 166 D5
Jessamine Rd SHEFN S5 145 J3
Jessell St DARN/MH S9 161 K2
Jessop St SHEF S1 9 G7
Jewitt Rd KIMB S61 128 C5
Joan Croft La BTLY DN5 46 C6
Joan La EDL/UDV S33 172 A4
MALT S66 150 C3
Joan Royd La STKB/PEN S36 78 F6
Job La BWTY DN10 155 M8
Jockell Dr RAW S62 129 K2
Jockey Rd STKB/PEN S36 79 M5
John Calvert Rd
HAN/WDH S13 179 H1
John Hibbard Av
HAN/WDH S13 163 K8 1
John Hibbard Cl
HAN/WDH S13 163 J8 1
John Hibbard Crs
HAN/WDH S13 163 J8
John Hibbard Ri
HAN/WDH S13 163 J8 2
Johnny Moor Long La
GLE DN14 14 A2
THNE DN8 14 A5
Johnson Ct CONI DN12 111 G4 3
Johnson La CHPT/GREN S35 126 F6
OWL S3 9 J2 1
Johnson St DOD/DAR S75 2 C4
OWL S3 9 J1
STKB/PEN S36 101 M6 1
Johnston's Rd HTFD DN7 49 G2
John St AWLS/ASK DN6 67 G1
BSLY S70 3 G7
BSLY S70 82 E2 5
CUD/GR S72 63 J6
DEARNE S63 64 B7
ECK/KIL S21 193 H4
HEM/SK/SE WF9 42 D5
MALT S66 149 J8
MEX/SWTN S64 108 E3
RHAM S60 6 C5
SHEFP/MNR S2 9 G9
WMB/DAR S73 84 A4
WRKS S80 198 C3
John Ward St HAN/WDH S13 163 H8
John West St STKB/PEN S36 101 M7
Joiner St OWL S3 9 J2
Jones Av WMB/DAR S73 83 M4
Jons Av HEM/SK/SE WF9 41 L5
Jordan Crs KIMB S61 146 C2
Jordanthorpe Gn SHEFS S8 191 G1
Jordanthorpe Pkwy SHEFS S8 190 E2
Jordanthorpe Vw SHEFS S8 177 G8 1
Josephine Rd KIMB S61 146 E1
Joseph La STKB/PEN S36 100 A3
Joseph Rd FUL S10 160 A2 3
Joseph St BSLY S70 3 G7
CUD/GR S72 62 E1
ECK/KIL S21 193 H4
RHAM S60 6 C2
Joshua Rd ABRD S7 160 C8
Josselin Ct CHPT/GREN S35 126 D2 2
Jossey La BTLY DN5 67 H7
Jowett House La DOD/DAR S75 57 M3
Jowitt Cl MALT S66 150 F4
Jowitt Rd ECC S11 175 M1
Jubb Cl RHAM/THRY S65 148 B3
Jubilee Cl BWTY DN10 137 M4
Jubilee Crs ECK/KIL S21 180 C8
Jubilee Rd DARN/MH S9 161 M1
DON DN1 5 J1
Jubilee St HOR/CROF WF4 19 K4
RHAM S60 6 E9
Judd Field La STKB/PEN S36 100 F1
Judith Rd AU/AST/KP S26 180 B1
Judy Rw BSLYN/ROY S71 61 G3
Julian Rd DARN/MH S9 145 M4
Julian Wy DARN/MH S9 145 M4
Julie Av HOR/CROF WF4 19 J2
Jumble La KIMB S61 127 J5
Jumble Rd ECC S11 174 D5
Junction Cl WMB/DAR S73 84 D6
Junction Rd ECC S11 160 A7

HAN/WDH S13 163 H8
HTFD DN7 48 C4
NROS/TKH DN11 113 J7
Junction St BSLY S70 3 L7
WMB/DAR S73 84 D6 5
June Rd HAN/WDH S13 179 H1
Juniper Ri ECK/KIL S21 194 A2

K

Kashmir Gdns DARN/MH S9 161 M2 5
Katherine Rd MALT S66 149 J8
Katherine St MALT S66 165 J1
Kathleen Gv DEARNE S63 86 D1
Kay Crs RAW S62 107 G7
Kaye Pl ST/HB/BR S6 8 A2
Kay's Ter BSLY S70 61 J8
Kay St HOY S74 104 F2
Kea Park Cl MALT S66 149 L2
Kearsley La CONI DN12 109 M7
Kearsley Rd SHEFP/MNR S2 160 E7
Keats Crs WRKN S81 198 F3
Keats Dr DIN S25 166 F7
Keats Gv STKB/PEN S36 79 H3
Keats Rd DONS/BSCR DN4 111 M1 7
ST/HB/BR S6 144 B1
Keble Martin Wy DEARNE S63 107 H1
Kedleston Rd WRKN S81 198 D1
Keenan Av HEM/SK/SE WF9 42 C6
Keeper La HOR/CROF WF4 38 B1
Keepers Cl NROS/TKH DN11 113 M5
Keeton Hall Rd AU/AST/KP S26 181 K4
Keeton's Hl SHEFP/MNR S2 8 F9 1
Keir Pl RAW S62 129 M1
Keir St BSLY S70 2 D4
Keir Ter BSLY S70 2 D4
Kelgate MOS S20 193 H1
Kelham Island OWL S3 9 G1
Kelham St DON DN1 4 E9
Kelly St DEARNE S63 86 C2
Kelsey Gdns DONS/BSCR DN4 113 J2
Kelsey Ter BSLY S70 3 H9
Kelso Dr DONS/BSCR DN4 89 H8
Kelvin Gv WMB/DAR S73 84 C5
Kelvin St MEX/SWTN S64 108 E2
RHAM/THRY S65 130 B6
Kemp Cl ECK/KIL S21 194 A1 5
Kemps Wy HOLM/MEL HD7 54 C5
Kempton Dr HTFD DN7 70 C3
Kempton Gdns
MEX/SWTN S64 109 G1
Kempton Park Rd BTLY DN5 89 H2
Kempwell Dr RAW S62 107 K7
Kenbourne Gv ABRD S7 160 C8 1
Kenbourne Rd ABRD S7 160 C8
Kendal Av DIN S25 182 C1
Kendal Cl BTLY DN5 88 E6 2
WRKN S81 184 C7
Kendal Crs BSLY S70 82 E3 5
CONI DN12 110 B5
Kendal Dr DEARNE S63 86 A6
DRON S18 190 C6
Kendal Green Rd BSLY S70 82 C3
Kendal Gv BSLYN/ROY S71 61 L7
Kendal Ri WKFDW/WTN WF2 20 E1
Kendal Rd BTLY DN5 67 L8
ST/HB/BR S6 143 M7
Kendal V BSLY S70 82 E3
Kendon Gdns THNE DN8 32 A7
Kendray St BSLY S70 3 G5
Kenilworth Cl BTLY DN5 89 H1 2
WRKS S80 198 E6
Kenilworth Dr WRKN S81 184 D1
Kenilworth Pl ECC S11 160 A7 1
Kenilworth Rd DONS/BSCR DN4 89 J8
Kenley Cl WRKN S81 184 B7
Kenmare Crs WHHL DN2 90 E3
Kennedy Cl STKB/PEN S36 78 B4
Kennedy Dr DEARNE S63 86 B4
Kennedy Rd SHEFS S8 176 C5
Kennel Dr RTFD DN22 187 G2
Kenneth Av HTFD DN7 48 C3
HTFD DN7 70 D3
Kenneth St RHAM/THRY S65 7 G2
Kenning Hall Cl
SHEFP/MNR S2 161 H8 1
Kenninghall Dr
SHEFP/MNR S2 161 H8
Kenninghall Mt
SHEFP/MNR S2 161 H8 2
Kenninghall Pl SHEFP/MNR S2 161 H8
Kenninghall Rd
SHEFP/MNR S2 161 H8
Kennington Av AWLS/ASK DN6 66 D2
Kennington Gv CONI DN12 111 G4
Kenrock Cl BTLY DN5 68 C6
Kensington Av STKB/PEN S36 78 E3
Kensington Rd DOD/DAR S75 2 C2
Kent Av RAW S62 107 J8
Kent Cl BSLYN/ROY S71 39 G3 1
WRKN S81 198 E1
Kent House Cl HACK/IN S12 178 C7
Kentmere Cl DRON S18 190 C6 4
Kent Rd DONS/BSCR DN4 111 M1
KIMB S61 128 C6 2
SHEFS S8 176 F1
Kents Gdns THNE DN8 32 B4
Kenwell Dr TOT/DORE S17 189 M2
Kenwood Av ABRD S7 160 C8 2
Kenwood Bank ECC S11 160 B7
Kenwood Cl BSLY S70 61 H7 2
Kenwood Park Rd ABRD S7 160 C7
Kenwood Ri MALT S66 149 G1 3
Kenwood Rd ABRD S7 160 B8
ECC S11 160 C7
Kenworthy Rd BSLY S70 60 D8 10
STKB/PEN S36 101 M7
Kenyon St HEM/SK/SE WF9 42 E4
OWL S3 8 E3
Keppel Dr KIMB S61 127 M5
Keppel Pl SHEFN S5 145 J1
Keppel Rd KIMB S61 127 M5
SHEFN S5 145 K1
Keppel View Rd KIMB S61 128 B7
Kepple Cl NROS/TKH DN11 113 K8
Keresforth Cl BSLY S70 2 B8
Keresforth Hall Rd BSLY S70 60 B8
Keresforth Hill Rd BSLY S70 2 B9 1
Keresforth Rd DOD/DAR S75 81 K1
Kerwin Cl TOT/DORE S17 175 G7
Kerwin Dr TOT/DORE S17 175 G7
Kerwin Rd TOT/DORE S17 175 G7
Kestrel Av KIMB S61 127 L2
Kestrel Cl ECK/KIL S21 179 M8 5
Kestrel Dr AWLS/ASK DN6 66 F1
ECK/KIL S21 192 F4
WKFDW/WTN WF2 20 B2
Kestrel Gn SHEFP/MNR S2 161 J5 1
Kestrel Ms WRKN S81 184 B8
Kestrel Ri BSLY S70 82 D7 1
Keswick BTLY DN5 67 L7
Keswick Cl ST/HB/BR S6 143 J7
Keswick Crs RHAM S60 146 F8
Keswick Pl DRON S18 190 B6
Keswick Rd DOD/DAR S75 37 L5
WRKN S81 184 C7
Keswick Wk BSLYN/ROY S71 61 M7
Keswick Wy DIN S25 182 D1 5
Kettlebridge Rd DARN/MH S9 161 L4
Kettlethorpe Hall Dr
WKFDW/WTN WF2 20 A1
Kettlethorpe Rd
WKFDW/WTN WF2 19 M2
Ketton Av SHEFS S8 176 E4
Ketton Wk DOD/DAR S75 2 A2
Kevin Gv MALT S66 149 M3
Kew Crs HACK/IN S12 177 K5
Kexbrough Dr DOD/DAR S75 37 G7
Key Av HOY S74 105 J1
Keyes Ri BWTY DN10 155 K7
Keyworth Pl HAN/WDH S13 178 E1
Keyworth Rd ST/HB/BR S6 144 A6 2
Khartoum Rd ECC S11 160 B7
Kibroyd Dr DOD/DAR S75 37 G8
Kid La WRKN S81 167 L2
Kieran Cl DIN S25 166 A5
Kier Hardie Av
NROS/TKH DN11 113 L7 2
Kilburn Rd DRON S18 190 A6
Kildale Gdns MOS S20 179 H8 2
Kildonan Gv HACK/IN S12 178 A4
Kilham La ARMTH DN3 92 D6
Killamarsh La ECK/KIL S21 194 E1
Kiln Bent Rd HOLM/MEL HD7 74 E1
Kilner Wy SHEFN S5 144 B4
Kilnhouse Bank La
HOLM/MEL HD7 52 F6
Kilnhurst Rd CONI DN12 108 D8
RAW S62 129 L1
RHAM/THRY S65 108 E8
Kiln La KBTN HD8 35 K2
Kiln Rd KIMB S61 128 D7
Kilton Cl WRKN S81 198 E3
Kilton Crs WRKN S81 198 E3
Kilton Gld WRKN S81 198 F3
Kilton Hl OWL S3 160 F1 5
WRKN S81 198 E2
WRKS S80 198 E4
Kilton Rd WRKS S80 198 E4
Kilton Ter WRKS S80 198 E4
Kilvington Av
HAN/WDH S13 161 M8 1
Kilvington Crs HAN/WDH S13 161 M8
Kilvington Rd HAN/WDH S13 161 M8
Kimberley St DARN/MH S9 161 K1
Kimberly Cl PONT WF8 24 F2 1
Kimberworth Park Rd
KIMB S61 128 D8 2
Kimberworth Rd KIMB S61 128 D8
Kinder Gdns SHEFN S5 144 F2
Kine Moor La STKB/PEN S36 80 B1
King Av MALT S66 150 F3
NROS/TKH DN11 113 J6
King Ecgbert Rd
TOT/DORE S17 189 J2
King Edward Crs THNE DN8 32 A6 3
King Edward Rd
DONS/BSCR DN4 89 M7
THNE DN8 31 M7
King Edwards Rd
NROS/TKH DN11 134 D8
King Edward St BSLYN/ROY S71 61 H1
HEM/SK/SE WF9 41 J1 6
Kingfield Rd ECC S11 160 B8
Kingfisher Cl WHHL DN2 68 F8 1
Kingfisher Ct NROS/TKH DN11 113 L6
Kingfisher Gv
WKFDW/WTN WF2 20 B2
Kingfisher Ri KIMB S61 127 L1 1
Kingfisher Rd AWLS/ASK DN6 66 F1
Kingfisher Wk WRKN S81 184 A8
WRKN S81 198 A1
King Georges Cl
NROS/TKH DN11 113 H7 1
King Georges Ct HTFD DN7 48 C5
King George Sq ARMTH DN3 69 K3
King George's Rd
NROS/TKH DN11 113 H6
King James St ST/HB/BR S6 160 B1
King Royd La HOR/CROF WF4 23 G1
Kings Cl FEA/AMT WF7 23 H2
HTFD DN7 48 F7
Kings Coppice TOT/DORE S17 189 H1
Kings Ct BSLY S70 83 G3
HEM/SK/SE WF9 22 F6
Kings Court Rd THNE DN8 32 A6 4
King's Crs CONI DN12 110 F4
Kings Cft HEM/SK/SE WF9 41 M5
Kingscroft Cl TOT/DORE S17 175 J7
Kingsdale WRKN S81 184 F7
Kingsforth La MALT S66 149 J7
Kingsforth Rd MALT S66 149 J8
Kingsley Av BTLY DN5 89 K3
WKFDW/WTN WF2 20 A1
Kingsley Cl BSLYN/ROY S71 60 E1 1
WKFDW/WTN WF2 20 A1
Kingsley Crs ARMTH DN3 91 M1
Kingsley Park Av ABRD S7 175 M3
Kingsley Park Gv ECC S11 175 M3
Kingsley Rd AWLS/ASK DN6 66 E2
Kingsmead Dr ARMTH DN3 92 B7
Kings Ms ECK/KIL S21 193 J4
King's Rd AWLS/ASK DN6 27 M7
CUD/GR S72 40 A6
DON DN1 5 J3
MEX/SWTN S64 108 F2
WMB/DAR S73 84 B5 2
King's St CUD/GR S72 62 E1
King's Ter AWLS/ASK DN6 27 M7
Kingston Cl ARMTH DN3 92 C6 1
WRKS S80 199 G7
Kingstone Pl BSLY S70 2 C9
Kingston Rd WHHL DN2 90 F3
WRKN S81 184 C1
WRKS S80 198 F7
Kingston St ATT S4 145 G8
King St AU/AST/KP S26 164 A7
BSLY S70 3 H7
CHPT/GREN S35 126 E1
DEARNE S63 64 C8
DEARNE S63 86 C2
DON DN1 5 H4 1
HEM/SK/SE WF9 22 F6
HOY S74 105 K1
KBTN HD8 34 E5
MEX/SWTN S64 108 B4 2
SHEF S1 9 J3
THNE DN8 31 M8
WRKS S80 198 C4
Kings Wy RHAM S60 147 L5
Kingsway DEARNE S63 64 A7
DOD/DAR S75 37 K6
HTFD DN7 48 C4
WMB/DAR S73 84 B5
WRKN S81 198 E3
Kingsway Cl
NROS/TKH DN11 113 L8 1
Kingsway Gv DEARNE S63 64 A7 3
Kingswood Av DIN S25 166 C3
MOS S20 178 E5
Kingswood Cl MOS S20 178 E5 4
WRKN S81 167 L1
Kingswood Crs HOY S74 83 J8
Kingswood Cft MOS S20 178 E5 5
Kingswood Gv MOS S20 178 E5
King's Wood La DIN S25 167 G1
Kingwell Crs BSLY S70 82 D1 3
Kingwell Cft BSLY S70 82 E2 6
Kingwell Ms BSLY S70 82 E2 7
Kingwell Rd BSLY S70 82 E2
Kinharvie Rd SHEFN S5 144 D4
Kinnaird Av SHEFN S5 145 G2 1
Kinnaird Pl SHEFN S5 145 G2
Kinnaird Rd SHEFN S5 145 G2
Kinsbourne Gn HTFD DN7 48 E8
Kinsey Rd CHPT/GREN S35 104 A8
Kinsley House Crs
HEM/SK/SE WF9 22 E5
Kinsley St HEM/SK/SE WF9 22 F6
Kipling Av DONS/BSCR DN4 111 K1
Kipling Cl DRON S18 191 G8
WRKN S81 198 F2
Kipling Rd ARMTH DN3 47 K7 4
Kirby La KIMB S61 105 H8
Kirby St MEX/SWTN S64 108 E2
Kirk Balk HOY S74 105 H1
Kirkbridge Wy
HEM/SK/SE WF9 42 D4 5
Kirkby Av BSLYN/ROY S71 38 E7
BTLY DN5 89 L1
HACK/IN S12 177 L3 4
Kirkby Cl HEM/SK/SE WF9 42 A4
Kirkby Dr HACK/IN S12 177 L3
Kirkbygate HEM/SK/SE WF9 41 J2
Kirkby La HOR/CROF WF4 17 G7
Kirkby Rd HACK/IN S12 177 L3
HEM/SK/SE WF9 41 J1
Kirkby Vw HACK/IN S12 177 L4
Kirkcroft Av ECK/KIL S21 180 B8
KIMB S61 127 L2
Kirkcroft Cl KIMB S61 127 K2 5
Kirkcroft Dr ECK/KIL S21 194 B1
Kirkcroft La ECK/KIL S21 194 B1
Kirk Cross Crs BSLYN/ROY S71 39 C5
Kirkdale Crs HAN/WDH S13 162 F6
Kirkdale Dr HAN/WDH S13 162 F6
HOR/CROF WF4 19 H1
Kirk Edge Av CHPT/GREN S35 143 H3
Kirk Edge Dr CHPT/GREN S35 143 G3
Kirk Edge Rd ST/HB/BR S6 142 A1
Kirkfield Cl DOD/DAR S75 58 D3
Kirkfield Wy BSLYN/ROY S71 39 G5
Kirkgate La CUD/GR S72 40 A1
Kirkham Cl BSLYN/ROY S71 61 G4
Kirkham Pl BSLYN/ROY S71 39 H8 5
Kirkhouse Green Rd HTFD DN7 29 L7
Kirklands Dr RAW S62 129 J1
Kirk La GLE DN14 30 B1
Kirklea KBTN HD8 34 A4
Kirklees Wy HOLM/MEL HD7 54 D4
Kirkpatrick Dr WRKN S81 183 M8
Kirkstall Cl BTLY DN5 89 H2
DIN S25 182 B4
RHAM S60 146 E6
Kirkstall Rd BSLYN/ROY S71 38 C8
ECC S11 160 A7
Kirkstead Abbey Ms KIMB S61 127 L4
Kirkstead Gdns HAN/WDH S13 163 J8
Kirkstead Rd KIMB S61 127 L8
Kirkstone Cl BTLY DN5 67 L7
Kirkstone Rd ST/HB/BR S6 144 A8
Kirk St ATT S4 161 G1
DONS/BSCR DN4 4 C6
Kirk Wy BSLYN/ROY S71 61 H4
Kirton La HTFD DN7 48 F3
Kirton Rd ATT S4 145 G8
Kitchin Rd WMB/DAR S73 83 M4
Kitson Dr BSLYN/ROY S71 61 H4
Kiveton Gdns AU/AST/KP S26 181 K4
Kiveton La AU/AST/KP S26 181 K1
Knabbs La STKB/PEN S36 80 E3
Knab Cl ECC S11 176 A2 1
Knab Cft ECC S11 176 A2
Knab Ri ECC S11 176 A2
Knab Rd ECC S11 176 A2
Knapton Av RAW S62 129 J1
Knaresboro Rd ABRD S7 176 A4
Knaresborough Cl
AU/AST/KP S26 164 A8 1
Knaresborough Rd CONI DN12 109 K6
Knaton Rd WRKN S81 168 C8
Knavesmire Gdns
DONS/BSCR DN4 91 H5 2
Knightscroft Pde
HEM/SK/SE WF9 42 E5
Knightsway WKFDW/WTN WF2 20 A1
Knollbeck Av WMB/DAR S73 84 E7
Knoll Beck Cl DEARNE S63 86 A3
Knoll Beck Crs WMB/DAR S73 84 E7
Knollbeck La WMB/DAR S73 84 E7
Knoll Cl STKB/PEN S36 102 A6
The Knoll DRON S18 191 H4
Knott End WRKN S81 168 C4
Knowle Cl ST/HB/BR S6 159 G1
Knowle Cft ECC S11 175 L2
Knowle Gn TOT/DORE S17 175 G8
Knowle La ECC S11 175 K2
Knowle Rd BSLY S70 82 F1
SHEFN S5 144 F1
Knowles Av STKB/PEN S36 102 B7
Knowles St STKB/PEN S36 79 K5
Knowle Top MOS S20 179 J8 2
Knowl Rd HOLM/MEL HD7 52 B3
Knowsley St BSLY S70 2 C6
Knutton Crs SHEFN S5 144 C1
Knutton Ri SHEFN S5 126 C8
Knutton Rd SHEFN S5 144 C1
Kye La AU/AST/KP S26 195 J1
Kyle Cl SHEFN S5 144 C3
Kyle Crs SHEFN S5 144 C3
Kynance Crs RHAM S60 146 F8

L

Laburnam BSLY S70 82 F3
Laburnum Av MALT S66 148 F1
THNE DN8 32 A5
Laburnum Cl
CHPT/GREN S35 126 E3 5
DIN S25 182 B3 1
WRKS S80 198 B6
Laburnum Dr ARMTH DN3 70 A8
Laburnum Gv CONI DN12 109 L6
ECK/KIL S21 194 A2
EPW DN9 114 F3
KBTN HD8 34 E6 1
STKB/PEN S36 101 M7
Laburnum Pde MALT S66 150 B2 1
Laburnum Pl BTLY DN5 67 M5 3
Laburnum Rd
DONS/BSCR DN4 111 K1
MALT S66 150 B2
MEX/SWTN S64 108 D1
WRKN S81 168 D3
Laceby Cl RHAM/THRY S65 131 H8
Laceby Ct BSLY S70 2 B9
Lacy St HEM/SK/SE WF9 23 G8 2
Ladies Spring Gv
TOT/DORE S17 175 L8 1
Ladock Cl BSLYN/ROY S71 3 L2
Ladybank Rd MOS S20 193 H1 1
Ladybank Vw ECK/KIL S21 193 H3
Ladybower Dr HATH/EY S32 172 E8
Ladycroft DEARNE S63 86 A5
Lady Cft DEARNE S63 107 J1
Lady Croft La WMB/DAR S73 84 A8
Ladycroft Rd ARMTH DN3 91 M3
Lady Field Rd AU/AST/KP S26 182 A6
Lady Gap La AWLS/ASK DN6 45 G2
Lady Ida's Dr ECK/KIL S21 192 E3
MOS S20 193 G2
Ladylea Cl WRKS S80 197 M5
Lady Mary Vw BTLY DN5 64 F8
Lady Oak Rd RHAM/THRY S65 130 A6
Ladyroyd Cft CUD/GR S72 61 M1
Lady's Br OWL S3 9 J2
Ladysmith Av ABRD S7 176 B1
Lady Wk WRKN S81 184 A8
Lady Wharncliffe's Rd
CHPT/GREN S35 125 H2
Ladywood Rd CUD/GR S72 62 F1
Lafflands La HOR/CROF WF4 21 L6
Laird Av ST/HB/BR S6 143 L6
Laird Dr ST/HB/BR S6 143 L6
Laird Rd ST/HB/BR S6 143 L6
Laithe Av HOLM/MEL HD7 53 G5
Laithe Bank Dr HOLM/MEL HD7 53 G5
Laithe Cft DOD/DAR S75 59 K8 1
Laithes Cl BSLYN/ROY S71 38 F8
Laithes Crs BSLYN/ROY S71 38 D8
Laithes La BSLYN/ROY S71 38 E8
Lake Cl CONI DN12 110 E6
Lakeen Rd WHHL DN2 90 E3
Lakeland Cl CUD/GR S72 62 A2 1
Lakeland Dr DIN S25 182 C1
Lakeland Wy WKFDW/WTN WF2 20 E1
Lake Rd AWLS/ASK DN6 67 G4
Lakeside Bvd DONS/BSCR DN4 90 E8
Lakeside Est HOR/CROF WF4 21 M5
Lake Vw WKFDW/WTN WF2 20 A3
Lambcote Wy MALT S66 150 F1 2
Lambcroft Vw HAN/WDH S13 179 G1
Lamb Dr SHEFN S5 144 B4
Lambecroft BSLYN/ROY S71 39 G6 1
Lambe Flatt DOD/DAR S75 37 G7 4
Lambert Fold DOD/DAR S75 59 L8 5
Lambert Rd BSLY S70 61 G8
Lamberts La RHAM/THRY S65 130 C4
Lambert St OWL S3 9 G3
Lambert Wk BSLY S70 61 G7 1
Lambeth Rd DONS/BSCR DN4 89 M8
Lamb Hl ST/HB/BR S6 141 M3
Lamb Hill Cl HAN/WDH S13 162 B8
Lamb La BSLYN/ROY S71 61 G2
DIN S25 167 G4
Lambra Rd BSLY S70 3 H6
Lambrell Av AU/AST/KP S26 181 G5
Lambrell Gn AU/AST/KP S26 181 G5 1
Lamb Rd SHEFN S5 144 B4
Lamma Well Rd
HOLM/MEL HD7 53 L5
Lanark Dr MEX/SWTN S64 87 G8
Lanark Gdns WHHL DN2 91 G2
Lancaster Av ARMTH DN3 69 K3
WHHL DN2 91 G3
Lancaster Cl NROS/TKH DN11 134 F8
Lancaster Crs NROS/TKH DN11 134 F8
Lancaster Dr BWTY DN10 136 D7
HTFD DN7 71 L7
Lancaster Ga BSLY S70 2 F4
Lancaster Rd STKB/PEN S36 101 M6
Lancaster St BSLY S70 2 C6
DEARNE S63 64 C6
OWL S3 160 D2 8
Lancaster Wk WRKN S81 184 C7
Lancastrian Wy WRKN S81 198 E1
Lancing Rd SHEFP/MNR S2 9 J9
SHEFP/MNR S2 160 F7 1
Land Ends Rd THNE DN8 31 K5
Landsdown Av
HEM/SK/SE WF9 41 L6
Landseer Cl DRON S18 190 C7
SHEFS S8 177 H5 2
Landseer Ct MALT S66 148 F1
Landseer Dr SHEFS S8 177 H5
Landseer Pl GLV S14 177 J5 3
Lane End CHPT/GREN S35 104 D8
Lane End Rd RHAM S60 147 L4
Lane Ends Cl HEM/SK/SE WF9 22 D3
Lane Hackings Gn KBTN HD8 34 C8
Laneham Cl DONS/BSCR DN4 113 H1
Lane Head Cl RAW S62 129 L1 2
Lane Head Ri DOD/DAR S75 37 L5
Lane Head Rd DOD/DAR S75 58 B4
ST/HB/BR S6 140 E3
TOT/DORE S17 189 G3
Laneside Cl DONS/BSCR DN4 4 A9 1
The Lanes RHAM/THRY S65 129 M8
The Lane ECK/KIL S21 194 B6
Lang Av BSLYN/ROY S71 61 J5
Langcliffe Cl DOD/DAR S75 37 L5 1
Lang Crs BSLYN/ROY S71 61 J5
Langdale Cl NROS/TKH DN11 134 F7
Langdale Dr BTLY DN5 67 K7
DRON S18 191 G4
NROS/TKH DN11 134 F7
Langdale Mt WKFDW/WTN WF2 20 E1
Langdale Rd AWLS/ASK DN6 44 F6
BSLYN/ROY S71 3 H6
DOD/DAR S75 59 J2 2
SHEFS S8 176 C2
WRKN S81 184 D8
Langdale Wy DIN S25 166 D8 2
Langdon Rd KIMB S61 128 C7
Langdon St ECC S11 160 D7
Langer St DONS/BSCR DN4 4 B8
Langford Cl DOD/DAR S75 59 L8
Langley Cl RHAM/THRY S65 130 B8
Langley La KBTN HD8 35 J5
Langleys Rd AWLS/ASK DN6 27 H6 1
Langley St WRKS S80 198 D5
Langsett Av ST/HB/BR S6 143 L5
Langsett Cl ST/HB/BR S6 144 B8
Langsett Crs ST/HB/BR S6 144 B8 5
Langsett Gv ST/HB/BR S6 160 B1 1
Langsett Ri ST/HB/BR S6 160 B1
Langsett Rd BSLYN/ROY S71 38 C8
ST/HB/BR S6 144 A7
WKFDW/WTN WF2 19 M2
Langsett Rd North
CHPT/GREN S35 125 G7
Langsett Rd South
CHPT/GREN S35 143 J1
Langthwaite La BTLY DN5 67 H5
HEM/SK/SE WF9 42 C5
Langthwaite Rd BTLY DN5 67 J6
HEM/SK/SE WF9 42 B5
Langton Gdns ARMTH DN3 92 C7 1
Lansbury Av
CHPT/GREN S35 126 D2 5
MALT S66 150 F4
NROS/TKH DN11 113 L6
Lansbury Pl RAW S62 130 A1 1
Lansbury Rd ECK/KIL S21 193 H4
Lansdowne Cl DEARNE S63 64 A8
Lansdowne Crs DOD/DAR S75 37 H8
MEX/SWTN S64 108 B5
Lansdowne Rd WHHL DN2 91 G2
Lanyon Wy BSLYN/ROY S71 3 M1
Lapwater Rd KIMB S61 128 D4
Lapwing V KIMB S61 127 L1 2
Larch Av ECK/KIL S21 194 A2
EPW DN9 114 D4
MALT S66 149 G2
Larch Cl WMB/DAR S73 84 E2
The Larches MEX/SWTN S64 108 A5
Larchfield Pl BSLYN/ROY S71 61 H2 2
Larchfield Rd
DONS/BSCR DN4 89 K8 5
Larch Gv CHPT/GREN S35 126 E3
CONI DN12 109 L7
Larch Hl DARN/MH S9 162 C4
Larch Pl BSLY S70 83 G1
Larch Rd ECK/KIL S21 192 F5
MALT S66 150 B1
Larkhill Cl RAW S62 129 L4
Lark Spinney WRKN S81 198 A1 1
Larkspur Cl ARMTH DN3 69 K6
MEX/SWTN S64 108 A7
Lark St ST/HB/BR S6 159 M1
Larwood WRKN S81 198 F1 2
Larwood Gv CONI DN12 111 G4 5
Latham Sq ECC S11 175 J2
Lathe Rd RHAM S60 148 A5
Lathkill Cl HAN/WDH S13 162 A8
Lathkill Rd HAN/WDH S13 162 A8
Latimer Cl AU/AST/KP S26 181 K5
Latin Gdns BTLY DN5 67 G8
Lauder Rd BTLY DN5 89 L1
Lauder St ATT S4 145 H6
Laudsdale Cl
RHAM/THRY S65 130 B8 2
Laudsdale Rd RHAM/THRY S65 130 A7
Laughton Common Rd
MALT S66 165 L3
Laughton Rd DARN/MH S9 145 M5 2
DIN S25 166 D7 1
DONS/BSCR DN4 4 C6
MALT S66 165 K1
Launce Rd SHEFN S5 144 D3
Laurel Av BSLY S70 61 H8
BTLY DN5 89 J2
MALT S66 149 G2
THNE DN8 32 A4
Laurel Cl DIN S25 182 B4

ECK/KIL S21 .... 193 G5
Laurel Dr ECK/KIL S21 .... 194 A3
Laurel Dr ARMTH DN3 .... 69 M8
Laurel Sq EPW DN9 .... 114 C3
Laurel Ter AWLS/ASK DN6 ...... 44 E5
DONS/BSCR DN4 .... 89 L8 🔲
Laurold Av HTFD DN7 .... 71 L1
Lavenham Pl AWLS/ASK DN6..... 44 C4
Laverack St HAN/WDH S13 ..... 162 D6
Laverdene Av TOT/DORE S17 .. 189 K2
Laverdene Cl TOT/DORE S17 .. 189 J3 🔲
Laverdene Dr TOT/DORE S17 .. 189 J3
Laverdene Rd TOT/DORE S17 .. 189 J3
Laverdene Wy TOT/DORE S17 . 189 K3 🔲
Laverock Wy SHEFN S5 .... 145 H2
Lavinia La CHPT/GREN S35 .... 126 B8
Law Common Rd
HOLM/MEL HD7 .... 76 C2
Lawn Av AWLS/ASK DN6 .... 66 D1
DON DN1 .... 5 J4
Lawndale AWLS/ASK DN6 .... 44 D5
Lawndale Fold DOD/DAR S75 ... 37 K7 🔲
Lawn Garth BTLY DN5 .... 67 K8
Lawn La AWLS/ASK DN6 .... 29 C2
Lawn Rd DON DN1 .... 5 J4
WRKN S81 .... 168 C7
The Lawns ECC S11 .... 175 M1
HOR/CROF WF4 .... 17 L1 🔲
The Lawn DRON S18 .... 190 F5
Lawrence Cl DOD/DAR S75 ..... 59 J4
MALT S66 .... 148 F2
Lawrence Dr MEX/SWTN S64 ... 108 A5
Law Slack Rd HOLM/MEL HD7 ... 76 B2
Lawson Rd FUL S10 .... 159 M5
Lawton La RHAM S60 .... 147 J4
Laxey Rd ST/HB/BR S6 .... 159 J2 🔲
Laxton Cl MALT S66 .... 150 B1
Laxton Rd BSLYN/ROY S71 ..... 38 D7
Laycock Av AU/AST/KP S26 .... 164 C8
Layden Dr BTLY DN5 .... 67 L6
Leabrook Rd DRON S18 .... 190 A6
Leach La MEX/SWTN S64 .... 108 E3
Lea Ct WRKS S80 .... 198 A5
Leadbeater Dr HACK/IN S12 ... 177 L2 🔲
Leadbeater Rd HACK/IN S12 ... 177 L2
Leader Rd ST/HB/BR S6 .... 143 M6
Lead HI WRKS S80 .... 198 C5
Leadley St DEARNE S63 .... 86 C2 🔲
Leadmill Rd SHEF S1 .... 9 J7
SHEFP/MNR S2 .... 9 J8
Leadmill St SHEF S1 .... 9 J7
Leaf Cl MALT S66 .... 150 F1
Leake Rd ST/HB/BR S6 .... 144 A5 🔲
Leak Hall Crs KBTN HD8 .... 56 D1
Leak Hall La KBTN HD8 .... 56 C1
Leamington Gdns WHHL DN2 . 91 G2 🔲
WHHL DN2 .... 91 G2 🔲
Leamington St FUL S10 .... 160 A3 🔲
Leapings La STKB/PEN S36 .... 78 D4
Lea Rd BSLYN/ROY S71 .... 38 F8
DRON S18 .... 190 E6
Lease Gate Rd RHAM S60 ..... 147 M5
Leas Gdns HOLM/MEL HD7 ..... 54 E6
The Leas BTLY DN5 .... 89 K2
The Lea MEX/SWTN S64 .... 107 M6
MOS S20 .... 179 H5
Leaton Cl ST/HB/BR S6 .... 143 H6
Leavy Greave FUL S10 .... 8 D5
Leavygreave Rd OWL S3 .... 8 A4
Leawood Pl ST/HB/BR S6 ..... 159 H1 🔲
Le Brun Sq WRKN S81 .... 184 C1
Ledbury Gdns BTLY DN5 .... 89 H2
Ledbury Rd BSLYN/ROY S71 .. 60 D1 🔲
Ledger Cl AU/AST/KP S26 ..... 181 C5
Ledsham Ct HOY S74 .... 105 M1 🔲
Ledsham Rd RHAM/THRY S65.... 7 M9
Ledstone Rd SHEFS S8 .... 176 C3
Lee Av STKB/PEN S36 .... 102 B6
Lee Brook La RAW S62 .... 106 C3
Lee Cft MALT S66 .... 151 G3
SHEF S1 .... 9 G3
Leedham Ct SHEFS S5 .... 145 K3
Leedham Rd RHAM/THRY S65.. 148 A3
SHEFN S5 .... 145 K3
Leeds Av DIN S25 .... 166 C8
Leeds Rd DARN/MH S9 .... 161 L1
WRKN S81 .... 183 K8
Lee House La STKB/PEN S36 .. 101 K7
Lee La DOD/DAR S75 .... 38 C5
STKB/PEN S36 .... 77 K3
STKB/PEN S36 .... 123 H4
Leeming Dr BWTY DN10 .... 154 D1
Lee Moor La ST/HB/BR S6 .... 142 D7
Lee Rd ST/HB/BR S6 .... 143 H6
Lees Av STKB/PEN S36 .... 79 H4
Lees Hall Av SHEFS S8 .... 176 E3
Lees Hall Pl SHEFS S8 .... 176 F2
Lees Hall Rd SHEFS S8 .... 176 F2
Lees House Ct SHEFS S8 .... 176 E3 🔲
Leger Wy DONS/BSCR DN4 ..... 90 E4
WHHL DN2 .... 69 G8
Legion Dr AU/AST/KP S26 .... 164 C8 🔲
Leicester Av WHHL DN2 .... 90 E4
Leicester Rd DIN S25 .... 166 E6
Leigh St DARN/MH S9 .... 145 L8
FEA/AMT WF7 .... 23 H2
Leighton Cl BSLYN/ROY S71 ... 3 C2
Leighton Dr GLV S14 .... 177 K4
Leighton Pl GLV S14 .... 177 K4
Leighton Rd GLV S14 .... 177 J2
Leighton Vw SHEFP/MNR S2 .. 177 J2
Leinster Av WHHL DN2 .... 90 E2
Leisure La KBTN HD8 .... 17 J7
Lemont Rd TOT/DORE S17 .... 189 J3
Lenacre La KBTN HD8 .... 16 B6
Lennox Rd ST/HB/BR S6 ...... 143 M6
WHHL DN2 .... 90 F2
Lenny Balk AWLS/ASK DN6 .... 43 J8
Lenton St SHEFP/MNR S2 .... 9 J8
Leonard Cl SHEFP/MNR S2 ... 161 L8
Leopold Av DIN S25 .... 166 D7 🔲
Leopold St BSLY S70 .... 2 D7
DIN S25 .... 166 D6
SHEF S1 .... 9 G4
Leppings La ST/HB/BR S6 ..... 144 A5
Lepton Gdns BSLY S70 .... 83 H1 🔲
Lescar La ECC S11 .... 160 A7

Lesley Rd DEARNE S63 .... 86 C2
Leslie Av CONI DN12 .... 109 L5
MALT S66 .... 150 B3
Leslie Rd BSLY S70 .... 61 H8
ST/HB/BR S6 .... 143 L6
Lesmond Crs CUD/GR S72 ...... 85 J1
Lestermoor Av
AU/AST/KP S26 .... 181 G5 🔲
Letard Dr RHAM S60 .... 147 G6
Levels La BWTY DN10 .... 116 B8
EPW DN9 .... 93 K7
Leverick Dr RAW S62 .... 108 A8
Leverstock Gn DONS/BSCR DN4 91 K8
Leverton Dr SHEFP/MNR S2 ..... 8 F9
Leverton Gdns SHEFP/MNR S2 .. 8 F9
Leverton Wy
RHAM/THRY S65 .... 130 C6 🔲
Leveson St ATT S4 .... 161 H2
Levet Rd DONS/BSCR DN4 ..... 91 K6
Lewdendale BSLY S70 .... 82 E3
Lewes Rd CONI DN12 .... 109 M6
Lewis Rd BSLYN/ROY S71 ..... 61 J6
HAN/WDH S13 .... 162 A8
Leybourne Rd KIMB S61 ...... 128 C6
Leyburn Cl DONS/BSCR DN4 .. 91 K8
Leyburn Dr AU/AST/KP S26 ... 164 A7
Leyburn Gv CHPT/GREN S35 . 126 E1 🔲
Leyburn Rd AWLS/ASK DN6 .... 44 D5
SHEFS S8 .... 176 D1
Ley End BSLY S70 .... 82 D3
Leyfield Ct ARMTH DN3 .... 92 A2
Leyfield Rd TOT/DORE S17 ... 175 H6
Leyland Av HTFD DN7 .... 49 C8
The Leylands DONS/BSCR DN4 111 K3
Leys Cl DONS/BSCR DN4 ...... 111 K3
Leys La AWLS/ASK DN6 .... 44 B6
DIN S25 .... 166 F6
KBTN HD8 .... 34 F1
The Leys HEM/SK/SE WF9 ...... 41 L6
Liberty Cl ST/HB/BR S6 ...... 159 J2 🔲
Liberty Dr ST/HB/BR S6 ...... 159 J2
Liberty HI ST/HB/BR S6 ...... 159 J2
Liberty La CHPT/GREN S35 ... 103 H4
Liberty Pl ST/HB/BR S6 ...... 159 J2
Liberty Rd ST/HB/BR S6 ...... 159 J2
Library Cl KIMB S61 .... 128 E4
Lichen Cl ARMTH DN3 .... 69 K6
Lichfield Cl WRKN S81 .... 184 E8
Lichfield Gdns CONI DN12 ... 110 E6
Lichfield Rd HTFD DN7 .... 48 E7
WHHL DN2 .... 90 D1
Lichfield Wy RHAM S60 ...... 147 H6
Lichford Rd SHEFP/MNR S2 .. 177 C1
Lidgate Crs ARMTH DN3 .... 92 A2
Lidgate La CUD/GR S72 .... 39 M4
Lidget Cl DONS/BSCR DN4 ..... 91 J8
Lidget La DEARNE S63 .... 64 D8
MALT S66 .... 131 C7
MALT S66 .... 149 J1
Lidgett La DIN S25 .... 166 D7
DOD/DAR S75 .... 104 B2
KBTN HD8 .... 34 D6
Lidgett Ri KBTN HD8 .... 34 D6
Lidgett Wy BSLYN/ROY S71 ... 39 G3
Liffey Av WHHL DN2 .... 90 E3
Lifford Pl HOY S74 .... 105 M2
WHHL DN2 .... 90 D2
Lifford St DARN/MH S9 ...... 146 C4
Lightwood Rd ECK/KIL S21 ... 192 C5
Lilac Av STKB/PEN S36 .... 101 M7
Lilac Cl DIN S25 .... 182 B3 🔲
Lilac Crs CONI DN12 .... 110 F6
HOY S74 .... 83 J8
Lilac Gv BWTY DN10 .... 136 D8
CONI DN12 .... 109 L6
DONS/BSCR DN4 .... 91 K7
EPW DN9 .... 114 E3
MALT S66 .... 149 G2
MALT S66 .... 150 B2
WRKN S81 .... 168 C8
Lilac Rd ARMTH DN3 .... 70 A8
MOS S20 .... 179 K4
SHEFN S5 .... 145 J4
Liley Av MIRF WF14 .... 16 A1
STKB/PEN S36 .... 78 A6
Lilian St South WRKN S81 .... 7 H4
Lillee Ct WRKN S81 .... 198 F2
Lilley St HEM/SK/SE WF9 ..... 41 H1
Lilley Ter HEM/SK/SE WF9 .... 41 M5
Lilford Rd ARMTH DN3 .... 92 C7
Lilly Hall Cl MALT S66 ...... 150 B1
Lilly Hall Rd MALT S66 ...... 150 C2
Lilydene Av CUD/GR S72 ...... 40 D8
Limb La TOT/DORE S17 .... 175 H7
Limbreck Ct BTLY DN5 .... 67 L6
Limbrick Cl ST/HB/BR S6 .... 143 M8
Limbrick Rd ST/HB/BR S6 ... 144 A8
Lime Av EPW DN9 .... 114 E3
WRKN S81 .... 167 L1
Lime Cl RHAM/THRY S65 ..... 130 D5
Lime Ct BTLY DN5 .... 89 H6 🔲
Lime Crs HEM/SK/SE WF9 ..... 42 C5
Limedale Vw ARMTH DN3 ..... 69 L1 🔲
Lime Gv BSLYN/ROY S71 ...... 59 G6
CHPT/GREN S35 .... 126 E3
HEM/SK/SE WF9 .... 42 C5
MALT S66 .... 150 F2
MEX/SWTN S64 .... 108 B6
Limegrove Rd MOS S20 .... 7 L9
Lime Gv STKB/PEN S36 .... 101 L7
Limekiln La MALT S66 .... 133 L8
NROS/TKH DN11 .... 133 J5
Limekilns DIN S25 .... 182 B1
Limelands DIN S25 .... 166 C7
Lime Rd ECK/KIL S21 .... 192 F6
Limes Av DOD/DAR S75 .... 38 A5
DOD/DAR S75 .... 59 M4
Limes Cl DOD/DAR S75 .... 38 A5
Limestone Ct WRKN S81 ...... 183 J4
Limestone Cottage La
ST/HB/BR S6 .... 143 M3
Lime St MOS S20 .... 179 K3
ST/HB/BR S6 .... 160 C1
Limesway DOD/DAR S75 .... 59 M4
MALT S66 .... 150 D2
Lime Tree Av ARMTH DN3 ...... 69 M8
DONS/BSCR DN4 .... 5 K7

ECK/KIL S21 .... 194 D1
WRKN S81 .... 168 C8
Limetree AU/AST/KP S26 ..... 181 G4
MALT S66 .... 165 K1
Lime Tree Ct DONS/BSCR DN4 .. 5 K7 🔲
Lime Tree Crs BWTY DN10 .... 136 D3
NROS/TKH DN11 .... 113 L7
RAW S62 .... 129 M1
Lime Tree Gv THNE DN8 .... 31 M7
Limpool Ct DONS/BSCR DN4 ... 91 K8
Limpsfield Rd DARN/MH S9 ... 145 L5
Linaker Rd ST/HB/BR S6 ..... 159 M2
Linburn Cl BSLYN/ROY S71 .... 38 E3
Linburn Rd SHEFS S8 .... 176 D5
Linby Rd BSLYN/ROY S71 ...... 38 D7
Lincoln Crs HEM/SK/SE WF9 .. 42 E3
Lincoln Gdns DEARNE S63 .... 86 B2 🔲
Lincoln Rd HTFD DN7 .... 71 L8
WHHL DN2 .... 90 D1
Lincoln St DARN/MH S9 ..... 145 M5 🔲
MALT S66 .... 150 E3
NROS/TKH DN11 .... 113 J6
RHAM S60 .... 6 E1
WRKS S80 .... 198 E5
Lincroft Dr RAW S62 .... 129 M4
Lindale Cl DIN S25 .... 182 D2
Lindale Gdns DEARNE S63 .... 86 D5
The Lindales DOD/DAR S75 ..... 2 A4
Linden Av DRON S18 .... 190 F4
MALT S66 .... 149 G2
SHEFS S8 .... 176 C5
Linden Cl HTFD DN7 .... 48 F7 🔲
Linden Ct CHPT/GREN S35 ... 126 F6
Linden Crs STKB/PEN S36 ... 101 M6
Linden Gv CONI DN12 .... 110 F6
MALT S66 .... 150 B2
Linden Rd CHPT/GREN S35 ... 126 F6
DEARNE S63 .... 106 F1
Linden Wk BTLY DN5 .... 67 L3
Lindholme Bank Rd HTFD DN7 .. 72 A5
Lindholme Dr NROS/TKH DN11 113 M6
Lindholme Gdns MOS S20 .... 179 G5 🔲
Lindhurst Rd BSLYN/ROY S71 . 38 C7
Lindisfarne Rd DRON S18 .... 190 F7 🔲
Lindley Ct EPW DN9 .... 115 J4
Lindley Crs DEARNE S63 ...... 64 B3
Lindley Rd EPW DN9 .... 115 J4
SHEFN S5 .... 145 H5 🔲
Lindley's Cft AU/AST/KP S26 181 K2
Lindley St RHAM/THRY S65 ..... 7 J5
Lindrick NROS/TKH DN11 ..... 152 E1
Lindrick Av MEX/SWTN S64 .. 108 C5
Lindrick Cl CUD/GR S72 ...... 40 A6
DONS/BSCR DN4 .... 113 C2
NROS/TKH DN11 .... 152 D1
WRKN S81 .... 168 D8
WRKN S81 .... 198 D2
Lindrick Dl WRKN S81 .... 183 C5
Lindrick Dr ARMTH DN3 .... 69 K8
Lindrick La NROS/TKH DN11 . 152 D2
Lindrick Rd HTFD DN7 .... 71 K1
WRKN S81 .... 183 J4
Lindsay Av SHEFS S5 .... 144 F3
Lindsay Cl SHEFN S5 .... 144 F2
Lindsay Crs SHEFN S5 .... 144 F2
Lindsay Dr SHEFN S5 .... 144 F2
Lindsay Pl AU/AST/KP S26 ... 164 B8
Lindsay Rd SHEFN S5 .... 144 F2
Lindsey Cl DONS/BSCR DN4 .. 113 H2
Lindsey Rd NROS/TKH DN11 .. 153 C2
Lindum Dr MALT S66 .... 149 G3
Lindum St DONS/BSCR DN4 ..... 4 C7
Lindwall Ct WRKN S81 .... 198 F2 🔲
Lingamore Leys DEARNE S63 .. 64 B6
Lingard Cl DOD/DAR S75 .... 2 D1 🔲
Lingard St DOD/DAR S75 .... 2 D2
Lingfield Cl MALT S66 ...... 149 J3
Lingfield Dr BTLY DN5 .... 89 H2
Ling Field Rd AWLS/ASK DN6 .. 66 A2
BTLY DN5 .... 65 M4
Lingfoot Av SHEFS S8 .... 190 F1
Lingfoot Cl SHEFS S8 ...... 190 F1 🔲
Lingfoot Crs SHEFS S8 ...... 190 F1
Lingfoot Dr SHEFS S8 .... 191 C1 🔲
Lingfoot Pl SHEFS S8 .... 190 F1
Ling House La HTFD DN7 ...... 47 M5
Lingmoor Cl DONS/BSCR DN4 . 111 J1
Lingodell Cl DIN S25 .... 166 C3
Lings La HTFD DN7 .... 70 F2
MALT S66 .... 149 H3
PONT WF8 .... 25 L7
The Lings ARMTH DN3 .... 92 B2
MALT S66 .... 149 H3
Lingthwaite DOD/DAR S75 ..... 59 L8 🔲
Link Rd RHAM/THRY S65 ..... 130 C5
Links Rd DRON S18 .... 190 F7
Links Vw DOD/DAR S75 .... 37 M5
Linkswood Av WHHL DN2 ...... 69 G8
The Link DOD/DAR S75 .... 81 L7
Linkway AWLS/ASK DN6 .... 27 H4 🔲
WHHL DN2 .... 90 F1
Linley La HACK/IN S12 ...... 178 C2 🔲
Linnet Gv WKFDW/WTN WF2 .. 20 B2
Linnet Mt KIMB S61 .... 127 K2
The Linnets WRKN S81 .... 184 B8
Linscott Rd SHEFS S8 .... 176 C5
Linshaws Rd HOLM/MEL HD7 ... 75 K2
Linthwaite La HOY S74 ...... 106 A2
RAW S62 .... 106 A4
Linton Cl BSLY S70 .... 59 M7
Liphill Bank Rd HOLM/MEL HD7 . 53 C2
Lipp Av ECK/KIL S21 .... 180 A8
Liquorice La WRKN S81 ...... 184 E3
Lisle Rd RHAM/THRY S65 .... 7 L8
Lismore Rd SHEFS S8 .... 176 F2
Lister Av DONS/BSCR DN4 ..... 89 M7
HACK/IN S12 .... 177 M3
RAW S62 .... 107 J8
Lister Cl HACK/IN S12 ..... 177 M4 🔲
Lister Ct WHHL DN2 .... 90 E2
Lister Crs HACK/IN S12 ..... 177 M4
Lister Dr HACK/IN S12 ...... 177 M4
Lister La OWL S3 .... 8 E1
Lister Pl HACK/IN S12 ..... 177 M4 🔲

Lister Rd ST/HB/BR S6 ...... 160 A1
Lister St RHAM/THRY S65 ...... 7 K5
Lister Wy HACK/IN S12 ...... 177 M3
Little Cake HOLM/MEL HD7 .... 54 D5
Little Common La ECC S11 ... 175 K4
GLE DN14 .... 10 D5
KIMB S61 .... 128 B8
RHAM S60 .... 148 C6
Littledale Rd DARN/MH S9 ... 161 M5
Littlefield La WMB/DAR S73 .. 84 D3
Littlefield Rd DIN S25 ..... 166 C1
Little Haynooking La
MALT S66 .... 150 D2
Little Hemsworth
HEM/SK/SE WF9 .... 41 J1
Littlehey Cl MALT S66 ...... 150 B1
Little La ATT S4 .... 145 K6 🔲
BTLY DN5 .... 88 E3
HACK/IN S12 .... 177 M1
HEM/SK/SE WF9 .... 24 F8
HEM/SK/SE WF9 .... 42 D4
HOLM/MEL HD7 .... 53 K2 🔲
HOLM/MEL HD7 .... 54 A1
KIMB S61 .... 127 L5
WHHL DN2 .... 69 G6
WRKN S81 .... 169 M5
WRKS S80 .... 196 F1
Little Leeds HOY S74 .... 105 J1 🔲
Little London Pl SHEFS S8 .. 176 C1 🔲
Little London Rd SHEFS S8 .. 176 C2
Little Matlock Gdns
ST/HB/BR S6 .... 159 H1
Little Matlock Wy
ST/HB/BR S6 .... 159 H1 🔲
Littlemoor ECK/KIL S21 ..... 193 J3
Littlemoor Av AU/AST/KP S26 181 C5
Littlemoor La DONS/BSCR DN4 .. 4 C9
Littlemoor St DONS/BSCR DN4 . 4 D8 🔲
Little New Cl DOD/DAR S75 .. 59 M4 🔲
Little Norton Av SHEFS S8 .. 176 E8
Little Norton Dr SHEFS S8 .. 176 E7
Little Norton La SHEFS S8 .. 176 E7
Little Norton Wy SHEFS S8 .. 176 E8
Little Wood Dr GLV S14 ..... 177 K4
Little Wood La AU/AST/KP S26 196 C7
Littlewood Rd THNE DN8 ...... 32 M8
Littlewood St DONS/BSCR DN4 .. 4 A7
Littlewood Wy MALT S66 ..... 150 F1
Littleworth Cl
NROS/TKH DN11 .... 113 M6 🔲
Littleworth La BSLYN/ROY S71 . 61 H4
NROS/TKH DN11 .... 113 M6
Littondale WRKN S81 .... 184 E8 🔲
Liverpool Av WHHL DN2 .... 90 D1
Liverpool St DARN/MH S9 ... 145 K8
Livesey St ST/HB/BR S6 ..... 144 B7
Livingstone Av WHHL DN2 .... 90 E2
Livingstone Crs BSLYN/ROY S71 60 F2
Livingstone Rd
CHPT/GREN S35 .... 126 C1
Livingston Rd DARN/MH S9 .. 161 J1 🔲
Llewelyn Crs AWLS/ASK DN6 .. 27 J8
Lloyd St ATT S4 .... 145 H6
RAW S62 .... 129 K4
Load Field Rd ST/HB/BR S6 .. 123 K6
Loakfield Dr SHEFN S5 ...... 126 D8
Lobelia Cl DIN S25 .... 182 B2
Lobelia Crs ARMTH DN3 .... 69 K4
Lobwood BSLY S70 .... 82 E2
Lobwood La BSLY S70 .... 82 F2 🔲
Locarno Rd THNE DN8 .... 32 B4
Lock Cl GLE DN14 .... 11 J3
Lockeaflash Crs BSLY S70 ... 83 H1
Locke Av BSLY S70 .... 2 E9
BSLY S70 .... 82 D1 🔲
Locke Rd DOD/DAR S75 .... 81 L1
Lockesley Av CONI DN12 ..... 109 L5
Locksley Dr MALT S66 ...... 165 H1
Lock St ST/HB/BR S6 .... 160 C1
Lockton Cl CHPT/GREN S35 .. 104 A7
Lockwood Av DIN S25 .... 182 B4
Lockwood Cl RHAM/THRY S65 . 148 A1
THNE DN8 .... 32 B8
Lockwood La BSLY S70 .... 60 D8
Lockwood Rd DEARNE S63 ..... 86 C1
DON DN1 .... 5 J1
RHAM/THRY S65 .... 130 A8
Lodge Dr RAW S62 .... 105 H6
Lodge Farm Cl DIN S25 ..... 182 B1
Lodge Hill Dr AU/AST/KP S26 180 F5
Lodge La AU/AST/KP S26 .... 180 B1
CHPT/GREN S35 .... 125 H2
DIN S25 .... 166 F2
FUL S10 .... 158 E5
HTFD DN7 .... 29 M8
KIMB S61 .... 127 K4
WKFDW/WTN WF2 .... 20 B3
Lodge Moor Rd FUL S10 ..... 158 C4
Lodge Rd DARN/MH S9 .... 146 F5
Lodges Cl HOR/CROF WF4 ..... 22 D7
Lodge St HEM/SK/SE WF9 ..... 23 H7
KBTN HD8 .... 34 A6
Lodge Wy RHAM S60 .... 147 G6
Lodore Rd DARN/MH S9 ...... 162 B3
Logan Rd DARN/MH S9 .... 162 D3
Loicher La CHPT/GREN S35 .. 127 H6
Lomas Cl ST/HB/BR S6 .... 143 C4
Lombard Cl DOD/DAR S75 ...... 2 E1
Lombard Crs WMB/DAR S73 .... 84 C2
London La AWLS/ASK DN6 ..... 28 F5
London Rd South SHEFS S8 .. 160 E8
London Wy KIMB S61 .... 127 J3
Longacre Cl MOS S20 .... 179 L6
Long Acre Vw MOS S20 ...... 179 L7
Longacre Wy MOS S20 .... 179 L7
Longcar La BSLY S70 .... 2 C9
Long Cswy BSLYN/ROY S71 .... 61 G4
HATH/EY S32 .... 173 G2

Long Cl DONS/BSCR DN4 ...... 113 H2
Long Close La HEM/SK/SE WF9 . 25 G8
HOLM/MEL HD7 .... 54 F1
Long Cft DOD/DAR S75 .... 37 M6
Longcroft Av DRON S18 ..... 189 M5
Longcroft Crs DRON S18 .... 190 A5
Long Croft Rd DRON S18 .... 190 A5
Longdale Dr HEM/SK/SE WF9 .. 42 C3
Long Dam La HOR/CROF WF4 ... 21 L3
Longdendale Trail GLSP SK13 . 96 C3
STKB/PEN S36 .... 97 L2
Long Edge La BTLY DN5 .... 67 J6
Longfellow Dr
RHAM/THRY S65 .... 147 M2
WRKN S81 .... 198 F3
Longfellow Rd
DONS/BSCR DN4 .... 112 A1
Longfield Cl WMB/DAR S73 ... 83 M3
Longfield Dr DOD/DAR S75 ... 37 M6
DONS/BSCR DN4 .... 113 H1
RHAM/THRY S65 .... 131 H7
Long Field Rd ARMTH DN3 .... 69 L4
Longfield Rd FUL S10 .... 159 M2
Longfields Crs HOY S74 ..... 105 H1
Longford Cl TOT/DORE S17 .. 189 L2 🔲
Longford Crs TOT/DORE S17 . 189 L2
Longford Dr TOT/DORE S17 .. 189 K3
Longford Rd TOT/DORE S17 .. 189 K3
Longford Spinney
TOT/DORE S17 .... 189 K3
Long Ga NROS/TKH DN11 ..... 133 K2
Longhurst WRKN S81 .... 198 F2
Long Ing Rd HOLM/MEL HD7 .. 53 L8
Longlands Av AU/AST/KP S26 181 G5
Longlands Dr DOD/DAR S75 .. 37 M7 🔲
RHAM/THRY S65 .... 130 E4
Long Lands La AWLS/ASK DN6 . 66 B3
Long La BTLY DN5 .... 88 F3
CHPT/GREN S35 .... 125 G8
CHPT/GREN S35 .... 143 G5
ECK/KIL S21 .... 192 A6
ECK/KIL S21 .... 194 C1
FUL S10 .... 159 K3
GLE DN14 .... 11 L3
HOR/CROF WF4 .... 16 B6
KBTN HD8 .... 35 K4
PONT WF8 .... 26 A6
RHAM S60 .... 163 K1
ST/HB/BR S6 .... 143 G6
ST/HB/BR S6 .... 158 A2
STKB/PEN S36 .... 79 K6
STKB/PEN S36 .... 101 H7
WRKN S81 .... 184 C1
Longley Av West SHEFS S5 .. 144 D5
Longley Cl DOD/DAR S75 ..... 59 J3 🔲
SHEFS S5 .... 144 F5
Longley Crs SHEFN S5 .... 144 F4
Longley Dr SHEFN S5 .... 144 F5
Longley Edge La
HOLM/MEL HD7 .... 53 M6
Longley Edge Rd
HOLM/MEL HD7 .... 53 M6
Longley Farm Vw SHEFN S5 .. 144 F5
Longley Hall Gv SHEFS S5 .. 145 G5
Longley Hall Ri SHEFN S5 .. 144 F5
Longley Hall Rd SHEFN S5 .. 144 F5
Longley Hall Wy SHEFN S5 .. 145 G4
Longley La HOLM/MEL HD7 .... 53 L6
SHEFN S5 .... 144 F5
Long Leys La CONI DN12 ..... 132 E2
Longley St DOD/DAR S75 ..... 59 J3
Long Line ECC S11 .... 174 F5
Longman Rd BSLY S70 .... 2 F2
Long Mdw BWTY DN10 .... 155 M4
Long Moor La KBTN HD8 .... 34 A6
Longridge Rd BSLYN/ROY S71 . 61 J3
Long Rd MALT S66 .... 165 J5
Longside Wy DOD/DAR S75 .... 59 J5
Longsight Rd DOD/DAR S75 ... 37 L6
Longstone Crs HACK/IN S12 . 178 B5
Longthwaite Cl DIN S25 .... 166 C3 🔲
Longton Rd ARMTH DN3 .... 69 L3 🔲
Lonsdale Av BSLYN/ROY S71 .. 61 M7
WHHL DN2 .... 90 F4
Lonsdale Cl DIN S25 .... 182 D1 🔲
Lonsdale Rd ST/HB/BR S6 ... 144 A8
Loosemore Dr HACK/IN S12 .. 177 K2
Lopham Cl OWL S3 .... 160 F2 🔲
Lopham St OWL S3 .... 160 F1 🔲
OWL S3 .... 160 F1 🔲
Lordens HI DIN S25 .... 166 E6
Lords Cl CONI DN12 .... 111 G3
Lord's Head La
DONS/BSCR DN4 .... 111 H3
Lord St BSLYN/ROY S71 ...... 61 G5
HTFD DN7 .... 48 C4 🔲
RHAM/THRY S65 .... 7 L3
Lorna Rd MEX/SWTN S64 ..... 108 E2
Lorne Cl DRON S18 .... 190 B5
Lorne Rd DEARNE S63 .... 63 M7
Lothian Rd WHHL DN2 .... 91 G2
Louden Cl KIMB S61 .... 127 M5
Louden Rd KIMB S61 .... 127 M5
Loughrigg Wk FEA/AMT WF7 .. 23 J2 🔲
Lounde Cl BTLY DN5 .... 89 G6
Lound La BTLY DN5 .... 65 K2
Lound Low Rd RTFD DN22 .... 171 M8
Lound Rd DARN/MH S9 .... 162 B4
Lound Side CHPT/GREN S35 .. 126 E1
Louth Rd ECC S11 .... 159 M8
Lovell St ATT S4 .... 161 H2
Loversall Cl DONS/BSCR DN4. 111 M2
Love St OWL S3 .... 9 H2
Lovetot Av AU/AST/KP S26 .. 164 B7
Lovetot Rd DARN/MH S9 ..... 161 J2 🔲
KIMB S61 .... 128 C5
Lowburn Rd HAN/WDH S13 .... 162 A8
Low Common ECK/KIL S21 .... 194 B8 🔲
Low Cft BSLYN/ROY S71 ...... 39 H4
Low Cudworth CUD/GR S72 .... 61 M2
Low Deeps La BWTY DN10 .... 116 C6
Lowedges Crs SHEFS S8 ..... 190 D1 🔲
Lowedges Dr SHEFS S8 ...... 190 D1 🔲
Lowedges Pl SHEFS S8 ...... 190 D1 🔲
Lowedges Rd SHEFS S8 ...... 190 D1
Lowe La DOD/DAR S75 .... 81 K4
Lowell Av DONS/BSCR DN4 ... 111 M1 🔲
Lower Boundary Rd BTLY DN5 . 46 F7

Lower Castlereagh St BSLY S70 2 F6
Lower Common La KBTN HD8 35 J6
Lower Denby La KBTN HD8 56 E4
Lower Dolcliffe Rd
MEX/SWTN S64 108 D2
Lower High Royds
DOD/DAR S75 37 L7
Lower Kenyon St THNE DN8 31 M7
Lower Malton Rd BTLY DN5 67 J8
Lower Maythorn La
HOLM/MEL HD7 55 G7
Lower Mdw HOLM/MEL HD7 53 H2 1
Lower Mill Cl DEARNE S63 86 A3
Lower Northcroft
HEM/SK/SE WF9 42 E4
Lower Northfield La
HEM/SK/SE WF9 42 A4
Lower Thomas St BSLY S70 2 F7
Lower Unwin St STKB/PEN S36 79 H5
Lower York St WMB/DAR S73 84 B4 2
Low Farm La FEA/AMT WF7 23 L1
Lowfield Av HACK/IN S12 178 C6
KIMB S61 129 G4
Lowfield Cl ARMTH DN3 69 M1 1
Lowfield Crs HEM/SK/SE WF9 23 J8
Lowfield Gv DEARNE S63 86 C6
Low Field La BWTY DN10 137 G6
Lowfield Mdw DEARNE S63 86 B6
Lowfield Rd DEARNE S63 86 B5
HEM/SK/SE WF9 23 J8
WHHL DN2 69 G8
Low Fisher Ga DON DN1 4 F3
Lowgate BTLY DN5 67 J8
GLE DN14 10 F6
Low Ga HEM/SK/SE WF9 42 E4
HOLM/MEL HD7 53 M3
Low Grange Rd DEARNE S63 64 A7
Low Grange Sq DEARNE S63 64 A7
Lowhill THNE DN8 31 K6
Lowhouse Rd SHEFN S5 127 J8
Low Laithes Vw
WMB/DAR S73 83 M3 1
Lowlands Cl BSLYN/ROY S71 61 H2
BTLY DN5 67 M4
Low La HTFD DN7 47 K2
KIMB S61 128 E7
MALT S66 150 A5
Low Levels Bank HTFD DN7 50 B7
THNE DN8 73 G1
Low Moor Crs HOR/CROF WF4 19 K4
Low Moor La HOR/CROF WF4 19 H6
STKB/PEN S36 100 A4
Low Pasture Cl DOD/DAR S75 59 L8
Low Rd BWTY DN10 154 E5
CHPT/GREN S35 125 H8
CONI DN12 110 A4
DONS/BSCR DN4 89 L8
ST/HB/BR S6 159 L1
STKB/PEN S36 80 B6
Low Rd East DONS/BSCR DN4 111 H1
Low Rd West DONS/BSCR DN4 111 G2
Lowry Dr DRON S18 190 D6
Low St DOD/DAR S75 81 M1
RTFD DN22 170 F5
WRKN S81 184 E2
Lowther Rd DON DN1 5 J1
ST/HB/BR S6 144 B6
Lowther Sq WRKN S81 168 C8 4
Lowton Wy MALT S66 149 L2
Lowtown Cl WRKS S80 198 E5 1
Lowtown St WRKS S80 198 E5
Lowtown Vw WRKS S80 198 E5
Low Vw DOD/DAR S75 59 J8
Low Wood Cl
MEX/SWTN S64 108 A6 3
Loxley Av WMB/DAR S73 84 A5
Loxley Mt AWLS/ASK DN6 27 G7
Loxley Rd BSLYN/ROY S71 61 K4
ST/HB/BR S6 142 A3
Loxley View Rd FUL S10 159 M2
Loy Cl KIMB S61 128 E4
Lucas St ATT S4 145 G8 3
Ludgate Cl NROS/TKH DN11 113 L8
Ludwell Hl BTLY DN5 87 J5
Lugano Gv WMB/DAR S73 84 C1
Luke La ST/HB/BR S6 143 K6
Lulworth Cl BSLY S70 3 L7 1
Lumb La CHPT/GREN S35 124 E7
Lumley Crs MALT S66 151 G3
Lumley Dr DIN S25 166 A5
NROS/TKH DN11 134 F8
Lumley St ATT S4 161 H3
DARN/MH S9 161 K3 1
Lump La CHPT/GREN S35 126 A6
Luna Cft HACK/IN S12 177 K5
Lunbreck Rd DONS/BSCR DN4 111 G2
Lund Av BSLYN/ROY S71 61 K4
Lund Cl BSLYN/ROY S71 61 K4
Lund Crs BSLYN/ROY S71 61 K4
Lundhill Cl WMB/DAR S73 84 C6
Lundhill Gv WMB/DAR S73 84 C7
Lund Hill La BSLYN/ROY S71 39 K3
Lundhill Rd WMB/DAR S73 84 C7
Lund La BSLYN/ROY S71 61 K4
Lund Rd CHPT/GREN S35 143 H2
Lundwood Cl MOS S20 179 G5 2
Lundwood Dr MOS S20 179 G5
Lundwood Gv MOS S20 179 G5
Lundy Rd DRON S18 190 E7
Lunn Rd CUD/GR S72 61 M1
Lupton Crs SHEFS S8 190 D1
Lupton Dr SHEFS S8 190 D1
Lupton Rd SHEFS S8 190 D1
Luterel Dr AU/AST/KP S26 164 B7
Lutterworth Dr AWLS/ASK DN6 66 E1
Lvy Ct CUD/GR S72 61 M1
Lych Gate Cl DONS/BSCR DN4 91 L8 2
Lydgate Cl HOLM/MEL HD7 54 C1
Lydgate Ct FUL S10 159 M4
Lydgate Hall Crs FUL S10 159 L4
Lydgate La FUL S10 159 L4
Lydgetts HOLM/MEL HD7 53 H2 2
Lyme St RHAM S60 6 C5
Lyminster Rd ST/HB/BR S6 144 A2
Lyminton La RHAM S60 163 J3
Lymister Av RHAM S60 147 K5
Lyncroft Cl RHAM S60 147 H7 2
Lyndale Av ARMTH DN3 69 J6
Lynden Av AWLS/ASK DN6 66 E2
Lyndhurst Cl AWLS/ASK DN6 27 J4
ECC S11 176 A1
THNE DN8 31 K7 2
Lyndhurst Crs ARMTH DN3 69 J4
Lyndhurst Dr AWLS/ASK DN6 27 H4
Lyndhurst Ri AWLS/ASK DN6 27 J4
Lyndhurst Rd ECC S11 176 A1 2
Lynmouth Rd ABRD S7 176 C2
Lynn Pl DARN/MH S9 145 M7 1
Lynton Av RHAM S60 147 L4
Lynton Dr ARMTH DN3 69 J4
Lynton Pl DOD/DAR S75 37 H7
Lynton Rd ECC S11 160 B7 10
Lynwood Cl DRON S18 190 B6 3
Lynwood Crs HEM/SK/SE WF9 22 D4
Lynwood Dr BSLYN/ROY S71 39 G6
MEX/SWTN S64 108 D2
WKFDW/WTN WF2 20 A1
Lyons Cl ATT S4 145 G8
Lyons St ATT S4 145 G8 2
Lytham Av BSLYN/ROY S71 61 H2
DIN S25 166 D8
Lyttleton Crs STKB/PEN S36 79 G6
Lytton Av SHEFN S5 144 C3
Lytton Cl DONS/BSCR DN4 111 M1
Lytton Crs SHEFN S5 144 C2
Lytton Dr SHEFN S5 144 C2
Lytton Rd SHEFN S5 144 C2

M

Mabel St RHAM/THRY S65 7 J6
Mable St WRKS S80 197 M3
Macaulay Cl WRKN S81 199 G3
Machin Dr RAW S62 107 G7
Machin Gv WRKN S81 184 A8
Machin La STKB/PEN S36 101 H5
Machins Ct DRON S18 190 E5 2
Machon Bank ABRD S7 176 C1
Machon Bank Rd ECC S11 176 B1
Mackenzie Crs
CHPT/GREN S35 126 B3
FUL S10 8 C7
Mackenzie St ECC S11 160 C7 1
Mackenzie Wy AU/AST/KP S26 181 H5
Mackie Hill Cl HOR/CROF WF4 19 H3 1
Macmanus Av RAW S62 107 K7 1
Macnaghten Rd
DOD/DAR S75 104 D2 1
Macro Rd WMB/DAR S73 84 C6
Madam La ARMTH DN3 47 J7
Madehurst Gdns
SHEFP/MNR S2 160 F8 2
Madehurst Ri
SHEFP/MNR S2 160 F8 3
Madehurst Rd SHEFP/MNR S2 160 F8
Madehurst Vw
SHEFP/MNR S2 160 F8 4
Madeley Rd HOR/CROF WF4 22 A6
Madingley Cl DONS/BSCR DN4 111 L2
Madison Dr BWTY DN10 154 D1
Mafeking Pl CHPT/GREN S35 126 E1
Magdalen Rd HOLM/MEL HD7 52 A2
Magellan Rd MALT S66 150 C1
Maggot La STKB/PEN S36 80 B5
Magna Cl MALT S66 148 E1
Magna Crs MALT S66 148 E1
Magna La RHAM/THRY S65 130 B6
Magnolia Cl ARMTH DN3 69 K4 2
CUD/GR S72 40 B5 1
DIN S25 182 B4
Magpie Cl WRKN S81 184 A8 3
Magpie Gv SHEFP/MNR S2 161 J5 2
Mahon Av RAW S62 129 K1
Maidstone Rd ST/HB/BR S6 144 B3
Maidwell Wy ARMTH DN3 69 J3
Main Av CONI DN12 110 F4
TOT/DORE S17 189 J3
Main Ga HOLM/MEL HD7 54 C5
Main Rd CHPT/GREN S35 124 F4
DARN/MH S9 162 A3 1
DRON S18 189 L7
DRON S18 191 J8
ECK/KIL S21 192 B8
ECK/KIL S21 192 C4
ECK/KIL S21 193 M6
HACK/IN S12 178 C8
Main St ARMTH DN3 91 M6
AU/AST/KP S26 164 A8
AU/AST/KP S26 164 A6
AU/AST/KP S26 164 C3
AWLS/ASK DN6 43 M6
BTLY DN5 88 F7
BWTY DN10 155 M8
CHPT/GREN S35 126 A7
CUD/GR S72 40 B1
DEARNE S63 86 C2
DIN S25 182 B2
EPW DN9 92 D8
GLE DN14 11 L3
HACK/IN S12 178 F3
HEM/SK/SE WF9 24 C5
HEM/SK/SE WF9 25 H7
HTFD DN7 30 E8
HTFD DN7 71 J1
KIMB S61 129 G4
MALT S66 149 H2
MEX/SWTN S64 108 D3
NROS/TKH DN11 111 M8
NROS/TKH DN11 153 H6
NROS/TKH DN11 153 J3
PONT WF8 26 B1
RAW S62 105 L6
RAW S62 129 L1
RHAM S60 6 D5
RHAM S60 163 H1
RHAM/THRY S65 131 H4
WMB/DAR S73 84 A4
WRKN S81 168 D1
Makin St MEX/SWTN S64 109 G2
Malcolm Cl BSLY S70 61 H7 3
Malham Cl BWTY DN10 136 D7
CUD/GR S72 40 A4
Malham Gdns MOS S20 179 H8
Malham Gv MOS S20 179 J8
Malham Pl CHPT/GREN S35 126 D1
Malham Tarn Ct
DONS/BSCR DN4 90 F7 1
Malincroft DOD/DAR S75 37 M7
Malinda St OWL S3 8 E1
Malin Rd RHAM/THRY S65 130 B7
ST/HB/BR S6 143 L8
Mallard Av ARMTH DN3 69 K1
WKFDW/WTN WF2 20 A2
Mallard Cl DONS/BSCR DN4 111 K1
KIMB S61 127 L2
Mallard Dr ECK/KIL S21 179 M8 6
The Mallards WRKN S81 184 A8 5
Mallin Dr CONI DN12 110 F7
Mallory Av RAW S62 129 J1
Mallory Dr MEX/SWTN S64 109 H1
Mallory Rd RHAM/THRY S65 130 A7
Mallory Wy CUD/GR S72 40 A8
Malpas Hl NROS/TKH DN11 152 D6
Maltby La MALT S66 132 D8
Maltby Rd WRKN S81 168 C1
Maltby St DARN/MH S9 145 L8
Malthouse Rd BSLYN/ROY S71 3 H6 2
Malting La ATT S4 9 L2
The Maltings RHAM S60 6 F7
WRKN S81 169 M4
Maltkiln Dr HOR/CROF WF4 18 D7
Maltkiln St RHAM S60 6 F6
Malton Dr AU/AST/KP S26 164 C8
Malton Pl BSLYN/ROY S71 38 C8 4
Malton Rd BTLY DN5 67 H8
HEM/SK/SE WF9 25 H7
WHHL DN2 90 F2
Malton St ATT S4 145 G8
Maltravers Cl SHEFP/MNR S2 161 J5 3
Maltravers Crs SHEFP/MNR S2 161 H4
Maltravers Pl
SHEFP/MNR S2 161 J3 1
SHEFP/MNR S2 161 J4 1
Maltravers Rd SHEFP/MNR S2 161 J4
Maltravers Ter SHEFP/MNR S2 161 J5
Maltravers Wy SHEFP/MNR S2 161 J4
Malvern Av BTLY DN5 89 J2 3
Malvern Cl DOD/DAR S75 59 M5 6
THNE DN8 49 L1 1
Malvern Rd DARN/MH S9 161 M2
WHHL DN2 91 G3
Malwood Wy MALT S66 150 F1
Manchester Rd FUL S10 159 J4
ST/HB/BR S6 157 H3
STKB/PEN S36 78 A6
STKB/PEN S36 101 K5
STKB/PEN S36 102 E8
Mandeville St DARN/MH S9 162 A2
Mangham La
NROS/TKH DN11 134 E7 2
Mangham Rd KIMB S61 129 H6
Mangham Wy KIMB S61 129 H6
Mannering Rd
DONS/BSCR DN4 111 J1 3
Manners St OWL S3 160 D1
Manor Ap KIMB S61 128 D8
Manor Av DEARNE S63 86 C2
Manor Cl ARMTH DN3 47 J8
AU/AST/KP S26 181 K2 1
AWLS/ASK DN6 27 G4
DEARNE S63 84 F8 2
HEM/SK/SE WF9 24 C5 1
HOR/CROF WF4 20 D8
MALT S66 150 D2
PONT WF8 26 B2
RAW S62 107 G7
WRKS S80 198 A5
Manor Ct RHAM/THRY S65 130 B7
Manor Crs CUD/GR S72 40 D7
DRON S18 190 D6
RHAM S60 146 F7
Manor Cft CUD/GR S72 40 B2
Manor Dr AU/AST/KP S26 181 K2
BTLY DN5 110 B2
CUD/GR S72 40 A1
HOR/CROF WF4 17 H4
KBTN HD8 34 E5
RHAM S60 148 A6
WHHL DN2 5 M5
Manor End BSLY S70 82 D2
Manor Est BTLY DN5 67 K3
Manor Farm AU/AST/KP S26 164 B5 1
Manor Farm Cl AWLS/ASK DN6 66 F1
BSLYN/ROY S71 39 H7
Manor Farm Ct MOS S20 179 L4 3
RHAM/THRY S65 130 D3
Manor Farm Dr
MEX/SWTN S64 108 A5
Manor Farm Gdns DIN S25 182 B3 3
Manor Farm La GLE DN14 29 L2
Manor Farm Ms MOS S20 179 L4 2
Manor Farm Rd
HOR/CROF WF4 19 J3
Manor Flds KIMB S61 128 C7
Manor Gdns BSLYN/ROY S71 61 L7
BTLY DN5 88 F6
HTFD DN7 49 G8 1
Manor Garth AWLS/ASK DN6 27 J3
Manor Gv BSLYN/ROY S71 38 F4
CUD/GR S72 40 D7
HEM/SK/SE WF9 41 L6
STV/CWN S43 194 E8
WRKS S80 198 A5
Manor House Cl HOY S74 105 J1
Manor House Ct BTLY DN5 67 K6 1
Manor House Rd KIMB S61 128 C7
Manor Laith Rd
SHEFP/MNR S2 161 H5
Manor La DIN S25 166 E5
MEX/SWTN S64 86 E7
SHEFP/MNR S2 161 J3
STKB/PEN S36 80 A6
Manor Oaks Cl SHEFP/MNR S2 161 J4
Manor Oaks Ct
SHEFP/MNR S2 161 H4 1
Manor Oaks Dr SHEFP/MNR S2 9 M4
Manor Oaks Gdns
SHEFP/MNR S2 9 M4
Manor Oaks Pl SHEFP/MNR S2 161 J5
Manor Oaks Rd SHEFP/MNR S2 9 M4
Manor Occupation Rd
BSLYN/ROY S71 38 F3
Manor Pk DOD/DAR S75 58 D8
Manor Park Av SHEFP/MNR S2 161 K6
Manor Park Centre
SHEFP/MNR S2 161 L5 3
Manor Park Cl SHEFP/MNR S2 161 K6
Manor Park Ct
SHEFP/MNR S2 161 K6 1
Manor Park Crs
SHEFP/MNR S2 161 K6
Manor Park Dr SHEFP/MNR S2 161 K6
Manor Park Pl SHEFP/MNR S2 161 K5
Manor Park Ri SHEFP/MNR S2 161 K5
Manor Park Rd
SHEFP/MNR S2 161 K5
Manor Park Wy
SHEFP/MNR S2 161 K6
Manor Pl RAW S62 129 L2 1
Manor Ri KBTN HD8 34 E6
NROS/TKH DN11 134 A1
Manor Rd ARMTH DN3 47 J7
AU/AST/KP S26 180 F3
AU/AST/KP S26 181 L6
AWLS/ASK DN6 27 K8
AWLS/ASK DN6 45 H7
BTLY DN5 67 L3 3
BTLY DN5 87 G6
BWTY DN10 154 E5
CUD/GR S72 61 L1
DEARNE S63 64 A7
DEARNE S63 84 E8
DIN S25 166 D5
ECK/KIL S21 194 B2
HTFD DN7 49 G8
KBTN HD8 35 L3
MALT S66 150 E2
MEX/SWTN S64 108 B5
RHAM S60 146 F7
STV/CWN S43 194 E8
Manor Sq DEARNE S63 63 M7
Manorstead KBTN HD8 34 E6
Manor St BSLYN/ROY S71 39 H7
Manor Vw CUD/GR S72 40 A5
MOS S20 179 J8 3
Manor Wy AU/AST/KP S26 181 K2
AWLS/ASK DN6 45 K1
HOY S74 105 J1
SHEFP/MNR S2 161 J4
Manse Cl DONS/BSCR DN4 91 L7
Mansel Av SHEFN S5 144 C1
Mansel Crs SHEFN S5 144 B1
Mansel Rd SHEFN S5 144 C1
Mansfield Crs ARMTH DN3 69 K8
AWLS/ASK DN6 44 F5
Mansfield Dr HACK/IN S12 177 M1
Mansfield Rd AU/AST/KP S26 180 B1
AU/AST/KP S26 180 D4
BSLYN/ROY S71 38 D7
DONS/BSCR DN4 4 D9
ECK/KIL S21 194 D1
HACK/IN S12 177 M1
WRKS S80 197 K8
WRKS S80 198 A5
Mansion Court Gdns THNE DN8 31 M7
Manston Wy WRKN S81 184 A7
Manton Crs WRKS S80 198 F6
Manton Dl WRKS S80 198 F6
Manton St SHEFP/MNR S2 9 J8
Manton Vls WRKS S80 199 G6
Manvers Cl AU/AST/KP S26 164 B8 2
DIN S25 166 C8 1
Manvers Pk DEARNE S63 108 A1
Manvers Rd AU/AST/KP S26 164 B8
MEX/SWTN S64 108 C2
MOS S20 179 K3
ST/HB/BR S6 144 A8
Manvers St WRKS S80 198 C4 3
Manvers Wy DEARNE S63 85 H7
Maori Av DEARNE S63 85 L5
Maple Av DONS/BSCR DN4 91 K7
EPW DN9 114 E3
MALT S66 150 B2
Maplebeck Dr DARN/MH S9 146 C5
Maplebeck Rd DARN/MH S9 146 C6
Maple Cl BSLY S70 3 M9
Maple Croft Crs SHEFN S5 145 K4
Maple Croft Rd SHEFN S5 145 K4
Maple Dr ECK/KIL S21 194 A2
EPW DN9 92 E8
MALT S66 148 F1
WRKN S81 184 D8
Maple Gv AU/AST/KP S26 164 D7
BWTY DN10 136 D8
CONI DN12 109 K7
DARN/MH S9 162 C4
STKB/PEN S36 101 M7
Maple Pl CHPT/GREN S35 126 E3
Maple Rd AU/AST/KP S26 181 G4
DOD/DAR S75 37 L6
DOD/DAR S75 104 B4
MEX/SWTN S64 108 D2
THNE DN8 32 A6
Mapperley Rd DRON S18 190 A6 3
Mappin's Rd RHAM S60 163 H2 1
Mappin St SHEF S1 8 E4
Mapplebeck Rd
CHPT/GREN S35 104 C8
Maran Av WMB/DAR S73 85 G2
Marbeck Cl DIN S25 166 B6
Marcham Dr MOS S20 179 L3 1
March Bank RHAM/THRY S65 130 E4
March Flatts Rd
RHAM/THRY S65 130 E5
March Ga CONI DN12 110 A6
March St CONI DN12 110 A5
DARN/MH S9 145 M8
March Vale Ri CONI DN12 109 M6
Marchwood Av ST/HB/BR S6 159 J1
Marchwood Dr ST/HB/BR S6 143 J8
Marchwood Rd ST/HB/BR S6 143 J8
Marcliff Cl MALT S66 148 D3
Marcliff Crs MALT S66 148 D3
Marcliff La MALT S66 148 D3
Marden Rd ABRD S7 176 C1 6
Margaret Cl AU/AST/KP S26 180 B1 1
WMB/DAR S73 84 D2
Margaret Rd WMB/DAR S73 84 C5
WMB/DAR S73 84 D2
Margaret St MALT S66 150 F4
SHEF S1 9 H8
Margate Dr ATT S4 145 H7
Margate St CUD/GR S72 40 E8
Margetson Crs SHEFN S5 144 D1
Margetson Dr SHEFN S5 144 C1
Margetson Rd SHEFN S5 144 D1
Marian Crs AWLS/ASK DN6 27 J8
Marian Rd ARMTH DN3 69 J5 1
Marigold Cl SHEFN S5 145 J4
Marina Ri WMB/DAR S73 84 C2
Marina Vw THNE DN8 49 M2
Marion Cl HEM/SK/SE WF9 41 L5
Marion Rd ST/HB/BR S6 143 M5
Marjorie St WRKS S80 197 L3
Mark Bottoms La
HOLM/MEL HD7 53 K1
Markbrook Dr CHPT/GREN S35 104 A7
Market Cl BSLYN/ROY S71 3 J6
Market Hl BSLY S70 2 F5
Market Pl AWLS/ASK DN6 27 L7
CONI DN12 110 F5
CUD/GR S72 39 M8
DON DN1 5 G4
Market Rd DON DN1 5 G3
Market Sq HAN/WDH S13 179 G1
Market St AWLS/ASK DN6 66 F5
BSLY S70 2 F5
CHPT/GREN S35 126 F2
CUD/GR S72 39 M8
DEARNE S63 64 A7
DEARNE S63 86 C2
ECK/KIL S21 193 H4
HAN/WDH S13 179 G1 1
HEM/SK/SE WF9 23 H8
HOLM/MEL HD7 53 L2
HOY S74 83 J8
MEX/SWTN S64 108 C4
MEX/SWTN S64 108 E3 2
RHAM S60 6 E4
STKB/PEN S36 79 H4
WRKS S80 198 D4
Markfield Dr MALT S66 148 F1
Markham Av ARMTH DN3 69 L8
AWLS/ASK DN6 45 G6
CONI DN12 109 L5
Markham Ct CONI DN12 109 L5 1
Markham Rd CONI DN12 110 F5
WRKN S81 168 C4
Markham Sq CONI DN12 111 G5
Markham Ter SHEFS S8 176 D1 4
Mark La FUL S10 174 E1
Mark St BSLY S70 2 E6
Marlborough Av BTLY DN5 89 K4
Marlborough Cl DEARNE S63 64 A7 6
DIN S25 166 B8 2
Marlborough Crs
AWLS/ASK DN6 27 M8
Marlborough Cft
HEM/SK/SE WF9 42 D3 1
Marlborough Ri
AU/AST/KP S26 180 C1
Marlborough Rd
AWLS/ASK DN6 27 M7
FUL S10 160 A4
THNE DN8 50 A1 3
WHHL DN2 5 M3
Marlcliffe Rd ST/HB/BR S6 143 L5
Marley Rd SHEFP/MNR S2 161 J6
Marlfield Cft CHPT/GREN S35 126 F7
Marlow Cl MALT S66 149 H3
WHHL DN2 91 G2 2
Marlowe Dr RHAM/THRY S65 147 M2
Marlowe Gdns WRKN S81 198 F3
Marlowe Rd ARMTH DN3 47 K8
RHAM/THRY S65 147 M2
Marlow Rd WHHL DN2 91 G2
Marmion Rd ECC S11 159 M8 1
Marples Cl SHEFS S8 160 D8 9
Marples Dr SHEFS S8 160 D8 10
Marquis Gdns ARMTH DN3 47 K8
Marr Grange La BTLY DN5 66 C8
Marrick Ct CHPT/GREN S35 126 D2 4
Marrion Rd RAW S62 129 L1
Marriott La SHEFS S8 176 B4
Marriott Pl RAW S62 107 H8
Marriott Rd MEX/SWTN S64 108 C3
SHEFS S8 176 B4
Marrison Dr ECK/KIL S21 194 A1
Marr Ter FUL S10 159 K6
Marsala Wk WMB/DAR S73 84 D1
Marsden Gv THNE DN8 31 L7
Marsden La OWL S3 8 E3
Marsden Rd STKB/PEN S36 102 A6 3
Marsden St KBTN HD8 34 E4
Marshall Av DONS/BSCR DN4 89 L8 2
HOR/CROF WF4 19 K4
Marshall Cl RAW S62 129 K3
Marshall Dr HEM/SK/SE WF9 42 C4
Marshall Gv DEARNE S63 107 K2 3
Marshall Mill Ct KBTN HD8 35 H6
Marshall Rd SHEFS S8 176 D5
Marsh Av DRON S18 190 F4
Marsh Cl MOS S20 193 G1
Marshfield BSLY S70 82 D6 1
Marsh Ga BTLY DN5 4 D2
Marsh Hl MALT S66 132 A6
Marsh Hill La GLE DN14 12 D8
Marsh House Rd ECC S11 175 K2
Marshland Rd THNE DN8 32 A6
Marsh La ARMTH DN3 47 G8
ARMTH DN3 47 G5
ARMTH DN3 69 G1
BTLY DN5 68 A3
FUL S10 159 K4
KBTN HD8 55 G1
THNE DN8 31 L3
Marsh Rd AWLS/ASK DN6 47 G3
BTLY DN5 89 M2
HOLM/MEL HD7 54 B4
Marsh St RHAM S60 6 D7
STKB/PEN S36 102 B6 3
WMB/DAR S73 84 B4
Marsh Vw ECK/KIL S21 192 F5
Marson Av AWLS/ASK DN6 66 D2
Marston Cl DRON S18 190 B7
Marston Crs BSLYN/ROY S71 60 D1
Marstone Crs TOT/DORE S17 189 J2
Marston Rd FUL S10 159 M3

Martin Beck La
NROS/TKH DN11 135 L7
Martin Cl AU/AST/KP S26 164 A6
BSLY S70 82 D7
Martin Ct ECK/KIL S21 193 G4
Martin Crs SHEFN S5 144 F1
Martin Cft DOD/DAR S75 58 D7 5
Martindale Wk
AWLS/ASK DN6 45 G7 2
Martin Gv WKFDW/WTN WF2 20 C1
Martin La BWTY DN10 136 D8
BWTY DN10 136 C7
BWTY DN10 136 B5
HOY S74 83 H6
Martin Ri ECK/KIL S21 193 G4
KIMB S61 127 L1
Martin's Rd BSLYN/ROY S71 61 J4
Martin St ST/HB/BR S6 8 D1
Martin Wells Rd CONI DN12 111 G6
Martlet Wy WRKS S80 198 E7 1
Marton Av HEM/SK/SE WF9 41 G1 4
Marton Dr HTFD DN7 48 F8
Marton Rd BTLY DN5 67 K2
Marvell Rd BTLY DN5 89 H1 3
Mary Ann Cl BSLYN/ROY S71 61 H5
Mary La WMB/DAR S73 84 F2
Mary Rd AWLS/ASK DN6 27 K8
Mary's Pl DOD/DAR S75 59 M5 7
Mary St CUD/GR S72 85 J1
DOD/DAR S75 59 H3
ECK/KIL S21 193 H4
RHAM S60 6 D3
SHEF S1 9 H8
WRKS S80 197 M3
Masbrough St RHAM S60 6 B5
Masefield Ct DIN S25 166 E7 1
Masefield Pl WRKN S81 198 F3
Masefield Rd DEARNE S63 85 G8 1
HAN/WDH S13 162 A8
WHHL DN2 69 G8
Masham Ct DONS/BSCR DN4 91 J7 2
Mason Av AU/AST/KP S26 164 B6
Mason Crs HAN/WDH S13 162 B8
Mason Dr AU/AST/KP S26 164 A6
Mason Gv HAN/WDH S13 178 B1
Mason Lathe Rd SHEFN S5 145 J2
Mason St DEARNE S63 86 C2 4
Masons Wy BSLY S70 83 G1
Mason Wy HOY S74 83 H8
Massey Rd HAN/WDH S13 179 H2
Mastall La BTLY DN5 68 C5
Masters Crs SHEFN S5 144 F2
Masters Rd SHEFN S5 144 F2
Mather Av DARN/MH S9 161 M5
Mather Ct DARN/MH S9 161 M4
Mather Crs DARN/MH S9 161 M4
Mather Dr DARN/MH S9 161 M4
Mather Rd DARN/MH S9 161 M4
Matherville KBTN HD8 34 E6
Matilda La SHEF S1 9 J7
Matilda St SHEF S1 9 J7
Matilda Wy SHEF S1 9 G6
Matlock Rd BSLYN/ROY S71 60 F1
FUL S10 160 A2
Mattersey Cl
DONS/BSCR DN4 113 J2 1
Mattersey Rd BWTY DN10 155 M8
RTFD DN22 170 F2
RTFD DN22 171 L7
Matthews Av DEARNE S63 107 H1
Matthews Cl DEARNE S63 107 H2
Matthews Dr MALT S66 148 F4 5
Matthews Fold SHEFS S8 177 G6 1
Matthews La SHEFS S8 177 G6
Matthew St OWL S3 8 F2
Maud's Br THNE DN8 50 F2
Mauncer Crs HAN/WDH S13 162 F8
Mauncer Dr HAN/WDH S13 162 F8
Mauncer La HAN/WDH S13 178 F1
Maun Wy SHEFN S5 145 G4
Maurice St RAW S62 129 K4
Mawfa Av SHEFS S8 177 H5
Mawfa Crs SHEFS S8 177 H5 3
Mawfa Dr SHEFS S8 177 H5
Mawfa Rd SHEFS S8 177 H5 4
Mawfield Rd DOD/DAR S75 59 K3
Mawson Green La GLE DN14 30 D1
Maxey Pl SHEFS S8 176 E1 6
Maxfield Av FUL S10 160 A4
Maxwell St ATT S4 161 G1
Maxwell Wy ATT S4 161 G1
May Av DONS/BSCR DN4 111 L1
Mayberry Dr DOD/DAR S75 58 D6
Maycock Av KIMB S61 128 B5
May Day Gn BSLY S70 3 G5
Mayfair Cl NROS/TKH DN11 153 K3
Mayfair Pl HEM/SK/SE WF9 23 H8
Mayfield AWLS/ASK DN6 27 L7
BSLYN/ROY S71 60 F3
STKB/PEN S36 79 M6
Mayfield Av HTFD DN7 48 F2
Mayfield Crs BSLY S70 82 C1 1
NROS/TKH DN11 113 K7
Mayfield Ri HOR/CROF WF4 21 L6
Mayfield Rd BTLY DN5 4 B1
FUL S10 158 E8
Mayfields BTLY DN5 67 H6
Mayfields Wy HEM/SK/SE WF9 41 M6
Mayflower Av BWTY DN10 154 E5
Mayflower Cl BWTY DN10 136 E7
Mayflower Rd
DONS/BSCR DN4 111 G2
Maynard Rd RHAM S60 148 A4
May Rd ST/HB/BR S6 143 M7
May Ter BSLY S70 2 A5
Maythorne Cl DOD/DAR S75 38 A7 4
May Tree Cl MOS S20 179 J6
Maytree Cl WMB/DAR S73 84 E3
May Tree Cft MOS S20 179 J6 1
May Tree La MOS S20 179 J6
Mcconnel Crs NROS/TKH DN11 113 H6
Mcintyre Rd STKB/PEN S36 101 M7
Mclaren Av HEM/SK/SE WF9 25 H7
Mclaren Crs MALT S66 150 E3
Mclintock Wy BSLY S70 2 D5
Meaburn Cl DONS/BSCR DN4 91 K8
Meade Dr WRKN S81 184 E8
Meadow Av CUD/GR S72 62 B3 1
RAW S62 107 H8
Meadow Bank HOLM/MEL HD7 54 A1
HOR/CROF WF4 22 A6
Meadow Bank Av ABRD S7 160 B8 5
Meadowbank Cl KIMB S61 146 E1 2
Meadow Bank Rd ABRD S7 160 B8
DARN/MH S9 146 A3
KIMB S61 146 B2
Meadow Cl AU/AST/KP S26 181 J4
DRON S18 191 G3 5
RHAM/THRY S65 130 C6
Meadow Ct BSLYN/ROY S71 39 H4
Meadowcourt DARN/MH S9 145 M5 4
Meadow Ct HEM/SK/SE WF9 42 F4
Meadow Crs BSLYN/ROY S71 39 H4
CUD/GR S72 40 E8 1
MOS S20 178 F8 1
Meadow Cft ARMTH DN3 69 L5
BTLY DN5 89 G7
CUD/GR S72 40 A4
HEM/SK/SE WF9 41 H2
MEX/SWTN S64 108 A7
Meadowcroft Cl RHAM S60 147 M7
Meadowcroft Gdns MOS S20 179 J7
Meadowcroft Gld MOS S20 179 J7 7
Meadowcroft Ri MOS S20 179 J7 8
Meadow Dirve
NROS/TKH DN11 135 G8
Meadow Dr BSLYN/ROY S71 61 H3
CHPT/GREN S35 126 C2
MEX/SWTN S64 108 A5
WRKS S80 198 A5
Meadowfield Cl
HEM/SK/SE WF9 22 E4 3
Meadowfield Dr HOY S74 105 J3
Meadow Field Rd ARMTH DN3 69 L1
Meadow Gate Av MOS S20 179 M4
Meadow Gate Cl MOS S20 179 M5 1
Meadow Gate La MOS S20 179 M6
Meadowgates DEARNE S63 86 A4
Meadow Gv TOT/DORE S17 189 J3
Meadow Grove Rd
TOT/DORE S17 189 H3
Meadowhall Rd DARN/MH S9 145 M5
KIMB S61 146 B2
Meadowhall Wy DARN/MH S9 146 A4
Meadowhead SHEFS S8 176 E8 2
Meadow Head Av SHEFS S8 176 C8
Meadow Head Dr SHEFS S8 176 D7
Meadow House Dr FUL S10 159 H6
Meadowland Ri CUD/GR S72 62 A2 2
Meadow La DOD/DAR S75 37 J8
MALT S66 150 E3
MEX/SWTN S64 108 E4
RAW S62 107 H8
WMB/DAR S73 84 F2
WRKN S81 169 J3
Meadow Lea WRKS S80 198 A5
Meadowpark Cft DIN S25 166 C7 2
Meadow Ri ARMTH DN3 47 L8 2
HEM/SK/SE WF9 41 G1
NROS/TKH DN11 134 A1
Meadow Rd BSLYN/ROY S71 39 H4
WRKS S80 198 A5
Meadows Morvern
HEM/SK/SE WF9 23 K8
The Meadows AU/AST/KP S26 181 J2
EPW DN9 117 M3
KBTN HD8 56 D2 1
Meadow St BSLYN/ROY S71 3 H3
DIN S25 166 A5
KIMB S61 146 E1
OWL S3 8 E2
Meadow Ter ECC S11 160 A7 2
The Meadow BTLY DN5 89 G6
Meadow V HOR/CROF WF4 18 E2
Meadow Vw BSLY S70 82 E2
KBTN HD8 34 F6
STKB/PEN S36 79 K1
Meadow View Cl HOY S74 105 H2
Meadow View Rd
MEX/SWTN S64 108 B7
SHEFS S8 176 D7
Meadow Wk ARMTH DN3 69 L4
HEM/SK/SE WF9 24 B4
Meadow Wy MEX/SWTN S64 108 D4
NROS/TKH DN11 153 K2
Meadstead Dr BSLYN/ROY S71 38 F4
The Meads SHEFS S8 176 F7
The Meadway TOT/DORE S17 175 H8
Meal Hill La HOLM/MEL HD7 54 D5
Meal Hill Rd HOLM/MEL HD7 52 D6
Mears Cl STKB/PEN S36 79 J4
Measham Dr HTFD DN7 48 E2
The Mede AWLS/ASK DN6 66 D2
Medina Wy DOD/DAR S75 59 J2
Medley Vw CONI DN12 110 B6
Medlock Cl HAN/WDH S13 162 E5
Medlock Crs HAN/WDH S13 162 E5
Medlock Cft HAN/WDH S13 162 E5
Medlock Dr HAN/WDH S13 162 E6
Medlock Rd HAN/WDH S13 162 E6 1
Medlock Wy HAN/WDH S13 162 E5
Medway Cl DOD/DAR S75 59 K2
Medway Pl WMB/DAR S73 84 D6 4
Meersbrook Av SHEFS S8 176 D2
Meersbrook Park Rd SHEFS S8 176 E1
Meersbrook Rd SHEFS S8 176 F2
Meetinghouse Cft
HAN/WDH S13 179 G1
Meetinghouse La
HAN/WDH S13 179 G1
SHEF S1 9 H3
Mekyll Cl MALT S66 148 F1 2
Melbeck Ct CHPT/GREN S35 126 C2 2
Melbourne Av AU/AST/KP S26 164 C7
DEARNE S63 85 M5
DRON S18 189 M6
FUL S10 160 A5
Melbourne Gv
NROS/TKH DN11 153 K3 3
Melbourne Rd
DONS/BSCR DN4 111 J1
STKB/PEN S36 101 L6
Melbourn Rd FUL S10 160 A2
Melciss Rd MALT S66 148 E3
Melford Cl DOD/DAR S75 37 M6 1
Melford Dr DONS/BSCR DN4 111 L3
Melfort Gln FUL S10 159 K4 2
Mell Av HOY S74 105 H1
Mellinder La BTLY DN5 88 A1
Melling Av BTLY DN5 89 K4
Mellington Cl SHEFS S8 177 G5
Mellish Rd WRKN S81 168 C5
Mellor La HOLM/MEL HD7 52 F3
Mellor Lea Farm Cha
CHPT/GREN S35 126 F5
Mellor Lea Farm Dr
CHPT/GREN S35 126 F5
Mellor Lea Farm Garth
CHPT/GREN S35 126 F5
Mellor Rd WMB/DAR S73 84 C5
Mellow Fields Rd DIN S25 166 B3
Mellwood Gv WMB/DAR S73 84 A7 2
Mellwood La HEM/SK/SE WF9 42 E4
Melrose Cl DONS/BSCR DN4 89 J8
MALT S66 165 H1
Melrose Gv RHAM S60 147 L5
Melrose Rd ATT S4 160 F1
Melrose Wy BSLYN/ROY S71 61 H5
Meltham House La
HOLM/MEL HD7 54 D3
Melton Av DEARNE S63 86 C2 3
WMB/DAR S73 84 F7
Melton Cl HEM/SK/SE WF9 42 E2 5
Meltonfield Cl ARMTH DN3 92 A2 3
Melton Gdns BTLY DN5 88 F6
Melton Gn DEARNE S63 107 G1
Melton Gv HACK/IN S12 178 E5
Melton High St DEARNE S63 107 G1
Melton Mill La BTLY DN5 87 K7
Melton Rd BTLY DN5 88 C6
HOR/CROF WF4 19 L3
Melton St MEX/SWTN S64 109 G3
WMB/DAR S73 84 F7 1
Melton Ter BSLY S70 83 G2 1
Melton Wood Gv BTLY DN5 88 F6 4
Melville St WMB/DAR S73 84 B4 3
Melvinia Crs DOD/DAR S75 60 B3
Melwood Ct ARMTH DN3 92 A3
Memorial Av WRKS S80 198 D5
Mendip Cl BTLY DN5 89 J2 4
DOD/DAR S75 59 M5 8
Mendip Ri RHAM S60 147 H7 3
Menson Dr HTFD DN7 48 F7
Merbeck Dr CHPT/GREN S35 104 C6
Merbeck Gv CHPT/GREN S35 104 C7 2
Mercel Av ARMTH DN3 70 A7
Mercia Cl WRKN S81 184 E8 5
Mercia Dr TOT/DORE S17 189 J1
Meredith Crs DONS/BSCR DN4 111 M1
Meredith Rd ST/HB/BR S6 143 M7
Mere La ARMTH DN3 69 L6
Merlin Cl AWLS/ASK DN6 66 F1
BSLY S70 82 D7
Merlin Wy KIMB S61 127 L1
SHEFN S5 145 G4
Merrill Rd DEARNE S63 64 A6
Merton La DARN/MH S9 145 M3
Merton Ri DARN/MH S9 145 M3
Merton Rd DARN/MH S9 145 M3 4
Metcalfe Av ECK/KIL S21 194 A1
Methley Cl SHEFP/MNR S2 177 K1
Methley St CUD/GR S72 61 M1
The Mews WRKN S81 169 L4
Mexborough Rd DEARNE S63 86 B6
Meynell Crs SHEFN S5 144 B3
Meynell Rd SHEFN S5 144 B3
Meyrick Dr DOD/DAR S75 37 H8
Michael Cft DEARNE S63 107 H1
Michael Rd BSLYN/ROY S71 61 J5
Michael's Est CUD/GR S72 40 E8
Mickelden Wy DOD/DAR S75 59 L6 4
Micklebring Gv CONI DN12 109 L7
Micklebring La MALT S66 132 D5
Micklebring Wy MALT S66 131 M8
Mickleden Edge STKB/PEN S36 99 J6
Micklethwaite Gv THNE DN8 32 A3 2
Micklethwaite Rd
HOR/CROF WF4 19 K4
THNE DN8 32 A3
Mickley La TOT/DORE S17 189 K3
Middle Av RAW S62 129 K1
Middle Bank DONS/BSCR DN4 90 C7
Middlebrook La THNE DN8 31 M8
Middleburn Cl BSLY S70 3 J9
Middlecliff Cl MOS S20 179 J6
Middlecliff Ct MOS S20 179 J6 2
Middlecliffe Dr STKB/PEN S36 77 H2
Middlecliff La CUD/GR S72 62 F7
CUD/GR S72 63 G7
Middlecliff Ri MOS S20 179 J6
Middle Dr RHAM S60 147 K6
Middlefield Cl TOT/DORE S17 175 G8
Middlefield Cft TOT/DORE S17 189 G1
Middle Field La HOR/CROF WF4 37 J1
Middlefield La PONT WF8 26 A2
Middle Field Rd DOD/DAR S75 59 H7
Middlefield Rd DONS/BSCR DN4 91 H8
RHAM S60 147 L5
Middlefields Dr RHAM S60 148 A6
Middlegate BTLY DN5 67 J6 1
Middle Hay Cl HACK/IN S12 177 J2
Middle Hay Pl HACK/IN S12 177 J2
Middle Hay Ri HACK/IN S12 177 J2
Middle Hay Vw GLV S14 177 J3
Middle La BTLY DN5 46 A4
CHPT/GREN S35 125 M6
RHAM/THRY S65 7 K3
ST/HB/BR S6 159 L1 2
Middle La South
RHAM/THRY S65 7 M5
Middle Ox Cl MOS S20 193 K1 2
Middle Ox Gdns MOS S20 193 K1
Middle Pl RHAM/THRY S65 129 M8
Middlesex St BSLY S70 3 G9
Middleton Av DIN S25 166 C7
Middleton La CHPT/GREN S35 126 B7
Middleton Rd RHAM/THRY S65 7 K4
Middle Wood La BWTY DN10 137 M1
Middlewood Rd ST/HB/BR S6 143 L4
Middlewood Rd North
CHPT/GREN S35 143 K2
Middlewoods DOD/DAR S75 59 L8 8
Midfield Rd FUL S10 159 L3
Midhill Rd SHEFP/MNR S2 160 F8
Midhope Cliff La
STKB/PEN S36 100 A2
Midhope Hall La
STKB/PEN S36 100 D3
Midhope La STKB/PEN S36 100 B3
Midhope Wy DOD/DAR S75 59 L6
Midhurst Gv DOD/DAR S75 59 J2
Midhurst Rd ST/HB/BR S6 143 M2
Midland Rd BSLYN/ROY S71 39 H3
KIMB S61 6 A4
KIMB S61 146 E1
MEX/SWTN S64 108 C4
Midland St BSLY S70 3 G5
RAW S62 129 J5
SHEF S1 9 H8
Midvale Av ST/HB/BR S6 160 C1
Midvale Cl ST/HB/BR S6 160 C2
Milano Ri WMB/DAR S73 84 D2
Milbanke St DON DN1 5 H2
Milburn Ct MOS S20 179 L6 8
Milburn Gv MOS S20 179 L6
Milcroft Crs HTFD DN7 48 F7 5
Milden Pl BSLY S70 60 E8
Milden Rd ST/HB/BR S6 143 L5
Mile End Av HTFD DN7 70 E2
Milefield La CUD/GR S72 40 C8
Milefield Vw CUD/GR S72 40 D8 2
Mile Oak Rd RHAM S60 147 K4
Miles Cl SHEFN S5 144 E6
Miles Rd CHPT/GREN S35 104 C8
SHEFN S5 144 D6
Mileswood Cl CUD/GR S72 63 H4 1
Milethorn La DON DN1 90 B2
Milford Av HOY S74 105 M1
Milford St DARN/MH S9 145 M7
Milgate St BSLYN/ROY S71 39 H3
Milgrove Crs CHPT/GREN S35 104 B7
Millais Ri MALT S66 130 F8
Millard Av HTFD DN7 48 E7
Millard La MALT S66 150 E3
Millars Wk HEM/SK/SE WF9 41 L6
Mill Cl AU/AST/KP S26 181 K3
DIN S25 166 B1
FEA/AMT WF7 23 L1
HEM/SK/SE WF9 41 L5
RHAM S60 6 C8
Mill Ct BSLY S70 82 E2 5
Milldale Rd TOT/DORE S17 189 K2
Milldyke Cl RHAM S60 148 B6 2
Miller Cl THNE DN8 50 A1
Miller Ct WKFDW/WTN WF2 19 M4
Miller Cft HAN/WDH S13 178 E1
Miller Dale Dr RHAM S60 147 H8 2
Miller Garth FEA/AMT WF7 23 L2
Miller Hl KBTN HD8 56 E2
Miller La STKB/PEN S36 100 F3
THNE DN8 50 A1
Miller Rd SHEFS S8 160 D8 11
Millers Dl BSLY S70 82 E3
Miller St STKB/PEN S36 102 D6 1
Mill Farm Dr WKFDW/WTN WF2 20 A3
Mill Field Ct ARMTH DN3 69 L1 3
Mill Field Rd HTFD DN7 30 D7
Millfield Rd BTLY DN5 68 A7
THNE DN8 31 M7
Mill Flds AU/AST/KP S26 181 J3
Millfield Vw WRKS S80 198 A5
Mill Gdns WRKS S80 198 A5
Mill Ga BTLY DN5 67 M7
Millgate FEA/AMT WF7 23 L2
Mill Hvn DIN S25 182 B2
Mill Hl RHAM S60 148 A6
WMB/DAR S73 83 M3
Mill Hill Cl BTLY DN5 89 K4
Mill Hill Rd HTFD DN7 71 G2
Mill Hills AU/AST/KP S26 181 K2
Millhouse La STKB/PEN S36 78 B4
Millhouses Ct ECC S11 175 M3
Millhouses Gln ECC S11 175 M3 1
Millhouses La ABRD S7 176 A4
Millhouses St HOY S74 105 J2
Millicent Sq MALT S66 150 E4 1
Millindale MALT S66 150 E3
Mill La AWLS/ASK DN6 44 D5
AWLS/ASK DN6 66 F1
BTLY DN5 87 G6
BWTY DN10 154 E4
DEARNE S63 107 G2
DIN S25 182 B2
DOD/DAR S75 37 J6
DONS/BSCR DN4 88 F8
DRON S18 190 F6
ECK/KIL S21 193 L5
FEA/AMT WF7 23 L2
HATH/EY S32 172 D8
HEM/SK/SE WF9 41 L6
HEM/SK/SE WF9 42 F3
HOR/CROF WF4 17 H4
HOR/CROF WF4 20 C8
HOR/CROF WF4 21 M6
RAW S62 105 K5
RHAM S60 163 H3
STKB/PEN S36 56 B7
STKB/PEN S36 78 D4
STKB/PEN S36 102 D6
STKB/PEN S36 123 K3
TOT/DORE S17 189 K2
Mill Lee La ST/HB/BR S6 141 L4
Mill Lee Rd ST/HB/BR S6 141 L4
Mill Meadow Gdns MOS S20 179 M6
Mill Meadow Vw WRKN S81 169 M4
Millmoor La RHAM S60 6 B5
Millmoor Rd WMB/DAR S73 84 D3
Millmount Rd HOY S74 105 K1
SHEFS S8 176 D2
Millrace Dr DEARNE S63 86 A3
Mill Rd CHPT/GREN S35 126 F6
ECK/KIL S21 193 H3
RHAM S60 163 H3
Mill Road Cl CHPT/GREN S35 126 E6
Millsands OWL S3 9 J2
Mills Dr HTFD DN7 71 L7
Mill Shaw La HOLM/MEL HD7 54 E6
Millside CUD/GR S72 40 A4
Millside Ct BTLY DN5 67 M7 2
Millside Wk CUD/GR S72 40 A4
Millstone Cl DRON S18 190 B5 1
FEA/AMT WF7 23 L2
Millstone Dr AU/AST/KP S26 164 B8
Millstones STKB/PEN S36 80 A6
Millstream Cl BTLY DN5 89 H6
Mill St ARMTH DN3 91 M1
HEM/SK/SE WF9 41 L5
KIMB S61 128 F3
RHAM S60 6 E7
WRKS S80 198 C3
Millthorpe Rd SHEFN S5 145 H3
Mill Vw DEARNE S63 85 M6
HEM/SK/SE WF9 41 G1
Millward St HOR/CROF WF4 21 L6 2
Millwood Rd
DONS/BSCR DN4 111 K2 1
Mill Wood Vw ST/HB/BR S6 143 G8
Milne Av NROS/TKH DN11 154 A3
Milne Dr NROS/TKH DN11 154 B3
Milne Gv NROS/TKH DN11 154 A3
Milner Av STKB/PEN S36 78 F4
Milner Cl MALT S66 149 J1
Milner Ga CONI DN12 110 C4
Milner Gate Ct CONI DN12 110 B5
Milne Rd NROS/TKH DN11 154 B3
Milner Rd DONS/BSCR DN4 89 K8 4
Milnes St BSLY S70 3 J8 1
Milne St DOD/DAR S75 59 J3
Milnrow Crs SHEFN S5 144 D1
Milnrow Dr SHEFN S5 144 D1
Milnrow Rd SHEFN S5 144 D1
Milton Av BTLY DN5 89 K3
Milton Cl DEARNE S63 84 F7
HOR/CROF WF4 19 H1
HOY S74 83 K8
KIMB S61 128 F3
Milton Ct MEX/SWTN S64 108 A4
Milton Crs HOY S74 105 J2
Milton Dr HEM/SK/SE WF9 22 F5
WRKN S81 198 F3
Milton Gv ARMTH DN3 69 K5 1
ARMTH DN3 91 M1
WMB/DAR S73 84 C5
Milton La SHEF S1 8 F7
Milton Rd ABRD S7 160 C8
ARMTH DN3 92 C6
AWLS/ASK DN6 45 G6
CHPT/GREN S35 126 B2
DIN S25 166 E7
HOY S74 105 J1 4
MEX/SWTN S64 108 E2
RHAM/THRY S65 7 J1
Milton St CUD/GR S72 63 H5
MALT S66 150 D3
MEX/SWTN S64 108 A4
OWL S3 8 E7
RHAM S60 6 D1
Milton Wk DON DN1 4 F6
WRKN S81 198 F3
Minden Cl MALT S66 148 F3
Minden Ct BTLY DN5 67 M7 3
Minna Rd OWL S3 144 F8
Minneymoor Hl CONI DN12 110 B4
Minneymoor La CONI DN12 110 B5
Minster Cl CHPT/GREN S35 127 G7
DONS/BSCR DN4 91 L8
Minster Rd CHPT/GREN S35 126 F7
Minster Wy BSLYN/ROY S71 61 H4
Minsthorpe La HEM/SK/SE WF9 42 E1
Minto Rd ST/HB/BR S6 143 M6
Mire La RTFD DN22 187 K1
Mission Fld WMB/DAR S73 84 E7
Misson Bank BWTY DN10 116 D3
EPW DN9 116 D2
Mitchell Cl BSLY S70 83 H2 3
HTFD DN7 48 E6
WRKN S81 184 C6
Mitchell Rd SHEFS S8 176 D5
WMB/DAR S73 84 A2
Mitchell's St BSLY S70 83 J2
Mitchell St OWL S3 8 D3
Mitchelson Av DOD/DAR S75 59 J8
Moat Cft BTLY DN5 67 K6 2
Moat Hills Ct BTLY DN5 67 L6
Moat La MALT S66 149 H6
Modd La HOLM/MEL HD7 53 K3
Modena Ct WMB/DAR S73 84 C1
Moffat Gdns WHHL DN2 69 H6
Moffatt Rd SHEFP/MNR S2 160 F8
Moira Cl HTFD DN7 48 F2
Molineaux Cl SHEFN S5 145 H2 2
Molineaux Rd SHEFN S5 145 G1
Molloy Pl SHEFS S8 176 E2 5
Molloy St SHEFS S8 176 E1 7
Molly Hurst La HOR/CROF WF4 19 K8
Mona Av FUL S10 160 A3
Mona Rd DONS/BSCR DN4 89 M7
FUL S10 160 A2
Monckton Rd NROS/TKH DN11 154 A3
SHEFN S5 145 K4
Moncrieffe Rd ABRD S7 176 C1
Monksbridge Rd DIN S25 166 A6
Monks Cl KIMB S61 128 A5
Monkspring BSLY S70 83 G2
Monks Wy BSLYN/ROY S71 61 H4
WRKN S81 183 K8
Monk Ter BSLYN/ROY S71 61 J2
Monkton Wy BSLYN/ROY S71 39 G2
Monkwood Rd RAW S62 107 H8
Monmouth Rd WHHL DN2 90 E1
WRKN S81 198 E1
Monmouth St FUL S10 8 D6
Monsal Crs BSLYN/ROY S71 38 E8
Monsal St DEARNE S63 64 A7
Montague Av CONI DN12 109 L4
Montague St CUD/GR S72 40 A7 2
DON DN1 5 H2
ECC S11 8 D9
Montagu Rd BTLY DN5 89 J5
Montagu St MEX/SWTN S64 108 F3 3
Monteney Crs SHEFN S5 126 E7
Monteney Gdns SHEFN S5 126 E8
Monteney Rd SHEFN S5 126 E8
Montfort Dr OWL S3 160 F1
Montgomery Av ABRD S7 160 C8
Montgomery Dr ABRD S7 160 C8 3
Montgomery Rd ABRD S7 160 C8
DEARNE S63 107 J1 4
Montgomery Terrace Rd
OWL S3 8 E1

ST/HB/BR S6 160 D2 11
Montrose WRKN S81 198 F2
Montrose Av DOD/DAR S75 37 K6
WHHL DN2 90 F2
Montrose Pl DRON S18 190 B5
Montrose Rd ECC S11 176 A2
Moonpenny Wy DRON S18 190 E6
Moonshine La SHEFN S5 144 D4
Moorbank Cl DOD/DAR S75 60 A3 2
FUL S10 159 H4
WMB/DAR S73 83 M3
Moorbank Dr FUL S10 159 J4
Moorbank Rd FUL S10 159 H4 1
WMB/DAR S73 83 M2
Moorbank Vw WMB/DAR S73 83 M2
Moorbridge Crs WMB/DAR S73 84 F6
Moorbrow HOLM/MEL HD7 54 A5
Moor Crs MOS S20 179 G8
Moorcrest Ri DOD/DAR S75 37 M5 1
Moorcroft Av FUL S10 158 F7
Moorcroft Cl FUL S10 158 F8
Moorcroft Dr FUL S10 158 F8
Moorcroft Rd FUL S10 158 F8 2
Moordale Vw RAW S62 108 A8
Moor Dike Rd HTFD DN7 71 L8
HTFD DN7 71 M3
Moor Edges Rd THNE DN8 32 B8
Moorend La DOD/DAR S75 80 E2
Moor End Rd FUL S10 160 A3
Moorends Rd THNE DN8 32 A1
Moore St SHEFP/MNR S2 8 F7
Moore Street Rbt OWL S3 8 E8
Moor Farm Av MOS S20 178 F7
Moor Farm Garth MOS S20 179 G7 1
Moor Farm Ri MOS S20 178 F7
Moorfield Av
RHAM/THRY S65 131 H8 2
Moorfield Cl RHAM/THRY S65 131 H8
Moorfield Crs HEM/SK/SE WF9 41 G1
Moorfield Dr ARMTH DN3 91 M2
Moorfield Gv
RHAM/THRY S65 131 H8 3
Moorfield Pl HEM/SK/SE WF9 41 G1
Moor Gap ARMTH DN3 92 B7
Moorgate Av FUL S10 8 A3
RHAM S60 7 G8
Moorgate Cha RHAM S60 7 G7
Moorgate Crs DRON S18 190 F7 2
Moorgate Gv RHAM S60 7 H9
Moorgate La RHAM S60 7 H8
Moorgate Rd RHAM S60 6 F6
RHAM S60 7 G8
Moorgate St RHAM S60 6 F4
Moor Green Cl DOD/DAR S75 59 L5
Moor Head SHEF S1 9 G6
Moorhouse Cl RHAM S60 148 B6 3
Moorhouse Ct HEM/SK/SE WF9 42 E6
Moorhouse Gap AWLS/ASK DN6 43 K6
Moorhouse La AWLS/ASK DN6 43 G7
DOD/DAR S75 37 G2
HOR/CROF WF4 22 A3
RHAM S60 148 A6
Moorhouse Vw
HEM/SK/SE WF9 42 F5
Moorland Av BSLY S70 59 M7
DOD/DAR S75 37 M5
Moorland Ct DEARNE S63 85 G7 1
Moorland Crs DOD/DAR S75 37 M5
Moorland Dr HOR/CROF WF4 19 K5
STKB/PEN S36 101 L6
Moorland Gv DONS/BSCR DN4 91 G6
Moorland Pl ST/HB/BR S6 159 G1
Moorland Rd HATH/EY S32 172 D8
Moorlands EPW DN9 117 M3
HOLM/MEL HD7 54 A4
MALT S66 148 D3
Moorlands Crs RHAM S60 148 A6
Moorland Ter CUD/GR S72 62 A2
Moorland Vw AU/AST/KP S26 164 C8
DEARNE S63 85 G7
DRON S18 191 L6 1
HACK/IN S12 177 L5
KBTN HD8 16 E8
KBTN HD8 35 L5
Moor La ARMTH DN3 69 J2
BSLY S70 104 D2
CONI DN12 131 M6
CUD/GR S72 63 J3
EPW DN9 94 D2
GLE DN14 11 M8
STKB/PEN S36 123 G3
THNE DN8 32 B5
THNE DN8 72 E1
WRKN S81 170 B5
Moor La North
RHAM/THRY S65 131 H7
Moor La South
RHAM/THRY S65 131 H8
Moor Oaks Rd FUL S10 160 A4
Moor Owners Rd THNE DN8 32 F8
Moor Rd DEARNE S63 107 K1 1
GLE DN14 14 E4
GLE DN14 14 A1
GLE DN14 14 C2
RHAM/THRY S65 147 M1
ST/HB/BR S6 142 D3
THNE DN8 50 C2
Moorshutt Rd HEM/SK/SE WF9 41 G1
Moorside FUL S10 158 E7
Moorside Av STKB/PEN S36 79 G5
Moorside Cl DOD/DAR S75 37 M7
MOS S20 179 G7
Moorside Crs HOR/CROF WF4 19 K5
Moorsyde Av FUL S10 159 M2
Moorsyde Crs FUL S10 159 M2
Moorthorpe Gdns MOS S20 178 E5
Moorthorpe Gn HACK/IN S12 178 D5
Moorthorpe Wy MOS S20 178 E5
MOS S20 179 G5
Moor Top Av FEA/AMT WF7 23 J2
Moor Top Dr HEM/SK/SE WF9 41 H2
Moor Top La HOR/CROF WF4 16 B6
Moortop Rd DRON S18 191 M6
Moor Top Rd NROS/TKH DN11 153 K2
Moortown Av DIN S25 166 E8
Moor Va MOS S20 178 D5
Moor Valley Cl HACK/IN S12 178 E6
Moor Vw ARMTH DN3 92 B7
HOR/CROF WF4 19 K2
Moorview KIMB S61 146 B1
Moor View Dr SHEFS S8 176 C5 2
Moor View Rd SHEFS S8 176 C5
Moor View Ter ECC S11 175 J2 2
Moorwinstow Cft
TOT/DORE S17 175 J8 2
Moorwood La ST/HB/BR S6 158 B3
TOT/DORE S17 188 F5
Moorwoods Av
CHPT/GREN S35 126 E1
Moorwoods La
CHPT/GREN S35 126 D2
Moray Pl DRON S18 190 B5
Mordaunt Rd SHEFP/MNR S2 177 K1
More Hall La STKB/PEN S36 124 E3
Morgan Av SHEFN S5 144 C4
Morgan Cl SHEFN S5 144 D4
Morgan Rd SHEFN S5 144 C5
Morland Cl GLV S14 177 K4
Morland Dr GLV S14 177 K4
Morland Pl GLV S14 177 K4
Morland Rd GLV S14 177 J4
Morley Cl DRON S18 190 A6
Morley Fold KBTN HD8 56 D2 2
Morley Pl CONI DN12 109 M6
Morley Rd KIMB S61 128 C6
WHHL DN2 90 C2
Morley St RAW S62 129 K3
ST/HB/BR S6 143 M8
Morpeth St OWL S3 8 E2
RHAM/THRY S65 7 G3 1
Morrall Rd SHEFN S5 126 D8
Morrell St MALT S66 150 E3
Morris Av RAW S62 107 K7
Morris Cl HEM/SK/SE WF9 22 F5
Morrison Av MALT S66 150 E1
Morrison Dr NROS/TKH DN11 113 K7
Morrison Pl WMB/DAR S73 84 E1
Morrison Rd WMB/DAR S73 84 D1
Morris Rd DONS/BSCR DN4 111 J1
Mortain Rd RHAM S60 147 K6
Mortains AU/AST/KP S26 181 K1
Morthen Hall La MALT S66 148 F8
Morthen La MALT S66 148 E7
RHAM S60 164 B1
Morthen Rd MALT S66 149 H7
Mortimer Dr STKB/PEN S36 79 G6
Mortimer Rd MALT S66 151 G3
ST/HB/BR S6 140 F3
STKB/PEN S36 100 F6
STKB/PEN S36 101 G2
Mortimer St SHEF S1 9 J7 1
Mortlake Rd SHEFN S5 145 H5 2
Mortomley Cl CHPT/GREN S35 104 C8
Mortomley La CHPT/GREN S35 104 C8
Morton Cl BSLYN/ROY S71 61 H2 3
Morton Gv WRKN S81 184 C6
Morton La ECK/KIL S21 192 A6
Morton Pl CHPT/GREN S35 126 A7
Morton Rd MEX/SWTN S64 108 F2
Morton Wood Gv
HOLM/MEL HD7 54 B4
Mosborough Hall Dr MOS S20 193 J2
Mosborough Moor MOS S20 178 F7
Mosbrough Rd HAN/WDH S13 161 M8
Moscar Cross Rd ST/HB/BR S6 156 F2
Moses Vw WRKN S81 183 J8
Mosgrove Cl WRKN S81 184 A8
Mosham Cl EPW DN9 115 H1
Mosham Rd EPW DN9 114 F2
Moss Cl MALT S66 148 F3
Mosscroft La HTFD DN7 71 H3
Mossdale WRKN S81 184 E7 2
Mossdale Av MOS S20 179 H8
Mossdale Cl BTLY DN5 67 J8
Moss Dr ECK/KIL S21 194 B2
Moss Edge Rd HOLM/MEL HD7 53 G7
Moss Gv HACK/IN S12 179 H3
Moss Hvn AWLS/ASK DN6 28 F6
Moss La AWLS/ASK DN6 47 G2
Mossley Rd STKB/PEN S36 101 G1
Moss Ri HOLM/MEL HD7 53 J2
Moss Rd AWLS/ASK DN6 28 A7
AWLS/ASK DN6 29 G6
TOT/DORE S17 188 F3
Moss Vw MOS S20 192 F1
Moss Wy HACK/IN S12 179 H4
MOS S20 179 H8
Mostyn Wk HOR/CROF WF4 19 K4
Motehall Dr SHEFP/MNR S2 161 L6
Motehall Pl SHEFP/MNR S2 161 M6
Motehall Rd SHEFP/MNR S2 161 L6
Motehall Wy SHEFP/MNR S2 161 L6 1
The Motte KIMB S61 128 D7
Mottram St BSLYN/ROY S71 3 G4
Mount Av CUD/GR S72 40 E7
CUD/GR S72 63 J6
HEM/SK/SE WF9 23 H7
WRKN S81 198 C2
Mountbatten Dr
CHPT/GREN S35 126 B2
Mount Cl BSLY S70 60 D8
Mount Crs HOY S74 105 H1
Mountenoy Rd RHAM S60 6 F7
Mountfields Wk
HEM/SK/SE WF9 41 M6 3
Mountford Cft
TOT/DORE S17 189 J2 2
Mount Pleasant BSLY S70 82 F3 2
CUD/GR S72 40 E7
DONS/BSCR DN4 89 L8 5
FEA/AMT WF7 23 K1
KBTN HD8 17 H8
Mount Pleasant Cl
CHPT/GREN S35 126 E1 2
Mount Pleasant Rd
DEARNE S63 107 K3
KIMB S61 6 A2
SHEFP/MNR S2 160 D7 6
THNE DN8 31 L5
Mount Rd CHPT/GREN S35 126 C1
CUD/GR S72 40 E7
OWL S3 144 D8
Mount Scar Vw
HOLM/MEL HD7 54 B3
Mount St BSLY S70 2 E8
BSLYN/ROY S71 61 K7
KIMB S61 6 A2
Mount Ter DEARNE S63 107 G1
WMB/DAR S73 84 A4
The Mount ARMTH DN3 69 L6
Mount Vernon Av BSLY S70 60 D8
Mount Vernon Crs BSLY S70 82 E1
Mount Vernon Rd BSLY S70 3 J9
Mount Vw CONI DN12 110 F6 1
Mount View Av SHEFS S8 176 E4
Mount View Gdns SHEFS S8 176 E4 2
Mount View Rd
HOLM/MEL HD7 54 C5
SHEFS S8 176 E5
Mousehole Cl RHAM/THRY S65 130 C6
Mousehole La
RHAM/THRY S65 130 C6
Mouse Park Ga
CHPT/GREN S35 125 K4
Mowbray Gdns
RHAM/THRY S65 130 A7
Mowbray Pl RHAM/THRY S65 130 A7
Mowbray Rd THNE DN8 50 A1
Mowbray St OWL S3 160 E2
RHAM/THRY S65 129 M7
Mowson Crs CHPT/GREN S35 143 H2
Mowson La CHPT/GREN S35 143 H2
Moxon Cl STKB/PEN S36 102 B7
Mucky La BSLYN/ROY S71 61 L6
STKB/PEN S36 101 L3
Muglet La MALT S66 150 F3
Mugup La HOLM/MEL HD7 54 C6
Muirfield WRKN S81 198 F1
Muirfield Av DONS/BSCR DN4 113 M1
MEX/SWTN S64 108 C5
Mulberry Av HOR/CROF WF4 21 M6
THNE DN8 32 A5
Mulberry Cl BTLY DN5 89 H2
RAW S62 129 K4 5
Mulberry Crs WRKN S81 168 D8
Mulberry Pl HOR/CROF WF4 21 M6
Mulberry Rd DIN S25 182 C1
ECK/KIL S21 192 F5
Mulberry St SHEF S1 9 J4
Mulberry Wy ARMTH DN3 91 M3 1
ECK/KIL S21 193 M2 1
Mulehouse Rd FUL S10 159 L3
Mundella Pl SHEFS S8 176 E4
Munro Cl ECK/KIL S21 194 B1
Munsbrough La KIMB S61 128 E5
Munsbrough Ri KIMB S61 128 F4
Murdoch Pl BSLYN/ROY S71 38 C8 5
Murdock Rd SHEFN S5 144 D3
Murrayfield Dr MOS S20 193 J1 6
Murray Rd ECC S11 175 M1
ECK/KIL S21 180 C8 1
RAW S62 129 L1
Musgrave Crs SHEFN S5 144 E6
Musgrave Dr SHEFN S5 144 E6
Musgrave Pl SHEFN S5 144 E6
Musgrave Rd SHEFN S5 144 D6
Musgrove Av RHAM/THRY S65 130 E5
Mushroom La FUL S10 8 B4
Muskoka Av ECC S11 175 J2
Muskoka Dr ECC S11 175 J1
Mutual St DONS/BSCR DN4 4 C7
Myers Av CHPT/GREN S35 125 H7
Myers Grove La ST/HB/BR S6 143 K8
Myers La CHPT/GREN S35 142 E4
Myers St WMB/DAR S73 84 A3
Mylnhurst Rd ECC S11 175 M3
Mylor Ct BSLYN/ROY S71 61 G4 4
Mylor Rd ECC S11 175 L1
Myrtle Crs MALT S66 149 G2
Myrtle Gv AU/AST/KP S26 181 G5
EPW DN9 92 E8
Myrtle Rd HTFD DN7 48 D7
SHEFP/MNR S2 160 E7
WMB/DAR S73 84 A4
Myrtle Springs HACK/IN S12 177 K2
Myrtle St DOD/DAR S75 2 B4
Myton Rd DARN/MH S9 161 L3

N

Nab La HTFD DN7 30 D8
Nairn Dr DRON S18 190 B6 4
Nairn St FUL S10 159 M4
Nancy Crs CUD/GR S72 62 F1 1
Nancy Rd CUD/GR S72 62 F1
Nanny Hl STKB/PEN S36 102 A6
Nanny Marr Rd WMB/DAR S73 84 F1
Nan Sampson Bank EPW DN9 94 B7
Napier Mt BSLY S70 82 D1
Napier St ECC S11 8 D9
Narrow La BTLY DN5 46 B2
BWTY DN10 136 F7
DIN S25 182 C2
NROS/TKH DN11 134 C5
Naseby Av BTLY DN5 89 H1
Naseby Cl HTFD DN7 70 E2 3
Naseby St DARN/MH S9 145 L5
Nash Cl WRKN S81 199 G3
Nathan Ct MOS S20 179 K6
Nathan Dr MOS S20 179 K5
Nathan Gv MOS S20 179 J5
Navan Rd SHEFP/MNR S2 161 L8
Navvy La BSLYN/ROY S71 21 H8
Naylor Gv CHPT/GREN S35 143 G1 1
DOD/DAR S75 59 K8
Naylor Rd CHPT/GREN S35 125 G8
CHPT/GREN S35 143 G1
Naylor St RAW S62 129 K4
Neale Rd WHHL DN2 68 F7
Nearcroft Rd KIMB S61 128 D7
Nearfield Rd DONS/BSCR DN4 113 H1
Needham Wy ECC S11 176 A2
Needlewood DOD/DAR S75 81 K1 3
Neepsend La OWL S3 160 E2 4
Neild Rd HOY S74 105 K1
Neill Rd ECC S11 160 A7
Nelson Av BSLYN/ROY S71 60 E3
Nelson Cl RHAM S60 147 H7
Nelson Pl CHPT/GREN S35 126 B2
Nelson Rd CONI DN12 110 F5
MALT S66 150 F2
ST/HB/BR S6 159 K1
Nelson St BSLY S70 2 F6 2
CUD/GR S72 40 C2
RHAM/THRY S65 7 H4
Nemesia Cl DIN S25 182 A3 1
Nene Gv EPW DN9 92 E8
Nene Wk WRKN S81 184 C8
Nesfield Wy SHEFN S5 145 H3
Nether Av CHPT/GREN S35 126 B6
ECK/KIL S21 194 A1
Nether Cantley La ARMTH DN3 91 M5
Nether Crs CHPT/GREN S35 126 B6
Nethercroft DOD/DAR S75 59 J2
Netherdene Rd DRON S18 190 E6
Nether Edge Rd ABRD S7 176 C2
Netherfield Av HOR/CROF WF4 18 B2
Netherfield Cl
STKB/PEN S36 102 D6 2
Netherfield Crs HOR/CROF WF4 18 B2
Netherfield La RAW S62 129 K3
Netherfield Pl
HOR/CROF WF4 18 B1 1
Netherfield Rd FUL S10 159 M2
Netherfields Crs DRON S18 190 E7
Netherfield Vw
RHAM/THRY S65 130 B7
Nethergate ST/HB/BR S6 158 F2
Nethergreen Av ECK/KIL S21 180 B8
Nethergreen Ct ECK/KIL S21 180 B8 1
Nethergreen Gdns
ECK/KIL S21 180 B8 2
Nethergreen Rd ECC S11 159 J7
Nether Hall Rd DON DN1 5 G4
Nether House La STKB/PEN S36 78 B8
Netherhouses
HOLM/MEL HD7 53 H2 3
Nether La CHPT/GREN S35 126 F5
Nether Ley Av CHPT/GREN S35 126 E2
Nether Ley Ct
CHPT/GREN S35 126 E2 4
Nether Ley Cft
CHPT/GREN S35 126 E2 5
Nether Ley Gdns
CHPT/GREN S35 126 E2 6
Nethermoor Av ECK/KIL S21 180 B8 3
Nethermoor Cl ECK/KIL S21 180 B8 4
Nethermoor Dr ECK/KIL S21 180 B8
MALT S66 149 G5
Nethermoor La ECK/KIL S21 180 B8
Nether Oak Cl MOS S20 179 M5 2
Nether Oak Dr MOS S20 179 M5
Nether Oak Vw MOS S20 179 M5 3
Nether Rd DOD/DAR S75 58 E6
Nether Shire La SHEFN S5 127 G8
Netherthorpe La ECK/KIL S21 194 A1
Netherthorpe Pl OWL S3 8 E1
Netherthorpe Rd OWL S3 8 D3
Nether Thorpe Rd WRKS S80 196 E2
Netherthorpe St OWL S3 8 E2 1
Netherthorpe Wy DIN S25 166 C8
Netherton Hall Gdns
HOR/CROF WF4 18 C1 4
Netherton La HOR/CROF WF4 18 B1
Netherton Pl WRKS S80 198 E6
Netherton Rd WRKS S80 198 E6
Netherwood Rd WMB/DAR S73 84 B2
Nettle Cft NROS/TKH DN11 135 G8
Nettleham Rd SHEFS S8 176 D4
Nettleholme HTFD DN7 48 F7
Neville Av BSLY S70 61 G8
Neville Cl BSLY S70 61 H8 2
HEM/SK/SE WF9 42 A4
OWL S3 160 F2
WMB/DAR S73 83 M3
Neville Ct WMB/DAR S73 83 M3
Neville Crs BSLY S70 61 H8
Neville Dr OWL S3 160 F1
Neville La HTFD DN7 29 L7
Neville Pits La GLE DN14 10 B6
Neville Rd KIMB S61 128 D6
Neville St RHAM S60 6 E3
Newall Crs HEM/SK/SE WF9 22 D4
Newall Dr BWTY DN10 155 L6
Newark Cl DOD/DAR S75 37 M5
Newark Rd MEX/SWTN S64 108 C2
Newark St DARN/MH S9 145 L8 1
NROS/TKH DN11 113 J6
Newbiggin Cl RAW S62 129 J3
Newbiggin Dr RAW S62 129 J3
Newbold Ter BTLY DN5 89 K1
Newbolt Rd DONS/BSCR DN4 111 M1
Newbould Crs MOS S20 179 L4
Newbould La FUL S10 160 A5
Newbridge Gv CONI DN12 111 G5 1
Newburn Dr DARN/MH S9 146 C5
Newbury Dr HEM/SK/SE WF9 42 E2
Newbury Rd FUL S10 159 M3 5
Newbury Wy BTLY DN5 89 H1 4
Newby Crs DONS/BSCR DN4 111 L2
Newcastle Av WRKS S80 198 B5
Newcastle Cl DIN S25 166 C8 2
Newcastle St SHEF S1 8 F4
WRKS S80 198 C5
New Chapel Av STKB/PEN S36 79 G6
New Cl DOD/DAR S75 58 D7
New Close La AWLS/ASK DN6 26 C8
Newcomen Rd BTLY DN5 4 A1
Newcroft Cl MOS S20 179 M4
New Cross Dr HAN/WDH S13 178 E1
New Cross Wy HAN/WDH S13 178 E1
Newdale Av CUD/GR S72 61 L2 1
New Droppingwell Rd
KIMB S61 145 M1
Newent La FUL S10 159 M3
Newfield Av BSLYN/ROY S71 61 H3
Newfield Crs DEARNE S63 107 H2
TOT/DORE S17 175 G8
Newfield Cft TOT/DORE S17 175 G7
Newfield Farm Cl
SHEFP/MNR S2 177 J2 1
Newfield Green Rd
SHEFP/MNR S2 177 H1
Newfield La TOT/DORE S17 175 G8
Newfields Av THNE DN8 32 A5
Newfields Cl THNE DN8 32 A5
Newfields Dr THNE DN8 32 A5
New Fold HOLM/MEL HD7 53 K3
New Ga HOLM/MEL HD7 54 A6
Newgate Cl CHPT/GREN S35 104 B8
Newgate St WRKS S80 198 D5
New Gn HTFD DN7 48 C3
New Hall Ap HOR/CROF WF4 17 J3
Newhall Av MALT S66 149 G5
New Hall Cl HOR/CROF WF4 19 J3
New Hall Crs STKB/PEN S36 101 K5 2
New Hall La HOR/CROF WF4 17 K3
Newhall La MALT S66 149 L4
New Hall La STKB/PEN S36 101 J6
Newhall Rd ARMTH DN3 69 L4
ATT S4 145 J7
DARN/MH S9 145 K8
New Hall Wy HOR/CROF WF4 17 K4
New Hl CONI DN12 110 A5
Newhill HEM/SK/SE WF9 41 M6 4
Newhill Rd BSLYN/ROY S71 60 E2
DEARNE S63 107 H2
New Holles Ct WRKS S80 198 D6
Newholme Dr THNE DN8 32 A4 1
New Ings ARMTH DN3 91 L1
New Ings La ARMTH DN3 47 H5
Newington Av CUD/GR S72 39 M7 2
Newington Dr AU/AST/KP S26 164 C8
Newington Rd BWTY DN10 137 G7
ECC S11 160 A7
New Inn La HTFD DN7 48 C2 2
New Laithe La HOLM/MEL HD7 53 M2
Newland Av CUD/GR S72 61 L2
MALT S66 150 D1
Newland Rd BSLYN/ROY S71 38 C8
Newlands Av AWLS/ASK DN6 44 C5
HACK/IN S12 177 L1
KBTN HD8 35 K5
Newlands Cl DONS/BSCR DN4 113 K1
Newlands Dr BTLY DN5 89 K2
HACK/IN S12 177 L1
Newlands Gv HACK/IN S12 177 M1
Newlands Rd HACK/IN S12 177 L1
New La BTLY DN5 88 E6
HEM/SK/SE WF9 42 E1
KBTN HD8 34 F6
NROS/TKH DN11 113 L6
New Lane Crs HEM/SK/SE WF9 24 E8
New Lodge Crs BSLYN/ROY S71 38 C8
Newlyn Dr BSLYN/ROY S71 3 L2
Newlyn Pl SHEFS S8 176 D4
Newlyn Rd SHEFS S8 176 D4
Newman Av BSLYN/ROY S71 39 G6
Newman Cl DARN/MH S9 145 M3 5
Newman Ct RHAM S60 147 L5
Newman Dr DARN/MH S9 145 L3
Newman Rd DARN/MH S9 145 L4
RHAM S60 147 L5
Newmarche Dr AWLS/ASK DN6 28 A7
Newmarch St DARN/MH S9 146 C4
Newmarket Rd
DONS/BSCR DN4 91 H5
New Mdw RAW S62 107 H7
New Mill Bank STKB/PEN S36 124 A2
New Mill Field Rd HTFD DN7 49 H8
HTFD DN7 71 H1
New Mill Rd HOLM/MEL HD7 53 M1
New Orchard La MALT S66 149 K8
New Orchard Rd MALT S66 149 J8
New Park Est HTFD DN7 48 E2
New Rd AWLS/ASK DN6 26 E7
AWLS/ASK DN6 27 K4
DEARNE S63 107 K1
DIN S25 166 D7
DIN S25 182 A1
DOD/DAR S75 37 L5
DOD/DAR S75 38 A6
DOD/DAR S75 57 M1
DOD/DAR S75 104 B2
DOD/DAR S75 104 D3
DRON S18 191 L6
HEM/SK/SE WF9 24 B5
HOR/CROF WF4 17 K1
HOR/CROF WF4 37 M1
HOY S74 84 B8
KIMB S61 145 M2
MALT S66 132 C4
NROS/TKH DN11 134 E8
NROS/TKH DN11 134 A1
ST/HB/BR S6 142 A4
ST/HB/BR S6 142 C5
STKB/PEN S36 57 J6
STKB/PEN S36 102 B6
STKB/PEN S36 123 K3
STV/CWN S43 194 F8
WRKN S81 167 K2
New Rw HOLM/MEL HD7 53 L2
New Row La STKB/PEN S36 56 C7
New Royd STKB/PEN S36 78 B4
Newsam Rd MEX/SWTN S64 108 B6
Newsham Rd SHEFS S8 176 D2
New Smithy Av
STKB/PEN S36 78 E3 2
New Smithy Dr STKB/PEN S36 78 E3
Newsome Av WMB/DAR S73 83 M4
New Station Rd
MEX/SWTN S64 108 C4
Newstead Av CHPT/GREN S35 125 H7
HACK/IN S12 178 C5
HEM/SK/SE WF9 22 E4
Newstead Cl DRON S18 190 A6 9
HACK/IN S12 178 C4 4
Newstead Crs HEM/SK/SE WF9 22 E3
Newstead Dr HACK/IN S12 178 C5
HEM/SK/SE WF9 22 E4
Newstead Gv HACK/IN S12 178 C4 5
HEM/SK/SE WF9 22 E4
Newstead La HOR/CROF WF4 22 C4
Newstead Pl HACK/IN S12 178 C4
Newstead Ri HACK/IN S12 178 C5
Newstead Rd BSLYN/ROY S71 38 C7
BTLY DN5 67 K6
HACK/IN S12 178 C4
Newstead Ter HEM/SK/SE WF9 22 E4
Newstead Vw HEM/SK/SE WF9 22 D4
Newstead Wy HACK/IN S12 178 C5
New St AWLS/ASK DN6 45 H6
BSLY S70 2 F7
BSLY S70 3 G6
BSLY S70 82 E3 6
BSLY S70 83 G3
BSLYN/ROY S71 39 G4
BSLYN/ROY S71 61 J7 2

BTLY DN5 .... 67 L7
CHPT/GREN S35 .... 104 B7
CUD/GR S72 .... 40 B1
CUD/GR S72 .... 62 E1
CUD/GR S72 .... 63 J6
DEARNE S63 .... 86 B8
DIN S25 .... 166 C3
DIN S25 .... 166 D6
DOD/DAR S75 .... 37 M6
DOD/DAR S75 .... 81 K1
DON DN1 .... 4 F8
EPW DN9 .... 115 J2
FEA/AMT WF7 .... 23 K2
HEM/SK/SE WF9 .... 23 C5
HEM/SK/SE WF9 .... 42 C4
KBTN HD8 .... 34 E6
KBTN HD8 .... 35 H6
KIMB S61 .... 127 K3
KIMB S61 .... 128 F3
MEX/SWTN S64 .... 109 H2
MOS S20 .... 179 L7
RAW S62 .... 129 K2
RHAM S60 .... 163 H1
SHEF S1 .... 9 H3
WMB/DAR S73 .... 83 M8
WMB/DAR S73 .... 84 C4
New Street Bus Link *MOS* S20 .... 179 L7
New Street La *SHEF/MNR* S2 .... 9 L3
Newthorpe Rd *AWLS/ASK* DN6 .... 27 C3
Newton Av *STKB/PEN* S36 .... 101 K5
Newton Cl *WRKN* S81 .... 184 A8
Newton Dr *BTLY* DN5 .... 89 K4
RHAM/THRY S65 .... 7 L5
Newton La *BTLY* DN5 .... 89 K4
SHEF S1 .... 9 H7
STKB/PEN S36 .... 101 K5
Newton Pl *KIMB* S61 .... 127 K4
Newton Rd *CHPT/GREN* S35 .... 126 C1
Newton St *BSLY* S70 .... 2 D5
RHAM/THRY S65 .... 7 L4
Newtown Av *BSLYN/ROY* S71 .... 38 F3
CUD/GR S72 .... 61 M2
Newtown Gn *CUD/GR* S72 .... 61 M2
Newtree Dr *NROS/TKH* DN11 .... 133 M1
Niagara Rd *ST/HB/BR* S6 .... 144 A4
Nicholas La *DEARNE* S63 .... 86 A2
Nicholas St *BSLY* S70 .... 2 D6
DOD/DAR S75 .... 59 J3
Nicholson Pl *SHEFS* S8 .... 176 F1
Nicholson Rd *DONS/BSCR* DN4 .... 4 A8
SHEFS S8 .... 176 L1
Nichols Rd *ST/HB/BR* S6 .... 159 L2
Nickerwood Dr
AU/AST/KP S26 .... 180 B1
Nidderdale Pl *MALT* S66 .... 149 G1
Nidderdale Rd *KIMB* S61 .... 128 D4
Nidd Rd *DARN/MH* S9 .... 161 L2
Nidd Rd East *DARN/MH* S9 .... 161 L2
Nightingale Ct *RHAM* S60 .... 6 F6
Nightingale Cft *KIMB* S61 .... 127 L1
Nightingale Gv *WRKN* S81 .... 184 B8
Nightingale Rd
CHPT/GREN S35 .... 126 B7
Nile St *FUL* S10 .... 160 A5
Ninelands Rd *EPW* DN9 .... 94 B7
Ninescores La *EPW* DN9 .... 94 B7
Ninevah La *HEM/SK/SE* WF9 .... 24 B4
Ninian Gv *DONS/BSCR* DN4 .... 91 J7
Noble St *HOY* S74 .... 105 K2
Nodder Rd *HAN/WDH* S13 .... 162 A8
Noehill Pl *SHEFP/MNR* S2 .... 161 M6
Noehill Rd *SHEFP/MNR* S2 .... 161 M6
Nookery Cl *MALT* S66 .... 150 F1
Nooking Cl *ARMTH* DN3 .... 92 A1
Nook La *ST/HB/BR* S6 .... 159 G1
STKB/PEN S36 .... 79 J6
The Nook *FUL* S10 .... 8 A2
STKB/PEN S36 .... 79 L1
Nora St *DEARNE* S63 .... 86 D1
Norborough Rd *DARN/MH* S9 .... 146 C5
WHHL DN2 .... 5 L1
Norbreck Av *AWLS/ASK* DN6 .... 28 A8
DONS/BSCR DN4 .... 111 G2
Norbrook Wy *RHAM* S60 .... 148 B6
Norburn Dr *ECK/KIL* S21 .... 194 B1
Norbury Cl *DRON* S18 .... 190 B6
Norcroft *BSLY* S70 .... 82 D1
Norcroft La *DOD/DAR* S75 .... 58 C4
Norfolk Av *NROS/TKH* DN11 .... 154 B3
Norfolk Cl *BSLYN/ROY* S71 .... 60 F3
Norfolk Dr *DIN* S25 .... 182 C1
NROS/TKH DN11 .... 154 A3
Norfolk Gv *NROS/TKH* DN11 .... 154 A3
Norfolk Hl *CHPT/GREN* S35 .... 126 A6
Norfolk La *SHEF* S1 .... 9 H5
Norfolk Park Av
SHEFP/MNR S2 .... 161 H7
Norfolk Park Dr *SHEFP/MNR* S2 .... 9 L9
Norfolk Park Rd *SHEFP/MNR* S2 .... 9 L8
Norfolk Pl *MALT* S66 .... 150 E2
Norfolk Rd *CUD/GR* S72 .... 63 J6
DONS/BSCR DN4 .... 111 M1
NROS/TKH DN11 .... 154 A3
SHEFP/MNR S2 .... 9 L6
Norfolk Rw *SHEF* S1 .... 9 H4
Norfolk St *RHAM/THRY* S65 .... 7 G3
SHEF S1 .... 9 H5
WRKS S80 .... 198 C5
Norfolk Wy *RHAM* S60 .... 147 L5
Norgreave Wy *MOS* S20 .... 179 J8
Norman Cl *BSLY* S70 .... 82 E2
BSLYN/ROY S71 .... 61 C3
Norman Cres *BTLY* DN5 .... 67 H8
NROS/TKH DN11 .... 113 J2
Normancroft Crs
SHEFP/MNR S2 .... 162 A6
Normancroft Dr
SHEFP/MNR S2 .... 161 M6
Normancroft Wy
SHEFP/MNR S2 .... 161 M6
Normandale Av *ST/HB/BR* S6 .... 143 H7
Normandale Rd *CUD/GR* S72 .... 63 H8
ST/HB/BR S6 .... 144 B8
Norman Rd *HTFD* DN7 .... 70 F1
Norman Rd *HTFD* DN7 .... 70 E1

Norman St *DARN/MH* S9 .... 145 L8
DEARNE S63 .... 64 C7
Normanton Gdns *ATT* S4 .... 145 L8
Normanton Gv *HAN/WDH* S13 .... 178 D1
Normanton Hl *HACK/IN* S12 .... 178 A1
Normanton Spring Ct
HAN/WDH S13 .... 178 C1
Normanton Spring Rd
HAN/WDH S13 .... 178 C2
Normanville Av *RHAM* S60 .... 146 F6
Nornay Cl *WRKN* S81 .... 169 L3
Norrel's Cft *RHAM* S60 .... 7 K9
Norridge Bottom
HOLM/MEL HD7 .... 53 L2
Norris Rd *ST/HB/BR* S6 .... 143 M7
Norroy St *ATT* S4 .... 161 H1
Norstead Crs *MALT* S66 .... 149 J1
Northampton Rd *WHHL* DN2 .... 91 G2
North Av *BWTY* DN10 .... 136 E7
HEM/SK/SE WF9 .... 42 D5
North Bridge Rd *BTLY* DN5 .... 4 D7
North Church St *SHEF* S1 .... 9 H3
North Cliff Rd *CONI* DN12 .... 109 M4
North Cl *BSLYN/ROY* S71 .... 39 G4
North Common Rd *THNE* DN8 .... 31 K3
Northcote Av *SHEFS* S8 .... 176 F1
Northcote Rd *SHEFS* S8 .... 176 F1
North Crs *ECK/KIL* S21 .... 180 C7
HEM/SK/SE WF9 .... 42 F3
RHAM/THRY S65 .... 7 M2
Northcroft AV *HEM/SK/SE* WF9 .... 42 E4
Northcroft Av *HEM/SK/SE* WF9 .... 42 E3
North Dr *KIMB* S61 .... 6 E1
North Eastern Rd *THNE* DN8 .... 31 L7
North End Dr *BTLY* DN5 .... 87 C5
Northern Av *SHEFP/MNR* S2 .... 161 J8
Northern Common *DRON* S18 .... 189 M4
North Farm Cl *AU/AST/KP* S26 .... 181 J8
North Farm Ct *AU/AST/KP* S26 .... 164 D8
North Fld *DOD/DAR* S75 .... 58 D7
Northfield Av *FUL* S10 .... 159 M2
HEM/SK/SE WF9 .... 41 M3
RAW S62 .... 107 K8
Northfield Cl *FUL* S10 .... 160 A2
Northfield Cl *MALT* S66 .... 148 F3
Northfield Dr *WRKN* S81 .... 183 J3
Northfield Gv *HEM/SK/SE* WF9 .... 41 M4
Northfield La *HEM/SK/SE* WF9 .... 41 M3
North Field La *MALT* S66 .... 148 E2
North Field Rd *AWLS/ASK* DN6 .... 43 J7
Northfield Rd *BTLY* DN5 .... 4 B1
FUL S10 .... 159 M3
RHAM S60 .... 6 F2
Northfield St *HEM/SK/SE* WF9 .... 41 M4
Northgate *CUD/GR* S72 .... 40 C1
NROS/TKH DN11 .... 134 E7
Northgate *THNE* DN8 .... 32 B3
North Hill Rd *SHEFN* S5 .... 144 D3
North Ings Rd *HTFD* DN7 .... 49 H7
Northlands *AU/AST/KP* S26 .... 181 J3
BSLYN/ROY S71 .... 39 G3
North La *GLE* DN14 .... 11 M8
GLE DN14 .... 12 C7
STKB/PEN S36 .... 57 K5
North Park La *AWLS/ASK* DN6 .... 45 H4
North Pitt St *KIMB* S61 .... 146 F1
North Pl *DOD/DAR* S75 .... 59 M4
RHAM/THRY S65 .... 7 M2
North Qd *SHEFN* S5 .... 145 H3
North Rd *ARMTH* DN3 .... 47 C7
BSLYN/ROY S71 .... 39 H3
RHAM/THRY S65 .... 129 M8
RTFD DN22 .... 187 M5
North Royds Wd
BSLYN/ROY S71 .... 39 D6
Northside Rd *DEARNE* S63 .... 107 K1
North St *CONI* DN12 .... 111 C5
DONS/BSCR DN4 .... 5 H8
HEM/SK/SE WF9 .... 41 M4
KIMB S61 .... 6 C2
MEX/SWTN S64 .... 108 C4
RAW S62 .... 107 M8
WMB/DAR S73 .... 84 E1
North Swaithe Cl *BTLY* DN5 .... 67 L5
Northumberland Av *HOY* S74 .... 83 J8
WHHL DN2 .... 90 F2
WRKN S81 .... 168 C8
Northumberland Rd *FUL* S10 .... 160 A4
Northumberland Wy
BSLYN/ROY S71 .... 61 K7
Northumbria Cl *WRKN* S81 .... 198 E1
North Wk *HEM/SK/SE* WF9 .... 23 H7
North Wy *WRKN* S81 .... 168 D8
Northwood *WRKN* S81 .... 198 E1
Norton & Kirk Smeaton Rd
PONT WF8 .... 26 B2
Norton Av *HACK/IN* S12 .... 177 K5
SHEFS S8 .... 177 G6
Norton Church Glebe
SHEFS S8 .... 176 F6
Norton Church Rd *SHEFS* S8 .... 176 F6
Norton Common La
AWLS/ASK DN6 .... 27 K4
Norton Common Rd
AWLS/ASK DN6 .... 27 M5
Norton Green Cl *SHEFS* S8 .... 177 G6
Norton Hammer La
SHEFS S8 .... 176 C3
Norton La *SHEFS* S8 .... 176 E4
Norton Lees Cl *SHEFS* S8 .... 176 E4
Norton Lees Crs *SHEFS* S8 .... 176 E3
Norton Lees La *SHEFS* S8 .... 176 D3
Norton Lees Rd *SHEFS* S8 .... 176 D3
Norton Lees Sq *SHEFS* S8 .... 176 E3
Norton Ms *SHEFS* S8 .... 177 G6
Norton Mill La *AWLS/ASK* DN6 .... 27 H5
Norton Park Av *SHEFS* S8 .... 176 F7
Norton Park Crs *SHEFS* S8 .... 176 E7
Norton Park Dr *SHEFS* S8 .... 176 E7
Norton Park Rd *SHEFS* S8 .... 176 E8
Norton Park Vw *SHEFS* S8 .... 176 E7
Norton Rd *DEARNE* S63 .... 85 H8
SHEFS S8 .... 177 J5
WHHL DN2 .... 90 F2
Norville Crs *WMB/DAR* S73 .... 84 F1

Norwich Rd *WHHL* DN2 .... 68 E8
Norwith Rd *DONS/BSCR* DN4 .... 113 H1
Norwood Av *EPW* DN9 .... 92 E1
HEM/SK/SE WF9 .... 41 M3
SHEFN S5 .... 144 F6
Norwood Cl *MALT* S66 .... 150 D1
SHEFN S5 .... 144 F6
Norwood Crs *AU/AST/KP* S26 .... 181 G8
ECK/KIL S21 .... 180 D8
Norwood Dr *BTLY* DN5 .... 67 L4
DOD/DAR S75 .... 59 J4
Norwood Grange Dr *SHEFN* S5 .... 144 F5
Norwood La *STKB/PEN* S36 .... 78 D2
Norwood Pl *ECK/KIL* S21 .... 180 D8
Nor Wood Rd *HEM/SK/SE* WF9 .... 41 H2
Norwood Rd *CONI* DN12 .... 109 M5
HTFD DN7 .... 48 D6
SHEFN S5 .... 144 F6
Norwood St *RHAM/THRY* S65 .... 130 B6
Nostell Fold *DOD/DAR* S75 .... 81 K1
Nostell La *HOR/CROF* WF4 .... 21 M5
Nostell Pl *DONS/BSCR* DN4 .... 113 H1
Nottingham Cliff *OWL* S3 .... 160 E1
Nottingham Cl *BSLYN/ROY* S71 .... 61 L8
BTLY DN5 .... 89 H1
DIN S25 .... 182 B4
Nottingham St *OWL* S3 .... 144 F8
RHAM/THRY S65 .... 7 C3
Notton La *HOR/CROF* WF4 .... 21 C8
Novello St *MALT* S66 .... 151 C3
Nowill Ct *SHEFS* S8 .... 176 E1
Nowill Pl *SHEFS* S8 .... 176 E1
Nunnery Crs *RHAM* S60 .... 163 G1
Nunnery Dr *SHEFP/MNR* S2 .... 161 K3
Nunnery Ter *SHEFP/MNR* S2 .... 161 J4
Nunthorpe Ct *HTFD* DN7 .... 48 F8
Nursery Crs *DIN* S25 .... 182 B1
Nursery Dr *CHPT/GREN* S35 .... 126 F7
RHAM S60 .... 163 G1
Nursery Gdns *BSLYN/ROY* S71 .... 61 J8
Nursery La *CHPT/GREN* S35 .... 126 F7
Nursery La *BSLY* S70 .... 88 E8
OWL S3 .... 9 J1
Nursery Rd *AU/AST/KP* S26 .... 164 A7
DIN S25 .... 166 C8
Nursery St *BSLY* S70 .... 2 F8
OWL S3 .... 9 H1
Nutfields Gv *HTFD* DN7 .... 48 D3
Nuttall Pl *SHEFP/MNR* S2 .... 161 H4
Nutwell Cl *DONS/BSCR* DN4 .... 113 J1
Nutwell La *ARMTH* DN3 .... 91 M1

O

Oak Av *DEARNE* S63 .... 107 L2
Oakbank Cl *MEX/SWTN* S64 .... 108 B7
Oakbank Cl *TOT/DORE* S17 .... 189 K7
Oakbrook Rd *ECC* S11 .... 159 K2
Oak Cl *ECK/KIL* S21 .... 194 A2
HOY S74 .... 105 G2
MALT S66 .... 148 F1
MEX/SWTN S64 .... 108 C2
WRKS S80 .... 198 C6
Oak Ct *BTLY* DN5 .... 89 H6
MEX/SWTN S64 .... 108 C2
Oak Crs *THNE* DN8 .... 31 M6
Oakcrest *DONS/BSCR* DN4 .... 113 M3
Oakdale *BSLY* S70 .... 82 F7
Oakdale Cl *ARMTH* DN3 .... 69 K6
Oakdale Pl *KIMB* S61 .... 146 F1
Oak Dale Rd *DONS/BSCR* DN4 .... 111 C3
Oakdale Rd *DIN* S25 .... 182 C2
ECC S11 .... 176 B1
KIMB S61 .... 146 D2
Oakdell *DRON* S18 .... 191 H4
Oakdene *NROS/TKH* DN11 .... 113 K4
Oaken Wood Cl *KIMB* S61 .... 127 L2
Oaken Wood Rd *KIMB* S61 .... 127 K2
Oakes Gn *DARN/MH* S9 .... 161 K1
Oakes Park Vw *SHEFS* S8 .... 177 H6
Oakes St *DARN/MH* S9 .... 145 M3
Oakfern Gv *CHPT/GREN* S35 .... 104 C3
Oakfield Gv *KBTN* HD8 .... 34 E6
Oakfield Pk *PONT* WF8 .... 24 F3
Oakfield Wk *DOD/DAR* S75 .... 59 M5
Oak Gv *CONI* DN12 .... 109 M6
Oak Grove Gn *TOT/DORE* S17 .... 189 J3
Oak Hall Pk *HOR/CROF* WF4 .... 19 L8
Oakham Dr *OWL* S3 .... 160 D1
Oakham Pl *DOD/DAR* S75 .... 2 A2
Oak Haven Av *CUD/GR* S72 .... 63 J6
Oakhill Rd *ABRD* S7 .... 176 B1
DRON S18 .... 191 C4
WHHL DN2 .... 90 F1
Oakholme Av *WRKN* S81 .... 198 C1
Oakholme Ms *ECC* S11 .... 160 A6
Oakholme Ri *WRKN* S81 .... 198 D1
Oakholme Rd *ECC* S11 .... 160 A6
Oakland Av *HTFD* DN7 .... 48 C8
Oakland Cl *WRKN* S81 .... 183 J2
Oakland Dr *HOR/CROF* WF4 .... 18 A2
Oakland Rd *HOR/CROF* WF4 .... 18 B2
ST/HB/BR S6 .... 143 M7
Oaklands *ARMTH* DN3 .... 114 A3
Oaklands Av *BSLYN/ROY* S71 .... 61 G3
Oaklands Cft *DONS/BSCR* DN4 .... 91 H7
NROS/TKH DN11 .... 153 H5
Oaklands Gdns
DONS/BSCR DN4 .... 91 H8
Oaklands Pl *DEARNE* S63 .... 107 J2
Oak La *GLE* DN14 .... 13 G4
Oak Lea *KIMB* S61 .... 128 F4
Oak Lea Av *DEARNE* S63 .... 85 G8
Oaklea Cl *DOD/DAR* S75 .... 37 M5
Oaklea Gv *BSLY* S70 .... 83 C3
Oak Leigh *DOD/DAR* S75 .... 58 C3
Oakley Rd *HAN/WDH* S13 .... 162 C5
Oak Lodge Rd *CHPT/GREN* S35 .... 104 A8
Oakmoor Rd *THNE* DN8 .... 32 B3
Oak Pk *FUL* S10 .... 159 M5
Oak Rd *ARMTH* DN3 .... 69 L7
CUD/GR S72 .... 40 B5
DEARNE S63 .... 64 C7
DEARNE S63 .... 107 L2
HACK/IN S12 .... 177 L5
MALT S66 .... 150 B2
MEX/SWTN S64 .... 108 C2
MOS S20 .... 179 K3
THNE DN8 .... 31 M6
Oaks Av *STKB/PEN* S36 .... 101 L6
Oak Scar La *HOLM/MEL* HD7 .... 54 B5
Oaks Cl *DEARNE* S63 .... 107 L3
RTFD DN22 .... 170 F2
Oaks Crs *BSLY* S70 .... 61 G7
Oaks Farm Dr *DOD/DAR* S75 .... 37 K7
Oaks Fold *SHEFN* S5 .... 145 J1
Oaks Fold Av *SHEFN* S5 .... 145 J2
Oaks Fold Rd *SHEFN* S5 .... 145 J2
Oaks La *BSLY* S70 .... 61 G7
BSLYN/ROY S71 .... 61 G6
SHEFN S5 .... 145 J2
ST/HB/BR S6 .... 142 A5
STKB/PEN S36 .... 101 G4
Oak St *BSLY* S70 .... 2 D6
CUD/GR S72 .... 62 F2
HEM/SK/SE WF9 .... 42 C6
MOS S20 .... 179 G7
SHEFS S8 .... 160 E8
Oaks Wood Dr *DOD/DAR* S75 .... 37 K7
Oak Ter *AU/AST/KP* S26 .... 163 M7
DONS/BSCR DN4 .... 4 F9
Oak Tree Av *CUD/GR* S72 .... 39 M8
Oak Tree Cl *DOD/DAR* S75 .... 37 H7
Oak Tree Dr *HEM/SK/SE* WF9 .... 41 K1
Oaktree La *HEM/SK/SE* WF9 .... 24 C4
Oak Tree Meadow
WKFDW/WTN WF2 .... 20 E1
Oak Tree Ri *WRKN* S81 .... 168 C8
Oak Tree Rd *ARMTH* DN3 .... 92 C6
BWTY DN10 .... 136 D8
Oakwell Cl *HEM/SK/SE* WF9 .... 22 E5
MALT S66 .... 150 E1
Oakwell Dr *AWLS/ASK* DN6 .... 28 A7
Oak Well La *BSLYN/ROY* S71 .... 3 J6
Oakwell Ter *BSLYN/ROY* S71 .... 3 J7
BSLYN/ROY S71 .... 3 K7
Oakwell Vw *BSLYN/ROY* S71 .... 3 K6
Oakwood Av *BSLYN/ROY* S71 .... 38 F3
SHEFN S5 .... 126 E8
Oakwood Cl *BSLY* S70 .... 83 G3
CHPT/GREN S35 .... 143 H2
RAW S62 .... 107 J8
Oakwood Crs *BSLYN/ROY* S71 .... 38 F4
HEM/SK/SE WF9 .... 41 K2
RHAM S60 .... 147 L4
Oakwood Dr *ARMTH* DN3 .... 92 B7
HEM/SK/SE WF9 .... 41 K2
RHAM S60 .... 147 L4
Oakwood Gv *RHAM* S60 .... 7 L9
Oakwood Ms *WRKS* S80 .... 198 A4
Oakwood Pk *GLE* DN14 .... 11 J3
Oakwood Rd *BSLYN/ROY* S71 .... 38 F3
DONS/BSCR DN4 .... 89 K8
Oakwood Rd East *RHAM* S60 .... 147 L4
Oakwood Rd West *RHAM* S60 .... 147 L4
Oakwood Sq *DOD/DAR* S75 .... 36 F7
Oakworth Cl *DOD/DAR* S75 .... 59 M4
MOS S20 .... 193 J1
Oakworth Dr *MOS* S20 .... 193 H1
Oakworth Gv *MOS* S20 .... 193 H1
Oakworth Vw *MOS* S20 .... 193 H1
Oates Av *RAW* S62 .... 129 L2
Oates Cl *KIMB* S61 .... 128 E8
Oates St *KIMB* S61 .... 128 E8
Oats Orch *MOS* S20 .... 193 H1
Oberon Crs *WMB/DAR* S73 .... 84 D1
Oborne Cl *RHAM/THRY* S65 .... 131 J7
Occupation La *HACK/IN* S12 .... 178 D4
Occupation Rd *RAW* S62 .... 105 H6
RAW S62 .... 129 J3
Ochre Dike Cl *MOS* S20 .... 179 J5
Ochre Dike La *MOS* S20 .... 179 H5
Octavia Cl *RHAM* S60 .... 147 G5
Oddfellows Rd *HATH/EY* S32 .... 172 E8
Oddy La *NROS/TKH* DN11 .... 134 C4
Odom Ct *SHEFS* S8 .... 176 F1
Offley La *HEM/SK/SE* WF9 .... 22 F1
Ogden Rd *WHHL* DN2 .... 69 H7
Oil Mill Fold *RHAM* S60 .... 6 F5
Oldale Cl *HAN/WDH* S13 .... 179 G1
Oldale Ct *HAN/WDH* S13 .... 179 G1
Oldale Gv *HAN/WDH* S13 .... 179 G1
Old Anna La Or Long La
STKB/PEN S36 .... 78 E3
Old Bar La *HOLM/MEL* HD7 .... 54 F7
Old Bawtry Rd *EPW* DN9 .... 115 H6
Old Blyth Rd *RTFD* DN22 .... 186 D7
Old Carpenter's Yd *HTFD* DN7 .... 48 B2
Old Coach Rd *WRKS* S80 .... 199 K8
Oldcoates Cl *DIN* S25 .... 166 D5
Oldcoates Rd *DIN* S25 .... 166 E4
Old Cross La *DEARNE* S63 .... 107 K1
Old Epworth Rd (East)
HTFD DN7 .... 49 J8
Old Farm Ct *MEX/SWTN* S64 .... 108 C1
Oldfield Av *CONI* DN12 .... 109 K5
ST/HB/BR S6 .... 159 H1
Oldfield Cl *ARMTH* DN3 .... 47 M3
HOY S74 .... 105 J1
HTFD DN7 .... 48 B4
Oldfield Crs *HTFD* DN7 .... 48 C5
Oldfield Gv *ST/HB/BR* S6 .... 159 H2
Old Field La *HTFD* DN7 .... 47 M5
Oldfield La *HTFD* DN7 .... 48 C4
KBTN HD8 .... 35 H5
Oldfield Rd *RHAM/THRY* S65 .... 130 B8
ST/HB/BR S6 .... 159 H2
THNE DN8 .... 50 A1
Oldfield Ter *ST/HB/BR* S6 .... 159 H2
Old Fulwood Rd *ECC* S11 .... 159 H8
Old Garden Dr *RHAM/THRY* S65 .... 7 L2
Old Ga *HOLM/MEL* HD7 .... 52 C8
Oldgate La *RHAM/THRY* S65 .... 130 C6
Old Hall Cl *BTLY* DN5 .... 89 C7
DIN S25 .... 166 B3
MALT S66 .... 149 H2
Old Hall Dr *MALT* S66 .... 149 H2
Old Hall La *KBTN* HD8 .... 35 J7
Old Hall Pl *BTLY* DN5 .... 89 H6
Old Hall Rd *AWLS/ASK* DN6 .... 44 E6
BTLY DN5 .... 89 H6
Old Hall Wk *CUD/GR* S72 .... 63 J6
Oldhay Cl *TOT/DORE* S17 .... 189 H1

Old Hay Gdns *TOT/DORE* S17 .... 189 G1
Old Hay La *TOT/DORE* S17 .... 189 G1
Old House Cl *WMB/DAR* S73 .... 84 A8
Old La *CHPT/GREN* S35 .... 142 E1
HOLM/MEL HD7 .... 52 A3
MOS S20 .... 179 L8
Old London Rd *RTFD* DN22 .... 187 G4
Old Manchester Rd
STKB/PEN S36 .... 77 J7
Old Manor Dr *STKB/PEN* S36 .... 79 M6
Old Mill Cl *HEM/SK/SE* WF9 .... 23 G8
Old Mill La *BSLY* S70 .... 2 F3
BSLYN/ROY S71 .... 3 J3
CHPT/GREN S35 .... 102 B1
Old Mill Rd *CONI* DN12 .... 110 B6
Old Mount Farm
HOR/CROF WF4 .... 19 L8
Old Park Av *SHEFS* S8 .... 176 B8
Old Park Rd *SHEFS* S8 .... 176 B8
Old Quarry Av *AU/AST/KP* S26 .... 180 F4
The Old Railway Yd *SHEFS* S8 .... 176 B4
Old Retford Rd *HAN/WDH* S13 .... 163 G6
Old Rd *BSLYN/ROY* S71 .... 60 C2
CONI DN12 .... 109 K7
HOLM/MEL HD7 .... 53 C5
HOR/CROF WF4 .... 17 K1
Oldroyd Av *CUD/GR* S72 .... 62 E1
Old School Cl *HOY* S74 .... 83 J8
Old School La *NROS/TKH* DN11 .... 111 M8
RHAM S60 .... 163 H1
Old Scotch Spring La
MALT S66 .... 133 J7
Old Sheffield Rd *RHAM* S60 .... 6 E7
Old St *AWLS/ASK* DN6 .... 43 K8
SHEFP/MNR S2 .... 9 M3
Old Thorne Rd *HTFD* DN7 .... 49 H7
Old Village St *AWLS/ASK* DN6 .... 44 E3
Old Warren V *RAW* S62 .... 107 L8
Oldwell Cl *TOT/DORE* S17 .... 189 H3
The Old Woodyard
HOR/CROF WF4 .... 18 A5
Old Wortley Rd *KIMB* S61 .... 128 C7
Old Yew Ga *CHPT/GREN* S35 .... 125 H5
Old Yew La *HOLM/MEL* HD7 .... 53 J5
Olive Cl *AU/AST/KP* S26 .... 164 B8
Olive Crs *HACK/IN* S12 .... 177 L5
Olive Grove Rd *SHEFP/MNR* S2 .... 160 F7
Olive Rd *MOS* S20 .... 179 H8
STKB/PEN S36 .... 101 M6
Oliver Rd *ABRD* S7 .... 176 A3
DONS/BSCR DN4 .... 89 L8
Olivers Dr *DARN/MH* S9 .... 162 B3
Olivers Mt *DARN/MH* S9 .... 162 C3
Oliver St *MEX/SWTN* S64 .... 108 D2
Olivers Wy *RHAM* S60 .... 148 A5
Olivet Rd *SHEFS* S8 .... 176 D5
Ollerton Rd *BSLYN/ROY* S71 .... 38 D7
Omega Bvd *THNE* DN8 .... 31 K8
Onchan Rd *ST/HB/BR* S6 .... 159 J2
Onesacre Rd *ST/HB/BR* S6 .... 124 A8
Onesmoor Bottom
ST/HB/BR S6 .... 124 C8
Onslow Rd *ECC* S11 .... 159 M8
Orange Cft *NROS/TKH* DN11 .... 134 F8
Orange St *SHEF* S1 .... 8 F4
Orange Wy *DIN* S25 .... 166 C8
Orchard Av *ARMTH* DN3 .... 69 J3
AWLS/ASK DN6 .... 27 H4
BSLYN/ROY S71 .... 61 G2
CHPT/GREN S35 .... 126 F8
DIN S25 .... 166 C2
DOD/DAR S75 .... 37 M6
DOD/DAR S75 .... 80 E2
HTFD DN7 .... 70 D2
RHAM S60 .... 163 H1
STV/CWN S43 .... 194 E3
Orchard Crs *SHEFN* S5 .... 126 F8
Orchard Cft *AU/AST/KP* S26 .... 180 F4
BWTY DN10 .... 136 E8
DOD/DAR S75 .... 81 L1
Orchard Dr *AWLS/ASK* DN6 .... 27 H4
CUD/GR S72 .... 40 B1
FEA/AMT WF7 .... 23 L2
HTFD DN7 .... 70 D2
Orchard Flatts Crs *KIMB* S61 .... 128 C5
Orchard Gdns *DIN* S25 .... 182 B1
Orchard Gv *HTFD* DN7 .... 48 E6
MALT S66 .... 150 F1
Orchard La *AU/AST/KP* S26 .... 180 F5
MOS S20 .... 179 K5
SHEF S1 .... 9 H4
THNE DN8 .... 32 B4
Orchard Lea Dr
AU/AST/KP S26 .... 164 B8
Orchard Lee *AU/AST/KP* S26 .... 195 J1
Orchard Pl *CUD/GR* S72 .... 62 A2
DEARNE S63 .... 107 H1
ECK/KIL S21 .... 194 B1
RHAM S60 .... 163 H1
Orchard Rd *ST/HB/BR* S6 .... 160 A1
Orchard Sq *DRON* S18 .... 190 B5
Orchard St *DEARNE* S63 .... 86 C3
DONS/BSCR DN4 .... 4 C9
SHEF S1 .... 9 H4
STKB/PEN S36 .... 102 D7
THNE DN8 .... 31 M8
WMB/DAR S73 .... 84 B4
The Orchard *AWLS/ASK* DN6 .... 27 G7
DIN S25 .... 182 C1
Orchard Ter *DOD/DAR* S75 .... 58 D3
Orchard Wk *EPW* DN9 .... 92 E8
Orchard Wy *DEARNE* S63 .... 64 B7
RHAM S60 .... 147 G8
Orchid Wy *DIN* S25 .... 182 A3
Orgreave Dr *HAN/WDH* S13 .... 163 G6
Orgreave La *HAN/WDH* S13 .... 162 E6
Orgreave Pl *HAN/WDH* S13 .... 162 F6
Orgreave Rd *RHAM* S60 .... 163 G2
HAN/WDH S13 .... 162 E6
Oriel Rd *FUL* S10 .... 159 G8
Oriel Wy *BSLYN/ROY* S71 .... 61 H4
Ormesby Cl *DRON* S18 .... 190 A6
Ormesby Crs *BTLY* DN5 .... 89 J2
Ormesby Wy *MALT* S66 .... 149 J2
Ormes Meadow *MOS* S20 .... 179 G5
Ormond Cl *SHEFS* S8 .... 190 F1
Ormond Dr *SHEFS* S8 .... 190 F1
Ormond Rd *SHEFS* S8 .... 190 F1

Ormond Wy SHEFS S8 176 F8
Ormsby Cl CHPT/GREN S35 102 D2
DONS/BSCR DN4 111 L3
Orpen Dr SHEFS S8 177 J5
Orpen Wy SHEFS S8 177 J5 4
Orwell Cl WMB/DAR S73 84 D6
Osbert Dr MALT S66 149 J8
Osberton Pl ECC S11 160 A7
Osberton St NROS/TKH DN11 112 A8
RAW S62 129 M1
RHAM/THRY S65 130 A6
Osbert Rd RHAM S60 147 M4
Osborne Av AU/AST/KP S26 164 C7
AWLS/ASK DN6 66 D2 1
Osborne Cl ECC S11 160 A8 1
Osborne Cft AU/AST/KP S26 195 K1
Osborne Dr AU/AST/KP S26 181 K2
Osborne Ms BSLY S70 3 K7
Osborne Rd AU/AST/KP S26 181 K5
ECC S11 160 A8
WHHL DN2 5 L2
Osborne St BSLY S70 3 K7
Osgathorpe Crs ATT S4 145 G7 3
Osgathorpe Dr ATT S4 145 H7
Osgathorpe Rd ATT S4 145 G7
Osmaston Rd SHEFS S8 176 D5 5
Osmond Dr BSLY S70 82 E2
Osmond Pl BSLY S70 82 E2 10
Osmond Wy BSLY S70 82 E2 11
Osmund Rd ECK/KIL S21 192 F4
Osprey Av BSLY S70 82 D7
Osprey Cl AWLS/ASK DN6 66 F1
Osprey Gdns SHEFP/MNR S2 161 J5 4
Osprey Rd AU/AST/KP S26 180 C1 2
Oswestry Rd SHEFN S5 145 G3
Oswin Av DONS/BSCR DN4 89 K7
Otley Cl CONI DN12 110 B5
Otter St DARN/MH S9 161 K1
Oughtibridge La
CHPT/GREN S35 125 J8
Oughton Wy ATT S4 145 H8
Oulton Av MALT S66 149 J1
Oulton Dr CUD/GR S72 40 A8
Oulton Ri MEX/SWTN S64 109 H1
Ouseburn Cft DARN/MH S9 161 L2
Ouseburn Rd DARN/MH S9 161 L2
Ouseburn St DARN/MH S9 161 L2 8
Ouse Rd DARN/MH S9 161 L2
Ouslethwaite Ct BSLY S70 82 C1
Outgang La DIN S25 166 A4
MALT S66 150 F4
Out La KBTN HD8 17 G8
Outram Rd SHEFP/MNR S2 161 J5
Oval Rd RHAM/THRY S65 129 M8
The Oval AWLS/ASK DN6 66 D1 1
CONI DN12 110 A4
DIN S25 182 C1
DONS/BSCR DN4 91 G6
HOR/CROF WF4 38 F1
HTFD DN7 48 D6
NROS/TKH DN11 134 F7
SHEFN S5 145 G4
WRKN S81 198 E3
Overcroft Ri TOT/DORE S17 189 G3
Overdale Av BSLY S70 82 F1
Overdale Gdns TOT/DORE S17 189 G1
Overdale Ri TOT/DORE S17 189 G1 1
Overdale Rd WMB/DAR S73 84 C6
Overend Cl GLV S14 177 H3
Overend Dr GLV S14 177 H3
Overend Rd GLV S14 177 H3
WRKS S80 198 C3
Overend Wy GLV S14 177 H3
Oversley Rd WHHL DN2 90 D1
Oversley St DARN/MH S9 146 C4
Overton Rd ST/HB/BR S6 143 M5
Owday La WRKN S81 183 M5
Owen Cl RHAM/THRY S65 7 H1
ST/HB/BR S6 144 B1 2
Owen Pl ST/HB/BR S6 144 B1
Owler Car La DRON S18 191 J3
SHEFS S8 191 J2
Owler Ga CHPT/GREN S35 124 F7
Owler La ATT S4 145 H6
Owler's La HEM/SK/SE WF9 24 D3
Owlings Pl ST/HB/BR S6 143 L7
Owlings Rd ST/HB/BR S6 143 L7
Owlthorpe Av MOS S20 178 F7
Owlthorpe Cl MOS S20 178 F7 1
Owlthorpe Dr MOS S20 178 F7
Owlthorpe Greenway
MOS S20 179 J6
Owlthorpe Gv MOS S20 178 F7
Owlthorpe La MOS S20 178 F7
Owlthorpe Ri MOS S20 178 F7
Owram St WMB/DAR S73 84 E2 2
Owston La AWLS/ASK DN6 45 H5
Owston Rd AWLS/ASK DN6 45 G7
Ox Carr ARMTH DN3 91 L1
Ox Close Av KIMB S61 128 C6
TOT/DORE S17 189 L2
Oxclose Dr DRON S18 190 A6 11
Oxclose La DRON S18 190 A6
Oxclose Park Rd MOS S20 179 K8
Oxclose Park Rd North
MOS S20 193 K1
Oxford Cl KIMB S61 129 G4 2
Oxford Dr NROS/TKH DN11 153 K2
Oxford Pl BSLYN/ROY S71 61 J7 3
DON DN1 4 F7
Oxford Rd WRKN S81 184 D1
Oxford St BSLY S70 3 J9
BSLYN/ROY S71 61 J7
HEM/SK/SE WF9 42 D5
MEX/SWTN S64 108 C2
NROS/TKH DN11 113 J6
RHAM/THRY S65 7 L2
ST/HB/BR S6 8 C2
Ox Hl MOS S20 193 L2
Ox Lee La HOLM/MEL HD7 54 C7
Oxley Cl STKB/PEN S36 101 L6
Oxley Gv RHAM S60 7 J9
Oxspring Bank SHEFN S5 144 B5
Oxspring La STKB/PEN S36 79 M4
Oxspring Rd STKB/PEN S36 79 H7
Oxted Rd DARN/MH S9 145 L5
Oxton Dr DONS/BSCR DN4 111 H1
Oxton Rd BSLYN/ROY S71 38 E7

P

Pack Horse Cl KBTN HD8 35 L3
Pack Horse Gn DOD/DAR S75 58 D7
Pack Horse La CHPT/GREN S35 104 C7
Packington Rd
DONS/BSCR DN4 91 L8
Packman La AU/AST/KP S26 181 M6
AU/AST/KP S26 196 A3
Packman Rd DEARNE S63 84 F8
Packman Wy DEARNE S63 106 F1
Packwood Cl MALT S66 150 E1
Paddock Cl BTLY DN5 89 J2
DOD/DAR S75 38 A6
Paddock Crs SHEFP/MNR S2 177 J2
Paddock Cft MEX/SWTN S64 107 M4
Paddock Gv CUD/GR S72 40 A8
Paddock Rd DOD/DAR S75 38 A6
The Paddocks AU/AST/KP S26 164 C8
BTLY DN5 89 H2
BTLY DN5 110 B1 2
EPW DN9 114 E1 1
RHAM/THRY S65 130 E5
WRKN S81 184 F8
The Paddock ARMTH DN3 47 J7 1
AWLS/ASK DN6 67 G1 3
HOR/CROF WF4 19 L8
KIMB S61 127 M3
NROS/TKH DN11 134 F8
WMB/DAR S73 84 A7
WMB/DAR S73 84 E1
Paddock Wy DRON S18 190 F5
Padley Cl DOD/DAR S75 59 J8 5
Padley Wy SHEFN S5 145 G3
Padua Ri WMB/DAR S73 84 D2
Pagdin Dr NROS/TKH DN11 153 J5
Page Hall Rd SHEFN S5 145 H6
Pagenall Dr AU/AST/KP S26 164 B7
Paget St DARN/MH S9 145 K8
Pagnell Av DEARNE S63 63 M8
Painthorpe La HOR/CROF WF4 19 K4
Palermo Fold WMB/DAR S73 84 D1 1
Palgrave Crs SHEFN S5 144 C3
Palgrave Rd SHEFN S5 144 B3
Pall Ml BSLY S70 2 F6
Palm Av ARMTH DN3 70 A8
Palmer Cl STKB/PEN S36 79 G6 1
Palmer Crs DRON S18 190 F6
Palmer Rd DARN/MH S9 162 A1
Palmer's Av HEM/SK/SE WF9 42 E5
Palmerston Av MALT S66 150 C1
Palmerston Rd FUL S10 8 B5
Palmer St DARN/MH S9 161 K2 2
DONS/BSCR DN4 5 J8
Palmers Wy MALT S66 165 H1
Palm Gv CONI DN12 109 L7
Palm Hollow Cl MALT S66 148 D3
Palm La ST/HB/BR S6 160 A1 3
Palm St DOD/DAR S75 2 C2
ST/HB/BR S6 160 A1
Pamela Dr DONS/BSCR DN4 111 G1
Pangbourne Rd DEARNE S63 64 A6
Pantry Gn BSLY S70 83 G3 2
Pantry Hl BSLY S70 83 G2
Pantry Well BSLY S70 83 G3 3
Paper Mill La NROS/TKH DN11 135 G7
Paper Mill Rd SHEFN S5 127 H8
The Parade RAW S62 107 J8 1
Paradise La SHEF S1 9 H3
Paradise Sq SHEF S1 9 H3 1
Paradise St SHEF S1 9 H3
Parish Wy BSLYN/ROY S71 61 H4
Paris Rd HOLM/MEL HD7 54 A3
Park Av ARMTH DN3 69 K8
AWLS/ASK DN6 45 G7
BSLY S70 2 E6
BSLYN/ROY S71 38 D8
BSLYN/ROY S71 39 H4
BTLY DN5 89 G6
CHPT/GREN S35 103 H4
CHPT/GREN S35 126 E3
CONI DN12 110 A6
CUD/GR S72 39 M8
CUD/GR S72 40 E7
CUD/GR S72 40 F4
DIN S25 166 C8
DRON S18 189 K7
DRON S18 190 F5
ECC S11 159 M7
HEM/SK/SE WF9 41 M5
KBTN HD8 35 K4
MEX/SWTN S64 108 E2
RHAM S60 148 A5
STKB/PEN S36 79 G4
Park Cl BTLY DN5 89 G6
DOD/DAR S75 38 A7
EPW DN9 117 M3
MEX/SWTN S64 108 A4
RHAM/THRY S65 130 D5
Park Ct DEARNE S63 64 B7
Park Crs BSLYN/ROY S71 39 H4
CHPT/GREN S35 126 F7
DONS/BSCR DN4 111 G2
FUL S10 8 B7
THNE DN8 49 M1
Park Crest HEM/SK/SE WF9 41 H1
Park Dr AU/AST/KP S26 163 M8
AWLS/ASK DN6 27 H6
BTLY DN5 89 G6
Parkdrive DOD/DAR S75 81 M3
Park Dr EPW DN9 117 M3
STKB/PEN S36 101 M6
WRKN S81 169 L4
Park Drive Wy
STKB/PEN S36 101 M5 3
Park Edge HATH/EY S32 172 D7
Park End Rd DEARNE S63 86 B3
Parker's La FUL S10 160 A4
TOT/DORE S17 175 G7
Parker's Rd FUL S10 160 A4
Parker St BSLY S70 2 D6
Park Farm DRON S18 190 A5
Park Farm Ms ECK/KIL S21 194 B6
Parkfield Ct RAW S62 129 K4 5
Parkfield Rd RHAM/THRY S65 7 J5
Parkgate HEM/SK/SE WF9 41 M6
Parkgate Av CONI DN12 109 L5
Parkgate Cl MOS S20 178 E7 2
Parkgate Cft MOS S20 178 E7 3
Parkgate Dr HACK/IN S12 178 E6
Park Grange Cl
SHEFP/MNR S2 161 G7
Park Grange Cft SHEFP/MNR S2 9 L9
Park Grange Dr
SHEFP/MNR S2 161 G7
Park Grange Mt
SHEFP/MNR S2 161 G7
Park Grange Rd SHEFP/MNR S2 9 L9
Park Grange Vw
SHEFP/MNR S2 161 H8
Park Gv BSLY S70 2 E8
MALT S66 149 H2
RAW S62 107 K8
STKB/PEN S36 101 M5 4
Parkhall La ECK/KIL S21 194 B5
Parkhead Cl BSLYN/ROY S71 38 E3
Parkhead Ct ECC S11 175 K3
Parkhead Crs ECC S11 175 K3
Park Head La HOLM/MEL HD7 53 J3
KBTN HD8 55 J2
Parkhead Rd ECC S11 175 K4
Park Hl AU/AST/KP S26 163 M8
DOD/DAR S75 36 F5
ECK/KIL S21 193 J4
Parkhill Crs ARMTH DN3 47 L8 3
Park Hill Dr WRKN S81 167 L3
Parkhill Rd ARMTH DN3 47 L8
Park Hill Rd WMB/DAR S73 84 C4
Park Hollow WMB/DAR S73 84 D5
Park House La DARN/MH S9 146 D6
Parkin House La STKB/PEN S36 78 B5
Parkinson St DON DN1 5 H1
Parkland Dr NROS/TKH DN11 113 M6
Parklands ARMTH DN3 69 K6
Parklands Av DIN S25 166 C7
Parklands Cl NROS/TKH DN11 113 L6
Parkland Wk EPW DN9 115 K1
Park La CHPT/GREN S35 102 D4
CONI DN12 131 L2
CONI DN12 131 L5
CUD/GR S72 62 F4
DIN S25 166 A5
DONS/BSCR DN4 91 G5
EPW DN9 115 J1
EPW DN9 117 L3
FUL S10 8 B7
GLE DN14 10 C5
GLE DN14 12 C3
HOR/CROF WF4 18 C8
KBTN HD8 34 E2
KBTN HD8 55 L2
RHAM/THRY S65 130 D5
STKB/PEN S36 79 H4
STKB/PEN S36 79 L8
Park Lane Cl HTFD DN7 70 D3
Park Lane Ct RHAM/THRY S65 130 D4
Park Lane Rd HTFD DN7 70 C3
Park Lodge Vw KBTN HD8 34 E6
Park Mill Wy KBTN HD8 35 K4
Park Mt RHAM/THRY S65 7 H5
Park Nook RHAM/THRY S65 130 C5
Park Pl RHAM/THRY S65 129 M8
WRKS S80 198 D6
Park Ri DRON S18 189 L7
Park Rd AWLS/ASK DN6 27 K8
BSLY S70 2 E9
BSLY S70 82 E3
BTLY DN5 67 L5 4
BWTY DN10 136 D8
CONI DN12 109 M6
CUD/GR S72 40 E8
CUD/GR S72 40 F4
DEARNE S63 64 A7
DEARNE S63 107 J2
DON DN1 5 H4
KBTN HD8 35 K4
MEX/SWTN S64 107 M5
MEX/SWTN S64 108 E2
RHAM/THRY S65 7 M3
ST/HB/BR S6 159 K1
THNE DN8 32 B4
Park Side HOLM/MEL HD7 54 C3
HOR/CROF WF4 17 G4
Parkside La ST/HB/BR S6 159 H2
Parkside Ms BSLY S70 82 E2 12
Parkside Rd HOY S74 104 F3
ST/HB/BR S6 144 A6
Parkson Rd RHAM S60 147 M5
Park Spring Dr SHEFP/MNR S2 161 G7
Park Spring Gv
SHEFP/MNR S2 161 G7
Park Spring Pl SHEFP/MNR S2 161 G7
Park Spring Rd CUD/GR S72 62 D3
Park Spring Wy
SHEFP/MNR S2 161 G7
Park Square Rbt ATT S4 9 K4
Parks Rd HTFD DN7 48 D7
Parkstone Crs MALT S66 149 M3
Parkstone Delph HACK/IN S12 177 L5
Parkstone Gv HTFD DN7 48 F7 5
Parkstone Wy WHHL DN2 69 G8 2
Park St AU/AST/KP S26 164 A8
BSLY S70 2 E8
KIMB S61 6 A3
RAW S62 129 K1
STV/CWN S43 194 F8 1
WMB/DAR S73 84 C5
WRKS S80 198 C5
Park Ter CHPT/GREN S35 126 F3
DON DN1 5 H4
The Park DOD/DAR S75 58 C3
Park Vale Dr RHAM/THRY S65 130 D5
Park Vw AU/AST/KP S26 181 J4
AWLS/ASK DN6 67 G2
Parkview BSLY S70 82 F2
Park Vw BSLYN/ROY S71 39 H3
CUD/GR S72 40 A4 1
CUD/GR S72 40 B5
CUD/GR S72 40 F4
DOD/DAR S75 59 K8
HEM/SK/SE WF9 22 F6
HOLM/MEL HD7 53 K2
MALT S66 150 F2
STV/CWN S43 194 F8
THNE DN8 49 M1
Park View Av MOS S20 179 J8
Park View Rd CHPT/GREN S35 126 E3
DOD/DAR S75 38 A6
KIMB S61 146 A2
ST/HB/BR S6 144 A6
Parkway ARMTH DN3 91 M2 3
Park Wy AWLS/ASK DN6 66 F1
Parkway Av DARN/MH S9 161 K3
Parkway Cl DARN/MH S9 161 K3
Parkway Dr DARN/MH S9 161 L3
Parkway North WHHL DN2 90 D1
Parkways HTFD DN7 48 F8
Parkway South WHHL DN2 90 E1
Parkwood Ri ARMTH DN3 69 L2
Parkwood Rd OWL S3 144 C8
Parkwood Rd North SHEFN S5 144 D6
ST/HB/BR S6 144 D6
Parliament St ECC S11 8 D9
Parma Ri WMB/DAR S73 84 C2
Parsley Hay Cl
HAN/WDH S13 162 D6 2
Parsley Hay Dr
HAN/WDH S13 162 D6 3
Parsley Hay Gdns
HAN/WDH S13 162 D6
Parsley Hay Rd HAN/WDH S13 162 D6
Parsonage Cl MOS S20 193 H1 4
Parsonage St ST/HB/BR S6 160 A1
Parson Cross Rd ST/HB/BR S6 144 A3
Parson La HOR/CROF WF4 19 L8
Partridge Cl ECK/KIL S21 192 F4
Partridge Flatt Rd
DONS/BSCR DN4 113 K1
Partridge Pl AU/AST/KP S26 180 C1
Partridge Ri DONS/BSCR DN4 113 K1
Partridge Rd ARMTH DN3 47 K8
Partridge Vw
SHEFP/MNR S2 161 J5 5
Pashley Cft WMB/DAR S73 83 M5
Pashley Rd THNE DN8 50 A1
Passfield Rd NROS/TKH DN11 113 L7
Passhouses Rd ATT S4 144 F7 1
Pasture Cl ARMTH DN3 91 L2
WRKN S81 168 E8
WRKS S80 198 A5
Pasture Gv ECK/KIL S21 193 G4
Pasture La BTLY DN5 109 M1
BWTY DN10 155 L2
DEARNE S63 85 H3
Pastures Rd MEX/SWTN S64 109 J2
The Pastures AU/AST/KP S26 181 J2
BWTY DN10 154 E1 1
Paternoster Rw SHEF S1 9 J6
Paterson Cl STKB/PEN S36 101 L5
Paterson Ct STKB/PEN S36 101 L5 1
Paterson Cft STKB/PEN S36 101 L5 2
Paterson Gdns STKB/PEN S36 101 L5
Paterson Rd DIN S25 166 E6
Patmore Rd SHEFN S5 145 H3
Patrick Stirling Ct DON DN1 4 F8
DONS/BSCR DN4 4 B9
Patterdale Cl DRON S18 190 C6 5
Patterdale Wy DIN S25 182 D1
Patte Roale Cl AWLS/ASK DN6 45 G6
Paul La HOR/CROF WF4 16 A4
Pavilion Cl CUD/GR S72 40 E4 2
Pavilion La RHAM S60 146 F5
Pavillion Cl CONI DN12 111 G4
Paw Hill La STKB/PEN S36 78 A7
Paxton Av AWLS/ASK DN6 45 H6
Paxton Crs ARMTH DN3 69 K8
Paxton La FUL S10 8 B6
Payler Cl SHEFP/MNR S2 161 L7
Payne Crs RAW S62 107 J8
Peacock Cl ECK/KIL S21 194 A1
KIMB S61 127 K1
Pea Fields La CHPT/GREN S35 103 K5
Peakdale Crs HACK/IN S12 178 C2
Peake Av CONI DN12 109 L5
Peake's Cft BWTY DN10 136 E8
Peak La MALT S66 150 C4
Peak Rd BSLYN/ROY S71 38 E8 2
Peaks Mt MOS S20 179 J4
Pearce Rd DARN/MH S9 162 A4
Pearce Wk DARN/MH S9 162 A4
Pearl St ECC S11 160 C7
Pearmain Dr MALT S66 132 B8
Pea Royd La STKB/PEN S36 102 A5
Pearson Crs WMB/DAR S73 83 M3
Pearson Pl SHEFS S8 176 D3
Pearson's Cl RHAM/THRY S65 148 A3
Pearson's Fld WMB/DAR S73 84 B4
Pearson St STKB/PEN S36 101 M5 5
Pear St ECC S11 8 D9
Peartree Av DEARNE S63 64 A7
Pear Tree Av MALT S66 149 G2
Pear Tree Cl CUD/GR S72 63 H5
ECK/KIL S21 194 A2
RHAM S60 147 H7
WRKN S81 183 J3 1
Peartree Field La PONT WF8 25 G3
Pear Tree La HEM/SK/SE WF9 23 H8 1
HTFD DN7 29 L8
Pear Tree Rd SHEFN S5 145 H1
Pearwood Crs
DONS/BSCR DN4 111 K2
Peasehill Cl BSLY S70 2 F7
Peashill St RAW S62 129 K2
Peastack La NROS/TKH DN11 134 D6
Peat Carr Bank EPW DN9 116 C1
Peatfield Rd ECK/KIL S21 180 D8
Peat Pits La CHPT/GREN S35 124 B7
Peck Hall La ST/HB/BR S6 142 A3
Peckham Rd
CHPT/GREN S35 126 D1 6
Peck Mill Vw AU/AST/KP S26 181 M6
Pedley Av MOS S20 179 J6
Pedley Cl MOS S20 179 J6 3
Pedley Dr MOS S20 179 J7 3
Pedley Gv MOS S20 179 J6
Peel Castle Rd THNE DN8 50 A1
Peel Cl MALT S66 150 C1
Peel Hill Rd THNE DN8 50 A1
Peel Pde BSLY S70 2 E5
Peel Pl BSLYN/ROY S71 3 J1
Peel Sq BSLY S70 2 F5
Peel St BSLY S70 2 E5
BSLY S70 3 H9
FUL S10 160 A5 3
Pelham St WRKS S80 198 E6
Pell La HOLM/MEL HD7 54 A1
Pell's Cl DON DN1 4 F5 2
Pembrey Ct MOS S20 179 L5
Pembroke Av
DONS/BSCR DN4 111 L1
Pembroke Crs CHPT/GREN S35 126 B1
Pembroke Dr WRKN S81 184 C1
Pembroke Ri BTLY DN5 89 H1
DIN S25 182 B3 4
Pembroke Rd DRON S18 190 E7
WRKN S81 183 K8 2
Pembroke St ECC S11 8 D9
KIMB S61 146 D1
Penarth Av HEM/SK/SE WF9 24 E8
Penarth Ter HEM/SK/SE WF9 24 D8
Pendeen Rd ECC S11 159 K7 4
Pendennis Av HEM/SK/SE WF9 42 C3
Pendlebury Gv HOY S74 105 G2 2
Pendle Cft MOS S20 179 M6 4
Pengeston Rd STKB/PEN S36 78 F5
Penistone Boundary Wk
STKB/PEN S36 58 A7
STKB/PEN S36 77 M2
STKB/PEN S36 78 B2
STKB/PEN S36 79 L2
Penistone La STKB/PEN S36 100 B2
Penistone Rd CHPT/GREN S35 126 B4
HOLM/MEL HD7 54 C8
HOLM/MEL HD7 54 D1
KBTN HD8 55 J1
KBTN HD8 56 A5
ST/HB/BR S6 123 J6
ST/HB/BR S6 144 C8
Penistone St DON DN1 5 H3
Penley St ECC S11 160 D7 7
Penlington Cl
HEM/SK/SE WF9 41 H2 1
Pennine Cl HOLM/MEL HD7 53 H2
Pennine Dr KBTN HD8 35 H5
Pennine Gdns MALT S66 150 B1 2
Pennine Ri KBTN HD8 35 H5
Pennine Rd THNE DN8 49 L1
Pennine Vw DOD/DAR S75 37 L5
HEM/SK/SE WF9 24 E7
STKB/PEN S36 101 M8
Pennine Wy DOD/DAR S75 59 M5
HEM/SK/SE WF9 23 K8
KBTN HD8 35 H5
STKB/PEN S36 118 A3
Pen Nook Cl STKB/PEN S36 102 B8
Pen Nook Ct STKB/PEN S36 102 C8 1
Pen Nook Dr STKB/PEN S36 102 C8
Pen Nook Gdns STKB/PEN S36 102 C8
Penns Rd SHEFP/MNR S2 177 G1
Penny Engine La ECK/KIL S21 193 J3
Penny Hl WRKN S81 167 J3
Penny Hill La AU/AST/KP S26 164 D3
Pennyholme Cl
AU/AST/KP S26 181 K5
Penny La TOT/DORE S17 189 G2
Penny Piece La DIN S25 182 B1
Penny Piece Pl DIN S25 182 B1
Penrhyn Rd ECC S11 160 A8
Penrhyn Wk BSLYN/ROY S71 61 L7
Penrith Cl SHEFN S5 144 C5
Penrith Crs SHEFN S5 144 C5
Penrith Gv BSLYN/ROY S71 61 K7
Penrith Rd SHEFN S5 144 C5
Penrose Beck Dr
FEA/AMT WF7 23 J2 2
Penrose Pl HAN/WDH S13 178 E1
WKFDW/WTN WF2 19 K2
Penthorpe Cl HACK/IN S12 177 M1 6
Pentland Dr WRKN S81 168 C8 5
Pentland Gdns MOS S20 179 H5
Pentland Rd DRON S18 190 B6
Penton St SHEF S1 9 G4 2
Penyghent Cl
CHPT/GREN S35 126 D1 7
Pepper Cl KIMB S61 128 B4
Pepper St HOY S74 83 J7
Percival St WRKN S81 198 C3
Percy St HEM/SK/SE WF9 41 M5
OWL S3 160 D2 12
RHAM/THRY S65 7 G4
Peregrine Dr BSLY S70 82 D7
Peregrine Wy
AU/AST/KP S26 195 J2 2
AU/AST/KP S26 195 J2 1
Perigree Rd SHEFS S8 176 C4
Periwood Av SHEFS S8 176 B4
Periwood Cl SHEFS S8 176 C4 3
Periwood Dr SHEFS S8 176 C4 2
Periwood Gv SHEFS S8 176 C4 5
Perkyn Rd SHEFN S5 127 G8
Perkyn Ter SHEFN S5 127 G8
Perran Gv BTLY DN5 89 K2
Perseverance St BSLY S70 2 C5
Persimmon Cl
NROS/TKH DN11 113 K8
Perth Cl MEX/SWTN S64 109 G1
Petal Cl MALT S66 150 F1
Peterborough Cl FUL S10 158 E7
Peterborough Dr FUL S10 158 E6
Peterborough Rd FUL S10 158 E6
Petersgate BTLY DN5 67 K7
Peter's Rd CONI DN12 110 F6
Peter St KIMB S61 128 C8
MALT S66 165 J1
Petre Dr ATT S4 145 J7
Petre St ATT S4 145 H8
Petworth Cft BSLYN/ROY S71 38 F3 3
Petworth Dr ECC S11 175 K5
Peveril Cl AU/AST/KP S26 181 J4
Peveril Crs BSLYN/ROY S71 38 E8 3
Peveril Rd ECC S11 159 M8
ECK/KIL S21 193 J3
Pexton Rd ATT S4 145 G7
Philadelphia Dr
ST/HB/BR S6 160 C2 3
Philadelphia Gdns
ST/HB/BR S6 160 C2

Philadelphia Gv
ST/HB/BR S6 160 C2 5
Philip Rd BSLY S70 61 H8
Phillimore Rd DARN/MH S9 161 M1
Phillips Rd ST/HB/BR S6 143 H6
Phoenix Av KBTN HD8 35 H1
Phoenix Ct HACK/IN S12 178 C6
Phoenix Gv RHAM S60 146 F6
Phoenix La DEARNE S63 64 C8
Phoenix Rd DARN/MH S9 146 C4
HACK/IN S12 178 C6
Piccadilly BTLY DN5 67 L7
Piccadilly Rd MEX/SWTN S64 108 A6
Pickburn La BTLY DN5 66 A4
Pickering Crs AU/AST/KP S26 180 A1
Pickering Gv THNE DN8 49 M1
Pickering Rd BTLY DN5 67 L4
OWL S3 144 D8
Pickering St DARN/MH S9 145 M7 2
Pickhill's Av DEARNE S63 86 D1
Pickles La KBTN HD8 34 F6
Pickmere Rd FUL S10 159 M3
Pickup Crs WMB/DAR S73 84 B6
Pickwick Dr RHAM S60 162 F1
Piece End CHPT/GREN S35 104 B7
Piece End Cl
CHPT/GREN S35 104 B7 5
The Pieces North RHAM S60 147 M7
The Pieces South RHAM S60 147 M7
Pighills La DRON S18 190 F3
Pike Lowe Gv DOD/DAR S75 38 B7
Pike Rd RHAM S60 147 G6
Pilgrim Ct WRKN S81 183 K8 3
Pilgrim Ri BWTY DN10 156 A8
Pilgrim St OWL S3 144 F8
Pilgrim Wy WRKS S80 198 D5
Pilley Gn DOD/DAR S75 104 B2
Pilley Hl DOD/DAR S75 81 K1 5
Pilley La DOD/DAR S75 104 B1
Pilling La KBTN HD8 34 F5
Pincheon Green La GLE DN14 12 E8
Pinchfield Ct MALT S66 148 F4
Pinchfield Holt MALT S66 148 F4
Pinchfield La MALT S66 148 F4
Pinchmill Hollow MALT S66 148 F5
Pinch Mill La RHAM S60 148 C6
Pindar Oaks Cottages BSLY S70 3 L8
Pindar Oaks St BSLY S70 3 J9
Pindar St BSLY S70 3 L8
Pine Av DIN S25 182 B4
Pine Cl BSLY S70 83 G1
ECK/KIL S21 194 A2
HOY S74 105 J2
MALT S66 149 G1
Pine Cft CHPT/GREN S35 126 E3
Pinecroft Wy CHPT/GREN S35 126 E3
Pinefield Av ARMTH DN3 69 L1
Pinefield Rd ARMTH DN3 69 L1
Pine Gv CONI DN12 109 L7
Pinehall Dr BSLYN/ROY S71 61 H3
Pine Hall Rd ARMTH DN3 69 L1
Pinehurst Ri MEX/SWTN S64 108 B5
Pine Rd DONS/BSCR DN4 91 K7
The Pines FUL S10 158 E7
Pine St HEM/SK/SE WF9 42 C6
Pine Tree Cl WRKS S80 198 C6
Pine Wk MEX/SWTN S64 108 B7
Pinewood Av ARMTH DN3 69 M7
DONS/BSCR DN4 111 J2 2
Pinewood Cl CUD/GR S72 63 H4
Pinfield Cl CUD/GR S72 63 J5
Pinfold Cl BSLYN/ROY S71 61 J7 4
EPW DN9 115 J4 5
HOR/CROF WF4 17 G5
MEX/SWTN S64 108 A5
NROS/TKH DN11 134 D8
Pinfold Ct ARMTH DN3 69 K1 1
Pinfold Dr WRKN S81 168 D8
Pinfold Hl BSLY S70 82 E1
Pinfold Lands MEX/SWTN S64 108 F3
Pinfold La AWLS/ASK DN6 27 H4
AWLS/ASK DN6 28 F7
BSLYN/ROY S71 39 G5
CHPT/GREN S35 80 D5
GLE DN14 11 J3
HOR/CROF WF4 17 G5
HTFD DN7 30 E5
NROS/TKH DN11 152 D1
NROS/TKH DN11 153 H5
OWL S3 144 E8
PONT WF8 26 B2
RHAM/THRY S65 7 H5 1
THNE DN8 31 L7
WMB/DAR S73 84 F2
Pinfold Pl NROS/TKH DN11 134 D8
Pinfold St ECK/KIL S21 193 H4
The Pinfold BTLY DN5 87 H3
Pinfold Vw GLE DN14 11 J3 2
Pingle Av ABRD S7 176 A4
Pingle La RHAM/THRY S65 131 G5
Pingle Ri KBTN HD8 34 E8
Pingle Rd ABRD S7 176 A4
ECK/KIL S21 180 C8
Pingles Crs RHAM/THRY S65 130 C5
Pinner Rd ECC S11 160 A8
Pinstone St SHEF S1 9 G6
Pipe House La RAW S62 107 K8 1
Piper Cl SHEFN S5 144 E4
Piper Ct SHEFN S5 144 E4 1
Piper Crs SHEFN S5 144 E4
Pipering La (East) BTLY DN5 67 K8
Pipering La (West) BTLY DN5 67 J8
Piper La AU/AST/KP S26 164 D8
Piper Rd SHEFN S5 144 F4
Piper Well La KBTN HD8 55 J1
Pipeyard La ECK/KIL S21 193 G4
Pippin Ct MALT S66 150 B1
Pipworth Gv SHEFP/MNR S2 162 A6
Pipworth La ECK/KIL S21 193 K3
Pisgah House Rd FUL S10 160 A4 5
Pitchford La FUL S10 159 H6
Pithouse La AU/AST/KP S26 180 A4
Pit La HAN/WDH S13 177 L1
KIMB S61 127 K4
RHAM S60 163 K3
Pitman Rd CONI DN12 109 J4
Pitsmoor Rd ATT S4 144 F8
OWL S3 160 E1
Pittam Cl ARMTH DN3 91 M1
Pitt Cl SHEF S1 8 E5
Pitt La SHEF S1 8 E5 3
Pitt St BSLY S70 2 E6
ECK/KIL S21 193 G5
KIMB S61 146 D1
MEX/SWTN S64 109 G2
SHEF S1 8 E5
WMB/DAR S73 84 C2
Pitt St West BSLY S70 2 D6 2
Plains La THNE DN8 73 J1
Plane Dr MALT S66 149 G3 1
Plane Tree Wy EPW DN9 114 D4
Planet Rd AWLS/ASK DN6 45 G8
Plank Ga CHPT/GREN S35 125 G3
STKB/PEN S36 102 E8
Plantation Av BSLYN/ROY S71 39 H4
DIN S25 166 D6
DIN S25 182 C1 1
DONS/BSCR DN4 113 M3
Plantation Cl AWLS/ASK DN6 28 A8
MALT S66 150 D1
Plantation Ct DIN S25 166 D6
Plantation Dr BWTY DN10 155 K6
Plantation Hl WRKN S81 198 F4
WRKN S81 198 E2
Plantation La WRKN S81 169 M8
Plantation Rd BTLY DN5 46 E8
SHEFS S8 176 E1 10
THNE DN8 31 M8
Plantin Ri MOS S20 179 J8 4
The Plantin MOS S20 179 J8
Plants Yd WRKS S80 198 C5
Platts Dr MOS S20 179 L3
Platts La CHPT/GREN S35 125 J8
ST/HB/BR S6 141 K7
Platt St OWL S3 160 E1
Pleasant Av CUD/GR S72 63 J5
Pleasant Cl HACK/IN S12 177 M1 3
Pleasant Rd HACK/IN S12 177 M1
Pleasant Vw CUD/GR S72 62 A3
Pleasley Rd RHAM S60 147 L6
Pledwick Crs WKFDW/WTN WF2 20 B1
Pledwick Dr WKFDW/WTN WF2 20 B2
Pledwick Gv WKFDW/WTN WF2 20 A2 1
Pledwick La WKFDW/WTN WF2 20 B2
Pledwick Ri WKFDW/WTN WF2 20 B1
Plimsoll St HEM/SK/SE WF9 23 H8
Plough Dr WRKN S81 168 D8 3
Plover Ct NROS/TKH DN11 113 L6
SHEFP/MNR S2 161 J5 5
Plover Cft KIMB S61 127 L1
Plover Dene WRKN S81 184 A8
Plover Dr BSLY S70 82 D7
Plowright Dr SHEFP/MNR S2 177 H2
Plowright Mt SHEFP/MNR S2 177 H2
Plowright Wy SHEFP/MNR S2 177 H2 2
Plumber St BSLY S70 2 D5
Plumbley Hall Ms MOS S20 193 G1
Plumbley Hall Rd MOS S20 179 G8 2
Plumbley La MOS S20 192 F1
Plum La OWL S3 9 H2
Plumper's Rd DARN/MH S9 146 B5 1
Plumpton Av MEX/SWTN S64 109 G1
Plumpton Gdns
DONS/BSCR DN4 113 L1
Plumpton La ST/HB/BR S6 141 L3
Plumpton Park Rd
DONS/BSCR DN4 113 L2
Plum St OWL S3 9 H2
Plumtree Hill Rd HTFD DN7 48 C1
Plumtree Rd BWTY DN10 154 A1
Plunket Rd WHHL DN2 5 M2
Plymouth Rd ABRD S7 176 C2
Poffinder Wood Rd HTFD DN7 49 H2
Pog La CHPT/GREN S35 102 F1
Pogmoor La DOD/DAR S75 59 L5
Pogmoor Rd DOD/DAR S75 59 M6
Pog Well La DOD/DAR S75 59 H5
Pole Hl SHEFS S8 176 E5
Poles Bank EPW DN9 95 H4
Polka Ct OWL S3 160 E1
Pollard Av SHEFN S5 144 C4
Pollard Crs SHEFN S5 144 C4
Pollard Rd SHEFN S5 144 C4
Pollard St KIMB S61 146 C1
Pollitt St DOD/DAR S75 2 D2
Pollyfox Wy DOD/DAR S75 59 J8
Polton Cl HTFD DN7 48 E2
Polton Toft HTFD DN7 48 E2 1
Pomona St ECC S11 8 D9
Pond Cl ST/HB/BR S6 159 H1
Pond Common La
STKB/PEN S36 101 M1
Pond Hl SHEF S1 9 K4
Pond Rd ST/HB/BR S6 159 H1
Pond St BSLY S70 2 F8
SHEF S1 9 J5
Ponker La KBTN HD8 34 C7
Ponker Nook La KBTN HD8 34 D6
Pontefract Rd BSLYN/ROY S71 3 J6
CUD/GR S72 40 A6 1
DEARNE S63 84 F8
HEM/SK/SE WF9 23 K6
Pontefract Ter
HEM/SK/SE WF9 41 J1 7
Pool Av AWLS/ASK DN6 27 L7
Pool Dr DONS/BSCR DN4 113 M1
Poole Pl DARN/MH S9 162 A3
Poole Rd DARN/MH S9 162 A3
Pool Hill La KBTN HD8 57 G2
Pools La BSLYN/ROY S71 39 J8
ECK/KIL S21 192 A8
Pool Sq SHEF S1 9 H4
Pope Av CONI DN12 109 K5
Poplar Av CUD/GR S72 40 A5
DEARNE S63 86 C2 6
MOS S20 179 K2
RHAM/THRY S65 130 C5
STKB/PEN S36 101 M7
Poplar Cl ARMTH DN3 92 B7
DRON S18 191 G8 2
ECK/KIL S21 194 A2
MEX/SWTN S64 108 D1
WRKS S80 198 B6
Poplar Dr DEARNE S63 107 K3
RHAM S60 146 F7
Poplar Gld MALT S66 148 F3
Poplar Gv AWLS/ASK DN6 27 L7
BSLYN/ROY S71 61 J3
CONI DN12 109 M6
DONS/BSCR DN4 111 G3
MEX/SWTN S64 108 B4 3
RHAM/THRY S65 131 J7
Poplar Pl ARMTH DN3 91 M1
Poplar Ri KBTN HD8 34 F6 1
MALT S66 150 B1 3
Poplar Rd AWLS/ASK DN6 44 F6
CHPT/GREN S35 125 G8
ECK/KIL S21 193 G5
HTFD DN7 48 D7
WMB/DAR S73 84 C6
Poplars Rd BSLY S70 3 M9
The Poplars BTLY DN5 87 G4
CONI DN12 109 M6
Poplar St CUD/GR S72 62 F2
Poplar Ter BSLYN/ROY S71 39 H3
BTLY DN5 67 M7 4
HEM/SK/SE WF9 42 E5
Poplar Wy RHAM S60 162 E2
Popple St ATT S4 145 J6
Poppyfields Wy ARMTH DN3 92 A8
Porter Brook Vw ECC S11 160 B7
Porter Ter DOD/DAR S75 59 M5 9
Portland Av AU/AST/KP S26 164 C8
Portland Cl DIN S25 166 C7
Portland Ct ST/HB/BR S6 160 C1
Portland La SHEF S1 8 E5
Portland Mdw RTFD DN22 187 L1
Portland Pl DON DN1 4 F6
HEM/SK/SE WF9 24 E8 1
MALT S66 150 E2
RTFD DN22 187 L1
WRKS S80 198 D3 1
Portland Rd MOS S20 179 L5
NROS/TKH DN11 113 K8
Portland St BSLY S70 3 L8
MEX/SWTN S64 108 B4
ST/HB/BR S6 160 C2 10
ST/HB/BR S6 160 C2 10
WRKS S80 198 C4 4
Portobello SHEF S1 8 E4
Portobello St SHEF S1 8 F4
Portsea Rd ST/HB/BR S6 143 M7
Pot House La STKB/PEN S36 101 M7
Potterdyke Av RAW S62 107 K7
Potter Hl KIMB S61 129 G4
Potter Hill La CHPT/GREN S35 104 A8
Potteric Carr Rd
DONS/BSCR DN4 5 K9
Potters Ga CHPT/GREN S35 104 A8
HOLM/MEL HD7 55 H7
Potters Nook WRKN S81 183 K8 4
Potter St WRKS S80 198 D5
Pottery Cl RAW S62 129 K2
Potts Crs CUD/GR S72 63 J5
Poucher St KIMB S61 146 A1
Poulton St BSLYN/ROY S71 61 H1
Powder Mill La BSLY S70 83 G4
Powell Dr ECK/KIL S21 194 A1
Powell St BSLY S70 82 F3
HEM/SK/SE WF9 42 B4
OWL S3 8 C3
Power Station Rd BTLY DN5 4 C2
Powley Rd ST/HB/BR S6 144 A2
Poxton Gv HEM/SK/SE WF9 42 C6
Poynton Av AU/AST/KP S26 164 C4
Poynton Dr DIN S25 166 D5 3
Poynton Wy AU/AST/KP S26 164 C4
Poynton Wood Crs
TOT/DORE S17 189 L1 1
Poynton Wood Gld
TOT/DORE S17 189 L1
Prescott Gv HTFD DN7 48 E7
Prescott Rd ST/HB/BR S6 143 L5
President Wy ATT S4 161 G2
Preston Av HOY S74 83 L8
Preston St SHEFP/MNR S2 160 E8 7
Preston Wy BSLYN/ROY S71 61 H1
Prestwich St DARN/MH S9 145 M3 2
Priest Croft La BSLYN/ROY S71 62 D7
Priestley Av DOD/DAR S75 37 G7
RAW S62 107 M8
Priestley Cl DONS/BSCR DN4 111 K2
Priestley St SHEFP/MNR S2 9 J9
Priest Royd DOD/DAR S75 37 L6
Primrose Av RHAM S60 147 H8 3
SHEFN S5 145 J3
WMB/DAR S73 84 D2
Primrose Cir
NROS/TKH DN11 113 L6 1
Primrose Cl ECK/KIL S21 180 C8
Primrose Crs MOS S20 179 K4 2
Primrose Dr CHPT/GREN S35 126 F7
Primrose Hl KIMB S61 6 D1
ST/HB/BR S6 160 C1 2
Primrose La ECK/KIL S21 180 C7
HOR/CROF WF4 19 H1
Primrose Wy HOY S74 105 J3 1
WRKN S81 198 E1 5
Primulas Cl DIN S25 182 A3 2
Prince Arthur St DOD/DAR S75 2 D3
Prince Charles Rd WRKN S81 184 B8
Prince of Wales Rd
DARN/MH S9 162 A4
SHEFP/MNR S2 161 M6 7
Prince's Crs CONI DN12 110 F4
Prince's Rd DONS/BSCR DN4 91 G6 1
Princess Anne Rd WRKN S81 198 C1
Princess Av HEM/SK/SE WF9 42 D5
HTFD DN7 48 C3
Princess Cl DEARNE S63 85 M5 2
Princess Ct SHEFP/MNR S2 161 M7 3
Princess Dr DEARNE S63 64 C8
STKB/PEN S36 102 A8
Princess Gdns WMB/DAR S73 84 B5
Princess Gv DOD/DAR S75 104 A2
Prince's Sq ARMTH DN3 69 K3 2
Princess Rd DEARNE S63 86 C2 7
DRON S18 190 E5
MEX/SWTN S64 108 F2
Princess St ATT S4 161 H2
AWLS/ASK DN6 66 F3
BSLY S70 2 E6
CUD/GR S72 62 E1 2
DEARNE S63 85 H8
DIN S25 166 A5
DOD/DAR S75 37 L6
HOY S74 104 F2
WMB/DAR S73 84 A4 3
Prince's St DON DN1 5 H5
RHAM S60 6 B4
Prince St MEX/SWTN S64 108 B3
Pringle Rd RHAM S60 146 F6
Printing Office St DON DN1 4 F5
Prior Rd CONI DN12 109 M6
Priorswell Rd WRKS S80 198 D5
Priory Av ECC S11 160 D7
Priory Cl BSLY S70 82 D5
CHPT/GREN S35 126 E6
CONI DN12 110 A4
WRKN S81 169 L4
Priory Ct AU/AST/KP S26 195 J2
Priory Crs BSLYN/ROY S71 61 J4
Priory Pl ABRD S7 160 D7
BSLYN/ROY S71 61 J3
DON DN1 4 F5
Priory Rd ABRD S7 160 C8
BSLYN/ROY S71 61 J3
CHPT/GREN S35 126 E6
Priory Rd Or Hall La
AWLS/ASK DN6 27 G3
Priory Wy AU/AST/KP S26 164 C8
Pritchard Cl HACK/IN S12 178 F4
Probert Av DEARNE S63 86 B2
Proctor Pl ST/HB/BR S6 144 A7
Progress Dr MALT S66 149 H3
Prospect Cl MALT S66 149 H3
Prospect Dr TOT/DORE S17 189 K2
WRKN S81 198 D1
Prospect Pl TOT/DORE S17 189 L1
Prospect Prec WRKN S81 198 E1 6
Prospect Rd BTLY DN5 67 L3
DEARNE S63 86 A4
DRON S18 191 G4
SHEFP/MNR S2 160 E8
SHEFS S8 160 E8
TOT/DORE S17 189 L2
Prospect St BSLY S70 2 D5
CUD/GR S72 39 M8
Providence Ct BSLY S70 2 F8
Providence Rd ST/HB/BR S6 159 M1
Providence St KIMB S61 129 G4
RHAM S60 6 C5
WMB/DAR S73 84 D3 1
Providential St HOR/CROF WF4 16 F4
Pryor Mede AU/AST/KP S26 195 J2
Psalter La ECC S11 159 M8
Psalters Dr STKB/PEN S36 79 L6
Psalters La KIMB S61 128 D8
Pump La KBTN HD8 16 A8
Purbeck Ct MOS S20 179 H5 2
Purbeck Gv MOS S20 179 H5
Purbeck Rd MOS S20 179 H5
Purcell Cl MALT S66 151 G3
Purslove Cl MALT S66 149 J3 2
Pye Av DOD/DAR S75 37 L7
Pye Bank Cl OWL S3 160 E1 1
Pye Bank Dr OWL S3 160 E1
Pye Bank Rd OWL S3 160 E1
Pym Rd MEX/SWTN S64 108 E2

Q

The Quadrant TOT/DORE S17 189 J2
Quail Ri SHEFP/MNR S2 161 J5 7
Quaker Cl DEARNE S63 107 H2
Quaker La BSLYN/ROY S71 61 K7
DONS/BSCR DN4 111 H1
Quantock Cl THNE DN8 49 L2
Quarry Bank DEARNE S63 106 F1
Quarry Bank Rd CUD/GR S72 61 M1 6
Quarry Cl DOD/DAR S75 37 H7 5
RHAM S60 146 E7
Quarryfield La MALT S66 132 D8
Quarry Field La MALT S66 148 F5
Quarry Flds MALT S66 148 F4
Quarry Gv WRKN S81 184 A8
Quarry Hl ECK/KIL S21 192 B5
HACK/IN S12 178 E7
RHAM S60 6 F5
Quarry Hill Rd DEARNE S63 107 J3
Quarry La ARMTH DN3 92 B7
AWLS/ASK DN6 66 E3
DIN S25 182 B1
ECC S11 176 A1
HEM/SK/SE WF9 24 E7
KIMB S61 6 C1
Quarry Mt HOR/CROF WF4 21 M6
Quarry Pl DIN S25 166 E6 2
Quarry Rd AWLS/ASK DN6 27 K4
DRON S18 191 L6 2
ECK/KIL S21 180 A8
HAN/WDH S13 162 C4
HOY S74 83 H6 1
TOT/DORE S17 189 J2
Quarry St BSLY S70 3 H7
BSLYN/ROY S71 60 E2 3
CUD/GR S72 39 M8
FEA/AMT WF7 23 K2
MEX/SWTN S64 108 F3
RAW S62 129 K1
Quarry Vale Gv HACK/IN S12 178 A3
Quarry Vale Rd HACK/IN S12 178 A3
Quay Rd THNE DN8 31 K6 1
Quayside THNE DN8 31 J6
Queen Av MALT S66 150 E3 3
NROS/TKH DN11 113 J6
Queen Elizabeth Crs
WRKS S80 197 L3
Queen Gdns WMB/DAR S73 84 B5
Queen Mary Cl
SHEFP/MNR S2 161 L8 1
Queen Mary Crs ARMTH DN3 69 K3
SHEFP/MNR S2 161 L7
Queen Mary Gv
SHEFP/MNR S2 161 K8 2
Queen Mary Ms
SHEFP/MNR S2 161 L8 2
Queen Mary Rd
SHEFP/MNR S2 161 K7
Queen Mary's Rd
NROS/TKH DN11 113 J6
Queen Mary St MALT S66 150 E4 2
Queens Av AU/AST/KP S26 181 G5
CUD/GR S72 63 H8
DOD/DAR S75 2 C3
MEX/SWTN S64 108 B3
Queensberry Rd WHHL DN2 91 G3
Queen's Ct BTLY DN5 89 L1 1
THNE DN8 31 L8
Queen's Crs BWTY DN10 136 E8
CONI DN12 110 F4
HOY S74 104 E2 1
HTFD DN7 48 C4 3
Queen's Dr BTLY DN5 89 L1
CUD/GR S72 39 M4
CUD/GR S72 40 A6
DOD/DAR S75 2 B2
DOD/DAR S75 59 K8
Queens Gdns DOD/DAR S75 2 B2
HOY S74 104 F2 6
Queensgate CHPT/GREN S35 126 B7 2
Queens Rd AU/AST/KP S26 164 A8
AWLS/ASK DN6 27 M7
AWLS/ASK DN6 45 G7
BSLYN/ROY S71 3 H5
CUD/GR S72 40 A6
CUD/GR S72 62 F1
DON DN1 5 J2
MOS S20 179 K3
SHEFP/MNR S2 160 E7
WRKN S81 168 C8
Queen's Rw OWL S3 8 F1
Queen's Ter MEX/SWTN S64 108 E2
Queen St BSLY S70 2 F5
CHPT/GREN S35 126 E1
DEARNE S63 64 C8
DEARNE S63 86 C2
DIN S25 166 D5
DONS/BSCR DN4 89 M7 4
ECK/KIL S21 193 J4
HEM/SK/SE WF9 42 D5
HOY S74 104 E2
KBTN HD8 34 E5
MEX/SWTN S64 108 B4
MOS S20 193 G1
RAW S62 107 L8
RHAM/THRY S65 7 L3
SHEF S1 9 H3
STKB/PEN S36 79 J4
THNE DN8 31 L8
WMB/DAR S73 84 F1
WRKS S80 198 D5
Queensway BSLY S70 82 F3
BSLYN/ROY S71 39 G3 2
DOD/DAR S75 2 B1
HOY S74 105 K1
RHAM S60 147 K5
WRKN S81 198 D3
Queen Victoria Rd
TOT/DORE S17 189 K2
Quern Wy WMB/DAR S73 84 E1
Quest Av WMB/DAR S73 83 M7
Quiet La ECC S11 174 F1
Quilter Rd MALT S66 151 G3
Quintec Ct RAW S62 129 J6
Quoit Gn DRON S18 190 F6

R

Raby St DARN/MH S9 146 C4
Race Common Av
STKB/PEN S36 79 G7
Racecommon La BSLY S70 60 B8
Racecommon Rd BSLY S70 2 D8
Racecourse Rd
MEX/SWTN S64 107 L4
Race La STKB/PEN S36 124 A2
Race St BSLY S70 2 E6 1
Racker Wy ST/HB/BR S6 143 M8
Rackford Rd DIN S25 182 C2
Radburn Rd NROS/TKH DN11 113 J8
Radcliffe La BTLY DN5 67 J6
Radcliffe Rd BSLYN/ROY S71 38 D7
BTLY DN5 67 L5
Radcliffe St KBTN HD8 34 D5
Radford Cl RHAM/THRY S65 131 J7
Radford Park Av
HEM/SK/SE WF9 41 M6
Radford St OWL S3 8 E3
WRKS S80 198 E6
Radley Av MALT S66 148 E2
Radnor Cl MOS S20 179 L5
Radnor Wy WHHL DN2 91 G2
Raeburn Cl GLV S14 177 J5
Raeburn Pl GLV S14 177 J4
Raeburn Rd GLV S14 177 J4
Raeburn Wy SHEFS S8 177 J5
Rag La CHPT/GREN S35 80 C8
Ragusa Dr NROS/TKH DN11 113 K8
Rail Mill Wy RAW S62 129 K5
Rails Rd ST/HB/BR S6 158 E3
Railway Av RHAM S60 163 G2
Railway Ter HEM/SK/SE WF9 22 E4
RHAM S60 6 D4 1
Railway Vw DEARNE S63 86 C2
Rainborough Ms DEARNE S63 84 F8 3
Rainborough Rd DEARNE S63 106 F1
Rainbow Av HACK/IN S12 178 F3
Rainbow Crs HACK/IN S12 179 G3
Rainbow Dr HACK/IN S12 179 G3
Rainbow Gv HACK/IN S12 179 G3
Rainbow Pl HACK/IN S12 179 G3
Rainbow Rd HACK/IN S12 179 G3
Rainbow Wy HACK/IN S12 178 F3
Raines Av WRKN S81 198 C1
Raines Park Rd WRKN S81 184 C8
Rainford Dr BSLYN/ROY S71 61 H1
Rainford Sq ARMTH DN3 69 K2 1
Rainton Gv DOD/DAR S75 59 M4
Rainton Rd DONS/BSCR DN4 5 J7
Raintree Ct BTLY DN5 89 K2
Raisen Hall Pl SHEFN S5 144 E5
Raisen Hall Rd SHEFN S5 144 D4
Rake Bridge Bank HTFD DN7 70 F5
Rake Head Rd HOLM/MEL HD7 52 C8

Rakes La CONI DN12 ... 133 G3
NROS/TKH DN11 ... 112 B5
Raleigh Ct WHHL DN2 ... 90 F4
Raleigh Dr CHPT/GREN S35 ... 126 B2
Raleigh Rd SHEFS S8 ... 176 F1
Raleigh Ter DONS/BSCR DN4 ... 111 J1
Raley St BSLY S70 ... 2 C8
Ralph Ellis Dr STKB/PEN S36 ... 101 M7
Ralston Ct MOS S20 ... 193 H1 5
Ralston Cft MOS S20 ... 193 J1 3
Ralston Gv MOS S20 ... 193 H1
Ramper Rd MALT S66 ... 149 M6
WRKN S81 ... 167 L4
Rampton Rd ABRD S7 ... 160 D8 12
Ramsden Av WRKN S81 ... 168 C4
Ramsden Crs WRKN S81 ... 168 D8 4
Ramsden Rd DONS/BSCR DN4 ... 4 B7
HOLM/MEL HD7 ... 53 G7
RHAM S60 ... 7 H7
Ramsey Rd FUL S10 ... 160 A3
Ramsker Dr ARMTH DN3 ... 91 M2
Ramskir La HTFD DN7 ... 48 D2
Ramsworth Cl BTLY DN5 ... 89 J2 5
Ranby Rd ECC S11 ... 159 M8
Randall Pl SHEFP/MNR S2 ... 160 D7
Randall St ECK/KIL S21 ... 192 F5 1
Randerson Dr MEX/SWTN S64 ... 108 C6
Rands La ARMTH DN3 ... 70 A8
Ranelagh Dr ECC S11 ... 175 M2
Ranfield Ct RHAM/THRY S65 ... 131 J7 1
Rangeley Rd ST/HB/BR S6 ... 159 L2
Ranmoor Cliffe Rd FUL S10 ... 159 J6
Ranmoor Crs FUL S10 ... 159 K6
Ranmoor Hl HATH/EY S32 ... 172 C7
Ranmoor Park Rd FUL S10 ... 159 K6
Ranmoor Ri FUL S10 ... 159 K6 2
Ranmoor Rd FUL S10 ... 159 K6
Ranskill Ct DARN/MH S9 ... 146 A8
Ranworth Rd MALT S66 ... 149 J2
Ranyard Rd DONS/BSCR DN4 ... 89 K8 5
Raseby Av MOS S20 ... 179 J5
Raseby Cl MOS S20 ... 179 J5
Raseby Pl MOS S20 ... 179 J5 2
Rasen Cl MEX/SWTN S64 ... 108 F1
Ratcliffe Rd ECC S11 ... 160 B7
Ratten Rw DOD/DAR S75 ... 81 J1
NROS/TKH DN11 ... 112 A8
Ravencar Rd ECK/KIL S21 ... 192 F4
Ravencarr Pl SHEFP/MNR S2 ... 161 L6
Ravencarr Rd SHEFP/MNR S2 ... 161 L6
Raven Dr KIMB S61 ... 127 L1
Ravenfield Cl MOS S20 ... 178 E5
Ravenfield Dr BSLYN/ROY S71 ... 60 E1
Ravenfield La RHAM/THRY S65 ... 131 G2
Ravenfield Rd ARMTH DN3 ... 92 A2
Ravenfield St CONI DN12 ... 109 K4
Ravenholt BSLY S70 ... 82 E3
Raven La CUD/GR S72 ... 39 L1
Raven Mdw MEX/SWTN S64 ... 108 A7
Raven Rd ABRD S7 ... 176 B1
Raven Royd BSLYN/ROY S71 ... 38 D6
Ravenscar Cl CONI DN12 ... 109 K4
Ravens Cl DOD/DAR S75 ... 37 M7 5
Ravenscourt BSLY S70 ... 82 F3
WRKN S81 ... 198 E1 7
Ravenscroft Av HAN/WDH S13 ... 162 C7
Ravenscroft Cl
HAN/WDH S13 ... 162 C7 1
Ravenscroft Ct
HAN/WDH S13 ... 162 C7 2
Ravenscroft Crs
HAN/WDH S13 ... 162 C7
Ravenscroft Dr HAN/WDH S13 ... 162 C7
Ravenscroft Gv
HAN/WDH S13 ... 162 C7 3
Ravenscroft Pl
HAN/WDH S13 ... 162 C7 4
Ravenscroft Rd HAN/WDH S13 ... 162 C8
Ravenscroft Wy
HAN/WDH S13 ... 162 C8
Ravensdale Rd DRON S18 ... 190 A6
Ravenshaw Cl DOD/DAR S75 ... 59 M4 3
Ravenshill Cl RTFD DN22 ... 170 F3
Ravensmead Ct DEARNE S63 ... 86 A5
Ravens Wk CONI DN12 ... 110 C5
Ravens Wy HOLM/MEL HD7 ... 54 C3
Ravenswood Dr EPW DN9 ... 92 E8
Ravensworth Rd DON DN1 ... 5 J7
The Ravine SHEFN S5 ... 127 J8
Raw La MALT S66 ... 133 J6
Rawmarsh Hl RAW S62 ... 129 K3
Rawmarsh Rd RHAM S60 ... 6 F1
Rawson Cl DONS/BSCR DN4 ... 91 K6 2
Rawson Rd NROS/TKH DN11 ... 134 D8
Rawsons Bank
CHPT/GREN S35 ... 126 F7
Rawson Spring Rd
ST/HB/BR S6 ... 144 B5
Rawson Spring Wy SHEFN S5 ... 144 B5
Raybould Rd KIMB S61 ... 128 D6 2
Rayls Ri AU/AST/KP S26 ... 181 K2
Rayls Rd AU/AST/KP S26 ... 181 K2
Raymond Av CUD/GR S72 ... 62 E1
Raymond Rd BSLY S70 ... 61 H8
BTLY DN5 ... 89 K1
Raymoth La WRKN S81 ... 184 C8
Raynald Rd SHEFP/MNR S2 ... 161 L6
Raynor Sike La
CHPT/GREN S35 ... 124 E7
Rayton Ct NROS/TKH DN11 ... 153 L3
Rayton La WRKN S81 ... 199 H4
Rayton Sp WRKN S81 ... 198 F4
Reader Crs MEX/SWTN S64 ... 108 B3
Reading Room La
CHPT/GREN S35 ... 103 H4
Reaper Crs CHPT/GREN S35 ... 126 C1
Reasbeck Ter BSLYN/ROY S71 ... 60 D2 1
Reasby Av RHAM/THRY S65 ... 131 H7
Rebecca Ms BSLY S70 ... 3 G8 1
Rebecca Rw BSLY S70 ... 3 G8
Recreation Av MALT S66 ... 165 K1
Recreation La
NROS/TKH DN11 ... 113 J6
Recreation Rd AWLS/ASK DN6 ... 66 F3 1
DEARNE S63 ... 85 K8
Rectory Cl BSLYN/ROY S71 ... 39 H6
DEARNE S63 ... 63 M7
ECK/KIL S21 ... 193 J3
STKB/PEN S36 ... 102 A6
WMB/DAR S73 ... 84 B5
Rectory Gdn KBTN HD8 ... 17 H8
Rectory Gdns AU/AST/KP S26 ... 181 K3
AU/AST/KP S26 ... 195 J1
CONI DN12 ... 110 E8
DON DN1 ... 5 K2
ECK/KIL S21 ... 194 B1
Rectory La DEARNE S63 ... 63 M7
EPW DN9 ... 115 H4
KBTN HD8 ... 17 H8
Rectory Ms BTLY DN5 ... 88 F7 4
Rectory Rd ECK/KIL S21 ... 194 B1
Rectory St RAW S62 ... 129 K3
Rectory Wy BSLYN/ROY S71 ... 61 H4 2
Redbourne Rd BTLY DN5 ... 67 M6
Redbrook Ct DOD/DAR S75 ... 60 A3 3
Redbrook Cft HACK/IN S12 ... 178 E4 3
Redbrook Gv MOS S20 ... 178 E4 5
Redbrook Rd DOD/DAR S75 ... 59 L3
Redbrook Vw DOD/DAR S75 ... 60 A3
Redbrook Wk DOD/DAR S75 ... 60 A3
Redcar Cl CONI DN12 ... 109 J5
Redcar Rd FUL S10 ... 160 A4
Redcliffe Cl DOD/DAR S75 ... 59 M3
Red Deer Park La
HOR/CROF WF4 ... 16 C2
Redfearn St BSLYN/ROY S71 ... 3 H3 2
Redfern Av MOS S20 ... 179 H6
Redfern Ct MOS S20 ... 179 H6 1
Redfern Dr MOS S20 ... 179 H6
Redfern Gv MOS S20 ... 179 H6
Red Fern Gv STKB/PEN S36 ... 101 M7
Redgrave Pl MALT S66 ... 148 F1
Redhall Cl ARMTH DN3 ... 69 L3
Red Hl AU/AST/KP S26 ... 181 K5
SHEF S1 ... 8 F3
Redhill Av BSLY S70 ... 61 G8
Redhill Ct NROS/TKH DN11 ... 111 M8
Red Hill La BTLY DN5 ... 65 G8
Red House La AWLS/ASK DN6 ... 44 E8
AWLS/ASK DN6 ... 66 B1
Redland Crs HEM/SK/SE WF9 ... 22 F5
THNE DN8 ... 32 A6
Redland Gv DOD/DAR S75 ... 37 M5
Redland Wy MALT S66 ... 150 C1
Red La ECC S11 ... 160 A6
WRKN S81 ... 184 E5
Redmarsh Av RAW S62 ... 107 J8
Redmires La FUL S10 ... 158 B6
Redmires Rd FUL S10 ... 157 L7
FUL S10 ... 159 G5
Red Oak La ST/HB/BR S6 ... 143 G8 1
Red Quarry La DIN S25 ... 167 J7
Redrock Rd RHAM S60 ... 147 L5
Redscope Crs KIMB S61 ... 128 B5
Redscope Rd KIMB S61 ... 128 B6
Redthorne Wy CUD/GR S72 ... 39 M4
Redthorn Rd HAN/WDH S13 ... 162 D7
Redthorpe Crest
DOD/DAR S75 ... 59 L3 2
Redwing Cl WRKN S81 ... 198 A1
Redwood Av BSLYN/ROY S71 ... 39 G4
ECK/KIL S21 ... 194 A2
Redwood Cl HOY S74 ... 105 H2
Redwood Dr MALT S66 ... 150 A2
Redwood Gln CHPT/GREN S35 ... 126 D3
Reedham Dr MALT S66 ... 149 J2
Reedholme La THNE DN8 ... 13 J7
Regent Av ARMTH DN3 ... 92 A2
Regent Crs BSLYN/ROY S71 ... 38 D8
Regent Cresent CUD/GR S72 ... 40 C2
Regent Gdns BSLY S70 ... 2 E3
Regent Gv BTLY DN5 ... 89 K2
NROS/TKH DN11 ... 113 K8
Regent Sq DON DN1 ... 5 H5
Regent St BSLY S70 ... 3 G4
CUD/GR S72 ... 40 C2
DONS/BSCR DN4 ... 89 L8
HEM/SK/SE WF9 ... 23 G8
HEM/SK/SE WF9 ... 42 C4
HOY S74 ... 104 E2
KIMB S61 ... 146 D1
SHEF S1 ... 8 E4
Regents Wy AU/AST/KP S26 ... 164 C8 4
Regent Ter OWL S3 ... 8 E4
Regina Crs CUD/GR S72 ... 40 C4
HOR/CROF WF4 ... 22 A6
Reginald Rd BSLY S70 ... 61 H8
WMB/DAR S73 ... 84 D5 2
Rembrandt Dr DRON S18 ... 190 C6
Remington Av SHEFN S5 ... 126 D8
Remington Dr SHEFN S5 ... 126 D8 2
Remington Rd SHEFN S5 ... 144 D1
Remount Rd KIMB S61 ... 128 B5
Remount Wy KIMB S61 ... 128 B5 1
Remple Av HTFD DN7 ... 71 L1
Remple Common Rd HTFD DN7 ... 71 K3
Remple La HTFD DN7 ... 71 L1
Renald La STKB/PEN S36 ... 57 J8
Renathorpe Rd SHEFN S5 ... 145 H1
Rencliffe Av RHAM S60 ... 147 K4
Reneville Cl RHAM S60 ... 6 F8
Reneville Ct SHEFN S5 ... 126 E7
Reneville Crs SHEFN S5 ... 126 E7
Reneville Dr SHEFN S5 ... 126 E7 1
Reneville Rd RHAM S60 ... 6 F8
Reney Av SHEFS S8 ... 190 B1
Reney Dr SHEFS S8 ... 190 B1
Reney Rd SHEFS S8 ... 176 C8
Renishaw Av RHAM S60 ... 147 M5
Renshaw Cl CHPT/GREN S35 ... 104 A7
Renshaw Rd ECC S11 ... 175 L1
Renville Cl RAW S62 ... 107 J8
Repton Pl DRON S18 ... 190 A6 12
Repton Rd AWLS/ASK DN6 ... 44 F7
Reresby Crs RHAM S60 ... 148 A5
Reresby Dr RHAM S60 ... 148 A5
Reresby Rd RHAM S60 ... 147 M5
RHAM/THRY S65 ... 130 E5
Reservoir Rd AU/AST/KP S26 ... 164 A3
FUL S10 ... 160 A4
Reservoir Vw KBTN HD8 ... 34 C5
Retford Rd HAN/WDH S13 ... 162 E6
WRKN S81 ... 169 M4
WRKN S81 ... 199 K5
WRKS S80 ... 198 E5
Retford Wk NROS/TKH DN11 ... 113 M6
Revel Garth KBTN HD8 ... 56 E2
Revell Cl RHAM/THRY S65 ... 130 B8
Revill Cl MALT S66 ... 150 D1
Revill Ct DIN S25 ... 166 D5 4
Revill La HAN/WDH S13 ... 179 G1
Rex Av ABRD S7 ... 175 M3
Reynard Crs ECK/KIL S21 ... 193 M7
Reynard La ST/HB/BR S6 ... 158 F2
Reynolds Cl DRON S18 ... 190 C7
MALT S66 ... 148 F2
Rhodes Av KIMB S61 ... 128 C5
Rhodes Dr RHAM S60 ... 148 A5
Rhodes St SHEFP/MNR S2 ... 9 L5
Rhyddings Av FEA/AMT WF7 ... 23 K2
Rhyddings Dr FEA/AMT WF7 ... 23 K3
Ribble Cft CHPT/GREN S35 ... 126 D1
Ribblesdale WRKN S81 ... 184 E7 3
Ribblesdale Dr HACK/IN S12 ... 178 D6
Ribble Wy SHEFN S5 ... 145 G4
Riber Av BSLYN/ROY S71 ... 38 E8
Riber Cl ST/HB/BR S6 ... 143 H8
Ribston Ct DARN/MH S9 ... 161 M3 1
Ribston Ms DARN/MH S9 ... 161 M3
Ribston Pl DARN/MH S9 ... 161 M3 2
Ribston Rd DARN/MH S9 ... 161 L3
Richard Av BSLYN/ROY S71 ... 60 E1
Richard La NROS/TKH DN11 ... 113 J6
Richard Rd BSLYN/ROY S71 ... 60 E1
DOD/DAR S75 ... 37 H7
RHAM S60 ... 7 H7
Richards Ct SHEFP/MNR S2 ... 176 F1 3
Richards Rd SHEFP/MNR S2 ... 160 E8
Richard St BSLY S70 ... 2 D6 3
Richards Wy RAW S62 ... 129 L1
Rich Farm Cl BTLY DN5 ... 68 B4
Rich Ga HOLM/MEL HD7 ... 53 M5
Richmond Av DOD/DAR S75 ... 37 H8 1
HAN/WDH S13 ... 162 C7
Richmond Dr AWLS/ASK DN6 ... 28 A7
Richmond Farm Ms
HAN/WDH S13 ... 162 B8 1
Richmond Gv HAN/WDH S13 ... 162 C7 3
Richmond Hall Av
HAN/WDH S13 ... 162 B7
Richmond Hall Crs
HAN/WDH S13 ... 162 B8 2
Richmond Hall Dr
HAN/WDH S13 ... 162 B7 1
Richmond Hall Rd
HAN/WDH S13 ... 162 B7
Richmond Hall Wy
HAN/WDH S13 ... 162 B8 3
Richmond Hill Rd BTLY DN5 ... 89 J5 1
HAN/WDH S13 ... 162 B8 4
Richmond La BTLY DN10 ... 154 D1
Richmond Park Av
HAN/WDH S13 ... 162 C5
KIMB S61 ... 146 B1
Richmond Park Cl
HAN/WDH S13 ... 162 C6 1
Richmond Park Crs
HAN/WDH S13 ... 162 C5
Richmond Park Cft
HAN/WDH S13 ... 162 B5
Richmond Park Dr
HAN/WDH S13 ... 162 C6
Richmond Park Gv
HAN/WDH S13 ... 162 B6
Richmond Park Ri
HAN/WDH S13 ... 162 B5
Richmond Park Rd
HAN/WDH S13 ... 162 C6
Richmond Park Vw
HAN/WDH S13 ... 162 C6
Richmond Park Wy
HAN/WDH S13 ... 162 C6
Richmond Pl HAN/WDH S13 ... 162 B8 5
Richmond Rd BTLY DN5 ... 67 H8
DEARNE S63 ... 64 A7
HAN/WDH S13 ... 162 C7
HAN/WDH S13 ... 178 A1
HEM/SK/SE WF9 ... 24 F8
KIMB S61 ... 146 C1
THNE DN8 ... 32 B3
WRKN S81 ... 184 D1
WRKS S80 ... 198 E6
Richmond St BSLY S70 ... 2 C6 1
OWL S3 ... 160 F1
Richworth Rd HAN/WDH S13 ... 162 D7
Ricknald Cl AU/AST/KP S26 ... 164 B5
Ridal Av STKB/PEN S36 ... 101 L5
Ridal Cl STKB/PEN S36 ... 101 L5
Ridal Cft STKB/PEN S36 ... 101 L5 3
Riddell Av WRKN S81 ... 168 C4
Riddings Cl HEM/SK/SE WF9 ... 41 H2
MALT S66 ... 165 K1 1
SHEFP/MNR S2 ... 161 L8
Riddings La BWTY DN10 ... 136 F4
Rider Rd ST/HB/BR S6 ... 144 A7
Ridge Balk La AWLS/ASK DN6 ... 66 D2
Ridge Cl KBTN HD8 ... 34 E6
Ridge Crs HOR/CROF WF4 ... 17 L1
Ridgehill Av HACK/IN S12 ... 177 L2
Ridgehill Gv HACK/IN S12 ... 177 M2
Ridge Rd AWLS/ASK DN6 ... 66 F5
ECK/KIL S21 ... 192 C5
RHAM/THRY S65 ... 7 H3
Ridgestone Av HEM/SK/SE WF9 ... 23 J8
The Ridge FUL S10 ... 159 G6
Ridge View Cl DARN/MH S9 ... 145 L4
Ridge View Dr DARN/MH S9 ... 145 L4
Ridgewalk Wy BSLY S70 ... 82 D1
Ridgeway DRON S18 ... 191 H4
RHAM/THRY S65 ... 130 A8
WRKN S81 ... 198 E1 3
Ridgeway Cescent
HACK/IN S12 ... 177 L2
Ridgeway Cl MALT S66 ... 149 L3
RHAM/THRY S65 ... 130 B8
Ridgeway Crs BSLYN/ROY S71 ... 39 G6
HACK/IN S12 ... 177 L1
Ridgeway Dr HACK/IN S12 ... 177 L1
Ridgeway Moor HACK/IN S12 ... 192 C1
Ridgeway Rd HACK/IN S12 ... 177 L2
RHAM S60 ... 146 F7
SHEFP/MNR S2 ... 177 L1 1
Ridgewood Av ARMTH DN3 ... 69 K6
Ridgill Av AWLS/ASK DN6 ... 44 E6
Ridgway Av WMB/DAR S73 ... 84 E1
Riding Cl DONS/BSCR DN4 ... 113 M1
MALT S66 ... 148 E2
Ridings Av BSLYN/ROY S71 ... 60 F2
The Ridings BSLYN/ROY S71 ... 61 G2 1
Ridingwood Ri KBTN HD8 ... 35 J5 5
Rig Cl KIMB S61 ... 128 D6
Rig Dr MEX/SWTN S64 ... 107 L4
Riggs High Rd ST/HB/BR S6 ... 158 D2
Riggs Low Rd ST/HB/BR S6 ... 158 D2
Riley Av DONS/BSCR DN4 ... 111 K1
Riley Rd DEARNE S63 ... 107 K2
Rimington Rd WMB/DAR S73 ... 84 B4
Rimini Ri WMB/DAR S73 ... 84 C2
Ringinglow Rd ECC S11 ... 174 F3
Ringstead Av FUL S10 ... 159 J5
Ringstead Crs FUL S10 ... 159 K5
Ringstone Gv CUD/GR S72 ... 40 E4
Ringway DEARNE S63 ... 85 M5
Ringwood WRKN S81 ... 198 E1 3
Ringwood Crs MOS S20 ... 179 L5
Ringwood Dr MOS S20 ... 179 L5
Ringwood Gv MOS S20 ... 179 L5
Ringwood Rd MOS S20 ... 179 L5 5
Ringwood Wy HEM/SK/SE WF9 ... 23 K8
Ripley Gv DOD/DAR S75 ... 59 M3
Ripley St ST/HB/BR S6 ... 144 A8
Ripon Av WHHL DN2 ... 90 D1
Ripon St DARN/MH S9 ... 161 K2
Ripon Wy AU/AST/KP S26 ... 164 A8
Rippon Ct RAW S62 ... 107 K8
Rippon Crs ST/HB/BR S6 ... 143 M7
Rippon Rd ST/HB/BR S6 ... 143 M7
Risedale Rd DEARNE S63 ... 86 D3 1
The Rise DIN S25 ... 182 C2
MEX/SWTN S64 ... 107 M5
Rishworth Av KBTN HD8 ... 35 H1
Rising St OWL S3 ... 160 F1
Rivelin Bank ST/HB/BR S6 ... 143 M8
Rivelin Mill Br ST/HB/BR S6 ... 158 E4
Rivelin Park Crs ST/HB/BR S6 ... 159 K1
Rivelin Park Dr ST/HB/BR S6 ... 159 K1
Rivelin Park Rd ST/HB/BR S6 ... 159 L2
Rivelin Rd ST/HB/BR S6 ... 159 L1
Rivelin St ST/HB/BR S6 ... 159 M1
Rivelin Ter ST/HB/BR S6 ... 159 L1
Rivelin Valley Rd ST/HB/BR S6 ... 158 E4
Riverdale Av ECC S11 ... 159 K7
Riverdale Dr FUL S10 ... 159 L6
Riverdale Rd BTLY DN5 ... 67 J7
ECC S11 ... 159 L7
Riverhead BTLY DN5 ... 88 F6
River La HTFD DN7 ... 30 F8 3
Riverside KBTN HD8 ... 35 J5
Riverside Cl ST/HB/BR S6 ... 143 K7
WMB/DAR S73 ... 85 G1 1
Riverside Dr BTLY DN5 ... 89 G6
Riverside Gdns DEARNE S63 ... 86 B6 3
EPW DN9 ... 92 D8
Riverside Wy RHAM S60 ... 6 C7
River Ter ST/HB/BR S6 ... 144 A7
River View Rd CHPT/GREN S35 ... 125 H8
River Wy EPW DN9 ... 92 D8
Riviera Pde BTLY DN5 ... 4 D1
Rix Rd MEX/SWTN S64 ... 108 B7
Roache Dr DEARNE S63 ... 86 A3
Roach Rd ECC S11 ... 160 A7
Roaine Dr HOLM/MEL HD7 ... 53 M4
Robert Av BSLYN/ROY S71 ... 61 H5
Robert Rd SHEFS S8 ... 176 D8
Roberts Av CONI DN12 ... 110 B6
Robertshaw Crs
STKB/PEN S36 ... 102 B6 4
Robertson Dr ST/HB/BR S6 ... 159 L1
Robertson Rd ST/HB/BR S6 ... 159 L2
Roberts Rd CONI DN12 ... 111 G6
DONS/BSCR DN4 ... 4 D8
Roberts St CUD/GR S72 ... 39 M8 2
WMB/DAR S73 ... 84 A5 2
Robert St BSLY S70 ... 82 E3 7
RHAM S60 ... 6 B4
Robey St ATT S4 ... 145 H6
Robinets Rd KIMB S61 ... 128 E4
Robin Hood Av
BSLYN/ROY S71 ... 39 H3 1
Robin Hood Cha ST/HB/BR S6 ... 143 G8
Robin Hood Crs ARMTH DN3 ... 69 L6 5
Robin Hood Rd ARMTH DN3 ... 69 L6
DARN/MH S9 ... 145 L3 1
Robin La BSLYN/ROY S71 ... 39 H3
HEM/SK/SE WF9 ... 40 E2
MOS S20 ... 179 K3
Robin Pl AU/AST/KP S26 ... 180 C1
Robins Cl AU/AST/KP S26 ... 164 C8
Robinson Dr WRKS S80 ... 198 C6
Robinson Rd SHEFP/MNR S2 ... 9 M6
Robinson St RHAM S60 ... 6 E8
Rob Royd DOD/DAR S75 ... 81 K1 6
Rob Royd La BSLY S70 ... 82 B1
Roche Cl BSLYN/ROY S71 ... 3 L2
Roche End AU/AST/KP S26 ... 181 J2
Rocher Av SHEFN S5 ... 126 C8
Rocher Cl SHEFN S5 ... 126 C8
Rocher Gv SHEFN S5 ... 126 C8
Rocher La CHPT/GREN S35 ... 124 A4
Rochester Cl FUL S10 ... 158 E6 1
WRKN S81 ... 184 E8
Rochester Dr FUL S10 ... 158 E6
Rochester Rd BSLYN/ROY S71 ... 60 F3
DIN S25 ... 182 B4
FUL S10 ... 158 E6
Rochester Rw BTLY DN5 ... 89 H2
Rockcliffe Dr NROS/TKH DN11 ... 111 M8
Rockcliffe Rd RAW S62 ... 129 K3
Rockfield Dr WRKN S81 ... 183 J4
Rockingham Cl BSLY S70 ... 104 C1
DRON S18 ... 190 A6 13
SHEF S1 ... 9 G7
Rockingham Ga SHEF S1 ... 9 G6
Rockingham La
HEM/SK/SE WF9 ... 24 C2
SHEF S1 ... 9 G4
Rockingham Rd DOD/DAR S75 ... 81 L2
MEX/SWTN S64 ... 107 L5
RAW S62 ... 129 L1
Rockingham Rw BSLY S70 ... 104 D1
Rockingham St BSLY S70 ... 104 D1
BSLYN/ROY S71 ... 60 C3
CUD/GR S72 ... 40 E8 2
HEM/SK/SE WF9 ... 22 F4 2
HOY S74 ... 104 E1
SHEF S1 ... 8 F4
Rockingham Wy SHEF S1 ... 9 G6
Rocklea Cl MEX/SWTN S64 ... 108 A5 1
Rockley Av BSLY S70 ... 82 C6
WMB/DAR S73 ... 83 M6
Rockley Crs BSLY S70 ... 82 C8
Rockley Dr WKFDW/WTN WF2 ... 19 M1
Rockley La BSLY S70 ... 82 B7
BTLY DN5 ... 45 K4
DOD/DAR S75 ... 82 A4
Rockley Mdw BSLY S70 ... 2 B9
BSLY S70 ... 60 A8
Rockley Nook WHHL DN2 ... 68 F8 2
Rockley Rd ST/HB/BR S6 ... 143 M5
Rockley Vw DOD/DAR S75 ... 104 B1
Rock Mt HOY S74 ... 105 K1 1
Rock Mount Rd DARN/MH S9 ... 145 M3
Rock Side Rd STKB/PEN S36 ... 78 E4
Rock St BSLY S70 ... 2 D4
OWL S3 ... 160 F2
Rockwood Cl
CHPT/GREN S35 ... 126 C2 3
DOD/DAR S75 ... 37 K7 4
Rockwood Crs HOR/CROF WF4 ... 19 H1
Rockwood Ri KBTN HD8 ... 34 E8
Roddis Cl DIN S25 ... 166 B6 1
Roden Wy RAW S62 ... 107 G7
Rodes Av CUD/GR S72 ... 63 J5
Rodger Rd HAN/WDH S13 ... 163 H8
Rodger St KIMB S61 ... 6 B2
Rodley La KBTN HD8 ... 17 H8
Rodman Dr HAN/WDH S13 ... 163 H7
Rodman St HAN/WDH S13 ... 163 H7
Rod Moor Rd TOT/DORE S17 ... 189 M3
Rodney Hl ST/HB/BR S6 ... 143 H7
Rod Side ST/HB/BR S6 ... 157 M2
Rodwood Av STV/CWN S43 ... 194 E8
Roebuck Hl HOY S74 ... 83 K7
Roebuck Rd ST/HB/BR S6 ... 8 A2
Roebuck St WMB/DAR S73 ... 84 C6
Roebuck Wy WRKS S80 ... 199 M7
Roeburn Cl DOD/DAR S75 ... 37 L5 2
Roe Croft Cl BTLY DN5 ... 89 K5
Roehampton Ri BSLYN/ROY S71 ... 61 K7
BTLY DN5 ... 89 J2 6
RHAM S60 ... 146 E6
Roe La ATT S4 ... 144 F7
Roger Rd BSLYN/ROY S71 ... 61 J5
Rojean Rd CHPT/GREN S35 ... 126 B7
Rokeby Dr SHEFN S5 ... 144 E1
Rokeby Rd SHEFN S5 ... 144 E1
Rolleston Av MALT S66 ... 150 C2
Rolleston Rd AWLS/ASK DN6 ... 44 F7
SHEFN S5 ... 145 G3
Rollet Cl SHEFP/MNR S2 ... 161 L7
Rollin Dr ST/HB/BR S6 ... 143 M6
Rolling Dales Cl MALT S66 ... 132 C8
Rolls Crs RAW S62 ... 107 G7
Roman Bank La BWTY DN10 ... 170 C2
Roman Ct KIMB S61 ... 146 C1 2
Roman Crs RAW S62 ... 129 J1
RHAM S60 ... 147 G6
Romandale Gdns
SHEFP/MNR S2 ... 162 A6
Roman Rdg AWLS/ASK DN6 ... 44 C8
AWLS/ASK DN6 ... 66 D3
Roman Ridge Rd DARN/MH S9 ... 145 M4
Roman Rd DOD/DAR S75 ... 37 H8
DONS/BSCR DN4 ... 5 K6
Roman St DEARNE S63 ... 64 C6
Romney Cl MALT S66 ... 148 F1
Romney Dr DRON S18 ... 190 C6
Romney Gdns
SHEFP/MNR S2 ... 176 F1 2
Romsdal Rd FUL S10 ... 160 A3 6
Romwood Av MEX/SWTN S64 ... 107 L4
Ronald Rd DARN/MH S9 ... 162 A3 5
DONS/BSCR DN4 ... 89 L8 6
Ronksley Crs SHEFN S5 ... 145 H1
Ronksley La ST/HB/BR S6 ... 158 A4
Ronksley Rd SHEFN S5 ... 145 H1
Roods La HOLM/MEL HD7 ... 52 E4
Rookdale Cl DOD/DAR S75 ... 59 M3
Rookery Bank
STKB/PEN S36 ... 102 D7 5
Rookery Cha STKB/PEN S36 ... 102 D7 3
Rookery Cl AU/AST/KP S26 ... 181 G4
STKB/PEN S36 ... 102 D7 6
Rookery Dell STKB/PEN S36 ... 102 D7 7
Rookery Ri STKB/PEN S36 ... 102 D8
Rookery Rd MEX/SWTN S64 ... 107 M5
The Rookery STKB/PEN S36 ... 102 D7
Rookery V STKB/PEN S36 ... 102 D7 8
Rookery Wy CHPT/GREN S35 ... 102 E1
Rook Hl BSLY S70 ... 83 G2
Roper Hl FUL S10 ... 158 B8
Roper House La
CHPT/GREN S35 ... 102 C1
Roper La CHPT/GREN S35 ... 80 D8
Rope Wk THNE DN8 ... 31 L8
Rosamond Av TOT/DORE S17 ... 189 L1
Rosamond Cl TOT/DORE S17 ... 189 L1
Rosamond Dr TOT/DORE S17 ... 189 L2
Rosamond Gld TOT/DORE S17 ... 189 L1 2
Rosamond Pl TOT/DORE S17 ... 189 L1 3
Rosa Rd FUL S10 ... 160 A3
Roscoe Bank ST/HB/BR S6 ... 159 J2
Roscoe Dr ST/HB/BR S6 ... 159 K2
Roscoe Mt ST/HB/BR S6 ... 159 K2
Roscoe Rd OWL S3 ... 8 F1
Rose Av DONS/BSCR DN4 ... 89 M7
HEM/SK/SE WF9 ... 24 D8
MOS S20 ... 179 K4
WMB/DAR S73 ... 62 D8
Roseberry Av HTFD DN7 ... 48 F8
Roseberry Cl HOY S74 ... 105 J3 2
Rosebery St KIMB S61 ... 146 E1
Rosebery Ter BSLY S70 ... 3 J7 2
Rose Cl HEM/SK/SE WF9 ... 24 E8
RHAM S60 ... 147 H8
Rose Ct DONS/BSCR DN4 ... 89 L7 1
MALT S66 ... 148 E3
Rose Crs BTLY DN5 ... 67 J8
RAW S62 ... 129 M1
Rosedale WRKN S81 ... 184 E7

Rosedale Av *RAW* S62 .... 129 K1
Rosedale Cl *HEM/SK/SE* WF9 ..... 24 F8 🔟
Rosedale Gdns *BSLY* S70 .... 2 B5
  ECC S11 .... 160 B7 🔟
Rosedale Rd *AU/AST/KP* S26 .... 164 C7
  BTLY DN5 .... 67 H8
  BTLY DN5 .... 67 L5
  ECC S11 .... 160 B7 🔟
  FUL S10 .... 8 B9
Rosedale Wy *MALT* S66 .... 149 G1
Rose Dr *MALT* S66 .... 148 F2
Rose Garth *BTLY* DN5 .... 89 L1 🔟
Rose Garth Av *AU/AST/KP* S26 .. 164 C7
Rosegarth Cl *BTLY* DN5 .... 67 J8 🔟
Rose Gv *HEM/SK/SE* WF9 .... 24 E8
  WMB/DAR S73 .... 83 M3
Rose Hl *DONS/BSCR* DN4 .... 91 G6
  MOS S20 .... 178 F7
Rose Hill Av *MOS* S20 .... 178 F7
Rose Hill Av *RAW* S62 .... 107 L8
Rose Hill Cl *MOS* S20 .... 178 F7
  STKB/PEN S36 .... 79 H5
Rosehill Ct *BSLY* S70 .... 2 F5
Rose Hill Dr *DOD/DAR* S75 .... 59 K8 🔟
  MOS S20 .... 178 F7
Rose Hill Ri *DONS/BSCR* DN4 .... 91 G5
Rosehill Rd *RAW* S62 .... 129 K1
Rose La *AWLS/ASK* DN6 .... 45 K1
  DIN S25 .... 165 M1
  FEA/AMT WF7 .... 23 H3
Roselle St *ST/HB/BR* S6 .... 144 A7 🔟
Rosemary Gv *BTLY* DN5 .... 110 B2 🔟
Rosemary Rd *MALT* S66 .... 148 E2
  MOS S20 .... 179 K3
Rose Pl *WMB/DAR* S73 .... 84 A3
Rose Tree Av *CUD/GR* S72 .... 39 M8
Rose Tree Ct *CUD/GR* S72 .... 39 M8
Rose Wy *ECK/KIL* S21 .... 194 B2
Rosewood Dr *ARMTH* DN3 .... 47 J8 🔟
Roslin Rd *FUL* S10 .... 160 A4
Roslyn Crs *HATH/EY* S32 .... 172 E8 🔟
Roslyn Rd *HATH/EY* S32 .... 172 E8
Rosser Av *HACK/IN* S12 .... 177 K5
Rossetti Gdns *WRKN* S81 .... 199 G4
Rossetti Mt *MALT* S66 .... 148 F1
Rossington Br
  DONS/BSCR DN4 .... 113 M3
Rossington Rd *ECC* S11 .... 160 A1
Rossington St *CONI* DN12 .... 109 K3
Rossiter Rd *KIMB* S61 .... 129 G3
Rosslyn Av *AU/AST/KP* S26 .... 164 C7
  FEA/AMT WF7 .... 23 K2
Rosslyn Cl *FEA/AMT* WF7 .... 23 K2 🔟
Rosslyn Crs *BTLY* DN5 .... 67 M5
Rosslyn Gv *FEA/AMT* WF7 .... 23 K2 🔟
Rossmoor Cl *EPW* DN9 .... 92 E8 🔟
Ross St *DARN/MH* S9 .... 162 B3
Rosston Rd *MALT* S66 .... 150 F2
Roston Cl *DRON* S18 .... 190 B6 🔟
Rotcher Rd *HOLM/MEL* HD7 .... 53 L3
Rothay Cl *DRON* S18 .... 190 C7
Rothay Rd *ATT* S4 .... 145 K6
Rothbury Cl *MOS* S20 .... 179 L5 🔟
Rothbury Ct *MOS* S20 .... 179 L5 🔟
Rothbury Wy *RHAM* S60 .... 147 G6 🔟
Rother Crs *RHAM* S60 .... 163 J3
Rotherham Baulk *WRKN* S81 ...... 167 K8
Rotherham Cl *ECK/KIL* S21 .... 180 D7
Rotherham La *DIN* S25 .... 166 A2
Rotherham Rd *AU/AST/KP* S26 ... 179 L3
  BSLYN/ROY S71 .... 60 C1
  CUD/GR S72 .... 63 J8
  CUD/GR S72 .... 85 H2
  DEARNE S63 .... 106 F7
  DIN S25 .... 166 A5
  ECK/KIL S21 .... 180 D7
  HAN/WDH S13 .... 162 F5
  MALT S66 .... 150 A2
  MOS S20 .... 179 K8
  NROS/TKH DN11 .... 152 D1
  RAW S62 .... 129 J6
  RHAM S60 .... 163 H1
  RHAM/THRY S65 .... 129 J6
Rotherham Rd North
  MOS S20 .... 179 K8 🔟
Rotherham Roundwalk
  KIMB S61 .... 128 F7
  RAW S62 .... 106 B7
  RHAM S60 .... 163 K1
Rotherham St *DARN/MH* S9 .... 145 L8 🔟
Rotherhill Cl *RHAM/THRY* S65 ...... 7 L2
Rothermoor Av
  AU/AST/KP S26 .... 181 G5
Rother Rd *RHAM* S60 .... 147 H4
Rotherside Rd *ECK/KIL* S21 .... 193 K3
Rotherstoke Cl *RHAM* S60 .... 7 H8
Rother St *WMB/DAR* S73 .... 84 E7
Rother Ter *RHAM* S60 .... 147 H4
Rothervale Cl *MOS* S20 .... 179 L3
Rother Valley Wy *MOS* S20 .... 179 L3
Rother View Rd *RHAM* S60 .... 6 F9
  RHAM S60 .... 147 H4
Rother Wy *MALT* S66 .... 149 L1
Rotherway *RHAM* S60 .... 147 J7
Rotherwood Av
  HAN/WDH S13 .... 163 H7
Rotherwood Cl *BTLY* DN5 .... 89 H1
Rotherwood Crs *MALT* S66 .... 165 J1
Rotherwood Rd *ECK/KIL* S21 ...... 180 C8
Rothesay Cl *BTLY* DN5 .... 89 K2 🔟
Roughbirchworth La
  STKB/PEN S36 .... 79 L7
Rough La *CHPT/GREN* S35 .... 103 G7
  CHPT/GREN S35 .... 125 M6
Roughwood Rd *KIMB* S61 .... 128 C5
Round Close Rd
  HOLM/MEL HD7 .... 75 M1
Roundel St *DARN/MH* S9 .... 161 K2
Round Green La *DOD/DAR* S75 ..... 81 M3
Round Hl *DOD/DAR* S75 .... 37 L7
Roundwood Cl *BSLY* S70 .... 82 E3 🔟
Roundwood Gv *RAW* S62 .... 129 L2
Roundwood Wy *WMB/DAR* S73 .... 84 C7
Rowan Cl *BSLY* S70 .... 3 H9
  CHPT/GREN S35 .... 126 E3 🔟
  EPW DN9 .... 114 E3 🔟
  THNE DN8 .... 32 A5

Rowan Ct *WHHL* DN2 .... 91 G1
Rowan Crs *WRKS* S80 .... 198 C6
Rowan Dr *DOD/DAR* S75 .... 59 M4
  MALT S66 .... 149 G2
Rowan Garth *BTLY* DN5 .... 89 L1 🔟
Rowan Mt *WHHL* DN2 .... 90 F1
Rowan Ri *MALT* S66 .... 150 B2
Rowan Rd *ECK/KIL* S21 .... 195 G6
The Rowans *EPW* DN9 .... 117 M3
Rowan Tree Dell
  TOT/DORE S17 .... 189 J4
Rowan Tree Rd *ECK/KIL* S21 ...... 193 M1
Rowborn Dr *CHPT/GREN* S35 ...... 143 K1
Rowdale Crs *HACK/IN* S12 .... 178 B2 🔟
Rowel La *ST/HB/BR* S6 .... 142 F8
Rowena Av *ARMTH* DN3 .... 69 K6
Rowena Dr *BTLY* DN5 .... 89 C1
  MALT S66 .... 149 J8
Rowena Rd *DON* DN12 .... 109 M5 🔟
Rowgate *KBTN* HD8 .... 55 L1
Rowlands Av
  HEM/SK/SE WF9 .... 24 E8 🔟
Rowland St *BSLYN/ROY* S71 .... 39 H3 🔟
  OWL S3 .... 160 E2 🔟
Rowley La *HEM/SK/SE* WF9 .... 42 E6
Rowms La *MEX/SWTN* S64 .... 108 D4
Rowsley St *SHEFP/MNR* S2 .... 9 J9
Roxby Cl *DONS/BSCR* DN4 .... 113 H2 🔟
Roxton Av *SHEFS* S8 .... 176 D7 🔟
Roxton Rd *SHEFS* S8 .... 176 C6
Royal Av *DON* DN1 .... 5 J3
Royal Ct *DOD/DAR* S75 .... 59 J1
  HOY S74 .... 105 K1
Royal Crs *WRKN* S81 .... 198 C6
Royale Cl *ECK/KIL* S21 .... 193 J4
Royal St *BSLY* S70 .... 2 F5
Royd Av *CUD/GR* S72 .... 61 M1
  DOD/DAR S75 .... 37 M6
  STKB/PEN S36 .... 78 B4
Royd Cl *BSLY* S70 .... 82 D3
Roydfield Cl *MOS* S20 .... 179 H5 🔟
Roydfield Dr *MOS* S20 .... 179 H5 🔟
Roydfield Gv *MOS* S20 .... 179 H5 🔟
Royd Field La *STKB/PEN* S36 .... 79 H7
Royd La *DOD/DAR* S75 .... 59 G4
  HOLM/MEL HD7 .... 53 J5
  STKB/PEN S36 .... 78 B3
  STKB/PEN S36 .... 78 B4
Royd Moor La *HEM/SK/SE* WF9 .... 23 M6
Royd Moor Rd *STKB/PEN* S36 ...... 78 B2
Royds Av *HOLM/MEL* HD7 .... 54 B1
  RHAM S60 .... 148 A5
Royds Cl *HOLM/MEL* HD7 .... 54 B1
Royds Close Crs
  RHAM/THRY S65 .... 130 C5
Royds Crs *WRKS* S80 .... 197 L2
Royds Dr *HOLM/MEL* HD7 .... 54 B1
Royds La *HOY* S74 .... 106 A2
Royds Moor Hl *RHAM* S60 .... 148 C6
Royds Pk *KBTN* HD8 .... 56 E1
The Royds *HOLM/MEL* HD7 .... 53 L2
  KBTN HD8 .... 35 L4
The Royd *STKB/PEN* S36 .... 102 B8
Roy Kilner Rd *WMB/DAR* S73 ..... 83 M3 🔟
Royles Cl *HEM/SK/SE* WF9 .... 42 A5 🔟
Royston Av *BTLY* DN5 .... 67 L8
  MOS S20 .... 178 E5
Royston Cl *MOS* S20 .... 178 E5
Royston Cft *MOS* S20 .... 178 E5 🔟
Royston Gv *MOS* S20 .... 178 E5 🔟
Royston Hl *HOY* S74 .... 105 H1
Royston La *BSLYN/ROY* S71 .... 39 G5
Royston Rd *CUD/GR* S72 .... 39 L6
Rubens Cl *DRON* S18 .... 190 D4
Rud Broom La *STKB/PEN* S36 ...... 78 F4
Ruddle La *MALT* S66 .... 132 D3
Ruddle Mill La *CONI* DN12 .... 133 H6
Rudgate La *GLE* DN14 .... 13 C8
Rudyard Rd *ST/HB/BR* S6 .... 144 A7
Rufford Av *BSLYN/ROY* S71 .... 38 E7
Rufford Ct *MOS* S20 .... 179 L5 🔟
Rufford Ri *DEARNE* S63 .... 86 A3
  MOS S20 .... 179 L5
Rufford Rd *DONS/BSCR* DN4 .... 5 M8
Rufford St *WRKS* S80 .... 198 F7
Rufus La *NROS/TKH* DN11 .... 113 H6
Rugby St *OWL* S3 .... 160 E1
Rugged Butts La *BWTY* DN10 ..... 137 L4
Rundle Dr *ABRD* S7 .... 160 C8
Rundle Rd *ABRD* S7 .... 160 C8
  STKB/PEN S36 .... 101 M6
Runnymede Rd *WHHL* DN2 .... 90 F4
Rupert Rd *ABRD* S7 .... 176 C2
Rural Crs *ARMTH* DN3 .... 92 B7
Rural La *ST/HB/BR* S6 .... 143 K5
Rushby St *ATT* S4 .... 145 J6
Rushdale Av *SHEFS* S8 .... 176 E2
Rushdale Mt *SHEFS* S8 .... 176 E2 🔟
Rushdale Rd *SHEFS* S8 .... 176 E2
Rushdale Ter *SHEFS* S8 .... 176 E2 🔟
Rushey Cl *RAW* S62 .... 107 J7
  WRKS S80 .... 198 F5
Rushley Av *TOT/DORE* S17 .... 175 H7
Rushley Cl *EPW* DN9 .... 114 E3 🔟
  TOT/DORE S17 .... 175 H7
Rushley Dr *TOT/DORE* S17 .... 175 H7
Rushley Rd *TOT/DORE* S17 .... 175 H8
Rushworth Cl *DOD/DAR* S75 .... 37 G7 🔟
Rushy La *STKB/PEN* S36 .... 123 K3
Rushy Moor Av *AWLS/ASK* DN6 ... 27 M7
Rushy Moor La *AWLS/ASK* DN6 ... 27 M7
Rushy Moor Rd *AWLS/ASK* DN6 ... 46 A1
Ruskin Av *MEX/SWTN* S64 .... 108 F1
Ruskin Cl *DEARNE* S63 .... 85 C8
Ruskin Dr *ARMTH* DN3 .... 47 J8
Ruskin Rd *DONS/BSCR* DN4 .... 111 L1 🔟
Ruskin Sq *SHEFS* S8 .... 176 E1
Russell Av *HOR/CROF* WF4 .... 19 K5
  NROS/TKH DN11 .... 153 H1
Russell Cl *BSLYN/ROY* S71 .... 60 F2
Russell Ct *ECC* S11 .... 175 L5 🔟
Russell Pl *MALT* S66 .... 150 E1
Russell St *OWL* S3 .... 9 G1
  RHAM/THRY S65 .... 7 H1

Russet Gv *BWTY* DN10 .... 136 E8
The Russets *WKFDW/WTN* WF2 ... 20 C1
Russett Ct *MALT* S66 .... 150 B1
Rustlings Rd *ECC* S11 .... 159 L1
Ruthin St *ATT* S4 .... 145 J7
Ruth Sq *FUL* S10 .... 8 C6
Ruthven Dr *DONS/BSCR* DN4 .... 89 H8
Ruthyn Av *STV/CWN* S43 .... 194 E8
Rutland Av *DON* DN25 .... 166 B8
Rutland Crs *NROS/TKH* DN11 ..... 153 K2
Rutland Dr *NROS/TKH* DN11 ...... 113 H6
Rutland La *NROS/TKH* DN11 ...... 113 H6
Rutland Pk *FUL* S10 .... 160 A5
Rutland Rd *HOR/CROF* WF4 .... 17 G4
  OWL S3 .... 160 E1
Rutland St *DON* DN1 .... 5 J3 🔟
  OWL S3 .... 160 E1
Rutland Wy *DOD/DAR* S75 .... 2 A2
Ryan Pl *RAW* S62 .... 129 K3
Rydal Dr *DEARNE* S63 .... 86 A6
  DRON S18 .... 190 B6
  STKB/PEN S36 .... 79 H3
Rydal Dr *WRKN* S81 .... 184 C7
Rydalhurst Av *ST/HB/BR* S6 ...... 143 K5
Rydall Pl *BTLY* DN5 .... 67 K7
Rydal Rd *AWLS/ASK* DN6 .... 45 G6
  DIN S25 .... 166 D8
  SHEFS S8 .... 176 C2
Rydal Wy *MEX/SWTN* S64 .... 109 G1
Ryebank *HOLM/MEL* HD7 .... 53 M3
Rye Bank *RHAM* S60 .... 148 B6
Rye Cl *STKB/PEN* S36 .... 79 K1
Rye Close La *HOLM/MEL* HD7 ...... 52 B3
Rye Cft *BSLYN/ROY* S71 .... 60 F1
  CONI DN12 .... 110 C5
  NROS/TKH DN11 .... 134 E7
Ryecroft Av *AWLS/ASK* DN6 .... 27 G4
  HOR/CROF WF4 .... 22 A5
Ryecroft Glen Rd
  TOT/DORE S17 .... 175 K8
Ryecroft La *HOLM/MEL* HD7 .... 54 A4
Ryecroft Rd *AWLS/ASK* DN6 .... 27 G4
  RAW S62 .... 130 A1
Ryecroft Vw *TOT/DORE* S17 ... 175 H7
Ryefield Gdns *ECC* S11 .... 175 L2
Ryefields *HOLM/MEL* HD7 .... 54 B3
Ryegate Crs *FUL* S10 .... 159 M4
Ryegate Rd *FUL* S10 .... 159 M5
Rye La *ST/HB/BR* S6 .... 142 F4
Ryeview Gdns *KIMB* S61 .... 128 F5
Ryhill Dr *HACK/IN* S12 .... 178 E5
Ryhill Pits La *HOR/CROF* WF4 ..... 21 H6
Ryle Rd *ABRD* S7 .... 176 C1
Rylstone Ct *HACK/IN* S12 .... 178 F5 🔟
Rylstone Gv *HACK/IN* S12 .... 178 F5
Rylstone Wk *BSLY* S70 .... 83 H1 🔟
Ryton Av *WMB/DAR* S73 .... 84 D6
Ryton Cl *MALT* S66 .... 150 E2
  WRKN S81 .... 169 M5
Ryton Flds *WRKN* S81 .... 169 M5
Ryton Pl *WRKS* S80 .... 198 C4
Ryton Rd *DIN* S25 .... 182 B2
Ryton St *WRKS* S80 .... 198 C4
Ryton Wy *DONS/BSCR* DN4 .... 113 L1

S

Sackerville Ter *ECK/KIL* S21 ...... 179 M8
Sackup La *DOD/DAR* S75 .... 37 K6
Sackville Rd *FUL* S10 .... 159 M3
Sackville St *BSLY* S70 .... 2 D3
Saddler Av *MOS* S20 .... 179 H6
Saddler Cl *MOS* S20 .... 179 H6 🔟
Saddler Gn *MOS* S20 .... 179 H6
Saddler Gv *MOS* S20 .... 179 H6
Saddler Ga *BSLY* S70 .... 2 F4
Sadler's Ga *WMB/DAR* S73 .... 84 A3 🔟
Saffron Cl *NROS/TKH* DN11 ...... 134 D8
Saffron Crs *NROS/TKH* DN11 .... 134 D8
Saffron Rd *NROS/TKH* DN11 ..... 134 D8
St Agnes' Rd *DONS/BSCR* DN4 .... 90 E5
St Aidan's Av *SHEFP/MNR* S2 .... 161 J6 🔟
St Aidan's Cl *SHEFP/MNR* S2 .... 161 J6 🔟
St Aidan's Dr *SHEFP/MNR* S2 .... 161 J6 🔟
St Aidan's Mt *SHEFP/MNR* S2 ... 161 J7 🔟
St Aidan's Pl *SHEFP/MNR* S2 .... 161 J7 🔟
St Aidan's Rd *SHEFP/MNR* S2 ... 161 J7 🔟
St Aidan's Wy *SHEFP/MNR* S2 .. 161 J7 🔟
St Albans Cl *FUL* S10 .... 159 L6 🔟
St Albans Ct *MALT* S66 .... 148 E3
St Albans Dr *FUL* S10 .... 158 F6
St Albans Rd *FUL* S10 .... 158 F6
St Alban's Wy *MALT* S66 .... 148 E3
St Andrew St *STKB/PEN* S36 ..... 102 C7 🔟
St Andrew's Cl *ABRD* S7 .... 160 B8 🔟
  MALT S66 .... 131 G4
  MEX/SWTN S64 .... 108 B6
St Andrews Crs *HOY* S74 .... 105 J1 🔟
St Andrews Dr *DOD/DAR* S75 ...... 37 L6
St Andrews Gv *HTFD* DN7 .... 48 E3 🔟
St Andrew's Rd *ABRD* S7 .... 160 B8
  CONI DN12 .... 109 M6
  HOY S74 .... 105 J1
St Andrew's Sq *DEARNE* S63 ...... 86 A5
St Andrew's Ter
  DONS/BSCR DN4 .... 5 J8
St Andrews Wk *RHAM* S60 .... 146 E6
St Andrew's Wy *ARMTH* DN3 ...... 69 L1
  BSLYN/ROY S71 .... 61 L8
St Annes Cl *WRKS* S80 .... 198 A4
St Anne's Dr *BSLYN/ROY* S71 ...... 39 H4
  WRKS S80 .... 198 A4
St Anne's Rd *DONS/BSCR* DN4 .... 90 E5
St Anne's St *HOR/CROF* WF4 .... 21 M6
St Annes Vw *WRKS* S80 .... 198 A4
St Annes Wy *WRKS* S80 .... 198 A5
St Ann's Rd *RHAM/THRY* S65 .... 7 H2
  STKB/PEN S36 .... 102 B6 🔟
St Anthony Rd *FUL* S10 .... 159 L1
St Augustine's Rd
  DONS/BSCR DN4 .... 91 G6
St Austell Dr *DOD/DAR* S75 .... 59 J3
St Barbara's Cl *MALT* S66 .... 150 C3 🔟
St Barbara's Rd *WMB/DAR* S73 ... 84 D2

St Barnabas La
  SHEFP/MNR S2 .... 160 E7 7️⃣
St Barnabas Rd
  SHEFP/MNR S2 .... 160 E7
St Bartholomew's Cl
  MALT S66 .... 150 C3 🔟
St Bartholomews Ri
  DONS/BSCR DN4 .... 91 H6 🔟
St Bede's Rd *RHAM* S60 .... 6 C4
St Catherine's Av
  DONS/BSCR DN4 .... 89 M7
St Catherine's Dr *HTFD* DN7 .... 70 C3 🔟
St Catherines Wy
  DOD/DAR S75 .... 59 M6 🔟
St Cecilia's Rd *DONS/BSCR* DN4 .. 90 E6
St Chad's Wy *BTLY* DN5 .... 89 G7
St Charles St *DARN/MH* S9 .... 161 J1
St Christophers Cl
  BSLYN/ROY S71 .... 61 L8 🔟
St Christopher's Crs *BTLY* DN5 .... 89 J1
St Clements Cl
  BSLYN/ROY S71 .... 61 L8 🔟
  BTLY DN5 .... 89 H1 🔟
St Cuthbert St *WRKS* S80 .... 198 D5
St David Rd *STKB/PEN* S36 .... 102 C7
St David's Cl *WRKN* S81 .... 198 E1
St David's Dr *BSLYN/ROY* S71 ..... 61 K7
  BTLY DN5 .... 89 H1
  STKB/PEN S36 .... 182 B4
  RHAM S60 .... 146 E6
St David's Rd *DON* DN12 .... 109 M5
St Dominic's Cl *BTLY* DN5 .... 88 F7
St Edmund's Av *MALT* S66 .... 165 J2
St Edwards Av *BSLY* S70 .... 2 C8
St Edwins Cl *HTFD* DN7 .... 48 E8
St Elizabeth Cl
  SHEFP/MNR S2 .... 160 F7 7️⃣
St Eric's Rd *DONS/BSCR* DN4 ...... 91 H7
St Francis Bvd
  BSLYN/ROY S71 .... 39 H8 🔟
St Francis Cl *MALT* S66 .... 131 G8
St George Ga *DON* DN1 .... 4 F4
St George Rd *STKB/PEN* S36 ...... 102 C7
St George's Av *HTFD* DN7 .... 70 D3
  MEX/SWTN S64 .... 107 M4
St George's Cl *OWL* S3 .... 8 D3
  THNE DN8 .... 50 B2 🔟
St Georges Cft *HOR/CROF* WF4 .... 22 B5
St Georges Dr *RHAM* S60 .... 146 E6 🔟
St Georges Ms
  WKFDW/WTN WF2 .... 19 L2
St George's Pk *BSLY* S70 .... 83 J8 🔟
  HOLM/MEL HD7 .... 54 B3
  THNE DN8 .... 50 B1
St George's Ter *SHEF* S1 .... 8 E4
St Georges Wk
  WKFDW/WTN WF2 .... 19 M1
St Giles Ga *BTLY* DN5 .... 89 H2
St Giles Sq *CHPT/GREN* S35 ...... 126 D2
St Helen Rd *STKB/PEN* S36 .... 102 C8 🔟
St Helen's Av *BSLYN/ROY* S71 ..... 60 F2
  HEM/SK/SE WF9 .... 23 G8
St Helens Cl *RHAM* S60 .... 163 K4
St Helen's La *BTLY* DN5 .... 87 J5
St Helen's Rd
  DONS/BSCR DN4 .... 90 E5 🔟
St Helen's Sq *ARMTH* DN3 .... 69 K3 🔟
St Helens St *HOY* S74 .... 105 L1
St Helens Wy *BSLYN/ROY* S71 ..... 61 K7
St Helier Dr *DOD/DAR* S75 .... 59 M5
St Hilda Av *BSLY* S70 .... 2 A5
St Hilda Cl *STKB/PEN* S36 .... 102 A5
St Hildas Cl *DEARNE* S63 .... 64 C6
St Hilda's Rd *DONS/BSCR* DN4 .... 90 E5
St James Av *DIN* S25 .... 182 B3
  HTFD DN7 .... 70 C2
St James Cl *ARMTH* DN3 .... 69 K3 🔟
  DEARNE S63 .... 107 L1
St James Ct *HOR/CROF* WF4 .... 22 B5
St James' Dr *RHAM/THRY* S65 ... 131 H5
St James' Gdns *DONS/BSCR* DN4 .. 4 D7
St James's Br *DONS/BSCR* DN4 .... 4 E7
St James St *DON* DN1 .... 4 D7
  SHEF S1 .... 9 H4
St James' Vw *RHAM/THRY* S65 .. 131 H4
St James Wk *HAN/WDH* S13 ...... 163 H7
St James Wy *HOR/CROF* WF4 .... 19 J2
St Joan Av *STKB/PEN* S36 .... 102 C8 🔟
St Johns Av *DOD/DAR* S75 .... 59 J3
  MALT S66 .... 149 G1
St Johns Cft
  NROS/TKH DN11 .... 133 M1 🔟
St John's Rd *BSLY* S70 .... 2 F8
  CONI DN12 .... 110 F5
  CUD/GR S72 .... 61 M1
  DIN S25 .... 166 C3
  DONS/BSCR DN4 .... 89 J7
  DRON S18 .... 191 J7
  MEX/SWTN S64 .... 108 A4
  RHAM/THRY S65 .... 129 L2
  SHEFP/MNR S2 .... 161 M3
  STKB/PEN S36 .... 102 D7
St John's Wk *BSLYN/ROY* S71 ...... 39 H4
St Joseph's Cl *DIN* S25 .... 166 D6
St Joseph's Rd *HAN/WDH* S13 ... 162 D5
St Julien's Mt *DOD/DAR* S75 .... 58 C3
St Julien's Wy *DOD/DAR* S75 ...... 58 C3
St Lawrence Rd *DARN/MH* S9 .... 146 C4
  HTFD DN7 .... 48 D8
St Leger Av *DIN* S25 .... 166 A5
St Leger Wy *DIN* S25 .... 166 D5 🔟
St Leonards *NROS/TKH* DN11 .... 134 E8
St Leonard's Av
  RHAM/THRY S65 .... 130 E5 🔟
St Leonard's Cl *DIN* S25 .... 166 C7
St Leonards Ct *SHEFN* S5 .... 144 F4
Saint Leonard's Cft
  RHAM/THRY S65 .... 130 D4 🔟
St Leonard's La *RHAM/THRY* S65 ... 7 K2

St Leonard's Lea *BTLY* DN5 .... 89 J1
St Leonard's Rd *RHAM/THRY* S65 ... 7 H3
St Leonards Wy
  BSLYN/ROY S71 .... 61 L8 🔟
St Luke's Cl *HTFD* DN7 .... 70 C3
St Lukes Wy *BSLYN/ROY* S71 ...... 61 G4 🔟
St Margaret Av *STKB/PEN* S36 ... 102 C7
St Margarets Av *BTLY* DN5 .... 87 G4 🔟
St Margaret's Dr
  MEX/SWTN S64 .... 107 M4
St Margaret's Rd
  CHPT/GREN S35 .... 126 F7
  DONS/BSCR DN4 .... 90 E6
St Mark Rd *STKB/PEN* S36 .... 102 C7
St Mark's Cl *WRKN* S81 .... 184 B7
St Mark's Crs *FUL* S10 .... 8 A6
St Martin Cl *STKB/PEN* S36 .... 102 C7
St Martin's Av *BTLY* DN5 .... 89 K2
  BWTY DN10 .... 136 D8
St Martins Cl *DOD/DAR* S75 .... 59 M5
  WRKN S81 .... 167 L1
  WRKN S81 .... 169 M5
St Mary's Crs *STKB/PEN* S36 ..... 102 C8
St Mary's Cl *CHPT/GREN* S35 .... 126 E6 🔟
  HEM/SK/SE WF9 .... 42 E5
St Mary's Crs *DON* DN1 .... 5 J2
  MEX/SWTN S64 .... 108 A3
  NROS/TKH DN11 .... 134 D8
St Mary's Dr *ARMTH* DN3 .... 92 A1
  HTFD DN7 .... 70 C3
  RHAM S60 .... 163 G1
St Mary's Gdn *BSLY* S70 .... 82 E5
St Mary's Ga *BSLY* S70 .... 2 F4
  NROS/TKH DN11 .... 134 D8
  SHEFP/MNR S2 .... 8 F8
St Mary's La *CHPT/GREN* S35 .... 126 E6
St Mary's Pl *BSLY* S70 .... 2 F4
St Mary's Rd *CONI* DN12 .... 111 G6
  DEARNE S63 .... 86 D1
  DON DN1 .... 5 J1
  HTFD DN7 .... 70 C2
  NROS/TKH DN11 .... 134 E8
  RAW S62 .... 129 L2
  SHEF S1 .... 9 H8
  SHEFP/MNR S2 .... 9 J8
  WMB/DAR S73 .... 84 A5
  WMB/DAR S73 .... 84 F2
St Mary's Sq *SHEFP/MNR* S2 .... 9 H8
St Mary's St *STKB/PEN* S36 .... 79 H4
St Mary's Vw *KIMB* S61 .... 128 F4
St Matthews Wy
  BSLYN/ROY S71 .... 61 G4
St Matthias Rd *STKB/PEN* S36 ... 102 C8
St Michael's Av *BSLYN/ROY* S71 .. 61 H1
  MEX/SWTN S64 .... 108 B3
  NROS/TKH DN11 .... 113 L5
St Michael's Cl
  CHPT/GREN S35 .... 126 F7 🔟
  DEARNE S63 .... 86 B2
  KBTN HD8 .... 17 H8 🔟
  THNE DN8 .... 50 B1
St Michael's Crs
  CHPT/GREN S35 .... 126 F7
St Michael's Dr *THNE* DN8 .... 50 B1
St Michael's Gdns *KBTN* HD8 ...... 17 G8
St Michael's Rd
  CHPT/GREN S35 .... 126 F7
  DONS/BSCR DN4 .... 90 F6
St Nicholas Cl *ARMTH* DN3 .... 69 J5 🔟
St Nicholas Rd *THNE* DN8 .... 31 M7
St Nicholas Wy *BWTY* DN10 ...... 154 C1 🔟
St Nicolas Rd *RAW* S62 .... 129 L1
St Oswald's Cl *EPW* DN9 .... 115 H4
St Oswald's Dr *ARMTH* DN3 .... 69 J5
  EPW DN9 .... 115 J4 🔟
St Owens Dr *DOD/DAR* S75 .... 59 M5 🔟
St Patrick Rd *STKB/PEN* S36 ...... 102 C7
St Patrick's Rd *WHHL* DN2 .... 90 E3
St Patrick's Wy *BTLY* DN5 .... 89 H1
St Paul Cl *AU/AST/KP* S26 .... 181 J2
  STKB/PEN S36 .... 102 C7
St Paul's Cl *HEM/SK/SE* WF9 .... 25 H7 🔟
St Paul's Pde *BSLYN/ROY* S71 ..... 61 K7
  BTLY DN5 .... 89 H2
St Peter Av *STKB/PEN* S36 .... 102 C7
St Peter's Cl *BTLY* DN5 .... 87 G3
  RHAM S60 .... 146 E7
  SHEF S1 .... 9 H3
St Peter's Ga *DEARNE* S63 .... 64 A6
St Peter's Rd *CONI* DN12 .... 109 M6
  DONS/BSCR DN4 .... 89 J8
  WRKS S80 .... 182 C8 🔟
St Peter's Ter *BSLY* S70 .... 3 J7
St Philip's La *OWL* S3 .... 8 E1
St Philip's Rd *OWL* S3 .... 8 E1
St Phillip's Cl *MALT* S66 .... 150 C3 🔟
St Quentin Cl *TOT/DORE* S17 .... 189 L2
St Quentin Dr *TOT/DORE* S17 .... 189 M2
St Quentin Mt *TOT/DORE* S17 ... 189 M2
St Quentin Ri *TOT/DORE* S17 .... 189 M2
St Quentin Vw *TOT/DORE* S17 ... 189 M2
St Ronan's Rd *ABRD* S7 .... 160 D8
Sepulchre Ga *DON* DN1 .... 4 F5
Sepulchre Ga West *DON* DN1 .... 4 E7
St Stephen's Dr
  AU/AST/KP S26 .... 164 B7
St Stephen's Rd *RHAM/THRY* S65 ... 7 H4
St Stephens Wk *BTLY* DN5 .... 89 J2
  OWL S3 .... 8 C3
St Thomas Rd *FUL* S10 .... 159 M4
St Thomas's Cl
  DONS/BSCR DN4 .... 111 J1
St Thomas's Rd *DOD/DAR* S75 .... 59 L3
St Thomas St *SHEF* S1 .... 8 F4 🔟
St Ursula's Rd *DONS/BSCR* DN4 .. 90 E5
St Veronica Rd
  STKB/PEN S36 .... 102 C8 🔟
St Vincent Av *AWLS/ASK* DN6 ...... 66 D1
  DON DN1 .... 5 J3
St Vincent Rd *DON* DN1 .... 5 J3
St Vincent's Av *ARMTH* DN3 .... 92 A8
St Wandrilles Cl
  CHPT/GREN S35 .... 126 F6
St Wilfrid's Rd *DONS/BSCR* DN4 .. 91 G6
  SHEFP/MNR S2 .... 160 E7
St Withold Av *MALT* S66 .... 165 J1
Salcombe Cl *DOD/DAR* S75 .... 38 A7
Salcombe Gv *BWTY* DN10 .... 136 D7

Sale Hl FUL S10 159 M5
Salerno Wy WMB/DAR S73 84 C1
Sales La GLE DN14 30 B2
Sale St HOY S74 104 E2
Salisbury Av DRON S18 190 E7
Salisbury Rd DONS/BSCR DN4 4 A8
DRON S18 190 F8
FUL S10 159 M4
MALT S66 150 D1
Salisbury St DOD/DAR S75 2 D2
Salmon St ECC S11 160 D7 3
Salt Box Gv CHPT/GREN S35 126 A7 1
Salt Box La CHPT/GREN S35 126 A8
Salter Hill La STKB/PEN S36 101 J1
Saltersbrook DEARNE S63 86 B2
Saltersbrook Rd WMB/DAR S73 62 D8
Salter's Wy STKB/PEN S36 79 H5
Salt Hl WRKN S81 167 M2
Salt Hill Rd WRKN S81 168 A4
Samson St SHEFP/MNR S2 9 M6
Samuel Cl SHEFP/MNR S2 161 H8 3
Samuel Dr SHEFP/MNR S2 161 H8 4
Samuel Pl SHEFP/MNR S2 161 H8
Samuel Rd DOD/DAR S75 59 M4
SHEFP/MNR S2 161 H8
Samuel Sq DOD/DAR S75 59 M4 4
Samuel St DONS/BSCR DN4 111 K1
Sanctuary Flds DIN S25 166 A8
Sandall Beat La WHHL DN2 91 H1
Sandall Beat Rd
DONS/BSCR DN4 90 F4
Sandall Carr Rd ARMTH DN3 69 J4
Sandall La ARMTH DN3 69 H3
Sandall Park Dr WHHL DN2 69 G8
Sandall Ri WHHL DN2 90 F1
Sandall Stones Rd ARMTH DN3 69 H4
Sandall Vw DIN S25 166 A4
Sandal Ri PONT WF8 24 E2 3
Sandal Rd CONI DN12 109 L6
Sandalwood Cl WHHL DN2 69 G7 1
Sandalwood Ri
MEX/SWTN S64 108 B7
Sandbeck Cl BSLYN/ROY S71 3 G1 1
Sandbeck Ct
NROS/TKH DN11 113 L7 3
Sandbeck La NROS/TKH DN11 151 M4
Sandbeck Pl ECC S11 160 B8
Sandbeck Rd DONS/BSCR DN4 5 M7
Sandbeck Wy MALT S66 149 L2
Sandbed Rd OWL S3 144 C8
Sandbergh Rd KIMB S61 128 C5
Sandby Ct SHEFS S8 177 J5 5
Sandby Cft SHEFS S8 177 J5 6
Sandby Dr SHEFS S8 177 J5
Sandcliffe Rd WHHL DN2 90 F1
Sandcroft Cl HOY S74 105 G2 3
Sandeby Dr RHAM/THRY S65 131 H8
Sanderson's Bank BWTY DN10 116 D3
Sanderson St DARN/MH S9 145 K8
Sandford Ct BSLY S70 2 D7
Sandford Grove Rd ABRD S7 176 C1
Sandford Rd DONS/BSCR DN4 111 L1
HEM/SK/SE WF9 42 E2
Sandhill Cl RAW S62 107 M8
Sandhill Gv CUD/GR S72 40 D6
Sandhill Ri EPW DN9 92 D8
Sandhill Rd RAW S62 129 M1
Sandhill St WRKS S80 198 C4
Sandhurst Rd DONS/BSCR DN4 91 L8
Sand La EPW DN9 94 D3
Sandmartins WRKN S81 184 A8
Sandown Cl ECK/KIL S21 192 F4 1
Sandown Gdns
DONS/BSCR DN4 91 H5
Sandown Rd MEX/SWTN S64 108 F1
Sandpiper Rd KIMB S61 127 K1
Sandpit Hl ARMTH DN3 92 B7
Sandringham Av RHAM S60 147 M6
Sandringham Cl
STKB/PEN S36 78 E3 5
Sandringham Crs WRKN S81 184 B8
Sandringham Pl
RHAM/THRY S65 131 H7
Sandringham Rd
DARN/MH S9 145 L3 2
WHHL DN2 90 E4
Sandrock Dr DONS/BSCR DN4 91 J8
Sandrock Rd NROS/TKH DN11 153 K2
Sands Cl GLV S14 177 J3
The Sands ST/HB/BR S6 141 L2
Sandstone Av DARN/MH S9 145 K5
Sandstone Cl DARN/MH S9 145 L4
Sandstone Dr DARN/MH S9 145 K5
Sandstone Rd DARN/MH S9 145 K5
Sandtoft Rd HTFD DN7 49 M7
Sandwith Rd AU/AST/KP S26 181 J2
Sandy Acres Cl MOS S20 179 K6
Sandy Acres Dr MOS S20 179 J6
Sandybridge La CUD/GR S72 39 M3
Sandycroft Crs
DONS/BSCR DN4 111 J1 5
Sandyfields Vw AWLS/ASK DN6 4 K6
Sandy Flat La MALT S66 148 F5
Sandygate DEARNE S63 107 K1
Sandy Ga HOLM/MEL HD7 54 A3
Sandygate Grange Dr FUL S10 159 J5
Sandygate Gv FUL S10 159 H5 5
Sandygate La HEM/SK/SE WF9 23 G8
Sandygate Pk FUL S10 159 G5
Sandygate Park Crs FUL S10 159 H5
Sandygate Park Rd FUL S10 159 H4
Sandygate Rd FUL S10 159 H5
Sandy La DONS/BSCR DN4 90 E6
MALT S66 149 K8
MALT S66 149 J4
WMB/DAR S73 84 J5
WRKS S80 198 C3
Sandymount NROS/TKH DN11 153 L2
Sandymount East
NROS/TKH DN11 153 L3 2
Sandymount Rd DEARNE S63 107 L2
Sandymount West
NROS/TKH DN11 153 L3 3
Sankey Sq DEARNE S63 86 B2
Santingley La HOR/CROF WF4 21 L1
Saracens La BWTY DN10 154 D5
Sarah St KIMB S61 6 A5
MEX/SWTN S64 108 E3
Sark Rd SHEFP/MNR S2 160 E8 3
Saundby Cl DONS/BSCR DN4 91 G8
Saunderson Rd STKB/PEN S36 78 F3
Saunders Pl SHEFP/MNR S2 161 J4 2
Saunders Rd SHEFP/MNR S2 161 J4
Saunders Rw WMB/DAR S73 84 A5
Savage La TOT/DORE S17 175 H8
Savile Av KBTN HD8 17 H8
Savile St KBTN HD8 17 H8
Savile St East ATT S4 161 H1
Savile Wk CUD/GR S72 40 F4
Saville Hall La DOD/DAR S75 81 K1 2
Saville La STKB/PEN S36 78 D4
Saville Rd DEARNE S63 107 J2
DOD/DAR S75 81 L1
KBTN HD8 34 E5
RHAM S60 147 M6
Saville St CUD/GR S72 39 M8
KBTN HD8 35 H6 1
RHAM/THRY S65 130 A6
Sawdon Rd ECC S11 8 C9
Sawn Moor Av MALT S66 165 K1
Sawn Moor Rd MALT S66 165 K2
Sawston Cl DONS/BSCR DN4 111 L3
Saxon Av HEM/SK/SE WF9 41 K5
Saxon Cl HEM/SK/SE WF9 25 J8
KBTN HD8 35 G1 2
Saxon Crs BSLY S70 82 E2
Saxon Gv HEM/SK/SE WF9 41 L6
Saxonlea Av SHEFP/MNR S2 162 A6
Saxonlea Ct SHEFP/MNR S2 162 A6
Saxonlea Crs SHEFP/MNR S2 162 A6
Saxonlea Dr SHEFP/MNR S2 161 M6 3
Saxon Mt HEM/SK/SE WF9 41 K5
Saxon Rd AU/AST/KP S26 181 K5
KIMB S61 146 B1
SHEFS S8 176 E1
Saxon Rw CONI DN12 110 C6
Saxon St CUD/GR S72 61 M1
DEARNE S63 64 C7
Saxon Wy NROS/TKH DN11 153 K3
Saxton Av DONS/BSCR DN4 91 G7
Saxton Cl HOY S74 83 M8
WRKS S80 198 B5
Saxton Dr RHAM S60 147 K6
Sayers Cl BTLY DN5 87 G5
Scafell Pl DIN S25 182 D1
Scaftworth Cl
DONS/BSCR DN4 113 G1
Scaly Ga HOLM/MEL HD7 54 E5
HOLM/MEL HD7 54 E2
Scammadine Cl RHAM S60 147 G7
Scarborough Cl DIN S25 166 C8 3
Scarborough La
NROS/TKH DN11 113 H6
Scarborough Rd DARN/MH S9 162 A2
MALT S66 148 F2
Scarbrough Crs MALT S66 150 E3 4
Scarfield Cl BSLYN/ROY S71 61 K7 5
Scarfold HOLM/MEL HD7 53 L2
Scargill Cft SHEF S1 9 H3
Scar Hole La HOLM/MEL HD7 54 E3
Scar La BSLYN/ROY S71 61 K7
Scarlett Oak Meadow
ST/HB/BR S6 159 G1 4
Scarll Rd DONS/BSCR DN4 4 A8
Scarsdale Cl DRON S18 190 F7
Scarsdale Cross DRON S18 190 F6 2
Scarsdale Rd DRON S18 190 F6
SHEFS S8 176 D4
Scarsdale St DIN S25 166 E6
Scawsby La BTLY DN5 66 F7
Scawthorpe Av BTLY DN5 67 H6
Sceptone Gv CUD/GR S72 40 A4
Schofield Dr WMB/DAR S73 84 E1
Schofield Pl WMB/DAR S73 84 E1 3
Schofield Rd STKB/PEN S36 102 B6
WMB/DAR S73 84 D1
Schofield St MEX/SWTN S64 108 D2
Schole Av STKB/PEN S36 79 G4
Schole Hill La STKB/PEN S36 78 F5
Scholes Gn KIMB S61 128 A4
Scholes La KIMB S61 127 L4
Scholes Moor Rd
HOLM/MEL HD7 54 A6
Scholes Rd HOLM/MEL HD7 54 C3
Scholes Vw CHPT/GREN S35 126 F6
Scholey Av WRKN S81 183 J4
Scholey Rd MALT S66 148 F2
Scholey St OWL S3 9 K1 2
Scholfield Crs MALT S66 150 F3 2
School Av MOS S20 179 J8
School Cl AU/AST/KP S26 180 F4
MOS S20 179 K8
Schoolfield Dr RAW S62 107 K8
School Green La FUL S10 158 F8
School Gv AU/AST/KP S26 164 C8
School Hl CUD/GR S72 39 M8 3
RHAM S60 147 M6
WKFDW/WTN WF2 19 M3
School La ARMTH DN3 91 M7
CHPT/GREN S35 102 A8
DRON S18 190 E6
ECK/KIL S21 192 C4
EPW DN9 114 E1
HATH/EY S32 172 E7
HOR/CROF WF4 21 M6
KBTN HD8 17 H8
KBTN HD8 56 E1
MALT S66 133 J7
RAW S62 129 J4
RHAM/THRY S65 130 D4
SHEFP/MNR S2 9 M5
SHEFS S8 176 D8 3
ST/HB/BR S6 159 G2
School Lane Cl SHEFS S8 177 G6
School Rd AU/AST/KP S26 180 E5
CHPT/GREN S35 104 C8
DIN S25 166 B3
FUL S10 159 M4
MALT S66 165 K1
MOS S20 179 M5 4
WRKN S81 168 C4
School St AU/AST/KP S26 164 A8
BSLY S70 61 H7
CUD/GR S72 39 M7 5
CUD/GR S72 63 H5
DEARNE S63 64 B7
DEARNE S63 86 A5
DIN S25 166 D6
DOD/DAR S75 2 C2
DOD/DAR S75 37 J6
DOD/DAR S75 38 A6
ECK/KIL S21 193 H4
HEM/SK/SE WF9 25 H7
HOLM/MEL HD7 53 L2
MOS S20 179 H8
RHAM/THRY S65 130 C5
WMB/DAR S73 84 A8
WMB/DAR S73 84 B4
WMB/DAR S73 84 F1
School Wk BWTY DN10 136 E8
CONI DN12 109 K3
CONI DN12 110 E8
MALT S66 150 D2
Scorcher Hills La
AWLS/ASK DN6 44 D3
Score Cft KBTN HD8 34 E5
Scotch Spring La MALT S66 151 K1
Scotia Cl SHEFP/MNR S2 161 K7 1
Scotia Dr SHEFP/MNR S2 161 K7 2
Scotland St OWL S3 8 F2
Scot La BWTY DN10 136 E8
DON DN1 5 G4
Scott Av BTLY DN5 87 G5
CONI DN12 109 L6
Scott Cl MALT S66 165 J1 3
WRKN S81 199 G3
Scott Crs ARMTH DN3 69 J4
Scott Hl BTLY DN5 88 F7
KBTN HD8 35 K4
Scott Rd ATT S4 145 G7
Scott St ATT S4 145 J7
Scott Wk MALT S66 150 B1
Scott Wy CHPT/GREN S35 126 D3
Scovell Av RAW S62 107 J8
Scowerdons Cl HACK/IN S12 178 D2
Scowerdons Dr HACK/IN S12 178 D2
Scraith Wood Dr SHEFN S5 144 B5
Scratta La WRKS S80 197 G5
Scrooby Cl NROS/TKH DN11 153 L3
Scrooby Dr RAW S62 129 G4
Scrooby La RAW S62 129 H4
Scrooby Pl RAW S62 129 G4
Scrooby Rd NROS/TKH DN11 153 M3
Scrooby St KIMB S61 129 G4
Seabrook Rd SHEFP/MNR S2 161 H5
Seagrave Av HACK/IN S12 177 M3
Seagrave Crs HACK/IN S12 177 L4
Seagrave Dr HACK/IN S12 177 L3
Seagrave Rd HACK/IN S12 177 L3
Searby Rd RHAM/THRY S65 131 H8
Seaton Cl SHEFP/MNR S2 161 K5
Seaton Crs SHEFP/MNR S2 161 K5
Seaton Gdns NROS/TKH DN11 113 K8
Seaton Pl SHEFP/MNR S2 161 K5
Seaton Wy SHEFP/MNR S2 161 K5
Sebastion Vw RHAM S60 147 G5
Seckar La HOR/CROF WF4 19 L7
Second Av AWLS/ASK DN6 67 G3
HEM/SK/SE WF9 22 E3
HEM/SK/SE WF9 24 E7
HEM/SK/SE WF9 41 K6
Second La DIN S25 182 C4
MALT S66 149 G5
Sedan St ATT S4 145 G8
Sedge Cl MALT S66 149 H3
Sedgefield Wy MEX/SWTN S64 108 F1
Sedgley Rd ST/HB/BR S6 144 B7
Sefton Rd ECC S11 159 J8
Selborne Rd FUL S10 159 L4
Selborne St RHAM/THRY S65 7 G1
Selbourne Cl DOD/DAR S75 59 J2 3
Selby Cl AU/AST/KP S26 164 A8
Selby Rd BSLYN/ROY S71 38 D8 2
GLE DN14 13 H6
SHEFN S5 145 H6
THNE DN8 31 K7
WHHL DN2 90 E2 1
Selhurst Crs DONS/BSCR DN4 91 J8
Selkirk Rd WHHL DN2 91 G1
Sellars Rd KIMB S61 128 C6
Sellers St SHEFS S8 160 D8 13
Selly Oak Gv SHEFS S8 191 G1
Selly Oak Rd SHEFS S8 191 G1 2
Selvage La GLE DN14 11 L4
Selwyn St RHAM/THRY S65 7 H1
Senior Rd DARN/MH S9 162 A3
DONS/BSCR DN4 4 B7
Sennen Cft BSLYN/ROY S71 3 M1
Serlby Dr AU/AST/KP S26 195 K2
Serlby La AU/AST/KP S26 195 J1
Serlby Rd NROS/TKH DN11 153 H5
Setcup La ECK/KIL S21 193 G5
Seth Ter BSLY S70 3 K7
Sevenairs Rd MOS S20 179 J4
Sevenfields Ct ST/HB/BR S6 143 L6
Sevenfields La ST/HB/BR S6 143 L6
Severn Ct FUL S10 8 A5
Severn Rd FUL S10 8 A5
Severnside Dr HAN/WDH S13 162 E8
Severnside Gdns
HAN/WDH S13 162 E8
Severnside Pl HAN/WDH S13 162 E8
Sewell Rd MOS S20 193 K1
Sexton Dr MALT S66 149 H3
Seymore Rd AU/AST/KP S26 180 B1
Seymour Rd MALT S66 150 F2 3
Shackleton Rd WHHL DN2 69 H6
Shackleton Vw STKB/PEN S36 79 H5
Shady Side DONS/BSCR DN4 4 B7
Shaftesbury Av WHHL DN2 90 F4
Shaftesbury Dr HOY S74 105 H2
Shaftesbury St BSLY S70 61 H7
Shaftholme La BTLY DN5 68 A1
Shaftholme Rd BTLY DN5 68 B2
Shafton Hall Dr CUD/GR S72 39 M4
Shafton Rd RHAM S60 147 M6
Shaftsbury Av AWLS/ASK DN6 66 D2
Shaftsbury Sq RHAM/THRY S65 7 G2
Shakespeare Av AWLS/ASK DN6 28 C4
BTLY DN5 89 K3
Shakespeare Crs DRON S18 191 G7
Shakespeare Dr DIN S25 166 E7
Shakespeare Rd BTLY DN5 67 M6 2
DEARNE S63 85 H8
RHAM/THRY S65 129 K7
Shakespeare St WRKN S81 198 F3
Shaldon Gv AU/AST/KP S26 164 B8
Shalesmoor OWL S3 8 F1
Shambles St BSLY S70 2 F5 1
Shardlow Gdns
DONS/BSCR DN4 113 K1
Sharlston Gdns
NROS/TKH DN11 113 M6
Sharman Cl DRON S18 191 L6
Sharpe Av SHEFS S8 176 C7
Sharpfield Av RAW S62 107 J7
Sharp Royd Nook
STKB/PEN S36 101 M2
Sharrard Cl HACK/IN S12 177 M2
Sharrard Dr HACK/IN S12 177 M2
Sharrard Gv HACK/IN S12 177 M1
Sharrard Rd HACK/IN S12 177 M2
Sharrow La ECC S11 160 C7
Sharrow St ECC S11 160 D7
Sharrow Vale Rd ECC S11 160 A7
Sharrow Vw ABRD S7 160 C7
Shaw Ct ARMTH DN3 92 A2
Shawfield Av HOLM/MEL HD7 53 H3
Shawfield Cl ARMTH DN3 69 L1
Shawfield Rd BSLYN/ROY S71 39 G8
BSLYN/ROY S71 61 G1
Shaw La AWLS/ASK DN6 28 E2
BSLY S70 2 C6
BSLYN/ROY S71 39 J6
DOD/DAR S75 38 A6
HOLM/MEL HD7 53 H3
STKB/PEN S36 100 B4
WHHL DN2 69 H7
Shaw Rd CONI DN12 110 F4
RHAM/THRY S65 129 L7
Shawsfield Rd RHAM S60 7 J9
Shaw St BSLY S70 2 C6
WRKS S80 198 C4 5
Shaw Wood Wy WHHL DN2 69 H8
Shay House La STKB/PEN S36 101 M7
Shay La HOLM/MEL HD7 52 C4
Shay Rd STKB/PEN S36 101 M6
The Shay DONS/BSCR DN4 91 J8
Sheaf Bank SHEFP/MNR S2 160 E8 5
Sheaf Cl CONI DN12 110 B6
Sheaf Ct BSLY S70 61 H8
Sheaf Crs DEARNE S63 86 B6
Sheaf Gdns SHEFP/MNR S2 9 K8
Sheaf Pl WRKN S81 184 C8
Sheaf St SHEF S1 9 K5
Sheards Cl DRON S18 190 D6
Sheards Dr DRON S18 190 C6 3
Sheards Wy DRON S18 190 C6
Shearman Av KIMB S61 128 C5
Shear Square Rbt SHEF S1 9 J6
Shearwood Rd FUL S10 8 B5
Sheep Bridge La
NROS/TKH DN11 113 M5
Sheep Cote La HTFD DN7 70 F4
Sheepcote Rd ECK/KIL S21 194 A1
Sheep Cote Rd
RHAM/THRY S65 148 B4
Sheep Dike La MALT S66 149 G7
Sheep Dip La HTFD DN7 48 D8
Sheephill Rd ECC S11 174 D6
Sheep La BTLY DN5 88 A6
Sheepwalk La HEM/SK/SE WF9 25 J7
PONT WF8 25 J7
Sheepwash La
NROS/TKH DN11 135 J6
Sheerien Cl BSLYN/ROY S71 38 C7
Sheffield La RHAM S60 163 G2
Sheffield Pkwy HAN/WDH S13 162 C4
SHEFP/MNR S2 161 H3
SHEFP/MNR S2 162 B5
Sheffield Rd BSLY S70 3 H7
BSLY S70 82 D8
CONI DN12 109 K7
CONI DN12 110 D4
DARN/MH S9 146 A6
DIN S25 182 C3
DIN S25 182 A2
DONS/BSCR DN4 110 F2
DRON S18 190 D4
ECK/KIL S21 180 A8
ECK/KIL S21 194 B7
HACK/IN S12 178 D5
HAN/WDH S13 163 L7
HAN/WDH S13 178 E1 2
HATH/EY S32 172 E8
HOLM/MEL HD7 54 C2
MOS S20 193 H2
RHAM S60 6 E7
STKB/PEN S36 102 A5
WRKN S81 169 K4
Sheldon Av CONI DN12 110 B6
Sheldon La ST/HB/BR S6 159 G1 5
Sheldon Rd ABRD S7 176 C1
STKB/PEN S36 101 M6
Sheldon Rw ATT S4 9 K2
Sheldon St SHEFP/MNR S2 9 G9
Sheldrake Cl KIMB S61 127 K2
Shelley Av DONS/BSCR DN4 111 M1
Shelley Cl STKB/PEN S36 79 H3
Shelley Dr ARMTH DN3 92 A2
BSLYN/ROY S71 3 K1
DIN S25 166 F7
DRON S18 191 G8
RHAM/THRY S65 147 M2
Shelley Gv BTLY DN5 89 K3 1
Shelley Ri AWLS/ASK DN6 66 E2
Shelley Rd RHAM/THRY S65 147 M1
Shelley St WRKS S80 198 E4
Shelley Wy DEARNE S63 85 G8 2
Shelley Woodhouse La
KBTN HD8 34 C7
Shenstone Dr RHAM/THRY S65 147 M3
Shenstone Rd
RHAM/THRY S65 147 M3
ST/HB/BR S6 143 M5
Shepcote La DARN/MH S9 146 A8
Shepcote Wy DARN/MH S9 146 A8
Shephard's Cl CONI DN12 109 K4
Shepherd Dr
CHPT/GREN S35 126 C1 5
Shepherd La DEARNE S63 64 B8
Shepherd's Av WRKN S81 198 D2
Shepherds Cft EPW DN9 115 K1
Shepherd St OWL S3 8 F2
Shepley Cft CHPT/GREN S35 126 C1 6
Sheppard Rd DONS/BSCR DN4 89 L8
Shepperson Rd ST/HB/BR S6 143 M6
Sherbourne Av MALT S66 149 J4
Sherburn Cl AWLS/ASK DN6 44 C5
Sherburn Ga CHPT/GREN S35 126 D1
Sherburn Rd BSLYN/ROY S71 38 C8
Sherde Rd ST/HB/BR S6 160 B1
Sheridan Av DONS/BSCR DN4 112 A1
Sheridan Ct BSLYN/ROY S71 3 L1
Sheridan Dr RHAM/THRY S65 148 A1
Sheridan Rd ARMTH DN3 47 K7 5
Sheringham Cl
CHPT/GREN S35 104 B8
Sherwood Av ARMTH DN3 69 K5 2
AWLS/ASK DN6 27 J8
BTLY DN5 89 H1
CONI DN12 109 L6
Sherwood Cl AWLS/ASK DN6 27 G6 2
Sherwood Crs RHAM/THRY S65 7 G5
WRKN S81 169 L5
Sherwood Dr AWLS/ASK DN6 44 C5
DONS/BSCR DN4 111 J2
WKFDW/WTN WF2 19 K2
Sherwood Gln SHEFS S8 175 M6
Sherwood Rd DRON S18 190 B6
ECK/KIL S21 180 C8
NROS/TKH DN11 113 L7
NROS/TKH DN11 153 K2
WRKS S80 198 D3
Sherwood St BSLYN/ROY S71 3 H5
Sherwood Wy CUD/GR S72 39 L6
Shetland Rd DRON S18 190 F7
Shield Av BSLY S70 82 D2
Shildon Gv THNE DN8 32 C4
Shining Cliff Ct BWTY DN10 136 D7
Ship Hl RHAM S60 6 F5
Shipman Balk MALT S66 132 C2
Shipman Ct MOS S20 179 H8 3
Shipton St ST/HB/BR S6 8 C1
Shirburn Gdns DONS/BSCR DN4 91 J6
Shirebrook Rd SHEFS S8 176 E1
Shirecliffe Cl OWL S3 144 F8
Shirecliffe La OWL S3 144 E8
Shirecliffe Rd SHEFN S5 144 E5
Shiregreen La SHEFN S5 145 J3
Shiregreen Ter SHEFN S5 145 H2
Shirehall Crs SHEFN S5 127 H8
Shirehall Rd SHEFN S5 145 H1
Shireoaks Common WRKN S81 183 L8
Shireoaks Rd DRON S18 191 G5
WRKN S81 197 M2
WRKS S80 197 M3
Shires Cl BTLY DN5 88 F6
Shirland Av BSLYN/ROY S71 60 E1
Shirland Ct DARN/MH S9 161 M2 6
Shirland La DARN/MH S9 161 K1
Shirland Ms DARN/MH S9 161 M2 7
Shirland Pl DARN/MH S9 161 M2 8
Shirley La AWLS/ASK DN6 46 A2
Shirley Rd DONS/BSCR DN4 4 B8
Shore Hall La STKB/PEN S36 78 C5
Shoreham Av RHAM S60 147 L6
Shoreham Dr RHAM S60 147 K6
Shoreham St SHEF S1 9 J6
SHEFP/MNR S2 9 H9
SHEFP/MNR S2 160 E7
Shore La FUL S10 159 L5
Shortbrook Bank MOS S20 179 J7 10
Shortbrook Cl MOS S20 179 J7
Shortbrook Cft MOS S20 179 K7 3
Shortbrook Dr MOS S20 179 J7
Shortbrook Rd MOS S20 179 J7
Shortbrook Wy MOS S20 179 J7
Shortfield Ct BSLYN/ROY S71 38 C7
Short Ga NROS/TKH DN11 133 L1
Short La DONS/BSCR DN4 90 F8
ST/HB/BR S6 158 C2
Shortridge St DARN/MH S9 161 K1
Short Rd WHHL DN2 91 G3
Shorts La TOT/DORE S17 188 F1
Short Wood Cl BSLY S70 82 D6
Shortwood La BTLY DN5 63 L3
Shrewsbury Cl
MEX/SWTN S64 108 D2 5
STKB/PEN S36 79 H4
Shrewsbury Rd
NROS/TKH DN11 153 M3
SHEFP/MNR S2 9 K7
STKB/PEN S36 79 H4
WRKS S80 198 F6
Shrewsbury Ter KIMB S61 146 D1
Shroggs Head Cl
WMB/DAR S73 84 F1 1
Shrogswood Rd
RHAM/THRY S65 148 B4
Shubert Cl HAN/WDH S13 162 F7
Shude Hl SHEF S1 9 K4
Sicey Av SHEFN S5 127 H7
Sicey La SHEFN S5 145 H1
Sicklebrook La DRON S18 191 J3
Sidcop Rd CUD/GR S72 39 M7
Siddall St OWL S3 8 E4
Sidings Ct DONS/BSCR DN4 90 C7
Sidling Hollow ST/HB/BR S6 142 A7
Sidney Rd WHHL DN2 90 F3
Sidney St MEX/SWTN S64 108 B4
SHEF S1 9 H7
Sidons Cl KIMB S61 128 C5 1
Siemens Cl DARN/MH S9 146 C5 1
Siena Cl WMB/DAR S73 84 C1
Sike Cl DOD/DAR S75 37 H6 2
Sike La HOLM/MEL HD7 54 B2
STKB/PEN S36 78 E6
WKFDW/WTN WF2 20 F2
Sikes Rd DIN S25 182 B2
Silkstone Cl DOD/DAR S75 104 B2
HACK/IN S12 178 C3
Silkstone Crs HACK/IN S12 178 C3
WKFDW/WTN WF2 20 A1
Silkstone Dr HACK/IN S12 178 B3
Silkstone La DOD/DAR S75 58 D5
Silkstone Ov THNE DN8 32 B4
Silkstone Pl HACK/IN S12 178 C3
Silkstone Rd HACK/IN S12 178 C3

Silkstone Vw *HOY* S74 83 J7
Silver Birch Av *FUL* S10 159 G8 1
Silver Birch Gv *EPW* DN9 115 K4 1
Silverdale Cl *ARMTH* DN3 92 C7
ECC S11 175 L2
Silverdale Crs *ECC* S11 175 L2
Silverdale Cft *ECC* S11 175 L3
Silverdale Dr *BSLYN/ROY* S71 61 H2
Silverdale Gdns *ECC* S11 175 M3 2
Silverdale Gld *ECC* S11 175 L3 1
Silverdale Rd *ECC* S11 175 L3
Silverdales *DIN* S25 166 E6
Silver Hill Rd *ECC* S11 175 M2
Silver Jubilee Cl *WHHL* DN2 91 G1
Silver Mill Rd *SHEFP/MNR* S2 160 E7 8
Silvermoor Dr
RHAM/THRY S65 131 H7
Silverstone Av *CUD/GR* S72 40 A8
Silver St *BSLY* S70 2 F7
DOD/DAR S75 81 K1
DON DN1 5 G4
HTFD DN7 48 C3
RHAM/THRY S65 130 C5
SHEF S1 9 H3
THNE DN8 31 M8
Silver Street Head *SHEF* S1 9 G3
Simcrest Av *ECK/KIL* S21 194 B2
Sime St *WRKS* S80 198 C3
Simmonite Rd *KIMB* S61 128 D6
Simons Wy *WMB/DAR* S73 83 M2
Simpson Pl *MEX/SWTN* S64 108 D2
Simpson Rd *HEM/SK/SE* WF9 42 F3 1
Sim Royd La *STKB/PEN* S36 57 H3
Sims St *SHEF* S1 9 G3
Singleton Crs *ST/HB/BR* S6 144 A8 1
Singleton Gv *ST/HB/BR* S6 144 A8 2
Singleton Rd *ST/HB/BR* S6 144 A8
Siskin Ct *WRKN* S81 184 A8
Sitka Cl *BSLYN/ROY* S71 38 F5
Sitwell Av *STKB/PEN* S36 101 L6
Sitwell Cl *WRKN* S81 198 F3
Sitwell Dr *RHAM* S60 147 L4
Sitwell Gv *MEX/SWTN* S64 108 B5
RHAM S60 147 L5
Sitwell La *MALT* S66 148 F4 1
Sitwell Park Rd
RHAM/THRY S65 148 B4
Sitwell Pl *SHEFP/MNR* S2 160 D7 1
Sitwell Rd *ABRD* S7 160 D7
WRKN S81 198 F3
Sitwell St *ECK/KIL* S21 193 G5
Sitwell V *RHAM* S60 147 K4
Sitwell Vw *RHAM* S60 148 B6
Sivilla Rd *MEX/SWTN* S64 108 B7
Siward St *HEM/SK/SE* WF9 22 E3
Sixrood La *AWLS/ASK* DN6 44 E2
Skellow Hall Gdns
AWLS/ASK DN6 44 D6
Skellow Rd *AWLS/ASK* DN6 45 G7
Skelton Av *DOD/DAR* S75 37 M6
Skelton Dr *HAN/WDH* S13 179 G2
Skelton Gv *HAN/WDH* S13 178 F1
Skelton La *HAN/WDH* S13 178 F1
MOS S20 179 K4
Skelton Ri *CHPT/GREN* S35 143 H1
Skelton Rd *SHEFS* S8 176 E2
Skelwith Cl *ATT* S4 145 K6
Skelwith Dr *ATT* S4 145 K6
Skelwith Rd *ATT* S4 145 K6
Skew Hill La *CHPT/GREN* S35 125 M7
Skiers View Rd *HOY* S74 105 G2
Skiers Wy *HOY* S74 105 G2
Skinnerthorpe Rd *ATT* S4 145 H6
Skinpit La *STKB/PEN* S36 79 L1
Skipton Cl *CONI* DN12 109 J4
Skipton Rd *ATT* S4 145 G7
AU/AST/KP S26 164 A8
Skipwith Cl *NROS/TKH* DN11 112 A5
Skipwith Gdns
NROS/TKH DN11 113 J7 1
Skye Edge Av *SHEFP/MNR* S2 161 H5
Skye Edge Rd *SHEFP/MNR* S2 161 H5
Slack Fields La
CHPT/GREN S35 124 F6
Slack La *CUD/GR* S72 39 M2
HOLM/MEL HD7 53 M3
WKFDW/WTN WF2 19 M3
Slacks La *MALT* S66 149 J4
Slack Top La *HOLM/MEL* HD7 55 G6
Slack Wk *WRKS* S80 198 C6
Slade Rd *MEX/SWTN* S64 108 A5
Slade Vw *DIN* S25 150 C8
Slaidburn Av *CHPT/GREN* S35 126 D1
Slant Ga *STKB/PEN* S36 78 B3
Slate St *SHEFP/MNR* S2 160 F8 5
Slayleigh Av *FUL* S10 159 G7
Slayleigh Delph *FUL* S10 159 G7
Slayleigh Dr *FUL* S10 159 H7
Slayleigh La *FUL* S10 159 G7
Slaynes La *BWTY* DN10 137 J7
Slay Pit La *HTFD* DN7 71 J1
Slaypit La *WRKS* S80 196 B1
Sleaford St *DARN/MH* S9 161 K1 5
Sledbrook Crs *STKB/PEN* S36 77 G1
Sledgate Dr *MALT* S66 148 D4
Sledgate La *MALT* S66 148 D4
Sledmere Rd *BTLY* DN5 89 J1
Sleep Hill La *AWLS/ASK* DN6 43 M1
HEM/SK/SE WF9 25 J8
Slinn St *FUL* S10 160 A3
Slitting Mill La *DARN/MH* S9 161 K1 6
Sloade La *HACK/IN* S12 178 B8
Smallage La *HAN/WDH* S13 163 L6
Smalldale Rd *HACK/IN* S12 178 B3
Smallfield La *ST/HB/BR* S6 123 J7
Small La *STKB/PEN* S36 57 M7
Smawell La *HOR/CROF* WF4 20 F8
Smeaton Cl *RHAM/THRY* S65 131 H7
Smeaton Rd *HEM/SK/SE* WF9 25 H7
Smeaton St *ECC* S11 160 D7 10
Smelter Wood Av
HAN/WDH S13 162 C8
Smelter Wood Cl
HAN/WDH S13 162 C8 1
Smelter Wood Crs
HAN/WDH S13 162 D8
Smelter Wood Dr
HAN/WDH S13 162 C8
Smelter Wood La
HAN/WDH S13 162 C8
Smelter Wood Pl
HAN/WDH S13 162 D8
Smelter Wood Ri
HAN/WDH S13 178 D1
Smelter Wood Rd
HAN/WDH S13 162 C8
Smelter Wood Wy
HAN/WDH S13 162 C8
Smillie Rd *NROS/TKH* DN11 113 L7
Smithey Cl *CHPT/GREN* S35 126 B1
Smithfield *OWL* S3 9 G2
Smithfield Rd *HACK/IN* S12 177 L5
Smithies La *BSLYN/ROY* S71 60 C3
Smithies Rd *MEX/SWTN* S64 108 A3
Smithies St *BSLYN/ROY* S71 60 C3
Smithley La *WMB/DAR* S73 83 L3
Smith Rd *STKB/PEN* S36 101 L6
Smith Sq *DONS/BSCR* DN4 89 K8
NROS/TKH DN11 153 K2
Smith St *CHPT/GREN* S35 126 E2
DONS/BSCR DN4 89 K8
WMB/DAR S73 84 C4 2
Smithy Bridge La
WMB/DAR S73 84 B8
Smithy Bridge Rd
ST/HB/BR S6 141 L3
Smithy Carr Av
CHPT/GREN S35 126 D2
Smithy Carr Cl
CHPT/GREN S35 126 D2
Smithy Cl *CHPT/GREN* S35 103 H3
KBTN HD8 34 E6
KIMB S61 128 D6
Smithy Cft *DRON* S18 190 A5
Smithy Fold La
CHPT/GREN S35 103 J8
Smithy Hl *CHPT/GREN* S35 80 E8
KBTN HD8 56 D4
Smithy La *HOLM/MEL* HD7 53 G5
HOR/CROF WF4 17 K3
KBTN HD8 34 E6
Smithy Mdw *HATH/EY* S32 172 E7
Smithy Moor Av
STKB/PEN S36 101 J4
Smithy Moor La *STKB/PEN* S36 101 J5
Smithy Wood Crs *SHEFS* S8 176 D3 5
Smithy Wood La *DOD/DAR* S75 81 K1
Smithy Wood Rd
CHPT/GREN S35 127 G3
SHEFS S8 176 C3
Snail Hl *RHAM* S60 6 F5
Snailsden Wy *DOD/DAR* S75 38 B7
Snaithing La *FUL* S10 159 J6
Snaithing Park Cl *FUL* S10 159 J6 2
Snaithing Park Rd *FUL* S10 159 J6
Snaith Rd *GLE* DN14 11 K1
Snake La *CONI* DN12 110 B6
Snape Hl *DRON* S18 190 E5
Snapehill Cl *DRON* S18 190 E4 2
Snapehill Crs *DRON* S18 190 E4
Snape Hill Dr *DRON* S18 190 F4 2
Snape Hill La *DRON* S18 190 E5
Snape Hill Rd *WMB/DAR* S73 84 F2
Snape La *NROS/TKH* DN11 153 L5
Snatchells La *GLE* DN14 30 C3
Snelston Cl *DRON* S18 190 A6 14
Snetterton Cl *CUD/GR* S72 40 A8 2
Snig Hl *SHEF* S1 9 J3
Snipe Park Rd
NROS/TKH DN11 153 M3
Snittle Rd *HOLM/MEL* HD7 53 M8
Snowberry Cl *MEX/SWTN* S64 108 A7
Snowden Ter *WMB/DAR* S73 84 B4
Snowdon La *ECK/KIL* S21 191 M4
Snowdon Wy *RHAM* S60 147 H8
Snow La *OWL* S3 9 G2
Snug La *HOLM/MEL* HD7 54 E6
Snydale Rd *CUD/GR* S72 39 M8
Soaper La *DRON* S18 190 E5
Soap House La *HAN/WDH* S13 163 J8
Sokell Av *WMB/DAR* S73 84 A5
Solly St *SHEF* S1 8 E3
Solway Ri *DRON* S18 190 B5
Somercotes Rd *HACK/IN* S12 178 B2
Somersby Av *BTLY* DN5 89 K3
Somerset Rd *DON* DN1 5 H7
OWL S3 160 F1
Somerset St *BSLY* S70 2 D4 1
CUD/GR S72 61 M1 5
MALT S66 150 F3 5
OWL S3 160 F1 5
Somerton Dr *DONS/BSCR* DN4 91 J8
HTFD DN7 71 K1
Somerville Ter *ST/HB/BR* S6 160 B1
Sorby Rd *AU/AST/KP* S26 163 M8
Sorby St *ATT* S4 161 G2
Sorby Wy *MALT* S66 148 F4
Sorrell La *HTFD* DN7 30 E5
Sorrel Rd *MALT* S66 149 G1
Sorrelsykes Cl *RHAM* S60 147 M7 1
Sorrento Wy *WMB/DAR* S73 84 D1
Sothall Cl *MOS* S20 179 K4
Sothall Ct *MOS* S20 179 K4 3
Sothall Gn *MOS* S20 179 K4
Sothall Ms *MOS* S20 179 K4 1
Sough Hall Av *KIMB* S61 127 K2
Sough Hall Cl *KIMB* S61 127 K2
Sough Hall Crs *KIMB* S61 127 K2
Sough Hall Rd *KIMB* S61 127 K3
Soughley La *CHPT/GREN* S35 102 E5
FUL S10 158 C7
Sour La *HTFD* DN7 30 F8
Sousa St *MALT* S66 151 G3
Southall St *SHEFS* S8 176 E1 11
Southard's La *AU/AST/KP* S26 196 C3
South Av *BWTY* DN10 136 E7
HEM/SK/SE WF9 42 C5
MEX/SWTN S64 107 M5
WRKS S80 198 F6
Southbourne Rd *ECC* S11 160 A5
Southbreck Ri *WRKS* S80 198 F6
South Cl *BSLYN/ROY* S71 39 G5
Southcote Dr *DRON* S18 190 B6
South Crs *DOD/DAR* S75 59 K8
ECK/KIL S21 180 C8
RHAM/THRY S65 129 M8
South Cft *CUD/GR* S72 40 A4
KBTN HD8 56 D4
Southcroft Gdns *SHEFS* S8 176 D1 5
Southdene *WRKN* S81 198 E1
South Dr *BSLYN/ROY* S71 39 G5
DEARNE S63 85 M6
South Drive Farm
AWLS/ASK DN6 44 E6
South End *THNE* DN8 50 A2
South End La *GLE* DN14 10 B7
Southend Pl *SHEFP/MNR* S2 161 J5
Southend Rd *SHEFP/MNR* S2 161 J6 2
Southern Wd *WRKS* S80 198 C7
Southey Av *SHEFN* S5 144 E4
Southey Cl *SHEFN* S5 144 D4 1
Southey Crs *MALT* S66 150 E2
SHEFN S5 144 D4
Southey Dr *SHEFN* S5 144 E4
Southey Green Cl *SHEFN* S5 144 D4 2
Southey Green Rd *SHEFN* S5 144 B3
Southey Hall Dr *SHEFN* S5 144 D4
Southey Hall Rd *SHEFN* S5 144 D4
Southey Hl *SHEFN* S5 144 C3
Southey Pl *SHEFN* S5 144 D4
Southey Ri *SHEFN* S5 144 D4
Southey Rd *MALT* S66 150 E2 1
Southfall Cl *RTFD* DN22 170 F2
South Farm Av *AU/AST/KP* S26 195 J1
Southfield Cl *THNE* DN8 50 A2
Southfield Crs *DEARNE* S63 63 M8
Southfield Dr *DRON* S18 191 G7
Southfield La *DEARNE* S63 63 M8
Southfield Mt *DRON* S18 191 G7 2
Southfield Rd *ARMTH* DN3 91 M1
CUD/GR S72 62 A3
THNE DN8 32 A8
Southfields Vw
HOR/CROF WF4 18 B2 2
Southgate *CUD/GR* S72 40 C1
DOD/DAR S75 2 B1
ECK/KIL S21 193 J4
HOY S74 105 J2
STKB/PEN S36 79 J5
Southgate Ct *ECK/KIL* S21 193 J4
South Grimesthorpe Rd
ATT S4 161 G1 4
Southgrove Rd *FUL* S10 8 A8
Southlands Cl *HEM/SK/SE* WF9 24 C5
Southlands Wy
AU/AST/KP S26 164 C8
South La *DOD/DAR* S75 57 M6
HOR/CROF WF4 18 B3
SHEF S1 9 G8
Southlea Av *HOY* S74 105 K2
Southlea Cl *HOY* S74 105 K2 1
Southlea Dr *HOY* S74 105 J2
Southlea Rd *HOY* S74 105 J1
Southmoor Av *ARMTH* DN3 91 L2
Southmoor La *ARMTH* DN3 91 L2
Southmoor Rd *CUD/GR* S72 41 H5
WRKS S80 198 F6
South Pde *BWTY* DN10 154 E2
DON DN1 5 J5
OWL S3 9 G1
THNE DN8 49 M1
WRKN S81 198 D3
South Pl *DOD/DAR* S75 59 M4
WMB/DAR S73 83 M4 1
South Precipitator Rd
ARMTH DN3 47 G7
South Rd *ARMTH* DN3 47 G7
CHPT/GREN S35 104 B8
DOD/DAR S75 59 K7
KIMB S61 128 C8
ST/HB/BR S6 160 A1
THNE DN8 32 B4
Southsea Rd *HAN/WDH* S13 178 E1
South St *AWLS/ASK* DN6 66 F5
BSLY S70 2 B5
DIN S25 166 D6
DOD/DAR S75 81 K1
DONS/BSCR DN4 5 H8
HEM/SK/SE WF9 41 J1
HOLM/MEL HD7 54 A1
HOR/CROF WF4 22 B6
KIMB S61 129 G4
KIMB S61 146 C2
MALT S66 165 K1 2
MOS S20 193 H1
RAW S62 129 L1
WMB/DAR S73 84 E2 5
South Street Pk *SHEFP/MNR* S2 9 L4
South Vale Dr
RHAM/THRY S65 130 D5
South Vw *BWTY* DN10 137 G6
HOLM/MEL HD7 54 D4
MOS S20 179 L8
WMB/DAR S73 84 E2
WRKN S81 198 D2
South View Cl *ST/HB/BR* S6 143 J6
South View Crs *ABRD* S7 160 D8 14
South View Ri *ST/HB/BR* S6 143 J6
South View Rd *ECC* S11 160 D7
HOY S74 105 H1
South View Ter *HOR/CROF* WF4 16 C3
RHAM S60 163 G2 2
Southwell Cl *WRKS* S80 198 E5
Southwell Ri *MEX/SWTN* S64 108 F1 2
Southwell Rd *ATT* S4 145 K6 4
RAW S62 129 M1
WHHL DN2 90 D1
Southwell St *DOD/DAR* S75 2 C4
Southwood Av *DRON* S18 190 E8
South Wood Dr *THNE* DN8 49 M2
Spa Brook Cl *HACK/IN* S12 178 D3
Spa Brooke Dr *HACK/IN* S12 178 D2
Spa La *HAN/WDH* S13 179 G2
Spa Lane Cft *HAN/WDH* S13 179 G1
Spalton Rd *RAW* S62 129 K3
Spansyke St *DONS/BSCR* DN4 4 D6
Sparken Cl *WRKS* S80 198 C7
Sparken Dl *WRKS* S80 198 C7
Sparken Hl *WRKS* S80 198 D6
Sparkfields *DOD/DAR* S75 37 M7
Spark La *DOD/DAR* S75 37 M7 4
Spartan Vw *MALT* S66 132 B8 1
Sparth La *HOLM/MEL* HD7 52 F3
Spa Ter *AWLS/ASK* DN6 27 L7
Spa View Av *HACK/IN* S12 178 D4
Spa View Dr *HACK/IN* S12 178 D4
Spa View Pl *HACK/IN* S12 178 D4
Spa View Rd *HACK/IN* S12 178 D4
Spa View Ter *HACK/IN* S12 178 D4 1
Spa View Wy *HACK/IN* S12 178 D4
Spa Well Crs *RHAM* S60 163 J2
Spa Well Gv *CUD/GR* S72 40 E4
Speedwell Pl *WRKS* S80 198 C3
Speetley Vw *STV/CWN* S43 194 F8
Speeton Rd *ST/HB/BR* S6 144 A8 5
Spencer Dr *RHAM/THRY* S65 131 H7
Spencer Gn *RHAM* S60 148 B6 4
Spencer Rd *SHEFP/MNR* S2 160 E8
Spencer St *BSLY* S70 2 E8
KBTN HD8 34 E5
MEX/SWTN S64 108 C2
Spennithorne Rd
AWLS/ASK DN6 44 C5
Spenser Rd *RHAM/THRY* S65 7 M7
Spey Cl *DOD/DAR* S75 38 A8
Spey Dr *EPW* DN9 92 E8
Spicer House La *STKB/PEN* S36 55 M8
Spilsby Cl *DONS/BSCR* DN4 113 L1
Spink Hall Cl *STKB/PEN* S36 102 A7 1
Spink Hall La *STKB/PEN* S36 101 M7
Spinkhill Av *HAN/WDH* S13 162 A7
Spinkhill Dr *HAN/WDH* S13 162 B7
Spinkhill La *ECK/KIL* S21 194 A5
Spinkhill Rd *ECK/KIL* S21 194 C3
HAN/WDH S13 162 B8
Spinney Cl *RHAM* S60 147 L4
Spinneyfield *RHAM* S60 147 L5
Spinney Hl *BTLY* DN5 88 F7
Spinneymead *RTFD* DN22 170 F2 1
The Spinney *ARMTH* DN3 69 L1
DONS/BSCR DN4 111 K2 2
WKFDW/WTN WF2 20 C1
Spitalfields *OWL* S3 9 J1
WRKN S81 169 M5
Spital Gv *NROS/TKH* DN11 113 L8
Spital Hl *ATT* S4 9 L1
Spital La *OWL* S3 161 G2
Spital Rd *WRKN* S81 170 A7
Spital St *OWL* S3 160 F2
Spittlerush La *PONT* WF8 26 E3
Spofforth Rd *DARN/MH* S9 161 L2 9
Spooner Dr *ECK/KIL* S21 194 A1
Spooner Rd *FUL* S10 160 A4
Spoon Gld *ST/HB/BR* S6 159 G1 6
Spoonhill Rd *ST/HB/BR* S6 159 K1
Spoon La *ST/HB/BR* S6 158 E1
Spoon Ms *ST/HB/BR* S6 159 G1
Spoon Wy *ST/HB/BR* S6 159 G1
Spotswood Cl *GLV* S14 177 J3 1
Spotswood Dr
SHEFP/MNR S2 177 J2 2
Spotswood Mt *GLV* S14 177 J2 3
Spotswood Pl *GLV* S14 177 H3
Spotswood Rd *SHEFS* S8 177 H3
Spout La *ST/HB/BR* S6 158 F1
Spout Spinney *ST/HB/BR* S6 158 F1
Springbank *WMB/DAR* S73 84 F2
Springbank Cl
BSLYN/ROY S71 39 G7 1
EPW DN9 115 K1
Spring Bank Cft
HOLM/MEL HD7 53 H3
Spring Bank Rd *CONI* DN12 109 M7
Spring Cl *ECK/KIL* S21 194 A8
Spring Close Dell *GLV* S14 177 K3
Spring Close Mt *GLV* S14 177 K3
Spring Close Vw *GLV* S14 177 J3
HACK/IN S12 177 M2
Spring Crs *BTLY* DN5 88 F6
Spring Cft *KIMB* S61 128 D6
Springcroft Dr *BTLY* DN5 67 J7
Spring Dr *WMB/DAR* S73 84 E7
Springfield *DEARNE* S63 85 L5 1
Springfield Av *ECC* S11 176 A2
HEM/SK/SE WF9 41 J1
HTFD DN7 49 G8
KBTN HD8 35 J5
Springfield Cl *ABRD* S7 176 A3
ARMTH DN3 92 A2 1
ECK/KIL S21 193 G4
KBTN HD8 35 J5
KIMB S61 129 H6
WMB/DAR S73 84 F2
WRKN S81 183 J3
Springfield Ct *BTLY* DN5 89 J2 7
Springfield Crs *HOY* S74 105 G2
PONT WF8 26 C2
WMB/DAR S73 84 F2
Springfield Dr *KBTN* HD8 55 L3
RHAM/THRY S65 130 E5
Springfield Gln *ECC* S11 175 M3
Springfield Mt
HEM/SK/SE WF9 42 C6 1
Springfield Pl *BSLY* S70 2 C5 1
Springfield Rd *ABRD* S7 176 A3
CONI DN12 111 G5
CUD/GR S72 40 D8
HOY S74 104 F2
MALT S66 148 E2
MEX/SWTN S64 108 C8
Springfield St *BSLY* S70 2 B5
Spring Gdns *BSLYN/ROY* S71 61 G3 4
BWTY DN10 136 E7
DON DN1 4 F5
HOLM/MEL HD7 53 J2
HOY S74 105 J1
Spring Grove Gdns
CHPT/GREN S35 124 F6
Spring Hl *FUL* S10 160 A3
Springhill Av *WMB/DAR* S73 84 E7
Spring Hill Cl *BTLY* DN5 88 F6 5
Spring Hill Rd *FUL* S10 160 A3
Spring House Rd *FUL* S10 160 A3 2
Spring La *BSLYN/ROY* S71 39 G7
BTLY DN5 88 F3
DOD/DAR S75 38 A3
HOLM/MEL HD7 53 H5
HOLM/MEL HD7 54 C2
SHEFP/MNR S2 161 J7
WRKN S81 197 J2
WRKS S80 197 K3
Springs Rd *BWTY* DN10 116 B8
Springstone Av
HEM/SK/SE WF9 23 J8
Spring St *BSLY* S70 2 F7
OWL S3 9 H2
RHAM/THRY S65 7 H3
Spring Vale Av *BSLY* S70 82 D3 5
Springvale Cl *MALT* S66 149 G5
MALT S66 150 D1 5
Springvale Ri *HEM/SK/SE* WF9 23 H7
Springvale Rd *CUD/GR* S72 63 J5
Spring Vale Rd
HEM/SK/SE WF9 42 A4 1
Springvale Rd *ST/HB/BR* S6 8 A2
Spring View Rd *FUL* S10 160 A3 8
Springville Gdns
HEM/SK/SE WF9 24 F8
Spring Wk *WRKS* S80 198 C6
Spring Water Av *HACK/IN* S12 178 D4
Spring Water Cl *HACK/IN* S12 178 E4 6
Spring Water Dr *HACK/IN* S12 178 D3
Springwell Av *MOS* S20 179 J3
Springwell Cl *MALT* S66 150 F1
Springwell Crs *MOS* S20 179 J3
Springwell Dr *MOS* S20 179 J3
Springwell Gdns
DONS/BSCR DN4 111 K1 5
Springwell Gv *MOS* S20 179 J3
Springwell La *DONS/BSCR* DN4 111 K2
NROS/TKH DN11 111 L5
Springwood Av
AU/AST/KP S26 164 A6
Springwood Cl *ARMTH* DN3 92 B7 2
CHPT/GREN S35 102 E1
Springwood La
CHPT/GREN S35 126 A1
Springwood Rd *BTLY* DN5 67 J7
HOY S74 105 G2
SHEFS S8 176 E1 12
Springwood Vw *STKB/PEN* S36 79 K5
Sprotbrough La *BTLY* DN5 66 B8
Sprotbrough Rd *BTLY* DN5 4 C1 1
Spruce Av *BSLYN/ROY* S71 38 F4
MALT S66 148 F2
Spruce Ct *WRKS* S80 197 M5
Spruce Crs *EPW* DN9 114 E4
Spruce Ri *ECK/KIL* S21 194 A2
Spry La *CUD/GR* S72 63 L4
Spur Crs *WRKS* S80 198 F6
Spurley Hey Gv *STKB/PEN* S36 102 A7
Spurr Gv *WKFDW/WTN* WF2 20 F1
Spurr St *SHEFP/MNR* S2 160 F7
The Square East *MALT* S66 131 G8
The Square *AU/AST/KP* S26 180 F5
BSLY S70 2 D8
CUD/GR S72 62 F1
RAW S62 105 H6
The Square West *MALT* S66 130 F8
Stable Cl *WRKN* S81 184 E8 6
Stables La *BTLY* DN5 87 G3
The Stables *MEX/SWTN* S64 107 M3
Stacey Crs *CUD/GR* S72 40 D8
Stacey Dr *RHAM/THRY* S65 130 C4 1
Stacey La *ST/HB/BR* S6 142 D6
Stacye Av *HAN/WDH* S13 179 H1
Stacye Ri *HAN/WDH* S13 179 H1
Stadium Cl *WRKN* S81 198 A1
Stadium Ct *RAW* S62 129 J5
Stadium Wy *DARN/MH* S9 161 K2
HEM/SK/SE WF9 42 F2
RHAM/THRY S65 129 K6
Stafford Cl *DRON* S18 190 A5 5
Stafford Crs *RHAM* S60 147 K6
Stafford Dr *RHAM* S60 147 K6
Stafford Gv *BSLY* S70 104 D2
Stafford La *SHEFP/MNR* S2 161 H5 2
Stafford Rd *AWLS/ASK* DN6 66 F2
SHEFP/MNR S2 161 H5
Staffordshire Cl *MALT* S66 150 F2 4
Stafford St *SHEFP/MNR* S2 9 L5
Stafford Wy
CHPT/GREN S35 126 D2 5
Stag Cl *RHAM* S60 148 A4
Stag Crs *RHAM/THRY* S65 148 A4
Stag La *RHAM* S60 147 M4
Stainborough Cl *DOD/DAR* S75 81 K1
Stainborough La *DOD/DAR* S75 81 J7
Stainborough Rd *DOD/DAR* S75 81 K1
Stainborough Vw *BSLY* S70 82 D2 1
DOD/DAR S75 104 B1 1
Staincross Common
DOD/DAR S75 37 M5
Staindrop Vw *CHPT/GREN* S35 126 E1
Stainforth Moor Rd *HTFD* DN7 71 M2
THNE DN8 72 E2
Stainforth Rd *ARMTH* DN3 47 L7
HTFD DN7 47 L6
Stainley Cl *DOD/DAR* S75 59 M3 2
Stainmore Av *MOS* S20 179 L5
Stainmore Cl *DOD/DAR* S75 58 D7 6
Stainton Cl *BSLYN/ROY* S71 60 C1
Stainton La *MALT* S66 132 F8
NROS/TKH DN11 133 K3
Stainton Rd *ECC* S11 159 M7
Stainton St *CONI* DN12 109 K4
Stair Rd *ATT* S4 145 G7
Stake Hill Rd *ST/HB/BR* S6 141 G8
Stake Lane Bank
HOLM/MEL HD7 53 M2
Stalker Lees Rd *ECC* S11 160 B7
Stalley Royd La
HOLM/MEL HD7 54 D4
Stambers Cl *WRKN* S81 183 J4
Stamford St *DARN/MH* S9 145 K8 5
Stamford Wy *DOD/DAR* S75 37 M5 2
Stampers Hl *DOD/DAR* S75 82 B5
Stanage Ri *HACK/IN* S12 178 B2
Stanbury Cl *DOD/DAR* S75 59 M4
Stancil La *NROS/TKH* DN11 112 E8
NROS/TKH DN11 134 E3
Standbridge Cl
WKFDW/WTN WF2 19 L2
Stand Bridge Garth
HOR/CROF WF4 19 K1
Standhill Crs *BSLYN/ROY* S71 38 C8
Standish Av *SHEFN* S5 144 E7
Standish Cl *SHEFN* S5 144 E6
Standish Crs *HEM/SK/SE* WF9 42 A3
Standish Dr *SHEFN* S5 144 E6

Standish Rd *SHEFN* S5 .... **144** E6
Standon Crs *DARN/MH* S9 .... **145** K2
Standon Dr *DARN/MH* S9 .... **145** K2
Standon Rd *DARN/MH* S9 .... **145** L2
Staneford Ct *MOS* S20 .... **179** H6
Stanford Cl *MALT* S66 .... **151** G3
Stanford Rd *DRON* S18 .... **190** A6 15
Stanhope Av *DOD/DAR* S75 .... **58** D2
Stanhope Gdns *DOD/DAR* S75 .... **2** B2
Stanhope Rd *DON* DN1 .... **5** J1
DON DN1 .... **90** C2
HACK/IN S12 .... **178** A2
Stanhope St *BSLY* S70 .... **2** C5
KBTN HD8 .... **35** H6 2
Stanhurst La *HTFD* DN7 .... **49** L5
Staniforth Av *ECK/KIL* S21 .... **192** F4
Staniforth Crs *AU/AST/KP* S26 .... **181** J2
Staniforth Rd *DARN/MH* S9 .... **161** L2
Stanley Gdns *DONS/BSCR* DN4 .... **4** D8
HTFD DN7 .... **48** C4
Stanley Gv *AU/AST/KP* S26 .... **164** D7 1
Stanley La *OWL* S3 .... **9** J1
Stanley Rd *BSLY* S70 .... **61** J7
BTLY DN5 .... **67** H8
CHPT/GREN S35 .... **126** C1
HTFD DN7 .... **48** C4 6
SHEFS S8 .... **176** F2
STKB/PEN S36 .... **102** A6 4
Stanley Sq *ARMTH* DN3 .... **69** K3 5
Stanley St *BSLY* S70 .... **2** D5
CUD/GR S72 .... **62** A2
ECK/KIL S21 .... **180** B8
OWL S3 .... **9** J1
WRKN S81 .... **198** C2
Stanley Ter *MALT* S66 .... **150** B3
Stannington Gln *ST/HB/BR* S6 .... **159** J1
Stannington Ri *ST/HB/BR* S6 .... **143** L8 1
Stannington Rd *ST/HB/BR* S6 .... **158** F1
Stannington View Rd *FUL* S10 .... **159** L3
Stanton Crs *HACK/IN* S12 .... **178** B3 1
Stan Va *PONT* WF8 .... **26** C1
Stanwell Av *DARN/MH* S9 .... **145** L3
Stanwell St *DARN/MH* S9 .... **145** L3
Stanwood Av *ST/HB/BR* S6 .... **159** K1
Stanwood Crs *ST/HB/BR* S6 .... **159** K1
Stanwood Dr *ST/HB/BR* S6 .... **159** K1 1
Stanwood Ms *ST/HB/BR* S6 .... **159** K1 2
Stanwood Rd *ST/HB/BR* S6 .... **159** K1
Staple Gn *RHAM/THRY* S65 .... **130** E5
Stapleton Rd *DONS/BSCR* DN4 .... **111** H2
Starkbridge La *GLE* DN14 .... **29** L1
Star La *BSLY* S70 .... **2** E5
Starling Gv *WRKN* S81 .... **198** A1
Starling Md *SHEFP/MNR* S2 .... **161** J5 5
Starnhill Cl *CHPT/GREN* S35 .... **127** G6
Statham Ct *WRKN* S81 .... **198** F2 2
Station Ap *HATH/EY* S32 .... **172** E8
Station Av *RTFD* DN22 .... **170** F2
Station Cl *EPW* DN9 .... **115** H3
Station La *CHPT/GREN* S35 .... **125** H8
DARN/MH S9 .... **145** L5
Station Rd *ARMTH* DN3 .... **69** K1
AU/AST/KP S26 .... **181** H5
AWLS/ASK DN6 .... **27** L7
AWLS/ASK DN6 .... **27** J4
AWLS/ASK DN6 .... **45** H7
BSLY S70 .... **2** C4
BSLY S70 .... **83** G3
BSLYN/ROY S71 .... **38** F3
BSLYN/ROY S71 .... **61** K2
BTLY DN5 .... **68** B5
BWTY DN10 .... **136** E7
BWTY DN10 .... **137** M4
BWTY DN10 .... **154** E5
CHPT/GREN S35 .... **126** F1
CHPT/GREN S35 .... **127** G6
CONI DN12 .... **110** A4
DARN/MH S9 .... **162** A3 6
DEARNE S63 .... **64** B7
DEARNE S63 .... **85** L7
DEARNE S63 .... **86** A5
DEARNE S63 .... **107** K1
DIN S25 .... **166** A4
DOD/DAR S75 .... **37** J6
DOD/DAR S75 .... **59** J8
ECK/KIL S21 .... **193** J4
ECK/KIL S21 .... **193** K5
ECK/KIL S21 .... **193** M1
ECK/KIL S21 .... **194** B5
EPW DN9 .... **115** J2
EPW DN9 .... **115** J4
HAN/WDH S13 .... **163** H8
HATH/EY S32 .... **172** E8
HEM/SK/SE WF9 .... **23** J8
HEM/SK/SE WF9 .... **42** E4
HOLM/MEL HD7 .... **53** L2
HOR/CROF WF4 .... **21** L6
HTFD DN7 .... **48** F7
HTFD DN7 .... **48** C5
KBTN HD8 .... **34** E3
MEX/SWTN S64 .... **108** E3
MOS S20 .... **179** H8 4
NROS/TKH DN11 .... **113** L6
RHAM S60 .... **6** B4
RHAM S60 .... **163** J3
RHAM S60 .... **163** G1
RTFD DN22 .... **170** F3
RTFD DN22 .... **187** J2
STKB/PEN S36 .... **102** E6
WMB/DAR S73 .... **84** C4
Station St *MEX/SWTN* S64 .... **108** B4
Station Wy *DIN* S25 .... **166** A4 1
Staton Av *MOS* S20 .... **179** L3
Staton La *DRON* S18 .... **191** L6
The Statutes *RHAM* S60 .... **6** D4
Staunton Rd *DONS/BSCR* DN4 .... **91** L8
Staveley La *ECK/KIL* S21 .... **192** E8
ECK/KIL S21 .... **193** J7
Staveley Rd *SHEFS* S8 .... **160** E8 10
Staveley St *CONI* DN12 .... **110** F4
Steade Rd *ABRD* S7 .... **160** D8
Steadfield Rd *HOY* S74 .... **104** F3 1
Steadfolds Cl *MALT* S66 .... **165** L1
Steadfolds La *DIN* S25 .... **165** L1
MALT S66 .... **165** K1
Steadfolds Ri *MALT* S66 .... **165** L1
Stead Ga *KBTN* HD8 .... **34** B5
The Steadlands *RAW* S62 .... **107** H8 2
Stead La *HOY* S74 .... **104** F2
Stead St *ECK/KIL* S21 .... **193** H4
Steele St *HOY* S74 .... **104** E2
Steel Hl *CHPT/GREN* S35 .... **126** A8
Steelhouse La *OWL* S3 .... **9** H2 1
Steel Rd *ECC* S11 .... **160** A7
Steel St *RHAM* S60 .... **146** E2
Steep La *STKB/PEN* S36 .... **79** K3
Steeple Av *HOR/CROF* WF4 .... **16** C3
Steetley La *WRKS* S80 .... **197** G5
Steeton Ct *HOY* S74 .... **105** L1
Stemp St *ECC* S11 .... **160** D7 11
Stenton Rd *SHEFS* S8 .... **176** D8
Stephen Dr *CHPT/GREN* S35 .... **125** M7
FUL S10 .... **159** K4
Stephen Hl *FUL* S10 .... **159** K4
Stephen Hill Rd *FUL* S10 .... **159** K4
Stephen La *CHPT/GREN* S35 .... **125** M7
Stepney St *SHEFP/MNR* S2 .... **9** L3
Stepping La *CHPT/GREN* S35 .... **125** M6
Sterndale Rd *ABRD* S7 .... **176** A4
Steven Cl *CHPT/GREN* S35 .... **126** D3
Steven Crs *CHPT/GREN* S35 .... **126** D2
Steven Pl *CHPT/GREN* S35 .... **126** D3
Stevenson Dr *DOD/DAR* S75 .... **59** J3
RHAM/THRY S65 .... **147** M2
Stevenson Rd *DARN/MH* S9 .... **161** J1
DONS/BSCR DN4 .... **111** M1
WRKN S81 .... **198** F3 1
Stevenson Wy *DARN/MH* S9 .... **161** J1
Stevens Rd *DONS/BSCR* DN4 .... **4** C9
Steventon Rd
RHAM/THRY S65 .... **130** E5
Stewart Cl *WRKN* S81 .... **184** C1 1
Stewart Rd *ECC* S11 .... **160** B7
WRKN S81 .... **184** C1
Stewarts Rd *RAW* S62 .... **129** L1
Stewart St *DON* DN1 .... **4** E6
Sticking La *MEX/SWTN* S64 .... **86** C8
Stirling Av *BWTY* DN10 .... **136** E7
Stirling Cl *HOY* S74 .... **105** L1 1
WRKN S81 .... **184** C7 3
Stirling Dr *WRKN* S81 .... **184** C1
Stirling St *DON* DN1 .... **4** F7
Stockarth Cl *CHPT/GREN* S35 .... **143** K3
Stockarth La *CHPT/GREN* S35 .... **143** J3
Stockbridge Av *BTLY* DN5 .... **67** L8 1
Stockbridge La *AWLS/ASK* DN6 .... **45** J4
BTLY DN5 .... **68** A5
Stockil Rd *DONS/BSCR* DN4 .... **5** K7
Stockingate *HEM/SK/SE* WF9 .... **41** M6
Stock Rd *SHEFP/MNR* S2 .... **161** J6
Stocks Green Ct
TOT/DORE S17 .... **189** G3
Stocks Green Dr
TOT/DORE S17 .... **189** H3 1
Stocks Hl *CHPT/GREN* S35 .... **126** E6
Stock's La *DOD/DAR* S75 .... **2** C4
RAW S62 .... **129** K2
STKB/PEN S36 .... **100** A3
Stocksmoor Rd *HOR/CROF* WF4 .... **18** A5
Stockton Cl *OWL* S3 .... **160** F2 11
Stockwell Av *AU/AST/KP* S26 .... **181** G6
Stockwell La *AU/AST/KP* S26 .... **180** F6
Stocthorn Gap
CHPT/GREN S35 .... **125** G5
Stoke St *DARN/MH* S9 .... **161** J2
Stoket La *AU/AST/KP* S26 .... **164** D2
Stokewell Rd *DEARNE* S63 .... **85** G8
Stoneacre Av *HACK/IN* S12 .... **178** F4
Stoneacre Cl *HACK/IN* S12 .... **178** F4 4
Stoneacre Dr *HACK/IN* S12 .... **178** F5
Stoneacre Ri *HACK/IN* S12 .... **178** F4
Stonebridge La *CUD/GR* S72 .... **63** K5
Stonecliffe Cl *SHEFP/MNR* S2 .... **161** L6
Stonecliffe Dr *STKB/PEN* S36 .... **101** M8
Stonecliffe Pl *SHEFP/MNR* S2 .... **161** L6
Stonecliffe Rd *SHEFP/MNR* S2 .... **161** L6
Stone Cl *AU/AST/KP* S26 .... **181** J5
DRON S18 .... **191** G4
RHAM/THRY S65 .... **131** H8
Stone Close Av *DONS/BSCR* DN4 .... **4** C7
Stone Ct *CUD/GR* S72 .... **40** C2
Stone Crs *MALT* S66 .... **148** F2
Stonecrest Ri
CHPT/GREN S35 .... **80** D8 2
Stonecroft Rd *TOT/DORE* S17 .... **189** J2
Stone Cross Dr *BTLY* DN5 .... **88** F5
Stonecross Gdns
DONS/BSCR DN4 .... **91** L7
Stonedale Cl *MOS* S20 .... **179** H8 5
Stone Delf *FUL* S10 .... **159** G6
Stone Font Gv *DONS/BSCR* DN4 .... **91** K8
Stonegarth Cl *CUD/GR* S72 .... **61** M1 6
Stonegate *THNE* DN8 .... **31** M8
Stonegate La *FEA/AMT* WF7 .... **23** J2 5
Stonegravels Wy *MOS* S20 .... **193** K1
Stone Grey Cl *NROS/TKH* DN11 .... **152** D1
Stone Gv *FUL* S10 .... **8** A6
Stone Hl *HTFD* DN7 .... **49** L8
Stonehill Cl *RTFD* DN22 .... **170** F2
Stone Hill Dr *AU/AST/KP* S26 .... **164** A8
Stonehill Ri *BTLY* DN5 .... **67** J7 1
CUD/GR S72 .... **61** M1
STKB/PEN S36 .... **79** G6
Stone Hill Rd *HTFD* DN7 .... **49** K8
Stone La *HAN/WDH* S13 .... **178** E2
Stonelea Cl *DOD/DAR* S75 .... **58** D7 7
Stone Lea Gv
HEM/SK/SE WF9 .... **42** E5 1
Stoneleigh *DIN* S25 .... **166** B4
Stoneleigh Cft *BSLY* S70 .... **60** D8 11
Stoneley Cl *HACK/IN* S12 .... **177** L6
Stoneley Crs *HACK/IN* S12 .... **177** M6
Stoneley Dell *HACK/IN* S12 .... **177** M6
Stoneley Dr *HACK/IN* S12 .... **177** M6
Stonelow Crs *DRON* S18 .... **191** H5
Stonelow Rd *DRON* S18 .... **190** F5
Stonely Brook
RHAM/THRY S65 .... **149** H1
Stone Moor Rd *STKB/PEN* S36 .... **101** L8
Stone Park Cl *MALT* S66 .... **150** F2 5
Stone Riding *CONI* DN12 .... **110** E6
Stone Rd *DRON* S18 .... **191** G3
Stone St *BSLYN/ROY* S71 .... **60** C3
MOS S20 .... **179** H8
Stonewood Ct *FUL* S10 .... **159** H5 4
Stonewood Gv *FUL* S10 .... **159** H5
Stoney Bank Dr
AU/AST/KP S26 .... **181** J5
Stoneybrook Cl *HOR/CROF* WF4 .... **18** D7
Stoney Ga *CHPT/GREN* S35 .... **104** B7
Stoney La *HOR/CROF* WF4 .... **19** K4
NROS/TKH DN11 .... **152** C1
Stoney Royd *BSLYN/ROY* S71 .... **38** D6
Stoney Well La *MALT* S66 .... **151** J3
Stony Croft La *AWLS/ASK* DN6 .... **44** E3
STKB/PEN S36 .... **100** E4
Stonyford Rd *WMB/DAR* S73 .... **84** D3
Stony Ga *HOLM/MEL* HD7 .... **53** J5
Stony La *NROS/TKH* DN11 .... **134** C5
ST/HB/BR S6 .... **142** D4
Stoops La *DONS/BSCR* DN4 .... **90** F8
Stoops Rd *DONS/BSCR* DN4 .... **91** H8
Stopes Rd *ST/HB/BR* S6 .... **158** E1
Store St *SHEFP/MNR* S2 .... **9** J9
Storey's Ga *WMB/DAR* S73 .... **83** M4
Storey St *MEX/SWTN* S64 .... **108** A4
Storrs Br *ST/HB/BR* S6 .... **142** E6
Storrs Bridge La *ST/HB/BR* S6 .... **142** E6
Storrs Carr *ST/HB/BR* S6 .... **142** D7
Storrs Hall Rd *ST/HB/BR* S6 .... **159** M1
Storrs La *BTLY* DN5 .... **46** A3
CHPT/GREN S35 .... **103** M5
ST/HB/BR S6 .... **142** F8
STKB/PEN S36 .... **80** A5
Storrs Mill La *BSLYN/ROY* S71 .... **62** C5
Storrs Wood Vw *CUD/GR* S72 .... **62** B3
Storth Av *FUL* S10 .... **159** J7
Storth La *AU/AST/KP* S26 .... **181** G4
AU/AST/KP S26 .... **181** J2
CHPT/GREN S35 .... **124** E5
FUL S10 .... **159** J6
Stortholme Ms *FUL* S10 .... **159** K6 3
Stotfold Dr *DEARNE* S63 .... **64** A7
Stotfold Rd *BTLY* DN5 .... **64** B4
Stothard Rd *FUL* S10 .... **159** M3
Stottercliffe Rd *STKB/PEN* S36 .... **78** F4
Stour La *ST/HB/BR* S6 .... **143** K5
Stovin Cl *DARN/MH* S9 .... **161** M1
Stovin Dr *DARN/MH* S9 .... **161** M1
Stovin Gdns *DARN/MH* S9 .... **145** M8
Stow Bridge La *RHAM* S60 .... **164** C1
Stowe Av *ABRD* S7 .... **176** A3
Stradbroke Av *HAN/WDH* S13 .... **162** B8
Stradbroke Cl *HAN/WDH* S13 .... **162** C8
Stradbroke Crs *HAN/WDH* S13 .... **162** C8
Stradbroke Dr *HAN/WDH* S13 .... **162** C8
Stradbroke Pl *HAN/WDH* S13 .... **162** C8
Stradbroke Rd *HAN/WDH* S13 .... **162** B8
Stradbroke Wy *HAN/WDH* S13 .... **162** C8
Strafford Av *BSLY* S70 .... **82** D1
HOY S74 .... **105** L1
Strafford Pl *KIMB* S61 .... **127** J2
Strafford Rd *KIMB* S61 .... **128** C5
Strafford St *DOD/DAR* S75 .... **37** G7
Strafford Wk *DOD/DAR* S75 .... **81** K1
Straight La *AWLS/ASK* DN6 .... **43** M3
DEARNE S63 .... **86** C2
Strands Ct *HOR/CROF* WF4 .... **18** C1
Stratford Rd *FUL* S10 .... **159** H6
Stratford Wy *MALT* S66 .... **149** J3
Strathavon Rd *WRKN* S81 .... **184** D1
Strathmore Dr *WRKN* S81 .... **184** D1
Strathmore Gdns
HEM/SK/SE WF9 .... **42** F3 2
Strathmore Gv *DEARNE* S63 .... **107** K1
Strathtay Rd *ECC* S11 .... **159** M8
Strauss Crs *MALT* S66 .... **150** F3
Strawberry Av *SHEFN* S5 .... **144** F1
Strawberry Gdns
BSLYN/ROY S71 .... **39** G3
Strawberry Lee La
TOT/DORE S17 .... **188** F2
Straw La *ST/HB/BR* S6 .... **160** C2 12
Streatfield Crs
NROS/TKH DN11 .... **113** J7
Street Farm Cl *AU/AST/KP* S26 .... **195** J1
Streetfield Crs *MOS* S20 .... **193** H1 6
Streetfields *MOS* S20 .... **193** J1
Street La *BTLY* DN5 .... **65** K5
RAW S62 .... **106** C5
Strelley Av *SHEFS* S8 .... **176** C6
Strelley Rd *BSLYN/ROY* S71 .... **38** C7 2
SHEFS S8 .... **176** B6
Stretton Cl *DONS/BSCR* DN4 .... **91** L7
Stretton Rd *BSLYN/ROY* S71 .... **60** E2
ECC S11 .... **160** A8
Strickland Rd *HEM/SK/SE* WF9 .... **25** H7
Strines Moor Rd
HOLM/MEL HD7 .... **54** A8
Stringer House La *KBTN* HD8 .... **16** E8
Stringers Cft *RHAM* S60 .... **148** B6 5
Stripe Rd *BWTY* DN10 .... **135** L5
Struan Rd *ECC* S11 .... **176** A2
Strutt Rd *OWL* S3 .... **144** E8
Stuart Gv *CHPT/GREN* S35 .... **126** E3
Stuart Rd *CHPT/GREN* S35 .... **126** F3
Stuart St *DEARNE* S63 .... **64** C7
Stubbin Cl *RAW* S62 .... **107** H8
Stubbin Fold *HOLM/MEL* HD7 .... **53** G4
Stubbing Ct *WRKS* S80 .... **198** B5
Stubbing House La
CHPT/GREN S35 .... **125** L8
Stubbing La *CHPT/GREN* S35 .... **142** F3 1
WRKS S80 .... **198** B4
Stubbin La *HOLM/MEL* HD7 .... **53** G4
KBTN HD8 .... **56** F1
RAW S62 .... **107** H7
SHEFN S5 .... **145** G3
Stubbin Rd *RAW* S62 .... **106** F8
Stubbins Hl *CONI* DN12 .... **111** G6
Stubbs Br *AWLS/ASK* DN6 .... **43** L5
Stubbs Crs *KIMB* S61 .... **128** D6
Stubbs La *AWLS/ASK* DN6 .... **27** H2
Stubbs Rd *PONT* WF8 .... **26** E2
WMB/DAR S73 .... **84** A5
Stubley Cl *DRON* S18 .... **190** C5
Stubley Cft *DRON* S18 .... **190** B5
Stubley Dr *DRON* S18 .... **190** C5
Stubley Hollow *DRON* S18 .... **190** C5
Stubley La *DRON* S18 .... **190** B5
Stubley Pl *DRON* S18 .... **190** C5
Studfield Crs *ST/HB/BR* S6 .... **143** K7
Studfield Dr *ST/HB/BR* S6 .... **143** K6
Studfield Gv *ST/HB/BR* S6 .... **143** K7
Studfield Hl *ST/HB/BR* S6 .... **143** K6
Studfield Ri *ST/HB/BR* S6 .... **143** K6
Studfield Rd *ST/HB/BR* S6 .... **143** K7
Studley Ct *DARN/MH* S9 .... **162** A3 7
Studmoor Rd *KIMB* S61 .... **128** B5
Stump Cross Gdns *DEARNE* S63 .... **85** M5
Stump Cross Rd *DEARNE* S63 .... **107** J2
Stumperlowe Av *FUL* S10 .... **159** J7 2
Stumperlowe Cl *FUL* S10 .... **159** J7 3
Stumperlowe Crescent Rd
FUL S10 .... **159** H7
Stumperlowe Cft *FUL* S10 .... **159** H6
Stumperlowe Hall Cha
FUL S10 .... **159** H6 2
Stumperlowe Hall Rd *FUL* S10 .... **159** H8
Stumperlowe La *FUL* S10 .... **159** H7
Stumperlowe Park Rd
FUL S10 .... **159** H7
Stumperlowe Vw *FUL* S10 .... **159** H6
Stupton Rd *DARN/MH* S9 .... **145** L5
Sturge Cft *SHEFP/MNR* S2 .... **176** F1 3
Sturton Cl *DONS/BSCR* DN4 .... **113** G1
Sturton Cft *RHAM/THRY* S65 .... **130** C6
Sturton Rd *ATT* S4 .... **145** G7
Stygate La *AWLS/ASK* DN6 .... **27** G5
Styrrup La *NROS/TKH* DN11 .... **152** F6
Styrrup Rd *NROS/TKH* DN11 .... **153** H5
Sudbury Dr *AU/AST/KP* S26 .... **164** C8
Sudbury St *OWL* S3 .... **8** E1
Sude Hl *HOLM/MEL* HD7 .... **54** C1
Sude Hill Ter *HOLM/MEL* HD7 .... **54** D1 2
Suffolk Av *NROS/TKH* DN11 .... **154** B3
Suffolk Cl *DIN* S25 .... **182** C1 2
Suffolk Gv *NROS/TKH* DN11 .... **154** B3
Suffolk Rd
DONS/BSCR DN4 .... **111** M1 10
NROS/TKH DN11 .... **154** A3
SHEF S1 .... **9** J6
Sugworth Rd *ST/HB/BR* S6 .... **140** E8
Sulby Gv *BSLY* S70 .... **83** H1
Sullivan Gv *HEM/SK/SE* WF9 .... **41** M6
Summerdale Rd *CUD/GR* S72 .... **61** L2
Summerfield *RHAM/THRY* S65 .... **7** H4
Summerfield Rd *DRON* S18 .... **190** F4
Summerfields Dr *EPW* DN9 .... **115** J1
Summerfield St *FUL* S10 .... **8** D8
Summer La *BSLYN/ROY* S71 .... **38** F3
DOD/DAR S75 .... **2** C3
KBTN HD8 .... **35** H1
TOT/DORE S17 .... **189** G3
WMB/DAR S73 .... **83** L5
Summerley Lower Rd
DRON S18 .... **191** J5
Summerley Rd *DRON* S18 .... **191** J5
Summer Rd *BSLYN/ROY* S71 .... **38** F3 4
Summer St *BSLY* S70 .... **2** D4
OWL S3 .... **8** C3
Summervale *HOLM/MEL* HD7 .... **53** L1 1
Summerwood La *DRON* S18 .... **190** D4
Summerwood Pl *DRON* S18 .... **190** D5
Sumner Rd *RHAM/THRY* S65 .... **7** J1
Sunderland Pl
NROS/TKH DN11 .... **134** F8
Sunderland St *ECC* S11 .... **8** D9
NROS/TKH DN11 .... **134** E8
Sunderland Ter *BSLY* S70 .... **3** K7
Sundew Cft *CHPT/GREN* S35 .... **104** B7 7
Sundew Gdns *CHPT/GREN* S35 .... **104** B6
Sundown Pl *HAN/WDH* S13 .... **162** D7
Sundown Rd *HAN/WDH* S13 .... **162** D7
Sunfield Av *WRKN* S81 .... **198** E3
Sunningdale Av *DOD/DAR* S75 .... **37** L6 5
Sunningdale Cl *ARMTH* DN3 .... **113** M1 2
MEX/SWTN S64 .... **108** B6
Sunningdale Dr *CUD/GR* S72 .... **40** A6
Sunningdale Mt *ECC* S11 .... **175** M2
Sunningdale Rd *DIN* S25 .... **166** D8
HTFD DN7 .... **71** K1
WHHL DN2 .... **90** E2 2
Sunny Av *HEM/SK/SE* WF9 .... **24** E8
HEM/SK/SE WF9 .... **42** F5
Sunny Bank *FUL* S10 .... **8** D8
HEM/SK/SE WF9 .... **22** E3
HOR/CROF WF4 .... **21** L6
HOY S74 .... **83** K8
Sunnybank *KBTN* HD8 .... **56** D2
Sunny Bank *WRKN* S81 .... **198** D3
Sunnybank Crs *RHAM* S60 .... **147** G7 1
Sunny Bank Dr *CUD/GR* S72 .... **61** M3
Sunny Bank Ri *HOY* S74 .... **105** L1 2
Sunny Bank Rd *DOD/DAR* S75 .... **58** D7
STKB/PEN S36 .... **124** A1
Sunny Bar *DON* DN1 .... **5** G4
Sunnybrook Cl *HOY* S74 .... **105** J3
Sunnyfield Dr *HEM/SK/SE* WF9 .... **22** E4
Sunnymead *KBTN* HD8 .... **35** H5
Sunnymede *WRKN* S81 .... **198** E1 10
Sunnymede Av *AWLS/ASK* DN6 .... **27** M7
Sunnymede Crs *AWLS/ASK* DN6 .... **27** M6
Sunnymede Ter *AWLS/ASK* DN6 .... **27** M7
Sunnyside *ARMTH* DN3 .... **69** J5
ARMTH DN3 .... **92** C7 2
WRKN S81 .... **198** D1
WRKS S80 .... **196** E8
Sunnyside Cl *DIN* S25 .... **182** C1
Sunnyvale Av *TOT/DORE* S17 .... **189** H3
Sunnyvale Mt *HEM/SK/SE* WF9 .... **42** C4
Sunnyvale Rd *TOT/DORE* S17 .... **189** H3
Surbiton St *DARN/MH* S9 .... **145** M7
Surrey Cl *BSLY* S70 .... **3** G9
Surrey La *SHEF* S1 .... **9** J6
Surrey Pl *SHEF* S1 .... **9** J5 2
Surrey St *DONS/BSCR* DN4 .... **89** M8
SHEF S1 .... **9** H5
Surtees Cl *MALT* S66 .... **132** C8 3
Sussex Cl *HEM/SK/SE* WF9 .... **23** H7
Sussex Rd *ATT* S4 .... **9** M1
CHPT/GREN S35 .... **126** E2
Sussex St *ATT* S4 .... **9** M2
Suthard Cross Rd *FUL* S10 .... **159** M3 6
Sutherland Cl *WRKN* S81 .... **168** D7 1
Sutherland Rd *ATT* S4 .... **161** G1
Sutherland St *ATT* S4 .... **161** H2 1
Sutton Av *BSLYN/ROY* S71 .... **38** D7
Sutton La *RTFD* DN22 .... **187** L3
Sutton Rd *ARMTH* DN3 .... **69** K2
AWLS/ASK DN6 .... **27** G7
AWLS/ASK DN6 .... **45** J2
Sutton St *OWL* S3 .... **8** D4
Suzanne Crs *HEM/SK/SE* WF9 .... **42** C4
Swaith Av *BTLY* DN5 .... **67** K8
Swaithedale *BSLY* S70 .... **83** G2
Swaithe Vw *BSLY* S70 .... **83** H2
Swale Cl *DEARNE* S63 .... **86** B5
Swaledale *WRKN* S81 .... **184** E8
Swaledale Rd *ABRD* S7 .... **176** B2
Swale Dr *CHPT/GREN* S35 .... **126** C2
Swale Gdns *DARN/MH* S9 .... **162** A3 8
Swale Rd *KIMB* S61 .... **128** E4
Swallow Cl *BSLY* S70 .... **82** D7
DOD/DAR S75 .... **37** H7
Swallow Ct *NROS/TKH* DN11 .... **113** L6
Swallow Garth
WKFDW/WTN WF2 .... **20** B2
Swallow Gv *WRKN* S81 .... **184** B8 3
Swallow Hill Rd *DOD/DAR* S75 .... **37** L8
Swallow La *AU/AST/KP* S26 .... **180** C1
Swallow Wood Ct
HAN/WDH S13 .... **178** E1
Swamp Wk *ST/HB/BR* S6 .... **144** B8
Swan Bank Ct *HOLM/MEL* HD7 .... **53** L3
Swan Bank La *HOLM/MEL* HD7 .... **53** L3
Swanbourne Pl *SHEFN* S5 .... **145** G3 2
Swanbourne Rd *SHEFN* S5 .... **145** G2
Swan Ct *WRKN* S81 .... **183** M8
Swanee Rd *BSLY* S70 .... **82** F1
Swannington Cl
DONS/BSCR DN4 .... **91** L8
Swan Rd *AU/AST/KP* S26 .... **180** C1
Swan St *BTLY* DN5 .... **67** M6 3
BWTY DN10 .... **154** E1
RHAM S60 .... **6** F6
Swan Syke Dr *AWLS/ASK* DN6 .... **27** J4
Swarcliffe Rd *DARN/MH* S9 .... **161** L2
Sweep La *HOLM/MEL* HD7 .... **53** M4
Sweyn Cft *BSLY* S70 .... **82** E2 13
Swifte Rd *RHAM* S60 .... **147** L4 1
Swift Ri *KIMB* S61 .... **127** L1
Swift Rd *CHPT/GREN* S35 .... **126** B7
Swift St *DOD/DAR* S75 .... **2** D3
Swift Wy *SHEFP/MNR* S2 .... **161** J5
WKFDW/WTN WF2 .... **20** A2
Swinburne Av *AWLS/ASK* DN6 .... **66** E2
DONS/BSCR DN4 .... **111** M1 11
Swinburne Cl *ARMTH* DN3 .... **47** K7 6
Swinburne Pl *RHAM/THRY* S65 .... **147** M2
Swinburne Rd
RHAM/THRY S65 .... **147** M2
Swine La *HOR/CROF* WF4 .... **22** A4
Swinnock La *CHPT/GREN* S35 .... **124** E5
Swinnow Rd *NROS/TKH* DN11 .... **154** A3
Swinston Hill Rd *DIN* S25 .... **166** E7
Swinton Rd *MEX/SWTN* S64 .... **108** D3
Swinton St *OWL* S3 .... **160** E2
Swithen Hl *DOD/DAR* S75 .... **36** F3
Sycamore Av *ARMTH* DN3 .... **70** A8
AU/AST/KP S26 .... **180** F5
CUD/GR S72 .... **39** M8 4
CUD/GR S72 .... **62** F2 1
DRON S18 .... **190** E4
MALT S66 .... **149** G2
Sycamore Cl *WRKS* S80 .... **198** C6
Sycamore Crs *BWTY* DN10 .... **136** D8
DEARNE S63 .... **107** K2 4
Sycamore Dr *BSLYN/ROY* S71 .... **38** E4
ECK/KIL S21 .... **194** A2
EPW DN9 .... **114** E3
Sycamore Farm Cl *MALT* S66 .... **148** F4 5
Sycamore Gn *KBTN* HD8 .... **34** C8
Sycamore Gv *CONI* DN12 .... **109** L6 1
DONS/BSCR DN4 .... **91** K7
Sycamore House Rd *SHEFN* S5 .... **145** K1
Sycamore La *HOR/CROF* WF4 .... **18** D7
Sycamore Rd *ARMTH* DN3 .... **47** J8
CHPT/GREN S35 .... **126** F7
HEM/SK/SE WF9 .... **41** G1
MEX/SWTN S64 .... **108** C2
RHAM/THRY S65 .... **129** M6
STKB/PEN S36 .... **101** L7
WRKN S81 .... **168** C8
The Sycamores *BTLY* DN5 .... **67** H6 1
Sycamore St *DOD/DAR* S75 .... **2** B4
MOS S20 .... **179** K3 1
MOS S20 .... **179** G7
Sycamore Vw *BTLY* DN5 .... **89** H6
Sycamore Wk *STKB/PEN* S36 .... **79** H4 2
Syday La *ECK/KIL* S21 .... **194** B6
Sydney Rd *ST/HB/BR* S6 .... **8** A2
Syke Cft *BSLYN/ROY* S71 .... **39** G2
Sykehouse La *ST/HB/BR* S6 .... **142** B8
Sykehouse Rd *GLE* DN14 .... **12** B8
Sykes Av *DOD/DAR* S75 .... **2** D3
Sykes Ct *MEX/SWTN* S64 .... **108** B6
Sykes St *BSLY* S70 .... **2** C9
Sylvan Cl *MALT* S66 .... **150** F1
Sylvester Av *DONS/BSCR* DN4 .... **4** E9
Sylvester Gdns *SHEF* S1 .... **9** H7
Sylvester St *SHEF* S1 .... **9** G8
Sylvestria Ct *NROS/TKH* DN11 .... **113** L6
Sylvia Cl *HAN/WDH* S13 .... **163** H8 3
Symes Gdns *DONS/BSCR* DN4 .... **91** K6
Symonds Av *RAW* S62 .... **107** G7
Symons Crs *SHEFN* S5 .... **144** D2

T

Tadcaster Cl *CONI* DN12 .... **109** J5
Tadcaster Crs *SHEFS* S8 .... **176** D3
Tadcaster Rd *SHEFS* S8 .... **176** D3
Tadcaster Wy *SHEFS* S8 .... **176** D3 4
Tait Av *CONI* DN12 .... **110** F7
Talbot Av *ARMTH* DN3 .... **47** K8
Talbot Crs *SHEFP/MNR* S2 .... **9** L6
Talbot Gdns *SHEFP/MNR* S2 .... **9** L6
Talbot Pl *SHEFP/MNR* S2 .... **9** M6
Talbot Rd *MEX/SWTN* S64 .... **108** D4
NROS/TKH DN11 .... **153** M3
SHEFP/MNR S2 .... **9** M5
STKB/PEN S36 .... **79** G4
WRKS S80 .... **198** E5
Talbot St *SHEFP/MNR* S2 .... **9** L6
Tallow Ms *KBTN* HD8 .... **34** E6
Talmont Rd *ECC* S11 .... **175** M1
Tamar Cl *DOD/DAR* S75 .... **59** J4

Tanfield Cl BSLYN/ROY S71 38 E3
Tanfield Rd ST/HB/BR S6 144 B6
Tanfield Wy MALT S66 148 F3
Tankersley La HOY S74 104 D3
Tank Rw BSLY S70 61 H6
Tannery Cl HAN/WDH S13 178 F1
Tannery St HAN/WDH S13 178 F1
Tan Pit Cl BTLY DN5 64 B3
Tanpit La AWLS/ASK DN6 27 H2
Tan Pit La BTLY DN5 64 B3
Tansley Dr DARN/MH S9 145 M3
Tansley St DARN/MH S9 145 M3
Tanyard Cft CUD/GR S72 40 E4 5
Tanyard Fold HOR/CROF WF4 19 L3
Taplin Rd ST/HB/BR S6 143 M7
Tapton Bank FUL S10 159 L5 1
Tapton Crescent Rd FUL S10 159 M5
Tapton Hill Rd FUL S10 159 L4
Tapton House Rd FUL S10 159 M5
Tapton Ms FUL S10 159 M4
Tapton Park Rd FUL S10 159 K6
Taptonville Crs FUL S10 160 A5 9
Taptonville Rd FUL S10 160 A4
Tarleton Cl ARMTH DN3 69 L3 2
Tarn Hows Wk FEA/AMT WF7 23 J2 1
Tasker Rd FUL S10 159 M4
Tasman Gv MALT S66 150 C1
Tatenhill Gdns
DONS/BSCR DN4 113 L1
Taunton Av DARN/MH S9 145 M4
Taunton Gdns MEX/SWTN S64 109 G1
Taunton Gv DARN/MH S9 145 M4 1
Taverner Cl CHPT/GREN S35 104 B6
Taverner Cft
CHPT/GREN S35 104 C7 5
Taverner Wy CHPT/GREN S35 104 C7
Tavistock Rd SHEFS S8 176 D1
Tavistock Wy
WKFDW/WTN WF2 19 K2
Tavy Cl DOD/DAR S75 59 J2 4
Tay Cl DRON S18 190 B5
Taylor Crs CUD/GR S72 62 E2
WRKN S81 183 J4
Taylor Dr WRKN S81 183 J4
Taylor Rw BSLY S70 3 H7
Taylors Cl RAW S62 129 J5
Taylors La RAW S62 129 J4
Taylor St CONI DN12 110 B5
T Benedict Ct
SHEFP/MNR S2 161 H7 1
Teague Pl WRKS S80 198 B4
Teal Ct WRKN S81 184 B8
Teapot Cnr BTLY DN5 64 B3
Teesdale Rd HACK/IN S12 178 D6
KIMB S61 128 D4
Teeside Cl BTLY DN5 89 H2
Telford Rd BTLY DN5 89 K2
Telson Cl MEX/SWTN S64 107 L4
Temperance St
MEX/SWTN S64 108 B4 4
Tempest Av WMB/DAR S73 62 E8
Tempest Rd HEM/SK/SE WF9 42 A3
Templar Cl MALT S66 165 H1 1
Temple Crs MALT S66 149 H3
Temple Gdns DONS/BSCR DN4 91 K8
Temple Rd RHAM S60 146 D4
Templestowe Ga CONI DN12 110 C5 5
Temple Wy BSLYN/ROY S71 61 H4 5
Ten Acre Rd KIMB S61 128 D7
Tenby Gdns DONS/BSCR DN4 89 L8
Tenby Gv WRKS S80 198 E5
Ten Lands La HOR/CROF WF4 21 K8
Tennyson Av ARMTH DN3 91 M1
AWLS/ASK DN6 27 G6
BTLY DN5 89 K3
MEX/SWTN S64 108 F1
THNE DN8 32 A8 2
Tennyson Cl DIN S25 166 E7 2
STKB/PEN S36 79 H3
Tennyson Dr WRKN S81 198 F3
Tennyson Ri DEARNE S63 85 G8
Tennyson Rd BSLYN/ROY S71 3 L1
BTLY DN5 67 M6
MALT S66 150 E3
RHAM/THRY S65 7 M6
RHAM/THRY S65 147 M1
ST/HB/BR S6 160 B1
Ten Pound Wk DONS/BSCR DN4 90 B7
Tenter Balk La AWLS/ASK DN6 66 E2
Tenter Cl KBTN HD8 34 E5
Tenterden Rd SHEFN S5 145 K4 2
Tenter Hl HOLM/MEL HD7 54 D3
Tenter La DONS/BSCR DN4 111 G1
STKB/PEN S36 101 L1
Tenter Rd DONS/BSCR DN4 111 G1
Tenters Gn BSLY S70 82 D3
Tenter St RHAM S60 6 C2
SHEF S1 9 G3
Terminus Rd ABRD S7 176 A4 1
Terrace Rd RAW S62 129 K3
Terrey Rd TOT/DORE S17 189 J2
Terry St DARN/MH S9 145 M8
Tetney Rd FUL S10 159 K6
Tewitt Rd BTLY DN5 67 L3 4
Teynham Dr SHEFN S5 144 D5
Teynham Rd SHEFN S5 144 C5
Thackeray Av RAW S62 107 M8
Thackeray Cl WRKN S81 198 F3
Thames St RHAM S60 6 D3
Thealby Gdns DONS/BSCR DN4 91 G8
Thellusson Av BTLY DN5 89 G1
Theobald Av DONS/BSCR DN4 5 L7
Theobald Cl DONS/BSCR DN4 5 K8
Theodore Rd AWLS/ASK DN6 27 J8
Thicket Dr MALT S66 150 F1
Thickett La STKB/PEN S36 79 J7
Thickwoods La STKB/PEN S36 99 M3
Thievesdale Av WRKN S81 184 D8 1
Thievesdale Cl WRKN S81 184 E8
Thievesdale La WRKN S81 184 E8
WRKN S81 185 H6
Thinholme La EPW DN9 117 M5
Third Av AWLS/ASK DN6 67 G3
HEM/SK/SE WF9 24 E7
Thirlmere Dr DIN S25 182 D1
DRON S18 190 E5
Thirlmere Gdns ARMTH DN3 69 K4 5
Thirlmere Rd BSLYN/ROY S71 3 J5
SHEFS S8 176 C2 5
Thirlwall Av CONI DN12 109 L5
Thirlwell Rd SHEFS S8 176 E1
Thirsk Cl CONI DN12 109 J5
Thistle Dr HEM/SK/SE WF9 24 D8
Thomas Rd HTFD DN7 48 D4
Thomas St AU/AST/KP S26 181 H5
BSLY S70 3 G7
BSLY S70 82 E3 9
CONI DN12 110 F6
HEM/SK/SE WF9 41 J1
MEX/SWTN S64 108 C8
MEX/SWTN S64 108 B4
SHEF S1 8 F6
WMB/DAR S73 84 F2 1
Thompson Av CONI DN12 110 E5
NROS/TKH DN11 153 K2
Thompson Cl MALT S66 132 C8
RAW S62 107 G7 1
Thompson Dr HTFD DN7 48 F8 5
MEX/SWTN S64 108 A6
Thompson Gdns
CHPT/GREN S35 104 A7 2
Thompson Hl CHPT/GREN S35 104 A8
Thompson House Gn
ST/HB/BR S6 140 F3
Thompson Nook HTFD DN7 48 F7 7
Thompson Rd FUL S10 8 A9
WMB/DAR S73 84 B5
Thompson Ter AWLS/ASK DN6 27 M7
Thomson Av DONS/BSCR DN4 89 K8
Thomson Cl DEARNE S63 107 K1
Thoresby Av BSLYN/ROY S71 60 F3
DONS/BSCR DN4 5 M8
Thoresby Cl AU/AST/KP S26 164 D8
Thoresby Rd ST/HB/BR S6 144 A8
Thorn Bank EPW DN9 95 G7
Thornborough Cl
SHEFP/MNR S2 161 G8 1
Thornborough Pl
SHEFP/MNR S2 161 G8 2
Thornborough Rd
SHEFP/MNR S2 160 F8
Thornbridge Av HACK/IN S12 178 B4
Thornbridge Cl HACK/IN S12 178 B4
Thornbridge Crs HACK/IN S12 178 C4
Thornbridge Dr HACK/IN S12 178 B4
Thornbridge Gv
HACK/IN S12 178 B4 2
Thornbridge La HACK/IN S12 178 C4 6
Thornbridge Pl HACK/IN S12 178 B4 3
Thornbridge Ri HACK/IN S12 178 C4
Thornbridge Rd HACK/IN S12 178 B4
Thornbridge Wy HACK/IN S12 178 C4
Thornbrook Cl
CHPT/GREN S35 126 F1
Thornbrook Gdns
CHPT/GREN S35 126 E1
Thornbrook Ms
CHPT/GREN S35 126 E1 5
Thornbury Hill La MALT S66 152 B7
Thorncliffe Gdns EPW DN9 92 E8 2
Thorncliffe La CHPT/GREN S35 104 D8
KBTN HD8 17 H8
Thorncliff La KBTN HD8 16 A8
Thorndale Ri RHAM S60 147 H7 9
Thorne & Dikesmarsh Rd
THNE DN8 31 L4
Thorne Cl BSLYN/ROY S71 38 C8 6
Thorne End Rd DOD/DAR S75 37 M5
Thornely Av DOD/DAR S75 59 K7
Thorne Rd ABRD S7 176 C2 6
ARMTH DN3 69 J6
BWTY DN10 136 F7
DON DN1 5 H4
EPW DN9 115 J1
HTFD DN7 48 C3
HTFD DN7 49 J7
Thorne Round Wk HTFD DN7 30 F8
Thorne Waste Drain Rd
THNE DN8 32 F6
Thorn Garth BTLY DN5 89 L1
Thornham Cl ARMTH DN3 91 M2 4
Thornham La ARMTH DN3 92 D1
Thornhill Av RHAM S60 146 F8
WHHL DN2 90 F1
Thornhill Edge RHAM S60 6 C3
Thornhill Pl DEARNE S63 107 J1 5
Thornhill Rd NROS/TKH DN11 153 H3
Thorn House La
CHPT/GREN S35 124 D4
Thorn La WHHL DN2 69 H5
Thornlea Ct CONI DN12 110 E6
Thornley Sq DEARNE S63 63 M7 2
Thorn Rd MEX/SWTN S64 108 B6
Thornseat Rd ST/HB/BR S6 140 E2
Thornsett Gdns TOT/DORE S17 175 K8
Thornsett Rd ECC S11 160 C7
Thornton Cl HEM/SK/SE WF9 41 H2 2
Thornton Dl WRKN S81 184 F8 1
Thorntondale Rd BTLY DN5 89 H1
Thornton Pl DRON S18 190 A6 16
Thornton Rd BSLY S70 3 M9
Thornton St KIMB S61 146 C2
Thornton Ter BSLY S70 61 G8 2
Thorntree Cl KIMB S61 127 K3 1
Thorntree La DOD/DAR S75 2 C2
GLE DN14 10 D4
Thorntree Rd KIMB S61 127 K4
Thornwell Gv CUD/GR S72 61 L1 2
Thornwell La KIMB S61 127 K1
Thorogate RAW S62 107 K8
Thorold Pl ARMTH DN3 69 K2
Thorp Av HOLM/MEL HD7 53 M3
Thorp Cl SHEFP/MNR S2 160 E7
Thorpe Av DRON S18 191 G3
Thorpe Bank ARMTH DN3 47 H8
Thorpe Dr MOS S20 179 J6
Thorpefield Cl KIMB S61 127 K2
Thorpefield Dr KIMB S61 127 K2
Thorpe Grange La BTLY DN5 46 B3
Thorpe Gn MOS S20 179 H5 5
Thorpehall Rd ARMTH DN3 69 L4
Thorpe House Av SHEFS S8 176 F3
Thorpe House Ri SHEFS S8 176 E3
Thorpe House Rd SHEFS S8 176 E3
Thorpe La AWLS/ASK DN6 46 E5
BTLY DN5 88 F6
HEM/SK/SE WF9 24 D4
WRKS S80 197 G1
Thorpe Mere Rd BTLY DN5 46 E8
Thorpe Mere Vw BTLY DN5 46 E7
Thorpe Rd AU/AST/KP S26 181 K8
BWTY DN10 155 L7
Thorpes Av KBTN HD8 34 E8
Thorpes Crs KBTN HD8 34 E6
Thorpe St KIMB S61 127 J2
Three Hills Cl
RHAM/THRY S65 130 D4 2
Three Nooks La CUD/GR S72 39 M6
Threshfield Wy HACK/IN S12 178 F4 5
Thrislington Sq THNE DN8 32 B3 5
Thrumpton Rd
BSLYN/ROY S71 38 D6 6
Thrush Av RHAM S60 147 H7 10
Thrush St ST/HB/BR S6 159 M1
Thruxton Cl CUD/GR S72 40 A7 4
Thrybergh Ct CONI DN12 109 M4 1
Thrybergh Hall Rd RAW S62 129 M1
Thrybergh La RHAM/THRY S65 130 F4
Thundercliffe Rd KIMB S61 127 M8
Thurgoland Bank
STKB/PEN S36 80 B7
Thurgoland Hall La
CHPT/GREN S35 80 D8
Thurlstone Rd STKB/PEN S36 78 F3
Thurnscoe Bridge La
DEARNE S63 86 B1
Thurnscoe La CUD/GR S72 63 K6
Thurnscoe Rd DEARNE S63 86 A5
Thurstan Av SHEFS S8 176 C7
Tiber Vw RHAM S60 147 G5 5
Tickhill Back La
NROS/TKH DN11 133 K5
Tickhill Rd BWTY DN10 136 D8
DONS/BSCR DN4 111 L1
MALT S66 150 F3
NROS/TKH DN11 153 J2
Tickhill Sq CONI DN12 109 K4
Tickhill St CONI DN12 109 K3
Tickhill Wy NROS/TKH DN11 113 M7
Tideswell Rd SHEFN S5 145 G4
Tideworth Hague La GLE DN14 30 C1
Tiercel Ms DIN S25 166 C6
Tilford Rd HAN/WDH S13 179 G1
Tillotson Cl SHEFS S8 176 E1 13
Tillotson Ri SHEFS S8 176 E1 14
Tiltshills La BTLY DN5 45 L8
Tilts La BTLY DN5 46 A8
BTLY DN5 68 B1
Timothy Wood Av BSLY S70 82 D7
Tindale Bank Rd EPW DN9 117 J7
Tingle Bridge Av WMB/DAR S73 84 A8
Tingle Bridge Crs
WMB/DAR S73 84 A8 5
Tingle Bridge La WMB/DAR S73 84 A8
Tingle Cl WMB/DAR S73 84 A8
Tinker Bottom ST/HB/BR S6 141 K6
Tinker La HOY S74 104 E1
RTFD DN22 186 E2
ST/HB/BR S6 159 M2
WRKN S81 186 C1
Tinker Rd RAW S62 129 L1
Tinker's Hl WRKN S81 184 F2
Tinsley Park Cl DARN/MH S9 146 A8
Tinsley Park Rd DARN/MH S9 145 M8
Tinsley Rd HOY S74 83 H8
Tinsworth Rd
WKFDW/WTN WF2 19 L3
Tipping La KBTN HD8 17 H8
Tippit La CUD/GR S72 62 A2
Tipton St DARN/MH S9 145 L5
Tithe Barn Av HAN/WDH S13 162 F8
Tithe Barn Cl HAN/WDH S13 163 G8
Tithe Barn Ct MEX/SWTN S64 86 D7 1
Tithe Barn La HAN/WDH S13 179 G1
THNE DN8 32 A8 5
Tithe Barn Wy HAN/WDH S13 162 F8
Tithe Laithe HOY S74 105 J1 6
Titterton Cl DARN/MH S9 161 L1
Titterton St DARN/MH S9 161 L1 2
Titus La KBTN HD8 34 B1
Tiverton Cl MEX/SWTN S64 108 B5 2
Tivy Dl DOD/DAR S75 58 C3
Tivy Dale Cl DOD/DAR S75 58 C3
Tivydale Dr DOD/DAR S75 37 J8
Tivy Dale Dr DOD/DAR S75 58 C3
Toadham La GLE DN14 10 C6
Toad La MALT S66 165 H2
Toby Wood La KBTN HD8 56 B2
Tockwith Rd DARN/MH S9 161 M2 5
Todmorden Cl CONI DN12 109 J4
Todwick Ct AU/AST/KP S26 181 K4
Todwick Rd AU/AST/KP S26 165 L7
SHEFS S8 176 C3
Toecroft La BTLY DN5 88 D6
Tofield Rd NROS/TKH DN11 111 L7
Tofts La ST/HB/BR S6 159 G3
STKB/PEN S36 101 K2
Toftstead ARMTH DN3 91 M2
Toftwood Av FUL S10 159 L3 1
Toftwood Rd FUL S10 159 M3
Togo St DEARNE S63 64 A8 1
Toll Bar Av HACK/IN S12 177 J2 5
Toll Bar Cl HACK/IN S12 177 J2
Tollbar Cl STKB/PEN S36 79 M7
Toll Bar Dr HACK/IN S12 177 J2
Toll Bar Rd MEX/SWTN S64 107 M4
RHAM/THRY S65 148 C3
Toll House Md MOS S20 179 G8
Tombridge Crs
HEM/SK/SE WF9 22 F6 2
Tom La FUL S10 159 H6
Tomlinson Rd HOY S74 105 K1
Tompson Hl CHPT/GREN S35 103 M8
Tom Wood Ash La
HEM/SK/SE WF9 25 H8
Tooker Rd RHAM S60 7 G6
Topcliffe Rd BSLYN/ROY S71 60 E2
Top Field La RHAM/THRY S65 130 B7
Top Hall Rd DONS/BSCR DN4 113 K2
Top La BTLY DN5 63 M3
HOR/CROF WF4 18 B6
HTFD DN7 47 L3
Top Orch HOR/CROF WF4 21 M6
Toppham Dr SHEFS S8 190 D1
Toppham Rd SHEFS S8 190 D1
Toppham Wy SHEFS S8 190 D1
Top Rd ARMTH DN3 47 K8
CHPT/GREN S35 143 H3
KBTN HD8 34 C8
Top Side CHPT/GREN S35 125 M6
Top St BWTY DN10 136 E8
HEM/SK/SE WF9 23 G8
Top Tree Wy RHAM/THRY S65 130 D4
Top View Crs CONI DN12 110 F7
Torbay Rd ATT S4 145 H8
Tor Cl BSLYN/ROY S71 60 E2
Torksey Cl DONS/BSCR DN4 113 J2 2
Torksey Rd SHEFN S5 145 H3
Torne Cl DONS/BSCR DN4 113 L1
Torne Vw EPW DN9 92 E7
Torry Ct HAN/WDH S13 179 G1
Tortmayns AU/AST/KP S26 181 J2
Torver Dr DEARNE S63 86 A6
Tor Wy RHAM S60 147 H8
Torwood Dr SHEFS S8 176 C8 2
Totley Brook Cl
TOT/DORE S17 189 H2 1
Totley Brook Cft
TOT/DORE S17 189 H2 2
Totley Brook Gln
TOT/DORE S17 189 H2 3
Totley Brook Gv
TOT/DORE S17 189 H2
Totley Brook Rd
TOT/DORE S17 189 H1
Totley Brook Wy
TOT/DORE S17 189 H2 4
Totley Cl BSLYN/ROY S71 38 F8
Totley Grange Cl
TOT/DORE S17 189 H3 2
Totley Grange Rd
TOT/DORE S17 189 H3
Totley Hall La TOT/DORE S17 189 H3
Totley La TOT/DORE S17 189 M2
Totties La HOLM/MEL HD7 54 B2
Towcester Wy MEX/SWTN S64 109 G1
Tower Av HEM/SK/SE WF9 24 E7
Tower Cl BTLY DN5 67 H6
SHEFP/MNR S2 161 G7 1
Tower Dr SHEFP/MNR S2 161 G7
Towers La HATH/EY S32 172 C7
Tower St BSLY S70 2 F9
Town End DRON S18 191 K6
Town End Av AU/AST/KP S26 164 B7
HOLM/MEL HD7 54 A1
Townend Av RHAM/THRY S65 130 C5
Townend Cl RHAM S60 163 J3
Townend La STKB/PEN S36 102 C8
Town End Rd CHPT/GREN S35 126 D7
HOLM/MEL HD7 53 M1
Townend St FUL S10 160 A3
Town End Vw HOLM/MEL HD7 53 M1
Town Field La CHPT/GREN S35 124 D4
Town Fields Av
CHPT/GREN S35 126 F7
Town Ga HOLM/MEL HD7 53 H2
HOLM/MEL HD7 53 L2
Towngate DOD/DAR S75 37 M6
DOD/DAR S75 58 D7
STKB/PEN S36 78 E3
Towngate Rd CHPT/GREN S35 143 G2
Town Hall St HOLM/MEL HD7 53 L2 5
Townhead Rd TOT/DORE S17 189 G1
Townhead St SHEF S1 9 G4
Town La KIMB S61 128 B5
Town Moor Av WHHL DN2 5 L3
Town St DARN/MH S9 146 B4
HEM/SK/SE WF9 23 G8
RHAM S60 6 E9
RTFD DN22 187 K1
Town View Av BTLY DN5 66 E7
Toyne St FUL S10 159 M3
Trafalgar Rd ST/HB/BR S6 144 A3
Trafalgar St AWLS/ASK DN6 45 G6
SHEF S1 8 F5
Trafford Ct DON DN1 4 E5 1
Trafford Rd AWLS/ASK DN6 27 H4
Trafford Wy DON DN1 4 E5
Tranker La WRKN S81 197 M1
Tranmoor Av DONS/BSCR DN4 91 J8
Tranmoor Ct HOY S74 104 F2 7
Tranmoor La ARMTH DN3 91 M2
Trans Pennine Trail
AWLS/ASK DN6 47 J2
BSLY S70 3 L7
BSLYN/ROY S71 39 J8
CHPT/GREN S35 102 D2
CHPT/GREN S35 103 J4
CONI DN12 109 L3
DARN/MH S9 145 K8
ECK/KIL S21 193 M6
HAN/WDH S13 162 C6
KIMB S61 146 D2
RAW S62 105 H4
Trap La ECC S11 175 J1
Travey Rd SHEFP/MNR S2 161 L8 5
Travis Av THNE DN8 32 A8
Travis Cl THNE DN8 32 A8
Travis Gdns DONS/BSCR DN4 4 A8
DONS/BSCR DN4 89 K6
Travis Gv THNE DN8 32 B8
Travis Pl FUL S10 8 D7
Tredis Cl BSLYN/ROY S71 3 L2
Treecrest Ri DOD/DAR S75 60 C3
Treefield Cl KIMB S61 128 E4
Treelands DOD/DAR S75 59 M4
Tree Root Wk FUL S10 8 A5
Treeton La AU/AST/KP S26 163 M4
RHAM S60 163 H2
Treetown Crs RHAM S60 163 J2
Treherne Rd RHAM/THRY S65 7 J7
Trelawney Wk BSLY S70 82 D2 2
Trent Cl CONI DN12 111 G4
Trent Gv DRON S18 190 F4
Trentham Cl RHAM S60 147 H7 11
Trenton Cl HAN/WDH S13 179 H1
Trenton Ri HAN/WDH S13 179 H1
Trent St DARN/MH S9 161 J1
WRKS S80 198 C3
Treswell Crs ST/HB/BR S6 144 A7 8
Trewan Ct BSLYN/ROY S71 3 M2
Tricket Rd CHPT/GREN S35 104 A7
Trickett Rd ST/HB/BR S6 144 A8
Trinity Dr KBTN HD8 56 D2
Trinity Mdw CHPT/GREN S35 80 D8 5
Trinity Rd AU/AST/KP S26 181 K5 1
Trinity St OWL S3 9 G2
Trippet La SHEF S1 9 G4
Tristford Cl RHAM S60 163 H1
Troon Rd HTFD DN7 48 F8
Troon Wk DIN S25 166 D7
Trouble Wood La ST/HB/BR S6 142 A3
Trough Dr RHAM/THRY S65 130 E5
Trough La HEM/SK/SE WF9 43 G4
Troutbeck Cl DEARNE S63 64 A8
Troutbeck Rd SHEFS S8 176 C3
Trowell Wy BSLYN/ROY S71 38 D7
Trueman Ct WRKN S81 198 F2 4
Trueman Gn MALT S66 150 C1
Trueman Ter BSLYN/ROY S71 61 J5 2
Truman Gv STKB/PEN S36 102 D6 5
Truman St BTLY DN5 67 L6
Trumfleet La AWLS/ASK DN6 28 F6
AWLS/ASK DN6 46 F1
Trundle La HTFD DN7 30 E8
Truro Av WHHL DN2 69 G7
Truro Ct BSLYN/ROY S71 3 M2
Truswell Av FUL S10 159 L3
Truswell Rd FUL S10 159 L4
Tudor Ct HEM/SK/SE WF9 42 D4
Tudor Rd AWLS/ASK DN6 67 G4
WHHL DN2 90 F3
Tudor St DEARNE S63 64 C7
NROS/TKH DN11 113 K7
Tudor Wy BSLY S70 82 E2
Tudworth Field Rd HTFD DN7 50 A5
Tudworth Rd HTFD DN7 49 L7
THNE DN8 49 M3
Tuffolds Cl SHEFP/MNR S2 161 L8
Tulip Tree Cl MOS S20 179 L2
Tullibardine Rd ECC S11 175 M1
Tumbling La BSLYN/ROY S71 61 K1
Tummon Rd SHEFP/MNR S2 161 J5
Tummon St KIMB S61 6 A5
Tune St BSLY S70 3 J8
WMB/DAR S73 84 A5
Tun La CUD/GR S72 22 B8
Tunwell Av SHEFN S5 126 F8
Tunwell Dr SHEFN S5 126 F8
Tunwell Greave SHEFN S5 126 F8
Tunwell Rd MALT S66 150 A6
Tup La HOR/CROF WF4 22 A7
Turf Moor Rd HTFD DN7 71 M2
Turie Av SHEFN S5 144 E1
Turie Crs SHEFN S5 144 E1
Turnberry WRKN S81 198 F1
Turnberry Ct BTLY DN5 67 L7 5
Turnberry Gv CUD/GR S72 40 A6 2
Turnberry Wy DIN S25 166 D8
Turner Av WMB/DAR S73 83 M4
Turner Cl DRON S18 190 D6 5
RAW S62 129 L3
Turner Dr WRKN S81 198 D3
Turner La RHAM S60 147 M6
Turner Rd WRKN S81 198 C3
Turner's Cl HOY S74 83 K8
Turners La FUL S10 160 A5 10
Turner St CUD/GR S72 63 J6
SHEFP/MNR S2 9 J6
Turnesc Gv DEARNE S63 64 B8
Turnpike Cft
CHPT/GREN S35 126 A6 1
Turnshaw Av AU/AST/KP S26 164 A6
Turnshaw Rd AU/AST/KP S26 164 D4
Tutbury Gdns DONS/BSCR DN4 91 L8
Tuxford Crs BSLYN/ROY S71 61 H5
The Twenty Lands RHAM S60 163 J4
Twentywell Dr
TOT/DORE S17 189 M1 1
Twentywell La TOT/DORE S17 175 L8
Twentywell Ri TOT/DORE S17 175 M8
Twentywell Rd TOT/DORE S17 189 M2
Twentywell Vw TOT/DORE S17 189 M2
Twibell St BSLYN/ROY S71 3 J2
Twickenham Cl MOS S20 193 J1 9
Twickenham Ct MOS S20 193 J1 10
Twickenham Crs MOS S20 193 J2
Twickenham Gld MOS S20 193 J1 11
Twickenham Gln MOS S20 193 K2 2
Twickenham Gv MOS S20 193 J1 12
Twitchill Dr HAN/WDH S13 178 F1
Two Acres WRKN S81 169 M5
Twyford Cl MEX/SWTN S64 107 L4
Tyas Pl MEX/SWTN S64 108 F2 1
Tyas Rd SHEFN S5 126 E8
Tyburn La KBTN HD8 34 F1
Tye Rd MOS S20 179 L4
Tylden Rd WRKS S80 197 M2 1
Tylden Wy WRKS S80 197 L2 1
Tyler St DARN/MH S9 145 M4
Tyler Wy DARN/MH S9 145 M4
Tylney Rd SHEFP/MNR S2 161 H6
Tynedale Ct ARMTH DN3 69 L3 5
Tynker Av MOS S20 179 L4
Tyzack Rd SHEFS S8 176 C5

U

Ughill Rd ST/HB/BR S6 141 K5
Ulley Crs HAN/WDH S13 161 M8
Ulley La AU/AST/KP S26 164 C4
Ulley Rd HAN/WDH S13 161 M8
Ulley Vw AU/AST/KP S26 164 B5
Ullswater Av MOS S20 193 J1
Ullswater Cl DEARNE S63 86 A6 2
DIN S25 166 C8
DRON S18 190 C5
MOS S20 193 J1
Ullswater Dr DRON S18 190 C6
Ullswater Pl DRON S18 190 C5
Ullswater Rd BSLYN/ROY S71 61 M7 5
MEX/SWTN S64 109 H1
Ulrica Dr MALT S66 165 J1
Ulverston Av AWLS/ASK DN6 28 A7
Ulverston Rd SHEFS S8 176 C3
Underbank La STKB/PEN S36 101 K3
Underbank Old Rd
HOLM/MEL HD7 53 M3

Undercliffe Rd ST/HB/BR S6 159 K1 3
Undergate Rd DIN S25 166 C5
Underhill BSLY S70 82 F3
Underhill La ST/HB/BR S6 143 M2
Underwood Av BSLY S70 82 F1
RTFD DN22 170 F4
Underwood Gdns WRKS S80 198 A4
Underwood Rd SHEFS S8 176 D3
Union Ct BSLY S70 3 H7
Union La SHEF S1 9 H6
Union Rd ECC S11 176 B1
THNE DN8 31 L8
Union St AU/AST/KP S26 181 J8
BSLY S70 3 G7
DON DN1 4 F6
HEM/SK/SE WF9 41 J1 3
KIMB S61 6 B4
SHEF S1 9 H6
Unity Pl RHAM S60 6 F5
Unsliven Rd STKB/PEN S36 101 J4
Unstone-dronfield By-pass
DRON S18 190 D4
Unstone Hl DRON S18 191 H7
Unstone St SHEFP/MNR S2 9 G9
Unwin Crs STKB/PEN S36 79 H5
Unwin St STKB/PEN S36 79 H5
Uplands Av DOD/DAR S75 37 G7
Uplands Rd ARMTH DN3 92 A1
Uplands Wy RAW S62 129 J1
Upper Albert Rd SHEFS S8 176 F2
Upper Allen St OWL S3 8 E3
Upper Ash Gv HEM/SK/SE WF9 42 E4
Upper Bank End Rd
HOLM/MEL HD7 53 M4
Upper Clara St KIMB S61 146 D1
Upper Cliffe Rd DOD/DAR S75 59 J7
Upper Common La KBTN HD8 35 K7
Upperfield Cl MALT S66 150 D1
Upper Field La DOD/DAR S75 36 B6
Upperfield Rd MALT S66 132 C8
Upper Folderings
DOD/DAR S75 59 K8 3
Upper Forest Rd
BSLYN/ROY S71 38 D7
Upper Ga HOLM/MEL HD7 54 C5
Upper Gate Rd ST/HB/BR S6 158 F2
Upper Hanover St OWL S3 8 D5
Upper Hatfield Pl
HOR/CROF WF4 22 B5
Upper High Royds
DOD/DAR S75 37 L7
Upper House Rd
HOLM/MEL HD7 54 A7
Upper Hoyland Rd HOY S74 83 G8
Upper Kenyon St THNE DN8 31 M7 2
Upper La HOR/CROF WF4 18 A3
KBTN HD8 35 H1
Upper Ley Ct
CHPT/GREN S35 126 E2 7
Upper Ley Dell
CHPT/GREN S35 126 E2 8
Upper Maythorn La
HOLM/MEL HD7 55 H7
Upper Mdw HOLM/MEL HD7 53 H2
Upper New St BSLY S70 3 G7
Upper Rye Cl RHAM S60 148 B6
Upper School La DRON S18 190 F7 5
DRON S18 190 E7 4
Upper Sheffield Rd BSLY S70 82 E1
Upperthong La HOLM/MEL HD7 53 J2
Upperthorpe ST/HB/BR S6 8 A1
Upperthorpe Gln ST/HB/BR S6 8 B1
Upperthorpe Hl EPW DN9 117 M3
Upperthorpe Rd ECK/KIL S21 194 B2
ST/HB/BR S6 8 D1
Upper Valley Rd SHEFS S8 176 F2
Upper Whiston La RHAM S60 148 A8
Upperwood Rd WMB/DAR S73 84 C1
Upper Wortley Rd KIMB S61 127 K4
Upton Cl MALT S66 132 C8
WMB/DAR S73 83 M3
Upwell Hl ATT S4 145 J6
Upwell La ATT S4 145 J6
Upwell St ATT S4 145 J6
Upwood Rd ST/HB/BR S6 143 M6
Urban Rd DONS/BSCR DN4 4 A8
Urch Cl CONI DN12 110 A6
Uttley Cl DARN/MH S9 161 M1
Uttley Cft DARN/MH S9 161 M1
Uttley Dr DARN/MH S9 161 M1
Uttoxeter Av MEX/SWTN S64 109 G1

V

Vaal St BSLY S70 3 M8
Vainor Rd ST/HB/BR S6 143 L5
Vale Av RHAM/THRY S65 130 D5
Vale Cl DRON S18 190 F6 3
Vale Crs RHAM/THRY S65 130 D5
Vale Gv ST/HB/BR S6 143 J7
Valentine Cl SHEFN S5 145 G2
Valentine Crs SHEFN S5 145 G2
Valentine Rd SHEFN S5 145 G2
Vale Rd HEM/SK/SE WF9 22 F6
OWL S3 144 D8
RHAM/THRY S65 130 D5
Valestone Av HEM/SK/SE WF9 23 J8
Valiant Gdns BTLY DN5 89 J4
Valley Av HEM/SK/SE WF9 42 F4
Valley Dr ARMTH DN3 92 B7
DEARNE S63 107 H1
ECK/KIL S21 180 B8 3
Valley Rd CHPT/GREN S35 126 C1
DOD/DAR S75 37 L6
ECK/KIL S21 180 B8
HACK/IN S12 179 G5
MEX/SWTN S64 107 M5
SHEFS S8 176 E1
WMB/DAR S73 84 C3
WRKN S81 184 C8
WRKN S81 198 C2
Valley St HEM/SK/SE WF9 42 D5
Valley Vw HEM/SK/SE WF9 42 F4
Valley View Cl ECK/KIL S21 193 G5 3
Valley Wy HOY S74 105 J1
Vancouver Dr DEARNE S63 85 M5
Varley Gdns MALT S66 148 F1 3
Varney Rd DEARNE S63 107 J2
Varsity Cl HTFD DN7 71 L8
Vaughan Av DON DN1 5 H3
Vaughan Rd AWLS/ASK DN6 27 H6
DOD/DAR S75 59 M4 3
Vaughton Hl STKB/PEN S36 102 E6
Vauxhall Cl DARN/MH S9 145 M3
Vauxhall Rd DARN/MH S9 145 M3
Velvet Wood Cl DOD/DAR S75 59 L4
Venetian Crs WMB/DAR S73 84 D2
Ventnor Cl DONS/BSCR DN4 89 K8 6
Ventnor Pl ABRD S7 160 D7 12
Venus Ct RHAM S60 147 G5
Verdant Wy SHEFN S5 145 H2
Verdon St OWL S3 160 F2
Verelst Av AU/AST/KP S26 164 B6
Vere Rd ST/HB/BR S6 144 A5
Verger Cl NROS/TKH DN11 113 L6
Vermuyden Rd THNE DN8 32 B4
Vernon Cl BSLY S70 60 D8
Vernon Crs BSLY S70 82 D2
Vernon Delph FUL S10 159 K4
Vernon Dr CHPT/GREN S35 126 D1
Vernon Rd BSLY S70 82 D2
RHAM/THRY S65 147 M4
TOT/DORE S17 189 J1
Vernon St BSLY S70 104 D1
BSLYN/ROY S71 3 H3
HOY S74 105 G2
Vernon St North BSLYN/ROY S71 3 H3
Vernon Ter FUL S10 159 L5
Vernon Wy DOD/DAR S75 59 M4
MALT S66 150 C1
Verona Ri WMB/DAR S73 84 E2
Vesey St RAW S62 129 K3
Vessey Rd WRKN S81 184 C8
Vicarage Cl CHPT/GREN S35 126 A7
DONS/BSCR DN4 91 L8
DRON S18 189 L7
HEM/SK/SE WF9 42 A4
HOY S74 105 J1 7
MEX/SWTN S64 109 G3
RHAM/THRY S65 130 B7
Vicarage Crs CHPT/GREN S35 126 A7
Vicarage Dr
NROS/TKH DN11 111 M8 1
Vicarage La BSLYN/ROY S71 39 G4
TOT/DORE S17 175 H8
Vicarage Rd CHPT/GREN S35 126 A7
DARN/MH S9 145 K8
Vicarage Wk STKB/PEN S36 79 H4
Vicarage Wy BTLY DN5 68 B5
Vicar Crs WMB/DAR S73 84 F2
Vicar La HAN/WDH S13 162 F8
SHEF S1 9 H3
Vicar Rd DEARNE S63 85 H8
WMB/DAR S73 84 F2
Vicar's Wk WRKS S80 198 D5
Vickers Av HEM/SK/SE WF9 42 C6
Vickers Dr SHEFN S5 145 H4
Vickers Rd CHPT/GREN S35 104 B8
SHEFN S5 145 H5
Victoria Av HTFD DN7 48 F7
RHAM/THRY S65 7 K5
Victoria Cl AU/AST/KP S26 181 J5 1
HTFD DN7 48 D5
STKB/PEN S36 101 M6
Victoria Ct AU/AST/KP S26 181 J5 2
BTLY DN5 67 M4
HEM/SK/SE WF9 24 E8
Victoria Crs BSLY S70 82 C8 2
DOD/DAR S75 2 D3
Victoria Crs West DOD/DAR S75 2 D4
Victoria La NROS/TKH DN11 113 J6
Victorian Crs WHHL DN2 5 L2
Victoria Quays Rbt ATT S4 9 M2
Victoria Rd AWLS/ASK DN6 45 K1
AWLS/ASK DN6 67 H1
BSLY S70 2 E3
BSLYN/ROY S71 39 H3
BTLY DN5 67 M5
CONI DN12 110 F4
DEARNE S63 85 H8
DONS/BSCR DN4 89 M7
FUL S10 8 C8
MEX/SWTN S64 108 E2
MOS S20 179 K3
RAW S62 129 K3
STKB/PEN S36 102 A6
WMB/DAR S73 84 A4
WRKS S80 198 D5
Victoria Springs
HOLM/MEL HD7 53 J3
Victoria Station Rd ATT S4 9 K2
Victoria St BSLY S70 2 E4
BSLY S70 61 H7
CUD/GR S72 39 M8
DEARNE S63 86 C2
DIN S25 166 E6
DRON S18 190 D5
FEA/AMT WF7 23 H2
HEM/SK/SE WF9 41 J1
HOLM/MEL HD7 53 L2
HOY S74 105 K1
KBTN HD8 35 J5
MALT S66 150 E4
MEX/SWTN S64 108 C5
MEX/SWTN S64 108 C8
OWL S3 8 E5
RHAM S60 6 B5
RHAM S60 163 H1
STKB/PEN S36 79 H4
STKB/PEN S36 101 M6
WMB/DAR S73 84 F1
Victoria Ter BSLY S70 3 J8
KBTN HD8 35 K5 3
Victoria Wy MALT S66 150 B1
Victor Rd HEM/SK/SE WF9 42 A5
TOT/DORE S17 175 K8
Victor St AWLS/ASK DN6 44 F7
HEM/SK/SE WF9 42 D5
ST/HB/BR S6 144 B8
Viewland Cl CUD/GR S72 62 A2
Viewlands DOD/DAR S75 80 E2
Viewlands Cl MALT S66 149 J3
STKB/PEN S36 79 H2
View Rd RHAM/THRY S65 7 M1
SHEFS S8 160 E8
STKB/PEN S36 78 E3
Viewtree Cl RAW S62 105 H6
Viking Av KBTN HD8 35 H1
Vikinglea Cl SHEFP/MNR S2 161 M7 4
Vikinglea Dr SHEFP/MNR S2 161 M7
Vikinglea Gld
SHEFP/MNR S2 161 M6 5
Vikinglea Rd SHEFP/MNR S2 161 M6
Viking Wy AU/AST/KP S26 181 K4 2
Villa Gdns BTLY DN5 67 L2
Village St AWLS/ASK DN6 66 F1
Villa Park Rd DONS/BSCR DN4 91 J7
Villa Rd AWLS/ASK DN6 66 F2
Villiers Cl SHEFP/MNR S2 177 J2
Villiers Dr SHEFP/MNR S2 177 J1
Vincent Rd BSLYN/ROY S71 61 K4 2
ECC S11 160 D7
RHAM/THRY S65 131 G8
Vine Cl BSLYN/ROY S71 61 G3
RHAM S60 6 C4
Vine Rd NROS/TKH DN11 135 G8
Vinery Cl KBTN HD8 35 K5
Vineyard Cl NROS/TKH DN11 134 D7
Viola Bank STKB/PEN S36 101 M6
Violet Av CONI DN12 110 F6
MOS S20 179 J4
Violet Bank Rd ABRD S7 176 C1 5
Vissett Cl HEM/SK/SE WF9 40 F1
Vissitt La HEM/SK/SE WF9 40 E1
Vivian Rd SHEFN S5 145 H5
Vizard Rd HOY S74 105 K1
Vulcan Pl WRKS S80 198 D4
Vulcan Rd DARN/MH S9 145 M6
Vulcan Wy HTFD DN7 71 L6

W

Waarburton KBTN HD8 35 G1
Wadbrough Rd FUL S10 8 A9
Waddington Rd DOD/DAR S75 59 M5
Wade Cl RHAM S60 7 J8
Wade Meadow ST/HB/BR S6 143 L6 1
Wade St ATT S4 145 J6 1
DOD/DAR S75 59 M5
Wadman Rd HOLM/MEL HD7 54 B4
Wadsley La ST/HB/BR S6 143 L5 1
Wadsley Park Crs
ST/HB/BR S6 143 L6
Wadsworth Av HACK/IN S12 178 A2
Wadsworth Cl HACK/IN S12 178 B2 1
Wadsworth Dr HACK/IN S12 178 B1
RAW S62 107 G7
Wadsworth Rd HACK/IN S12 178 A2 3
MALT S66 149 H3
Wadworth Av
NROS/TKH DN11 113 M6
Wadworth Cl BTLY DN5 87 G4
Wadworth Hall La
NROS/TKH DN11 111 L8
Wadworth Hl NROS/TKH DN11 112 A6
Wadworth Ri RHAM/THRY S65 130 C6
Wadworth St CONI DN12 109 L4
Waggon La HEM/SK/SE WF9 24 F8
Waggon Rd KIMB S61 128 F4
Wain Ct WRKN S81 184 F8
Waingate OWL S3 9 J3
Wainwright Av HAN/WDH S13 162 B7
WMB/DAR S73 83 M4
Wainwright Crs HAN/WDH S13 162 A7
Wainwright Pl
WMB/DAR S73 83 M4 2
Wainwright Rd DONS/BSCR DN4 5 K7
KIMB S61 128 D6 3
Wakefield Rd BSLYN/ROY S71 38 D8
BSLYN/ROY S71 38 C7
BSLYN/ROY S71 60 D1
DOD/DAR S75 38 B6
FEA/AMT WF7 23 H2
HEM/SK/SE WF9 22 E4
KBTN HD8 35 K4
KBTN HD8 56 C2
Wake Rd ABRD S7 160 C8
Walbank Rd ARMTH DN3 92 A1
Walbert Av DEARNE S63 64 A8
Walbrook BSLY S70 82 F3
Walden Av BTLY DN5 67 J6
Walden Rd SHEFP/MNR S2 160 F8
Walden Stubbs Rd
AWLS/ASK DN6 27 H3
Walders Av ST/HB/BR S6 143 L5
Walders La STKB/PEN S36 124 A1
Walesmoor Av AU/AST/KP S26 181 G5
Wales Pl ST/HB/BR S6 160 B1
Wales Rd AU/AST/KP S26 180 F5
Waleswood Rd
AU/AST/KP S26 180 A3
Waleswood Vw
AU/AST/KP S26 180 B1
Walford Rd ECK/KIL S21 194 A1
Walker Cl CHPT/GREN S35 126 A7
Walker Edge ST/HB/BR S6 123 L4
Walker La RHAM/THRY S65 7 H4
Walker Rd DOD/DAR S75 104 D2 2
KIMB S61 128 D6
Walkers La ECK/KIL S21 194 B1
Walker St MEX/SWTN S64 108 C4
OWL S3 9 K1
RAW S62 129 M1
Walker Vw RAW S62 129 M1
Walkley Bank Cl ST/HB/BR S6 160 A1
Walkley Bank Rd ST/HB/BR S6 159 M1
Walkley Crescent Rd
ST/HB/BR S6 159 M1
Walkley La ST/HB/BR S6 144 A7
Walkley Rd ST/HB/BR S6 160 A1
Walkley St ST/HB/BR S6 160 B2
Walkley Ter ST/HB/BR S6 159 L1
Walk Royd Hl DOD/DAR S75 36 F5
The Walk BSLY S70 104 C1
Wallace Rd DONS/BSCR DN4 111 J1
OWL S3 160 D1
Waller Rd ST/HB/BR S6 159 L2
Wallingbrook Ri WRKS S80 197 M5
Walling Cl DARN/MH S9 145 M5
Walling Rd DARN/MH S9 145 M5 3
Wallingwells La WRKN S81 183 L1
Wall Nook La KBTN HD8 55 H1
Wallroyds KBTN HD8 56 C2
Walls La STV/CWN S43 195 J7
WRKS S80 195 L7
Wall St BSLY S70 2 F8
Walmsley Dr HEM/SK/SE WF9 24 F8
Walney Fold BSLYN/ROY S71 61 H1 3
Walnut Av EPW DN9 114 E3
NROS/TKH DN11 134 F8
WRKN S81 183 K8
Walnut Dr DIN S25 166 D7
ECK/KIL S21 194 A2 2
Walnut Gv MEX/SWTN S64 108 D1
Walnut Pl CHPT/GREN S35 126 D3
Walnut Rd THNE DN8 31 M6
Walnut St HEM/SK/SE WF9 42 D6
Walnut Tree Hl
NROS/TKH DN11 112 A8
Walpole Cl DONS/BSCR DN4 111 K2
Walpole Gv AU/AST/KP S26 164 B6
Walseker La AU/AST/KP S26 181 G8
Walsham Dr BTLY DN5 89 J2
Walshaw Rd CHPT/GREN S35 143 H2
Walters Rd MALT S66 150 F2
Walter St RHAM S60 6 C3
ST/HB/BR S6 144 B8 7
Waltham Dr AWLS/ASK DN6 44 C5
Waltham Gdns MOS S20 179 L5 10
Waltham St BSLY S70 3 H7
Waltheof Rd SHEFP/MNR S2 161 L7
Waltin Rd HOLM/MEL HD7 53 K6
Walton Cl CHPT/GREN S35 104 A7 3
DRON S18 190 A5
Walton Rd FUL S10 8 A9
HEM/SK/SE WF9 25 H7
Walton St DOD/DAR S75 2 A1
Walton St North DOD/DAR S75 2 A1
DOD/DAR S75 59 M4
Wannop St RAW S62 129 K4
Wansfell Rd ATT S4 145 K6
The Wapping RHAM/THRY S65 109 H8
Warburton Cl
SHEFP/MNR S2 161 G8 3
Warburton Gdns
SHEFP/MNR S2 161 G8 4
Warburton Rd SHEFP/MNR S2 161 G8
Ward Bank Rd HOLM/MEL HD7 53 L3
Warde-aldam Crs MALT S66 148 E2
Warde Av DONS/BSCR DN4 111 K1
Warden Cl DONS/BSCR DN4 91 L7
Warden St RHAM S60 147 H4
Ward La STV/CWN S43 194 F4
Wardlow Rd HACK/IN S12 178 B2
Ward Pl SHEFP/MNR S2 160 D7 13
Ward Place La HOLM/MEL HD7 53 K4
Wardsend Rd SHEFN S5 144 B5
Wardsend Rd North
ST/HB/BR S6 144 A4
Ward St OWL S3 9 G1
STKB/PEN S36 79 H5
Wareham Ct MOS S20 179 L5 11
Wareham Gv DOD/DAR S75 59 L7
Warehouse La DEARNE S63 107 J1
Warminster Cl SHEFS S8 176 E3
Warminster Crs SHEFS S8 176 F3
Warminster Dr SHEFS S8 176 F4 1
Warminster Pl SHEFS S8 176 F5
Warminster Rd SHEFS S8 176 E3
Warmsworth Halt CONI DN12 110 F3
Warmsworth Rd
DONS/BSCR DN4 111 J1
Warner Av DOD/DAR S75 59 M5
Warner Pl DOD/DAR S75 2 A3
Warner Rd DOD/DAR S75 59 M5
ST/HB/BR S6 143 M6
Warnington Dr ARMTH DN3 113 M3
DONS/BSCR DN4 113 L2
Warning Tongue La
ARMTH DN3 91 M8
Warren Av RAW S62 107 J8
Warren Cl BSLYN/ROY S71 39 H2
DONS/BSCR DN4 111 G1
WHHL DN2 90 E3
WRKN S81 183 J3
Warren Crs BSLY S70 60 D8
ECK/KIL S21 192 C5
Warren Dr KIMB S61 128 D7
Warreners Dr RHAM/THRY S65 130 D5
Warren Gdns CHPT/GREN S35 104 E7
Warren Hl KIMB S61 128 D7
Warren House Cl MALT S66 149 H1
Warren La CHPT/GREN S35 104 F7
DOD/DAR S75 38 A3
DONS/BSCR DN4 113 K2
HOY S74 104 D6
Warren Mt KIMB S61 128 D7
Warrenne Cl HTFD DN7 48 E8 2
Warrenne Rd HTFD DN7 48 E8
Warren Pl BSLY S70 3 G9
BSLY S70 60 D8 12
Warren Quarry La BSLY S70 3 G8
Warren Ri DRON S18 191 G4
Warren Rd MALT S66 148 F2
THNE DN8 50 A1
Warren St ATT S4 161 H2
Warren V MEX/SWTN S64 107 L6
RAW S62 107 L8
Warren Vale Rd
MEX/SWTN S64 107 L4
Warren Vw HOY S74 105 G3
Warrington Rd FUL S10 8 A3
Warris Cl KIMB S61 128 C6
Warris Pl SHEFP/MNR S2 161 H4
Warsop Rd BSLYN/ROY S71 38 C6
Warwick Av WRKN S81 184 D1
Warwick Cl HTFD DN7 71 K1
Warwick Rd BSLYN/ROY S71 3 M1
WHHL DN2 90 F2
Warwick St FUL S10 160 A3 3
RHAM/THRY S65 7 G6
Warwick St South
RHAM/THRY S65 7 H6 2
Warwick Ter FUL S10 160 A3 10
Warwick Wy DIN S25 182 C1
Wasdale Av MOS S20 193 J1 13
Wasdale Cl MOS S20 193 J1
Washfield Crs RHAM S60 163 J3
Washfield La RHAM S60 163 J4
Washford Rd DARN/MH S9 161 J1
Washington Av CONI DN12 109 K5
WMB/DAR S73 83 M5
Washington Cl DIN S25 166 C7 3
Washington Gv BTLY DN5 67 L8
Washington Rd AWLS/ASK DN6 66 F2
CHPT/GREN S35 126 F6
DEARNE S63 86 B3
ECC S11 8 E9
ECC S11 160 D7
Washington St
MEX/SWTN S64 108 F2
Washpit New Rd
HOLM/MEL HD7 53 L5
Wasteneys Rd AU/AST/KP S26 181 K2
Watch House La BTLY DN5 89 K1
Watchit Hole La PONT WF8 25 G3
Watchley La BTLY DN5 64 F5
Watch St HAN/WDH S13 163 H7
Water Bank EPW DN9 95 G5
Waterdale DON DN1 5 G6
Waterdale Cl BTLY DN5 89 H7 1
Waterdale Rd BSLY S70 82 D3
Waterfield Ms MOS S20 179 J6 4
Waterfield Pl BSLYN/ROY S71 61 J7 5
Waterford Rd OWL S3 144 C8
Water Hall La STKB/PEN S36 79 H3
Waterhall Vw STKB/PEN S36 79 H3 1
Waterhouse Cl
RHAM/THRY S65 130 C6
Watering Place Rd
STKB/PEN S36 78 E4 2
Water La HEM/SK/SE WF9 41 K3
HOR/CROF WF4 19 L7
HTFD DN7 48 C2
NROS/TKH DN11 152 E2
PONT WF8 26 C1
RAW S62 105 L4
RHAM S60 6 E6
TOT/DORE S17 175 K8
WRKN S81 184 E1
Waterloo Rd BSLY S70 2 D6
Waterloo Wk OWL S3 160 D2 15
Watermead DEARNE S63 86 B6
Watermeade ECK/KIL S21 192 F5
Water Mdw WRKS S80 198 B6
Water Rw HOLM/MEL HD7 54 C1 2
Water Royd Dr DOD/DAR S75 59 K8
Waterside THNE DN8 31 J7
Waterside Gdns
CHPT/GREN S35 125 H8
Waterside Rd THNE DN8 31 K6 2
Waterslack Rd
NROS/TKH DN11 153 M3
Water Slacks Cl
HAN/WDH S13 178 F1 3
Water Slacks Dr
HAN/WDH S13 178 F1
Water Slacks Rd
HAN/WDH S13 178 F1
Watersmeet Rd
ST/HB/BR S6 143 M8
Water St HOLM/MEL HD7 53 H4
KBTN HD8 35 H6 3
OWL S3 9 H2
RHAM S60 6 F3
Waterthorpe Cl MOS S20 179 K7 4
Waterthorpe Crs MOS S20 179 K7
Waterthorpe Gdns MOS S20 179 J7
Waterthorpe Gld MOS S20 179 J7
Waterthorpe Gln MOS S20 179 K7 3
Waterthorpe Greenway
MOS S20 179 H4
Waterthorpe Ri MOS S20 179 K7
Waterton Cl HEM/SK/SE WF9 42 B4 1
WKFDW/WTN WF2 20 E1
Waterton La HTFD DN7 71 G5
Water Way Garth CLE DN14 11 J3 3
Watery La HOLM/MEL HD7 52 D7
Watery St OWL S3 8 E1
Wath Rd ABRD S7 176 C1
DEARNE S63 85 M6
HOY S74 105 L3
MEX/SWTN S64 108 B1
WMB/DAR S73 84 D6
Wath Wood Bottom
DEARNE S63 107 J4
Wath Wood Dr DEARNE S63 107 K4
Wath Wood Rd DEARNE S63 107 K3
Watkinson Gdns MOS S20 179 J5
Watnall Rd BSLYN/ROY S71 38 D7 2
Watson Cl KIMB S61 128 D7
Watson Gln KIMB S61 128 A7
Watson Rd FUL S10 8 A6
FUL S10 160 A5 11
KIMB S61 128 D7
WRKS S80 198 D4
Watsons Cft HTFD DN7 48 F3 2
Watson St HOY S74 104 F2 3
Watt La FUL S10 159 K5
Waulkmill Cl HEM/SK/SE WF9 24 E8
Wavell Crs BWTY DN10 155 L6
Waveney Dr DOD/DAR S75 59 J4 1
Waverley Av AU/AST/KP S26 181 J4
CONI DN12 110 A5
DONS/BSCR DN4 89 J8
MALT S66 165 K1
Waverley Ct BTLY DN5 67 L3
Waverley Pl WRKS S80 198 E7
Waverley Rd DARN/MH S9 162 A3 3
Waverley Vw RHAM S60 163 G2
Waverley Wy WRKS S80 198 E7
Waycliffe BSLYN/ROY S71 61 G4
Wayford Av MALT S66 149 J1
Wayland Av BSLY S70 82 D2
Wayland Rd ECC S11 160 B7
Weakland Cl HACK/IN S12 178 D5
Weakland Crs HACK/IN S12 178 D4
Weakland Dr HACK/IN S12 178 D4
Weakland Wy HACK/IN S12 178 D4 2
Weatherall Pl AWLS/ASK DN6 44 D5
Weather Hill La HOLM/MEL HD7 53 J7
Weaver Cl DOD/DAR S75 59 J4
Weavers Cl CHPT/GREN S35 126 A6
Weavers Cft EPW DN9 117 M3
Weavers Wk KBTN HD8 34 F8
Webb Av STKB/PEN S36 102 C7

Webbs Av ST/HB/BR S6 159 J1
Webster Cl KIMB S61 128 B7 2
Webster Crs KIMB S61 128 B7
Webster St DARN/MH S9 145 M6 1
Wedgewood Cl RAW S62 129 K2
Weedon St DARN/MH S9 145 M5
Weet Shaw La CUD/GR S72 39 L6
Weetwood Dr ECC S11 175 M2 1
Weetwood Rd RHAM S60 147 L5
Weigh La SHEFP/MNR S2 9 M5 1
Weir Cl EPW DN9 117 M3
Weir Head DARN/MH S9 145 M6
Weir Rd EPW DN9 117 M3
Weirside WRKN S81 168 D1
Welbeck Cl DRON S18 190 A5
Welbeck Dr AU/AST/KP S26 164 D8
Welbeck Rd DONS/BSCR DN4 5 L6
NROS/TKH DN11 153 L2 1
Welbeck St DOD/DAR S75 2 C3 1
WRKS S80 198 D3
Welbury Gdns MOS S20 193 J1
Welby Pl SHEFS S8 176 D3
Welfare Av CONI DN12 109 L5
Welfare Rd AWLS/ASK DN6 66 F4
DEARNE S63 64 A7
Welfare Vw DEARNE S63 86 B3
Welham Dr RHAM S60 7 G8
Welland Cl OWL S3 160 D1
WRKN S81 184 C8
Welland Ct DOD/DAR S75 59 J4
Welland Crs HOY S74 105 L1
Wellbeck Rd ST/HB/BR S6 159 M1
Wellbourne Cl CHPT/GREN S35 127 G3
Wellcarr Rd SHEFS S8 176 E5
Wellcliffe Cl MALT S66 149 G1
Wellcroft Cl WHHL DN2 91 G1
Well Dr RHAM/THRY S65 130 E5
Wellesley Cl WRKN S81 184 B7
Wellesley Rd FUL S10 8 B5
Wellfield Av HOR/CROF WF4 16 C2
Wellfield Cl HACK/IN S12 178 C6
HOR/CROF WF4 16 C2 1
ST/HB/BR S6 8 B1
Wellfield Crs WRKN S81 183 J4
Wellfield Gv STKB/PEN S36 79 H2
Wellfield Rd DOD/DAR S75 2 C2
KIMB S61 128 C5
ST/HB/BR S6 8 B1
Wellgate CONI DN12 110 A5
DOD/DAR S75 37 M6
RHAM/THRY S65 6 F4
Wellgate Mt RHAM/THRY S65 7 G5
Well Green Rd ST/HB/BR S6 158 F2
Wellhead Rd SHEFS S8 176 E1 15
Well Hill Gv BSLYN/ROY S71 39 G3 3
Well Hill Rd CHPT/GREN S35 102 D3
HOLM/MEL HD7 53 M4
Well House La STKB/PEN S36 78 F1
Well Houses La
CHPT/GREN S35 103 H2
Wellhouse Wy STKB/PEN S36 79 H2
Wellingley La NROS/TKH DN11 134 D5
Wellington Av DIN S25 166 B8
Wellington Cl BSLYN/ROY S71 60 F3
Wellington Crs BSLY S70 83 G2
Wellington Gv BTLY DN5 67 L8
BWTY DN10 136 D7 1
Wellingtonia Dr AWLS/ASK DN6 27 G6
Wellington Rd CONI DN12 110 F5
HTFD DN7 71 L7
ST/HB/BR S6 159 J2
Wellington St BSLY S70 3 G6 2
DEARNE S63 86 C2 3
MEX/SWTN S64 108 E2
SHEF S1 8 F6
Welling Wy KIMB S61 128 C8
Well La AU/AST/KP S26 164 A5
BSLYN/ROY S71 61 G2
NROS/TKH DN11 112 A8
RHAM S60 147 M6 3
RHAM S60 148 B8
RHAM S60 163 J3
ST/HB/BR S6 143 K5
Well Meadow Dr OWL S3 8 E3
Well Meadow St OWL S3 8 E2
Well Pl SHEFS S8 176 E1 16
Well Rd SHEFS S8 176 E1 17
Wells Mt KBTN HD8 55 L1
Wells Rd WHHL DN2 90 D1
Wells St CUD/GR S72 61 M1
DOD/DAR S75 37 J7 2
The Wells DIN S25 182 B2
Well St BSLY S70 2 D6
Wellsyke Rd AWLS/ASK DN6 45 H8
Wellthorne Av STKB/PEN S36 56 C6
Wellthorne La STKB/PEN S36 56 B6
Well View Rd KIMB S61 128 B7
The Wellway MALT S66 130 F8
Welney Pl ST/HB/BR S6 144 A3
Welton Cl DONS/BSCR DN4 113 G1
Welwyn Cl HACK/IN S12 177 M3 1
Welwyn Rd HACK/IN S12 177 M3
Wembley Av CONI DN12 109 L5
Wembley Cl WHHL DN2 91 G2 3
Wembley Rd THNE DN8 32 A4
WRKN S81 168 D4 1
Wenchirst La GLE DN14 30 E4
Wendan Rd THNE DN8 49 M1
Wendel Gv HOY S74 105 M1 1
Wenlock St HAN/WDH S13 162 D6 4
Wensley Cl ATT S4 145 J6
Wensley Crs DONS/BSCR DN4 91 K8
Wensley Cft ATT S4 145 J5
Wensleydale WRKN S81 184 E7
Wensley Dale Dr RHAM S60 147 H8
Wensleydale Rd BTLY DN5 67 H8
KIMB S61 128 D4
Wensley Gdns ATT S4 145 J5
Wensley Gn ATT S4 145 J5
Wensley Rd BSLYN/ROY S71 38 C8
Wensley St ATT S4 145 J5
DEARNE S63 63 M7
Went Br AWLS/ASK DN6 27 M2
Wentbridge La PONT WF8 25 G1
Wentdale PONT WF8 26 C1
Went La HOR/CROF WF4 22 E1
Went Vw PONT WF8 24 E2
Wentworth Av AU/AST/KP S26 180 D1
ECC S11 175 L5 3
KBTN HD8 35 G1
Wentworth Cl HOR/CROF WF4 19 K8
KIMB S61 127 J2
Wentworth Ct BWTY DN10 154 E1
RAW S62 128 F3
Wentworth Crs DOD/DAR S75 38 A7 3
STKB/PEN S36 79 H4
Wentworth Dr DOD/DAR S75 38 A7 6
HEM/SK/SE WF9 42 A4
KBTN HD8 35 G1
RAW S62 129 K3
Wentworth Gdns
MEX/SWTN S64 108 A7
Wentworth Mdw
STKB/PEN S36 79 G3
Wentworth Ms
STKB/PEN S36 79 H4 3
Wentworth Pl KIMB S61 128 A5
Wentworth Rd DOD/DAR S75 37 G7
DOD/DAR S75 38 A7
DRON S18 190 A6
HOY S74 83 H6
HOY S74 83 L8
HOY S74 105 L4
KIMB S61 127 K2
RAW S62 107 H7
STKB/PEN S36 79 G3
WHHL DN2 90 C2
Wentworth St BSLY S70 82 C8
BSLYN/ROY S71 2 F1
Wentworth Ter
HEM/SK/SE WF9 22 F4
Wentworth Vw HOY S74 105 K2 2
WMB/DAR S73 84 B6
Wentworth Wy DIN S25 166 E8
DOD/DAR S75 81 K1
DOD/DAR S75 104 B3
Wescoe Av CUD/GR S72 63 J6
Wesley Av AU/AST/KP S26 164 B7
Wesley Ct KIMB S61 127 K2
Wesley La FUL S10 159 M4 3
Wesley Pl DIN S25 182 B3 3
Wesley Rd AU/AST/KP S26 181 H4
CHPT/GREN S35 104 A8
Wesley St BSLY S70 3 G6
HEM/SK/SE WF9 42 C5
Wesley Ter KBTN HD8 56 D1
Wessenden Cl DOD/DAR S75 59 L6 5
Wessex Cl WRKN S81 198 E1 11
Wessex Gdns TOT/DORE S17 189 H2
Wessex Rd WRKN S81 198 E1
West Av AWLS/ASK DN6 66 D3
DEARNE S63 85 M6
DONS/BSCR DN4 89 L8
HEM/SK/SE WF9 24 E8
HEM/SK/SE WF9 42 F3
HTFD DN7 48 D3
RAW S62 129 K1
WMB/DAR S73 83 M4
West Bank HTFD DN7 48 B2
Westbank Cl DRON S18 190 F3
Westbank Dr DIN S25 182 A3
West Bank Ri DIN S25 182 B3
West Bar SHEF S1 9 H3
West Bawtry Rd RHAM S60 147 H6
Westbourne Cl
WKFDW/WTN WF2 20 A1 1
Westbourne Gdns
DONS/BSCR DN4 111 K1 4
Westbourne Gv DOD/DAR S75 2 C1
Westbourne Rd ECC S11 160 A5
Westbourne Ter BSLY S70 2 B5
Westbridge Rd STV/CWN S43 194 E8
Westbrook Bank ECC S11 160 B7
Westbrook Rd
CHPT/GREN S35 126 E2
Westbury Av CHPT/GREN S35 126 F3
Westbury Cl DOD/DAR S75 59 M3
Westbury St DARN/MH S9 161 K2
Westby Cl RHAM/THRY S65 131 J7
Westby Crs RHAM S60 147 M6
West Circuit ARMTH DN3 67 M8
West Cl KIMB S61 128 C7
West Ct THNE DN8 49 M1
West Crs STKB/PEN S36 79 L5
STKB/PEN S36 101 L6
Westcroft Crs MOS S20 179 J7
Westcroft Dr MOS S20 179 J7
Westcroft Gdns MOS S20 179 J7
Westcroft Gln MOS S20 179 J8 5
Westcroft Gv MOS S20 179 J8
Westcroft Rd HEM/SK/SE WF9 23 H8
West Don St ST/HB/BR S6 160 C1
West Edge Rd PONT WF8 25 K1
West End GLE DN14 11 J3
STV/CWN S43 194 E8
West End Av BSLYN/ROY S71 38 E4
BTLY DN5 67 L8
HOLM/MEL HD7 54 A1
STKB/PEN S36 78 B4
West End Crs BSLYN/ROY S71 38 E4
West End Gdns GLE DN14 11 J3
Westend La GLE DN14 10 B4
West End La NROS/TKH DN11 113 H5
West End Rd AWLS/ASK DN6 27 G4
DEARNE S63 106 F1
West End Vw ECK/KIL S21 193 G5
Westerdale WRKN S81 184 E7
Westerdale Rd BTLY DN5 89 H1
Western Av DIN S25 166 D7
Western Bank FUL S10 8 C4 1
Western Cl DIN S25 166 D7
Western Rd FUL S10 159 M3
RHAM/THRY S65 7 M3
Western St BSLY S70 2 E3
Western Ter WMB/DAR S73 84 A4
Westerton Dr MALT S66 149 J3
Westfield Av AU/AST/KP S26 164 A6
HACK/IN S12 179 G4
KBTN HD8 34 D6
STKB/PEN S36 78 E3
West Field Bank STV/CWN S43 194 E8
Westfield Centre MOS S20 179 J7
Westfield Cl NROS/TKH DN11 134 D8
Westfield Crs AWLS/ASK DN6 27 L7
DEARNE S63 63 M7
HOR/CROF WF4 21 L6
MOS S20 179 H7
Westfield Dr KBTN HD8 34 D6
WRKN S81 198 E2
Westfield Gv HACK/IN S12 178 F4 6
Westfield La BTLY DN5 86 F4
ECK/KIL S21 192 B7
HEM/SK/SE WF9 42 D6
West Field La HOLM/MEL HD7 54 A1
Westfield La HTFD DN7 30 A6
KBTN HD8 16 C7
PONT WF8 26 C4
STKB/PEN S36 78 E3
STV/CWN S43 194 D8
Westfield Northway MOS S20 179 J7
Westfield Rd ARMTH DN3 91 L1 1
DEARNE S63 84 E8 2
DRON S18 191 G7
ECK/KIL S21 194 A2
HEM/SK/SE WF9 23 H8
HTFD DN7 30 A7
HTFD DN7 49 G8
MALT S66 149 H2
NROS/TKH DN11 134 D8
RAW S62 129 J3
Westfields BSLY S70 82 E3
BSLYN/ROY S71 38 E3
Westfield Southway MOS S20 179 J7
Westfield St BSLY S70 2 C5
Westfield Ter SHEF S1 8 F5
Westfield Vls HTFD DN7 49 G7 2
West Garth Cl DIN S25 166 D6 1
West Ga HOLM/MEL HD7 53 K7
MEX/SWTN S64 109 G2
NROS/TKH DN11 152 D1
Westgate BSLY S70 2 E5
BSLYN/ROY S71 60 F3
HEM/SK/SE WF9 41 G1
RHAM S60 6 F5
STKB/PEN S36 79 H5
WRKS S80 198 C5
Westgate Vw WRKS S80 198 C5 4
West Green Dr ARMTH DN3 69 J3
West Gv BSLYN/ROY S71 38 E3
WHHL DN2 90 E2
West Hl KIMB S61 146 A1
Westhill La SHEF S1 8 E5
Westholme Rd DONS/BSCR DN4 4 D8
West Kirk La CUD/GR S72 63 J8
West Laith Ga DON DN1 4 F5
Westland Cl MOS S20 179 J6
Westland Gdns MOS S20 179 H6
Westland Gv MOS S20 179 J7 11
Westland Rd MOS S20 179 J6
West La AU/AST/KP S26 163 M6
GLE DN14 29 K2
MALT S66 149 L6
ST/HB/BR S6 141 K6
ST/HB/BR S6 142 D5
Westminster Cl FUL S10 158 F6 1
WRKN S81 184 E8
Westminster Crs FUL S10 158 F6
WHHL DN2 91 G2 4
Westminster Dr HTFD DN7 70 C3
West Moor Crs DOD/DAR S75 59 L6
West Moor La ARMTH DN3 70 B8
West Moor Rd
HEM/SK/SE WF9 22 E5 1
Westmoreland St
ST/HB/BR S6 160 C2 13
Westmorland Ct
NROS/TKH DN11 154 B3
Westmorland Dr WRKN S81 168 C7
Westmorland St
DONS/BSCR DN4 111 K1
Westmorland Wy BTLY DN5 88 E6
Westmount Av DEARNE S63 85 G7 2
Westnall Rd SHEFN S5 127 H8
Westnall Ter SHEFN S5 127 H8
Westoff La CUD/GR S72 22 A8
Westongales Wy BTLY DN5 67 L7 4
Weston Rd DONS/BSCR DN4 111 M1
Weston St OWL S3 8 D3
Westover Rd FUL S10 159 J5
West Park Dr AU/AST/KP S26 163 M8
West Pinfold BSLYN/ROY S71 39 G4
Westpit Hl DEARNE S63 84 E8
West Pl BTLY DN5 67 M6
West Qd SHEFN S5 145 H4
West Rd DOD/DAR S75 59 M5
MEX/SWTN S64 108 D2
THNE DN8 32 B4
West Service Rd ARMTH DN3 47 G7 1
Westside Gra
DONS/BSCR DN4 89 L7 2
West St BSLY S70 82 F3
BSLYN/ROY S71 39 H3
BWTY DN10 137 M5
CONI DN12 110 A5
CUD/GR S72 40 C2
DEARNE S63 86 C1 1
DEARNE S63 107 J1
DIN S25 182 B3
DON DN1 4 E5
DRON S18 190 D5 1
ECK/KIL S21 193 G5
HEM/SK/SE WF9 23 G8
HEM/SK/SE WF9 41 K5
HEM/SK/SE WF9 42 F3
HOR/CROF WF4 22 A6
HOY S74 105 G1
MALT S66 149 K8
MEX/SWTN S64 108 D3
MOS S20 179 K4
NROS/TKH DN11 153 L2
SHEF S1 8 F5
THNE DN8 49 M1
WMB/DAR S73 84 A4
WMB/DAR S73 84 E2
WRKS S80 198 C5
West Street La SHEF S1 9 G4
Westthorpe Fields Rd
ECK/KIL S21 194 A3
Westthorpe Rd ECK/KIL S21 194 B2
West Vale Gv RHAM/THRY S65 130 D5
West Vw CUD/GR S72 62 A2
FEA/AMT WF7 23 H2
STV/CWN S43 194 E8
West View Cl TOT/DORE S17 189 K1 4
West View Crs DEARNE S63 86 A3
West View La TOT/DORE S17 189 K1 5
West View Rd KIMB S61 146 A2
MEX/SWTN S64 108 E3
Westville Rd DOD/DAR S75 2 C2
West Wy BSLY S70 3 G6
Westway WRKN S81 184 E8
Westwell Pl MOS S20 193 H1
Westwick Crs TOT/DORE S17 176 B8
Westwick Gv SHEFS S8 176 B8
Westwick Rd SHEFS S8 176 B8
Westwood Ct BSLY S70 2 E3
CHPT/GREN S35 104 B7
Westwood Dr WRKS S80 197 M4
Westwood La CHPT/GREN S35 103 M4
Westwood New Rd
DOD/DAR S75 104 B4
Westwood Rd ECC S11 159 K7
Wetherby Cl BTLY DN5 89 H2
Wetherby Ct DARN/MH S9 162 A3
Wetherby Dr AU/AST/KP S26 164 A8
MEX/SWTN S64 108 F1
Wet Moor La DEARNE S63 85 K8
Wet Shaw La ST/HB/BR S6 141 H5
Whaley Rd DOD/DAR S75 59 K2
Whams Rd STKB/PEN S36 77 J5
Wharf Cl MEX/SWTN S64 108 C4 2
Wharfedale WRKN S81 184 E7
Wharfedale Crs KBTN HD8 34 F6
Wharfedale Dr
CHPT/GREN S35 126 C2
Wharfedale Rd DOD/DAR S75 59 L4
Wharf Rd DARN/MH S9 146 B4
DON DN1 5 H1
MEX/SWTN S64 108 C7
Wharf St ATT S4 9 L3
BSLYN/ROY S71 3 J2
BWTY DN10 136 E8
MEX/SWTN S64 108 C4
Wharncliffe DOD/DAR S75 81 L1 2
Wharncliffe Av
AU/AST/KP S26 164 C7 1
CHPT/GREN S35 124 F4
DEARNE S63 107 K1 2
Wharncliffe Cl HOY S74 105 H3
RAW S62 107 H7 1
Wharncliffe Rd
CHPT/GREN S35 104 B8 1
FUL S10 8 D7
HOR/CROF WF4 19 L3
WKFDW/WTN WF2 19 L2
Wharncliffe St BSLY S70 2 D5
BSLYN/ROY S71 39 H7 1
DONS/BSCR DN4 4 B7 1
Wharton Av AU/AST/KP S26 164 B6
Wheatacre Rd STKB/PEN S36 102 A6
Wheata Dr SHEFN S5 126 E8
Wheata Pl SHEFN S5 126 E8
Wheata Rd SHEFN S5 144 E1
Wheat Cft CONI DN12 110 C5
WRKN S81 184 F8 2
Wheatcroft Rd RAW S62 129 M1
Wheatfield Cl ARMTH DN3 69 L1
Wheatfield Crs SHEFN S5 145 H1
Wheatfield Dr DEARNE S63 64 B8 3
NROS/TKH DN11 134 F7
Wheathill St RHAM S60 6 E6
Wheatley Cl BSLYN/ROY S71 60 D3 1
Wheatley Gv HAN/WDH S13 162 C6
Wheatley Hall Rd WHHL DN2 69 H6
WHHL DN2 90 D1
Wheatley Hill La KBTN HD8 35 J7
Wheatley La DON DN1 5 H2 2
Wheatley Pl CONI DN12 109 K4 1
Wheatley Ri DOD/DAR S75 37 M5 3
Wheatley Rd BSLY S70 61 J8 2
BTLY DN5 67 L5
KIMB S61 128 C6
MEX/SWTN S64 108 C8
Wheatley St CONI DN12 109 K4
Wheeldon St SHEF S1 8 E4
Wheel La CHPT/GREN S35 126 B7
CHPT/GREN S35 143 H1
The Wheel CHPT/GREN S35 126 C7
Wheldrake Rd SHEFN S5 145 H5
Whernside Av
CHPT/GREN S35 126 D1 3
Whinacre Cl SHEFS S8 190 F1 3
Whinacre Pl SHEFS S8 190 F1
Whinby Cft DOD/DAR S75 59 K8 4
Whinby Rd DOD/DAR S75 59 H7
Whin Cl HEM/SK/SE WF9 41 H2
Whinfell Cl AWLS/ASK DN6 66 F1
Whinfell Ct ECC S11 175 J5
Whin Gdns DEARNE S63 64 B6
Whin Hill Rd DONS/BSCR DN4 91 H7
Whinmoor Cl DOD/DAR S75 58 D6
Whinmoor Dr DOD/DAR S75 58 D6
Whin Moor La DOD/DAR S75 58 A7
Whinmoor Rd CHPT/GREN S35 104 A8
SHEFN S5 145 K4 3
Whinmoor Vw DOD/DAR S75 58 D6
Whinmoor Wy DOD/DAR S75 58 D7
Whinny Haugh La
NROS/TKH DN11 152 F2
Whinside Crs DEARNE S63 64 A6
The Whins RAW S62 129 G2
Whiphill Cl DONS/BSCR DN4 91 J8 3
Whiphill La ARMTH DN3 92 A2
Whiphill Top La ARMTH DN3 92 C7
Whirlow Court Rd ECC S11 175 K5
Whirlowdale Cl ECC S11 175 K5 2
Whirlowdale Crs ECC S11 175 M4
Whirlowdale Ri ECC S11 175 K5 3
Whirlowdale Rd ABRD S7 175 L5
ECC S11 175 K5
Whirlow Gv ECC S11 175 K5
Whirlow La ECC S11 175 K4 4
Whirlow Ms ECC S11 175 K4 5
Whirlow Park Rd ABRD S7 175 K6
Whisperwood Dr
DONS/BSCR DN4 111 M3
Whiston Brook Vw RHAM S60 148 A6
Whiston Gra RHAM S60 147 L6
Whiston Gn RHAM S60 147 M7 2
Whiston Gv RHAM S60 7 J9
Whiston V RHAM S60 147 M7
Whitaker Cl NROS/TKH DN11 113 K8
Whitbeck Cl NROS/TKH DN11 111 M8
Whitbourne Cl
BSLYN/ROY S71 60 D2 2
Whitburn Rd DON DN1 5 H7
Whitby Rd DARN/MH S9 161 M3 3
DARN/MH S9 162 A2 7
NROS/TKH DN11 153 L2
Whitcomb Dr NROS/TKH DN11 113 K8
White Apron St
HEM/SK/SE WF9 41 M5
White Av WRKN S81 168 C4
White Cft SHEF S1 8 F3
Whitecroft Crs RHAM S60 147 G7
White Cross Av CUD/GR S72 61 M2
White Cross Ct CUD/GR S72 62 A2 3
White Cross Gdns CUD/GR S72 40 B1
White Cross La BSLY S70 83 H2
NROS/TKH DN11 111 L6
White Cross Mt CUD/GR S72 62 A2 4
White Cross Ri BSLY S70 83 H2
White Cross Rd CUD/GR S72 61 M2
White Ga DIN S25 182 D1 3
White Gate Rd HOLM/MEL HD7 53 H6
Whitehall Rd KIMB S61 128 D3
White Hart Fold
HEM/SK/SE WF9 42 F1 1
White Hart Yd WRKS S80 198 C5 3
Whitehead Av STKB/PEN S36 102 B7
Whitehead Cl DIN S25 166 C7
White Hill Av BSLY S70 59 L6
Whitehill Av RHAM S60 147 G7
Whitehill Dr RHAM S60 147 G8
White Hill Gv BSLY S70 59 M6 3
Whitehill La RHAM S60 147 G6
Whitehill Rd RHAM S60 147 G7
White Hill Ter BSLY S70 59 L6 6
White House Cl HTFD DN7 48 E8 3
HTFD DN7 48 C2 3
Whitehouse Ct
NROS/TKH DN11 154 A3
White House Dr
NROS/TKH DN11 154 A3
Whitehouse La ST/HB/BR S6 160 B1
White House Rd
NROS/TKH DN11 154 A3
Whitehouse Rd ST/HB/BR S6 160 B1
White House Vw ARMTH DN3 47 J7
White La BTLY DN5 65 J3
CHPT/GREN S35 104 F8
HACK/IN S12 177 L4
THNE DN8 31 K8
Whitelea Gv MEX/SWTN S64 108 D3
White Lee La CHPT/GREN S35 123 M4
Whitelee Rd MEX/SWTN S64 108 C3
Whiteley La ECC S11 159 G8
White Ley Rd AWLS/ASK DN6 26 C6
Whiteley Wood Cl ECC S11 159 J8
Whiteley Wood Rd ECC S11 175 J1
Whitelow La TOT/DORE S17 174 E8
White Moss Cl FEA/AMT WF7 23 K1
White Rose Ct BTLY DN5 68 A6
White Rose Wy
DONS/BSCR DN4 90 C7
DONS/BSCR DN4 112 D1
White's La SHEFP/MNR S2 161 H4
White Thorns Cl SHEFS S8 190 F1 6
White Thorns Dr SHEFS S8 190 F2
White Thorns Vw SHEFS S8 190 F1
White Walls La HOLM/MEL HD7 52 D4
Whitewater La
NROS/TKH DN11 153 G8
WRKN S81 169 J2
Whiteways Cl ATT S4 145 H7
Whiteways Dr ATT S4 145 H7 2
Whiteways Gv ATT S4 145 H7
Whiteways Rd ATT S4 145 H7
White Wells Gdns
HOLM/MEL HD7 54 B4
White Wells Rd HOLM/MEL HD7 54 B4
Whitewood Cl
BSLYN/ROY S71 38 F4 2
Whitfield Gdns WRKN S81 183 H3
Whitfield Rd FUL S10 159 G8
RAW S62 107 G7
Whiting St SHEFS S8 176 E1 18
Whitley Carr CHPT/GREN S35 126 C5
Whitley La CHPT/GREN S35 126 B6
Whitley Rd STKB/PEN S36 77 K1
Whitley Vw CHPT/GREN S35 126 F5
Whitley View Rd KIMB S61 145 M2
Whitley Wy HOR/CROF WF4 16 C2
Whitney Cl DONS/BSCR DN4 111 J2 3
Whitsun Dl WRKN S81 184 F8
Whittier Rd DONS/BSCR DN4 111 L1
Whittington St DON DN1 5 H1
Whitton Cl DONS/BSCR DN4 113 G1
RTFD DN22 170 F2
Whitwell Crs STKB/PEN S36 101 M6
Whitwell La STKB/PEN S36 101 L7
Whitwell Rd AU/AST/KP S26 196 E4
WRKS S80 196 E3
Whitwell St DARN/MH S9 162 B3
Whitwell Vw
NROS/TKH DN11 113 M6 2
Whitworth La DARN/MH S9 145 L8
Whitworth Rd FUL S10 159 J6
Whitworth St DEARNE S63 86 C2 2
Whitworth Wy DEARNE S63 85 J8
Whybourne Ter RHAM S60 7 G6 1
Whyn Vw DEARNE S63 64 A7 3
Wicker OWL S3 9 K1
Wicker La OWL S3 9 K2
Wickersley Rd RHAM/THRY S65 7 M9
Wickett Hern Rd ARMTH DN3 92 B1
Wicket Wy CONI DN12 111 G4
Wickfield Cl HACK/IN S12 178 D2
Wickfield Dr HACK/IN S12 178 C3
Wickfield Gv HACK/IN S12 178 C2
Wickfield Pl HACK/IN S12 178 C2
Wickfield Rd HACK/IN S12 178 D3
Wickins La HOLM/MEL HD7 53 H1
Wickleden Ga HOLM/MEL HD7 54 B4
Wicklow Rd WHHL DN2 90 E2
Widdop Cl HAN/WDH S13 162 B7
Widdop Cft HAN/WDH S13 162 B7
Widford Gn HTFD DN7 70 E1
Wigfield Dr BSLY S70 82 D2
Wigfull Rd ECC S11 160 A6

Wignall Av MALT S66 148 D3
Wigthorpe La WRKN S81 184 E3
Wike Gate Cl THNE DN8 50 B1 1
Wike Gate Gv THNE DN8 50 B1 2
Wike Gate Rd THNE DN8 32 B8
Wike Rd BSLYN/ROY S71 61 J5
Wilberforce Rd DIN S25 182 B2
WHHL DN2 69 H6
Wilbrook Ri DOD/DAR S75 59 L3
Wilby La BSLY S70 3 J7
Wilcox Cl ST/HB/BR S6 144 B2
Wilcox Rd ST/HB/BR S6 144 A2
Wild Av RAW S62 107 G8
Wildene Dr MEX/SWTN S64 108 E1
Wildflower Cl NROS/TKH DN11 113 J8
Wilding Cl KIMB S61 128 C7
Wilding Wy KIMB S61 128 C7
Wildspur Gv HOLM/MEL HD7 54 C3
Wilford Rd BSLYN/ROY S71 38 C6
Wilfred Cl DARN/MH S9 161 L2 10
Wilfred Dr DARN/MH S9 161 L2
Wilfred St RHAM S60 6 F5
Wilfrid Rd DARN/MH S9 161 L2
Wilkinson Av
NROS/TKH DN11 113 L7 4
THNE DN8 32 A5
Wilkinson La FUL S10 8 D5
Wilkinson Rd HOY S74 105 L2
Wilkinson St BSLY S70 3 H8 1
FUL S10 8 C5
Willan Dr RHAM S60 163 G2
Willbury Dr HACK/IN S12 177 L1
Willey St OWL S3 9 K2
William Bradford Cl
BWTY DN10 137 G6
William Cl MOS S20 193 H1 7
William Crs MOS S20 179 H8
William La NROS/TKH DN11 113 H6
Williamson Rd ECC S11 160 B8
Williams Rd BTLY DN5 89 K1
Williams St WRKN S81 168 C4
William St BSLY S70 82 E2
DEARNE S63 86 A2
DEARNE S63 107 K1
ECK/KIL S21 193 H4
FUL S10 8 D7
MEX/SWTN S64 108 C4
RAW S62 129 L3
RHAM/THRY S65 7 H5
WMB/DAR S73 84 A4 4
Willingham Cl MOS S20 179 L6
Willingham Gdns MOS S20 179 L5 12
Willington Rd AWLS/ASK DN6 44 E6
SHEFN S5 145 G3
Willis Rd ST/HB/BR S6 143 M6
Willman Rd BSLYN/ROY S71 61 K4
Willoughby St ATT S4 145 H5
Willow Av DONS/BSCR DN4 91 K7
RAW S62 129 L2
THNE DN8 31 M5
WRKN S81 168 C8
Willow Bank BSLYN/ROY S71 60 B3
Willow Beck HOR/CROF WF4 20 E8
Willow Bridge La HTFD DN7 47 J1
Willow Bridge Rd BTLY DN5 4 D1
Willowbrook AWLS/ASK DN6 44 D5
Willow Brook Rd DOD/DAR S75 37 L7
Willow Cl CUD/GR S72 39 M8 5
DIN S25 182 B4
GLE DN14 11 L3
HOY S74 105 G2
MALT S66 149 G1
RHAM S60 147 H8
WRKS S80 198 C6
Willow Ct MALT S66 148 F2
Willow Crs CHPT/GREN S35 126 E3
EPW DN9 114 D3
MALT S66 132 E5
THNE DN8 31 M6
Willowdale Cl BTLY DN5 89 H7
Willow Dene Rd CUD/GR S72 40 E8 5
Willow Dr CONI DN12 111 G4
DARN/MH S9 162 C4
HEM/SK/SE WF9 41 G2
MALT S66 149 G1
MEX/SWTN S64 108 D2
Willow Garth GLE DN14 11 L4 1
HEM/SK/SE WF9 42 F5
RAW S62 129 L1
Willowgarth Av RHAM S60 147 G8
Willowgarth Cl HOR/CROF WF4 21 L7
Willow Garth La AWLS/ASK DN6 27 M6
Willow Gv AU/AST/KP S26 164 D7 2
GLE DN14 11 L4 2
THNE DN8 32 A5
Willow La DEARNE S63 86 B6
GLE DN14 11 L4
NROS/TKH DN11 113 L6
Willowlees Ct
DONS/BSCR DN4 91 J8 4
Willow Pl MALT S66 132 E5
Willow Ri KBTN HD8 34 D6
Willow Rd ARMTH DN3 70 A8
AWLS/ASK DN6 27 H6
DEARNE S63 64 B7
DEARNE S63 107 L3
ECK/KIL S21 194 A2
MALT S66 150 B2
STKB/PEN S36 101 M8
THNE DN8 31 M6
The Willows KIMB S61 128 B5
Willow St CONI DN12 110 B5
Willow Wk BTLY DN5 67 L4 1
Wilmington Dr
DONS/BSCR DN4 90 D8
Wilsden Gv DOD/DAR S75 59 M3 5
Wilsic La NROS/TKH DN11 134 B5
Wilsic Rd NROS/TKH DN11 133 L1
Wilson Av RAW S62 129 J1
STKB/PEN S36 79 H5 5
Wilson Cl BWTY DN10 155 L7
Wilson Dr RHAM/THRY S65 130 C6
Wilson Gv BSLYN/ROY S71 61 J3
Wilson Pl SHEFS S8 176 E1 13
Wilson Rd DRON S18 191 G3
ECC S11 160 A7
STKB/PEN S36 102 D7
Wilson St DRON S18 190 F7 4
OWL S3 160 E1
WMB/DAR S73 83 M4
Wilthorpe Av DOD/DAR S75 60 A3
Wilthorpe Crs DOD/DAR S75 60 A3
Wilthorpe Farm Rd
DOD/DAR S75 60 A3
Wilthorpe Gdns HACK/IN S12 178 E4 7
Wilthorpe Gn DOD/DAR S75 60 A3 4
Wilthorpe La DOD/DAR S75 59 M3 4
Wilthorpe Rd DOD/DAR S75 59 L3
Wilton Cl RAW S62 129 K2
Wilton Ct KIMB S61 128 E8
Wilton Gdns KIMB S61 128 E8
Wilton La KIMB S61 146 E1
Wilton Pl FUL S10 8 C7
Wiltshire Rd WHHL DN2 91 G3
Wimberry Av DIN S25 182 C2
Wincanton Cl MEX/SWTN S64 108 F1
Winchester Av FUL S10 158 F7
WHHL DN2 90 E1
Winchester Cl WRKN S81 184 E8
Winchester Crs FUL S10 158 F8
Winchester Dr FUL S10 158 F7 2
Winchester Ms
NROS/TKH DN11 154 A2
Winchester Rd FUL S10 158 F7
HTFD DN7 48 E7
Winchester Wy
BSLYN/ROY S71 61 L8 4
BTLY DN5 89 H1
RHAM S60 146 E6
Wincobank Av SHEFN S5 145 J4
Wincobank Cl SHEFN S5 145 K4 4
Wincobank La ATT S4 145 K6
Wincobank Rd SHEFN S5 145 K4
Windam Dr ARMTH DN3 47 K7
Winden Cl HOR/CROF WF4 19 H1
Windermere Av DRON S18 190 C6
NROS/TKH DN11 153 K3 4
WHHL DN2 91 G2 5
Windermere Cl
AWLS/ASK DN6 44 E6 4
WRKN S81 184 C7 4
Windermere Ct DIN S25 182 C1
Windermere Crs ARMTH DN3 69 K3 6
Windermere Gra CONI DN12 110 F6 2
Windermere Rd BSLYN/ROY S71 3 J5
SHEFS S8 176 C2 7
STKB/PEN S36 79 H3
Winders Pl WMB/DAR S73 84 B5 5
Windgate Hl CONI DN12 110 B4
Windham Cl BSLYN/ROY S71 3 G2
Windhill Av DOD/DAR S75 37 L4
MEX/SWTN S64 109 G2
Windhill Crs DOD/DAR S75 37 L4
MEX/SWTN S64 109 G1
Windhill Dr DOD/DAR S75 37 L4
Windhill La DOD/DAR S75 37 L4
Wind Hill La STKB/PEN S36 100 F7
Windhill Mt DOD/DAR S75 37 K4
Windhill Ter MEX/SWTN S64 109 G1
The Windings DEARNE S63 64 C8
Windle Edge STKB/PEN S36 97 L1
Windle Rd DONS/BSCR DN4 4 A8
Windle Sq ARMTH DN3 69 K3 7
Windlestone Sq THNE DN8 32 C4
Windmere Av DEARNE S63 86 C3
Windmill Av CONI DN12 110 B6
CUD/GR S72 40 D7
Windmill Balk La
AWLS/ASK DN6 66 F3
Windmill Crs KBTN HD8 34 F6
Windmill Dr NROS/TKH DN11 133 M1
Windmill Greenway MOS S20 193 J2
Windmill Hill La
CHPT/GREN S35 126 C3
KBTN HD8 16 D7
Windmill La AWLS/ASK DN6 26 F5
KBTN HD8 55 H4
SHEFN S5 145 J4
WRKS S80 198 E7
Windmill Rd DIN S25 182 C1
WMB/DAR S73 83 M5
Windmill Vw HOLM/MEL HD7 54 A4
Windsor Av DOD/DAR S75 37 G7
STKB/PEN S36 78 E3
Windsor Cl AWLS/ASK DN6 28 A7
BTLY DN5 87 G5
MALT S66 149 H1
Windsor Ct HTFD DN7 70 C3
Windsor Crs BSLYN/ROY S71 3 L1
CUD/GR S72 63 H8
Windsor Dr BTLY DN5 87 G4
DOD/DAR S75 59 K8 5
DRON S18 190 A6
KBTN HD8 34 F6 2
MEX/SWTN S64 109 G1
Windsor Gdns WRKN S81 184 C1
Windsor Ri AU/AST/KP S26 180 C1
Windsor Rd CONI DN12 109 M4 2
HEM/SK/SE WF9 41 K1
KIMB S61 127 K3
SHEFS S8 176 D1
WHHL DN2 5 L2
WRKN S81 184 B8
WRKN S81 184 C1
Windsor Sq DEARNE S63 64 C7
Windsor St ATT S4 161 H1 5
DEARNE S63 64 C7
HEM/SK/SE WF9 42 E5
HOY S74 83 H8
Windsor Wk BTLY DN5 89 J1
DIN S25 182 A4
Windy Bank ST/HB/BR S6 141 J1
Windy House La
SHEFP/MNR S2 161 K8
Windy Rdg AU/AST/KP S26 164 A6
Winfield Rd DEARNE S63 107 K2
Wingerworth Av SHEFS S8 176 B8
Wingfield Av WRKN S81 198 D1
Wingfield Cl DRON S18 190 A7
KIMB S61 128 E4
Wingfield Crs HACK/IN S12 178 A2
Wingfield Rd BSLYN/ROY S71 60 E1
KIMB S61 128 C4
Winifred St RHAM S60 6 C3
WRKS S80 197 L3
Winkley Ter SHEFN S5 145 J2
Winlea Av RHAM/THRY S65 148 C3
Winn Cl ST/HB/BR S6 143 M4
Winn Dr ST/HB/BR S6 143 M4
Winnery Cl NROS/TKH DN11 134 E7 5
Winney Bank La
HOLM/MEL HD7 53 M2
Winney Hl AU/AST/KP S26 195 J2
Winney La AU/AST/KP S26 195 J3
Winn Gdns ST/HB/BR S6 143 M4
Winn Gv ST/HB/BR S6 143 L4
Winnipeg Rd BTLY DN5 67 M6
Winsford Rd ST/HB/BR S6 144 A2
Winster Cl BSLY S70 82 D7
Winster Gv WRKN S81 184 D7
Winster Rd ST/HB/BR S6 144 A6
Winston Av STKB/PEN S36 101 K5
Winston Gn BWTY DN10 155 K6
Winter Av BSLYN/ROY S71 39 G2
DOD/DAR S75 2 A3
Winter Hill La KIMB S61 128 C8
Winterhill Rd KIMB S61 146 B1
Winter Rd DOD/DAR S75 2 A4
Wintersett La HOR/CROF WF4 21 L3
Winter St OWL S3 8 C3
Winter Ter DOD/DAR S75 2 A3
Winterton Cl
DONS/BSCR DN4 113 H1 1
Winterton Gdns HACK/IN S12 179 G4
Winterwell Rd DEARNE S63 85 G8
Winton Cl BSLY S70 3 J9 2
Winton Rd WHHL DN2 90 F3
Wiseton Rd ECC S11 160 A6
Wisewood Av ST/HB/BR S6 143 L7
Wisewood La ST/HB/BR S6 143 L7
Wisewood Pl ST/HB/BR S6 143 L7
Wisewood Rd ST/HB/BR S6 143 L7
Witham Ct DOD/DAR S75 59 J4
Witham Rd FUL S10 160 A5
Withens Av ST/HB/BR S6 143 M5
Withens Ct DOD/DAR S75 37 L6
Withyside KBTN HD8 56 E1
Witmore St HEM/SK/SE WF9 42 E4
Witney St SHEFP/MNR S2 160 E7 9
Wivelsfield Rd DONS/BSCR DN4 89 H8
Woburn Cl DONS/BSCR DN4 111 J2
Woburn Pl DOD/DAR S75 81 K1 3
ECC S11 175 K5
Wolfe Dr ST/HB/BR S6 144 B2 1
Wolfe Rd ST/HB/BR S6 144 B2
Wolfstones Rd HOLM/MEL HD7 53 G1
Wollaton Av TOT/DORE S17 189 L2
Wollaton Cl BSLYN/ROY S71 38 C7
Wollaton Dr TOT/DORE S17 189 L2 4
Wollaton Rd TOT/DORE S17 189 K3
Wolseley Rd SHEFS S8 160 D8
Wolsey Av WHHL DN2 90 F3
Wolverley Rd HAN/WDH S13 178 E1
Wombwell Av DEARNE S63 107 H2 1
Wombwell La BSLY S70 61 K8
WMB/DAR S73 83 H5
Wombwell Rd HOY S74 83 J8
Wong La NROS/TKH DN11 134 D8
NROS/TKH DN11 152 D1
Wood Acres DOD/DAR S75 59 L3
Woodall La AU/AST/KP S26 195 G1
Woodall Rd ECK/KIL S21 194 D2
RHAM/THRY S65 148 A2
Woodall Rd South
RHAM/THRY S65 148 A2
Woodbank Crs SHEFS S8 176 D2
Woodbank Rd ST/HB/BR S6 158 D3
Woodbine Rd DARN/MH S9 145 K8
Woodbourn Hl DARN/MH S9 161 K3
Woodbourn Rd DARN/MH S9 161 K3
Woodburn Dr CHPT/GREN S35 126 F2
Woodbury Cl DARN/MH S9 145 L2
Woodbury Rd DARN/MH S9 145 L2
Wood Cliffe ECC S11 174 F1
Wood Cl CHPT/GREN S35 127 G3
HEM/SK/SE WF9 22 E5
RAW S62 107 J8
RHAM/THRY S65 131 G7
Woodcock Cl KIMB S61 128 D5
Woodcock Pl SHEFP/MNR S2 161 H4
Woodcock Rd HOY S74 105 J2
Woodcock Wy AWLS/ASK DN6 44 F8 1
Wood Cft KIMB S61 128 D6
Woodcross Av DONS/BSCR DN4 91 L8
Wood End Av STKB/PEN S36 79 G6
Woodend Cl ST/HB/BR S6 143 L8
Woodend Dr ST/HB/BR S6 143 L8
Woodfall La ST/HB/BR S6 141 M2
Woodfarm Av ST/HB/BR S6 159 K1
Woodfarm Cl ST/HB/BR S6 159 J1
Woodfarm Dr ST/HB/BR S6 159 J1
Woodfarm Pl ST/HB/BR S6 159 J1
Woodfield Av MEX/SWTN S64 108 F2
Woodfield Cl WMB/DAR S73 84 E1
Woodfield Pk
WKFDW/WTN WF2 20 E1
Woodfield Rd ARMTH DN3 92 A2
AWLS/ASK DN6 26 D7
DEARNE S63 106 F1
DONS/BSCR DN4 111 M1
FUL S10 159 M3
PONT WF8 25 M7
Wood Flds MALT S66 149 J3
Wood Fold OWL S3 144 E8
Woodfoot Rd RHAM S60 147 K6
Woodford Rd ARMTH DN3 47 K7
Woodgarth Ct AWLS/ASK DN6 27 G7
Woodgrove Rd DARN/MH S9 145 M2
RHAM/THRY S65 130 A8
Woodhall Cl HOR/CROF WF4 17 L1 3
WMB/DAR S73 84 E1
Woodhall Dr FEA/AMT WF7 23 K1
Woodhall Ri MEX/SWTN S64 108 B5 3
Woodhall Rd WMB/DAR S73 84 E2
Woodhead Dr HOY S74 83 H6
Woodhead La HOY S74 83 J6
Woodhead Rd
CHPT/GREN S35 103 H6
HOLM/MEL HD7 74 B2
SHEFP/MNR S2 160 E7
Woodholm Pl ECC S11 175 M2 2
Woodholm Rd ECC S11 175 M2
Woodhouse Av MOS S20 179 K3
Woodhouse Cl RAW S62 107 H7 2
Woodhouse Ct MOS S20 179 J2
Woodhouse Crs MOS S20 179 K3
Woodhouse Gn MALT S66 149 J8
Woodhouse Green Rd
HTFD DN7 30 B8
Woodhouse La DOD/DAR S75 37 M2
HOLM/MEL HD7 53 H6
HTFD DN7 70 E3
KBTN HD8 17 K8
MOS S20 179 K2
WRKN S81 168 E7
Woodhouse Rd HACK/IN S12 177 M1
HOY S74 105 H2
WHHL DN2 90 C1
Woodland Av DIN S25 182 C2 1
WRKS S80 198 F6 1
Woodland Cl HOR/CROF WF4 19 K5
MALT S66 148 F4
RHAM S60 162 F2
Woodland Dr BSLY S70 59 M7
DIN S25 182 C2
HACK/IN S12 177 M5 1
KBTN HD8 34 F6
WKFDW/WTN WF2 20 B1
WRKN S81 198 C1
Woodland Gdns MALT S66 150 F2
Woodland Gv DEARNE S63 107 K3
Woodland Pl TOT/DORE S17 189 K2
Woodland Ri STKB/PEN S36 80 E2
Woodland Rd DEARNE S63 107 K3
SHEFS S8 176 F4
Woodlands Av MOS S20 179 K2
Woodlands Cl
AU/AST/KP S26 164 B6 1
KBTN HD8 56 E1
Woodlands Crs
HEM/SK/SE WF9 23 J7
MEX/SWTN S64 107 L5
Woodlands Ri AWLS/ASK DN6 27 G6
Woodlands Rd AWLS/ASK DN6 66 F3
HOY S74 83 J7
The Woodlands WRKN S81 169 M1
Woodlands Vw CUD/GR S72 63 J5 1
HOY S74 83 J8
WMB/DAR S73 83 L7
Woodland Ter CUD/GR S72 62 F2
Woodland Vw CUD/GR S72 61 M2
HACK/IN S12 177 M5
MEX/SWTN S64 109 G3 5
STKB/PEN S36 80 E2
Woodland View Rd
ST/HB/BR S6 159 L1 5
Woodland Wy
RHAM/THRY S65 148 A3
Wood La BSLYN/ROY S71 39 G6
CONI DN12 110 F8
CUD/GR S72 62 E1
DOD/DAR S75 38 C5
HOLM/MEL HD7 53 L1
HOR/CROF WF4 19 L4
HTFD DN7 30 F7
KBTN HD8 56 C1
MALT S66 133 J6
MALT S66 149 G4
MALT S66 165 G2
NROS/TKH DN11 111 K5
RHAM S60 146 E8
RHAM S60 163 K4
ST/HB/BR S6 159 K1
THNE DN8 31 H5
Wood Lane Cl ST/HB/BR S6 159 J1
Woodlea Gdns DONS/BSCR DN4 91 K8
Woodlea Gv ARMTH DN3 91 M1
Woodlea Wy WHHL DN2 69 G8 5
Woodleigh Crs FEA/AMT WF7 23 K1
Woodleys Av RAW S62 107 J7
Woodman Dr MEX/SWTN S64 107 L5
Woodmoor Cl HOR/CROF WF4 19 J3 1
Woodmoor Dr HOR/CROF WF4 19 H3
Woodmoor Ri HOR/CROF WF4 19 H2
Wood Moor Rd
HEM/SK/SE WF9 23 K8
Woodmoor Rd
WKFDW/WTN WF2 19 L2
Woodmoor St
BSLYN/ROY S71 39 H7 2
Wood Mt HOR/CROF WF4 17 K1
Woodnook Gv ECK/KIL S21 192 C5
Woodpecker Cl
AU/AST/KP S26 180 C1
Wood Rd KIMB S61 128 D6
ST/HB/BR S6 143 M7
Woodrove Av HAN/WDH S13 161 M8
Woodrove Cl HAN/WDH S13 161 M8
Woodroyd Av BSLYN/ROY S71 39 G6
Woodroyd Cl BSLYN/ROY S71 39 G6
Wood Royd Hill La
HOLM/MEL HD7 54 F8
Wood Royd Rd STKB/PEN S36 102 B6
Wood Seats CHPT/GREN S35 126 B4
Woodseats Cl SHEFS S8 176 C3
Woodseats House Rd
SHEFS S8 176 D5
Woodseats Rd SHEFS S8 176 C3
Woodsetts La WRKN S81 183 L6
Woodsetts Rd DIN S25 182 C1
WRKN S81 183 K1
Woodsett Wk CONI DN12 110 C4
Woodside KBTN HD8 56 E1
Woodside Av DEARNE S63 107 K2
DRON S18 189 L7
ECK/KIL S21 180 D8
Woodside Ct AWLS/ASK DN6 66 E3 1
MALT S66 149 G4
Woodside La CHPT/GREN S35 126 A6
EPW DN9 94 F4
OWL S3 160 E1 2
Woodside Rd AWLS/ASK DN6 66 E3
BTLY DN5 67 J7
WRKN S81 183 K8
Woodside Vw DRON S18 189 L7
HOLM/MEL HD7 53 H3
NROS/TKH DN11 153 M3
Woodside Wk KIMB S61 128 E5
Wood Spring Ct ATT S4 145 J7
Wood's Riding DONS/BSCR DN4 91 H3
Woodstock Rd ABRD S7 176 C1
DOD/DAR S75 60 B3
DONS/BSCR DN4 111 J1
ST/HB/BR S6 143 J6
Wood St BSLY S70 3 G8
CUD/GR S72 40 C1
DON DN1 5 G5
KBTN HD8 34 D5
KBTN HD8 35 H6
MEX/SWTN S64 108 D2
RHAM/THRY S65 130 C5
ST/HB/BR S6 160 C1
WMB/DAR S73 84 A5
Wood Syke DOD/DAR S75 59 L8
Wood Ter RHAM S60 147 H4
Woodthorpe Cl
SHEFP/MNR S2 161 L7
Woodthorpe Crs
HAN/WDH S13 162 A7 5
Woodthorpe Rd
HAN/WDH S13 162 A8
Woodvale Rd ECC S11 159 M6
Woodview BTLY DN5 88 F6 6
Wood Vw CONI DN12 110 C6
CONI DN12 111 G4
HOY S74 105 L2
Woodview La DOD/DAR S75 59 M4 6
Wood View Pl RHAM S60 147 H4
Woodview Rd ST/HB/BR S6 144 A8
Woodview Ter ECC S11 159 J7 4
Wood Wk BSLYN/ROY S71 39 G2
HOY S74 83 J7
MEX/SWTN S64 108 D1
WMB/DAR S73 83 L7
The Woodway MALT S66 130 F8
Woofindin Av ECC S11 159 J8
Woofindin Rd ECC S11 159 H8
Woolcroft Dr HOLM/MEL HD7 54 A1
Wooldale Cliff Rd
HOLM/MEL HD7 53 M1
Wooldale Cl MOS S20 178 E5
Wooldale Cft MOS S20 178 E5
Wooldale Dr MOS S20 178 E5
Wooldale Gdns MOS S20 178 E5
Wooley Av WMB/DAR S73 84 A5
Woolgreaves Av
WKFDW/WTN WF2 20 B1
Woolgreaves Cft
WKFDW/WTN WF2 20 B1
Woolgreaves Dr
WKFDW/WTN WF2 20 B1
Woolgreaves Garth
WKFDW/WTN WF2 20 B1
Woolley Colliery Rd
DOD/DAR S75 37 J4
Woolley Edge La
DOD/DAR S75 37 J2
Woolley Low Moor La
HOR/CROF WF4 19 H5
Woolley Park Gdns
HOR/CROF WF4 19 L8
Woolley Rd STKB/PEN S36 101 L6
Woolley Vw HOR/CROF WF4 19 K5
Woolley Wood Rd SHEFN S5 127 J8
Wool Row La KBTN HD8 34 A2
Woolstocks La DOD/DAR S75 58 C4
Wootton Ct RHAM/THRY S65 130 C5 3
Worcester Av WHHL DN2 68 D8
Worcester Cl FUL S10 158 F6 2
WRKN S81 184 E8 7
Worcester Dr FUL S10 158 F6
Worcester Rd FUL S10 158 E6
Wordsworth Av AWLS/ASK DN6 27 G6
DIN S25 166 E7 3
DONS/BSCR DN4 111 M1
SHEFN S5 144 C4
STKB/PEN S36 79 G5
Wordsworth Cl SHEFN S5 144 C1
Wordsworth Crs SHEFN S5 144 C3
Wordsworth Dr BTLY DN5 89 K3
RHAM/THRY S65 7 M5
SHEFN S5 144 C3
Wordsworth Pl DRON S18 191 G8
Wordsworth Rd
BSLYN/ROY S71 60 F3
DEARNE S63 85 G8
Work Bank La STKB/PEN S36 78 F3
Workhouse La OWL S3 9 H2
Worksop Rd AU/AST/KP S26 164 B8
DARN/MH S9 161 L1
DIN S25 182 D4
NROS/TKH DN11 152 D2
WRKN S81 169 L5
WRKN S81 183 J3 2
WRKS S80 182 C8
WRKS S80 196 E8
Wormley Hill La GLE DN14 31 H3
Worral Av RHAM S60 163 J3
Worral Cl BSLY S70 82 D1
Worral Ct ARMTH DN3 69 L5 2
Worrall Dr CHPT/GREN S35 143 H2
Worrall Rd CHPT/GREN S35 126 C1
CHPT/GREN S35 143 H3
WKFDW/WTN WF2 19 L3
Worry Goose La RHAM S60 148 A5
Worsborough Vw
DOD/DAR S75 104 B1
Worsbrough Rd BSLY S70 82 D7
HOY S74 83 H6
Worsley Cl BSLY S70 82 F1
Worsley Pl AWLS/ASK DN6 44 D5
Worthing Crs CONI DN12 110 B5
Worthing Rd DARN/MH S9 161 J3
Wortley Av MEX/SWTN S64 108 B5
WMB/DAR S73 83 M3
Wortley Dr CHPT/GREN S35 125 J8
Wortley Ms KIMB S61 127 J3
Wortley Pl HEM/SK/SE WF9 23 G8
Wortley Rd CHPT/GREN S35 102 E5
CHPT/GREN S35 104 A7
KIMB S61 128 C7
KIMB S61 128 E8 2
STKB/PEN S36 102 D6
Wortley St BSLY S70 2 F6
Wortley Vw HOY S74 83 H6
Wostenholm Rd ABRD S7 160 D8
Wragby Rd ECC S11 159 L7
Wragg La AU/AST/KP S26 179 M2
Wragg Rd SHEFP/MNR S2 161 J5
Wrancarr La AWLS/ASK DN6 46 E1

Wrangbrook La
HEM/SK/SE WF9 .... 43 G1
Wrangbrook Rd
HEM/SK/SE WF9 .... 25 H7
Wreakes La DRON S18 .... 190 D5
Wren Bank SHEFP/MNR S2 ... 161 J5 🔢
Wren Ct WRKN S81 .... 184 A8
Wren Garth WKFDW/WTN WF2 ... 20 A2
Wren Park CI HACK/IN S12 ... 178 C7
Wrens Wy BSLY S70 .... 82 D7
Wright Crs WMB/DAR S73 ... 84 B5
Wrightson Av
DONS/BSCR DN4 .... 111 G2
Wrightson Ter BTLY DN5 ...... 89 M1 🔢
Wright St DIN S25 .... 182 C1
Wroot Rd EPW DN9 .... 115 M1
Wroxham CI MALT S66 .... 149 J2 🔢
Wroxham Dr MALT S66 .... 149 J2
MALT S66 .... 149 J2
Wulfric CI SHEFP/MNR S2 ... 161 K7
Wulfric PI SHEFP/MNR S2 ... 161 K7
Wulfric Rd ECK/KIL S21 ...... 193 G4

SHEFP/MNR S2 .... 161 L7
Wyatt Av ECC S11 .... 176 A1
Wybourn House Rd
SHEFP/MNR S2 .... 161 J4 🔢
Wybourn Ter
SHEFP/MNR S2 .... 161 J4 🔢
Wychwood CI
DONS/BSCR DN4 .... 111 K3
Wychwood Cft MOS S20 .... 179 L5 🔢
Wychwood Gln MOS S20 .... 179 L5 🔢
Wychwood Gv MOS S20 .... 179 L5 🔢
Wycombe St BSLYN/ROY S71 ... 61 J5 🔢
Wyedale Cft MOS S20 .... 179 K3
Wyming Brook Dr FUL S10 ... 157 M5
The Wynd ECK/KIL S21 .... 193 M8
Wynford Dr HEM/SK/SE WF9 ... 42 E4
Wyn Gv WMB/DAR S73 .... 84 E8
Wynlea Dr WRKN S81 .... 168 D1
Wynmoor Crs WMB/DAR S73 ... 84 B5
Wynyard Rd ST/HB/BR S6 ...... 143 M6
Wyvern Gdns TOT/DORE S17 ... 189 J1

Y

Yarborough Ter BTLY DN5 ...... 89 M2
Yardley Sq OWL S3 .... 8 C3 🔢
Yarmouth St DARN/MH S9 ... 145 M6 🔢
Yarwell Dr MALT S66 .... 150 C1
Yates CI MALT S66 .... 148 E4
Yealand CI AWLS/ASK DN6 ...... 66 F1
Yearling Cha MEX/SWTN S64 ... 107 M4
Yeoman CI WRKS S80 .... 198 E6
Yeomans Rd ST/HB/BR S6 ... 160 C2 🔢
Yeomans Wy DIN S25 .... 182 B3
Yewdale BSLY S70 .... 82 F2
Yew Greave Crs SHEFN S5 ... 126 D8
Yew La CHPT/GREN S35 .... 126 E7
SHEFN S5 .... 126 D8
Yews Av BSLY S70 .... 82 F2
Yews CI CHPT/GREN S35 ...... 143 H3
Yews La BSLY S70 .... 3 M9
BSLY S70 .... 82 F1
ST/HB/BR S6 .... 142 B7
Yews PI BSLY S70 .... 3 M9

Yew Tree Av DIN S25 .... 182 D2
Yew Tree Crs NROS/TKH DN11 ... 113 L5
Yew Tree Dr BWTY DN10 .... 136 D8
DARN/MH S9 .... 146 D6
ECK/KIL S21 .... 194 A2 🔢
EPW DN9 .... 114 F3
Yew Tree La HOLM/MEL HD7 ... 53 G4
Yew Tree Rd MALT S66 .... 150 A1
Yewtrees La STKB/PEN S36 ... 123 M2
Yoredale Av CHPT/GREN S35 ... 126 D1
York Gdns DONS/BSCR DN4 ... 91 H6
York La MALT S66 .... 148 F8
York PI WRKN S81 .... 183 K8 🔢
York Ri AU/AST/KP S26 .... 164 A8
York Rd BTLY DN5 .... 4 C1
BTLY DN5 .... 67 H7
DARN/MH S9 .... 162 A2
HTFD DN7 .... 48 E7
NROS/TKH DN11 .... 134 F8
NROS/TKH DN11 .... 153 L5
RHAM/THRY S65 .... 7 H2
STKB/PEN S36 .... 101 M6 🔢
York St BSLY S70 .... 2 E6
CUD/GR S72 .... 61 L1

DEARNE S63 .... 64 C6
HEM/SK/SE WF9 .... 41 J2
HOY S74 .... 83 J8
MEX/SWTN S64 .... 108 D2
NROS/TKH DN11 .... 113 J5
SHEF S1 .... 9 H3
WMB/DAR S73 .... 84 B4
Young St DON DN1 .... 5 G5
SHEF S1 .... 8 F8
Youlgreave Dr HACK/IN S12 ... 178 B2
Yvonne Gv WMB/DAR S73 ... 83 M4

Z

Zamor Crs MALT S66 .... 165 J2
Zetland Rd HOY S74 .... 105 M2
WHHL DN2 .... 5 M2
Zion Dr DOD/DAR S75 .... 37 M6
Zion PI DARN/MH S9 .... 161 K1

Index - featured places

Abbeydale Grange School
ABRD S7 .... 176 B3
Abbeydale Park Sports Club
TOT/DORE S17 ...... 175 L8
Abbeydale Primary School
ABRD S7 .... 176 D1
Abbey Lane Primary School
SHEFS S8 .... 176 C5
Abbey School
KIMB S61 .... 128 B8
A C E Business Centre
ATT S4 .... 9 K2
Ackworth Mill Dam School
FEA/AMT WF7 .... 23 L2
Acorn Business Park
SHEFS S8 .... 176 C3
Acres Hill Primary School
DARN/MH S9 .... 161 M4
Adwick Comprehensive School
AWLS/ASK DN6 ...... 66 F3
Adwick Leisure Centre
AWLS/ASK DN6 ...... 66 F3
Adwick Park Junior School
AWLS/ASK DN6 ...... 66 F3
Adwick Road Surgery
MEX/SWTN S64 ...... 108 A2
Adwick Washington
First School
AWLS/ASK DN6 ...... 67 G3
Akwaaba Surgery
CHPT/GREN S35 ...... 126 F3
The Alhambra Shopping Centre
BSLY S70 .... 3 G6
All Saints Church
of England School
DIN S25 .... 166 B2
All Saints RC School
SHEFP/MNR S2 ...... 9 L8
All Saints School
BTLY DN5 .... 65 G2
Amber Business Centre
RHAM S60 .... 6 F2
Ambler Junior School
DONS/BSCR DN4 ...... 111 K1
Anchorage School
BTLY DN5 .... 89 J1
Anns Grove Primary School
SHEFS S8 .... 160 E8
Anston Brook Junior School
DIN S25 .... 182 B2
Anston Park Junior
& Infant School
DIN S25 .... 166 C8
Apperknowle County
Primary School
DRON S18 .... 191 K6
Arbourthorne Junior School
SHEFP/MNR S2 ...... 177 H1
Ardsley Oaks Junior
& Infant School
BSLY S70 .... 61 K7
Arksey County Junior
& Infant School
BTLY DN5 .... 68 B5
Armthorpe High School
ARMTH DN3 .... 69 L8
Armthorpe Southfield Infant
& Junior School
ARMTH DN3 .... 91 M2
The Armthorpe Surgery
ARMTH DN3 .... 91 L1
Art Gallery & Museum
RHAM/THRY S65 ...... 7 J4
Ashdell Preparatory School
FUL S10 .... 159 M5
Ash Hill Middle School
HTFD DN7 .... 48 E8
Ashley Industrial Estate
RHAM S60 .... 6 F1
Ashmount Industrial Park
HEM/SK/SE WF9 ...... 23 G5
Ashville Medical Centre
BSLY S70 .... 61 H7
Ashwood Road Junior
& Infant School
RAW S62 .... 129 K4
Asian Mosque Centre
SHEFP/MNR S2 ...... 160 E8
Askern CP School
BTLY DN5 .... 67 L2
Askern Health Centre
AWLS/ASK DN6 ...... 27 L7
Askern Spa Junior School
AWLS/ASK DN6 ...... 45 K1
Askern Swimming Pool
AWLS/ASK DN6 ...... 27 J7
Aston Comprehensive School
AU/AST/KP S26 ...... 164 A6
Aston Fence Junior
& Infant School
HAN/WDH S13 ...... 163 L7

Aston Hall Cricket Club
AU/AST/KP S26 ...... 164 E8
Aston Lodge School
AU/AST/KP S26 ...... 180 C1
Aston Springwood
Junior School
AU/AST/KP S26 ...... 164 C7
Aston Swallownest Junior
& Infant School
AU/AST/KP S26 ...... 163 M7
Athersley North
Primary School
BSLYN/ROY S71 ...... 38 C7
Athersley South Junior School
BSLYN/ROY S71 ...... 38 D8
Athletic Club
HEM/SK/SE WF9 ...... 22 F4
Athron Industrial Estate
DON DN1 .... 5 H2
Atlas Business Park
CHPT/GREN S35 ...... 127 G6
Auckley County
Primary School
EPW DN9 .... 114 E1
Aughton Junior
& Infant School
AU/AST/KP S26 ...... 164 B6
Austerfield Park Golf Club
BWTY DN10 .... 137 H2
The Avenue Medical Practice
SHEFS S8 .... 176 B8
Badsley Moor Lane Jmi School
RHAM/THRY S65 ...... 147 M1
Badsworth C of E
Junior & Infant School
HEM/SK/SE WF9 ...... 24 C5
Balby Carr School
DONS/BSCR DN4 ...... 112 A1
Balby Waverley First School
DONS/BSCR DN4 ...... 111 J1
Ballifield Primary School
HAN/WDH S13 ...... 162 E7
Bank End Junior
& Infant School
FEA/AMT WF7 ...... 23 K2
Bankwood Lane
Industrial Estate
NROS/TKH DN11 ...... 113 H5
Bankwood Primary School
SHEFS S8 .... 177 H2
Barlborough Hall School
STV/CWN S43 ...... 194 F6
Barlborough Primary School
STV/CWN S43 ...... 194 F8
Barnburgh Primary School
BTLY DN5 .... 87 G5
Barnby Dun Primary School
ARMTH DN3 .... 47 K8
Barnsley Borough Council
BSLY S70 .... 3 G5
Barnsley Christian School
BSLY S70 .... 2 F6
Barnsley College
BSLY S70 .... 2 F3
Barnsley College
DOD/DAR S75 ...... 2 F2
Barnsley College
DOD/DAR S75 ...... 60 B3
Barnsley County Court
BSLY S70 .... 2 F4
Barnsley District
General Hospital
DOD/DAR S75 ...... 2 A2
Barnsley Football Club
BSLYN/ROY S71 ...... 3 K5
Barnsley Magistrates Court
BSLY S70 .... 2 F4
Barnsley Metropolitan
Borough Council
BSLY S70 .... 2 F4
Barnsley Metropolitan
Borough Council
BSLY S70 .... 2 E3
Barnsley Metropolitan
Borough Council
BSLY S70 .... 2 D8
Barnsley Metropolitan
Borough Council
BSLY S70 .... 3 G3
Barnsley Metropolitan
Borough Council
BSLY S70 .... 82 D2
Barnsley Metropolitan
Borough Council
BSLYN/ROY S71 ...... 3 H5
Barnsley Metropolitan
Borough Council
BSLYN/ROY S71 ...... 3 J2
Barnsley Metropolitan
Borough Council
BSLYN/ROY S71 ...... 38 D8

Barnsley Metropolitan
Borough Council
BSLYN/ROY S71 ...... 39 G3
Barnsley Metropolitan
Borough Council
DEARNE S63 .... 86 A5
Barnsley Metropolitan
Borough Council
DEARNE S63 .... 86 C3
Barnsley Metropolitan
Borough Council
DOD/DAR S75 ...... 37 H7
Barnsley Metropolitan
Borough Council
DOD/DAR S75 ...... 104 A1
Barnsley Metropolitan Borough
Council
WMB/DAR S73 ...... 84 C4
Barnsley Municipal Golf Club
DOD/DAR S75 ...... 38 A5
Barnsley Private Clinic
DOD/DAR S75 ...... 2 E2
The Basement Gallery
FUL S10 .... 159 G8
Baslow Road Surgery
TOT/DORE S17 ...... 189 J2
Bassetlaw District
General Hospital
WRKN S81 .... 198 E2
Bassetlaw Leisure Centre
WRKS S80 .... 198 E3
Bawtry Health Centre
BWTY DN10 .... 136 E8
Beauchief Golf Club House
SHEFS S8 .... 175 M6
Becca House Surgery
HEM/SK/SE WF9 ...... 23 H8
Beevor Industrial Estate
BSLYN/ROY S71 ...... 3 M5
Beighton Health Centre
MOS S20 .... 179 K3
Belgrave Medical Centre
SHEFP/MNR S2 ...... 160 E7
Bell Lane Junior
& Infant School
FEA/AMT WF7 ...... 23 K2
Bentley Colliery Cricket Club
BTLY DN5 .... 67 M5
Bentley Health Centre
BTLY DN5 .... 67 L6
Bentley High Street
Primary School
BTLY DN5 .... 67 M7
Bentley Sunnyfields
Infant School
BTLY DN5 .... 67 J8
Bentley Sunnyfields
Junior School
BTLY DN5 .... 67 K8
Bents Green Special School
ECC S11 .... 175 J2
Bircotes Sports Centre
NROS/TKH DN11 ...... 153 M2
Birdsedge First School
KBTN HD8 .... 55 L3
Birdwell Health Centre
BSLY S70 .... 104 D1
Birdwell Primary School
BSLY S70 .... 82 D8
Birkdale Preparatory School
FUL S10 .... 8 A8
Birkdale School
ECC S11 .... 160 A6
Birkhill Primary School
ECK/KIL S21 ...... 192 F5
Birkwood First School
CUD/GR S72 .... 62 A2
Birley First School
HACK/IN S12 ...... 178 B4
Birley Health Centre
HACK/IN S12 ...... 178 B5
Birley Middle School
HACK/IN S12 ...... 178 B4
Birley Primary School
HACK/IN S12 ...... 178 B4
Birley Spa Primary School
HACK/IN S12 ...... 178 D3
Blackburn County Junior Mixed
School
KIMB S61 .... 145 M1
Bluebell Medical Centre
SHEFN S5 .... 145 K4
Bluestone Middle School
SHEFP/MNR S2 ...... 161 H7
Bluestone Primary School
SHEFP/MNR S2 ...... 161 H7
Blyth C of E Primary School
WRKN S81 .... 169 M5
Blyth Cricket Club
WRKN S81 .... 169 L4
Bolton Medical Centre
DEARNE S63 .... 85 M5

Bolton Upon Dearne
Infant School
DEARNE S63 .... 86 A5
Bootham Lane
Industrial Estate
HTFD DN7 .... 48 E6
Bracken Moor Sports Club
STKB/PEN S36 ...... 102 A7
Bradfield Dungworth
Primary School
ST/HB/BR S6 ...... 142 C6
Bradfield School
CHPT/GREN S35 ...... 143 G2
Bradmarsh Business Park
RHAM S60 .... 6 D7
Bramley Grange Jmi School
MALT S66 .... 149 H1
Bramley Sunnyside Jmi School
MALT S66 .... 149 G1
Brampton Ellis Infant School
DEARNE S63 .... 107 G1
Brampton Health Centre
WMB/DAR S73 ...... 84 E7
Brantwood Independent
School for Girls
ABRD S7 .... 160 B7
Brierley C of E Junior
& Infant School
CUD/GR S72 .... 40 E4
Brinsworth Clinic
RHAM S60 .... 146 F6
Brinsworth
Comprehensive School
RHAM S60 .... 146 E7
Brinsworth Medical Centre
RHAM S60 .... 146 E6
Brinsworth Whitehill
Jm School
RHAM S60 .... 147 G8
Broad Elms School
ECC S11 .... 175 K3
Broadway School
BSLY S70 .... 2 A8
Brodsworth Hall
BTLY DN5 .... 65 M4
Brook House Junior School
MOS S20 .... 179 M4
Broomhill Clinic
FUL S10 .... 160 A5
Broomhill Infant School
FUL S10 .... 160 A5
Broomhill Medical Surgery
FUL S10 .... 159 M5
Broom Lane Medical Centre
RHAM S60 .... 147 L4
Broom Valley Junior
& Infant School
RHAM S60 .... 7 H8
Brunswick Primary School
HAN/WDH S13 ...... 163 H8
Burncross Surgery
CHPT/GREN S35 ...... 126 D2
Burns Medical Centre
DONS/BSCR DN4 ...... 91 J7
The Burns Practice
WHHL DN2 .... 5 J5
Burntwood School
HEM/SK/SE WF9 ...... 42 A4
Burntwood Sports
& Leisure Centre
CUD/GR S72 .... 41 G5
Burton Road Junior
& Infant School
BSLYN/ROY S71 ...... 3 K1
The Business Centre
RHAM S60 .... 6 D8
The Business Centre
RHAM S60 .... 6 F4
Byron Wood Primary School
ATT S4 .... 144 F8
Camms Endowed
C of E Primary School
MOS S20 .... 193 H3
Campsmount School
AWLS/ASK DN6 ...... 26 F5
Canklow Meadows
Industrial Estate
RHAM S60 .... 147 G6
Canklow Woods Junior & Infant
School
RHAM S60 .... 147 H5
Cannon Hall Museum
& Country Park
DOD/DAR S75 ...... 58 A2
Cantley Hawthorn First School
DONS/BSCR DN4 ...... 91 J6
Cantley Hawthorn
Junior School
DONS/BSCR DN4 ...... 91 J6
Cantley Health Centre
DONS/BSCR DN4 ...... 91 K8

Carbrook Hall Industrial Estate
DARN/MH S9 .... 145 M6
Carcroft Health Centre
AWLS/ASK DN6 ...... 45 G7
Carcroft Industrial Estate
AWLS/ASK DN6 ...... 45 H8
Carfield Primary School
SHEFS S8 .... 176 E2
Caribbean Sports Club
CHPT/GREN S35 ...... 127 G7
Carlton Industrial Estate
BSLYN/ROY S71 ...... 39 G7
Carlton Junior & Infant School
BSLYN/ROY S71 ...... 39 H7
Carlton Phoenix
Industrial Estate
WRKS S80 .... 198 E3
Carrfield Junior
& Infant School
DEARNE S63 .... 86 A4
Carrfield Medical Centre
SHEFP/MNR S2 ...... 176 F1
Carterknowle & Dore Medical
Practice
ABRD S7 .... 176 C2
Carter Knowle Junior School
ABRD S7 .... 176 B2
Castle Market
ATT S4 .... 9 K3
Cathedral Church
of St Peter & St Paul
SHEF S1 .... 9 H3
Cawthorne C of E Junior
& Infant School
DOD/DAR S75 ...... 58 C3
Cawthorne Victoria
Jubilee Museum
DOD/DAR S75 ...... 58 C2
Cedar Special School
DONS/BSCR DN4 ...... 111 K1
Central Business Park
RHAM S60 .... 6 D4
Central Sheffield
University Hospitals
FUL S10 .... 8 A4
Chapelthorpe Surgery
HOR/CROF WF4 ...... 19 K3
Chapeltown Surgery
CHPT/GREN S35 ...... 126 F3
Charnock Hall
Primary School
HACK/IN S12 ...... 177 M5
Charter Gallery Museum
CONI DN12 .... 109 M5
Chaucer School
SHEFN S5 .... 144 C2
Chestnut House Surgery
THNE DN8 .... 31 M7
Childrens Hospital N H S Trust
FUL S10 .... 8 B5
Child Welfare & School Clinic
RHAM/THRY S65 ...... 7 K1
Church Drive Surgery
CUD/GR S72 .... 40 D4
Cifford C of E
Grammar School
ECC S11 .... 160 B7
City Museum
& Mappin Art Gallery
FUL S10 .... 8 B4
Civic Building
RHAM/THRY S65 ...... 6 F3
Civic Theatre
BSLY S70 .... 3 G6
Claremont Hospital
FUL S10 .... 159 H5
Claycliffe Business Park
DOD/DAR S75 ...... 59 J2
Clayfield Industrial Estate
DONS/BSCR DN4 ...... 111 L1
Clifford Lister Business Centre
MALT S66 .... 148 E3
Clifton Comprehensive School
RHAM/THRY S65 ...... 7 L3
The Clinic
KBTN HD8 .... 17 G8
Clough House Medical Centre
SHEFP/MNR S2 ...... 9 H8
Club House
AWLS/ASK DN6 ...... 44 E3
Coit Primary School
CHPT/GREN S35 ...... 126 E3
Coleridge Road Jmi School
RHAM/THRY S65 ...... 7 L1
College Lane Surgery
FEA/AMT WF7 ...... 23 K1
College of Technology
RHAM/THRY S65 ...... 6 F4
College Pines Golf Club
WRKS S80 .... 198 E8

Colonnades Centre
   DON DN1 .... 4 F5
Concord Middle School
   SHEFN S5 .... 145 J3
Conisbrough Castle
   CONI DN12 .... 110 C4
Contour Health Centre
   RHAM S60 .... 6 F6
Cooper Gallery
   BSLY S70 .... 2 F4
Cope Street Surgery
   BSLY S70 .... 3 J9
Copley School
   BTLY DN5 .... 88 F7
Coroners Court
   DON DN1 .... 4 F6
Cortonwood County
   Primary School
   WMB/DAR S73 .... 84 E7
Costhorpe Industrial Estate
   WRKN S81 .... 168 C6
County Primary School
   ARMTH DN3 .... 69 L5
County Primary School
   BWTY DN10 .... 137 M5
Crigglestone Sports Club
   HOR/CROF WF4 .... 19 K3
The Crookes Practice
   FUL S10 .... 160 A3
Crown Court
   DON DN1 .... 5 G6
Crown Court
   OWL S3 .... 9 H2
Crucible Theatre
   SHEF S1 .... 9 J5
Cudworth Churchfield School
   CUD/GR S72 .... 39 M8
The Culvert Gallery
   ECC S11 .... 160 B7
Cumberworth
   C of E First School
   KBTN HD8 .... 55 M1
Cupola Gallery
   ST/HB/BR S6 .... 144 A5
Curlew Junior School
   WHHL DN2 .... 69 H6
The Curtain Gallery
   ECC S11 .... 160 B7
Cusworth Hall
   BTLY DN5 .... 89 H3
Dalton Foljambe Infant School
   RHAM/THRY S65 .... 130 C6
Dalton Health Centre
   RHAM/THRY S65 .... 130 B6
Dane Royd Junior
   & Infant School
   HOR/CROF WF4 .... 19 J8
Danum Grammar School
   WHHL DN2 .... 91 J7
Darfield C of E Junior School
   WMB/DAR S73 .... 84 F1
Darfield Cricket Club
   WMB/DAR S73 .... 84 F2
Darfield Health Centre
   WMB/DAR S73 .... 84 F2
Darfield Valley Primary School
   WMB/DAR S73 .... 84 D3
Darnall Health Centre
   DARN/MH S9 .... 162 A2
Darnall Road Surgery
   DARN/MH S9 .... 161 M2
Darton High School
   DOD/DAR S75 .... 36 F7
Darton Junior & Infant School
   DOD/DAR S75 .... 37 K7
Darton Kexborough
   Infant School
   DOD/DAR S75 .... 36 F7
Davy Gallery
   NROS/TKH DN11 .... 134 E8
Dead Earnest Theatre
   ST/HB/BR S6 .... 160 A1
Dearne Goldthorpe
   Junior & Infant School
   DEARNE S63 .... 86 C2
Dearne Highgate
   Junior & Infant School
   DEARNE S63 .... 86 A2
Dearne High School
   DEARNE S63 .... 86 C3
Dearne Valley Health Centre
   KBTN HD8 .... 35 H8
Deepcar Junior School
   STKB/PEN S36 .... 102 C7
Deerlands Special School
   SHEFN S5 .... 144 F2
Deer Park Surgery
   ST/HB/BR S6 .... 159 J1
Denaby Lane Industrial Estate
   CONI DN12 .... 109 J4
Denby C of E First School
   KBTN HD8 .... 56 C4
Denby Dale Industrial Park
   KBTN HD8 .... 56 D1
Derbyshire County Council
   ECK/KIL S21 .... 193 J4
Devonshire Green
   Medical Centre
   SHEF S1 .... 8 F5
Dinnington Business Centre
   DIN S25 .... 166 C5
Dinnington Clinic
   DIN S25 .... 166 D7
Dinnington
   Comprehensive School
   DIN S25 .... 166 D5
Dinnington Rugby Club
   DIN S25 .... 166 F6
Dinnington
   St Josephs RC School
   DIN S25 .... 166 D6
Dobcroft Infant School
   ECC S11 .... 175 M3
Dobcroft Junior School
   ECC S11 .... 175 M4
Dodworth C of E Junior School
   DOD/DAR S75 .... 81 J1
Dodworth Health Centre
   DOD/DAR S75 .... 59 K8
Dodworth Junior School
   DOD/DAR S75 .... 59 K8

Doncaster Area Health
   Authority
   CONI DN12 .... 109 M5
Doncaster Area Health
   Authority
   DON DN1 .... 5 H5
Doncaster Area Health
   Authority
   MEX/SWTN S64 .... 108 F3
Doncaster Balby Central
   First School
   DONS/BSCR DN4 .... 4 C9
Doncaster Civic Theatre
   DON DN1 .... 5 H5
Doncaster College
   BTLY DN5 .... 87 M7
Doncaster College
   DON DN1 .... 4 F3
Doncaster Golf Course
   DONS/BSCR DN4 .... 113 L3
Doncaster Health Authority
   DONS/BSCR DN4 .... 90 B7
Doncaster Health Authority
   DONS/BSCR DN4 .... 111 M2
Doncaster Magistrates Court
   DON DN1 .... 4 F6
Doncaster Metropolitan
   Borough Council
   ARMTH DN3 .... 69 J5
Doncaster Metropolitan
   Borough Council
   BTLY DN5 .... 4 D2
Doncaster Metropolitan
   Borough Council
   CONI DN12 .... 110 A5
Doncaster Metropolitan
   Borough Council
   DON DN1 .... 4 F7
Doncaster Metropolitan
   Borough Council
   DON DN1 .... 4 F5
Doncaster Metropolitan
   Borough Council
   DON DN1 .... 5 H4
Doncaster Metropolitan
   Borough Council
   DON DN1 .... 5 J6
Doncaster Metropolitan
   Borough Council
   DONS/BSCR DN4 .... 91 J7
Doncaster Metropolitan
   Borough Council
   MEX/SWTN S64 .... 109 G2
Doncaster Metropolitan
   Borough Council
   NROS/TKH DN11 .... 113 H6
Doncaster Museum
   & Art Gallery
   DON DN1 .... 5 H5
Doncaster Road Infant School
   MEX/SWTN S64 .... 109 G3
Doncaster Road Jmi School
   RHAM/THRY S65 .... 7 L1
Doncaster Road Junior School
   MEX/SWTN S64 .... 109 G3
Doncaster Road
   Primary School
   BSLY S70 .... 3 J7
Doncaster Rovers Football Club
   DONS/BSCR DN4 .... 90 E5
Doncaster Royal Infirmary &
   Montagu Hospital NHS Trust
   WHHL DN2 .... 5 M1
Doncaster & South Humber
   Healthcare NHS Trust
   DONS/BSCR DN4 .... 111 M2
Doncaster Town Cricket Club
   WHHL DN2 .... 5 K5
Don Valley High School
   BTLY DN5 .... 67 H7
Dore Junior & Infant School
   TOT/DORE S17 .... 189 H1
Dovercourt Surgery
   SHEFP/MNR S2 .... 161 J6
Dr Chambers & Partners
   CHPT/GREN S35 .... 104 B7
Dr John Bingham
   Junior & Infant School
   SHEFS S8 .... 190 E2
Dr John Worrall School
   DARN/MH S9 .... 145 L8
Dronfield County
   Junior School
   DRON S18 .... 190 E6
Dronfield Health Centre
   DRON S18 .... 190 E6
Dronfield Infant School
   DRON S18 .... 190 E6
The Dronfield School
   DRON S18 .... 190 C5
Dronfield Sports Centre
   DRON S18 .... 190 D6
Duke Medical Centre
   SHEFP/MNR S2 .... 9 M6
Dukeries Art Gallery
   WRKS S80 .... 198 C3
Dukeries Clinic
   WRKS S80 .... 198 D5
Dukeries Industrial Estate
   WRKN S81 .... 198 A1
Dunsville Health Centre
   HTFD DN7 .... 70 C3
Dykeshall Medical Centre
   ST/HB/BR S6 .... 143 M6
Eastwood Trading Estate
   RHAM/THRY S65 .... 129 L6
Ecclesall Infant School
   ECC S11 .... 175 K1
Ecclesall Medical Centre
   ECC S11 .... 175 L2
Ecclesfield
   Comprehensive School
   CHPT/GREN S35 .... 126 E4
Ecclesfield Health Centre
   CHPT/GREN S35 .... 126 F6
Ecclesfield Parish Council
   CHPT/GREN S35 .... 104 C8
Eckington Health Centre
   ECK/KIL S21 .... 193 J4
Eckington Junior School
   ECK/KIL S21 .... 193 H4

Eckington School
   ECK/KIL S21 .... 192 E4
Edenthorpe Surgery
   ARMTH DN3 .... 69 K5
Edlington School
   CONI DN12 .... 110 F7
Edlington Victoria
   Primary School
   CONI DN12 .... 110 E4
Edward Sheerien School
   BSLYN/ROY S71 .... 60 F1
Ellers Middle School
   DONS/BSCR DN4 .... 90 F7
Ellesmere Teaching School
   ATT S4 .... 161 G1
Emley First School
   KBTN HD8 .... 17 H8
Emley Moor Business Park
   KBTN HD8 .... 34 F1
Emmett Carr Surgery
   ECK/KIL S21 .... 193 M7
Eppic Theatre
   CHPT/GREN S35 .... 126 A6
Fairfield School of Art
   BSLY S70 .... 2 E4
Falkland House Surgery
   ECC S11 .... 175 L1
Far Lane Medical Centre
   ST/HB/BR S6 .... 143 M6
Ferham House Clinic
   KIMB S61 .... 146 E1
Fernbank Special School
   AWLS/ASK DN6 .... 67 G1
Fernham Junior & Infant School
   KIMB S61 .... 6 A5
Finningley Airfield
   EPW DN9 .... 114 F5
Finningley C of E School
   EPW DN9 .... 115 K4
Fire Police Museum
   OWL S3 .... 9 G3
Firs Hill Junior School
   ATT S4 .... 144 F7
Firth Park Medical Centre
   SHEFN S5 .... 145 H4
Firth Park School
   SHEFN S5 .... 145 G4
Flanderwell Junior
   & Infant School
   MALT S66 .... 148 F1
Flockton C of E School
   HOR/CROF WF4 .... 17 G4
The Flockton Surgery
   HOR/CROF WF4 .... 16 F5
The Foulstone School
   WMB/DAR S73 .... 84 F1
Foxhill Medical Centre
   ST/HB/BR S6 .... 144 B1
Fox Hill Primary School
   ST/HB/BR S6 .... 144 B1
Frame Gallery
   RHAM S60 .... 6 F3
Frenchgate Centre
   DON DN1 .... 4 F4
Fullerton House School
   CONI DN12 .... 109 K4
The Gables School
   WMB/DAR S73 .... 84 B5
The Gallery
   DON DN1 .... 5 G4
Gawber Junior & Infant School
   DOD/DAR S75 .... 59 L4
Gilthwaites First School
   KBTN HD8 .... 34 F1
Gladys Buxton School
   DRON S18 .... 191 G5
Gleadless Clinic
   HACK/IN S12 .... 177 M4
Gleadless Primary School
   HACK/IN S12 .... 177 M2
Globe Business Centre
   OWL S3 .... 160 D2
Goldthorpe Health Centre
   DEARNE S63 .... 86 B3
Goldthorpe Industrial Estate
   DEARNE S63 .... 85 M3
Goldthorpe RC Jmi School
   DEARNE S63 .... 86 C1
Gooseacre Primary School
   DEARNE S63 .... 64 A6
Grange Gate Junior School
   BSLYN/ROY S71 .... 61 J5
Grange Lane Industrial Estate
   BSLYN/ROY S71 .... 61 J5
Graves Art Gallery
   SHEF S1 .... 9 J5
Greasborough Health Centre
   KIMB S61 .... 128 F4
Greasborough Junior
   & Infant School
   KIMB S61 .... 128 F4
Great Houghton Clinic
   CUD/GR S72 .... 63 J6
Green Arbour School
   MALT S66 .... 165 J1
Greengate Lane
   Primary School
   CHPT/GREN S35 .... 104 C8
Greenhill Health Centre
   SHEFS S8 .... 190 C1
Greenhill Primary School
   SHEFS S8 .... 176 C8
Greenlands Junior School
   DARN/MH S9 .... 162 A3
Green Lane Middle School
   THNE DN8 .... 50 B1
Greenside Surgery
   KIMB S61 .... 128 F4
Green Top First School
   THNE DN8 .... 49 M1
Greenway Natural
   Health Centre
   TOT/DORE S17 .... 189 H3
Grenoside Primary School
   CHPT/GREN S35 .... 126 A6
Greystones First School
   ECC S11 .... 159 L8
Greystones Medical Centre
   ECC S11 .... 159 M8
Greystones Primary School
   ECC S11 .... 159 M8

Grimethorpe Hall
   CUD/GR S72 .... 40 D7
Grimethorpe Ladywood
   First School
   CUD/GR S72 .... 62 F7
Grove Street Junior
   & Infant School
   BSLYN/ROY S71 .... 3 J5
Guildhall Industrial Estate
   ARMTH DN3 .... 69 J4
Gunthwaite Hall
   STKB/PEN S36 .... 56 F5
Hackenthorpe Medical Centre
   HACK/IN S12 .... 178 E4
Hade Edge Primary School
   HOLM/MEL HD7 .... 53 M7
Haggonfields County
   Primary School
   WRKS S80 .... 197 L3
Halfway Infant School
   MOS S20 .... 179 J8
Halfway Junior School
   MOS S20 .... 179 J8
Hallam Primary School
   FUL S10 .... 159 G6
Hallamshire Business Park
   FUL S10 .... 8 D8
The Hallamshire Gallery
   ECC S11 .... 159 M8
Hallamshire Natural
   Health Centre
   ECC S11 .... 160 A7
Hall Cross Comprehensive
   School
   DON DN1 .... 5 J4
Handsworth Branch Clinic
   HAN/WDH S13 .... 162 D6
Handsworth Road
   Medical Centre
   HAN/WDH S13 .... 162 D6
Hanover Medical Centre
   FUL S10 .... 8 D7
Harrison Drive Business Centre
   WRKS S81 .... 168 C3
Harthill Junior
   & Infant School
   AU/AST/KP S26 .... 195 J2
Harworth C of E
   Primary School
   NROS/TKH DN11 .... 153 K3
Harworth Medical Centre
   NROS/TKH DN11 .... 153 L2
Harworth Park Industrial
   Estate
   NROS/TKH DN11 .... 153 L5
Hatfield Comprehensive
   School
   HTFD DN7 .... 48 F8
Hatfield County
   Primary School
   HTFD DN7 .... 48 E7
Hatfield & Dunsville
   County Primary School
   HTFD DN7 .... 70 E2
Hatfield Primary School
   SHEFS S5 .... 145 H2
Hatfield Woodhouse
   County Primary School
   HTFD DN7 .... 71 L1
Hathersage Swimming Pool
   HATH/EY S32 .... 172 E8
Havercroft Health Centre
   HOR/CROF WF4 .... 21 M7
Havercroft Junior
   & Infant School
   HOR/CROF WF4 .... 21 M7
Hayfield Comprehensive School
   EPW DN9 .... 114 D3
Heaf Gardens Industrial Estate
   SHEFP/MNR S2 .... 9 J8
Healthcare Surgery
   SHEFN S5 .... 144 B3
The Health Centre
   CONI DN12 .... 110 F5
Heather Garth Junior
   & Infant School
   DEARNE S63 .... 85 M4
Heeley Business Centre
   SHEFP/MNR S2 .... 160 E7
Heeley Green Surgery
   SHEFP/MNR S2 .... 176 F1
Heeley Retail Park
   SHEFS S8 .... 176 D4
Hellaby Industrial Estate
   MALT S66 .... 149 L1
Hemingfield Ellis C of E Junior &
   Infant School
   WMB/DAR S73 .... 84 A7
Hemsworth Fitzwilliam School
   HEM/SK/SE WF9 .... 22 F3
Hemsworth Grove Lea Junior
   & Infant School
   HEM/SK/SE WF9 .... 23 H8
Hemsworth Primary School
   GLV S14 .... 177 H5
Hemsworth R U F C
   HEM/SK/SE WF9 .... 23 K8
Hemsworth Town Council
   HEM/SK/SE WF9 .... 23 H8
Hepworth Junior & Infant School
   HOLM/MEL HD7 .... 54 C6
Herdings Primary School
   GLV S14 .... 177 J5
Herries School
   SHEFN S5 .... 144 C5
Herringthorpe Junior
   & Infant School
   RHAM/THRY S65 .... 147 M3
Hesley Hall School
   NROS/TKH DN11 .... 135 K3
Hexthorpe First School
   DONS/BSCR DN4 .... 4 B7
Hexthorpe Primary School
   DONS/BSCR DN4 .... 4 B8
Hickleton Golf Club
   DEARNE S63 .... 64 F7
Highfields County
   Primary School
   AWLS/ASK DN6 .... 66 F5
Highfields Junior School
   WMB/DAR S73 .... 84 A4

High Greave Jmi School
   RHAM/THRY S65 .... 130 A7
High Green Health Centre
   CHPT/GREN S35 .... 104 B7
High Green Primary School
   CHPT/GREN S35 .... 104 B7
High School
   HTFD DN7 .... 48 F8
High Storrs School
   ECC S11 .... 175 K1
Highwoods Infant School
   MEX/SWTN S64 .... 108 C1
Hill Brow Surgery
   DOD/DAR S75 .... 37 L6
Hill House Preparatory School
   DON DN1 .... 5 K3
Hill Primary School
   DEARNE S63 .... 64 D6
Hillsborough Health Centre
   ST/HB/BR S6 .... 144 A8
Hillsborough Primary School
   ST/HB/BR S6 .... 144 A6
Hill Top Junior & Infant School
   CONI DN12 .... 110 E6
Hinchliffe Mill County School
   HOLM/MEL HD7 .... 53 G5
Hinde House School
   SHEFN S5 .... 145 J3
HM Prison
   BTLY DN5 .... 4 D4
Holgate School
   BSLY S70 .... 2 B6
Hollies Medical Centre
   ECC S11 .... 160 B8
Hollis Hospital
   TOT/DORE S17 .... 175 J5
Hollywood Bowling
   DARN/MH S9 .... 146 A7
Holmescarr Junior
   Mixed School
   NROS/TKH DN11 .... 113 J6
Holme School
   HOLM/MEL HD7 .... 52 C6
Holmfirth Craft Market
   HOLM/MEL HD7 .... 53 K2
Holt House Infant School
   ABRD S7 .... 176 B3
Holy Cross Deanery C of E
   Junior & Infant School
   BSLYN/ROY S71 .... 60 F1
Holy Family CP School
   HTFD DN7 .... 48 D3
Holy Family RC Primary School
   WRKS S80 .... 198 D1
Holyrood RC Junior
   & Infant School
   BSLY S70 .... 2 C7
Houghton Main Welfare
   & Sports Club
   CUD/GR S72 .... 63 J8
Howarth Junior
   & Infant School
   RHAM S60 .... 147 G8
Hoyland Common
   Primary School
   HOY S74 .... 104 E2
Hoyland Elsecar C of E
   Junior & Infant School
   HOY S74 .... 105 M2
Hoyland Greenfield Junior
   & Infant School
   HOY S74 .... 105 K1
Hoyland St Helens RC Junior
   & Infant School
   HOY S74 .... 105 H1
Hoyland Sports Centre
   HOY S74 .... 105 G1
H S B C Sports Club
   TOT/DORE S17 .... 175 H6
Hucklow Primary School
   SHEFN S5 .... 145 J3
Huddersfield Technical College
   HOLM/MEL HD7 .... 53 L1
Hungerhill Comprehensive
   School
   ARMTH DN3 .... 69 K5
Hunningley Junior
   & Infant School
   BSLY S70 .... 61 J8
Hunters Bar Junior
   & Infant School
   ECC S11 .... 160 A7
I B T E Museum of
   Telecommunications
   WRKS S80 .... 198 D5
Industrial Centre
   MEX/SWTN S64 .... 108 E3
Industrial Estate
   HEM/SK/SE WF9 .... 42 B5
Intake High School
   WHHL DN2 .... 91 J2
Intake Junior & Infant School
   HACK/IN S12 .... 177 M1
Ironbridge Industrial Estate
   HAN/WDH S13 .... 163 G7
Ivanhoe Junior
   & Infant School
   CONI DN12 .... 109 L6
Jamiyat Tabliq Ul Islam
   Mosque
   DARN/MH S9 .... 161 J1
Jaunty Springs Health Centre
   HACK/IN S12 .... 177 M1
Jessop Hospital for Women
   OWL S3 .... 8 D1
Jordanthorpe Health Centre
   SHEFS S8 .... 190 F1
Junction 34 Industrial Estate
   DARN/MH S9 .... 146 B6
Kayes First School
   KBTN HD8 .... 35 K5
Keir House Surgery
   BSLY S70 .... 2 D3
Kelham Island Museum
   OWL S3 .... 9 G1
Kelvin Grove Surgery
   WMB/DAR S73 .... 84 C5
Kendray Hospital
   BSLY S70 .... 61 G2
Kendray Infant School
   BSLY S70 .... 61 G8

Keresforth Primary School
DOD/DAR S75 .... 81 L1
Kettlethorpe High School
WKFDW/WTN WF2 .... 20 A1
Kexborough Junior School
DOD/DAR S75 .... 36 F7
Khan Medical Centre
NROS/TKH DN11 .... 153 L3
Killamarsh County
Junior & Infant School
ECK/KIL S21 .... 180 C8
Killamarsh Leisure Centre
ECK/KIL S21 .... 180 B8
Killamarsh Medical Centre
ECK/KIL S21 .... 180 A8
Kilnhurst Business Park
MEX/SWTN S64 .... 130 C1
Kilnhurst Junior
& Infants School
MEX/SWTN S64 .... 108 D8
Kilton Forest Golf Club
WRKN S81 .... 198 F1
Kilton Industrial Estate
WRKS S80 .... 198 E4
Kimberworth Comprehensive
School
KIMB S61 .... 146 D1
Kimberworth Infants School
KIMB S61 .... 128 D8
Kimberworth Park Clinic
KIMB S61 .... 128 C6
Kimberworth Park Medical
Centre
KIMB S61 .... 128 C7
King Ecgbert Secondary
School
TOT/DORE S17 .... 189 H1
King Edward First School
THNE DN8 .... 32 A7
King Edward Vii School
FUL S10 .... 8 A7
Kingfisher First School
WHHL DN2 .... 68 E8
Kingthorne Group Practice
ARMTH DN3 .... 69 K5
Kingthorne Group Practice
DON DN1 .... 5 J3
Kinsley Industrial Estate
HEM/SK/SE WF9 .... 23 G6
Kirk Balk School
HOY S74 .... 105 G1
Kirkby Avenue Primary School
BTLY DN5 .... 89 L1
Kirk Sandall Infant School
ARMTH DN3 .... 69 K4
Kirk Sandall Junior School
ARMTH DN3 .... 69 K4
Kirk Smeaton C of E
Primary School
PONT WF8 .... 26 B1
Kirton Lane Primary School
HTFD DN7 .... 48 E3
Kitchen Gallery
RHAM S60 .... 6 F5
Kiveton Park Group Practice
AU/AST/KP S26 .... 181 H5
Kiveton Park Infant School
AU/AST/KP S26 .... 181 J5
Lacewood Primary School
DEARNE S63 .... 86 B5
Lakeside First School
DONS/BSCR DN4 .... 5 M9
The Lakeside Surgery
WRKN S81 .... 168 D5
Langold Dyscarr Junior School
WRKN S81 .... 168 B4
Langold Health Centre
WRKN S81 .... 168 D4
Lantern Theatre
ABRD S7 .... 160 C7
Larwood Health Centre
WRKN S81 .... 198 F1
Laughton Junior
& Infant School
DIN S25 .... 166 B3
Lawn Road Industrial Estate
WRKN S81 .... 168 C7
Lecture Theatre
SHEF S1 .... 8 E4
Lenthall School
DRON S18 .... 190 F4
Lilly Hall Junior
& Middle School
MALT S66 .... 150 C2
Limpsfield Junior School
DARN/MH S9 .... 145 L5
Lindrick Golf Club
WRKN S81 .... 183 H5
Listerdale Shopping Centre
RHAM/THRY S65 .... 148 C3
The Little Gallery
RAW S62 .... 105 M6
Littlemoor First School
AWLS/ASK DN6 .... 45 J1
Little Theatre
DEARNE S63 .... 64 A8
Littleworth Lane Infant School
BSLYN/ROY S71 .... 61 H4
Lobwood Junior
& Infant School
BSLY S70 .... 82 E2
Lodge Moor Medical Centre
FUL S10 .... 158 E6
Longcar Junior
& Infant School
BSLY S70 .... 2 D7
Lound Infant School
CHPT/GREN S35 .... 126 D1
Lound Junior School
CHPT/GREN S35 .... 126 E1
Lowedges Primary School
SHEFS S8 .... 190 D1
Loxley Primary School
ST/HB/BR S6 .... 143 H6
Lundwood Medical Centre
BSLYN/ROY S71 .... 61 H5
The Lyceum Theatre
SHEF S1 .... 9 J5
Lydgate Infant School
FUL S10 .... 159 L4
Lydgate Junior School
FUL S10 .... 159 L5

Mackie Hill Junior
& Infant School
HOR/CROF WF4 .... 19 H3
Makki Mosque
SHEFS S8 .... 176 E1
Malin Bridge Primary School
ST/HB/BR S6 .... 143 M7
Maltby Comprehensive
School
MALT S66 .... 150 D2
Maltby Crags Junior
& Infant School
MALT S66 .... 150 D3
Maltby Hall Infant School
MALT S66 .... 150 D2
Maltby Health Centre
MALT S66 .... 150 D2
Maltby Manor Junior
& Infant School
MALT S66 .... 150 E2
Maltby Redwood Jmi School
MALT S66 .... 150 A2
Maltby Sports Centre
MALT S66 .... 150 D2
Manor Clinic
SHEFP/MNR S2 .... 177 K1
Manor Lodge Middle School
SHEFP/MNR S2 .... 161 J6
Manor Lodge Primary School
SHEFP/MNR S2 .... 161 J6
Manor Middle School
HTFD DN7 .... 49 G7
Manor Park Medical Centre
SHEFP/MNR S2 .... 161 L5
Manor Top Medical Centre
HACK/IN S12 .... 177 L1
Manton Infant School
WRKS S80 .... 199 G6
Manton Junior School
WRKS S80 .... 198 F6
Maple Industrial Estate
DOD/DAR S75 .... 38 B7
Mapplewell Health Centre
DOD/DAR S75 .... 37 M7
Market Hall
DON DN1 .... 5 G3
Market Junior School
HOY S74 .... 83 J8
Marlcliffe Primary School
ST/HB/BR S6 .... 143 M5
Marshgate Industrial Estate
BTLY DN5 .... 4 D3
Marsh Lane Primary School
ECK/KIL S21 .... 192 C4
Mattersey Primary School
BWTY DN10 .... 155 M8
Mayflower Gallery
RTFD DN22 .... 170 F3
Mayflower Junior
& Infant School
BWTY DN10 .... 136 E8
Mayflower Junior School
BWTY DN10 .... 136 E7
The Mcauley School
DONS/BSCR DN4 .... 91 L7
Meadow Bank
Industrial Estate
KIMB S61 .... 146 D1
Meadowhall Centre
DARN/MH S9 .... 146 A4
Meadowhall Junior School
KIMB S61 .... 146 C1
Meadowhall Retail Park
DARN/MH S9 .... 146 A4
Meadowhead School
SHEFS S8 .... 176 E8
Meadows Junior School
AU/AST/KP S26 .... 181 G4
Meadowview Industrial Estate
ARMTH DN3 .... 70 D1
Meersbrook Bank
Primary School
SHEFS S8 .... 176 D2
Melrose Surgery
OWL S3 .... 160 F1
Merlin Theatre
ABRD S7 .... 160 B8
Merlin Theatre
ST/HB/BR S6 .... 143 J6
Metrodomesports
& Leisurecomplexl
BSLYN/ROY S71 .... 3 J4
Mexborough Business Centre
MEX/SWTN S64 .... 108 F2
Mexborough
Comprehensive School
MEX/SWTN S64 .... 108 D1
Mexborough Windhill
Junior & Infant School
MEX/SWTN S64 .... 109 G1
Mill Road Surgery
CHPT/GREN S35 .... 126 F6
Mill Trading Estate
BSLYN/ROY S71 .... 3 M5
Minsthorpe Community College
HEM/SK/SE WF9 .... 42 D3
Minsthorpe Swimming Pool
HEM/SK/SE WF9 .... 42 E3
Monk Bretton Health Centre
BSLYN/ROY S71 .... 61 G3
Monksbridge Trading Estate
DIN S25 .... 166 A5
Monkwood Health Centre
RAW S62 .... 107 J8
Montagu Hospital
MEX/SWTN S64 .... 108 E1
Monteney Middle
& Primary School
SHEFN S5 .... 126 E8
Montgomery House
Medical Centre
ST/HB/BR S6 .... 160 C2
Montgomery Theatre
SHEF S1 .... 9 H4
Monument
DON DN1 .... 5 J5
Moorends Clinic
THNE DN8 .... 32 A4
Moorends Marshland
First School
THNE DN8 .... 32 B4

Moorgate Business Centre
RHAM S60 .... 7 G5
Moorgate Mosque
& Community Centre
RHAM S60 .... 6 F5
Moortop Special School
FEA/AMT WF7 .... 23 K3
Morley Place Junior School
CONI DN12 .... 109 L5
Mosborough Medical Centre
MOS S20 .... 179 G8
Mosborough Primary School
MOS S20 .... 179 H8
Mosque
OWL S3 .... 160 F1
Mosque
RHAM S60 .... 6 C4
Mossbrook Special School
SHEFS S8 .... 177 D2
Moss Road Infant School
AWLS/ASK DN6 .... 27 M7
The Mount Group Practice
DON DN1 .... 5 K3
Mount Osborne Industrial Park
BSLYN/ROY S71 .... 3 L6
Mount St Marys College
ECK/KIL S21 .... 194 A5
Mount Vernon Hospital
BSLY S70 .... 82 D1
Museum
ECC S11 .... 160 A7
Myers Grove School
ST/HB/BR S6 .... 143 L8
National Coal Mining
Museum for England
HOR/CROF WF4 .... 17 J2
National Music Centre
SHEF S1 .... 9 J6
The Nelson Practice
BTLY DN5 .... 67 J8
Nether Edge Hospital
ECC S11 .... 176 B1
Nether Green Infant School
FUL S10 .... 159 H7
Nether Green Junior School
FUL S10 .... 159 J7
Netherthorpe Primary School
OWL S3 .... 8 E2
Netherton Sitlington
Junior & Infant School
HOR/CROF WF4 .... 18 C1
Newfield School
SHEFS S8 .... 177 G4
The New Indoor Market
MALT S66 .... 150 E2
Newman Special School
RHAM S60 .... 147 L6
New Street Health Centre
BSLY S70 .... 2 F7
New Surgery
MEX/SWTN S64 .... 108 F3
Newton Business Centre
BTLY DN5 .... 89 K4
New Village Primary School
BTLY DN5 .... 67 M5
Nightingale Primary School
DONS/BSCR DN4 .... 111 J1
Nook Lane Junior School
ST/HB/BR S6 .... 143 G8
Norfolk Middle School
SHEFP/MNR S2 .... 161 J7
Norfolk Park Health Centre
SHEFP/MNR S2 .... 161 G7
North Anston Business Centre
DIN S25 .... 166 A7
North Border County
Secondary School
NROS/TKH DN11 .... 153 M2
North Border Infant School
NROS/TKH DN11 .... 153 M3
North Border Junior School
NROS/TKH DN11 .... 153 M3
Northcliffe School
CONI DN12 .... 109 L4
North East Derbyshire
District Council
DRON S18 .... 190 E6
North East Derbyshire
District Council
DRON S18 .... 190 F6
Northfield Junior School
DRON S18 .... 191 G4
Northfield School
HEM/SK/SE WF9 .... 42 A4
Northlands Community
Health Centre
SHEFN S5 .... 144 D3
North Notts College of Further
Education
WRKN S81 .... 198 D2
Northstead Surgery
BWTY DN10 .... 136 D8
Norton County Junior
& Infant School
AWLS/ASK DN6 .... 27 G4
Norton Free Primary School
SHEFS S8 .... 177 G6
Norton Oakes Cricket Club
SHEFS S8 .... 177 H6
Nortonthorpe Hall School
KBTN HD8 .... 35 H6
Nortonthorpe Industrial Estate
KBTN HD8 .... 35 H6
Notre Dame School
FUL S10 .... 159 L6
Nottingham County
Health Clinic
WRKN S81 .... 184 D1
Oakes Park Special School
SHEFS S8 .... 177 G5
Oakfield Junior School
WMB/DAR S73 .... 84 B5
Oak Tree School
FEA/AMT WF7 .... 23 K3
Oakwell Business Centre
BSLYN/ROY S71 .... 3 L6
Oakwood Surgery
DONS/BSCR DN4 .... 91 J8
Oakwood Swimming Baths
RHAM S60 .... 147 K4
Odeon Cinema
BSLY S70 .... 3 G4

Odeon Cinema
DON DN1 .... 5 H5
Odeon Cinema
SHEF S1 .... 9 J4
Old College of Technology
BSLY S70 .... 2 F4
Old Forge Business Park
SHEFP/MNR S2 .... 160 E8
Old Hall Comprehensive
School
KIMB S61 .... 128 C8
Ora Gallery
ECC S11 .... 160 B7
Orchard Infant School
BTLY DN5 .... 88 F7
Oughtibridge Primary School
CHPT/GREN S35 .... 125 H8
Our Lady of Sorrows RC
School
ARMTH DN3 .... 69 L8
Our Lady RC Primary School
BTLY DN5 .... 67 M6
Our Ladys & St Josephs RC
JMI School
DEARNE S63 .... 107 K1
Owlthorpe Surgery
MOS S20 .... 178 E5
Owston Skellow First School
AWLS/ASK DN6 .... 44 F5
Oxspring Junior
& Infant School
STKB/PEN S36 .... 79 M6
Parkgate Business Park
RAW S62 .... 129 K5
Parkgate Medical Centre
RAW S62 .... 129 K3
Park Health Centre
SHEFP/MNR S2 .... 9 L5
Park Hill Primary School
SHEFP/MNR S2 .... 9 L5
Park Infant School
WHHL DN2 .... 90 D1
Park Primary School
WHHL DN2 .... 90 D1
Park Road Infant School
MEX/SWTN S64 .... 108 E1
Park Street Junior
& Infant School
WMB/DAR S73 .... 84 C5
Parson Cross C of E
Primary School
ST/HB/BR S6 .... 144 B3
Peacock Trading Estate
ST/HB/BR S6 .... 144 C7
Penistone Grammar School
STKB/PEN S36 .... 79 G2
Penistone Group Practice
STKB/PEN S36 .... 79 H4
Penistone Sports Centre
STKB/PEN S36 .... 79 G3
Penistone Springvale
JMI School
STKB/PEN S36 .... 79 K4
Penistone Thurlstone
JMI School
STKB/PEN S36 .... 78 E3
The Petersgate
Medical Centre
BTLY DN5 .... 67 J7
Peveril School of Art
ECC S11 .... 159 M7
Pheasant Bank Junior School
NROS/TKH DN11 .... 113 J6
Phillimore Park
School
DARN/MH S9 .... 161 M1
Phoenix Surgery
DON DN1 .... 5 H5
Phoenix Theatre
BWTY DN10 .... 136 E8
Picture Drome
Cinema Museum
HOLM/MEL HD7 .... 53 K2
Pipworth Junior School
SHEFP/MNR S2 .... 161 M6
Pitsmoor Dental Health Centre
ATT S4 .... 144 F8
Pitsmoor Surgery
OWL S3 .... 144 E8
Platts Common
Industrial Estate
HOY S74 .... 83 H8
Plumb Estates
ARMTH DN3 .... 69 H5
Plumtree Farm Estate
NROS/TKH DN11 .... 154 A2
Pollington Balne C of E School
GLE DN14 .... 11 J4
Ponds Forge International
Sports Centre
SHEF S1 .... 9 K4
Pontefract Road Junior &
Infant School
CUD/GR S72 .... 39 M7
Porter Croft School
ECC S11 .... 8 C9
Portland Business Park
HAN/WDH S13 .... 162 C6
Primary School
HTFD DN7 .... 48 E8
Prince Edward Middle School
SHEFP/MNR S2 .... 161 L8
Prince Edward Primary School
SHEFP/MNR S2 .... 161 L8
Prince of Wales Road
Medical Centre
DARN/MH S9 .... 162 A4
Priory Business Park
HEM/SK/SE WF9 .... 22 F3
Priory School
DONS/BSCR DN4 .... 91 J8
Prospect Hill Junior & Infant
School
WRKN S81 .... 198 F1
Public Baths
DEARNE S63 .... 107 K1
Public Baths
ST/HB/BR S6 .... 8 C1
Public Swimming Baths
ECK/KIL S21 .... 193 M1

Pye Bank Trinity C of E Junior
School
OWL S3 .... 160 F1
Queens Medical Centre
MALT S66 .... 150 E2
Queens Road Clinic
BSLYN/ROY S71 .... 3 H5
Queen Street Junior & Infant
School
MEX/SWTN S64 .... 108 B4
Railwaymens Sports Club
BSLYN/ROY S71 .... 39 J3
Ranby C of E Primary School
RTFD DN22 .... 186 E8
Ranby House Preparatory
School
RTFD DN22 .... 186 F8
Ranskill Primary School
RTFD DN22 .... 170 F2
Ravenfield Junior & Infant
School
RHAM/THRY S65 .... 131 H6
Rawmarsh Leisure Centre
RAW S62 .... 129 L3
Rawmarsh Monkwood
Jmi School
RAW S62 .... 107 J8
Rawmarsh Thorogate
Junior & Infant School
RAW S62 .... 107 K8
Redbrook Business Park
DOD/DAR S75 .... 59 M2
Redscope Junior
& Infant School
KIMB S61 .... 128 C6
Reflex Theatre
SHEFS S8 .... 176 E1
Regent Square Group Practice
DON DN1 .... 5 J4
Register Office
DON DN1 .... 5 J6
Reignhead Primary School
MOS S20 .... 179 K4
Renishaw Primary School
ECK/KIL S21 .... 193 M7
Richard Newman Infant School
BSLYN/ROY S71 .... 38 D8
The Richmond Fellowship
MEX/SWTN S64 .... 108 B4
Richmond Hill Junior
& Infant School
BTLY DN5 .... 89 J4
Richmond Medical Centre
HAN/WDH S13 .... 162 B8
Ridgeway Medical Centre
RHAM/THRY S65 .... 130 A8
Ridgeway Primary School
HACK/IN S12 .... 178 C7
Ridgewood Comprehensive
School
BTLY DN5 .... 89 G1
Rivelin Primary School
ST/HB/BR S6 .... 143 M8
Riverside Business Park
KBTN HD8 .... 35 H5
Robin Hood Golf Club
AWLS/ASK DN6 .... 45 J4
Rockingham Business Park
BSLY S70 .... 104 D1
Rockingham College of Further
Education
DEARNE S63 .... 107 J1
Rockingham Junior & Infant
School
KIMB S61 .... 128 D4
Rockley Mount School
BSLY S70 .... 2 A9
Rose Court Surgery
MALT S66 .... 148 E3
Rosedale Middle School
BTLY DN5 .... 67 H8
Rosedale Road Infant School
BTLY DN5 .... 67 H8
Rossington Comprehensive
School
NROS/TKH DN11 .... 113 L3
Rossington Hall School
NROS/TKH DN11 .... 136 B1
Rossington Parish Council
NROS/TKH DN11 .... 113 H6
Rossington Swimming Pool
NROS/TKH DN11 .... 113 K5
Rotherham Borough Council
MALT S66 .... 165 J1
Rotherham Civic Theatre
RHAM/THRY S65 .... 7 G4
Rotherham College of Arts &
Technology
RHAM/THRY S65 .... 7 G3
Rotherham County Court
RHAM S60 .... 7 G5
Rotherham District General
Hospital
RHAM S60 .... 147 K5
Rotherham Health Authority
RHAM S60 .... 147 J5
Rotherham Health Authority
RHAM/THRY S65 .... 7 M4
Rotherham Magistrates Court
RHAM S60 .... 6 E4
Rotherham Metropolitan
Borough Council
MALT S66 .... 149 H2
Rotherham Metropolitan
Borough Council
MALT S66 .... 165 J1
Rotherham Metropolitan
Borough Council
RAW S62 .... 129 J2
Rotherham Metropolitan
Borough Council
RHAM S60 .... 6 F5
Rotherham Metropolitan
Borough Council
RHAM S60 .... 6 E2
Rotherham Metropolitan
Borough Council
RHAM/THRY S65 .... 7 G4
Rotherham Metropolitan
Borough Council
RHAM/THRY S65 .... 7 G2

Rotherham Priority
 Health Trust
 RHAM/THRY S65 .... 7 G4
Rotherham Road
 Medical Centre
 BSLYN/ROY S71 .... 60 E1
Rotherham Rugby Club
 RHAM/THRY S65 .... 7 J6
Rotherham Town Cricket Club
 RHAM/THRY S65 .... 7 J6
Rotherham Town Hall
 RHAM S60 .... 6 F5
Rotherham United
 Football Club
 RHAM S60 .... 6 B5
Rotunda Business Centre
 CHPT/GREN S35 .... 104 D8
Roughwood Junior School
 KIMB S61 .... 128 C5
Rowan School
 TOT/DORE S17 .... 189 J1
Rowena Infant School
 CONI DN12 .... 109 M5
Royal Hallamshire Hospital
 FUL S10 .... 8 B6
Royston Clinic
 BSLYN/ROY S71 .... 39 G4
Royston Comprehensive
 School
 BSLYN/ROY S71 .... 39 G3
Royston Meadstead
 Junior School
 BSLYN/ROY S71 .... 38 F4
Royston Midland Junior
 & Infant School
 BSLYN/ROY S71 .... 39 G3
Royston St John Baptist C E (A)
 Primary School
 BSLYN/ROY S71 .... 39 G4
RSPCA Centre
 BWTY DN10 .... 136 C2
Rudston Preparatory School
 RHAM/THRY S65 .... 7 K7
Ruskin Gallery
 SHEF S1 .... 9 H5
Rustlings Road Medical Centre
 ECC S11 .... 159 L7
Rutland Business Park
 OWL S3 .... 160 D1
Ryecroft Infant School
 RAW S62 .... 129 L1
Ryhill County Primary School
 HOR/CROF WF4 .... 21 M6
Ryton Park Primary School
 WRKS S80 .... 198 D5
Sacred Heart R C Primary
 School
 ST/HB/BR S6 .... 144 A8
St Aidans C of E First School
 KBTN HD8 .... 34 E6
St Albans Junior & Infant
 School
 MALT S66 .... 148 F3
St Albans RC School
 CONI DN12 .... 109 L4
St Andrews C of E Methodist
 Aided School
 DRON S18 .... 190 B6
St Annes Infant School
 WRKS S80 .... 198 B5
St Ann Medical Centre
 RHAM/THRY S65 .... 6 F4
St Anns Surgery
 KIMB S61 .... 128 C6
St Augustines County Junior
 School
 WRKN S81 .... 198 F3
St Bedes Primary School
 KIMB S61 .... 128 C7
St Bernards RC School
 RHAM/THRY S65 .... 130 A7
St Catherines RC Primary
 School
 OWL S3 .... 144 E7
St Francis Xavier RC School
 DONS/BSCR DN4 .... 4 E8
St Georges Church
 SHEF S1 .... 8 E4
St Georges Hospital
 OWL S3 .... 8 C3
St Giles C of E (Aided) Primary
 School
 ECK/KIL S21 .... 194 A1
St Helens Junior & Infant
 School
 BSLYN/ROY S71 .... 61 J1
St James C of E Junior & Infant
 School
 HOR/CROF WF4 .... 19 J1
St James Swimming Pool
 DON DN1 .... 5 G6
St John Fisher RC Junior
 & Infants School
 HACK/IN S12 .... 178 E4
St Johns C of E Infants School
 STKB/PEN S36 .... 79 G5
St Johns C of E (Park) Primary
 School
 SHEFP/MNR S2 .... 161 H4
St Johns C of E Primary School
 WRKN S81 .... 184 C8
St Johns C of E School
 MEX/SWTN S64 .... 108 F1
St John the Baptist C of E
 (Aided) Junior School
 STKB/PEN S36 .... 79 G5
St Josephs Junior & Infants
 School
 RAW S62 .... 129 K2
St Josephs School
 NROS/TKH DN11 .... 113 K6
St Lukes C of E School
 WRKN S81 .... 183 K7
St Maries R C Primary School
 FUL S10 .... 159 L6
St Marys Catholic School
 CONI DN12 .... 110 E5
St Mary School
 FUL S10 .... 160 A2
St Marys C of E Junior & Infant
 School
 DOD/DAR S75 .... 2 B4

St Marys C of E Junior & Infant
 School
 RAW S62 .... 129 K2
St Marys C of E Primary School
 ST/HB/BR S6 .... 160 B1
St Marys High Green RC Primary
 School
 CHPT/GREN S35 .... 104 C7
St Marys RC School
 RHAM/THRY S65 .... 148 A1
St Marys School
 DONS/BSCR DN4 .... 91 H7
St Marys School
 DRON S18 .... 191 K7
St Matthews Infant School
 DOD/DAR S75 .... 2 B3
St Michaels C of E School
 HATH/EY S32 .... 172 E7
St Michaels C of E School
 NROS/TKH DN11 .... 113 M6
St Michaels RC Comprehensive
 School
 BSLYN/ROY S71 .... 38 F8
St Michaels RC Junior
 & Infant School
 WMB/DAR S73 .... 84 D3
St Oswalds RC Primary School
 SHEFP/MNR S2 .... 161 J5
St Patricks Primary School
 NROS/TKH DN11 .... 153 M3
St Patricks RC School
 SHEFN S5 .... 145 G3
St Peters RC Primary School
 DONS/BSCR DN4 .... 90 E6
St Theresas School
 SHEFP/MNR S2 .... 161 M8
St Thomas More RC Primary
 School
 CHPT/GREN S35 .... 126 B8
St Thomas of Canterbury RC
 Primary School
 SHEFS S8 .... 176 D7
Saint Vincent Medical Centre
 DON DN1 .... 5 J3
St Wilfreds C of E (A) Junior
 & Infant School
 ARMTH DN3 .... 92 B7
St Wilfrids RC Primary School
 ABRD S7 .... 176 A3
Sandall Wood School
 WHHL DN2 .... 91 H2
Sandhill J M I School
 RAW S62 .... 130 A1
Sandhill Primary School
 CUD/GR S72 .... 63 J6
The Sandringham Practice
 WHHL DN2 .... 90 F2
Sarahs Gallery
 NROS/TKH DN11 .... 134 E8
Savoy Squash Club
 KBTN HD8 .... 34 E5
Scawsby College
 BTLY DN5 .... 89 G1
Scawsby Health Centre
 BTLY DN5 .... 89 J1
Scawthorpe Clinic
 BTLY DN5 .... 67 J8
Scholes Cricket Club
 HOLM/MEL HD7 .... 54 B4
Scholes Junior & Infant School
 HOLM/MEL HD7 .... 54 B4
Scissett Middle School
 KBTN HD8 .... 35 H5
Scissett Swimming Baths
 KBTN HD8 .... 35 J5
Serlby Park Golf Club
 BWTY DN10 .... 154 C8
Shafton Two Gates Junior
 & Infant School
 CUD/GR S72 .... 40 A5
Shardlows Sports Club
 CHPT/GREN S35 .... 126 F5
Sharrow Junior School
 ECC S11 .... 160 D7
Shawlands Junior & Infant
 School
 BSLY S70 .... 2 C7
Shaw Lane Industrial Estate
 WHHL DN2 .... 69 J7
Shaw Wood Junior & Infant
 School
 ARMTH DN3 .... 69 L7
Sheaf Gardens Industrial Estate
 SHEFP/MNR S2 .... 9 J8
Sheaf Market
 SHEF S1 .... 9 K3
Sheffield Area Health Authority
 Sports & Social Club
 ECC S11 .... 159 H8
Sheffield Area Health Authority
 (Teaching)
 FUL S10 .... 8 B5
Sheffield City Council
 ATT S4 .... 144 F8
Sheffield City Council
 ATT S4 .... 145 G7
Sheffield City Council
 ATT S4 .... 161 G2
Sheffield City Council
 CHPT/GREN S35 .... 126 B8
Sheffield City Council
 DARN/MH S9 .... 146 A6
Sheffield City Council
 DARN/MH S9 .... 162 A3
Sheffield City Council
 HACK/IN S12 .... 178 C4
Sheffield City Council
 HAN/WDH S13 .... 178 F1
Sheffield City Council
 MOS S20 .... 179 J5
Sheffield City Council
 OWL S3 .... 8 E4
Sheffield City Council
 OWL S3 .... 160 E1
Sheffield City Council
 SHEF S1 .... 9 H4
Sheffield City Council
 SHEF S1 .... 9 J3
Sheffield City Council
 SHEFN S5 .... 127 J8
Sheffield City Council
 SHEFP/MNR S2 .... 9 L4

Sheffield City Council
 SHEFP/MNR S2 .... 160 F7
Sheffield City Council
 SHEFP/MNR S2 .... 161 J4
Sheffield City Council
 SHEFP/MNR S2 .... 161 L8
Sheffield City Council
 SHEFP/MNR S2 .... 177 H2
Sheffield City Council
 SHEFS S8 .... 176 E2
Sheffield City Council
 SHEFS S8 .... 190 C1
Sheffield City Council
 ST/HB/BR S6 .... 8 C1
Sheffield City Council
 ST/HB/BR S6 .... 8 D1
Sheffield City Council
 ST/HB/BR S6 .... 144 A7
The Sheffield College
 MOS S20 .... 179 K7
The Sheffield College
 SHEFN S5 .... 126 D8
The Sheffield College
 SHEFP/MNR S2 .... 9 L8
The Sheffield College
 SHEFS S8 .... 176 F8
Sheffield Eagles RLFC
 DARN/MH S9 .... 161 L1
Sheffield Hallam University
 FUL S10 .... 8 B8
Sheffield Hallam University
 FUL S10 .... 8 B6
Sheffield Hallam University
 SHEF S1 .... 9 J5
Sheffield Health Authority
 CHPT/GREN S35 .... 125 H8
Sheffield Health Authority
 SHEFN S5 .... 145 H3
Sheffield High School
 ECC S11 .... 160 A5
Sheffield Magistrates Court
 SHEF S1 .... 9 J3
Sheffield Medical Centre
 OWL S3 .... 161 G2
Sheffield Natural Health Centre
 SHEFS S8 .... 160 D8
Sheffield Sports Stadium Ltd
 ST/HB/BR S6 .... 144 B6
Sheffield Technology Park
 DARN/MH S9 .... 161 K1
Sheffield United AFC
 SHEFP/MNR S2 .... 9 H9
Sheffield United Cricket Club
 DARN/MH S9 .... 146 D6
Sheffield Wednesday Football
 Club
 ST/HB/BR S6 .... 144 A5
Shelley High School
 KBTN HD8 .... 34 C5
Shirecliffe Junior School
 SHEFN S5 .... 144 C5
Shire Green Medical Centre
 SHEFN S5 .... 145 J1
Shireoaks Business Centre
 WRKN S81 .... 197 L1
Shireoaks Miners Welfare
 & Sports Club
 WRKN S81 .... 197 K1
Shooters Grove Primary School
 ST/HB/BR S6 .... 143 K8
Shopping Centre
 BSLY S70 .... 3 G5
Shopping Centre
 RAW S62 .... 129 J2
Shortbrook Primary School
 MOS S20 .... 179 K7
Shrewsbury Hospital
 SHEFP/MNR S2 .... 9 M6
Sikh Temple
 ATT S4 .... 145 G8
Sikh Temple
 DON DN1 .... 5 G6
Silverdale School
 ECC S11 .... 175 J2
Sir Edmund Hillary County
 Primary School
 WRKN S81 .... 198 E3
Sir Harold Jackson Primary
 School
 TOT/DORE S17 .... 189 M2
Sitwell Junior & Infants School
 RHAM S60 .... 147 M4
Skelmanthorpe Business Park
 KBTN HD8 .... 34 E5
The Sloan Practice
 SHEFS S8 .... 177 H5
Sothall Medical Centre
 MOS S20 .... 179 K5
Sothall Snooker & Leisure
 Centre
 MOS S20 .... 179 K4
South Cantley Middle School
 DONS/BSCR DN4 .... 113 K1
South Elmsall Ash Grove Junior
 & Infant School
 HEM/SK/SE WF9 .... 42 E3
South Elmsall Health Centre
 HEM/SK/SE WF9 .... 42 D4
Southey Green Medical Centre
 SHEFN S5 .... 144 D4
Southey Hill Surgery
 SHEFN S5 .... 144 D3
South Kirkby Common Road
 School
 HEM/SK/SE WF9 .... 41 L6
South Kirkby First School
 HEM/SK/SE WF9 .... 42 C4
South Yorkshire Business Centre
 RAW S62 .... 129 J5
Springfield Primary School
 OWL S3 .... 8 E6
Springwood Junior & Infant
 School
 HOY S74 .... 105 H2
Sprotbrough Health Centre
 BTLY DN5 .... 89 J5
Stag Medical Centre
 RHAM/THRY S65 .... 148 A4
Stainforth Middle School
 HTFD DN7 .... 48 C3
Stairfoot Health Centre
 BSLY S70 .... 61 H8

Standbridge Primary School
 WKFDW/WTN WF2 .... 19 L2
Staniland Yacht Club
 THNE DN8 .... 31 K8
Stanley Street County Primary
 School
 WRKN S81 .... 198 C2
Stannington Health Centre
 ST/HB/BR S6 .... 159 G1
Stannington Infant School
 ST/HB/BR S6 .... 159 G1
Station Road Industrial Estate
 WMB/DAR S73 .... 84 C4
Station Road Junior & Infant
 School
 CONI DN12 .... 110 A4
Steed Court Business Park
 HEM/SK/SE WF9 .... 25 G7
Stirling First School
 DON DN1 .... 4 F7
Stirling Junior School
 DON DN1 .... 5 G7
Stockingate First School
 HEM/SK/SE WF9 .... 41 L8
Stockingate Surgery
 HEM/SK/SE WF9 .... 41 M5
Stocksbridge Golf Club
 STKB/PEN S36 .... 102 B8
Stocksbridge High School
 STKB/PEN S36 .... 101 M6
Stocksbridge Junior School
 STKB/PEN S36 .... 101 M7
Stocksbridge Leisure Centre
 STKB/PEN S36 .... 101 L6
Stocksbridge Rugby Club
 STKB/PEN S36 .... 101 M5
Stonelow Junior School
 DRON S18 .... 190 F5
Storm House School
 DEARNE S63 .... 86 A8
Stradbroke Primary School
 HAN/WDH S13 .... 162 B8
Sues Health Centre
 BSLYN/ROY S71 .... 38 E7
Summerfields Junior & Infants
 School
 BSLYN/ROY S71 .... 38 E3
Summer Lane Primary School
 DOD/DAR S75 .... 2 B3
Sunday School
 DEARNE S63 .... 63 M7
Superbowl Two Thousand
 KIMB S61 .... 128 C7
Superintendent Swimming
 Baths
 CHPT/GREN S35 .... 126 E2
Sutton Cum Lound C of E
 School
 RTFD DN22 .... 187 L1
Swallownest Health Centre
 AU/AST/KP S26 .... 164 B8
Swinton Brookfield Primary
 School
 MEX/SWTN S64 .... 108 B5
Swinton Comprehensive School
 MEX/SWTN S64 .... 108 A5
Swinton Fitzwilliam Infants
 School
 MEX/SWTN S64 .... 107 M5
Swinton Meadows Business Park
 MEX/SWTN S64 .... 108 D4
Swinton Meadows
 Industrial Estate
 MEX/SWTN S64 .... 108 D4
Swinton Milton Special School
 MEX/SWTN S64 .... 108 A4
Swinton Swimming Pool
 MEX/SWTN S64 .... 108 B4
Sycamore Hall
 Preparatory School
 DONS/BSCR DN4 .... 89 L8
Tapton Secondary School
 FUL S10 .... 159 L5
Tates Gallery
 DARN/MH S9 .... 162 A3
Tates Gallery
 ST/HB/BR S6 .... 144 A7
Technical College
 WRKN S81 .... 184 E4
Templeborough Business
 Centre
 RHAM S60 .... 6 D8
Tertiary College
 ECK/KIL S21 .... 193 H4
Thomas Rotherham College
 RHAM S60 .... 7 H7
Thornbridge School
 HACK/IN S12 .... 178 B5
Thorne Golf Club
 THNE DN8 .... 49 K2
Thorne Grammar School
 THNE DN8 .... 32 A7
Thorne Health Centre
 THNE DN8 .... 31 M8
Thorne South Common
 First School
 THNE DN8 .... 50 A1
Thorne Swimming Baths
 THNE DN8 .... 32 A8
Thornhill Industrial Estate
 KIMB S61 .... 6 D1
Thornhill Jmi School
 RHAM S60 .... 6 C3
Thorpe Hesley Clinic
 KIMB S61 .... 127 K3
Thorpe Hesley Infant School
 KIMB S61 .... 127 J3
Thorpe Hesley Junior School
 KIMB S61 .... 127 K3
Thrybergh Comprehensive
 School
 RHAM/THRY S65 .... 130 D4
Thrybergh Fullerton Church of
 England J & I School
 RHAM/THRY S65 .... 130 D4
Thrybergh Medical Centre
 RHAM/THRY S65 .... 130 D5
Thrybergh St Gerards RC M & I
 School
 RHAM/THRY S65 .... 130 B5
Thurcroft Infant School
 MALT S66 .... 165 J1

Thurcroft Junior Mixed School
 MALT S66 .... 165 K1
Thurgoland C of E Primary
 School
 CHPT/GREN S35 .... 80 D8
Thurnscoe Business Centre
 DEARNE S63 .... 64 C8
Thurnscoe Business Park
 DEARNE S63 .... 64 C8
Thurnscoe Gooseacre J M School
 DEARNE S63 .... 64 A6
Tickfield Eastfield Primary
 School
 NROS/TKH DN11 .... 134 E7
Tickhill C of E School
 NROS/TKH DN11 .... 134 D8
Tinsley Junior School
 DARN/MH S9 .... 146 C5
Todwick Jmi School
 AU/AST/KP S26 .... 181 J2
Tornedale Infant School
 NROS/TKH DN11 .... 113 K6
Totley All Saints C of E
 Primary School
 TOT/DORE S17 .... 189 G3
Totley Primary School
 TOT/DORE S17 .... 189 H3
Town Fields Primary School
 WHHL DN2 .... 5 K3
Trafalgar House Medical Centre
 ST/HB/BR S6 .... 144 B3
Tramways Medical Centre
 ST/HB/BR S6 .... 144 A7
Travis County Primary School
 HTFD DN7 .... 49 G7
Treeton C of E Junior
 & Infant School
 RHAM S60 .... 163 J3
U C I Cinema
 MOS S20 .... 179 J4
University of Sheffield
 ECC S11 .... 159 M6
University of Sheffield
 FUL S10 .... 8 B5
University of Sheffield
 FUL S10 .... 8 C6
University of Sheffield
 FUL S10 .... 8 C6
University of Sheffield
 FUL S10 .... 160 A4
University of Sheffield
 OWL S3 .... 8 C4
University of Sheffield
 SHEF S1 .... 8 F4
Unstone Junior School
 DRON S18 .... 191 J8
Untitled Gallery
 SHEF S1 .... 9 J6
Upperthong Junior
 & Infant School
 HOLM/MEL HD7 .... 53 J3
Upper Whitley Junior
 & Infant School
 HOR/CROF WF4 .... 16 C3
Upperwood Junior
 & Infant School
 WMB/DAR S73 .... 84 D1
Upton A R L F C
 HEM/SK/SE WF9 .... 24 F7
Upton Clinic
 HEM/SK/SE WF9 .... 25 H7
Upton Surgery
 HEM/SK/SE WF9 .... 25 G7
Valley Medical Centre
 STKB/PEN S36 .... 101 M5
Verdon Recreation Centre
 OWL S3 .... 160 F2
Victoria Middle School
 CONI DN12 .... 110 F4
Victoria Primary School
 DEARNE S63 .... 107 L1
The Village Surgery
 MALT S66 .... 165 K3
Wadworth County
 Primary School
 NROS/TKH DN11 .... 134 A1
Wakefield College
 HEM/SK/SE WF9 .... 23 J8
Wakefield Golf Club
 WKFDW/WTN WF2 .... 20 C1
Wakefield Independent
 Junior School
 HOR/CROF WF4 .... 22 D1
Wakefield Metropolitan District
 Council
 HEM/SK/SE WF9 .... 23 H8
Wakefield Metropolitan District
 Council
 HEM/SK/SE WF9 .... 42 D5
Wales High School
 AU/AST/KP S26 .... 181 G4
Wales Junior & Infant School
 AU/AST/KP S26 .... 180 F5
Walkley Medical Centre
 FUL S10 .... 160 A1
Walk Talk Galleries
 ECC S11 .... 159 M7
Waltheof School
 SHEFP/MNR S2 .... 161 M5
Ward Green Junior School
 BSLY S70 .... 82 D2
Warmsworth Primary School
 DONS/BSCR DN4 .... 111 G1
Warren House Surgery
 BSLY S70 .... 3 H8
Watergate Centre
 DON DN1 .... 5 G5
Waterton Park Golf Club
 WKFDW/WTN WF2 .... 21 G1
Wath C of E Jmi School
 DEARNE S63 .... 85 J3
Wath Park Infant School
 DEARNE S63 .... 107 J2
Wath Pope Pius R C
 Secondary School
 DEARNE S63 .... 107 L3
Wath R U F C
 DEARNE S63 .... 85 K8
Wath Upon Dearne
 Comprehensive School
 DEARNE S63 .... 107 K2

Wath West Industrial Estate
DEARNE S63 .... **85** G7
Waverley Junior School
DONS/BSCR DN4 .... **111** J1
Welfare Clinic
ECK/KIL S21 .... **193** H4
Wellgate Infant School
DOD/DAR S75 .... **37** M6
Wentworth Castle College of Education
DOD/DAR S75 .... **81** K4
Wentworth C of E School
RAW S62 .... **105** L6
West Bretton Junior & Infant School
HOR/CROF WF4 .... **18** D7
Westfield Health Centre
MOS S20 .... **179** J7
West Melton J & I School
DEARNE S63 .... **85** G8
Weston Park Hospital N H S Trust
FUL S10 .... **8** A5
West Road First School
THNE DN8 .... **32** B4
Westside Gallery
ECC S11 .... **8** C9
Westways Middle Primary School
FUL S10 .... **160** A3
Wharncliffe Side Primary School
CHPT/GREN S35 .... **124** E5
Wheatley Hall Business Centre
WHHL DN2 .... **68** E8

Whiston Grange School
RHAM S60 .... **147** L6
Whiston Junior & Infant School
RHAM S60 .... **147** M6
Whiston Worry Goose Jmi School
RHAM S60 .... **148** B6
White House Surgery
SHEFP/MNR S2 .... **161** M7
Whitelea Grove Trading Estate
MEX/SWTN S64 .... **108** C3
Whiteley Wood Clinic
ECC S11 .... **159** J8
White Rose Surgery
HEM/SK/SE WF9 .... **42** D4
Whiteways Junior School
ATT S4 .... **145** H7
Whitley Hall Cricket Club
CHPT/GREN S35 .... **126** C6
Wickersley Comprehensive School
MALT S66 .... **149** G3
Wickersley Health Centre
MALT S66 .... **148** F2
William Levick Infant School
DRON S18 .... **190** A5
William Levick Primary School
DRON S18 .... **190** A5
Wilsic Hall School
NROS/TKH DN11 .... **133** L3
Wilthorpe Junior School
DOD/DAR S75 .... **60** A3
Wincobank Surgery
DARN/MH S9 .... **145** M3

Windmill Hill Primary School
CHPT/GREN S35 .... **126** D3
Wingfield Comprehensive School
KIMB S61 .... **128** E5
Wisewood Secondary School
ST/HB/BR S6 .... **143** K6
Wombwell Aldham Junior & Infant School
WMB/DAR S73 .... **83** L4
Wombwell Clinic
WMB/DAR S73 .... **84** A4
Wombwell Cricket Club
WMB/DAR S73 .... **83** M5
Wombwell High School
WMB/DAR S73 .... **84** C6
Wombwell Jump Junior & Infant School
HOY S74 .... **83** K8
Wombwell Public Baths
WMB/DAR S73 .... **84** B5
Woodfield First School
DONS/BSCR DN4 .... **111** M1
Woodgrove Surgery
DEARNE S63 .... **107** K1
Woodhouse Clinic
HAN/WDH S13 .... **178** F1
Woodhouse Medical Centre
HAN/WDH S13 .... **178** F1
Woodlands East RC School
AWLS/ASK DN6 .... **67** G3
Woodlands First School
AWLS/ASK DN6 .... **66** E3
Woodlands Middle School
AWLS/ASK DN6 .... **66** E3

Woodseats Medical Centre
SHEFS S8 .... **176** D5
Woodseats Primary School
SHEFS S8 .... **176** D4
Woodsetts Infant School
WRKN S81 .... **183** J3
Woodsetts Junior & Infant School
WRKN S81 .... **183** J3
Woodside Surgery
AWLS/ASK DN6 .... **66** E4
Woodstock Bower Group Practice
KIMB S61 .... **146** E1
Woodthorpe Community Primary School
HAN/WDH S13 .... **162** A8
Woolley Hall College
HOR/CROF WF4 .... **19** M8
Works
ARMTH DN3 .... **69** H3
Works
RHAM/THRY S65 .... **130** A4
Worksop College
WRKS S80 .... **198** F8
Worksop Cricket & Sports Club
WRKS S80 .... **198** C4
Worksop Hartland Comprehensive School
WRKS S80 .... **198** D7
Worksop Leisure Centre
WRKN S81 .... **198** C2
Worksop Portland Comprehensive School
WRKS S80 .... **198** D7

Worksop Redlands County Primary School
WRKS S80 .... **198** B3
Worksop Valley Comprehensive School
WRKN S81 .... **198** C2
Worsbrough Bridge RC School
BSLY S70 .... **82** F2
Worsbrough C of E Junior & Infant School
BSLY S70 .... **82** D6
Worsbrough Common County Primary School
BSLY S70 .... **82** D1
Worsbrough Health Centre
BSLY S70 .... **82** F2
Worsbrough High School
BSLY S70 .... **83** H3
Worsbrough Mill Museum
BSLY S70 .... **82** E4
W R C C Clinic
HTFD DN7 .... **48** C4
Wybourn Primary School
SHEFP/MNR S2 .... **161** H4
Yewlands School
CHPT/GREN S35 .... **126** C8
Yews Day Hospital
CHPT/GREN S35 .... **143** H3
York House Medical Centre
SHEFP/MNR S2 .... **161** K7
Yorkshire Neurology Clinic
MALT S66 .... **148** E3
Yorkshire Sculpture Park
HOR/CROF WF4 .... **18** C8

Page 60
A3 1 Huddersfield Rd 2 Moorbank Cl 3 Redbrook St 4 Wilthorpe Gn
A4 1 Cottesmore Cl 2 Grenville Pl 3 Ketton Wk 4 Queensway
A5 1 Helensburgh Cl 2 The Lindales 3 Myrtle St 4 Sycamore St
A6 1 South St
A8 1 Keresforth Hill Rd
B3 1 Dearnley Vw
B4 1 Carrington St 2 Lingard St 3 Thorntree La 4 Westbourne Gv
B5 1 Buckden Rd 2 Darley Ter 3 Hilton St 4 Johnson St 5 Keir St 6 Lingard Ct 7 Newton St 8 Rock St 9 Somerset St 10 Southwell St 11 Summer St
B6 1 Dean St 2 Hindle St 3 Knowsley St 4 McIntock Wy 5 Nicholas St 6 Perseverance St 7 Pitt St West 8 Richard St 9 Richmond St 10 Springfield Pl 11 Stanhope St 12 Stanley St 13 Waterloo Rd 14 Well St 15 Westfield St
B7 1 Cranbrook St 2 Fife St 3 Helena Ct 4 Leopold St 5 Sandford Ct
B8 1 Dyson St 2 Ellington Ct 3 Kingstone Pl
C4 1 Burton St 2 Cavendish Rd 3 Lombard Ct 4 Wentworth St
C5 1 Aireton Rd 2 Churchfield 3 Church La 4 Church St 5 Eastgate 6 Lancaster Ga 7 Rosehill Ct 8 Sadler Ga 9 St Mary's Ga 10 St Mary's Pl 11 Victoria St 12 Westwood Ct
C6 1 Beaconsfield St 2 Fenton St 3 George Sq 4 Graham's Orch 5 Holden Ct 6 Lower Castlereagh St 7 Mark St 8 Nelson St 9 Peel Sq 10 Plumber St 11 Royal St 12 Wortley St 13 York St
C7 1 Fleming Pl 2 Lower Thomas St
C8 1 California Ter 2 Highstone V
D1 1 Ledbury Rd
D2 1 Reasbeck Ter 2 Whitbourne Cl
D3 1 Wheatley Cl
D4 1 Aylesford Cl 2 Leighton Cl 3 Sandbeck Cl 4 Windham Cl
D5 1 Denton St 2 Hanson St 3 Harborough Hill Rd 4 Redfearn St 5 Vernon St North
D6 1 Burleigh Ct 2 Burlington Ar 3 Cheapside 4 Freemans Yd 5 Hayes Cft 6 Malthouse Rd 7 May Day Gn 8 Midland St 9 Pall Mall 10 Sherwood St 11 Wesley St
D7 1 Britannia Cl 2 Buckley St 3 Copper Cl 4 Denison Ct 5 Duke Crs 6 Duke St 7 Freeman St 8 Providence Ct 9 Quarry St 10 Rebecca Ms 11 Rosebery Ter 12 Taylor Rw 13 Upper New St 14 Warren St
D8 1 California Crs 2 Chestnut Pl 3 Dickinson Pl 4 Dickinson Rd 5 Essex Rd 6 Frederic Rd 7 Hornby St 8 Howard St 9 Kelsey Ter 10 Kenworthy Rd 11 Stoneleigh Cft 12 Warren Pl
E1 1 Kingsley Cl
E2 1 Dunmere Cl 2 Edgecliffe Rd 3 Quarry St
E4 1 Wharf St
E6 1 Crasmere Rd 2 Grenville St 3 Market Cl 4 Thirlmere Rd 5 Windermere Rd
E7 1 Clifton St 2 Cold Cft 3 Henshall St 4 Milnes St 5 Oakwell Ter 6 Osborne Ms 7 St Peter's Ter 8 Seth Ter 9 Sunderland St 10 Victoria Ter 11 Willby La
F1 1 Crown Av 2 Crown St 3 Harriet Ct 4 Winton Cl
F1 1 Haddon Rd
F2 1 Browning Cl
F3 1 Edinburgh Cl
F4 1 Carbis Cl 2 Haworth Cl 3 Roche Cl 4 Sennen Cft 5 Sheridan Ct 6 Trewan Ct
F6 1 Beevor Ct
F7 1 Applehurst Bank 2 Evelyn Ter 3 Lulworth Ct 4 Pindar Oaks Cottages 5 Pindar St

Page 61
G2 1 The Ridings
G3 1 Farm Cl 2 Hunt Ct 3 Norman Cl 4 Spring Gdns
G4 1 Bude Ct 2 Chapter Wy 3 Cliffe La 4 Mylor Ct 5 St Lukes Wy
G7 1 Lambert Wk
G8 1 Colley Pl 2 Thornton Ter
H1 1 Edenfield Cl 2 Formby Ct 3 Longridge Rd 4 Walney Fold
H2 1 Blundell St 2 Larchfield Rd 3 Morton Cl
H4 1 Brookvale 2 Rectory Wy 3 Temple Wy
H7 1 Doncaster Rd 2 Kenwood Cl 3 Malcolm St
I7 1 Hunningley La 2 Neville Ct
J3 1 Abbey Sq 2 Hickson Dr
J7 1 Darrington Cl
J5 1 Harwood Ter 2 Trueman Ter 3 Wycombe St
L1 1 Co-operative St 2 Thornwell Vw
L2 1 Newdale Av
L7 1 Ambleside Gv 2 Eskdale Rd 3 Hillside
L8 1 St Christophers Cl 2 St Clements Cl 3 St Leonards Wy 4 Winchester Wy
M1 1 Churchfield Av 2 Churchfield Cres 3 Churchfield Ter 4 Quarry Bank Rd 5 Somerset St 6 Stonegarth Cl
M2 1 Edgelands Ri 2 Newtown Cl
M7 1 Buttermere Wy 2 Crummock Wy 3 Ullswater Dr

Page 67
M7 1 Beech Cl 2 Millside Ct 3 Nasmyth Cl 4 Poplar Ter

Page 81
K1 1 Chatsworth Ri 2 Hardwick Cl 3 Needlewood 4 Nostell Fold 5 Pilley Hl 6 Rob Royd 7 Saville Hall La 8 Woburn Pl

Page 82
E2 1 Blackburn St 2 Brockfield Cl 3 Croft St 4 Henry St 5 John St 6 Kingwell Cft 7 Kingwell Ms 8 Mill Ct 9 Norman Cl 10 Osmond Pl 11 Osmond Wy 12 Parkside Ms 13 Sweyn Cft

Page 84
D5 1 Badsworth Rd 2 Reginald Rd
D6 1 Brampton Vw 2 Derwent Pl 3 Junction St 4 Medway Pl
E1 1 Clarehurst Rd 2 Fensome Wy 3 Scofield Ct
E2 1 Havelock St 2 Owram St 3 South St
E8 1 Butterfield Rd
E8 1 Hurley Cft 2 Westfield Rd
F1 1 Shroggs Head Cl
F2 1 Thomas St
G3 1 Melton St
F8 1 Hall Cl 2 Manor Ct 3 Rainborough Ms

Page 89
J2 1 Farmhill Cl 2 Gramplan Cl 3 Malvern Av 4 Mendip Cl 5 Ramsworth Cl 6 Roshampton Ri 7 Springfield Ct
K2 1 Charnock Dr 2 Farthing Gale Ms 3 Fernlea Cl 4 Rothesay Cl
L7 1 Rose Ct 2 Westside Gra
M1 1 Wrightson Ter
M3 1 Elwis St
M5 1 Denison Rd 2 Littlewood St
M6 1 Firth St 2 Littlemoor St 3 Stanley Gdns 4 Stevens Rd 5 Westholme Rd
M7 1 Burton Ter 2 Cookson St 3 Great Central Av 4 Queen St

Page 90
A4 1 Chancery Pl 2 Factory La 3 Pell's Cl 4 Portland Pl 5 Printing Office St 6 St Sepulchre Ga 7 Trafford Ct 8 West Laith Ga
B3 1 Allerton St 2 Athron St 3 Copley Rd 4 Harrington St 5 High Fisher Ga 6 Market Rd
F1 1 Adlard Rd
F7 1 Norton Rd
F7 1 Malham Tarn Ct
F8 1 Clayworth Dr

Page 108
D2 1 Beaconsfield St 2 Blenheim St 3 Catherine St 4 Cowood St 5 Shrewsbury Cl
F3 1 Adwick Cl 2 Adwick Rd 3 Montagu St

Page 111
M7 1 Barrie Rd 2 Browning Av 3 Burns Rd 4 Crookes Rd 5 Gray Gdns 6 Gurney Rd 7 Keats Rd 8 Lowell Av 9 Norfolk Rd 10 Suffolk Av

Page 126
D1 1 Blackburn Cft 2 Chamberlain St 3 Habershon Dr 4 Hodder Ct 5 Ingleborough Cft 6 Peckham Rd 7 Penyghent Cl 8 Whernside Av
D2 1 Dickenson Ct 2 Josselin Ct 3 Lansbury Av 4 Marrick Ct 5 Stafford Wy
E3 1 Cherry Wk 2 Firtree Ri 3 Laburnum Ct

Page 129
J1 1 Carlisle St 2 Eastwood La 3 Elliott Ct 4 Henry St 5 Kenneth St 6 Nottingham St 7 Rawson St
K1 1 Cromer Cl 2 Hardie Pl

Page 144
A7 1 Brier St 2 Cannock St 3 Cheadle St 4 Hillsborough Pl 5 Hillsborough Rd 6 Holme Cl 7 Roselle St 8 Treswell Cr
B7 1 Bilston St 2 Blackburne St 3 Burnaby Gn 4 Cuthbert Bank Rd 5 Langsett Crs 6 Normandale Rd 7 Walter St

Page 145
G7 1 Cawston Rd 2 Gayton Rd 3 Osgathorpe Crs
G8 1 Ella Rd 2 Grimesthorpe Rd 3 Lucas St 4 Lyons St
H6 1 Bolsover Rd East 2 Heathcote St
J7 1 Earl Marshal Rd 2 Whiteways Dr
M3 1 Asquith St 2 Chapman St 3 Elmview Rd 4 Merton Rd
M5 1 Bubwith Rd 2 Laughton Rd 3 Lincoln St 4 Meadowcourt 5 Walling Rd
M6 1 Webster St 2 Yarmouth St
M7 1 Lynn Pl 2 Pickering St

Page 147
H1 1 College St 2 The Crofts 3 Domine La 4 Down's Rw 5 Quarry Hl 6 Snail Hl 7 Stanley St 8 The Statutes 9 Unity Pl
H7 1 Blackbird Av 2 Buckingham Wy 3 Chaffinch Av 4 Chatsworth Ri 5 Cherry Tree Cl 6 Fairburn Gdns 7 Lyncroft Cl 8 Meridip Ri 9 Thorndale Ri 10 Thrush Av 11 Trentham St
J1 1 Catherine St 2 Chatham St 3 Doncaster Ga 4 Douglas St 5 Morpeth St 6 Percy St 7 Summerfield 8 Whybourne Gv
K1 1 Clifton La 2 Ellesmere Rd 3 Gordon Ter 4 Granville St 5 Harcourt Ter
K2 1 Carrington St 2 Frances St 3 Garfield Mt 4 Mabel St
M5 1 East Bawtry Rd
M6 1 Brook St 2 Hollow Ga 3 St Leonards
M7 1 Sorrelsykes Cl 2 Whiston Gv

Page 150
F2 1 Heatherdale Rd 2 Howard Rd 3 Seymour Rd 4 Staffordshire Cl 5 Stone Park Cl

Page 159
J2 1 Fairbarn Rd 2 Hall Park Mt 3 Laxey Rd 4 Liberty Cl 5 Onchan Rd
C3 1 St Stephen's Wk 2 Yardley Sq

Page 160
A1 1 Elliottville St 2 Gresham Rd 3 Palm La
A2 1 Bank House Rd 2 Eastfield Rd 3 Joseph Rd 4 Northfield Cl
A3 1 Ainsley Rd 2 Clementson Rd 3 Cobden Pl 4 Conduit La 5 Learnington St 6 Romsdal Rd 7 Spring House Rd 8 Spring View Rd 9 Warwick St 10 Warwick Ter
A4 1 Churchill Rd 2 Coombe Rd 3 Highnam Crescent Rd 4 Pisgah House Rd
A5 1 Ashdell 2 Ashdell La 3 Ashgate La 4 Caxton Rd 5 Chandos St 6 Hoole La 7 Nile St 8 Peel St 9 Taptonville Rd 10 Turners La 11 Watson Rd
A6 1 Betjeman Gdns 2 Oakholme Ms
A7 1 Kenilworth Pl 2 Meadow Ter
A8 1 Osborne Ct
B1 1 Langsett Gv
B2 1 Alpine Rd 2 Birkendale Vw 3 Bransby St 4 Daniel Hill St 5 Upperthorpe Gln
B3 1 Barber Cres 2 Barber Pl 3 The Coach Houses 4 Crookesmoor Rd 5 Elliot Rd 6 Ivy Dr 7 Ivy Gv 8 Moorgate Av 9 Warrington Rd
B5 1 Broomgrove Crs 2 College La 3 Paxton La 4 St Mark's Crs
B6 1 Cemetery Av
B7 1 Ashford Rd 2 Berresford Rd 3 Bruce Rd 4 Dyson Pl 5 Eastwood Rd 6 Gordon Rd 7 Harefield Rd 8 Hickmott Rd 9 Jarrow Rd 10 Lynton Rd 11 Rosedale Gdns 12 Rosedale Rd
B8 1 Cherry Tree Dell 2 Cherry Tree Rd 3 Cherry Tree Rd 4 Meadow Bank Av 5 St Andrew's Dr
C1 1 Gilpin St 2 Primrose Hl
C3 1 Blake Grove Rd 2 Brandeth Rd 3 Brandreth Cl 4 Burlington Ct 5 Carnarvon St 6 Daniel Hill Ter 7 Gilpin La 8 Philadelphia Dr 9 Philadelphia Gn 10 Portland St 11 Shipton St 12 Straw La 13 Westmoreland St 14 Yeomans Rd
C4 1 Brightmore Dr 2 Conway St 3 Durham Rd 4 Duke La 5 Faved Rd 6 Hounsfield La 7 Hounsfield Rd 8 Leavygreave Rd 9 Western Bank 10 Wilkinson La 11 Wilkinson St
C5 1 Broomspring Cl 2 Broomspring La 3 Exeter Wy 4 Gloucester Crs 5 Hanover St 6 Holberry Cl 7 Holberry Gdns 8 Mackenzie Crs 9 Monmouth St 10 Ruth So 11 Upper Hanover St
C6 1 Parliament St 2 Pembroke St 3 Sawdon Rd 4 Sunderland St
C7 1 Mackenzie St
C8 1 Kenbourne Gv 2 Kenwood Rd 3 Montgomery Dr
D1 1 Haddon St
D2 1 Bedford St 2 Dixon St 3 Downing La 4 Dun Fds 5 Dun La 6 Henry St 7 Infirmary Rd 8 Lancaster St 9 Lister La 10 Matthew St 11 Montgomery Terrace Rd 12 Percy St 13 St Phillip's Rd 14 Sudbury St 15 Waterloo Wk
D3 1 Blue Boy St 2 Brocco St 3 Brownell St 4 Burnt Tree La 5 Craven St 6 Ellison St 7 Morpeth St 8 Netherthorpe St 9 Queen's Rw 10 Well Meadow Dr 11 Well Meadow St
D4 1 Abney St 2 Broad La 3 Broad Lane Ct 4 Canning St 5 Charlotte La 6 Chester St 7 Congress St 8 Convent Pl 9 Devonshire La 10 Devonshire St 11 Orange St 12 Pitt St 13 Portland La 14 Red Hl 15 Regent St 16 St George's Ter 17 St Thomas St 18 Siddall St 19 Wheeldon St
D4 1 Castle Gn 2 Harts Head 3 Haymarket 4 Johnson La 5 Lady's Br 6 Meetinghouse La 7 Shude Hl 8 Waingate 9 Wharf St 10 Willey St
D5 1 Bath St 2 Broomhall St 3 Broomspring La 4 Cavendish Ct 5 Chester La 6 Evans St 7 Exeter Pl 8 Headford Ms 9 Headford St
D6 1 Beeley St 2 Exeter Dr 3 Hermitage St 4 Keeton's Hl 5 Leverton Gdns 6 St Mary's Sq
D7 1 Asher Rd 2 Bennett St 3 Crowther Pl 4 Croydon St 5 Grosvenor Sq 6 Mount Pleasant Rd 7 Penley St 8 Salmon St 9 Sitwell Pl 10 Smeaton St 11 Stemp St 12 Ventnor Pl 13 Ward Pl
D8 1 Ainsty Rd 2 Aizlewood Rd 3 Alcester Rd 4 Brookfield Rd 5 Cutts Ter 6 Dalton Ct 7 Farrar Rd 8 Herschell Rd 9 Marples Cl 10 Marples Dr 11 Miller Rd 12 Rampton Rd 13 Sellers St 14 South View Crs
E1 1 Pye Bank Cl 2 Woodside La
E3 1 Bower Spring 2 Cupola 3 Lee Cft 4 North Church St 5 Paradise La 6 Paradise Sq 7 Paradise St 8 Plum La 9 Silver Street Head 10 Water St 11 Workhouse La
E5 1 Cambridge St 2 Clay La 3 Cumberland Wy 4 Duke La 5 Proggatt La 6 Hallam La 7 Jessop St 8 Matilda Wy 9 Moor Head 10 Newton La 11 Rockingham La 12 Rockingham Ga 13 Rockingham Wy 14 Union La 15 Union St
E6 1 Ascot St 2 Baron St 3 Countess Rd 4 Forge La 5 Hereford St 6 Midland St
E7 1 Alderson Rd North 2 Atkin Pl 3 Batt St 4 Belgrave Sq 5 Harrington Rd 6 Holland St 7 St Barnabas La 8 Silver Mill Rd 9 Witney St
E8 1 Alderney Rd 2 Fieldhead Rd 3 Gifford Rd 4 Glover Rd 5 Guernsey Rd 6 Jersey Rd 7 Preston St 8 Sark St 9 Sheaf Bank 10 Staveley Rd
F1 1 Cranworth Pl 2 Cranworth Rd 3 Kilton Hl 4 Lopham St
F2 1 Andrew La 2 Andrew St 3 Denholme Cl 4 Lopham Cl 5 Nursery La 6 Scholey St 7 Spitalfields
F5 1 Bakers Hl 2 Cadman La 3 Esperanto Pl 4 Fitzalan Sq 5 Gilbert St 6 High St 7 Mulberry St
F6 1 Brittain St 2 Cross Turner St 3 Fornham St 4 Granville St 5 Leadmill Rd
F7 1 Cream St 2 Cromford St 3 Leadmill Rd 4 Lenton St 5 Manton St 6 Sheaf Gdns

Page 161
G1 1 Bressingham Cl 2 Ditchingham St 3 Harleston St 4 South Grimesthorpe Rd
G2 1 Dorking St
G3 1 Blast La 2 Cadman St 3 Effingham La 4 Malting La 5 New Street La 6 Stepney St
C7 1 Thornborough Cl 2 Thornborough Pl 3 Warburton Cl 4 Warburton Rd 5 Woodthorpe Cres
C8 1 Claywood Rd
D7 1 Castledale Cft 2 Castledale Pl 3 Princess St 4 Vikinglea Cl
D8 1 Anson St 2 Blackwell Cl 3 Blackwell Ct 4 Crown Pl 5 High Street La 6 Manor Oaks Gdns 7 Rhodes St 8 Talbot Rd 9 Weigh La
H1 1 Babur Rd 2 Norroy St 3 Windsor St
H2 1 Sutherland St
H4 1 Manor Oaks Ct
H5 1 Ingram Ct 2 Stafford Rd

Page 162
A3 1 The Avenue 2 Catcliffe Rd 3 Jeffcock Rd 4 Main Rd 5 Ronald Rd 6 Station Rd 7 Studley Ct 8 Swale Gdns 9 Waverley Rd
A6 1 Castlebeck Cft 2 Danebrook Cl 3 Danebrook Ct 4 Normancroft Crs
A7 1 Angleton Cl 2 Angleton Gdns 3 Angleton Gn 4 Angleton Ms 5 Aughton Dr 6 Woodthorpe Rd
G2 1 Coates St 2 Glencoe Dr 3 Glencoe Pl 4 Robinson Rd 5 Samson St 6 Talbot Gdns 7 Talbot St 8 Sturge Cft
G6 1 Claywood Rd
C8 1 Tower Cl

Page 166
D5 1 Clarke Ct 2 Oldcoates Cl 3 Poynton Dr 4 Revill Ct 5 St Leger Wy
G1 1 Greystock St 2 Livingston Rd
J2 1 Baldwin St 2 Bessemer Pl 3 Lovetot Rd
J3 1 Maltravers Rd
J4 1 Maltravers Rd 2 Saunders Pl 3 Wyborn House Rd 4 Wyborn Ter
J5 1 Kestrel Gn 2 Magpie Gv 3 Osprey Gdns 4 Partridge Vw 5 Plover Ct 6 Quail Ri 7 Starling Mead 8 Wren Bank
J6 1 St Aidan's Rd 2 Southend Rd
J7 1 Brimmesfield Dr 2 Guildford Vw 3 St Aidan's Mt 4 St Aidan's Rd
J8 1 Cradock Ms
K1 1 Bodmin St 2 Chippingham St 3 Heppenstall La 4 Sleaford St 5 Slitting Mill La
K2 1 Arras Ct 2 Palmer St
K3 1 Lumley St
K6 1 Manor Park Ct
K7 1 Scotia Cl 2 Scotia Dr
K8 1 Babington Ct 2 Queen Mary Gv
L1 1 Chapel La 2 Titterton St
L2 1 Bray St 2 Cattai St 3 Chinley St 4 Faranden Rd 5 Fearnehough St 6 Garth Cl 7 Harry Firth Cl 8 Ouseburn St 9 Spofforth Rd 10 Wilfred Ct
L6 1 Motehall Wy
L7 1 Archdale Pl 2 Fretson Rd 3 Hastilar Rd
L8 1 Queen Mary Rd 2 Queen Mary Ms 3 Travey Rd
M2 1 Basford Cl 2 Bramham Ct 3 Bramham Rd 4 Flaxby Rd 5 Kashmir Gdns 6 Shirland La 7 Shirland Ms 8 Shirland Pl 9 Tockwith Rd
M4 1 Ribston Ct 2 Ribston Pl 3 Whitby Rd

Page 176
A1 1 Bannerdale Rd 2 Lyndhurst Rd
A2 1 Knab Cl
A4 1 Terminus Rd
A6 1 Foids Dr
B1 1 Brentwood Av
B4 1 Hutchinson La 2 Hutchinson Rd
B8 1 Hemper Gv
C1 1 Archibald Rd 2 Gatefield Rd 3 Herbert Rd 4 Marden Rd 5 Violet Bank Rd
C3 1 Norton Hammer La
C5 1 Booker Rd
C7 1 Abbey Brook Ct
D1 1 Allenby Cl 2 Torwood Dr
D5 1 Belper Rd 2 Empire Rd 3 Little London Pl 4 Markham Ter
D7 1 The Greenway 2 Roxton Av
E2 1 Brooklyn Pl 2 Brooklyn Rd 3 Cross Park Rd 4 Cyprus Rd 5 Molloy Pl 6 Rushdale Rd 7 Rushdale Ter
E3 1 Lees House Ct
E4 1 Hartford Cl 2 Mount View Gdns 3 Norton Lees Cl
F4 1 Warminster Dr
F6 1 Norton Church Glebe
F7 1 Norton Park Av
F8 1 Hazlebarrow Ct

Page 177
C1 1 Abney Cl 2 Derby Pl 3 Hallyburton Cl 4 Hallyburton Rd 5 Hartopp Cl
G2 1 Callow Mt
G6 1 Matthews Fold
G8 1 Hazleborough Gv 2 Jordanthorpe Vw

Page 178
H1 1 East Bank Cl 2 East Bank Wy 3 Gleadless Rd 4 Hartopp Dr
H2 1 Farmstead Cl 2 Plowright Wy
H5 1 Constable Wy 2 Landseer Cl 3 Mawfa Cr 4 Mawfa Rd
J2 1 Oakes Park Vw
J5 1 Newfield Farm Cl 2 Spotswood Dr 3 Spotswood Mt 4 Toll Bar Av
J5 1 Constable Cl 2 Gibbons Wy 3 Landseer Cl 4 Orpen Wy 5 Sandby Ct 6 Sandby Cft
K1 1 Dagnam Cl
K2 1 Ashleigh Ct 2 Grassmoor Ct
K3 1 Gleadless Bank
L1 1 Ridgeway Rd
L2 1 Chatsworth Park Av 2 Chatsworth Park Dr 3 Chatsworth Park Gr 4 Durlstone Cl 5 Leadbeater Dr
L3 1 Crispin Cl 2 Crispin Rd 3 Hollinsend Rd 4 Kirkby Av
L4 1 Gleadless Mt 2 Herdings Cl 3 Little Wood Rd
L6 1 Abbots Meadow 2 Bramshill Ct 3 Collingbourne Dr 4 Hursley Cl 5 Inglewood Av 6 Inglewood Cl 7 Inglewood Dell 8 Milburn Cl
M1 1 Applegarth Cl 2 Bagshaw's Rd 3 Holbrook Dr 4 Penthorpe Cl 5 Pleasant Cl
M3 1 Welwyn Cl
M4 1 Basegreen Pl 2 Lister Cl 3 Lister Pl
M5 1 Meadow Gate Cl 2 Nether Oak Cl 3 Nether Oak Vw 4 School Rd
M6 1 Bedgebury Cl 2 Bennone Dr 3 Farmoor Gdns 4 Pendle Cft
M7 1 Cutler Cl 2 Havercroft Ter 3 Kestrel Cl 4 Maillard Rd

Page 179
H8 1 Church Ms 2 Kildale Gdns 3 Shipman Ct 4 Stonedale Cl
J7 1 Birchwood Cl 2 Birchwood Gdns 3 Birchwood Ri 4 Birchwood Wy 5 Challoner Gn 6 Garland Mt 7 Meadowcroft Cl 8 Meadowcroft Gld 9 Pedley Dr 10 Shortbrook Bank 11 Westland Gv
J8 1 Horton Cl 2 Knowle Top 3 Manor Vw 4 Plantin Ri 5 Westcroft Gn
K7 1 Eastcroft Cl 2 Eastcroft Wy 3 Shortbrook Cft 4 Waterthorpe Cl 5 Waterthorpe Gln
L5 1 Byron Rd 2 Charnwood Cl 3 Grizedale Cl 4 Hartland Av 5 Hartland Ct 6 Ringwood Rd 7 Rothbury Cl 8 Rothbury Ct 9 Waltham Gdns 10 Wareham Ct 11 Wychwood Cl 12 Wychwood Gln 13 Wychwood Gv 14 Wychwood Cl

Page 189
M1 1 Twentywell Dr

Page 190
A6 1 Allestree Dr 2 Barley Ms 3 Belton Cl 4 Burnaston Cl 5 Chaddesden Cl 6 Hazelwood Cl 7 Ivan Brook Cl 8 Mapperley Rd 9 Newstead Cl 10 Ormesby Cl 11 Oxclose Dr 12 Repton Pl 13 Rockingham Cl 14 Sneliston Cl 15 Stanford Rd 16 Thornton Cl
B6 1 Buckingham Cl 2 Burbage Cl 3 Chatsworth Cl 4 Millstone Cl
C6 1 Gardom Cl 2 Hayfield Cl 3 Lynwood Cl 4 Nairn Dr 5 Norbury Cl 6 Roston Cl
D6 1 Farwater La 2 Garth Wy 3 Gosforth Crs 4 Gosforth Cl 5 Turner Cl
F4 1 Derwent Cl 2 Snape Hill La
F5 1 Alexandra Rd 2 Egerton Rd
F6 1 Hallowes Ct 2 Scarsdale Cross 3 Vale Cl

Page 193
E1 1 Ambleside Cl 2 Borrowdale Av 3 Borrowdale Cl 4 Ennerdale Av 5 Ennerdale Cl 6 Murrayfield Dr 7 Oakworth Cl 8 Twickenham Cl 9 Twickenham Ct 10 Twickenham Cres 11 Twickenham Gld 12 Twickenham Glen 13 Wasdale Av

Page 198
E1 1 Beechcroft 2 Coventry Dr 3 Northumbria Cl 4 Northwood 5 Primrose Wy 6 Prospect Prec 7 Ravenscourt 8 Ridgeway 9 Ringwood 10 Summerwde 11 Wessex Cl

Notes